Spell it right
Dictionary

edited by **Bill Trumble**

with

Jonathan Blaney
Judith Wood
Richard Jones

OXFORD
UNIVERSITY PRESS

OXFORD
UNIVERSITY PRESS

Great Clarendon Street, Oxford OX2 6DP

Oxford University Press is a department of the University of Oxford.
It furthers the University's objective of excellence in research, scholarship,
and education by publishing worldwide in

Oxford New York

Athens Auckland Bangkok Bogotá Buenos Aires
Cape Town Chennai Dar es Salaam Delhi Florence Hong Kong Istanbul
Karachi Kolkata Kuala Lumpur Madrid Melbourne Mexico City Mumbai
Nairobi Paris São Paulo Shanghai Singapore Taipei Tokyo Toronto Warsaw

with associated companies in Berlin Ibadan

Oxford is a registered trade mark of Oxford University Press
in the UK and in certain other countries

British Library Cataloguing in Publication Data
Data available

ISBN 0–19–860369x

10 9 8 7 6 5 4 3 2 1

Designed by Jane Stevenson
Typeset in Charter and Meta
by Morton Word Processing Ltd
Printed in Great Britain by
Mackays of Chatham plc, Chatham, Kent

Preface

The **Spell it right Dictionary** is a brand new kind of dictionary. It focuses on the two areas where help tends to be most needed: spelling, and meanings of difficult words. It is designed for people who want to find this kind of information quickly, and who are less interested in the full range of information about familiar everyday words and phrases that a standard dictionary contains.

There are thousands of helpful notes on spelling and grammar, giving you clear practical tips on how to improve your spelling and command of English and how to avoid making mistakes; whether it is to sort out easily confused meanings (*intense* or *intensive*?), grammatical points (*between you and me* or *between you and I*?), or problem spellings (*irritable* or *irritible*?).

As you would expect in a dictionary, you can also look up words you don't know the meaning of. The definitions are written in straightforward English and the layout of the page is very open and clear, so it is always easy to find what you are looking for. What you won't find are definitions for very familiar words such as 'face' and 'fact': these have been deliberately left out to make more room for the spelling and usage help.

Help is also given on how to pronounce words, using a simple system in which, for example, the pronunciation of *acoustic* is given as uh-**koo**-stik.

All in all, **Spell it right** is designed to give you practical help where you need it—quickly.

How to use the Spell it right Dictionary

part of speech (verb, noun, adjective, etc.)

entry word

how the word is typically used

forms of the verb (inflections)

abide »*verb* (**abides, abiding, abided**)
❶ **abide by** accept or obey a rule or decision. ❷ (in informal English) put up with: *he could not abide conflict.*

label showing how the word is used

accede »*verb* (**accedes, acceding, acceded**)
❶ agree to a demand or request. ❷ take up an office or position.
— SAY uhk-**seed**

sense number

pronunciation help

plural form of the noun

Adonis »*noun* (plural **Adonises**) an extremely handsome young man.
— SAY uh-**doh**-nis

> **i** *Adonis* was the name of a beautiful youth in Greek mythology

information note

centrifugal »*adjective* (in physics) moving away from a centre.
— SAY sen-tri-**fyoo**-g'l

label showing which subject the entry deals with

> ✓ **al** not **el**: centrifugal

spelling notes

entry with no definition given

Christmas (plural **Christmases**)
Christmassy

word derived from the entry word

> ✓ remember the **t** of **Christ**: **Christmas** do not double the **s** (or use an apostrophe) in making the plural: **Christmases**

comparative and superlative forms of the adjective

number indicating different words with the same spelling

close¹ (adjective: **closer, closest**) [near]
closely
closeness

brief explanation of words to distinguish similar entries

close² (verb: **closes, closing, closed**) [shut]

label showing where the word is used

eggplant »*noun* (in American English) =
AUBERGINE.

cross reference to another entry

Pronunciations

Pronunciations are given for any word which might cause difficulty, but not for everyday words which everyone is familiar with, such as *table* or *large*. They are given by writing the word out again as it is spoken, using the system shown below. The part of the pronunciation printed in bold is the syllable that is stressed.

List of Symbols

VOWELS	EXAMPLES	CONSONANTS	EXAMPLES
a	as in **cat**	b	as in **bat**
ah	as in **calm**	ch	as in **chin**
air	as in **hair**	d	as in **day**
ar	as in **bar**	f	as in **fat**
aw	as in **law**	g	as in **get**
ay	as in **say**	h	as in **hat**
e	as in **bed**	j	as in **jam**
ee	as in **meet**	k	as in **king**
eer	as in **beer**	kh	as in **loch**
er	as in **her**	l	as in **leg**
ew	as in **few**	m	as in **man**
i	as in **pin**	n	as in **not**
I	as in **eye**	ng	as in **sing**, **finger**
o	as in **top**	nk	as in **thank**
oh	as in **most**	p	as in **pen**
oi	as in **join**	r	as in **red**
oo	as in **soon**	s	as in **sit**
oor	as in **poor**	sh	as in **shop**
or	as in **corn**	t	as in **top**
ow	as in **cow**	th	as in **thin**
oy	as in **boy**	*th*	as in **this**
u	as in **cup**	v	as in **van**
uh	as in **along**	w	as in **will**
uu	as in **book**	y	as in **yes**
y	as in **cry**	z	as in **zebra**
yoo	as in **unit**	*zh*	as in **vision**
yoor	as in **Europe**		
yr	as in **fire**		

Note on trademarks and proprietary status

Aa

aardvark »*noun* an African mammal with a tubular snout and a long tongue, which feeds on ants and termites.

aback »*adverb* (**take someone aback**) shock or surprise someone.

abacus »*noun* (plural **abacuses**) a frame with rows of wires along which beads are slid, used for counting.
– **SAY** a-buh-kuhss

abandon (verb: **abandons, abandoning, abandoned**)
abandonment

abase »*verb* (**abases, abasing, abased**) (**abase yourself**) behave in a very humble way.
abasement

abashed »*adjective* embarrassed or ashamed.

abasing

abate »*verb* (**abates, abating, abated**) (of something bad) become less severe or widespread.
abatement

abattoir »*noun* a slaughterhouse.
– **SAY** a-buh-twar

 one **b** and two **t's**: **abattoir** is a French word

abbess »*noun* (plural **abbesses**) a woman who is the head of a nunnery or convent.

abbey »*noun* (plural **abbeys**) a building lived in by a community of monks or nuns.

abbot »*noun* a man who is the head of a monastery or community of monks.

 note there is only one **t**: **abbot**

abbreviate (verb: **abbreviates, abbreviating, abbreviated**)

abbreviation

abdicate »*verb* (**abdicates, abdicating, abdicated**) ❶ give up the role of king or queen. ❷ fail to fulfil a responsibility.
abdication

abdomen »*noun* ❶ the part of the body containing the digestive and reproductive organs; the belly. ❷ the rear part of the body of an insect, spider, or crustacean.
– **SAY** ab-duh-muhn

 b before **d**: **abdomen**

abdominal »*adjective* having to do with the abdomen.
– **SAY** ab-**dom**-in'l

 i not **e**: **abdominal**

abduct »*verb* (**abducts, abducting, abducted**) take someone away by force or trickery.
abductee
abduction
abductor

aberrant »*adjective* not normal or acceptable.
– **SAY** uh-**berr**-uhnt
aberrance
aberrantly

aberration »*noun* ❶ an act or happening which is not normal or acceptable. ❷ an unexpected silly mistake.
– **SAY** a-buh-**ray**-sh'n

✓ one **b**, two **r's**: **aberration**

abet »*verb* (**abets, abetting, abetted**) encourage or help someone to do something wrong: *he was guilty of aiding and abetting others.*
abetter

✓ double the **t** in **abetted, abetting**, and **abetter**

abeyance »*noun* (**in abeyance**) temporarily not occurring or in use.
– **SAY** uh-**bay**-uhnss

abhor »*verb* (**abhors, abhorring, abhorred**) detest.
– **SAY** uhb-**hor**

✓ double the **r** in **abhorred** and **abhorring**

abhorrent »*adjective* disgusting or hateful.
– **SAY** uhb-**horr**-uhnt
abhorrence

abhorring

abhors

abide »*verb* (**abides, abiding, abided**) ❶ (**abide by**) accept or obey a rule or decision. ❷ (in informal English) put up with: *he could not abide conflict.*

ability (plural **abilities**)

a

abject »*adjective* ❶ very unpleasant and wretched: *abject poverty.* ❷ completely without pride or dignity: *an abject apology.*
abjectly
abjectness

abjure »*verb* (abjures, abjuring, abjured) swear to give up a belief or claim.

ablaze

able (adjective: abler, ablest)

ablutions »*plural noun* (mainly used in a humorous way) the act of washing yourself.

ably

abnegate »*verb* (abnegates, abnegating, abnegated) give up or refuse something that you want or that is your duty.
– SAY ab-ni-gayt
abnegation

abnormal

abnormality (plural abnormalities)

abnormally

aboard

abode »*noun* a house or home.

abolish »*verb* (abolishes, abolishing, abolished) put an end to a custom, law, or institution.

abolition
abolitionist

abominable »*adjective* ❶ seen as morally wrong. ❷ (in informal English) very bad; terrible.
abominably

abominate »*verb* (abominates, abominating, abominated) detest; loathe.

abomination »*noun* ❶ something that you hate or find disgusting. ❷ a feeling of hatred.

aboriginal »*adjective* ❶ existing in a country from the earliest times or from before the arrival of colonists. ❷ (Aboriginal) having to do with the Australian Aboriginals.
» *noun* (Aboriginal) a member of one of the native peoples of Australia.

Aborigine »*noun* an Australian aboriginal.
– SAY ab-uh-**ri**-ji-nee

> ☑ to make the plural, just add **s** (Aborigines): do not use **ies**

abort »*verb* (aborts, aborting, aborted) ❶ end a pregnancy early to stop the baby from developing and being born. ❷ undergo a natural abortion. ❸ end something early because of a problem or fault.

abortion »*noun* ❶ the deliberate ending of a human pregnancy. ❷ the natural ending of a pregnancy before the fetus is able to survive on its own.
abortionist

abortive »*adjective* failing to achieve the intended result; unsuccessful.
abortively

aborts

abound »*verb* (abounds, abounding, abounded) ❶ exist in large numbers or amounts. ❷ (abound in or with) have a specified thing in large numbers or amounts.

about

about-face

about-turn

above

abracadabra

abrade »*verb* (abrades, abrading, abraded) scrape or wear away.
– SAY uh-**brayd**

abrasion »*noun* ❶ the process of scraping or wearing away. ❷ an area of scraped skin.

abrasive »*adjective* ❶ able to polish or clean a hard surface by rubbing or grinding. ❷ harsh or rough in manner.
» *noun* an abrasive substance used for polishing or cleaning.
abrasively
abrasiveness

abreast

abridge »*verb* (abridges, abridging, abridged) shorten a text or film.
abridgement

> ☑ do not drop the **e** when spelling **abridgement**

abroad

abrogate »*verb* (abrogates, abrogating, abrogated) cancel or do away with a law or agreement.
– SAY ab-ruh-gayt

abrupt
abruptly
abruptness

abscess »*noun* (plural abscesses) a swelling containing pus.

> ☑ remember, **s** and **c** in the middle: **abscess**

abscond »*verb* (absconds, absconding, absconded) leave quickly and secretly to escape from custody or avoid arrest.
absconder

abseil »*verb* (abseils, abseiling, abseiled) climb down a rock-face using a rope wrapped round the body and fixed at a higher point.

– say ab-sayl
abseiler

> ☑ **abseil** is a German word, and the ending is **-seil**, not **-sail**

absence

absent (verb: **absents, absenting, absented**)
absently

absentee »*noun* a person who is absent.
absenteeism

absenting

absently

absent-minded
absent-mindedly
absent-mindedness

absents

absinthe »*noun* a green liqueur flavoured with aniseed.

absolute
absolutely

absolute zero »*noun* the lowest temperature physically possible (minus 273.15 degrees Celsius).

absolution »*noun* formal forgiveness of a person's sins.

absolve »*verb* (**absolves, absolving, absolved**) formally declare that someone is free from guilt, blame, or sin.

absorb (verb: **absorbs, absorbing, absorbed**)

absorbent
absorbency

> ☑ **ent** not **ant**: absorbent

absorbing

absorbs

absorption

> ☑ after the **r**, **p** not **b**: absorption

abstain »*verb* (**abstains, abstaining, abstained**) ❶ stop yourself from doing or indulging in something. ❷ formally choose not to vote.
abstainer

abstemious »*adjective* not letting yourself have much food, alcohol, or enjoyment.
– say uhb-stee-mi-uhss
abstemiously
abstemiousness

abstention »*noun* ❶ a deliberate choice not to vote. ❷ abstinence.
– say uhb-sten-sh'n

abstinence »*noun* the avoidance of doing or indulging in something.
– say ab-sti-nuhnss
abstinent

abstract »*adjective* ❶ having to do with ideas or qualities rather than physical or concrete things. ❷ (of art) using colour and shapes to create an effect rather than attempting to represent real life accurately.
» *verb* (**abstracts, abstracting, abstracted**) take out or remove.
» *noun* a summary of a book or article.
abstraction
abstractly

abstruse »*adjective* complicated and hard to understand.
– say uhb-strooss
abstrusely
abstruseness

absurd
absurdity
absurdly

abundance

abundant
abundantly

abuse (verb: **abuses, abusing, abused**)
abuser

abusive
abusively
abusiveness

abut »*verb* (**abuts, abutting, abutted**) (of a building) be next to or touching.
abutment

> ☑ double the **t** in abutted and abutting

abysmal
– say uh-biz-m'l
abysmally

> ☑ unlike abyss, abysmal is spelled with only one **s**

abyss »*noun* (plural **abysses**) a very deep hole or pit.
– say uh-biss

AC »*abbreviation* alternating current.

acacia »*noun* a tree or shrub with yellow or white flowers, found in warm climates.
– say uh-kay-shuh

academia »*noun* the academic environment or community.
– say a-kuh-dee-mi-uh

academic »*adjective* having to do with education or study.
» *noun* a teacher or scholar in a university or college.
academically

academy »*noun* (plural **academies**) ❶ a place where people study or are trained in a particular field. ❷ a society of scholars, artists, or scientists.

a a cappella »*adjective & adverb* (of music) sung without being accompanied by instruments.
– say a kuh-**pel**-luh

> ☑ two words, not one, and remember the double p: **a cappella** (an Italian phrase meaning 'in chapel style')

accede »*verb* (accedes, acceding, acceded) ❶ agree to a demand or request. ❷ take up an office or position.
– say uhk-**seed**

accelerate (verb: accelerates, accelerating, accelerated)
acceleration

> ☑ double c, single l: **accelerate**

accelerator

> ☑ -or not -er: **accelerator**

accent (verb: accents, accenting, accented)

accentuate »*verb* (accentuates, accentuating, accentuated) make a particular feature more noticeable.
accentuation

accept (verb: accepts, accepting, accepted) [agree to receive or do]

> ℹ do not confuse **accept** with **except**, which means 'not including'

acceptable
acceptability
acceptably

acceptance

accepted

accepting

acceptor

> ☑ -or not -er: **acceptor**

accepts

access (verb: accesses, accessing, accessed) [way of entering a place]

> ☑ double c, double s: **access** do not confuse **access** with **excess**, which means 'too much'

accessible
accessibility
accessibly

> ☑ -ible not -able: **accessible**

accessing

accession »*noun* ❶ the gaining of an important position or rank. ❷ a new item added to a library or museum collection.

accessory »*noun* (plural accessories) ❶ a thing which can be added to or worn with something else to make it more useful or attractive. ❷ (in law) a person who helps someone commit a crime without taking part in it.

> ☑ double c, double s, and ory not ary: **accessory**

accident

accidental
accidentally

acclaim »*verb* (acclaims, acclaiming, acclaimed) praise enthusiastically and publicly.
» *noun* enthusiastic public praise.

acclamation »*noun* loud and enthusiastic approval or praise.

acclimatize »*verb* (acclimatizes, acclimatizing, acclimatized) get used to a new climate or new conditions.
acclimatization

> ☑ many people prefer the alternative spellings **acclimatise**, **acclimatises**, etc., and **acclimatisation**: both s and z spellings are correct

accolade »*noun* something given as a special honour or as a reward for excellence.
– say ak-kuh-**layd**

accommodate (verb: accommodates, accommodating, accommodated)
accommodation

> ☑ double c, double m: **accommodate**, **accommodation**

accompanied

accompanies

accompaniment »*noun* ❶ a musical part which accompanies an instrument, voice, or group. ❷ something that accompanies something else.

> ☑ i not y: **accompaniment**

accompanist »*noun* a person who plays a musical accompaniment.

accompany (verb: accompanies, accompanying, accompanied)

accomplice »*noun* a person who helps someone commit a crime.
– say uh-**kum**-pliss

accomplish (verb: accomplishes, accomplishing, accomplished)

accomplishment

accord »*verb* (accords, according, accorded) ❶ give power or recognition to someone. ❷ be in agreement or consistent with something.
» *noun* ❶ agreement in opinion or feeling. ❷ an official agreement or treaty.

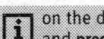
accordance

accorded

according

accordingly

accordion »*noun* a musical instrument that you play by stretching and squeezing it with the hands and pressing buttons or keys.
– SAY uh-**kor**-di-uhn
accordionist

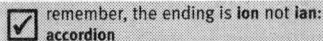
remember, the ending is **ion** not **ian**: **accordion**

accords

accost »*verb* (**accosts, accosting, accosted**) approach someone and speak to them boldly or aggressively.

account (verb: **accounts, accounting, accounted**)

accountable »*adjective* required or expected to give reasons for actions or decisions.
accountability
accountably

accountant
accountancy

accounted

accounting

accounts

accoutrement »*noun* an extra item of dress or equipment.
– SAY uh-**koo**-truh-muhnt

accredit »*verb* (**accredits, accrediting, accredited**) ❶ give someone the credit for something. ❷ officially authorize.
accreditation

accretion »*noun* ❶ a growth or increase by a gradual build-up. ❷ something formed or added gradually.
– SAY uh-**kree**-sh'n

accrue »*verb* (**accrues, accruing, accrued**) ❶ (of money) be received in regular or increasing amounts. ❷ collect or receive payments or benefits.
– SAY uh-**kroo**
accrual

accumulate (verb: **accumulates, accumulating, accumulated**)
accumulation
accumulative

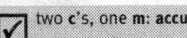
two **c**'s, one **m**: **accumulate**

accumulator »*noun* ❶ a large rechargeable electric cell. ❷ a bet placed on a series of events, the winnings and stake from each being placed on the next.

accurate
accuracy
accurately

on the difference between **accurate** and **precise**, see the note at PRECISE

accursed

accusation

accusatory »*adjective* conveying an accusation.
– SAY uh-**kyoo**-zuh-tuh-ri

accuse (verb: **accuses, accusing, accused**)
accuser

accustom »*verb* (**accustoms, accustoming, accustomed**) ❶ make someone used to something. ❷ (**accustomed to**) used to something.

do not double the **m** in **accustomed** and **accustoming**

ace

acerbic »*adjective* sharp and direct: *acerbic comments.*
– SAY uh-**ser**-bik
acerbically
acerbity

acetate »*noun* a type of chemical compound made from acetic acid.
– SAY **a**-si-tayt

acetic acid »*noun* the acid that gives vinegar its characteristic taste.
– SAY uh-**see**-tik

acetone »*noun* a colourless liquid used as a solvent.
– SAY **a**-si-tohn

acetylene »*noun* a gas which burns with a bright flame, used in welding.
– SAY uh-**set**-i-leen

ache (verb: **aches, aching, ached**)

drop the **e** when spelling **aching**

achieve (verb: **achieves, achieving, achieved**)
achievable
achievement
achiever

the usual rule is **i** before **e** except after **c**: **achieve**

Achilles heel »*noun* a person's weak point.
– SAY uh-**kil**-leez

spell **Achilles** with a capital **A**: *Achilles* was a hero in Greek myth whose mother dipped him in the River Styx when he was a baby, making it impossible to hurt any part of his body except for the heel she held him by

Achilles tendon »*noun* the tendon which connects the calf muscles to the heel.

aching

> ☑ no e: aching

achy [suffering from aches]

> ☑ the ending is simply y, not ey: achy

acid »*noun* (in chemistry) a substance which can neutralize alkalis, turn litmus red, and often dissolve metals.
» *adjective* ❶ having the properties of an acid. ❷ sharp-tasting or sour. ❸ (of a remark) bitter or cutting.
acidic

acidify »*verb* (acidifies, acidifying, acidified) make something acid.
acidification

acidity

acidly

acid rain »*noun* rainfall made acid by pollution from the burning of fossil fuels.

acknowledge (verb: acknowledges, acknowledging, acknowledged)

acknowledgement

> ☑ acknowledgement can also be spelled acknowledgment, with one e less: both spellings are correct

acknowledges

acknowledging

acme »*noun* the highest point of achievement or excellence.
– SAY ak-mi

acne »*noun* a skin condition which causes red pimples.

acolyte »*noun* an assistant or follower.
– SAY ak-uh-lyt

acorn

acoustic »*adjective* ❶ having to do with sound or hearing. ❷ not electrically amplified: *an acoustic guitar.*
» *noun* ❶ (also **acoustics**) the aspects of a room or building that affect how well it transmits sound. ❷ (**acoustics**) the part of physics concerned with sound.
– SAY uh-**koo**-stik
acoustically

acquaint »*verb* (acquaints, acquainting, acquainted) ❶ make someone aware of or familiar with. ❷ (be **acquainted with**) know personally.

> ☑ remember the c. It is one of a set of words that begin with acqu, not aqu: acquaint, acquaintance.

acquaintance

acquainted

acquainting

acquaints

acquiesce »*verb* (acquiesces, acquiescing, acquiesced) accept something without protest.
– SAY ak-wi-ess
acquiescence
acquiescent

> ☑ acq not aq: acquiesce

acquire (verb: acquires, acquiring, acquired)
acquirer

> ☑ remember the c: acquire, acquisition

acquisition

acquisitive »*adjective* too interested in gaining money or material things.
acquisitively
acquisitiveness

acquit »*verb* (acquits, acquitting, acquitted) ❶ formally decide that someone is not guilty of a criminal charge. ❷ (**acquit yourself**) behave or perform in a particular way.
acquittal

> ☑ acq not aq: acquit, acquittal

acre »*noun* a unit of land area equal to 4,840 square yards (0.405 hectare).
– SAY ay-ker
acreage

acrid »*adjective* unpleasantly bitter or sharp.
– SAY ak-rid
acridity

acrimonious »*adjective* angry and bitter.
– SAY ak-ri-**moh**-ni-uhss
acrimoniously

acrimony »*noun* bitterness or ill feeling.
– SAY ak-ri-muh-ni

acrobat »*noun* an entertainer who performs feats gymnastic feats.

acrobatic
acrobatically

acronym »*noun* a word formed from the first letters of other words (e.g. *Aids, laser, quango*).
– SAY ak-ruh-nim

across

acrostic »*noun* a poem or puzzle in which certain letters in each line form a word or words.
– SAY uh-**kross**-tik

acrylic »*adjective* (of synthetic fabric, plastic, paint, etc.) made using a particular acid.
– say a-**kril**-ik

act (verb: **acts, acting, acted**)

actinium »*noun* a rare radioactive metallic chemical element.
– say ak-**tin**-iuhm

action (verb: **actions, actioning, actioned**)
actionable

activate »*verb* (**activates, activating, activated**) cause something to act or work.
activation
activator

active
actively

activist »*noun* a person who campaigns for political or social change.
activism

activity (plural **activities**)

> ☑ plural: drop the **y** and add **ies**:
> **activities**

actor

actress (plural **actresses**)

acts

actual

actuality »*noun* (plural **actualities**) actual reality or fact, as opposed to what was intended or expected.

actually

actuary »*noun* (plural **actuaries**) a person who compiles and analyses statistics in order to calculate insurance risks and premiums.
– say ak-tyoo-uh-ri
actuarial

actuate »*verb* (**actuates, actuating, actuated**) ❶ cause a machine to function. ❷ motivate someone to do something.
actuation

acuity »*noun* sharpness of thought, vision, or hearing.
– say uh-**kyoo**-i-ti

acumen »*noun* the ability to make good judgements and take quick decisions.
– say ak-yoo-muhn

acupuncture »*noun* a kind of medical treatment in which very thin needles are inserted into the skin.
acupuncturist

acute »*adjective* ❶ (of something bad) critical; serious. ❷ sharp-witted or shrewd. ❸ (of a physical sense or faculty) highly developed.

acute accent »*noun* a mark (′) placed over letters in some languages to indicate pronunciation (e.g. in *fiancée*).

acute angle »*noun* an angle less than 90 degrees.

acutely

acuteness

AD »*abbreviation* Anno Domini, used to indicate a date of a certain number of years after Christ's birth.

> ℹ **AD** is placed *before* a number, as in *AD 375*, but *after* words, as in *the third century AD*

adage »*noun* a proverb or saying expressing a general truth.
– say ad-ij

adagio (in music) »*adverb & adjective* in slow time.
»*noun* (plural **adagios**) a piece of music to be played in slow time.
– say uh-**dah**-ji-oh

> ☑ the plural of **adagio**, an Italian word, has **os** not **oes**: **adagios**

adamant »*adjective* refusing to be persuaded or to change your mind.
adamantly

Adam's apple

adapt (verb: **adapts, adapting, adapted**)

adaptable
adaptability

adaptation

adapted

adapter another way of spelling **ADAPTOR**.

adapting

adaption

adaptive

adaptor

> ☑ **adaptor** can also be spelled **adapter**

adapts

add (verb: **adds, adding, added**)

addendum »*noun* (plural **addenda**) an extra item added at the end of a book or text.
– say uh-**den**-duhm

> ☑ like many other words ending in **um** derived from Latin, **addendum** has a plural ending in **a**: **addenda**

adder »*noun* a poisonous snake with a dark zigzag pattern on its back.

addict

addicted

addiction
addictive

adding

addition

additional
additionally

additive »*noun* a substance added to improve or preserve something.

addled »*adjective* ❶ (of an egg) rotten. ❷ confused or intoxicated.

address (plural **addresses**; verb: **addresses**, **addressing**, **addressed**)
addressee

> ✓ remember the double **d**: **address**

adds

adduce »*verb* (**adduces**, **adducing**, **adduced**) refer to something as evidence.
– sᴀʏ uh-**dyooss**

adenoids »*plural noun* a mass of tissue between the back of the nose and the throat, which in some young people becomes enlarged and hinders speech or breathing.
– sᴀʏ ad-uh-noydz

adept »*adjective* very skilled or able.
»*noun* a person who is very skilled at something.
adeptly
adeptness

adequate
adequacy
adequately

adhere »*verb* (**adheres**, **adhering**, **adhered**) stick firmly to something.
adherence

adherent »*noun* a person who supports a particular party, person, or set of ideas.
»*adjective* sticking firmly to an object or surface.

> ✓ the ending is **ent** not **ant**: **adherent**

adheres

adhering

adhesion

adhesive »*adjective* sticky.
»*noun* a substance which causes things to stick.
adhesively
adhesiveness

ad hoc »*adjective & adverb* created or done for one particular occasion only.

> ⓘ **ad hoc** is a Latin phrase literally meaning 'to this'

adieu »*exclamation* (an old word) goodbye.

ad infinitum »*adverb* endlessly; forever.
– sᴀʏ ad in-fi-**ny**-tuhm

> ⓘ **ad infinitum** is a Latin phrase literally meaning 'to infinity'

adipose »*adjective* having to do with fatty body tissue.
– sᴀʏ ad-i-pohss

adjacent

adjective »*noun* a word used to describe a noun or to make its meaning clearer, such as *sweet*, *red*, or *technical*.
adjectival

adjoin (verb: **adjoins**, **adjoining**, **adjoined**)

adjourn »*verb* (**adjourns**, **adjourning**, **adjourned**) ❶ break off a meeting until later. ❷ postpone a decision.
adjournment

adjudge (verb: **adjudges**, **adjudging**, **adjudged**)

adjudicate »*verb* (**adjudicates**, **adjudicating**, **adjudicated**) ❶ make a formal judgement. ❷ judge a competition.
adjudication
adjudicator

adjunct »*noun* an additional and supplementary part.

adjure »*verb* (**adjures**, **adjuring**, **adjured**) solemnly urge someone to do something.
– sᴀʏ uh-**joor**

adjust (verb: **adjusts**, **adjusting**, **adjusted**)
adjustability
adjustable
adjuster
adjustment

adjutant »*noun* a military officer who helps a senior officer with administrative work.
– sᴀʏ a-juu-tuhnt

ad-lib »*verb* (**ad-libs**, **ad-libbing**, **ad-libbed**) speak in public without preparing your words beforehand.
»*noun* an unprepared remark or speech.

> ⓘ a shortened form of the Latin phrase *ad libitum* 'according to pleasure'

administer »*verb* (**administers**, **administering**, **administered**) ❶ organize or put into effect. ❷ give out or apply a drug or remedy.

administrate »*verb* (**administrates**, **administrating**, **administrated**) manage the affairs of an organization or company.

administration

administrative

administrator

admirable
admirably

admiral

Admiralty »*noun* the British government department formerly in charge of the Royal Navy.

admire (verb: admires, admiring, admired)
admiration
admirer

admissible »*adjective* ❶ acceptable or valid. ❷ having the right to be allowed in to a place.
admissibility

✓ -ible not -able: admissible

admission

admit (verb: admits, admitting, admitted)
admittance

admix »*verb* (admixes, admixing, admixed) mix with something else.
admixture

admonish »*verb* (admonishes, admonishing, admonished) ❶ reprimand firmly. ❷ urge or warn seriously.
admonishment

admonition »*noun* a reprimand or warning.
– say ad-muh-**ni**-sh'n
admonitory

ad nauseam »*adverb* so frequently that people become bored or angry.
– say ad **naw**-zi-am

ℹ️ ad nauseam is a Latin phrase literally meaning 'to sickness'

ado »*noun* trouble; fuss.

adobe »*noun* a kind of clay used to make sun-dried bricks.
– say uh-**doh**-bi

adolescent »*adjective* in the process of developing from a child into an adult. »*noun* an adolescent boy or girl.
adolescence

Adonis »*noun* (plural Adonises) an extremely handsome young man.
– say uh-**doh**-nis

ℹ️ Adonis was the name of a beautiful youth in Greek mythology

adopt »*verb* (adopts, adopting, adopted) ❶ legally take someone else's child and bring it up as your own. ❷ take up or follow a course of action, attitude, etc.
adoptable
adoptee
adopter
adoption

adoptive »*adjective* (of a parent) having adopted a child.

ℹ️ children are **adopted**, their parents are **adoptive**

adopts

adorable »*adjective* very lovable or charming.
adorably

adore »*verb* (adores, adoring, adored) love and respect deeply.
adoration
adorer

adorn »*verb* (adorns, adorning, adorned) make something more attractive or beautiful; decorate.
adornment

adrenal glands »*plural noun* a pair of glands above the kidneys which produce adrenalin and other hormones.
– say uh-**dree**-nuhl

adrenalin »*noun* a hormone produced in response to stress, that increases rates of blood circulation, breathing, and metabolism.
– say uh-**dre**-nuh-lin

✓ scientists usually spell this word with a final **e**: **adrenaline**

Adriatic »*adjective* referring to the arm of the Mediterranean Sea between Italy and the Balkans.
– say ay-dri-**at**-ik

adrift

adroit »*adjective* clever or skilful in using the hands or mind.
– say uh-**droyt**

adulation »*noun* excessive admiration.
adulatory

adult

adulterate »*verb* (adulterates, adulterating, adulterated) make poorer in quality by adding another substance.
adulteration

adulterer »*noun* a person who has committed adultery.

adulteress »*noun* (plural adulteresses) a female adulterer.

adultery »*noun* sex between a married person and someone who is not their husband or wife.
adulterous

adulthood

adumbrate »*verb* (adumbrates, adumbrating, adumbrated) ❶ give a faint or general idea of. ❷ be a warning of.
– say ad-um-**brayt**
adumbration

advance (verb: advances, advancing, advanced)
advancement

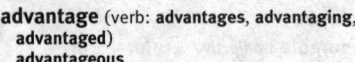

advantage (verb: **advantages, advantaging, advantaged**)
advantageous

advent »*noun* ❶ the arrival of an important person or thing. ❷ (**Advent**) (in Christian belief) the coming or second coming of Jesus. ❸ (**Advent**) the period of time leading up to Christmas.

adventitious »*adjective* happening by chance.
– sᴀʏ ad-vuhn-**ti**-shuhss
adventitiously

adventure

adventurer »*noun* ❶ a person willing to take risks or use dishonest methods for their own gain: *a political adventurer.* ❷ a person who enjoys or seeks adventure.

adventuress »*noun* (plural **adventuresses**) a female adventurer.

adventurous
adventurously
adventurousness

adverb »*noun* a word that makes the meaning of an adjective, verb, or other adverb more specific (e.g *gently, very, fortunately*).
adverbial

adversarial »*adjective* having to do with conflict or opposition.
– sᴀʏ ad-ver-**sair**-i-uhl
adversarially

adversary »*noun* (plural **adversaries**) an opponent or enemy.
– sᴀʏ **ad**-ver-suh-ri

adverse »*adjective* harmful; unfavourable: *adverse publicity.*
adversely

> ℹ️ do not confuse **adverse** with **averse**, which means 'strongly disliking or opposed', as in *I am not averse to helping out*

adversity »*noun* (plural **adversities**) difficulty; misfortune.

advert[1] »*noun* an advertisement.
– sᴀʏ **ad**-vert

advert[2] »*verb* (**adverts, adverting, adverted**) refer to something.
– sᴀʏ uhd-**vert**

advertise (verb: **advertises, advertising, advertised**)
advertiser

> ☑️ unlike most verbs ending in **ise**, **advertise** cannot be spelled with an **ize** ending

advertisement

> ☑️ remember to keep the final **e** of **advertise** in **advertisement**

advertiser
advertises
advertising
adverts
advice

advisable »*adjective* to be recommended; sensible.
advisability

advise (verb: **advises, advising, advised**)
advisedly
adviser

> ☑️ **advise** cannot be spelled with an **ize** ending

advisory »*adjective* having the power to make recommendations but not to make sure that they are carried out.

advocaat »*noun* a liqueur made with eggs, sugar, and brandy.
– sᴀʏ **ad**-vuh-kah

> ☑️ double **a** before the **t**: **advocaat** is a Dutch word literally meaning 'an advocate or lawyer'

advocate »*noun* ❶ a person who publicly supports or recommends a particular cause or policy. ❷ a person who pleads a case on someone else's behalf. ❸ (in Scotland) a barrister.
» *verb* (**advocates, advocating, advocated**) publicly recommend or support.
advocacy

adze »*noun* a tool similar to an axe, with an arched blade.

Aegean »*adjective* referring to the part of the Mediterranean Sea between Greece and Turkey.
– sᴀʏ i-**jee**-uhn

aegis »*noun* the protection, backing, or support of someone.
– sᴀʏ **ee**-jiss

aeon »*noun* an extremely long period of time.
– sᴀʏ **ee**-on

> ☑️ scientists often use the American spelling, with just **e** rather than **ae**: **eon** (this pattern is followed in other British and American spellings, e.g. an*ae*mia/an*e*mia)

aerate »*verb* (**aerates, aerating, aerated**) introduce air into something.
aeration
aerator

> ☑️ **aer** not **air**, and **ate** not **iate**: **aerate, aerated**

aerial »*noun* a device that sends out or receives radio or television signals.
» *adjective* ❶ existing or taking place in the air. ❷ involving the use of aircraft.

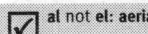 al not el: **aerial**

aerobatics »*noun* exciting and daring flying performed for display.
aerobatic

aerobic »*adjective* ❶ (of exercise) intended to increase the amount of oxygen you breathe in and make it move around the body more quickly. ❷ (in biology) using oxygen from the air.
– SAY air-**oh**-bik
aerobically

☑ **aerobic** is one of a group of words based on Greek *aēr* 'air' and therefore spelled with an **e**: **aerobic, aerodrome, aerosol,** etc.

aerobics »*noun* aerobic exercises.

aerodrome »*noun* an airfield.

aerodynamic »*adjective* ❶ relating to aerodynamics. ❷ having a shape which moves through the air quickly.
aerodynamically

aerodynamics »*noun* ❶ the study of the movement of solid bodies through the air. ❷ the aspects of an object which make it good or bad at moving through the air.

aeronautics »*noun* the study or practice of travel through the air.
aeronautic
aeronautical

aeroplane »*noun* a powered flying vehicle with fixed wings.

☑ **aer** not **air**: **aeroplane**. Note that the American equivalent is **airplane**.

aerosol »*noun* a substance sealed in a container under pressure and released as a fine spray.

aerospace

aesthete »*noun* a person who appreciates art and beauty.
– SAY eess-**theet**

aesthetic »*adjective* ❶ having to do with beauty or the appreciation of beauty. ❷ having a pleasant appearance.
» *noun* ❶ (aesthetics) a set of principles relating to the nature of beauty. ❷ the set of principles behind the work of an artist or movement: *the Cubist aesthetic.*
– SAY eess-**thet**-ik
aesthetically

☑ the correct spellings are **aesthete, aesthetic, aesthetics,** although in

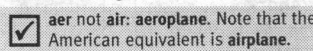 America they are sometimes spelled with **es**: **esthete, esthetic, esthetics**

aether another way of spelling ETHER.

☑ the old spelling **aether** is only used to refer to the air or sky, not in the chemical meaning of **ether**

aetiology »*noun* the investigation of causes, especially of disease.
– SAY ee-ti-**ol**-uhji
aetiological

afar »*adverb* at or to a distance.

affable »*adjective* good-natured and friendly.
affability
affably

affair

affect »*verb* (affects, affecting, affected) ❶ make a difference to; have an effect on: *the changes will affect everyone.* ❷ touch the feelings of. ❸ pretend to have a particular feeling. ❹ wear something or behave in a particular way in an attempt to impress people: *he affected an upper-class frostiness.*

ℹ do not confuse **affect** with **effect**, which is used both as a noun meaning 'a result' (*the substance has a painkilling effect*) and as a verb meaning 'bring about a result' (*she effected a cost-cutting exercise*)

affectation »*noun* behaviour that is artificial and designed to impress people.
– SAY af-fek-**tay**-sh'n

affected »*adjective* artificial and designed to impress people.
affectedly

affecting

affection »*noun* a feeling of fondness or liking.

affectionate »*adjective* readily showing affection.
affectionately

affects

affidavit »*noun* a written statement that a person swears is true and that can be used as evidence in a law court.
– SAY af-fi-**day**-vit

☑ double f: **affidavit** is a Latin word meaning 'he has stated on oath'

affiliate »*verb* (affiliates, affiliating, affiliated) officially link a person or group to an organization.
» *noun* an affiliated person or group.
– SAY uh-**fil**-i-ayt [verb], uh-**fil**-i-uht [noun]
affiliation

a

affinity »*noun* (plural **affinities**) ❶ a natural liking or understanding. ❷ a close relationship between people or things with similar qualities.

affirm »*verb* (**affirms, affirming, affirmed**) state firmly or publicly.
affirmation

affirmative »*adjective* agreeing with a statement, or consenting to a request.
» *noun* a statement or word indicating agreement, such as 'yes'.
affirmatively

affirmed

affirming

affirms

affix »*verb* (**affixes, affixing, affixed**) attach or fasten something to something else.
– SAY uh-**fiks**

afflict »*verb* (**afflicts, afflicting, afflicted**) cause pain or suffering to someone: *she was afflicted with a skin disease.*
affliction

> **i** do not confuse **afflict** with **inflict**, which means 'be the cause of', as in *they inflicted serious injuries on three men*

affluent »*adjective* wealthy.
affluence

afford (verb: **affords, affording, afforded**)
affordability
affordable

afforest »*verb* (**afforests, afforesting, afforested**) change land into forest.
– SAY uh-**for**-rist
afforestation

affray »*noun* (an old word) a breach of the peace by fighting in a public place.

affront »*noun* an action or remark that offends someone.
» *verb* (**affronts, affronting, affronted**) offend someone.

Afghan [of Afghanistan]

> **✓** remember the h: **Afghan**

Afghan hound »*noun* a silky-haired dog used for hunting.

aficionado »*noun* (plural **aficionados**) a person who knows a lot about an activity or subject and is very keen on it.
– SAY uh-fi-shuh-**nah**-doh

> **✓** single f: **aficionado** is a Spanish word originally meaning 'person who is fond of bullfighting'

afield »*adverb* to or at a distance.

aflame »*adjective* in flames.

afloat

afoot »*adverb & adjective* in preparation or progress.

aforementioned »*adjective* previously mentioned.

afraid

afresh »*adverb* in a new or different way.

African

African American »*noun* an American of African origin; an American black person.
» *adjective* relating to African Americans.

Afrikaans »*noun* a language of southern Africa derived from Dutch.
– SAY af-ri-**kahns**

Afrikaner »*noun* an Afrikaans-speaking white person in South Africa.
– SAY af-ri-**kah**-ner

Afro-Caribbean »*noun* a person of African descent living in or coming from the Caribbean.
» *adjective* relating to Afro-Caribbeans.

aft »*adverb & adjective* at, near, or towards the stern of a ship or tail of an aircraft.

after

afterbirth »*noun* the placenta and other material discharged from the womb after a birth.

aftercare

after-effect »*noun* an effect that occurs after its cause has gone.

afterlife »*noun* a supposed life after death.

aftermath »*noun* the consequences of an unpleasant or disastrous event.

afternoon

aftershave

aftershock »*noun* a smaller earthquake immediately following a large one.

aftertaste

afterthought

afterward

afterwards

again

against

agape »*adjective* (of a person's mouth) wide open.

agate »*noun* an ornamental stone marked with bands of colour.
– SAY **ag**-uht

agave »*noun* an American plant with narrow spiny leaves.
– SAY uh-**gay**-vi

age (verb: **ages, ageing** or **aging, aged**)

aged

ageing

☑ more often spelled with an **e**, although both **ageing** and **aging** are correct

ageless »*adjective* not ageing or appearing to age.
agelessness

agency (plural **agencies**)

☑ plural: drop the **y** and add **ies**: **agencies**

agenda »*noun* ❶ a list of items to be discussed at a meeting. ❷ a list of matters to be dealt with.

ⓘ **agenda** is the plural of the Latin word **agendum**, but in English it is used as a singular noun with the plural **agendas**

agent

agent provocateur »*noun* (plural **agents provocateurs**) a person who tempts suspected criminals to commit a crime and therefore be convicted.
– sᴀʏ a-*zh*on pruh-vo-kuh-**ter**

ⓘ as in the original French, the plural has the same pronunciation as the singular, with both **s**'s silent

age-old »*adjective* having existed for a very long time.

ages

agglomerate »*verb* (**agglomerates, agglomerating, agglomerated**) collect or form into a mass.
– sᴀʏ uh-**glom**-uh-rayt
agglomeration

agglutinate »*verb* (**agglutinates, agglutinating, agglutinated**) firmly stick together to form a mass.
– sᴀʏ uh-**gloo**-ti-nayt
agglutination

aggrandize »*verb* (**aggrandizes, aggrandizing, aggrandized**) make someone or something more powerful, important, or impressive.
– sᴀʏ uh-**gran**-dyz
aggrandizement

☑ double **g**: aggrandize
many people prefer the alternative spellings **aggrandise, aggrandises**, etc., and **aggrandisement**: both **s** and **z** spellings are correct

aggravate »*verb* (**aggravates, aggravating, aggravated**) ❶ make something worse. ❷ (in informal English) annoy or exasperate someone.
aggravation

ⓘ the use of **aggravate** to mean 'annoy or exasperate' is not regarded as correct English

aggregate »*noun* ❶ a whole or total formed by combining several separate items. ❷ pieces of broken stone or gravel used to make concrete.
» *adjective* formed or calculated by combining items together.
» *verb* (**aggregates, aggregating, aggregated**) combine into a whole.
– sᴀʏ ag-gri-guht [noun and adjective], ag-gri-gayt [verb]
aggregation

aggression »*noun* hostile or violent behaviour or attitudes.

aggressive »*adjective* ❶ very angry or hostile. ❷ too forceful.
aggressively
aggressiveness

aggressor »*noun* a person or country that attacks another without being provoked.

aggrieved »*adjective* resentful because you feel you have been treated unfairly.

☑ the usual rule is **i** before **e** except after **c**: aggrieved

aghast »*adjective* filled with horror or shock.
– sᴀʏ uh-**gahst**

agile »*adjective* ❶ able to move quickly and easily. ❷ quick-witted or shrewd.
agilely
agility

aging another way of spelling AGEING.

agitate »*verb* (**agitates, agitating, agitated**) ❶ make someone troubled or nervous. ❷ campaign to arouse public concern about an issue. ❸ stir or disturb a liquid briskly.
agitation

agitator »*noun* a person who urges others to protest or rebel.

AGM »*abbreviation* annual general meeting.

agnostic »*noun* a person who thinks that it is impossible to know whether or not God exists.
– sᴀʏ ag-**noss**-tik
agnosticism

ago

agog »*adjective* very eager to hear or see something.

agonies

agonize »*verb* (**agonizes, agonizing, agonized**) worry greatly about something.

☑ many people prefer the alternative spellings **agonise, agonising**, etc.: both **s** and **z** spellings are correct

agony »*noun* (plural **agonies**) extreme suffering.

☑ plural: drop the **y** and add **ies**: **agonies**

agoraphobia »*noun* abnormal fear of open or public places.
– SAY ag-uh-ruh-**foh**-bi-uh
agoraphobic

☑ the beginning is **agora-**, from the Greek word *agora* 'public open space', not **agro-**: **agoraphobia**

agrarian »*adjective* having to do with agriculture.
– SAY uh-**grair**-i-uhn

agree (verb: **agrees**, **agreeing**, **agreed**)

agreeable »*adjective* ❶ pleasant. ❷ willing to agree to something. ❸ acceptable.
agreeableness
agreeably

agreed

agreeing

agreement

agrees

agriculture »*noun* the science or practice of farming.
agricultural
agriculturally

aground »*adjective & adverb* (with reference to a ship) on or on to the bottom in shallow water.

ague »*noun* (an old word) malaria or some other illness involving fever and shivering.
– SAY **ay**-gyoo

ahead

AI »*abbreviation* artificial intelligence.

aid (verb: **aids**, **aiding**, **aided**)

aide »*noun* an assistant to a political leader.

aided

aide-de-camp »*noun* (plural **aides-de-camp**) a military officer acting as a personal assistant to a senior officer.
– SAY ayd-duh-**kom**

ⓘ as in the original French, the plural has the same pronunciation as the singular, with a silent **s**

aiding

Aids »*noun* a disease, caused by the HIV virus and transmitted in body fluids, which breaks down a person's natural defences against infection.

ⓘ the word **Aids** is an acronym standing for 'acquired immune deficiency syndrome'

aids

aikido »*noun* a Japanese martial art that uses locks, holds, throws, and the opponent's own movements.
– SAY I-kee-doh

ail »*verb* (**ails**, **ailing**, **ailed**) (an old word) cause someone to be ill or have problems.

ⓘ do not confuse **ail** and **ails** with **ale** and **ales**, which refer to beer

aileron »*noun* a hinged part of an aircraft's wing, used to control balance.
– SAY **ayl**-uh-ron

ailing

ailment »*noun* a minor illness.

ails

aim (verb: **aims**, **aiming**, **aimed**)

aimless

aims

ain't

ⓘ **ain't**, used to mean 'is not', 'are not', or 'am not', is not good English and should never be used in writing or formal speech

air (verb: **airs**, **airing**, **aired**) [the atmosphere; a manner or impression; a short tune]

ⓘ do not confuse **air** with **heir**, which sounds the same but means 'person who will inherit something when another person dies'

airbase

airborne

 ☑ do not forget the **e**: **airborne**

airbrush »*noun* an artist's device for spraying paint using compressed air.
» *verb* (**airbrushes**, **airbrushing**, **airbrushed**) paint or alter with an airbrush.

air conditioning
air-conditioned

aircraft (plural **aircraft**)

aircrew

aired

Airedale »*noun* a large black-and-tan terrier.

ⓘ from *Airedale* in Yorkshire

airer

airfield

air force

air-freshener

air gun

airily

airiness

airing

airless

airlift (verb: **airlifts, airlifting, airlifted**)

airline

airliner

airlock

airmail

airman (plural **airmen**)

airplane »*noun* (in American English) = AEROPLANE.

airplay

airport

air raid

airs

air-sea rescue

airship

airspace »*noun* the part of the air above a particular country.

airstrip

airtight

airtime »*noun* time during which a broadcast is being transmitted.

airwaves »*plural noun* the radio frequencies used for broadcasting.

airway »*noun* ❶ the passage by which air reaches the lungs. ❷ a recognized route followed by aircraft.

airwoman (plural **airwomen**)

airworthy »*adjective* (of an aircraft) safe to fly.
  airworthiness

airy (adjective: **airier, airiest**)
  airily
  airiness

> ✓ drop the **y** and add **ier** or **iest** to spell **airier** or **airiest**

airy-fairy »*adjective* vague and unrealistic or impractical.

aisle »*noun* a passage between rows of seats in a church or other public building or between shelves in a shop.
– **SAY** *rhymes with* mile

> ℹ do not confuse **aisle** with **isle**, meaning 'island', which sounds the same

aitch »*noun* the letter H.

ajar »*adverb & adjective* (of a door or window) slightly open.

aka »*abbreviation* also known as.

akimbo »*adverb* with hands on the hips and elbows turned outwards.

akin »*adjective* ❶ of similar character. ❷ related by blood.

alabaster »*noun* a white, semi-transparent mineral that is often carved into ornaments.
» *adjective* smooth and white: *pale, alabaster skin.*

a la carte »*adjective & adverb* (of a menu) offering dishes that are separately priced, rather than part of a set meal.

> ✓ **a la carte** can also be written **à la carte**, with a grave accent on the **a** (as in the original French): it means literally 'according to the card'

alacrity »*noun* brisk eagerness or enthusiasm.
– **SAY** uh-**lak**-ri-ti

Aladdin's cave »*noun* a place filled with lots of interesting or precious items.

> ✓ single **l**, double **d**: **Aladdin**

a la mode »*adverb & adjective* up to date; fashionable.
– **SAY** ah lah **mohd**

> ✓ **a la mode** can also be written **à la mode**, with a grave accent on the **a** (as in the original French): it means literally 'in the fashion'

alarm (verb: **alarms, alarming, alarmed**)

alarmist »*noun* a person who exaggerates a danger and causes needless alarm.
» *adjective* causing needless alarm.

alarms

alas

Albanian

albatross »*noun* (plural **albatrosses**) a very large seabird with long, narrow wings.
– **SAY** al-buh-tross

> ✓ remember the double **s** at the end: **albatross**

albeit »*conjunction* though.
– **SAY** awl-**bee**-it

> ✓ spell as one word, **albeit**, rather than *all be it*

albino »*noun* (plural **albinos**) a person or animal born without pigment in the skin and hair (which are white) and the eyes (which are usually pink).
– **SAY** al-**bee**-noh

> ✓ the plural of **albino** has **os** not **oes**: **albinos**

album

albumen »*noun* egg white.
– **SAY** al-byuu-muhn

alchemy »*noun* a medieval form of chemistry concerned particularly with

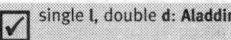

a

trying to change ordinary metals into gold.
– **say** al-kuh-mi
alchemist

alcohol
alcoholic

alcoholism »*noun* addiction to alcoholic drink.

alcopop »*noun* a ready-mixed fizzy drink containing alcohol.

alcove »*noun* a recess in the wall of a room.

al dente »*adjective & adverb* (of food) cooked so as to be still firm when bitten.
– **say** al **den**-tay

> ℹ️ an Italian phrase literally meaning 'to the tooth'

alder »*noun* a tree which produces catkins, related to the birch.

alderman »*noun* (plural **aldermen**) (mainly a historical term) a member of a council below the rank of Mayor.

ale [kind of beer]

> ℹ️ do not confuse **ale** and **ales** with **ail** and **ails** meaning 'cause someone to be ill'

alert (verb: **alerts, alerting, alerted**)
alertly
alertness

A level »*noun* the advanced level of the GCE examination.

Alexander technique »*noun* a system designed to promote well-being through the control of posture.

alfalfa »*noun* a plant like clover with bluish flowers, used as food for animals.
– **say** al-**fal**-fuh

alfresco »*adverb & adjective* in the open air.
– **say** al-**fress**-koh

> ℹ️ from the Italian phrase *al fresco* meaning 'in the fresh air'

algae »*plural noun* simple plants that do not have true stems, roots, and leaves, e.g. seaweed.
– **say** al-jee or al-gee

> ℹ️ the singular form of **algae** is **alga** and is most often used by scientists; the word comes from Latin *alga*, meaning 'seaweed'

algebra »*noun* the part of mathematics in which letters and other symbols are used to represent numbers and quantities.
– **say** al-ji-bruh

Algerian

algorithm »*noun* a procedure or set of rules used in a mathematical calculation or other complicated operation.
– **say** al-guh-ri-*th*'m

> ☑️ -rithm not -rhythm: algorithm

alias »*adverb* also known as.
» *noun* (plural **aliases**) a false identity.
– **say** ay-li-uhss

> ℹ️ **alias** is a Latin word meaning 'at another time, otherwise'

alibi »*noun* (plural **alibis**) a piece of evidence that someone was elsewhere when a crime was committed.
– **say** a-li-bI

> ℹ️ the word **alibi** refers to something that proves a person could not have committed a crime; do not use it to mean 'an excuse for not doing something'

> ☑️ the plural has **is** not **ies** at the end: alibis

alien »*adjective* ❶ belonging to a foreign country. ❷ unfamiliar and unattractive: *principles that are alien to them.* ❸ from another world.
» *noun* ❶ a foreigner. ❷ a being from another world.
– **say** ay-li-uhn
alienness

> ☑️ the ending is **en** not **an**: alien

alienate »*verb* (**alienates, alienating, alienated**) ❶ make someone feel isolated. ❷ lose the support or sympathy of.
alienation

alienness

alight[1] »*verb* (**alights, alighting, alighted**) ❶ get down from a vehicle. ❷ (**alight on**) happen to notice.

alight[2] »*adverb & adjective* ❶ on fire. ❷ shining brightly.

align »*verb* (**aligns, aligning, aligned**) ❶ place something in a straight line or in the correct position in relation to others. ❷ (**align yourself with**) be on the side of.
alignment

> ☑️ single **l**, and **ign** not **ine**: align, alignment

alike

alimentary canal »*noun* the passage along which food passes through the body.

alimony »*noun* financial support for a husband or wife after separation or divorce.
– **say** a-li-muh-ni

alive

alkali »*noun* (plural **alkalis**) a substance which can neutralize acids and turn litmus blue, and can often burn the skin.
– SAY al-kuh-lI
alkaline

☑ the plural has **is** not **ies** at the end: **alkalis**

all

Allah »*noun* the name of God among Muslims and Arab Christians.
– SAY al-luh

allay »*verb* (**allays**, **allaying**, **allayed**) reduce or end fear, worry, or difficulty.
– SAY uh-lay

all-clear »*noun* a signal that danger or difficulty is over.

allegation »*noun* a claim that someone has done something illegal or wrong.

allege »*verb* (**alleges**, **alleging**, **alleged**) claim that someone has done something illegal or wrong.
– SAY uh-lej
allegedly

☑ -**lege** not -**ledge**: **allege**, **alleged**

allegiance »*noun* loyalty to a person of higher status or to a group or cause.
– SAY uh-lee-juhnss

alleging

allegory »*noun* (plural **allegories**) a story, poem, or picture which contains a hidden meaning.
– SAY al-li-guh-ri
allegorical

allegretto »*adverb & adjective* (in music) to be played at a fairly brisk tempo.
– SAY al-li-gret-toh

allegro »*adverb & adjective* (in music) to be played at a brisk tempo.
– SAY uh-lay-groh

alleluia another way of spelling HALLELUJAH.

Allen screw »*noun* (trademark) a screw with a hexagonal socket in the head.

allergen »*noun* a substance that causes an allergic reaction.
– SAY al-ler-juhn

allergenic »*adjective* likely to cause an allergic reaction.
– SAY al-ler-jen-ik

allergic »*adjective* caused by or having an allergy.
– SAY al-ler-jik

allergy »*noun* (plural **allergies**) a medical condition that makes you feel unwell when you come into contact with a particular substance.

– SAY al-ler-ji

☑ plural: drop the **y** and add **ies**: **allergies**

alleviate »*verb* (**alleviates**, **alleviating**, **alleviated**) make a pain or problem less severe.
– SAY uh-lee-vi-ayt
alleviation

alley

alleyway

alliance

☑ **ance** not **ence**: **alliance**

allied

☑ use a capital **a** in **Allied** when referring to Britain and its allies in the First and Second World Wars

allies

alligator

all-in »*adjective* including everything.

alliteration »*noun* the occurrence of the same letter or sound at the beginning of words next to or close to each other.
– SAY uh-lit-uh-ray-sh'n
alliterative

☑ double **l** but two single **t**'s: **alliteration**

allocate (verb: **allocates**, **allocating**, **allocated**)
allocation

allot »*verb* (**allots**, **allotting**, **allotted**) give out as a share or assign to.

☑ remember the double **l**, and do not confuse **allot** with **a lot** meaning 'a large amount'

allotment »*noun* ❶ a small plot of rented land for growing vegetables or flowers. ❷ the action of allotting or an amount of something allotted.

allots

allotted

allotting

allow (verb: **allows**, **allowing**, **allowed**)
allowable

allowance

allowed

ⓘ do not confuse **allowed** meaning 'permitted' with **aloud** meaning 'out loud'

allowing

allows

alloy »*noun* ❶ a mixture of two or more metals. ❷ an inferior metal mixed with a precious one.

» *verb* (**alloys, alloying, alloyed**) ❶ mix metals to make an alloy. ❷ spoil by adding something inferior.
– say al-loy [noun], uh-**loy** [verb]

all right » *adjective* ❶ satisfactory; acceptable. ❷ permitted.
» *adverb* fairly well.

> ℹ️ use **all right** rather than **alright** in formal writing

all-round

all-rounder » *noun* a person with a wide range of skills.

allspice » *noun* the dried fruit of a Caribbean tree, used as a spice in cookery.

all-time » *adjective* not having been bettered or beaten: *the all-time record.*

allude » *verb* (**alludes, alluding, alluded**) (**allude to**) ❶ hint at. ❷ mention in passing.
– say uh-**lood**

> ℹ️ do not confuse **allude** with **elude** meaning 'evade or escape from'

allure » *noun* powerful attractiveness or charm.

alluring

allusion » *noun* an indirect reference to something.

> ℹ️ do not confuse **allusion** with **illusion** meaning 'something which seems real or true but is not'

ally » *noun* (plural **allies**) ❶ a person, organization, or country that cooperates with another. ❷ (**the Allies**) the countries that fought with Britain in the First and Second World Wars.
» *verb* (**allies, allying, allied**) ❶ side with. ❷ combine one resource with another in a way that benefits both.
– say al-**II** [noun], uh-**II** [verb]

> ✅ plural: drop the **y** and add **ies: allies**

alma mater » *noun* the school, college, or university that a person once attended.
– say al-muh **mah**-ter or **may**-ter

> ℹ️ **alma mater** means 'bountiful mother' in Latin

almanac » *noun* ❶ a calendar that gives important dates and information about the sun, moon, tides, etc. ❷ a book published every year and containing useful information for that year.
– say al-muh-nak

> ✅ **almanac** can also be spelled **almanack**. The **ack** spelling is mainly used in titles, such as *Whitaker's Almanack.*

almighty » *adjective* ❶ having unlimited or very great power. ❷ (in informal English) enormous.
» *noun* (**the Almighty**) God.

almond

almost

alms » *plural noun* (a historical term) charitable gifts of money or food to the poor.
– say ahmz

almshouse » *noun* a house built for poor people to live in.

aloe » *noun* a tropical plant whose bitter juice is used in medicine.
– say a-loh

aloe vera » *noun* a jelly-like substance obtained from a kind of aloe, used as a soothing treatment for the skin.
– say a-loh **veer**-uh

> ℹ️ **aloe vera** means 'true aloe' in Latin

aloft » *adjective & adverb* up in or into the air.

alone

along

alongside

aloof » *adjective* cool and distant.
aloofness

alopecia » *noun* abnormal loss of hair.
– say a-luh-**pee**-shuh

aloud

> ℹ️ do not confuse **aloud** meaning 'out loud' with **allowed** meaning 'permitted'

alpaca » *noun* a long-haired South American mammal related to the llama.
– say al-**pak**-uh

alpha » *noun* the first letter of the Greek alphabet (A, α).

alphabet

alphabetical
alphabetically

alpine » *adjective* ❶ relating to or found on high mountains. ❷ (**Alpine**) relating to the Alps.

already

alright another way of spelling **ALL RIGHT**.

> ℹ️ when writing, use the spelling **all right** rather than **alright**

Alsatian » *noun* a German shepherd dog.

> ✅ **atian** not **ation: Alsatian**

also

also-ran » *noun* a loser in a race or contest.

altar »*noun* **❶** the table in a Christian church at which the bread and wine are blessed in communion services. **❷** a table on which offerings to a god or goddess are made.

> ☑ ar not er: altar

alter (verb: **alters, altering, altered**)
alteration

altercation »*noun* a noisy disagreement.
– SAY awl-ter-**kay**-sh'n

altered

alter ego »*noun* **❶** a person's alternative personality. **❷** a close friend who is very like yourself.
– SAY awl-ter ee-goh

> ℹ **alter ego** is a Latin phrase meaning 'other self'

altering

alternate »*verb* (**alternates, alternating, alternated**) **❶** (of two things or people) repeatedly follow one another in turn. **❷** keep changing between two states.
»*adjective* **❶** every other. **❷** (of two things) each following and succeeded by the other in a regular pattern.
– SAY awl-ter-nayt [verb], awl-**ter**-nuht [adjective]
alternately
alternation

> ℹ do not use **alternate** to mean **alternative**: this use is American

alternating current »*noun* an electric current that reverses its direction many times a second, as opposed to a *direct current*.

alternation

alternative »*adjective* **❶** (of one or more things) available as another possibility. **❷** different from what is usual or traditional: *alternative medicine.*
»*noun* one of two or more available possibilities.
alternatively

> ℹ be careful how you use **alternative** in formal situations. Some people say that you can only have two alternatives (because the word **alternative** comes from Latin *alter* 'other of two'), and that strictly speaking it is wrong to refer to three (or more) alternatives.

alternative medicine »*noun* treatment regarded as unorthodox by the medical profession, such as herbalism.

alternator »*noun* a dynamo that generates an alternating current.

alters

although

> ☑ remember, one l: although

altimeter »*noun* an instrument which indicates the altitude that has been reached.
– SAY al-ti-mee-ter

altitude »*noun* the height of an object or point above sea level or ground level.

alto »*noun* (plural **altos**) the highest adult male or lowest female singing voice.
– SAY **al**-toh

> ☑ the plural of **alto** has **os** not **oes**: altos

altogether

> ℹ use **altogether** to mean 'completely' or 'on the whole', as in *things were now altogether different*. Otherwise **all** and **together** should be treated as separate words, as in *the glue that holds them all together*.

altruism »*noun* unselfish concern for others.
– SAY al-troo-iz'm
altruist
altruistic

aluminium »*noun* a lightweight silvery-grey metal.
– SAY al-yoo-**min**-i-uhm

> ☑ nium not num: aluminium (the spelling **aluminum** is American)

alumna »*noun* (plural **alumnae**) a female alumnus.
– SAY uh-**lum**-nuh [singular], uh-**lum**-nee [plural]

> ☑ make the plural by adding an **e** (like the original Latin): alumnae

alumnus »*noun* (plural **alumni**) a former student of a particular school, college, or university.
– SAY uh-**lum**-nuhss [singular], uh-**lum**-nI [plural]

> ℹ the feminine form of **alumnus** is **alumna**

> ☑ make the plural by changing the **us** ending to **i** (like the original Latin): alumni

always

Alzheimer's disease »*noun* a disease of older people, which affects the functioning of the brain.
– SAY alts-hy-merz

> ☑ e before i: Alzheimer's (the disease is named after the German neurologist Alois *Alzheimer*)

AM »*abbreviation* amplitude modulation.

am

a.m. »*abbreviation* before noon.

> ℹ️ from the Latin phrase *ante meridiem*

amalgam »*noun* ❶ a mixture or blend of two or more things. ❷ an alloy of mercury with another metal.
– SAY uh-**mal**-guhm

amalgamate »*verb* (**amalgamates, amalgamating, amalgamated**) combine two or more things to form one organization or structure.
– SAY uh-**mal**-guh-mayt
amalgamation

amanuensis »*noun* (plural **amanuenses**) a literary assistant.
– SAY uh-man-yoo-**en**-siss [singular], uh-man-yoo-**en**-seez [plural]

> ✅ make the plural by changing the **-is** ending to **-es** (like the original Latin): **amanuenses**

amaryllis »*noun* (plural **amaryllis**) a plant with large trumpet-shaped flowers.
– SAY am-uh-**ril**-liss

> ✅ **yll** in the middle: **amaryllis**

amass »*verb* (**amasses, amassing, amassed**) build up over time.

amateur

amateurish

amateurism

amatory »*adjective* having to do with love or desire.
– SAY am-uh-tuh-ri

amaze (verb: **amazes, amazing, amazed**)
amazement

amazing
amazingly

Amazon »*noun* ❶ one of a legendary race of female warriors. ❷ a very tall, strong woman.
– SAY am-uh-zuhn

Amazonian »*adjective* ❶ relating to the River Amazon. ❷ (of a woman) very tall and strong.
– SAY am-uh-**zoh**-ni-uhn

ambassador

> ✅ double s, and **-or** not **-er** at the end: **ambassador**

amber »*noun* ❶ a hard clear fossilized resin used in jewellery. ❷ a honey-yellow colour.

ambergris »*noun* a waxy substance produced by sperm whales, which is used in making perfume.
– SAY am-ber-greess

ambiance another way of spelling **AMBIENCE**.

ambidextrous »*adjective* able to use the right and left hands equally well.
– SAY am-bi-**deks**-truhss
ambidexterity

> ✅ remember, **trous** not **terous**: **ambidextrous** (but **ter** in **ambidexterity**)

ambience »*noun* the character and atmosphere of a place.
– SAY am-bi-uhnss

> ✅ **ambience** can also be spelled **ambiance**. This is the French spelling, and the word is sometimes pronounced am-bi-onss.

ambient »*adjective* ❶ relating to the surroundings of something. ❷ (of music) quiet and relaxing.
– SAY am-bi-uhnt

ambiguity »*noun* (plural **ambiguities**) uncertain or inexact meaning.
– SAY am-bi-**gyoo**-i-ti

ambiguous »*adjective* ❶ having more than one meaning. ❷ not clear or decided.
– SAY am-**big**-yoo-uhss
ambiguously

> ℹ️ do not confuse **ambiguous** with **ambivalent**: **ambiguous** refers to mixed meanings, while **ambivalent** means 'having mixed feelings about someone or something'

ambit »*noun* the scope or extent of something.

ambition

ambitious
ambitiously

ambivalent »*adjective* having mixed feelings about something or someone.
– SAY am-**biv**-uh-luhnt
ambivalence
ambivalently

> ℹ️ do not confuse **ambivalent** with **ambiguous**: **ambivalent** refers to mixed feelings, while **ambiguous** means 'having more than one meaning'

amble (verb: **ambles, ambling, ambled**)

ambrosia »*noun* ❶ (in mythology) the food of the gods. ❷ something very pleasing to taste or smell.
– SAY am-**broh**-zi-uh
ambrosial

ambulance

ambulatory »*adjective* relating to walking or able to walk or move.
– SAY am-byoo-luh-tri

ambush »*noun* a surprise attack by people lying in wait in a hidden position.
»*verb* (**ambushes, ambushing, ambushed**) attack in such a way.

ameba American spelling of **AMOEBA**.

ameliorate »*verb* (**ameliorates, ameliorating, ameliorated**) make something better.
– SAY uh-**mee**-li-uh-rayt
amelioration

amen »*exclamation* said at the end of a prayer or hymn, meaning 'so be it'.
– SAY ah-men or ay-men

amenable »*adjective* ❶ willing to be persuaded. ❷ (**amenable to**) able to be affected by something.
– SAY uh-**meen**-uh-b'l
amenability

 amen- not amean-: **amenable**

amend »*verb* (**amends, amending, amended**) make minor improvements to something.

do not confuse **amend** and **emend**: **amend** means 'make minor improvements to', while **emend** means 'correct and revise a text'

amendment »*noun* a minor improvement.

amends

amenity »*noun* (plural **amenities**) a useful or desirable feature of a place.
– SAY uh-**mee**-ni-ti

American

American Indian »*noun* a member of one of the native peoples of America.

see the note at **NATIVE AMERICAN**

Americanism »*noun* a word or phrase originating in the US.

amethyst »*noun* a violet or purple precious stone which is a variety of quartz.
– SAY am-uh-thist

 yst not ist: **amethyst**

amiable »*adjective* (of a person) friendly and pleasant in manner.
– SAY ay-mi-uh-b'l
amiability
amiably

amicable »*adjective* (of a situation or relationship) friendly and without disagreement.

– SAY am-i-kuh-b'l
amicably

amid »*preposition* in the middle of.

amidships »*adverb & adjective* in the middle of a ship.

amidst »*preposition* = **AMID**.

amino acid »*noun* one of a group of natural substances which combine to form proteins.
– SAY uh-**mee**-noh

amir another way of spelling **EMIR**.

amiss »*adjective* not quite right; inappropriate.
»*adverb* wrongly or inappropriately.

amity »*noun* friendly relations.
– SAY **am**-i-ti

ammeter »*noun* an instrument for measuring electric current in amperes.
– SAY **am**-mi-ter

ammonia »*noun* a strong-smelling gas which is used to make a cleaning fluid.
– SAY uh-**moh**-ni-uh

 double **m**, single **n**: **ammonia**

ammonite »*noun* an extinct sea creature with a spiral shell, found as a fossil.
– SAY **am**-uh-nyt

ammunition

double **m**, single **n**: **ammunition**

amnesia »*noun* loss of memory.
– SAY am-**nee**-zi-uh

amnesiac »*noun* a person who has lost their memory.
»*adjective* having to do with amnesia.
– SAY am-**nee**-zi-ak

amnesty »*noun* (plural **amnesties**) ❶ a pardon given to people who have committed an offence against the government. ❷ a period during which people who admit to committing an offence are not punished.

amniotic fluid »*noun* the fluid which surrounds an unborn baby in the womb.
– SAY **am**-ni-ott-ik

amoeba »*noun* (plural **amoebas** or **amoebae**) a microscopic animal that is made up of a single cell and can change its shape.
– SAY uh-**mee**-buh [singular], uh-**mee**-bee [plural]

 moe not me: **amoeba** (the spelling **ameba** is American)
the plural can be spelled either with an **s** or with an **e** (as in Latin): **amoebas** or **amoebae**

amok »*adverb* (**run amok**) behave in an uncontrolled way.
– **SAY** uh-**mok**

 amok can also be spelled **amuck**

among

amongst

amoral »*adjective* not concerned with whether something is right or wrong.
– **SAY** ay-**mo**-ruhl
amorality

i do not confuse **amoral** with **immoral**: **amoral** means 'not concerned with whether something is right or wrong', while **immoral** means 'contrary to or defying accepted ideas of right and wrong'

amorous »*adjective* showing or feeling sexual desire.
amorously
amorousness

amorphous »*adjective* without a clear shape or form.
– **SAY** uh-**mor**-fuhss

amortize »*verb* (**amortizes, amortizing, amortized**) gradually pay off a debt.
– **SAY** uh-**mor**-tyz
amortization

 many people prefer the alternative spellings **amortise, amortises,** etc.: both **s** and **z** spellings are correct

amount (verb: **amounts, amounting, amounted**)

amperage »*noun* the strength of an electric current in amperes.
– **SAY** am-**puh**-rij

ampere »*noun* a basic unit of electric current.
– **SAY** am-**pair**

i the **ampere** is named after the French physicist André-Marie *Ampère*

ampersand »*noun* the sign &, standing for *and*.
– **SAY** am-per-sand

amphetamine »*noun* a drug used illegally as a stimulant.
– **SAY** am-**fet**-uh-meen

amphibian »*noun* an animal such as a frog or toad, which lives in the water when young and on the land as an adult.

amphibious »*adjective* living in or suited for both land and water.
– **SAY** am-**fib**-i-uhss

amphitheatre »*noun* a round, open building used for performing plays or for sports, with tiers of seats surrounding a central space.

– **SAY** am-fi-thee-uh-ter

 remember, **amphi** not **ampi**: **amphitheatre**

ample (adjective: **ampler, amplest**)
amply

amplification

amplify »*verb* (**amplifies, amplifying, amplified**) ❶ increase the strength of a sound or an electrical signal. ❷ explain something in more detail.
amplification
amplifier

amplitude »*noun* ❶ the maximum amount by which a vibration such as an alternating current varies from its average intensity. ❷ great size or extent.

amply

ampoule »*noun* a small glass capsule containing liquid used in giving an injection.
– **SAY** am-**pool**

 poule not **pule**: **ampoule** (the spelling **ampule** is American)

amputate »*verb* (**amputates, amputating, amputated**) cut off a limb in a surgical operation.
– **SAY** am-**pyoo**-tayt
amputation

amputee »*noun* a person who has had a limb cut off.

amuck another way of spelling **AMOK**.

amulet »*noun* a small piece of jewellery worn for good luck or protection against evil.
– **SAY** am-**yoo**-lit

amuse (verb: **amuses, amusing, amused**)
amusement
amuses
amusing
amusingly

an

i **an** should be used with words beginning with *h* when the *h* is not pronounced, such as *an heir* and *an hour*. When the *h* is pronounced it is better to use **a**, as in *a hotel*.

anabolic steroid »*noun* a synthetic hormone used to build up muscle.
– **SAY** an-uh-**bol**-ik

anachronism »*noun* a thing which seems to belong to a time other than the one in which it exists.
– **SAY** uh-**nak**-ruh-ni-z'm
anachronistic

anaconda »*noun* a very large water snake found in tropical South America.

– say an-uh-**kon**-duh

anaemia »*noun* a shortage of red cells or haemoglobin in the blood, causing people to feel tired and often to look pale.
– say uh-**nee**-mi-uh

> ✓ **anae** not **ane: anaemia** and **anaemic** (the spellings **anemia** and **anemic** are American)

anaemic »*adjective* ❶ suffering from anaemia. ❷ having little colour or vitality.

anaerobic »*adjective* not using oxygen from the air.
– say an-air-**oh**-bik

> ✓ spelled with **aer** not **air**, and opposite in meaning to **aerobic: anaerobic**

anaesthetic »*noun* a drug or gas that stops you feeling pain.
– say an-iss-**thet**-ik

> ✓ **anae** not **ane: anaesthetic** (the spelling **anesthetic** is American)

anaesthetise another way of spelling ANAESTHETIZE.

anaesthetist »*noun* a medical specialist who gives anaesthetics.
– say uh-**neess**-thuh-tist

anaesthetize »*verb* (**anaesthetizes, anaesthetizing, anaesthetized**) give an anaesthetic to a person or animal.
– say uh-**neess**-thuh-tyz

> ✓ many people prefer the alternative spellings **anaesthetise, anaesthetises,** etc. : both **s** and **z** spellings are correct. The American spelling is **anesthetize**.

anagram »*noun* a word or phrase formed by rearranging the letters of another.
– say **an**-uh-gram

> ✓ there is no **me** at the end of **anagram**

anal »*adjective* having to do with the anus.
– say **ay**-nuhl

analgesic »*noun* a pain-relieving drug.
– say an-uhl-**jee**-zik

analog American spelling of ANALOGUE.

analogies

analogous »*adjective* similar to and able to be compared with something else.
– say uh-**nal**-uh-guhss

analogue »*noun* a person or thing that is similar to and can be compared with something else.
»*adjective* using a variable physical property, such as voltage, to represent information, rather than binary digits.
– say **an**-uh-log

> ✓ **logue** not **log: analogue** (the spelling **analog** is American)

analogy »*noun* (plural **analogies**) a way of explaining something by comparing it to something else.
– say uh-**nal**-uh-ji

analyse (verb: **analyses, analysing, analysed**)

> ✓ **se** not **ze: analyse** (the spelling **analyze** is American)

analysis (plural **analyses**)
– say uh-**nal**-i-siss [singular], uh-**nal**-i-seez [plural]

> ✓ make the plural by changing the **-is** ending to **-es** (as in Latin): **analyses**

analyst »*noun* a person who carries out analysis.

> ✓ **yst** not **ist: analyst**

analytical »*adjective* having to do with analysis.
analytically

analyze American spelling of ANALYSE.

anarchic »*adjective* not controlled or governed by any rules or principles.
– say uh-**nar**-kik

anarchist »*noun* a person who believes that all government should be abolished and that society should be organized on a cooperative basis.
– say **an**-uhr-kist
anarchism
anarchistic

anarchy »*noun* a state of disorder due to lack of government or control.
– say **an**-uhr-ki

anathema »*noun* something that you hate: *racism was anathema to her.*
– say uh-**na**-thuh-muh

anatomical »*adjective* having to do with the structure of the body.
– say an-uh-**tom**-i-k'l
anatomically

anatomy »*noun* (plural **anatomies**) ❶ the scientific study of the structure of the human body. ❷ the structure of the body of a person, animal, or plant. ❸ a detailed examination or analysis.
anatomist

ancestor

> ✓ **-or** not **-er: ancestor**

ancestral »*adjective* having to do with or inherited from an ancestor or ancestors: *their ancestral home.*
– say an-**sess**-truhl

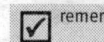
ancestry »*noun* (plural **ancestries**) a person's ancestors or ethnic origins.

anchor (verb: **anchors, anchoring, anchored**)

☑ remember the **h**: anchor

anchorage »*noun* a place where ships can anchor safely.

anchored

anchoring

anchorman »*noun* (plural **anchormen**) a person who presents a live television or radio programme and coordinates the contributions of other people involved.

anchors

anchorwoman (plural **anchorwomen**)

anchovy »*noun* (plural **anchovies**) a sea fish like a small herring, with a strong flavour.
– say an-chuh-vi

ancient
   anciently

☑ **ie** not **ei**: ancient (this is an exception to the rule '*i* before *e* except after *c*')

ancillary »*adjective* ❶ providing support to the main activities of an organization. ❷ additional; extra.
– say an-**sil**-luh-ri

☑ double **l**: ancillary

and

ℹ it is often said to be bad writing style to begin a sentence with **and** (or **but** or **because**). However, writers down the centuries have used **and, but,** and **because** to start sentences. Provided there is a good reason for it, this should not be seen as a mistake.

andante (in music) »*adverb & adjective* in a moderately slow time.
»*noun* a piece of music to be played in a moderately slow time.
– say an-**dan**-tay

androgynous »*adjective* partly male and partly female.
– say an-**dro**-ji-nuhss
   androgyny

☑ **gy** not **gi**: androgynous, androgyny

android »*noun* (in science fiction) a robot with a human appearance.

anecdotal »*adjective* (of a story) not backed up by facts.
– say an-ik-**doh**-t'l

anecdote »*noun* a short entertaining story about a real incident or person.
– say an-ik-**doht**

☑ there is no **k** in anecdote

anemia American spelling of ANAEMIA.

anemic American spelling of ANAEMIC.

anemometer »*noun* an instrument for measuring the speed of the wind.
– say an-i-**mom**-i-ter

anemone »*noun* a plant with brightly coloured flowers that have dark centres.
– say uh-**nem**-uh-ni

☑ **n** then **m** then **n**: anemone
   remember, there is no **i** in the plural: anemones

anesthetic etc. American spelling of ANAESTHETIC etc.

aneurysm »*noun* a swelling of the wall of an artery.
– say **an**-yuu-ri-z'm

☑ aneurysm can also be spelled aneurism

anew »*adverb* ❶ in a new or different way. ❷ once more; again.

angel [heavenly being]

☑ **el** not **le**: angel

angelfish

angelic
   angelically

angelica »*noun* the stalks of a sweet-smelling plant, preserved in sugar and used in cake decoration.
– say an-**jel**-li-kuh

anger (verb: **angers, angering, angered**)

angina »*noun* severe pain in the chest caused by an inadequate supply of blood to the heart.
– say an-**jy**-nuh

angle (verb: **angles, angling, angled**) [space between lines; position from which something is viewed]

☑ **le** not **el**: angle

angler

angles

Anglican »*adjective* relating to the Church of England.
   Anglicanism

anglicize »*verb* (**anglicizes, anglicizing, anglicized**) make something English.
   anglicization

☑ 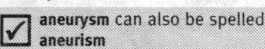 many people prefer the alternative spellings **anglicise, anglicises,** etc., and **anglicisation**: both **s** and **z** spellings are correct

angling

Anglophile »*noun* a person who greatly admires England or Britain.

Anglo-Saxon

angora »*noun* ❶ a breed of cat, goat, or rabbit with long, soft hair. ❷ fabric made from the hair of the angora goat or rabbit.
– sᴀʏ ang-**gor**-uh

angostura »*noun* the bitter bark of a South American tree, used as a flavouring.
– sᴀʏ ang-guh-**styoor**-uh

angry (adjective: **angrier**, **angriest**)
angrily

angst »*noun* a strong feeling of anxiety about life in general.

> ⓘ **angst** is a German word meaning 'fear'

anguish »*noun* severe mental or physical pain or suffering.
anguished

angular »*adjective* ❶ having angles or sharp corners. ❷ (of a person) lean and bony. ❸ placed or directed at an angle.
– sᴀʏ **ang**-gyuu-ler
angularity

> **ar** nor **er**: ang**ular**

animal

animate »*verb* (**animates**, **animating**, **animated**) ❶ bring life or fresh energy to. ❷ make drawings or models into an animated film.
» *adjective* living.
– sᴀʏ **an**-i-mayt [verb], **an**-i-muht [adjective]
animated
animatedly
animator

animation

animator

animism »*noun* the belief that all things in nature, such as plants, winds, and hills, have a soul.
– sᴀʏ **an**-i-mi-z'm
animist

animosity »*noun* (plural **animosities**) a feeling of hatred or dislike.
– sᴀʏ an-i-**moss**-i-ti

animus »*noun* animosity.
– sᴀʏ **an**-i-muhss

aniseed »*noun* the strongly flavoured seed of a plant called the **anise**.

ankle

anklet »*noun* a chain or band worn round the ankle.

annals »*plural noun* a historical record of events year by year.
– sᴀʏ **an**-nuhlz

> ✓ double n: annals

anneal »*verb* (**anneals**, **annealing**, **annealed**) heat metal or glass and allow it to cool slowly, so as to toughen it.
– sᴀʏ uh-**neel**

annex »*verb* (**annexes**, **annexing**, **annexed**) ❶ take possession of another country's land. ❷ add something as an extra part.
» *noun* (plural **annexes**) ❶ a building attached or near to a main building, used for additional space. ❷ an addition to a document.
– sᴀʏ an-**neks** [verb], **an**-neks [noun]
annexation

> ✓ the noun **annex** can also be spelled **annexe**: both spellings are correct

annihilate »*verb* (**annihilates**, **annihilating**, **annihilated**) destroy completely.
– sᴀʏ uh-**ny**-i-layt
annihilation
annihilator

> ✓ don't forget the **h**: annihilate

anniversary (plural **anniversaries**)

> ✓ the ending is **ary** not **ery**: anniversary plural: drop the **y** and add **ies**: anniversaries

Anno Domini »*adverb* full form of **AD**.

> ⓘ **Anno Domini** is a Latin phrase meaning 'in the year of the Lord'

annotate »*verb* (**annotates**, **annotating**, **annotated**) add explanatory notes to.
– sᴀʏ **an**-nuh-tayt
annotation

announce (verb: **announces**, **announcing**, **announced**)
announcement
announcer

> ✓ double n: announce

annoy (verb: **annoys**, **annoying**, **annoyed**)
annoyance

annoying
annoyingly

annoys

annual »*adjective* ❶ happening once a year. ❷ calculated over or covering a year. ❸ (of a plant) living for a year or less.
» *noun* a book published once a year.
annually

annuity »*noun* (plural **annuities**) a fixed sum of money paid to someone each year.
– SAY uh-**nyoo**-i-ti

annul »*verb* (**annuls, annulling, annulled**) declare a law, marriage, or other legal contract to be no longer valid.
– SAY uh-**nul**
annulment

 two n's, one l: **annul, annulment,** but double the l in **annulled** and **annulling**

annular »*adjective* ring-shaped.

annulled

annulling

annuls

Annunciation »*noun* (in Christian belief) the announcement by the angel Gabriel to the Virgin Mary that she was to be the mother of Jesus.

anode »*noun* an electrode with a positive charge (the opposite of *cathode*).
– SAY **an**-ohd

anodized »*adjective* (of metal) coated with a protective layer by the action of an electric current.
– SAY **an**-uh-dyzd

 anodized can also be spelled with an s: **anodised**

anodyne »*adjective* unlikely to cause offence or disagreement; bland.
» *noun* a painkilling drug.
– SAY **an**-uh-dyn

 yne not ine: **anodyne**

anoint »*verb* (**anoints, anointing, anointed**) dab or smear water or oil on someone as part of a religious ceremony.

 an- not ann-: **anoint**

anomalies

anomalous »*adjective* differing from what is standard or normal.

anomaly »*noun* (plural **anomalies**) something that departs from what is standard or normal.
– SAY uh-**nom**-uh-li

 plural: drop the y and add ies: **anomalies**

anon »*adverb* soon; shortly.

anonymity »*noun* the state of being anonymous.
– SAY an-uh-**nim**-iti

anonymous »*adjective* ❶ having a name that is not publicly known. ❷ having no outstanding or individual features: *her*

anonymous flat.
anonymously

 nym not **nim: anonymous**

anorak

 there is no c in **anorak**

anorexia »*noun* a disorder in which a person refuses to eat because they are afraid of becoming fat.
– SAY an-uh-**rek**-siuh
anorexic

another

answer (verb: **answers, answering, answered**)

answerable

answered

answering

answers

ant [small insect]

antacid »*adjective* (of a medicine) reducing excess acid in the stomach.
– SAY an-**tass**-id

antagonise another way of spelling ANTAGONIZE.

antagonism »*noun* open hostility or opposition.
– SAY an-**tag**-uh-ni-z'm

antagonist »*noun* an opponent or enemy.
antagonistic

antagonize »*verb* (**antagonizes, antagonizing, antagonized**) make someone feel hostile towards you.

 many people prefer the alternative spellings **antagonise, antagonises,** etc. : both s and z spellings are correct

Antarctic

 the ending is **-arctic** not **-artic: Antarctic**

ante »*noun* a stake put up by a player in poker or brag before receiving cards.
– SAY **an**-ti

 ante is Latin for 'before'

anteater

antecedent »*noun* ❶ a thing that occurs or exists before another. ❷ (**antecedents**) a person's ancestors.
» *adjective* coming before in time or order.
– SAY an-ti-**see**-duhnt

 ante- not **anti-,** and c not s in the middle: **antecedent**

antedate »*verb* (antedates, antedating, antedated) come or exist before something else.

> ✓ **ante-** not **anti-** in **antedate** and **antediluvian**

antediluvian »*adjective* ❶ belonging to the time before Noah's Flood. ❷ ridiculously old-fashioned.
– SAY an-ti-di-**loo**-vi-uhn

antelope

> ✓ **ante-** not **anti-**: **antelope**

antenatal »*adjective* before birth; during or relating to pregnancy.

> ✓ **ante-** not **anti-**: **antenatal**

antenna »*noun* (plural **antennae** or **antennas**) ❶ one of a pair of long, thin feelers on the head of an insect or other creature. ❷ an aerial.
– SAY an-**ten**-nuh [singular], an-**ten**-nee [plural]

> ✓ the plural can either be spelled with an **e** (like the original Latin) or with an **s**: **antennae** or **antennas**

antepenultimate »*adjective* last but two in a series.

> ✓ **ante-** not **anti-**: **antepenultimate**

anterior »*adjective* at or near the front.

ante-room »*noun* a small room leading to a more important one.

anthem

anther »*noun* the part of a flower's stamen that contains the pollen.

anthill

anthology »*noun* (plural **anthologies**) a collection of poems or other pieces of writing or music.

> ✓ plural: drop the **y** and add **ies**: **anthologies**

anthracite »*noun* hard coal that burns with little flame and smoke.
– SAY an-thruh-syt

> ✓ **-cite** not **-site**: **anthracite**

anthrax »*noun* a serious disease of sheep and cattle that can be transmitted to humans.
– SAY an-thraks

anthropoid »*adjective* having to do with apes that are like people in general form, such as gorillas or chimpanzees.

anthropology »*noun* the study of human origins, societies, and cultures.

– SAY an-thruh-**pol**-uh-ji
anthropological
anthropologist

anthropomorphic »*adjective* treating a god, animal, or object as if it is human.
– SAY an-thruh-puh-**mor**-fik

antibiotic »*noun* a medicine that destroys bacteria or slows down their growth.

antibody »*noun* (plural **antibodies**) a protein produced in the blood in reaction to harmful substances, which it then destroys.

> ✓ plural: drop the **y** and add **ies**: **antibodies**

Antichrist »*noun* an enemy of Jesus that some people believe will appear before the end of the world.

anticipate (verb: **anticipates**, **anticipating**, **anticipated**)
anticipatory

anticipation

anticipatory

anticlimax
anticlimactic

> ✓ no hyphen in **anticlimax** or **anticlockwise**

anticlockwise

antics »*plural noun* foolish, outrageous, or amusing behaviour.

> ✓ there is no **k** in **antics**

anticyclone »*noun* an area of high atmospheric pressure around which air slowly circulates, usually resulting in calm, fine weather.

antidepressant »*noun* a drug used to treat depression.

> ✓ double **s**, and **ant** not **ent** at the end: **antidepressant**

antidote »*noun* a medicine taken to undo the effect of a poison.

> ✓ **anti-** not **ante-**: **antidote**

antifreeze »*noun* a liquid added to water to prevent it from freezing, used in the radiator of a motor vehicle.

> ✓ no hyphen in **antifreeze**

antigen »*noun* a harmful substance which causes the body to produce antibodies.
– SAY an-ti-jen

anti-hero »*noun* (plural **anti-heroes**) a central character in a story, film, or play who, unlike a conventional hero, is ordinary or unpleasant.

anti-heroine »*noun* a female anti-hero.

antihistamine »*noun* a drug that undoes the effects of histamine and is used in treating allergies.

antimacassar »*noun* a piece of cloth put over the back of a chair to protect it from grease and dirt.
– SAY an-ti-muh-**kass**-er

> ✓ single **c**, double **s**: anti**macassar**

antimatter »*noun* matter consisting of particles with the same mass as normal matter but opposite electric or magnetic properties.

> ✓ no hyphen in anti**matter**

antimony »*noun* a brittle silvery-white metal.
– SAY an-ti-muh-ni

antinomy »*noun* (plural **antinomies**) a paradox.
– SAY an-**tin**-uh-mi

antioxidant »*noun* a substance that prevents oxidation taking place.

> ✓ **ant** not **ent**: anti**ox**idant

antipathy »*noun* (plural **antipathies**) a strong feeling of dislike.
– SAY an-ti-**puh**-thi
antipathetic

antiperspirant »*noun* a substance applied to the skin to prevent or reduce sweating.

> ✓ **ant** not **ent**: antiperspir**ant**

antiphon »*noun* a short sentence sung or recited before or after a psalm or canticle.
– SAY **an**-ti-fuhn

Antipodes »*plural noun* (**the Antipodes**) Australia and New Zealand.
– SAY an-**ti**-puh-deez
Antipodean

antiquarian »*adjective* relating to the collection or study of antiques, rare books, or antiquities.
» *noun* a person who studies or collects antiquarian items.
– SAY an-ti-**kwair**-i-uhn

antiquary »*noun* (plural **antiquaries**) an antiquarian.

antiquated »*adjective* old-fashioned or outdated.

antique

> ✓ don't forget the **u**: anti**que**

antiquity »*noun* (plural **antiquities**) ❶ the distant past. ❷ an object from the distant past.

> ✓ plural: drop the **y** and add **ies**: anti**quities**

antirrhinum »*noun* (plural **antirrhinums**) a snapdragon.
– SAY an-ti-**ry**-nuhm

> ✓ double **r** and an **h**: anti**rrhinum**

anti-Semitism »*noun* hostility to or prejudice against Jews.
anti-Semite
anti-Semitic

antiseptic »*adjective* preventing the growth of germs that cause disease or infection.
» *noun* an antiseptic substance.

antisocial »*adjective* ❶ doing things in a way that is unacceptable or annoying to other people. ❷ not wanting to mix with other people.

> ℹ do not confuse **antisocial** with **unsociable**, which means 'not enjoying the company of or engaging in activities with others', and **unsocial**, which means 'socially inconvenient'

antithesis »*noun* (plural **antitheses**) ❶ a person or thing that is the direct opposite of another. ❷ the putting together of contrasting ideas or words to produce an effect.
– SAY an-ti-**thuh**-siss [singular], an-**ti**-thuh-seez [plural]

> ✓ make the plural by changing the **-is** ending to **-es** (as in Latin): anti**theses**

antithetical »*adjective* opposed to or incompatible with each other.
– SAY an-ti-**thet**-i-k'l

antler

antonym »*noun* a word opposite in meaning to another.
– SAY **an**-tuh-nim

> ✓ **nym** not **nim**: anto**nym**

anus »*noun* (plural **anuses**) the opening in the bottom through which solid waste matter leaves the body.

> ✓ one **n** and one **s**: an**us** (**annus** is the Latin for 'year')

anvil »*noun* an iron block on which metal is hammered and shaped.

anxiety (plural **anxieties**)

> ✓ plural: drop the **y** and add **ies**: anxi**eties**

anxious
anxiously

any

anybody

anyhow

anyone

> ℹ the two-word phrase **any one** is not the same as the word **anyone** and the two forms cannot be used in place of each other. Use **anyone** to mean 'any person or people', as in *anyone could do it* or *I couldn't see anyone*; **any one** means 'any single', as in *not more than twelve new members are admitted in any one year*.

anything

anyway

anywhere

aorta »*noun* the main artery supplying blood from the heart to the rest of the body.
– SAY ay-or-tuh

apace »*adverb* quickly.

Apache »*noun* (plural **Apache** or **Apaches**) a member of an American Indian people living chiefly in New Mexico and Arizona.
– SAY uh-pa-chi

> ✓ there is no t: **Apache**

apart

apartheid »*noun* the system of racial segregation and discrimination formerly in force in South Africa.
– SAY uh-par-tayt

> ✓ notice the **h** in the middle and the **eid** at the end: **apartheid**

apartment

> ✓ there is only one p: **apartment**

apathetic »*adjective* not interested or enthusiastic.

apathy »*noun* lack of interest or enthusiasm.

ape (verb: **apes, aping, aped**)

aperitif »*noun* an alcoholic drink taken before a meal.
– SAY uh-pe-ri-teef

> ✓ notice the final f: **aperitif** (from the French *apéritif*)

aperture »*noun* ❶ an opening, hole, or gap. ❷ the variable opening by which light enters a camera.

apes

apex »*noun* (plural **apices**) the top or highest point.

– SAY ay-peks [singular], ay-pi-seez [plural]

aphelion »*noun* (plural **aphelia**) the point in a planet's orbit at which it is furthest from the sun.
– SAY ap-hee-li-uhn

aphid »*noun* a small insect that feeds on the sap of plants.
– SAY ay-fid

aphorism »*noun* a short witty remark which contains a general truth.
– SAY af-uh-ri-z'm

aphrodisiac »*noun* a food, drink, or drug that makes people very keen to have sex.
– SAY af-ruh-diz-i-ak

apiary »*noun* (plural **apiaries**) a place where bees are kept.
– SAY ay-pee-uh-ri

apices plural of APEX.

apiece »*adverb* for or by each one.

> ℹ do not confuse **apiece** with the two words **a piece**

aping

aplenty »*adjective* in large amounts.

aplomb »*noun* calm self-confidence.
– SAY uh-plom

> ✓ do not forget the **b** at the end of the word: **aplomb**

apocalypse »*noun* a terrible event in which everything is destroyed.
– SAY uh-po-kuh-lips

apocalyptic »*adjective* having far-reaching or disastrous consequences.

apocryphal »*adjective* (of information) widely circulated but unlikely to be true.
– SAY uh-pok-ri-ful

apogee »*noun* ❶ the point in the orbit of a moon or a satellite at which it is furthest from the earth. ❷ the highest point of something.

apolitical »*adjective* not interested or involved in politics.

apologetic
apologetically

apologies

apologise another way of spelling APOLOGIZE.

apologist »*noun* a person who speaks in defence of something controversial.

apologize (verb: **apologizes, apologizing, apologized**)

> ✓ many people prefer the alternative spellings **apologise, apologises**, etc.: both **s** and **z** spellings are correct

apology (plural **apologies**)

✓ plural: drop the **y** and add **ies**: **apologies**

apoplectic »*adjective* (in informal English) extremely angry.
– SAY a-puh-**plek**-tik

✓ **ct** not **x**: apoplectic

apoplexy »*noun* (plural **apoplexies**) (an old word) unconsciousness or inability to feel or move, caused by a shock, stress, etc.
– SAY a-puh-plek-si

apostasy »*noun* abandonment of a belief or principle.
– SAY uh-**poss**-tuh-si

✓ the ending is not **acy** but **asy**: apostasy

apostate »*noun* a person who abandons a belief or principle.
– SAY a-puh-stayt

apostle »*noun* ❶ (**Apostle**) one of the twelve chief disciples of Jesus. ❷ a follower or supporter.

✓ use a capital **A** when referring to the Apostles of Jesus

apostolic »*adjective* having to do with the Apostles.
– SAY a-puh-**sto**-lik

apostrophe »*noun* a punctuation mark (') used to show either possession (as in *my friend's sister*) or the omission of letters or numbers (as in *I'm* and *June '99*).
– SAY uh-**poss**-truh-fi

ℹ the apostrophe should be placed before the **s** with singular nouns (*the student's book*: one student) and after the **s** with plural nouns ending in *s* (*the students' books*: more than one student)

apothecary »*noun* (plural **apothecaries**) (a historical term) a person who prepared and sold medicines.
– SAY uh-**poth**-uh-kuh-ri

apotheosis »*noun* (plural **apotheoses**) the highest level in the development of something.
– SAY uh-po-thi-**oh**-siss [singular], uh-po-thi-**oh**-seez [plural]

✓ make the plural by changing the **-is** ending to **-es** (as in Latin): apotheoses

appal (verb: **appals, appalling, appalled**)

✓ two **p**'s, one **l**: appal, appals, but double the **l** in appalled and appalling

appalling
 appallingly

appals

apparatus (plural **apparatuses**)

✓ two **p**'s but only one **r**: apparatus

apparel »*noun* clothing.
– SAY uh-**pa**-ruhl

✓ two **p**'s but only one **r**: apparel

apparent
 apparently

✓ two **p**'s but only one **r**, and the ending is **ent** not **ant**: apparent

apparition »*noun* a remarkable thing making a sudden appearance, especially a ghost.

✓ two **p**'s but only **r**: apparition

appeal (verb: **appeals, appealing, appealed**)
appealing
 appealingly
appeals
appear (verb: **appears, appearing, appeared**)

✓ remember, the word ends with **ear**, not **eer**: appear

appearance

✓ two **p**'s, one **r**, and **ance** not **ence** at the end: appearance

appeared
appearing
appears
appease »*verb* (**appeases, appeasing, appeased**) make someone calm or less hostile by agreeing to their demands.
 appeasement
appellation »*noun* a name or title.
– SAY ap-puh-**lay**-sh'n

✓ double **p**, double **l**: appellation

append »*verb* (**appends, appending, appended**) add something to the end of a document or piece of writing.

appendage »*noun* a thing that is attached to something larger or more important.

appendectomy »*noun* (plural **appendectomies**) a surgical operation to remove someone's appendix.
– SAY a-pen-**dek**-tuh-mi

appended
appendices
appendicitis »*noun* a condition in which the appendix becomes infected and inflamed.
appending
appendix »*noun* (plural **appendices** or **appendixes**) ❶ a small tube of tissue

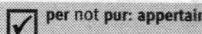

attached to the lower end of the large intestine. ❷ a section of additional information at the end of a book.

appends

appertain »*verb* (appertains, appertaining, appertained) be related, relevant, or appropriate to something.
– SAY ap-per-**tayn**

> ✓ per not pur: appertain

appetiser another way of spelling APPETIZER.

appetising another way of spelling APPETIZING.

appetite

> ✓ double p, followed by e not i: appetite

appetizer »*noun* a small dish of food or a drink taken before a meal to stimulate the appetite.

> ✓ this word can also be spelled appetiser: both spellings are correct

appetizing

> ✓ this word can also be spelled appetising: both spellings are correct

applaud (verb: applauds, applauding, applauded)

> ✓ this word ends in aud not ord: applaud

applause

apple

appliance

> ✓ ance not ence: appliance

applicable »*adjective* able to be applied.
applicability

applicant

application

applicator »*noun* a device for putting something into or on to something.

applied

applies

applique »*noun* decorative needlework in which fabric shapes are sewn or fixed on to a background.
– SAY uh-**plee**-kay

> ✓ this word can also be written appliqué, with an acute accent on the e (as in the original French)

apply (verb: applies, applying, applied)

> ✓ change the y to ie when writing applies or applied

appoint (verb: appoints, appointing, appointed)
appointee

> ✓ double p: appoint, appointment

appointment

appoints

apportion »*verb* (apportions, apportioning, apportioned) share out.
apportionment

apposite »*adjective* appropriate.
– SAY ap-puh-zit

> ✓ do not forget the final e: apposite

apposition »*noun* a grammatical relationship in which a word or phrase is placed next to another so as to qualify or explain it (e.g. *my friend Sue*).

appraisal »*noun* ❶ an assessment of the quality or value of something. ❷ a formal assessment of an employee's performance.

> ✓ remember, ai not i or a alone: appraisal

appraise »*verb* (appraises, appraising, appraised) assess the quality or value of something.

> ℹ do not confuse **appraise** with **apprise**: appraise means 'assess', as in *the two men stepped back to appraise their handiwork*, while **apprise** means 'inform', as in *I apprised him of what had happened*

appreciable »*adjective* large or important enough to be noticed.
appreciably

appreciate (verb: appreciates, appreciating, appreciated)

appreciation

appreciative
appreciatively

apprehend »*verb* (apprehends, apprehending, apprehended) ❶ seize or arrest someone for doing something unlawful or wrong. ❷ understand.

apprehension »*noun* ❶ worry or fear about what might happen. ❷ understanding.

apprehensive »*adjective* worried or afraid about what might happen.
apprehensively

apprentice »*noun* a person learning a skilled practical trade from an employer.
»*verb* (apprentices, apprenticing, apprenticed) be employed as an apprentice.
apprenticeship

✓ double **p**, and the ending is **ice**, not **ise**: apprentice, apprenticeship

apprise »*verb* (apprises, apprising, apprised) inform someone of something: *I apprised him of what had happened.*

ℹ do not confuse **apprise** with **appraise**: apprise means 'inform', while appraise means 'assess', as in *the two men stepped back to appraise their handiwork*

✓ **apprise** cannot be spelled with an **ize** ending

approach (verb: approaches, approaching, approached)

approachable

approached

approaches

approaching

approbation »*noun* approval.

appropriate »*adjective* acceptable and right for the situation that is taking place; suitable.
» *verb* (appropriates, appropriating, appropriated) ❶ take for your own use without permission. ❷ set money aside for a special purpose.
– SAY uh-**proh**-pri-uht [adjective], uh-**proh**-pri-ayt [verb]
appropriately
appropriateness
appropriation

approval

approve (verb: approves, approving, approved)
approvingly

✓ remember the double **p** in **approve** and **approval**

approximate »*adjective* almost but not completely accurate; rough.
» *verb* (approximates, approximating, approximated) be roughly equal or similar to something.
– SAY uh-**prok**-si-muht [adjective], uh-**prok**-si-mayt [verb]
approximately

approximation

appurtenances »*plural noun* the things you need for a particular activity.
– SAY uh-**per**-ti-nuhn-siz

✓ spelled with a **u**, not **e**, after the double **p**: appurtenances

APR »*abbreviation* annual (or annualized) percentage rate.

apres-ski »*noun* parties and entertainments which take place after a day's skiing.

– SAY ap-ray-skee

✓ often spelled with a grave accent on the **e**: après-ski is a French phrase meaning 'after skiing'

apricot

April

April Fool's Day

a priori »*adjective & adverb* based on theory rather than observation.
– SAY ay pry-**or**-I

ℹ a Latin phrase meaning 'from what is before'

apron

apropos »*preposition* with reference to.
– SAY a-pruh-**poh**

ℹ **apropos** (with a silent **s**) is from the French phrase *à propos* 'with regard to this purpose'. It can be used with or without *of* following: you can say *apropos something* or *apropos of something*.

apse »*noun* (plural apses) a large recess with a domed or arched roof at the eastern end of a church.
– SAY apss

apt
aptly
aptness

ℹ the comparative and superlative are usually **more** and **most apt**, not **apter** and **aptest**

aptitude »*noun* a natural ability.

aptly

aptness

aqualung »*noun* a breathing apparatus for divers.

aquamarine »*noun* ❶ a light bluish-green precious stone. ❷ a light bluish-green colour.

✓ **aquamarine**, **aquarium**, and other words derived from Latin *aqua* 'water', begin with **aq** not **acq**

aquaplane »*verb* (aquaplanes, aquaplaning, aquaplaned) (of a vehicle) slide uncontrollably on a wet surface.

aquarium »*noun* (plural aquaria or aquariums) a water-filled glass tank in which fish and other aquatic creatures are kept.

✓ the plural can be either **aquaria** (like the original Latin) or **aquariums**

Aquarius »*noun* a constellation and a sign of the zodiac (the Water Carrier, 19 January–18 February).

aquatic »*adjective* ❶ relating to water. ❷ living in or near water.

– say uh-**kwat**-ik

> aqua not acqua: aquatic

aqueduct »*noun* a long channel or bridge which carries water across country.
– say ak-wuh-**dukt**

> aque, not aqua or aqui-: aqueduct

aqueous »*adjective* relating to or containing water.
– say ay-kwee-uhss

aquiline »*adjective* (of a person's nose) curved like an eagle's beak.
– say **ak**-wi-lyn

Arab

arabesque »*noun* ❶ a ballet position in which one leg is extended horizontally backwards and the arms are outstretched. ❷ an ornamental design of intertwined flowing lines.
– say a-ruh-**besk**

Arabian

Arabic

Arabic numerals »*plural noun* the figures 0, 1, 2, 3, 4, 5, 6, 7, 8, and 9.

arable »*adjective* (of land) able to be ploughed and used for growing crops.
– say a-ruh-b'l

> single r: arable

arachnid »*noun* a creature of a kind including spiders, scorpions, mites, and ticks.
– say uh-**rak**-nid

arachnophobia »*noun* extreme fear of spiders.
– say uh-rak-nuh-**foh**-bi-uh

> note the o in the middle of the word: arachnophobia

arbiter »*noun* ❶ a person who settles a dispute. ❷ a person who has influence in a particular area: *an arbiter of taste.*
– say **ar**-bi-ter

> -er, not -re (or -or) at the end: arbiter

arbitrary »*adjective* ❶ not seeming to be based on any plan or system. ❷ (of power) used without restraint or kindness.
– say ar-bi-truh-ri or ar-bi-tri
arbitrarily

> remember, the ending is trary: arbitrary

arbitrate »*verb* (arbitrates, arbitrating, arbitrated) act as an arbitrator to settle a dispute.

arbitration

arbitrator »*noun* an independent person officially appointed to settle a dispute.

arbor American spelling of ARBOUR.

arboreal »*adjective* ❶ relating to trees. ❷ living in trees.
– say ar-**bor**-i-uhl

arboretum »*noun* (plural **arboretums** or **arboreta**) a garden in which trees are grown for scientific study or display to the public.
– say ar-buh-**ree**-tuhm

> the plural can be either arboreta (like the original Latin) or arboretums

arboriculture »*noun* the cultivation of trees and shrubs.

arbour »*noun* a shady place in a garden, with a canopy of trees or climbing plants.

> -our not -or: arbour (the spelling arbor is American)

arc »*noun* ❶ a curve forming part of the circumference of a circle. ❷ a curving passage through the air. ❸ a glowing electrical discharge between two points.
» *verb* (arcs, arcing, arced) move in an arc.

> do not confuse arc with ark, meaning 'the ship built by Noah in the Bible'

arcade

arcane »*adjective* secret and mysterious.
– say ar-**kayn**

arced past of ARC.
– say arkt

arch¹ (verb: arches, arching, arched) [a curved structure]

arch² »*adjective* suggesting in a playful way that you know more than you are revealing.

archaeology »*noun* the study of ancient history through the digging up of old sites and studying what is found there.
archaeological
archaeologist

> ae, not simply e, in front of the ology: archaeology. The spelling archeology is American.

archaic »*adjective* ❶ very old or old-fashioned. ❷ belonging to an earlier period.
– say ar-**kay**-ik

archaism »*noun* an old or old-fashioned word or style.
– say **ar**-kay-i-z'm

archangel »*noun* an angel of high rank.
– say **ark**-ayn-j'l

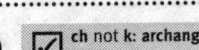

✓ ch not k: archangel

archbishop »*noun* a bishop of the highest rank.

archdeacon »*noun* a senior Christian priest.

arched

arch-enemy (plural **arch-enemies**)

archeology American spelling of **ARCHAEOLOGY**.

archer
archery

arches

archetypal »*adjective* serving as an archetype; very typical.
– SAY ar-ki-**ty**-p'l

✓ the ending is **typal**, not **typical**

archetype »*noun* ❶ a very typical example of something. ❷ an original model which others follow.
– SAY ar-ki-typ

✓ **arche** not **archi**: archetype

arching

archipelago »*noun* (plural **archipelagos** or **archipelagoes**) a group of many islands.
– SAY ar-ki-**pel**-uh-goh

✓ the plural of **archipelago** can have **os** or **oes**: archipelagos or archipelagoes

architect

✓ remember the **ch** in the middle: **architect**

architecture
architectural

architrave »*noun* ❶ the frame around a doorway or window. ❷ (in classical architecture) a main beam resting across the tops of columns.
– SAY ar-ki-trayv

archive »*noun* a collection of historical documents or records.
» *verb* (**archives**, **archiving**, **archived**) place in an archive.
– SAY ar-kyv
archival

✓ ch not **k** in the middle: **archive**

archivist »*noun* a person who is in charge of archives.
– SAY ar-ki-vist

archway

arcing [formation of an arc]
– SAY ar-king

arcs

Arctic »*adjective* relating to the regions around the North Pole.

✓ remember the first **c**: **Arctic** (an **artic** is a lorry)

ardent »*adjective* feeling passionate about something.
ardently

✓ ent not ant: ardent

ardor American spelling of **ARDOUR**.

ardour »*noun* passionate feelings.

✓ -our: ardour. The spelling **ardor** is American.

arduous »*adjective* difficult and tiring.

✓ there are two **u's**: arduous

are

area

arena

aren't [are not]

ℹ **aren't** may be used to mean 'am not' in questions such as *I'm right, aren't I?* It is not good English, however, to use **aren't** to mean 'am not' outside questions: *I aren't going* is incorrect.

✓ be careful to put the apostrophe where a letter has been left out, that is between the **n** and **t** of **not**: aren't

areola »*noun* (plural **areolae**) the circular area of darker skin surrounding a nipple.
– SAY uh-**ree**-uh-luh [singular], uh-**ree**-uh-lee [plural]

ℹ do not confuse **areola** with **aureole**, which refers to a bright area around the sun or moon

✓ make the plural by adding an **e** (as in the original Latin): areolae

arete »*noun* a sharp mountain ridge.
– SAY uh-**ret**

✓ **arete** can also be written **arête**, with a circumflex accent on the **e** (as in the original French)

Argentine
Argentinian

argon »*noun* an unreactive gas present in small amounts in the air.
– SAY ar-gon

argot »*noun* the jargon or slang of a particular group.
– SAY ar-goh

✓ although it is not pronounced, there is a **t** at the end of the word: argot (as in the original French)

arguable
  arguably

argue (verb: argues, arguing, argued)

argument

argumentative

aria »*noun* a song for a solo singer in an opera.
  – SAY ah-ri-uh

arid »*adjective* very dry because there is little or no rain.
  aridity

Aries »*noun* a constellation and a sign of the zodiac (the Ram, 21 March–20 April).
  – SAY air-eez

> ✓ remember the **i**, but it comes after the **r**, not before: **Aries**. Do not confuse **Aries** with *Ares* (pronounced the same), who was a Greek war god, equivalent to Mars.

arise (verb: arises, arising, arose; past participle arisen)

aristocracy (plural aristocracies)

> ✓ plural: drop the **y** and add **ies**: **aristocracies**

aristocrat

aristocratic

arithmetic »*noun* the use of numbers in counting and calculation.
  »*adjective* relating to arithmetic.
  – SAY uh-**rith**-muh-tik [noun], a-rith-**met**-ik [adjective]
  arithmetical

ark »*noun* (in the Bible) the ship built by Noah to save his family and two of every kind of animal from the Flood.

> ✓ do not confuse **ark** with **arc** meaning 'a curve'

arm (verb: arms, arming, armed)

armada »*noun* a fleet of warships.
  – SAY ar-**mar**-duh

> ✓ use a capital **A** when referring to the Spanish **Armada** defeated by the English fleet in 1588

armadillo »*noun* (plural armadillos) an insect-eating mammal of Central and South America, with a body covered in bony plates.
  – SAY ar-muh-**dil**-loh

> ✓ the plural of **armadillo**, a Spanish word meaning 'little armed man', has **os** not **oes**: **armadillos**

Armageddon »*noun* ❶ (in the Bible) the final battle between good and evil before the Day of Judgement. ❷ a terrible war with a catastrophic ending.

– SAY ar-muh-**ged**-duhn

> ✓ one **g** and two **d**'s: **Armageddon**

armament »*noun* ❶ military weapons and equipment. ❷ the equipping of military forces for war.
  – SAY ar-muh-muhnt

> ✓ **ent** not **ant**: **armament**

armature »*noun* ❶ the rotating coil of a dynamo or electric motor. ❷ a piece of iron placed across the poles of a magnet to preserve its power.
  – SAY ar-muh-cher

armchair

armed

Armenian

armies

arming

armistice »*noun* an agreement to stop fighting.
  – SAY ar-**miss**-tiss

armor American spelling of ARMOUR.

armored American spelling of ARMOURED.

armorer American spelling of ARMOURER.

armorial »*adjective* having to do with coats of arms.

armory American spelling of ARMOURY.

armour
  armoured

> ✓ -**our**: armour, armoured (the spellings armor and armored are American, as are armorer and armory)

armourer »*noun* a person who makes, supplies, or looks after weapons or armour.

armoury »*noun* (plural armouries) a store or supply of arms.

armpit

arms

arm-wrestle (verb: arm-wrestles, arm-wrestling, arm-wrestled)

army (plural armies)

> ✓ plural: drop the **y** and add **ies**: **armies**

aroma »*noun* a pleasant smell.

aromatherapy »*noun* the use of aromatic oils for healing or to enhance pleasant feelings.
  aromatherapist

aromatic »*adjective* having an aroma.

arose past of ARISE.

around

a

ⓘ on the difference in use between **around** and **round**, see the note at **ROUND**

arouse »*verb* (**arouses, arousing, aroused**)
❶ bring about a feeling or response in someone. ❷ excite someone sexually. ❸ awaken someone from sleep.
arousal

arpeggio »*noun* (plural **arpeggios**) the notes of a musical chord played in quick succession.
– SAY ar-**pej**-ji-oh

✓ the plural of **arpeggio**, an Italian word, has **os** not **oes: arpeggios**

arraign »*verb* call someone before a court to answer a criminal charge.
– SAY uh-**rayn**
arraignment

✓ note the silent **g** before the **n: arraign**

arrange (verb: **arranges, arranging, arranged**)
arranger

arrangement

arranger

arranges

arranging

arrant »*adjective* utter; complete.

ⓘ do not confuse **arrant** with **errant**, which means 'going astray' or 'wandering'

array »*noun* ❶ an impressive display or range. ❷ an ordered arrangement of troops.
» *verb* (**arrays, arraying, arrayed**) ❶ display or arrange in a neat or impressive way. ❷ clothe someone: *they were arrayed in Hungarian national dress.*

arrears »*plural noun* money owed that should already have been paid.

✓ do not forget the **r** before the **s: arrears**

arrest (verb: **arrests, arresting, arrested**)
arrival

arrive (verb: **arrives, arriving, arrived**)

arrogant »*adjective* behaving in an unpleasant way because you think that you are more important or clever than other people.
arrogance
arrogantly

arrogate »*verb* (**arrogates, arrogating, arrogated**) take or claim something that you have no right to.
– SAY **ar**-ruh-gayt

arrow

arrowroot »*noun* a kind of starch used as a thickener in cookery.

arse

arsenal »*noun* a store of weapons and ammunition.

arsenic »*noun* a brittle grey element from which a highly poisonous white powder is obtained.

arson »*noun* the crime of deliberately setting fire to property.
arsonist

art

art deco »*noun* a decorative style of the 1920s and 1930s, which made much use of geometric shapes.
– SAY art **dek**-oh

artefact »*noun* a useful or decorative man-made object.
– SAY **ar**-ti-fakt

✓ use an **e**, not an **i: artefact** (the spelling **artifact** is American)

arterial »*adjective* relating to an artery or arteries.
– SAY ar-**teer**-i-uhl

artery »*noun* (plural **arteries**) ❶ one of the tubes through which blood flows from the heart around the body. ❷ an important transport route.

✓ plural: drop the **y** and add **ies: arteries**

artesian well »*noun* a well drilled down into a layer of rock, from which water rises through natural pressure.
– SAY ar-**tee**-zh'n

artful »*adjective* cunningly clever.
artfully

✓ -**ful** not -**full: artful**

arthritis »*noun* painful inflammation and stiffness of the joints.
– SAY ar-**thry**-tiss
arthritic

arthropod »*noun* an animal with a body that is divided into segments and with the skeleton on the outside, such as an insect, spider, crab, or lobster.
– SAY **ar**-thruh-pod

artichoke »*noun* a vegetable consisting of the unopened flower head of a plant like a thistle.
– SAY **ar**-ti-chohk

✓ **arti** not **arte: artichoke**

article

articled clerk »*noun* a law student employed as a trainee.

articulate »*adjective* ❶ fluent and clear in speech. ❷ having joints or jointed segments.
» *verb* (**articulates, articulating, articulated**) ❶ pronounce words distinctly. ❷ express an idea or feeling clearly.
– SAY ar-**tik**-yuu-luht [adjective], ar-**tik**-yuu-layt [verb]
articulacy
articulately

articulated »*adjective* having sections connected by a flexible joint or joints.

articulately

articulates

articulating

articulation

artier

artiest

artifact American spelling of ARTEFACT.

artifice »*noun* the clever use of tricks to deceive people.
– SAY **ar**-ti-fiss

artificer »*noun* a person who is skilled in making or planning things.

artificial
artificiality
artificially

artillery

artiness

artisan »*noun* a skilled worker who makes things by hand.
– SAY **ar**-ti-zan

✓ s not z: **artisan**

artist

artiste »*noun* a professional singer or dancer.
– SAY ar-**teest**

artistic
artistically

artistry

artless »*adjective* straightforward and sincere.

art nouveau »*noun* a decorative style of the late 19th and early 20th centuries, with intricate designs and flowing curves.
– SAY ar or art noo-**voh**

artwork

arty (adjective: **artier, artiest**)
artiness

Aryan »*noun* ❶ a member of an ancient people of Europe and Asia. ❷ (in Nazi thinking) a white person not of Jewish descent.
» *adjective* relating to Aryans.
– SAY **air**-i-uhn

✓ yan not ian: **Aryan**

as

asbestos »*noun* a fibrous grey-white mineral that does not burn.

✓ no double s in **asbestos**

ascend (verb: **ascends, ascending, ascended**)

ascendant »*adjective* ❶ rising in power or status. ❷ (of a planet or sign of the zodiac) just above the eastern horizon.
ascendancy

✓ ant not ent: **ascendant**

ascended

ascending

ascends

ascension »*noun* ❶ the action of reaching a higher position or status. ❷ (**the Ascension**) the rising of Jesus into heaven after the Resurrection.

✓ sion not tion: **ascension**

ascent »*noun* ❶ the action of going up. ❷ an upward slope.

ⓘ do not confuse **ascent** with **assent**, which means 'approval' or 'agreement'

ascertain »*verb* (**ascertains, ascertaining, ascertained**) find something out for certain.
– SAY ass-er-**tayn**
ascertainable

✓ asc not ass: **ascertain**

ascetic »*adjective* choosing to live without pleasures and luxuries.
» *noun* an ascetic person.
– SAY uh-**set**-ik
asceticism

ascribe »*verb* (**ascribes, ascribing, ascribed**) regard something as being caused by: *he ascribed his breakdown to exhaustion.*
ascription

asexual »*adjective* ❶ without sex or sexual organs. ❷ not having sexual qualities or feelings.
– SAY ay-**sek**-shoo-uhl
asexually

ash (plural **ashes**)

ashamed

ashen »*adjective* very pale from shock, fear, or illness.

ashes

ashore

ashram »*noun* a Hindu religious retreat or community.
– SAY ash-ruhm

Asian

Asiatic

> ℹ️ use **Asian** to describe people or things from Asia: **Asiatic** is chiefly used by scientists to describe diseases, animals, etc. coming from Asia

aside

asinine »*adjective* extremely stupid or foolish.
– SAY ass-i-nyn

> ✓ **asinine** comes from the Latin word for 'ass', *asinus*, and should be spelled with only one **s**

ask (verb: **asks**, **asking**, **asked**)

askance »*adverb* with a suspicious or disapproving look.
– SAY uh-**skanss**

asked

askew

asking

asks

aslant

asleep

asp »*noun* a poisonous snake of southern Europe and Africa.

asparagus

> ✓ the ending is **us** not **ous**: **asparagus**

aspect [a particular feature or appearance]

> ℹ️ do not confuse **aspect** with **expect** meaning 'believe something is likely to happen'

aspen »*noun* a poplar tree with small rounded leaves.

asperity »*noun* harshness in the way you say or do something.
– SAY uh-**spe**-ri-ti

aspersion »*noun* a remark which is critical of someone's character or reputation: *I don't think anyone is casting aspersions on you.*
– SAY uh-**sper**-sh'n

> ✓ **sion** not **tion**: **aspersion**

asphalt »*noun* a black substance like tar, used in surfacing roads or roofs.
– SAY ass-falt

> ✓ remember, there is no **ash** in **asphalt**

asphyxia »*noun* a condition in which someone cannot get enough oxygen and becomes unconscious or dies.
– SAY uh-**sfik**-si-uh

asphyxiate »*verb* (**asphyxiates**, **asphyxiating**, **asphyxiated**) kill someone or make them unconscious by depriving them of oxygen.
asphyxiation

> ✓ remember, **y** not **i**: **asphyxiate**, **asphyxia**, etc.

aspic »*noun* a savoury jelly made with meat stock.

aspidistra »*noun* a plant with broad tapering leaves.
– SAY ass-pi-**diss**-truh

aspirant »*noun* a person with ambitions to do or be something.
– SAY **ass**-pi-ruhnt

aspirate »*verb* (**aspirates**, **aspirating**, **aspirated**) ❶ pronounce a word with the sound of *h* at the start. ❷ (mainly in medicine) extract fluid by suction from something.
»*noun* the sound of *h*.
– SAY **ass**-pi-rayt [verb], **ass**-pi-ruht [noun]

aspiration »*noun* ❶ a hope or ambition. ❷ the pronouncing of a word with an *h*.
aspirational

aspire »*verb* (**aspires**, **aspiring**, **aspired**) have a strong desire to achieve or become something: *she aspired to be an actress.*

aspirin »*noun* a medicine used to relieve pain and reduce fever and inflammation.

> ✓ remember the **i** in the middle: it is spelled **aspirin** although pronounced ass-prin

aspiring

ass (plural **asses**)

assail »*verb* (**assails**, **assailing**, **assailed**) ❶ attack someone violently. ❷ (of an unpleasant feeling) come over someone strongly.

assailant »*noun* an attacker.

> ✓ **ant** not **ent**: **assailant**

assassin »*noun* a person who assassinates someone.

assassinate »*verb* (**assassinates**, **assassinating**, **assassinated**) murder a

political or religious leader.
assassination

> ✓ remember, double **s**, double **s**:
> **assassinate**

assault (verb: **assaults, assaulting, assaulted**)

> ✓ remember the **u**: **assault** has nothing
> to do with **salt**

assay »*noun* the testing of a metal to see
how pure it is.
» *verb* (**assays, assaying, assayed**) test a
metal for purity.
– SAY ass-ay or uh-**say**

> ℹ be careful not to confuse **assay** with
> **essay**, which means 'a piece of
> writing on a topic' or 'try to do something'

assegai »*noun* (plural **assegais**) a kind of
spear used by southern African peoples.
– SAY ass-uh-gy

assemblage »*noun* ❶ a collection or
gathering of things or people.
❷ something made of pieces fitted
together.
– SAY uh-**sem**-blij

assemble (verb: **assembles, assembling,
assembled**)
assembler

assembly (plural **assemblies**)

> ✓ plural: drop the **y** and add **ies**:
> **assemblies**

assent »*noun* approval or agreement.
» *verb* (**assents, assenting, assented**) agree
to a request or suggestion.

> ℹ do not confuse **assent** with **ascent**,
> which means 'the action of going up'

assert »*verb* (**asserts, asserting, asserted**)
❶ confidently state that something is true.
❷ make other people recognize your
rights. ❸ (**assert yourself**) be confident
and forceful.

assertion

assertive »*adjective* speaking and doing
things in a confident and forceful way.
assertively
assertiveness

asserts

assess »*verb* (**assesses, assessing,
assessed**) make a judgement about the
value or quality of something.
assessment
assessor

> ✓ double **s**, double **s**: **assess**

asset »*noun* ❶ a useful or valuable thing
or person. ❷ (**assets**) property owned by
a person or company.

assiduity »*noun* careful attention to what
you are doing.
– SAY ass-i-**dyoo**-i-ti

assiduous »*adjective* showing great care
and thoroughness.
– SAY uh-**sid**-yoo-uhss
assiduously

assign »*verb* (**assigns, assigning, assigned**)
❶ give someone a task or duty. ❷ set
something aside for a purpose. ❸ regard
something as belonging to.

assignation »*noun* a secret arrangement
to meet.
– SAY a-sig-**nay**-sh'n

assigned

assigning

assignment »*noun* a piece of work that
someone has been asked to do.

assigns

assimilate »*verb* (**assimilates, assimilating,
assimilated**) ❶ take in and understand
information. ❷ absorb people or ideas
into a society or culture. ❸ absorb and
digest food.
assimilation

> ✓ double **s** but only one **m** or **l**:
> **assimilate, assimilation**

assist (verb: **assists, assisting, assisted**)
assistance
assistant

> ✓ **ant** not **ent**: **assistant**

assisted
assisting
assists

assize »*noun* (also **assizes**) (a historical
term) a court which sat at intervals in each
county of England and Wales.
– SAY uh-**syz**

associate (verb: **associates, associating,
associated**)
– SAY uh-**soh**-si-ayt or uh-**soh**-shi-ayt [verb],
uh-**soh**-si-uht or uh-**soh**-shi-uht [noun
and adjective]

association
associational

associative

assonance »*noun* a rhyming of vowel
sounds (as in *hide* and *time*) or of
consonants but not vowels (as in *cold* and
killed).
– SAY ass-uh-nuhnss

assorted

assortment

assuage »*verb* (assuages, assuaging, assuaged) ❶ make an unpleasant feeling less intense. ❷ relieve thirst or an appetite or desire.
– **SAY** uh-swayj

assume (verb: assumes, assuming, assumed)

> **assume** and **presume** both mean 'suppose something to be true'. However, **assume** is used where something is taken for granted without proof, while **presume** is used when the supposition is based on evidence.

assumption

assurance »*noun* ❶ a statement made to make someone feel confident about something. ❷ self-confidence. ❸ life insurance.

> in the field of life insurance, **assurance** and **insurance** do not mean the same thing. **Assurance** refers to policies where a payment is guaranteed, either after a fixed term or on the death of the insured person; **insurance** refers to policies where a payment is made only if, for example, someone dies or has an accident within a limited period.

> ☑ **ance** not **ence: assurance**

assure (verb: assures, assuring, assured)

assured »*adjective* ❶ confident in yourself and your abilities. ❷ protected against change or ending.
assuredly

assures

assuring

asterisk »*noun* a symbol (*) used as a distinguishing mark or pointer in text.

> ☑ **isk** not **ix: asterisk** (*Asterix* is a character in a cartoon strip)

astern »*adverb* behind or towards the rear of a ship or aircraft.

asteroid »*noun* a small rocky planet orbiting the sun.

asthma »*noun* a medical condition causing difficulty in breathing.
– **SAY** ass-muh
asthmatic

> ☑ although it is not pronounced, there is a **th** in the middle of the word: **asthma**

astigmatism »*noun* a fault in the curved shape of someone's eye, which prevents them from seeing clearly.
– **SAY** uh-stig-muh-ti-z'm

astir »*adjective* ❶ in a state of excited movement. ❷ awake and out of bed.

astonish (verb: astonishes, astonishing, astonished)
astonishment

astound (verb: astounds, astounding, astounded)

astrakhan »*noun* the dark curly fleece of young lambs from central Asia, used to make coats and hats.
– **SAY** ass-truh-kan

> ☑ there is an **h** after the **k: astrakhan** (named after the Russian city of *Astrakhan*)

astral »*adjective* relating to the stars.

astray »*adverb* away from the correct course.

astride

astringent »*adjective* ❶ causing body tissue to contract. ❷ sharp or severe.
»*noun* an astringent lotion used medically or as a cosmetic.
– **SAY** uh-strin-juhnt
astringency

> ☑ **ent** not **ant: astringent**

astrology »*noun* study of the positions of the stars and planets carried out by people who think these influence human affairs.
astrologer
astrological

> 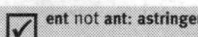 do not confuse **astrology** with **astronomy** which is the science of stars, planets, and the universe

astronaut

> ☑ **-naut**, not **-naught** or **-nought: astronaut**

astronomer

astronomical »*adjective* ❶ relating to astronomy. ❷ extremely large: *he wanted an astronomical fee.*
astronomically

astronomy »*noun* the science of stars, planets, and the universe.
astronomer

> do not confuse **astronomy** with **astrology**, which is concerned with the supposed influence of the stars and planets on human affairs

astrophysics »*noun* the branch of astronomy concerned with the physical nature of stars and planets.
astrophysicist

astute »*adjective* good at making accurate judgements.

astutely
astuteness

asunder »*adverb* apart.

asylum »*noun* (plural **asylums**)
❶ protection from danger. ❷ protection given to someone who has fled their country for political reasons. ❸ (old-fashioned) an institution for people who are mentally ill.
– SAY a-sI-luhm

asymmetrical »*adjective* having no symmetry.
asymmetric
asymmetrically

 be careful when spelling **asymmetrical**: single **s**, double **m**

asymmetry »*noun* the condition of having no symmetry.
– SAY ay-sim-mi-tri

at

atavistic »*adjective* inherited from the earliest human beings: *atavistic fears*.
– SAY at-uh-**viss**-tik
atavism

 ata not atta: **atavistic**

ate past of EAT.

atelier »*noun* a workshop or studio.
– SAY uh-**tel**-i-ay

 atelier is a French word, hence the pronunciation of the ending **ier**

atheism »*noun* disbelief in the existence of a god or gods.
– SAY ay-thi-iz'm
atheist
atheistic

athlete

 there is no **e** after the **h**: **athlete**

athlete's foot »*noun* a form of ringworm infection affecting the feet.

athletic
athletically
athleticism

athwart »*preposition & adverb* across from side to side.
– SAY uh-**thwort**

Atlantic »*adjective* having to do with the Atlantic Ocean.

atlas »*noun* a book of maps or charts.

ATM »*abbreviation* automated teller machine.

atmosphere
atmospheric

atoll »*noun* a ring-shaped coral reef or chain of islands.
– SAY a-tol

 only one **t** but two **l**'s: **atoll**

atom »*noun* ❶ the smallest particle of a chemical element that can exist. ❷ a very small amount of something.

atom bomb

atomic »*adjective* ❶ relating to an atom or atoms. ❷ relating to nuclear energy or nuclear weapons: *an atomic bomb*.

atomic number »*noun* the number of protons in the nucleus of the atom of a chemical element.

atomize »*verb* (**atomizes, atomizing, atomized**) convert something into very fine particles or droplets.
atomizer

 many people prefer the alternative spellings **atomise, atomising**, etc., and **atomiser**: both **s** and **z** spellings are correct

atonal »*adjective* not written in any musical key.
– SAY ay-**toh**-n'l

atone »*verb* (**atones, atoning, atoned**) do something to show you are sorry for something that happened in the past.
– SAY uh-**tohn**
atonement

atop

atrium »*noun* (plural **atria**) ❶ a central hall rising through several storeys and having a glass roof. ❷ an open central court in an ancient Roman house. ❸ one of the two upper cavities of the heart.
– SAY ay-tri-uhm [singular], ay-tri-uh [plural]

 like many other words ending in **um** derived from Latin, **atrium** has a plural ending in **a**: **atria**

atrocious

atrocity »*noun* (plural **atrocities**) an extremely wicked or cruel act.

 plural: drop the **y** and add **ies**: **atrocities**

atrophy »*verb* (**atrophies, atrophying, atrophied**) (of a part of the body) waste away.
» *noun* the condition of wasting away.
– SAY a-truh-fi

attach (verb: **attaches, attaching, attached**)
attachable

 ach not atch: **attach**

a

attache »*noun* a person attached to an ambassador's staff in a specific field of activity: *a military attache.*
– SAY uh-**tash**-ay

> ✓ attache can also be written attaché, with an acute accent on the e (as in the original French)

attache case »*noun* a small, flat briefcase for carrying documents.

> ✓ can also be written attaché case, with an acute accent over the e

attached

attaches

attaching

attachment

attack (verb: **attacks, attacking, attacked**)
attacker

attain »*verb* (**attains, attaining, attained**)
❶ succeed in doing. ❷ reach.
attainable

attainment »*noun* ❶ the achieving of something. ❷ an achievement.

attains

attar »*noun* a sweet-smelling oil made from rose petals.
– SAY **at**-tar

attempt (verb: **attempts, attempting, attempted**)

attend (verb: **attends, attending, attended**)
attendee
attender

attendance

> ✓ ance not ence: attendance

attendant

> ✓ ant not ent: attendant

attended

attendee

attender

attending

attends

attention

> ✓ the ending is tion, not sion: attention

attentive »*adjective* ❶ paying close attention. ❷ considerate and helpful.
attentively
attentiveness

attenuate »*verb* (**attenuates, attenuating, attenuated**) ❶ make something weaker. ❷ make something thin or thinner.
– SAY uh-**ten**-yoo-ayt
attenuation

attest »*verb* (**attests, attesting, attested**)
❶ provide or act as clear evidence of something. ❷ declare something to be true.
attestation

attic »*noun* a space or room inside the roof of a building.

> ✓ no k at the end: attic

attire »*noun* clothes of a particular kind: *business attire.*
»*verb* (**attires, attiring, attired**) dress someone in clothes of a particular kind: *she was attired in an elaborate evening gown.*

attitude

attorney »*noun* (plural **attorneys**) a person who is appointed to act for someone else in legal matters.
– SAY uh-**ter**-ni

> ✓ the plural of attorney simply adds an s: attorneys

Attorney General »*noun* (plural **Attorneys General**) the chief legal officer in some countries.

> ✓ General is an adjective, so make the plural by adding s to Attorney: Attorneys General

attract (verb: **attracts, attracting, attracted**)

attraction

attractive
attractively
attractiveness

attracts

attribute »*verb* (**attributes, attributing, attributed**) (**attribute to**) say or believe that something is the result of: *the moth's rarity is attributed to pollution.*
»*noun* a quality or feature of something.
– SAY uh-**trib**-yoot [verb], **at**-tri-byoot [noun]
attributable
attribution

attrition »*noun* ❶ gradual wearing down through prolonged attack or pressure. ❷ wearing away by friction.
– SAY uh-**tri**-sh'n

attune »*verb* (**attunes, attuning, attuned**) make someone familiar and comfortable with a new situation.

atypical »*adjective* not typical; uncharacteristic.
– SAY ay-**tip**-ik'l

aubergine »*noun* a purple fruit shaped like a large egg, eaten as a vegetable.
– SAY **oh**-ber-*zh*een

aubretia »*noun* a trailing plant with purple, pink, or white flowers.
– SAY aw-**bree**-shuh

> ☑ **bretia** not **brietia**: **aubretia**. Strictly speaking, the correct botanical name is *Aubrieta*.

auburn »*noun* a reddish-brown colour.
– SAY aw-**bern**

> ☑ do not forget the **r** after the **u**: **auburn**

auction (verb: **auctions, auctioning, auctioned**)
auctioneer

audacious »*adjective* bold and daring.
– SAY aw-**day**-shuhss
audaciously

audacity »*noun* ❶ the willingness to take bold risks. ❷ rude and disrespectful behaviour.
– SAY aw-**da**-si-ti

audible »*adjective* able to be heard.
audibility
audibly

audience

> ☑ the ending is **ence** not **ance**: **audience**

audio »*adjective* relating to sound, especially when recorded, transmitted, or reproduced: *audio equipment.*

audio-visual »*adjective* using both sight and sound.

audit »*noun* an official inspection of an organization's accounts.
» *verb* (**audits, auditing, audited**) inspect the accounts of.
– SAY aw-**dit**

> ☑ do not double the **t** in **audited** and **auditing**

audition »*noun* an interview for a performer in which they give a practical demonstration of their skill.
» *verb* (**auditions, auditioning, auditioned**) assess or be assessed by an audition.

auditor »*noun* a person who carries out an audit.

auditorium »*noun* (plural **auditoriums** or **auditoria**) the part of a theatre or hall in which the audience sits.

> ☑ the plural can be either **auditoria** (like the original Latin) or **auditoriums**

auditory »*adjective* relating to hearing.

> ☑ **ory** not **ary**: **auditory**

audits

au fait »*adjective* completely familiar with something.
– SAY oh **fay**

> ℹ **au fait** comes from a French phrase meaning 'to the point'

auger »*noun* a tool for boring holes.
– SAY aw-**ger**

> ℹ do not confuse **auger** with **augur**, which means 'be a sign of a likely outcome' (as in *this augurs well*)

aught »*pronoun* (an old word) anything at all: *for aught I know she might be in danger.*
– SAY awt

> ℹ do not confuse **aught** with the verb **ought** meaning 'have a duty or obligation to do something'

augment »*verb* (**augments, augmenting, augmented**) increase the amount or value of something.
– SAY awg-**ment**
augmentation

au gratin »*adjective* (of food) sprinkled with breadcrumbs or grated cheese and browned.
– SAY oh **gra**-tan

> ℹ **au gratin** is a French phrase meaning 'by grating'

augur »*verb* (**augurs, auguring, augured**) be a sign of a likely outcome: *the end of the cold war seemed to augur well.*
– SAY aw-**ger**

> ℹ do not confuse **augur** with **auger**, which refers to a kind of tool used for boring

augury »*noun* (plural **auguries**) a sign of what will happen in the future.
– SAY aw-**gyoo**-ri

August [eighth month]

august »*adjective* inspiring respect and admiration.
– SAY aw-**gust**

auk »*noun* a black and white seabird with short wings.

auld lang syne »*noun* times long ago.

> ℹ **auld lang syne** is a phrase in Scottish dialect meaning literally 'old long since'

aunt [female relative]

au pair »*noun* a foreign girl employed to look after children and help with housework in exchange for board and lodging.
– SAY oh **pair**

> ℹ **au pair** is a French phrase meaning 'on equal terms'

aura »*noun* (plural **aurae** or **auras**) the distinctive feeling that seems to surround a particular place or person.
– SAY aw-ruh [singular], aw-ree [plural]

> ☑ the plural can be spelled either with an **e** (as in Latin) or an **s**: **aurae** or **auras**

aural »*adjective* having to do with the ear or hearing.
– SAY aw-ruhl

> ⓘ do not confuse **aural** with **oral**, which means 'spoken' or 'having to do with the mouth': both words have the same pronunciation

aureole »*noun* a circle of light around the sun or moon.
– SAY aw-ri-ohl

> ☑ aur-, not or- or ar-: **aureole**. Do not confuse **aureole** with **oriole**, a kind of bird, or **areola**, which refers to the area of darker skin around a nipple.

au revoir »*exclamation* goodbye.
– SAY aw ruh-**vwar**

auricle »*noun* ❶ the external part of the ear. ❷ one of the two upper cavities of the heart.
– SAY o-ri-k'l

aurora »*noun* (plural **auroras** or **aurorae**) streamers of coloured light sometimes seen in the night sky near the north or south poles; the northern or southern lights.

> ☑ the plural can be spelled either with an **e** (like the original Latin) or an **s**: **aurorae** (SAY aw-**raw**-ree) or **auroras**

aurora australis »*noun* the aurora near the south pole; the southern lights.
– SAY aw-**raw**-ruh aw-**stray**-liss

aurora borealis »*noun* the aurora near the north pole; the northern lights.
– SAY aw-**raw**-ruh bo-ri-**ay**-liss

auspices »*plural noun* (**under the auspices of**) with the support or protection of a person or organization.
– SAY awss-piss-iz

auspicious »*adjective* giving hope that there is a good chance of success.
– SAY aw-**spi**-shuhss
auspiciously

Aussie (plural **Aussies**)

austere »*adjective* ❶ severe or strict in appearance or manner. ❷ lacking comforts, luxuries, or decoration.
– SAY aw-**steer** or o-**steer**
austerity

> ☑ the ending is **ere** not **eer**: **austere**

Australasian »*adjective* relating to Australasia, a region made up of Australia, New Zealand, and neighbouring islands in the Pacific.

Australian

Austrian

authentic »*adjective* known to be real; genuine.
authentically
authenticity

authenticate »*verb* (**authenticates**, **authenticating**, **authenticated**) prove or show that something is authentic.
authentication

authenticity

author
authorship

authoress (plural **authoresses**)

authorise another way of spelling AUTHORIZE.

authoritarian »*adjective* demanding that people should strictly obey authority and rules.
» *noun* an authoritarian person.
– SAY aw-tho-ri-**tair**-i-uhn

authoritative »*adjective* ❶ true or accurate and so able to be trusted. ❷ commanding and self-confident. ❸ supported by authority; official.
authoritatively

> ☑ **tative**, not simply **tive**: **authoritative**

authority (plural **authorities**)

> ☑ plural: drop the **y** and add **ies**: **authorities**

authorize »*verb* (**authorizes**, **authorizing**, **authorized**) give official permission for.
authorization

> ☑ many people prefer the alternative spellings **authorise**, **authorises**, etc., and **authorisation**: both **s** and **z** spellings are correct

authorship

autism »*noun* a mental condition in which the sufferer has great difficulty in communicating.
– SAY aw-ti-z'm
autistic

autobiography »*noun* (plural **autobiographies**) an account of a person's life written by that person.
autobiographical

> ☑ plural: drop the **y** and add **ies**: **autobiographies**

autocracy »*noun* (plural **autocracies**) ❶ a system of government in which one

person has total power. ❷ a state governed in this way.
– SAY aw-**tok**-ruh-si

autocrat »*noun* ❶ a ruler who has absolute power. ❷ a person who expects others to obey them.
autocratic

autograph (verb: **autographs, autographing, autographed**)

automata plural of AUTOMATON.
– SAY aw-**tom**-uh-tuh

automate »*verb* (**automates, automating, automated**) convert a process or machine so that it can operate automatically.

automatic
automatically

automating

automation

automaton »*noun* (plural **automata** or **automatons**) a moving mechanical device that looks like a human being.
– SAY aw-**tom**-uh-tuhn [singular], aw-**tom**-uh-tuh [plural]

> ℹ️ the plural can be either **automata** (like the original Greek) or **automatons**

automobile

automotive »*adjective* having to do with motor vehicles.
– SAY aw-tuh-**moh**-tiv

autonomous »*adjective* self-governing or independent.
autonomously

autonomy »*noun* ❶ self-government. ❷ freedom of action.
– SAY aw-**ton**-uh-mi

autopilot »*noun* a device for keeping an aircraft on a set course without the pilot having to control it.

autopsy »*noun* (plural **autopsies**) an examination of a dead body to discover the cause of death.
– SAY aw-**top**-si

> ✅ **p** before **s**: **autopsy**

autumn
autumnal

> ✅ watch for the silent **n** at the end of **autumn** (no longer silent in **autumnal**)

auxiliary »*adjective* providing extra help and support.
»*noun* (plural **auxiliaries**) an auxiliary person or thing.
– SAY awg-**zil**-yuh-ri

> ✅ 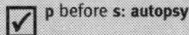 **li** not **ll** in the middle: **auxiliary** plural: drop the **y** and add **ies**: **auxiliaries**

avail »*verb* (**avails, availing, availed**) (**avail yourself of**) use or take advantage of.
»*noun* use or benefit: *his protests were to no avail.*

available
availability

availed

availing

avails

avalanche

> ✅ **ch** not **sh**, and remember the final **e**: **avalanche**

avant-garde »*adjective* (in the arts) new and experimental.
– SAY a-von **gard**

> ℹ️ a French phrase literally meaning 'vanguard, first part of an army'

avarice »*noun* extreme greed for wealth or material things.
– SAY **av**-uh-ris

avaricious »*adjective* very greedy for wealth or material things.
– SAY av-uh-**ri**-shuhss

avatar »*noun* (in Hindu belief) a god or goddess appearing in bodily form on earth.
– SAY **av**-uh-tar

avenge »*verb* (**avenges, avenging, avenged**) repay something bad that has been done to you by harming the person that did it.
avenger

avenue

aver »*verb* (**avers, averring, averred**) declare that something is the case.
– SAY uh-**ver**

average (verb: **averages, averaging, averaged**)

> ✅ remember the first **e**, and the ending is **age**, not **idge**: **average**

averred

averring

avers

averse »*adjective* strongly disliking or opposed to something: *I am not averse to helping out.*

> ℹ️ do not confuse **averse** with **adverse**, which means 'unfavourable' or 'harmful', as in *adverse publicity*

aversion »*noun* a strong dislike.

> ✅ **sion** not **tion**: **aversion**

avert »*verb* (averts, averting, averted)
❶ turn away your eyes. ❷ prevent something unpleasant happening.

avian »*adjective* having to do with birds.

aviary »*noun* (plural **aviaries**) a large enclosure for keeping birds in.

aviation »*noun* the activity of operating and flying aircraft.

aviator

avid »*adjective* keenly interested or enthusiastic.
avidly

avocado »*noun* (plural **avocados**) a pear-shaped fruit with pale green flesh and a large stone.

> ✓ **avo** not **ava**: avocado is a Spanish word. Spell the plural with **os** not **oes**: avocados.

avocet »*noun* a black and white wading bird with an upturned bill.

avoid (verb: avoids, avoiding, avoided)
avoidable
avoidably
avoidance

avoirdupois »*noun* the system of weights based on a pound of 16 ounces.
– **say** av-war-dyoo-**pwah**

> ℹ️ avoirdupois comes from a French phrase meaning 'goods of weight'

avow »*verb* (avows, avowing, avowed)
openly state or confess.

avuncular »*adjective* like an uncle in being kind and friendly towards a younger person.
– **say** uh-**vung**-kyuu-ler

await (verb: awaits, awaiting, awaited)

awake (verb: awakes, awaking, awoke; past participle **awoken**)

awaken (verb: awakens, awakening, awakened)

awakes

awaking

award (verb: awards, awarding, awarded)

aware
awareness

awash »*adjective* covered or flooded with water.

away

awe »*noun* a feeling of great respect mixed with fear.
awed

awesome

> ✓ remember the **e** of awe: awesome

awful
awfully
awfulness

> ✓ **-ful** not **-full**: awful

awhile »*adverb* for a short time.

> ℹ️ do not confuse **awhile** (*stand here awhile*) with **a while**, meaning 'a period of time' (*we chatted for a while*)

awkward
awkwardly
awkwardness

> ✓ **awk** not **auk**: awkward

awl »*noun* a small pointed tool used for making holes.

awning »*noun* a sheet of canvas on a frame, used for shelter.

awoke past of **AWAKE**.

awoken past participle of **AWAKE**.

AWOL »*abbreviation* absent without official leave.
– **say** ay-wol

awry »*adverb & adjective* away from the expected course or position.
– **say** uh-**rI**

axe (verb: axes, axing, axed)

axes plural of **AXIS**.

axing

axiom »*noun* a statement regarded as being obviously true.
– **say** ak-si-uhm
axiomatic

axis »*noun* (plural **axes**) ❶ an imaginary line around which an object or shape rotates. ❷ a fixed line against which points on a graph are measured. ❸ a small group of allied countries.
– **say** ak-sis [singular], ak-seez [plural]

axle

> ✓ **le** not **el**: axle

ayatollah »*noun* a religious leader in Iran.
– **say** I-uh-**tol**-luh

> ✓ don't forget the **h** at the end: ayatollah

aye »*exclamation* (old-fashioned or dialect) yes.
– **say** *rhymes with* my

azalea »*noun* a shrub with brightly coloured flowers.
– **say** uh-**zay**-li-uh

Azerbaijani (plural **Azerbaijanis**)
– **say** a-zuh-by-**jah**-ni

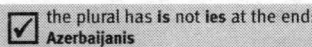 the plural has **is** not **ies** at the end: **Azerbaijanis**

azimuth »*noun* (in astronomy) the direction of a star measured horizontally as an angle from due north or south.
– SAY az-i-muhth

Aztec »*noun* a member of an American Indian people that ruled Mexico before the Spanish conquest of the 16th century. **b**

azure »*noun* a bright blue colour like a cloudless sky.
– SAY az-yuur

Bb

BA »*abbreviation* Bachelor of Arts.

baa (plural **baas**; verb: **baas, baaing, baaed**) [cry of a sheep]

babble (verb: **babbles, babbling, babbled**) [talk rapidly in a confused way] **babbler**

babe

babel »*noun* a confused noise made by a lot of people speaking together.
– SAY bay-b'l

 el not **le**: **babel** (in the Bible, God stopped the building of the *Tower of Babel* by making the builders speak different languages)

babied

babies

baboon »*noun* a large monkey with a long snout, large teeth, and a pink rump.

baby (plural **babies**; verb: **babies, babying, babied**)

 change the **y** to **i** in forming the plural (**babies**) and making the past tense of the verb 'to baby someone', to treat them as a baby (**babied**)

baby boom »*noun* a temporary sharp rise in the birth rate, especially the one which came just after the Second World War.

babyhood

babying

babyish

Babylonian »*noun* a person from the ancient city or kingdom of Babylon in Mesopotamia.
»*adjective* relating to Babylon.
– SAY ba-bi-loh-ni-uhn

babysit (verb: **babysits, babysitting, babysat**) **babysitter**

baccalaureate »*noun* an examination taken in some countries to qualify for higher education.
– SAY ba-kuh-lor-i-uht

☑ double **c**, one **l**: **baccalaureate**

baccarat »*noun* a gambling card game in which players bet against a banker.
– SAY bak-kuh-rah

☑ remember the final **t**: **baccarat** is a French word and the **t** is silent

bacchanalian »*adjective* (of a party or celebration) drunken and wild.
– SAY bak-kuh-nay-li-uhn

☑ remember the **h**: **bacchanalian**. The word comes from *Bacchus*, the Roman god of wine.

bachelor **bachelorhood**

☑ no **t**: **bachelor**

bacillus »*noun* (plural **bacilli**) a bacterium with a simple shape like a rod.
– SAY buh-sil-luhss [singular], buh-sil-lee [plural]

☑ make the plural by changing the **us** ending to **i** (like the original Latin): **bacilli**

back (verb: **backs, backing, backed**) **backer** **backless**

backbencher »*noun* an MP who does not hold a government or opposition post and who sits behind the front benches in the House of Commons.

backbiting

backbone

backchat

backcloth »*noun* = BACKDROP.

backdate (verb: **backdates, backdating, backdated**)

backdrop »*noun* ❶ a painted cloth hung at the back of a theatre stage as part of the scenery. ❷ the setting or background for a scene or event.

backed

backer

backfire (verb: **backfires, backfiring, backfired**)

backgammon »*noun* a game in which two players move their pieces around a board according to the throw of dice.

background

backhand »*noun* (in tennis and similar games) a stroke played with the back of the hand facing in the direction of the stroke.

backhanded

backhander

backing

backlash

backless

backlog

backpack (verb: **backpacks, backpacking, backpacked**)
  backpacker

back-pedal (verb: **back-pedals, back-pedalling, back-pedalled**)

backroom

backs

back-seat driver

backside

backslash »*noun* (plural **backslashes**) a backward-sloping diagonal line (\).

backslide (verb: **backslides, backsliding, backslid**)

backspace »*noun* a typewriter or computer key used to move the carriage or cursor backwards.
»*verb* (**backspaces, backspacing, backspaced**) move a typewriter carriage or computer cursor backwards.

backstage

backstreet

backstroke

back-to-back

backtrack (verb: **backtracks, backtracking, backtracked**)

back-up

backward
  backwardly
  backwardness

backwards

backwash

backwater

backwoods

backwoodsman (plural **backwoodsmen**)

backyard

bacon

bacteria »*plural noun* (singular **bacterium**) a group of microscopic organisms, many kinds of which can cause disease.
  bacterial

> ℹ️ **bacteria** is actually a Latin plural and should always be used with a plural verb, e.g. *the bacteria were multiplying*. If you are referring to one organism or type of organism, use the singular form **bacterium**, as in *this bacterium causes disease*.

bacteriology »*noun* the study of bacteria.
– SAY bak-teer-i-**ol**-uh-ji
  bacteriological
  bacteriologist

bacterium singular of **BACTERIA**.

bad (adjective: **worse, worst**)
  badly
  badness

baddy (plural **baddies**)

> ☑️ **baddy** can also be spelled **baddie**

bade old-fasioned past of **BID**.

badge

badger »*noun* a mammal with a grey and black coat and a white-striped head.
» *verb* (**badgers, badgering, badgered**) pester someone to do something.

badinage »*noun* witty conversation.
– SAY bad-i-nahz*h*

badlands »*plural noun* poor land with very little soil.

badly (adverb: **worse, worst**)

badminton »*noun* a game in which the players hit a shuttlecock across a high net with rackets.

badness

bad-tempered

baffle (verb: **baffles, baffling, baffled**)
  bafflement

baffling
  bafflingly

bag (verb: **bags, bagging, bagged**)

bagatelle »*noun* ❶ a game in which you hit small balls into numbered holes on a board. ❷ something trivial.
– SAY ba-guh-**tel**

49

✓ one **g**, double **l**, and an **e** at the end: **bagatelle**

bagel »*noun* a ring-shaped bread roll with a heavy texture.
– SAY **bay**-g'l

✓ **el** not **le**: **bagel**

baggage

bagged

baggier

baggiest

bagginess

bagging

baggy (adjective: **baggier**, **baggiest**)
bagginess

bagpipes
bagpiper

bags

baguette »*noun* a long, narrow French loaf of bread.
– SAY ba-**get**

✓ remember the **u**, and the ending is **ette**: **baguette** is a French word

Bahraini (plural **Bahrainis**)
– SAY bah-**ray**-ni

✓ the plural has **is** not **ies** at the end: **Bahrainis**

bail[1] »*noun* ❶ the release of an accused person on condition that a sum of money is left with the court, which will be returned as long as the person attends their trial. ❷ money paid to release an accused person.
»*verb* (**bails**, **bailing**, **bailed**) set free an accused person on payment of bail.

ℹ️ do not confuse **bail**, referring to setting free an accused person on condition that money is paid, or **bails** in cricket, with **bale** and **bales** referring to bundles of paper, hay, etc. But see also the note at **BAIL**[3].

bail[2] »*noun* (in cricket) one of the two small wooden crosspieces which rest on the stumps.

bail[3] »*verb* (**bails**, **bailing**, **bailed**) ❶ scoop water out of a boat. ❷ (**bail out**) make an emergency jump out of an aircraft using a parachute. ❸ (**bail someone out**) rescue someone from a difficulty.

✓ in these senses **bail**, **bails**, **bailed**, etc. can also be spelled **bale**, **bales**, **baled**

bailey »*noun* (plural **baileys**) the outer wall of a castle.

bailiff »*noun* ❶ a person who delivers writs and seizes the property of people who owe money for rent. ❷ a landlord's agent.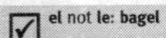

bailing

bailiwick »*noun* ❶ a district over which a bailiff has authority. ❷ (**your bailiwick**) your territory or subject.

bails

bait (verb: **baits**, **baiting**, **baited**) [food used to catch fish or other animals; taunt or tease]

✓ do not confuse **baited** with **bated** (as in the phrase *with bated breath*)

baize »*noun* a thick green material used for covering snooker and card tables.

✓ remember the **i**: **baize**

bake (verb: **bakes**, **baking**, **baked**)

Bakelite »*noun* (trademark) an old kind of plastic which is brittle and dark brown.

✓ **Bakelite** is usually spelled with a capital **B**: it was named after the Belgian-born American chemist Leo H. *Baekeland*, who invented it

baker

bakery (plural **bakeries**)

bakes

baking

baking soda »*noun* sodium bicarbonate.

balaclava »*noun* a close-fitting woollen hat covering the head and neck except for the face.
– SAY ba-luh-**klah**-vuh

balalaika »*noun* a Russian musical instrument like a guitar with a triangular body and three strings.
– SAY ba-luh-**ly**-kuh

balance (verb: **balances**, **balancing**, **balanced**)
balancer

balcony »*noun* (plural **balconies**) ❶ an enclosed platform projecting from the outside of a building. ❷ the highest level of seats in a theatre or cinema.

✓ plural: drop the **y** and add **ies**: **balconies**

bald

balderdash »*noun* nonsense.

balding

baldric »*noun* (a historical term) a belt for a sword, worn over one shoulder and reaching down to the opposite hip.
– SAY **borl**-drik

cunningly, no k: **baldric**

b

bale[1] »*noun* a large bundle of paper, hay, or cotton.
» *verb* (**bales, baling, baled**) make up into bales.
baler

 do not confuse **bale** meaning 'bundle' with **bail** meaning 'release an accused person on payment of a money deposit' or 'wooden crosspiece on a wicket in cricket'. But see also the note at **BAIL**[3].

bale[2] another way of spelling **BAIL**[3].

baleen »*noun* whalebone.
– SAY buh-**leen**

baleen whale »*noun* one of the kinds of whale that have plates of whalebone in the mouth for straining plankton from the water.

baleful »*adjective* threatening to cause harm.
balefully

 -ful not -full: **baleful**

baler

bales

baling

balk another way of spelling **BAULK**.

Balkan »*adjective* relating to the countries on the peninsula in SE Europe surrounded by the Adriatic, Ionian, Aegean, and the Black Seas.

ball (verb: **balls, balling, balled**)

ballad »*noun* ❶ a poem or song telling a story. ❷ a slow sentimental or romantic song.
balladeer

ball-and-socket joint

ballast »*noun* ❶ a heavy substance carried by a ship or hot-air balloon to keep it stable. ❷ gravel or coarse stone used to form the base of a railway track or road.

ballboy

ballcock »*noun* a valve which automatically tops up a cistern when liquid is drawn from it.

balled

ballerina

ballet
balletic

ballgirl

balling

ballistic »*adjective* having to do with to the flight through the air of missiles, bullets, or similar objects.
– SAY buh-**liss**-tik

 ball- not bull-: **ballistic**

ballistic missile »*noun* a missile which is fired and then falls on to its target by gravity.

ballistics »*noun* the science of missiles and firearms.

balloon (verb: **balloons, ballooning, ballooned**)
balloonist

ballot »*noun* ❶ a way of voting on something secretly by putting paper slips in a box. ❷ (**the ballot**) the total number of such votes recorded.
» *verb* (**ballots, balloting, balloted**) ask someone to vote secretly about something.

 do not double the **t** in **balloted** and **balloting**

ballpark »*noun* ❶ a baseball ground. ❷ a general area or approximate range of values.

ballpoint »*noun* a pen with a tiny ball as its writing point.

ballroom

balls

ballyhoo »*noun* excessive publicity or fuss.

balm »*noun* ❶ a sweet-smelling ointment used to heal or soothe the skin. ❷ something that soothes or heals.
– SAY bahm

balmy »*adjective* (**balmier, balmiest**) (of the weather) pleasantly warm.
– SAY **bah**-mi

 do not confuse **balmy** with **barmy**, which is an informal word meaning 'foolish'

balsa »*noun* very lightweight wood from a tropical American tree, used for making models.
– SAY **bawl**-suh

balsam »*noun* a scented resin obtained from some trees and shrubs, used in perfumes and medicines.
– SAY **bawl**-suhm

balsamic vinegar »*noun* dark, sweet Italian vinegar.
– SAY bawl-**sam**-ik

balti »*noun* (plural **baltis**) a type of Pakistani cooking in which the food is cooked in a small two-handled pan.

 the plural has **is** not **ies** at the end: **baltis**

Baltic »*adjective* relating to the Baltic sea or those countries (Estonia, Latvia, and Lithuania) on its eastern shores.

baluster »*noun* a short pillar forming part of a series supporting a rail.
– SAY ba-luh-ster

> ✓ single l, and the ending is er not re: **baluster**

balustrade »*noun* a railing supported by balusters.
– SAY ba-luh-**strayd**

bamboo »*noun* a giant tropical grass with hollow woody stems.

bamboozle »*verb* (**bamboozles, bamboozling, bamboozled**) (in informal English) ❶ cheat or deceive. ❷ confuse.

ban (verb: **bans, banning, banned**)

banal »*adjective* boring because too ordinary and predictable.
– SAY buh-**nahl**

banality (plural **banalities**)

banana

band (verb: **bands, banding, banded**)

bandage (verb: **bandages, bandaging, bandaged**)

bandanna »*noun* a large coloured handkerchief.
– SAY ban-**dan**-nuh

> ✓ **bandanna** can also be spelled **bandana**, with only one n: both spellings are correct

B. & B. »*abbreviation* bed and breakfast.

bandeau »*noun* (plural **bandeaux**) ❶ a narrow band worn round the head. ❷ a woman's strapless top.
– SAY ban-doh [singular], ban-dohz [plural]

> ✓ the plural of **bandeau** is **bandeaux** (as in the original French)

banded [marked with bands]

bandicoot »*noun* an insect-eating marsupial found in Australia and New Guinea.
– SAY ban-di-koot

bandied past of **BANDY**[2].

bandier

bandies

bandiest

banding

bandit
  banditry

> ℹ the normal plural is **bandits**, although you sometimes come across the Italian form **banditti**

bandolier »*noun* a shoulder belt with loops or pockets for carrying bullets.
– SAY ban-duh-**leer**

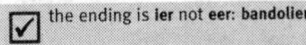

> ✓ the ending is **ier** not **eer: bandolier**

bands

bandsaw »*noun* a power saw having a moving steel belt with a toothed edge.

bandstand

bandwagon »*noun* an activity or cause that has suddenly become fashionable or popular.

> ✓ only one **g: bandwagon**

bandwidth »*noun* ❶ a range of frequencies used in telecommunications. ❷ the ability of a computer network to transmit signals.

bandy[1] »*adjective* (**bandier, bandiest**) (of a person's legs) curved outwards so that the knees are wide apart.

bandy[2] »*verb* (**bandies, bandying, bandied**) use an idea or word often in casual talk.

bane »*noun* a cause of great distress or annoyance.

> ✓ **ane** not **ain: bane**

bang (verb: **bangs, banging, banged**)

banger

banging

Bangladeshi (plural **Bangladeshis**)

> ✓ the plural of **Bangladeshi** simply adds an s, not **es: Bangladeshis**

bangle

banish »*verb* (**banishes, banishing, banished**) ❶ make someone leave a place as a punishment. ❷ get rid of; drive away.
banishment

banister »*noun* ❶ the upright posts and handrail at the side of a staircase. ❷ a single upright post at the side of a staircase.

> ✓ **banister** can also be spelled **bannister**, with two n's: both spellings are correct

banjo »*noun* (plural **banjos** or **banjoes**) a musical instrument like a guitar, with a circular body and a long neck.
banjoist

> ✓ the plural of **banjo** can have **os** or **oes: banjos** or **banjoes**

bank (verb: **banks, banking, banked**)

banker

banking

banknote »*noun* a piece of paper money.

bankroll »*verb* (**bankrolls, bankrolling, bankrolled**) (in informal English) provide with money.

bankrupt »*adjective* ❶ officially declared not to have the money to pay debts. ❷ completely lacking in a particular good quality or value: *morally bankrupt.*
» *noun* a bankrupt person.
» *verb* (**bankrupts, bankrupting, bankrupted**) make someone bankrupt.

bankruptcy (plural **bankruptcies**)

> ✓ remember to keep the **t**: **bankruptcy** plural: drop the **y** and add **ies**: **bankruptcies**

bankrupted

bankrupting

bankrupts

banks

banned

banner

banning

bannister another way of spelling **BANISTER**.

bannock »*noun* (in Scotland and northern England) a round, flat loaf.

banns »*plural noun* a public announcement of an intended marriage read out in a parish church.

> ✓ **banns** has two **n**'s, unlike **bans** meaning 'forbids' or 'orders which forbid'

banquet »*noun* a formal meal for many people.
» *verb* (**banquets, banqueting, banqueted**) take part in a banquet.
– SAY bang-kwit

> ✓ do not double the **t** in **banqueting** and **banqueted**

banquette »*noun* a padded bench along a wall.
– SAY bang-ket

bans

> ℹ see the note at **BANNS**

banshee »*noun* (in Irish legend) a female spirit whose wailing warns of a death.

> ✓ two **e**'s at the end: **banshee**

bantam »*noun* a chicken of a small breed.

bantamweight »*noun* a boxing weight coming between flyweight and featherweight.

banter »*noun* friendly teasing between people.

» *verb* (**banters, bantering, bantered**) make friendly teasing remarks.

Bantu »*noun* (plural **Bantu** or **Bantus**) ❶ a member of a large group of peoples living in central and southern Africa. ❷ the group of languages spoken by these peoples.
– SAY ban-**too**

> ℹ **Bantu** is a very offensive word in South African English, although it is a standard term outside South Africa with reference to language

banyan »*noun* an Indian fig tree with spreading branches from which roots grow downwards to the ground and form new trunks.
– SAY ban-yan or **ban**-yuhn

bap »*noun* a soft, round, flattish bread roll.

baptise another way of spelling **BAPTIZE**.

baptism »*noun* the Christian ceremony of sprinkling a person with water or dipping them in it to show that they have entered the Church.
baptismal

Baptist »*noun* a member of a Christian group believing that only adults should be baptized.

baptize »*verb* (**baptizes, baptizing, baptized**) ❶ perform the ceremony of baptism on a person. ❷ give someone a name or nickname.

> ✓ many people prefer the alternative spellings **baptise, baptises**, etc.: both **s** and **z** spellings are correct

bar (verb: **bars, barring, barred**)

barb

Barbadian »*noun* a person from Barbados.
» *adjective* relating to Barbados.
– SAY bah-**bay**-di-uhn

barbarian

> ✓ **-bar-** in the middle, not **-bair-** or **-bear-**: **barbarian**

barbaric

barbarism

barbarous
barbarously

barbecue (verb: **barbecues, barbecuing, barbecued**)

> ✓ be very careful with the spelling of **barbecue**. The beginning is not **barber-** or **barbi-**, and the ending is not **-que**: **barbecue**.

barbed »*adjective* ❶ having a barb or barbs. ❷ (of a remark) spiteful.

barbed wire

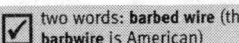
two words: **barbed wire** (the spelling **barbwire** is American)

barbel »*noun* ❶ a long, thin growth hanging from the mouth or snout of some fish. ❷ a freshwater fish with barbels.
– SAY **bar**-b'l

barbell »*noun* a long metal bar with discs of different weights attached at each end, used for weightlifting.

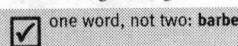
one word, not two: **barbell**

barber

barbershop »*noun* close harmony singing by a group of four men without musical backing.

barbican »*noun* a double tower above a gate or drawbridge of a castle.
– SAY **bar**-bi-kuhn

barbiturate »*noun* a kind of sedative drug.
– SAY bar-**bit**-yuu-ruht

barbwire American spelling of **BARBED WIRE**.

bar chart »*noun* a diagram in which different quantities are shown by rectangles of different heights.

bar code »*noun* a set of stripes printed on a product, able to be read by a computer.

bard »*noun* ❶ (an old word) a poet. ❷ (the **Bard**) Shakespeare.
bardic

bare (verb: **bares**, **baring**, **bared**) [without clothes; reveal]
barely
bareness

bareback »*adverb & adjective* on a horse without a saddle.

bared

barefaced »*adjective* done openly and without shame: *a barefaced lie*.

barely

bareness

bares

bargain (verb: **bargains**, **bargaining**, **bargained**)

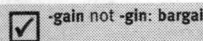
-**gain** not -**gin**: **bargain**

barge (verb: **barges**, **barging**, **barged**)

bargee »*noun* a person in charge of or working on a barge.
– SAY bar-**jee**

bargepole »*noun* a long pole used to push a barge along.

barges

barging

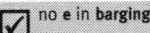
no **e** in **barging**

bar graph »*noun* = **BAR CHART**.

baring

baritone »*noun* a man's singing voice between tenor and bass.

there is only one **r** in **baritone**

barium »*noun* a chemical element that is a soft white metal.
– SAY **bair**-i-uhm

barium meal »*noun* a mixture which is swallowed so that the stomach or intestines can be seen on an X-ray.

bark (verb: **barks**, **barking**, **barked**)

barker »*noun* a person at a fair who calls out to passers-by to persuade them to visit a sideshow.

barking

barks

barley »*noun* a type of cereal plant with bristly heads.

ley not **ly**: **barley**

barley sugar »*noun* an orange sweet made of boiled sugar.

barmaid

barman (plural **barmen**)

barmier

barmiest

bar mitzvah »*noun* a religious ceremony in which a Jewish boy aged 13 takes on the responsibilities of an adult.
– SAY bar **mitz**-vuh

two words, not one: **bar mitzvah**. It is a Hebrew phrase meaning 'son of the commandment'.

barmy »*adjective* (**barmier**, **barmiest**) (in informal English) foolish or crazy.

do not confuse **barmy** with **balmy**, used to describe pleasantly warm weather

barn

barnacle »*noun* a small shellfish which fixes itself to things underwater.
– SAY **bar**-nuh-k'l

barn dance »*noun* a party with country dancing.

barn owl »*noun* a pale-coloured owl with a heart-shaped face.

barnstorming »*adjective* done in a very showy, forceful, and successful way.

barometer »*noun* an instrument that measures the pressure of the atmosphere, used to forecast the weather.
– SAY buh-**rom**-i-ter
barometric

✓ this is one of the words that ends in -meter rather than -metre: barometer

baron »*noun* ❶ a man belonging to the lowest rank of the British nobility. ❷ (in the middle ages) a man who held lands or property from the king or queen or a lord.
baronial SAY buh-**roh**-ni-uhl

✓ only one **r** and one **n**: baron, baroness, baronet

baroness (plural **baronesses**)

baronet »*noun* a man who holds a title below that of baron.

baroque »*adjective* in a highly decorated style of European architecture, art, and music popular during the 17th and 18th centuries.
– SAY buh-**rok**

✓ there is only one **r**: baroque

barque »*noun* a sailing ship with three masts.
– SAY bark

✓ **que** not **k**: barque (**bark** is an old spelling sometimes used as a poetic word for a boat)

barrack »*verb* (**barracks, barracking, barracked**) ❶ provide soldiers with somewhere to stay. ❷ shout insulting comments at a performer or speaker.

barracks »*noun* buildings for housing soldiers.

barracuda »*noun* a large predatory fish found in tropical seas.
– SAY ba-ruh-**koo**-duh

✓ two **r**'s but only one **c** and one **d**: barracuda

barrage »*noun* ❶ a continuous attack by heavy guns. ❷ an overwhelming number of questions or complaints. ❸ a barrier across a river to control the water level.
»*verb* (**barrages, barraging, barraged**) bother someone with lots of questions or complaints.
– SAY ba-**rahz**h

barred [prohibited; marked with bars]

barrel

✓ double **r**, single **l**: barrel

barren »*adjective* ❶ (of land) too poor to produce vegetation. ❷ (of a female animal) unable to bear young. ❸ bleak and lifeless.
barrenly
barrenness

barricade (verb: **barricades, barricading, barricaded**)
– SAY ba-ri-**kayd**

barrier

barrier reef »*noun* a coral reef close to the shore but separated from it by a channel of deep water.

barring

barrister »*noun* a lawyer qualified to argue a case in court.
– SAY ba-**riss**-ter

✓ double **r** in barrister

barrow

bars

bartender

barter »*verb* (**barters, bartering, bartered**) exchange goods or services for other goods or services.
»*noun* trading by exchange.

basal »*adjective* forming or belonging to a base.
– SAY **bay**-s'l

basalt »*noun* a kind of dark rock that comes from volcanoes.
– SAY ba-**sawlt**

base¹ (verb: **bases, basing, based**) [lowest part; use as a foundation]

base² »*adjective* (**baser, basest**) ❶ bad or immoral: *the electorate's baser instincts.* ❷ (an old word) of low social class.

baseball

based

baseless »*adjective* not based on fact; untrue.

baseline »*noun* ❶ a starting point for comparisons. ❷ (in tennis and volleyball) the line marking each end of a court.

basement

base metal »*noun* a common non-precious metal.

baser

bases¹ plural of BASE¹.
– SAY **bay**-siz

bases² plural of BASIS.
– SAY **bay**-seez

basest

bash (verb: **bashes, bashing, bashed**)

bashful »*adjective* shy and easily embarrassed.
bashfully
bashfulness

-ful not -full: **bashful**

bashing

BASIC »*noun* a computer programming language.

basic

basically

the ending is **cally**, not **cly**: **basically**

basics

basil »*noun* a herb used in cooking.

basilica »*noun* a large church or hall having two rows of columns inside and a curved end with a dome.
– SAY buh-**zil**-i-kuh

basilisk »*noun* a mythical reptile that could kill people by looking at or breathing on them.
– SAY **baz**-i-lisk

basin

basing

basis (plural **bases**) [underlying principles or foundation]

make the plural by changing the **-is** ending to **-es** (as in Latin): **bases** (SAY **bay**-seez)

bask »*verb* (**basks, basking, basked**) ❶ lie in the sun for pleasure. ❷ (**bask in**) take great pleasure in something.

basket

basketball

basketry »*noun* ❶ the craft of basket-making. ❷ baskets collectively.

basketwork

basking

basking shark »*noun* a shark which feeds on plankton and swims slowly close to the surface.

basks

basmati »*noun* a kind of long-grain Indian rice.
– SAY baz-**mah**-ti

Basque »*noun* ❶ a member of a people living in the western Pyrenees in France and Spain. ❷ the language of this people.

basque »*noun* a woman's close-fitting bodice.

bas-relief »*noun* (in art) low relief.
– SAY bass-**ri**-leef

bas-relief has only one **s**, not two (**bas** being the French word for 'low')

bass¹ »*noun* (plural **basses**) ❶ the lowest adult male singing voice. ❷ the deep,

low-frequency part of a sound. ❸ a bass guitar or double bass.
– SAY bayss

bass² »*noun* (plural **bass** or **basses**) a sea or freshwater fish with spiny fins, used for food.
– SAY bass

basset hound »*noun* a hunting dog with a long body, short legs, and long, drooping ears.

bassist »*noun* a musician who plays a double bass or bass guitar.
– SAY **bay**-sist

bassoon »*noun* a large bass woodwind instrument of the oboe family.
bassoonist

double **s** and double **o**: **bassoon**

bastard »*noun* ❶ (an old word) a person whose parents were not married. ❷ (in informal English) an unpleasant person.
» *adjective* no longer in its pure or original form.

bastardize »*verb* (**bastardizes, bastardizing, bastardized**) make something less good by adding new elements.
bastardization

many people prefer the alternative spellings **bastardise, bastardises**, etc., and **bastardisation**: both **s** and **z** spellings are correct

bastardy »*noun* (an old word) illegitimacy.

baste »*verb* (**bastes, basting, basted**) ❶ pour fat or juices over meat while it cooks. ❷ sew with long, loose stitches to prepare something for permanent sewing.
– SAY *rhymes with* taste

bastion »*noun* ❶ a part of a fortification that sticks out. ❷ something that protects or preserves particular principles or activities: *the town was a bastion of Conservatism.*

bat (verb: **bats, batting, batted**)

batch

bated »*adjective* (**with bated breath**) in great suspense.

the spelling is **ated** not **aited**: **bated**

bath (verb: **baths, bathing, bathed**) [large container of water in which you wash; wash in a bath]

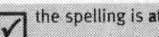
the inflected forms **bathed** and **bathing** are spelled the same as the inflections of the verb **bathe**, although pronounced differently

Bath bun »*noun* a round currant bun topped with icing or sugar.

> ✓ capital **B**: named after the town of *Bath* in SW England

bathe (verb: **bathes, bathing, bathed**) [wash by immersion in water; swim]
– ꜱᴀʏ bay*th*
bather
bathing

> ✓ remember to drop the **e** in the word **bathing**. The inflected forms **bathed** and **bathing** are therefore spelled the same for the two verbs **bath** and **bathe**, although pronounced differently.

bathed past of **BATH** or **BATHE**.

bathing present participle of **BATH** or **BATHE**.

bathos »*noun* (in literature) a change from an important and serious mood to a trivial or ridiculous one.
– ꜱᴀʏ bay-thoss

bathrobe

bathroom

baths

batik »*noun* a method of producing coloured designs on cloth by waxing the parts that you do not want to be dyed.
– ꜱᴀʏ ba-teek

baton »*noun* ❶ a thin stick used to conduct an orchestra or choir. ❷ a short stick passed from runner to runner in a relay race. ❸ a stick carried and twirled by a drum major.

> ⓘ do not confuse **baton** with **batten** meaning 'a strip used for strengthening something'

bats

batsman (plural **batsmen**) »*noun* a player who bats in cricket.

battalion »*noun* a large body of troops, forming part of a brigade.
– ꜱᴀʏ buh-tal-i-uhn

> ✓ two **t**'s, one **l**: batt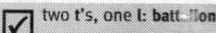lion

batted

batten »*noun* a long wooden or metal strip for strengthening or securing something.

> ⓘ do not confuse **batten** with **baton** referring to a stick

Battenberg cake »*noun* an oblong marzipan-covered sponge cake in two colours.

batter (verb: **batters, battering, battered**)
battered
batteries
battering

battering ram »*noun* a heavy object rammed against a door to break it down.

batters

battery (plural **batteries**)

> ✓ plural: drop the **y** and add **ies**: **batteries**

battier

battiest

battiness

batting

battle (verb: **battles, battling, battled**)
battler

battleaxe

battlecruiser

battled

battledress

battlefield

battleground

battlement »*noun* a wall with gaps for firing through, forming part of a fortification.

battler

battles

battleship

battling

batty (adjective: **battier, battiest**)
battiness

bauble »*noun* a small, showy trinket.
– ꜱᴀʏ baw-b'l

> ✓ **bau** not **baw**: **bauble**

baulk »*verb* (**baulks, baulking, baulked**)
❶ (**baulk at**) hesitate to accept an idea.
❷ thwart or hinder: *he raised every objection to baulk this plan.*
– ꜱᴀʏ bawlk

> ✓ **baulk** can also be spelled **balk**: both spellings are correct

bauxite »*noun* a rock resembling clay, from which aluminium is obtained.
– ꜱᴀʏ bawk-syt

bawdy »*adjective* (**bawdier, bawdiest**) indecent in an amusing way.
bawdiness

bawl (verb: **bawls, bawling, bawled**) [shout or cry noisily]

bay (verb: **bays, baying, bayed**)

bayonet »*noun* a long blade fixed to a rifle for hand-to-hand fighting.
»*verb* (**bayonets, bayoneting, bayoneted**) stab someone with a bayonet.

> ✓ do not double the **t** in **bayoneting** and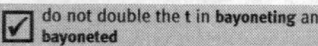
> **bayoneted**

bays

bazaar »*noun* ❶ a market in a Middle Eastern country. ❷ a sale of goods to raise funds.
– **SAY** buh-**zar**

> ✓ one **z**, double **a**: **bazaar**. Do not confuse the spellings of **bazaar** and **bizarre** meaning 'strange'

bazooka »*noun* a short-range rocket launcher used against tanks.

BBC »*abbreviation* British Broadcasting Corporation.

BC »*abbreviation* before Christ, used to indicate a date of a certain number of years before Christ's birth.

> ℹ **BC** is placed *after* a number, as in *72 BC*

be

beach (verb: **beaches, beaching, beached**) [seashore]

> ✓ do not confuse the spelling of **beach** with that of the **beech** tree

beachcomber »*noun* a person who searches beaches for valuable things.

> ✓ remember the second **b**: **beachcomber**

beached

beaches

beaching

beacon »*noun* ❶ a fire lit on the top of a hill as a signal. ❷ a light acting as a signal for ships or aircraft.

bead (verb: **beads, beading, beaded**)

beadle »*noun* ❶ a ceremonial officer of a church, college, etc. ❷ (a historical term) a parish officer dealing with petty offenders.

beads

beady »*adjective* (of a person's eyes) small, round, and observant.

beagle »*noun* a small short-legged hound.

beak

beaker

beam (verb: **beams, beaming, beamed**)

bean

beanbag

beanfeast »*noun* (in informal English) a party with lots of food and drink.

beanpole

bear (verb: **bears, bearing, bore**; past participle **borne**) [carry; put up with; kind of animal]

> ℹ do not confuse **bear** with **bare** meaning 'naked' or 'reveal'

bearable
bearably

beard »*noun* a growth of hair on the chin and lower cheeks of a man's face.
» *verb* (**beards, bearding, bearded**) boldly confront or challenge someone formidable.

bearer

bearing

bearish »*adjective* expecting share prices to fall; not confident (the opposite of *bullish*).
bearishly
bearishness

bear market »*noun* a stock market in which share prices are falling.

bears

bearskin »*noun* a tall cap of black fur worn for ceremonies by certain troops.

beast

beastly
beastliness

beast of burden »*noun* an animal used for carrying loads.

beat (verb: **beats, beating, beat**; past participle **beaten**)
beater

beatific »*adjective* feeling or expressing blissful happiness.
– **SAY** bee-uh-**tif**-ik
beatifically

beatify »*verb* (**beatifies, beatifying, beatified**) (in the Roman Catholic Church) announce that a dead person is in a state of bliss, the first step towards making them a saint.
– **SAY** bi-**at**-i-fI
beatification

> ✓ do not confuse with **beautify**: **beatify** has no **u**

beating

beatnik »*noun* a young person in the 1950s and 1960s who rejected conventional society.

> ✓ **ik** not **ic**: **beatnik**

beats

beau »*noun* (plural **beaux** or **beaus**) (old-fashioned) a boyfriend.
– **SAY** boh [singular], bohz [plural]

> ℹ **beau** is a French word meaning 'handsome'

Beaufort scale »*noun* a scale of wind speed ranging from force 0 to force 12.
– **SAY** **boh**-fert

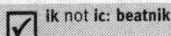

Beaujolais »*noun* a light red wine from SE France.
– SAY boh-*zh*uh-lay

beautician »*noun* a person whose job is to give beauty treatments.

beautiful
beautifully

 remember the **u** before the **t**, and **-ful** not **-full** at the end: **beautiful**

beautify »*verb* (**beautifies, beautifying, beautified**) make beautiful.
beautification

 remember the **u**: **beautify**. To be **beatified** is not the same at all.

beauty (plural **beauties**)

 plural: drop the **y** and add **ies**: **beauties**

beaux plural of BEAU.

beaver »*noun* a large rodent that lives partly in water.
» *verb* (**beavers, beavering, beavered**) (**beaver away**) (in informal English) work hard.

becalmed »*adjective* (of a sailing ship) unable to move due to lack of wind.

became past of BECOME.

because

ℹ️ on starting a sentence with **because**, see the note at AND

beck

beckon (verb: **beckons, beckoning, beckoned**)

become (verb: **becomes, becoming, became**; past participle **become**)

becoming »*adjective* ❶ (of clothing) looking good on someone. ❷ in good taste; polite and restrained.
becomingly

becquerel »*noun* (in physics) a unit of radioactivity.
– SAY bek-kuh-rel

 remember the **c**: **becquerel**. It was named after the French physicist Antoine-Henri *Becquerel*.

bed (verb: **beds, bedding, bedded**)

bedbug

bedchamber

bedclothes

bedded

bedding

bedeck »*verb* (**bedecks, bedecking, bedecked**) decorate something richly.

bedevil »*verb* (**bedevils, bedevilling, bedevilled**) cause continual trouble to someone or something.

✅ double the **l** in **bedevilling** and **bedevilled** (the spelling with a single **l** is American)

bedfellow

bedlam »*noun* a scene of great confusion and noise.
– SAY bed-luhm

bedlinen

Bedouin »*noun* (plural **Bedouin**) an Arab living as a nomad in the desert.
– SAY bed-oo-in

bedpan

bedpost

bedraggled »*adjective* untidy.

✅ remember to double the **g**: **bedraggled**

bedridden »*adjective* unable to get out of bed because of sickness or old age.

bedrock »*noun* ❶ a layer of solid rock under soil. ❷ the central principles on which something is based.

bedroom

beds

bedside

bedsit »*noun* a rented room which contains a combined bedroom and living room, with cooking facilities.
bedsitter

bedsore »*noun* a sore caused by lying in bed in one position for a long time.

bedspread

bedstead »*noun* the framework of a bed.

bed-wetting

bee [insect producing honey]

beech »*noun* a large tree with grey bark and pale wood.

✅ do not confuse the spelling of **beech** with **beach** meaning 'shore of sand or pebbles'

beechnut

beef (verb: **beefs, beefing, beefed**)

beefburger

beefeater »*noun* a Yeoman Warder or Yeoman of the Guard in the Tower of London.

beefed

beefier

beefiest

beefiness

beefing

beefs

beefsteak »*noun* a thick slice of steak.

beefy »*adjective* (beefier, beefiest) muscular or strong.
beefiness

beehive

bee-keeping
bee-keeper

beeline »*noun* (make a beeline for) hurry straight to.

Beelzebub »*noun* the Devil.
– SAY bi-el-zi-bub

 Beelzebub is a Hebrew word meaning 'lord of flies'

been

beep (verb: beeps, beeping, beeped)
beeper

beer

beeswax »*noun* wax produced by bees to make honeycombs, used for wood polishes and candles.

beet »*noun* a plant with a fleshy root, grown as food and for making into sugar.

ee not ea: **beet**

beetle

beetroot

befall »*verb* (befalls, befalling, befell; past participle **befallen**) (usually of something bad) happen to someone: *a tragedy befell his daughter.*

befit »*verb* (befits, befitting, befitted) be appropriate for someone.
befitting

double the t in **befitting** and **befitted**

before

beforehand

befriend (verb: befriends, befriending, befriended)

befuddle »*verb* (befuddles, befuddling, befuddled) muddle or confuse.

beg (verb: begs, begging, begged)

began past of BEGIN.

begat see BEGET.

beget »*verb* (begets, begetting, begot or begat; past participle **begotten**) (an old word) ❶ produce a child. ❷ cause something.
– SAY bi-get

remember to double the t in **begetting** and **begotten**
begat is an older version of the past tense **begot**

beggar

 ar not er: **beggar**

beggarly »*adjective* ❶ meagre and ungenerous. ❷ poverty-stricken.

begin (verb: begins, beginning, began; past participle **begun**)
beginner

remember to double the n in **beginning** and **beginner**

begonia »*noun* a plant with brightly coloured flowers.
– SAY bi-goh-ni-uh

begot past of BEGET.

begotten past participle of BEGET.

begrudge »*verb* (begrudges, begrudging, begrudged) ❶ feel envious that someone possesses or enjoys something. ❷ give something reluctantly or resentfully.

beguile »*verb* (beguiles, beguiling, beguiled) charm or trick.

don't forget the u: **beguile**

begun past participle of BEGIN.

behalf

behave (verb: behaves, behaving, behaved)

behaviour
behavioural

remember the u: **behaviour** (**behavior** is the American spelling)

behead (verb: beheads, beheading, beheaded)

beheld past and past participle of BEHOLD.

behemoth »*noun* a huge creature or monster.
– SAY bi-hee-moth

behest »*noun* a person's order or command: *they had assembled at his behest.*
– SAY bi-hest

behind

behindhand

behold »*verb* (behold, beholding, beheld) (an old word) see or observe.
beholder

beholden »*adjective* (beholden to) owing something to someone because they have done you a favour.

beholder

beholding

behove »*verb* (it behoves someone to do) it is right or appropriate for someone to do.
– SAY bi-hohv

beige »*noun* a pale sandy colour.

b being

✓ e before i: **beige** does not follow the usual rule

bejewelled »*adjective* decorated with jewels.

✓ double l: **bejewelled** (the spelling **bejeweled** is American)

Belarussian
– SAY bel-uh-**rush**-uhn

✓ the country is **Belarus**, with an **a**, hence **Belarussian**, although the older spelling **Belorussian** is still used

belated
belatedly
belatedness

belay »*verb* (**belays**, **belaying**, **belayed**)
❶ fix a rope round a rock, pin, or other object to secure it. ❷ (in nautical slang) stop!
– SAY bi-**lay**

belch (verb: **belches**, **belching**, **belched**)

beleaguered »*adjective* ❶ under siege. ❷ in difficulties; harassed.

✓ ue after the g: **beleaguered**

belfry »*noun* (plural **belfries**) the place in a bell tower or steeple in which bells are housed.

Belgian [from Belgium]

✓ -an not -un: **Belgian**

Belial »*noun* the Devil.
– SAY bee-li-uhl

ℹ **Belial** is a Hebrew word meaning 'worthlessness'

belie »*verb* (**belies**, **belying**, **belied**) ❶ fail to give a true idea of. ❷ show that something is untrue or unjustified.

belief

✓ i before e: **belief**

belies

believe (verb: **believes**, **believing**, **believed**)
believable
believer

✓ the usual rule is **i** before **e**, except after **c**: **believe**

Belisha beacon »*noun* an orange ball containing a flashing light, mounted on a post at each end of a zebra crossing.
– SAY buh-**lee**-shuh

✓ one l, followed by an **i**: **Belisha** (named after the British Minister of Transport Leslie Hore-*Belisha*)

belittle »*verb* (**belittles**, **belittling**, **belittled**) dismiss as unimportant.

✓ two t's: **belittle**

Belizean [of Belize]
– SAY be-**leez**-i-uhn

✓ zean, not zan or zian: **Belizean**

bell [object that rings]

belladonna »*noun* a poisonous plant (deadly nightshade), or a drug made from it.
– SAY bel-luh-**don**-nuh

✓ two l's, two n's: **belladonna**

belle »*noun* a beautiful girl or woman.

bellicose »*adjective* aggressive and ready to fight.
– SAY **bel**-li-kohss
bellicosity

bellies

belligerent »*adjective* ❶ hostile and aggressive. ❷ engaged in a war or conflict.
belligerence
belligerently

✓ two l's and ent, not ant: **belligerent**

bellow (verb: **bellows**, **bellowing**, **bellowed**) [give a deep roar]

✓ double l in **bellow**; do not confuse it with **below**

bellows »*plural noun* a device consisting of a bag with two handles, used for blowing air into a fire.

bell-ringing

belly (plural **bellies**)
bellied

✓ plural: drop the **y** and add **ies**: **bellies**

bellyache (in informal English) »*noun* a stomach pain.
» *verb* (**bellyaches**, **bellyaching**, **bellyached**) complain noisily or often.

bellyflop »*noun* a dive into water in which you land flat on your front.

bellyful

✓ -ful not -full: **bellyful**

belong (verb: **belongs**, **belonging**, **belonged**)
belongings
belongs

Belorussian older spelling of BELARUSSIAN.

beloved

below [at a lower level than]

> ✓ do not confuse the spellings of **below** and **bellow** meaning 'make a loud roar'

belt (verb: **belts, belting, belted**)

beluga »*noun* ❶ a small white Arctic whale. ❷ a very large sturgeon from which caviar is obtained.
– **say** buh-**loo**-guh

belying present participle of **BELIE.**

bemoan »*verb* (**bemoans, bemoaning, bemoaned**) express sadness or regret about something.

bemused »*adjective* confused or bewildered.
bemusement

bench

benchmark »*noun* a standard or point of reference.

bench press »*noun* an exercise in which you lie on a bench with your feet on the floor and raise a weight with both arms.

bend (verb: **bends, bending, bent**)
bendy

bendy (adjective: **bendier, bendiest**)

beneath

Benedictine »*noun* ❶ a monk or nun of a Christian order following the rule of St Benedict. ❷ (trademark) a liqueur originally made by Benedictine monks in France.
– **say** ben-i-**dik**-teen

benediction »*noun* ❶ the speaking of a blessing. ❷ the state of being blessed.

benefaction »*noun* a donation.
– **say** ben-i-**fak**-shuhn

benefactor »*noun* a person who gives money or other help.

> ✓ **bene-** not **beni-** and **-or** not **-er**: **benefactor**

benefice »*noun* an arrangement in which a Christian priest is paid and given accommodation for being in charge of a parish.
– **say** ben-i-**fiss**

beneficial »*adjective* favourable or advantageous.
beneficially

> ✓ **bene** not **beni** and **cial** not **shal**: **beneficial**

beneficiary »*noun* (plural **beneficiaries**) a person who benefits from something.

benefit (verb: **benefits, benefiting, benefited**)

> ✓ do not double the t in **benefiting** and **benefited** (the spellings **benefitting** and **benefitted** are American)

benevolent »*adjective* ❶ well meaning and kindly. ❷ (of an organization) charitable rather than profit-making.
– **say** bi-**nev**-uh-luhnt
benevolence
benevolently

> ✓ **bene** not **beni** and **ent** not **ant**: **benevolent**

Bengali »*noun* (plural **Bengalis**) ❶ a person from Bengal. ❷ the language of Bangladesh and West Bengal.
»*adjective* relating to Bengal.
– **say** ben-**gaw**-li

> ✓ the plural has **is** not **ies** at the end: **Bengalis**

benighted »*adjective* ignorant or primitive.

> ✓ there is no k in **benighted**, which has to do with **night** not **knights**

benign »*adjective* ❶ cheerful and kindly. ❷ favourable; not harmful. ❸ (of a tumour) not malignant.
benignity
benignly

> ✓ **ign** not **ine**: **benign**

Beninese (plural **Beninese**) [of Benin]
– **say** ben-i-**neez**

bent past and past participle of **BEND.**

benzene »*noun* (in chemistry) a volatile liquid hydrocarbon present in coal tar and petroleum.
– **say** **ben**-zeen

> ✓ be careful to spell the chemical **benzene** with the ending **ene**, not **ine**. **Benzine** is an old word for a kind of petroleum mixture.

bequeath »*verb* (**bequeaths, bequeathing, bequeathed**) ❶ leave property to someone by a will. ❷ hand down or pass on.
– **say** bi-**kwee**th

bequest »*noun* ❶ the action of bequeathing something. ❷ something that is bequeathed.

berate »*verb* (**berates, berating, berated**) scold or criticize someone angrily.

bereave »*verb* (**be bereaved**) be deprived of a close relation or friend through their death.
bereavement

> ✓ **ea** in the middle: **bereave**

bereft »*adjective* ❶ (**bereft of**) deprived of something; without. ❷ lonely and abandoned.

beret »*noun* a flat round cap of felt or cloth.
– SAY be-ray

bergamot »*noun* ❶ an oily substance found in Seville oranges, used as flavouring in Earl Grey tea. ❷ a herb of the mint family.
– SAY ber-guh-mot

beriberi »*noun* a disease causing inflammation of the nerves and heart failure, due to a lack of vitamin B_1.
– SAY be-ri-be-ri

berk [stupid person]

✓ spell **berk** with an **e**, not an **i** or a **u**

berry (plural **berries**)

✓ plural: drop the **y** and add **ies**: **berries**

berserk »*adjective* out of control; wild and frenzied.
– SAY buh-zerk

✓ don't forget the first **r**: **berserk**

berth »*noun* ❶ a place in a harbour where a ship can stay. ❷ a bunk on a ship or train.
»*verb* (**berths, berthing, berthed**) moor in a berth.

ℹ do not confuse **berth** with **birth**, meaning 'the process of being born'

beryl »*noun* a transparent pale green, blue, or yellow gemstone.

beryllium »*noun* a hard, grey metallic element.
– SAY buh-**ril**-li-uhm

✓ two **ll**'s in **beryllium**

beseech »*verb* (**beseeches, beseeching, besought** or **beseeched**) ask in a pleading way.

beset »*verb* (**besets, besetting, beset**) trouble or worry someone continuously.

✓ notice that the past of **beset** is also **beset**

beside
besides

besiege »*verb* (**besieges, besieging, besieged**) ❶ surround a place with armed forces so as to force it to surrender. ❷ worry or overwhelm someone with requests or complaints.
besieger

✓ the usual rule is **i** before **e** except after **c**: **besiege**

besmirch »*verb* (**besmirches, besmirching, besmirched**) damage someone's reputation.
– SAY bi-smerch

besotted »*adjective* so much in love with someone that you stop acting sensibly.
– SAY bi-**sot**-tid

besought past and past participle of **BESEECH**.

bespeak »*verb* (**bespeaks, bespeaking, bespoke**; past participle **bespoken**) be evidence of something.

bespectacled

bespoke[1] »*adjective* made to a customer's requirements.

bespoke[2] past of **BESPEAK**.

bespoken past participle of **BESPEAK**.

best (verb: **bests, besting, bested**)

bestial »*adjective* savagely cruel.
– SAY bess-ti-uhl
bestially

✓ **best-**, not **beast-**, in **bestial** and **bestiality**

bestiality »*noun* ❶ savagely cruel behaviour. ❷ sex between a person and an animal.

besting

bestir »*verb* (**bestirs, bestirring, bestirred**) (**bestir yourself**) rouse yourself to action.

bestow »*verb* (**bestows, bestowing, bestowed**) give an honour, right, or gift to someone.

bestride »*verb* (**bestrides, bestriding, bestrode**; past participle **bestridden**) put a leg on either side of something.

bests
best-seller
best-selling

bet (verb: **bets, betting, bet** or **betted**)

ℹ a person who bets is a **bettor**, not a **better**

beta »*noun* the second letter of the Greek alphabet (B, β).
– SAY bee-tuh

✓ only one **e**: **beta**

beta blocker »*noun* a drug used to treat high blood pressure and angina.

betake »*verb* (**betakes, betaking, betook**; past participle **betaken**) (**betake yourself to**) go somewhere.

bete noire »*noun* (plural **betes noires**) a person or thing that you particularly dislike.
– SAY bet nwar [singular and plural]

> ✅ **bete noire** can also be written **bête noire**, with a circumflex accent on the **e**: it was originally a French phrase meaning 'black beast'

bethink »*verb* (**bethinks, bethinking, bethought**) (**bethink yourself**) (an old word) come to think.

betide »*verb* (**betide, betiding, betided**) happen to someone: *woe betide anyone who questions her authority.*

betoken »*verb* (**betokens, betokening, betokened**) be a warning or sign of something.

betook past of **BETAKE**.

betray (verb: **betrays, betraying, betrayed**)
betrayal
betrayer

betrothed »*adjective* engaged to be married.
– SAY bi-troh*th*d
betrothal

bets

betted

better (verb: **betters, bettering, bettered**)
betterment »*noun* improvement.

betting

bettor »*noun* a person who bets.

> ✅ surprisingly, this is spelled **-or**, not **-er**: **bettor**

between

> ℹ it is correct to say **between you and me** but incorrect to say **between you and I**, because **between** is a preposition and should be followed by an object pronoun such as **me** or **him** rather than a subject pronoun such as **I** or **he**

betwixt »*preposition & adverb* (an old word) between.

bevel »*noun* an edge cut at an angle in wood or glass.
»*verb* (**bevels, bevelling, bevelled**) cut the edge of wood or glass at an angle.
– SAY rhymes with level

> ✅ there is a double **l** in **bevelling** and **bevelled**

beverage »*noun* a drink.

bevies plural of **BEVY**.

bevvy »*noun* (plural **bevvies**) (in informal English) an alcoholic drink.

> ✅ do not confuse **bevvy** with **bevy** 'a large group'

bevy »*noun* (plural **bevies**) a large group.
– SAY bev-i

> ✅ do not confuse **bevy** with **bevvy**, an informal word meaning 'a drink'

bewail »*verb* (**bewails, bewailing, bewailed**) be very sorry or sad about.

beware

bewilder »*verb* (**bewilders, bewildering, bewildered**) puzzle or confuse someone.
bewilderment

bewitch »*verb* (**bewitches, bewitching, bewitched**) ❶ put a magic spell on someone. ❷ attract and delight.

beyond

bhaji »*noun* (plural **bhajis**) an Indian dish of vegetables fried in batter.
– SAY baa-ji

> ✅ as in other words from Indian languages, such as **bhang** and **bhangra**, there is an **h** after the first **b**: **bhaji**

bhang »*noun* the leaves and flower tops of cannabis.
– SAY bang

bhangra »*noun* a type of popular music combining Punjabi folk traditions with Western pop music.
– SAY bahng-gruh

Bhutanese (plural **Bhutanese**) [of Bhutan]
– SAY boo-tuh-neez

biannual »*adjective* occurring twice a year.
biannually

> ℹ do not confuse **biannual** with **biennial**, which means 'taking place every two years'

bias »*noun* (plural **biases**) ❶ a feeling for or against a person or thing that is based on prejudice rather than sound reason. ❷ a direction diagonal to the grain of a fabric.

> ✅ the plural of **bias** adds **es** and does not double the **s**: **biases**

biased »*adjective* having a feeling for or against someone or something based on prejudice rather than sound reason.

> ✅ there is only one **s**: **biased**

biathlon »*noun* a sporting event which combines cross-country skiing and rifle shooting.
– SAY by-ath-lon

> ✅ in **biathlon**, as well as *decathlon* and *triathlon*, there is no **a** before the **lon**: **biathlon**

bib

b

bible

✓ use a capital **B** when referring to the holy book of the Christian and Jewish religions

biblical

bibliography »*noun* (plural **bibliographies**) a list of the books referred to in a piece of work or written on a particular subject.
– say bib-li-**og**-ruh-fi
bibliographic

✓ plural: drop the **y** and add **ies**: **bibliographies**

bibliophile »*noun* a person who collects books.
– say **bib**-li-oh-fyl

bibulous »*adjective* fond of drinking alcohol.
– say **bib**-yuu-luhss

bicameral »*adjective* (of a parliament) having two separate bodies.
– say by-**kam**-uh-ruhl

bicarbonate

bicentenary »*noun* (plural **bicentenaries**) a two-hundredth anniversary.

bicentennial »*noun* = BICENTENARY.

✓ note the double **n** at the end: **bicentennial**

biceps »*noun* (plural **biceps**) a large muscle in the upper arm which flexes the arm and forearm.
– say **by**-seps

ℹ the plural of **biceps** is the same as the singular: **biceps**

bicker (verb: **bickers**, **bickering**, **bickered**)

bicycle (verb: **bicycles**, **bicycling**, **bicycled**)
bicyclist

bid (verb: **bids**, **bidding**, **bid** or in old use **bade**)
bidder
bidding

biddable »*adjective* obedient.

bidder

bidding

bide »*verb* (**bides**, **biding**, **bided**) (**bide your time**) wait patiently for a good opportunity.

bidet »*noun* a low basin that you sit on to wash your bottom.
– say bee-day

✓ there is a **t** at the end, which is not pronounced because the word comes from French: **bidet**

biding

bids

biennial »*adjective* ❶ taking place every other year. ❷ (of a plant) living for two years.
– say by-**en**-ni-uhl
biennially

ℹ do not confuse **biennial** with **biannual**, which means 'occurring twice a year'

bier »*noun* a platform on which a coffin or dead body is placed before burial.
– say beer

✓ although it is pronounced the same as the drink, it is spelled **ie**: **bier**

bifocal »*adjective* (of a lens) made in two sections, one with a focus for seeing distant things and one for seeing things that are close.
»*noun* (**bifocals**) a pair of glasses with bifocal lenses.

big (adjective: **bigger**, **biggest**)
biggish
bigness

bigamy »*noun* the crime of marrying someone when you are already married to someone else.
– say **bi**-guh-mi
bigamist
bigamous

big bang »*noun* the rapid expansion of matter and space which is thought to have started the formation of the universe.

Big Brother »*noun* a person who has total control over other people's lives.

ℹ **Big Brother** comes from the name of the head of state in George Orwell's novel *Nineteen Eighty-four*

big dipper »*noun* a roller coaster.

big end »*noun* the larger end of the connecting rod in a piston engine.

bigger

biggest

biggish

bight »*noun* a long inward curve in a coastline.

ℹ do not confuse **bight** with **bite** meaning 'cut with your teeth'

bigness

bigot »*noun* a person with prejudiced views who does not listen to the opinions of other people.
– say **bi**-guht
bigoted
bigotry

✓ only one **g** and one **t**: **bigot**

bigwig »*noun* (in informal English) an important person.

bijou »*adjective* small and elegant.
– SAY bee-zhoo

✓ **ou** at the end: **bijou** is a French word meaning literally 'jewel'

bike (verb: **bikes, biking, biked**)
  biker

bikini (plural **bikinis**)

✓ the plural of **bikini** simply adds an **s**, not **es**: **bikinis**

bilateral »*adjective* involving two countries or groups of people.
  bilaterally

bilberry »*noun* (plural **bilberries**) a small blue edible berry.

✓ there is only one **l** in **bilberry**

bile »*noun* ❶ a bitter fluid which is produced by the liver and helps digestion. ❷ anger.

bilge »*noun* ❶ the bottom of a ship's hull. ❷ (in informal English) nonsense.

bilge water »*noun* dirty water that collects in the bottom of a ship's hull.

bilingual »*adjective* ❶ speaking two languages fluently. ❷ expressed in two languages.

bilious »*adjective* ❶ feeling sick. ❷ relating to bile.

✓ there is only one **l**: **bilious**

bill (verb: **bills, billing, billed**)

billabong »*noun* (in Australian English) a branch of a river forming a backwater or stagnant pool.

billboard »*noun* a large board for displaying advertising posters.

billed

billet »*noun* a private house used as temporary lodgings for soldiers.
  »*verb* (**be billeted**) (of a soldier) stay in a particular place.

✓ do not double the **t** in **billeting** and **billeted**

billet-doux »*noun* (plural **billets-doux**) (old-fashioned) a love letter.
– SAY bil-li-**doo** [singular], bil-li-**dooz** [plural]

✓ the plural of **billet-doux** adds an **s** to **billet**: **billets-doux**. It comes from a French phrase meaning 'sweet note'.

billhook »*noun* a tool with a curved blade, used for pruning.

billiards

billiard table

billies

billing

billion »*cardinal number* ❶ a thousand million; 1,000,000,000. ❷ (old-fashioned) a million million; 1,000,000,000,000.
  billionth

billionaire

✓ single **n**: **billionaire**

billionth

billow »*verb* (**billows, billowing, billowed**) ❶ (of smoke, cloud, or steam) roll outward. ❷ fill with air and swell outwards: *her dress billowed out behind her.*
  billowy

bills

billy »*noun* (plural **billies**) a metal cooking pot with a lid and handle, used in camping.

billy goat »*noun* a male goat.

bimbo »*noun* (plural **bimbos**) (used in an insulting way) an attractive but unintelligent woman.

✓ the plural of **bimbo**, 'little child' in Italian, has **os** not **oes**: **bimbos**

bin (verb: **bins, binning, binned**)

binary »*adjective* ❶ composed of or involving two things. ❷ (in mathematics) relating to a system of numbers which has two as its base and uses only the digits 0 and 1.
– SAY by-nuh-ri

✓ **ary** not **ery**: **binary**

bind (verb: **binds, binding, bound**)

binder

binding

binds

bindweed »*noun* a plant that has trumpet-shaped flowers and twines itself round things.

binge »*noun* a short period of uncontrolled eating or drinking.
  »*verb* (**binges, bingeing, binged**) eat or drink in an uncontrolled way.

✓ do not drop the **e** when spelling **bingeing**

bingo

binman (plural **binmen**)

binnacle »*noun* a casing that holds a ship's compass.

binned

binning

binocular »*adjective* for or using both eyes.
– say bi-**nok**-yuu-ler

☑ there is just one n: binocular

binoculars

☑ there is only one **n** and the ending is **ulars**, not **liers**: binoculars

bins

bint

biochemistry »*noun* the study of the chemical processes that take place in living things.
biochemical
biochemist

biodegradable »*adjective* able to be decomposed by bacteria or other living things.

☑ -able not -ible: biodegradable

biodiversity »*noun* the variety of plant and animal life in the world or in a particular environment.

biography »*noun* (plural biographies) an account of a person's life written by someone else.
biographer
biographical

☑ plural: drop the y and add ies: biographies

biological
biologically

biology »*noun* the scientific study of the life and structure of plants and animals.
biologist

bionic »*adjective* (of an artificial body part) electronically powered.

biopsy »*noun* (plural biopsies) an examination of tissue taken from the body, to discover the presence or cause of a disease.
– say by-op-si

☑ plural: drop the y and add ies: biopsies

biorhythm »*noun* a recurring cycle in the functioning of an organism, such as the daily cycle of sleeping and waking.

biosphere »*noun* the parts of the earth occupied by living things.

biotechnology »*noun* the use of living cells and bacteria in industry and medicine.

bipartisan »*adjective* involving the cooperation of two political parties.

bipartite »*adjective* involving two separate parties.

biped »*noun* an animal that walks on two feet.
– say by-ped

bipedal »*adjective* (of an animal) walking on two legs.
– say by-pee-d'l

biplane »*noun* an early type of aircraft with two pairs of wings, one above the other.

bipolar »*adjective* having to do with two poles or extremes.
– say by-**poh**-ler

birch »*noun* ❶ a slender tree with thin, peeling bark. ❷ (the birch) (in the past) the punishment of being beaten with a bundle of birch twigs.

bird

birdcage

birdie »*noun* (plural birdies) (in golf) a score of one stroke under par at a hole.

☑ in golf, birdie ends with ie, not y

birding »*noun* birdwatching.
birder

bird of paradise »*noun* a brightly coloured tropical bird.

bird of prey »*noun* a bird such as an eagle, hawk, or owl, that eats small animals or birds.

bird's-eye view »*noun* a view from above.

birdsong

birdwatching
birdwatcher

biriani »*noun* an Indian dish made with seasoned rice and meat, fish, or vegetables.
– say bi-ri-ah-ni

☑ biriani can also be spelled biriyani or biryani: all three spellings are correct

biro »*noun* (plural biros) (trademark) a ballpoint pen.

☑ the plural of biro has os not oes: biros. It was named after its Hungarian inventor, László *Biró*.

birth [the process of being born]

ℹ do not confuse birth with berth, 'a place in a harbour for a ship'

birth control »*noun* the use of contraception to prevent unwanted pregnancies.

birthday

birthmark

birthplace

birth rate »*noun* the number of live births per thousand of population per year.

birthright »*noun* ❶ a right or privilege that a person has through being born into a particular family or place. ❷ a basic right belonging to all human beings.

birth sign »*noun* the sign of the zodiac through which the sun is passing when a person is born.

biryani another way of spelling BIRIANI.

biscuit

☑ do not forget the u before the final i: **biscuit**

bisect »*verb* (**bisects**, **bisecting**, **bisected**) divide something into two parts.
bisection

☑ unlike **dissect**, with which it is sometimes confused, **bisect** has only one s

bisexual »*adjective* ❶ sexually attracted to both men and women. ❷ (in biology) having both male and female organs.
» *noun* a bisexual person.
bisexuality

bishop »*noun* (in the Christian Church) a senior minister who is in charge of a diocese (a district).

bishopric »*noun* the office or diocese of a bishop.

☑ there is no k at the end: **bishopric**

bismuth »*noun* a brittle reddish-grey metal resembling lead.
– SAY biz-muhth

bison »*noun* (plural **bison**) a wild ox with a humped back and shaggy hair.

☑ the plural of **bison** is the same as the singular: **bison**

bisque »*noun* ❶ a rich soup made from lobster or other shellfish. ❷ a light brown colour.
– SAY bisk

bistro »*noun* (plural **bistros**) a small, inexpensive restaurant.
– SAY bee-stroh

☑ the plural of **bistro**, a French word, has os not oes: **bistros**

bit[1] [small piece; mouthpiece of a bridle]

bit[2] »*noun* the smallest unit of information used by a computer, described as being either a 0 or a 1.

bit[3] past of BITE.

bitch »*noun* ❶ a female dog. ❷ (in informal English) a spiteful or unpleasant woman.

» *verb* (**bitches**, **bitching**, **bitched**) (in informal English) make spiteful comments.

bitchy
bitchily
bitchiness

bite (verb: **bites**, **biting**, **bit**; past participle **bitten**) [cut with teeth]
biter

ℹ️ do not confuse **bite** with **bight**, which means 'a long curve in a coastline'

biting

bit part »*noun* a small acting role in a play or a film.

bitten past participle of BITE.

bitter
bitterly
bitterness

bittern »*noun* a marshland bird with a booming call.

bitterness

bittersweet »*adjective* ❶ sweet with a bitter aftertaste. ❷ bringing pleasure mixed with sadness.
» *noun* a plant (woody nightshade), with poisonous red fruit.

bitty (adjective: **bittier**, **bittiest**)
bittiness

bitumen »*noun* a black sticky substance obtained from oil, used for covering roads and roofs.
– SAY bit-yuu-muhn

bituminous »*adjective* having to do with or containing bitumen.
– SAY bi-tyoo-mi-nuhss

☑ min not men: **bituminous**

bivalve »*noun* a creature with a hinged double shell, such as an oyster, cockle, or mussel.

bivouac »*noun* a temporary open-air camp without tents.
» *verb* (**bivouacs**, **bivouacking**, **bivouacked**) stay overnight in such a camp.
– SAY bi-voo-ak

☑ there is no k in **bivouac** and **bivouacs**, but a k is added to **bivouacking** and **bivouacked**

bizarre [strange]
bizarrely

☑ one z, two r's: **bizarre**. Do not confuse the spellings of **bizarre** and **bazaar** meaning 'a market'.

blab »*verb* (**blabs**, **blabbing**, **blabbed**) (in informal English) give away a secret.

b

blabber »*verb* (blabbers, blabbering, blabbered) (in informal English) talk carelessly or in an annoying way.

blabbing

blabs

black (verb: blacks, blacking, blacked; adjective: blacker, blackest)

blackish

blackly

blackness

> ℹ️ to refer to African peoples and their descendants, **black** is the word most generally accepted in Britain today, instead of **coloured** or **Negro**

blackball »*verb* (blackballs, blackballing, blackballed) prevent someone from joining a club, traditionally by voting against them by placing a black ball in a ballot box.

black belt »*noun* a black belt given to an expert in judo, karate, and other martial arts.

blackberry (plural blackberries)

> ✓ plural: drop the **y** and add **ies**: **blackberries**

blackbird

blackboard

black box »*noun* a machine that records what is happening to the controls in an aircraft during the flight.

blackcurrant

> ✓ **ant** not **ent**: **blackcurrant**

black economy »*noun* buying and selling of goods that takes place without the government knowing about it and without being taxed.

blacked

blacken (verb: blackens, blackening, blackened)

blacker

blackest

blackguard »*noun* (old-fashioned) a man who is dishonest or treats others badly. – *say* blag-gerd

> ✓ although it is not pronounced this way, it is written **black-**: **blackguard**

blackhead »*noun* a lump of oily matter blocking a pore in the skin.

black hole »*noun* an area in space where gravity is so strong that nothing, not even light, can escape.

blacking

blackish

blackjack »*noun* a gambling card game similar to pontoon.

blacklist »*noun* a list of people who cannot be trusted or who are out of favour.

» *verb* (blacklists, blacklisting, blacklisted) put on a blacklist.

blackly

black magic »*noun* magic in which evil spirits are called on.

blackmail »*noun* ❶ the demanding of money from someone in return for not giving away secret information about them. ❷ the use of threats or other pressure to influence someone.

» *verb* (blackmails, blackmailing, blackmailed) use blackmail on someone. **blackmailer**

> ✓ **-mail** not **-male**: **blackmail**

black market »*noun* an illegal trade in goods that are scarce or officially controlled.
black marketeer

blackness

blackout

black pudding »*noun* a black sausage containing pork, dried pig's blood, and suet.

blacks

black sheep »*noun* a person who is different from the rest of their family and who is considered bad or embarrassing.

blacksmith »*noun* a person who makes and repairs things made of iron.

blackthorn »*noun* a thorny bush that has blue-black fruits (called sloes).

black widow »*noun* a very poisonous American spider with a black body and red markings.

bladder »*noun* ❶ a bag-like organ in the abdomen in which urine collects before it is passed from the body. ❷ an inflated or hollow flexible bag or chamber.

> ✓ double **d**: **bladder**

blade

blag »*verb* (blags, blagging, blagged) (in informal English) ❶ get something by clever talk or lying. ❷ steal something in a violent robbery.
blagger

blame (verb: blames, blaming, blamed)

blameless

blames

blameworthy

b

blaming

blanch »*verb* (**blanches, blanching, blanched**) ❶ make or become white or pale. ❷ prepare vegetables by putting them briefly in boiling water.
– SAY blahnch

> ℹ️ do not confuse **blanch** with **blench**, which means 'flinch'

blancmange »*noun* a sweet dessert like a jelly, made with cornflour and milk.
– SAY bluh-**mon***zh*

> ✓ **blancmange** is from French and begins with **blanc** meaning 'white'; the ending **mange** comes from French *manger* 'eat'

bland »*adjective* ❶ not having strong qualities and therefore uninteresting. ❷ showing little emotion: *bland assurances that things were going well.*
blandly
blandness

blandishments »*plural noun* nice things said to someone in order to persuade them to do something.

blandly
blandness

blank (verb: **blanks, blanking, blanked**)
blankly
blankness

blanket (verb: **blankets, blanketing, blanketed**)

> ✓ do not double the **t** in **blanketing, blanketed**

blanking
blankly
blankness
blanks

blank verse »*noun* poetry that does not rhyme.

blare (verb: **blares, blaring, blared**)

blarney »*noun* talk intended to be charming or flattering.

> ✓ don't forget the **e** before the **y**: **blarney**

blase »*adjective* unimpressed by something because you have experienced it often before.
– SAY blah-zay

> ✓ **blase** can also be written **blasé**, with an acute accent on the **e** (as in the original French)

blaspheme »*verb* (**blasphemes, blaspheming, blasphemed**) speak rudely about God or use the name of God as a swear word.

– SAY blass-**feem**
blasphemer

blasphemies

blaspheming

blasphemous »*adjective* rude or disrespectful about God.
– SAY blass-fuh-muhss
blasphemously

> ✓ **phem** not **phim**: **blasphemous**

blasphemy »*noun* (plural **blasphemies**) rude or disrespectful talk about God.
– SAY blass-fuh-mi

blast (verb: **blasts, blasting, blasted**)
blaster

blast furnace »*noun* a furnace for extracting metal from ore, using blasts of hot compressed air.

blasting

blasts

blatant »*adjective* open and unashamed.
blatancy
blatantly

> ✓ **ant** not **ent**: **blatant**

blather »*verb* (**blathers, blathering, blathered**) talk at length without making much sense.
» *noun* rambling talk.

blaze (verb: **blazes, blazing, blazed**)

blazer

blazes

blazing

blazon »*verb* (**blazons, blazoning, blazoned**) ❶ display or proclaim something in a way that catches people's attention. ❷ (in heraldry) describe or depict a coat of arms.
» *noun* a coat of arms.
– SAY blay-zuhn

bleach (verb: **bleaches, bleaching, bleached**)

bleak »*adjective* (**bleaker, bleakest**) ❶ bare and exposed to the weather. ❷ dreary and unwelcoming. ❸ (of a situation) not hopeful.
bleakly
bleakness

> ✓ there is no **c** before the **k**: **bleak**

bleary (adjective: **blearier, bleariest**)
blearily

bleat »*verb* (**bleats, bleating, bleated**) ❶ (of a sheep or goat) make a weak, wavering

b

cry. ❷ speak or complain in a weak or foolish way.
» *noun* a bleating sound.

> ☑ ea not ee: b**lea**t

bleed (verb: **bleeds, bleeding, bled**)

bleep (verb: **bleeps, bleeping, bleeped**)
bleeper

blemish (verb: **blemishes, blemishing, blemished**)

blench »*verb* (**blenches, blenching, blenched**) flinch suddenly out of fear or pain.

> ℹ do not confuse **blench** with **blanch**, meaning 'make or become white' and 'put vegetables briefly in boiling water'

blend (verb: **blends, blending, blended**)
blender

blenny »*noun* (plural **blennies**) a small coastal sea fish with spiny fins and no scales.

bless (verb: **blesses, blessing, blessed**)

blessed
blessedly
blessedness

blesses

blessing

blew past of **BLOW**.

> ☑ do not confuse the spelling of **blew** with that of the colour **blue**

blight »*noun* ❶ a plant disease caused by fungi. ❷ a thing that spoils or damages something.
» *verb* (**blights, blighting, blighted**) ❶ infect something with blight. ❷ spoil or destroy something.

blighter »*noun* (in informal English) a person who you think is stupid or who you feel sorry for.

blighting

blights

Blighty »*noun* (in informal English) (used by soldiers serving abroad) Britain or England.

> ℹ **Blighty** is an Urdu word meaning 'foreign, European'

blimey

blind (verb: **blinds, blinding, blinded**)
blindly
blindness

blindfold (verb: **blindfolds, blindfolding, blindfolded**)

blinding
blindingly

blindly

blind man's buff »*noun* a game in which a blindfold player tries to catch others while being pushed about by them.

blindness

blinds

blind spot »*noun* ❶ a small area of the retina of the eye that is insensitive to light. ❷ an area where a person's view is obstructed. ❸ an area in which a person shows an inability to understand or judge properly.

blindworm »*noun* = **SLOW-WORM**.

blink (verb: **blinks, blinking, blinked**)

blinker »*noun* ❶ (**blinkers**) a pair of leather flaps attached to a horse's bridle to prevent the horse seeing sideways. ❷ a vehicle indicator light that flashes on and off.
» *verb* (**blinkers, blinkering, blinkered**) ❶ put blinkers on a horse. ❷ cause someone to have a narrow outlook.

blinking

blinks

blip

bliss

blissful
blissfully

> ☑ -ful not -full: bliss**ful**

blister (verb: **blisters, blistering, blistered**)

blistering

blisters

blithe »*adjective* ❶ without thought or care: *a blithe ignorance of the facts.* ❷ very happy.
– SAY blythe
blithely

> ☑ remember the **e** at the end: blith**e**

blithering »*adjective* (in informal English) complete: *a blithering idiot.*

blitz »*noun* (plural **blitzes**) ❶ a sudden fierce military attack. ❷ (**the Blitz**) the German air raids on Britain in 1940–41. ❸ (in informal English) a sudden and concentrated effort.
» *verb* (**blitzes, blitzing, blitzed**) ❶ make a sudden fierce attack on. ❷ overwhelm or completely defeat.

blitzkrieg »*noun* a fierce military campaign intended to bring about a rapid victory.
– SAY blits-kreeg

> ☑ i before **e**: blitzkrieg is a German word meaning 'lightning war'

blizzard

 double **z**: **blizzard**

bloat »*verb* (**bloats**, **bloating**, **bloated**) make something swell up.
bloated

bloater »*noun* a salted and smoked herring.

bloating

bloats

blob
blobby

bloc »*noun* a group of countries with similar political systems who support each other.

 no **k** at the end: **bloc**

block (verb: **blocks**, **blocking**, **blocked**)
blocker

blockade »*noun* a blocking of the way in or out of a place to prevent people or goods from entering or leaving it.
» *verb* (**blockades**, **blockading**, **blockaded**) block the way in or out of a place.

blockage

block and tackle »*noun* a lifting mechanism consisting of ropes, a pulley block, and a hook.

blockbuster »*noun* a film or book that is a great commercial success.

block capitals »*plural noun* plain capital letters.

blocked

blocker

blockhouse »*noun* a reinforced concrete shelter used as an observation point.

blocking

blocks

bloke

blokeish

 blokeish can also be spelled **blokish**: both spellings are correct

blonde

 blonde may also be spelled **blond**, without the **e**, and both spellings may be used to refer to either women or men. In French, though, **blonde** refers to women and **blond** to men.

blood (verb: **bloods**, **blooding**, **blooded**)

bloodbath »*noun* an event in which many people are killed violently.

blood-curdling »*adjective* horrifying.

blooded [given a first experience of something]

blood group »*noun* one of the various types into which human blood is classified.

bloodhound »*noun* a large hound with a very good sense of smell, used in tracking.

bloodied [made bloody]

bloodier

bloodies

bloodiest

blooding

bloodless

bloodletting »*noun* ❶ violence during a war or conflict. ❷ (a historical term) the surgical removal of some of a patient's blood.

bloodline »*noun* a set of ancestors.

blood money »*noun* ❶ money paid to compensate the family of someone who has been killed. ❷ money paid to a hired killer.

bloods

bloodshed »*noun* the killing or wounding of people.

bloodshot »*adjective* (of the eyes) having tiny red blood vessels visible in the whites.

blood sport »*noun* a sport involving the hunting, wounding, or killing of animals.

bloodstock »*noun* thoroughbred horses.

bloodstream

bloodsucker
bloodsucking

bloodthirsty »*adjective* taking pleasure in killing and violence.

blood vessel »*noun* a vein, artery, or capillary carrying blood through the body.

bloody (adjective: **bloodier**, **bloodiest**; verb: **bloodies**, **bloodying**, **bloodied**)

Bloody Mary »*noun* (plural **Bloody Marys**) a drink consisting of vodka and tomato juice.

bloody-minded »*adjective* deliberately unhelpful.

bloom (verb: **blooms**, **blooming**, **bloomed**)

bloomer »*noun* a large bread loaf with diagonal slashes on a rounded top.

bloomers »*plural noun* (mainly a historical term) women's loose-fitting trousers or underpants, gathered at the knee or ankle.

blooming

blooms

blossom (verb: **blossoms**, **blossoming**, **blossomed**)

 two **s**'s, one **m**: **blossom**

b

blot (verb: **blots, blotting, blotted**)

> ☑ double the **t** in **blotting** and **blotted**

blotch (verb: **blotches, blotching, blotched**)
blotchy

blots

blotted

blotter »*noun* a pad of blotting paper.

blotting

blouse

blouson »*noun* a short loose-fitting jacket.
– SAY bloo-zon

blow (verb: **blows, blowing, blew**; past participle **blown**)

blow-by-blow »*adjective* (of a description of an event) giving all the details in order.

blower

blowfly »*noun* (plural **blowflies**) a large fly which lays its eggs on meat and carcasses.

blowhole »*noun* ❶ the nostril of a whale or dolphin on the top of its head. ❷ a hole in ice for breathing or fishing through.

blowier

blowiest

blowing

blowlamp

blown past participle of BLOW.

blowout »*noun* ❶ an occasion when a vehicle tyre bursts or an electric fuse melts. ❷ (in informal English) a large meal.

blowpipe »*noun* a weapon consisting of a long tube through which an arrow or dart is blown.

blows

blowsy »*adjective* (of a woman) coarse, untidy, and red-faced.
– SAY *rhymes with* drowsy

> ☑ **blowsy** can also be spelled **blowzy**: both spellings are correct

blowtorch

blowy »*adjective* (**blowier, blowiest**) windy or windswept.

blowzy another way of spelling BLOWSY.

blub (verb: **blubs, blubbing, blubbed**)

> ☑ double the **b** in **blubbing** and **blubbed**

blubber[1] »*noun* the fat of sea mammals, especially whales and seals.
blubbery

blubber[2] »*verb* (**blubbers, blubbering, blubbered**) (in informal English) sob noisily and uncontrollably.

> ☑ two **b**'s in the middle, and only one **r**: **blubber**

blubbery

blubbing

blubs

bludgeon »*noun* a thick, heavy stick used as a weapon.
» *verb* (**bludgeons, bludgeoning, bludgeoned**)
❶ hit someone with a thick, heavy stick.
❷ bully someone into doing something.

> ☑ remember the **d** before the **g**, and the **eon** ending: **bludgeon**

blue (adjective: **bluer, bluest**) [colour]
blueness

> ☑ do not confuse the spelling of **blue** with that of **blew**, past of *blow*

bluebell

blueberry (plural **blueberries**)

blue-blooded »*adjective* from a royal or aristocratic family.

bluebottle »*noun* a common blowfly with a metallic-blue body.

blue-chip »*adjective* (of a company or shares) considered to be a reliable investment.

blue-collar »*adjective* relating to manual work or workers.

blue-eyed

blueish another way of spelling BLUISH.

blueness

Blue Peter »*noun* a blue flag with a white square in the centre, raised by a ship about to leave port.

blueprint »*noun* ❶ a technical drawing or plan. ❷ a model that others can follow.

bluer

blues »*noun* ❶ slow, sad music of black American origin. ❷ (**the blues**) (in informal English) feelings of sadness or depression.
bluesy

bluest

bluestocking »*noun* an intellectual or literary woman.

bluesy

blue tit »*noun* a common songbird with a blue cap and yellow underparts.

bluff[1] (verb: **bluffs, bluffing, bluffed**) [attempt to deceive]

bluff[2] »*adjective* frank and direct in a good-natured way.

bluff[3] »*noun* a steep cliff, bank, or headland.

bluish »*adjective* having a blue tinge.

73

blunder » bobble

 bluish can also be spelled **blueish**: both spellings are correct

blunder (verb: **blunders**, **blundering**, **blundered**)

blunderbuss »*noun* (plural **blunderbusses**) (a historical term) a gun with a short, wide barrel, firing balls or lead bullets.

 double s: **blunderbuss**

blundered

blundering

blunders

blunt (verb: **blunts**, **blunting**, **blunted**)
  bluntly
  bluntness

blur (verb: **blurs**, **blurring**, **blurred**)

 double the r in **blurring** and **blurred**

blurb »*noun* a short description written to promote a book, film, or other product.

blurred

blurrier

blurriest

blurring

blurry (adjective: **blurrier**, **blurriest**)

blurs

blurt »*verb* (**blurts**, **blurting**, **blurted**) say something suddenly and without thinking.

blush (verb: **blushes**, **blushing**, **blushed**)

blusher »*noun* a cosmetic used to give a warm reddish tinge to the cheeks.

blushes

blushing

bluster »*verb* (**blusters**, **blustering**, **blustered**) ❶ talk loudly or aggressively but without having any effect. ❷ (of wind or rain) blow or beat fiercely and noisily.
»*noun* loud and empty talk.
  blustery

BMA »*abbreviation* British Medical Association.

B-movie »*noun* a low-budget film supporting a main film in a cinema programme.

BMX »*abbreviation* a sturdy bicycle designed for cross-country racing.

 BMX is short for *bicycle motocross*

boa »*noun* ❶ a large snake which winds itself round its prey and crushes it to death. ❷ a long, thin stole of feathers or fur worn around a woman's neck.

boar »*noun* (plural **boar** or **boars**) ❶ a wild pig with tusks. ❷ an uncastrated male pig.

 do not confuse the spellings of **boar** and **bore** meaning 'drill a hole; make someone bored'

board (verb: **boards**, **boarding**, **boarded**)

boarder »*noun* ❶ a pupil who lives in school during term time. ❷ a person who forces their way on to a ship in an attack.

boarding

boardroom »*noun* a room in which a board of directors meets regularly.

boards

boast (verb: **boasts**, **boasting**, **boasted**)

boastful
  boastfully

 -ful not -full: **boastful**

boasting

boasts

boat (verb: **boats**, **boating**, **boated**)

boater »*noun* a flat-topped straw hat with a brim.

boathook »*noun* a long pole with a hook and a spike at one end, used for moving boats.

boating

boatload

boatman (plural **boatmen**)

boat people »*plural noun* refugees who have left a country by sea.

boats

boatswain »*noun* a ship's officer in charge of equipment and the crew.
– SAY boh-s'n

 boatswain can also be spelled **bo'sun** or **bosun**: all three spellings are correct

bob¹ »*noun* ❶ a quick, short movement up and down. ❷ a short hairstyle hanging evenly all round. ❸ a weight on a pendulum, plumb line, or kite-tail. ❹ a bobsleigh.
»*verb* (**bobs**, **bobbing**, **bobbed**) ❶ make a quick, short movement up and down. ❷ curtsy briefly. ❸ cut a person's hair in a bob.

 double the second b in **bobbing** and **bobbed**

bob² »*noun* (plural **bob**) (in informal English) a shilling.

bobbin »*noun* a cylinder, cone, or reel holding thread.

bobble »*noun* a small ball made of strands of wool.
  bobbly

bobby »*noun* (plural **bobbies**) (in informal English) a police officer.

> ☑ plural: drop the **y** and add **ies**: **bobbies**

bobsleigh »*noun* a sledge with brakes and a steering mechanism, used for racing down an ice-covered run.

> ☑ **bobsleigh** does not follow the usual rule **i** before **e**, except after **c**

bode »*verb* (**bodes, boding, boded**) (**bode well** or **ill**) be a sign of a good or bad outcome.

bodge »*verb* (**bodges, bodging, bodged**) (in informal English) make or repair something badly or clumsily.

bodice »*noun* ❶ the upper part of a woman's dress. ❷ a woman's sleeveless undergarment.

bodies

bodily

boding

bodkin »*noun* a thick, blunt needle with a large eye.

body (plural **bodies**)

> ☑ plural: drop the **y** and add **ies**: **bodies**

bodybuilder

bodyguard

> ☑ don't forget the **u** after the **g**: **bodyguard**

body language »*noun* the showing of your feelings through the way in which you move or hold your body.

body politic »*noun* the people of a nation or society considered as an organized group of citizens.

bodysuit

bodywork »*noun* the metal outer shell of a vehicle.

Boer »*noun* a member of the Dutch people who settled in southern Africa.
» *adjective* relating to the Boers.
– **SAY** *rhymes with* more *or* mower

boffin »*noun* (in informal English) a scientist.

bog (verb: **bogs, bogging, bogged**)

bogey »*noun* (plural **bogeys**) ❶ an evil or mischievous spirit. ❷ a cause of fear or alarm. ❸ (in informal English) a piece of mucus in the nose. ❹ (in golf) a score of one stroke over par at a hole.

> ☑ the ending is **ey**, not simply **y**: **bogey** do not confuse **bogey** with **bogie**, referring to a frame with wheels supporting a railway vehicle

bogeyman »*noun* an evil spirit.

> ☑ **bogeyman** can also be spelled **bogyman**: both spellings are correct

bogged

boggier

boggiest

bogginess

bogging

boggle »*verb* (**boggles, boggling, boggled**) ❶ be astonished or baffled. ❷ (**boggle at**) hesitate to do something.

boggy (adjective: **boggier, boggiest**) **bogginess**

bogie »*noun* (plural **bogies**) a supporting frame with wheels, fitted on a pivot beneath the end of a railway vehicle.

bogs

bog-standard »*adjective* (in informal English) ordinary; basic.

bogus »*adjective* not genuine or true.

Bohemian »*noun* a person who is involved in the arts and who lives in an unconventional way.
» *adjective* unconventional.
– **SAY** boh-hee-mi-uhn
Bohemianism

boil (verb: **boils, boiling, boiled**)

boiler

boiler suit »*noun* a pair of overalls worn for dirty manual work.

boiling

boiling point »*noun* the temperature at which a liquid boils.

boils

boisterous »*adjective* noisy, lively, and high-spirited.
boisterously
boisterousness

> ☑ do not forget the **e** before the **r**: **boisterous**

bold (adjective: **bolder, boldest**) [brave]
boldly
boldness

> ☑ do not confuse **bolder** with **boulder**, which means 'a large rock'

bole »*noun* a tree trunk.

bolero »*noun* (plural **boleros**) ❶ a Spanish dance. ❷ a woman's short open jacket.
– **SAY** buh-**lair**-oh [the dance], bol-uh-roh [the jacket]

> ☑ the plural of **bolero** has **os** not **oes**: **boleros**

Bolivian

boll »*noun* the rounded seed capsule of plants such as cotton or flax.
– SAY *rhymes with* hole

bollard »*noun* ❶ a short post used to prevent traffic from entering an area. ❷ a short post on a ship or quayside for securing a rope.

bollocks

Bolshevik »*noun* (a historical term) a member of the communist majority group within the Russian Social Democratic Party, which seized power in the Revolution of 1917.
– SAY bol-shi-vik
Bolshevism

> ☑ there is no **c** before the **k**: **Bolshevik**

bolshie »*adjective* (in informal English) bad-tempered and uncooperative.

> ☑ **bolshie** can also be spelled **bolshy**

bolster »*noun* a long, firm pillow.
»*verb* (**bolsters, bolstering, bolstered**) support or strengthen: *campaigns to bolster the president's image.*

bolt (verb: **bolts, bolting, bolted**)

bolt hole »*noun* a place to escape to and hide in.

bolting

bolts

bomb (verb: **bombs, bombing, bombed**)

bombard (verb: **bombards, bombarding, bombarded**)
bombardment

bombardier »*noun* ❶ a rank of non-commissioned officer in some artillery regiments, equivalent to corporal. ❷ a member of a bomber crew in the US air force responsible for releasing bombs.
– SAY bom-buh-**deer**

> ☑ do not forget the **r** before the **d**: **bombardier**

bombarding

bombardment

bombards

bombast »*noun* language that sounds impressive but has little meaning.
bombastic

Bombay duck »*noun* dried fish eaten as an accompaniment with curries.

Bombay mix »*noun* an Indian spiced snack made up of lentils, peanuts, and deep-fried strands of flour.

bombazine »*noun* a twill dress fabric of worsted and silk or cotton.

– SAY bom-buh-zeen

bombed

bomber

bomber jacket »*noun* a short zipped jacket that is gathered at the waist and cuffs.

bombing

bombs

bombshell »*noun* ❶ a great surprise and shock. ❷ (in informal English) a very attractive woman.

bona fide »*adjective* genuine; real.
– SAY boh-nuh fy-di

> ℹ a Latin phrase meaning 'with good faith'

bona fides »*noun* ❶ honesty and trustworthiness. ❷ evidence which proves that a person is what they claim to be.
– SAY boh-nuh fy-deez

bonanza »*noun* a sudden supply of money or good luck, or of something else that is very welcome.

bon appetit »*exclamation* used to wish someone an enjoyable meal.
– SAY bon a-puh-**tee**

> ☑ **bon appetit** can also be written **bon appétit**, with an acute accent on the **e** (it is from a French phrase meaning 'good appetite')

bonbon »*noun* a sweet.

bond (verb: **bonds, bonding, bonded**)

bondage »*noun* ❶ the state of being a slave or having no freedom. ❷ sexual activity that involves the tying up of one partner.

> ☑ **age** not **ege**: **bondage**

bonded

bonding

bonds

bone (verb: **bones, boning, boned**)
boneless

bone china »*noun* white porcelain that contains a mineral derived from bone.

boned

bone dry »*adjective* completely dry.

bone idle »*adjective* very idle.

boneless

bonemeal »*noun* ground bones used as a fertilizer.

bones

bonfire »*noun* an open-air fire lit to burn rubbish or as a celebration.

bongo »*noun* (plural **bongos** or **bongoes**) one of a pair of small drums that are held between the knees.

 the plural of **bongo** can have **os** or **oes**: **bongos** or **bongoes**

bonhomie »*noun* good-natured friendliness.
– SAY bon-uh-mee

 although it is not pronounced, there is an **h** in **bonhomie**

bonier

boniest

boning

bonk (verb: **bonks**, **bonking**, **bonked**)

bonkers »*adjective* (in informal English) insane; crazy.

bonking

bonks

bon mot »*noun* (plural **bons mots**) a clever or witty remark.
– SAY bon **moh** [singular], bon **moh** or bon moh*z* [plural]

 bon mot is a French phrase meaning 'good word', and to make the plural you add **s** to both words: **bons mots**

bonnet

bonny »*adjective* (**bonnier**, **bonniest**) physically attractive and healthy-looking.

 bonny can also be spelled **bonnie**: both spellings are correct

bonsai »*noun* the Japanese art of growing miniature ornamental trees.
– SAY bon-sI

bonus (plural **bonuses**)

 do not double the **s** to form the plural; simply add **es**: **bonuses**

bon vivant »*noun* (plural **bon vivants** or **bons vivants**) a person who enjoys a sociable and luxurious lifestyle.
– SAY bon vee-**von** [singular and plural]

 strictly, the plural of the French phrase **bon vivant** is **bons vivants**

bon viveur »*noun* (plural **bon viveurs** or **bons viveurs**) = BON VIVANT.
– SAY bon vee-**ver** [singular and plural]

 bon viveur is not an authentic French phrase, and the plural can have one or two **s**'s

bon voyage »*exclamation* have a good journey.
– SAY bon voy-**yah***z*h

 a French phrase meaning 'good journey'

bony (adjective: **bonier**, **boniest**)

 ny not ney: **bony**

boo (verb: **boos**, **booing**, **booed**)

boob (verb: **boobs**, **boobing**, **boobed**)

boobed

boobies

boobing

boobs

boob tube »*noun* a woman's tight-fitting strapless top.

booby »*noun* (plural **boobies**) ❶ (in informal English) a stupid person. ❷ a large tropical seabird. ❸ (**boobies**) (in informal English) a woman's breasts.

booby prize »*noun* a prize given to the person who comes last in a contest.

booby trap »*noun* ❶ an object containing a hidden explosive device. ❷ a trap or similar device set up as a joke to take someone by surprise.
booby-trapped

booed

boogie »*noun* (plural **boogies**) ❶ a style of blues played on the piano with a strong, fast beat. ❷ (in informal English) a dance to pop or rock music.
» *verb* (**boogies**, **boogieing**, **boogied**) (in informal English) dance to pop or rock music.

 the ending is **ie**, not **y**: **boogie**
do not drop the **e** in **boogieing**

boogie-woogie

booing

book (verb: **books**, **booking**, **booked**)

bookbinder

bookcase

booked

bookend

bookie »*noun* (plural **bookies**) (in informal English) a bookmaker.

booking

bookish »*adjective* devoted to reading and studying.

bookkeeping »*noun* the keeping of records of financial dealings.

 note that there are two **k**'s in **bookkeeping**

booklet

bookmaker »*noun* a person who takes bets on races and other events, calculates odds, and pays out winnings.

bookmark

books

bookshelf (plural **bookshelves**)

bookworm »*noun* (in informal English) a person who loves books.

boom[1] (verb: **booms**, **booming**, **boomed**) [loud deep sound; period of prosperity]

boom[2] »*noun* ❶ a pivoted beam at the foot of a sail. ❷ a movable arm carrying a microphone or film camera. ❸ a floating beam used to form a barrier across the mouth of a harbour.

boomerang

> ☑ two o's but only one m: **boomerang**

boon »*noun* a thing that is very helpful.

boor »*noun* a rough and bad-mannered person.
boorish

> ☑ do not confuse the spelling of **boor** with **boar** meaning 'a wild pig' or **bore** meaning 'drill a hole' or 'make someone bored'

boos

boost »*verb* (**boosts**, **boosting**, **boosted**) help something to improve or become more successful.
»*noun* a source of help or encouragement.

booster

boosting

boosts

boot (verb: **boots**, **booting**, **booted**)

bootee [child's shoe]

> ☑ do not confuse **bootee** with **booty**, meaning 'stolen goods'
> **bootee** can also be spelled **bootie**

booth »*noun* ❶ a small temporary structure used for selling goods or staging shows at a market or fair. ❷ an enclosed compartment that gives you privacy when telephoning, voting, etc.

bootie another way of spelling **BOOTEE**.

booting

bootlace

bootleg »*adjective* (of alcoholic drink or a recording) made or distributed illegally.
bootlegger
bootlegging

> ☑ there are two g's in the words **bootlegger** and **bootlegging**

boots

bootstrap

booty »*noun* valuable stolen goods.

> ☑ do not confuse the spelling of **booty** with **bootee** (which can also be spelled **bootie**), meaning 'a child's shoe'

booze (verb: **boozes**, **boozing**, **boozed**)
boozy

booze-up

boozing

boozy

bop (in informal English) »*noun* a dance to pop music.
» *verb* (**bops**, **bopping**, **bopped**) dance to pop music.
bopper

> ☑ double the p in **bopping**, **bopped**, and **bopper**

borage »*noun* a plant with bright blue flowers and hairy leaves.
– SAY bo-rij

borax »*noun* a white mineral used in making glass and in soldering or smelting.

> ☑ there is no **e** at the end: **borax**

bordello »*noun* (plural **bordellos**) a brothel.
– SAY bor-**del**-oh

> ☑ the plural of **bordello**, an Italian word, has **os** not **oes**: **bordellos**

border (verb: **borders**, **bordering**, **bordered**)
borderer

borderland

borderline

borders

bore[1] (verb: **bores**, **boring**, **bored**) [drill a hole; uninteresting thing]

> ☑ do not confuse the spelling of **bore** with **boor** meaning 'a bad-mannered person', or **boar** meaning 'a wild pig'
> drop the **e** to spell **boring**

bore[2] past of **BEAR**. [carried]

bored

> ℹ say **bored by** or **bored with something** rather than **bored of**

boredom

borehole »*noun* a deep, narrow hole in the ground made to find water or oil.

borer

bores

boring
boringly

> ☑ there is no **e** in **boring**

born [having started life]

> ℹ do not confuse **born** with **borne**, which means 'carried'

born-again »*adjective* newly converted to Christianity or some other cause.

borne past participle of **BEAR**.

b

ℹ️ do not confuse **borne**, meaning 'carried', with **born**, which means 'having started life'

boron »*noun* a chemical element used in making alloy steel and in nuclear reactors.

borough »*noun* ❶ (in Britain) a town with a corporation and privileges granted by a royal charter. ❷ a part of London or New York City which has its own local council.

✓ unless you are referring to a Scottish town, use the spelling **borough** rather than **burgh**

borrow (verb: **borrows, borrowing, borrowed**)
borrower

borstal »*noun* (a historical term) a type of prison for young offenders.
– SAY **bor**-st'l

borzoi »*noun* (plural **borzois**) a large Russian dog with a narrow head.
– SAY **bor**-zoy

✓ the plural of **borzoi** simply adds an **s**, not **es**: **borzois**

Bosnian
bosom

✓ single **s** in **bosom**

boss (verb: **bosses, bossing, bossed**)

bossa nova »*noun* a dance like the samba, from Brazil.
– SAY bos-suh **noh**-vuh

bossed
bosses
bossiness
bossing
bossy (adjective: **bossier, bossiest**)
bossiness

bosun another way of spelling **BOATSWAIN**.

botanic
botanical
botanically

botany »*noun* the scientific study of plants.
– SAY **bot**-uh-ni
botanist

botch »*verb* (**botches, botching, botched**) (in informal English) do something badly or carelessly.

both

bother (verb: **bothers, bothering, bothered**)

bothersome »*adjective* annoying.

Botswanan
– SAY bot-**swah**-nuhn

bottle (verb: **bottles, bottling, bottled**)

bottleneck »*noun* a narrow section of road where the flow of traffic is restricted.

bottles
bottling
bottom
bottomless

bottom line »*noun* (in informal English) the most important factor.

botulism »*noun* a dangerous form of food poisoning.
– SAY bot-**yuu**-li-z'm

✓ there is only one **t**: **botulism**

boudoir »*noun* a woman's bedroom or small private room.
– SAY **boo**-dwar

ℹ️ a French word which literally means 'sulking-place'

bouffant »*adjective* (of hair) styled so as to stand out from the head in a rounded shape.
– SAY **boo**-fon

✓ the final **t** is not pronounced because **bouffant** comes from French

bougainvillea »*noun* a tropical climbing plant with brightly coloured bracts surrounding the flowers.
– SAY boo-guhn-**vil**-li-uh

✓ the correct Latin spelling is **villea**, not **villaea**: **bougainvillea**

bough »*noun* a main branch of a tree.
– SAY *rhymes with* cow

ℹ️ do not confuse **bough** with **bow**, which means 'bend the head' or 'front end of a ship'

bought

bouillon »*noun* thin soup or stock.
– SAY **boo**-yon

✓ notice the **oui** in **bouillon**: it is a French word

boulder [rock]

✓ do not confuse the spelling of **boulder** with **bolder**, which means 'braver'

boules »*noun* a French game similar to bowls.
– SAY bool

✓ **boules** is the plural of French *boule*, and the **s** is silent

boulevard »*noun* a wide street.
– SAY **boo**-luh-vard

bounce (verb: **bounces, bouncing, bounced**)

✓ drop the **e** to spell **bouncing**

bouncer

bounces

bouncing

bouncy

bound[1] (verb: **bounds, bounding, bounded**) [leap; boundary; restrict]

bound[2] past and past participle of **BIND**.

boundary (plural **boundaries**)

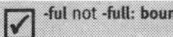
> **ary** not **ery**: **boundary**
> plural: drop the **y** and add **ies**: **boundaries**

bounded

bounder »*noun* (old-fashioned) a man who behaves dishonourably.

bounding

boundless

bounds

bounteous »*adjective* (an old word) given or giving generously.

bounties

bountiful »*adjective* ❶ plentiful. ❷ giving generously.

> **-ful** not **-full**: **bountiful**

bounty »*noun* (plural **bounties**) ❶ a reward paid for killing or capturing someone. ❷ something given or occurring in generous amounts. ❸ generosity: *people along the Nile depend on its bounty.*

bouquet »*noun* ❶ a bunch of flowers. ❷ the characteristic scent of a wine or perfume.
– SAY boo-**kay**

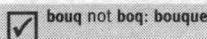
> **bouq** not **boq**: **bouquet**

bourbon »*noun* an American whisky made from maize and rye.
– SAY ber-**buhn**

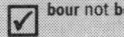
> **bour** not **ber** or **bur**: **bourbon**

bourgeois »*adjective* having to do with the middle class, especially in being concerned with wealth and social status.
– SAY boor-*zh*wah

> no **e** at the end: **bourgeois**
> (**bourgeoise** is strictly feminine)

bourgeoisie »*noun* the middle class.
– SAY boor-*zh*wah-zee

> **ie** at the end: **bourgeoisie** (like **bourgeois**, a French word)

bourse »*noun* a stock market in a non-English-speaking country.
– SAY *rhymes with* course

bout »*noun* ❶ a short period of intense activity or illness. ❷ a wrestling or boxing match.

boutique »*noun* a small shop selling fashionable clothes.
– SAY boo-**teek**

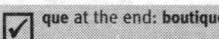
> **que** at the end: **boutique**

bovine »*adjective* ❶ having to do with cattle. ❷ sluggish or stupid.
» *noun* an animal of the cattle group.
– SAY boh-vyn

bow[1] [knot; weapon]
– SAY *rhymes with* toe

bow[2] (verb: **bows, bowing, bowed**) [bend the head; a bend of the head; front of a ship]
– SAY *rhymes with* cow

> ℹ️ do not confuse **bow** with **bough**, which means 'a branch of a tree'

bowdlerize »*verb* (**bowdlerizes, bowdlerizing, bowdlerized**) remove parts of a text that might shock or offend people.
– SAY bowd-luh-ryz

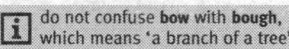
> many people prefer the alternative spellings **bowdlerise, bowdlerises,** etc.: both **s** and **z** spellings are correct

bowed

bowel »*noun* ❶ the intestine. ❷ (**bowels**) the deepest inner parts of something.
– SAY *rhymes with* towel

> there is only one **l**: **bowel**

bower »*noun* a pleasant shady place under trees.
– SAY *rhymes with* tower

bowerbird »*noun* an Australasian bird noted for the male's habit of building an elaborate bower to attract the female.

bowie knife »*noun* a long knife with a double-edged blade at its point.
– SAY *rhymes with* snowy

bowing

bowl (verb: **bowls, bowling, bowled**)

bow-legged »*adjective* having legs that curve outwards at the knee.

bowler

bowline »*noun* a simple knot for forming a loop at the end of a rope.
– SAY boh-lin

bowling

bowls

bows

bowsprit »*noun* a pole sticking out from a ship's bow, to which the ropes supporting the front mast are tied.
– say boh-sprit

bow window »*noun* a curved bay window.

box[1] (plural **boxes**; verb: **boxes, boxing, boxed**) [container; fight]

box[2] »*noun* a shrub with small, round glossy leaves.

boxer

boxes

boxing

Boxing Day

box office »*noun* a place at a theatre or cinema where tickets are sold.

boxroom »*noun* a very small room.

boxy »*adjective* ❶ roughly square in shape. ❷ (of a room or space) cramped.

boy
boyhood
boyish

boycott »*verb* (**boycotts, boycotting, boycotted**) refuse to have dealings with a person, organization, or country as a punishment or protest.
» *noun* an act of boycotting.

 double t: **boycott**

boyfriend

boyhood

boyish

Boy Scout

boysenberry »*noun* (plural **boysenberries**) a large red blackberry-like fruit.
– say boy-z'n-buh-ri

bra (plural **bras**)

brace (verb: **braces, bracing, braced**)

bracelet

braces

brachiosaurus »*noun* (plural **brachiosaurus**) a huge plant-eating dinosaur with forelegs much longer than the hind legs.
– say bra-ki-uh-**sor**-uhss

bracing

bracken »*noun* a tall fern with coarse fronds.

 -en not -in: **bracken**

bracket (verb: **brackets, bracketing, bracketed**)

 do not double the t in **bracketing** and **bracketed**

brackish »*adjective* (of water) slightly salty.

bract »*noun* a leaf with a flower in the angle where it meets the stem.

brad »*noun* a nail with a rectangular cross section and a small head.

bradawl »*noun* a tool for boring holes, resembling a screwdriver.

 awl not all: **bradawl**

brag (verb: **brags, bragging, bragged**)

braggart »*noun* a person who brags.
– say brag-gert

 double g, and art not ert: **braggart**

bragged

bragging

brags

Brahman »*noun* (plural **Brahmans**) a member of the highest Hindu caste, that of the priesthood.
– say brah-muhn

 don't forget the h before the m: **Brahman**

Brahmin »*noun* = BRAHMAN.
– say brah-min

braid (verb: **braids, braiding, braided**)

 aid not ade: **braid**

Braille »*noun* a written language for the blind using raised dots.
– say brayl

 double l and an e at the end: **Braille** is named after the French educationist Louis *Braille*

brain

brainchild »*noun* (in informal English) an idea or invention thought up by a particular person.

brain death »*noun* brain damage which cannot be reversed and which causes a person to stop breathing independently.
brain-dead

brainier

brainiest

brainless
brainlessly
brainlessness

brainstorm »*noun* ❶ (in informal English) a moment in which you are suddenly unable to think clearly. ❷ a group discussion to produce ideas.
» *verb* (**brainstorms, brainstorming, brainstormed**) have a discussion to produce ideas.

brain-teaser »*noun* (in informal English) a problem or puzzle.

brainwash »*verb* (**brainwashes, brainwashing, brainwashed**) cause someone to change their attitudes and beliefs by putting pressure on them or by repeating the same thing over and over.

brainwave »*noun* ❶ an electrical impulse in the brain. ❷ (in informal English) a sudden clever idea.

brainy (adjective: **brainier, brainiest**)

braise »*verb* (**braises, braising, braised**) fry food lightly and then stew it slowly in a closed container.

> ✓ don't forget the **i** between the **a** and the **s**: **braise**, and do not confuse **braise** with **braze**, which means 'join metal parts together'

brake (verb: **brakes, braking, braked**) [device for stopping vehicle; slow or stop a vehicle]

> ✓ do not confuse the spelling of **brake** with **break**, which means 'separate into pieces; stop working; a pause or gap'

brake drum »*noun* a broad, short cylinder attached to a wheel, against which the brake shoes press to cause braking.

brake horsepower »*noun* an imperial unit equal to one horsepower, expressing the power available at the shaft of an engine.

brake shoe »*noun* a long curved block which presses on to a brake drum.

bramble »*noun* ❶ a blackberry bush or similar prickly shrub. ❷ the fruit of the blackberry.

brambling »*noun* a finch with a white rump.

Bramley »*noun* (plural **Bramleys**) a large English cooking apple with green skin.

bran

branch (verb: **branches, branching, branched**)

brand (verb: **brands, branding, branded**)

brandies

branding

brandish »*verb* (**brandishes, brandishing, brandished**) wave something as a threat or in anger or excitement.

brands

brandy »*noun* (plural **brandies**) a strong alcoholic spirit made from wine or fermented fruit juice.

brash »*adjective* (**brasher, brashest**) very confident in a rather rude or aggressive way.

brashly
brashness

brass

brasserie »*noun* (plural **brasseries**) an inexpensive French or French-style restaurant.
– SAY **brass**-uh-ri

> ✓ double **s** and **ie** not **y** at the end: **brasserie**

brassica »*noun* a plant of the family that includes cabbage, swede, and rape.
– SAY **bras**-ik-uh

> ✓ double **s**: **brassica**

brassier [more brassy]

brassiere »*noun* a bra.
– SAY **braz**-i-er

> ⓘ do not confuse **brassiere** with **brazier**, which means 'a portable heater holding lighted coals'

brassiest

brass rubbing »*noun* reproduction of the design on a brass in a church by rubbing chalk or other substance over paper laid on it.

brassy (adjective: **brassier, brassiest**)

brat
brattish

bravado »*noun* boldness intended to impress or intimidate people.
– SAY bruh-**vah**-doh

brave (adjective: **braver, bravest**; verb: **braves, braving, braved**)
bravely
bravery

bravo »*exclamation* shouted to express approval for a performer.
– SAY brah-**voh**

bravura »*noun* ❶ great skill; brilliance. ❷ the display of great daring.
– SAY bruh-**vyoor**-uh

brawl (verb: **brawls, brawling, brawled**)
brawler

> ✓ **awl** not **all**: **brawl**

brawn »*noun* physical strength as opposed to intelligence.

brawny (adjective: **brawnier, brawniest**)

bray »*noun* the loud, harsh cry of a donkey.
»*verb* (**brays, braying, brayed**) make such a sound.

braze »*verb* (**brazes, brazing, brazed**) join metal parts together using an alloy of copper and zinc.
»*noun* a brazed joint.

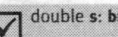

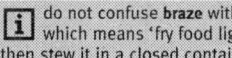

> ℹ️ do not confuse **braze** with **braise** which means 'fry food lightly and then stew it in a closed container'

brazen »*adjective* bold and shameless.
» *verb* (**brazens, brazening, brazened**) (**brazen it out**) endure a difficult situation without seeming to be ashamed.
brazenly

brazes

brazier »*noun* ❶ a portable heater holding lighted coals. ❷ a worker in brass.
– SAY bray-zi-er

> ℹ️ do not confuse **brazier** with **brassiere**, which means 'a bra'

Brazilian

brazing

breach »*verb* (**breaches, breaching, breaches**) ❶ make a hole in; break through. ❷ break a rule or agreement.
» *noun* ❶ a gap made in a barrier. ❷ an action that breaks a rule or agreement. ❸ a disagreement.

> ✓ do not confuse the spellings of **breach** and **breech**, which means 'the back part of a rifle or gun barrel'

bread

breadcrumb

breaded »*adjective* (of food) coated with breadcrumbs and fried.

breadline

breadth

breadwinner »*noun* a person who supports their family with the money they earn.

break (verb: **breaks, breaking, broke**; past participle **broken**) [separate into pieces; stop working; a pause or gap]
breakable
breaker

> ✓ do not confuse the spelling of **break** with **brake**, which refers to a device for slowing or stopping a vehicle

breakage

breakaway

break-dancing »*noun* an energetic and acrobatic style of street dancing.

breakdown

breaker

breakfast (verb: **breakfasts, breakfasting, breakfasted**)

break-in

breaking

breakneck »*adjective* dangerously fast.

breaks

breakthrough

breakwater »*noun* a barrier built out into the sea to protect a coast or harbour from the force of waves.

bream »*noun* (plural **bream**) a greenish-bronze freshwater fish.

> ✓ **ea** not **ee**: **bream**

breast (verb: **breasts, breasting, breasted**)

breastbone

breasted

breastfeed (verb: **breastfeeds, breastfeeding, breastfed**)

breasting

breastplate »*noun* a piece of armour covering the chest.

breasts

breaststroke

breath
breathable

> ✓ no **e** at the end: **breath** is a noun referring to air taken into the lungs, whereas **breathe** is a verb meaning 'take air into the lungs'

breathalyse »*verb* (**breathalyses, breathalysing, breathalysed**) test how much alcohol a driver has in their breath by making them breathe into a portable device.
breathalyser

> ✓ **yse** not **yze** or **ise**: **breathalyse**. **Breathalyze** and **breathalyzer** (trademark) are American spellings.

breathe (verb: **breathes, breathing, breathed**)
breather
breathing

> ✓ don't forget the **e** at the end: **breathe** is a verb meaning 'take air into the lungs', whereas **breath** is a noun referring to air taken into the lungs

breathless
breathlessly
breathlessness

breathtaking
breathtakingly

breathy »*adjective* having a noticeable sound of breathing: *a breathy laugh*.

bred past and past participle of **BREED**.

breech »*noun* the back part of a rifle or gun barrel.

> ✓ do not confuse the spelling of **breech** with **breach**, which means 'break through'

breech birth »*noun* a birth in which the baby's buttocks or feet are delivered first.

breeches »*plural noun* short trousers fastened just below the knee.

breed (verb: **breeds**, **breeding**, **bred**)
breeder
breeding

breeze (verb: **breezes**, **breezing**, **breezed**)

breeze block »*noun* a lightweight building brick made from cinders, sand, and cement.

breezed

breezes

breezier

breeziest

breezily

breezing

breezy (adjective: **breezier**, **breeziest**)
breezily

brethren »*plural noun* ❶ (an old word) brothers. ❷ fellow Christians or members of a male religious order.

Breton »*noun* ❶ a person from Brittany. ❷ the language of Brittany.
– SAY bre-tuhn

> ✓ only one **t**: Breton

breve »*noun* ❶ a musical note twice as long as a semibreve. ❷ a mark (˘) indicating a short or unstressed vowel.
– SAY *rhymes with* sleeve

> ✓ only one **e** between the **r** and the **v**: breve

breviary »*noun* (plural **breviaries**) a book containing the service for each day, used in the Roman Catholic Church.
– SAY bree-vi-uh-ri

brevity »*noun* ❶ concise and exact use of words. ❷ shortness of time.
– SAY brev-i-ti

brew (verb: **brews**, **brewing**, **brewed**)
brewer

brewery (plural **breweries**)

> ✓ plural: drop the **y** and add **ies**: breweries

brewing

brews

briar »*noun* a prickly scrambling shrub.

> ✓ briar can also be spelled **brier**: both spellings are correct

bribe (verb: **bribes**, **bribing**, **bribed**)
bribery

bric-a-brac »*noun* various objects of little value.

> ✓ there are no **k**'s in bric-a-brac
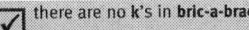

brick (verb: **bricks**, **bricking**, **bricked**)

brickbat »*noun* ❶ a piece of brick used as a missile. ❷ a critical remark.

bricked

bricking

bricklayer

bricks

bridal [relating to a bride]

> ✓ do not confuse the spelling of **bridal** with **bridle**, which means refers to headgear used to control a horse

bride

bridegroom

bridesmaid

bridge (verb: **bridges**, **bridging**, **bridges**)

> ✓ drop the **e** when spelling **bridging**

bridgehead »*noun* a strong position gained by an army inside enemy territory.

bridges

bridging

bridle »*noun* the headgear used to control a horse.
» *verb* (**bridles**, **bridling**, **bridled**) ❶ put a bridle on. ❷ bring under control. ❸ show resentment or anger.

> ✓ do not confuse the spelling of **bridle** with **bridal**, which means 'relating to a bride'

bridleway »*noun* a path along which horse riders have right of way.

bridling

Brie »*noun* a kind of soft, mild, creamy cheese.
– SAY bree

brief (adjective: **briefer**, **briefest**; verb: **briefs**, **briefing**, **briefed**)
briefly

> ✓ the usual rule is **i** before **e**, except after **c**: brief

briefcase

briefed

briefer

briefest

briefing

briefly

briefs

brier another way of spelling **BRIAR**.

brig »*noun* a sailing ship with two masts.

brigade »*noun* ❶ a subdivision of an army, made up of battalions and forming part of a division. ❷ (in informal English) a particular group of people: *the anti-smoking brigade.*

brigadier »*noun* a rank of officer in the British army, above colonel and below major general.
– SAY bri-guh-deer

> ✓ ier not eer: brigadier

brigand »*noun* a member of a gang of bandits.
– SAY brig-uhnd

> ✓ only one g: brigand

brigantine »*noun* a kind of sailing ship with two masts.
– SAY brig-uhn-teen

> ✓ ine not een: brigantine

bright (adjective: **brighter**, **brightest**)
brightly
brightness

brighten (verb: **brightens**, **brightening**, **brightened**)

brighter

brightest

brightly

brightness

brilliance

brilliancy »*noun* brilliance.

brilliant
brilliantly

> ✓ double l, and ant not ent: brilliant

brim (verb: **brims**, **brimming**, **brimmed**)
brimful

> ✓ double the m in brimming and brimmed

brimstone »*noun* (an old word) sulphur.

brindle »*adjective* (of an animal) brownish with streaks of another colour.

brindled »*adjective* = BRINDLE.

brine »*noun* salt water.

bring (verb: **brings**, **bringing**, **brought**)
bringer

brink »*noun* ❶ the edge of land before a steep slope or a body of water. ❷ the stage just before a new situation.

brinkmanship »*noun* the pursuing of a dangerous course of action to the limits of safety before stopping.

briny »*adjective* salty, like seawater.
– SAY *rhymes with tiny*

brio »*noun* energy or liveliness in performing something.

– SAY bree-oh

brioche »*noun* a small, round, sweet French roll.
– SAY bree-osh

> ✓ ch not sh, and an e at the end: brioche

briquette »*noun* a block of compressed coal dust or peat used as fuel.
– SAY bri-ket

> ✓ q not ck in the middle: briquette. It can also be spelled briquet: both spellings are correct.

brisk
briskly
briskness

brisket »*noun* meat from the breast of a cow.

> ✓ -et not -it: brisket

briskly

briskness

bristle (verb: **bristles**, **bristling**, **bristled**)
bristly

> ✓ drop the e when spelling bristling and bristly

Brit

Britannia »*noun* the personification of Britain, usually as a helmeted woman with a shield and trident.
– SAY bri-tan-yuh
Britannic

> ✓ single t, double n: Britannia

British
Britishness

Briton »*noun* ❶ a British person. ❷ a person from southern Britain before and during Roman times.

> ✓ note the -on ending: Briton

brittle
brittleness

> ✓ double t: brittle

broach »*verb* (**broaches**, **broaching**, **broached**) ❶ raise a subject for discussion. ❷ pierce or open a container to draw out liquid.

> ✓ do not confuse the spelling of broach with brooch, which means 'an ornament pinned to clothing'

broad
broadly

broadcast (verb: **broadcasts**, **broadcasting**, **broadcast**; past participle **broadcast** or **broadcasted**)
broadcaster

broadcloth »*noun* a fine cloth of wool or cotton.

broaden (verb: **broadens**, **broadening**, **broadened**)

broadleaf »*noun* (plural **broadleaves**) a tree with fairly wide flat leaves, as opposed to a conifer.
broadleaved

broadloom »*noun* carpet woven in wide widths.

broadly

broad-minded

broadsheet »*noun* a newspaper printed on large sheets of paper.

broadside »*noun* ❶ a strongly worded critical attack. ❷ (a historical term) a firing of all the guns from one side of a warship.

broadsword »*noun* a sword with a wide blade.

brocade »*noun* a rich fabric woven with a raised pattern.

 ade not aid: brocade

broccoli

two **c**'s, one **l**: **broccoli** is an Italian word

brochure

broderie anglaise »*noun* open embroidery on fine white cotton or linen.
– SAY broh-duh-ri **onng**-glayz

broderie anglaise is French for 'English embroidery'

brogue »*noun* ❶ a strong outdoor shoe with perforated patterns in the leather. ❷ a strong regional accent.

remember the **u** after the **g**: **brogue**

broil »*verb* (**broils**, **broiling**, **broiled**) cook meat or fish using direct heat.
broiler

broke past of BREAK.

broken past participle of BREAK.

broken-down

broken-hearted

broker »*noun* a person who buys and sells things for others.
»*verb* (**brokers**, **brokering**, **brokered**) arrange a deal or plan.
brokerage

brolly »*noun* (plural **brollies**) (in informal English) an umbrella.

bromide »*noun* a compound of bromine.
– SAY broh-myd

bromine »*noun* a dark red liquid chemical element.
– SAY broh-meen

bronchi plural of BRONCHUS.

bronchial »*adjective* relating to the air passages of the lungs.
– SAY brong-ki-uhl

bronchitis »*noun* inflammation of the air passages of the lungs.

bronchus »*noun* (plural **bronchi**) one of the major air passages of the lungs which spread out from the windpipe.
– SAY brong-kuhss [singular], brong-kee [plural]

make the plural by changing the **us** ending to **i** (as in Latin): **bronchi**

bronco »*noun* (plural **broncos**) a wild or half-tamed horse of the western US.

the plural of **bronco** has **os** not **oes**: **broncos**

brontosaurus »*noun* (plural **brontosaurus**) a huge plant-eating dinosaur with a long neck and tail.
– SAY bron-tuh-sor-uhs

bronze (verb: **bronzes**, **bronzing**, **bronzed**)

Bronze Age »*noun* a period that came after the Stone Age and before the Iron Age, when weapons and tools were made of bronze.

bronzed

bronzes

bronzing

brooch [ornament pinned to clothing]

do not confuse the spelling of **brooch** with **broach**, which means 'raise a subject for discussion'

brood »*noun* a family of young animals born or hatched at the same time.
»*verb* (**broods**, **brooding**, **brooded**) ❶ think deeply about an unpleasant subject. ❷ (**brooding**) appearing darkly menacing. ❸ (of a bird) sit on eggs to hatch them.

broody »*adjective* (**broodier**, **broodiest**) ❶ (of a hen) wishing to hatch eggs. ❷ (in informal English) (of a woman) having a strong desire to have a baby. ❸ thoughtful and unhappy.

brook[1] »*noun* a small stream.
brooklet

brook[2] **»verb** (**brooks, brooking, brooked**) tolerate or allow: *she would brook no criticism.*

broom

broomstick

broth **»noun** soup made of meat or vegetable chunks cooked in stock.

brothel **»noun** a house where men visit prostitutes.

brother
brotherly

brotherhood

brother-in-law (plural **brothers-in-law**)

> 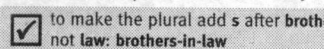 to make the plural add **s** after **brother** not **law**: **brothers-in-law**

brotherly

brougham **»noun** (a historical term) ❶ a horse-drawn carriage with a roof and an open driver's seat in front. ❷ a motor car with an open driver's seat.
– **say** broo-uhm

brought past and past participle of **BRING**.

brouhaha **»noun** a noisy and overexcited reaction.
– **say** broo-hah-hah

> **ou** not **oo**: **brouhaha**

brow
browed

browbeat **»verb** (**browbeats, browbeating, browbeat**; past participle **browbeaten**) bully someone with words or looks.

browed

brown (adjective: **browner, brownest**; verb: **browns, browning, browned**)
brownish
browny

brownie **»noun** (plural **brownies**) ❶ a small square of rich chocolate cake. ❷ a kind elf that supposedly does housework secretly. ❸ (**Brownie**) a member of the junior branch of the Guides Association.

> the ending is **ie** not **y**: **brownie** (**browny** is an adjective meaning 'somewhat brown')

browning

brownish

browns

Brownshirt **»noun** a member of a Nazi military force with brown uniforms.

browny [somewhat brown]

browse **»verb** (**browses, browsing, browsed**) ❶ look at goods or text in a leisurely way. ❷ look at information on a computer.

❸ (of an animal) feed on leaves, twigs, etc.
»noun an act of browsing.
browsable

> 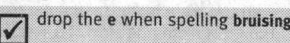 drop the **e** to spell **browsing** and **browsable**

browser **»noun** ❶ a person or animal that browses. ❷ a computer program used for navigating the World Wide Web.

browses

browsing

brucellosis **»noun** a disease of cattle which can sometimes infect humans.
– **say** broo-suh-**loh**-siss

> double **l**: **brucellosis** is caused by a bacterium named *Brucella*

bruise (verb: **bruises, bruising, bruised**)
bruiser
bruising

> drop the **e** when spelling **bruising**

bruit **»verb** (an old word) (**bruits, bruiting, bruited**) spread a report or rumour widely.
– **say** *rhymes with* fruit

> do not confuse **bruit** with **brute**, which means 'a violent person or animal'

Brummie **»noun** (plural **Brummies**) (in informal English) a person from Birmingham.

brunch **»noun** a late morning meal eaten instead of breakfast and lunch.

Bruneian [of Brunei]
– **say** broo-**ny**-uhn

> **e** before **i** in **Brunei** and **Bruneian**

brunette **»noun** a woman or girl with dark brown hair.

> **ette** at the end, not **et**: **brunette** (the spelling **brunet** is American)

brunt **»noun** the chief impact of something bad.

bruschetta **»noun** toasted Italian bread covered in olive oil.
– **say** bruu-**sket**-uh

brush (verb: **brushes, brushing, brushed**)
brushy

brushwood **»noun** undergrowth, twigs, and small branches.

brushy

brusque **»adjective** rather rude and abrupt.
– **say** bruusk
brusquely
brusqueness

☑ **que** at the end: **brusque**

Brussels sprout

brut »*adjective* (of sparkling wine) very dry.
– SAY rhymes with loot

brutal
brutality
brutally

brutalize »*verb* (brutalizes, brutalizing, brutalized) ❶ make someone brutal by frequently exposing them to violence. ❷ treat someone brutally.
brutalization

☑ many people prefer the alternative spellings **brutalise, brutalises,** etc., and **brutalisation**: both **s** and **z** spellings are correct

brute [violent person or animal]
brutish

ℹ️ do not confuse **brute** with **bruit**, which means 'spread a rumour widely', or **brut**, which refers to very dry sparkling wine

☑ drop the **e** when spelling **brutish**

bryony »*noun* a climbing hedgerow plant with red berries.
– SAY bry-uh-ni

BSc »*abbreviation* Bachelor of Science.

BSE »*abbreviation* bovine spongiform encephalopathy, a fatal disease of cattle.

B-side »*noun* the less important side of a pop single.

BST »*abbreviation* British Summer Time.

BT »*abbreviation* British Telecom.

bubble (verb: bubbles, bubbling, bubbled)

☑ drop the **e** to form **bubbling**

bubble and squeak »*noun* cooked cabbage fried with cooked potatoes.

bubbled

bubblegum

bubbles

bubbling

bubbly

bubonic plague »*noun* a form of plague passed on by rat fleas.

buccaneer »*noun* ❶ (a historical term) a pirate. ❷ a recklessly adventurous person.
buccaneering

☑ there are two **c**'s and two **e**'s, but only one **n**: **buccaneer**

buck (verb: bucks, bucking, bucked)

bucket
bucketful

bucking

buckle (verb: buckles, buckling, buckled)

☑ drop the **e** when spelling **buckling**

buckram »*noun* coarse cloth used to bind books.

bucks

buckshot »*noun* lead shot used in shotgun shells.

buckskin »*noun* ❶ the skin of a male deer. ❷ thick smooth cotton or woollen fabric.

buck teeth »*plural noun* upper teeth that stick out over the lower lip.

buckthorn »*noun* a thorny shrub with black berries.

buck-toothed

buckwheat »*noun* a plant whose seeds are used for animal feed or made into flour.

bucolic »*adjective* relating to country life.
– SAY byoo-kol-ik

bud (verb: buds, budding, budded)

☑ double the **d** when spelling **budding** and **budded**

Buddhism »*noun* a religion based on the teachings of Buddha (563–460 BC) in India.
Buddhist

☑ note the **h** after the double **d**:
Buddhism, Buddhist

budding

buddleia »*noun* a shrub with clusters of lilac, white, or yellow flowers.
– SAY bud-li-uh

☑ **eia** at the end: **buddleia**

buddy (plural buddies)

budge (verb: budges, budging, budged)

☑ drop the **e** when spelling **budging**

budgerigar »*noun* a small Australian parakeet.

budges

budget »*noun* ❶ an estimate of income and spending for a set period of time. ❷ the amount of money needed or available for a purpose. ❸ (**Budget**) a regular estimate of national income and spending put forward by a finance minister.
» *verb* (budgets, budgeting, budgeted) plan to spend a particular amount of money.

b

» *adjective* inexpensive.
budgetary

> ✓ do not double the t in **budgeting** or
> **budgeted**

budgie »*noun* (plural **budgies**) (in informal
English) a budgerigar.

budging

buds

buff »*noun* ❶ a yellowish-beige colour. ❷ a
person who knows a lot about a particular
subject: *a film buff*.
» *verb* (**buffs, buffing, buffed**) polish
something with a soft cloth.

buffalo (plural **buffalo** or **buffaloes**)

> ✓ the plural of **buffalo** is either the
> same (as in *herds of buffalo*) or adds
> **es: buffaloes**

buffed

buffer »*noun* ❶ shock-absorbing devices at
the end of a railway track or on a railway
vehicle. ❷ a person or thing that lessens
the impact of harmful effects: *family and
friends can provide a buffer against stress.*

buffet[1] »*noun* ❶ a meal made up of several
dishes from which you serve yourself. ❷ a
room or counter selling light meals or
snacks.
– **SAY** buf-fay

> ✓ although it is not pronounced, there
> is a t at the end: **buffet**

buffet[2] »*verb* (**buffets, buffeting, buffeted**)
strike something repeatedly and violently.
– **SAY** buf-fit

> ✓ do not double the t in **buffeting** and
> **buffeted**

buffing

buffoon »*noun* a ridiculous but amusing
person.
buffoonery

buffs

bug (verb: **bugs, bugging, bugged**)

bugbear »*noun* something that causes
anxiety or irritation.

bug-eyed »*adjective* with bulging eyes.

bugged

bugger (verb: **buggers, buggering,
buggered**)

buggery »*noun* anal sex.

bugging

buggy »*noun* (plural **buggies**) ❶ a small
motor vehicle with an open top. ❷ (a
historical term) a light horse-drawn vehicle
for one or two people.

bugle »*noun* a brass instrument like a small
trumpet.
bugler

bugs

build (verb: **builds, building, built**)
builder

building

building society »*noun* a financial
organization which pays interest on
members' investments and lends money
for mortgages.

builds

build-up

built past and past participle of **BUILD**.

built-in

built-up

bulb

bulbous »*adjective* ❶ round or bulging in
shape. ❷ (of a plant) growing from a
bulb.

> ✓ **ous** at the end: **bulbous**

Bulgarian

bulgar wheat »*noun* a cereal food made
from whole wheat which has been boiled
then dried.

> ✓ **bulgar** can also be spelled **bulgur**:
> both spellings are correct

bulge (verb: **bulges, bulging, bulged**)
bulging
bulgy

> ✓ drop the e when spelling **bulging** and
> **bulgy**

bulgur wheat another way of spelling
BULGAR WHEAT.

bulgy

bulimia »*noun* a disorder which causes
bouts of overeating, followed by fasting or
vomiting.
– **SAY** buu-**lim**-i-uh
bulimic SAY buu-**lim**-ik

> ✓ **bu** not **bou**, and **lim** not **lem**: **bulimia**

bulk (verb: **bulks, bulking, bulked**)

bulkhead »*noun* a barrier between
separate areas inside a ship, aircraft, etc.

bulkier

bulkiest

bulkiness

bulking

bulks

bulky (adjective: **bulkier, bulkiest**)
bulkiness

bull

bulldog

bulldoze (verb: **bulldozes, bulldozing, bulldozed**)

 drop the **e** when spelling **bulldozing**

bulldozer

bulldozes

bulldozing

bullet

bulletin »*noun* ❶ a short official statement or summary of news. ❷ a regular newsletter or report.

there is only one **t: bulletin**

bulletin board »*noun* a noticeboard.

bulletproof

bullfighting
  bullfight
  bullfighter

bullfinch »*noun* a finch with a pink breast.

double **l** in **bullfinch** and **bullfrog**, but strangely this is not the usual spelling of **bulrush**

bullfrog »*noun* a very large frog with a deep croak.

bullied

bullies

bullion »*noun* gold or silver in bulk before being made into coins.
– SAY buul-li-uhn

bullish »*adjective* expecting share prices to rise; aggressively confident (the opposite of *bearish*).
  bullishly
  bullishness

bullock »*noun* a castrated male animal of the cattle group.

bullring »*noun* an arena where bullfights are held.

bullrush see **BULRUSH**.

bullseye

bullshit (verb: **bullshits, bullshitting, bullshitted**)
  bullshitter

bully (plural **bullies**; verb: **bullies, bullying, bullied**)

 plural: drop the **y** and add **ies: bullies**

bulrush »*noun* a tall reed-like waterside plant.

bulrush is usually spelled with a single **l**, although **bullrush** is also correct

bulwark »*noun* ❶ a defensive wall. ❷ an extension of a ship's sides above deck level.
– SAY buul-werk

 there is only one **l** in **bulwark**

bum (verb: **bums, bumming, bummed**)

bumble (verb: **bumbles, bumbling, bumbled**)
  bumbler

drop the **e** when spelling **bumbling**

bumblebee

bumbled

bumbler

bumbles

bumbling

bumf »*noun* (in informal English) useless or boring printed information.

can also be spelled with **ph: bumf** or **bumph**

bummed

bummer

bumming

bump (verb: **bumps, bumping, bumped**)

bumper

bumph another way of spelling **BUMF**.

bumpier

bumpiest

bumpiness

bumping

bumpkin »*noun* an unsophisticated person from the countryside.

remember the **p: bumpkin**

bumps

bumptious »*adjective* irritatingly forceful and confident.
  bumptiously
  bumptiousness

do not forget the **p: bumptious**

bumpy (adjective: **bumpier, bumpiest**)
  bumpiness

bums

bun

bunch (verb: **bunches, bunching, bunched**)
  bunchy

bundle (verb: **bundles, bundling, bundled**)

 drop the **e** in **bundling**

bunfight »*noun* (mainly used in a humorous way) a grand tea party or other function.

bung (verb: **bungs, bunging, bunged**)

bungalow

bunged

bungee »*noun* a long rubber band used for securing luggage and for bungee jumping.
– SAY bun-ji

> ✓ gee not jee: bungee

bungee jumping »*noun* the sport of leaping from a high place, held by a bungee around the ankles.
bungee jumper

bunging

bungle (verb: **bungles, bungling, bungled**)
bungler

> ✓ drop the e when spelling **bungling**

bungs

bunion »*noun* a painful swelling on the big toe.

> ✓ single n: **bunion**

bunk (verb: **bunks, bunking, bunked**)
bunker
bunking
bunks

bunkum »*noun* (old-fashioned) nonsense.

bunny (plural **bunnies**)

Bunsen burner »*noun* a small gas burner used in laboratories.

> ✓ capital B, and **-en** not **-on**: named after the German chemist Robert *Bunsen*

bunting »*noun* ❶ a small bird with brown streaked plumage. ❷ flags and streamers used as decorations.

buoy »*noun* an anchored float used to mark dangerous and safe areas of water.
» *verb* (**be buoyed** or **buoyed up**) be cheered up and made more confident.
– SAY boy

> ✓ the u comes before the o: **buoy**

buoyant »*adjective* ❶ able to keep afloat. ❷ cheerful and optimistic.
buoyancy
buoyantly

> ✓ u before o: **buoyant**

burble (verb: **burbles, burbling, burbled**)

> ✓ drop the e when spelling **burbling**

burbot »*noun* a freshwater fish of the cod family.
– SAY ber-buht

burden (verb: **burdens, burdening, burdened**)

> ✓ **den** not **don**: burden

burdensome

burdock »*noun* a plant with large leaves and prickly flowers.

bureau »*noun* (plural **bureaux** or **bureaus**)
❶ an office for carrying out particular business: *a news bureau.* ❷ a government department. ❸ (in British English) a writing desk with an angled top that opens downwards to form a writing surface.
❹ (in American English) a chest of drawers.
– SAY byoor-oh

> ✓ the plural of **bureau** can be **bureaux** (as in the original French) or **bureaus**

bureaucracy »*noun* (plural **bureaucracies**)
❶ a system of government in which most decisions are taken by state officials.
❷ excessively complicated administrative procedure.
– SAY byuu-**rok**-ruh-si

> ✓ remember, **eau** not **o** in the middle of these words: **bureaucracy, bureaucrat**

bureaucrat »*noun* an official who is thought to be too concerned with following guidelines rigidly.
bureaucratic

bureau de change »*noun* (plural **bureaux de change**) a place where you can exchange foreign money.
– SAY byoo-roh duh **shonzh** [singular and plural]

> ✓ add an **x** to **bureau** to make the plural: **bureaux de change** (as in French)

bureaus plural of BUREAU.

bureaux plural of BUREAU.

burette »*noun* a glass tube with a tap at one end, used for delivering known amounts of a liquid.
– SAY byuu-**ret**

> ✓ **ette** not **et**: burette (the spelling **buret** is American)

burgeon »*verb* (**burgeons, burgeoning, burgeoned**) grow or increase rapidly.
– SAY ber-juhn

> ✓ **geon** not **gon** at the end: **burgeon**

burger [hamburger]

> ℹ do not confuse **burger** with **burgher**, which means 'a citizen of a town'

burgess »*noun* (plural **burgesses**) (mainly a historical term) **❶** a Member of Parliament for a borough, corporate town, or university. **❷** (in America and formerly in Britain) a magistrate or member of the governing body of a town.

burgh »*noun* (in Scotland) a borough or chartered town.
– SAY **bur**-uh

> ✓ see the note at **BOROUGH**

burgher »*noun* (an old word) a citizen of a town or city.
– SAY **ber**-guh

> ⓘ do not confuse **burgher** with **burger**, which means 'hamburger'

burglar

> ✓ **glar** at the end, not **galer**: bur**glar**

burglary (plural **burglaries**)

> ✓ plural: drop the **y** and add **ies**: bur**glaries**

burgle (verb: **burgles, burgling, burgled**)

> ✓ drop the **e** when spelling bur**gling**

burgundy »*noun* (plural **burgundies**) **❶** a red wine from Burgundy in east central France. **❷** a deep red colour.
– SAY **ber**-guhn-di

burial

Burkinan [of Burkina Faso]
– SAY ber-**keen**-uhn

burl »*noun* a lump in wool or cloth.

burlap »*noun* coarse canvas woven from jute or hemp.

> ✓ **bur** not **ber**: **bur**lap

burlesque »*noun* **❶** a comically exaggerated imitation of something. **❷** (in American English) a variety show.
»*verb* (**burlesques, burlesquing, burlesqued**) imitate something in a comically exaggerated way.
– SAY ber-**lesk**

> ✓ **que** at the end, not **k**: burles**que** drop the **e** when spelling burles**quing**

burly »*adjective* (**burlier, burliest**) (of a man) large and strong.
burliness

Burmese (plural **Burmese**)

burn (verb: **burns, burning, burned** or **burnt**)
burner
burning

> ⓘ the past of **burn** can be either **burned** or **burnt**: both words are correct

burnish »*verb* (**burnishes, burnishing, burnished**) polish something by rubbing it.

burnout »*noun* physical or mental collapse. **b**

burnt past of **BURN**.

burp

burr »*noun* **❶** a strong pronunciation of the letter *r*. **❷** a prickly seed case or flower head that clings to clothing and animal fur.

> ✓ double **r**: bur**r**

burrito »*noun* (plural **burritos**) a Mexican dish made up of a rolled tortilla filled with minced beef or beans.
– SAY bu-**ree**-toh

> ✓ two **r**'s but only one **t**: bu**rr**i**t**o

burrow (verb: **burrows, burrowing, burrowed**)
burrower

bursar »*noun* a person who manages the financial affairs of a college or school.

> ✓ **ar** not **er**: burs**ar**

bursary »*noun* (plural **bursaries**) a grant.

burst (verb: **bursts, bursting, burst**)

Burundian
– SAY bu-**run**-di-uhn

bury (verb: **buries, burying, buried**)

bus (plural **buses**; verb: **buses** or **busses, busing** or **bussing, bused** or **bussed**)

> ✓ note that the verb **bus** can have either a single or double **s** in **buses**, **busses**, etc.

busby »*noun* (plural **busbies**) a tall fur hat worn by certain military regiments.

> ⓘ the term **busby** is often applied to the tall fur cap worn ceremonially by the guards at Buckingham Palace in London, but this is correctly called a **bearskin**

bused

buses

bush

bushbaby »*noun* (plural **bushbabies**) a small African mammal with very large eyes.

bushel »*noun* a measure of capacity equal to 8 gallons (36.4 litres).

> ✓ **el** not **ell**: bush**el**

bushier

bushiest

bushily

bushiness

Bushman »*noun* (plural **Bushmen**) ❶ a member of a southern African people inhabiting very dry areas. ❷ (**bushman**) a person who lives or travels in the Australian bush.

bushwhack »*verb* (**bushwhacks, bushwhacking, bushwhacked**) ❶ (mainly in Australian English) live or travel in the bush. ❷ (in American English) ambush someone.
bushwhacker

 spell with **wh**: **bushwhack**

bushy (adjective: **bushier, bushiest**)
bushily
bushiness

busied

busier

busies

busiest

busily

business (plural **businesses**) [trade]

 single **s** and single **n**, followed by double **s**: **business**

businesslike

businessman (plural **businessmen**)

businesswoman (plural **businesswomen**)

busing

busk »*verb* (**busks, busking, busked**) play music in the street in the hope of being given money by passers-by.
busker

busman »*noun* (plural **busmen**) a bus driver.

bussed

busses

bussing

bust[1] »*noun* ❶ a woman's breasts. ❷ a sculpture of a person's head, shoulders, and chest.

bust[2] (verb: **busts, busting, busted** or **bust**) [break; broken]

bustard »*noun* a large swift-running bird.

 ard not **erd**: **bustard**

busted

bustier[1] »*noun* a close-fitting strapless top for women.
– say **buss**-ti-ay

bustier[2] [more busty]

bustiest

busting

bustle[1] (verb: **bustles, bustling, bustled**) [move energetically; excited activity]
bustling

 drop the **e** when spelling **bustling**

bustle[2] »*noun* a pad or frame formerly worn under a skirt to puff it out behind.

bustled

bustles

bustling

busts

bust-up

busty »*adjective* (**bustier, bustiest**) (in informal English) (of a woman) having large breasts.

busy (adjective: **busier, busiest**; verb: **busies, busying, busied**)
busily
busyness

 drop the **y** to spell **busier, busiest, busies, busied,** and **busily**

busybody (plural **busybodies**)

busy Lizzie »*noun* a plant with many red, pink, or white flowers.

busyness [state of being busy]

but

 on starting a sentence with **but**, see the note at **AND**

butane »*noun* a flammable gas used as a fuel.
– say **byoo**-tayn

butch »*adjective* (in informal English) aggressively masculine.

butcher (verb: **butchers, butchering, butchered**)
butchery

butler

butt (verb: **butts, butting, butted**)

butter (verb: **butters, buttering, buttered**)

butter bean »*noun* a large flat edible bean.

buttercream »*noun* a mixture of butter and icing sugar used to ice cakes.

buttercup

butterfat »*noun* the natural fat found in milk and dairy products.

butterfly (plural **butterflies**)

 plural: drop the **y** and add **ies**: **butterflies**

buttermilk »*noun* the slightly sour liquid left after butter has been churned.

butterscotch »*noun* a sweet made with butter and brown sugar.

buttery »*adjective* containing, tasting like, or covered with butter.
» *noun* (plural **butteries**) a room in a college where food is kept and sold to students.

buttie another way of spelling **BUTTY**.

butties

buttock

button (verb: **buttons, buttoning, buttoned**)

> ✓ do not double the **n** in **buttoned** and **buttoning**

buttonhole (verb: **buttonholes, buttonholing, buttonholed**)

buttoning

buttons

buttress »*noun* (plural **buttresses**) ❶ a projecting support built against a wall. ❷ a projecting part of a hill or mountain.
» *verb* (**buttresses, buttressing, buttressed**) support or strengthen something.

butty »*noun* (plural **butties**) (in informal English) a sandwich.

> ✓ **butty** can also be spelled **buttie**

buxom »*adjective* (of a woman) attractively plump and large-breasted.
– **SAY** buk-suhm

buy (verb: **buys, buying, bought**)

buyer

buying

buyout »*noun* the buying of a controlling share in a company.

buys

buzz (verb: **buzzes, buzzing, buzzed**)

buzzard »*noun* a large bird of prey which soars in wide circles.

buzzed

buzzer

buzzes

buzzing

buzzword »*noun* a technical word or phrase that has become fashionable.

by

bye »*noun* ❶ the moving of a competitor straight to the next round of a competition because they have no opponent. ❷ (in cricket) a run scored from a ball that passes the batsman without being hit.

bye-law another way of spelling **BY-LAW**.

by-election »*noun* an election held during a government's term of office to fill a vacant seat.

byeline another way of spelling **BYLINE** (in sense 'part of goal line to either side of the goal'.

bygone »*adjective* belonging to an earlier time.

bygones

by-law »*noun* ❶ a law made by a local authority. ❷ a rule made by a company or society to control its members.

> ✓ **by-law** can also be spelled **bye-law**: both spellings are correct

byline »*noun* ❶ a line in a newspaper naming the writer of an article. ❷ (in soccer) the part of the goal line to either side of the goal.

> ✓ sense 2 can be spelled **byline** or **byeline**: both spellings are correct

bypass (plural **bypasses**; verb: **bypasses, bypassing, bypassed**)

by-product »*noun* a product produced in the process of making something else.

byre »*noun* (an old word) a cowshed.
– **SAY** *rhymes with* wire

byroad

bystander »*noun* a person who is present at an event but does not take part.

byte »*noun* a unit of information stored in a computer, equal to eight bits.

byway »*noun* a minor road or path.

byword »*noun* ❶ a notable example of something: *his name became the byword for luxury.* ❷ a saying.

Byzantine »*adjective* ❶ relating to Byzantium (now Istanbul) or the Eastern Orthodox Church. ❷ excessively complicated and detailed. ❸ very devious or underhand.
– **SAY** bi-**zan**-tyn

Cc

cab

cabal »*noun* a secret political group or faction.
– SAY kuh-**bal**

cabaret »*noun* entertainment held in a nightclub or restaurant while the audience sit at tables.
– SAY **kab**-uh-ray

> ☑ the ending is **et**, with a silent **t** (as in the original French): **cabaret**

cabbage

> ☑ remember, the ending is **age** not **idge**: **cabbage**

cabby »*noun* (plural **cabbies**) (in informal English) a taxi driver.

> ☑ **cabby** can also be spelled **cabbie**: both spellings are correct, and the plural of either form is **cabbies**

caber »*noun* a tree trunk used in the Scottish Highland sport of tossing the caber.
– SAY **kay**-ber

cabin

> ☑ remember, there is only one **b**: **cabin**

cabinet

cabinetmaker »*noun* a skilled joiner who makes furniture.

cable

cable car »*noun* a small carriage that hangs from a moving cable and travels up and down a mountainside.

cable television »*noun* a system in which television programmes are transmitted by cable.

caboodle »*noun* (**the whole caboodle**) (in informal English) the whole number of people or things in question.

cacao »*noun* the seeds or beans of a tropical American tree, from which cocoa and chocolate are made.
– SAY kuh-**kah**-oh

> ☑ do not confuse **cacao** with **cocoa**, which refers to a powder or drink made from cacao

cache »*noun* a hidden store of things: *a cache of gold coins.*
– SAY kash

> ℹ do not confuse **cache** with **cash** meaning 'money'

cachet »*noun* prestige or fame.
– SAY **ka**-shay

> ☑ the ending is **et**, with a silent **t** (as in the original French): **cachet**

cackle (verb: **cackles, cackling, cackled**)

cacophony »*noun* (plural **cacophonies**) a clashing mixture of sounds.
– SAY kuh-**kof**-uh-ni
cacophonous

cactus »*noun* (plural **cacti** or **cactuses**) a plant with a thick fleshy stem bearing spines but no leaves.

> ☑ the plural can be spelled either with an **i** (as in Latin) or **es**: **cacti** (SAY **kak**-ty) or **cactuses**

cad »*noun* (old-fashioned) a man who behaves dishonourably.
caddish

cadaver »*noun* (mainly in medicine) a dead body.
– SAY kuh-**da**-ver

cadaverous »*adjective* very pale and thin.
– SAY kuh-**dav**-er-ruhss

caddie »*noun* (plural **caddies**) a person who carries a golfer's clubs during a match.
» *verb* (**caddies, caddying, caddied**) work as a caddie.

> ☑ **caddie** can also be spelled **caddy**, which can mean in addition 'small storage container'

caddish

caddy »*noun* (plural **caddies**) ❶ a small storage container. ❷ another way of spelling **CADDIE**.

caddying

cadence »*noun* ❶ the rise and fall in pitch of the voice. ❷ a sequence of notes or chords making up the close of a musical phrase.
– SAY **kay**-duhnss

cadenza »*noun* a difficult solo passage in a musical work.
– SAY kuh-**den**-zuh

cadet
  cadetship

cadge »*verb* (**cadges, cadging, cadged**) (in informal English) ask for or get something to which you are not entitled.
  cadger

cadmium »*noun* a silvery-white metal resembling zinc.

cadre »*noun* a small group of people trained for a particular purpose or at the centre of a political organization.
– SAY **kah**-der

> ✓ re not er: **cadre**

Caesar »*noun* a title of Roman emperors.

> ✓ ae not ea: **Caesar**

Caesarean section »*noun* an operation for delivering a child by cutting through the wall of the mother's abdomen.
– SAY si-**zair**-i-uhn

> ✓ Cae not Ce, and ean not ian: **Caesarean** (**Cesarean** is American)

caesium »*noun* a soft, silvery, extremely reactive metallic chemical element.
– SAY **see**-zi-um

> ✓ **caesium** is spelled **cesium** in America

cafe »*noun* a small restaurant selling light meals and drinks.
– SAY **ka**-fay

> ✓ **cafe** is sometimes spelled with an acute accent on the **e**: **café** (as in the original French)

cafeteria »*noun* a self-service restaurant.

cafetiere »*noun* a coffee pot containing a plunger with which you push the grounds to the bottom before pouring the coffee.
– SAY ka-fuh-**tyair**

> ✓ this word can also be spelled with a grave accent on the middle **e**: **cafetière** (as in the original French)

caffeine »*noun* a stimulating substance found in tea and coffee.
– SAY **kaf**-feen
  caffeinated

> ✓ **e** before **i**, and do not forget the **e** at the end: **caffeine**

caftan another way of spelling **KAFTAN**.

cage (verb: **cages, caging, caged**)

cagey »*adjective* cautiously reluctant to speak.

cagily
caginess

> ✓ the ending is **ey**, not simply **y**: **cagey** remember that the **ey** becomes **i** in **cagily** and **caginess**

C

caging

cagoule »*noun* a lightweight, hooded, waterproof jacket.
– SAY kuh-**gool**

> ✓ spell **cagoule** with a **c**, not a **k**, and the ending is **oule**, not **ool** or **oul**. **Cagoule** is a French word meaning 'cowl'.

cahoots »*plural noun* (in **cahoots**) (in informal English) making secret plans together.
– SAY kuh-**hoots**

Cain »*noun* (**raise Cain**) create trouble or a commotion.

> ✓ spell **Cain** with a capital **c**: in the Bible, *Cain* was the eldest son of Adam and Eve and murderer of his brother Abel

cairn »*noun* a mound of rough stones built as a memorial or landmark.

cajole »*verb* (**cajoles, cajoling, cajoled**) persuade someone to do something by flattering them.
– SAY kuh-**johl**
  cajolery

> ✓ there is no **d**: **cajole**

Cajun »*noun* a member of a French-speaking community in Louisiana in the south-eastern US.
» *adjective* relating to the Cajuns.
– SAY **kay**-juhn

> ✓ there is no **y** in **Cajun**: the word is a shortening of **Acadian**, referring to *Acadia*, a former French colony in Canada where the Cajuns originated

cake (verb: **cakes, caking, caked**)

calabash »*noun* a water container made from the dried shell of a gourd.
– SAY **kal**-uh-bash

calabrese »*noun* a bright green variety of broccoli.
– SAY **kal**-uh-breez

> ℹ **calabrese** is an Italian word meaning literally 'from Calabria (in southern Italy)'

calamine »*noun* a pink powder used to make a soothing lotion or ointment.
– SAY **kal**-uh-myn

calamity »*noun* (plural **calamities**) an event causing great and sudden damage or

distress.
calamitous

✓ single **l**, single **m**: **calamity**
plural: drop the **y** and add **ies**:
calamities

calcareous »*adjective* containing lime;
chalky.
– say kal-**kair**-i-uhss

calcified »*adjective* hardened by the
addition of calcium salts.
– say **kal**-si-fíd

calcite »*noun* a white or colourless mineral
consisting of calcium carbonate.
– say **kal**-syt

calcium »*noun* a soft grey metallic
chemical element.

calculate (verb: **calculates, calculating,
calculated**)
calculable

calculation

calculator

calculus »*noun* (plural **calculi** or **calculuses**)
❶ the branch of mathematics concerned
with problems involving rates of change.
❷ (in medicine) a stone formed in the
kidney or gall bladder.
– say kal-**kyuu**-luhss [singular], kal-**kyuu**-lí
[plural]

✓ the plural can be formed with an **i**, as
in Latin, or by adding **es**: **calculi** or
calculuses

caldron American spelling of **CAULDRON**.

Caledonian »*adjective* relating to Scotland
or the Scottish Highlands.
– say ka-li-**doh**-ni-uhn

calendar [chart showing days, weeks, and
months of a year]

✓ remember, the ending is **ar**, not **er**:
calendar

calender »*noun* a machine in which cloth
or paper is pressed by rollers to glaze or
smooth it.

calf (plural **calves**)

caliber American spelling of **CALIBRE**.

calibrate »*verb* (**calibrates, calibrating,
calibrated**) ❶ mark a gauge or instrument
with units of measurement. ❷ compare
the readings of an instrument with those
of a standard.
– say ka-li-**brayt**
calibration

✓ only one **l** in **calibrate** and **calibration**

calibre »*noun* ❶ the diameter of the inside
of a gun barrel, or of a bullet or shell.

❷ quality or ability: *they could not afford
to lose a man of his calibre.*
– say **ka**-li-ber

✓ the ending is **bre**, not **ber**: **calibre**
(**caliber** is the American spelling)

calico »*noun* (plural **calicoes** or **calicos**) ❶ a
type of plain white or unbleached cotton
cloth. ❷ (in American English) printed
cotton fabric.
– say **ka**-li-koh

✓ the plural of **calico** can have **oes** or
os: **calicoes** or **calicos**

caliper »*noun* ❶ (also **calipers**) a
measuring instrument with two hinged
legs. ❷ a metal support for a person's leg.
– say **ka**-li-per

✓ can also be spelled with a double **l**:
both **caliper** and **calliper** are correct

calisthenics American spelling of
CALLISTHENICS.

calk American spelling of **CAULK**.

call (verb: **calls, calling, called**)

call centre »*noun* an office in which large
numbers of telephone calls are handled
for an organization.

called

caller

call girl »*noun* a prostitute who accepts
appointments by telephone.

calligraphy »*noun* decorative handwriting.
– say kuh-**lig**-ruh-fi
calligrapher
calligraphic

✓ double **l**: **calligraphy**

calling

calliper another way of spelling **CALIPER**.

callisthenics »*plural noun* gymnastic
exercises to achieve fitness and grace of
movement.
– say kal-liss-**then**-iks

✓ spell **callisthenics** with two **l**'s
(**calisthenics** is the American spelling)

callous »*adjective* insensitive and cruel.
»*noun* (plural **callouses**) another way of
spelling **CALLUS**.
– say **kal**-luhss
calloused
callously
callousness

callow »*adjective* (of a young person)
inexperienced and immature.

calls

callus »*noun* (plural **calluses**) an area of
thickened and hardened skin.

– say **kal**-luhss
callused

> ✓ **callus** meaning 'hardened skin' can also be spelled **callous**; both **callus** and **callous** are correct in this sense, but for the adjective meaning 'insensitive and cruel', the only correct spelling is **callous**

calm (adjective: **calmer**, **calmest**; verb: **calms**, **calming**, **calmed**)
calmly
calmness

calorie »*noun* (plural **calories**) a unit for expressing how much energy food will produce (technically, equal to the amount of energy needed to raise the temperature of 1 kilogram of water by 1 degree Celsius).
– say **ka**-luh-ri

> ✓ remember, this word ends in **ie**, not **y**: **calorie**

calorific »*adjective* relating to the amount of energy contained in food or fuel.
– say ka-luh-**riff**-ik

calumny »*noun* (plural **calumnies**) the making of false and damaging statements about someone.
– say **ka**-luhm-ni

calve »*verb* (**calves**, **calving**, **calved**) give birth to a calf.

calves plural of **CALF**.

calving

Calvinism »*noun* the form of Protestantism of John Calvin, centring on the belief that God has decided everything that happens in advance.
Calvinist
Calvinistic

calypso »*noun* (plural **calypsos**) a kind of West Indian song with improvised words on a topical theme.
– say kuh-**lip**-soh

> ✓ the plural of **calypso** has **os** not **oes**: **calypsos**

calyx »*noun* (plural **calyces** or **calyxes**) the ring of small leaves (sepals) which form a protective layer around the bud of a flower.
– say **kay**-liks [singular], **kay**-li-seez [plural]

cam »*noun* ❶ a projecting part on a wheel or shaft, which comes into contact with another part while rotating and makes it move. ❷ a camshaft.

camaraderie »*noun* trust and friendship between people.
– say kam-uh-**rah**-duh-ri

> ✓ **cam** not **com**, and the ending is **erie** not **ery**: **camaraderie**. Although it is

related in meaning to **comrade**, **camaraderie** is a French word and is spelled differently.

camber »*noun* a slightly curved shape of a horizontal surface e.g. a road.
cambered

Cambodian

Cambrian »*adjective* ❶ Welsh. ❷ relating to the geological period from about 570 to 510 million years ago.

cambric »*noun* a lightweight white linen or cotton fabric.
– say **kam**-brik

camcorder »*noun* a portable combined video camera and video recorder.

came past of **COME**.

camel

camellia »*noun* an evergreen shrub with large, bright flowers and shiny leaves.
– say kuh-**mee**-li-uh or kuh-**mel**-li-uh

> ✓ despite its common pronunciation, **camellia** has one **e** and two **l**'s

Camembert »*noun* a rich, soft, creamy cheese originally made near Camembert in Normandy.
– say **kam**-uhm-bair

cameo »*noun* (plural **cameos**) ❶ a piece of jewellery consisting of a carving of a head against a differently coloured background. ❷ a short descriptive piece of writing. ❸ a small part in a play or film played by a well-known actor.
– say **kam**-i-oh

> ✓ the plural of **cameo** has **os** not **oes**: **cameos**

camera

camerawork

Cameroonian

> ✓ sometimes also spelled **Camerounian**

camisole »*noun* a woman's loose-fitting undergarment for the upper body.
– say **kam**-i-sohl

camomile another way of spelling **CHAMOMILE**.

camouflage (verb: **camouflages**, **camouflaging**, **camouflaged**)

> ✓ do not forget the **u**: **camouflage**

camp¹ (verb: **camps**, **camping**, **camped**) [place where tents are set up; temporary lodging; stay in a camp]

camp² »*adjective* ❶ (of a man) theatrically effeminate. ❷ deliberately exaggerated and theatrical in style.

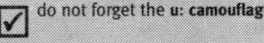

» *noun* camp behaviour or style.
» *verb* (**camps**, **camping**, **camped**) (**camp it up**) behave in a camp way.

campaign (verb: **campaigns**, **campaigning**, **campaigned**)
campaigner

> ✓ remember the silent **g** in **campaign**

campanile »*noun* a bell tower.
– SAY kam-puh-**nee**-lay

> ℹ **campanile** is an Italian word

campanology »*noun* the art of bell-ringing.
– SAY kam-puh-**nol**-uh-ji
campanologist

campanula »*noun* a plant with blue, purple, or white bell-shaped flowers.
– SAY kam-**pan**-yu-luh

camped

camper

campfire

camphor »*noun* a white substance with a sweet smell and bitter taste, occurring in some essential oils.
– SAY **kam**-fer

camping

campion »*noun* a plant with pink or white flowers with notched petals.

camps

campsite

campus »*noun* (plural **campuses**) the grounds and buildings of a university or college.

camshaft »*noun* a shaft with one or more cams attached to it.

can[1] [be able to]

> ℹ **can** is mainly used to mean 'be able to', as in the sentence *can he move?* = is he physically able to move? When asking to be allowed to do something, it is better to say **may** (*May we leave now?* rather than *Can we leave now?*), as **can** is thought to be less correct or less polite in such cases.

can[2] (verb: **cans**, **canning**, **canned**) [cylindrical metal container]

Canadian

canal »*noun* ❶ a water-filled channel made for boats to travel on or to convey water to fields. ❷ a tubular passage in a plant or animal carrying food, liquid, or air.

canalize »*verb* (**canalizes**, **canalizing**, **canalized**) ❶ convert a river into a canal.

❷ convey through a duct or channel.
❸ give a direction or purpose to.

> ✓ many people prefer the alternative spellings **canalise**, **canalises**, etc.: both **s** and **z** spellings are correct

canape »*noun* a small piece of bread or pastry with a savoury topping.
– SAY kan-uh-pay

> ✓ **canape** can also be written **canapé**, with an acute accent on the **e** (as in the original French)

canard »*noun* a false rumour or story.
– SAY ka-**nard**

canary »*noun* (plural **canaries**) a small bright yellow bird with a tuneful song.

> ✓ plural: drop the **y** and add **ies**: **canaries**

canasta »*noun* a card game using two packs and usually played by two pairs of partners.
– SAY kuh-**nass**-tuh

cancan »*noun* a lively, high-kicking stage dance originating in 19th-century Parisian music halls.

cancel (verb: **cancels**, **cancelling**, **cancelled**)
cancellation

> ✓ double the **l** in **cancelled**, **cancelling**, and **cancellation**. Spellings with a single **l**, such as **cancelation**, are common in American English.

Cancer »*noun* a constellation and sign of the zodiac (the Crab, 21 June–21 July).

cancer »*noun* ❶ a disease caused by an uncontrolled spreading of abnormal cells in a part of the body. ❷ a tumour.
❸ something evil or destructive that is hard to contain or destroy.
cancerous

candelabrum »*noun* (plural **candelabra**) a large branched candlestick or holder for several candles or lamps.
– SAY kan-di-**lah**-bruhm [singular], kan-di-**lah**-bruh [plural]

> ✓ like many other words ending in **um** derived from Latin, **candelabrum** has a plural ending in **a**: **candelabra**

candid »*adjective* truthful and straightforward; frank.
candidly

> ℹ do not confuse **candid** with **candied**, which means 'preserved in sugar syrup'

candidate
candidacy
candidature

candied »*adjective* (of fruit) preserved in a sugar syrup.

> ℹ️ do not confuse **candied** with **candid**, which means 'truthful and straightforward', as in *a candid discussion*

candies

candle

> ☑️ **le** not **el**: **candle**

candlestick

candlewick »*noun* a thick, soft cotton fabric with a raised, tufted pattern.

candour »*noun* the quality of being open and honest.

> ☑️ **-our** not **-or**: **candour** (the spelling **candor** is American)

candy (plural **candies**)

candyfloss »*noun* a mass of pink or white fluffy spun sugar wrapped round a stick.

candy-striped »*adjective* patterned with alternating stripes of white and another colour.

cane (verb: **canes**, **caning**, **caned**)

canine »*adjective* having to do with a dog or dogs.
» *noun* a pointed tooth next to the incisors.
– ꜱᴀʏ **kay**-nyn

caning

canister »*noun* a round or cylindrical container.

> ☑️ only one **n**: **canister**

canker »*noun* ❶ a disease of trees and plants, caused by a fungus. ❷ a condition in animals that causes open sores.
cankerous

cannabis »*noun* a drug obtained from the hemp plant; marijuana.

> ☑️ double **n**: **cannabis**

canned

cannelloni »*plural noun* rolls of pasta stuffed with a meat or vegetable mixture, cooked in a cheese sauce.
– ꜱᴀʏ kan-nuh-**loh**-ni

> ☑️ double **n** double **l**: **cannelloni** is an Italian word meaning 'large tubes'

cannery »*noun* (plural **canneries**) a factory where food is canned.

cannibal »*noun* a person who eats the flesh of other human beings.
cannibalism
cannibalistic

> ☑️ two **n**'s but only one **l**: **cannibal**

cannibalize »*verb* (**cannibalizes**, **cannibalizing**, **cannibalized**) use a machine as a source of spare parts for others.
cannibalization

> ☑️ many people prefer the alternative spellings **cannibalise**, **cannibalises**, etc.: both **s** and **z** spellings are correct

cannier

canniest

cannily

canning

cannon (plural **cannon** or **cannons**) [large, heavy gun]

> ℹ️ do not confuse **cannon** with a double **n**, referring to a gun, with **canon** with a single **n**, meaning 'a member of the clergy', 'a general rule', 'a set of authentic works', etc.

cannonade »*noun* a period of continuous heavy gunfire.
– ꜱᴀʏ kan-nuh-**nayd**

cannonball

> ☑️ double **n**: **cannonball**

cannon fodder »*noun* soldiers seen merely as a resource to be used up in war.

cannot

> ℹ️ both the one-word form **cannot** and the two-word form **can not** are correct; however, **cannot** is far more usual

canny »*adjective* (**cannier**, **canniest**) shrewd, especially in financial matters.
cannily

canoe (verb: **canoes**, **canoeing**, **canoed**)
canoeist

> ☑️ do not drop the **e** when spelling **canoeing** and **canoeist**

canon »*noun* ❶ a general rule or principle by which something is judged. ❷ a Church decree or law. ❸ the authentic works of a particular author or artist or a group of literary works considered to be of the highest quality. ❹ a member of the clergy on the staff of a cathedral. ❺ a piece of music in which a theme is taken up by two or more parts that overlap.

> ☑️ single **n** in the middle: **canon** (not to be confused with **cannon** referring to a large gun)

canonical »*adjective* ❶ according to canon law. ❷ accepted as being authentic or established as a standard.
– ꜱᴀʏ kuh-**non**-i-k'l

c

canonize »*verb* (**canonizes**, **canonizing**, **canonized**) (in the Roman Catholic Church) officially declare a dead person to be a saint.
canonization

> ✓ many people prefer the alternative spellings **canonise**, **canonises**, etc., and **canonisation**: both **s** and **z** spellings are correct

canon law »*noun* the laws of the Christian Church.

canoodle (verb: **canoodles**, **canoodling**, **canoodled**)

> ✓ drop the **e** when spelling **canoodling**

canopy »*noun* (plural **canopies**) ❶ a cloth covering over a throne or bed. ❷ a roof-like covering or shelter. ❸ the expanding, umbrella-like part of a parachute.
canopied

cans

cant[1] »*noun* ❶ insincere talk about moral or religious matters. ❷ (used in a disapproving way) the language typical of a particular group: *thieves' cant.*

cant[2] »*verb* (**cants**, **canting**, **canted**) tilt or slope.
» *noun* a slope or tilt.

can't [can not]

> ✓ be careful to put the apostrophe where a letter has been left out, that is between the **n** and **t** of **not**: **can't**

cantaloupe »*noun* a small round melon with orange flesh.
– SAY **kan**-tuh-loop

> ✓ **canta-** not **cante-**, and the ending is **-loupe** not **-lope** or **-loop**: **cantaloupe**

cantankerous »*adjective* bad-tempered and uncooperative.
– SAY kan-**tang**-kuh-ruhss

> ✓ **er** not **ar** in the middle: **cantankerous**

cantata »*noun* a musical composition with a solo voice and usually a chorus and orchestra.
– SAY kan-**tah**-tuh

canteen

canter (verb: **canters**, **cantering**, **cantered**)

canticle »*noun* a hymn or chant forming a regular part of a church service.
– SAY **kan**-ti-k'l

> ✓ there is no **k** in **canticle**

cantilever »*noun* a long projecting beam or girder fixed at only one end, used for building bridges.
– SAY **kan**-ti-lee-ver

canto »*noun* (plural **cantos**) one of a number of parts of a long poem.
– SAY **kan**-toh

> ✓ the plural of **canto**, which means 'song' in Italian, has **os** not **oes**: **cantos**

canton »*noun* a political or administrative subdivision of a country, especially in Switzerland.
– SAY **kan**-ton

Cantonese »*noun* (plural **Cantonese**) ❶ a person from Canton (another name for Guangzhou), a city in China. ❷ a form of Chinese spoken mainly in SE China and Hong Kong.
» *adjective* relating to Canton or Cantonese.
– SAY kan-tuh-**neez**

cantonment »*noun* a military station in British India.
– SAY kan-**ton**-muhnt

cantor »*noun* ❶ a person who leads the prayers in a synagogue. ❷ a person who sings solo verses to which the choir or congregation respond in a Christian service.
– SAY **kan**-tor

> ✓ **-or** not **-er**: **cantor**

cantos

canvas (plural **canvases** or **canvasses**) [strong, coarse cloth]

> ✓ **canvas** referring to strong cloth has only a single **s**, except that the plural form **canvasses** is accepted as a correct alternative to **canvases**

canvass »*verb* (**canvasses**, **canvassing**, **canvassed**) ❶ visit someone to seek their vote in an election. ❷ question someone to find out their opinion. ❸ propose an idea or plan for discussion.
canvasser

> ✓ be careful to keep the double **s** in **canvass** meaning 'seek support, discover opinion', and words derived from it such as **canvasser** and **canvassing**

canvasses plural of CANVAS.

canvassing

canyon

cap (verb: **caps**, **capping**, **capped**)

> ✓ double the **p** in **capping** and **capped**

capability (plural **capabilities**)

✓ plural: drop the **y** and add **ies**: **capabilities**

capable
  capably

capacious »*adjective* having a lot of space inside; roomy.

✓ **cious** not **tious**: **capacious**

capacitance »*noun* the ability to store electric charge.
– SAY kuh-**pass**-i-tuhnss

✓ **ance** not **ence**: **capacitance**

capacities

capacitor »*noun* a device used to store electric charge.

✓ **-or** not **-er**: **capacitor**

capacity (plural **capacities**)

✓ plural: drop the **y** and add **ies**

caparison »*verb* (**be caparisoned**) be clothed in rich decorative coverings.
– SAY kuh-**pa**-ri-s'n

cape
  caped

caper (verb: **capers, capering, capered**)

capercaillie »*noun* (plural **capercaillies**) a large grouse of forests in northern Europe.
– SAY kap-er-**kay**-li

✓ double **l** and **ie** at the end: **capercaillie**

capered

capering

capers »*plural noun* the flower bud of a southern European shrub, pickled for use in cooking.

Cape Verdean [of Cape Verde]

capillaries

capillarity »*noun* the tendency of a liquid in a narrow tube or pore to rise or fall as a result of surface tension.

capillary »*noun* (plural **capillaries**) ❶ a very narrow blood vessel that forms part of a network between the arteries and veins. ❷ (also **capillary tube**) a tube with a very narrow diameter.
– SAY kuh-**pil**-luh-ri

capillary action »*noun* = CAPILLARITY.

capital [chief city; wealth; head of pillar]

✓ **al** not **le**: **capital**, and do not confuse it with **capitol**, used in America to refer to legislative buildings

capital gain »*noun* a profit from the sale of property or an investment.

capitalise another way of spelling CAPITALIZE.

capitalism »*noun* a system in which a country's trade and industry are controlled by private owners for profit.
  capitalist

capitalize »*verb* (**capitalizes, capitalizing, capitalized**) ❶ (**capitalize on**) take advantage of. ❷ convert into or provide with financial capital. ❸ write in capital letters or with a capital first letter.
  capitalization

✓ many people prefer the alternative spellings **capitalise, capitalises**, etc., and **capitalisation**: both **s** and **z** spellings are correct

capital punishment »*noun* the punishment of a crime by death.

capitation »*noun* the payment of money to a doctor, school, etc., the amount of which depends on the number of people involved.

capitol »*noun* ❶ (in the US) a building housing a law-making body. ❷ (**the Capitol**) the seat of the US Congress in Washington DC.
– SAY **kap**-i-t'l

✓ **ol** not **al**: **capitol**

capitulate »*verb* (**capitulates, capitulating, capitulated**) give in to an opponent or an unwelcome demand.
– SAY kuh-**pit**-yuu-layt
  capitulation

✓ drop the **e** when spelling **capitulating** and **capitulation**

capon »*noun* a domestic cock that has been castrated and fattened for eating.
– SAY **kay**-puhn

capped

capping

cappuccino »*noun* (plural **cappuccinos**) coffee made with milk that has been frothed up with pressurized steam.
– SAY kap-puh-**chee**-noh

✓ double **p**, double **c**: **cappuccino**. It is an Italian word, and the plural has **os** not **oes**: **cappuccinos**.

caprice »*noun* a sudden change of mood or behaviour.
– SAY kuh-**preess**

capricious »*adjective* prone to sudden changes of mood or behaviour.
– SAY kuh-**pri**-shuhss

cious not **tious**: **capricious**

Capricorn »*noun* a constellation and a sign of the zodiac (the Goat, 21 December–19 January).
– SAY **kap**-ri-korn

capri pants »*plural noun* close-fitting tapered trousers for women.
– SAY kuh-**pree**

caps

capsicum »*noun* (plural **capsicums**) a sweet pepper or chilli pepper.
– SAY **kap**-si-kuhm

capsize »*verb* (**capsizes**, **capsizing**, **capsized**) (of a boat) overturn in the water.

 capsize cannot be spelled with an **ise** ending

capstan »*noun* a broad revolving cylinder used for winding a rope or cable.
– SAY **kap**-stuhn

capstone »*noun* a stone put on top of a wall, tomb, or other structure.

capsule

captain (verb: **captains**, **captaining**, **captained**)
captaincy

 don't forget the second **a**: **captain**

caption »*noun* ❶ a title or explanation accompanying an illustration or cartoon. ❷ a piece of text appearing as part of a film or television broadcast.
» *verb* (**captions**, **captioning**, **captioned**) provide a caption for a picture.

captious »*adjective* prone to petty fault-finding.
– SAY **kap**-shuhss

captivate (verb: **captivates**, **captivating**, **captivated**)
captivation

 drop the **e** when spelling **captivating**

captive
captivity

captor »*noun* a person who captures another.

 -or not **-er**: **captor**

capture (verb: **captures**, **capturing**, **captured**)

 drop the **e** when spelling **capturing**

Capuchin »*noun* ❶ a friar belonging to a strict branch of the Franciscan order.

❷ (**capuchin**) a South American monkey with a cap of hair like a hood.
– SAY **kap**-uh-chin

capybara »*noun* a large South American rodent which looks like a long-legged guinea pig.
– SAY ka-pi-**bah**-ruh

car

carafe »*noun* a wide-necked glass bottle for serving wine.
– SAY kuh-**raf**

 fe not **ff**: **carafe**

carambola »*noun* a golden-yellow fruit which is shaped like a star when cut through.
– SAY ka-ruhm-**boh**-luh

caramel »*noun* ❶ sugar or syrup heated until it turns brown. ❷ soft toffee made with sugar and butter.

 one **r**, one **m**: **caramel**

caramelize »*verb* (**caramelizes**, **caramelizing**, **caramelized**) turn or be turned into caramel.

 many people prefer the alternative spellings **caramelise**, **caramelises**, etc.: both **s** and **z** spellings are correct

carapace »*noun* the hard upper shell of a tortoise, lobster, or related animal.
– SAY ka-ruh-**payss**

carat »*noun* ❶ a unit of weight for precious stones and pearls, equivalent to 200 milligrams. ❷ a measure of the purity of gold, pure gold being 24 carats.
– SAY **ka**-ruht

 single **r**, and **-at** not **-ot** or **-et** at the end: **carat** (**carrots** and **carets** are different)

caravan
caravanner
caravanning

caravanserai »*noun* (plural **caravanserais**) ❶ (a historical term) an inn with a central courtyard in the desert regions of Asia or North Africa. ❷ a group of people travelling together.
– SAY ka-ruh-**van**-suh-ry

 ai not **y**: **caravanserai**

caravel »*noun* (a historical term) a small, fast Spanish or Portuguese ship of the 15th–17th centuries.
– SAY ka-ruh-**vel**

 caravel can also be spelled **carvel**

103

caraway » carded

caraway »*noun* a Mediterranean plant whose seeds are used as a spice.
– **say** ka-ruh-way

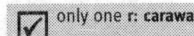 only one r: **caraway**

carbide »*noun* a compound of carbon with a metal or other element.

carbine »*noun* a light automatic rifle.

carbohydrate »*noun* a substance (e.g. sugar and starch) containing carbon, hydrogen, and oxygen, found in food and used to give energy.

 hyd not **hid**: **carbohydrate**

carbolic acid »*noun* the compound phenol, used as a disinfectant.

carbon »*noun* a chemical element found in all organic compounds, which has two main pure forms (diamond and graphite).

carbonaceous »*adjective* consisting of or containing carbon or its compounds.
– **say** kar-buh-**nay**-shuhss

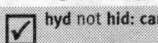 **ceous** not **tious**: **carbonaceous**

carbonara »*noun* a pasta sauce made with bacon or ham, egg, and cream.
– **say** kar-buh-**nah**-ruh

carbonate »*noun* a compound containing carbon and oxygen together with a metal.
– **say** **kar**-buh-nayt

carbonated »*adjective* (of a drink) fizzy because it contains dissolved carbon dioxide.

carbon copy »*noun* ❶ a copy made with carbon paper. ❷ a person or thing identical to another.

carbon dating »*noun* a way of finding out how old an organic object is by measuring the amount of radioactive carbon-14 that it contains.

carbon dioxide »*noun* a gas produced by people and animals breathing out, and also by burning carbon, which is absorbed by plants in photosynthesis.

carbonic acid »*noun* a very weak acid formed when carbon dioxide dissolves in water.

Carboniferous »*adjective* relating to the geological period from about 363 to 290 million years ago, when many coal deposits were formed.
– **say** kar-buh-**nif**-uh-ruhss

carbonize »*verb* (**carbonizes, carbonizing, carbonized**) convert into carbon, by heating or burning.
carbonization

many people prefer the alternative spellings **carbonise, carbonises,** etc., and **carbonisation**: both **s** and **z** spellings are correct

carbon monoxide »*noun* a poisonous flammable gas formed when carbon is incompletely burned.

carbon paper »*noun* thin paper coated with carbon, used for making a copy of a document.

carborundum »*noun* a very hard black solid consisting of silicon and carbon, used for grinding, smoothing, and polishing.
– **say** kar-buh-**run**-duhm

carboy »*noun* a large rounded glass bottle with a narrow neck, used for holding acids.

carbuncle »*noun* ❶ a large abscess or boil in the skin. ❷ a polished garnet.
– **say** **kar**-bung-k'l

there is no **k** in **carbuncle**

carburettor »*noun* a device in an internal-combustion engine for mixing air with a fine spray of liquid fuel.
– **say** kar-buh-**ret**-ter

the ending is **-or** not **-er**, and remember the double **t**: **carburettor** (the spelling with a single **t** is American)

carcass

carcass can also be spelled **carcase**: both spellings are correct

carcinogen »*noun* a substance capable of causing cancer.
– **say** kar-**sin**-uh-juhn
carcinogenic

carcinoma »*noun* (plural **carcinomas** or **carcinomata**) a cancer of the skin or of the lining of the internal organs.
– **say** kar-si-**noh**-muh [singular], kar-si-**noh**-muh-tuh [plural]

in medicine the Latin or Greek plural **carcinomata** is often used, but the form with **s** is also correct

card (verb: **cards, carding, carded**)

cardamom »*noun* the seed and pods of a SE Asian plant, used as a spice.
– **say** **kar**-duh-muhm

 mom not **mum**: **cardamom**

cardboard

card-carrying »*adjective* registered as a member of a political party or trade union.

carded

cardiac »*adjective* having to do with the heart.
– sᴀʏ **kar**-di-ak

cardigan

-an not -en: **cardigan**

cardinal »*noun* an important Roman Catholic clergyman who has the power to elect the Pope.
» *adjective* most important.

al not el: **cardinal**

cardinal number »*noun* a number expressing quantity (such as one, two, three, etc.), rather than order (first, second, third, etc.).

cardinal point »*noun* one of the four main points of the compass (north, south, east, and west).

carding

cardiograph »*noun* an instrument for recording heart movements.
– sᴀʏ **kar**-di-uh-grahf

cardiology »*noun* the branch of medicine concerned with the heart.
– sᴀʏ kar-di-**ol**-uh-ji
cardiologist

cardiovascular »*adjective* having to do with the heart and blood vessels.
– sᴀʏ kar-di-oh-**vass**-kyuu-ler

ar not er: **cardiovascular**

cardoon »*noun* a tall thistle-like plant with edible leaves and roots.

cards

care (verb: **cares, caring, cared**)

drop the e when spelling **caring**

careen »*verb* (**careens, careening, careened**) ❶ (with reference to a ship) tilt to one side. ❷ move in an uncontrolled way.
– sᴀʏ kuh-**reen**

career (verb: **careers, careering, careered**)

careerist »*noun* a person whose main concern is to progress in their career.
careerism

careers

carefree

careful
carefully
carefulness

-ful not -full: **careful**

careless
carelessly
carelessness

carer

caress (verb: **caresses, caressing, caressed**)

single r, double s: **caress**

caret »*noun* a mark (∧, ⟨) placed below a line of text to indicate that something is to be inserted.
– sᴀʏ ka-**ruht**

-et not -at: **caret** (a **carat** is a unit describing the weight of gemstones or the purity of precious metal)

caretaker

careworn »*adjective* tired and unhappy because of prolonged worry.

cargo »*noun* (plural **cargoes** or **cargos**) goods carried on a ship, aircraft, or truck.

the plural of **cargo** can have **oes** or **os**: **cargoes** or **cargos**

Caribbean
– sᴀʏ ka-rib-**bee**-uhn or kuh-**rib**-bi-uhn

ⓘ there are two ways of pronouncing **Caribbean**: British people put the stress on the **be**, while in the US and the Caribbean itself the stress is on the **rib**

one r and two b's: **Caribbean**

caribou »*noun* (plural **caribou**) (in American English) a reindeer.

ou not oo: **caribou**

caricature »*noun* a picture in which a person's distinctive features are amusingly exaggerated.
» *verb* (**caricatures, caricaturing, caricatured**) make a caricature of someone.
– sᴀʏ **ka**-ri-kuh-tyoor
caricaturist

car not char: **caricature**

caries »*noun* decay and crumbling of a tooth or bone.
– sᴀʏ **kair**-eez

carillon »*noun* a set of bells sounded from a keyboard or by an automatic mechanism.
– sᴀʏ ka-**ril**-lyuhn

one r, two l's: **carillon**

carmine »*noun* a vivid crimson colour.
– sᴀʏ **kar**-myn

carnage »*noun* the killing of a large number of people.

– **say** kar-nij

carnal »*adjective* relating to sexual needs and activities.
 carnality

carnation

 ion not ian: carnation

carnelian »*noun* a dull red or pink semi-precious stone.
– **say** kar-**nee**-li-uhn

 carnelian can also be spelled cornelian

carnival

carnivore »*noun* a carnivorous animal.
– **say** kar-ni-vor

carnivorous »*adjective* eating a diet of meat.
– **say** kar-**niv**-uh-ruhss

✓ vorous not verous: carnivorous

carob »*noun* the pod of an Arabian tree, from which a substitute for chocolate is made.
– **say** ka-ruhb

carol (verb: **carols, carolling, carolled**)
 caroller

✓ double the l when spelling **carolling, carolled,** and **caroller** (the spellings with a single l are American)

carotene »*noun* an orange or red substance found in carrots and many other plants, important in forming vitamin A.
– **say** ka-ruh-teen

✓ one r, one t: carotene

carotid »*adjective* relating to the two main arteries carrying blood to the head and neck.
– **say** kuh-**rot**-id

carouse »*verb* (**carouses, carousing, caroused**) drink alcohol and enjoy yourself with others in a noisy, lively way.
– **say** kuh-**rowz**
 carouser

✓ drop the e when spelling **carousing**

carousel »*noun* ❶ a merry-go-round at a fair. ❷ a rotating device for baggage collection at an airport.
– **say** ka-ruh-**sel**

✓ remember the u before the s: carousel

carouser

carouses

carousing

carp[1] »*noun* (plural **carp**) an edible freshwater fish.

carp[2] »*verb* (**carps, carping, carped**) complain or find fault continually.

carpal »*adjective* relating to the bones in the wrist.
» *noun* a bone in the wrist.
– **say** kar-p'l

ℹ️ do not confuse **carpal** with **carpel,** which means 'the female reproductive organ of a flower'

carped

carpel »*noun* the female reproductive organ of a flower, consisting of an ovary, a stigma, and usually a style.
– **say** kar-p'l

ℹ️ do not confuse **carpel** with **carpal,** which refers to the bones in the wrist

carpenter
 carpentry

carpet (verb: **carpets, carpeting, carpeted**)

✓ do not double the t when spelling **carpeting** and **carpeted**

carpetbagger »*noun* ❶ a politician who tries to get elected in an area where they have no local connections. ❷ a person who exploits a situation unscrupulously.

carpeting

carpets

carpi plural of **CARPUS.**

carping

carport »*noun* an open-sided shelter for a car, projecting from the side of a house.

carps

carpus »*noun* (plural **carpi**) the group of small bones in the wrist.
– **say** kar-puhss [singular], kar-pI [plural]

✓ make the plural by changing the us ending to i (as in Latin): carpi

carrageen »*noun* an edible red seaweed.
– **say** kar-ruh-geen

✓ two r's, one g, two e's: carrageen. It is an Irish word and is sometimes spelled with an h: carragheen.

carrel »*noun* a small cubicle with a desk for a reader in a library.
– **say** kar-ruhl

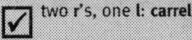 two r's, one l: carrel

carriage

 remember the a before the g: carriage

carriage clock »*noun* a portable clock in a rectangular case with a handle on top.

carriageway

carried

carrier

carrier pigeon »*noun* a homing pigeon trained to carry messages.

carries

carrion »*noun* the decaying flesh of dead animals.

> ✓ double r: **carrion**

carrot [vegetable]
carroty

> ✓ double r: **carrot**. Not to be confused with **carat** and **caret**.

carry (verb: **carries, carrying, carried**)

carrycot

carrying

carry-on

cart (verb: **carts, carting, carted**)

carte blanche »*noun* complete freedom to act as you wish.
– SAY kart **blahnsh**

> ℹ **carte blanche** is French for 'blank paper'

carted

cartel »*noun* an association of manufacturers or suppliers formed to keep prices high and restrict competition.
– SAY kar-**tel**

Cartesian coordinates »*plural noun* a system for describing the position of a point by reference to its distance from lines which intersect at right angles.
– SAY kar-**tee**-zi-uhn

> ℹ named after the 17th-century French philosopher René *Descartes*

carthorse

cartilage »*noun* firm, flexible tissue which covers the ends of joints and forms structures such as the external ear.
– SAY kar-ti-lij

> ✓ **lage** not **lidge**: **cartilage**

cartilaginous »*adjective* made of cartilage.
– SAY kar-ti-**laj**-i-nuhss

carting

cartography »*noun* the science or practice of drawing maps.
– SAY kar-**tog**-ruh-fi
 cartographer
 cartographic

carton

cartoon
 cartoonist

cartouche »*noun* ❶ a drawing or carving showing a scroll with rolled-up ends. ❷ an oval or oblong containing Egyptian hieroglyphs representing the name and title of a monarch.
– SAY kar-**toosh**

cartridge

> ✓ remember the **d**: **cartridge**

cartridge paper »*noun* thick, rough-textured drawing paper.

carts

cartwheel (verb: **cartwheels, cartwheeling, cartwheeled**)

carve (verb: **carves, carving, carved**)

> ✓ drop the **e** when spelling **carving**

carvel another way of spelling CARAVEL.
– SAY kar-v'l

carver

carvery »*noun* (plural **carveries**) a buffet or restaurant where cooked joints are carved as required.

carves

carving

Casanova »*noun* a man known for seducing many women.
– SAY ka-suh-**noh**-vuh

casbah another way of spelling KASBAH.

cascade »*noun* ❶ a small waterfall. ❷ a mass of something that falls, hangs, or occurs in large quantities: *a cascade of blossoms*.
»*verb* (**cascades, cascading, cascaded**) pour downwards rapidly and in large quantities.

> ✓ drop the **e** when spelling **cascading**

case (verb: **cases, casing, cased**)

casebook

cased

case history »*noun* a record of a person's background or medical history kept by a doctor or social worker.

casein »*noun* the main protein present in milk and cheese.
– SAY kay-seen

> ✓ **casein** does not follow the usual rule, **i** before **e**, except after **c**

caseload »*noun* the number of cases being dealt with by a doctor, lawyer, or social worker at one time.

casement »*noun* a window hinged at the side so that it opens like a door.

cases

case study »*noun* ❶ a detailed study of the development of a person, group, or situation over a period of time. ❷ a particular instance used to illustrate a general principle.

cash (verb: **cashes**, **cashing**, **cashed**) **cashless**

cash and carry »*noun* a system of wholesale trading in which goods are paid for in full and taken away by the person who buys them.

cashback »*noun* ❶ a cash refund offered to encourage people to buy something. ❷ a service that allows a shop customer to withdraw cash when buying something with a debit card.

cash crop »*noun* a crop produced for sale rather than for use by the grower.

cashed

cashes

cashew »*noun* the edible kidney-shaped nut of a tropical American tree.
– **SAY** ka-shoo

cash flow »*noun* the total amount of money passing into and out of a business.

cashier[1] »*noun* a person responsible for paying out and receiving money in a shop, bank, or business.

cashier[2] »*verb* (**cashiers**, **cashiering**, **cashiered**) dismiss someone from the armed forces.

cashing

cashless

cashmere »*noun* fine soft wool from a breed of Himalayan goat.

 -mere not -meer: **cashmere**

cashpoint

cash register »*noun* a machine used in shops for adding up and recording the amount of each sale and storing the money received.

casing

casino »*noun* (plural **casinos**) a public building or room for gambling.

✓ the plural of **casino**, which means 'little house' in Italian, has **os** not **oes**: **casinos**

cask

casket »*noun* ❶ a small ornamental box or chest for holding valuable objects. ❷ a coffin.

Cassandra »*noun* a person who makes gloomy predictions.

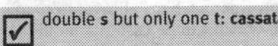 *Cassandra* in Greek mythology was doomed to prophecy truthfully but never be believed

cassata »*noun* an ice cream dessert containing dried fruit and nuts.
– **SAY** kuh-**sah**-tuh

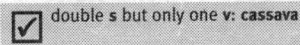 double s but only one t: **cassata**

cassava »*noun* the root of a tropical American tree, used as food.
– **SAY** kuh-**sah**-vuh

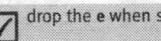 double s but only one v: **cassava**

casserole »*noun* ❶ a large dish with a lid, used for cooking food slowly in an oven. ❷ a kind of stew cooked slowly in an oven.
» *verb* (**casseroles**, **casseroling**, **casseroled**) cook food in a casserole.

✓ drop the e when spelling **casseroling**

cassette

✓ double s and double t: **cassette**

cassock »*noun* a long garment worn by Christian priests and members of church choirs.

cassowary »*noun* (plural **cassowaries**) a very large bird that cannot fly, found in New Guinea.
– **SAY** kass-uh-wuh-ri

cast (verb: **casts**, **casting**, **cast**) [throw]

ℹ️ do not confuse **cast** with **caste**, which means 'a class of Hindu society'

castanets »*plural noun* a pair of small curved pieces of wood, clicked together by the fingers to accompany Spanish dancing.

castaway

caste »*noun* one of the classes of Hindu society.

castellated »*adjective* (of a building) having battlements.
– **SAY** kass-tuh-lay-tid

✓ double l: **castellated**

caster »*noun* ❶ a person or machine that casts. ❷ another way of spelling **CASTOR**.

caster sugar »*noun* white sugar in fine grains.

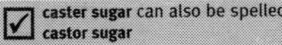 caster sugar can also be spelled **castor sugar**

castigate »*verb* (**castigates**, **castigating**, **castigated**) tell someone off severely.
– SAY kass-ti-gayt
castigation

casting

casting vote »*noun* an extra vote used by a chairperson to decide an issue when votes on each side are equal.

cast iron »*noun* a hard alloy of iron and carbon which can be cast in a mould.
»*adjective* (**cast-iron**) firm and unchangeable.

> ☑ add a hyphen if you use this word as an adjective, as in *a cast-iron guarantee*

castle

cast-off

castor »*noun* ❶ a small swivelling wheel fixed to the legs or base of a piece of furniture. ❷ a small container with holes in the top, used for sprinkling salt, sugar, etc.

> ☑ **castor** can also be spelled **caster**: both spellings are correct

castor oil »*noun* oil from the seeds of an African shrub, used as a laxative.

castor sugar another way of spelling CASTER SUGAR.

castrate »*verb* (**castrates**, **castrating**, **castrated**) ❶ remove someone's testicles. ❷ make something less powerful or vigorous.
castration

castrato »*noun* (plural **castrati**) (a historical term) a male singer castrated in boyhood so as to retain a soprano or alto voice.
– SAY ka-**strah**-toh [singular], ka-**strah**-tee [plural]

> ☑ **castrato**, like many terms in music, is an Italian word and adds an **i** to form the plural **castrati**

casts

casual [relaxed]
casually
casualness

> ☑ do not confuse the spelling of **casual** with **causal**, which means 'relating to a cause'

casualty (plural **casualties**)

casuistry »*noun* the use of clever but false reasoning.
– SAY ka*zh*-oo-iss-tri
casuist

cat

cataclysm »*noun* a violent upheaval or disaster.

– SAY kat-uh-kli-z'm
cataclysmic

> ☑ **ysm** not **ism** at the end: **cataclysm**

catacomb »*noun* an underground cemetery consisting of tunnels with recesses for tombs.
– SAY kat-uh-koom

> ☑ there is only one **o**: **catacomb**

Catalan »*noun* ❶ a person from Catalonia in north east Spain. ❷ the language of Catalonia.
»*adjective* relating to Catalonia.
– SAY kat-uh-lan

catalepsy »*noun* a medical condition in which a person becomes unconsciousness and their body goes rigid.
– SAY kat-uh-lep-si
cataleptic

catalogue (verb: **catalogues**, **cataloguing**, **catalogued**)

> ☑ **logue** not **log**: **catalogue** (the spellings **catalog**, **catalogs**, etc. are American)

catalyse »*verb* (**catalyses**, **catalysing**, **catalysed**) cause or speed up a reaction by acting as a catalyst.
– SAY kat-uh-lyz

> ☑ **yse** not **yze**: **catalyse** (the spellings **catalyze**, **catalyzes**, etc. are American)

catalysis »*noun* the speeding up of a chemical reaction by a catalyst.
– SAY kuh-**tal**-i-siss

catalyst »*noun* ❶ a substance that increases the rate of a chemical reaction while remaining unchanged itself. ❷ a person or thing that triggers an event.
– SAY kat-uh-list

> ☑ **yst** not **ist**: **catalyst**

catalytic »*adjective* relating to a catalyst or its action.
– SAY kat-uh-**lit**-ik

catalytic converter »*noun* a device in a motor vehicle which converts exhaust gases into less polluting ones.

catalyze American spelling of CATALYSE.

catamaran »*noun* a boat with twin hulls in parallel.
– SAY kat-uh-muh-ran

catapult (verb: **catapults**, **catapulting**, **catapulted**)

> ☑ **ult** not **ault** at the end: **catapult**

cataract »*noun* ❶ a large waterfall. ❷ a medical condition in which the lens of the

eye becomes cloudy, resulting in blurred vision.
– SAY kat-uh-rakt

catarrh »*noun* excessive mucus in the nose or throat.
– SAY kuh-**tar**

> ✓ double r followed by h at the end: **catarrh**

catastrophe »*noun* a sudden event that causes great damage or suffering.
– SAY kuh-**tass**-truh-fi
catastrophic

> ✓ phe not phy: **catastrophe**

catatonia »*noun* a disturbed condition in which a person may experience periods of unconsciousness or overactivity.
– SAY kat-uh-**toh**-ni-uh
catatonic

> ✓ there is only one n in **catatonia** and **catatonic**

cat burglar »*noun* a thief who enters a building by climbing to an upper storey.

catcall »*noun* a shrill whistle or shout of mockery or disapproval.
»*verb* (**catcalls**, **catcalling**, **catcalled**) make a catcall.

catch (verb: **catches**, **catching**, **caught**)
catcher

catch-all »*noun* a term or category intended to cover all possibilities.

catcher

catches

catchier

catchiest

catching

catchline »*noun* ❶ a short, eye-catching headline or title. ❷ an advertising slogan.

catchment »*noun* ❶ the area from which a hospital's patients or a school's pupils are drawn. ❷ the area from which rainfall flows into a river, lake, or reservoir.

catchpenny »*adjective* outwardly attractive so as to sell quickly.

catchphrase »*noun* a well-known sentence or phrase.

catch-22 »*noun* a difficult situation from which there is no escape because it involves conditions which conflict with each other.

> ℹ from the name of a novel by Joseph Heller in which the hero asks to be relieved from flying bombing missions on grounds of insanity, but is considered to be sane because of this request

catchword »*noun* a word or phrase commonly used to sum up a particular thing or idea.

catchy »*adjective* (**catchier**, **catchiest**) (of a tune or phrase) appealing and easy to remember.

catechise another way of spelling CATECHIZE.

catechism »*noun* a summary of the principles of Christian religion in the form of questions and answers, used for teaching.
– SAY kat-i-ki-z'm

> ✓ ch not k in the middle: **catechism**

catechist »*noun* a Christian teacher.

catechize »*verb* (**catechizes**, **catechizing**, **catechized**) teach someone by using a catechism.

> ✓ many people prefer the alternative spellings **catechise**, **catechises**, etc.: both s and z spellings are correct

categoric »*adjective* = CATEGORICAL.

categorical »*adjective* completely clear and direct.
categorically

> ✓ cate not cata: **categorical**
> double the l in **categorically**

categories

categorize »*verb* (**categorizes**, **categorizing**, **categorized**) place something in a category.
categorization

> ✓ many people prefer the spellings **categorise**, **categorises**, etc., and **categorisation**: both s and z spellings are correct

category »*noun* (plural **categories**)

> ✓ plural: drop the y and add ies: **categories**

cater (verb: **caters**, **catering**, **catered**)
caterer

caterpillar

> ✓ ar not er at the end: **caterpillar**

caterwaul »*verb* (**caterwauls**, **caterwauling**, **caterwauled**) make a shrill howling or wailing noise.
– SAY kat-er-wawl

> ✓ do not double the l to spell **caterwauling**, and **caterwauled**

catfish »*noun* a freshwater or marine fish with whisker-like growths round the mouth.

C

catgut »*noun* material used for the strings of musical instruments, made of the dried intestines of sheep or horses.

catharsis »*noun* the process of releasing pent-up emotions through an experience like watching a film.
– SAY kuh-**thar**-siss
cathartic

cathedral

Catherine wheel »*noun* a firework in the form of a spinning coil.

> ⓘ named after St *Catherine*, who was tortured on a spiked wheel

catheter »*noun* a tube that is inserted into the bladder or another body cavity, for draining fluid.
– SAY kath-i-ter

> ✓ eter not iter: catheter

cathode »*noun* an electrode with a positive charge (the opposite of *anode*).
– SAY kath-ohd

cathode ray tube »*noun* a tube in which beams of electrons produce a luminous image on a screen, as in a television.

catholic »*adjective* ❶ including a wide variety of things: *catholic tastes*. ❷ (**Catholic**) Roman Catholic.
» *noun* (**Catholic**) a Roman Catholic.
Catholicism

catkin »*noun* a spike of small soft flowers hanging from trees such as willow and hazel.

catmint

catnap »*noun* a short sleep during the day.
» *verb* (**catnaps**, **catnapping**, **catnapped**) have a catnap.

> ✓ double the p in catnapping and catnapped

cat-o'-nine-tails »*noun* (a historical term) a rope whip with nine knotted cords.

cat's cradle »*noun* a game in which patterns are formed in a loop of string held between the fingers of each hand.

catseye »*noun* (trademark) one of a series of reflective studs marking the lanes or edges or a road.

cat's paw »*noun* a person used by another to carry out an unpleasant task.

catsuit »*noun* a woman's close-fitting one-piece garment with trouser legs.

cattery »*noun* (plural **catteries**) a place where cats are kept while their owners are away.

cattier

cattiest

cattle

cattle grid »*noun* a metal grid covering a trench across a road, allowing vehicles to pass over but not animals.

catty »*adjective* (**cattier**, **cattiest**) spiteful.

catwalk

Caucasian »*adjective* ❶ relating to peoples from Europe, western Asia, and parts of India and North Africa. ❷ white-skinned; of European origin.
» *noun* a Caucasian person.
– SAY kaw-**kay**-zi-uhn or kaw-**kay**-zh'n

> ✓ Cau not Caw: Caucasian

caucus »*noun* (plural **caucuses**) ❶ a meeting of a committee of a political party to decide policy. ❷ a group of people within a larger organization who have shared concerns.
– SAY **kaw**-kuhss

> ✓ to make the plural add **es** but do not double the **s**: caucuses

caudal »*adjective* having to do with the tail or the rear part of the body.
– SAY **kaw**-duhl

caught past and past participle of **CATCH**.

caul »*noun* a membrane that encloses an unborn baby in the womb.
– SAY *rhymes with* ball

> ✓ aul not all: caul

cauldron »*noun* a large metal cooking pot.

> ✓ remember the u: cauldron (caldron is an American spelling)

cauliflower »*noun* a variety of cabbage with a large white edible flower head.

> ✓ caul not col: cauliflower

caulk »*noun* a waterproof substance used to fill cracks and seal joins.
– SAY kawk

> ✓ do not forget the u: caulk (calk is an American spelling)

causal »*adjective* relating to or being a cause: *a causal connection between smoking and lung cancer*.
causally

> ✓ do not confuse the spelling of causal with casual, which means 'relaxed'

causality »*noun* the relationship between a cause and the effect it produces.

causation »*noun* ❶ the process of causing an effect. ❷ = **CAUSALITY**.

causative »*adjective* causing an effect: *HIV is the causative agent of Aids*.

cause (verb: **causes, causing, caused**)

> ☑ drop the e when spelling **causing**

cause celebre »*noun* (plural **causes celebres**) something which causes great public interest and discussion.
– SAY kohz se-**leb**-ruh [singular and plural]

> ☑ the plural of **cause celebre** adds an s to both words: **causes celebres**
> **cause celebre** can also be written **cause célèbre**, with acute and grave accents (as in the original French phrase, which means 'famous case')

caused

causes

causeway »*noun* a raised road or track across low or wet ground.

causing

caustic »*adjective* ❶ able to burn through or wear away living tissue by chemical action. ❷ sarcastic in a hurtful way.
– SAY **kaw**-stik

caustic soda »*noun* a substance used in making paper and soap and in other industrial processes.

cauterize »*verb* (**cauterizes, cauterizing, cauterized**) burn the skin or flesh of a wound to stop bleeding or prevent infection.
– SAY **kaw**-tuh-ryz

> ☑ many people prefer the spellings **cauterise, cauterises**, etc.: both s and z spellings are correct

caution (verb: **cautions, cautioning, cautioned**)

cautionary »*adjective* acting as a warning.

> ☑ ary not ery: **cautionary**

cautioned

cautioning

cautions

cautious
   cautiously

cava »*noun* a Spanish sparkling wine made in the same way as champagne.
– SAY **kah**-vuh

cavalcade »*noun* a procession of vehicles or people on horseback.
– SAY ka-vuhl-**kayd**

cavalier »*noun* (**Cavalier**) (a historical term) a supporter of King Charles I in the English Civil War.
»*adjective* showing a lack of real concern: *the cavalier treatment of mental illness.*

> ☑ i before **e**, except after **c**: **cavalier**

cavalry »*noun* (plural **cavalries**) (in the past) soldiers who fought on horseback.

cavalryman (plural **cavalrymen**)

cave (verb: **caves, caving, caved**)
   caver
   caving

caveat »*noun* a warning.
– SAY **ka**-vi-at

caveat emptor »*noun* the principle that the buyer is responsible for checking the quality and suitability of goods before purchase.

> ⓘ the Latin phrase *caveat emptor* means 'let the buyer beware'

caved

caveman (plural **cavemen**)

cavern »*noun* a large cave.

cavernous »*adjective* like a cavern in being huge, spacious, or gloomy.
– SAY **ka**-ver-nuhss

caves

cavewoman (plural **cavewomen**)

caviar »*noun* the pickled roe of the sturgeon (a large fish).
– SAY **ka**-vi-ar

> ☑ **caviar** can also be spelled **caviare**, with an **e** on the end: both spellings are correct

cavies plural of **CAVY**.

cavil »*verb* (**cavils, cavilling, cavilled**) make unnecessary complaints.
»*noun* an unnecessary complaint.
– SAY **ka**-vuhl

> ☑ double the **l** to spell **cavilling** and **cavilled** (the spellings **caviling** and **caviled** are American)

caving

cavity »*noun* (plural **cavities**) ❶ a hollow space inside something solid. ❷ a decayed part of a tooth.

> ☑ plural: drop the **y** and add **ies**: **cavities**

cavity wall »*noun* a wall made with two layers of bricks with a space between them.

cavort »*verb* (**cavorts, cavorting, cavorted**) jump or dance around excitedly.

cavy »*noun* (plural **cavies**) a kind of guinea pig from South America.
– SAY **kay**-vi

caw »*verb* (**caws, cawing, cawed**) make a harsh cry like a crow.

cayenne »*noun* a hot-tasting red powder made from dried chillies.
– SAY kay-**en**

 enne not **en** at the end: **cayenne**

CB »*abbreviation* Citizens' Band (radio).
CCTV »*abbreviation* closed-circuit television.
CD »*abbreviation* compact disc.
CD-ROM »*noun* a compact disc storing large amounts of information, used in a computer.

 ROM stands for 'read-only memory'

cease (verb: **ceases, ceasing, ceased**)
ceasefire
ceaseless
   ceaselessly
ceases
ceasing
cedar »*noun* a tall spreading evergreen tree.

 ar not **er**: **cedar**

cede »*verb* (**cedes, ceding, ceded**) give up power or territory.
– SAY seed

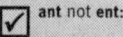 do not confuse **ceding** with **seeding**, which refers to spreading seed or to giving a sports competitor a favoured position in a draw

cedilla »*noun* a mark (¸) written under the letter *c* to show that it is pronounced like an *s* (e.g. *façade*).
– SAY si-**dil**-luh

ceding
ceilidh »*noun* a social event with Scottish or Irish folk music and dancing.
– SAY kay-li

 although it is not pronounced, there is a **dh** at the end: **ceilidh**

ceiling [top surface of a room]

 the usual rule is **i** before **e** except after **c**: **ceiling**

celandine »*noun* a yellow flower related to the buttercup.
– SAY sel-uhn-dyn

celebrant »*noun* a priest who performs the service of Holy Communion in a church.

 ant not **ent**: **celebrant**

celebrate (verb: **celebrates, celebrating, celebrated**)
   celebration
   celebratory

celebrity (plural **celebrities**)

 plural: drop the **y** and add **ies**: **celebrities**

celeriac »*noun* a vegetable with a large edible root.
– SAY suh-**lair**-i-ak

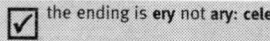 there is no **k** at the end: **celeriac**

celerity »*noun* (an old word) speed of movement.
– SAY si-**le**-ri-ti

celery [vegetable]

 the ending is **ery** not **ary**: **celery**

celestial »*adjective* ❶ relating to heaven. ❷ relating to the sky or outer space.
– SAY si-**less**-ti-uhl

celiac disease American spelling of COELIAC DISEASE.

celibate »*adjective* not married or in a sexual relationship.
– SAY sel-i-buht
   celibacy

cell [small room; basic unit]
cellar
cello »*noun* (plural **cellos**) an instrument like a large violin, held upright on the floor between the legs of the seated player.
– SAY chel-loh
   cellist

 the plural of **cello** has **os** not **oes**: **cellos**

cellophane »*noun* (trademark) a thin transparent wrapping material.
– SAY sel-luh-fayn

cellphone »*noun* a mobile phone.
cellular »*adjective* ❶ relating to or made up of cells. ❷ (of a mobile phone system) using a number of short-range radio stations to cover the area it serves.
– SAY sel-yuu-ler

 double **l**, and **lar** not **ler**: **cellular**

cellulite »*noun* fat that builds up under the skin, causing a dimpled effect.
– SAY sel-yuu-lyt

celluloid »*noun* a kind of transparent plastic formerly used for cinema film.
cellulose »*noun* a substance found in all plant tissues, used in making paint, plastics, and man-made fibres.
– SAY sel-yuu-lohz

Celsius »*noun* a scale of temperature on which water freezes at zero and boils at 100 degrees.
– SAY sel-si-uhss

> ℹ **Celsius** rather than **centigrade** is the accepted scientific term for giving temperatures (*25° Celsius*, not *25° centigrade*). The scale was named after the Swedish scientist Anders *Celsius*.

Celt »*noun* a member of a people who lived in Britain and elsewhere in Europe before the Romans arrived.
– SAY kelt

Celtic »*noun* a group of languages including Irish, Scottish Gaelic, Welsh, Breton, Manx, and Cornish.
»*adjective* relating to Celtic languages or to the Celts.
– SAY kel-tik

> ℹ when referring to language, peoples, and culture, pronounce **Celt** and **Celtic** with an initial **k** sound. Only use the **s** sound in the names of sports teams such as Celtic FC.

cement (verb: **cements, cementing, cemented**)

cemetery (plural **cemeteries**)

> ✓ the ending is **ery** not **ary**: **cemetery** plural: drop the **y** and add **ies**: **cemeteries**

cenotaph »*noun* a monument built to honour soldiers killed in a war.
– SAY sen-uh-tahf

Cenozoic »*adjective* relating to the geological era from about 65 million years ago to the present.
– SAY see-nuh-zoh-ik

censer »*noun* a container in which incense is burnt.

censor »*noun* a person who examines material that is to be published and bans unacceptable parts.
»*verb* (**censors, censoring, censored**) ban unacceptable parts of a document or film.
censorship

> ℹ do not confuse **censor** with **censure**, which means 'express strong disapproval of someone or something'

censorious »*adjective* severely critical.
– SAY sen-sor-i-uhss

censure »*verb* (**censures, censuring, censured**) express strong disapproval of someone or something.
»*noun* strong disapproval or criticism.
– SAY sen-sher

> ℹ do not confuse **censure** with **censor**, which means 'ban unacceptable parts of a document or film'

census »*noun* (plural **censuses**) an official count or survey of a population.

> ✓ **census** ends with **sus**, not **cus**, and do not double the final **s** in the plural: **censuses**

cent [hundredth of a dollar]

centaur »*noun* (in Greek mythology) a creature with a man's head, arms, and upper body and a horse's lower body and legs.
– SAY sen-tor

> ✓ **-aur** not **-or**: **centaur**

centenarian »*noun* a person who has reached one hundred years of age.
– SAY sen-ti-nair-i-uhn

centenary »*noun* (plural **centenaries**) the hundredth anniversary of an event.
– SAY sen-tee-nuh-ri

centennial »*adjective* relating to a hundredth anniversary.
»*noun* a hundredth anniversary.

> ✓ double **n** in the middle: **centennial**

center American spelling of CENTRE.

centerboard American spelling of CENTREBOARD.

centerfold American spelling of CENTREFOLD.

centerpiece American spelling of CENTREPIECE.

centigrade »*adjective* measured by the Celsius scale of temperature.

> ℹ use **Celsius** rather than **centigrade** when giving temperatures: see the note at CELSIUS

centilitre »*noun* a volume of one hundredth of a litre.

centime »*noun* one hundredth of a franc in French and other currencies.
– SAY son-teem

centimetre »*noun* a length of one hundredth of a metre.

> ✓ **re** not **er**: **centimetre** (the spelling **centimeter** is American)

centipede

central
  centrality
  centrally

centralize »*verb* (**centralizes, centralizing, centralized**) bring something under the control of a central authority.
centralism

centralist
centralization

✓ many people prefer the spellings **centralise**, **centralises**, etc., and **centralisation**: both **s** and **z** spellings are correct

centrally

central nervous system »*noun* the system of nerve tissues in the brain and spinal cord in vertebrates.

central reservation »*noun* the strip of land between the carriageways of a motorway or dual carriageway.

centre (verb: **centres, centring, centred**)

✓ **re** not **er**: **centre** (the spelling **center** is American)
drop the **e** to spell **centring**

centreboard »*noun* a board lowered through the keel of a sailing boat to reduce sideways movement.

✓ spell **centreboard**, **centrefold**, etc. with **re** not **er** in the middle (spellings like **centerboard** and **centerfold** are American)

centred

centrefold »*noun* the two middle pages of a magazine, usually containing illustrations or a special feature.

centre of gravity »*noun* the central point in an object, about which its mass is evenly distributed.

centrepiece »*noun* an object or item that is designed to have people's attention focused on it.

✓ **re** not **er** in the middle: **centrepiece** (the spelling **centerpiece** is American)

centres

centrifugal »*adjective* (in physics) moving away from a centre.
– SAY sen-tri-**fyoo**-g'l

✓ **al** not **el**: **centrifugal**

centrifugal force »*noun* (in physics) a force which appears to cause something travelling round a central point to fly outwards from its circular path.

centrifuge »*noun* a machine with a container which can spin rapidly, used to separate liquids from solids.
– SAY **sen**-tri-fyooj

centring

centripetal »*adjective* (in physics) moving towards a centre.
– SAY sen-tri-**pee**-t'l

centripetal force »*noun* (in physics) a force which causes something travelling

round a central point to move inwards from its circular path.

centrist »*noun* a person having moderate political views or policies.
centrism

✓ **tri** not **trei**: **centrist**

centurion »*noun* a commander of one hundred men in the army of ancient Rome.

✓ **-on** not **-an**: **centurion**

century (plural **centuries**)

✓ plural: drop the **y** and add **ies**: **centuries**

cep »*noun* a mushroom with a smooth brown cap.
– SAY sep

cephalic »*adjective* relating to the head.
– SAY si-**fal**-ik or ki-**fal**-ik

ceramic »*adjective* made of fired clay.

ceramics »*noun* the art of making ceramic articles.

cereal [edible grass]

ℹ do not confuse **cereal** with **serial**, which means 'taking place in a series'

cerebellum »*noun* (plural **cerebellums** or **cerebella**) the part of the brain at the back of the skull.
– SAY se-ri-**bel**-luhm

✓ the plural can be either **cerebella** (like the original Latin) or **cerebellums**

cerebra plural of CEREBRUM.

cerebral »*adjective* ❶ relating to the brain. ❷ intellectual rather than emotional or physical.
– SAY se-ri-bruhl or suh-**ree**-bruhl

✓ **al** not **el**, and remember the **r** after the **b**: **cerebral**

cerebral palsy »*noun* a condition in which a person has difficulty in controlling their muscles, caused by brain damage before or at birth.

cerebrum »*noun* (plural **cerebra**) the main, front part of the brain.
– SAY se-ri-bruhm [singular], se-ri-bruh [plural]

✓ like many other words ending in **um** derived from Latin, **cerebrum** has a plural ending in **a**: **cerebra**

ceremonial »*adjective* having to do with ceremonies.
» *noun* = CEREMONY.
ceremonially

ceremonious »*adjective* done in a formal and grand way.
ceremoniously

ceremony (plural **ceremonies**)

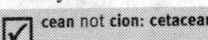 plural: drop the **y** and add **ies**: **ceremonies**

cerise »*noun* a light, clear red colour.
– SAY suh-**reess**

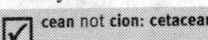 ise not ice: **cerise**

cerium »*noun* a silvery-white metallic chemical element.
– SAY **seer**-i-uhm

cert [certain thing]

certain

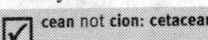 remember the **a**: **certain**

certainly

certainty (plural **certainties**)

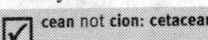 plural: drop the **y** and add **ies**: **certainties**

certifiable »*adjective* ❶ needing to be certified as insane. ❷ able to be officially confirmed.

certificate
certification

certify »*verb* (**certifies, certifying, certified**) ❶ declare or confirm in a certificate or other official document. ❷ officially declare someone insane.

certitude »*noun* a feeling of complete certainty.

cerulean »*adjective* deep blue like a clear sky.
– SAY si-**roo**-li-uhn

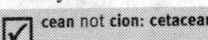 -lean not -laean: **cerulean**

cervical »*adjective* relating to the cervix.
– SAY **ser**-vi-k'l or ser-**vy**-k'l

cervical smear »*noun* a specimen of cells from the neck of the womb spread on a microscope slide for examination for signs of cancer.

cervix »*noun* (plural **cervices**) ❶ the narrow neck-like passage forming the lower end of the womb. ❷ the neck.
– SAY **ser**-viks [singular], **ser**-vi-seez [plural]

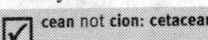 make the plural by changing the **x** ending to **ces** (as in Latin): **cervices**

Cesarean American spelling of **CAESAREAN**.

cesium American spelling of **CAESIUM**.

cessation »*noun* the stopping of something.

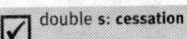 double **s**: **cessation**

cession »*noun* the formal giving up of rights or territory by a state.

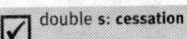 do not confuse **cession** with **session**, which means 'a period devoted to a particular activity'

cesspit »*noun* a cesspool.

cesspool »*noun* an underground tank or covered pit where sewage is collected.

cetacean »*noun* the name in zoology for a whale or dolphin.
– SAY si-**tay**-sh'n

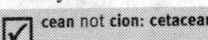 cean not cion: **cetacean**

CFC »*abbreviation* chlorofluorocarbon, a gas used in refrigerators and aerosols that is harmful to the ozone layer.

Chablis »*noun* a dry white wine from Chablis in France.
– SAY **shab**-lee

cha-cha »*noun* a modern ballroom dance performed to a Latin American rhythm.

chaconne »*noun* a musical composition in a series of varying sections in slow triple time.
– SAY shuh-**kon**

Chadian [of Chad]

chador »*noun* a piece of dark cloth worn by Muslim women around the head and upper body, so that only part of the face can be seen.
– SAY **chah**-dor

chafe »*verb* (**chafes, chafing, chafed**) ❶ make something sore or worn by rubbing against it. ❷ rub a part of the body to warm it. ❸ become impatient because you are prevented from acting freely.

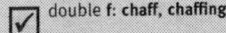 one **f**: **chafe**
drop the **e** when spelling **chafing**

chafer »*noun* a large flying beetle.

chafes

chaff »*noun* ❶ husks of grain that have been separated from the seed. ❷ hay and straw cut up as food for cattle. ❸ light-hearted joking.
»*verb* (**chaffs, chaffing, chaffed**) tease.

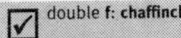 double **f**: **chaff, chaffing**

chaffinch »*noun* a finch, the male of which has a bluish head, pink underparts, and dark wings.

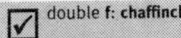 double **f**: **chaffinch**

chaffing

chaffs

chafing

chagrin »*noun* a feeling of annoyance or shame at having failed.
»*verb* (**be chagrined**) feel annoyed or ashamed.
– SAY sha-**grin** or sha-grin

> ✓ **ch** not **sh**: **chagrin** (take care not to confuse with **shagreen** meaning 'sharkskin; untanned leather')

chain (verb: **chains, chaining, chained**)

chain gang »*noun* a group of convicts chained together while working outside the prison.

chaining

chain letter »*noun* a letter sent to a number of people, all of whom are asked to make copies and send these to other people, who then do the same.

chain mail »*noun* (a historical term) armour made of small metal rings linked together.

chain reaction »*noun* ❶ a chemical reaction in which the products of the reaction cause further changes. ❷ a series of events, each caused by the previous one.

chains

chainsaw

chain-smoke »*verb* (**chain-smokes, chain-smoking, chain-smoked**) smoke cigarettes one after the other.

chair (verb: **chairs, chairing, chaired**)

chairlift

chairman »*noun* (plural **chairmen**) a person in charge of a meeting or organization.

chairperson »*noun* a chairman or chairwoman.

chairs

chairwoman »*noun* (plural **chairwomen**) a woman in charge of a meeting or organization.

chaise »*noun* (a historical term) a two-wheeled horse-drawn carriage for one or two people.
– SAY shayz

> ✓ don't forget the **i** before the **s**: **chaise**

chaise longue »*noun* (plural **chaises longues**) a sofa with a backrest at only one end.
– SAY shayz **longg** [singular and plural]

> ✓ remember the **ue** on the end: **chaise longue**. It is a French phrase and the plural has an **s** after both words: **chaises longues**.

chalcedony »*noun* (plural **chalcedonies**) a type of quartz with very small crystals.
– SAY kal-sed-uh-ni

chalet »*noun* ❶ a wooden house with overhanging eaves, found in the Swiss Alps. ❷ a wooden cabin used by holidaymakers.
– SAY sha-lay

> ✓ there is a **t** at the end, which is not pronounced because the word comes from French: **chalet**

chalice »*noun* ❶ (a historical term) a goblet. ❷ the wine cup used in Holy Communion.
– SAY cha-liss

> ✓ single **l**, and the ending is -**ice** not -**is**: **chalice**

chalk (verb: **chalks, chalking, chalked**)

chalky

challenge (verb: **challenges, challenging, challenged**)

challenger

challenging

> ✓ double **l**: **challenge**

chamaeleon another way of spelling CHAMELEON.

chamber

chamberlain »*noun* (a historical term) a person who looked after the household of a king or queen, or a noble.
– SAY chaym-ber-lin

> ✓ remember the **a** between the **l** and the **i**: **chamberlain**

chambermaid

chamber music »*noun* classical music played by a small group of musicians.

Chamber of Commerce »*noun* a local association to promote the interests of the business community.

chamber pot »*noun* a bowl kept in a bedroom and used as a toilet.

chambray »*noun* a gingham cloth with white weft threads and coloured warp threads.
– SAY sham-bray

> ✓ **ray** not **rey**: **chambray**

chameleon »*noun* a small lizard that can change colour according to its surroundings.
– SAY kuh-**mee**-li-uhn

> ✓ **chameleon** can also be spelled **chamaeleon,** with an **a** after the **m**

chamfer »*verb* (**chamfers, chamfering, chamfered**) (in carpentry) cut an angled edge on a piece of wood.
– **SAY** sham-fer

chamois »*noun* (plural **chamois**) ❶ a wild antelope that lives in the mountains of southern Europe. ❷ soft leather made from the skin of sheep, goats, or deer.
– **SAY** sham-wah [antelope], plural sham-wah or sham-wahz; sham-mi [leather], plural sham-miz

> ☑ don't forget the **o** after the **m**: **chamois**

chamomile »*noun* a plant with white and yellow flowers, used in herbal medicine.
– **SAY** kam-uh-myl

> ☑ **chamomile** can also be spelled **camomile**, without the **h**: both spellings are correct

champ »*verb* (**champs, champing, champed**) munch noisily.

champagne »*noun* a white sparkling wine from the Champagne region of France.
– **SAY** sham-**payn**

> ☑ remember the **g**: **champagne**

champed
champing
champion (verb: **champions, championing, championed**)
championship

> ☑ **-ship** not **-chip**: **championship**

champs
chance (verb: **chances, chancing, chanced**)
chancel »*noun* the part of a church near the altar, reserved for the clergy and choir.
– **SAY** chahn-s'l

chancellery »*noun* (plural **chancelleries**) the post or department of a chancellor.
– **SAY** chahn-suh-luh-ri

> ☑ double **l** and **ery** not **ory**: **chancellery**

chancellor »*noun* ❶ a senior state or legal official. ❷ (**Chancellor**) the head of the government in some European countries.

> ☑ **-or** not **-er**: **chancellor**

Chancellor of the Exchequer »*noun* (in the UK) the government minister in charge of the country's finances.

chancer »*noun* (in informal English) a person who cunningly makes the most of any opportunity.

Chancery »*noun* (plural **Chanceries**) (in the UK) the Lord Chancellor's court, a division of the High Court of Justice.

chancier
chanciest
chancre »*noun* a painless ulcer that develops on the genitals in venereal disease.
– **SAY** shang-ker

> ☑ **cre** not **cer**: **chancre**

chancy »*adjective* (**chancier, chanciest**) (in informal English) risky.

> ☑ **cy** not **cey**: **chancy**

chandelier »*noun* a large hanging light with branches for several light bulbs or candles.
– **SAY** shan-duh-leer

> ☑ **del** not **dal**: **chandelier**

chandler »*noun* a dealer in supplies and equipment for ships.
– **SAY** chahnd-ler
chandlery

change (verb: **changes, changing, changed**)
changeless
changer
changeable

> ☑ remember the first **e**: **changeable**

changed
changeless
changeling »*noun* a child believed to have been secretly left by fairies in exchange for the parents' real child.

changeover
changer
changes
changing
channel (verb: **channels, channelling, channelled**)

> ☑ double the **l** when spelling **channelling** and **channelled** (the spellings with a single **l** are American)

chant (verb: **chants, chanting, chanted**)

Chanukkah another way of spelling **HANUKKAH**.

chaos »*noun* complete disorder and confusion.

chaos theory »*noun* the branch of science concerned with very complex systems which appear unpredictable because tiny changes can have major effects.

chaotic »*adjective* in a state of complete confusion and disorder.
– SAY kay-**ot**-ik
chaotically

C **chap**

chaparral »*noun* (in America) vegetation consisting chiefly of tangled shrubs and thorny bushes.
– SAY sha-puh-**ral**

 one p, two r's in **chaparral**, which is a Spanish word referring to small oak trees

chapatti »*noun* (plural **chapattis**) (in Indian cookery) a flat cake of wholemeal bread.
– SAY chuh-**pah**-ti or chuh-**pat**-ti

 one p, two t's: **chapatti**

chapel

chaperone »*noun* (old-fashioned) an older woman in charge of an unmarried girl at social occasions.
»*verb* (**chaperones, chaperoning, chaperoned**) accompany and look after someone younger.
– SAY **shap**-uh-rohn

 drop the second **e** when spelling **chaperoning**, but don't forget it elsewhere: **chaperone**

chaplain »*noun* a minister of the church attached to a chapel in a private house or an institution, or to a military unit.
chaplaincy

 don't forget the second **a**: **chaplain**

chaplet »*noun* an ornamental circular band worn on the head.

chapped »*adjective* (of the skin) cracked and sore through exposure to cold weather.

chapter

char[1] »*verb* (**chars, charring, charred**) partially burn something so as to blacken the surface.

 double the **r** in **charring** and **charred**

char[2] »*noun* (in informal English) a charwoman.

char[3] »*noun* (in informal English) tea.

char[4] another way of spelling CHARR.

charabanc »*noun* an early form of bus.
– SAY sha-ruh-bang

 there is no **k** in **charabanc**

character
characterful
characterless

characterise another way of spelling CHARACTERIZE.

characteristic
characteristically

characterize »*verb* (**characterizes, characterizing, characterized**) ❶ describe the character of. ❷ be characteristic of: *the rugged hills that characterize this part of Wales.*
characterization

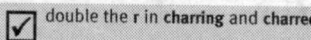 many people prefer the alternative spellings **characterise, characterises**, etc., and **characterisation**: both **s** and **z** spellings are correct

characterless

charade »*noun* a pretence that something is true when it is clearly not.
– SAY shuh-**rahd**

charades »*noun* a game of guessing a word or phrase from written or acted clues.

charcoal

chard »*noun* a vegetable with large leaves and thick white or red leaf stalks.

Chardonnay »*noun* ❶ a grape used for making champagne and other white wines. ❷ a wine made from this grape.
– SAY **shah**-duh-nay

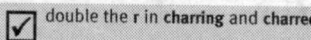 remember the double **n** in **Chardonnay**

charge (verb: **charges, charging, charged**)
chargeable

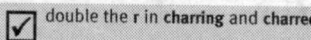 drop the **e** when spelling **charging**

charge card »*noun* a kind of credit card issued by a large shop.

charged

charge d'affaires »*noun* (plural **charges d'affaires**) ❶ an ambassador's deputy. ❷ the diplomatic representative of a state in a minor country.
– SAY shar-*zhay* da-**fair** [singular and plural]

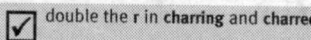 **charge d'affaires** can also be written **chargé d'affaires**, with an acute accent above the **e** (as in the original French)

charger »*noun* ❶ a device for charging a battery. ❷ a horse ridden by a knight or cavalryman.

charges
charges d'affaires
charging

chargrill »*verb* (**chargrills, chargrilling, chargrilled**) grill food quickly at a very high heat.

chariot »*noun* a two-wheeled horse-drawn vehicle, used in ancient warfare and racing.
charioteer

charisma »*noun* attractiveness or charm that inspires admiration or enthusiasm in other people.
– SAY kuh-**riz**-muh

charismatic

charitable
charitably

charity (plural **charities**)

> ☑ plural: drop the **y** and add **ies**: **charities**

charlatan »*noun* a person who claims to have knowledge or skills that they do not really have.
– SAY **shar**-luh-tuhn
charlatanism

> ☑ there are no **e**'s in **charlatan**

charleston »*noun* a 1920s dance in which you turn your knees inwards and kick out your lower legs.

> ☑ don't forget the **e**: **charleston**

charm (verb: **charms, charming, charmed**)
charmer
charming
charmingly
charmless

charr »*noun* (plural **charr**) a trout-like northern freshwater or marine fish.

> ☑ **charr** can also be spelled **char**, with only one **r**: both spellings are correct

charred

charring

chars

chart (verb: **charts, charting, charted**)

charter »*noun* ❶ an official document stating that a ruler or government allows an institution to exist and setting out its rights. ❷ a document listing and describing the functions of an organization. ❸ the hiring of an aircraft, ship, or motor vehicle.
»*verb* (**charters, chartering, chartered**)
❶ hire an aircraft, ship, or motor vehicle.
❷ grant a charter to an institution.

chartered »*adjective* (of an accountant, engineer, etc.) qualified as a member of a professional body that has a royal charter.

charter flight »*noun* a flight by an aircraft chartered for a specific journey.

charting

Chartism »*noun* a UK movement (1837–48) for social and parliamentary reform, the principles of which were set out in *The People's Charter*.
Chartist

chartreuse »*noun* a pale green or yellow liqueur.
– SAY shah-**trerz**

charts

charwoman »*noun* (plural **charwomen**) (old-fashioned) a woman employed as a cleaner in a house or office.

chary »*adjective* cautiously reluctant: *leaders are chary of reform.*
– SAY **chair**-i

chase (verb: **chases, chasing, chased**)
chaser

chasm »*noun* ❶ a deep crack in the earth. ❷ a marked difference between people or between their opinions.

chassis »*noun* (plural **chassis**) ❶ the framework forming the base of a vehicle. ❷ the outer structural framework of a piece of audio, radio, or computer equipment.
– SAY **sha**-si [singular], **sha**-siz [plural]

> ☑ don't forget the **s** at the end: **chassis**

chaste »*adjective* ❶ having sex only with your husband or wife, or not at all. ❷ not expressing sexual interest; demure and modest.

> remember the **e** at the end: **chaste**

chasten »*verb* (**chastens, chastening, chastened**) make someone feel subdued and less confident about something.
– SAY **chay**-s'n

chastise »*verb* (**chastises, chastising, chastised**) tell someone off in a very strict manner.
chastisement

> ☑ **chastise** cannot be spelled with an **ize** ending

chastity »*noun* the state of being chaste.

chasuble »*noun* a long sleeveless garment worn over other robes by a priest when celebrating Mass.
– SAY **chaz**-yuu-b'l

chat (verb: **chats, chatting, chatted**)

> 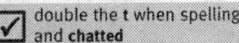 double the **t** when spelling **chatting** and **chatted**

chateau »*noun* (plural **chateaux**) a large French country house or castle.
– SAY sha-toh [singular], sha-toh or sha-tohz [plural]

> ✓ **chateau** can also be written **château**, with a circumflex accent on the first **a** (as in the original French)

chatelaine »*noun* (old-fashioned) a woman in charge of a large house.
– SAY sha-tuh-layn

> ✓ remember the **i** between the **a** and **n**: **chatelaine**
> like **chateau**, it is sometimes written with a circumflex accent: **châtelaine**

chatline »*noun* a telephone service which allows conversation among a number of separate callers.

chat room »*noun* an area on the Internet or other computer network where users can communicate with each other.

chats

chatted

chattel »*noun* a personal possession.
– SAY chat-t'l

> ✓ two **t**'s, and the ending is **el** not **le**: **chattel**

chatter (verb: **chatters, chattering, chattered**)

> ✓ two **t**'s, one **r**: **chatter**

chatterbox

chattered

chattering

chatters

chattier

chattiest

chatting

chatty (adjective: **chattier, chattiest**)

chauffeur »*noun* a person employed to drive someone around in a car.
» *verb* (**chauffeurs, chauffeuring, chauffeured**) be a driver for someone.

> ✓ remember the **u**'s before the **ff** and the **r**: **chauffeur**

chauvinism »*noun* ❶ an aggressive belief that your own country or group is better than others. ❷ a belief held by some men that men are superior to women.
– SAY shoh-vin-iz'm

chauvinist »*noun* a person who considers their own country, sex, or group to be better than others.
» *adjective* having to do with chauvinists or chauvinism.
chauvinistic

cheap [inexpensive]
cheaply
cheapness

> ℹ do not confuse **cheap** with **cheep**, meaning 'the cry of a young bird'

cheapen (verb: **cheapens, cheapening, cheapened**)

cheaply

cheapness

cheapskate »*noun* (in informal English) a person who hates to spend money.

cheat (verb: **cheats, cheating, cheated**)

Chechen [of Chechnya]
– SAY che-chen

check¹ (verb: **checks, checking, checked**) [examine the accuracy or condition of; an act of checking]
checker

check² [pattern of small squares]

check³ American spelling of CHEQUE.

checked

checker

checkers »*plural noun* ❶ American spelling of CHEQUERS. ❷ (in American English) the game of draughts.

checking

checklist

checkmate »*noun* ❶ a chess position of check from which a king cannot escape. ❷ a final defeat or deadlock.
» *verb* (**checkmates, checkmating, checkmated**) ❶ put a king into checkmate. ❷ defeat or thwart: *US aid would help them to checkmate invasion.*

checkout

checkpoint

checks

check-up

Cheddar [cheese]

> ✓ **ar** not **er**: **Cheddar**

cheek

cheekbone

cheeky (adjective: **cheekier, cheekiest**)
cheekily
cheekiness

cheep (verb: **cheeps, cheeping, cheeped**) [cry of a young bird]

> ℹ do not confuse **cheep** with **cheap**, which means 'inexpensive'

cheer (verb: **cheers, cheering, cheered**)

cheerful
cheerfully
cheerfulness

☑ -ful not -full: **cheerful**

cheerier

cheeriest

cheering

cheerio

cheerleader »*noun* (in North America) a girl belonging to a group that performs organized chanting and dancing at sporting events.

cheerless »*adjective* gloomy; depressing.

cheers

cheery »*adjective* (**cheerier**, **cheeriest**) happy and optimistic.

cheese

cheeseboard

cheeseburger

cheesecake

cheesecloth »*noun* thin, loosely woven cotton cloth.

cheesed off »*adjective* (in informal English) annoyed or discontented.

cheesemonger

cheesy »*adjective* (**cheesier**, **cheesiest**) ❶ like cheese. ❷ (in informal English) sentimental or of poor quality.

cheetah »*noun* a large spotted cat that can run very fast, found in Africa and parts of Asia.
– SAY **chee**-tuh

☑ don't forget the **h**: **cheetah**

chef

chemical
　　chemically

chemise »*noun* a woman's loose-fitting dress, nightdress, or undergarment.
– SAY shuh-**meez**

chemist

chemistry »*noun* ❶ the branch of science concerned with the nature and properties of substances and how they react with each other. ❷ attraction or interaction between two people.

chemotherapy »*noun* the treatment of disease, especially cancer, by the use of chemicals.
– SAY kee-moh-**the**-ruh-pi

chenille »*noun* fabric with a long velvety pile.
– SAY shuh-**neel**

☑ one **n**, two **l**'s: **chenille**

cheque »*noun* a written order to a bank to pay a stated sum from an account to a specified person.

☑ **que** not **ck**: **cheque** (the spelling with **ck** is American)

cheque card »*noun* a card issued by a bank to guarantee payment of a customer's cheques.

chequered »*adjective* ❶ divided into or marked with chequers. ❷ marked by periods of varied fortune: *a chequered career.*

☑ **cheque-** not **check-**: **chequered**

chequers »*noun* a pattern of alternately coloured squares.

☑ **chequ-** not **check-**: **chequers** (the spelling with **ck** is American)

cherish »*verb* (**cherishes**, **cherishing**, **cherished**) ❶ protect and care for lovingly. ❷ keep in your mind: *I will always cherish memories of those days.*

Cherokee »*noun* (plural **Cherokee** or **Cherokees**) a member of an American Indian people formerly inhabiting much of the southern US.
– SAY che-ruh-**kee**

cheroot »*noun* a cigar with both ends open.
– SAY shuh-**root**

cherry (plural **cherries**)

☑ plural: drop the **y** and add **ies**: **cherries**

cherry-pick »*verb* (**cherry-picks**, **cherry-picking**, **cherry-picked**) choose the best things or people from those available.

cherub »*noun* ❶ (plural **cherubim** or **cherubs**) a type of angel, shown in art as a chubby child with wings. ❷ (plural **cherubs**) a beautiful or innocent-looking child.
cherubic SAY chuh-**roo**-bik

☑ single **r**: **cherub**. The plural form **cherubim** comes from Hebrew.

chervil »*noun* a herb with an aniseed flavour.
– SAY **cher**-vil

chess »*noun* a board game for two players, the object of which is to put the opponent's king under a direct attack, leading to checkmate.

chessboard

chest

chesterfield »*noun* a sofa with a back of the same height as the arms.

chestnut

✓ remember the **t** in the middle: **chestnut**

chesty »*adjective* (in informal English) having a lot of catarrh in the lungs.

chevron »*noun* a V-shaped line or stripe, worn on the sleeve of a military uniform to show rank or length of service.

chew (verb: **chews, chewing, chewed**)
chewable
chewer

chewier

chewiest

chewing

chews

chewy (adjective: **chewier, chewiest**)

chez »*preposition* at the home of.
– SAY shay

✓ **chez** is French, with a silent final **z**

chi »*noun* the twenty-second letter of the Greek alphabet (X, χ).
– SAY kee

Chianti »*noun* (plural **Chiantis**) a dry red Italian wine.
– SAY ki-an-ti

✓ don't forget the **h** after the **c**: **Chianti**

chiaroscuro »*noun* the treatment of light and shade in drawing and painting.
– SAY ki-ah-ruh-skoor-oh

ℹ️ **chiaroscuro** is an Italian word, from *chiaro* 'clear, bright' and *oscuro* 'dark, obscure'

chic »*adjective* (**chicer, chicest**) smart and fashionable.
» *noun* stylishness and elegance.
– SAY sheek

✓ the comparative and superlative forms are **chicer** and **chicest**, but because they can look rather strange, some people spell them with a hyphen, **chic-er** and **chic-est**

chicane »*noun* a sharp double bend in a motor-racing track.
– SAY shi-kayn

chicanery »*noun* the use of cunning tricks to get what you want.

chicer [more chic]

✓ see the note at CHIC

chicest [most chic]

✓ see the note at CHIC

chick

chicken (verb: **chickens, chickening, chickened**)

chickenpox »*noun* a disease causing a mild fever and itchy inflamed pimples.

chickpea »*noun* a yellowish seed eaten as a pulse.

chickweed »*noun* a small white-flowered plant, often growing as a garden weed.

chicory »*noun* (plural **chicories**) ❶ a plant with a root which is added to or used instead of coffee. ❷ (in American English) endive.
– SAY chi-kuh-ri

chide »*verb* (**chides, chiding, chided**) tell someone off.
– SAY chyd

ℹ️ the past tense of **chide** is normally **chided**: **chid** is old-fashioned

chief
chiefdom
chiefly

✓ the usual rule is **i** before **e** except after **c**: **chief**

chief of staff »*noun* (plural **chiefs of staff**) the senior staff officer of an armed service or command.

chieftain

✓ remember, the ending is **-ain**, not **-an**: **chieftain**

chieftaincy (plural **chieftaincies**)

✓ remember the **i** in **tain**: **chieftaincy**

chiffchaff »*noun* a common warbler with a repetitive call.

chiffon »*noun* a light, see-through fabric of silk or nylon.
– SAY shif-fon

chihuahua »*noun* a very small dog with smooth hair and large eyes.
– SAY chi-wah-wuh

chilblain »*noun* a painful, itching swelling on a hand or foot caused by poor circulation in the skin when exposed to cold.

✓ only one **l** in **chil**: **chilblain**

child (plural **children**)
childbirth
childcare
childhood
childish
childishly
childishness
childless

childlike
childminder
childproof
children
Chilean
chili American spelling of CHILLI.
chill (verb: **chills, chilling, chilled**)
　chiller
chilli »*noun* (plural **chillies**) a small hot-tasting pod of a kind of capsicum, used in cookery and as a spice.

> ☑ double l: **chilli** (the spelling **chili** is American)

chilli con carne »*noun* a stew of minced beef and beans flavoured with chilli.
– SAY chil-li kon **kar**-ni

> ℹ **chilli con carne** is Spanish, meaning 'chilli with meat'

chillier
chillies
chilliness
chilling
chills
chilly »*adjective* (**chillier, chilliest**) ❶ just too cold to be comfortable. ❷ unfriendly.
　chilliness
chimaera another way of spelling CHIMERA.
chime (verb: **chimes, chiming, chimed**)
chimera »*noun* ❶ (in Greek mythology) a female monster with a lion's head, a goat's body, and a serpent's tail. ❷ an impossible hope or dream.
– SAY ky-**meer**-uh
　chimerical

> ☑ **chimera** can also be spelled **chimaera**, which is more like the original Greek word *khimaira*: both forms are correct

chimes
chiming
chimney (plural **chimneys**)

> ☑ make the plural by simply adding **s**, not **ies**: **chimneys**

chimp
chimpanzee
chin
china »*noun* ❶ a fine white ceramic material. ❷ household objects made from china.
china clay »*noun* kaolin.
chinchilla »*noun* a small South American rodent with soft grey fur and a long bushy tail.
– SAY chin-**chil**-luh

Chinese (plural **Chinese**)
Chinese wall »*noun* a barrier to the passage of information.
Chinese whispers »*noun* a game in which a message is altered by being passed around in a whisper.
chink »*noun* ❶ a narrow opening or crack. ❷ a beam of light entering through a chink. ❸ a light, high-pitched ringing sound.
» *verb* (**chinks, chinking, chinked**) make a light, high-pitched ringing sound.
chinless
chinos »*noun* casual trousers made from a smooth cotton fabric.
– SAY chee-nohz

> ☑ the ending is **os** not **oes**: **chinos**

chintz »*noun* patterned cotton fabric with a glazed finish, used for curtains and upholstery.
　chintzy
chip (verb: **chips, chipping, chipped**)
chipboard
chipmunk »*noun* a burrowing squirrel with light and dark stripes running down its body.

> ☑ -**munk** not -**monk**: **chipmunk**

chipolata »*noun* a small thin sausage.

> ☑ one p, one l: **chipolata**

chipped
chipper »*adjective* cheerful and lively.
chippie another way of spelling CHIPPY.
chipping
chippy »*noun* (plural **chippies**) (in informal English) a fish-and-chip shop.

> ☑ **chippy** can also be spelled **chippie**, with the same plural form **chippies**

chips
chiropody »*noun* care and treatment of the feet.
– SAY ki-**rop**-uh-di
　chiropodist
chiropractic »*noun* a system of complementary medicine based on the manipulation of the joints, especially those of the spinal column.
– SAY ky-roh-**prak**-tik
　chiropractor
chirp (verb: **chirps, chirping, chirped**)
chirpy (adjective: **chirpier, chirpiest**)
　chirpily
　chirpiness

chirrup (verb: **chirrups, chirruping, chirruped**)

chisel (verb: **chisels, chiselling, chiselled**)

> ☑ double the **l** in **chiselled** and **chiselling** (the spellings **chiseled** and **chiseling** are American)

chit »*noun* a short note recording a sum owed.

chit-chat (verb: **chit-chats, chit-chatting, chit-chatted**)

chivalrous »*adjective* acting in a polite and charming way towards women.
– **SAY** shi-vuhl-ruhss
chivalrously

chivalry »*noun* ❶ an honourable code of behaviour adopted by knights in medieval times. ❷ polite behaviour on the part of a man towards women.
– **SAY** shi-vuhl-ri

chives »*noun* a plant with long thin leaves that taste of onions and are used as a herb.

chivvy »*verb* (**chivvies, chivvying, chivvied**) keep telling someone to do something.

> ☑ two **v**'s, not one: **chivvy**

chloride

chlorinate »*verb* (**chlorinates, chlorinating, chlorinated**) treat water with chlorine.
– **SAY** klor-in-ayt
chlorination

chlorine »*noun* a poisonous green gaseous chemical element.
– **SAY** klor-een

> ☑ do not forget the **h** in **chlorine** and related words such as **chlorinated** and **chloroform**

chloroform »*noun* a liquid used to dissolve things and formerly as an anaesthetic.
»*verb* (**chloroforms, chloroforming, chloroformed**) use this liquid to make someone unconscious.

chlorophyll »*noun* a green pigment in plants which allows them to absorb sunlight and use it in photosynthesis.
– **SAY** klo-ruh-fil

> ☑ starts with a **ch** and ends with a double **l**: **chlorophyll**

chock »*noun* a wedge or block placed against a wheel to prevent it from moving.

chock-a-block »*adjective* crammed full.

> ☑ do not forget the **k** of **block**: **chock-a-block**

chocolate

> ☑ remember the **o** in the middle and the **e** at the end: **chocolate**

chocolatey

> ☑ this adjective can also be spelled **chocolaty**: both spellings are correct

choice (adjective: **choicer, choicest**)

choir »*noun* ❶ an organized group of singers. ❷ the part of a church between the altar and the nave.
– **SAY** *rhymes with* wire

> ☑ you still sometimes come across the old spelling **quire**, which besides meaning the same as **choir** can also refer to a number of sheets of paper

choirboy

choirgirl

choke (verb: **chokes, choking, choked**)
choker

cholera »*noun* an infectious disease causing severe vomiting and diarrhoea.
– **SAY** ko-luh-ruh

> ☑ **cholera** starts with **ch** and has a single **l**

cholesterol »*noun* a substance which is present in most body tissues but which, when there is too much of it in the blood, is believed to cause disease of the arteries.
– **SAY** kuh-less-tuh-rol

> ☑ the ending is **sterol**, not **strol**: **cholesterol**

chomp (verb: **chomps, chomping, chomped**)

choose (verb: **chooses, choosing, chose**; past participle **chosen**)

choosy (adjective: **choosier, choosiest**)
choosiness

> ☑ **sy** not **sey**: **choosy**

chop (verb: **chops, chopping, chopped**)

chopper

choppier

choppiest

choppiness

chopping

choppy »*adjective* (**choppier, choppiest**) (of the sea) having many small waves.
choppiness

chops

chopsticks

chop suey »*noun* a Chinese-style dish of meat with bean sprouts, bamboo shoots, and onions.
– **SAY** chop soo-i

choral »*adjective* sung by a choir or chorus.

chorale »*noun* a simple, stately hymn tune.
– SAY kuh-**rahl**

☑ remember the final **e**, and do not confuse **chorale** with **corral** 'a pen for livestock'

chord »*noun* ❶ a group of three or more notes sounded together in harmony. ❷ a straight line joining the ends of a curved line.

ⓘ do not confuse **chord** with **cord**, which refers to thin string, rope, or flex

chore »*noun* an unpleasant task, or one that has to be done regularly.

choreograph »*verb* (**choreographs, choreographing, choreographed**) compose the sequence of steps for a ballet or dance routine.
– SAY **ko**-ri-uh-grahf
choreographer SAY ko-ri-**og**-ruh-fer
choreography SAY ko-ri-**og**-ruh-fi

chorister »*noun* a choirboy or choirgirl.
– SAY **ko**-riss-ter

chortle »*verb* (**chortles, chortling, chortled**) laugh loudly, with the sound coming from deep in the throat.

chorus (plural **choruses**; verb: **choruses, chorusing, chorused**)

☑ do not double the **s** in spelling **choruses, chorused**, etc.

chose past of CHOOSE.

chosen past participle of CHOOSE.

chough »*noun* a black bird of the crow family with a curved red or yellow bill.
– SAY chuf

choux pastry »*noun* very light pastry made with egg, used for eclairs and profiteroles.
– SAY shoo

☑ remember the **x**: **choux** is a French word meaning 'cabbages' or 'rosettes'

chowder »*noun* a rich soup containing fish, clams, or corn with potatoes and onions.

chow mein »*noun* a Chinese-style dish of fried noodles with shredded meat or seafood and vegetables.
– SAY chow **mayn**

Christ

christen »*verb* (**christens, christening, christened**) ❶ give a name to a baby while they are being baptised. ❷ (in informal English) use for the first time.

Christendom »*noun* (old-fashioned) the worldwide body of Christians.

christened

christening
christens
Christian
Christianity

Christian name »*noun* a forename given at baptism.

ⓘ the term **Christian name** is not appropriate for people who are not Christian or of Christian upbringing. Use **given name, first name**, or **forename** instead.

Christmas (plural **Christmases**)
Christmassy

☑ remember the **t** of **Christ**: **Christmas** do not double the **s** (or use an apostrophe) in making the plural: **Christmases**

Christmas time
Christmas tree

chromatic »*adjective* ❶ (in music) using notes that do not belong to the key in which the passage is written. ❷ (of a musical scale) going up or down by semitones. ❸ relating to or produced by colour.
– SAY kruh-**ma**-tik

chromatography »*noun* (in chemistry) a technique for separating a mixture by passing it through a medium in which the components move at different rates.
– SAY kroh-muh-**tog**-ruh-fi

chrome »*noun* a hard, bright metal coating made from chromium.

☑ do not forget the **h**: **chrome**

chromium »*noun* a hard white metal used in stainless steel and other alloys.

chromosome »*noun* (in biology) a thread-like structure in a cell nucleus, carrying the genes.

☑ **chromo** not **chroma**: **chromosome**

chronic »*adjective* ❶ (of an illness or problem) lasting for a long time. ❷ having a long-lasting illness or bad habit. ❸ (in informal English) very bad.
chronically

chronicle »*noun* a record of historical events made as or in the order in which they happened.
»*verb* (**chronicles, chronicling, chronicled**) record a series of events in detail.
chronicler

☑ the ending is **le** not **al**: **chronicle**

chronograph »*noun* an instrument for recording time very accurately.

chronological »*adjective* **❶** relating to the time and order in which things happen. **❷** (of a record of events) starting with the earliest and following the order in which they occurred.
chronologically

chronology »*noun* (plural **chronologies**) **❶** the study of records to establish the dates of past events. **❷** the arrangement of events or dates in the order of their occurrence.
– SAY kruh-**nol**-uh-ji

chronometer »*noun* an instrument for measuring time.
– SAY kruh-**nom**-i-ter

chrysalis »*noun* (plural **chrysalises**) a butterfly or moth when it is changing from a larva to the adult form, inside a hard case.
– SAY **kriss**-uh-liss

> ✓ single **s**, single **l**: **chrysalis** just add **es** to make the plural: **chrysalises**

chrysanthemum »*noun* (plural **chrysanthemums**) a garden plant with brightly coloured flowers.
– SAY kri-**santh**-i-muhm

> ✓ the beginning is **chrys**, the middle is **anthe**, and the ending is **mum**: **chrysanthemum**

chub »*noun* a thick-bodied river fish.

chubby »*adjective* (**chubbier**, **chubbiest**) plump and rounded.
chubbiness

chuck (verb: **chucks**, **chucking**, **chucked**)
chucker

chuckle (verb: **chuckles**, **chuckling**, **chuckled**)

chuff (verb: **chuffs**, **chuffing**, **chuffed**) [make the sound of a steam train]

chuffed »*adjective* (in informal English) delighted.

chuffing

chuffs

chug (verb: **chugs**, **chugging**, **chugged**)

chukka »*noun* one of six periods into which a game of polo is divided.

> ✓ **kk** not **ck**: the game of polo developed in Asia and **chukka** is a Hindi word meaning 'a circle or wheel'

chum
chummy

chump

chunk

chunky (adjective: **chunkier**, **chunkiest**)
chunkiness

church

churchgoer

churchman (plural **churchmen**)

churchwarden »*noun* one of two people in a Church of England parish who are elected to represent the congregation.

churchwoman (plural **churchwomen**)

churchyard

churl »*noun* an unfriendly or rude person.

churlish »*adjective* unfriendly and rude.
churlishly
churlishness

churn »*noun* **❶** a machine for making butter by shaking milk or cream. **❷** a large metal milk can.
»*verb* (**churns**, **churning**, **churned**) **❶** shake milk or cream in a churn to produce butter. **❷** (of liquid) move about vigorously. **❸** (**churn out**) produce something mechanically and in large quantities.

chute »*noun* **❶** a sloping channel for moving things to a lower level. **❷** a slide leading into a swimming pool.

> ℹ do not confuse **chute** with **shoot** meaning 'fire a gun', 'move rapidly', 'new part of a plant', etc.

chutney »*noun* (plural **chutneys**) a spicy sauce made of fruits or vegetables with vinegar, spices, and sugar.

chutzpah »*noun* shameless audacity.
– SAY **khuuts**-puh

> ✓ **chutzpah** (a Yiddish word) begins with **ch** and ends with **ah**

CIA »*abbreviation* Central Intelligence Agency.

ciabatta »*noun* a flat Italian bread made with olive oil.
– SAY chuh-**bah**-tuh

> ✓ **ci** not **ch**: **ciabatta**

cicada »*noun* an insect found in warm countries which makes a shrill droning noise.
– SAY si-**kah**-duh

CID »*abbreviation* Criminal Investigation Department.

cider »*noun* an alcoholic drink made from apple juice.

cigar

cigarette

> ✓ the ending is **ette**, not **et**: **cigarette**

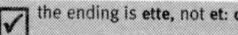

cilium »*noun* (plural **cilia**) (in biology) a microscopic hair-like structure, occurring on the surface of some cells.
– SAY sil-i-uhm [singular], sil-i-uh [plural]

> ✓ like many other words ending in **um** derived from Latin, **cilium** has a plural ending in **a**: **cilia**

cill another way of spelling SILL.

> ✓ **sill** is considered to be the correct spelling

C.-in-C. »*abbreviation* Commander-in-Chief.

cinch »*noun* (in informal English) something very easy or certain.

cinder »*noun* a piece of partly burnt coal or wood.

cine »*adjective* cinematographic.

cinema

cinematic »*adjective* relating to the cinema or like a film shown in a cinema.
cinematically

cinematography »*noun* the skilled use of the camera in film-making.
cinematographer

cinnamon »*noun* a spice made from the dried and rolled bark of an Asian tree.

> ✓ the ending is **mon**: **cinnamon**

cinquefoil »*noun* a plant having yellow flowers with five petals and leaves with five leaflets.
– SAY singk-foyl

cipher »*noun* ❶ a code. ❷ a key to a code. ❸ an unimportant person or thing.

> ✓ **cipher** can also be spelled **cypher**: both spellings are correct

circa »*preposition* approximately (used mainly with dates).
– SAY ser-kuh

circadian »*adjective* (of biological processes) happening on a twenty-four-hour cycle.
– SAY ser-kay-di-uhn

circle (verb: **circles, circling, circled**)

circlet »*noun* a circular band worn on the head as an ornament.

circling

circuit

circuit-breaker »*noun* an automatic safety device for stopping the flow of current in an electric circuit.

circuitous »*adjective* (of a route) long and indirect.

– SAY ser-kyoo-i-tuhss
circuitously
circuitousness

> ✓ the ending is **tous**, not **tious**: **circuitous**

circuitry »*noun* electric circuits collectively.
– SAY ser-ki-tri

circular
circularity

circularize »*verb* (**circularizes, circularizing, circularized**) distribute letters, leaflets, etc. to a number of recipients.

> ✓ many people prefer the alternative spellings **circularise, circularises**, etc.: both **s** and **z** spellings are correct

circulate (verb: **circulates, circulating, circulated**)

circulation

circulatory »*adjective* relating to the circulation of something, especially blood.
– SAY ser-kyoo-luh-tri or serk-yoo-lay-tuh-ri

circumcise »*verb* (**circumcises, circumcising, circumcised**) ❶ cut off a boy's or man's foreskin. ❷ cut off a girl's or woman's clitoris.
circumcision

> ✓ **circumcise** cannot be spelled with an **ize** ending

circumference »*noun* ❶ the boundary which encloses a circle. ❷ the distance around something.

> ✓ **ference** not **frence** or **ferance**: **circumference**

circumflex »*noun* (plural **circumflexes**) an accent (ˆ) placed over a vowel in some languages to show a change in the sound.

circumlocution »*noun* a way of saying something which uses more words than are necessary.
– SAY ser-kuhm-luh-**kyoo**-sh'n
circumlocutory

circumnavigate »*verb* (**circumnavigates, circumnavigating, circumnavigated**) sail all the way around something.
circumnavigation

circumscribe »*verb* (**circumscribes, circumscribing, circumscribed**) restrict the freedom or movements of someone.
circumscription

circumspect »*adjective* thoughtful and cautious about something.
circumspection
circumspectly

circumstance

circumstantial »*adjective* (of evidence) consisting of facts that make something

C

seem likely but do not prove it.
circumstantially

circumvent »*verb* (**circumvents, circumventing, circumvented**) find a way around an obstacle.
– SAY ser-kuhm-**vent**
circumvention

circus (plural **circuses**)

> ✓ do not double the **s** in **circuses**

cirrhosis »*noun* a disease of the liver.
– SAY si-**roh**-siss

> ✓ double **r** followed by an **h**: **cirrhosis**

cirrus »*noun* cloud forming wispy streaks high in the sky.
– SAY **sir**-ruhss

> ✓ like other cloud words, **cirrus** is from Latin, and the ending is **us** not **ous**. It is unusual to need a plural, but if you do it would be **cirri** (SAY **sir**-ree).

cissy another way of spelling SISSY.

Cistercian »*noun* a monk or nun of an order that is a stricter branch of the Benedictines.
– SAY si-**ster**-sh'n

> ✓ **cian** not **sian** or **tian**: **Cistercian**

cistern »*noun* ❶ a tank connected to a toilet, in which the water for flushing it is stored. ❷ an underground reservoir for rainwater.

citadel »*noun* a fortress protecting or overlooking a city.

citation »*noun* ❶ a quotation from or reference to a book or author. ❷ a mention of a praiseworthy act in an official report. ❸ a note accompanying an award, giving reasons for it.
– SAY sy-**tay**-sh'n

cite »*verb* (**cites, citing, cited**) make a quotation from or reference to a book or author.

> ℹ️ do not confuse **cite** with **site**, which means 'a place where something is located'

> ✓ drop the **e** when spelling **citing**

cities

citing

citizen
citizenship

citric acid »*noun* a sharp-tasting acid present in the juice of lemons and other sour fruits.

citron »*noun* the lemon-like fruit of an Asian tree.

citronella »*noun* a sweet-smelling natural oil used as an insect repellent and in perfume.

> ✓ one **n**, two **l**'s: **citronella**

citrus »*noun* (plural **citruses**) a fruit of a group that includes the citron, lemon, lime, orange, and grapefruit.

city (plural **cities**)

> ✓ plural: drop the **y** and add **ies**: **cities**

cityscape »*noun* a city landscape.

city slicker »*noun* a sophisticated person living in a city.

city state »*noun* a city and surrounding territory that forms an independent state.

civet »*noun* ❶ a cat native to Africa and Asia. ❷ a strong perfume obtained from the civet.
– SAY **siv**-it

> ✓ **-et** not **-it**: **civet**

civic »*adjective* having to do with a city or town.

civics »*plural noun* the study of the rights and duties of citizenship.

civil »*adjective* ❶ relating to the lives of ordinary people rather than to military or church matters. ❷ (of a court) dealing with personal legal matters rather than criminal offences. ❸ polite.
civilly

civil engineer »*noun* an engineer who designs public roads, bridges, dams, etc.

civilian »*noun* a person not in the armed services or the police force.
» *adjective* relating to a civilian.

civilisation

civilise another way of spelling CIVILIZE.

civility »*noun* (plural **civilities**) politeness.

> ✓ plural: drop the **y** and add **ies**: **civilities**

civilization »*noun* ❶ an advanced stage of human development in which people in a society behave well towards each other and share a common culture. ❷ the society, culture, and way of life of a particular area or period.

> ✓ **civilization** can also be spelled **civilisation**

civilize »*verb* (**civilizes, civilizing, civilized**) ❶ bring a person or group of people to an

advanced stage of social development.
❷ (**civilized**) polite and good-mannered.

> ✓ many people prefer the alternative spellings **civilise, civilises**, etc.: both **s** and **z** spellings are correct

civil liberties »*plural noun* a person's rights to freedom of action and speech within the law.

Civil List »*noun* (in the UK) an annual allowance voted by Parliament for the royal family's household expenses.

civilly

civil rights »*plural noun* the rights of citizens to political and social freedom.

civil servant »*noun* a member of the civil service.

civil service »*noun* the departments that carry out the work of the government.

civil war »*noun* a war between groups of people within the same country.

Civvy Street »*noun* (in informal English) civilian life.

CJD »*abbreviation* Creutzfeldt–Jakob disease, a fatal disease which affects the brain and is thought to be linked to BSE.

clack (verb: **clacks, clacking, clacked**) [sharp sound]

clad past and past participle of **CLOTHE**.

cladding »*noun* a protective or insulating covering or coating.

> ✓ double **d**: **cladding**

claim (verb: **claims, claiming, claimed**)

claimant »*noun* a person who makes a claim.

> ✓ **ant** not **ent**: **claimant**

claimed

claiming

claims

clairvoyant »*noun* a person who claims that they can see into the future or communicate with people who are dead or far away.
» *adjective* claiming to have these powers.
– SAY klair-**voy**-uhnt
  clairvoyance

> ✓ **clair** not **clar**, and **ant** not **ent**: **clairvoyant**

clam »*noun* a large shellfish with a hinged double shell.
» *verb* (**clams, clamming, clammed**) (**clam up**) stop talking suddenly.

> ✓ double the **m** in **clamming** and **clammed**

clamber (verb: **clambers, clambering, clambered**)

clammy »*adjective* (**clammier, clammiest**) ❶ unpleasantly damp and sticky. ❷ (of air) cold and damp.

clamour »*noun* ❶ a loud and confused noise. ❷ a loud protest or demand.
» *verb* (**clamours, clamouring, clamoured**) (of a group) make a clamour.
  clamorous

> ✓ **-our** not **-or** (except in **clamorous**): **clamour** (the other spellings with **-or** are American)

clamp (verb: **clamps, clamping, clamped**)

clampdown

clamped

clamping

clamps

clan »*noun* a group of related families, especially in the Scottish Highlands.

clandestine »*adjective* done secretly.
– SAY klan-**dess**-tin

> ✓ don't forget the **e** at the end: **clandestine**

clang (verb: **clangs, clanging, clanged**)
  clanger

clangour »*noun* a continuous clanging sound.
– SAY **klang**-ger

> ✓ **-our** not **-or**: **clangour** (the spelling without the **u** is American)

clangs

clank (verb: **clanks, clanking, clanked**)

clannish »*adjective* tending to exclude others outside the group.

> ✓ double **n**: **clannish**

clansman »*noun* (plural **clansmen**) a male member of a clan.

clap (verb: **claps, clapping, clapped**)

> ✓ double the **p** in **clapping** and **clapped**

clapped-out »*adjective* (in informal English) worn out from age or heavy use.

clapper »*noun* the moving part inside a bell.

clapperboard »*noun* hinged boards that are struck together at the beginning of filming so that the picture and sound machinery can be matched.

clapping

claps

claptrap »*noun* nonsense.

claque »*noun* ❶ a group of people hired to applaud or heckle a performer. ❷ a group of slavish followers.
– SAY klak

> ✓ **que** not **ck**: **claque**

claret »*noun* ❶ a red wine from Bordeaux in France. ❷ a purplish-red colour.
– SAY kla-ruht

clarify »*verb* (**clarifies**, **clarifying**, **clarified**) ❶ make something easier to understand. ❷ melt butter to separate out the impurities.
clarification

clarinet »*noun* a woodwind instrument with holes stopped by keys and a mouthpiece with a single reed.
clarinettist

> ✓ one **r**, one **n**: **clarinet**. Double the **t** in **clarinettist** (the spelling with a single **t** in the middle is American).

clarion »*noun* (a historical term) a war trumpet.
» *adjective* loud and clear.
– SAY kla-ri-uhn

clarity »*noun* ❶ the state or quality of being clear and easily understood. ❷ transparency or purity.

clash (verb: **clashes**, **clashing**, **clashed**)

clasp (verb: **clasps**, **clasping**, **clasped**)

class (plural **classes**; verb: **classes**, **classing**, **classed**)

classic »*adjective* ❶ judged over a period of time to be of the highest quality. ❷ typical.
» *noun* ❶ a work of art which is generally agreed to be of high quality. ❷ (**Classics**) the study of ancient Greek and Latin literature, philosophy, and history.

classical »*adjective* ❶ relating to the cultures of ancient Greece or Rome. ❷ (of a form of art or a language) representing the highest standard within a long-established form. ❸ (of music) belonging to a long-established form or style or (more specifically) written in the European tradition between approximately 1750 and 1830.

classicism »*noun* the use of a simple and elegant style characteristic of the art, architecture, or literature of ancient Greece and Rome.

> ✓ **cism** not **sism**: **classicism**

classicist »*noun* a person who studies Classics.

classier

classiest

classify (verb: **classifies**, **classifying**, **classified**)
classification
classified

classing

classless »*adjective* ❶ (of a society) not divided into social classes. ❷ not showing characteristics of a particular social class.

classmate

classroom

classy »*adjective* (**classier**, **classiest**) stylish and sophisticated.

clatter (verb: **clatters**, **clattering**, **clattered**)

clause »*noun* ❶ a group of words that includes a subject and a verb and forms part of a sentence. ❷ a part of a treaty, bill, or contract.

claustrophobia »*noun* extreme fear of being in a small or enclosed space.
– SAY kloss-truh-**foh**-bi-uh
claustrophobic

> ✓ **tro** not **tra**: **claustrophobia**

clavichord »*noun* a small early keyboard instrument with a soft tone.
– SAY klav-i-kord

> ✓ don't forget the **h** between the **c** and the **o**: **clavichord**

clavicle »*noun* the collarbone.

claw (verb: **claws**, **clawing**, **clawed**)

claw hammer »*noun* a hammer with one side of the head split and curved.

clawing

claws

clay

claymore »*noun* (a historical term) a large Scottish sword.

clay pigeon »*noun* a saucer-shaped piece of baked clay thrown up in the air as a target for shooting.

clean (adjective: **cleaner**, **cleanest**; verb: **cleans**, **cleaning**, **cleaned**)
cleaner
cleanly

clean-cut

cleaned

cleaner

cleanest

cleaning

cleanliness
– SAY klen-li-nuhss

cleanly

cleans

cleanse (verb: **cleanses**, **cleansing**, **cleansed**)
– SAY klenz

clean-shaven

cleansing

clear (adjective: **clearer**, **clearest**; verb: **clears**, **clearing**, **cleared**)
clearly

clearance »*noun* ❶ the action or the process of being cleared. ❷ official authorization for something to take place. ❸ clear space allowed for a thing to move past or under another.

> ✓ **ance** not **ence**: **clearance**

clear-cut »*adjective* sharply defined; easy to see or understand.

cleared

clearer

clearest

clearing

clearing house »*noun* a bankers' establishment where cheques and bills from member banks are exchanged.

clearly

clears

clear-sighted »*adjective* able to think clearly and make good judgements.

clearway »*noun* a main road other than a motorway on which vehicles are not allowed to stop.

cleat »*noun* ❶ a T-shaped or similar projection to which a rope may be attached. ❷ a projecting wedge on a tool, the sole of a boot, etc., to prevent slippage.

cleavage »*noun* ❶ a sharp division; a split. ❷ the hollow between a woman's breasts.

cleave[1] »*verb* (**cleaves**, **cleaving**, **clove** or **cleft** or **cleaved**; past participle **cloven** or **cleft** or **cleaved**) ❶ split along a natural grain or line. ❷ divide; split.

cleave[2] »*verb* (**cleaves**, **cleaving**, **cleaved**) ❶ stick fast to something. ❷ become strongly involved with or emotionally attached to someone.

cleaver »*noun* a tool with a heavy broad blade, used for chopping meat.

cleaves

cleaving

clef »*noun* (in music) a symbol placed at the end of a stave, to show the pitch of the notes written on it.

cleft past participle of **CLEAVE**[1]. »*adjective* split, divided, or partly divided into two.

» *noun* ❶ a split in rock or the ground. ❷ an indentation in a person's forehead or chin, or a hollow between parts of the body.

cleft palate »*noun* a split in the roof of the mouth which is present from birth.

clematis »*noun* an ornamental climbing plant.
– SAY **klem**-uh-tiss

clement »*adjective* ❶ (of weather) mild. ❷ merciful.
clemency

clementine »*noun* an orange-red variety of tangerine.
– SAY **klem**-uhn-tyn

clench »*verb* (**clenches**, **clenching**, **clenched**) ❶ close your fist or hold your teeth together tightly, in response to stress or anger. ❷ (of a set of muscles) contract sharply. ❸ grasp something tightly.

clerestory »*noun* (plural **clerestories**) the part high up above the nave and transepts in a large church, which has windows which light the space below.
– SAY **kleer**-stor-i

clergy »*noun* (plural **clergies**) the priests and ministers who carry out religious duties in the Christian Church.
– SAY **kler**-ji

clergyman (plural **clergymen**)

clergywoman (plural **clergywomen**)

cleric »*noun* a priest or religious leader.
– SAY **kle**-rik

clerical »*adjective* ❶ relating to the normal work of an office clerk. ❷ having to do with the clergy.

clerk »*noun* ❶ a person employed in an office or bank to keep records or accounts and to do other routine work. ❷ a person in charge of the records of a local council or court.

clever (adjective: **cleverer**, **cleverest**)
cleverly
cleverness

cliche »*noun* a phrase or an idea that has been used too much and is no longer fresh or interesting.
– SAY **klee**-shay
cliched

> ✓ **cliche** may also be spelled **cliché**, with an acute accent over the e (as in the original French)

click (verb: **clicks**, **clicking**, **clicked**)

client »*noun* a person using the services of a professional person or organization.

clientele »*noun* the clients or customers of a shop, restaurant, or professional service.
– SAY klee-on-**tel**

☑ don't forget the **e** at the end:
clientele. It is a French word,
sometimes written **clientèle** with a grave
accent.

cliff

cliffhanger »*noun* a situation in a story or
series of events that is exciting because its
outcome is uncertain.

climacteric »*noun* (in medicine) the period
in someone's life when their fertility has
started to decline; (in women) the
menopause.
– **say** kly-**mak**-tuh-rik

climactic »*adjective* forming an exciting
climax.
– **say** kly-**mak**-tik

ℹ️ do not confuse **climactic**, 'forming a
climax', with **climatic**, which means
'relating to climate'

climate »*noun* ❶ the general weather
conditions in an area over a long period.
❷ a general attitude or feeling among
people.

climatic »*adjective* relating to climate.
– **say** kly-**mat**-ik

ℹ️ do not confuse **climatic** with **climactic**,
which means 'forming a climax'

climax »*noun* (plural **climaxes**) ❶ the most
intense, exciting, or important point of
something. ❷ an orgasm.
»*verb* (**climaxes, climaxing, climaxed**) reach
a climax.

climb (verb: **climbs, climbing, climbed**)
[ascend]
climber
climbing

☑ do not confuse the spellings of **climb**
and **clime** meaning 'a region
considered in terms of its climate'

clime »*noun* a region considered in terms
of its climate: *sunnier climes*.

☑ do not confuse the spellings of **clime**
and **climb** meaning 'ascend'

clinch »*verb* (**clinches, clinching, clinched**)
❶ settle a contract or contest. ❷ settle
something that has been uncertain or
undecided.
»*noun* ❶ a tight hold in a struggle or
scuffle. ❷ a tight embrace.
clincher

cling (verb: **clings, clinging, clung**)

cling film »*noun* a thin plastic film used to
wrap or cover food.

clingier

clingiest

clinging

clings

clingy (adjective: **clingier, clingiest**)

clinic »*noun* a place where specialized
medical treatment or advice is given.

clinical »*adjective* ❶ relating to the
observation and treatment of patients
(rather than theoretical studies).
❷ efficient and showing no emotion.
❸ (of a place) bare, functional, and clean.

clink (verb: **clinks, clinking, clinked**)

clinker »*noun* the stony remains from
burnt coal or from a furnace.

clinking

clinks

clip (verb: **clips, clipping, clipped**)

☑ double the **p** in **clipping** and **clipped**

clip art »*noun* pre-drawn pictures and
symbols provided with word-processing
software and drawing packages.

clipboard

clipped

clipper »*noun* a fast sailing ship of 19th-
century design.

clippers »*noun* an instrument for clipping.

clipping

clips

clique »*noun* a small group of people who
spend time together and do not allow
others to join them.
– **say** *rhymes with* seek
cliquey
cliquish

☑ the ending is **que**: **clique**. The **e** is
dropped in **cliquish** but not in **cliquey**.

clitoris »*noun* (plural **clitorises**) a small
sensitive part of the female genitals at the
front end of the vulva.
– **say** kli-**tuh**-riss

ℹ️ a Greek plural **clitorides** (**say** kli-tuh-
ri-deez) is sometimes used in
medical writing

cloak (verb: **cloaks, cloaking, cloaked**)

cloak-and-dagger »*adjective* concealed or
mysterious.

cloaked

cloaking

cloakroom

cloaks

clobber (verb: **clobbers, clobbering,
clobbered**)

cloche »*noun* ❶ a glass or plastic cover for
protecting outdoor plants. ❷ a woman's
bell-shaped hat.

– **SAY** klosh

✓ don't forget the **e** at the end: **cloche**

clock (verb: **clocks, clocking, clocked**)

clockwise

clockwork

clod »*noun* a lump of earth.

clodhopper »*noun* (in informal English) ❶ a large, heavy shoe. ❷ a foolish, awkward, or clumsy person.

clog (verb: **clogs, clogging, clogged**)

cloisonne »*noun* enamel work in which different colours are separated by strips of flattened wire placed edgeways on a metal backing.
– **SAY** klwah-zon-ay

✓ **cloisonne** can also be spelled **cloisonné**, with an acute accent above the **e** (as in the original French)

cloister »*noun* a covered passage round an open court in a convent, monastery, college, or cathedral.

cloistered »*adjective* ❶ having or enclosed by a cloister. ❷ protected from the outside world.

clomp (verb: **clomps, clomping, clomped**)

clone »*noun* ❶ an animal or plant created from the cells of another, to which it is genetically identical. ❷ a copy or double.
»*verb* (**clones, cloning, cloned**) ❶ create something as a clone. ❷ make an identical copy of something.

clop (verb: **clops, clopping, clopped**)

✓ double the **p** in **clopping** and **clopped**

close[1] (adjective: **closer, closest**) [near]
closely
closeness

close[2] (verb: **closes, closing, closed**) [shut]

closed-circuit television »*noun* a television system used to observe people within a building, shopping centre, etc., in which signals are sent by cable.

closed shop »*noun* a place of work where all employees must belong to a particular trade union.

closer

closes

close season »*noun* a period when fishing or hunting is officially forbidden or when a particular sport is not played.

closest

closet »*noun* a tall cupboard or wardrobe.
»*adjective* secret.

»*verb* (**closets, closeting, closeted**) shut away in private to talk to someone or to be alone.

✓ do not double the **t** in **closeting** and **closeted**

close-up

closing

closure »*noun* ❶ the closing of something. ❷ a device that closes or seals.

clot »*noun* ❶ a lump that is formed when a thick liquid substance dries or becomes thicker. ❷ (in informal English) a foolish or clumsy person.
»*verb* (**clots, clotting, clotted**) form into clots.

✓ double the **t** in **clotting** and **clotted**

cloth »*noun* (plural **cloths**) ❶ fabric made from a soft fibre such as wool or cotton. ❷ a piece of cloth for a particular purpose. ❸ (**the cloth**) ministers of the Church.

clothe »*verb* (**clothes, clothing, clothed** or **clad**) ❶ provide someone with clothes. ❷ (**be clothed in**) be dressed in.

✓ drop the **e** when spelling **clothing**

clothes

✓ remember the **e** to distinguish **clothes** 'things to wear' from **cloths** 'pieces of fabric'

clothier »*noun* a person who makes or sells clothes or cloth.
– **SAY** kloh-*th*i-er

clothing

cloths

clots

clotted

clotted cream »*noun* thick cream obtained by heating milk slowly and then allowing it to cool while the cream rises to the top in lumps.

clotting

cloud (verb: **clouds, clouding, clouded**)

cloudburst »*noun* a sudden violent rainstorm.

cloud cuckoo land »*noun* a state of unrealistic fantasy.

clouded

cloudier

cloudiest

clouding

cloudless

clouds

cloudy (adjective: **cloudier, cloudiest**)

clout (in informal English) **»noun** ❶ a heavy blow. ❷ influence or power.
» verb (**clouts, clouting, clouted**) hit hard.

clove[1] **»noun** ❶ the dried flower bud of a tropical tree, used as a spice. ❷ one of the small bulbs making up a larger bulb of garlic or a shallot.

clove[2] past of **CLEAVE**[1].

clove hitch »noun a knot by which a rope is secured to a spar or another rope.

cloven past participle of **CLEAVE**[1].

cloven hoof »noun the divided hoof of animals such as cattle, sheep, goats, antelopes, and deer.

clover »noun a plant with white or pink flowers and leaves with three lobes.

clown (verb: **clowns, clowning, clowned**)
clownish

cloying »adjective disgusting or sickening because too sweet or sentimental.

club (verb: **clubs, clubbing, clubbed**)
clubber

> ✓ double the **b** in **clubbing, clubbed,** and **clubber**

clubbable »adjective sociable and popular.

clubbed

clubber

clubbing

club class »noun the class of seating on an aircraft designed for business travellers.

club foot »noun a deformed foot which is twisted so that the sole cannot be placed flat on the ground.

clubhouse

clubs

club sandwich »noun a sandwich consisting typically of chicken and bacon, tomato, and lettuce, layered between three slices of bread.

cluck (verb: **clucks, clucking, clucked**)

clue

clued-up »adjective well informed about a particular subject.

clueless »adjective not able to understand or do something.

clump (verb: **clumps, clumping, clumped**)

clumpy »adjective (of shoes or boots) heavy and inelegant.

clumsy (adjective: **clumsier, clumsiest**)
clumsily

clung past and past participle of **CLING**.

clunk (verb: **clunks, clunking, clunked**)

cluster (verb: **cluster, clustering, clustered**)

clutch (verb: **clutches, clutching, clutched**)

clutter (verb: **clutters, cluttering, cluttered**)

CO »abbreviation Commanding Officer.

Co. »abbreviation ❶ company. ❷ county.

c/o »abbreviation care of.

coach (verb: **coaches, coaching, coached**)

coachload

coachwork »noun the bodywork of a road or railway vehicle.

coagulant »noun a substance that causes a liquid to change to thicken or become solid.
– SAY koh-ag-yoo-luhnt

> ✓ ant not ent: coagulant

coagulate »verb (**coagulates, coagulating, coagulated**) (of a liquid) thicken or become solid.
– SAY koh-ag-yoo-layt
coagulation

coal

coalesce »verb (**coalesces, coalescing, coalesced**) come or bring something together to form a single mass or whole.
– SAY koh-uh-less
coalescence

coalface

coalfield »noun a large area containing deposits of coal.

coalition »noun a government made up of two political parties who have agreed to work together.
– SAY koh-uh-li-sh'n

coal tar »noun a thick black liquid distilled from coal.

coal tit »noun a small songbird with a grey back and a black cap and throat.

> ✓ coal not cole: coal tit

coarse (adjective: **coarser, coarsest**)
[rough]
coarsely
coarseness

> ℹ do not confuse **coarse** with **course,** which means 'a direction'

coarse fish »plural noun freshwater fish other than salmon and trout.

coarsely

coarsen (verb: **coarsens, coarsening, coarsened**)

coarseness

coarser [more coarse]

coarsest

coast (verb: **coasts**, **coasting**, **coasted**)
coastal

coaster »*noun* a small mat for a glass.

coastguard »*noun* an organization or person that keeps watch over coastal waters.

coasting

coastline

coasts

coat (verb: **coats**, **coating**, **coated**)

coating

coat of arms »*noun* a design used on a shield and elsewhere as a special symbol of a family, city, or organization.

coats

coat-tail »*noun* one of the flaps formed by the back of a tailcoat.

coax »*verb* (**coaxes**, **coaxing**, **coaxed**)
❶ gently persuade to do something.
❷ gently guide or move something.
– ꜱᴀʏ kohks

 ax not **axe**: **coax**

coaxial »*adjective* (of a cable) having two wires, one wrapped around the other but separated by insulation.
– ꜱᴀʏ koh-**ak**-si-uhl

coaxing

cob »*noun* ❶ a loaf of bread. ❷ the central part of an ear of maize.

cobalt »*noun* a silvery-white metal.
– ꜱᴀʏ koh-bolt

 alt not **olt**: **cobalt**

cobber »*noun* (in informal Australian English) a companion or friend.

cobble[1] »*noun* a small round stone used to cover road surfaces.
cobbled

cobble[2] »*verb* (**cobbles**, **cobbling**, **cobbled**)
(**cobble together**) make something up roughly from materials that happen to be available.

 drop the **e** to spell **cobbling**

cobbler »*noun* ❶ a person whose job is mending shoes. ❷ a fruit pie with a cake-like crust.

cobbles

cobblestone

cobbling

cobnut »*noun* a hazelnut or filbert.

cobra »*noun* a highly poisonous snake native to Africa and Asia.

– ꜱᴀʏ koh-bruh

cobweb

coca »*noun* a tropical American shrub grown for its leaves, which are the source of cocaine.
– ꜱᴀʏ koh-kuh

cocaine
– ꜱᴀʏ koh-**kayn**

 do not forget the **i**: **cocaine**

coccyx »*noun* (plural **coccyxes**) a small triangular bone at the base of the spine.
– ꜱᴀʏ kok-siks [singular], **kok**-sik-siz [plural]

 note the double **c** in the middle: **coccyx**
a Greek plural **coccyges** (ꜱᴀʏ kok-si-jeez) is sometimes used in medical writing

cochineal »*noun* a scarlet dye used for colouring food.
– ꜱᴀʏ koch-i-**neel**

cochlea »*noun* (plural **cochleae**) the spiral cavity of the inner ear.
– ꜱᴀʏ kok-li-uh [singular], **kok**-li-ee [plural]

 the plural of **cochlea** is spelled with an **e** (like the original Latin): **cochleae**

cock (verb: **cocks**, **cocking**, **cocked**)

cockade »*noun* a rosette or knot of ribbons worn on a hat as part of a uniform.
– ꜱᴀʏ kok-**ayd**

cock-a-hoop »*adjective* extremely pleased.

cock-a-leekie »*noun* a soup traditionally made in Scotland with chicken and leeks.

cock and bull story »*noun* (in informal English) an unbelievable story.

cockatoo »*noun* a parrot with a crest.
– ꜱᴀʏ kok-uh-**too**

cockcrow »*noun* dawn.

cocked

cockerel

 there is only one **l**: **cockerel**

cocker spaniel

cock-eyed

cockfighting »*noun* the illegal sport of setting two cocks to fight each other.

cockier

cockiest

cocking

cockle »*noun* an edible shellfish with a ribbed shell.

cockney (plural **cockneys**)
– ꜱᴀʏ kok-ni

✓ the plural of **cockney** simply adds an s: **cockneys**

cockpit

cockroach

cocks

cockscomb »*noun* the crest or comb of a domestic cock.

ℹ️ do not confuse **cockscomb** with **coxcomb**, which is an old word meaning 'a vain and conceited man'. The two terms were originally the same word.

cocksure »*adjective* confident in an arrogant way.

cocktail

cock-up (plural **cock-ups**)

cocky (adjective: **cockier**, **cockiest**)

cocoa

✓ note the **oa** at the end: **cocoa**

coconut

✓ o not oa in the middle: **coconut**

coconut shy

cocoon »*noun* ❶ a silky case spun by the larva of many insects, which protects it while it is turning into an adult. ❷ something that envelops you in a protective or comforting way.
»*verb* (**cocoons**, **cocooning**, **cocooned**) wrap in a cocoon.
– **say** kuh-koon

✓ single c in the middle, followed by double o: **cocoon**

COD »*abbreviation* cash on delivery.

cod

coda »*noun* an extra passage marking the end of a piece of music.
– **say** koh-duh

coddle »*verb* (**coddles**, **coddling**, **coddled**) give someone too much care and attention.

✓ drop the e when spelling **coddling**

code (verb: **codes**, **coding**, **coded**)

✓ drop the e when spelling **coding**

codeine »*noun* a painkilling drug obtained from morphine.
– **say** koh-deen

✓ the ending is **eine** not **een**, with i after e: **codeine**

codes

codex »*noun* (plural **codices** or **codexes**) an ancient manuscript text in the form of a book.
– **say** koh-deks [singular], koh-di-seez or koh-dek-siz [plural]

✓ the plural of **codex** can be either **codices** (as in Latin) or **codexes**: both are correct

codfish

codger »*noun* (in informal English) an elderly man.

codicil »*noun* a part added to a will that explains or alters an earlier part.
– **say** koh-di-sil

✓ there is only one l: **codicil**

codify »*verb* (**codifies**, **codifying**, **codified**) arrange a set of rules as a formal code.
– **say** koh-di-fl

coding

cod liver oil

codpiece »*noun* (a historical term) a pouch worn by a man over his trousers, covering the area of the penis.

codswallop

co-education »*noun* the teaching of both boys and girls together in the same schools.
co-educational

coefficient »*noun* ❶ (in mathematics) a quantity which is placed before another which it multiplies (e.g. 4 in $4x^2$). ❷ (in physics) a number that represents some physical property.
– **say** koh-i-fi-sh'nt

coelacanth »*noun* a large sea fish, formerly thought to be extinct, having a tail with three lobes.
– **say** seel-uh-kanth

✓ note the **coe** at the beginning: **coelacanth**

coeliac disease »*noun* a condition in which the small intestine is very sensitive to gluten and cannot digest food properly.
– **say** see-li-ak

✓ **coe** not **ce**: **coeliac** (the spelling **celiac** is American)

coerce »*verb* (**coerces**, **coercing**, **coerced**) force someone to do something that they do not want to do.
– **say** koh-erss
coercion
coercive

✓ drop the e when spelling **coercing**, **coercion**, and **coercive**

coeval »*adjective* having the same age.

» *noun* a person of roughly the same age as you are.
– **say** koh-ee-vuhl

coexist »*verb* (**coexists, coexisting, coexisted**) ❶ exist at the same time or in the same place. ❷ be together in harmony.
coexistence

C. of E. »*abbreviation* Church of England.

coffee

 ff followed by ee: **coffee**

coffee-table book »*noun* a large book with high-quality illustrations.

coffer »*noun* a small chest for holding money or valuable items.

coffin

cog »*noun* ❶ a wheel or bar with projections on its edge, which transfers motion by engaging with projections on another wheel or bar. ❷ one of these projections.

cogent »*adjective* (of an argument) clear, logical, and convincing.
– **say** koh-juhnt
cogency
cogently

 ent not ant: **cogent**

cogitate »*verb* (**cogitates, cogitating, cogitated**) think carefully about something.
– **say** koj-i-tayt
cogitation

 drop the e when spelling **cogitating**

cognac »*noun* brandy made in Cognac in western France.
– **say** kon-yak

although it is not pronounced, there is a **g** in the middle: **cognac**

cognisance another way of spelling **COGNIZANCE**.

cognition »*noun* the acquiring of knowledge through thought, experience, and the senses.
– **say** kog-**ni**-sh'n

cognitive »*adjective* having to do with cognition.

cognizance »*noun* knowledge or awareness.
– **say** kog-ni-zuhnss

cognizance can also be spelled **cognisance**: both spellings are correct
ance not **ence**: **cognizance**

cognoscenti »*plural noun* people who are well informed about a particular subject.
– **say** kon-yuh-**shen**-ti

although it is not pronounced, there is a **g** before the first **n**: **cognoscenti**. It is an Italian word meaning 'people who know'.

cogwheel

cohabit »*verb* (**cohabits, cohabiting, cohabited**) live together and have a sexual relationship without being married.
cohabitation

do not double the **t** to spell **cohabiting** and **cohabited**

cohere »*verb* (**coheres, cohering, cohered**) hold firmly together; form a whole.
– **say** koh-**heer**

drop the **e** when spelling **cohering**

coherent »*adjective* ❶ (of an argument or theory) logical and consistent. ❷ able to speak clearly and logically.

ent not ant: **coherent**

cohesion

cohesive »*adjective* holding or making something hold together.

cohort »*noun* ❶ an ancient Roman military unit equal to one tenth of a legion. ❷ a band of people.
– **say** koh-hort

coif »*noun* a close-fitting cap worn by nuns under a veil.
» *verb* (**coifs, coiffing, coiffed**) arrange someone's hair.
– **say** koyf [noun], kwahf or kwof [verb]

double the **f** when spelling **coiffed** and **coiffing**

coiffure »*noun* a person's hairstyle.
– **say** kwah-**fyoor**
coiffured

coil (verb: **coils, coiling, coiled**)

coin (verb: **coins, coining, coined**)

coinage

age not ege: **coinage**

coincide (verb: **coincides, coinciding, coincided**)
– **say** koh-in-**syd**

coincidence
– **say** koh-**in**-si-duhnss
coincidental

 ence not ance: **coincidence**

coined

coining
coins

Cointreau »*noun* (trademark) a liqueur with an orange flavour.
– SAY kwun-troh

coir »*noun* fibre from the outer husk of a coconut, used in potting compost and for making ropes and matting.
– SAY koy-uh

coitus »*noun* sexual intercourse.
– SAY koh-i-tuhss
coital

coitus interruptus »*noun* sexual intercourse in which the man withdraws his penis before he ejaculates so that the woman does not become pregnant.
– SAY in-ter-**rup**-tuhss

coke[1] »*noun* a solid fuel made by heating coal in the absence of air.

coke[2] »*noun* (in informal English) cocaine.

col »*noun* the lowest point of a ridge between two mountain peaks.

> ☑ only one l: col is a French word literally meaning 'neck'

cola »*noun* a brown carbonated drink containing a flavouring made from cola nuts.

colander »*noun* a bowl with holes in it, used to strain off liquid from food.
– SAY kul-uhn-der

> ☑ col- not cul-, and -and- not -ind-: colander

cold
coldly
coldness

cold-blooded

cold-call »*verb* (cold-calls, cold-calling, cold-called) visit or telephone someone without their agreement in an attempt to sell them goods or services.

cold cream »*noun* a cream for cleaning and softening the skin.

cold frame »*noun* a frame with a glass top in which small plants are grown and protected.

cold-hearted
coldly
coldness

cold sore »*noun* an inflamed blister beside the mouth, caused by a virus.

cold turkey »*noun* unpleasant feelings experienced by someone who has suddenly stopped taking a drug to which they are addicted.

cold war »*noun* a state of hostility between the countries of the Soviet bloc and the Western powers after the Second World War.

coleslaw »*noun* a dish of shredded raw cabbage and carrots mixed with mayonnaise.

> ☑ cole- not cold-: coleslaw

colic »*noun* severe pain in the abdomen caused by wind or obstruction in the intestines.
colicky

> ☑ single l and no k in colic, although there is a k in colicky

coliseum »*noun* a large theatre, cinema, or stadium.

> ☑ colis not coloss: coliseum (the name colosseum is applied only to the amphitheatre in Rome)

collaborate »*verb* (collaborates, collaborating, collaborated) ❶ work together on an activity. ❷ cooperate with your country's enemy.
– SAY kuh-**lab**-uh-rayt
collaboration
collaborative
collaborator

> ☑ double l, and bor not ber: collaborate

collage »*noun* a form of art in which various materials are arranged and stuck to a backing.
– SAY kol-lah*zh*

collagen »*noun* a protein found in animal tissue.
– SAY kol-luh-juhn

collapse (verb: collapses, collapsing, collapsed)

> ☑ drop the e when spelling collapsing

collapsible

> ☑ -ible not -able: collapsible

collar

> ☑ the ending is ar not er: collar

collarbone »*noun* one of the pair of bones joining the breastbone to the shoulder blades.

collate »*verb* (collates, collating, collated) collect and combine texts or information.
– SAY kuh-**layt**
collation

collateral »*noun* something that you promise to give up if you are unable to repay a loan.
» *adjective* additional but less important; secondary.
– say kuh-**lat**-uh-ruhl

colleague

✓ note the **gue** at the end: **colleague**

collect[1] (verb: **collects, collecting, collected**) [gather together]
– say kuh-**lekt**

collect[2] »*noun* a short prayer used in church on a particular day.
– say **kol**-lekt

collectable

✓ **collectable** can also be spelled **collectible**: both spellings are correct

collected

collectible another way of spelling **COLLECTABLE**.

collecting

collection

collective »*adjective* ❶ done by or belonging to all the members of a group. ❷ taken as a whole.
» *noun* a small business or project owned and shared by the people who work for it.
collectively

collective bargaining »*noun* negotiation of conditions of employment by an organized body of employees.

collectively

collective noun »*noun* a noun that refers to a group of individuals (e.g. *staff, family*).

collectivism »*noun* the giving of priority to a group over each individual in it.

collector

✓ -**or** not -**er**: **collector**

collects

college

✓ there is no **d** in **college**

collegiate »*adjective* ❶ having to do with a college or college students. ❷ (of a university) composed of different colleges.
– say kuh-**lee**-ji-uht

collide (verb: **collides, colliding, collided**)

collie »*noun* (plural **collies**) a sheepdog with a pointed nose and long hair.

✓ the ending is **ie**, not **y**: **collie**

collier »*noun* a coal miner.
– say **kol**-li-er

colliery »*noun* (plural **collieries**) a coal mine.

collision

colloquia plural of **COLLOQUIUM**.

colloquial »*adjective* (of language) used in ordinary conversation.
– say kuh-**loh**-kwi-uhl
colloquially

colloquialism »*noun* a colloquial word or phrase.

colloquially

colloquium »*noun* (plural **colloquiums** or **colloquia**) an academic conference or seminar.
– say kuh-**loh**-kwi-uhm

✓ the plural can be either **colloquia** (like the original Latin) or **colloquiums**

colloquy »*noun* (plural **colloquies**) a conference or conversation.
– say **kol**-luh-kwi

collude »*verb* (**colludes, colluding, colluded**) have a secret plan with someone.
– say kuh-**lood**

collusion »*noun* secret cooperation designed to cheat or deceive someone.

collywobbles

colobus »*noun* (plural **colobus**) a slender African monkey with silky fur.
– say **kol**-uh-buhss

cologne »*noun* a type of light perfume.
– say kuh-**lohn**

✓ do not forget the **g**: **cologne**

Colombian [of Colombia]
– say kuh-**lum**-bi-uhn

✓ **lom** not **lum**: **Colombian**

colon[1] »*noun* a punctuation mark (:) used before a list of items, a quotation, or an expansion or explanation.

colon[2] »*noun* the main part of the large intestine, which leads to the rectum.
colonic

colonel »*noun* a rank of officer in the army and in the US air force, above a lieutenant colonel.

✓ be careful writing this word which is pronounced **ker-nuhl**, but is spelled very differently: **colonel**

colonial »*adjective* having to do with a colony or colonialism.
» *noun* a person who lives in a colony.

colonialism »*noun* the practice of acquiring and controlling another country and occupying it with settlers.
  colonialist

colonic

colonies

colonise another way of spelling **COLONIZE**.

colonist »*noun* an inhabitant of a colony.

colonize »*verb* (**colonizes, colonizing, colonized**) ❶ make a colony in a territory. ❷ take over a place for your own use.
  colonization

> ✓ many people prefer the alternative spellings **colonise, colonises**, etc., and **colonisation**: both **s** and **z** spellings are correct

colonnade »*noun* a row of evenly spaced columns supporting a roof.
– SAY kol-uh-**nayd**

> ✓ single **l** but double **n**: **colonnade**

colony (plural **colonies**)

> ✓ plural: drop the **y** and add **ies**: **colonies**

color American spelling of **COLOUR**.

Colorado beetle »*noun* an American beetle whose larvae destroy potato plants.

coloration »*noun* the colours and markings of a plant or animal.

> ✓ **coloration** can also be spelled **colouration**: both spellings are correct

coloratura »*noun* singing in opera which involves a very elaborate version of the melody.
– SAY kol-uh-ruh-**tyoor**-uh

colored American spelling of **COLOURED**.

colorful American spelling of **COLOURFUL**.

coloring American spelling of **COLOURING**.

colorist American spelling of **COLOURIST**.

colorless American spelling of **COLOURLESS**.

colossal

> ✓ single **l**, double **s**: **colossal**

colosseum see the note at **COLISEUM**.

colossus »*noun* (plural **colossi** or **colossuses**) a person or thing of enormous size.
– SAY kuh-**loss**-uhss [singular], kuh-**loss**-I or kuh-**loss**-uhss-iz [plural]

> ✓ the plural can be formed with an **i** (as in Latin) or by adding **es**: **colossi** or **colossuses**

colostomy »*noun* (plural **colostomies**) a surgical operation in which the large

intestine is shortened and the cut end is diverted to an opening in the wall of the abdomen.
– SAY kuh-**loss**-tuh-mi

colour (verb: **colours, colouring, coloured**)

> ✓ remember the **u**: **colour** (**color, colors**, etc. are American spellings)

colouration another way of spelling **COLORATION**.

colour-blind

coloured

> ℹ in reference to skin colour, **coloured** is now normally considered to be offensive

colour-fast »*adjective* dyed in colours that will not fade or be washed out.

colourful
  colourfully

> ✓ -**ful** not -**full**: **colourful**

colouring

colourist »*noun* an artist or designer who uses colour in a special or skilful way.

colourless

colours

colour sergeant »*noun* a rank of officer in the Royal Marines, below warrant officer.

colt »*noun* a young male horse.

coltish »*adjective* energetic but awkward in movement or behaviour.

coltsfoot »*noun* a plant with yellow flowers and heart-shaped leaves.

columbine »*noun* a plant with purplish-blue flowers.
– SAY kol-uhm-byn

column
  columnar

> ✓ watch for the silent **n** at the end of **column** (no longer silent in **columnar** and **columnist**)

columnist

coma »*noun* a state of long-lasting deep unconsciousness.
– SAY koh-muh

Comanche »*noun* (plural **Comanche** or **Comanches**) a member of an American Indian people of the south-western US.
– SAY kuh-**man**-chi

> ✓ **che**, not **chee** at the end: **Comanche**

comatose »*adjective* of or in a state of coma.
– SAY koh-muh-**tohss**

comb (verb: **combs, combing, combed**)

combat (verb: combats, combating, combated or combats, combatting, combatted)

 the verb can either keep a single t: combating and combated, or double the t: combatting, combatted (both spellings are correct)

combatant »*noun* a person or group engaged in fighting during a war.
» *adjective* engaged in fighting.
– SAY kom-buh-tuhnt

 ant not ent: combatant

combated

combating

combative »*adjective* ready or eager to fight or argue.
– SAY kom-buh-tiv

combats

combatted

combatting

combat trousers »*plural noun* loose trousers with large pockets halfway down each leg.

combe »*noun* a short valley or hollow on a hillside or coastline.
– SAY koom

 combe can also be spelled coombe: both spellings are correct

combed

combination

combine (verb: combines, combining, combined)

combine harvester

combing

combo »*noun* (plural combos) a small jazz, rock, or pop band.

 the plural of combo has os not oes: combos

combs

combust »*verb* (combusts, combusting, combusted) catch fire or burn.
– SAY kuhm-bust

combustible »*adjective* able to catch fire and burn easily.

 -ible not -able: combustible

combusting

combustion »*noun* the process of burning.

combusts

come (verb: comes, coming, came; past participle come)

comeback

comedian

comedic »*adjective* having to do with comedy.
– SAY kuh-mee-dik

comedienne »*noun* a female comedian.
– SAY kuh-mee-di-en

comedies

comedown

comedy »*noun* (plural comedies) ❶ a film, play, or other entertainment intended to make people laugh. ❷ a light-hearted play in which the characters finally triumph over difficult situations.

 plural: drop the y and add ies: comedies

comely »*adjective* (comelier, comeliest) (an old word) pleasant to look at.
– SAY kum-li
comeliness

come-on

comes

comestibles »*plural noun* items of food.
– SAY kuh-mess-ti-b'lz

comet »*noun* an object moving around the solar system which consists of ice and dust and sometimes shows a long tail.
cometary

comeuppance »*noun* (get your comeuppance) get the punishment or fate that you deserve.

comfier

comfiest

comfort (verb: comforts, comforting, comforted)

comfortable
comfortably

comforted

comforter

comforting

comforts

comfy »*adjective* (comfier, comfiest) (in informal English) comfortable.

comic »*adjective* ❶ causing laughter; amusing. ❷ having to do with comedy.
» *noun* ❶ a comedian. ❷ a children's magazine that contains cartoons.

comical
comically

coming

comity »*noun* friendly relations between countries.
– SAY kom-i-ti

 note that this is a different word from committee

comma »*noun* a punctuation mark (,) showing a pause between parts of a sentence or separating items in a list.

command (verb: **commands, commanding, commanded**)

commandant »*noun* an officer in charge of a force or institution.
– SAY kom-uhn-dant

commanded

commandeer »*verb* (**commandeers, commandeering, commandeered**) officially take possession of something for military purposes.
– SAY kom-uhn-**deer**

commander

commander-in-chief (plural **commanders-in-chief**)

commanding

commandment »*noun* a rule held to be laid down by God, especially one of the Ten Commandments.

commando »*noun* (plural **commandos**) ❶ a soldier trained for carrying out raids. ❷ a unit of such troops.

> ☑ the plural of **commando**, a Portuguese word, has **os** not **oes**: **commandos**

commands

commemorate »*verb* (**commemorates, commemorating, commemorated**) honour the memory of a person or event.
commemoration

> ☑ the first **m** is double, but not the second: **commemorate**

commemorative »*adjective* acting as a mark or memorial of an event or person.
– SAY kuh-**mem**-muh-ruh-tiv

commence (verb: **commences, commencing, commenced**)
commencement

commend »*verb* (**commends, commending, commended**) ❶ praise formally or officially. ❷ present something as being suitable or good; recommend.

commendable »*adjective* deserving praise.
commendably

commendation

commended

commending

commends

commensurable »*adjective* ❶ able to be measured by the same standard.
❷ (**commensurable to**) proportionate to.
– SAY kuh-**men**-shuh-ruh-b'l

commensurate »*adjective* corresponding or in proportion: *salary will be commensurate with age and experience.*
– SAY kuh-**men**-shuh-ruht

comment (verb: **comments, commenting, commented**)

commentary »*noun* (plural **commentaries**) ❶ the expression of opinions about an event or situation. ❷ a spoken description of an event as it happens, broadcast on radio or television. ❸ a set of explanatory notes on a text.

> ☑ double **m**, and the ending is **ary**: **commentary**
> plural: drop the **y** and add **ies**: **commentaries**

commentate (verb: **commentates, commentating, commentated**)

commentator

> ☑ **-or** not **-er**: **commentator**

commented

commenting

comments

commerce »*noun* the activity of buying and selling, especially on a large scale.

commercial
commerciality
commercially

commercialise another way of spelling **COMMERCIALIZE**.

commercialism »*noun* emphasis on making as much profit as possible.

commerciality

commercialize »*verb* (**commercializes, commercializing, commercialized**) manage something in a way designed to make a profit.
commercialization

> ☑ many people prefer the alternative spellings **commercialise, commercialises**, etc., and **commercialisation**: both **s** and **z** spellings are correct

commercially

commingle »*verb* (**commingles, commingling, commingled**) mix; blend.
– SAY kom-**ming**-g'l

> ☑ double **m**: **commingle**

commiserate »*verb* (**commiserates, commiserating, commiserated**) express sympathy or pity; sympathize.
– SAY kuh-**miz**-uh-rayt
commiseration

double m, single s: **commiserate**, **commiseration**

commissar »*noun* a Communist official responsible for political education.
– SAY kom-mi-**sar**

commission (verb: **commissions**, **commissioning**, **commissioned**)

 remember, double m and double s: **commission**

commissionaire »*noun* a uniformed door attendant at a hotel, theatre, or other building.
– SAY kuh-mi-shuh-**nair**

 only a single n in **commissionaire**

commissioned

commissioner »*noun* ❶ a member of a commission. ❷ a representative of the supreme authority in an area.

commissioning

commissions

commit (verb: **commits**, **committing**, **committed**)

 commit and **commits** have a double m and single t, but remember to double the t in **committed** and **committing**

commitment

 double m, but single t: **commitment**

commits

committal »*noun* the sending of someone to prison or psychiatric hospital, or for trial.

committed

committee

 committee has a double m, double t, and double e
do not confuse **committee**, which refers to a group of people appointed for a particular purpose, with **comity**, which means 'peaceful relations between countries'

committing

commode »*noun* a piece of furniture containing a concealed chamber pot.

commodify »*verb* (**commodifies**, **commodifying**, **commodified**) treat something as a commodity.
– SAY kuh-**mod**-i-fI
commodification

commodious »*adjective* roomy and comfortable.
– SAY kuh-**moh**-di-uhss

commodity »*noun* (plural **commodities**)
❶ a raw material or agricultural product that can be bought and sold. ❷ something useful or valuable.
– SAY kuh-**mod**-i-ti

 two m's in **commodity**
plural: drop the y and add **ies**: **commodities**

commodore »*noun* ❶ the naval rank above captain but below rear admiral. ❷ the president of a yacht club.

common (adjective: **commoner**, **commonest**)
commonly
commonness

commonality »*noun* the sharing of features.

 the ending of **commonality** is **ality**, not **alty**; **commonalty** is an old word meaning 'the common people'

common denominator »*noun* ❶ (in mathematics) a number that can be divided exactly by all the numbers below the line in a set of fractions. ❷ a feature shared by all members of a group.

commoner[1] »*noun* an ordinary person as opposed to the aristocracy.

commoner[2] [more common]

commonest

common law »*noun* the part of the law established by custom and legal precedent rather than by legislation.

 add a hyphen if you use this word as an adjective, as in *common-law marriage*

commonly

common market »*noun* a group of countries that impose few duties on trade with one another.

 use capital initials (**the Common Market**) when referring to the European Union

commonness

commonplace »*adjective* ordinary.
»*noun* ❶ a usual or ordinary thing. ❷ a trivial saying or topic.

Commons »*plural noun* the House of Commons.

common sense
commonsensical

Commonwealth »*noun* ❶ the association consisting of the UK together with countries that used to be part of the British Empire. ❷ (**commonwealth**) an independent state or community.

commotion »*noun* a state of confused and noisy disturbance.

communal »*adjective* shared or done by all members of a community.
– **say** kuh-**myoo**-n'l
 communally

commune[1] »*noun* a group of people living together and sharing possessions and responsibilities.
– **say** kom-myoon

commune[2] »*verb* (**communes, communing, communed**) be in communion: *he spent an hour communing with nature.*
– **say** kuh-**myoon**

communicable »*adjective* (of a disease) able to be passed on to others.

communicant »*noun* a person who receives Holy Communion.

communicate (verb: **communicates, communicating, communicated**)
 communicator

> ✓ remember the double **m** in **communicate** and **communication**

communication

communicative »*adjective* willing or eager to talk or pass on information.
– **say** kuh-**myoo**-ni-kuh-tiv

communicator

communing

communion »*noun* ❶ the sharing of intimate thoughts and feelings. ❷ the service of Christian worship at which bread and wine are made holy and shared; the Eucharist.

communiqué »*noun* an official announcement or statement.
– **say** kuh-**myoo**-ni-kay

> ✓ **communique** can also be written **communiqué**, with an acute accent on the **e** (as in the original French)

communism »*noun* ❶ a political system in which all property is owned by the community. ❷ a system of this kind derived from Marxism, followed in China and formerly in Russia.

communist

community (plural **communities**)

> ✓ plural: drop the **y** and add **ies: communities**

commutator »*noun* an attachment which ensures that electric current flows as direct current.
– **say** kom-yuu-tay-ter

commute »*verb* (**commutes, commuting, commuted**) ❶ regularly travel some distance between your home and place of work. ❷ reduce a sentence given to an offender to a less severe one.
 commuter

Comoran [of the Comoro Islands]

compact »*adjective* ❶ closely and neatly packed together; dense. ❷ having all the necessary parts fitted into a small space.
» *verb* (**compacts, compacting, compacted**) press something together into a small space.
» *noun* ❶ a small case containing face powder, a mirror, and a powder puff. ❷ a formal agreement.
– **say** kuhm-**pakt** [adjective and verb], kom-pakt [noun]
 compaction
 compactly
 compactness
 compactor

companies

companion »*noun* ❶ a person that you spend time or travel with. ❷ one of a pair of things intended to complement or match each other.

companionable »*adjective* friendly and sociable.
 companionably

companionship

companionway »*noun* a set of steps leading from a ship's deck down to a cabin or lower deck.

company (plural **companies**)

> ✓ plural: drop the **y** and add **ies: companies**

comparable »*adjective* able to be compared with another; similar.
– **say** kom-puh-ruh-b'l
 comparability
 comparably

> the correct pronunciation is with the stress on the first syllable rather than the second: com**parable**, not com**parable**

comparative »*adjective* ❶ measured or judged by comparison; relative. ❷ involving comparison between two or more subjects. ❸ (of an adjective or adverb) expressing a higher degree of a quality, but not the highest possible (e.g. *braver*).
– **say** kuhm-**pa**-ruh-tiv
 comparatively

> ✓ **ative** not **itive: comparative**

comparator »*noun* ❶ a device for comparing something measurable with a reference or standard. ❷ a standard for comparison.
– **say** kuhm-**pa**-ruh-tuh

compare (verb: compares, comparing, compared)

comparison

compartment

compartmentalize »*verb* (compartmentalizes, compartmentalizing, compartmentalized) divide something into categories or sections.
compartmentalization

✓ many people prefer the alternative spellings **compartmentalise**, **compartmentalises**, etc., and **compartmentalisation**: both **s** and **z** spellings are correct

compass »*noun* (plural **compasses**) ❶ an instrument containing a pointer which shows the direction of magnetic north. ❷ an instrument for drawing circles, consisting of two arms linked by a movable joint. ❸ range or scope.

compassion »*noun* sympathetic pity and concern for the sufferings of others.

✓ **ss** not **sh** in the middle: **compassion**

compassionate
compassionately

compatible »*adjective* ❶ able to exist or be used together. ❷ (of two people) able to have a harmonious relationship; well suited. ❸ consistent or in keeping with something.
compatibility

✓ the ending is **-ible** not **-able**: **compatible**

compatriot »*noun* a person from the same country; a fellow citizen.
– SAY kuhm-pat-ri-uht

compel »*verb* (compels, compelling, compelled) ❶ force someone to do something. ❷ make something happen.

✓ there is only one **l** in **compel** and **compels**, but two in **compelled** and **compelling**

compelling
compellingly

compels

compendia

compendious »*adjective* presenting the facts in a comprehensive but concise way.
compendiously

compendium »*noun* (plural **compendiums** or **compendia**) ❶ a collection of information about a subject. ❷ a collection of similar items.

✓ the plural can be either **compendia** (like the original Latin) or **compendiums**

compensate (verb: compensates, compensating, compensated)
compensation
compensatory

compere »*noun* a person who introduces the different acts that are performing in one show.
» *verb* (comperes, compering, compered) act as a compere in a show.
– SAY kom-pair

✓ **compere** can also be written **compère**, with a grave accent on the **e** (as in the original French)

compete (verb: competes, competing, competed)

competent »*adjective* ❶ having the necessary skill or knowledge to do something successfully. ❷ satisfactory, though not outstanding: *she spoke competent French.*
competence
competency
competently

competition

competitive
competitively
competitiveness

competitor

compilation

compile »*verb* (compiles, compiling, compiled) produce a book, report, etc. by assembling material from other sources.
compiler

complacent »*adjective* smug and uncritically satisfied with yourself.
complacency
complacently

ℹ do not confuse **complacent** with **complaisant**, which means 'willing to please'

complain (verb: complains, complaining, complained)

✓ the ending is **ain**, not **ane** or **ayn**: **complain**

complainant »*noun* (in law) a plaintiff.

complained

complaining

complains

complaint »*noun* ❶ an act of complaining. ❷ a reason to be dissatisfied. ❸ an illness or medical condition, especially a minor one.

complaisant »*adjective* willing to please others or to accept their behaviour without protest.
– **say** kuhm-**play**-z'nt
complaisance

> **i** do not confuse **complaisant** with **complacent**, meaning 'smug and self-satisfied'

compleat old spelling of **COMPLETE**.

complement »*noun* ❶ a thing that contributes extra features to something else so as to improve it. ❷ the number or quantity that makes something complete.
» *verb* (**complements**, **complementing**, **complemented**) add to something in a way that improves it.

> **i** do not confuse **complement** and **compliment**. As a verb, **complement** means 'add to in a way that improves' (as in *she selected a green sweater to complement her blonde hair*), while **compliment** means 'politely congratulate or praise' (as in *he complimented her on her appearance*).

complementary »*adjective* combining so as to form a complete whole or to enhance each other.
complementarity

> **i** do not confuse **complementary** (as in *complementary colours*, which combine to make white) with **complimentary**, which means 'giving praise' (*complimentary remarks*) or 'given without charge' (*complimentary tickets*)

complementary medicine »*noun* medical treatment that is not part of scientific medicine but may be used alongside it, e.g. acupuncture.

complemented
complementing
complements

complete (verb: **completes**, **completing**, **completed**)
completely
completeness
completion

> **✓** you sometimes come across the old spelling **compleat** used in titles, as in Izaak Walton's book *The Compleat Angler* (1653)

complex (plural **complexes**)
complexity

complexion »*noun* ❶ the condition of the skin of a person's face. ❷ the general character of something.
complexioned

> **✓** spell **complexion** with an **x**, not **ct**

complexity

compliance »*noun* the action of complying with a request, rule, etc.
– **say** kuhm-**ply**-uhnss

compliant »*adjective* ❶ tending to be excessively obedient. ❷ obeying rules.
compliantly

complicate »*verb* (**complicates**, **complicating**, **complicated**) make something more intricate or confusing.
complicated
complicatedly

complication

complicit »*adjective* involved with others in doing something unlawful.
– **say** kuhm-**pli**-sit

complicity »*noun* involvement with others in doing something unlawful.

> **✓** remember that **complicit** and **complicity** are spelled with a **c**, not an **s**, before the **it**

complied
complies

compliment »*noun* ❶ a remark that expresses praise or admiration. ❷ (**compliments**) formal greetings.
» *verb* (**compliments**, **complimenting**, **complimented**) politely congratulate or praise someone.

> **i** do not confuse **compliment** and **complement**. As a verb, **compliment** means 'politely congratulate or praise' (as in *he complimented her on her appearance*), while **complement** means 'add to in a way that improves' (as in *she selected a green sweater to complement her blonde hair*).

complimentary »*adjective* ❶ praising or approving: *complimentary remarks*. ❷ given free of charge: *complimentary tickets*.

> **i** do not confuse **complimentary** with **complementary**, which means 'combining so as to form a complete whole or to enhance each other' (as in *complementary colours*, which combine to make white)

complimented
complimenting
compliments

comply »*verb* (**complies**, **complying**, **complied**) ❶ do what someone wants or tells you to do. ❷ meet specified standards.

component

 ent not **ant: component**

comportment »*noun* behaviour or bearing.

compose (verb: **composes, composing, composed**)
composer

composite »*adjective* made up of various parts.
» *noun* a thing made up of several parts.
– SAY kom-puh-zit

composition

compos mentis »*adjective* having full control of your mind.

 compos mentis is a Latin phrase, often used in the negative form **non compos mentis**, 'not having full control of your mind'

compost »*noun* decayed organic material added to soil as a fertilizer.

composure »*noun* the state of being calm and self-controlled.

compound (verb: **compounds, compounding, compounded**)

comprehend (verb: **comprehends, comprehending, comprehended**)

comprehensible »*adjective* able to be understood; intelligible.
comprehensibility

 -ible not **-able: comprehensible**

comprehension

comprehensive »*adjective* ❶ including or dealing with all or nearly all aspects of something. ❷ (of secondary education) in which children of all abilities are educated in one school. ❸ (of a victory or defeat) by a large margin.
» *noun* a comprehensive school.
comprehensively
comprehensiveness

compress »*verb* (**compresses, compressing, compressed**) ❶ flatten something by pressure; force into less space. ❷ squeeze or press two things together.
» *noun* (plural **compresses**) an absorbent pad pressed on to part of the body to relieve inflammation or stop bleeding.
– SAY kuhm-**press** [verb], **kom**-press [noun]

compression
compressional

compressor »*noun* ❶ a tool for compressing something. ❷ a machine used to supply air at increased pressure.

 -or not **-er: compressor**

comprise »*verb* (**comprises, comprising, comprised**) ❶ be made up of; consist of. ❷ (**be comprised of**) make up; constitute.

ℹ **comprise** means 'consist of' (*the country comprises twenty states*) and should not be used to mean 'constitute or make up' (as in *twenty states comprise the country*). However, a passive use of **comprise** (as in *the country is comprised of twenty states*) is now common and means the same as the traditional active sense. The use of **comprise of**, e.g. in *the property comprises of three bedrooms*, is not standard English.

✓ **comprise** cannot be spelled with an **-ize** ending

compromise »*noun* ❶ an agreement reached by each side giving way on some points. ❷ an intermediate state between conflicting opinions.
» *verb* (**compromises, compromising, compromised**) ❶ give way on some points in order to settle a dispute. ❷ accept something that is against your principles or is less good than you would like. ❸ cause someone danger or embarrassment by behaving in an indiscreet or reckless way.

✓ unlike most words ending in **ise**, **compromise** cannot be spelled with an **ize** ending

compromising

comptroller »*noun* a controller of financial affairs.
– SAY kuhn-**troh**-ler or komp-**troh**-ler

ℹ **comptroller** is an old spelling of **controller**, used in some official titles

compulsion »*noun* ❶ pressure to do something. ❷ an irresistible urge to behave in a certain way.

compulsive »*adjective* ❶ done because of an irresistible urge. ❷ unable to stop yourself doing a particular thing. ❸ irresistibly exciting.
compulsively
compulsiveness

compulsory »*adjective* required by law or a rule; obligatory.
compulsorily
compulsoriness

✓ **ory** not **ary: compulsory**

compunction »*noun* a feeling of guilt about doing something wrong: *he had no compunction about letting her worry.*

computable

computation
computational

compute (verb: **computes**, **computing**, **computed**)
computable

computer

> ✓ remember, the ending is **-er**, not **-or**: **computer**

computerize (verb: **computerizes**, **computerizing**, **computerized**)
computerization

> ✓ many people prefer the alternative spellings **computerise**, **computerises**, etc., and **computerisation**: both **s** and **z** spellings are correct

computer-literate »*adjective* good at using computers.
computer literacy

computes

computing

comrade »*noun* **❶** (among men) a person who shares your activities or is a fellow member of an organization. **❷** a fellow soldier.
– say kom-rayd or kom-rad
comradely
comradeship

> ✓ it is easy to forget the **e** in **comrade** and **comradeship**, especially if you hear the words pronounced in the American way with the second syllable rhyming with *bad*

con (verb: **cons**, **conning**, **conned**)

> ✓ single **n** in **con** and **cons**; double the **n** in **conned** and **conning**

concatenation »*noun* a series of interconnected things.
– say kon-ka-ti-**nay**-sh'n

concave »*adjective* curving inwards (the opposite of *convex*).
– say kon-kayv
concavity say kuhn-**ka**-vi-ti

conceal »*verb* (**conceals**, **concealing**, **concealed**) prevent from being seen or known.
concealment

> ✓ the ending is **-ceal**, not **-seal** or **-cele**: **conceal**

concede »*verb* (**concedes**, **conceding**, **conceded**) **❶** finally admit that something is true. **❷** give up a possession, advantage, or right. **❸** admit defeat in a contest. **❹** allow an opponent to score a goal or point.

> ✓ **cede** not **ceed**: **concede**

conceit »*noun* **❶** excessive pride in yourself. **❷** an artistic effect. **❸** a fanciful idea.

> ✓ **e** before **i**: **conceit**, **conceited**

conceited »*adjective* excessively proud of yourself.

conceivable »*adjective* able to be imagined or understood.
conceivably

conceive »*verb* (**conceives**, **conceiving**, **conceived**) **❶** become pregnant with a child. **❷** imagine.

> ✓ **conceive** and **conceivable** follow the usual rule that **i** comes before **e** except after **c**

concentrate (verb: **concentrates**, **concentrating**, **concentrated**)

> ✓ **c** not **s** in **concentrate** and **concentration**

concentration

concentric »*adjective* (of circles or arcs) sharing the same centre.
concentrically

concept »*noun* an abstract idea.

conception

> ✓ **tion** not **cion**: **conception**

conceptual »*adjective* having to do with concepts.
conceptually

conceptualize »*verb* (**conceptualizes**, **conceptualizing**, **conceptualized**) form an idea of something in your mind.
conceptualization

> ✓ many people prefer the alternative spellings **conceptualise**, **conceptualises**, etc., and **conceptualisation**: both **s** and **z** spellings are correct

conceptually

concern (verb: **concerns**, **concerning**, **concerned**)

> ✓ **cern** not **sern**: **concern**, **concerning**, etc.

concerned

concerning

concert »*noun* **❶** a musical performance given in public. **❷** agreement or harmony.
– say kon-sert

concerted »*adjective* **❶** jointly arranged or carried out: *a concerted campaign*. **❷** done in a determined way: *a concerted effort*.
– say kuhn-**ser**-tid

concerti plural of **concerto**.

concertina »*noun* a small musical instrument which you play by stretching and squeezing it and pressing buttons.
» *verb* (**concertinas, concertinaing, concertinaed** or **concertina'd**) compress in folds like those of a concertina.

concerto »*noun* (plural **concertos** or **concerti**) a musical composition for an orchestra and one or more solo instruments.
– SAY kuhn-**cher**-toh [singular], kuhn-**cher**-ti [plural]

> ✓ the plural can be spelled either with an **i** (as in the original Italian) or **os**: **concerti** or **concertos**

concession
concessionary

concessionaire »*noun* the holder of a concession or grant.

> ✓ single **n**, not double, in **concessionaire**

conch »*noun* (plural **conchs** or **conches**) a tropical shellfish with a large spiral shell.
– SAY kongk or konch [singular], kongks or **kon**-chiz [plural]

concierge »*noun* a resident caretaker of a block of flats or small hotel.
– SAY kon-si-**air**zh

> ✓ a French word, **concierge** does not follow the usual rule, and **i** comes before **e**, even though it is after **c**

conciliate »*verb* (**conciliates, conciliating, conciliated**) ❶ make someone calm and content. ❷ try to bring the two sides in a dispute together.
– SAY kuhn-**sil**-i-ayt
conciliation

> ✓ **cil** not **cill** or **sil**: **conciliate**

concise »*adjective* giving a lot of information clearly and in few words.
concisely
concision

conclave »*noun* ❶ a private meeting. ❷ (in the Roman Catholic Church) the assembly of cardinals for the election of a pope.
– SAY **kong**-klayv

conclude (verb: **concludes, concluding, concluded**)

conclusion

conclusive »*adjective* decisive or convincing.
conclusively

concoct »*verb* (**concocts, concocting, concocted**) ❶ make a dish by combining ingredients. ❷ invent or devise a story or plan.
– SAY kuhn-**kokt**
concoction

concomitant »*adjective* naturally accompanying or associated with something else.
» *noun* a concomitant thing.
– SAY kuhn-**kom**-i-tuhnt

> ✓ **ant** not **ent**: **concomitant**

concord »*noun* agreement; harmony.

concordance »*noun* an alphabetical list of the important words in a text.
– SAY kuhn-**kor**-duhnss

> ✓ **ance** not **ence**: **concordance**

concordat »*noun* an agreement or treaty.
– SAY kuhn-**kor**-dat

concourse »*noun* a large open area inside or in front of a public building.

concrete (verb: **concretes, concreting, concreted**)

> ✓ **-crete** not **-create**: **concrete**

concretion »*noun* a hard solid mass formed by a build-up of matter.

concubine »*noun* (mainly a historical term) a woman who lives with a man but has lower status than his wife or wives.
– SAY **kong**-kyuu-byn

concur »*verb* (**concurs, concurring, concurred**) ❶ agree. ❷ happen at the same time.
– SAY kuhn-**ker**

> ✓ double the **r** in **concurring** and **concurred**

concurrent »*adjective* existing or happening at the same time.

> ✓ double **r**, and **ent** not **ant**: **concurrent**

concussion »*noun* ❶ temporary unconsciousness or confusion caused by a blow on the head. ❷ a violent shock, as from a heavy blow.
concussed

condemn (verb: **condemns, condemning, condemned**)
condemnation

> ✓ don't forget the silent **n** at the end of **condemn** (no longer silent in **condemnation**)

condensation »*noun* ❶ water from humid air collecting as droplets on a cold surface. ❷ the conversion of a vapour or gas to a liquid.

condense »*verb* (**condenses, condensing, condensed**) ❶ make something more concentrated. ❷ change from a gas or vapour to a liquid. ❸ express a piece of writing or speech in fewer words.

condenser

condenses

condensing

condescend »*verb* (**condescends, condescending, condescended**) ❶ show that you feel superior to someone. ❷ do something despite seeing it as being below your dignity.
condescending

> ✓ **-scend** not **-send**: condescend

condescension »*noun* an attitude or way of behaving that suggests you think that you are better than other people.
– SAY kon-di-**sen**-sh'n

condiment »*noun* a seasoning or relish for food, such as salt or mustard.

condition (verb: **conditions, conditioning, conditioned**)

conditional
conditionally

conditioned

conditioner

conditioning

conditions

condole »*verb* (**condoles, condoling, condoled**) (**condole with**) express sympathy for.
– SAY kuhn-**dohl**

condolence »*noun* an expression of sympathy.

> ✓ **ence** not **ance**: condolence

condoles

condoling

condom

condominium »*noun* (plural **condominiums**) ❶ the joint control of a state's affairs by other states. ❷ (in American English) a building containing a number of individually owned flats or houses.
– SAY kon-duh-**min**-i-uhm

condone »*verb* (**condones, condoning, condoned**) accept or forgive an offence or wrongdoing.
– SAY kuhn-**dohn**

condor »*noun* a very large American vulture with a bare head and black plumage.

conducive »*adjective* (**conducive to**) contributing or helping towards.

> ✓ **cive** not **sive**: conducive

conduct (verb: **conducts, conducting, conducted**)

conductance »*noun* the degree to which a material conducts electricity.

> ✓ **ance** not **ence**: conductance

conducted

conducting

conduction »*noun* the transmission of heat or electricity directly through a substance.

conductivity »*noun* the degree to which a particular material conducts electricity or heat.
conductive

conductor

> ✓ **-or** not **-er**: conductor

conducts

conduit »*noun* ❶ a channel for moving water from one place to another. ❷ a tube or trough protecting electric wiring.
– SAY kon-dit or kon-dyuu-it

cone

coney another way of spelling CONY.

confabulate »*verb* (**confabulates, confabulating, confabulated**) have a conversation.
– SAY kuhn-**fab**-yuu-layt
confabulation

confect »*verb* (**confects, confecting, confected**) make something elaborate.
– SAY kuhn-**fekt**

confection »*noun* ❶ an elaborate sweet dish or delicacy. ❷ something put together elaborately.

confectionery »*noun* (plural **confectioneries**) sweets and chocolates.
confectioner

> ✓ **ery** not **ary**: confectionery

confederacy »*noun* (plural **confederacies**) ❶ an alliance of groups or states. ❷ (**the Confederacy**) the Confederate states of the US.

confederate »*adjective* ❶ joined by an agreement or treaty. ❷ (**Confederate**) having to do with the southern states which separated from the US in 1860–1.
»*verb* (**confederates, confederating, confederated**) bring into an alliance.

– SAY kuhn-**fed**-uh-ruht [adjective], kuhn-**fed**-uh-rayt [verb]

confederation »*noun* ❶ an alliance of states or groups. ❷ a union of states with some political power belonging to a central authority.

confer »*verb* (**confers, conferring, conferred**) ❶ grant a title, degree, benefit, or right. ❷ have discussions.
– SAY kuhn-**fer**

> double the r in **conferring** and **conferred**

conference »*noun* a formal meeting for discussion or debate.

confess (verb: **confesses, confessing, confessed**)

confession

confessional »*noun* ❶ an enclosed box in a church, in which a priest sits to hear confessions. ❷ a confession.

confessor »*noun* a priest who hears confessions.

> ☑ **-or** not **-er: confessor**

confetti

> ☑ one f, two t's: **confetti** is an Italian word, literally meaning 'sweets'

confidant »*noun* a person in whom you confide.
– SAY kon-fi-dant or kon-fi-**dant**

> ☑ **ant** not **ent: confidant**

confidante »*noun* a female confidant.
– SAY kon-fi-dant or kon-fi-**dant**

confide »*verb* (**confides, confiding, confided**) tell someone about a secret or private matter.
– SAY kuhn-**fyd**

confidence

confident
confidently

> ☑ **ent** not **ant: confident**

confidential »*adjective* intended to be kept secret.
confidentiality
confidentially

confidently

confides

confiding

configuration »*noun* an arrangement of parts in a particular form or figure.
– SAY kuhn-fi-guh-**ray**-sh'n

configure »*verb* (**configures, configuring, configured**) ❶ arrange or set up in a particular way. ❷ arrange a computer system so as to fit it for a particular task.

confine »*verb* (**confines, confining, confined**) ❶ (**confine to**) restrict someone or something to certain limits. ❷ (**be confined to**) be unable to leave a particular place due to illness or disability.
– SAY kuhn-**fyn**
confinement

confined »*adjective* (of a space) enclosed; cramped.

confines[1] »*noun* limits or boundaries.
– SAY kon-fynz

confines[2] present of **CONFINE** [as in *he confines*].

confining

confirm (verb: **confirms, confirming, confirmed**)

confirmation »*noun* ❶ the action of confirming. ❷ the rite at which a baptized person is admitted as a full member of the Christian Church.

confirmed

confirming

confirms

confiscate »*verb* (**confiscates, confiscating, confiscated**) take or seize someone's property with authority.
– SAY kon-fi-**skayt**

conflagration »*noun* a large and destructive fire.
– SAY kon-fluh-**gray**-sh'n

conflate »*verb* (**conflates, conflating, conflated**) combine into one.

conflict (verb: **conflicts, conflicting, conflicted**)

confluence »*noun* the junction of two rivers.
– SAY kon-floo-uhnss

conform »*verb* (**conforms, conforming, conformed**) ❶ follow rules or standards. ❷ be similar in form or type.

conformist »*noun* a person who behaves in a conventional or expected way.
»*adjective* conventional.

conformity »*noun* ❶ compliance with conventions, rules, or laws. ❷ similarity in form or type.

confound »*verb* (**confounds, confounding, confounded**) ❶ surprise or bewilder. ❷ prove someone wrong. ❸ defeat a plan, aim, or hope.

confront (verb: **confronts, confronting, confronted**)
confrontation

Confucian »*adjective* relating to the Chinese philosopher Confucius.
– SAY kuhn-**fyoo**-sh'n

confuse (verb: **confuses, confusing, confused**)

confused

confuses

confusing
  confusingly

confusion

confute »*verb* (**confutes, confuting, confuted**) prove someone to be wrong.

conga »*noun* a Latin American dance performed by people in single file.
– SAY kong-guh

the ending is a not er: conga (a conger is an eel)

congeal »*verb* (**congeals, congealing, congealed**) become semi-solid.
– SAY kuhn-**jeel**

congenial »*adjective* suited or pleasing to your tastes.
– SAY kuhn-**jee**-ni-uhl

congenital »*adjective* ❶ (of a disease or abnormality) present from birth. ❷ having a particular quality as part of your character: *a congenital liar.*
– SAY kuhn-**jen**-i-t'l

conger »*noun* a predatory eel found in coastal waters.
– SAY **kong**-ger

the ending is er not a: conger (a conga is a dance)

congested »*adjective* ❶ so crowded that it is difficult or impossible to move. ❷ abnormally full of blood. ❸ blocked with mucus.
  congestion

conglomerate »*noun* ❶ something consisting of a number of different and distinct things. ❷ a large corporation formed by the merging of separate firms.
»*verb* (**conglomerates, conglomerating, conglomerated**) gather into or form a conglomerate.
– SAY kuhn-**glom**-muh-ruht [noun], kuhn-**glom**-muh-rayt [verb]
  conglomeration

one m, one r: conglomerate

Congolese (plural **Congolese**) [of the Congo]

congratulate (verb: **congratulates, congratulating, congratulated**)
  congratulatory

congratulation

congratulatory

congregate »*verb* (**congregates, congregating, congregated**) gather into a crowd or mass.

no double g in congregate

congregation »*noun* ❶ a group of people assembled for religious worship. ❷ a gathering or collection of people or things.
  congregational

congress »*noun* (plural **congresses**) ❶ a formal meeting or series of meetings between representatives of different groups. ❷ (**Congress**) a national law-making body.
  congressional

congressman (plural **congressmen**)

congresswoman (plural **congresswomen**)

congruent »*adjective* ❶ in agreement or harmony. ❷ (in mathematics) (of shapes) identical in form.
– SAY **kong**-groo-uhnt
  congruence

ent not ant: congruent

conic »*adjective* of a cone.
– SAY **kon**-ik

conical »*adjective* shaped like a cone.

conies

conifer »*noun* a tree that has cones and evergreen needle-like leaves.
– SAY **kon**-i-fer or **kohn**-i-fer
  coniferous

conjecture »*noun* a guess.
»*verb* (**conjectures, conjecturing, conjectured**) guess.
– SAY kuhn-**jek**-cher

conjoin »*verb* (**conjoins, conjoining, conjoined**) join; combine.

conjugal »*adjective* relating to marriage or the relationship between husband and wife.
– SAY **kon**-juu-g'l

jugal not dugal: conjugal

conjugate »*verb* (**conjugates, conjugating, conjugated**) give the different forms of a verb.
– SAY **kon**-juu-gayt
  conjugation

conjunction »*noun* ❶ a word used to connect words or clauses (e.g. *and*, *if*). ❷ an instance of two or more events occurring at the same point in time or space.

junct not juct: **conjunction**

conjunctivitis »*noun* inflammation of the membranes of the eye.
– SAY kuhn-jungk-ti-**vy**-tiss

conjure »*verb* (**conjures, conjuring, conjured**) ❶ cause to appear by or as if by magic. ❷ call something to the mind.

conjurer another way of spelling **CONJUROR**.

conjuring »*noun* the performing of seemingly magical tricks.

conjuror »*noun* a performer of conjuring tricks.

 conjuror can also be spelled **conjurer**

conk (verb: **conks, conking, conked**)

conker »*noun* the dark brown nut of a horse chestnut tree.

conking

conks

con man (plural **con men**)

connect (verb: **connects, connecting, connected**)
connector

connection

 connection can also be spelled **connexion**: both spellings are correct

connective »*adjective* connecting.

connective tissue »*noun* bodily tissue that connects, supports, binds, or separates other tissues or organs.

connector

connects

conned

connexion another way of spelling **CONNECTION**.

conning

connive »*verb* (**connives, conniving, connived**) ❶ (**connive at** or **in**) secretly allow something wrong to be done. ❷ conspire.
– SAY kuh-**nyv**
connivance

connoisseur »*noun* an expert judge in matters of taste.
– SAY kon-nuh-**ser**

double n, double s, and remember the **i** in **noiss**: **connoisseur**

connotation »*noun* an idea or feeling suggested by a word in addition to its main meaning.
– SAY kon-nuh-**tay**-sh'n

connote »*verb* (**connotes, connoting, connoted**) (of a word) suggest something in addition to its main meaning.
– SAY kuh-**noht**

connote does not mean the same as **denote**: denote refers to the main meaning of something, while **connote** refers to extra ideas or feelings suggested by that thing

connubial »*adjective* having to do with marriage.
– SAY kuh-**nyoo**-bi-uhl

conquer (verb: **conquers, conquering, conquered**) [overcome]
conqueror

conquest

conquistador »*noun* (plural **conquistadores** or **conquistadors**) a Spanish conqueror of Mexico or Peru in the 16th century.
– SAY kon-**kwiss**-tuh-dor

a Spanish word, **conquistador** is sometimes pronounced kon-**kiss**-tuh-dor, and the plural **conquistadores** kon-kiss-tuh-**dor**-ayz

cons

consanguinity »*noun* descent from the same ancestor.
– SAY kon-sang-**gwin**-i-ti
consanguineous

conscience »*noun* a person's moral sense of right and wrong.

do not confuse **conscience** with **conscious** 'aware of and responding to your surroundings'

don't forget the **c** after the **s**: **conscience**

conscientious »*adjective* ❶ careful and thorough in carrying out your work or duty. ❷ relating to a person's conscience.
– SAY kon-shi-**en**-shuhss
conscientiously

conscientious objector »*noun* a person who refuses to serve in the armed forces for moral reasons.

conscious [aware]
consciously
consciousness

do not confuse **conscious** with **conscience**, 'a person's sense of right and wrong'

remember the **c** after the first **s**: **conscious**

conscript »*verb* (**conscripts, conscripting, conscripted**) call someone up for compulsory military service.

» *noun* a conscripted person.
conscription

consecrate »*verb* (**consecrates, consecrating, consecrated**) ❶ make or declare something holy. ❷ officially make someone a priest. ❸ (in Christian belief) make bread or wine into the body and blood of Christ.
– SAY kon-si-krayt
consecration

 sec not sac: **consecrate**

consecutive »*adjective* following in unbroken or logical sequence.
– SAY kuhn-**sek**-yuu-tiv

consensual »*adjective* relating to or involving consent or consensus.
– SAY kuhn-**sen**-syoo-uhl

 there is no **t** in **consensual**

consensus »*noun* (plural **consensuses**) general agreement.
– SAY kuhn-**sen**-suhss

 sen not **cen**: **consensus**

consent (verb: **consents, consenting, consented**)

consequence

 don't forget the **u** after the **q**: **consequence**

consequent »*adjective* following as a consequence.
consequently

conservancy »*noun* (plural **conservancies**) an organization concerned with the preservation of natural resources.
– SAY kuhn-ser-vuhn-si

conservation »*noun* ❶ preservation or restoration of the natural environment. ❷ preservation and repair of historical sites and objects. ❸ careful use of a resource: *energy conservation*.
conservationist

conservative »*adjective* ❶ opposed to change and holding traditional values. ❷ (**Conservative**) of the Conservative Party. ❸ (of an estimate) deliberately low for the sake of caution.
» *noun* a conservative person.
conservatism

ℹ use a capital **C** when referring to the Conservative Party (*the Conservative position on Europe*), but a small **c** in other cases (*a conservative estimate*; *religious conservatives*)

conservatoire »*noun* a college for the study of classical music.

– SAY kuhn-ser-vuh-twar

 don't forget the **e** at the end: **conservatoire**

conservatory »*noun* (plural **conservatories**) a room with a glass roof and walls, attached to a house.

 plural: drop the **y** and add **ies**: **conservatories**

conserve »*verb* (**conserves, conserving, conserved**) protect something from being harmed or overused.
» *noun* fruit jam.

consider (verb: **considers, considering, considers**)

considerable
considerably

considerate »*adjective* careful not to harm or inconvenience others.

consideration

considered

considering

considers

consign »*verb* (**consigns, consigning, consigned**) ❶ deliver something into someone's possession or care. ❷ send goods by a public carrier. ❸ (**consign to**) put someone or something in a place so as to be rid of them.

 sign not **sine**: **consign**

consignment

consigns

consist (verb: **consists, consisting, consisted**)

consistency »*noun* (plural **consistencies**) ❶ the state of being consistent. ❷ the degree of thickness of a substance.

 ency not **ancy**: **consistency**
plural: drop the **y** and add **ies**: **consistencies**

consistent
consistently

 ent not **ant**: **consistent**

consisting

consistory »*noun* (plural **consistories**) (in the Roman Catholic Church) the council of cardinals.
– SAY kuhn-**siss**-tuh-ri

consists

consolation »*noun* ❶ comfort received after a loss or disappointment. ❷ a source of such comfort.
– SAY kon-suh-**lay**-sh'n

consolation prize »*noun* a prize given to a competitor who just fails to win.

console[1] »*verb* (**consoles, consoling, consoled**) comfort someone who is unhappy or disappointed about something.
– SAY kuhn-**sohl**

console[2] »*noun* ❶ a panel or unit accommodating a set of controls. ❷ a small machine for playing computerized video games.
– SAY **kon**-sohl

consoled

consoles

consolidate »*verb* (**consolidates, consolidating, consolidated**) ❶ make stronger or more solid. ❷ combine into a single unit.
– SAY kuhn-**sol**-i-dayt
consolidation

consoling

consomme »*noun* a clear soup made with concentrated stock.
– SAY kuhn-**som**-may

> ✓ **consomme** can also be spelled **consommé**, with an acute accent above the **e** (as in the original French)

consonance »*noun* agreement or compatibility.
– SAY **kon**-suh-nuhnss

> ✓ **ance** not **ence**: **consonance**

consonant »*noun* a letter of the alphabet representing a sound in which the breath is completely or partly obstructed.
» *adjective* (**consonant with**) in agreement or harmony with.
– SAY **kon**-suh-nuhnt

> ✓ **ant** not **ent**: **consonant**

consort »*noun* ❶ a wife, husband, or companion. ❷ a small group of musicians performing together.
» *verb* (**consorts, consorting, consorted**) (**consort with**) habitually associate with.
– SAY **kon**-sort [noun], kuhn-**sort** [verb]

consortia

consorting

consortium »*noun* (plural **consortia** or **consortiums**) an association of several companies.

> ✓ the plural can be either **consortia** (like the original Latin) or **consortiums**

consorts

conspicuous »*adjective* ❶ clearly visible. ❷ attracting notice: *conspicuous bravery.*

– SAY kuhn-**spik**-yoo-uhss
conspicuously

> ✓ **cuous**, not **cious** or **cous**: **conspicuous**

conspiracy »*noun* (plural **conspiracies**) ❶ a secret plan by a group to do something unlawful or harmful. ❷ the action of conspiring.

> ✓ plural: drop the **y** and add **ies**: **conspiracies**

conspire »*verb* (**conspires, conspiring, conspired**) ❶ jointly make secret plans to commit a wrongful act. ❷ (of circumstances) seem to be working together to bring about something bad.
conspirator
conspiratorial

constable »*noun* (in the UK and some other police forces) a police officer of the lowest rank.

constabulary »*noun* (plural **constabularies**) a police force.
– SAY kuhn-**stab**-yuu-luh-ri

constant
constancy
constantly

> ✓ **ant** not **ent**: **constant**

constellation »*noun* a group of stars forming a recognized pattern.

> ✓ double **l**: **constellation**

consternation »*noun* anxiety or dismay.

constipated »*adjective* affected with constipation.

constipation »*noun* difficulty in emptying the bowels.

constituency »*noun* (plural **constituencies**) ❶ a body of voters in a particular area who elect a representative to a law-making body. ❷ the area represented in this way.
– SAY kuhn-**stit**-yoo-uhn-si

> ✓ plural: drop the **y** and add **ies**: **constituencies**

constituent »*adjective* being a part of a whole.
» *noun* ❶ a member of a constituency. ❷ a part of a whole.

constitute »*verb* (**constitutes, constituting, constituted**) ❶ be a part of a whole. ❷ be or be equivalent to. ❸ establish something by law.
– SAY **kon**-sti-tyoot

constitution »*noun* ❶ a body of principles according to which a state or organization is governed. **❷** composition or formation. **❸** a person's physical or mental state.

constitutional »*adjective* **❶** relating to or in accordance with a constitution. **❷** relating to a person's physical or mental state.
» *noun* (old-fashioned) a walk taken regularly to maintain good health.

constrain »*verb* (constrains, constraining, constrained) **❶** force someone to do a particular thing. **❷** severely restrict or limit.

constraint »*noun* **❶** a limitation or restriction. **❷** strict control of your behaviour.

constrict »*verb* (constricts, constricting, constricted) **❶** make or become narrower; tighten. **❷** stop someone moving or acting freely.
constriction

constrictor »*noun* a snake that kills by squeezing and choking its prey.

 -or not -er: **constrictor**

constricts

construct (verb: constructs, constructing, constructed)
constructor

construction
constructional

constructive »*adjective* serving a useful purpose.
constructively

constructor

constructs

construe »*verb* (construes, construing, construed) interpret something in a particular way.

 drop the **e** when spelling **construing**

consul »*noun* **❶** an official based in a foreign city and protecting their country's citizens and interests there. **❷** (in ancient Rome) one of two elected officials who ruled the republic jointly for a year.
consular

consulate »*noun* the place where a consul works.

consult (verb: consults, consulting, consulted)
consultation
consultative

consultancy »*noun* (plural consultancies) **❶** the work of being a consultant. **❷** a company giving expert advice in a particular field.

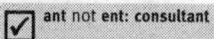 plural: drop the **y** and add **ies**: **consultancies**

consultant »*noun* **❶** a person who provides expert advice professionally. **❷** a senior hospital doctor.

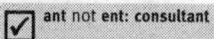 ant not ent: **consultant**

consultation
consultative
consulted
consulting
consults

consume »*verb* (consumes, consuming, consumed) **❶** eat or drink. **❷** use up. **❸** (especially of a fire) completely destroy. **❹** (of a feeling) absorb someone completely.

consumer »*noun* a person who buys a product or uses a service.

consumerism »*noun* **❶** protection of the interests of consumers. **❷** the preoccupation of society with acquiring goods.
consumerist

consumes

consuming

consummate »*verb* (consummates, consummating, consummated) **❶** make a marriage or relationship complete by having sex. **❷** complete a transaction.
» *adjective* showing great skill and flair.
– say kon-syuu-mayt [verb], kuhn-sum-muht or kon-sum-muht [adjective]
consummation

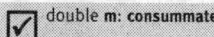 double m: **consummate**

consumption »*noun* **❶** the process of consuming. **❷** an amount consumed. **❸** (old-fashioned) a wasting disease, especially tuberculosis.
consumptive

contact (verb: contacts, contacting, contacted)

contact lens »*noun* a plastic lens placed on the surface of the eye to help you see better.

contacts

contagion »*noun* the passing of a disease from one person to another by close contact.
– say kuhn-**tay**-juhn

contagious »*adjective* **❶** (of a disease) spread by contact between people or organisms. **❷** having a contagious disease.

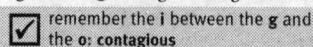 remember the **i** between the **g** and the **o**: **contagious**

contain (verb: **contains, containing, contained**)
container

containment »*noun* the action of keeping something harmful under control.

contains

contaminant »*noun* a substance which contaminates something.

contaminate »*verb* (**contaminates, contaminating, contaminated**) make something impure by exposing it to a poisonous or polluting substance.
contamination

contemplate »*verb* (**contemplates, contemplating, contemplated**) ❶ look at thoughtfully. ❷ think about. ❸ think deeply and at length.
– say kon-tuhm-**playt**

contemplation

contemplative »*adjective* showing or involving contemplation.
– say kuhn-**tem**-pluh-tiv
contemplatively

contemporaneous »*adjective* existing at or occurring in the same period of time.
– say kuhn-tem-puh-**ray**-ni-uhss
contemporaneously

> ✓ **por** not **per** in the middle:
> **contemporaneous**

contemporary »*adjective* ❶ living or occurring at the same time. ❷ belonging to or occurring in the present. ❸ modern in style.
»*noun* (plural **contemporaries**) a person living or working at the same time as another.

> ✓ **porary** not **pory**: **contemporary**
> plural: drop the **y** and add **ies**:
> **contemporaries**

contempt »*noun* ❶ the feeling that someone or something is worthless or beneath consideration. ❷ the offence of disobeying or being disrespectful to a court of law.

> ✓ don't forget the **p**: **contempt**

contemptible »*adjective* deserving contempt.
contemptibly

> ✓ **-ible** not **-able**: **contemptible**

contemptuous »*adjective* showing contempt.
contemptuously

contend »*verb* (**contends, contending, contended**) ❶ (**contend with** or **against**) struggle to deal with a difficulty. ❷ (**contend for**) struggle to achieve. ❸ put forward a particular view in an argument.
contender

content[1] (verb: **contents, contenting, contented**) [happy; happiness; satisfy]
– say kuhn-**tent**
contentment

content[2] [material included]
– say **kon**-tent

contented

contenting

contention »*noun* ❶ heated disagreement. ❷ a point of view that is expressed.

contentious »*adjective* ❶ causing or likely to cause disagreement or controversy. ❷ liking to cause arguments.
contentiously

contentment

contents

contest (verb: **contests, contesting, contested**)

contestant

> ✓ **ant** not **ent**: **contestant**

contested

contesting

contests

context »*noun* ❶ the circumstances surrounding an event, statement, or idea. ❷ the parts that come immediately before and after a word or passage and make its meaning clearer.
contextual
contextually

contiguous »*adjective* ❶ sharing a border. ❷ next or together in sequence.
– say kuhn-**tig**-yoo-uhss
contiguity

continence

continent[1] »*noun* ❶ one of the world's main continuous expanses of land (Europe, Asia, Africa, North and South America, Australia, Antarctica). ❷ the mainland of Europe as distinct from the British Isles.

> ✓ **continent** is often spelled with a capital **C** when referring to Europe

continent[2] »*adjective* ❶ able to control movements of the bowels and bladder. ❷ restrained; self-disciplined.
continence

continental »*adjective* ❶ forming or belonging to a continent. ❷ (also **Continental**) coming from or like mainland Europe.

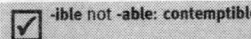

» *noun* (also **Continental**) a person from mainland Europe.

 continental is often spelled with a capital **C** when referring to Europe

continental drift »*noun* the very gradual movement of the continents across the earth's surface over millions of years.

continental shelf »*noun* an area of seabed around a large land mass where the sea is shallow.

contingency »*noun* (plural **contingencies**) **❶** a future event which is possible but cannot be predicted with certainty. **❷** a plan made in case a particular thing happens.
– SAY kuhn-**tin**-juhn-si

contingent »*adjective* **❶** depending on chance. **❷** (**contingent on**) dependent on.
» *noun* a group of people forming part of a larger group.
– SAY kuhn-**tin**-juhnt

 ent not **ant**: conting**ent**

continua plural of **CONTINUUM**.

continual [constantly happening]
continually

ℹ️ **continual** should not be used in the same way as **continuous**: see the note at **CONTINUOUS**

continuance

continuation

continue (verb: **continues**, **continuing**, **continued**)

✓ drop the **e** to spell **continuing**

continuity »*noun* (plural **continuities**) **❶** unbroken existence or operation. **❷** an unbroken connection or line of development. **❸** organization of a film or television programme so that the plot makes sense and clothing, scenery, etc. remain the same in different scenes.
– SAY kon-ti-**nyoo**-i-ti

continuous [without interruption]
continuously

ℹ️ **continuous** and **continual** do not mean exactly the same thing: *continuous fighting* means 'fighting that goes on without interruption', whereas *continual fighting* means 'fighting that happens at frequent intervals'

continuum »*noun* (plural **continua**) a continuous sequence in which the elements change gradually.

✓ like many other words ending in **um** derived from Latin, **continuum** has a plural ending in **a**: **continua**

contort »*verb* (**contorts**, **contorting**, **contorted**) twist or bend something out of its normal shape.

contortion

contortionist »*noun* an entertainer who twists and bends their body into unnatural positions.

contorts

contour »*noun* **❶** an outline of the shape or form of something. **❷** (also **contour line**) a line on a map joining points of equal height.
» *verb* (**contours**, **contouring**, **contoured**) **❶** mould something into a specific shape. **❷** (**contoured**) (of a map or diagram) marked with contours.

contraband »*noun* goods that have been imported or exported illegally.
– SAY **kon**-truh-band

contraception »*noun* the use of contraceptives.

contraceptive »*adjective* preventing a woman becoming pregnant.
» *noun* a device or drug used to prevent a woman becoming pregnant.

contract (verb: **contracts**, **contracting**, **contracted**)
contractual

contraction

contractor

✓ **-or** not **-er**: contract**or**

contracts

contractual

✓ **ual** not **ural**: contract**ual**

contradict »*verb* (**contradicts**, **contradicting**, **contradicted**) **❶** deny that a statement is true by saying the opposite. **❷** challenge someone by making a statement opposing one made by them.

contradiction »*noun* **❶** a combination of statements, ideas, or features which are opposed to one another. **❷** saying the opposite to something already said.

contradictory »*adjective* **❶** inconsistent with or opposing each other. **❷** containing inconsistent elements.

contradicts

contradistinction »*noun* distinction made by contrasting two things.

contraflow »*noun* an arrangement by which the lanes of a dual carriageway or motorway normally carrying traffic in one direction become two-directional.

contralto »*noun* (plural **contraltos**) the lowest female singing voice.
– **SAY** kuhn-**tral**-toh

> ☑ the plural of **contralto**, an Italian word, has **os** not **oes**: **contraltos**

contraption

contrapuntal »*adjective* (in music) of or in counterpoint.
– **SAY** kon-truh-**pun**-t'l

contrariwise »*adverb* in the opposite way.
– **SAY** kuhn-**trair**-i-wyz

contrary »*adjective* ❶ opposite in nature, direction, or meaning. ❷ (of two or more statements, beliefs, etc.) opposed to one another. ❸ deliberately inclined to do the opposite of what is expected or desired.
» *noun* (**the contrary**) the opposite.
– **SAY** kon-truh-ri or [in sense 'deliberately inclined to do the opposite' only] kuhn-**trair**-i

contrast »*noun* ❶ the state of being noticeably different from something else when placed or considered together. ❷ a thing or person noticeably different from another. ❸ the amount of difference between tones in a television picture, photograph, etc.
» *verb* (**contrasts, contrasting, contrasted**) ❶ be noticeably different. ❷ compare two things to emphasize their differences.
contrastive

contravene »*verb* (**contravenes, contravening, contravened**) ❶ do something that breaks a law, treaty, etc. ❷ conflict with a right, principle, etc.
– **SAY** kon-truh-**veen**
contravention

contretemps »*noun* (plural **contretemps**) a minor disagreement.
– **SAY** kon-truh-ton [singular], kon-truh-tonz [plural]

> ☑ **contre** not **contra**: **contretemps**. It is a French word: the singular and plural are spelled the same, **contretemps**, but they are pronounced differently.

contribute (verb: **contributes, contributing, contributed**)
contribution
contributor

contributory
– **SAY** kuhn-**trib**-yuu-tuh-ri

> ☑ **ory** not **ary**: **contributory**

con trick »*noun* (in informal English) a confidence trick.

contrite »*adjective* sorry for something that you have done.
– **SAY** kuhn-**tryt** or **kon**-tryt
contrition

contrivance »*noun* ❶ the action of contriving. ❷ a clever device or scheme.

> ☑ **ance** not **ence**: **contrivance**

contrive »*verb* (**contrives, contriving, contrived**) ❶ skilfully devise or plan something. ❷ manage to do something foolish.
– **SAY** kuhn-**tryv**

contrived »*adjective* deliberately created rather than arising spontaneously.

contrives

contriving

control (verb: **controls, controlling, controlled**)
controller

> ☑ double the **l** to spell **controlling, controlled**, and **controller**

controversial »*adjective* causing or likely to cause controversy.
controversially

> ☑ **contra** not **contro**: **controversial**

controversy »*noun* (plural **controversies**) debate or disagreement about a matter which arouses strong opinions.
– **SAY** kon-truh-ver-si or kuhn-**trov**-er-si

> ☑ the ending is **sy**, not **sey**: **controversy** plural: drop the **y** and add **ies**: **controversies**

contusion »*noun* (in medicine) a bruise.

conundrum »*noun* (plural **conundrums**) ❶ a confusing and difficult problem or question. ❷ a riddle.
– **SAY** kuh-**nun**-druhm

> ☑ the plural of **conundrum** simply adds an **s**: **conundrums**

conurbation »*noun* an area consisting of several towns merging together or with a city.
– **SAY** kon-er-**bay**-sh'n

> ☑ **conu** not **connu**: **conurbation**

convalesce »*verb* (**convalesces, convalescing, convalesced**) gradually get better after an illness or injury.
– **SAY** kon-vuh-**less**

> ☑ do not forget the **c** after the **s**: **convalesce**

convalescent »*adjective* recovering from an illness or injury.

» *noun* a convalescent person.
convalescence

convalesces

convalescing

convection »*noun* the process by which heat moves through a gas or liquid as the warmer part rises and the cooler part sinks.

convector »*noun* a heater that circulates warm air by convection.

 -or not **-er: convector**

convene »*verb* (**convenes, convening, convened**) ❶ call people together for a meeting. ❷ come together for a meeting.
– SAY kuhn-**veen**

convener »*noun* a person who convenes meetings of a committee.

 convener can also be spelled **convenor**: both spellings are correct

convenes

convenience

 ven in the middle: **convenience, convenient**

convenient
conveniently

convening

convenor another way of spelling **CONVENER.**

convent »*noun* a building where nuns live.

convention »*noun* ❶ a way in which something is usually done. ❷ socially acceptable behaviour. ❸ an agreement between countries. ❹ a large meeting or conference.

conventional
conventionally

converge »*verb* (**converges, converging, converged**) ❶ come together from different directions. ❷ (**converge on**) come from different directions and meet at.
convergent

 ent not **ant: convergent**

conversant »*adjective* (**conversant with**) familiar with or knowledgeable about.

 ant not **ent: conversant**

conversation
conversational

conversationalist »*noun* a person who is good at or likes conversation.

converse[1] »*verb* (**converses, conversing, conversed**) hold a conversation.
– SAY kuhn-**verss**

converse[2] »*noun* something that is the opposite of another.
» *adjective* opposite.
– SAY kon-**verss**
conversely

conversed

conversely

converses

conversing

conversion »*noun* ❶ the action of converting. ❷ (in British English) a building that has been converted to a new purpose. ❸ (in rugby) a successful kick at goal after a try.

convert (verb: **converts, converting, converted**)

convertible

 -ible not **-able: convertible**

converting

converts

convex »*adjective* curving outwards (the opposite of *concave*).
– SAY kuhn-**veks** or **kon**-veks

convey »*verb* (**conveys, conveying, conveyed**) ❶ transport or carry to a place. ❷ communicate an idea or feeling.

conveyance »*noun* ❶ the action of conveying. ❷ a means of transport. ❸ the legal process of transferring property from one owner to another.
conveyancing

 ance not **ence: conveyance**

conveyed

conveying

conveyor belt

 -or not **-er: conveyor belt**

conveys

convict (verb: **convicts, convicting, convicted**)

conviction »*noun* ❶ an instance of being convicted of a criminal offence. ❷ a firmly held belief or opinion. ❸ the quality of showing that you believe strongly in what you are saying.

convicts

convince (verb: **convinces, convincing, convinced**)

convincing
convincingly

convivial »*adjective* ❶ (of an atmosphere or event) friendly and lively. ❷ (of a person) cheerfully sociable.

– SAY kuhn-**viv**-i-uhl

convocation »*noun* a large formal meeting.
– SAY kon-vuh-**kay**-sh'n

convoke »*verb* (**convokes, convoking, convoked**) call together a meeting.
– SAY kuhn-**vohk**

convoluted »*adjective* **❶** (of an argument or account) extremely complex. **❷** intricately folded, twisted, or coiled.
– SAY kon-vuh-**loo**-tid

> ☑ single **l**: **convoluted**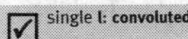

convolution »*noun* **❶** a coil or twist. **❷** the state of being coiled or twisted. **❸** (**convolutions**) something complex and difficult to follow.

convolvulus »*noun* (plural **convolvuluses**) a twining plant with trumpet-shaped flowers.
– SAY kuhn-**volv**-yuu-luhss

> ☑ do not double the **s** in the plural **convolvuluses**

convoy »*noun* a group of ships or vehicles travelling together under armed protection.

convulse »*verb* (**convulses, convulsing, convulsed**) **❶** suffer convulsions. **❷** (**be convulsed**) make sudden, uncontrollable movements because of emotion, laughter, etc.
– SAY kuhn-**vulss**

convulsion »*noun* **❶** a sudden, irregular movement of the body caused by involuntary contraction of muscles. **❷** (**convulsions**) uncontrollable laughter. **❸** a violent upheaval.

convulsive
convulsively

cony »*noun* (plural **conies**) (in informal English) a rabbit.

> ☑ **cony** can also be spelled **coney** (plural **coneys**)

coo (verb: **coos, cooing, cooed**)

> ☑ do not add an **e** when spelling **cooing**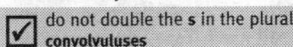

cook (verb: **cooks, cooking, cooked**)

cookbook

cooked

cooker

cookery

cookie (plural **cookies**)

cooking

cooks

cool (adjective: **cooler, coolest**; verb: **cools, cooling, cooled**)
coolly
coolness

> ☑ double the **l** in **coolly**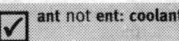

coolant »*noun* a fluid used to cool an engine or other device.

> ☑ **ant** not **ent**: **coolant**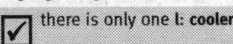

cooled

cooler »*noun* a device or container for keeping things cool.

> ☑ there is only one **l**: **cooler**

coolest

coolie »*noun* (plural **coolies**) (old-fashioned) an unskilled labourer in an Asian country.
– SAY **koo**-li

cooling

cooling tower »*noun* a concrete tower with an open top, used for cooling water or condensing steam from an industrial process.

coolly

coolness

cools

coombe another way of spelling COMBE.

coop »*noun* a cage or pen for poultry.
»*verb* (**coops, cooping, cooped**) (**coop up**) confine in a small space.

co-op »*noun* (in informal English) a cooperative organization.

cooper »*noun* a person who makes or repairs casks and barrels.

cooperate (verb: **cooperates, cooperating, cooperated**)
– SAY koh-**op**-uh-rayt
cooperation

> ☑ **cooperate, cooperates,** and related words can also be spelled with a hyphen: **co-operate, co-operates,** etc.

cooperative
cooperatively
cooperativeness

> ☑ **cooperative** can also be spelled with a hyphen: **co-operative**

cooping

coops

co-opt »*verb* (**co-opts, co-opting, co-opted**) **❶** appoint someone as a member of a committee or other body. **❷** adopt an idea or policy for your own use.

coordinate »*verb* (**coordinates, coordinating, coordinated**) ❶ bring the different elements of something together so that it works well. ❷ (**coordinate with**) negotiate with others to work together effectively. ❸ match or harmonize different elements attractively.
» *noun* ❶ (in mathematics) one of a group of numbers used to indicate the position of a point, line, or plane. ❷ (**coordinates**) matching items of clothing.
– say koh-**or**-di-nayt [verb], koh-**or**-di-nuht [noun]
coordinator

> **coordinate, coordinates,** etc. and **coordinator** can also be spelled with a hyphen: **co-ordinate, co-ordinates, co-ordinator**

coordination

coordinator

coot »*noun* a waterbird with black plumage and a white bill.

cop (verb: **cops, copping, copped**)

> double the **p** when spelling **copping** and **copped**

cope[1] (verb: **copes, coping, coped**) [deal with something]

cope[2] »*noun* a long cloak worn by a priest on ceremonial occasions.

copeck another way of spelling **KOPEK**.

coped

copes

copied

copier

copies

co-pilot

coping[1] »*noun* the top line of bricks or stones in a wall.

coping[2] present participle of **COPE**[1].

copious »*adjective* abundant; plentiful.
copiously

copped

copper
coppery

copperplate »*noun* an elaborate style of handwriting.

coppery

coppice »*noun* an area of woodland in which the trees or shrubs are periodically cut back to ground level.
coppiced
coppicing

copping

copra »*noun* dried coconut kernels, from which oil is obtained.

– say kop-ruh

cops

copse »*noun* a small group of trees.

> do not forget the **e** at the end: **copse**

Copt »*noun* ❶ an Egyptian in the periods of Greek and Roman rule. ❷ a member of the Coptic Church, the Christian Church in Egypt.
Coptic

copulate »*verb* (**copulates, copulating, copulated**) mate or have sex.
– say kop-yuu-layt
copulation

copy (plural **copies**; verb: **copies, copying, copied**)

> plural: drop the **y** and add **ies**: **copies**

copybook »*noun* a book containing models of handwriting for learners to imitate.
» *adjective* done in exactly the proper way.

copy-edit »*verb* (**copy-edits, copy-editing, copy-edited**) edit text by checking that it is consistent and accurate.
copy editor

copying

copyist »*noun* a person who makes copies.

copyright »*noun* the exclusive right to publish, perform, film, or record literary, artistic, or musical material.

> **-right** not **-write**: **copyright**

copywriter »*noun* a person who writes the text of advertisements or publicity material.

coq au vin »*noun* a casserole of chicken pieces cooked in red wine.
– say kok oh van

> a French phrase meaning 'cock in wine'

coquette »*noun* a woman who flirts.
– say ko-ket
coquetry
coquettish

> note the double **t** in **coquette** and **coquettish**, but single **t** in **coquetry**

coracle »*noun* a small, round boat made of wickerwork covered with a watertight material.
– say ko-ruh-k'l

> there is no **k**: **coracle**

coral [hard substance made by living organisms in warm seas]

☑ there is only one **r** and one **l** in **coral**

coralline »*adjective* ❶ derived or formed from coral. ❷ pinkish-red.
– sᴀʏ ko-ruh-lyn

☑ double **l** in **coralline**

cor anglais »*noun* (plural **cors anglais**) a woodwind instrument of the oboe family.
– sᴀʏ kor **ong**-glay [singular and plural]

☑ the plural of **cor anglais** adds an **s** to **cor**: **cors anglais** (it is from a French phrase meaning 'English horn')

corbel »*noun* a projection jutting out from a wall to support a structure above it.
– sᴀʏ kor-b'l

cord [string or rope]

ℹ do not confuse **cord** with **chord**, which means 'a group of musical notes sounded together'

cordial »*adjective* ❶ warm and friendly. ❷ sincere.
»*noun* ❶ a sweet fruit-flavoured drink, sold in concentrated form. ❷ = LIQUEUR.
cordiality
cordially

cordite »*noun* a kind of explosive.

cordless

cordon »*noun* a line or circle of police, soldiers, or guards forming a barrier.
»*verb* (**cordons, cordoning, cordoned**) (**cordon off**) close off by means of a cordon.

☑ the ending is **don**, not **den**: **cordon** do not double the **n** in **cordoned** and **cordoning**

cordon bleu »*adjective* (in cookery) of the highest class.
– sᴀʏ kor-don **bler**

☑ **bleu** not **blue**: **cordon bleu** (it is from a French phrase meaning 'blue ribbon')

cordoned

cordoning

cordons

corduroy
– sᴀʏ kor-duh-roy

☑ **dur** not **der**: **corduroy**

core (verb: **cores, coring, cored**) [central part of something; take out the core of something]

ℹ do not confuse **core** with **corps**, which is pronounced the same: **corps** means 'a part of an army'

cored

cores

co-respondent »*noun* a person named in a divorce case as having committed adultery with the respondent.

☑ **co-respondent** can also be spelled without the hyphen: **corespondent** (both spellings are correct, but be careful not to double the r)

corgi »*noun* (plural **corgis**) a dog with short legs and a pointed face.

☑ the plural of **corgi** has **-is**, not **-ies**: **corgis**

coriander »*noun* a plant used as a herb in cookery.
– sᴀʏ ko-ri-**an**-der

coring

Corinthian »*adjective* relating to an ornate style of classical architecture distinguished by flared columns decorated with leaves at the top.

cork (verb: **corks, corking, corked**)

corkage »*noun* a charge made by a restaurant for serving wine that has been brought in by a customer.

corked

corking

corks

corkscrew (verb: **corkscrews, corkscrewing, corkscrewed**)

corm »*noun* an underground part of certain plants.

cormorant »*noun* a diving seabird with a long hooked bill and black plumage.
– sᴀʏ kor-muh-ruhnt

☑ **ant** not **ent**: **cormorant**

corn

corncob »*noun* the central part of an ear of maize, to which the grains are attached.

corncrake »*noun* a bird inhabiting coarse grasslands, with a distinctive rasping call.

corn dolly »*noun* a model of a human figure, made of straw.

cornea »*noun* the transparent layer forming the front of the eye.
– sᴀʏ kor-ni-uh

corned beef

cornelian another way of spelling CARNELIAN.
– sᴀʏ kor-nee-li-uhn

corner (verb: **corners, cornering, cornered**)

cornerstone »*noun* ❶ a stone that forms the base of a corner of a building. ❷ a vital part.

cornet »*noun* ❶ a brass instrument resembling a trumpet but shorter and wider. ❷ a cone-shaped wafer for holding ice cream.

 cornflakes

cornflour »*noun* ground maize flour, used for thickening sauces.

cornflower »*noun* a plant with deep blue flowers.

cornice »*noun* a decorative border round the wall of a room just below the ceiling.
– sᴀʏ **kor**-niss

cornier

corniest

Cornish

Cornish pasty »*noun* a pasty containing meat and vegetables.

cornucopia »*noun* a plentiful supply of good things.
– sᴀʏ kor-nyuu-**koh**-pi-uh

corny »*adjective* (**cornier, corniest**) trivial or very sentimental.

corolla »*noun* the petals of a flower.
– sᴀʏ kuh-**rol**-luh

> ✓ single **r** but double **l**: **corolla**

corollary »*noun* (plural **corollaries**) ❶ a logical conclusion. ❷ a direct consequence or result.
– sᴀʏ kuh-**rol**-luh-ri

corona »*noun* (plural **coronae**) ❶ the gases surrounding the sun or a star. ❷ a small circle of light seen round the sun or moon.
– sᴀʏ kuh-**roh**-nuh [singular], kuh-**roh**-nee [plural]
coronal

> ✓ **corona** is Latin for 'crown', and the plural is formed with an **e**: **coronae**

coronary »*adjective* having to do with the heart, in particular with the arteries which supply it with blood.
»*noun* (plural **coronaries**) a blockage of the flow of blood to the heart.
– sᴀʏ **ko**-ruh-nuh-ri

> ✓ the ending is **ary**, not **ory** or **nry**: **coronary**

coronation »*noun* the ceremony of crowning a sovereign.

coroner »*noun* an official who holds inquests into violent, sudden, or suspicious deaths.
– sᴀʏ **ko**-ruh-ner

> ✓ **-er** not **-or**: **coroner**

coronet »*noun* ❶ a small or simple crown. ❷ a decorative band put around the head.
– sᴀʏ ko-ruh-net

> single **t** at the end: **coronet**

corpora plural of **corpus**.

corporal[1] »*noun* a rank of officer in the army, below sergeant.

corporal[2] »*adjective* relating to the human body.

corporal punishment »*noun* physical punishment, such as caning.

corporate »*adjective* ❶ relating to a business corporation. ❷ of or shared by all members of a group.

corporation »*noun* ❶ a large company, or group of companies acting as a single unit. ❷ (in Britain) a group of people elected to govern a city, town, or borough.

corporation tax »*noun* tax paid by companies on their profits.

corporeal »*adjective* relating to a person's body; physical rather than spiritual.
– sᴀʏ kor-**por**-i-uhl

corps »*noun* (plural **corps**) ❶ a large unit of an army. ❷ a branch of an army with a particular kind of work. ❸ a body of people engaged in a particular activity.
– sᴀʏ kor [singular], korz [plural]

> ℹ do not confuse **corps** with **core**, which is pronounced the same: **core** means 'the central part of something; remove the central part of something'. The plural of **corps** is the same as the singular: **corps** (but the two words are pronounced differently).

corps de ballet »*noun* ❶ the members of a ballet company who dance together as a group. ❷ the lowest rank of dancers in a ballet company.
– sᴀʏ kor duh **bal**-lay

corpse »*noun* a dead body, especially of a human.

corpulent »*adjective* (of a person) fat.
– sᴀʏ **kor**-pyuu-luhnt
corpulence

> **-lent** not **-lant**: **corpulent**

corpus »*noun* (plural **corpora** or **corpuses**) a collection of written texts.
– sᴀʏ **kor**-puhss [singular], **kor**-puh-ruh or **kor**-puhss-iz [plural]

> ✓ the plural of **corpus** can be either **corpora** (as in Latin) or **corpuses**: both are correct

corpuscle »*noun* a red or white blood cell.

– say kor-pus-s'l

> ✓ do not forget the **c** after the **s**: **corpuscle**

corral (mainly in American English) »*noun* a pen for livestock on a farm or ranch.
» *verb* (**corrals, corralling, corralled**) ❶ drive livestock into a corral. ❷ gather a group together.
– say kuh-**rahl**

> ✓ double the **l** to spell **corralling** and **corralled**, and do not confuse **corral** with **coral** 'hard substance made by living organisms in warm seas' or **chorale** 'a simple hymn tune'

correct (verb: **corrects, correcting, corrected**)
correctly
correctness

correction

corrective »*adjective* designed to correct something undesirable.

correctly

correctness

corrects

correlate »*verb* (**correlates, correlating, correlated**) be in a situation in which one thing affects or depends on another.
– say kor-ruh-layt or kor-ri-layt

> ✓ double **r** but single **l: correlate**

correlation »*noun* ❶ a situation in which one thing affects or depends on another. ❷ the process of correlating two or more things.

correlative »*adjective* having a correlation.
– say kuh-**rel**-uh-tiv

correspond (verb: **corresponds, corresponding, corresponded**)

correspondence »*noun* ❶ the fact of corresponding. ❷ letters sent or received.

> ✓ **ence** not **ance: correspondence**

correspondence course »*noun* a course of study in which student and tutors communicate by post.

correspondent »*noun* ❶ a person who writes letters. ❷ a journalist who reports on a particular subject.

> ✓ **ent** not **ant**, and double **r: correspondent** (a **corespondent** is not the same at all)

corresponding
corresponds
corridor

> ✓ there is no **door: corridor**

corrie »*noun* (plural **corries**) a steep-sided mountain valley.

corroborate »*verb* (**corroborates, corroborating, corroborated**) confirm or give support to a statement or theory.
– say kuh-**rob**-uh-rayt
corroboration
corroborative

> ✓ two **r**'s, one **b**, then one **r: corroborate**

corrode »*verb* (**corrodes, corroding, corroded**) ❶ (with reference to metal or other hard material) wear or be worn away slowly by chemical action. ❷ gradually weaken or destroy.
– say kuh-**rohd**

> ✓ double **r: corrode**

corrosion »*noun* the process of corroding, or damage caused by this.
– say kuh-**roh**-*zh*'n

corrosive »*adjective* tending to cause corrosion.

corrugate »*verb* ❶ contract into wrinkles or folds. ❷ (**corrugated**) shaped into alternate ridges and grooves.
– say **kor**-ruh-gayt
corrugation

> ✓ two **r**'s, one **g: corrugate**

corrupt »*adjective* ❶ willing to act dishonestly in return for money or other reward. ❷ evil or immoral. ❸ (of a text or computer data) unreliable because of errors or alterations.
» *verb* (**corrupts, corrupting, corrupted**) make corrupt.
corruptible
corruptly

> ✓ double **r: corrupt**

corruption

corruptly

corrupts

corsage »*noun* a spray of flowers worn pinned to a woman's clothes.
– say kor-**sah**z*h*

corsair »*noun* (an old word) a pirate.
– say kor-**sair**

corset »*noun* a tight-fitting undergarment worn to shape a woman's figure or to support a person's back.
corsetry

cortege »*noun* a solemn funeral procession.
– SAY kor-te*zh*

 cortege can also be spelled **cortège**, with a grave accent above the **e** (as in the original French)

cortex »*noun* (plural **cortices**) the outer layer of an organ or structure.
– SAY kor-teks [singular], kor-ti-seez [plural]
cortical

 make the plural by changing the **ex** ending to **ices** (as in Latin): **cortices**

cortisone »*noun* a steroid hormone used to treat inflammation and allergy.
– SAY kor-ti-zohn

 -sone not **-zone**: **cortisone**

corundum »*noun* an extremely hard form of aluminium oxide, used for grinding, smoothing, and polishing.
– SAY kuh-run-duhm

coruscating »*adjective* flashing or sparkling.
– SAY ko-ruh-skay-ting

corvette »*noun* a small warship designed for escorting convoys.
– SAY kor-vet

 double **t** and **e** at the end: **corvette**

cos »*noun* a variety of lettuce with crisp narrow leaves.
– SAY koss

cosecant »*noun* (in a right-angled triangle) the ratio of the hypotenuse to the side opposite an acute angle.
– SAY koh-see-kuhnt or koh-sek-uhnt

cosh »*noun* a thick heavy stick or bar used as a weapon.
»*verb* (**coshes, coshing, coshed**) hit someone on the head with a cosh.

cosied

cosier

cosies

cosiest

cosily

cosine »*noun* (in a right-angled triangle) the ratio of the side next to a particular acute angle to the hypotenuse.
– SAY koh-syn

 -sine not **-sign**: **cosine**

cosiness

cosmetic »*adjective* ➊ (of treatment) intended to improve a person's appearance. ➋ improving something only outwardly.
»*noun* a substance put on the face or body to make them more attractive.
cosmetically

cosmic »*adjective* relating to the universe.
cosmically

cosmic rays »*plural noun* harmful radiation reaching the earth from space, consisting of subatomic particles.

cosmogony »*noun* (plural **cosmogonies**) the study of the origin of the earth and the solar system.
– SAY koz-mog-uh-ni
cosmogonic

cosmology »*noun* (plural **cosmologies**) the science of the origin and development of the universe.
cosmological
cosmologist

cosmonaut »*noun* a Russian astronaut.

 -naut not **-not**: **cosmonaut**

cosmopolitan »*adjective* ➊ made up of people from many different countries and cultures. ➋ familiar with and at ease in many different countries.
– SAY koz-muh-pol-i-tuhn

 -an not **-en**: **cosmopolitan**

cosmos »*noun* the universe seen as a well-ordered whole.

Cossack »*noun* a member of a people of southern Russia, Ukraine, and Siberia, famous for being good horseriders.
– SAY koss-ak

 double **s** and **ck** at the end: **Cossack**

cosset »*verb* (**cossets, cosseting, cosseted**) care for and protect someone in an excessively soft-hearted way.

 double **s**, single **t**: **cosset**
do not double the **t** in **cosseting** and **cosseted**

cost (verb: **costs, costing, cost** or **costed** in the sense 'estimate the cost of')

co-star (verb: **co-stars, co-starring, co-starred**)

Costa Rican

costed

cost-effective »*adjective* effective or productive in relation to its cost.

cost-efficient »*adjective* cost-effective.

costermonger »*noun* (old-fashioned) a person who sells fruit and vegetables from a handcart in the street.

– sᴀʏ koss-ter-mung-ger

costing

costive »*adjective* (old-fashioned) constipated.

costly (adjective: **costlier, costliest**)

cost price »*noun* the price at which goods are bought by a retailer.

costs

costume
   costumed

costume jewellery »*noun* jewellery made with inexpensive materials or imitation gems.

costumier »*noun* a person who makes or supplies theatrical or fancy-dress costumes.
– sᴀʏ koss-**tyoo**-mi-er

 ✓ mier not **mer: costumier**

cosy (plural **cosies**; adjective: **cosier, cosiest**; verb: **cosies, cosying, cosied**)
   cosily
   cosiness

 ✓ s not **z: cosy** (the spelling with a **z** is American)

cot

cotangent »*noun* (in a right-angled triangle) the ratio of the side (other than the hypotenuse) next to a particular acute angle to the side opposite the angle.
– sᴀʏ koh-**tan**-juhnt

cot death »*noun* the unexplained death of a baby in its sleep.

coterie »*noun* (plural **coteries**) a small exclusive group of people with shared interests or tastes.
– sᴀʏ **koh**-tuh-ri

 ✓ ie not **y: coterie**

cotoneaster »*noun* a shrub with small leaves and red berries.
– sᴀʏ kuh-toh-ni-**ass**-ter

cottage

cottage cheese »*noun* soft, lumpy white cheese made from the curds of skimmed milk.

cottage industry »*noun* a business or manufacturing activity carried on in people's homes.

cottage pie »*noun* a dish of minced meat topped with browned mashed potato.

cottager »*noun* a person living in a cottage.

cotter pin »*noun* ❶ a metal pin used to fasten two parts of a mechanism together.

❷ a split pin that is opened out after being passed through a hole.

cotton (verb: **cottons, cottoning, cottoned**)
   cottony

 ✓ do not double the **n** in **cottoned, cottoning**, and **cottony**

cotyledon »*noun* the first leaf that grows from a seed.
– sᴀʏ ko-ti-**lee**-duhn

couch (verb: **couches, couching, couched**)
– sᴀʏ kowch

couch grass »*noun* a coarse grass with long creeping roots.
– sᴀʏ kowch or kooch

couching

couch potato »*noun* (in informal English) a person who spends a great deal of time watching television.

cougar »*noun* (in American English) a puma.
– sᴀʏ **koo**-ger

 ✓ ar not **er: cougar**

cough (verb: **coughs, coughing, coughed**)

could

couldn't [could not]

✓ be careful to put the apostrophe where a letter has been left out, that is between the **n** and **t** of **not: couldn't**

coulis »*noun* (plural **coulis**) a thin fruit or vegetable puree, used as a sauce.
– sᴀʏ **koo**-li

coulomb »*noun* the basic unit of electric charge.
– sᴀʏ **koo**-lom

✓ don't forget the **b** at the end: **coulomb** (named after the French military engineer Charles-Augustin de *Coulomb*)

council [administrative or advisory body]

ⓘ do not confuse **council** with **counsel**, which means 'advice' or 'advise'

councillor »*noun* a member of a council.

✓ double **l**, and **-or** not **-er: councillor** (the spelling with a single **l** is American)

council tax »*noun* (in the UK) a tax charged on households by local authorities, based on the estimated value of a property.

counsel (verb: **counsels, counselling, counselled**) [advice; advise]

ⓘ do not confuse **counsel** with **council**, which means 'an administrative or advisory body' double the l in **counselling** and **counselled** (the spellings with a single l are American)

counsellor »*noun* ❶ a person trained to give advice on personal or psychological problems. ❷ a senior officer in the diplomatic service.

 double l, and **-or** not **-er: counsellor** (the spelling with a single l is American)

counsels

count (verb: **counts, counting, counted**)
  countable

countdown

counted

countenance »*noun* a person's face or expression.
  »*verb* (**countenances, countenancing, countenanced**) tolerate or allow.

 nance not **nence: countenance**

counter[1] [shop fitting; token]

counter[2] »*verb* (**counters, countering, countered**) speak or act in opposition or response to: *he helped to counter an invasion*.
  »*adverb* (**counter to**) in the opposite direction or in opposition to.
  »*adjective* opposing.
  »*noun* an act which opposes something else.

counteract »*verb* (**counteracts, counteracting, counteracted**) act against something so as to reduce its force or cancel it out.

counter-attack (verb: **counter-attacks, counter-attacking, counter-attacked**)

counter-attraction

counterbalance »*noun* ❶ a weight that balances another. ❷ something that has an equal but opposite effect to something else.
  »*verb* (**counterbalances, counterbalancing, counterbalanced**) have an equal but opposite effect on something.

counterclockwise

counterculture

countered

counter-espionage »*noun* activities designed to prevent spying by an enemy.

counterfeit »*adjective* made in exact imitation of something valuable so as to deceive or cheat people.
  »*noun* a forgery.

»*verb* (**counterfeits, counterfeiting, counterfeited**) imitate something dishonestly.
– SAY **kown**-ter-fit
  counterfeiter

 counterfeit does not follow the usual rule **i** before **e**, except after **c**

counterfoil »*noun* the part of a cheque, ticket, etc. that is kept as a record by the person issuing it.

countering

countermand »*verb* (**countermands, countermanding, countermanded**) cancel an order.

countermeasure »*noun* an action taken to counteract a danger or threat.

counterpane »*noun* a bedspread.

 pane not **pain: counterpane**

counterpart »*noun* a person or thing that corresponds to another.

counterpoint »*noun* ❶ the playing of two or more tunes at the same time. ❷ a tune played at the same time as another. ❸ an idea or theme contrasting with the main element.
  »*verb* (**counterpoints, counterpointing, counterpointed**) emphasize something by contrast.

counterpoise »*noun* a counterbalance.
  »*verb* (**counterpoises, counterpoising, counterpoised**) counterbalance.

counterproductive »*adjective* having the opposite of the desired effect.

counters

countersign »*verb* (**countersigns, countersigning, countersigned**) sign a document already signed by another person.

countersink »*verb* (**countersinks, countersinking, countersunk**) insert a screw or bolt so that the head doesn't stick out from the surface.

countertenor »*noun* the highest male adult singing voice.

countervail »*verb* (**countervails, countervailing, countervailed**) counteract something with something else of equal force.
– SAY **kown**-ter-**vayl**

 vail not **vale: countervail**

counterweight »*noun* a counterbalancing weight.

countess (plural **countesses**)

counties

counting

countless

count noun »*noun* a noun that can form a plural and, in the singular, can be used with *a*, e.g. *books*, *a book*.

countries

countrified »*adjective* characteristic of the country or country life.

country (plural **countries**)

☑ plural: drop the **y** and add **ies**: **countries**

country and western »*noun* country music.

country dance »*noun* a traditional type of English dance performed by couples facing each other in long lines.

countryman (plural **countrymen**)

country music »*noun* a form of popular music from the rural southern US, featuring ballads and dance tunes.

countryside

countrywoman (plural **countrywomen**)

counts

county (plural **counties**)

☑ plural: drop the **y** and add **ies**: **counties**

county town »*noun* the main town of a county, where its council is based.

coup »*noun* (plural **coups**) ❶ a coup d'etat. ❷ a successful move: *the deal is a major coup for the company.*
– sᴀʏ koo [singular], kooz [plural]

coup de grace »*noun* (plural **coups de grace**) a final blow or shot given to kill a wounded person or animal.
– sᴀʏ koo duh **grahss** [singular and plural]

☑ **coup de grace** can also be spelled **coup de grâce**, with a circumflex accent above the **e** (as in the original French)
when forming the plural, add **s** after **coup**: **coups de grace**

coup d'etat »*noun* (plural **coups d'etat**) a sudden violent seizing of power from a government.
– sᴀʏ koo day-**tah** [singular and plaural]

☑ **coup d'etat** can also be spelled **coup d'état**, with an acute accent over the **e** (as in the original French)
when forming the plural add **s** after **coup**: **coups d'etat**

coupe »*noun* a car with a fixed roof, two doors, and a sloping rear.
– sᴀʏ koop or **koo**-pay

☑ **coupe** can also be spelled **coupé**, with an acute accent over the **e** (as in the original French)

couple (verb: **couples**, **coupling**, **coupled**)
coupler

couplet »*noun* a pair of rhyming lines of poetry one after another.

coupling

coupon

courage

courageous
courageously

courgette »*noun* a long, thin vegetable with green skin and soft white flesh.
– sᴀʏ koor-**zhet**

☑ don't forget the **u** and the double **t**: **courgette**

courier »*noun* ❶ a messenger employed to deliver goods or documents quickly. ❷ a person employed to guide and help a group of tourists.
– sᴀʏ kuu-ri-er

course (verb: **courses**, **coursing**, **coursed**) [direction taken; stage of meal; flow]

ℹ do not confuse **course** with **coarse**, which means 'rough'

coursebook

coursed

courses

coursework

coursing

court (verb: **courts**, **courting**, **courted**)

court card »*noun* a playing card that is a king, queen, or jack of a suit.

courted

courteous »*adjective* polite and considerate.
– sᴀʏ ker-ti-uhss
courteously

☑ don't forget the first **o**: **courteous**

courtesan »*noun* a prostitute with wealthy or upper-class clients.
– sᴀʏ kor-ti-zan

☑ **tes** not **tis**: courtesan

courtesy »*noun* (plural **courtesies**) ❶ polite and considerate behaviour. ❷ a polite speech or action.
– sᴀʏ ker-tuh-si

☑ **cou** not **cu**: courtesy
plural: drop the **y** and add **ies**: **courtesies**

courthouse

C

courtier »*noun* a king or queen's companion or adviser.
– SAY kor-ti-er

courting

courtly »*adjective* (**courtlier, courtliest**) very dignified and polite.

court martial »*noun* (plural **courts martial** or **court martials**) a court for trying members of the armed services accused of breaking military law.
» *verb* (**court-martial**) (**court-martials, court-martialling, court-martialled**) try someone by court martial.

> ✓ double the l in **court-martialling** and **court-martialled** (the spellings with a single l are American)
> to make the plural add **s** after **court** or after **martial**, but not after both: **courts martial** or **court martials**

courtroom

courts

courtship »*noun* ❶ a period during which a couple develop a romantic relationship. ❷ the process of trying to win a person's love or support.

courtyard

couscous »*noun* a North African dish of steamed or soaked semolina, served with spicy meat or vegetables.
– SAY **kuuss**-kuuss or **kooss**-kooss

> ✓ no hyphen in **couscous**

cousin

couture »*noun* the designing and making of fashionable clothes to a particular customer's requirements.
– SAY koo-**tyoor**

couturier »*noun* a person who designs and sells couture clothes.
– SAY koo-**tyoo**-ri-ay

couturiere »*noun* a woman who designs and sells couture clothes.
– SAY koo-tyoo-ri-**air**

> ✓ **couturiere** can also be spelled **couturière**, with a grave accent above the **e** (as in the original French)

cove »*noun* a small sheltered bay.

coven »*noun* a group of witches who meet regularly.
– SAY **kuv**-uhn

covenant »*noun* ❶ a formal agreement. ❷ an agreement saying that you will make regular payments to a charity. ❸ an agreement believed to be the basis of a relationship of commitment between God and his people.

» *verb* (**covenants, covenanting, covenanted**) agree or pay by covenant.
– SAY **kuv**-uh-nuhnt

> ✓ ant not ent: **covenant**

cover (verb: **covers, covering, covered**)

coverage

cover charge »*noun* a service charge per person added to the bill in a restaurant.

covered

covering

coverlet »*noun* a bedspread.

cover note »*noun* a temporary certificate showing that a person has a current insurance policy.

covers

covert »*adjective* not done openly; secret.
» *noun* a thicket in which game can hide.
– SAY **kuv**-ert or **koh**-vert [adjective], **kuv**-ert [noun]
covertly

cover-up

covet »*verb* (**covets, coveting, coveted**) long to possess something belonging to someone else.
– SAY **kuv**-it

> ✓ do not double the t in **coveting** and **coveted**

covetous »*adjective* longing to possess something.
covetously

covets

covey »*noun* (plural **coveys**) a small flock of game birds.
– SAY **kuv**-i

cow[1] [animal]

cow[2] »*verb* (**cows, cowing, cowed**) frighten someone into doing what you want.

coward

cowardice

cowardly

cowboy

cowed

cower (verb: **cowers, cowering, cowered**)

cowgirl

cowhide

cowing

cowl »*noun* ❶ a large loose hood forming part of a monk's habit. ❷ a hood-shaped covering for a chimney or ventilation shaft.

> ✓ there is no e in **cowl**

cowlick »*noun* a lock of hair hanging over the forehead.

cowling »*noun* a removable cover for a vehicle or aircraft engine.

cowpat

cowrie »*noun* (plural **cowries**) a shellfish that has a glossy shell with a long, narrow opening.
– SAY kow-ri

 cowrie can also be spelled **cowry**: both spellings are correct

cows

cowshed

cowslip »*noun* a wild plant with clusters of sweet-smelling yellow flowers.

cox »*noun* a coxswain.
»*verb* (**coxes, coxing, coxed**) act as a coxswain for a rowing crew.

coxcomb »*noun* (an old word) a vain and conceited man.
– SAY koks-kohm

 x not cks: coxcomb. See also the note at COCKSCOMB.

coxed

coxes

coxing

coxswain »*noun* a person whose job it is to steer a rowing boat.
– SAY kok-suhn

 be careful writing this word which is pronounced and spelled very differently: **coxswain**

coy »*adjective* (**coyer, coyest**) ❶ pretending to be shy or modest. ❷ reluctant to give details about something sensitive.
coyly
coyness

coyote »*noun* a wolf-like wild dog found in North America.
– SAY koy-oht or koy-**oh**-ti

coypu »*noun* (plural **coypus**) a large South American rodent resembling a beaver.
– SAY koy-pyoo

cozen »*verb* (**cozens, cozening, cozened**) (an old word) trick or deceive.
– SAY kuz-uhn

cozy American spelling of **cosy**.

CPS »*abbreviation* Crown Prosecution Service.

crab

crabbed »*adjective* ❶ (of writing) hard to read or understand. ❷ bad-tempered.

crabby »*adjective* (**crabbier, crabbiest**) bad-tempered.

crabwise »*adverb & adjective* sideways.

crack (verb: **cracks, cracking, cracked**)

crackdown

cracked

cracker

crackerjack

cracking

crackle (verb: **crackles, crackling, crackled**)
crackling
crackly

crackpot »*noun* an eccentric or foolish person.
»*adjective* eccentric; impractical.

cracks

cradle (verb: **cradles, cradling, cradled**)

craft (verb: **crafts, crafting, crafted**)

craftier

craftiest

craftily

craftiness

crafting

crafts

craftsman (plural **craftsmen**)
craftsmanship

craftswoman (plural **craftswomen**)

crafty (adjective: **craftier, craftiest**)
craftily
craftiness

crag »*noun* a steep or rugged cliff or rock face.
craggy

cram (verb: **crams, cramming, crammed**)

 double the **m** in cramming and crammed

crammer »*noun* a college that gives concentrated preparation for examinations.

cramming

cramp »*noun* ❶ painful involuntary tightening of a muscle or muscles. ❷ a tool for clamping two objects together.
»*verb* (**cramps, cramping, cramped**) restrict the development of something.

cramped »*adjective* ❶ uncomfortably small or crowded. ❷ (of handwriting) small and difficult to read.

cramping

crampon »*noun* a metal plate with spikes, fixed to a boot for climbing on ice or rock.

cramps

crams

cranberry (plural **cranberries**)

crane »*noun* ❶ a tall machine used for moving heavy objects by suspending them

from a projecting arm. ❷ a wading bird with long legs and a long neck.
» *verb* (**cranes, craning, craned**) stretch out your neck to see something.

crane fly »*noun* a daddy-long-legs.

cranes

cranesbill »*noun* a plant with purple or violet flowers with five petals.

crania plural of **CRANIUM**.

cranial »*adjective* relating to the skull or cranium.
– SAY kray-ni-uhl

craning

cranium »*noun* (plural **craniums** or **crania**) the part of the skull enclosing the brain.
– SAY kray-ni-uhm

> ✓ the plural can be either **crania** (like the original Latin) or **craniums**

crank »*noun* ❶ a part of a shaft that is bent at right angles, so as to produce movement when the shaft turns. ❷ an eccentric person.
» *verb* (**cranks, cranking, cranked**) ❶ turn a crankshaft or handle. ❷ (**crank up**) increase the intensity of something. ❸ (**crank out**) produce something regularly and routinely.

crankcase

crankier

crankiest

cranking

cranks

crankshaft »*noun* a shaft driven by a crank.

cranky »*adjective* (**crankier, crankiest**) ❶ eccentric; odd. ❷ bad-tempered; irritable.

cranny »*noun* (plural **crannies**) a small, narrow space or opening.

> ✓ plural: drop the **y** and add **ies**: **crannies**

crap (verb: **craps, crapping, crapped**)
crappy

> ✓ double the **p** in **crapping, crapped**, and **crappy**

crape »*noun* black silk, formerly used for mourning clothes.

> ℹ do not confuse **crape** with **crepe**: see the note at **CREPE**

crapped

crapping

crappy

craps

crapulous »*adjective* relating to the drinking of alcohol or to drunkenness.
– SAY krap-yuu-luhss
crapulent

crash (verb: **crashes, crashing, crashed**)

crash-land (verb: **crash-lands, crash-landing, crash-landed**)

crass »*adjective* very thoughtless and stupid.
crassly
crassness

crate (verb: **crates, crating, crated**)

crater

crates

crating

cravat »*noun* a strip of fabric worn by men round the neck and tucked inside a shirt.
– SAY kruh-vat

crave (verb: **craves, craving, craved**)

craven »*adjective* cowardly.

craves

craving

craw »*noun* (old-fashioned) the part of a bird's throat where food is prepared for digestion.

crawl (verb: **crawls, crawling, crawled**)
crawler

crayfish »*noun* a freshwater or marine shellfish resembling a small lobster.

crayon »*noun* a stick of coloured chalk or wax, used for drawing.
» *verb* (**crayons, crayoning, crayoned**) draw with a crayon or crayons.

> ✓ do not double the **n** in **crayoned** and **crayoning**

craze »*noun* a widespread but short-lived enthusiasm for something.

crazed »*adjective* ❶ wildly insane. ❷ covered with a network of fine cracks.

crazy (adjective: **crazier, craziest**)
crazily
craziness

> ✓ drop the **y** and add **ier** or **iest** to spell **crazier** or **craziest**

creak (verb: **creaks, creaking, creaked**)
[harsh squeaking sound]

> ℹ do not confuse **creak** with **creek**, which refers to a stretch of water

creaky (adjective: **creakier, creakiest**)
creakily
creakiness

cream (verb: **creams, creaming, creamed**)

creamer »*noun* a cream or milk substitute for adding to coffee or tea.

creamery »*noun* (plural **creameries**) a factory where butter and cheese are produced.

creamier

creamiest

creaminess

creaming

creams

creamy (adjective: **creamier**, **creamiest**)
creaminess

crease »*noun* ❶ a line or ridge produced by folding or pressing something. ❷ (in cricket) one of a number of lines marked on the pitch.
» *verb* (**creases**, **creasing**, **creased**) make or become crumpled.

create (verb: **creates**, **creating**, **created**)

creation

creative »*adjective* using the imagination or original ideas in order to create something.
creatively
creativity

creator »*noun* ❶ a person or thing that creates. ❷ (the Creator) God.

✓ -or not -er: creator

creature »*noun* a living being, in particular an animal rather than a person.

creche »*noun* a place where babies and young children are looked after while their parents are at work.
– SAY kresh

✓ creche can also be written crèche, with a grave accent on the e (as in the original French)

credal »*adjective* relating to a creed.
– SAY kree-d'l

✓ note that while creed has two e's, credal has only one

credence »*noun* ❶ acceptance that something is true: *he gave no credence to the witness's statement.* ❷ credibility.
– SAY kree-duhnss

✓ there is no double e, and the ending is ence not ance: credence

credential »*noun* ❶ a qualification, achievement, or quality used to indicate how suitable a person is for something: *his academic credentials cannot be doubted.* ❷ (**credentials**) documents that prove a person's identity or qualifications.
– SAY kri-den-sh'l

credibility »*noun* the quality of being credible.

ⓘ do not confuse credibility with credulity, which means 'the quality of being too ready to believe things'

credible »*adjective* able to be believed; convincing.
credibly

ⓘ do not confuse credible with creditable, which means 'deserving recognition and praise'

credit (verb: **credits**, **crediting**, **credited**)

creditable »*adjective* deserving recognition and praise.
creditably

ⓘ do not confuse creditable with credible, which means 'able to be believed'

credited

crediting

creditor »*noun* a person or company to whom money is owed.

credits

creditworthy »*adjective* suitable to receive financial credit.
creditworthiness

credo »*noun* (plural **credos**) a statement of a person's beliefs or aims.
– SAY kree-doh or kray-doh

✓ the plural of credo (a Latin word meaning literally 'I believe') has os not oes: credos

credulity »*noun* the tendency to be too ready to believe things.
– SAY kri-dyoo-li-ti

ⓘ do not confuse credulity with credibility, which means 'the quality of being credible'

credulous »*adjective* too ready to believe things.
– SAY kred-yuu-luhss

ⓘ do not confuse credulous with credible, which means 'believable'

creed »*noun* ❶ a system of religious belief; a faith. ❷ a statement of beliefs or principles: *liberalism was more than a political creed.*

creek »*noun* a narrow stretch of water running inland from the coast.

ⓘ do not confuse creek with creak meaning 'harsh squeaking sound'

creel »*noun* a large basket for carrying fish.

creep (verb: **creeps**, **creeping**, **crept**)
creeper

creepy (adjective: **creepier**, **creepiest**)
creepiness

cremate »*verb* (**cremates, cremating, cremated**) dispose of a dead body by burning it to ashes.
cremation

crematorium »*noun* (plural **crematoria** or **crematoriums**) a building where dead people are cremated.

> ✓ the plural can be either **crematoria** (like the original Latin) or **crematoriums**

creme brulee »*noun* (plural **cremes brulees** or **creme brulees**) a dessert of custard topped with caramelized sugar.
– **say** krem broo-**lay** [singular], krem broo-**lay** or krem broo-**layz** [plural]

> ✓ **creme brulee** is sometimes written with accents, as in French *crème brûlée*, 'burnt cream'

creme caramel »*noun* (plural **cremes caramel** or **creme caramels**) a custard dessert made with whipped cream and eggs and topped with caramel.
– **say** krem ka-ruh-**mel** [singular], krem ka-ruh-**mel** or krem ka-ruh-**melz** [plural]

> ✓ like other phrases involving the French word *crème* 'cream', **creme caramel** is often written with a grave accent

creme de la creme »*noun* the best person or thing of a particular kind.
– **say** krem duh la **krem**

> ℹ a French phrase meaning 'cream of the cream', and sometimes written with grave accents: **crème de la crème**

creme de menthe »*noun* a green liqueur flavoured with peppermint.
– **say** krem duh **month**

> ℹ from French *crème de menthe* 'cream of mint'

creme fraiche »*noun* a type of thick cream with buttermilk, sour cream, or yogurt.
– **say** krem **fresh**

> ✓ also written **crème fraiche**, as in the original French (meaning 'fresh cream')

Creole »*noun* ❶ a person of mixed European and black descent. ❷ a descendant of French settlers in the southern US. ❸ a combination of a European language and an African language.
– **say** kree-ohl

creosote »*noun* a dark brown oil obtained from coal tar, painted on to wood to preserve it.

> ✓ spelled **creo** not **crea**: **creosote**

crepe »*noun* ❶ a light, thin fabric with a wrinkled surface. ❷ hard-wearing wrinkled rubber used for the soles of shoes. ❸ a thin pancake.
– **say** krayp or [in sense 'pancake' only] krep

> ✓ **crepe** is sometimes written with a circumflex accent (**crêpe**), as in the original French. It should not be confused with **crape**, which refers to black silk (**crape** is a variant spelling of **crepe**).

crepe paper »*noun* thin, crinkled paper.

crept past and past participle of **CREEP**.

crepuscular »*adjective* resembling or relating to twilight.
– **say** kri-**pus**-kyuu-ler

crescendo »*noun* (plural **crescendos** or **crescendi**) ❶ a gradual increase in loudness in a piece of music. ❷ a climax. »*adverb & adjective* (in music) gradually becoming louder.
– **say** kri-**shen**-doh

> ℹ form the plural with **os**, not **oes**: **crescendos**. In music the Italian plural **crescendi** (**say** kri-**shen**-di) is also used.

crescent »*noun* a narrow curved shape tapering to a point at each end, like the moon seen just before or just after it is new.

> ✓ watch for the **sc** in the middle: **crescent**

cress »*noun* a plant with hot-tasting leaves, eaten in salads.

crest (verb: **crests, cresting, crested**) **crested**

crestfallen »*adjective* sad and disappointed.

Cretaceous »*adjective* relating to the geological period from about 146 to 65 million years ago.
– **say** kri-**tay**-shuhss

cretin »*noun* a stupid person.
– **say** **kret**-in
cretinous

Creutzfeldt–Jakob disease »*noun* full form of **CJD**.
– **say** kroyts-felt-**yak**-ob

crevasse »*noun* a deep open crack in a glacier or ice field.
– **say** kri-**vass**

> ℹ a **crevasse** is a crack in a glacier or ice field, whereas a **crevice** is in rock or a wall

crevice »*noun* a narrow opening or crack in rock or a wall.
– **say** **kre**-viss

crew[1] (verb: **crews, crewing, crewed**)
[people who work on a ship, aircraft, etc.]

crew[2] past of **CROW**.

crew cut »*noun* a very short haircut for men and boys.

> ☑ add a hyphen if you use this word as an adjective, as in *crew-cut boys*

crewed

crewing

crews

crib »*noun* **❶** (mainly in American English) a child's cot. **❷** something copied from another person's work. **❸** the card game cribbage.
» *verb* (**cribs, cribbing, cribbed**) copy something dishonestly.

> ☑ double the **b** in **cribbed** and **cribbing**

cribbage »*noun* a card game for two players.

cribbed

cribbing

cribs

crick »*noun* a painful stiff feeling in the neck or back.
» *verb* (**cricks, cricking, cricked**) twist or strain the neck or back.

cricket
cricketer
cricketing

cricking

cricks

cried past and past participle of **CRY**.

crier [person who cries]

> ☑ spell **crier** with an **i**, not a **y**

cries

crime

criminal
criminality
criminally

criminology »*noun* the scientific study of crime and criminals.
criminologist

crimp »*verb* (**crimps, crimping, crimped**) press something into small folds or ridges.
crimper

crimson

cringe »*verb* (**cringes, cringing, cringed**) **❶** shrink back or cower in fear. **❷** have a sudden feeling of embarrassment or disgust.

crinkle (verb: **crinkles, crinkling, crinkled**)
crinkly

crinoline »*noun* a petticoat stiffened with hoops, formerly worn to make a long skirt stand out.
– SAY **krin**-uh-lin

cripple (verb: **cripples, crippling, crippled**)

> ℹ do not refer to a person as **a cripple**: it can be offensive and you should use a term such as 'a disabled person' instead

crisis »*noun* (plural **crises**) **❶** a time of severe difficulty or danger. **❷** a time when a difficult or important decision must be made.
– SAY **krI**-siss [singular], **krI**-seez [plural]

> ☑ make the plural by changing the **-is** ending to **-es** (as in Latin): **crises**

crisp (adjective: **crisper, crispest**)
crisply
crispness

crispbread »*noun* a thin crisp biscuit made from rye or wheat.

crisper

crispest

crispier

crispiest

crisply

crispness

crispy (adjective: **crispier, crispiest**)

criss-cross (verb: **criss-crosses, criss-crossing, criss-crossed**)

criterion »*noun* (plural **criteria**) a standard by which something may be judged or decided.
– SAY kry-**teer**-i-uhn

> ℹ **criterion** is a singular word (*a further criterion needs to be considered*) and the plural is **criteria** (*further criteria*). Be careful not to use **criteria** as if it were a singular.

critic

critical
criticality
critically

criticise another way of spelling **CRITICIZE**.

criticism

criticize (verb: **criticizes, criticizing, criticized**)

> ☑ many people prefer the alternative spellings **criticise, criticises**, etc.: both **s** and **z** spellings are correct

critique »*noun* a critical assessment.
– SAY kri-**teek**

croak (verb: **croaks, croaking, croaked**)
croaky

Croat »*noun* a person from Croatia.
– SAY kroh-at

Croatian

crochet »*noun* a craft in which yarn is made into fabric with a hooked needle.
» *verb* (**crochets, crocheting, crocheted**) make something in this way.
– SAY kroh-shay; **kroh**-shay-ing [crocheting], **kroh**-shayd [crocheted]

croci see **CROCUS**.

crock
crocked

crockery

crocodile

 croco not croca: crocodile

crocus »*noun* (plural **crocuses**) a small plant with bright yellow, purple, or white flowers.

the normal plural of **crocus** is **crocuses**; the Latin plural **croci** (SAY kroh-kee) is now only used humorously

croft »*noun* a small rented farm in Scotland or northern England.
crofter
crofting

croissant »*noun* a crescent-shaped flaky bread roll.
– SAY krwass-on

 a French word, **croissant** has an i and the s is double

crone »*noun* an ugly old woman.

crony »*noun* (plural **cronies**) (used in an insulting way) a close friend or companion.
– SAY kroh-ni
cronyism

the ending is simply y, not **ey**: **crony** plural: drop the y and add **ies**: **cronies**

crook »*noun* ❶ a shepherd's or bishop's hooked staff. ❷ a bend at a person's elbow. ❸ (in informal English) a criminal or dishonest person.
» *verb* (**crooks, crooking, crooked**) bend a finger or leg.

crooked
crookedly
crookedness

crooking

crooks

croon »*verb* (**croons, crooning, crooned**) hum, sing, or speak in a soft, low voice.
crooner

crop (verb: **crops, cropping, cropped**)

cropper »*noun* (**come a cropper**) (in informal English) fall or fail heavily.

cropping

crops

croquet »*noun* a game in which wooden balls are driven through hoops with a mallet.
– SAY kroh-kay

croquette »*noun* a small cake or roll of vegetables, meat, or fish, fried in breadcrumbs.
– SAY kroh-**ket**

crosier another way of spelling **CROZIER**.

cross (plural **crosses**; verb: **crosses, crossing, crossed**; adjective: **crosser, crossest**)

crossbar

crossbow

cross-breed »*noun* an animal or plant produced by crossing two different species, breeds, or varieties.
» *verb* (**cross-breeds, cross-breeding, cross-bred**) breed in this way.

cross-check (verb: **cross-checks, cross-checking, cross-checked**)

cross-country

cross-dressing »*noun* the wearing of clothing typical of the opposite sex.
cross-dresser

crossed

crosser

crosses

crossest

cross-examine »*verb* (**cross-examines, cross-examining, cross-examined**) question a witness called by the other party in a court of law.
cross-examination

cross-eyed

cross-fertilize »*verb* (**cross-fertilizes, cross-fertilizing, cross-fertilized**) ❶ fertilize a plant using pollen from another plant of the same species. ❷ stimulate the development of something with an exchange of ideas.
cross-fertilization

the alternative spellings **cross-fertilise** and **cross-fertilisation** are also correct

crossfire

cross-hatch »*verb* (**cross-hatches, cross-hatching, cross-hatched**) shade an area with many intersecting parallel lines.

crossing

cross-legged

crossover

crosspiece

cross-question »*verb* (**cross-questions, cross-questioning, cross-questioned**) cross-examine; question someone in great detail.

cross-refer (verb: **cross-refers, cross-referring, cross-referred**)

cross reference »*noun* a reference to another text or part of a text, given to provide further information.

cross-referred

cross-referring

cross-refers

crossroads

cross section »*noun* **❶** a surface exposed by making a straight cut through a solid object at right angles to its length. **❷** a sample of a larger group.

crossways »*adverb* = **CROSSWISE.**

crosswind

crosswise »*adverb* **❶** in the form of a cross. **❷** diagonally.

crossword

crotch »*noun* the part of the body between the legs.

> ℹ️ the word **crutch** can mean the same as **crotch**, but it can also refer to supports used for walking by a lame person

crotchet »*noun* a musical note that lasts half as long as a minim.

> ✅ remember the first **t**: **crotchet** (**crochet** is a craft in which yarn is made into fabric with a hooked needle)

crotchety »*adjective* irritable.

crouch (verb: **crouches, crouching, crouched**)

croup »*noun* **❶** an illness of children, with coughing and breathing difficulties. **❷** the rump of a horse.
– **SAY** kroop

croupier »*noun* the person in charge of a gambling table in a casino.
– **SAY** kroo-pi-ay or kroo-pi-er

crouton »*noun* a small piece of fried or toasted bread served with soup or used as a garnish.
– **SAY** kroo-ton

> ✅ remember the **ou**: **crouton**

crow (verb: **crows, crowing, crowed or crew**)

crowbar »*noun* an iron bar with a flattened end, used as a lever.

crowd (verb: **crowds, crowding, crowded**) [large number of people; come together as a crowd]

crowded

crowed past of **CROW.**

crowfoot »*noun* a water plant with white or yellow flowers.

crowing

crown (verb: **crowns, crowning, crowned**)

Crown Court »*noun* (in England and Wales) a court which deals with serious cases referred from the magistrates' courts.

crowned

crowning

crowns

crows

crow's-nest »*noun* a platform on a ship's mast for a lookout to watch from.

crozier »*noun* a hooked staff carried by a bishop.
– **SAY** kroh-zi-er or kroh-*zh*er

> ✅ can also be spelled with an **s**: both **crozier** and **crosier** are correct

crucial »*adjective* decisive or critical: *negotiations were at a crucial stage.*
crucially

crucible »*noun* a container in which metals or other substances may be melted or heated.
– **SAY** kroo-si-b'l

> ✅ **c** not **s**; **-ible** not **-able**: **crucible**

crucified

crucifies

crucifix »*noun* (plural **crucifixes**) a small cross with a figure of Jesus on it.
– **SAY** kroo-si-fiks

crucifixion

> ✅ **x** not **ct**: **crucifixion**. It is normally spelled with a capital **C** when referring to Jesus's death: **the Crucifixion.**

cruciform »*adjective* shaped like a cross.
– **SAY** kroo-si-form

crucify »*verb* (**crucifies, crucifying, crucified**) **❶** execute someone by nailing or binding them to a cross. **❷** (in informal English) criticize someone severely.

crud

crude »*adjective* (**cruder, crudest**) **❶** in a natural state; not yet processed. **❷** rough or simple: *a pair of crude huts.* **❸** coarse or vulgar.
crudely
crudeness
crudity

crudites »*plural noun* mixed raw vegetables served with a dip.
– SAY kroo-di-tay

☑ **crudites** can also be written **crudités**, with an acute accent on the **e** (as in the original French). The final **s** is silent.

crudity

cruel »*adjective* (**crueller, cruellest**)
❶ taking pleasure in the suffering of others. ❷ causing pain or suffering.
cruelly

☑ double the **l** in **crueller** and **cruellest** (**crueler** and **cruelest** are American spellings)

cruelty (plural **cruelties**)

☑ plural: drop the **y** and add **ies**: **cruelties**

cruet »*noun* ❶ a small container for salt, pepper, oil, or vinegar. ❷ a stand holding such containers.
– SAY kroo-it

cruise »*verb* (**cruises, cruising, cruised**)
❶ move slowly around without a precise destination. ❷ travel smoothly at a moderate speed.
»*noun* a voyage on a ship taken as a holiday.

☑ do not forget the **i**, and **cruise** and related words such as **cruiser** are always spelled with an **s**, not a **z**

cruise missile »*noun* a low-flying missile fitted with a computer to guide it to its target.

cruiser

cruiserweight »*noun* a weight in boxing coming between middleweight and heavyweight.

cruises

cruising

crumb »*noun* ❶ a small piece of bread, cake, or biscuit. ❷ a very small amount of something.

☑ do not forget the final **b: crumb**

crumble (verb: **crumbles, crumbling, crumbled**)

crumbly (adjective: **crumblier, crumbliest**)

crummy »*adjective* (**crummier, crummiest**) (in informal English) bad or unpleasant.

crumpet »*noun* ❶ a soft, flat cake with an open texture, eaten toasted and buttered. ❷ (in informal English) women regarded as objects of sexual desire.

crumple (verb: **crumples, crumpling, crumpled**)

crunch (verb: **crunches, crunching, crunched**)

crunchy (adjective: **crunchier, crunchiest**)

crusade »*noun* ❶ (**the Crusades**) a series of medieval military expeditions made by Europeans against Muslims in the Middle East. ❷ an energetic organized campaign: *a crusade against crime.*
»*verb* (**crusades, crusading, crusaded**) lead or take part in a crusade.
crusader

crush (verb: **crushes, crushing, crushed**)
crusher

crust (verb: **crusts, crusting, crusted**)

crustacean »*noun* an animal of a kind including crabs, lobsters, and shrimps, with a hard shell.
– SAY kruss-**tay**-sh'n

crusted

crustier

crustiest

crusting

crusts

crusty (adjective: **crustier, crustiest**)

crutch »*noun* ❶ a long stick with a crosspiece at the top, used as a support by a lame person. ❷ a person's crotch.

crux »*noun* (plural **cruxes**) the most important point that is being discussed: *the crux of the matter is that attitudes have changed.*

cry (plural **cries**; verb: **cries, crying, cried**)
crier

crybaby (plural **crybabies**)

crying

cryogenics »*noun* the branch of physics concerned with very low temperatures.
– SAY kry-uh-**jen**-iks
cryogenic

☑ **cry** not **cri**: **cryogenics** (**cryo**- comes from a Greek word meaning 'frost')

crypt »*noun* an underground room beneath a church, used as a chapel or burial place.

cryptic »*adjective* mysterious or obscure in meaning: *a cryptic message.*
– SAY **krip**-tik
cryptically

cryptography »*noun* the art of writing or solving codes.
cryptographer
cryptographic

crystal

crystalline »*adjective* having the form of a crystal or crystals.
– SAY kriss-tuh-lyn

> ☑ double l in the middle of **crystalline** and **crystallize**

crystallize »*verb* (**crystallizes, crystallizing, crystallized**) ❶ make into or form crystals. ❷ make or become definite and clear. **crystallization**

> ☑ many people prefer the alternative spellings **crystallise, crystallises**, etc., and **crystallisation**: both **s** and **z** spellings are correct

CS gas »*noun* a powerful form of tear gas used in the control of riots.

cub

Cuban [of Cuba]

cubbyhole »*noun* a small enclosed space or room.

cube (verb: **cubes, cubing, cubed**)

cube root »*noun* the number which produces a given number when cubed.

cubes

cubic »*adjective* ❶ having the shape of a cube. ❷ involving the cube of a quantity: *a cubic metre*.

cubicle

> ☑ **le** not **al**: **cubicle**

cubing

cubism »*noun* an early 20th-century style of painting in which objects are shown as made up of regular lines and shapes. **cubist**

cubit »*noun* an ancient measure of length, approximately equal to the length of a forearm.
– SAY kyoo-bit

cuboid »*adjective* having the shape of a cube.
»*noun* a solid which has six rectangular faces at right angles to each other.

cuckold »*noun* a man whose wife has committed adultery.
»*verb* (**cuckolds, cuckolding, cuckolded**) make a married man a cuckold.
– SAY kuk-ohld

cuckoo (plural **cuckoos**)

cucumber

cud »*noun* partly digested food returned from the first stomach of cattle or similar animals to the mouth for further chewing.

cuddle (verb: **cuddles, cuddling, cuddled**)

cuddly (adjective: **cuddlier, cuddliest**)

cudgel »*noun* a short thick stick used as a weapon.
»*verb* (**cudgels, cudgelling, cudgelled**) beat with a cudgel.

– SAY ku-juhl

> don't forget the **d**: **cudgel** double the **l** when spelling **cudgelling** and **cudgelled** (the spellings with a single **l** are American)

cue »*noun* ❶ a signal to an actor to enter or to begin their speech or performance. ❷ a signal or prompt for action. ❸ a long wooden rod for striking the ball in snooker, billiards, or pool.
»*verb* (**cues, cueing** or **cuing, cued**) ❶ give a cue to. ❷ set a piece of audio or video equipment in readiness to play a particular part of a recording. ❸ use a cue to strike the ball.

> ☑ do not confuse the spelling of **cue** with **queue**, which means 'a line of people or vehicles'

cuff [1] »*noun* the end part of a sleeve, where the material of the sleeve is turned back or a separate band is sewn on.

cuff [2] »*verb* (**cuffs, cuffing, cuffed**) strike with an open hand.
»*noun* a blow given with an open hand.

cufflink

cuffs

cuing

cuirass »*noun* (plural **cuirasses**) (a historical term) a piece of armour consisting of breastplate and a similar plate at the back.
– SAY kwi-rass

cuisine »*noun* a style of cooking, especially as typical of a country or region.
– SAY kwi-zeen

cul-de-sac »*noun* (plural **cul-de-sacs**) a street or passage closed at one end.

> ☑ **cul-de-sac** is a French expression translated as 'bottom of a sack'. Strictly speaking, the correct plural is **culs-de-sac**, but no-one says that.

culinary »*adjective* having to do with cooking.
– SAY cul-i-nuh-ri

> ☑ **ary** not **ery**: **culinary**

cull »*verb* (**culls, culling, culled**) ❶ reduce the numbers of animals by selective slaughter. ❷ select a few things from a large range.
»*noun* a selective slaughter of animals.

culminate »*verb* (**culminates, culminating, culminated**) reach a climax or point of highest development: *the disorders which culminated in World War II*.
– SAY kul-mi-nayt
culmination

culottes »*plural noun* women's wide-legged knee-length trousers.
– SAY kyuu-**lots**

 one l, two t's: **culottes**

culpable »*adjective* deserving blame.
– SAY kul-puh-b'l
culpability
culpably

culprit

cult
cultish
cultist

cultivable »*adjective* (of land) able to be cultivated.

 vable not **vatable**: **cultivable**

cultivar »*noun* a plant variety that has been produced by selective breeding.
– SAY kul-ti-var

 var not **ver**: **cultivar**

cultivate (verb: **cultivates**, **cultivating**, **cultivated**)
cultivated
cultivation
cultivator

cultural
culturally

 al not **el**: **cultural**

culture
cultured

culvert »*noun* a tunnel carrying a stream or open drain under a road or railway.
– SAY kul-vert

cum »*preposition* combined with: *a study-cum-bedroom*.

cumbersome »*adjective* ❶ difficult to carry or use on account of its size or weight. ❷ complicated and therefore time-consuming.

cumbrous »*adjective* cumbersome.

 there is no **e** in **cumbrous**

cumin »*noun* the strong-smelling seeds of a plant, used as a spice.
– SAY kum-in or kyoo-min

 cumin can also be spelled **cummin**: both spellings are correct

cummerbund »*noun* a sash worn around the waist as part of a man's formal evening suit.
– SAY kum-mer-bund

 double **m**, and **-und** not **-and** at the end: **cummerbund**

cummin another way of spelling **CUMIN**.

cumulative »*adjective* increasing by successive additions: *the cumulative effect of years of drought*.
– SAY kyoo-myuu-luh-tiv
cumulatively

 one **m**, one **l**: **cumulative**

cumulonimbus »*noun* cloud forming a towering mass with a flat base, as in thunderstorms.
– SAY kyoo-myuu-loh-**nim**-buhss

cumulus »*noun* (plural **cumuli**) cloud forming rounded masses heaped on a flat base.

 lus not **lous**: **cumulus**. It is unusual to need a plural, but if you do it is **cumuli** (SAY kyoo-myuu-lee)

cuneiform »*adjective* (of ancient writing systems) using wedge-shaped characters.
– SAY kyoo-ni-form

 cunei not **cuni**: **cuneiform**

cunnilingus »*noun* stimulation of a woman's genitals using the tongue or lips.
– SAY kun-ni-**ling**-guhss

cunning
cunningly

cunt

cup (verb: **cups**, **cupping**, **cupped**)

 double the **p** in **cupping** and **cupped**

cupboard

Cupid »*noun* ❶ the Roman god of love. ❷ (**cupid**) a picture or statue of a naked winged child carrying a bow.

cupidity »*noun* greed for money or possessions.
– SAY kyoo-**pid**-i-ti

cupola »*noun* a rounded dome that forms or decorates a roof or ceiling.
– SAY kyoo-puh-luh

 ola not **ula**: **cupola**

cupro-nickel »*noun* an alloy of copper and nickel used in 'silver' coins.

cur »*noun* an aggressive mongrel dog.

curable

curacy »*noun* (plural **curacies**) the position of a curate.

curare »*noun* a paralysing poison obtained from South American plants.
– SAY kyuu-**rah**-ri

181

curate[1] »*noun* a member of the clergy who works as as assistant to a parish priest.
– SAY kyoor-uht

curate[2] »*verb* (**curates, curating, curated**) select, organize, and look after the items in a collection or exhibition.
– SAY kyoo-**rayt**
curation

curative »*adjective* able to cure disease.

> ✓ rat not ret: **curative**

curator »*noun* a keeper of a museum or other collection.
curatorial

> ✓ **-or** not **-er: curator**

curb »*noun* ❶ something that limits or restrains something. ❷ a type of bit with a strap or chain attached which passes under a horse's lower jaw.
»*verb* (**curbs, curbing, curbed**) keep in check.

> ℹ do not confuse **curb** with **kerb,** which means 'a stone edging to a pavement'. In America **curb** is used as an alternative spelling of **kerb**.

curd »*noun* (also **curds**) a soft, white substance formed when milk coagulates, used as for making cheese.

curdle »*verb* (**curdles, curdling, curdled**) form curds or lumps.

cure (verb: **cures, curing, cured**)
curable
curer

curfew »*noun* ❶ a regulation requiring people to remain indoors between specified hours of the night. ❷ the time at which a curfew begins.
– SAY ker-fyoo

Curia »*noun* the court of the Pope at the Vatican, by which the Roman Catholic Church is governed.
– SAY kyoor-i-uh

curie »*noun* (plural **curies**) a unit of radioactivity.
– SAY kyoor-i

> ℹ named after the French physicists Pierre and Marie *Curie*

curing

curio »*noun* (plural **curios**) an object that is interesting because it is rare or unusual.
– SAY kyoor-i-oh

> ✓ the plural of **curio** has **os** not **oes: curios**

curiosity »*noun* (plural **curiosities**) ❶ a strong desire to know or learn something. ❷ a unusual or interesting object or fact.

> ✓ there is no **u** between the **o** and **s: curiosity**
> plural: drop the **y** and add **ies: curiosities**

curious
curiously

curl (verb: **curls, curling, curled**)
curly

curler

curlew »*noun* a large wading bird with a long bill that curves downwards.
– SAY ker-lyoo

curlicue »*noun* a decorative curl or twist.
– SAY ker-li-kyoo

> ✓ **ue** not **ew: curlicue**

curling[1] »*noun* a game played on ice, in which you slide large circular flat stones towards a mark.

curling[2] present participle of **CURL**.

curls

curly

curmudgeon »*noun* a bad-tempered person.
– SAY ker-**muj**-uhn
curmudgeonly

> ✓ don't forget the **d** before the **g: curmudgeon**

currant [dried fruit]

> ✓ **ant** not **ent: currant**
> do not confuse with **current,** which means 'happening now' or 'flow of water or electricity'

currency »*noun* (plural **currencies**) ❶ a system of money in general use in a country. ❷ the state or period of being current.

> ✓ plural: drop the **y** and add **ies: currencies**

current [happening now; flow of water or electricity]

> ✓ **ent** not **ant: current**
> do not confuse with **currant** which means 'a type of dried fruit'

current account »*noun* an account with a bank or building society from which you may withdraw money at any time.

currently

curriculum »*noun* (plural **curricula** or **curriculums**) the subjects that make up a course of study in a school or college.
– SAY kuh-**rik**-yuu-luhm
curricular

✓ the plural can be either **curricula** (like the original Latin) or **curriculums**

curriculum vitae »*noun* (plural **curricula vitae**) a brief account of a person's qualifications and previous occupations, sent with a job application.
– SAY kuh-**rik**-yuu-luhm **vee**-tI or **vy**-tee

ⓘ **curriculum vitae** means 'course of life' in Latin, and the plural is made with an **a** replacing the **um**: **curricula vitae**

curried

curry[1] (plural **curries**) [Indian dish]

curry[2] »*verb* (**curries, currying, curried**) groom a horse with a curry-comb.

curry-comb »*noun* a hand-held implement with jagged ridges, used for grooming horses.

currying

curse (verb: **curses, cursing, cursed**) [words bringing harm; affliction; swear]
cursed

cursive »*adjective* (of handwriting) written with the letters joined.
– SAY **ker**-siv

cursor »*noun* ❶ a movable indicator on a computer screen identifying the point where input from the user will take effect. ❷ the sliding part used to locate points on a slide rule.

✓ **-or** not **-er**: **cursor**

cursory »*adjective* hasty and therefore not thorough.
– SAY **ker**-suh-ri
cursorily

✓ **ory** not **ery**: **cursory**

curt »*adjective* rudely brief.
curtly
curtness

curtail »*verb* (**curtails, curtailing, curtailed**) reduce or restrict.
– SAY ker-**tayl**
curtailment

✓ **-tail** not **-tale**: **curtail**

curtain (verb: **curtains, curtaining, curtained**)

✓ don't forget the **a**: **curtain**

curtain call »*noun* the appearance of a performer on stage after a performance to acknowledge the audience's applause.

curtained
curtaining

curtain-raiser »*noun* an event happening just before a longer or more important one.

curtains

curtly

curtness

curtsy (plural **curtsies**; verb: **curtsies, curtsying, curtsied**)

✓ **curtsy** can also be spelled **curtsey**, in which case the plural is **curtseys** and the verb forms **curtseys, curtseying**, and **curtseyed**

curvaceous »*adjective* having an attractively curved shape.
– SAY ker-**vay**-shuhss

✓ **ceous** not **cious**: **curvaceous**

curvature »*noun* the fact of being curved or the degree to which something is curved.
– SAY **ker**-vuh-cher

curve (verb: **curves, curving, curved**)

curvet »*noun* a horse's short energetic leap.
»*verb* (**curvets, curvetting** or **curveting, curvetted** or **curveted**) (of a horse) make such a leap.
– SAY ker-**vet**

✓ **curvetting** and **curvetted** can also be spelled **curveting** or **curveted**, with a double or single **t**: both spellings are correct

curvier

curviest

curvilinear »*adjective* contained by or consisting of a curved line or lines.
– SAY ker-vi-**lin**-i-er

curviness

curving

curvy (adjective: **curvier, curviest**)
curviness

cushier

cushiest

cushion (verb: **cushions, cushioning, cushioned**)

cushy »*adjective* (**cushier, cushiest**) (in informal English) easy and undemanding.

cusp »*noun* ❶ a pointed end where two curves meet, such as each of the ends of a crescent moon. ❷ a cone-shaped projection on the surface of a tooth. ❸ the initial point of an astrological sign or house. ❹ a point of changing from one state to another: *those on the cusp of adulthood.*

cuss (in informal English) »*noun* (plural **cusses**) an annoying or stubborn person or animal.
» *verb* (**cusses**, **cussing**, **cussed**) swear or curse.

cussed »*adjective* (in informal English) stubborn and awkward.
– **SAY** kuss-id
  cussedness

cusses

cussing

custard

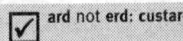 ard not erd: **custard**

custodial »*adjective* having to do with custody: *she got a custodial sentence.*
– **SAY** kuss-**toh**-di-uhl

custodian »*noun* a person who is responsible for looking after something.

custody »*noun* ❶ protective care. ❷ imprisonment.
– **SAY** kuss-tuh-di

custom

customary »*adjective* in accordance with custom; usual.
  customarily

 ary not ery: **customary**

custom-built »*adjective* made to a particular customer's order.

customer

customize »*verb* (**customizes**, **customizing**, **customized**) modify something to suit a person or task.

many people prefer the alternative spellings **customise**, **customises**, etc.: both **s** and **z** spellings are correct

custom-made »*adjective* custom-built.

customs »*plural noun* ❶ the charges made by a government on imported goods. ❷ the official department that administers and collects customs charges.

cut (verb: **cuts**, **cutting**, **cut**)

double the **t** in **cutting**

cutaneous »*adjective* having to do with the skin.
– **SAY** kyoo-**tay**-ni-uhss

don't forget the **e**: **cutaneous**

cutaway

cutback

cute (adjective: **cuter**, **cutest**)
  cutely
  cuteness

cut glass »*noun* glass with decorative patterns cut into it.

cuticle »*noun* ❶ the dead skin at the base of a fingernail or toenail. ❷ the epidermis of the body.
– **SAY** kyoo-ti-k'l

cutlass »*noun* (plural **cutlasses**) a short sword with a slightly curved blade, formerly used by sailors.
– **SAY** kut-luhss

-**lass** not -**less**: **cutlass**

cutler »*noun* a maker or seller of cutlery.

cutlery

cutlet »*noun* ❶ a lamb or veal chop from just behind the neck. ❷ a flat cake of minced meat, nuts, etc., covered in breadcrumbs and fried.

cut-off

cut-out

cut-price

cuts

cutter »*noun* ❶ a person or thing that cuts. ❷ a light, fast patrol boat or sailing boat. ❸ a ship's boat used for carrying light stores or passengers.

cut-throat »*adjective* ruthless and fierce: *cut-throat competition.*

cut-throat razor »*noun* a razor with a long blade which folds like a penknife.

cutting

cutting edge »*noun* the most advanced stage; the forefront.

add a hyphen if you use this word as an adjective, as in *cutting-edge design*

cuttlefish »*noun* a sea creature resembling a squid, that squirts out a black liquid when attacked.

CV »*abbreviation* curriculum vitae.

cwm »*noun* a steep-sided mountain valley in Wales.
– **SAY** kuum

cyan »*noun* a greenish-blue colour.
– **SAY** sy-uhn

cyanide »*noun* a highly poisonous compound containing a metal combined with carbon and nitrogen atoms.

cyanosis »*noun* a bluish discoloration of the skin due to poor circulation or a lack of oxygen in the blood.
– **SAY** sy-uh-**noh**-siss

cybernetics »*noun* the science of communications and automatic control systems in both machines and living

things.
cybernetic

cyberphobia »*noun* extreme or irrational fear of computers or technology.

cyberspace »*noun* the hypothetical environment in which communication over computer networks occurs.

cybersquatting »*noun* the registering of well-known names as Internet domain names, in the hope of selling them to the owner at a profit.

cyborg »*noun* (in science fiction) a person who has mechanical elements built into the body to extend their normal physical abilities.
– **SAY** sy-borg

cyclamen »*noun* a plant having pink, red, or white flowers with petals that curve backwards.
– **SAY** sik-luh-muhn

 men not **min**: cyclamen

cycle (verb: **cycles, cycling, cycled**)

cyclic »*adjective* ❶ occurring in cycles. ❷ (in chemistry) having a molecule containing one or more rings of atoms.
– **SAY** syk-lik or sik-lik
cyclical

cycling

cyclist

cyclone »*noun* ❶ a system of winds rotating inwards to an area of low atmospheric pressure. ❷ a violent tropical storm.
– **SAY** sy-klohn
cyclonic

 -one not **-oan**: cyclone

cyclopean »*adjective* having to do with a Cyclops.
– **SAY** sy-kluh-**pee**-uhn or sy-**kloh**-pi-uhn

 ean not **ion**: cyclopean

Cyclops »*noun* (plural **Cyclops** or **Cyclopes**) (in Greek mythology) a member of a race of one-eyed giants.
– **SAY** sy-klops [singular], sy-klops or sy-**kloh**-peez [plural]

cygnet »*noun* a young swan.

ℹ️ do not confuse **cygnet** with **signet**, which means 'a small seal'

cylinder
cylindrical

cymbal [musical instrument]

ℹ️ do not confuse **cymbal** with **symbol**, which means 'a mark or character representing something'

cynic »*noun* ❶ a person who believes that people always act from selfish motives. ❷ a person who raises doubts about something. ❸ (**Cynic**) a member of an ancient Greek school of philosophers who despised wealth and pleasure.
– **SAY** si-nik
cynicism SAY si-ni-si-z'm

cynical »*adjective* ❶ believing that people always act from selfish motives. ❷ doubtful or sneering. ❸ concerned only with your own interests: *a cynical professional foul.*
cynically

cynicism

cynosure »*noun* a person or thing that is the centre of attention or admiration.
– **SAY** si-nuh-zyoor or sy-nuh-zyoor

cypher another way of spelling **CIPHER**.

cypress »*noun* (plural **cypresses**) an evergreen coniferous tree with small dark leaves.

 ess not **us**: cypress

Cypriot »*noun* a person from Cyprus. »*adjective* relating to Cyprus.

Cyrillic »*adjective* having to do with the alphabet used for Russian, Ukrainian, Bulgarian, and related languages.
– **SAY** si-**ril**-lik

 double l: Cyrillic

cyst »*noun* an abnormal sac or cavity in the body, containing fluid.
– **SAY** sist

cystic »*adjective* ❶ having to do with cysts. ❷ relating to the urinary bladder or the gall bladder.

cystic fibrosis »*noun* a serious inherited disorder which causes too much mucus to be produced and leads to the blockage of tubes in the body.

cystitis »*noun* inflammation of the urinary bladder.
– **SAY** si-**sty**-tiss

cytology »*noun* the branch of biology concerned with the structure and function of cells.
– **SAY** sy-**tol**-uh-ji
cytological
cytologist

cytoplasm »*noun* the material of a living cell, excluding the nucleus.

– **say** sy-toh-pla-z'm
  cytoplasmic

czar see the note at **TSAR**.

Czech
– **say** chek

Czechoslovak »*noun* a person from the

former country of Czechoslovakia, now divided between the Czech Republic and Slovakia.

» *adjective* relating to Czechoslovakia.
– **say** chek-uh-**sloh**-vak
  Czechoslovakian

d

Dd

DA »*abbreviation* (in America) district attorney.

dab (verb: **dabs, dabbing, dabbed**)

dabble (verb: **dabbles, dabbling, dabbled**)
  dabbler

dabs

dace »*noun* (plural **dace**) a small freshwater fish related to the carp.

dachshund »*noun* a dog with a long body and very short legs.
– **say** daks-huund or dak-suhnd

> ✓ two h's: **dachshund**. It is a German word meaning literally 'badger dog'.

dad

Dada »*noun* an early 20th-century artistic movement which made fun of conventions and emphasized illogical and absurd things.
– **say** dah-dah
  Dadaism
  Dadaist

daddy (plural **daddies**)

daddy-long-legs

dado »*noun* (plural **dados**) a waist-high decorative rail or moulding round the wall of a room.

> ✓ the plural of **dado**, an Italian word, has **os** not **oes**: **dados**

daffodil

> ✓ two f's, one l: **daffodil**

daft (adjective: **dafter, daftest**)
  daftness

dagger

daguerreotype »*noun* an early kind of photograph made using silver-coated copper plates.
– **say** duh-**ger**-ruh-typ

> ✓ named after the French pioneer of photography L.-J.-M. *Daguerre*. Notice the spelling, which keeps the final **e** of his name: **daguerreotype**.

dahlia »*noun* a garden plant with large, brightly coloured flowers.
– **say** day-li-uh

Dail »*noun* the lower House of Parliament in the Republic of Ireland.
– **say** doyl

> ✓ **Dail** can also be written **Dáil**, with an acute accent on the **a** (as in Irish)

daily (plural **dailies**)

dainty (adjective: **daintier, daintiest**)
  daintily
  daintiness

daiquiri »*noun* (plural **daiquiris**) a cocktail containing rum and lime juice.
– **say** da-kuh-ri

> ✓ make the plural by adding **s** not **es**: **daiquiris**

dairy (plural **dairies**)

> ✓ **a** before **i**: a **dairy** is a place where milk is collected and stored, while a **diary** is a book for keeping a daily record

dais »*noun* (plural **daises**) a low platform that supports a throne, or that people stand on to make a speech.
– **say** day-iss or dayss

> ✓ **a** before **i**: **dais**

daisy (plural **daisies**)

dal another way of spelling **DHAL**.

dale »*noun* a valley, especially one in northern England.

dally »*verb* (**dallies, dallying, dallied**) ❶ do something in a very leisurely way. ❷ treat someone or something in a casual way: *the company has been dallying with the*

idea of opening a new office.
dalliance

Dalmatian »*noun* a large dog with short
white hair and dark spots.
– sᴀʏ dal-**may**-sh'n

> ☑ the spelling is **atian** not **ation**,
> because it is named after *Dalmatia* (a
> region of Croatia)

dam (verb: **dams**, **damming**, **dammed**)
[barrier holding back water]

> ☑ do not confuse the verb **dam**,
> meaning 'hold back water by a
> barrier', with **damn** meaning 'condemn' or
> 'curse'

damage (verb: **damages**, **damaging**,
damaged)
damaging

damask »*noun* a rich heavy fabric with a
pattern woven into it.
– sᴀʏ **dam**-uhsk

dame

dammed

damming

damn »*verb* (**damns**, **damning**, **damned**)
❶ (**be damned**) (in Christian belief) be
condemned by God to eternal punishment
in hell. ❷ harshly condemn or curse.

> ☑ remember the silent **n**, and be
> careful not to confuse **damn** with
> **dam**, which refers to an artificial barrier
> holding back water. *A dammed river* has a
> dam built across it, whereas *a damned
> river* is one you are annoyed with.

damnable »*adjective* very bad or
unpleasant.
– sᴀʏ **dam**-nuh-b'l
damnably

damnation »*noun* the state of eternal
punishment in hell.

damned

damning

damns

damp (adjective: **damper**, **dampest**; verb:
damps, **damping**, **damped**)
dampness

damp course »*noun* a layer of waterproof
material in a wall near the ground, to
prevent rising damp.

damped

dampen (verb: **dampens**, **dampening**,
dampened)
dampener

damper

damping

damp-proof

damps

damp squib »*noun* something that turns
out to be much less impressive than
expected.

dams

damsel »*noun* (an old word) a young
unmarried woman.
– sᴀʏ **dam**-zuhl

damson »*noun* a small purple-black fruit
like a plum.
– sᴀʏ **dam**-zuhn

dan »*noun* one of the ten degrees of
advanced skill in judo or karate.

dance (verb: **dances**, **dancing**, **danced**)
dancer
dancing

dandelion

> ☑ **e** not **y**: **dandelion**

dander »*noun* (**get your dander up**) lose
your temper.

dandies

dandified »*adjective* ❶ (of a man) too
concerned about personal appearance.
❷ self-consciously elaborate: *dandified
courtesy.*

dandle »*verb* (**dandles**, **dandling**, **dandled**)
gently bounce a young child on your
knees or in your arms.

dandruff

dandy »*noun* (plural **dandies**) a man who is
too concerned with a stylish and
fashionable appearance.

Dane »*noun* a person from Denmark.

danger

dangerous
dangerously

dangle (verb: **dangles**, **dangling**, **dangled**)
dangler
dangly

Danish »*adjective* relating to Denmark or
the Danes.
» *noun* the language of Denmark.

dank »*adjective* (**danker**, **dankest**) damp
and cold.
dankness

dapper »*adjective* (of a man) neat in dress
and appearance.

dapple »*verb* (**dapples**, **dappling**, **dappled**)
mark with spots or small patches.
» *noun* a patch of colour or light.

dare (verb: **dares**, **daring**, **dared**)

daredevil »*noun* a person who enjoys
doing dangerous things.

dares

daring »*adjective* fearlessly bold.
» *noun* adventurous courage.
  daringly

dark (adjective: **darker**, **darkest**)
  darkly
  darkness

Dark Ages »*plural noun* the period in
  Europe between the fall of the Roman
  Empire and the Middle Ages, 500–1100,
  thought of as being uncultured.

darken (verb: **darkens**, **darkening**,
  darkened)

darker

darkest

dark horse »*noun* a person who is
  secretive about themselves.

darkly

darkness

darkroom

darling

darn »*verb* (**darns**, **darning**, **darned**) mend
  knitted material by interweaving yarn
  across it.

dart (verb: **darts**, **darting**, **darted**)

dartboard

darted

darting

darts

Darwinism »*noun* the theory of the
  evolution of species by natural selection,
  put forward by the English natural
  historian Charles Darwin.
  Darwinian
  Darwinist

dash (verb: **dashes**, **dashing**, **dashed**)

dashboard

dashed

dashes

dashing

dastardly »*adjective* (mainly used in a
  humorous way) wicked and cruel.
  – SAY dass-terd-li

data »*noun* ❶ facts or statistics used for
  reference or analysis. ❷ information
  operated on by a computer.
  – SAY day-tuh

> ℹ️ **data** is the plural of the Latin word
> **datum**. Scientists use it as a plural
> noun, taking a plural verb (for example,
> *the data were classified*). In everyday use,
> however, **data** is often treated as a
> singular noun, as in *data was collected
> over a number of years.*

database »*noun* a structured set of data
  held in a computer.

datable

> ✓ you can also spell this word with an
> extra e: both **datable** and **dateable** are
> correct

data protection »*noun* legal control over
  access to data stored in computers.

date (verb: **dates**, **dating**, **dated**)

dateable another way of spelling **DATABLE**.

dated »*adjective* appearing old-fashioned.

dates

dating

datum »*noun* (plural **data**) a piece of
  information.
  – SAY day-tuhm

> ℹ️ see the note at **DATA**

daub (verb: **daubs**, **daubing**, **daubed**)
  dauber

daughter

daughter-in-law (plural **daughters-in-law**)

daunt »*verb* (**be daunted**) feel intimidated
  or apprehensive: *some people are daunted
  by technology.*
  daunting

dauntless »*adjective* fearless and
  determined.

davit »*noun* a small crane on a ship.
  – SAY da-vit or day-vit

dawdle (verb: **dawdles**, **dawdling**, **dawdled**)
  dawdler

dawn (verb: **dawns**, **dawning**, **dawned**)

dawn chorus »*noun* the early-morning
  singing of birds.

dawned

dawning

dawns

day

daybreak

daydream (verb: **daydreams**, **daydreaming**,
  daydreamed)
  daydreamer

daylight

daytime

day-to-day

daze (verb: **dazes**, **dazing**, **dazed**)

dazzle (verb: **dazzles**, **dazzling**, **dazzled**)
  dazzler
  dazzling

DC »*abbreviation* direct current.

D-Day »*noun* the day (6 June 1944) in the
  Second World War on which Allied forces
  invaded northern France.

DDT »*noun* an insecticide, now banned in many countries.

> **i** **DDT** is an abbreviation of the chemical name *dichlorodiphenyltrichloroethane*

deacon »*noun* ❶ a Christian minister just below the rank of priest. ❷ (in some Protestant Churches) a person who assists a minister.

deaconess »*noun* (plural **deaconesses**) a woman with the duties of a deacon.

deactivate »*verb* (**deactivates**, **deactivating**, **deactivated**) stop something working by disconnecting or destroying it.
deactivation

dead (adjective: **deader**, **deadest**)
deadness

deadbeat »*noun* an idle or aimless person.

deadbolt »*noun* a bolt fastened by turning a knob or key, rather than by a spring action.

deaden (verb: **deadens**, **deadening**, **deadened**)

deader

deadest

dead heat »*noun* a race in which two or more competitors are exactly level.

dead letter »*noun* a law or treaty which is no longer applied in practice.

deadlier

deadliest

deadline »*noun* the time or date by which you have to complete something.

deadliness

deadlock »*noun* ❶ a situation in which no one can make any progress. ❷ a lock operated by a key.
deadlocked

deadly (adjective: **deadlier**, **deadliest**)
deadliness

deadpan »*adjective* not showing any emotion; expressionless.

dead reckoning »*noun* a way of finding out your position by estimating the direction and distance travelled.

deadweight »*noun* ❶ the weight of a motionless person or thing. ❷ the total weight which a ship can carry.

deaf (adjective: **deafer**, **deafest**)
deafness

deafen (verb: **deafens**, **deafening**, **deafened**)
deafening
deafeningly

deafer

deafest

deal (verb: **deals**, **dealing**, **dealt**)

dealer
dealership

dealing

deals

dealt past and past participle of **DEAL**.

dean »*noun* ❶ the head of a cathedral's governing body. ❷ the head of a university department or of a medical school. ❸ a college officer who deals with matters of discipline and welfare.

> **i** do not confuse **dean** with **dene**, which means 'a deep, narrow, wooded valley'

deanery »*noun* (plural **deaneries**) ❶ the status or position of a dean. ❷ the official residence of a dean.

dear (adjective: **dearer**, **dearest**) [much loved; expensive]
dearly

dearth »*noun* a lack of something: *a dearth of datable men.*
– **SAY** derth

death

death knell »*noun* ❶ the ringing of a bell to mark a death. ❷ an event that signals the end of something.

deathless

deathly »*adjective* (**deathlier**, **deathliest**) suggesting death: *a deathly hush.*

death rate »*noun* the number of deaths per one thousand people per year.

death-watch beetle »*noun* a beetle whose grubs bore into wood and that makes a ticking sound which people used to think was an omen of death.

debacle »*noun* a total failure or disaster.
– **SAY** day-**bah**-k'l

> ✓ **debacle** is sometimes written **débacle**, with an acute accent on the **e** (as in the original French)

debar »*verb* (**debars**, **debarring**, **debarred**) officially prevent someone from doing something.
debarment

> ✓ double the **r** in **debarred** and **debarring**

debase »*verb* (**debases**, **debasing**, **debased**) make something worse in quality, value, or character.
debasement

debatable »*adjective* open to discussion or argument.

> ✓ no **e** before **-able**: debatable

debate (verb: **debates, debating, debated**)
debater

debauch »*verb* (**debauches, debauching, debauched**) lead someone into immorality or overindulgence.
– SAY di-**bawch**
debauched

debauchery »*noun* overindulgence in physical pleasures.

debauches

debauching

debenture »*noun* a certificate issued by a company acknowledging a debt on which a fixed rate of interest is being paid.
– SAY di-**ben**-cher

debilitate »*verb* (**debilitates, debilitating, debilitated**) weaken someone severely.
debilitation

debility »*noun* physical weakness.

debit »*noun* ❶ an entry in an account recording a sum owed. ❷ a payment that has been made or that is owed.
»*verb* (**debits, debiting, debited**) (of a bank) remove money from a customer's account.

> ☑ one b and one t: **debit, debits, debited**

debonair »*adjective* (of a man) confident, stylish, and charming.
– SAY deb-uh-**nair**

> ☑ unlike French *débonnaire*, **debonair** is spelled with a single **n** and no final **e**

debouch »*verb* (**debouches, debouching, debouched**) come out from a confined space into a wide, open area.
– SAY di-**bowch** or di-**boosh**

debrief »*verb* (**debriefs, debriefing, debriefed**) question someone in detail about a mission they have completed.
debriefing

debris »*noun* ❶ scattered items or pieces of rubbish. ❷ loose broken pieces of rock.
– SAY **deb**-ree or **day**-bree

debt

debtor »*noun* a person who owes money.

debug »*verb* (**debugs, debugging, debugged**) remove errors from computer hardware or software.
debugger

debunk »*verb* (**debunks, debunking, debunked**) show that something believed in by many people is false or exaggerated.

debut »*noun* a person's first appearance in a role.
»*verb* (**debuts, debuting, debuted**) make a debut.
– SAY **day**-byoo or **day**-boo

> ☑ **debut** and words related to it are sometimes written with an acute accent on the **e**, as in French *début*

debutant »*noun* a person making a debut.
– SAY **deb**-yoo-tont or **day**-byoo-tont

debutante »*noun* a young upper-class woman making her first appearance in society.
– SAY **deb**-yuh-tahnt or **day**-byoo-tahnt

debuted

debuting

debuts

decade »*noun* a period of ten years.
– SAY **dek**-ayd or di-**kayd**

> ℹ️ traditionalists prefer to pronounce **decade** with the stress on the first syllable (**dek**-ayd), rather than making it sound like *decayed*

decadent »*adjective* ❶ immoral and interested only in pleasure. ❷ luxuriously self-indulgent.
– SAY **dek**-uh-duhnt
decadence
decadently

decaffeinated »*adjective* (of tea or coffee) having had most or all of its caffeine removed.
– SAY dee-**kaf**-fi-nay-tid

> ☑ be careful to keep the double **f** and **ein** of **caffeine**: **decaffeinated**

decagon »*noun* a figure with ten straight sides and angles.
– SAY **dek**-uh-guhn

decahedron »*noun* (plural **decahedra** or **decahedrons**) a solid figure with ten plane faces.

> ☑ the plural can be either **decahedra** (like the original Greek) or **decahedrons**

decal »*noun* a design transferred from special paper on to glass, porcelain, etc.
– SAY **dee**-kal

decalitre »*noun* a volume of 10 litres.

decametre »*noun* a length of 10 metres.

decamp »*verb* (**decamps, decamping, decamped**) go away suddenly or secretly.

decant »*verb* (**decants, decanting, decanted**) pour liquid from one container into another.
– SAY di-**kant**

decanter »*noun* a glass container with a stopper, which wine or spirits are poured into before being served.

decanting

decants

decapitate »*verb* (**decapitates**, **decapitating**, **decapitated**) cut off the head of someone or something.
– SAY di-**kap**-i-tayt
decapitation

decathlon »*noun* an athletic contest in which each competitor takes part in the same ten events.
– SAY di-**kath**-luhn
decathlete

decay »*verb* (**decays**, **decaying**, **decayed**) ❶ rot; decompose. ❷ become weaker or less good.
»*noun* ❶ the state or process of decaying. ❷ rotten matter or tissue.

decease »*noun* (mainly in legal or official use) death.

deceased (mainly in legal or official use)
»*adjective* recently dead.
»*noun* (**the deceased**) the recently dead person in question.

deceit »*noun* ❶ the practice of deceiving. ❷ something done or said to deceive others.

> ✓ **deceit** and **deceitful** follow the usual rule: **i** before **e** except after **c**

deceitful
deceitfully
deceitfulness

> ✓ -**ful** not -**full**: **deceitful**

deceive (verb: **deceives**, **deceiving**, **deceived**)
deceiver

> ✓ **i** before **e** except after **c**: **deceive**

decelerate »*verb* (**decelerates**, **decelerating**, **decelerated**) slow down.
deceleration

December

decency (plural **decencies**)

decennial »*adjective* lasting for or happening every ten years.
– SAY di-**sen**-i-uhl

> ✓ double **n** in **decennial**

decent
decently

decentralize »*verb* (**decentralizes**, **decentralizing**, **decentralized**) transfer authority from central to local government.
decentralization

> ✓ many people prefer the spellings **decentralise**, **decentralises**, etc.: both **s** and **z** spellings are correct

deception

deceptive »*adjective* giving a false impression.
deceptively

> ℹ **deceptively** can mean both one thing and also its complete opposite. A *deceptively smooth surface* is one which looks smooth but in fact is not smooth at all, while a *deceptively spacious room* is one that does not look spacious but is in fact more spacious than it appears.

decibel »*noun* a unit of measurement expressing the intensity of a sound or the power of an electrical signal.
– SAY **dess**-i-bel

decide (verb: **decides**, **deciding**, **decided**)

decided »*adjective* definite; clear: *a decided improvement.*
decidedly

decider

decides

deciding

deciduous »*adjective* (of a tree) shedding its leaves every year (the opposite of *evergreen*).
– SAY di-**sid**-yoo-uhss

decilitre »*noun* a volume of one tenth of a litre.

decimal »*adjective* having to do with a system of numbers based on the number ten.
»*noun* a fractional number in the decimal system, written with figures either side of a full point.

decimalization »*noun* the conversion of a system of coinage or weights and measures to a decimal system.

decimal point »*noun* a full point placed after the figure representing units in a decimal fraction.

decimate »*verb* (**decimates**, **decimating**, **decimated**) ❶ kill or destroy a large proportion of a group. ❷ drastically reduce the strength of something.
– SAY **dess**-i-mayt
decimation

> ℹ **decimate** originally meant 'kill one in every ten of a group of soldiers', a reference to a form of collective punishment in the Roman army. Some people think that this is the only correct meaning, and that the meanings given here are incorrect.

decimetre »*noun* a length of one tenth of a metre.

decipher »*verb* (**deciphers**, **deciphering**, **deciphered**) ❶ convert something from

code into normal language. ❷ succeed in understanding something that is hard to interpret.
– SAY di-**sy**-fer
decipherable
decipherment

decision

decisive »*adjective* ❶ settling an issue quickly: *decisive evidence.* ❷ able to make decisions quickly.
– SAY di-**sy**-siv
decisively
decisiveness

deck (verb: **decks, decking, decked**)

deckchair

decked

deckhand

decking

decks

declaim »*verb* (**declaims, declaiming, declaimed**) speak or recite in a dramatic or passionate way.

> ✓ **-claim** not **-clame**: **declaim**

declamation »*noun* the action or art of declaiming.
declamatory

> ✓ **-clam-** not **-claim-**: **declamation**

declaration

declarative »*adjective* ❶ making a declaration: *declarative statements.* ❷ (of a sentence or phrase) taking the form of a simple statement.
– SAY di-**kla**-ruh-tiv

declare (verb: **declares, declaring, declared**)
declarer

> ✓ **clare** not **clair**: **declare**

declassify »*verb* (**declassifies, declassifying, declassified**) officially declare information or documents to be no longer secret.
declassification

declension »*noun* the changes in the form of a noun, pronoun, or adjective that identify its grammatical case, number, and gender.
– SAY di-**klen**-shuhn

> ✓ **sion** not **tion**: **declension**

declination »*noun* ❶ (in astronomy) the position of a point in the sky equivalent to latitude on the earth. ❷ the angle that a compass needle makes with true north.
– SAY dek-li-**nay**-sh'n

decline (verb: **declines, declining, declined**)

declivity »*noun* (plural **declivities**) a downward slope.
– SAY di-**kliv**-i-ti

decoction »*noun* the concentrated essence of a substance, produced by heating or boiling.

decode »*verb* (**decodes, decoding, decoded**) ❶ convert a coded message into understandable language. ❷ convert audio or video signals from analogue to digital.
decoder

decolletage »*noun* a low neckline on a woman's garment.
– SAY day-kol-**tah**z*h*

> ✓ **decolletage** can also be spelled **décolletage**, with an acute accent above the **e** (as in the original French)

decollete »*adjective* having a low neckline. »*noun* a decolletage.
– SAY day-**kol**-tay

> ✓ **decollete** can also be spelled **décolleté**, with acute accents above the first and final **e**'s (as in the original French)

decommission »*verb* (**decommissions, decommissioning, decommissioned**) ❶ take a ship out of service. ❷ take a nuclear reactor or weapon out of use and make it safe.

> ✓ double m, double s: **decommission**

decompose »*verb* (**decomposes, decomposing, decomposed**) ❶ decay. ❷ break down a substance into its elements.
decomposition

decompress »*verb* (**decompresses, decompressing, decompressed**) ❶ reduce pressure on. ❷ expand compressed computer data to its normal size.
– SAY dee-kuhm-**press**
decompressor

> ✓ one m, two s's: **decompress**

decompression »*noun* ❶ reduction in air pressure. ❷ a gradual reduction of air pressure on a person who has been experiencing high pressure while diving. ❸ the process of decompressing computer data.

decompression sickness »*noun* a serious condition that results when a diver surfaces too quickly.

decongestant »*adjective* (of a medicine) used to relieve a blocked nose.

– **SAY** dee-kuhn-**jess**-tuhnt

✓ ant not ent: **decongestant**

deconstruct »*verb* (**deconstructs, deconstructing, deconstructed**) take something apart to expose its workings.
– **SAY** dee-kuhn-**strukt**

decontaminate »*verb* (**decontaminates, decontaminating, decontaminated**) remove dangerous substances from something.
decontamination

decor »*noun* the furnishing and decoration of a room.
– **SAY** day-kor

✓ **decor** can also be written **décor**, with an acute accent on the **e** (as in the original French)

decorate (verb: **decorates, decorating, decorated**)

decoration

decorative
decoratively
decorativeness

decorator

✓ -or not -er: **decorator**

decorous »*adjective* in good taste; polite and restrained.
– **SAY** dek-uh-ruhss
decorously
decorousness

decorum »*noun* polite and socially acceptable behaviour.
– **SAY** di-kor-uhm

decoupage »*noun* the decoration of a surface with paper cut-outs.
– **SAY** day-koo-**pahzh** or dek-oo-pahzh

✓ **decoupage** can also be spelled **découpage**, with an acute accent over the **e** (as in the original French)

decoy (verb: **decoys, decoying, decoyed**)

decrease (verb: **decreases, decreasing, decreased**)

decree »*noun* **①** an official order that has the force of law. **②** a judgement of certain law courts.
»*verb* (**decrees, decreeing, decreed**) order by decree.

ℹ do not confuse **decrees** and **decreed** with **decries** and **decried**, which mean 'publicly declares/declared something to be wrong'

decree absolute »*noun* (plural **decrees absolute**) (in English law) a final order by a court which officially ends a marriage.

✓ to make the plural add **s** after **decree** only: **decrees absolute**

decree nisi »*noun* (plural **decrees nisi**) (in English law) an order by a court that states the date on which a marriage will end, unless a good reason to prevent a divorce is produced.
– **SAY** di-kree ny-sy

✓ to make the plural add **s** after **decree** only: **decrees nisi** (nisi is a Latin word meaning 'unless')

decrement »*noun* a reduction or diminution (the opposite of *increment*).
– **SAY** dek-ri-muhnt

decrepit »*adjective* **①** worn out or ruined because of age or neglect. **②** elderly and infirm.
– **SAY** di-**krep**-it
decrepitude

decried

decries

decriminalize »*verb* (**decriminalizes, decriminalizing, decriminalized**) stop treating something as illegal.
decriminalization

✓ many people prefer the alternative spellings **decriminalise, decriminalises**, etc., and **decriminalisation**: both **s** and **z** spellings are correct

decry »*verb* (**decries, decrying, decried**) publicly declare something to be wrong or evil.
– **SAY** di-**kry**

ℹ do not confuse **decries** and **decried** with **decrees** and **decreed**, which mean 'orders/ordered by decree'

decrypt »*verb* (**decrypts, decrypting, decrypted**) decode (a message).
– **SAY** dee-**kript**
decryption

✓ ypt not ipt: **decrypt**

dedicate (verb: **dedicates, dedicating, dedicated**)
dedicatory

dedication

dedicatory

deduce »*verb* (**deduces, deducing, deduced**) reach a logical conclusion by thinking about the information or evidence that is available.

deduct »*verb* (**deducts, deducting, deducted**) take an amount away from a total.

deductible »*adjective* able to be deducted.

✓ **-ible** not **-able: deductible**

deducting

deduction »*noun* ❶ the action of deducting. ❷ an amount that is or may be deducted. ❸ a method of reasoning in which a general principle is used to draw a particular conclusion.
deductive

deducts

deed

deed poll »*noun* a legal deed made and carried out by one party only.

deejay »*noun* (in informal English) a disc jockey.

deem »*verb* (**deems, deeming, deemed**) consider in a specified way.

deep (adjective: **deeper, deepest**)

deepen (verb: **deepens, deepening, deepened**)

deeper

deepest

deep freeze »*noun* a freezer.
deep-frozen

deep-fried

deep-fries

deep-frozen

deep-fry »*verb* (**deep-fries, deep-frying, deep-fried**) fry food in enough fat or oil to cover it completely.

deeply

deep-rooted »*adjective* firmly established.

deep-seated »*adjective* firmly established.

deer (plural **deer**) [animal]

deerstalker »*noun* a soft cloth cap, with peaks in front and behind and ear flaps which can be tied together over the top.

✓ **-stalk-** not **-stock-: deerstalker**

deface »*verb* (**defaces, defacing, defaced**) spoil the surface or appearance of.
defacement

de facto »*adjective* existing in fact, whether legally accepted or not: *a de facto one-party system*.
– **SAY** day **fak**-toh or dee **fak**-toh

ℹ **de facto** means 'of fact' in Latin

defame »*verb* (**defames, defaming, defamed**) damage the good reputation of.
defamation
defamatory

✓ drop the **e** when spelling **defaming, defamation,** and **defamatory**

default »*noun* ❶ failure to do what you are supposed to do. ❷ an option adopted by a computer program or other mechanism when no alternative is specified.
» *verb* (**defaults, defaulting, defaulted**) ❶ fail to do what you are supposed to do. ❷ (**default to**) go back automatically to a default option.
defaulter

defeat (verb: **defeats, defeating, defeated**)

defeatist »*noun* a person who gives in to failure too easily.
» *adjective* showing ready acceptance of failure.
defeatism

defeats

defecate »*verb* (**defecates, defecating, defecated**) discharge waste matter from the bowels.
– **SAY** **def**-i-kayt or **dee**-fi-kayt
defecation

✓ one **f**, one **c: defecate**

defect[1] [a fault]
– **SAY** **dee**-fekt

defect[2] »*verb* (**defects, defecting, defected**) abandon your country or cause in favour of an opposing one.
– **SAY** di-**fekt**
defection
defector

defective »*adjective* imperfect or faulty.

defector

✓ **-or** not **-er: defector**

defects

defence

✓ **-ence** not **-ense: defence** (the spelling with an **s** is American)

defenceless

defend (verb: **defends, defending, defended**)
defendable
defender

defendant »*noun* a person sued or accused in a court of law.

✓ **-ant** not **-ent: defendant**

defended

defender

defending

defends

defense American spelling of **DEFENCE**.

defensible »*adjective* ❶ able to be justified by argument. ❷ able to be protected.

☑ **-ible** not **-able**: defensible

defensive
  defensively
  defensiveness

defer »*verb* (defers, deferring, deferred)
  ❶ put something off to a later time.
  ❷ humbly give in to someone.
  – SAY di-**fer**

ℹ do not confuse **defer** with **differ**, which means 'be different'

☑ double the **r** in **deferring** and **deferred**

deference »*noun* humble respect.

deferential »*adjective* respectful.
  deferentially

deferment »*noun* the action of putting something off until later.

deferral »*noun* = DEFERMENT.

deferred

deferring

defers

defiant
  defiance
  defiantly

☑ **ant** not **ent**: defiant

defibrillator »*noun* a device for restarting a heartbeat by giving a controlled electric shock.
  – SAY dee-fib-ri-**lay**-ter

☑ double **l**, and the ending is **-or** not **-er**: defibrillator

deficiency »*noun* (plural deficiencies) ❶ a lack or shortage of something. ❷ a failing or shortcoming.

☑ plural: drop the **y** and add **ies**: deficiencies

deficient »*adjective* ❶ not having enough of a specified quality or ingredient. ❷ insufficient: *the documentary evidence is deficient.*
  – SAY di-**fi**-shuhnt

deficit »*noun* ❶ the amount by which something falls short. ❷ the amount by which money spent is greater than money earned in a particular period of time.
  – SAY **def**-i-sit

defied

defies

defile[1] »*verb* (defiles, defiling, defiled)
  ❶ make something dirty. ❷ treat something sacred with disrespect.
  – SAY di-**fyl**

defile[2] »*noun* a steep-sided narrow gorge or passage.
  – SAY di-**fyl** or dee-fyl

define (verb: defines, defining, defined)
  definable

definite [clearly stated; certain]
  definiteness

ℹ do not confuse **definite** with **definitive**, which means 'decisive and with authority'

☑ **ite** not **ate**: definite

definite article »*noun* the word *the*.

definitely

☑ **itely** not **ately**: definitely

definition

definitive »*adjective* ❶ (of a conclusion or agreement) decisive and with authority. ❷ (of a text) the most accurate and trusted of its kind.
  definitively

ℹ do not confuse **definitive** with **definite**, which means 'clearly stated; certain'

deflate »*verb* (deflates, deflating, deflated)
  ❶ let air or gas out of a tyre, balloon, etc.
  ❷ cause someone to feel suddenly depressed. ❸ reduce price levels in an economy.

deflation »*noun* ❶ the action or process of deflating. ❷ reduction of the general level of prices in an economy.
  deflationary

deflect (verb: deflects, deflecting, deflected)
  deflection
  deflector

deflower »*verb* (deflowers, deflowering, deflowered) (old-fashioned) have sex with a woman who is a virgin.

defoliant »*noun* a chemical used to remove the leaves from trees and plants.

☑ **ant** not **ent**: defoliant

defoliate »*verb* (defoliates, defoliating, defoliated) remove leaves from trees or plants.
  – SAY dee-**foh**-li-ayt
  defoliation

deforest »*verb* (deforests, deforesting, deforested) clear an area of trees.
  deforestation

deform »*verb* (deforms, deforming, deformed) distort the shape or form of.
  deformation
  deformed

deformity »*noun* (plural **deformities**) ❶ a deformed part. ❷ the state of being deformed.

> ✓ plural: drop the **y** and add **ies**: **deformities**

deforms

defraud »*verb* (**defrauds**, **defrauding**, **defrauded**) illegally obtain money from someone by deception.

defray »*verb* (**defrays**, **defraying**, **defrayed**) provide money to pay a cost.

defrock »*verb* (**defrocks**, **defrocking**, **defrocked**) remove the official status of a Christian priest as a punishment for an offence.

defrost (verb: **defrosts**, **defrosting**, **defrosted**)

deft »*adjective* (**defter**, **deftest**) quick and neatly skilful.
deftly
deftness

defunct »*adjective* no longer existing or functioning.
– **say** di-**fungkt**

> ✓ -**funct** not -**funked**: defunct

defuse »*verb* (**defuses**, **defusing**, **defused**) ❶ remove the fuse from an explosive device in order to prevent it from exploding. ❷ reduce the danger or tension in a difficult situation.

> ⚠ do not confuse **defuse** with **diffuse**, which means 'spread over a wide area'

defy (verb: **defies**, **defying**, **defied**)

> ✓ change the **y** to **i** in **defies** and **defied**

degenerate »*adjective* having very low moral standards.
» *noun* a morally degenerate person.
» *verb* (**degenerates**, **degenerating**, **degenerated**) become worse or weaker.
degeneracy
degenerately
degeneration

degenerative »*adjective* (of a disease) causing gradual deterioration.

degrade »*verb* (**degrades**, **degrading**, **degraded**) ❶ cause someone to lose dignity or self-respect. ❷ make worse in character or quality. ❸ make something break down or deteriorate chemically.
degradable
degradation

degree

dehumanize »*verb* (**dehumanizes**, **dehumanizing**, **dehumanized**) remove the positive human qualities from.

> ✓ many people prefer the alternative spellings **dehumanise**, **dehumanises**, etc.: both **s** and **z** spellings are correct

d

dehumidify »*verb* (**dehumidifies**, **dehumidifying**, **dehumidified**) remove moisture from the air or a gas.
dehumidifier

dehydrate »*verb* (**dehydrates**, **dehydrating**, **dehydrated**) ❶ cause someone to lose a large amount of water from their body. ❷ remove water from food in order to preserve it.
dehydration

> ✓ hyd not hid: dehydrate

de-ice (verb: **de-ices**, **de-icing**, **de-iced**)
de-icer

deify »*verb* (**deifies**, **deifying**, **deified**) make into or worship as a god.
– **say** day-i-fl or dee-i-fl
deification

deign »*verb* (**deigns**, **deigning**, **deigned**) (**deign to do**) do something that you think you are too important to do.
– **say** dayn

> ✓ don't forget the **g**: deign

deism »*noun* belief in the existence of an all-powerful creator who does not intervene in the universe.
– **say** day-i-z'm or dee-i-z'm
deist

deity »*noun* (plural **deities**) ❶ a god or goddess. ❷ divine status or nature.
– **say** day-i-ti or dee-i-ti

> ✓ plural: drop the **y** and add **ies**: deities

deja vu »*noun* a feeling of having already experienced the present situation.
– **say** day-zhah **voo**

> ✓ **deja vu** can also be spelled **déjà vu**, with an acute accent over the **e** and a grave accent over the **a** (as in the original French phrase meaning 'already seen')

dejected »*adjective* sad and dispirited.
dejectedly

dejection

de jure »*adverb* rightfully; by right.
» *adjective* rightful.
– **say** day **joo**-ray

> ⚠ **de jure** is a Latin phrase meaning 'of law'

delay (verb: **delays**, **delaying**, **delayed**)

d

delectable »*adjective* lovely, delightful, or delicious.
delectably

delectation »*noun* pleasure and delight.
– SAY dee-lek-**tay**-sh'n

delegate »*noun* ❶ a person sent to represent others. ❷ a member of a committee.
» *verb* (**delegates, delegating, delegated**) ❶ entrust a task or responsibility to a less important person. ❷ authorize someone to act as a representative.
– SAY **del**-i-guht [noun], **del**-i-gayt [verb]

delegation »*noun* ❶ a body of delegates. ❷ the process of delegating.

delete (verb: **deletes, deleting, deleted**)
deletion

deleterious »*adjective* causing harm or damage.
– SAY de-li-**tee**-ri-uhss

deletes

deleting

deletion

delft »*noun* glazed earthenware decorated in blue on a white background.

✓ f not ph: **delft** (named after the town of *Delft* in the Netherlands)

deli »*noun* (plural **delis**) (in informal English) = **DELICATESSEN**.

✓ **deli** is spelled with a single l. The plural has **is** not **ies**: **delis**.

deliberate (verb: **deliberates, deliberating, deliberated**)
deliberately
deliberateness

✓ **ber** not **bar**: **deliberate**

deliberation »*noun* ❶ long and careful consideration. ❷ slow and careful movement or thought.

deliberative »*adjective* having to do with consideration or discussion: *a deliberative assembly.*

delicacy »*noun* (plural **delicacies**) ❶ delicate quality or structure. ❷ discretion and tact. ❸ a high-quality or expensive food.

✓ plural: drop the y and add **ies**: **delicacies**

delicate
delicately

delicatessen »*noun* a shop selling cooked meats, cheeses, and unusual or foreign prepared foods.
– SAY de-li-kuh-**tess**-uhn

✓ double s: **delicatessen**

delicious
deliciously
deliciousness

delight (verb: **delights, delighting, delighted**)
delighted
delightedly

✓ **-light** not **-lite**: **delight**

delightful
delightfully

✓ **-ful** not **-full**: **delightful**

delighting

delights

delimit »*verb* (**delimits, delimiting, delimited**) determine the limits or boundaries of an area, policy, etc.
– SAY di-**lim**-it

✓ do not double the t in **delimiting** and **delimited**

delineate »*verb* (**delineates, delineating, delineated**) describe or indicate something precisely.
– SAY di-**lin**-i-ayt
delineation

✓ don't forget the e between the n and the a: **delineate**

delinquency »*noun* (plural **delinquencies**) ❶ minor crime. ❷ neglect of your duty.

delinquent »*adjective* ❶ tending to commit crime. ❷ failing in your duty.
» *noun* a delinquent person.
– SAY di-**ling**-kwuhnt

deliquesce »*verb* (**deliquesces, deliquescing, deliquesced**) (of a solid) become liquid by absorbing moisture.
– SAY de-li-**kwess**
deliquescence
deliquescent

✓ **esce** not **ess**: **deliquesce**

delirious »*adjective* ❶ suffering from delirium. ❷ extremely excited or happy.
deliriously

delirium »*noun* a disturbed state of mind in which a person becomes very restless, has illusions, and is unable to think clearly.
– SAY di-**li**-ri-uhm

✓ **lir** not **ler**: **delirium**

197

deliver » demerara sugar

deliver (verb: **delivers, delivering, delivered**)
deliverable
deliverer

deliverance »*noun* the process of being rescued or set free.

> ☑ **ance** not **ence**: deliverance

delivered
deliverer
deliveries
delivering
delivers
delivery (plural **deliveries**)

> ☑ plural: drop the **y** and add **ies**: deliveries

dell »*noun* a small valley.

Delphic »*adjective* deliberately difficult to understand: *Delphic utterances*.
– sᴀʏ del-fik

> ⓘ from the ancient Greek oracle at *Delphi*

delphinium »*noun* (plural **delphiniums**) a garden plant that has tall spikes of blue flowers.
– sᴀʏ del-**fin**-i-uhm

delta »*noun* ❶ the fourth letter of the Greek alphabet (Δ, δ). ❷ a triangular patch of land where the mouth of a river has split into several channels.

delta wing »*noun* a triangular aircraft wing.

delude »*verb* (**deludes, deluding, deluded**) persuade someone to believe something that is not true.
– sᴀʏ di-**lood**

deluge »*noun* ❶ a severe flood or very heavy fall of rain. ❷ a great quantity of something arriving at the same time: *a deluge of complaints*.
»*verb* (**deluges, deluging, deluged**) ❶ overwhelm someone with a great quantity of something. ❷ flood.
– sᴀʏ del-yooj

delusion »*noun* a belief or impression that is not real.
delusional
delusive

de luxe »*adjective* luxurious; of a superior kind.

> ⓘ **de luxe** is a French phrase meaning 'of luxury'

delve »*verb* (**delves, delving, delved**) ❶ reach inside a container and search for something. ❷ research intensively into something. ❸ (an old word) dig.

demagnetize »*verb* (**demagnetizes, demagnetizing, demagnetized**) make something no longer magnetic.

> ☑ many people prefer the alternative spellings **demagnetise, demagnetises**, etc.: both **s** and **z** spellings are correct

demagogue »*noun* a political leader who appeals to the desires and prejudices of the public.
– sᴀʏ dem-uh-gog
demagogic
demagoguery

> ☑ **gogue** not **gog**: demagogue

demand (verb: **demands, demanding, demanded**)

demanding »*adjective* requiring much skill or effort.
demandingly

demands

demarcate »*verb* (**demarcates, demarcating, demarcated**) set the boundaries of something.
– sᴀʏ dee-mar-kayt

> ☑ **-marc-** not **-mark-**: demarcate

demarcation »*noun* ❶ the action of fixing boundaries. ❷ a dividing line.

dematerialize »*verb* (**dematerializes, dematerializing, dematerialized**) stop being physically present.

> ☑ many people prefer the alternative spellings **dematerialise, dematerialises**, etc.: both **s** and **z** spellings are correct

demean »*verb* (**demeans, demeaning, demeaned**) make someone lose dignity or respect.
– sᴀʏ di-**meen**

demeanour »*noun* the way a person behaves or appears.

> ☑ **-our** not **-or**: demeanour (the spelling without the **u** is American)

demented »*adjective* ❶ suffering from dementia. ❷ (in informal English) wild and irrational.
dementedly

dementia »*noun* a mental disorder in which a person is unable to remember things or think clearly, and develops changes in personality.
– sᴀʏ di-**men**-shuh

demerara sugar »*noun* a type of light brown cane sugar.
– sᴀʏ dem-uh-**rair**-uh

d

d

✓ **mer** not **mar**: the sugar came originally from *Demerara* in Guyana

demerit »*noun* a fault or disadvantage.

demersal »*adjective* living close to the seabed.
– say di-**mer**-suhl

demesne »*noun* ❶ (a historical term) land attached to a manor. ❷ (an old word) a domain.
– say di-**mayn** or di-**meen**

✓ be careful when writing this word which is pronounced and spelled very differently: **demesne**

demigod »*noun* a lesser or partial god.

demigoddess (plural **demigoddesses**)

demijohn »*noun* a narrow-necked bottle holding from 3 to 10 gallons of liquid.

✓ don't forget the **h**: **demijohn**

demilitarize »*verb* (**demilitarizes, demilitarizing, demilitarized**) remove all military forces from an area.
demilitarization

✓ many people prefer the alternative spellings **demilitarise, demilitarises,** etc., and **demilitarisation**: both **s** and **z** spellings are correct

demi-monde »*noun* a group of people considered to be on the fringes of respectable society.
– say de-mi-**mond**

ℹ **demi-monde** means 'half-world' in French

demise »*noun* ❶ a person's death. ❷ the end or failure of something.
– say di-**myz**

demisemiquaver »*noun* a note having the time value of half a semiquaver.
– say dem-i-**sem**-i-kway-ver

demist »*verb* (**demists, demisting, demisted**) clear condensation from.
– say dee-**mist**
demister

demo »*noun* (plural **demos**) ❶ a political demonstration. ❷ a demonstration recording or piece of software.

✓ the plural of **demo** has **os** not **oes**: **demos**

demob »*verb* (**demobs, demobbing, demobbed**) (in informal English) demobilize.
– say dee-**mob**

✓ double the **b** in **demobbing** and **demobbed**

demobilize »*verb* (**demobilizes, demobilizing, demobilized**) take troops out of active service.
– say dee-**moh**-bi-lyz
demobilization

✓ many people prefer the alternative spellings **demobilise, demobilises,** etc., and **demobilisation**: both **s** and **z** spellings are correct

demobs

democracy »*noun* (plural **democracies**) ❶ a form of government in which the people have a say in who should hold power and how they should use it. ❷ a state governed in such a way. ❸ control of a group by the majority of its members.
– say di-**mok**-ruh-si

✓ plural: drop the **y** and add **ies**: **democracies**

democrat

democratic
democratically

democratize »*verb* (**democratizes, democratizing, democratized**) introduce a democratic system or democratic ideas to.
democratization

✓ many people prefer the alternative spellings **democratise, democratises,** etc., and **democratisation**: both **s** and **z** spellings are correct

demography »*noun* the study of the structure of human populations using records of the numbers of births, deaths, instances of disease, etc.
– say di-**mog**-ruh-fi
demographer
demographic

demolish (verb: **demolishes, demolishing, demolished**)
demolition

demon

demonetize »*verb* (**demonetizes, demonetizing, demonetized**) make a coin or precious metal no longer valid as money.
– say dee-**mun**-i-tyz or dee-**mon**-i-tyz
demonetization

✓ many people prefer the alternative spellings **demonetise, demonetises,** etc., and **demonetisation**: both **s** and **z** spellings are correct

demoniac »*adjective* demonic.
– say di-**moh**-ni-ak
demoniacal

demonic »*adjective* having to do with demons or evil spirits.

- **say** di-**mon**-ik
  demonically

demonize »*verb* (**demonizes**, **demonizing**, **demonized**) portray someone as wicked and threatening.
  demonization

> ✓ many people prefer the alternative spellings **demonise**, **demonises**, etc., and **demonisation**: both **s** and **z** spellings are correct

demonology »*noun* the study of demons or belief in demons.

demonstrable »*adjective* clearly apparent or able to be proved.
- **say** di-**mon**-struh-b'l or de-muhn-struh-b'l
  demonstrably

demonstrate (verb: **demonstrates**, **demonstrating**, **demonstrated**)
  demonstrator

demonstration

demonstrative »*adjective* ❶ tending to show your feelings openly. ❷ demonstrating something. ❸ (of a determiner or pronoun) indicating the person or thing referred to (e.g. *this, that, those*).
- **say** di-**mon**-struh-tiv
  demonstratively

demonstrator

demoralize »*verb* (**demoralizes**, **demoralizing**, **demoralized**) make someone lose confidence or hope.
  demoralization

> ✓ many people prefer the alternative spellings **demoralise**, **demoralises**, etc., and **demoralisation**: both **s** and **z** spellings are correct

demote »*verb* (**demotes**, **demoting**, **demoted**) move someone to a less senior position.
  demotion

demotic »*adjective* (of language) used by ordinary people.
- **say** di-**mot**-ik

demoting

demotion

demotivate »*verb* (**demotivates**, **demotivating**, **demotivated**) make someone less eager to work or make an effort.
  demotivation

demur »*verb* (**demurs**, **demurring**, **demurred**) show reluctance.
»*noun* the showing of reluctance: *they accepted without demur.*
- **say** di-**mer**
  demurral

> ✓ double the **r** in **demurring**, **demurred**, and **demurral**

demure »*adjective* (of a woman) reserved, modest, and shy.
- **say** di-**myoor**
  demurely

demurral

demurred

demurring

demurs

demystify »*verb* (**demystifies**, **demystifying**, **demystified**) make a subject less difficult to understand.
  demystification

den

denationalize »*verb* (**denationalizes**, **denationalizing**, **denationalized**) transfer a company from public to private ownership.
  denationalization

> ✓ many people prefer the alternative spellings **denationalise**, **denationalises**, etc., and **denationalisation**: both **s** and **z** spellings are correct

denature »*verb* (**denatures**, **denaturing**, **denatured**) ❶ alter the natural qualities of. ❷ make alcohol unfit for drinking by adding poisonous or foul-tasting substances.
- **say** dee-**nay**-cher
  denaturation

dene »*noun* a deep, narrow, wooded valley.

> ℹ do not confuse **dene** with **dean**, which means 'head of a cathedral chapter'

dengue »*noun* a tropical disease transmitted by mosquitoes, causing fever and pain in the joints.
- **say** **deng**-gi

> ✓ remember the **u**: **dengue** (a Swahili word)

deniable
  deniability

denial

> ✓ **al** not **el**: **denial**

denied

denier »*noun* a unit of measurement for the fineness of textile fibre.
- **say** **den**-yer

denies

denigrate »*verb* (**denigrates**, **denigrating**, **denigrated**) criticize someone unfairly.
- **say** **den**-i-grayt
  denigration

✓ **nig** not **neg**: denigrate

denim

denizen »*noun* an inhabitant or occupant.
– SAY den-i-zuhn

✓ **zen** not **sen**: denizen

denominate »*verb* (**denominates, denominating, denominated**) call; name.
– SAY di-nom-i-nayt

✓ single **n**'s, single **m**: denominate

denomination »*noun* ❶ a recognized branch of a church or religion. ❷ the face value of a banknote, coin, postage stamp, etc. ❸ a name or designation.

denominational »*adjective* relating to a particular religious denomination.

denominator »*noun* the number below the line in a fraction, for example 4 in ¼.

✓ **-or** not **-er**: denominator

denote »*verb* (**denotes, denoting, denoted**) ❶ be a name or symbol for something. ❷ be an indication of something.

ℹ **denote** does not mean the same as **connote**: **denote** refers to what something stands for, while **connote** refers to extra ideas or feelings suggested by that thing

denouement »*noun* the final part of a story, in which matters are explained or resolved.
– SAY day-**noo**-mon

✓ there is an **e** between the **u** and the **m**: denouement. It is a French word and is sometimes written **dénouement**, with an acute accent on the first **e**.

denounce »*verb* (**denounces, denouncing, denounced**) publicly declare that someone is wrong or evil.
denouncement

dense (adjective: **denser, densest**)
densely

✓ **se** not **ce**: dense

density »*noun* (plural **densities**) ❶ the degree to which something is dense. ❷ the quantity of people or things in a given area.

✓ plural: drop the **y** and add **ies**: densities

dent (verb: **dents, denting, dented**)
dental
dented

dentine »*noun* hard dense bony tissue forming the bulk of a tooth.
– SAY den-teen

✓ don't forget the **e** on the end: dentine (the spelling without the **e** is American)

denting
dentist
dentistry

dentition »*noun* the arrangement or condition of the teeth in a particular species or individual.
– SAY den-**ti**-sh'n

dents

denture »*noun* a removable plate or frame holding one or more false teeth.
– SAY den-cher

denude »*verb* (**denudes, denuding, denuded**) make something bare or empty.
denudation

denunciation »*noun* the action of denouncing.
– SAY di-nun-si-ay-sh'n

✓ **nunc** not **nounc**: denunciation

deny (verb: **denies, denying, denied**)
deodorant

✓ **-odor-** not **-odour-**: deodorant

deodorize »*verb* (**deodorizes, deodorizing, deodorized**) remove or conceal an unpleasant smell in a place.

✓ many people prefer the alternative spellings **deodorise, deodorises**, etc.: both **s** and **z** spellings are correct

deoxygenate »*verb* (**deoxygenates, deoxygenating, deoxygenated**) remove oxygen from.
– SAY dee-**ok**-si-juh-nayt

deoxyribonucleic acid »*noun* = DNA.
– SAY di-ok-si-ry-boh-nyoo-**klay**-ik

depart (verb: **departs, departing, departed**)
department
departmental
departmentally

departs
departure

depend (verb: **depends, depending, depended**)

dependable
dependability
dependably

dependant »*noun* a person who relies on another for financial support.

✓ the noun **dependant** can also be spelled **dependent**: both spellings are correct. However, the adjective **dependent**, which means 'determined by; relying on', is always spelled with **ent** at the end.

depended
dependence

dependency »*noun* (plural **dependencies**)
❶ a country or province controlled by another. **❷** the state of being dependent.

✓ **ency** not **ancy**: **dependency** plural: drop the **y** and add **ies**: **dependencies**

dependent »*adjective* **❶** (**dependent on**) determined by. **❷** relying on someone or something for support. **❸** (**dependent on**) unable to do without.
» *noun* another way of spelling **DEPENDANT**.
dependence
dependently

✓ the adjective is spelled with the ending **ent**, not **ant**: **dependent**. The noun can be spelled with either **ent** or **ant** at the end.

depending
depends

depict (verb: **depicts, depicting, depicted**)
depiction

depilate »*verb* (**depilates, depilating, depilated**) remove the hair from.
– SAY dep-i-layt
depilation
depilator

depilatory »*adjective* used to remove unwanted hair.
» *noun* (plural **depilatories**) a cream or lotion used to remove unwanted hair.
– SAY di-**pil**-uh-tri

deplete »*verb* (**depletes, depleting, depleted**) **❶** reduce the number or quantity of. **❷** use up supplies.
– SAY di-**pleet**
depletion

deplorable »*adjective* shockingly bad.
– SAY di-**plor**-uh-b'l
deplorably

deplore »*verb* (**deplores, deploring, deplored**) strongly disapprove of something.

deploy »*verb* (**deploys, deploying, deployed**) **❶** bring or move forces into position for military action. **❷** use a resource or quality effectively.
– SAY di-**ploy**
deployment

depopulate »*verb* (**depopulates, depopulating, depopulated**) greatly reduce the population of an area.
depopulation

deport »*verb* (**deports, deporting, deported**) expel a foreigner or immigrant from a country.
deportation
deportee

deportment »*noun* **❶** the way a person stands and walks. **❷** (in American English) a person's behaviour or manners.

deports

depose »*verb* (**deposes, deposing, deposed**) remove someone from office suddenly and forcefully.

deposit (verb: **deposits, depositing, deposited**)
depositor

✓ do not double the **t** in **depositing** and **deposited**

deposition »*noun* **❶** the action of deposing someone from office. **❷** (in law) the giving of sworn evidence. **❸** (in law) a sworn statement to be used as evidence. **❹** the action of depositing.
– SAY de-puh-**zi**-shuhn or dee-puh-**zi**-shuhn

depository »*noun* (plural **depositories**) a place where things are stored.

depot

✓ don't forget the silent **t** at the end: **depot**

deprave »*verb* (**depraves, depraving, depraved**) lead someone away from what is natural or right; corrupt.
– SAY di-**prayv**
depravity SAY di-**prav**-i-ti

deprecate »*verb* (**deprecates, deprecating, deprecated**) express disapproval of: *it has become fashionable to deprecate opponents of any government project.*
– SAY **dep**-ri-kayt
deprecation
deprecatory

ℹ do not confuse **deprecate**, which means 'express disapproval of', with **depreciate**, which means 'decrease in value'

depreciate »*verb* (**depreciates, depreciating, depreciated**) decrease in value over a period of time: *the latest cars will depreciate heavily in the first year.*
– SAY di-**pree**-shi-ayt
depreciation
depreciatory

ℹ do not confuse **depreciate**, which means 'decrease in value', with **deprecate**, which means 'express disapproval of'

d

depredations »*plural noun* acts that cause harm or damage.
– **say** dep-ri-**day**-sh'nz

> ✓ pred not prad: depredations

depress »*verb* (depresses, depressing, depressed) ❶ make someone feel utterly dejected. ❷ make something less active: *alcohol depresses the nervous system.* ❸ push or pull down.

depressant »*adjective* slowing down the natural processes of the body.

> ✓ ant not ent: depressant

depressed

depresses

depressing

depression

depressive »*adjective* tending to causing depression.
» *noun* a person who tends to suffer from depression.

depressurize »*verb* (depressurizes, depressurizing, depressurized) release the pressure inside a compartment or container.
depressurization

> ✓ many people prefer the alternative spellings **depressurise, depressurises,** etc., and **depressurisation**: both **s** and **z** spellings are correct

deprivation »*noun* ❶ hardship resulting from not having enough of the things necessary for life. ❷ the action of depriving.
– **say** dep-ri-**vay**-sh'n

deprive (verb: deprives, depriving, deprived)

depth
depthless

deputation »*noun* a group of people who are sent to do something on behalf of a larger group.

depute »*verb* (deputes, deputing, deputed) ❶ instruct someone to perform a task that you are responsible for. ❷ give authority or a task to someone.
– **say** di-**pyoot**

deputies

deputize »*verb* (deputizes, deputizing, deputized) temporarily act on behalf of someone else.
– **say** dep-yuu-tyz

> ✓ many people prefer the alternative spellings **deputise, deputises,** etc.: both **s** and **z** spellings are correct

deputy »*noun* (plural deputies) a person appointed to do the work of a more senior person in that person's absence.

> ✓ plural: drop the **y** and add **ies**: deputies

derail »*verb* (derails, derailing, derailed) ❶ cause a train to leave the tracks. ❷ obstruct a process by diverting it from its intended course: *an attempt to derail the negotiations.*
derailment

> ✓ do not double the **l** in **derailing, derailed,** and **derailment**

derange »*verb* (deranges, deranging, deranged) ❶ make someone insane. ❷ throw something into disorder.
derangement

Derby »*noun* (plural Derbies) ❶ an annual flat race at Epsom in Surrey for three-year-old horses, founded by the 12th Earl of Derby. ❷ (derby) a sports match between two rival teams from the same area.
– **say** dar-bi

> ✓ der not dar: Derby

deregulate »*verb* (deregulates, deregulating, deregulated) remove regulations or restrictions from something.
deregulation

derelict »*adjective* in a very poor condition as a result of disuse and neglect.
» *noun* a person without a home, job, or property.
– **say** der-i-likt

> ✓ dere not deri, and ct not cked: derelict

dereliction »*noun* ❶ an abandoned and run-down state. ❷ (dereliction of duty) shameful failure to do something you are supposed to do.

deride »*verb* (derides, deriding, derided) express contempt for; ridicule.
– **say** di-**ryd**

de rigueur »*adjective* required by etiquette or current fashion.
– **say** duh ri-**ger**

> ✓ don't forget the **u** after the **g**: de **rigueur** is a French phrase meaning 'in strictness'

derision »*noun* scornful ridicule or mockery.
– **say** di-**ri**-zh'n

derisive »*adjective* expressing contempt or ridicule.

– say di-**ry**-siv or di-**ry**-ziv
derisively
derisiveness

derisory »*adjective* ridiculously small or inadequate.
– say di-**ry**-suh-ri or di-**ry**-zuh-ri

> ℹ️ there is a difference between **derisory** and **derisive**: **derisory** means 'ridiculously small or inadequate' (*a derisory pay rise*), whereas **derisive** means 'expressing contempt' (*a derisive laugh*)

derivation »*noun* ❶ the deriving of something from a source. ❷ the formation of a word from another word or from a root in the same or another language.

derivative »*adjective* imitating the work of another artist, writer, etc.; not original. »*noun* ❶ something which is derived from another source. ❷ (in mathematics) an expression representing the rate of change of one quantity in relation to another.
– say di-**riv**-uh-tiv

derive »*verb* (**derives, deriving, derived**) (**derive from**) ❶ obtain something from a source. ❷ arise or originate from.

dermatitis »*noun* inflammation of the skin as a result of irritation or an allergic reaction.
– say der-muh-**ty**-tiss

dermatology »*noun* the branch of medicine concerned with skin disorders.
dermatological
dermatologically
dermatologist

dermis »*noun* the thick layer of the skin below the epidermis.
– say **der**-miss

derogate »*verb* (**derogates, derogating, derogated**) ❶ (**derogate from**) detract from something. ❷ (**derogate from**) deviate from a set of rules. ❸ speak critically about something.
– say **der**-uh-gayt
derogation

> ☑️ one **r**, one **g**: **derogate**

derogatory »*adjective* critical or disrespectful.
– say di-**rog**-uh-tri

derrick »*noun* ❶ a kind of crane with a movable pivoted arm. ❷ the framework over an oil well for holding the drilling machinery.
– say **der**-rik

> ☑️ double **r**, and **ick** not **ek** at the end: **derrick**

derring-do »*noun* (old-fashioned) action displaying heroic courage.
– say der-ring-**doo**

dervish »*noun* a member of a Muslim religious group vowed to poverty and known for their wild rituals.
– say **der**-vish

desalinate »*verb* (**desalinates, desalinating, desalinated**) remove salt from seawater.
– say dee-**sal**-i-nayt
desalination

descant »*noun* an independent melody sung or played above a basic melody.
– say **dess**-kant

descend (verb: **descends, descending, descended**)

> ☑️ don't forget the **c** after the **s**: **descend**

descendant »*noun* a person or animal that is descended from a particular ancestor.

> ☑️ **ant** not **ent**: **descendant**. **Descendent** is an adjective and means 'descending', whereas **descendent** is a noun meaning 'someone descended from an ancestor'.

descended

descendent »*adjective* descending.

descending

descends

descent »*noun* ❶ an act of descending. ❷ a downward slope. ❸ a person's origin or nationality.

> ☑️ remember the **c**: **descent**

describe (verb: **describes, describing, described**)
describable
describer

description

descriptive
descriptively

descry »*verb* (**descries, descrying, descried**) (an old word) catch sight of something.
– say di-**skry**

desecrate »*verb* (**desecrates, desecrating, desecrated**) treat something sacred with violent disrespect.
– say **dess**-i-krayt
desecration

> ☑️ **sec** not **sac**: **desecrate**

desegregate »*verb* (**desegregates, desegregating, desegregated**) end racial segregation in a place.
desegregation

d

✓ greg not grag: de**seg**regate

deselect »*verb* (**deselects, deselecting, deselected**) reject an existing MP as a candidate in a forthcoming election.
deselection

desensitize »*verb* (**desensitizes, desensitizing, desensitized**) make someone or something less sensitive.
desensitization

✓ many people prefer the alternative spellings **desensitise, desensitises,** etc., and **desensitisation**: both **s** and **z** spellings are correct

desert[1] (verb: **deserts, deserting, deserted**) [abandon]
– *SAY* di-**zert**
desertion

✓ single **s**: de**s**ert. Do not confuse **desert** meaning 'abandon' with **dessert** meaning 'the sweet course'.

desert[2] [waterless area]
– *SAY* **dez**-ert

✓ single **s**: de**s**ert. Do not confuse **desert** meaning 'a waterless area' with **dessert** meaning 'the sweet course'.

deserted

deserter »*noun* a member of the armed forces who illegally runs away from military service.

deserting

desertion

deserts[1] »*plural noun* the reward or punishment that a person deserves.
– *SAY* di-**zerts**

deserts[2] present of **DESERT**[1] [as in *he deserts*].

deserve (verb: **deserves, deserving, deserved**)
deservedly

deshabille »*noun* the state of being only partly or scantily clothed.
– *SAY* day-za-bee-**yay** or dess-uh-**beel**

✓ **deshabille** is sometimes written **déshabillé**, with acute accents above the **e**'s (as in the original French). It can also be spelled **dishabille**.

desiccate »*verb* (**desiccates, desiccating, desiccated**) remove the moisture from something.
– *SAY* **dess**-i-kayt

✓ one **s**, two **c**'s: de**s**i**cc**ate

desideratum »*noun* (plural **desiderata**) something that is needed or wanted.

– *SAY* di-zi-duh-**raa**-tuhm [singular], di-zi-duh-**raa**-tuh [plural]

✓ like many other words ending in **um** derived from Latin, **desideratum** has a plural ending in **a**: desiderat**a**

design (verb: **designs, designing, designed**)
designer

designate »*verb* (**designates, designating, designated**) ❶ officially give a particular status or name to something. ❷ appoint someone to a particular position.
» *adjective* appointed to a position but not yet having taken it up.
– *SAY* **dez**-ig-nayt [verb], **dez**-ig-nuht [adjective]

ℹ when used as an adjective, **designate** should be placed after the noun, as in *the Director designate*

designation »*noun* ❶ the action of designating. ❷ an official title or description.

designed

designer

designing

designs

desirable
desirability
desirably

✓ there is no **e** after the **r**: desirable

desire (verb: **desires, desiring, desired**)

desirous »*adjective* strongly wishing to have something.
– *SAY* di-zy-ruhss

desist »*verb* (**desists, desisting, desisted**) stop doing something.

desk

desktop

desolate »*adjective* ❶ bleak and dismally empty. ❷ very unhappy.
» *verb* (**desolates, desolating, desolated**) make someone very unhappy.
– *SAY* **dess**-uh-luht [adjective], **dess**-uh-layt [verb]
desolation

despair (verb: **despairs, despairing, despaired**)

✓ **des** not **dis**: despair

despatch another way of spelling **DISPATCH**.

desperado »*noun* (plural **desperadoes** or **desperados**) (old-fashioned) a desperate or reckless criminal.
– *SAY* dess-puh-**rah**-doh

☑ the plural of **desperado** can have **oes** or **os**: **desperadoes** or **desperados**

desperate
desperately
desperation

☑ **per** not **par**: **desperate**

despicable
despicably

despise (verb: **despise, despising, despised**)

☑ **despise** cannot be spelled with an **ize** ending

despite

despoil »*verb* (**despoils, despoiling, despoiled**) steal valuable possessions from a place.

despondent »*adjective* very sad and without much hope.
despondency
despondently

☑ **ent** not **ant**: **despondent**

despot »*noun* a ruler with unlimited power.
– SAY **dess**-pot
despotic
despotism

dessert [sweet course eaten at the end of a meal]
– SAY di-**zert**

☑ double **s**: **dessert**. Do not confuse **dessert** with **desert**, which means 'a waterless area' or 'abandon'.

dessertspoon

destabilize »*verb* (**destabilizes, destabilizing, destabilized**) make a country or government unstable.
destabilization

☑ many people prefer the alternative spellings **destabilise, destabilises,** etc., and **destabilisation**: both **s** and **z** spellings are correct

destination

destined

destiny (plural **destinies**)

☑ plural: drop the **y** and add **ies**: **destinies**

destitute »*adjective* extremely poor and without a home or other things necessary for life.
– SAY **dess**-ti-tyoot
destitution

destroy (verb: **destroys, destroying, destroyed**)
destroyer

destructible

☑ **-ible** not **-able**: **destructible**

destruction

destructive
destructively
destructiveness

desuetude »*noun* a state of disuse.
– SAY di-**syoo**-i-tyood or **dess**-wi-tyood

desultory »*adjective* ❶ without much purpose or enthusiasm. ❷ going constantly from one subject to another in a half-hearted way.
– SAY **dess**-uhl-tuh-ri or **dez**-uhl-tuh-ri
desultorily

☑ don't forget the **o** between the **t** and the **r**: **desultory**

detach (verb: **detaches, detaching, detached**)
detachable
detached

☑ only one **t**: **detach**, not **tatch**

detachment »*noun* ❶ the state of being uninvolved or aloof. ❷ a group of troops, ships, etc. sent away on a mission. ❸ the action of detaching.

detail (verb: **details, detailing, detailed**)
detailed

detain (verb: **detains, detaining, detained**)
detainer
detainment

detainee »*noun* a person who is kept in custody.

detaining

detainment

detains

detect (verb: **detects, detecting, detected**)
detectable
detection

detective

detector

☑ **-or** not **-er**: **detector**

detects

detente »*noun* the easing of hostility or strained relations between countries.
– SAY day-**tahnt**

☑ **detente** may also be spelled **détente**, with an acute accent above the first **e** (as in the original French)

detention

deter (verb: deters, deterring, deterred)

 double the r in **deterring** and **deterred**

detergent

deteriorate (verb: deteriorates, deteriorating, deteriorated)
deterioration

determinant »*noun* a factor which determines the nature or outcome of something: *force of will was the main determinant of his success.*
– **SAY** di-**ter**-mi-nuhnt

 ant not **ent**: determinant

determination

determine »*verb* (determines, determining, determined) ❶ be the main factor in deciding something: *it is biological age that determines our looks.* ❷ firmly decide. ❸ ascertain or establish by research or calculation.
determinable

determined
determinedly

determiner »*noun* ❶ a person or thing that determines. ❷ a word that comes before a noun to show how the noun is being used, e.g. *a, the, every.*

determines

determining

determinism »*noun* the belief that people's lives are determined by factors outside their control.
determinist
deterministic

deterred

deterrent »*noun* a thing that deters or is intended to deter.
– **SAY** di-**ter**-ruhnt
deterrence

 double **r**, and **ent** not **ant** at the end: deterrent

deterring

deters

detest (verb: detests, detesting, detested)

detestable

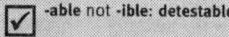 **-able** not **-ible**: detestable

detestation »*noun* intense dislike.
– **SAY** dee-tess-**tay**-sh'n

detested

detesting

detests

dethrone »*verb* (dethrones, dethroning, dethroned) remove a ruler from power.
dethronement

detonate »*verb* (detonates, detonating, detonated) explode or cause to explode.
detonation

detonator »*noun* a device used to detonate an explosive.

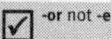 **-or** not **-er**: detonator

detour »*noun* a long or roundabout route taken to avoid something or to visit something along the way.
»*verb* (detours, detouring, detoured) take a detour.

detox (in informal English) »*noun* detoxification.
»*verb* (detoxes, detoxing, detoxed) detoxify.

detoxify »*verb* (detoxifies, detoxifying, detoxified) ❶ remove poisonous substances from something. ❷ stop taking or help someone to stop taking drink or drugs.
detoxification

detoxing

detract »*verb* (detracts, detracting, detracted) (**detract from**) make something seem less valuable or impressive.
detraction

detractor »*noun* a person who speaks critically about someone or something.

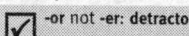 **-or** not **-er**: detractor

detracts

detriment »*noun* harm or damage: *she dieted to the detriment of her health.*
– **SAY** det-ri-muhnt
detrimental

detritus »*noun* debris or waste material.
– **SAY** di-**try**-tuhss

deuce »*noun* the score of 40 all in tennis, at which two consecutive points are needed to win the game.
– **SAY** dyooss

deus ex machina »*noun* an unexpected event saving a seemingly hopeless situation.
– **SAY** day-uuss eks **mak**-i-nuh or dee-uhss eks muh-**shee**-nuh

> **i** **deus ex machina** is a Latin phrase meaning 'god from the machinery'. It originally referred to an actor playing a god in ancient theatre, who was suspended above the stage and intervened in the play's outcome.

Deutschmark »*noun* the basic unit of money of Germany.

– **say** doych-mark

> ✓ tsch not tch: Deutschmark

devalue »*verb* (**devalues**, **devaluing**, **devalued**) ❶ make something seem less important than it really is. ❷ reduce the official value of a currency in relation to other currencies.
devaluation

devastate (verb: **devastates**, **devastating**, **devastated**)
devastation
devastator

devastating
devastatingly

devastation

devastator

develop (verb: **develops**, **developing**, **developed**)
developer
developing

> ✓ there is no **e** at the end: **develop**, **develops**

development
developmental
developmentally

develops

deviant »*adjective* different from what is considered normal.
»*noun* a deviant person.
deviance

deviate »*verb* (**deviates**, **deviating**, **deviated**) depart from an established course or from normal standards: *you must not deviate from the agreed route.*
deviation

device [a thing made for a particular purpose]

> ℹ️ do not confuse **device** with **devise**, which means 'plan or invent'

devil

deviled American spelling of **DEVILLED**.

devilish »*adjective* ❶ evil and cruel. ❷ mischievous: *a devilish grin.*
devilishly

> ✓ only one **l**: **devilish**

devilled »*adjective* cooked with hot seasoning.

> ✓ double **l**: **devilled** (**deviled** is the American spelling)

devilment »*noun* reckless mischief.

devilry »*noun* ❶ wicked activity. ❷ reckless mischief.

devil's advocate »*noun* a person who expresses an unpopular opinion in order to provoke debate.

devious »*adjective* ❶ behaving in a cunning way to get what you want. ❷ (of a route or journey) indirect.
deviously
deviousness

devise (verb: **devises**, **devising**, **devised**) [plan or invent]
deviser

> ✓ **devise** cannot be spelled with an **ize** ending
> do not confuse **devise** with **device**, which means 'a thing made for a particular purpose'

devoid »*adjective* (**devoid of**) entirely without.
– **say** di-**voyd**

devolution »*noun* the transferring of power by central government to local or regional governments.
– **say** dee-vuh-**loo**-sh'n or dev-uh-**loo**-sh'n
devolutionary

devolve »*verb* (**devolves**, **devolving**, **devolved**) ❶ transfer power to a lower level. ❷ (**devolve on** or **to**) (of responsibility) pass to a particular person.
– **say** di-**volv**

Devonian »*adjective* relating to the geological period from about 409 to 363 million years ago.
– **say** di-**voh**-ni-uhn

devore »*noun* a velvet fabric with a pattern formed by burning the pile away with acid.
– **say** duh-**vor**-ay

> ✓ **devore** can also be spelled **devoré**, with an acute accent over the **e** (as in the original French)

devote (verb: **devotes**, **devoting**, **devoted**)
devoted
devotedly

devotee »*noun* ❶ a person who is very enthusiastic about someone or something. ❷ a follower of a particular religion or god.
– **say** dev-oh-**tee**

devotes

devoting

devotion »*noun* ❶ great love or loyalty. ❷ religious worship.
devotional

devotions »*plural noun* prayers or religious observances.

devour (verb: **devours**, **devouring**, **devoured**)
devourer

devout »*adjective* ❶ deeply religious.
❷ earnestly sincere: *my devout hope.*
– sᴀʏ di-**vowt**
   devoutly
   devoutness

dew [drops of moisture]

dewberry »*noun* (plural **dewberries**) the
blue-black fruit of a trailing bramble.

dewlap »*noun* a fold of loose skin hanging
from the neck or throat of an animal or
bird.

dew point »*noun* the air temperature
below which dew can form.

dewy »*adjective* ❶ wet with dew. ❷ (of a
person's skin) appearing soft and shining.

dexterity »*noun* skill in performing tasks.
– sᴀʏ dek-**ster**-i-ti

dexterous »*adjective* showing neat skill.
– sᴀʏ dek-stuh-ruhss
   dexterously

> ☑️ **dexterous** can also be spelled
> **dextrous**, without the second **e**: both
> spellings are correct

dhal »*noun* (in Indian cookery) split pulses.
– sᴀʏ dahl

> ☑️ **dhal** can also be spelled **dal**, without
> the **h**: both spellings are correct

dharma »*noun* (in Indian religion) the
eternal law of the universe.
– sᴀʏ **dar**-muh

diabetes »*noun* an illness in which the
body cannot absorb sugar and starch
properly because it does not have enough
of the hormone insulin.
– sᴀʏ dy-uh-**bee**-teez

diabetic

diabolic »*adjective* having to do with the
Devil.

diabolical »*adjective* ❶ having to do with
the Devil. ❷ (in informal English) very bad.
   diabolically

diabolism »*noun* worship of the Devil.
– sᴀʏ dy-**ab**-uh-liz'm
   diabolist

diaconal »*adjective* relating to a deacon or
deacons.
– sᴀʏ dy-**ak**-uh-nuhl

> ☑️ **dia** not **dea**: diaconal

diacritic »*noun* a sign written above or
below a letter to indicate a difference in
pronunciation from the same letter when
unmarked.
– sᴀʏ dy-uh-**krit**-ik

diadem »*noun* a jewelled crown or
headband worn as a symbol of power or
authority.
– sᴀʏ **dy**-uh-dem

diaeresis »*noun* (plural **diaereses**) a mark
(¨) placed over a vowel to indicate that it
is sounded separately, as in *naïve.*
– sᴀʏ dy-**eer**-i-siss [singular], dy-**eer**-i-seez
[plural]

> ☑️ **diae-** not **die-**: diaeresis (the spelling
> without the **a** is American)
> make the plural by changing the **-is** ending
> to **-es** (as in Latin): **diaereses**

diagnose (verb: **diagnoses, diagnosing,
diagnosed**)

diagnosis (plural **diagnoses**)

> ☑️ make the plural by changing the **-is**
> ending to **-es** (as in Latin): **diagnoses**

diagnostic »*adjective* having to do with
diagnosis.
– sᴀʏ dy-uhg-**noss**-tik
   diagnostically

diagonal »*adjective* ❶ (of a straight line)
joining opposite corners of a rectangle,
square, or other figure. ❷ straight and at
an angle; slanting.
»*noun* a diagonal line.
   diagonally

diagram
   diagrammatic
   diagrammatically

> ☑️ double the **m** in diagrammatic

dial (verb: **dials, dialling, dialled**)

> ☑️ double the **l** in dialling and dialled
> (the spellings with a single **l** are
> American)

dialect »*noun* a form of a language used in
a particular region or by a particular social
group.
– sᴀʏ **dy**-uh-lekt
   dialectal

dialectic »*noun* (also **dialectics**) the art of
investigating or debating the truth of
opinions.
»*adjective* having to do with dialectic or
dialectics.
– sᴀʏ dy-uh-**lek**-tik
   dialectical

dialled

dialling

dialog American spelling of **DIALOGUE**.

dialog box »*noun* a small area on a
computer screen in which the user is
prompted to provide information or select
commands.

✓ in British English **dialog box** can also be spelled **dialogue box**

dialogue

✓ don't forget the **ue** at the end: **dialogue**. In computing, the American spelling **dialog** is often used.

dials

dialysis »*noun* (plural **dialyses**) ❶ (in chemistry) the separation of particles in a liquid on the basis of differences in their ability to pass through a membrane. ❷ the purifying of blood by this technique, in cases of kidney failure.
– SAY dy-**al**-i-siss [singular], dy-**al**-i-seez [plural]

✓ make the plural by changing the **-is** ending to **-es** (as in Latin): **dialyses**

diamante »*adjective* decorated with artificial jewels.
– SAY dy-uh-**mon**-tay

✓ **diamante** can also be spelled **diamanté**, with an acute accent above the **e** (as in the original French)

diameter »*noun* a straight line passing from side to side through the centre of a circle or sphere.
– SAY dy-**am**-i-ter

✓ **met** not **mit**: **diameter**

diametrical »*adjective* ❶ (of opposites) complete. ❷ having to do with a diameter.
– SAY dy-uh-**met**-ri-k'l
diametric
diametrically

diamond

✓ don't forget the **a**: **diamond**

diamond jubilee »*noun* the sixtieth anniversary of a notable event.

diamond wedding »*noun* the sixtieth anniversary of a wedding.

diamorphine »*noun* heroin.
– SAY dy-**mor**-feen

diaper »*noun* (in American English) a baby's nappy.
– SAY **dy**-per

diaphanous »*adjective* light, delicate, and semi-transparent.
– SAY dy-**af**-uh-nuhss

diaphragm »*noun* ❶ a dome-shaped layer of muscle separating the thorax from the abdomen in mammals. ❷ a taut flexible membrane in mechanical or sound systems. ❸ a thin contraceptive cap fitting over the cervix.

– SAY **dy**-uh-fram

✓ don't forget the **g** before the **m**: **diaphragm**

diaries
diarist
diarrhoea »*noun* a condition in which you have frequent liquid bowel movements.
– SAY dy-uh-**ree**-uh

✓ two **r**'s, and **hoea** not **hea** at the end: **diarrhoea** (the spelling with **hea** is American)

diary (plural **diaries**)

✓ **i** before **a**: a **diary** is a book for keeping a daily record, while a **dairy** is a place where milk is collected and stored
plural: drop the **y** and add **ies**: **diaries**

diaspora »*noun* ❶ the dispersion of the Jews beyond Israel. ❷ the dispersion of any people from their traditional homeland.
– SAY dy-**ass**-puh-ruh

diastole »*noun* the phase of the heartbeat when the heart muscle relaxes and the chambers fill with blood.
– SAY dy-**ass**-tuh-li
diastolic

diatonic »*adjective* involving only the musical notes of the major or minor scale, without additional sharps, flats, etc.
– SAY dy-uh-**ton**-ik

diatribe »*noun* a speech or piece of writing forcefully attacking someone.
– SAY dy-uh-**tryb**

dibber »*noun* a dibble.

dibble »*noun* a pointed hand tool for making holes in the ground for seeds or young plants.

dice (plural **dice**; singular also **die**; verb: **dices**, **dicing**, **diced**)

ℹ historically, **dice** is the plural of **die**, but in modern English **dice** is used as both the singular and the plural

dicey »*adjective* (**dicier**, **diciest**) (in informal English) difficult or risky.

✓ the ending is **ey**, not simply **y**: **dicey** drop the **ey** and add **ier** or **iest** to spell **dicier** or **diciest**

dichotomy »*noun* (plural **dichotomies**) a separation or contrast between two things: *the false dichotomy between education and entertainment.*
– SAY dy-**kot**-uh-mi
dichotomous

dicier

diciest

d

dicing

dick

Dickensian »*adjective* like the novels of Charles Dickens, especially in terms of the urban poverty that they portray.
– SAY di-**ken**-zi-uhn

dicker »*verb* (**dickers, dickering, dickered**) ❶ argue or bargain in a petty way. ❷ toy or fiddle with something.

dickhead

dicky »*adjective* (in informal English) not strong, healthy, or working properly.

dicta plural of **DICTUM**.

dictate (verb: **dictates, dictating, dictated**)
dictation

dictator »*noun* a ruler with total power over a country.
– SAY dik-**tay**-ter
dictatorial
dictatorship

> ✅ -or not -er: **dictator**

diction »*noun* ❶ the choice and use of words in speech or writing: *poetic diction.* ❷ a person's way of pronouncing words.

dictionary

> ✅ ary not ery: **dictionary**
> plural: drop the **y** and add **ies**: **dictionaries**

dictum »*noun* (plural **dicta** or **dictums**) ❶ a formal announcement made by someone in authority. ❷ a short statement that expresses a general principle.

> ✅ the plural can be either **dicta** (like the original Latin) or **dictums**

did

didactic »*adjective* intended to teach or give moral instruction.
– SAY di-**dak**-tik or dy-**dak**-tik
didacticism

diddle »*verb* (**diddles, diddling, diddled**) (in informal English) cheat or swindle someone.

didgeridoo »*noun* an Australian Aboriginal wind instrument in the form of a long wooden tube, which produces a deep sound when blown.
– SAY di-juh-ri-**doo**

> ✅ ger not jer: **didgeridoo**

didn't [did not]

> ✅ be careful to put the apostrophe where a letter has been left out, that is between the **n** and **t** of **not**: **didn't**

die[1] (verb: **dies, dying, died**) [stop living]

die[2] »*noun* ❶ singular of **DICE**. ❷ (plural **dies**) a device for cutting or moulding metal or for stamping a design onto coins or medals.

> ℹ the traditional singular **die** for a small cube with numbered faces is now uncommon, and **dice** is used for both the singular and the plural

die-cast »*adjective* formed by pouring molten metal into a mould.

died

diehard »*noun* a person who obstinately supports something in spite of opposition or changing circumstances.

dielectric »*adjective* that does not conduct electricity; insulating.
» *noun* an insulator.
– SAY dy-i-**lek**-trik

dieresis American spelling of **DIAERESIS**.

dies

diesel »*noun* ❶ a type of engine in which heat produced by compressing air is used to ignite the fuel. ❷ a form of petroleum used as fuel in diesel engines.

> ✅ i before e: **diesel** (named after the German engineer Rudolf *Diesel*)

diet[1] (verb: **diets, dieting, dieted**) [kinds of food eaten; restrict food intake in order to lose weight]
dieter

> ✅ do not double the **t** in **dieting, dieted**, and **dieter**

diet[2] »*noun* ❶ a law-making assembly in certain countries. ❷ (a historical term) a regular meeting of the states of a confederation.

dietary »*adjective* having to do with diets or dieting.

> ✅ ary not ery: **dietary**

dieted

dieter

dietetics »*noun* the branch of knowledge concerned with the diet and its effects on health.
– SAY dy-uh-**tet**-iks
dietetic

dietician another way of spelling **DIETITIAN**.

dieting

dietitian »*noun* an expert on diet and nutrition.
– SAY dy-uh-**ti**-sh'n

> ✅ **dietitian** can also be spelled **dietician**: both spellings are correct

diets

differ (verb: **differs**, **differing**, **differed**)

> ⓘ do not confuse **differ** with **defer**, which means 'put off until later' or 'humbly give in to someone'

> ✓ two **f**'s, one **r**: **differ**

difference

> ✓ double **f**, and **ence** not **ance**: **difference**

different
differently

> ⓘ **different** can be followed by **from**, **to**, or **than**: in British English **different from** is generally thought of as the correct use, while **different than** is mainly American

differential »*adjective* having to do with or depending on a difference: *the differential achievements of boys and girls.*
» *noun* ❶ a difference in wages between industries or between categories of worker. ❷ (in mathematics) a minute difference between successive values of a variable. ❸ a gear that allows a vehicle's driven wheels to revolve at different speeds when going around corners.
– **SAY** dif-fuh-**ren**-sh'l
differentially

differentiate »*verb* (**differentiates**, **differentiating**, **differentiated**) ❶ recognize things as being different from each other. ❷ cause to appear different. ❸ (in mathematics) transform a function into its derivative.
– **SAY** dif-fuh-**ren**-shi-ayt
differentiation

> ✓ **tiate** not **tate**: **differentiate**

differently
difficult
difficulty (plural **difficulties**)

> ✓ plural: drop the **y** and add **ies**: **difficulties**

diffident »*adjective* not having much self-confidence.
diffidence
diffidently

> ✓ double **f**: **diffident**

diffract »*verb* cause a beam of light to be spread out as a result of passing through a narrow opening or across an edge.
diffraction

diffuse »*verb* (**diffuses**, **diffusing**, **diffused**) ❶ spread over a wide area: *technologies diffuse rapidly.* ❷ (with reference to a gas or liquid) become or cause to become intermingled with a substance by movement.
» *adjective* ❶ spread out over a large area; not concentrated. ❷ not clearly or briefly expressed.
diffusely
diffuser

> ⓘ do not confuse **diffuse** with **defuse**, which means 'remove the fuse from' or 'reduce the danger or tension in'

diffusion »*noun* ❶ the action of spreading over a wide area. ❷ the intermingling of substances by the natural movement of their particles.
diffusive

dig (verb: **digs**, **digging**, **dug**)

digest »*verb* (**digests**, **digesting**, **digested**) ❶ break down food in the stomach and intestines so that it can be absorbed by the body. ❷ reflect on and absorb information.
» *noun* a summary or collection of material or information.
digestible

digestion

digestive »*adjective* relating to the digestion of food.
» *noun* a semi-sweet biscuit made with wholemeal flour.

digests

digger

digging

digit »*noun* ❶ one of the numbers from 0 to 9. ❷ a finger or thumb.
– **SAY** di-jit

> ✓ only one **g**: **digit**

digital »*adjective* ❶ having to do with information represented as a series of binary digits, as in a computer. ❷ (of a clock or watch) showing the time by displaying numbers electronically. ❸ having to do with a finger or fingers.
digitally

digitalis »*noun* a drug prepared from foxglove leaves, used to stimulate the heart muscle.
– **SAY** di-ji-**tay**-liss

digitally

digitize »*verb* (**digitizes**, **digitizing**, **digitized**) convert pictures or sound into a digital form that can be processed by a computer.
digitization
digitizer

d

☑ many people prefer the alternative spellings **digitise**, **digitises**, etc., **digitisation**, and **digitiser**: both **s** and **z** spellings are correct

dignified

dignify »*verb* (**dignifies**, **dignifying**, **dignified**) make something impressive or worthy of respect.

dignitary »*noun* (plural **dignitaries**) a very important or high-ranking person.
– SAY dig-ni-tuh-ri

☑ plural: drop the **y** and add **ies**: **dignitaries**

dignity »*noun* (plural **dignities**) ❶ the state of being worthy of respect. ❷ a calm or serious manner. ❸ a sense of pride in yourself.

digraph »*noun* a combination of two letters representing one sound, as in *ph*.
– SAY dy-grahf

digress »*verb* (**digresses**, **digressing**, **digressed**) temporarily leave the main subject in speech or writing.
– SAY dy-**gress**
digression

☑ one **g**, two **s**'s: **digress**

digs

dihedral »*adjective* having or contained by two plane faces.
– SAY dy-hee-druhl

dike another way of spelling DYKE.

diktat »*noun* an order given by someone in power without popular consent.
– SAY dik-tat

☑ **dik** not **dic**: **diktat** (a German word)

dilapidated »*adjective* old and in poor condition.
– SAY di-**lap**-i-day-tid
dilapidation

☑ **dil** not **del**: **dilapidated**

dilate »*verb* (**dilates**, **dilating**, **dilated**) ❶ make or become wider, larger, or more open: *her eyes dilated with horror*. ❷ (**dilate on**) speak or write at length on.
– SAY dy-**layt** or di-**layt**
dilation

ⓘ do not confuse **dilate** with **dilute**, which means 'make weaker or thinner'

dilatory »*adjective* ❶ slow to act. ❷ intended to cause delay.
– SAY di-luh-tri
dilatoriness

☑ **ory** not **ary**: **dilatory**

dildo »*noun* (plural **dildos** or **dildoes**) an object shaped like an erect penis, used for sexual stimulation.

dilemma »*noun* a difficult situation in which a choice has to be made between alternatives.
– SAY di-**lem**-muh or dy-**lem**-muh

ⓘ **dilemma** should not be used to mean simply 'a difficult situation or problem'

dilettante »*noun* (plural **dilettanti** or **dilettantes**) a person who dabbles in a subject for enjoyment but without serious study.
– SAY di-li-**tan**-tay [singular], di-li-**tan**-ti [plural]
dilettantism

☑ single **l**, double **t**: **dilettante** is an Italian word
make the plural by changing the **e** ending to **i** (like the Italian) or by adding **s**: **dilettanti** or **dilettantes**

diligent »*adjective* showing care or effort in a task or duty.
diligence
diligently

dill »*noun* a herb used in cookery and medicine.

dilly-dally (verb: **dilly-dallies**, **dilly-dallying**, **dilly-dallied**)

dilute »*verb* (**dilutes**, **diluting**, **diluted**) ❶ make a liquid thinner or weaker by adding water or another liquid. ❷ weaken something by modifying it or adding other elements.
»*adjective* (of a liquid) diluted; weak.
dilution

ⓘ do not confuse **dilute** with **dilate**, which means 'become wider, larger, or more open'

dim (adjective: **dimmer**, **dimmest**; verb: **dims**, **dimming**, **dimmed**)
dimly
dimness

☑ double the **m** in **dimmed** and **dimming**

dime »*noun* (in American English) a ten-cent coin.

dimension »*noun* ❶ a measure of how long, broad, high, etc. something is. ❷ an aspect or feature: *we modern types lack a spiritual dimension*.
– SAY di-**men**-sh'n or dy-**men**-sh'n
dimensional

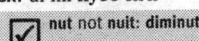 sion not tion: **dimension**

diminish (verb: **diminishes, diminishing, diminished**)

diminuendo »*adverb & adjective* (in music) with a decrease in loudness.
– **say** di-min-yoo-**en**-doh

diminution »*noun* a reduction.
– **say** di-mi-**nyoo**-sh'n

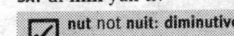 nut not nuit: **diminution**

diminutive »*adjective* extremely or unusually small.
» *noun* a shortened form of a name, used informally.
– **say** di-**min**-yuh-tiv

☑ nut not nuit: **diminutive**

dimly
dimmed
dimmer
dimmest
dimming
dimness
dimple (verb: **dimples, dimpling** [**dimpled**])
dims

dim sum »*noun* a Chinese dish of small dumplings containing various fillings.

dimwit
   dim-witted

din

dinar »*noun* the basic unit of money of Yugoslavia and certain Middle Eastern and North African countries.
– **say** dee-nar

☑ ar not er: **dinar**

dine (verb: **dines, dining, dined**)

☑ do not double the **n** in **dining** and **dined**

diner [person who dines; roadside restaurant]

dines

dinette »*noun* a small room or part of a room used for eating meals.
– **say** dy-**net**

☑ double **t** and **e** at the end: **dinette**

dinghy »*noun* (plural **dinghies**) ❶ a small open sailing boat. ❷ a small inflatable rubber boat.

☑ remember the **h** after the **g**: **dinghy** plural: drop the **y** and add **ies**: **dinghies**

dingier
dingiest
dinginess
dingle »*noun* a deep wooded valley.
dingo »*noun* (plural **dingoes** or **dingos**) a wild Australian dog.
– **say** ding-goh

☑ the plural of **dingo** can have **oes** or **os**: **dingoes** and **dingos**

dingy »*adjective* (**dingier, dingiest**) gloomy and drab.
– **say** din-ji

dining

dinky »*adjective* (**dinkier, dinkiest**) (in informal English) attractively small and neat.

dinner [main meal of the day]

☑ double **n**: **dinner**

dinosaur

dint »*noun* (**by dint of**) by means of.

diocese »*noun* (plural **dioceses**) a district for which a bishop is responsible.
– **say** dy-uh-siss [singular], dy-uh-seez or dy-uh-seez-iz [plural]
   diocesan

diode »*noun* an electrical device that has two terminals and allows current to flow in one direction only.
– **say** dy-ohd

Dionysiac »*adjective* Dionysian.
– **say** dy-uh-**niss**-i-ak

Dionysian »*adjective* ❶ relating to Dionysus, the Greek god of fertility and wine. ❷ wild and uninhibited.
– **say** dy-uh-**niss**-i-uhn

diorama »*noun* a model representing a scene with three-dimensional figures against a painted background.
– **say** dy-uh-**rah**-muh

dioxide

dioxin »*noun* a highly poisonous substance produced as a by-product in some manufacturing processes.
– **say** dy-**ok**-sin

dip (verb: **dips, dipping, dipped**)

☑ double the **p** in **dipped** and **dipping**

diphtheria »*noun* a serious infectious disease causing inflammation of the mucous membranes, especially in the throat.
– **say** dip-**theer**-i-uh

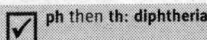 ph then th: **diphtheria**

d

d

diphthong »*noun* a sound formed by the combination of two vowels in a single syllable (as in *coin*).
– SAY dif-thong

> ☑ ph then th: diphthong

diplodocus »*noun* (plural **diplodocus**) a huge plant-eating dinosaur with a long slender neck and tail.
– SAY di-**plod**-uh-kuhss [singular and plural]

diploma »*noun* a certificate awarded to someone who has successfully completed a course of study.

diplomacy »*noun* ❶ the management of relations between countries. ❷ skill and tact in dealing with people.

diplomat »*noun* an official who represents a country abroad.

diplomatic »*adjective* ❶ having to do with diplomacy. ❷ tactful.
diplomatically

dipole »*noun* ❶ a pair of equal and oppositely charged or magnetized poles separated by a distance. ❷ an aerial consisting of a horizontal metal rod with a connecting wire at its centre.
– SAY **dy**-pohl
dipolar

dipped

dipper »*noun* ❶ a songbird able to dive into fast-flowing streams to feed. ❷ a ladle.

dipping

dippy »*adjective* (in informal English) foolish or eccentric.

dips

dipsomania »*noun* alcoholism.
– SAY dip-suh-**may**-ni-uh
dipsomaniac

dipstick »*noun* a rod for measuring the depth of a liquid.

diptych »*noun* a painting on two hinged wooden panels, forming an altarpiece.
– SAY **dip**-tik

> ☑ ych not ic: diptych

dire »*adjective* (direr, direst) ❶ extremely serious or urgent. ❷ (in informal English) of a very poor quality.
direly
direness

direct (verb: directs, directing, directed)
directly
directness

direct action »*noun* the use of public forms of protest rather than negotiation to achieve your aims.

direct current »*noun* an electric current flowing in one direction only, as opposed to an *alternating current*.

direct debit »*noun* an arrangement by which a bank transfers money from your account to pay a particular person or organization.

directed

directing

direction
directional
directionless

directive »*noun* an official instruction.

directly

directness

director
directorial
directorship

> ☑ -or not -er: director

directorate »*noun* ❶ the board of directors of a company. ❷ a section of a government department in charge of a particular activity.

director-general »*noun* (plural **directors-general**) the chief executive of a large organization.

> ☑ make the plural by adding an **s** after director only: directors-general

directorial

directorship

directory »*noun* (plural **directories**) a book that lists individuals or organizations with details such as addresses and telephone numbers.

> ☑ plural: drop the **y** and add **ies**: directories

directs

direct speech »*noun* the reporting of speech by repeating the actual words of a speaker (e.g. *'I'm going'*, she said), as opposed to *reported speech*.

direly

direness

direr

direst

dirge »*noun* ❶ a lament for the dead. ❷ a mournful song or piece of music.

dirigible »*noun* an airship.
– SAY di-**rij**-i-b'l

✓ rig not ridg: **dirigible**

dirk »*noun* a short dagger of a kind formerly carried by Scottish Highlanders.

dirndl »*noun* a full, wide skirt gathered into a tight waistband.
– **SAY** dern-d'l

✓ there is no **e** in **dirndl**

dirt

dirty (adjective: **dirtier**, **dirtiest**; verb: **dirties**, **dirtying**, **dirtied**)
dirtily
dirtiness

disability (plural **disabilities**)

✓ plural: drop the **y** and add **ies**: **disabilities**

disable »*verb* (**disables**, **disabling**, **disabled**) **❶** (of a disease, injury, or accident) limit someone in their movements, senses, or activities. **❷** put something out of action.
disabled
disablement

ℹ️ **disabled** should be used to refer to people with physical or mental disabilities, instead of other terms which can offend, such as **crippled**, **defective**, or **handicapped**

disabuse »*verb* (**disabuses**, **disabusing**, **disabused**) persuade someone that an idea or belief is mistaken: *he disabused me of my fanciful notions.*
– **SAY** diss-uh-**byooz**

disadvantage (verb: **disadvantages**, **disadvantaging**, **disadvantaged**)
disadvantageous

disaffected »*adjective* unhappy with the people in authority or with the organization you belong to, and no longer willing to support them.
disaffection

disagree (verb: **disagrees**, **disagreeing**, **disagreed**)
disagreement

✓ do not drop the second **e** when spelling **disagreeing**

disagreeable »*adjective* **❶** unpleasant. **❷** bad-tempered.
disagreeably

✓ double **e**: **disagreeable**

disagreed
disagreeing
disagreement

disagrees

disallow »*verb* (**disallows**, **disallowing**, **disallowed**) declare that something is not valid.

✓ one **s**, two **l**'s: **disallow**

d

disappear (verb: **disappears**, **disappearing**, **disappeared**)
disappearance

✓ one **s**, two **p**'s: **disappear**

disappoint (verb: **disappoints**, **disappointing**, **disappointed**)

✓ one **s**, two **p**'s: **disappoint**

disappointing
disappointingly
disappointment
disappoints

disapprobation »*noun* strong disapproval.
– **SAY** diss-ap-ruh-**bay**-sh'n

✓ two **p**'s, one **b**: **disapprobation**

disapprove (verb: **disapproves**, **disapproving**, **disapproved**)
disapproval

✓ double **p**: **disapprove**

disapproving
disapprovingly

disarm »*verb* (**disarms**, **disarming**, **disarmed**) **❶** take a weapon or weapons away from someone. **❷** give up or reduce armed forces or weapons. **❸** remove the fuse from a bomb. **❹** win over a hostile or suspicious person.

disarmament
disarmed
disarming
disarms

disarrange »*verb* (**disarranges**, **disarranging**, **disarranged**) make something untidy or disordered.

disarray »*noun* a state of disorder or confusion.

disassemble »*verb* (**disassembles**, **disassembling**, **disassembled**) take something to pieces.

disassociate »*verb* (**disassociates**, **disassociating**, **disassociated**) = **DISSOCIATE**.

disassociation
disaster
disastrous
disastrously

trous not **terous**: **disastrous**

disavow »*verb* (**disavows**, **disavowing**, **disavowed**) deny that you are responsible for or in favour of something.
disavowal

disband »*verb* (**disbands**, **disbanding**, **disbanded**) (with reference to an organized group) break up.

disbar »*verb* (**disbars**, **disbarring**, **disbarred**) expel a barrister from the Bar.
disbarment

 double the **r** in **disbarring** and **disbarred**

disbelief

disbelieve (verb: **disbelieves**, **disbelieving**, **disbelieved**)
disbeliever

 the usual rule is **i** before **e**, except after **c**: **disbelieve**

disburse »*verb* (**disburses**, **disbursing**, **disbursed**) pay out money from a fund.
– SAY diss-**berss**
disbursement

i do not confuse **disburse** with **disperse**, which means 'go in different directions'

disc

generally speaking, the British spelling is **disc** and the US spelling is **disk**. However, the spelling for senses relating to computers is nearly always **disk**.

discard (verb: **discards**, **discarding**, **discarded**)

discern »*verb* (**discerns**, **discerning**, **discerned**) ❶ recognize or be aware of: *I can discern no difference between the two policies.* ❷ see or hear with difficulty.
– SAY di-**sern**
discernible
discerning

 sc not **ss**: **discern**

discernment

discerns

discharge (verb: **discharges**, **discharging**, **discharged**)

disciple »*noun* ❶ a follower of Jesus during his life, especially one of the twelve Apostles. ❷ a follower of a teacher, leader, or philosophy.
– SAY di-**sy**-puhl

disc- not **diss-**: **disciple**

disciplinarian »*noun* a person who enforces firm discipline.

disciplinary »*adjective* having to do with discipline.
– SAY diss-i-**plin**-uh-ri

discipline (verb: **disciplines**, **disciplining**, **disciplined**)

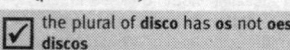 **disc-** not **diss-**, and only one **p**: **discipline**

disc jockey

disclaim »*verb* (**disclaims**, **disclaiming**, **disclaimed**) refuse to acknowledge that you are responsible for or interested in something.

disclaimer »*noun* a statement disclaiming responsibility for something.

disclaiming

disclaims

disclose »*verb* (**discloses**, **disclosing**, **disclosed**) ❶ make secret or new information known. ❷ allow to be seen.

disclosure »*noun* ❶ the disclosing of information. ❷ a secret that is disclosed.

disco (plural **discos**)

the plural of **disco** has **os** not **oes**: **discos**

discography »*noun* (plural **discographies**) a descriptive catalogue of musical recordings.
– SAY diss-**kog**-ruh-fi

discolour »*verb* (**discolours**, **discolouring**, **discoloured**) make or become stained or otherwise changed in colour.
discoloration

-colour not **-color** (except in **discoloration**): **discolour** (the other spellings without the **u** are American)

discomfit »*verb* (**discomfits**, **discomfiting**, **discomfited**) make someone uneasy or embarrassed.
– SAY diss-**kum**-fit
discomfiture

do not double the **t** in **discomfiting**, **discomfited**, and **discomfiture**

discomfort (verb: **discomforts**, **discomforting**, **discomforted**)

discompose »*verb* (**discomposes**, **discomposing**, **discomposed**) disturb or agitate.
discomposure

disconcert »*verb* (**disconcerts**, **disconcerting**, **disconcerted**) unsettle or upset.
– SAY diss-kuhn-**sert**

☑ cert not **sert: disconcert**

disconnect (verb: **disconnects, disconnecting, disconnected**)
disconnection

disconsolate »*adjective* very unhappy and unable to be consoled.
– SAY diss-**kon**-suh-luht
disconsolately

☑ sol not **sul: disconsolate**

discontent
discontented
discontentment

discontinue »*verb* (**discontinues, discontinuing, discontinued**) stop doing, providing, or making something.
discontinuation

☑ drop the e when spelling **discontinuing** and **discontinuation**

discontinuity (plural **discontinuities**)

discontinuous »*adjective* having intervals or gaps; not continuous.
discontinuously

discord »*noun* ❶ lack of agreement or harmony. ❷ lack of harmony between musical notes sounding together.

☑ -cord not **-chord: discord**

discordant »*adjective* ❶ not in harmony or agreement: *discordant opinions.* ❷ (of a sound or sounds) harsh and unpleasant.
discordance

discotheque »*noun* = DISCO.
– SAY diss-kuh-tek

☑ don't forget the h: **discotheque** is a French word, and it is sometimes written with a grave accent on the first e (**discothèque**)

discount (verb: **discounts, discounting, discounted**)

discourage (verb: **discourages, discouraging, discouraged**)
discouragement

discourse »*noun* ❶ written or spoken communication or debate. ❷ a formal discussion of a topic.
»*verb* (**discourses, discoursing, discoursed**) speak or write about something with authority.

discourteous »*adjective* rude and lacking consideration for others.
discourteously

discourtesy (plural **discourtesies**)

☑ plural: drop the y and add **ies: discourtesies**

discover (verb: **discovers, discovering, discovered**)
discoverer

discovery (plural **discoveries**)

☑ plural: drop the y and add **ies: discoveries**

d

discredit »*verb* (**discredits, discrediting, discredited**) ❶ make someone seem less trustworthy or honourable. ❷ make something seem false or unreliable.
»*noun* damage to someone's reputation.

☑ do not double the t in **discrediting** and **discredited**

discreditable »*adjective* bringing discredit; shameful.
discreditably

discredited

discrediting

discredits

discreet »*adjective* careful not to attract attention or give offence.
discreetly

ⓘ do not confuse **discreet** with **discrete**, which means 'separate, distinct'

discrepancy »*noun* (plural **discrepancies**) a failure to correspond between facts: *there's a discrepancy between your story and his.*
– SAY diss-**krep**-uhn-si

☑ plural: drop the y and add **ies: discrepancies**

discrete »*adjective* individually separate and distinct.
discretely

ⓘ do not confuse **discrete** with **discreet**, which means 'careful not to attract attention or give offence'

discretion »*noun* ❶ the quality of being discreet. ❷ the freedom to decide what should be done in a particular situation.

discretionary »*adjective* done or used according to the judgement of a particular person.

discriminate »*verb* (**discriminates, discriminating, discriminated**) ❶ recognize a difference. ❷ treat people unfairly on the grounds of race, sex, or age.
– SAY diss-**krim**-i-nayt
discriminating
discriminative

discrimination »*noun* ❶ the action of discriminating against people. ❷ recognition of the difference between one thing and another. ❸ good judgement or taste.

discriminative

discriminatory »*adjective* showing discrimination or prejudice.

discursive »*adjective* wandering from subject to subject.
– SAY diss-ker-siv
  discursively
  discursiveness

discus »*noun* (plural **discuses**) a heavy thick-centred disc thrown in athletic contests.

> ✓ do not double the **s** in the plural: **discuses**

discuss (verb: **discusses**, **discussing**, **discussed**) [talk about]

> ✓ double **s** at the end: **discuss**

discussion

disdain »*noun* the feeling that someone or something does not deserve consideration or respect.
» *verb* (**disdains**, **disdaining**, **disdained**) consider or treat with disdain.
  disdainful
  disdainfully

disease
  diseased

> ✓ -**ease** not -**ese**: **disease**

disembark »*verb* (**disembarks**, **disembarking**, **disembarked**) leave a ship, aircraft, or train.
  disembarkation

disembodied »*adjective* ❶ separated from or existing without the body: *a disembodied head floating in space.* ❷ (of a sound) lacking any obvious physical source.

disembowel »*verb* (**disembowels**, **disembowelling**, **disembowelled**) cut open and remove the internal organs of.

> ✓ double the **l** in **disembowelling** and **disembowelled** (the spellings with a single **l** are American)

disempower »*verb* (**disempowers**, **disempowering**, **disempowered**) make someone less powerful or confident.

disenchant »*verb* (**disenchants**, **disenchanting**, **disenchanted**) make someone disillusioned.
  disenchantment

disenfranchise »*verb* (**disenfranchises**, **disenfranchising**, **disenfranchised**)
❶ deprive someone of the right to vote.
❷ deprive someone of a right or privilege.

> ✓ **disenfranchise** cannot be spelled with an **ize** ending

disengage »*verb* (**disengages**, **disengaging**, **disengaged**) ❶ release or detach: *I disengaged his hand from mine.* ❷ remove troops from an area of conflict.
  disengagement

disentangle »*verb* (**disentangles**, **disentangling**, **disentangled**) free something from entanglement.

disestablish »*verb* (**disestablishes**, **disestablishing**, **disestablished**) take away the official status of a national Church.
  disestablishment

disfavour »*noun* ❶ disapproval or dislike. ❷ the state of being disliked.

> ✓ -**our** not -**or**: **disfavour** (the spelling with -**or** is American)

disfigure »*verb* (**disfigures**, **disfiguring**, **disfigured**) spoil the appearance of.
  disfigurement

disgorge »*verb* (**disgorges**, **disgorging**, **disgorged**) ❶ cause something to pour out: *a bus disgorged a group of youths.* ❷ bring up food from the stomach.

disgrace (verb: **disgraces**, **disgracing**, **disgraced**)

disgraceful
  disgracefully

> ✓ -**ful** not -**full**: **disgraceful**

disgraces

disgracing

disgruntled »*adjective* angry or dissatisfied.
  disgruntlement

disguise (verb: **disguises**, **disguising**, **disguised**)

disgust (verb: **disgusts**, **disgusting**, **disgusted**)
  disgusted
  disgustedly

disgusting
  disgustingly

disgusts

dish (verb: **dishes**, **dishing**, **dished**)

dishabille another way of spelling **DESHABILLE**.

disharmony »*noun* lack of harmony.

dishearten »*verb* (**disheartens**, **disheartening**, **disheartened**) cause someone to lose determination or confidence.

dished

dishes

dishevelled »*adjective* untidy in appearance.

– SAY di-**shev**-v'ld
dishevelment

> ✓ double l: **dishevelled** (the spelling with only one l is American)

dishier

dishiest

dishing

dishonest
dishonestly
dishonesty

dishonour »*noun* a state of shame or disgrace.
» *verb* (**dishonours, dishonouring, dishonoured**) ❶ bring dishonour to. ❷ fail to honour an agreement or cheque.

> ✓ **-our** not **-or**: **dishonour** (the spelling with **-or** is American)

dishonourable
dishonourably

dishonoured

dishonouring

dishonours

dishwasher

dishy »*adjective* (**dishier, dishiest**) (in informal English) good-looking; attractive.

disillusion »*noun* disappointment from discovering that your beliefs are mistaken or unrealistic.
» *verb* (**disillusions, disillusioning, disillusioned**) cause someone to experience disillusion.
disillusionment

> ✓ double l: **disillusion**

disincentive »*noun* a factor that discourages someone from doing a particular thing.

> ✓ **-cent-** not **-sent-**: **disincentive**

disinclination »*noun* a reluctance to do something.

disinclined »*adjective* reluctant; unwilling.

disinfect (verb: **disinfects, disinfecting, disinfected**)
disinfection

disinfectant

> ✓ **ant** not **ent**: **disinfectant**

disinfected

disinfecting

disinfection

disinfects

disinformation »*noun* information which is intended to mislead people.

disingenuous »*adjective* not sincere, especially in pretending ignorance about something.
– SAY diss-in-**jen**-yoo-uhss
disingenuously
disingenuousness

> ✓ **genuous**, not **genious** or **genous**: **disingenuous**

disinherit »*verb* (**disinherits, disinheriting, disinherited**) deprive someone of an inheritance.

> ✓ do not double the t in **disinheriting** and **disinherited**

disintegrate (verb: **disintegrates, disintegrating, disintegrated**)
disintegration

disinter »*verb* (**disinters, disinterring, disinterred**) dig up something buried.
– SAY diss-in-**ter**

> ✓ double the r in **disinterring** and **disinterred**

disinterest »*noun* ❶ impartiality. ❷ lack of interest.

disinterested »*adjective* not influenced by self-interest; impartial.
disinterestedly

> ℹ do not confuse **disinterested** with **uninterested**: **disinterested** means 'impartial' (as in *a banker is under an obligation to give disinterested advice*), while **uninterested** means 'not interested' (as in *a man uninterested in money*)

disinterred

disinterring

disinters

disjointed »*adjective* lacking a logical sequence or clear connection; disconnected.

disjunction »*noun* a difference or lack of agreement between things that you might expect to be the same.

disk see the note at **DISC**.

disk drive »*noun* a device which allows a computer to read from and write on to computer disks.

diskette »*noun* a floppy disk.

dislikable

> ✓ **dislikable** can also be spelled **dislikeable**: both spellings are correct

dislike (verb: **dislike, disliking, disliked**)

dislocate »*verb* (**dislocates, dislocating, dislocated**) ❶ put a bone out of its proper position in a joint. ❷ stop something from working properly; disrupt.
dislocation

dislodge »*verb* (dislodges, dislodging, dislodged) remove something from a fixed position.

disloyal
disloyally
disloyalty

dismal »*adjective* ❶ causing or showing gloom or depression. ❷ (in informal English) disgracefully bad.
dismally

dismantle »*verb* (dismantles, dismantling, dismantled) take something to pieces.
dismantlement

dismay (verb: dismays, dismaying, dismayed)

dismember »*verb* (dismembers, dismembering, dismembered) ❶ tear or cut the limbs from a person or animal. ❷ divide up a territory or organization.
dismemberment

dismiss (verb: dismisses, dismissing, dismissed)
dismissal

dismissive »*adjective* showing that you feel something is not worthy of serious consideration.
dismissively

dismount »*verb* (dismounts, dismounting, dismounted) get off or down from a horse or bicycle.

disobedient
disobedience
disobediently

disobey (verb: disobeys, disobeying, disobeyed)

disorder (verb: disorders, disordering, disordered)

disorderly »*adjective* ❶ untidy or disorganized. ❷ involving a breakdown of peaceful and law-abiding behaviour.

disorders

disorganized
disorganization

> ☑ disorganized and disorganization can also be spelled disorganised and disorganisation: both s and z spellings are correct

disorientate »*verb* (disorientates, disorientating, disorientated) confuse someone so that they lose their bearings.
disorientation

> ☑ -orient- not -orent-: disorientate

disown »*verb* (disowns, disowning, disowned) refuse to acknowledge any connection with someone.

disparage »*verb* (disparages, disparaging, disparaged) speak critically or negatively about someone or something.
– SAY diss-pa-rij
disparagement
disparaging
disparagingly

disparate »*adjective* ❶ very different from one another. ❷ containing elements that are very different from one another: *a culturally disparate country.*
– SAY diss-puh-ruht

disparity »*noun* (plural disparities) a great difference.

dispassionate »*adjective* not influenced by strong emotion; rational and impartial.
dispassionately

> ☑ double s in the middle: dispassionate

dispatch »*verb* (dispatches, dispatching, dispatched) ❶ send someone or something off to a destination or for a purpose. ❷ deal with a task or problem quickly and efficiently. ❸ kill.
» *noun* ❶ the action of dispatching. ❷ an official report on the latest situation in state or military affairs. ❸ a report sent in from abroad by a journalist.
❹ promptness and efficiency.
dispatcher

> ☑ dispatch can also be spelled despatch: both spellings are correct

dispel »*verb* (dispels, dispelling, dispelled) make a doubt, feeling, or belief disappear.

> ☑ double the l in dispelling and dispelled

dispensable »*adjective* able to be replaced or done without.

> ☑ -able not -ible: dispensable

dispensary »*noun* (plural dispensaries) a room where medicines are prepared and provided.

dispensation »*noun* ❶ special permission not to obey a rule or usual requirement. ❷ a religious or political system of a particular time: *the capitalist dispensation.* ❸ the action of dispensing.

dispense »*verb* (dispenses, dispensing, dispensed) ❶ distribute or supply something to a number of people. ❷ (of a chemist) prepare and supply medicine according to a prescription. ❸ (dispense with) get rid of or manage without.
dispenser

disperse »*verb* (disperses, dispersing, dispersed) ❶ go or move apart in different

directions or over a wide area: *the crowd dispersed.* ❷ (of gas, smoke, etc.) thin out and eventually disappear.
dispersal

ℹ️ do not confuse **disperse** with **disburse**, which means 'pay out money from a fund'

dispersion »*noun* ❶ the action of dispersing. ❷ the action of splitting light into parts with different wavelengths.

dispirited »*adjective* disheartened or depressed.
dispiriting

displace »*verb* (**displaces, displacing, displaced**) ❶ move something from its proper or usual position. ❷ take over the position or role of: *machines are coming along to displace the typists.*

displacement »*noun* ❶ the action of displacing. ❷ the amount by which something is displaced. ❸ the volume or weight of water displaced by a floating ship, used as a measure of the ship's size.

displaces

displacing

display (verb: **displays, displaying, displayed**)

displease (verb: **displeases, displeasing, displeased**)

displeasure

disport »*verb* (**disports, disporting, disported**) (**disport yourself**) enjoy yourself in an unrestrained way.

disposable »*adjective* ❶ (of an article) intended to be used once and then thrown away. ❷ (of income or financial assets) available to be used as required.

disposal »*noun* the action of disposing.

dispose »*verb* (**disposes, disposing, disposed**) ❶ (**dispose of**) get rid of. ❷ arrange in a particular position. ❸ (**be disposed**) be inclined to do or think something. ❹ (**disposed**) having a specified attitude: *they were favourably disposed towards him.*
disposer

disposition »*noun* ❶ a person's natural qualities of character. ❷ an inclination or tendency. ❸ the way in which something is arranged.

dispossess »*verb* (**dispossesses, dispossessing, dispossessed**) deprive someone of a possession.
dispossession

✓ double **s** in the middle and at the end: **dispossess**

disproportionate »*adjective* too large or too small in comparison with something else.
disproportionately

disprove »*verb* (**disproves, disproving, disproved**) prove something to be false.

disputable »*adjective* open to question.

disputation »*noun* debate or argument.

disputatious »*adjective* fond of arguing.

✓ **tious** not **cious**: **disputatious**

dispute »*verb* (**disputes, disputing, disputed**) ❶ argue about. ❷ question whether something is true or valid. ❸ compete for.
» *noun* an argument or disagreement.

disqualify (verb: **disqualifies, disqualifying, disqualified**)
disqualification

disquiet »*noun* a feeling of anxiety.
» *verb* (**disquiets, disquieting, disquieted**) make someone anxious.

✓ do not double the **t** in **disquieting** and **disquieted**

disquisition »*noun* a long or complex discussion of a topic.

disregard »*verb* (**disregards, disregarding, disregarded**) pay no attention to.
» *noun* the action of disregarding something: *his disregard for truth.*

disrepair »*noun* poor condition due to being neglected.

disreputable »*adjective* not respectable in appearance or character.

disrepute »*noun* the state of having a bad reputation.

disrespect
disrespectful
disrespectfully

disrobe »*verb* (**disrobes, disrobing, disrobed**) undress.

disrupt (verb: **disrupts, disrupting, disrupted**)
disruption

disruptive

disrupts

diss »*verb* (**disses, dissing, dissed**) (in informal English) speak disrespectfully to or of someone.

dissatisfied »*adjective* not content or happy.
dissatisfaction

ℹ️ do not confuse **dissatisfied** and **unsatisfied**: if you are **dissatisfied** you are unhappy because what you have is not

d

what you want; whereas, if you are **unsatisfied** you do not have enough of something you want or need

dissect »*verb* (dissects, dissecting, dissected) ❶ methodically cut up a body, part, or plant in order to study its internal parts. ❷ analyse something in great detail.
– SAY di-**sekt** or dy-**sekt**
dissection

> ✓ unlike **bisect**, with which it is sometimes confused, **dissect** has a double **s**

dissed

dissemble »*verb* (dissembles, dissembling, dissembled) hide or disguise your motives or feelings.
dissembler

disseminate »*verb* (disseminates, disseminating, disseminated) spread information widely.
dissemination

> ✓ two **s**'s, one **m**, one **n**: **disseminate**

dissension »*noun* disagreement that causes trouble within a group.

> ✓ **sion** not **tion**: **dissension**

dissent »*verb* (dissents, dissenting, dissented) ❶ express disagreement with a widely held view. ❷ disagree with the doctrine of an established Church.
» *noun* disagreement with a widely held view.
dissenter

dissentient »*adjective* opposing a widely held opinion.
– SAY di-**sen**-shi-uhnt or di-**sen**-shuhnt

dissenting

dissents

dissertation »*noun* a long essay, especially one written for a university degree or diploma.

disservice »*noun* a harmful action.

disses

dissident »*noun* a person who opposes official policy.
» *adjective* in opposition to official policy.
dissidence

dissimilar »*adjective* not similar; different.
dissimilarity

dissimulate »*verb* (dissimulates, dissimulating, dissimulated) hide or disguise your thoughts or feelings.
dissimulation

> ✓ two **s**'s, one **m**, one **l**: **dissimulate**

dissing

dissipate »*verb* (dissipates, dissipating, dissipated) ❶ dispel or disperse: *the steam dissipated in the air.* ❷ waste money, energy, or resources. ❸ (**dissipated**) indulging too much in physical pleasures.

> ✓ two **s**'s, one **p**: **dissipate**

dissipation »*noun* ❶ luxurious and self-indulgent living. ❷ the action of dissipating.

dissociate »*verb* (dissociates, dissociating, dissociated) ❶ disconnect or separate. ❷ (**dissociate yourself from**) declare that you are not connected with someone or something.
dissociation

dissolute »*adjective* indulging too much in physical pleasures.
– SAY diss-uh-**loot**

dissolution »*noun* ❶ the formal closing down or ending of an assembly, official body, or agreement. ❷ the action of dissolving or decomposing. ❸ dissolute living.

> ✓ two **s**'s, one **l**: **dissolution**

dissolve »*verb* (dissolves, dissolving, dissolved) ❶ (with reference to a solid) disperse in a liquid so as to form a solution. ❷ close down or end an assembly or agreement. ❸ (**dissolve into** or **in**) give way to strong emotion.

dissonant »*adjective* lacking harmony; discordant.
dissonance

> ✓ **ant** not **ent**: **dissonant**

dissuade »*verb* (dissuades, dissuading, dissuaded) persuade or advise someone not to do something.
– SAY di-**swayd**
dissuasion

distaff »*noun* a spindle on to which wool or flax is wound for spinning.
– SAY **diss**-tahf

distaff side »*noun* (old-fashioned) the female side of a family.

distance (verb: distances, distancing, distanced)

distant
distantly

distaste
distasteful
distastefully

distemper »*noun* ❶ a kind of paint used on walls. ❷ a disease affecting dogs, causing fever and coughing.

distend »*verb* (**distends, distending, distended**) swell because of internal pressure.
distensible
distension

distil »*verb* (**distils, distilling, distilled**) ❶ purify a liquid by heating it so that it vaporizes, then condensing the vapour and collecting the resulting liquid. ❷ make spirits in this way. ❸ extract the most important aspects of: *my notes were distilled into a book.*
distillation

☑ double the l in **distilling** and **distilled**, but not in **distils** (the spelling **distill** is American)

distiller »*noun* a person or company that manufactures spirits.

distillery »*noun* (plural **distilleries**) a place where spirits are manufactured.

distilling

distils

distinct »*adjective* ❶ recognizably different: *there are two distinct types of the disease.* ❷ able to be perceived clearly by the senses.
distinctly
distinctness

distinction »*noun* ❶ a marked difference or contrast. ❷ the action of distinguishing. ❸ outstanding excellence. ❹ a special honour or recognition.

distinctive »*adjective* characteristic of a person or thing and distinguishing it from others: *the car's distinctive design.*
distinctively
distinctiveness

distinctly

distinctness

distinguish »*verb* (**distinguishes, distinguishing, distinguished**) ❶ recognize the difference between two people or things. ❷ manage to see or hear. ❸ be an identifying characteristic of: *what distinguishes sport from games?* ❹ (**distinguish yourself**) make yourself worthy of respect.
distinguishable

distinguished »*adjective* ❶ dignified in appearance. ❷ worthy of great respect.

distinguishes

distinguishing

distort »*verb* (**distorts, distorting, distorted**) ❶ pull or twist something out of shape.

❷ give a misleading account of.
distorted
distortion

distract (verb: **distracts, distracting, distracted**)

distraction

distracts

distraught »*adjective* very worried and upset.

☑ remember the **gh**: **distraught**

distress (verb: **distresses, distressing, distressed**)
distressing
distressingly

distribute »*verb* (**distributes, distributing, distributed**) ❶ hand or share out to a number of people. ❷ (**be distributed**) be spread over an area. ❸ supply goods to retailers.
distributable

distribution »*noun* ❶ the action of distributing. ❷ the way in which something is distributed.

distributive »*adjective* relating to distribution.

distributor »*noun* ❶ a company that supplies goods to retailers. ❷ a device in a petrol engine for passing electric current to each spark plug in turn.

☑ -or not -er: **distributor**

district »*noun* an area of a town or region, regarded as a unit for administrative purposes or because of a particular feature.

district attorney »*noun* (in the US) a public official who acts as prosecutor for the state or the federal government in court in a particular district.

district nurse »*noun* (in the UK) a nurse who treats patients in their homes, operating within a particular district.

distrust (verb: **distrusts, distrusting, distrusted**)
distrustful

disturb (verb: **disturbs, disturbing, disturbed**)

disturbance

☑ ance not ence: **disturbance**

disturbed

disturbing
disturbingly

disturbs

disunited »*adjective* not united.
disunity

disuse »*noun* the state of not being used; neglect.
disused

ditch (verb: **ditches, ditching, ditched**)

dither »*verb* (**dithers, dithering, dithered**) be indecisive.
» *noun* (in informal English) a state of agitation or indecision.
dithery

ditties

ditto »*noun* ❶ the same thing again (used in lists). ❷ a symbol consisting of two apostrophes (,,) placed under the item to be repeated.

ditty »*noun* (plural **ditties**) a short simple song.

diuretic »*adjective* (of a drug) making you pass more urine.
– **say** dy-uh-**ret**-ik

diurnal »*adjective* ❶ of or during the daytime. ❷ daily.
– **say** dy-**er**-n'l

diva »*noun* a celebrated female opera singer.
– **say** dee-vuh

Divali another way of spelling **DIWALI**.

divan »*noun* ❶ a bed consisting of a base and mattress but no footboard or headboard. ❷ a long, low sofa without a back or arms.
– **say** di-van

dive (verb: **dives, diving, dived**)

> ℹ️ in British English, the past tense of **dive** is **dived**, but in American English it is **dove**

dive-bomb (verb: **dive-bombs, dive-bombing, dive-bombed**)

dived

diver

diverge »*verb* (**diverges, diverging, diverged**) ❶ (of a route or line) separate from another route and go in a different direction. ❷ (**diverge from**) depart from: *I diverged from my prepared remarks.*
divergence

divergent »*adjective* different.

diverges

diverging

divers »*adjective* (an old word) various; several: *in divers places.*

diverse »*adjective* widely varied.

diversify »*verb* (**diversifies, diversifying, diversified**) ❶ make or become more varied. ❷ (of a company) expand its range of products or field of operation.
diversification

diversion »*noun* ❶ the action of diverting something from its course. ❷ an alternative route for use when the usual road is closed. ❸ something intended to distract attention. ❹ a recreation or pastime.
diversionary

diversity »*noun* (plural **diversities**) ❶ the state of being varied. ❷ a range of different things.

> ✅ plural: drop the **y** and add **ies**: **diversities**

divert »*verb* (**diverts, diverting, diverted**) ❶ change the direction or course of something. ❷ distract someone or their attention. ❸ amuse or entertain.

divertissement »*noun* a minor entertainment.
– **say** dee-vair-**teess**-mon

> ✅ a French word, **divertissement** has a double **s** and an **e** before the **m**

diverts

dives

divest »*verb* (**divests, divesting, divested**) (**divest of**) ❶ deprive someone of: *they are unlikely to be divested of power.* ❷ free or rid yourself of something.
– **say** dy-**vest** or di-**vest**
divestment

divide (verb: **divides, dividing, divided**)

dividend »*noun* ❶ a sum of money that is divided among a number of people, such as the part of a company's profits paid to its shareholders. ❷ (**dividends**) benefits. ❸ (in mathematics) a number to be divided by another number.

divider

divides

dividing

divination »*noun* the use of supernatural means to find out about the future or the unknown.

divine[1] »*adjective* ❶ having to do with God or a god. ❷ (in informal English) excellent.
divinely

divine[2] »*verb* (**divines, divining, divined**) ❶ discover something by guesswork or intuition. ❷ have supernatural insight into the future.
diviner

diving

divinity »*noun* (plural **divinities**) ❶ the state of being divine. ❷ a god or goddess. ❸ the study of religion; theology.

divisible »*adjective* ❶ capable of being divided. ❷ (of a number) containing another number a number of times without a remainder.

> ✓ -**ible** not -**able**: **divisible**

division
divisional

divisive »*adjective* causing disagreement or hostility between people.
– SAY di-**vy**-siv
divisively
divisiveness

divisor »*noun* a number by which another number is to be divided.

> ✓ -**or** not -**er**: **divisor**

divorce (verb: **divorces**, **divorcing**, **divorced**)

divorcee »*noun* a divorced person.
– SAY di-vor-**see**

divorces

divorcing

divot »*noun* a piece of turf cut out of the ground.
– SAY di-**vuht**

> ✓ one **v**, one **t**: **divot**

divulge »*verb* (**divulges**, **divulging**, **divulged**) reveal information.
– SAY dy-**vulj** or di-**vulj**

divvy »*verb* (**divvies**, **divvying**, **divvied**) (in informal English) share out.

Diwali »*noun* a Hindu festival with lights, held in October and November to celebrate the end of the monsoon.
– SAY di-**wah**-li

> ✓ **Diwali** can also be spelled **Divali**: both spellings are correct

Dixie »*noun* the Southern states of the US.
Dixieland

DIY »*abbreviation* do it yourself.

dizzy (adjective: **dizzier**, **dizziest**; verb: **dizzies**, **dizzying**, **dizzied**)
dizzily
dizziness

DJ »*abbreviation* disc jockey.

djellaba »*noun* a loose woollen hooded cloak traditionally worn by Arabs.
– SAY jel-**luh**-buh

> ✓ **djellaba** can also be spelled with an h on the end: **djellabah**

Djiboutian [of Djibouti in NE Africa]

– SAY ji-**boo**-ti-uhn

DNA »*noun* deoxyribonucleic acid, a substance carrying genetic information that is found in the cells of nearly all animals and plants.

DNA fingerprinting »*noun* = GENETIC FINGERPRINTING.

do (verb: **does**, **doing**, **did**; past participle **done**)
doable
doer

Dobermann »*noun* a large breed of dog with powerful jaws.
– SAY doh-**ber**-muhn

> ✓ double n: **Dobermann**. The full name of the breed is **Dobermann pinscher** (*pinscher* being the German for 'terrier').

docile »*adjective* ready to accept control or instruction; submissive.
docilely
docility

dock (verb: **docks**, **docking**, **docked**)

docker »*noun* a person employed in a port to load and unload ships.

docket »*noun* a document accompanying a batch of goods that lists its contents, certifies payment of duty, or entitles the holder to delivery.

docking

dockland

docks

dockyard

doctor (verb: **doctors**, **doctoring**, **doctored**)

doctoral »*adjective* relating to a doctorate.

doctorate »*noun* the highest degree awarded by a university.

doctored

doctoring

doctors

doctrinaire »*adjective* very strict in applying beliefs or principles.
– SAY dok-tri-**nair**

> ✓ **naire**, not **nair** or **nare**: **doctrinaire** is a French word

doctrine »*noun* a set of beliefs or principles held and taught by a religious, political, or other group.
doctrinal SAY dok-**try**-n'l

docudrama »*noun* a television film based on a dramatized version of real events.

document (verb: **documents**, **documenting**, **documented**)

documentary »*adjective* ❶ consisting of documents and other material. ❷ using

film, photographs, and sound recordings of real events to provide a factual report.
» *noun* (plural **documentaries**) a documentary film or television or radio programme.

> ☑ plural: drop the **y** and add **ies**: **documentaries**

documentation »*noun* documents providing official information, evidence, or instructions.

documented

documenting

documents

docusoap »*noun* a documentary following people in a particular occupation or location over a period of time.

dodder »*verb* (**dodders**, **doddering**, **doddered**) be slow and unsteady.
doddery

doddle

dodecagon »*noun* a shape with twelve straight sides and angles.
– SAY doh-**dek**-uh-guhn

dodecahedron »*noun* (plural **dodecahedra** or **dodecahedrons**) a three-dimensional shape with twelve faces.
– SAY doh-de-kuh-**hee**-druhn

> ☑ the plural can be either **dodecahedra** (like the original Greek) or **dodecahedrons**

dodge (verb: **dodges**, **dodging**, **dodged**)

dodgem »*noun* a small electric car with rubber bumpers, driven at a funfair with the aim of bumping other such cars.

dodger

dodges

dodgier

dodgiest

dodging

dodgy (adjective: **dodgier**, **dodgiest**)

dodo »*noun* (plural **dodos** or **dodoes**) a large extinct flightless bird formerly found on Mauritius.
– SAY doh-doh

> ☑ the plural of **dodo** can have **os** or **oes**: **dodos** or **dodoes**

doe »*noun* ❶ a female deer or reindeer. ❷ the female of some other animals, such as a rabbit or hare.

doer

does present of **DO** [as in *he does*].

doesn't [does not]

> ☑ be careful to put the apostrophe where a letter has been left out, that is between the **n** and **t** of **not**: **doesn't**

doff »*verb* (**doffs**, **doffing**, **doffed**) remove your hat when greeting someone.

dog (verb: **dogs**, **dogging**, **dogged**)

doge »*noun* (a historical term) the chief magistrate of Venice or Genoa.
– SAY dohj

dog-eared »*adjective* having worn or battered corners.

dogfight »*noun* a close combat between military aircraft.

dogfish »*noun* a small shark with a long tail, living close to the seabed.

dogged »*adjective* very persistent.
– SAY dog-gid
doggedly
doggedness

doggerel »*noun* badly written verse.
– SAY dog-guh-ruhl

> ☑ two **g**'s, one **r**, one **l**: **doggerel**

doggies

dogging

doggy (plural **doggies**)

doggy-paddle »*noun* a simple swimming stroke like that of a dog.

doghouse

dogleg »*noun* a sharp bend.

dogma »*noun* a principle or set of principles that is intended to be accepted without question.

dogmatic »*adjective* ❶ firmly putting forward your opinions and expecting that other people will accept them. ❷ relating to dogma.
dogmatically
dogmatism

do-gooder »*noun* a well-meaning but unrealistic or interfering person.

dogs

dogsbody »*noun* (plural **dogsbodies**) (in informal English) a person who is given boring, menial tasks.

dog-tired »*adjective* extremely tired.

dogtooth »*noun* a small check pattern with notched corners.

dogwood »*noun* a flowering shrub or small tree with red stems, colourful berries, and hard wood.

doily »*noun* (plural **doilies**) a small ornamental mat made of lace or paper.

> doi not doy; ly not ley: **doily**

doing present of **DO** [as in *he is doing*].

doldrums »*plural noun* (**the doldrums**) ❶ a state of being inactive or feeling depressed. ❷ a region of the Atlantic Ocean where there is little or no wind.

dole »*verb* (**doles, doling, doled**) (**dole out**) distribute.
» *noun* (in British English) benefit paid by the state to unemployed people: *I ended up on the dole*.

doleful »*adjective* sad or depressing.
dolefully

✓ **-ful** not **-full: doleful**

doles

doling

doll (verb: **dolls, dolling, dolled**)

dollar

dollar sign »*noun* the sign $.

dolled

dollies

dolling

dollop

dolls

doll's house

dolly (plural **dollies**)

dolorous »*adjective* very sad or distressed.
– **SAY** dol-uh-ruhss

dolphin

dolphinarium »*noun* (plural **dolphinariums** or **dolphinaria**) an aquarium in which dolphins are kept.

✓ the plural can be either **dolphinaria** (like the original Latin) or **dolphinariums**

dolt »*noun* a stupid person.

domain »*noun* ❶ an area controlled by a ruler or government. ❷ an area of activity or knowledge.
– **SAY** duh-**mayn**

dome
domed

domestic »*adjective* ❶ relating to a home or family. ❷ for use in the home. ❸ (of an animal) tame and kept by humans. ❹ existing or occurring within a country; not foreign: *China's domestic affairs*.
domestically

domesticate »*verb* (**domesticates, domesticating, domesticated**) tame an animal and keep it as a pet or on a farm.
domestication

domesticity »*noun* home or family life.

domicile (in legal or official use) »*noun* ❶ the country in which a person lives permanently. ❷ a person's home.
» *verb* (**be domiciled**) be living in a particular country or place.
– **SAY** dom-i-syl

domiciliary »*adjective* in someone's home: *a domiciliary visit*.
– **SAY** dom-i-**sil**-i-uh-ri

dominant »*adjective* ❶ most important, powerful, or influential. ❷ (of a high place or object) overlooking others. ❸ (of a gene) appearing in offspring even if a contrary gene is also inherited.
dominance
dominantly

✓ **ant** not **ent: dominant**

dominate (verb: **dominates, dominating, dominated**)
domination

domineering »*adjective* arrogantly trying to control other people.

dominion »*noun* ❶ supreme power or control. ❷ the territory of a sovereign or government.

domino (plural **dominoes**)

✓ the plural of **domino** has **oes** not **os: dominoes**

don[1] »*noun* a university teacher, especially at Oxford or Cambridge.

don[2] »*verb* (**dons, donning, donned**) put on an item of clothing.

donate (verb: **donates, donating, donated**)
donation

done past participle of **DO**.

doner kebab »*noun* a Turkish dish of spiced lamb cooked on a spit and served in slices.

✓ there is only a single **n** in **doner**, which is from the Turkish word *döner* meaning 'rotating'

donkey (plural **donkeys**)

donned

donning

donnish »*adjective* like a college don, particularly in having a fussy manner.

donor »*noun* a person who donates something.

dons

don't [do not]

✓ be careful to put the apostrophe where a letter has been left out, that is between the **n** and **t** of **not: don't**

donut American spelling of **DOUGHNUT**.

doodle »*verb* (doodles, doodling, doodled) scribble absent-mindedly.
» *noun* a drawing made absent-mindedly.

doom »*noun* death, destruction, or another terrible fate.
» *verb* (**be doomed**) be fated to fail or be destroyed.

doomsday »*noun* the last day of the world's existence.

door

doorbell

do-or-die

doorman »*noun* (plural **doormen**) a man who is on duty at the entrance to a large building.

doormat

doormen

doorstep

doorstop

doorway

dope (verb: **dopes**, **doping**, **doped**)

dopey

> ✓ the ending is **ey**, not simply **y**: **dopey**

doping

doppelganger »*noun* a ghost or double of a living person.
– SAY dop-puhl-gang-er or dop-puhl-geng-er

> ✓ **doppelganger** is a German word, and is sometimes written with an umlaut: **doppelgänger**. The correct German pronunciation is **dop**-puhl-geng-er.

Doppler effect »*noun* (in physics) the apparent change in the frequency of sound or light waves as the source and an observer move towards or away from each other.

> ✓ double **p**: the effect is named after the Austrian physicist J. C. *Doppler*

Doric »*adjective* relating to a style of classical architecture distinguished by plain columns with a square slab on top.
– SAY do-rik

dork

dormant »*adjective* ❶ (of an animal) in a deep sleep. ❷ (of a plant or bud) alive but not growing. ❸ (of a volcano) temporarily inactive.
dormancy

> ✓ **mant** not **ment**: **dormant**

dormer window »*noun* a window set vertically into a sloping roof.

dormice

dormitory (plural **dormitories**)

dormouse »*noun* (plural **dormice**) a small mouse-like rodent with a bushy tail.

dorsal »*adjective* having to do with the upper side or back (the opposite of *ventral*).

dosage »*noun* the size of a dose of medicine or radiation.

dos and don'ts

dose »*noun* ❶ a quantity of a medicine or drug taken at one time. ❷ an amount of radiation received or absorbed at one time.
» *verb* (**doses**, **dosing**, **dosed**) give a dose of medicine to someone.

dosh

dosing

doss »*verb* (**dosses**, **dossing**, **dossed**) (in informal English) ❶ sleep in rough or makeshift conditions. ❷ spend time idly.

dossier »*noun* a collection of documents about a person or subject.
– SAY doss-i-er or doss-i-ay

dossing

dot (verb: **dots**, **dotting**, **dotted**)

dotage »*noun* the period of life in which a person is old and weak.
– SAY doh-tij

dot-com »*noun* a company that conducts its business on the Internet.

> ℹ often written **dot.com** with a full stop, *.com* being the typical ending of a commercial Internet address

dote »*verb* (**dotes**, **doting**, **doted**) (**dote on**) be excessively fond of someone.

dots

dotted

dottier

dottiest

dottiness

dotting

dotty (adjective: **dottier**, **dottiest**)
dottiness

double (verb: **doubles**, **doubling**, **doubled**)
doubly

double agent »*noun* an agent who pretends to act as a spy for one country while in fact acting for its enemy.

double-barrelled

double bass »*noun* the largest and lowest-pitched instrument of the violin family.

double-breasted »*adjective* (of a jacket or coat) having a large overlap at the front and two rows of buttons.

double-check (verb: **double-checks, double-checking, double-checked**)

double-cross (verb: **double-crosses, double-crossing, double-crossed**)

doubled

double-dealing »*noun* deceitful behaviour.

double-decker »*noun* a bus with two levels.

double-edged

double entendre »*noun* a word or phrase with two meanings, one of which is usually rude.
– **say** doo-b'l on-**ton**-druh

> double entendre is an old French phrase meaning 'double understanding', and the plural **double entendres** is pronounced the same as the singular

double glazing
double-glazed

double-jointed »*adjective* (of a person) having unusually flexible joints.

double negative »*noun* a negative statement with two negative elements (e.g. *I don't know nothing* or *I never saw nobody*).

> double negatives are usually not good English. They are incorrect because the two negative elements cancel each other out to make a positive statement, so that *I don't know nothing* strictly means *I know something*. If you don't mean this you should say *I don't know anything*.

doubles

doublespeak »*noun* language that is deliberately unclear or has more than one meaning.

double standard »*noun* a rule or principle applied unfairly in different ways to different people.

doublet »*noun* ❶ a man's short close-fitting padded jacket, worn from the 14th to the 17th century. ❷ a pair of similar things.

double take »*noun* a delayed reaction to something unexpected.

doublethink »*noun* the acceptance of conflicting opinions or beliefs at the same time.

doubling

doubloon »*noun* (a historical term) a Spanish gold coin.

doubly

doubt (verb: **doubts, doubting, doubted**)
doubter

doubtful
doubtfully

> ✓ -ful not -full: doubtful

doubting

doubting Thomas »*noun* (plural **doubting Thomases**) a person who refuses to believe something without proof.

doubtless »*adverb* very probably.

doubts

douche »*noun* a jet of water applied to part of the body to clean it or as therapy.
– **say** doosh

dough »*noun* ❶ a thick mixture of flour and liquid, for baking into bread or pastry. ❷ (in informal English) money.

doughiness

doughnut »*noun* a small fried cake or ring of sweetened dough.

> ✓ spell out **dough** in full: **doughnut** (donut is an American spelling)

doughty »*adjective* (**doughtier, doughtiest**) (an old word) brave and determined.
– **say** dow-ti

doughy »*adjective* like dough, or containing too much dough.
– **say** doh-i
doughiness

dour »*adjective* (**dourer, dourest**) very severe, stern, or gloomy.
– **say** *rhymes with* tower
dourly
dourness

> do not confuse **dour** with **dower**, which refers to a widow's share of her late husband's estate

douse »*verb* (**douses, dousing, doused**) ❶ drench with liquid. ❷ extinguish a fire or light.
– **say** dowss

> ✓ can also be spelled **dowse**: both **douse** and **dowse** are correct

dove¹ »*noun* ❶ a bird with a cooing voice, very similar to a pigeon. ❷ a person who favours a policy of peace and negotiation (the opposite of *hawk*).
dovish

dove² American past tense of **DIVE**.
– **say** dohv

dovecote »*noun* a shelter with nest holes for domesticated pigeons.
– SAY duv-kot

 remember the final **e: dovecote**

dovetail »*noun* a wedge-shaped joint made by interlocking two pieces of wood.
» *verb* (**dovetails, dovetailing, dovetailed**) ❶ join by means of a dovetail. ❷ fit together easily or conveniently.

dovish

dowager »*noun* ❶ a widow who has a title or property from her late husband. ❷ (in informal English) a dignified elderly woman.
– SAY dow-uh-jer

dowdy »*adjective* (**dowdier, dowdiest**) (especially of a woman) unfashionable and dull in appearance.
dowdiness

dowel »*noun* a rod or peg used for holding together components.
dowelling

 double the **l** in **dowelling**

dower »*noun* a widow's share for life of her late husband's estate.
– SAY *rhymes with* tower

ⓘ do not confuse **dower** with **dour** meaning 'very stern or gloomy'

down (verb: **downs, downing, downed**)

down-and-out »*noun* a homeless and very poor person.

downbeat »*adjective* ❶ gloomy. ❷ relaxed and low-key.

downcast »*adjective* ❶ (of eyes) looking downwards. ❷ discouraged; dejected.

downed

downer

downfall

downgrade (verb: **downgrades, downgrading, downgraded**)

downhearted

downhill

downier

downiest

downing

download »*verb* (**downloads, downloading, downloaded**) copy data from one computer system to another or to a disk.

downmarket »*adjective & adverb* at or towards the cheap and low quality end of the market.

down payment »*noun* an initial payment made when buying on credit.

downplay »*verb* (**downplays, downplaying, downplayed**) make something appear less important than it really is.

downpour »*noun* a heavy fall of rain.

downright

downriver

downs

downsize »*verb* (**downsizes, downsizing, downsized**) reduce the size of a workforce by making people redundant.

Down's syndrome »*noun* a medical disorder arising from a genetic defect, causing mental and physical abnormalities.

ⓘ **Down's syndrome** is the accepted modern term for this condition. Avoid older words such as **mongol** and **mongolism**, which will cause offence.

downstairs

downstream

down-to-earth

downtown

downtrodden »*adjective* treated badly by those in power.

downturn

downward
downwardly

downwards

downwind

downy »*adjective* (**downier, downiest**) covered with fine soft hair or feathers.

dowry »*noun* (plural **dowries**) property or money brought by a bride to her husband on their marriage.
– SAY dow-ri

dowse[1] »*verb* (**dowses, dowsing, dowsed**) search for underground water or minerals with a pointer which is supposedly moved by unseen influences.
– SAY dowz
dowser

dowse[2] another way of spelling **douse**.

doyen »*noun* the most respected or prominent person in a particular field: *the doyen of British physicists*.
– SAY doy-yen

doyenne »*noun* a female doyen.
– SAY doy-yen

doze »*verb* (**dozes, dozing, dozed**) sleep lightly.
» *noun* a short light sleep.

dozen
dozenth

dozes

dozier

doziest

doziness

dozing

dozy (adjective: **dozier**, **doziest**)
doziness

drab »*adjective* (**drabber**, **drabbest**) dull and uninteresting.
» *noun* a dull light brown colour.
drably
drabness

✓ double the **b** in **drabber** and **drabbest**

draconian »*adjective* (of laws) excessively harsh.
– **SAY** druh-**koh**-ni-uhn

draft »*noun* ❶ a rough version of a piece of writing. ❷ a written order requesting a bank to pay a specified sum. ❸ (**the draft**) (in American English) compulsory recruitment for military service.
» *verb* (**drafts**, **drafting**, **drafted**) ❶ prepare a rough version of a text. ❷ select someone for a particular purpose. ❸ (**be drafted**) (in American English) be conscripted for military service.

ℹ️ make sure that you distinguish correctly between **draft** and **draught**. A **draft** is a preliminary version or an order to pay money, whereas a **draught** is a current of air or an act of drinking. In American English the spelling **draft** is used for all these meanings.

draftsman »*noun* (plural **draftsmen**) a person who drafts legal documents.

ℹ️ do not confuse a **draftsman** with a **draughtsman**, who makes detailed drawings or is skilled at drawing. In America, both are called **draftsmen**.

drafty »*adjective* American spelling of **DRAUGHTY**.

drag (verb: **drags**, **dragging**, **dragged**)

dragnet »*noun* ❶ a net drawn through water or across ground to trap fish or game. ❷ a systematic search for criminals.

dragon

dragonfly »*noun* (plural **dragonflies**) a long-bodied insect with two pairs of large transparent wings.

dragoon »*noun* a member of one of several British cavalry regiments.
» *verb* (**dragoons**, **dragooning**, **dragooned**) force someone into doing something.

drag queen »*noun* a man who dresses up in showy women's clothes.

drag race »*noun* a short race between two cars to see which can accelerate fastest from a standstill.

drags

dragster »*noun* a car used in drag racing.

drain (verb: **drains**, **draining**, **drained**)

drainage

drained

draining

drainpipe

drains

drake »*noun* a male duck.

dram »*noun* a small drink of spirits.

drama »*noun* ❶ a play. ❷ plays as a literary form. ❸ an exciting series of events.

dramatic
dramatically

dramatise another way of spelling **DRAMATIZE**.

dramatis personae »*plural noun* the characters of a play, novel, or story.
– **SAY** dra-muh-tiss per-**soh**-nee

ℹ️ **dramatis personae** is a Latin phrase meaning 'persons of the drama'

dramatist »*noun* a person who writes plays.

dramatize »*verb* (**dramatizes**, **dramatizing**, **dramatized**) ❶ present a novel or story as a play. ❷ make something seem more exciting or serious than it really is.
dramatization

✓ many people prefer the alternative spellings **dramatise**, **dramatises**, etc., and **dramatisation**: both **s** and **z** spellings are correct

drank past of **DRINK**.

drape »*verb* (**drapes**, **draping**, **draped**) ❶ arrange cloth or clothing loosely on or round something. ❷ rest part of your body on something in a relaxed way.
» *noun* (**drapes**) long curtains.

draper »*noun* a person who sells fabrics.

drapery »*noun* (plural **draperies**) cloth, curtains, or clothing hanging in loose folds.

drapes

draping

drastic »*adjective* having a strong or far-reaching effect.
drastically

✓ the ending of **drastically** is **ally**, not just **ly**

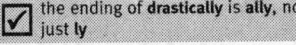

draught »*noun* ❶ a current of cool air indoors. ❷ an act of drinking or breathing in. ❸ (old-fashioned) a quantity of a medicinal liquid: *a sleeping draught.* ❹ the depth of water needed to float a particular ship.

> ℹ️ make sure that you distinguish correctly between **draught** and **draft**. A **draught** is chiefly a current of air or an act of drinking, whereas a **draft** is a preliminary version or an order to pay money. In American English, the spelling **draft** is used for all these meanings.

draught animal »*noun* an animal used for pulling heavy loads.

draught beer »*noun* beer served from a cask.

draughts »*noun* a game for two players played on a chequered board.

draughtsman »*noun* (plural **draughtsmen**) ❶ a person who makes detailed technical plans or drawings. ❷ an artist skilled at drawing.
draughtsmanship

> ℹ️ do not confuse a **draughtsman** with a **draftsman**, who drafts legal documents. In America, both are called **draftsmen**.

draughty »*adjective* uncomfortable because of draughts of cold air.

> ☑️ spell **draughty** with **ugh**, not **f**: the spelling **drafty** is American

draw (verb: **draws**, **drawing**, **drew**; past participle **drawn**) [make a picture; pull, attract, or move; game with scores equal]

> ℹ️ do not confuse **draw** with **drawer** (a sliding storage compartment)

drawback »*noun* a disadvantage or problem.

drawbridge »*noun* a bridge which is hinged at one end so that it can be raised.

drawer [sliding storage compartment]

drawers »*plural noun* (an old word) knickers or underpants.

drawing

drawing room »*noun* a room in a private house in which guests can be received.

drawl »*verb* (**drawls**, **drawling**, **drawled**) speak in a slow, lazy way with long vowel sounds.
» *noun* a drawling accent.

drawn past participle of **DRAW**.

drawn-out

draws

drawstring »*noun* a string in the seam of a garment or bag, which can be pulled to tighten or close it.

dray »*noun* a low truck or cart for delivering barrels or other heavy loads.

dread »*verb* (**dreads**, **dreading**, **dreaded**) think about something with great fear or anxiety.
» *noun* great fear or anxiety.

dreadful
dreadfully

> ☑️ **-ful** not **-full**: **dreadful**

dreading

dreadlocks »*plural noun* a Rastafarian hairstyle in which the hair is twisted into tight braids or ringlets.
dreadlocked

> ☑️ remember, there is an **a** in **dreadlocks** and **dreads**

dreadnought »*noun* (a historical term) a type of battleship of the early 20th century.

> ☑️ the ending is **nought**, not **naught**: **dreadnought**

dreads

dream (verb: **dreams**, **dreaming**, **dreamed** or **dreamt**)
dreamer
dreamless
dreamlike

dreamy (adjective: **dreamier**, **dreamiest**)
dreamily
dreaminess

dreary (adjective: **drearier**, **dreariest**)
drearily
dreariness

dredge »*verb* (**dredges**, **dredging**, **dredged**) ❶ clean out the bed of a harbour or river. ❷ (**dredge up**) bring something unwelcome and forgotten to people's attention.
» *noun* an apparatus for bringing up objects from a river or seabed by scooping or dragging.
dredger

dregs »*noun* ❶ the small amount of a liquid left in a container, together with any sediment. ❷ the most worthless parts: *the dregs of society.*

drench (verb: **drenches**, **drenching**, **drenched**)

dress (verb: **dresses**, **dressing**, **dressed**)

dressage »*noun* the training of a horse to perform a series of controlled movements at the rider's command.

– say dress-ah*zh*

dressed

dresser

dresses

dressier

dressiest

dressing

dressing-down »*noun* a severe reprimand.

dressmaker

dress rehearsal »*noun* a final rehearsal in which everything is done as it would be in a real performance.

dressy »*adjective* (**dressier, dressiest**) (of clothes) smart or formal.

drew past of DRAW.

dribble (verb: **dribbles, dribbling, dribbled**)

dribs and drabs

dried

drier[1] another way of spelling DRYER.

drier[2] [more dry]

dries

driest

drift (verb: **drifts, drifting, drifted**)
    drifter

drift net »*noun* a large fishing net kept upright and allowed to drift in the sea.

drifts

driftwood

drill

drily »*adverb* in a matter-of-fact or ironically humorous way.

> ☑ **drily** can also be spelled **dryly**: both spellings are correct

drink (verb: **drinks, drinking, drank**; past participle **drunk**)
    drinkable
    drinker

drink-driving

drinker

drinking

drinks

drip (verb: **drips, dripping, dripped**)

> ☑ double the **p** in **dripped** and **dripping**

drip-dry

drip-feed »*verb* (**drip-feeds, drip-feeding, drip-fed**) put fluid into something drop by drop.

dripped

drippiness

dripping »*noun* fat that has dripped from roasting meat.

» *adjective* extremely wet.

drippy »*adjective* (**drippier, drippiest**) (in informal English) weak or sentimental.
    drippiness

drips

drive (verb: **drives, driving, drove**; past participle **driven**)

drivel »*noun* nonsense.

> ☑ only one **v** and one **l**: **drivel**

driven

driver

drives

driveshaft »*noun* a rotating shaft which transmits power in an engine.

driving

drizzle (verb: **drizzles, drizzling, drizzled**)
    drizzly

drogue »*noun* ❶ a device towed behind a boat or aircraft to reduce speed or improve stability. ❷ a small parachute used as a brake or to pull out a larger parachute.
– say drohg

droll »*adjective* (**droller, drollest**) amusing in a strange or quaint way.
    drollery
    drollness
    drolly say drohl-li

dromedary »*noun* (plural **dromedaries**) an Arabian camel, with one hump.
– say drom-i-duh-ri

drone »*verb* (**drones, droning, droned**) ❶ make a low continuous humming sound. ❷ talk for a long time in a boring way.
» *noun* ❶ a low continuous humming sound. ❷ a male bee which does no work but can fertilize a queen.

drool (verb: **drools, drooling, drooled**)

droop (verb: **droops, drooping, drooped**)

droopy (adjective: **droopier, droopiest**)
    droopily
    droopiness

drop (verb: **drops, dropping, dropped**)

> ☑ double the **p** in **dropping** and **dropped**

droplet

dropout

dropper

droppings

dropsy »*noun* old-fashioned term for OEDEMA.

dross »*noun* rubbish.

drought »*noun* a prolonged period of abnormally low rainfall; a shortage of water.
– **SAY** drowt

✓ **ou** not **au: drought** (**draught** means 'current of air', 'act of drinking', etc.)

drove[1] past of **DRIVE**.

drove[2] »*noun* ❶ a flock of animals being driven. ❷ a large number of people doing the same thing.

drown (verb: **drowns, drowning, drowned**)

drowsy (adjective: **drowsier, drowsiest**)
drowsily
drowsiness

drub »*verb* (**drubs, drubbing, drubbed**) hit or beat repeatedly.
drubbing

✓ double the **b** in **drubbed** and **drubbing**

drudge »*noun* a person made to do hard, menial, or dull work.

drudgery »*noun* hard, menial, or dull work.

drug (verb: **drugs, drugging, drugged**)
druggist
druggy

druggie [drug addict]

drugging

druggist

druggy [caused or affected by drugs]

drugs

drugstore

Druid »*noun* a priest in the ancient Celtic religion.
– **SAY** droo-id

drum (verb: **drums, drumming, drummed**)

✓ double the **m** in **drumming** and **drummed**

drumbeat

drum majorette »*noun* ❶ the female leader of a marching band. ❷ a female member of such a band.

drummed

drummer

drumming

drums

drumstick

drunk

drunken
drunkenly
drunkenness

drupe »*noun* a fleshy fruit with a central stone, e.g. a plum or olive.
– **SAY** droop

dry (adjective: **drier, driest**; verb: **dries, drying, dried**)
dryness

✓ drop the **y** and add **ier** or **iest** to spell **drier** or **driest**

dryad »*noun* (in Greek mythology) a nymph living in a tree or wood.

dry-clean »*verb* (**dry-cleans, dry-cleaning, dry-cleaned**)
dry-cleaner

dryer [device for drying]

✓ **dryer** can also be spelled **drier**

dry ice »*noun* ❶ solid carbon dioxide. ❷ white mist produced with this as a theatrical effect.

drying

dryly another way of spelling **DRILY**.

dryness

dry rot »*noun* a fungus that causes wood to decay in poorly ventilated conditions.

drystone »*adjective* (of a stone wall) built without using mortar.

DSS »*abbreviation* (in the UK) Department of Social Security.

DTI »*abbreviation* (in the UK) Department of Trade and Industry.

DTP »*abbreviation* desktop publishing.

dual »*adjective* consisting of two parts or aspects.

✓ **al** not **el: dual.** Do not confuse **dual** with **duel** meaning 'combat between two people'.

dualism »*noun* ❶ division into two contrasted aspects, such as good and evil. ❷ the state of having two parts or aspects.
dualist

duality »*noun* (plural **dualities**) ❶ the state of having two parts or aspects. ❷ an opposition between two concepts or aspects.

dub[1] »*verb* (**dubs, dubbing, dubbed**) ❶ give an unofficial name to. ❷ knight someone by the touching of the shoulder with a sword.

✓ double the **b** in **dubbing** and **dubbed**

dub[2] »*verb* (**dubs, dubbing, dubbed**) ❶ provide a film with a soundtrack in a different language from the original. ❷ add sound effects or music to a film or a recording.

dubbin »*noun* prepared grease used for softening and waterproofing leather.

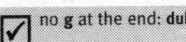 no **g** at the end: **dubbin**

dubbing

dubiety »*noun* uncertainty.
– **say** dyoo-by-i-ti

dubious »*adjective* ❶ hesitating or
doubting. ❷ not to be relied upon. ❸ of
questionable value.
– **say** dyoo-bi-uhss
dubiously

dubs

ducal »*adjective* relating to a duke or
dukedom.
– **say** dyoo-k'l

ducat »*noun* a former European gold coin.
– **say** duk-uht

duchess (plural **duchesses**)

 there is no **t** in **duchess**

duchy »*noun* (plural **duchies**) the territory
of a duke or duchess.
– **say** duch-i

duck (plural **duck** or **ducks**; verb: **ducks**,
ducking, **ducked**)

duck-billed platypus

duckboards »*plural noun* wooden slats
joined together to form a path over
muddy ground.

ducked

ducking

duckling

ducks

duckweed »*noun* a tiny plant that floats on
the surface of still water.

duct »*noun* ❶ a tube or passageway for air,
cables, etc. ❷ a tube in the body through
which fluid passes.

ductile »*adjective* (of a metal) able to be
drawn out into a thin wire.
– **say** duk-tyl
ductility

dud

dude

dudgeon »*noun* deep resentment.
– **say** duj-uhn

✓ don't forget the **d** before the **g**:
dudgeon

due [owing; proper; a right; etc.]

duel »*noun* ❶ (a historical term) a pre-
arranged contest with deadly weapons
between two people to settle a point of
honour. ❷ a contest between two parties.
» *verb* (**duels**, **duelling**, **duelled**) fight a duel.
duellist

✓ **el** not **al**: **duel** (**dual** means 'having
two parts or aspects', as in *dual
carriageway*)
double the **l** in **duelling** and **duelled** (the
spellings with a single **l** are American)

duet »*noun* ❶ a performance by two
singers, musicians, or dancers. ❷ a
musical composition for two performers.
» *verb* (**duets**, **duetting**, **duetted**) perform a
duet.

✓ double the **t** in **duetting** and **duetted**

duff (verb: **duffs**, **duffing**, **duffed**)

duffel »*noun* a coarse woollen cloth.

✓ **duffel** (from *Duffel* in Belgium) can
also be spelled with **le**, so **duffle bag**
and **duffle coat** are also correct

duffel bag »*noun* a cylinder-shaped canvas
bag closed by a drawstring.

duffel coat »*noun* a hooded coat made of a
coarse woollen material.

duffer

duffing

duffle another way of spelling **DUFFEL**.

duffs

dug past and past participle of **DIG**.

dugong »*noun* (plural **dugong** or **dugongs**)
a sea cow found in the Indian Ocean.
– **say** doo-gong or dyoo-gong

dugout »*noun* ❶ a trench that is roofed
over as a shelter for troops. ❷ a low
shelter at the side of a sports field for a
team's coaches and substitutes.

duke
dukedom

dulcet »*adjective* (of a sound) sweet and
soothing.
– **say** dul-sit

✓ **cet** not **set**: **dulcet**

dulcimer »*noun* a musical instrument
which you play by hitting the strings with
small hammers.
– **say** dul-si-mer

dull (adjective: **duller**, **dullest**; verb: **dulls**,
dulling, **dulled**)
dullness

dullard »*noun* a slow or stupid person.
– **say** dul-lerd

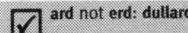 **ard** not **erd**: **dullard**

dulled
duller
dullest

dulling

dullness

dulls

duly »*adverb* in accordance with what is required or expected.

dumb »*adjective* ❶ not able to speak. ❷ temporarily unable or unwilling to speak. ❸ (in informal English) stupid. » *verb* (**dumbs, dumbing, dumbed**) (**dumb down**) (in informal English) make or become less intellectually challenging.

> ℹ️ avoid **dumb** in the sense meaning 'not able to speak', as it is likely to cause offence; use alternatives such as **speech-impaired**

dumb-bell »*noun* a short bar with a weight at each end, used for exercise.

dumbfounded »*adjective* greatly astonished.

> 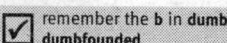 remember the **b** in **dumb**: **dumbfounded**

dumbshow »*noun* gestures used to communicate something without speech.

dumbstruck »*adjective* so shocked or surprised as to be unable to speak.

dumb waiter »*noun* a small lift for carrying food and crockery between floors.

dumdum »*noun* a kind of soft-nosed bullet that expands on impact.

dummy (plural **dummies**; verb: **dummies, dummying, dummied**)

> 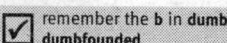 plural: drop the **y** and add **ies**: **dummies**

dump (verb: **dumps, dumping, dumped**)

dumped

dumper

dumpier

dumpiest

dumping

dumpling »*noun* a small savoury ball of dough boiled in water or in a stew.

dumps

dumpy »*adjective* (**dumpier, dumpiest**) short and stout.

dun »*noun* a dull greyish-brown colour.

dunce »*noun* a person who is slow at learning.

dunderhead »*noun* (in informal English) a stupid person.

dune »*noun* a mound or ridge of sand formed by the wind.

dung

dungarees

dungeon »*noun* a strong underground prison cell.

> 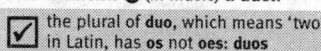 **dun** not **dud**: **dungeon**

dunghill

dunk »*verb* (**dunks, dunking, dunked**) ❶ dip food into a drink or soup before eating it. ❷ immerse something in water. ❸ score in basketball by shooting the ball down through the basket with the hands above the rim.

dunlin »*noun* a small sandpiper.

dunnock »*noun* a songbird with a grey head and a reddish-brown back.

duo »*noun* (plural **duos**) ❶ a pair of people or things, especially in music or entertainment. ❷ (in music) a duet.

> 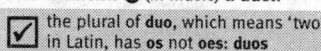 the plural of **duo**, which means 'two' in Latin, has **os** not **oes**: **duos**

duodecimal »*adjective* relating to a system of counting that has twelve as a base.
– **SAY** dyoo-oh-**des**-i-m'l

duodenum »*noun* (plural **duodenums** or **duodena**) the first part of the small intestine immediately beyond the stomach.
– **SAY** dyoo-uh-**dee**-nuhm

> 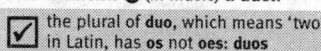 the plural can be either **duodena** (like the original Latin) or **duodenums**

duopoly »*noun* (plural **duopolies**) a situation in which two suppliers dominate a market.
– **SAY** dyoo-**op**-uh-li

dupe »*verb* (**dupes, duping, duped**) deceive; trick.
» *noun* a person who is tricked or deceived.

duple »*adjective* (in music) (of rhythm) based on two main beats to the bar.
– **SAY** dyoo-p'l

duplex »*adjective* having two parts.
» *noun* ❶ (in American English) a residential building divided into two apartments. ❷ (in American & Australian English) a semi-detached house.
– **SAY** dyoo-pleks

duplicate (verb: **duplicates, duplicating, duplicated**)
duplication
duplicator

duplicitous »*adjective* deceitful.

> 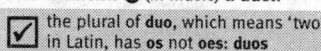 **cit** not **sit**: **duplicitous**

duplicity »*noun* deceitfulness.
– **SAY** dyoo-**pli**-si-ti

durable »*adjective* ❶ hard-wearing. ❷ (of goods) not for immediate consumption

and so able to be kept.
durability

duration »*noun* the time during which something continues.

duress »*noun* threats or violence used to force a person to do something: *confessions extracted under duress.*
– SAY dyuu-**ress**

> ✓ one r, two **s**'s: **duress**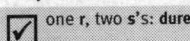

during

durum wheat »*noun* a kind of hard wheat, yielding flour that is used to make pasta.
– SAY dyoo-ruhm

dusk »*noun* the darker stage of twilight.

dusky »*adjective* (**duskier, duskiest**) darkish in colour.

dust (verb: **dusts, dusting, dusted**)

dustbin

dust bowl »*noun* an area where vegetation has been lost and soil reduced to dust and eroded.

dustcart

dusted

duster

dustier

dustiest

dustiness

dusting

dust jacket »*noun* a removable paper cover on a book.

dustman (plural **dustmen**)

dustpan

dusts

dust-up »*noun* (in informal English) a fight or quarrel.

dusty (adjective: **dustier, dustiest**)
dustiness

Dutch [of the Netherlands]

Dutch auction »*noun* a method of selling in which the price is reduced until a buyer is found.

Dutch courage »*noun* confidence gained from drinking alcohol.

dutiable »*adjective* on which duty needs to be paid.
– SAY dyoo-ti-uh-b'l

duties

dutiful »*adjective* conscientiously doing your duty.
dutifully

> ✓ -ful not -full: **dutiful**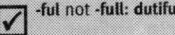

duty »*noun* (plural **duties**) ❶ a moral or legal obligation. ❷ a task required as part of your job. ❸ a payment charged on the import, export, manufacture, or sale of goods.

> ✓ plural: drop the **y** and add **ies**: **duties**

d

duty-bound »*adjective* morally or legally obliged.

duty-free

duvet »*noun* a thick quilt used instead of an upper sheet and blankets.
– SAY doo-vay

> ✓ a French word, **duvet** has a **t** at the end, which is not pronounced

DVD »*abbreviation* digital versatile disc.

dwarf (plural **dwarfs** or **dwarves**; verb: **dwarfs, dwarfing, dwarfed**)

> ℹ️ when used to mean 'an abnormally small person', **dwarf** is normally considered offensive

dwarfism »*noun* the condition of being unusually short or small.

dwarfs

dwarves

dwell »*verb* (**dwells, dwelling, dwelt** or **dwelled**) ❶ live in or at a place. ❷ (**dwell on** or **upon**) think at length about.
dweller
dwelling

dwelt past and past participle of DWELL.

dwindle »*verb* (**dwindles, dwindling, dwindled**) gradually lessen or fade.

dye (verb: **dyes, dyeing, dyed**) [substance used to colour something; colour something using a dye]
dyer

> ✓ do not drop the **e** in **dyeing**

dyestuff »*noun* a substance used as or yielding a dye.

dying present participle of DIE[1].

dyke »*noun* ❶ a barrier built to prevent flooding from the sea. ❷ an earthwork serving as a boundary or defence: *Offa's Dyke.* ❸ a ditch or water-filled channel. ❹ (in informal English) a lesbian.

> ✓ **dyke** can also be spelled in **dike**: both spellings are correct

dynamic »*adjective* ❶ (of a process or system) characterized by constant change or activity. ❷ full of energy and new ideas. ❸ (in physics) relating to forces that produce motion.

» *noun* an energizing force.
dynamically

✓ one n, one m: **dynamic**

dynamics »*plural noun* ❶ the study of the forces involved in movement. ❷ the forces which stimulate change within a system or process. ❸ the varying levels of volume of sound in a musical performance.

dynamism »*noun* the quality of being dynamic.

dynamite »*noun* ❶ a high explosive made of nitroglycerine. ❷ (in informal English) an extremely impressive or dangerous person or thing.
» *verb* (**dynamites, dynamiting, dynamited**) blow something up with dynamite.

dynamo »*noun* (plural **dynamos**) a machine for converting mechanical energy into electrical energy.

✓ the plural of **dynamo** has os not oes: **dynamos**

dynasty »*noun* (plural **dynasties**) ❶ a line of hereditary rulers. ❷ a succession of powerful people from the same family.
– SAY di-nuh-sti
dynastic SAY di-**nass**-tik

✓ plural: drop the y and add **ies**: **dynasties**

dyne »*noun* (in physics) a force which would give a mass of one gram an acceleration of one centimetre per second per second.

dysentery »*noun* a disease of the intestines which results in severe diarrhoea.
– SAY **diss**-uhn-tri

✓ **dys** not **dis** or **diss**, and the ending is **ery** not **ary** or **try**: **dysentery**

dysfunctional »*adjective* ❶ not operating properly. ❷ unable to deal with normal social relations.
dysfunction
dysfunctionally

✓ **dys** not **dis**: **dysfunctional** and **dyslexic** belong to a group of words based on the Greek prefix *dus*- meaning 'bad' or 'difficult'

dyslexia »*noun* a disorder involving difficulty in learning to read words and letters.
– SAY diss-**lek**-si-uh
dyslexic

dyspepsia »*noun* indigestion.
– SAY diss-**pep**-si-uh

dyspeptic »*adjective* ❶ suffering from indigestion. ❷ irritable.

dyspraxia »*noun* a disorder of the brain in childhood causing difficulty in coordination and movement.
– SAY diss-**prak**-si-uh

dysprosium »*noun* a soft silvery-white metallic chemical element.
– SAY diss-**proh**-zi-uhm

dystopia »*noun* an imaginary place or society in which everything is bad (the opposite of *utopia*).
– SAY diss-**toh**-pi-uh
dystopian

dystrophy »*noun* a disorder in which an organ or tissue of the body wastes away.
– SAY **diss**-truh-fi

Ee

each

each-way »*adjective & adverb* (of a bet) backing a horse to win or to finish in the first three.

eager
eagerly
eagerness

eagle

eagle-eyed »*adjective* very observant.

eaglet

ear

earache

eardrum

earhole

earl »*noun* a British nobleman ranking above a viscount.
earldom

Earl Grey »*noun* a kind of China tea flavoured with bergamot.

early (adjective: **earlier, earliest**)

☑ drop the **y** and add **ier** or **iest** to spell **earlier** or **earliest**

earmark »*noun* a mark made on the ear of a domesticated animal to indicate who owns it.
» *verb* (**be earmarked**) be chosen for a particular purpose.

earmuffs

earn (verb: **earns, earning, earned**)
earner

earnest »*adjective* extremely serious.
earnestly
earnestness

☑ **ear** not **er: earnest** (**Ernest** is a man's name)

earning

earnings

earns

earphone

earpiece »*noun* the part of a telephone or other device for listening that is applied to the ear during use.

earplug

earring

☑ note the double **r: earring**

earshot »*noun* the distance over which you can hear or be heard.

earth (verb: **earths, earthing, earthed**)

earthbound

earthen »*adjective* ❶ made of compressed earth. ❷ (of a pot) made of baked or fired clay.

earthenware »*noun* pottery made of fired clay.

earthier [more earthy]

earthiest

earthing

earthling »*noun* (in science fiction) a person from the earth.

earthly

earthquake

earths

earth sciences »*plural noun* the branches of science concerned with the physical composition of the earth and its atmosphere.

earthwork »*noun* a large man-made bank of earth.

earthworm

earthy »*adjective* (**earthier, earthiest**) ❶ resembling soil. ❷ direct and unembarrassed about sexual subjects or bodily functions.

earwax

earwig

ease (verb: **eases, easing, eased**)

easel »*noun* a wooden frame on legs used by artists for holding the picture they are working on.

eases

easier

easiest

easily

easiness

easing

east
eastbound

Easter

easterly

eastern

Eastern Church »*noun* = ORTHODOX CHURCH.

easterner

east-north-east

east-south-east

eastward

eastwards

easy (adjective: **easier, easiest**)
easily
easiness

☑ drop the **y** and add **ier** or **iest** to spell **easier** or **easiest**

easy-going

eat (verb: **eats, eating, ate**; past participle **eaten**)

eatable

☑ **-able** not **-ible: eatable**

eaten past participle of EAT.

eater

eatery »*noun* (plural **eateries**) (in informal English) a restaurant or cafe.

eating

eats

eau de cologne »*noun* (plural **eaux de cologne**) = COLOGNE.
– SAY oh duh kuh-**lohn** [singular and plural]

☑ the plural of **eau de cologne** adds an **x** to **eau: eaux de cologne** (it is a French phrase meaning 'water of Cologne')

eau de Nil »*noun* a pale greenish colour.
– SAY oh duh **neel**

 a French phrase meaning 'water of the Nile'

eau de toilette »*noun* (plural **eaux de toilette**) a dilute form of perfume.

– **say** oh duh twah-**let** [singular and plural]

> ✓ this is a French phrase, and the plural of **eau de toilette** adds an **x** to eau: **eaux de toilette**

eau de vie »*noun* (plural **eaux de vie**) brandy.
– **say** oh duh vee [singular and plural]

> ✓ the plural of **eau de vie** adds an **x** to eau: **eaux de vie** (it is a French phrase meaning 'water of life')

eaux de cologne plural of EAU DE COLOGNE.

eaux de toilette plural of EAU DE TOILETTE.

eaux de vie plural of EAU DE VIE.

eaves »*plural noun* the part of a roof that meets or overhangs the walls of a building.

eavesdrop »*verb* (**eavesdrops**, **eavesdropping**, **eavesdropped**) secretly listen to a conversation.
eavesdropper

ebb »*noun* the movement of the tide out to sea.
»*verb* (**ebbs**, **ebbing**, **ebbed**) ❶ (of the tide) move away from the land. ❷ (**ebb away**) (of an emotion or quality) gradually lessen or reduce.

ebony »*noun* ❶ heavy blackish or very dark brown wood from a tree of tropical and warm regions. ❷ a very dark brown or black colour.
– **say** eb-uh-ni

ebullient »*adjective* cheerful and full of energy.
– **say** i-**bul**-yuhnt or i-**buul**-yuhnt
ebullience
ebulliently

> ✓ ent not ant at the end: **ebullient**

EC »*abbreviation* European Community.

eccentric »*adjective* unconventional and slightly strange.
»*noun* an eccentric person.
– **say** ik-**sen**-trik or ek-**sen**-trik
eccentrically

> ✓ note the double **c**: **eccentric**

eccentricity »*noun* (plural **eccentricities**) ❶ the quality of being eccentric. ❷ an eccentric act or habit.
– **say** ek-sen-**triss**-i-ti

> ✓ plural: drop the **y** and add **ies**: **eccentricities**

ecclesiastical »*adjective* relating to the Christian Church or its clergy.
– **say** i-klee-zi-**ass**-ti-k'l

ECG »*abbreviation* electrocardiogram or electrocardiograph.

echelon »*noun* a level or rank in an organization, profession, or society.
– **say** esh-uh-lon

echo (plural **echoes**; verb: **echoes**, **echoing**, **echoed**)
echoey

> ✓ the plural of **echo** has **oes** not **os**: **echoes**

echoic »*adjective* of or like an echo.
– **say** e-**koh**-ik

echoing

echolocation »*noun* the location of objects by reflected sound, used by animals such as dolphins and bats.

eclair »*noun* a cake of light pastry filled with cream and topped with chocolate icing.

> ✓ **eclair** comes from a French word meaning 'lightning' and is sometimes written **éclair**, with an acute accent on the **e**

eclat »*noun* a notably brilliant or successful effect.
– **say** ay-**klah**

> ✓ **eclat** can also be written **éclat**, with an acute accent on the **e** (as in the original French)

eclectic »*adjective* taking ideas from a wide range of sources.
– **say** i-**klek**-tik
eclectically
eclecticism

> ✓ do not forget the **c** before the **t**: **eclectic**

eclipse »*noun* ❶ an occasion when one planet, the moon, etc. passes between another and the observer, or in front of a planet's source of light. ❷ a sudden loss of significance or power.
»*verb* (**eclipses**, **eclipsing**, **eclipsed**) ❶ (of a planet, the moon, etc.) obscure the light coming from or shining on another. ❷ make less significant or powerful.

ecliptic »*noun* the sun's apparent circular path among the stars during the year.
– **say** i-**klip**-tik

E. coli »*noun* the bacteria commonly found in the intestines of humans, some kinds of which can cause severe food poisoning.
– **say** ee koh-**lI**

> ℹ **E. coli** is short for the Latin name *Escherichia coli*

ecology »*noun* the study of how animals and plants relate to one another and to their surroundings.
– SAY i-**kol**-uh-ji
  ecological
  ecologically
  ecologist

e-commerce »*noun* commercial transactions conducted on the Internet.

economic »*adjective* ❶ relating to economics or the economy. ❷ profitable or concerned with profitability.

> ℹ️ although they overlap, **economic** and **economical** have somewhat different meanings: **economic** generally refers to economics and profitability (*economic policy* | *many organizations must become larger if they are to remain economic*), whereas **economical** generally refers to the careful or effective use of money or resources (*a small, economical car* | *he was economical in all areas of life*)

economical »*adjective* ❶ giving good value in relation to the resources used or money spent. ❷ careful in the use of resources or money.
  economically

economics »*plural noun* the study of the production, consumption, and transfer of wealth.

economies

economise another way of spelling ECONOMIZE.

economist

economize »*verb* (**economizes, economizing, economized**) spend less; be economical.

> ✓ many people prefer the alternative spellings **economise, economises,** etc.: both s and z spellings are correct

economy (plural **economies**)

> ✓ plural: drop the **y** and add **ies**: **economies**

ecosystem »*noun* all the plants and animals of a particular area considered in terms of how they interact with their environment.

ecotourism »*noun* tourism directed towards unspoiled natural environments and intended to support conservation efforts.
  ecotourist

eco-warrior »*noun* a person who engages in protest activities aimed at protecting the environment from damage.

ecru »*noun* the light cream or beige colour of unbleached linen.

– SAY ay-kroo or e-**kroo**

> ✓ **ecru** can also be written **écru**, with an acute accent on the **e** (as in the original French)

ecstasy »*noun* (plural **ecstasies**) ❶ an overwhelming feeling of great happiness or joyful excitement. ❷ an emotional or religious frenzy. ❸ (**Ecstasy**) an illegal drug that produces feelings of excitement and happiness.
  ecstatic
  ecstatically

> ✓ no **x**: there is a **cs** at the beginning and an **s** at the end: **ecstasy** plural: drop the **y** and add **ies**: **ecstasies**

ectopic pregnancy »*noun* a pregnancy in which the fetus develops outside the womb.
– SAY ek-**top**-ik

ectoplasm »*noun* a substance that is thought by some people to come out of the body of a medium during a seance.
– SAY **ek**-toh-pla-z'm

Ecuadorian

ecumenical »*adjective* ❶ representing a number of different Christian Churches. ❷ wishing for the world's Christian Churches to be united.
– SAY ee-kyoo-**men**-i-k'l or ek-yoo-**men**-i-k'l

eczema »*noun* a condition in which patches of skin become rough and inflamed.
– SAY **eks**-i-muh

> ✓ do not forget the **e** after the **z**: **eczema**

Edam »*noun* a round yellow Dutch cheese with a red wax coating.
– SAY ee-dam

> ✓ **Edam** has a capital **E**: it is named after *Edam* in the Netherlands

eddy »*noun* (plural **eddies**) a circular movement of water causing a small whirlpool.
» *verb* (**eddies, eddying, eddied**) (of water, air, etc.) move in a circular way.

edelweiss »*noun* a mountain plant with small white flowers.
– SAY **ay**-duhl-vyss

> ✓ note there is a **w** not a **v** in the middle: **edelweiss** is a German word

edema American spelling of OEDEMA.

Eden »*noun* ❶ (in the biblical account of the Creation) the place where Adam and Eve lived. ❷ a place of unspoilt happiness or beauty.

edge (verb: **edges, edging, edged**)

drop the final **e** to spell **edging**

edgeways
edgewise
edgier
edgiest
edgily
edginess
edging

edgy »*adjective* (**edgier**, **edgiest**) tense, nervous, or irritable.
  edgily
  edginess

edible »*adjective* fit to be eaten.
  edibility

 -ible not **-able**: **edible**

edict »*noun* an official order.
– SAY ee-dikt

edification

edifice »*noun* a large, imposing building.
– SAY ed-i-fiss

edify »*verb* (**edifies**, **edifying**, **edified**) teach someone something that is educational or morally improving.
– SAY ed-i-fI
  edification
  edifying

edit »*verb* (**edits**, **editing**, **edited**) ❶ prepare written material for publication by correcting or shortening it. ❷ prepare material for a recording or broadcast. ❸ be editor of a newspaper or magazine. »*noun* a change made as a result of editing.

 do not double the **t** when spelling **editing** and **edited**

edition
editor

 -or not **-er**: **editor**

editorial »*adjective* relating to the editing of material.
»*noun* a newspaper article giving the editor's opinion on an issue.
  editorially

edits

educate (verb: **educates**, **educating**, **educated**)
  educative
  educator

education
  educational
  educationally
  educationist

educative

educator

Edwardian »*adjective* relating to the reign of King Edward VII (1901–10).

EEC »*abbreviation* European Economic Community.

eel

e'er »*adverb* (a poetic term) ever.
– SAY air

 be careful to put the apostrophe where a letter has been left out, that is, between the two **e**'s of **ever**: **e'er**

eerie »*adjective* (**eerier**, **eeriest**) strange and frightening.
  eerily
  eeriness

 do not confuse **eerie** with **eyrie**, which means 'a large nest of a bird of prey'

efface »*verb* (**effaces**, **effacing**, **effaced**)
❶ rub off a mark from a surface.
❷ (**efface yourself**) make yourself appear unimportant.
– SAY i-fayss
  effacement

effect (verb: **effects**, **effecting**, **effected**) [a result, bring about a result]

 do not confuse **effect** with **affect** meaning 'make a difference to'

effective
  effectively
  effectiveness

effects

effectual »*adjective* producing the intended result; effective.
– SAY i-fek-choo-uhl or i-fek-tyoo-uhl
  effectually

effeminate »*adjective* (of a man) looking, behaving, or sounding like a woman.
– SAY i-fem-i-nuht
  effeminacy
  effeminately

effervesce »*verb* (**effervesces**, **effervescing**, **effervesced**) (of a liquid) give off bubbles.

 note the **sc** at the end: **effervesce**

effervescent »*adjective* ❶ (of a liquid) giving off bubbles; fizzy. ❷ lively and enthusiastic.
  effervescence

 ent not **ant**: **effervescent**

effervesces
effervescing

effete »*adjective* ❶ weak; feeble. ❷ (of a man) effeminate.

– say i-**feet**
effetely
effeteness

efficacious »*adjective* effective.
– say ef-fi-**kay**-shuhss
efficaciously
efficaciousness

efficacy »*noun* effectiveness.
– say **ef**-fi-kuh-si

efficiency (plural **efficiencies**)

efficient
efficiently

effigy »*noun* (plural **effigies**) a sculpture or statue of a person.
– say **ef**-fi-ji

> ✓ plural: drop the **y** and add **ies**:
> **effigies**

effloresce »*verb* (**effloresces**, **efflorescing**, **effloresced**) ❶ turn to a fine powder on exposure to air. ❷ (of salts) come to the surface of a material and crystallize.
– say ef-fluh-**ress**
efflorescence
efflorescent

effluence »*noun* ❶ a substance that flows out. ❷ the action of flowing out.
– say **ef**-floo-uhnss

effluent »*noun* liquid waste or sewage discharged into a river or the sea.

effluvium »*noun* (plural **effluvia**) an unpleasant or harmful odour or discharge.
– say i-**floo**-vi-uhm

> ✓ like many other words ending in **um** derived from Latin, **effluvium** has a plural ending in **a**: **effluvia**

effort

effortless
effortlessly
effortlessness

effrontery »*noun* rude and disrespectful behaviour.
– say i-**frun**-tuh-ri

> ✓ **ery** not **ary**: **effrontery**

effusion »*noun* ❶ an instance of giving off a liquid, light, or smell. ❷ an instance of unrestrained speech or writing.

effusive »*adjective* expressing pleasure or approval in a warm and emotional way.
effusively

e.g. »*abbreviation* for example.

> ℹ **e.g.** stands for the Latin phrase *exempli gratia* 'for the sake of an example'

egalitarian »*adjective* believing that all people are equal and deserve equal rights and opportunities.
» *noun* an egalitarian person.
– say i-gal-i-**tair**-i-uhn
egalitarianism

egg (verb: **eggs**, **egging**, **egged**)
eggy

egghead

egging

eggplant »*noun* (in American English) = AUBERGINE.

eggs

eggshell

eggy

ego »*noun* (plural **egos**) ❶ a person's sense of their own value and importance. ❷ the part of the mind that is responsible for a person's sense of who they are.

> ✓ the plural of **ego** (the Latin word for 'I') has **os** not **oes**: **egos**

egocentric »*adjective* self-centred.
egocentricity

egoism »*noun* ❶ the philosophy that self-interest should be the basis for behaviour. ❷ = EGOTISM.
egoist

egomania »*noun* obsessive egotism.
egomaniac

egotism »*noun* the quality of being excessively conceited or absorbed in yourself.
egotist
egotistical

ego trip »*noun* something that a person does to make themselves feel important.

egregious »*adjective* outstandingly bad.
– say i-**gree**-juhss
egregiously
egregiousness

egress »*noun* (plural **egresses**) ❶ going out of a place. ❷ a way out.
– say **ee**-gress

egret »*noun* a kind of heron with white plumage.
– say **ee**-grit

Egyptian

Egyptology
Egyptologist

eider »*noun* a duck with black-and-white plumage that lives in northern countries.
– say **I**-der

eiderdown »*noun* a quilt filled with down or some other soft material.

eight
eightfold

eighteen
eighteenth

eightfold

eighth
eighthly

✓ there are two **h**'s: **eighth**

eighth note »*noun* (in music) a quaver.

eighty (plural **eighties**)
eightieth

eirenic »*adjective* aiming or aimed at peace.
– SAY I-**ren**-ik or I-**ree**-nik

eisteddfod »*noun* (plural **eisteddfods** or **eisteddfodau**) a Welsh festival of music and poetry.
– SAY I-steth-vod [singular], I-steth-vodz or I-steth-vod-I [plural]

ℹ **eisteddfod** is a Welsh word; the plural can either be the English form **eisteddfods** or the Welsh form **eisteddfodau**

either

ejaculate »*verb* (**ejaculates, ejaculating, ejaculated**) ❶ (of a man or male animal) eject semen from the penis at the moment of orgasm. ❷ (old-fashioned) say something quickly and suddenly.
– SAY i-**jak**-yuu-layt
ejaculation

eject »*verb* (**ejects, ejecting, ejected**) ❶ force or throw out violently or suddenly. ❷ (of a pilot) escape from an aircraft by means of an ejection seat. ❸ make someone leave a place.
ejection

ejector seat »*noun* a seat that can throw the pilot out of the aircraft in an emergency.

ejects

eke »*verb* (**ekes, eking, eked**) (**eke out**) ❶ make a supply of something last a long time. ❷ make a living with difficulty.

✓ **eke** is not to be confused with the comic-book exclamation **eek!**

elaborate (verb: **elaborates, elaborating, elaborated**)
elaborately
elaboration

✓ b**or** not b**our**: **elaborate**

elan »*noun* energy and flair.
– SAY ay-**lan** or ay-**lon**

✓ **elan** can also be written **élan**, with an acute accent on the **e** (as in the original French)

eland »*noun* a spiral-horned African antelope.
– SAY ee-luhnd

elapse »*verb* (**elapses, elapsing, elapsed**) (of time) pass.

elastic
elasticated
elasticity

✓ there is no **k** at the end: **elastic**

elated »*adjective* extremely happy and excited.
– SAY i-**lay**-tid

elation »*noun* great happiness and excitement.

elbow (verb: **elbows, elbowing, elbowed**)

elder[1] [of a greater age; older person; senior figure]

elder[2] »*noun* a small tree or shrub with white flowers and bluish-black or red berries.

elderberry (plural **elderberries**)

elderflower

elderly
elderliness

eldest

elect »*verb* (**elects, electing, elected**) ❶ choose someone to hold a position by voting. ❷ choose to do something.
»*adjective* ❶ chosen or singled out. ❷ elected to a position but not yet in office: *the President Elect*.

electable

✓ -**able** not -**ible**: **electable**

elected

electing

election

electioneering »*noun* the action of campaigning to be elected.

elective »*adjective* ❶ using or chosen by election. ❷ (of study, treatment, etc.) chosen; not compulsory.

elector »*noun* a person who has the right to vote in an election.

✓ -**or** not -**er**: **elector**

electoral »*adjective* relating to elections or electors.

electorate »*noun* the people who are entitled to vote in an election.

electric

electrical
electrically

electrician

electricity

electrify »*verb* (**electrifies**, **electrifying**, **electrified**) ❶ charge something with electricity. ❷ convert something to use electrical power.
electrifying

electrocute »*verb* (**electrocutes**, **electrocuting**, **electrocuted**) injure or kill someone by electric shock.
electrocution

electrode »*noun* a conductor through which electricity enters or leaves something.

electrolysis »*noun* ❶ the separation of a liquid into its chemical parts by passing an electric current through it. ❷ the removal of hair roots or small blemishes on the skin by means of an electric current.
– SAY i-lek-**trol**-i-siss

electrolyte »*noun* a liquid or gel that an electric current can pass through, e.g. in a battery.
– SAY i-**lek**-truh-lyt

> ✓ the ending is **lyte**, not **lite**: **electrolyte**

electromagnet »*noun* a piece of metal made into a magnet by passing an electric current through a surrounding coil.

electromagnetic »*adjective* relating to the interaction of electric currents or fields and magnetic fields.
electromagnetism

electromotive force »*noun* a voltage that tends to produce an electric current.

electron »*noun* a particle with a negative charge, found in all atoms.

electronic »*adjective* ❶ having parts such as microchips and transistors that control and direct electric currents. ❷ relating to electrons or electronics. ❸ carried out by means of a computer.
electronically

electronic publishing »*noun* the production of texts in a form that can be input into a computer, rather than on paper.

electronics »*plural noun* ❶ the study of the behaviour and movement of electrons. ❷ circuits or devices using transistors, microchips, etc.

electroplated »*adjective* coated with a layer of metal by the process of electrolysis.

electrostatic »*adjective* relating to stationary electric charges or fields as opposed to electric currents.

elects

elegant
elegance
elegantly

elegiac »*adjective* ❶ characteristic of an elegy. ❷ wistfully mournful.
– SAY el-i-jy-uhk

> ✓ be careful to spell **elegiac** correctly: the ending is **iac**, not **aic**

elegy »*noun* (plural **elegies**) a mournful poem, usually a lament for a dead person.
– SAY el-i-ji

element

elemental »*adjective* ❶ fundamental. ❷ of or like the primitive forces of nature: *elemental hatred*.

elementary »*adjective* ❶ relating to the most basic aspects of a subject. ❷ straightforward and uncomplicated.

> ✓ the ending is **tary**, not **try**: **elementary**

elephant

elephantiasis »*noun* a medical condition, usually caused by parasites, in which an arm or leg becomes very swollen.
– SAY e-li-fuhn-ty-uh-siss

elephantine »*adjective* of or like an elephant.
– SAY el-i-**fan**-tyn

elevate »*verb* (**elevates**, **elevating**, **elevated**) ❶ lift to a higher position. ❷ raise to a higher level or status.
elevated

elevation

elevator

eleven

eleven-plus

elevenses

eleventh

elf (plural **elves**)

elfin »*adjective* of or like an elf; small and delicate.

elicit »*verb* (**elicits**, **eliciting**, **elicited**) produce or draw out a response or reaction.
– SAY i-**liss**-it

> ℹ do not confuse **elicit** with **illicit**, which means 'unlawful'

eligible »*adjective* ❶ satisfying the conditions to do or receive something: *you may be eligible for a refund*. ❷ desirable as a husband or wife.
eligibility

> ✓ the ending is **-ible**, not **-able**: **eligible**

eliminate »*verb* (**eliminates, eliminating, eliminated**) ❶ completely remove or get rid of. ❷ stop considering someone or something as a potential participant. ❸ exclude a competitor from a sporting competition by beating them.
elimination
eliminator

> ☑ single **l**, and **min** not **man** in the middle: **eliminate**

elision »*noun* the omission of a sound or syllable in speech.
– SAY i-li-*zh*'n

elite »*noun* a group of people regarded as the best in a particular society or organization.
– SAY i-**leet** or ay-**leet**

> ☑ **elite** and **elitism** are sometimes written with an acute accent on the e, as in French *élite*

elitism »*noun* ❶ the belief that a society should be run by an elite. ❷ the superior attitude or behaviour associated with an elite.
elitist

elixir »*noun* a potion believed to make people live for ever or have other magical effects.
– SAY i-**lik**-seer

> ☑ **lix** not **lex**: **elixir**

Elizabethan »*adjective* relating to the reign of Queen Elizabeth I (1558–1603).

elk »*noun* (plural **elk** or **elks**) a large deer with a growth of skin hanging from the neck.

ellipse »*noun* (plural **ellipses**) a regular oval shape.

ellipsis »*noun* (plural **ellipses**) ❶ the omission of words from speech or writing. ❷ a set of dots (...) indicating an omission.
– SAY i-**lip**-siss [singular], i-**lip**-seez [plural]

> ☑ make the plural by changing the **-is** ending to **-es** (as in Latin): **ellipses**. This is spelled the same as the plural of **ellipse**, but pronounced differently.

elliptical »*adjective* ❶ having the form of an ellipse. ❷ (of speech or text) having a word or words deliberately left out.

elm

El Nino »*noun* (plural **El Ninos**) abnormal ocean currents, wind, and weather affecting the Pacific and other parts of the world every few years.
– SAY el **neen**-yoh

> ☑ the name **El Nino** is Spanish and means 'the Christ child'. It is often written with a tilde over the second **n**, as in Spanish *El Niño*.

elocution »*noun* the skill of clear and expressive speech.
– SAY el-uh-**kyoo**-sh'n

elongate »*verb* (**elongates, elongating, elongated**) make or become longer.
elongated
elongation

elope »*verb* (**elopes, eloping, eloped**) run away secretly in order to get married.
elopement

eloquent »*adjective* ❶ fluent or persuasive in speaking or writing. ❷ clearly expressive.
– SAY el-uh-**kwuhnt**
eloquence
eloquently

else

elsewhere

elucidate »*verb* (**elucidates, elucidating, elucidated**) make something clear; explain.
elucidation

elude »*verb* (**eludes, eluding, eluded**) ❶ cleverly escape from or avoid something. ❷ fail to be understood or achieved by: *the logic of this eluded her.*

elusive »*adjective* difficult to find, catch, or achieve.

> ⓘ do not confuse **elusive** with **illusive**, which means 'illusory, not real'

elver »*noun* a young eel.

elves

Elysian »*adjective* relating to Elysium or the Elysian Fields, the heavenly place in Greek mythology where heroes were taken after death.
– SAY i-**liz**-i-uhn

emaciated »*adjective* abnormally thin and weak.
emaciation

email »*noun* the sending of electronic messages from one computer user to another via a network.
» *verb* (**emails, emailing, emailed**) mail or send using email.

> ☑ **email** is often spelled with a hyphen, **e-mail** or **E-mail**

emanate »*verb* (**emanates, emanating, emanated**) issue or spread out from a source: *warmth emanated from the fireplace.*
– SAY em-uh-**nayt**
emanation

emancipate »*verb* (**emancipates, emancipating, emancipated**) ❶ set free from restrictions. ❷ free someone from slavery.
– SAY i-**man**-si-payt
emancipation

 spelled with a **c**, not an **s**: **emancipate**

emasculate »*verb* (**emasculates, emaculating, emasculated**) ❶ make something weaker or less effective. ❷ deprive a man of his male role or identity.
– SAY i-**mass**-kyuu-layt
emasculation

embalm »*verb* (**embalms, embalming, embalmed**) specially treat a dead body in order to preserve it from decay.
embalmer

embankment »*noun* ❶ a wall or bank built to prevent flooding by a river. ❷ a bank of earth or stone built to carry a road or railway over low ground.

embargo »*noun* (plural **embargoes**) an official ban, especially on trade with a particular country.
» *verb* (**embargoes, embargoing, embargoed**) impose an embargo on something.

 add an **e** to make the plural (**embargoes**) and the past tense (**embargoed**)

embark »*verb* (**embarks, embarking, embarked**) ❶ go on board a ship or aircraft. ❷ (**embark on**) begin a new project or course of action.
embarkation

embarrass »*verb* (**embarrasses, embarrassing, embarrassed**) ❶ make someone feel awkward or ashamed. ❷ (**be embarrassed**) be in financial difficulties.
embarrassing
embarrassment

 remember, there are two **r**'s and two **s**'s in **embarrass, embarrassing**, etc.

embassy »*noun* (plural **embassies**) the official residence or offices of an ambassador.

 plural: drop the **y** and add **ies**: **embassies**

embattled »*adjective* ❶ prepared for battle, especially by being surrounded by enemy forces. ❷ facing many difficulties.

embed »*verb* (**embeds, embedding, embedded**) fix something firmly in a surrounding mass.

 em not im: **embed** (the spelling **imbed** is mainly American)
double the **d** in **embedded** and **embedding**

embellish »*verb* (**embellishes, embellishing, embellished**) ❶ make something more attractive by decorating it. ❷ add extra details to a story.

 embellish begins with an **e**, not an **i**, and has a double **l**

ember »*noun* a piece of burning wood or coal in a dying fire.

embezzle »*verb* (**embezzles, embezzling, embezzled**) steal money that you have been given responsibility for.
embezzlement
embezzler

 le not **el**: **embezzle**

embittered »*adjective* bitter or resentful.

emblazon »*verb* (**emblazons, emblazoning, emblazoned**) conspicuously display a design on something: *he wore a jacket emblazoned with the company logo.*
– SAY im-**blay**-z'n

emblem

emblematic »*adjective* representing a particular quality or idea.

embody »*verb* (**embodies, embodying, embodied**) ❶ give a tangible or visible form to an idea or quality. ❷ include or contain a part.
embodiment

embolden »*verb* (**emboldens, emboldening, emboldened**) make someone braver or more confident.

embolism »*noun* (in medicine) blockage of an artery by a clot of blood or an air bubble.
– SAY em-buh-li-z'm

emboss »*verb* (**embosses, embossing, embossed**) carve a raised design on something.

embrace (verb: **embraces, embracing, embraced**)

embrocation »*noun* a liquid medication rubbed on the body to relieve pain from strains.
– SAY em-bruh-**kay**-sh'n

embroider »*verb* (**embroiders, embroidering, embroidered**) ❶ sew decorative needlework patterns on something. ❷ add false or exaggerated details to a story.

embroidery (plural **embroideries**)

embroil »*verb* (embroils, embroiling, embroiled) involve someone deeply in a conflict or difficult situation.

> ☑ em not im: embroil

embryo »*noun* (plural embryos) an unborn or unhatched offspring in the early stages of development.
– SAY em-bri-oh

> ☑ be careful to spell **embryo** and **embryonic** with a **y**
> the plural has **os** not **oes**: embryos

embryonic »*adjective* ❶ relating to an embryo. ❷ at a rudimentary stage.
– SAY em-bri-on-ik

emend »*verb* (emends, emending, emended) correct and revise a text.
emendation

> ℹ do not confuse **emend** and **amend**: **emend** means 'correct and revise', while **amend** means 'make minor improvements to'

emerald »*noun* ❶ a green precious stone. ❷ a bright green colour.

emerge (verb: emerges, emerging, emerged)
emergence

emergency (plural emergencies)

> ☑ plural: drop the **y** and add **ies**: emergencies

emergent »*adjective* in the process of coming into being.

> ☑ ent not ant: emergent

emerges

emerging

emeritus »*adjective* retired but allowed to retain a title as an honour: *an emeritus professor.*
– SAY i-me-ri-tuhss

emery board »*noun* a strip of thin wood or card coated with a rough material and used as a nail file.

emetic »*adjective* causing vomiting.
– SAY i-met-ik

emigrant »*noun* a person who emigrates.

> ℹ an **emigrant**, who leaves the country, is the opposite of an **immigrant**, who comes in

emigrate »*verb* (emigrates, emigrating, emigrated) leave your own country in order to live in another.
emigration

emigre »*noun* a person who has emigrated.
– SAY em-i-gray

> ☑ **emigre** can also be written émigré, with acute accents on the **e**'s (as in the original French)

eminence »*noun* ❶ the quality of being very accomplished and respected in a particular area. ❷ an important or distinguished person.

eminent »*adjective* ❶ very accomplished and respected; distinguished. ❷ outstanding or conspicuous: *the eminent reasonableness of their claim.*
eminently

emir »*noun* a title of some Muslim rulers.
– SAY e-meer

> ☑ **emir** can also be spelled **amir**

emissary »*noun* (plural emissaries) a person sent as a diplomatic representative on a special mission.
– SAY em-i-suh-ri

emission »*noun* ❶ the action of emitting something. ❷ a substance which is emitted.

emit »*verb* (emits, emitting, emitted) ❶ discharge or send out something. ❷ make a sound.

> ☑ double the **t** in emitted and emitting

emollient »*adjective* ❶ softening or soothing the skin. ❷ attempting to avoid confrontation; calming.
– SAY i-mol-li-uhnt
emollience

emolument »*noun* a salary or fee received for holding a job or position.
– SAY i-mol-yuu-muhnt

emote »*verb* (emotes, emoting, emoted) show emotion in an exaggerated way.

emotion

emotional
emotionally

emotive

> ℹ **emotive** and **emotional** do not mean the same thing: **emotive** means 'arousing strong feeling' (as in *an emotive issue*), while **emotional** tends to mean 'showing strong feeling' (as in *an emotional response*)

empathize »*verb* (empathizes, empathizing, empathized) understand and share the feelings of someone else.

> ☑ many people prefer the alternative spellings **empathise**, **empathises**, etc.: both **s** and **z** spellings are correct

empathy »*noun* the ability to empathize with someone.

– **say** em-puh-thi

> i strictly, **empathy** does not mean the same thing as **sympathy**: if you have **empathy** for someone you understand and share their feelings, whereas if you have **sympathy** for them you feel sorry for them because they are suffering some misfortune

emperor

emphasis »*noun* (plural **emphases**)
❶ special importance or value given to something. ❷ stress placed on a word or words in speaking.
– **say** em-fuh-siss [singular], em-fuh-seez [plural]

> ✓ make the plural by changing the **-is** ending to **-es** (as in Latin): **emphases**

emphasize »*verb* (**emphasizes, emphasizing, emphasized**) give special importance or prominence to something.

> ✓ many people prefer the alternative spellings **emphasise, emphasises,** etc.: both **s** and **z** spellings are correct

emphatic »*adjective* ❶ showing or giving emphasis. ❷ definite and clear: *an emphatic win*.
emphatically

emphysema »*noun* a condition that affects the lungs, causing breathlessness.
– **say** em-fi-**see**-muh

empire

empirical »*adjective* based on observation or experience rather than theory or logic.
empirically

empiricism »*noun* the theory that all knowledge comes from experience and observation.
– **say** em-**pi**-ri-si-z'm
empiricist

emplacement »*noun* a structure or platform where a gun is placed for firing.

employ (verb: **employs, employing, employed**)
employable
employee
employer
employment

emporium »*noun* (plural **emporia** or **emporiums**) a large store selling a wide variety of goods.

> ✓ the plural can be either **emporia** (like the original Latin) or **emporiums**

empower »*verb* (**empowers, empowering, empowered**) ❶ give authority or power to someone. ❷ give strength and confidence to someone.
empowerment

empress (plural **empresses**)

empty (adjective: **emptier, emptiest**; verb: **empties, emptying, emptied**; plural **empties**)
emptiness

empty-handed

empty-headed

emptying

EMU »*abbreviation* Economic and Monetary Union.

emu »*noun* a flightless Australian bird similar to an ostrich.

emulate »*verb* (**emulates, emulating, emulated**) try to equal or surpass someone or something.
– **say** em-**yuu**-layt
emulation

emulsify »*verb* (**emulsifies, emulsifying, emulsified**) combine two liquids into an emulsion.
emulsification
emulsifier

emulsion »*noun* ❶ a smooth liquid in which particles of oil or fat are evenly distributed. ❷ a type of paint for walls and ceilings. ❸ a light-sensitive coating for photographic film.

> ✓ the ending is **sion**, not **tion: emulsion**

enable »*verb* (**enables, enabling, enabled**) ❶ provide with the ability or means to do something. ❷ make something possible.

enact »*verb* (**enacts, enacting, enacted**) ❶ pass a law. ❷ act out a role or play.
enactment

enamel »*noun* ❶ a layer of coloured glass applied to metal, glass, or pottery for decoration or protection. ❷ the hard substance that covers the crown of a tooth. ❸ a paint that dries to give a hard coat.
enamelled

> ✓ spell **enamelled** with two **l**'s (the spelling **enameled** is American)

enamoured »*adjective* (**enamoured of, with,** or **by**) filled with love or admiration for someone or something.
– **say** i-**nam**-erd

> ✓ **-our** not **-or: enamoured** (the spelling **enamored** is American)

en bloc »*adverb* all together, or all at once.
– **say** on **blok**

> ✓ **en bloc** (no **k**) is a French phrase meaning 'in a block'

e

encamp »*verb* (**encamps, encamping, encamped**) settle in or establish a camp.
encampment

encapsulate »*verb* (**encapsulates, encapsulating, encapsulated**) ❶ symbolize or sum up. ❷ summarize clearly in few words.
encapsulation

encase »*verb* (**encases, encasing, encased**) enclose or cover in a case.

encephalitis »*noun* an infection of the brain which makes it inflamed.
– **SAY** en-sef-uh-**ly**-tiss or en-kef-uh-**ly**-tiss

enchant »*verb* (**enchants, enchanting, enchanted**) ❶ delight or charm someone. ❷ put under a spell.
enchanter
enchantment

enchanting »*adjective* delightfully charming or attractive.
enchantingly

enchantress (plural **enchantresses**)

enchants

enchilada »*noun* a tortilla filled with meat or cheese and served with chilli sauce.
– **SAY** en-chi-**lah**-duh

encircle »*verb* (**encircles, encircling, encircled**) form a circle around something or someone.
encirclement

enclave »*noun* a small area of one country's territory surrounded by another country.
– **SAY** en-klayv

enclose (verb: **encloses, enclosing, enclosed**)

> ✓ use **en-**, not **in-**, to spell **enclose** and **enclosure**. **Inclose** and **inclosure** are now old-fashioned.

enclosure »*noun* ❶ a closed-off area. ❷ a document or object put in an envelope together with a letter.

encode »*verb* (**encodes, encoding, encoded**) convert something into a coded form.
encoder

encomium »*noun* (plural **encomiums** or **encomia**) a speech or piece of writing expressing praise.
– **SAY** en-**koh**-mi-uhm [singular], en-**koh**-mi-uh [plural]

> ✓ the plural can be either **encomia** (like the original Latin) or **encomiums**

encompass »*verb* (**encompasses, encompassing, encompassed**) ❶ surround and hold something. ❷ include comprehensively.

encore »*noun* a short extra performance given at the end of a concert in response to calls by the audience.
– **SAY** ong-kor

> ℹ **encore** is the French word for 'again'

encounter »*verb* (**encounters, encountering, encountered**) unexpectedly meet or be faced with someone or something.
»*noun* ❶ an unexpected or casual meeting. ❷ a confrontation.

encourage »*verb* (**encourages, encouraging, encouraged**) ❶ give support, confidence, or hope to someone. ❷ help the development of something.
encouragement
encouraging

encroach »*verb* (**encroaches, encroaching, encroached**) ❶ gradually intrude on a person's territory, rights, etc. ❷ advance gradually beyond expected or acceptable limits: *the sea has encroached all round the coast.*
encroachment

en croute »*adjective & adverb* in a pastry crust.
– **SAY** on kroot

> ✓ **en croute** is sometimes spelled with a circumflex accent on the **u**: **en croûte** (as in the original French)

encrust »*verb* (**encrusts, encrusting, encrusted**) cover with a hard crust.
encrustation

> ✓ use **en-**, not **in-**, to spell **encrust**. **Incrust** is now old-fashioned.

encrypt »*verb* (**encrypts, encrypting, encrypted**) convert a message into code.
– **SAY** en-**kript**
encryption

encumber »*verb* (**encumbers, encumbering, encumbered**) be a burden to someone.

encumbrance »*noun* a burden or impediment.

> ✓ the ending is **brance**, not **berance**: **encumbrance**

encyclopedia »*noun* a book or set of books giving information on many subjects.
encyclopedic

> ✓ as with other words such as **medieval**, the simpler **e** spelling is now more usual than **ae**: **encyclopedia** and **encyclopedic** rather than **encyclopaedia** and **encyclopaedic**

end (verb: **ends, ending, ended**)

endanger »*verb* (**endangers, endangering, endangered**) put in danger.
endangered

endear »*verb* (**endears, endearing, endeared**) make someone loved or liked by: *Flora's spirit endeared her to everyone.*
endearing

endearment »*noun* ❶ love or affection. ❷ a word or phrase expressing affection.

endears

endeavour »*verb* try hard to do or achieve something.
» *noun* ❶ an attempt to achieve something. ❷ concentrated hard work and effort.
– SAY in-**dev**-er or en-**dev**-er

> ✓ remember, **deav** not **dev**, and the ending is **-our** not **-or**: **endeavour** (the spelling **endeavor** is American)

ended

endemic »*adjective* ❶ (of a disease or condition) regularly found among particular people or in a certain area. ❷ (of a plant or animal) native to a certain area.
– SAY en-**dem**-ik

endgame »*noun* the final stage of a game such as chess or bridge.

ending

endive »*noun* a plant with bitter leaves, eaten in salads.
– SAY en-**dyv** or en-**div**

endless
endlessly

endocrine »*adjective* (of a gland) secreting hormones or other products directly into the blood.
– SAY en-duh-**kryn** or en-duh-**krin**

endorphin »*noun* a painkilling hormone within the brain and nervous system.
– SAY en-**dor**-fin

endorse »*verb* (**endorses, endorsing, endorsed**) ❶ publicly state that you approve of something or someone. ❷ sign a cheque on the back so that it can be paid into an account. ❸ mark details of a driving offence on a driving licence.
endorsement

> ✓ **en-** not **in-**: **endorse, endorsement**

endow »*verb* (**endows, endowing, endowed**) ❶ give someone your property, or leave it to them in your will. ❷ donate a large sum of money to an institution, from which they will be able to receive a regular income. ❸ (**be endowed with**) have as a natural quality or characteristic: *he was endowed with great physical strength.*

endowment »*noun* ❶ property or a regular income that has been given or left to a person or an institution. ❷ a quality or ability that you are born with.

endowment mortgage »*noun* a mortgage linked to an endowment insurance policy which is intended to repay the sum borrowed when the policy reaches the end of its term.

endows

endpaper »*noun* a leaf of paper at the beginning or end of a book, fixed to the inside of the cover.

ends

endurance »*noun* ❶ the ability to do or cope with something painful or difficult over a long period of time. ❷ the ability to last for a long time before wearing out.

endure »*verb* (**endures, enduring, endured**) ❶ patiently suffer something painful and prolonged. ❷ tolerate. ❸ remain in existence: *these cities have endured through time.*

endways

endwise

enema »*noun* (plural **enemas** or **enemata**) a procedure in which fluid is injected into the rectum to clean it out.
– SAY en-i-**muh** [singular], i-**nem**-uh-tuh [plural]

> ✓ in medicine the Latin or Greek plural **enemata** is sometimes used, but the form with **s** is more usual

enemy (plural **enemies**)

> ✓ plural: drop the **y** and add **ies**: **enemies**

energetic
energetically

energies

energize »*verb* (**energizes, energizing, energized**) give energy and enthusiasm to a person or group.

> ✓ many people prefer the alternative spellings **energise, energises**, etc.: both **s** and **z** spellings are correct

energy (plural **energies**)

> ✓ plural: drop the **y** and add **ies**: **energies**

enervate »*verb* (**enervates, enervating, enervated**) cause someone to feel drained of energy.
– SAY **en**-er-vayt
enervation

> ✓ only one **n**: **enervate**

enfant terrible »*noun* (plural **enfants terribles**) a person whose controversial attitude shocks or annoys others.
– **SAY** on-fon te-**ree**-bluh [singular and plural]

 plural: add **s** after both **enfant** and **terrible: enfants terribles**
enfant terrible is French for 'terrible child'

enfeeble »*verb* (**enfeebles, enfeebling, enfeebled**) weaken.
enfeeblement

enfilade »*noun* a volley of gunfire directed along a line from end to end.
– **SAY** en-fi-**layd** or **en**-fi-layd

enfold »*verb* (**enfolds, enfolding, enfolded**) envelop: *silence enfolded them.*

enforce (verb: **enforces, enforcing, enforced**)
enforceable
enforcement
enforcer

 en- not **in-: enforce**

enfranchise »*verb* (**enfranchises, enfranchising, enfranchised**) **❶** give a person or people the right to vote. **❷** (a historical term) free a slave.
– **SAY** in-**fran**-chyz
enfranchisement

 enfranchise cannot be spelled with an **ize** ending

engage »*verb* (**engages, engaging, engaged**) **❶** attract or involve someone's interest or attention. **❷** (**engage in** or **with**) become involved in. **❸** employ or hire someone. **❹** enter into a contract to do something. **❺** enter into combat with someone. **❻** (of a part of a machine or engine) move into position so as to begin to operate.

engaged

engagement

engages

engaging »*adjective* charming and attractive.
engagingly

engender »*verb* (**engenders, engendering, engendered**) give rise to.
– **SAY** in-**jen**-der

engine

engineer »*noun* **❶** a person qualified in engineering. **❷** a person who maintains or controls an engine or machine. **❸** a person who makes something happen.
»*verb* (**engineers, engineering, engineered**) **❶** design and build. **❷** skilfully arrange for something to occur.

engineering

engineers

English

Englishman (plural **Englishmen**)

Englishness

Englishwoman (plural **Englishwomen**)

engorge »*verb* (**engorges, engorging, engorged**) swell or cause to swell with a fluid.
– **SAY** in-**gorj**

engrain another way of spelling **INGRAIN**.

engrained another way of spelling **INGRAINED**.

engrave »*verb* (**engraves, engraving, engraved**) **❶** carve a text or design on a hard surface. **❷** (**be engraved on** or **in**) be permanently fixed in your mind.
engraver

engraving »*noun* **❶** a print made from an engraved plate or block. **❷** the process of carving a design on a hard surface.

engross »*verb* (**engrosses, engrossing, engrossed**) absorb all of someone's attention.
– **SAY** in-**grohss**

engulf »*verb* (**engulfs, engulfing, engulfed**) (of a natural force) sweep over someone or something and completely surround or cover them.

enhance »*verb* (**enhances, enhancing, enhanced**) increase the quality, value, or extent of something.
– **SAY** in-**hahnss**
enhancement
enhancer

enigma »*noun* a mysterious or puzzling person or thing.
– **SAY** i-**nig**-muh
enigmatic
enigmatically

enjoin »*verb* (**enjoins, enjoining, enjoined**) instruct or urge someone to do something.

enjoy (verb: **enjoys, enjoying, enjoyed**)
enjoyment

enjoyable
enjoyably

enjoyed

enjoying

enjoyment

enjoys

enlarge »*verb* (**enlarges, enlarging, enlarged**) **❶** make or become bigger. **❷** (**enlarge on** or **upon**) speak or write about something in greater detail.
enlargement
enlarger

enlighten »*verb* (enlightens, enlightening, enlightened) ❶ give someone greater knowledge and understanding. ❷ (enlightened) reasonable, tolerant, and well-informed.
enlightenment

enlist »*verb* (enlists, enlisting, enlisted) ❶ enrol or be enrolled in the armed services. ❷ ask for a person's help in doing something.
enlistment

enliven »*verb* (enlivens, enlivening, enlivened) ❶ make something more interesting. ❷ make someone more cheerful or animated.

en masse »*adverb* all together.
– SAY on mass

> ✓ en not on, and an e at the end: en masse is a French phrase meaning 'in a mass'

enmesh »*verb* (enmeshes, enmeshing, enmeshed) entangle.

enmity »*noun* (plural enmities) hostility.

> ✓ enm not emn: enmity

ennoble »*verb* (ennobles, ennobling, ennobled) ❶ give someone a noble rank or title. ❷ give someone greater dignity.
ennoblement

> ✓ double n: ennoble

ennui »*noun* a feeling of listlessness, boredom, and dissatisfaction.
– SAY on-wee

> ✓ double n: ennui (a French word)

enormity »*noun* (plural enormities) ❶ (the enormity of) the extreme seriousness of something bad. ❷ great size or scale: *the enormity of Einstein's intellect*. ❸ a serious crime or sin.

enormous
enormously

enough

enquire (verb: enquires, enquiring, enquired)
enquirer

> ℹ traditionally, in British English, enquire means 'ask', while inquire is used more specifically to mean 'make a formal investigation'

enquiry (plural enquiries)

> ✓ plural: drop the y and add ies: enquiries

enrage (verb: enrages, enraging, enraged)

enrapture »*verb* (enraptures, enrapturing, enraptured) give intense pleasure or joy to someone.

enrich »*verb* (enriches, enriching, enriched) ❶ improve the quality or value of something. ❷ make wealthier.
enrichment

enrol »*verb* (enrols, enrolling, enrolled) officially register or recruit someone as a member or student.
– SAY in-rohl
enrolment

> ✓ double the l in enrolling and enrolled, but not in enrols and enrolment (the spelling of these with two l's is American)

en route »*adverb* on the way.
– SAY on root

> ✓ en not on: en route is a French phrase

ensconce »*verb* (ensconces, ensconcing, ensconced) establish someone in a comfortable, safe, or secret place.
– SAY in-skonss

ensemble »*noun* ❶ a group of musicians, actors, or dancers who perform together. ❷ a passage for a whole choir or group of instruments. ❸ a group of items viewed as a whole: *her ensemble of tweed and cashmere*.
– SAY on-som-buhl

enshrine »*verb* (enshrines, enshrining, enshrined) ❶ place a precious object in an appropriate receptacle. ❷ preserve a right, tradition, or idea in a form that ensures it will be respected.

enshroud »*verb* (enshrouds, enshrouding, enshrouded) envelop something completely and hide it from view.
– SAY in-shrowd

ensign »*noun* ❶ a flag showing a ship's nationality. ❷ the lowest rank of commissioned officer in the US and some other navies.
– SAY en-syn

> ✓ -sign not -sine: ensign

enslave »*verb* (enslaves, enslaving, enslaved) ❶ make someone a slave. ❷ cause someone to lose freedom of choice or action: *youngsters enslaved by drugs*.
enslavement

ensnare »*verb* (ensnares, ensnaring, ensnared) catch someone or something in or as in a trap.

ensue »*verb* (ensues, ensuing, ensued) happen afterwards or as a result.

☑ drop the **e** in **ensuing**

en suite »*adjective & adverb* (of a bathroom) immediately next to a bedroom and forming a single unit with it.
– SAY on **sweet**

ℹ️ **en suite** is a French phrase meaning 'in sequence'

ensure »*verb* (**ensures, ensuring, ensured**) ❶ make certain that something will occur or be so. ❷ (**ensure against**) make sure that a problem does not occur.

ℹ️ unlike **insure**, **ensure** does not mean 'provide compensation in the event of damage to property'; however in more general senses **ensure** and **insure** mean the same thing

entail »*verb* (**entails, entailing, entailed**) involve something as an inevitable part or consequence: *a situation which entails considerable risks.*

entangle »*verb* (**entangles, entangling, entangled**) ❶ cause something to become tangled. ❷ involve someone in complicated circumstances.
entanglement

entente »*noun* a friendly understanding between states or factions.
– SAY on-**tont**

ℹ️ from French **entente cordiale**, which means 'friendly understanding'

enter (verb: **enters, entering, entered**)

enterprise »*noun* ❶ a project or undertaking. ❷ bold resourcefulness. ❸ a business or company.

☑ **ise** not **ize**: **enterprise**

enterprising »*adjective* showing initiative and resourcefulness.
enterprisingly

enters

entertain (verb: **entertains, entertaining, entertained**)

entertainer

entertaining
entertainingly

entertainment

entertains

enthral »*verb* (**entrals, enthralling, enthralled**) fascinate someone and hold their attention.
– SAY in-**thrawl**

☑ one **l** in **enthral** and **enthrals**, two in **enthralled** and **enthralling** (the spelling of the first two also with two **l**'s is American)

enthrone »*verb* (**enthrones, enthroning, enthroned**) ceremonially install a king, queen, or bishop on a throne.
enthronement

enthuse »*verb* (**enthuses, enthusing, enthused**) ❶ express your great enthusiasm for something. ❷ make someone enthusiastic.
– SAY in-**thyooz**

enthusiasm

enthusiast
enthusiastic
enthusiastically

enthusing

entice »*verb* (**entices, enticing, enticed**) attract someone by offering them something desirable.
enticement

entire
entirely

entirety »*noun* the whole of something.

☑ **ety** not **ity**: **entirety**

entities

entitle »*verb* (**entitles, entitling, entitled**) ❶ give someone a right to do or have something. ❷ give a title to a book, play, etc.
entitlement

entity »*noun* (plural **entities**) a thing which exists separately from other things.
– SAY **en**-ti-ti

entomb »*verb* (**entombs, entombing, entombed**) ❶ place someone in a tomb. ❷ bury someone or something in or under something.
entombment

entomology »*noun* the study of insects.
– SAY en-tuh-**mol**-uh-ji
entomological
entomologist

entourage »*noun* a group of people surrounding an important person.
– SAY on-toor-ah*zh*

entrails »*plural noun* a person's or animal's intestines or internal organs.

entrance[1] [way in to a place]

entrance[2] »*verb* (**entrances, entrancing, entranced**) ❶ fill someone with wonder and delight. ❷ cast a spell on someone.
– SAY in-**trahnss**

entrant »*noun* a person who enters, joins, or takes part in something.

entrap »*verb* (**entraps, entrapping, entrapped**) ❶ catch a person or animal in a trap. ❷ trick someone into committing a

crime in order to have them prosecuted.
entrapment

> ✓ one **p** in **entraps** and **entrapment**, two in **entrapping** and **entrapped**

entreat »*verb* (**entreats**, **entreating**, **entreated**) ask someone earnestly or anxiously to do something.

entreaty »*noun* (plural **entreaties**) an earnest or humble request.

> ✓ plural: drop the **y** and add **ies**: **entreaties**

entree »*noun* ❶ the main course of a meal. ❷ a dish served between the fish and meat courses at a formal dinner. ❸ the right to enter a place or social group.
– say **on**-tray

> ✓ **entree** can also be spelled **entrée**, with an acute accent above the **e** (as in the original French)

entrench »*verb* (**entrenches**, **entrenching**, **entrenched**) ❶ establish something so firmly that change is difficult: *prejudice is entrenched in our society.* ❷ establish a military force in fortified positions.
entrenchment

entrepreneur »*noun* a person who is successful in setting up businesses.
– say on-truh-pruh-**ner**
entrepreneurial

> ✓ **entre-** not **enter-** at the beginning, **-pren-** not **-pen-** in the middle: **entrepreneur** (a French word)

entries

entropy »*noun* (in physics) a quantity expressing how much of a system's thermal energy is unavailable for conversion into mechanical work.
– say **en**-truh-pi

entrust (verb: **entrusts**, **entrusting**, **entrusted**)

entry (plural **entries**)

> ✓ plural: drop the **y** and add **ies**: **entries**

entry-level »*adjective* suitable for a beginner or first-time user.

entwine »*verb* (**entwines**, **entwining**, **entwined**) wind or twist together.

E-number »*noun* a code number starting with the letter E, given to food additives numbered according to EU instructions.

enumerate »*verb* (**enumerates**, **enumerating**, **enumerated**) mention a number of things one by one.
– say i-**nyoo**-muh-rayt
enumeration

> ✓ one **n**, one **m**: **enumerate**

enunciate »*verb* (**enunciates**, **enunciating**, **enunciated**) ❶ say or pronounce something clearly. ❷ set something out clearly and precisely.
– say i-**nun**-si-ayt
enunciation

envelop (verb: **envelops**, **enveloping**, **enveloped**) [cover or surround something]
envelopment

> ✓ unlike the noun **envelope**, the verb **envelop** has no **e** at the end. An **e** is added in **enveloped** but not in **envelops** and **enveloping**.

envelope [flat paper container]

enveloped

enveloping

envelopment

envelops

enviable »*adjective* arousing or likely to arouse envy.
– say en-vi-uh-b'l
enviably

envied

envies

envious »*adjective* feeling or showing envy.
enviously

environment »*noun* ❶ the surroundings or conditions in which a person, animal, or plant lives or operates. ❷ (**the environment**) the natural world.
environmental
environmentally

> ✓ remember the **n** before **ment**: **environment**

environmentalist »*noun* a person who is concerned with the protection of the environment.
environmentalism

environmentally

environs »*plural noun* the surrounding area or district.

envisage »*verb* (**envisages**, **envisaging**, **envisaged**) ❶ see something as a possibility. ❷ form a mental picture of something.
– say in-**viz**-ij

envision »*verb* (**envisions**, **envisioning**, **envisioned**) visualize; envisage.

envoy »*noun* a messenger or representative.
– say **en**-voy

envy »*noun* (plural **envies**) ❶ a feeling of wanting something that belongs to

someone else and that you cannot have.
② (**the envy of**) a thing belonging to
someone else that people would like to
but cannot have.
» verb (**envies, envying, envied**) wish that
you had the same possessions or
opportunities as someone.

enzyme **»noun** a substance produced by a
living thing which helps a chemical
change within the body without being
changed itself.
– **SAY** en-zym

✓ zyme not **zime**: **enzyme**

Eocene **»adjective** relating to the geological
period from 56.5 to 35.4 million years
ago.
– **SAY** ee-oh-seen

eon American and scientific spelling of
AEON.

epaulette **»noun** an ornamental shoulder
piece on a military uniform.
– **SAY** e-puh-**let**

✓ a French word, **epaulette** has **tte** at
the end

ephemera **»plural noun** items of short-lived
interest or usefulness.
– **SAY** i-**fem**-uh-ruh or i-**feem**-uh-ruh

✓ one **m**, one **r**: **ephemera**

ephemeral **»adjective** lasting or living for a
very short time.

epic **»noun** **①** a long poem about the
actions of great men and women or the
past history of a nation. **②** a long film,
book, etc. that portrays the actions of
great men and women or covers a long
period of time.
» adjective **①** having to do with an epic.
② heroic or grand in scale or character.

epicene **»adjective** having male and female
characteristics or no characteristics of
either sex.
– **SAY** ep-i-seen

epicentre **»noun** the point on the earth's
surface directly above the origin of an
earthquake.

epicure **»noun** a person who takes
particular pleasure in good food and
drink.
– **SAY** e-pi-kyoor
epicurean

epidemic **»noun** **①** a widespread
occurrence of an infectious disease in a
community at a particular time. **②** a
sudden, widespread occurrence of

something undesirable: *an epidemic of
violent crime.*

✓ one **p**, one **d**, one **m**: **epidemic**

epidemiology **»noun** the study of the
spread and control of diseases.
– **SAY** ep-i-dee-mi-**ol**-uh-ji
epidemiologist

epidermis **»noun** **①** the surface layer of an
animal's skin, overlying the dermis. **②** the
outer layer of tissue in a plant.
epidermal

epidural **»noun** an anaesthetic introduced
into the space around the outermost
membrane of the spinal cord.
– **SAY** e-pi-**dyoor**-uhl

epiglottis **»noun** a flap of cartilage at the
root of the tongue, that prevents food
entering the windpipe.

✓ one **p**, two **t**'s: **epiglottis**

epigram **»noun** **①** a concise and witty
saying. **②** a short witty poem.
epigrammatic

✓ no **me** at the end: **epigram**

epigraph **»noun** **①** an inscription on a
building, statue, or coin. **②** a short
quotation introducing a book or chapter.

epilation **»noun** the removal of hair by the
roots.
– **SAY** e-pi-**lay**-sh'n
epilator

epilepsy **»noun** a disorder of the nervous
system that causes periodic loss of
consciousness or convulsions.
– **SAY** e-pi-lep-si
epileptic

epilogue **»noun** a section at the end of a
book or play which comments on what
has happened.
– **SAY** e-pi-log

✓ **ue** at the end: **epilogue** (the spelling
epilog is American)

epiphany **»noun** (plural **epiphanies**)
① (**Epiphany**) (in the bible) the time when
the Magi visited the infant Jesus and
realized he was the son of God. **②** a
sudden and inspiring revelation.
– **SAY** i-**pif**-uh-ni

episcopacy **»noun** **①** government of a
Church by bishops. **②** the bishops of a
region or church as a group.
– **SAY** i-**piss**-kuh-puh-si

episcopal **»adjective** having to do with a
bishop or bishops.
– **SAY** i-**piss**-kuh-puhl

episcopalian »*adjective* having to do with episcopacy or an episcopal Church.
» *noun* a supporter of government of a Church by bishops.
– SAY i-piss-kuh-**pay**-li-uhn
episcopalianism

episcopate »*noun* ❶ the office or term of office of a bishop. ❷ the bishops of a church or region as a group.
– SAY i-**piss**-kuh-puht

episiotomy »*noun* (plural **episiotomies**) a surgical cut made at the opening of the vagina during childbirth, to aid a difficult delivery.
– SAY i-pi-si-**ot**-uh-mi

episode

episodic »*adjective* ❶ made up of a series of separate events. ❷ occurring at irregular intervals.
– SAY e-pi-**sod**-ik

epistemology »*noun* the branch of philosophy that deals with knowledge.
– SAY i-piss-ti-**mol**-uh-ji

epistle »*noun* ❶ a letter. ❷ (**Epistle**) a book of the New Testament in the form of a letter from an Apostle.

epistolary »*adjective* ❶ relating to the writing of letters. ❷ (of a literary work) in the form of letters.
– SAY i-**piss**-tuh-luh-ri

> ✓ **ary** not **ery**: epistolary

epitaph »*noun* words written in memory of a person who has died.

epithet »*noun* a word or phrase describing someone or something's character or most important quality.

epitome »*noun* the perfect example of a quality or type.
– SAY i-**pit**-uh-mi

> ✓ **tome** not **tomy**: epitome

epitomize »*verb* (**epitomizes**, **epitomizing**, **epitomized**) be a perfect example of something.

> ✓ many people prefer the alternative spellings **epitomise**, **epitomises**, etc.: both **s** and **z** spellings are correct

epoch »*noun* a long and distinct period of time: *the Victorian epoch.*
– SAY **ee**-pok or **e**-pok
epochal

epoch-making »*adjective* of major importance; historic.

eponym »*noun* ❶ a word or phrase based on someone's name. ❷ a person after whom something is named.

– SAY ep-uh-nim

> ✓ **nym** not **nim**: eponym

eponymous »*adjective* ❶ (of a person) giving their name to something. ❷ (of a thing) named after a particular person.
– SAY i-**pon**-i-muhss

epoxy »*noun* (plural **epoxies**) a type of strong glue made from synthetic polymers.
– SAY i-**pok**-si

epsilon »*noun* the fifth letter of the Greek alphabet (E, ε).
– SAY **ep**-si-lon or ep-**sy**-lon

Epsom salts »*plural noun* crystals of magnesium sulphate used as a laxative.

equable »*adjective* ❶ calm and even-tempered. ❷ not varying greatly: *an equable climate.*
– SAY **ek**-wuh-b'l

equal (verb: **equals**, **equalling**, **equalled**)

> ✓ double the **l** in **equalling** and **equalled** (the spellings with a single **l** are American)

equalise another way of spelling EQUALIZE.

equality

equalize (verb: **equalizes**, **equalizing**, **equalized**)
equalization
equalizer

> ✓ many people prefer the alternative spellings **equalise**, **equalises**, etc., **equalisation**, and **equaliser**: both **s** and **z** spellings are correct

equalled
equalling
equally

> ℹ do not use the words **equally as** together, as in the sentence *follow-up discussion is equally as important*: just use either **equally** or **as** alone

equals

equanimity »*noun* calmness; evenness of temper.
– SAY ek-wuh-**nim**-i-ti or ee-kwuh-**nim**-i-ti

equate »*verb* (**equates**, **equating**, **equated**) ❶ consider one thing as equal to another. ❷ make two or more things the same in quantity or value: *we must equate supply and demand.*
– SAY i-**kwayt**

equation »*noun* ❶ the process of equating one thing with another. ❷ a statement that the values of two mathematical expressions are equal (indicated by the sign =). ❸ a formula representing the

changes which occur in a chemical reaction.
– SAY i-**kway**-zh'n

equator »*noun* an imaginary line around the earth at equal distances from the poles, dividing the earth into northern and southern hemispheres.
– SAY i-**kway**-ter

-or not -er: equator

equatorial »*adjective* having to do with the equator.
– SAY ek-wuh-**tor**-i-uhl

equerry »*noun* (plural **equerries**) an officer of the British royal household who assists members of the royal family.
– SAY **ek**-wuh-ri

equestrian »*adjective* relating to horse riding.
» *noun* a person on horseback.
– SAY i-**kwess**-tri-uhn

-an not -en: equestrian

equestrianism »*noun* the skill or sport of horse riding.

equestrienne »*noun* a woman on horseback.
– SAY i-**kwess**-tri-**en**

equidistant »*adjective* at equal distances.

equilateral »*adjective* having all its sides of the same length: *an equilateral triangle.*

equilibrium »*noun* (plural **equilibria**) ❶ a state in which opposing forces are balanced. ❷ the state of being physically balanced. ❸ a calm state of mind.
– SAY ee-kwi-**lib**-ri-uhm or ek-wi-**lib**-ri-uhm

like many other words ending in **um** derived from Latin, **equilibrium** has a plural ending in **a**: **equilibria**

equine »*adjective* ❶ relating to horses. ❷ resembling a horse: *her somewhat equine features.*
– SAY **ek**-wyn or **ee**-kwyn

equinoctial »*adjective* ❶ having to do with the equinox. ❷ at or near the equator.
– SAY ee-kwi-**nok**-sh'l or ek-wi-**nok**-sh'l

equinox »*noun* the time or date (twice each year, about 22 September and 20 March) when day and night are of equal length.
– SAY **ee**-kwi-noks or **ek**-wi-noks

equip (verb: **equips, equipping, equipped**)

double the **p** in **equipping** and **equipped**

equipment

equipoise »*noun* balance of forces or interests: *this temporary equipoise of power.*
– SAY **ek**-wi-poyz or **ee**-kwi-poyz

equipped

equipping

equips

equitable »*adjective* fair and impartial.
– SAY **ek**-wi-tuh-b'l
equitably

equitation »*noun* the art and practice of horse riding.
– SAY ek-wi-**tay**-sh'n

equity »*noun* (plural **equities**) ❶ the quality of being fair and impartial. ❷ (in law) a system of natural justice to be used alongside existing laws. ❸ the value of the shares issued by a company.

equivalent »*adjective* equal in value, amount, function, meaning, etc.
» *noun* a person or thing that is equivalent to another.
equivalence
equivalently

equivocal »*adjective* unclear in meaning or intention.
– SAY i-**kwiv**-uh-k'l
equivocally

equivocate »*verb* (**equivocates, equivocating, equivocated**) use language that can be understood in more than one way in order to conceal the truth or avoid committing yourself.
– SAY i-**kwiv**-uh-kayt
equivocation

era »*noun* a long and distinct period of time: *the Mesozoic era.*
– SAY **eer**-uh

eradicate »*verb* (**eradicates, eradicating, eradicated**) remove or destroy completely.
– SAY i-**rad**-i-kayt
eradication
eradicator

one r, one d: eradicate

erase »*verb* (**erases, erasing, erased**) ❶ rub out something written in pencil with a piece of rubber or plastic. ❷ remove all traces of something.
erasable
eraser
erasure

erbium »*noun* a soft silvery-white metallic chemical element.

ere »*preposition & conjunction* (an old word) before (in time).
– SAY air

erect (verb: **erects, erecting, erected**)
erector

 er not err: erect

erectile »*adjective* able to become erect.
– SAY i-**rek**-tyl

erecting

erection

erector

erects

ergo »*adverb* therefore.

ergo is a Latin word

ergonomics »*noun* the study of people's efficiency in their working environment.
– SAY er-guh-**nom**-iks
ergonomic

Erin »*noun* (an old word) Ireland.
– SAY e-rin

Eritrean [of Eritrea]
– SAY e-ri-**tray**-uhn

ermine »*noun* (plural **ermine** or **ermines**)
❶ a stoat. ❷ the white winter fur of the stoat.
– SAY er-min

erode »*verb* (**erodes, eroding, eroded**)
❶ gradually wear or be worn away.
❷ gradually destroy: *this humiliation has eroded Jean's confidence.*
– SAY i-**rohd**

erogenous »*adjective* (of a part of the body) sensitive to sexual stimulation.
– SAY i-**roj**-i-nuhss

gen not gin: erogenous

erosion »*noun* the process of eroding or the result of being eroded.
– SAY i-**roh**-zh'n
erosive

erotic »*adjective* having to do with sexual desire or excitement.
– SAY i-**rot**-ik
erotically

erotica »*noun* erotic literature or art.

erotically

eroticise another way of spelling EROTICIZE.

eroticism »*noun* ❶ the quality of being erotic. ❷ sexual desire or excitement.

eroticize »*verb* (**eroticizes, eroticizing, eroticized**) give erotic qualities to something.

 many people prefer the alternative spellings **erotise, erotises**, etc.: both **s** and **z** spellings are correct

err »*verb* (**errs, erring, erred**) ❶ make a mistake. ❷ do wrong.

errand [short journey to deliver or collect something]

errant »*adjective* ❶ straying from the accepted course or standards. ❷ (an old word) travelling in search of adventure: *a knight errant.*
– SAY e-ruhnt

 ant not ent: errant

errata plural of ERRATUM.

erratic »*adjective* moving or doing something in an irregular or uneven way.
– SAY ir-**rat**-ik
erratically

 two r's, one t: erratic

erratum »*noun* (plural **errata**) ❶ a mistake in a book or printed document. ❷ (**errata**) a list of corrected errors added to a publication.
– SAY e-**rah**-tuhm or e-**ray**-tuhm

like many other words ending in **um** derived from Latin, **erratum** has a plural ending in **a**: **errata**

erred

erring

erroneous »*adjective* incorrect.
– SAY i-**roh**-ni-uhss
erroneously

neous not nious: erroneous

error

errs

ersatz »*adjective* ❶ (of a product) artificial and not as good as the real thing. ❷ not genuine.
– SAY **er**-sats or **er**-zats

ers not erts or erz: ersatz (a German word meaning 'replacement')

Erse »*noun* the Scottish or Irish Gaelic language.

erstwhile »*adjective* former.

erudite »*adjective* having or showing knowledge gained from reading or study.
– SAY e-**roo**-dyt
eruditely
erudition

erupt (verb: **erupts, erupting, erupted**)
[break out suddenly]

do not confuse **erupt** with **irrupt**, which means 'enter forcibly or suddenly'

eruption
eruptive

erupts

escalate »*verb* (escalates, escalating, escalated) ❶ increase rapidly. ❷ become more serious.
escalation

escalator

 -or not -er: escalator

escalope »*noun* a thin slice of meat coated in breadcrumbs and fried.
– SAY i-**ska**-luhp or i-**skol**-uhp

escapade »*noun* an adventure.

escape (verb: escapes, escaping, escaped)
escapee
escaper

escape clause »*noun* a clause in a contract which gives the conditions under which one party can be freed from an obligation.

escaped

escapee

escapement »*noun* a mechanism that connects and regulates the movement of a clock or watch.

escaper

escapes

escaping

escapism »*noun* the doing of enjoyable things that stop you thinking about unpleasant realities.
escapist

 there is no e after the p: escapism

escapologist »*noun* an entertainer whose act consists of breaking free from ropes and chains.
– SAY ess-kuh-**pol**-uh-jist
escapology

escarpment »*noun* a long, steep slope at the edge of an area of high land.
– SAY i-**skarp**-muhnt

eschatology »*noun* the part of theology concerned with death, judgement, and destiny.
– SAY ess-kuh-**tol**-uh-ji
eschatological

 remember the ch: eschatology

eschew »*verb* (eschews, eschewing, eschewed) deliberately avoid doing or indulging in something.
– SAY iss-**choo**

escort (verb: escorts, escorting, escorted)

escritoire »*noun* a small writing desk with drawers.
– SAY ess-kri-**twar**

✓ note the oire ending: escritoire is a French word

escudo »*noun* (plural escudos) the basic unit of money of Portugal.

✓ the plural of escudo has os not oes: escudos

escutcheon »*noun* a shield or emblem bearing a coat of arms.

Eskimo (plural Eskimo or Eskimos)

ℹ although some people consider the word Eskimo to be offensive, it is still widely used as there is no other term which correctly covers both the Inuit and Yupik peoples

✓ the plural of Eskimo can be the same or has os (not oes) at the end: Eskimo or Eskimos

esophagus etc. American spelling of OESOPHAGUS etc.

esoteric »*adjective* intended for or understood by only a small number of people with a specialized knowledge.
– SAY e-suh-**te**-rik or ee-suh-**te**-rik
esoterically

✓ there is no k at the end: esoteric

ESP »*abbreviation* extrasensory perception.

espadrille »*noun* a light canvas shoe with a plaited fibre sole.
– SAY ess-puh-**dril**

✓ ille not ill: espadrille is a French word

especial

especially [in particular]

ℹ although especially and specially can both mean 'particularly', they are not exactly the same. Only especially means 'in particular, chiefly', as in *he hated them all, especially Thomas*, and only specially means 'for a special purpose', as in *the car was specially made for the occasion*.

Esperanto »*noun* an artificial language intended to be used as an international way of communicating.
– SAY ess-puh-**ran**-toh

espied

espies

espionage »*noun* the practice of spying or of using spies.
– SAY ess-pi-uh-nah*zh*

esplanade »*noun* a long, open, level area used for leisurely walking.

– **SAY** ess-pluh-**nayd** or ess-pluh-nayd

espousal »*noun* the action of espousing.

espouse »*verb* (**espouses**, **espousing**, **espoused**) support or adopt a particular belief or way of doing things.
– **SAY** i-**spowz** or e-**spowz**

espresso »*noun* (plural **espressos**) strong black coffee made by forcing steam through ground coffee beans.
– **SAY** ess-**press**-oh

 es not **ex**: espresso is an Italian word. Spell the plural with **os** not **oes**: **espressos**.

esprit de corps »*noun* a feeling of pride and loyalty that unites the members of a group.
– **SAY** e-spree duh **kor**

a French phrase meaning 'spirit of the body'

espy »*verb* (**espies**, **espying**, **espied**) catch sight of something.

Esquire »*noun* a polite title placed after a man's name when no other title is used.

essay »*noun* a piece of writing on a particular subject.
»*verb* (**essays**, **essaying**, **essayed**) attempt to do something: *Donald essayed a smile.*
essayist

essence

ence not **ance**: essence

essential
essentially

essential oil »*noun* a natural oil extracted from a plant, used in making perfume or in aromatherapy.

establish (verb: **establishes**, **establishing**, **established**) [set up]

establishment »*noun* ❶ the action of establishing something. ❷ a business organization, public institution, or household.

estate

estate agent »*noun* a person whose business is selling and renting out houses and flats for clients.
estate agency

estate car »*noun* a car which has a large storage area behind the seats and an extra door at the rear.

esteem »*noun* respect and admiration.
»*verb* (**esteems**, **esteeming**, **esteemed**) respect and admire someone.

ester »*noun* (in chemistry) an organic compound formed by a reaction between an acid and an alcohol.

– **SAY** ess-ter

esthetic etc. American spelling of **AESTHETIC** etc.

estimable »*adjective* deserving respect and admiration.

estimate (verb: **estimates**, **estimating**, **estimated**)
estimation

Estonian

estranged »*adjective* ❶ feeling less close to or familiar with something. ❷ (of someone's husband or wife) no longer living with them.
estrangement

estrogen etc. American spelling of **OESTROGEN** etc.

estuary »*noun* (plural **estuaries**) the mouth of a large river where it becomes affected by tides.
– **SAY** ess-**tyuh**-ri
estuarine

 note the **a** after the **u**: estuary

Estuary English »*noun* an English accent containing features of received pronunciation and London speech.

ETA »*abbreviation* estimated time of arrival.

eta »*noun* the seventh letter of the Greek alphabet (**H**, **η**).
– **SAY** ee-tuh

e-tailer »*noun* a retailer who sells goods over the Internet.

et al. »*abbreviation* and others.

et al. is short for the Latin phrase **et alii** 'and others'

etc. »*abbreviation* et cetera.

et cetera »*adverb* and other similar things; and so on.
– **SAY** et **set**-uh-ruh

avoid the mistake of pronouncing **et cetera** as **ek** rather than **et**
et cetera is a Latin phrase meaning 'and the rest'

etch »*verb* (**etches**, **etching**, **etched**) ❶ engrave metal, glass, or stone by applying a protective coating, drawing on this with a needle, and then covering the surface with acid to attack the exposed parts. ❷ cut a text or design on a surface. ❸ cause something to be clearly defined.
etching

eternal »*adjective* lasting or existing forever.
eternally

eternity »*noun* (plural **eternities**)
❶ unending time. ❷ (in informal English) an undesirably long period of time.

> ☑ plural: drop the **y** and add **ies**: **eternities**

ethane »*noun* a flammable gas present in petroleum and natural gas.
– **SAY** ee-thayn or e-thayn

ethanol »*noun* = ETHYL ALCOHOL.
– **SAY** eth-uh-nol

ether »*noun* ❶ a highly flammable liquid used as an anaesthetic and as a solvent. ❷ the upper regions of air.
– **SAY** ee-ther

> ☑ when used to refer to the air or sky, **ether** can also be spelled **aether** (this spelling cannot be used for the chemical meaning)

ethereal »*adjective* ❶ extremely delicate and light. ❷ heavenly or spiritual.
– **SAY** i-**theer**-i-uhl
ethereally

> ☑ the ending is **eal** not **ial**: **ethereal**

ethic »*noun* a set of moral principles.

> ☑ there is no **k** at the end: **ethic**

ethical »*adjective* ❶ having to do with beliefs and principles about what is right and wrong. ❷ morally correct.
ethically

ethics »*noun* ❶ a set of beliefs and principles stating what is right and wrong or how an activity should be carried out. ❷ the branch of philosophy concerned with moral principles.

Ethiopian

ethnic »*adjective* ❶ having to do with a group of people from the same national or cultural background. ❷ referring to a person's origin by birth rather than by present nationality. ❸ belonging to a non-Western cultural tradition.
ethnically
ethnicity

> ☑ there is no **k** at the end: **ethnic**

ethnic cleansing »*noun* the expelling or killing of members of one ethnic or religious group in an area by those of another.

ethnicity

ethnic minority »*noun* a group within a community which has a different ethnic origin from the main population.

ethnography »*noun* the scientific description of peoples and cultures.

ethnology »*noun* the study of the characteristics of different peoples and the differences and relationships between them.

ethology »*noun* the science of animal behaviour.
– **SAY** ee-**thol**-uh-ji

ethos »*noun* the characteristic spirit of a culture, era, or community.
– **SAY** ee-**thoss**

ethyl alcohol »*noun* the chemical name for alcohol.
– **SAY** ee-thyl or eth-uhl

etiolated »*adjective* (of a plant) pale and weak due to a lack of light.
– **SAY** ee-ti-uh-lay-tid

etiquette »*noun* the code of polite behaviour in a society.
– **SAY** et-i-ket

> ☑ ette not et: **etiquette**

etymology »*noun* (plural **etymologies**) an account of the origins and the developments in meaning of a word.
– **SAY** e-ti-**mol**-uh-ji
etymological
etymologically

EU »*abbreviation* European Union.

eucalyptus »*noun* an evergreen Australasian tree valued for its wood, oil, gum, and resin.
– **SAY** yoo-kuh-**lip**-tuhss

> ℹ the best plural is 'eucalyptus trees'. A eucalyptus is sometimes known as a **eucalypt** (plural **eucalypts**).

Eucharist »*noun* ❶ the Christian ceremony commemorating the Last Supper, in which consecrated bread and wine are consumed. ❷ the consecrated bread and wine used in this ceremony.
– **SAY** yoo-kuh-rist
Eucharistic

eugenics »*noun* the science of ways of increasing the occurrence of desirable characteristics in a population by choosing which people become parents.
– **SAY** yoo-**jen**-iks

eulogies

eulogise another way of spelling EULOGIZE.

eulogistic

eulogize »*verb* (**eulogizes**, **eulogizing**, **eulogized**) praise someone highly.
– **SAY** yoo-luh-jyz

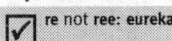 many people prefer the alternative spellings **eulogise**, **eulogises**, etc.: both **s** and **z** spellings are correct

eulogy »*noun* (plural **eulogies**) a speech or piece of writing that praises someone highly.
– SAY yoo-luh-ji
eulogistic

eunuch »*noun* a man who has had his testicles removed.
– SAY yoo-nuhk

euphemism »*noun* a less direct word used instead of one that is harsh or blunt when referring to something unpleasant or embarrassing.
– SAY yoo-fuh-mi-z'm
euphemistic
euphemistically

euphonic

euphonious »*adjective* sounding pleasant.
– SAY yoo-foh-ni-uhss
euphoniously

euphonium »*noun* a brass musical instrument resembling a small tuba.
– SAY yoo-foh-ni-uhm

euphony »*noun* the quality of being pleasing to the ear.
– SAY yoo-fuh-ni
euphonic

euphoria »*noun* a feeling of intense happiness.
– SAY yoo-for-i-uh
euphoric
euphorically

Eurasian »*adjective* ❶ of mixed European (or European-American) and Asian parentage. ❷ relating to Eurasia (the land mass of Europe and Asia together).

eureka »*exclamation* a cry of joy or satisfaction when you discover something.
– SAY yuu-ree-kuh

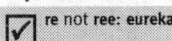 **re** not **ree**: eureka

euro »*noun* (plural **euros**) the single European currency, introduced in the European Union in 1999.

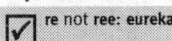 the plural of **euro** has **os** not **oes**: euros

Eurocentric »*adjective* seeing European culture as the most important.
Eurocentrism

Eurocrat »*noun* (mainly used in an insulting way) a bureaucrat in the administration of the European Union.

European

europium »*noun* a soft silvery-white metallic element.

Euro-sceptic »*noun* a person who is opposed to increasing the powers of the European Union.

Eustachian tube »*noun* a narrow passage leading from the pharynx to the cavity of the middle ear.
– SAY yoo-stay-sh'n

euthanasia »*noun* the painless killing of a patient suffering from an incurable disease or in an irreversible coma.
– SAY yoo-thuh-nay-zi-uh

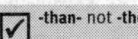 -**than**- not -**then**-: euthanasia

evacuate (verb: **evacuates**, **evacuating**, **evacuated**)
evacuation

evacuee »*noun* a person who is evacuated from a place of danger.

evade »*verb* (**evades**, **evading**, **evaded**) ❶ escape or avoid. ❷ avoid giving a direct answer to a question. ❸ avoid paying tax or duty.

evaluate »*verb* (**evaluates**, **evaluating**, **evaluated**) form an idea of the amount or value of something.
evaluation
evaluative
evaluator

evanescent »*adjective* soon passing out of sight, memory, or existence.
– SAY ev-uh-ness-uhnt
evanescence

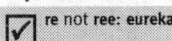 -**scent** not -**sent**: evanescent

evangelical »*adjective* ❶ having to do with the teaching of the gospel or Christianity. ❷ having to do with a tradition within Protestant Christianity which emphasizes Biblical authority and personal conversion. ❸ showing very strong support for something.
» *noun* a member of the evangelical tradition in the Christian Church.
evangelically

evangelise another way of spelling EVANGELIZE.

evangelist »*noun* ❶ a person who sets out to convert others to the Christian faith. ❷ the writer of one of the four Gospels. ❸ a passionate supporter of something.
evangelism
evangelistic

evangelize »*verb* (**evangelizes**, **evangelizing**, **evangelized**) ❶ set out to convert people to Christianity. ❷ preach the gospel.
evangelization

✓ many people prefer the alternative
spellings **evangelise, evangelising,**
etc.: both **s** and **z** spellings are correct

evaporate (verb: **evaporates, evaporating,
evaporated**)
evaporation

✓ **-por-** not **-pour-: evaporate**

evasion »*noun* the action of avoiding
something.

evasive »*adjective* ❶ avoiding committing
yourself or revealing things about
yourself. ❷ (of an action) intended to
avoid or escape something.
evasively
evasiveness

eve »*noun* ❶ the day or period of time
immediately before an event or occasion.
❷ evening.

even (verb: **evens, evening, evened**)
evenly
evenness

even-handed »*adjective* fair and impartial.
even-handedly
even-handedness

evening

evening primrose »*noun* a plant with pale
yellow flowers that open in the evening.

evening star »*noun* the planet Venus, seen
shining in the western sky after sunset.

evenly

even money »*noun* (in betting) odds
offering an equal chance of winning or
losing.

evenness

evens

evensong »*noun* a Christian service of
evening prayers, psalms, and canticles.

event

eventful
eventfully

✓ **-ful** not **-full: eventful**

eventide »*noun* (an old word) evening.

eventing »*noun* a riding competition in
which competitors must take part in each
of several contests.

eventual
eventually

eventuality »*noun* (plural **eventualities**) a
possible event or outcome.

✓ plural: drop the **y** and add **ies:
eventualities**

eventually

eventuate »*verb* (**eventuates, eventuating,
eventuated**) ❶ occur as a result.
❷ (**eventuate in**) lead to as a result.

ever

evergreen »*adjective* (of a plant) retaining
green leaves throughout the year (the
opposite of *deciduous*).

everlasting
everlastingly

evermore

every

everybody

everyday

Everyman »*noun* an ordinary or typical
human being.

ℹ **Everyman** has a capital **E** because it
was originally the name of a
character in a medieval play

everyone

everything

everywhere

evict »*verb* (**evicts, evicting, evicted**) expel
someone legally from a property.
eviction

evidence »*noun* ❶ information indicating
whether something is true or valid. ❷ the
information used in a law court to
establish facts.
» *verb* (**evidences, evidencing, evidenced**) be
or show evidence of something.

✓ **ence** not **ance: evidence**

evident
evidently

✓ **ent** not **ant: evident**

evidential »*adjective* having to do with
evidence.

evidently

evil
evilly

✓ double the **l** to spell **evilly**

evince »*verb* (**evinces, evincing, evinced**)
reveal the presence of something.

eviscerate »*verb* (**eviscerates, eviscerating,
eviscerated**) remove a person's intestines.
– **SAY** i-**viss**-uh-rayt

✓ do not forget the **c** after the **s:
eviscerate**

evocation

evocative »*adjective* bringing strong
images, memories, or feelings to mind.

– say i-vok-uh-tiv
evocatively

evoc not evok: **evocative**

evoke »*verb* (**evokes, evoking, evoked**)
❶ bring a feeling or memory into someone's mind. ❷ obtain a response.
– say i-vohk
evocation

c not k in **evocation**

evolution »*noun* ❶ the process by which different kinds of animals and plants develop from earlier forms. ❷ gradual development.
evolutionary

evolutionist »*noun* a person who accepts the theories of evolution and natural selection.

evolve »*verb* (**evolves, evolving, evolved**)
❶ develop gradually. ❷ (of an organism) develop from earlier forms by evolution.

ewe »*noun* a female sheep.

ewer »*noun* a large jug with a wide mouth.
– say yoo-er

ex »*noun* (plural **exes**) (in informal English) a former husband, wife, boyfriend, or girlfriend.

exacerbate »*verb* (**exacerbates, exacerbating, exacerbated**) make something that is already bad worse.
– say ig-zass-er-bayt
exacerbation

exact (verb: **exacts, exacting, exacted**)
exactly
exactness

exacting »*adjective* making great demands on your endurance or skill.

exaction »*noun* ❶ the action of demanding something: *the exaction of payment from debtors.* ❷ a sum of money demanded.

exactitude »*noun* the quality of being exact.

exactly

exactness

exacts

exaggerate (verb: **exaggerates, exaggerating, exaggerated**)
exaggeratedly
exaggeration

double g: **exaggerate**

exalt »*verb* (**exalts, exalting, exalted**)
❶ praise someone or something highly.
❷ give someone or something a higher rank or status.

exaltation »*noun* ❶ extreme happiness.
❷ the action of exalting.

exalted »*adjective* ❶ having high rank or status. ❷ (of an idea) noble.

exalting

exalts

exam

examination

examine (verb: **examines, examining, examined**)
examinee
examiner

example

exasperate »*verb* (**exasperates, exasperating, exasperated**) irritate someone intensely.
exasperated
exasperating
exasperation

excavate »*verb* (**excavates, excavating, excavated**) ❶ make a hole or channel by digging. ❷ dig material out from the ground. ❸ carefully remove earth from an area in order to find buried remains.
excavation
excavator

exceed (verb: **exceeds, exceeding, exceeded**)

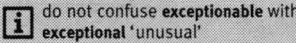
eed not ede: **exceed**

exceedingly

exceeds

excel (verb: **excels, excelling, excelled**)

double the l to spell **excelling** and **excelled**

excellence

Excellency »*noun* (plural **Excellencies**) (**His, Your**, etc. **Excellency**) a title or form of address for ambassadors and some other high officials.

excellent
excellence

excelling

excels

except (verb: **excepts, excepting, excepts**)
excepting

do not forget the c in **except**, and do not confuse **except** with **accept**, which means 'agree to receive or do'

exception

exceptionable »*adjective* causing disapproval or offence.

do not confuse **exceptionable** with **exceptional** 'unusual'

e

exceptional [unusual]
exceptionally

> ℹ️ do not confuse **exceptional** with **exceptionable**, which means 'causing disapproval or offence'

excepts

excerpt »*noun* a short extract from a film or piece of music or writing.
» *verb* (**excerpts, excerpting, excerpted**) take a short extract from a text.

> ✓ do not forget the **c** after the **x** or the **p** before the **t**: **excerpt**

excess (plural **excesses**) [too much]

> ✓ do not confuse **excess** with **access**, which means 'a way of getting to something'

excessive
excessively

exchange (verb: **exchanges, exchanging, exchanged**)
exchangeable
exchanger

exchange rate »*noun* the value at which one currency may be exchanged for another.

exchanges

exchequer »*noun* ❶ a royal or national treasury. ❷ (**Exchequer**) the account at the Bank of England into which public money is paid.

> ✓ **-chequer** not **-checker**: **exchequer**

excise¹ »*noun* a tax imposed on certain goods, commodities, and licences.

excise² »*verb* (**excises, excising, excised**) ❶ cut something out surgically. ❷ remove a section from a text or piece of music.
excision

> ✓ **excise** cannot be spelled with an **ize** ending

excitable
excitability
excitably

> ✓ **-table** not **-teable**: **excitable**

excite (verb: **excites, exciting, excited**)
excitation
excited
excitedly

excitement

excites

exciting
excitingly

exclaim (verb: **exclaims, exclaiming, exclaimed**)

exclamation

> ✓ **exclam-** not **exclaim-**: **exclamation**

exclamation mark »*noun* a punctuation mark (!).

exclamatory

> ✓ **ory** not **ery**: **exclamatory**

exclude (verb: **excludes, excluding, excluded**)
excluder
excluding

exclusion

exclusive
exclusively
exclusiveness
exclusivity

excommunicate »*verb* (**excommunicates, excommunicating, excommunicated**) officially bar someone from the sacraments and services of the Christian Church.
– SAY eks-kuh-**myoo**-ni-kayt
excommunication

excoriate »*verb* (**excoriates, excoriating, excoriated**) ❶ (in medicine) damage or remove part of the surface of the skin. ❷ criticize severely.
– SAY ek-**skor**-i-ayt
excoriation

excrement »*noun* waste material passed from the body through the bowels.
– SAY **eks**-kri-muhnt
excremental

excrescence »*noun* an abnormal growth protruding from a body or plant.
– SAY eks-**kress**-uhnss

> ✓ note the **c** after the **s**: **excrescence**

excreta »*noun* waste material that is passed out of the body.
– SAY ek-**skree**-tuh

excrete »*verb* (**excretes, excreting, excreted**) pass waste material from the body.
excretion
excretory

> ✓ **ete** not **eet**: **excrete**

excruciating »*adjective* ❶ intensely painful. ❷ very embarrassing, awkward, or tedious.
excruciatingly

exculpate »*verb* (**exculpates, exculpating, exculpated**) say that someone is not guilty of doing something wrong.

– say eks-kul-payt

excursion »*noun* a short journey or trip taken for pleasure.

excuse (verb: **excuses, excusing, excused**)
excusable
excusably

ex-directory

execrable »*adjective* extremely bad or unpleasant.
– say ek-si-kruh-b'l
execrably

 -able not -ible: execrable

execrate »*verb* (**execrates, execrating, execrated**) feel great hatred for someone or something.
– say ek-si-krayt
execration

execute (verb: **executes, executing, executed**)
executable

execution

executioner

executive »*adjective* having the power to put plans, actions, or laws into effect.
» *noun* ❶ a senior manager in a business organization. ❷ a group of people who run an organization or business. ❸ (**the executive**) the branch of a government responsible for putting plans, actions, or laws into effect.

executor »*noun* a person appointed by someone to carry out the terms of their will.
– say ig-zek-yuu-ter

 -or not -er: executor

executrix »*noun* (plural **executrices** or **executrixes**) a female executor.
– say ig-zek-yoo-triks [singular], ig-zek-yoo-tri-seez or ig-zek-yoo-triks-iz [plural]

exemplar »*noun* a person or thing serving as a typical example or a good model.
– say eg-zem-pler

 ar not er: exemplar

exemplary »*adjective* ❶ representing the best of its kind: *exemplary behaviour.* ❷ (of a punishment) serving as a warning.

exemplify »*verb* (**exemplifies, exemplifying, exemplified**) be or give a typical example of something.
exemplification

exempt »*adjective* not having to do or pay something that other people have to do or pay.
» *verb* (**exempts, exempting, exempted**) make someone exempt.
exemption

 remember the **p** in **exempt** and **exemption**

exercise (verb: **exercises, exercising, exercised**) [physical activity; use or apply a right or power]

unlike most verbs ending in **ise**, **exercise** cannot be spelled with an **ize** ending
do not confuse **exercise** with **exorcize** meaning 'drive out evil spirits'

exert »*verb* (**exerts, exerting, exerted**) ❶ use a force, influence, or quality to make something happen. ❷ (**exert yourself**) make a physical or mental effort.
exertion

exes plural of EX.

exeunt »*verb* (in a play) a stage direction telling actors to leave the stage.
– say ek-si-uhnt

ℹ **exeunt** is a Latin word meaning 'they go out'

exfoliant »*noun* a cosmetic for exfoliating the skin.

exfoliate »*verb* (**exfoliates, exfoliating, exfoliated**) ❶ shed or be shed from a surface in scales or layers. ❷ rub the skin with a grainy substance to remove dead cells.
exfoliation
exfoliator

ex gratia »*adverb & adjective* (of payment) given as a gift or favour, not as a legal requirement.
– say eks gray-shuh

ℹ a Latin phrase meaning 'from favour'

exhale »*verb* (**exhales, exhaling, exhaled**) ❶ breathe out. ❷ give off vapour or fumes.
exhalation

exhaust (verb: **exhausts, exhausting, exhausted**)
exhausted
exhausting
exhaustion

exhaustive »*adjective* covering all aspects fully.
exhaustively
exhaustiveness

exhausts

e

exhibit (verb: **exhibits, exhibiting, exhibited**)
exhibitor

> ✓ do not double the **t** in **exhibiting** and **exhibited**

exhibition

exhibitionism »*noun* extravagant behaviour that is intended to make people notice you.
exhibitionist

exhibitor

exhibits

exhilarate »*verb* (**exhilarates, exhilarating, exhilarated**) make someone feel very happy or animated.
exhilaration

> ✓ remember the **h**: **exhilarate**

exhort »*verb* (**exhorts, exhorting, exhorted**) strongly urge someone to do something.
exhortation

exhume »*verb* (**exhumes, exhuming, exhumed**) dig out from the ground something that has been buried.
– say ek-**syoom** or ig-**zyoom**
exhumation

exigency »*noun* (plural **exigencies**) an urgent need or demand.
– say ek-si-**juhn**-si or ig-**zi**-juhn-si

exigent »*adjective* pressing; urgent: *exigent demands.*

exiguous »*adjective* very small or few.
– say eg-**zig**-yoo-uhss

exile »*noun* ❶ the state of being barred from your own country. ❷ a person who lives in exile.
»*verb* (**exiles, exiling, exiled**) expel and bar someone from their own country.

exist (verb: **exists, existing, existed**)

existence
existent

> ✓ the ending is **ence** not **ance**: **existence**

existential »*adjective* ❶ having to do with existence. ❷ concerned with existentialism.
– say eg-zi-**sten**-sh'l
existentially

existentialism »*noun* a theory in philosophy which says that each human being exists as a free individual, with responsibility for their own actions, in a world that otherwise has no meaning.
existentialist

existing

exists

exit (verb: **exits, exiting, exited**)

> ✓ do not double the **t** to spell **exiting** and **exited**

exodus »*noun* (plural **exoduses**) a mass departure of people.

ex officio »*adverb & adjective* as a result of a person's position or status: *the chairman was an ex officio member of the committee.*
– say eks uh-**fish**-i-oh

> ℹ a Latin phrase meaning 'out of duty'

exonerate »*verb* (**exonerates, exonerating, exonerated**) ❶ declare someone free from blame. ❷ release someone from a duty.
exoneration

exorbitant »*adjective* (of an amount charged) unreasonably high.
exorbitantly

> ✓ there is no **h** in **exorbitant**

exorcize »*verb* (**exorcizes, exorcizing, exorcizes**) drive an evil spirit from a person or place.
exorcism
exorcist

> ✓ many people prefer the alternative spellings **exorcise, exorcises**, etc.: both **s** and **z** spellings are correct. Do not confuse **exorcize** or **exorcise** with **exercise**.

exotic »*adjective* ❶ coming from or characteristic of a distant foreign country. ❷ strikingly colourful or unusual: *an exotic outfit.*
exotically
exoticism

exotica »*plural noun* things considered exotic.
– say eg-**zot**-i-kuh

exotically

exoticism

expand »*verb* (**expands, expanding, expanded**) ❶ make or become larger or more extensive. ❷ (**expand on**) give a fuller account of something.
expandable
expanded

expanse »*noun* a wide continuous area of something: *the green expanse of forest.*

expansion »*noun* the action or an instance of expanding.
expansionary

expansive »*adjective* ❶ covering a wide area. ❷ relaxed, friendly, and communicative.

expansively
expansiveness

expat »*noun* = EXPATRIATE.

expatiate »*verb* (**expatiates, expatiating, expatiated**) speak or write in detail on a subject.
– SAY ek-**spay**-shi-ayt
expatiation

expatriate »*noun* a person who lives outside their native country.
– SAY eks-**pat**-ri-uht

expect (verb: **expects, expecting, expected**) [think likely to happen or arrive; require]

> ℹ️ do not confuse **expect** with **aspect** meaning 'a particular feature or appearance'

expectant »*adjective* ❶ believing or hoping that something is about to happen. ❷ pregnant.
expectancy
expectantly

expectation

expected

expecting

expectorant »*noun* a medicine which helps to bring up phlegm from the air passages, used to treat coughs.

expectorate »*verb* (**expectorates, expectorating, expectorated**) cough or spit out phlegm from the throat or lungs.
expectoration

expects

expedient »*adjective* ❶ useful or helpful for a particular purpose. ❷ useful in achieving something, rather than morally correct.
»*noun* a means of achieving something.
expediency
expediently

> ✅ **ent** not **ant**: **expedient**

expedite »*verb* (**expedites, expediting, expedited**) make something happen more quickly: *he promised to expedite economic reforms.*
– SAY eks-pi-dyt
expediter

expedition »*noun* ❶ a journey with a particular purpose, made by a group of people. ❷ promptness in doing something.
expeditionary

expeditious »*adjective* quick and efficient: *an expeditious investigation.*
expeditiously

expel »*verb* (**expels, expelling, expelled**)
❶ force someone or something out.
❷ force a pupil to leave a school.

> ✅ single **l** in **expel** and **expels**, double **l** in **expelled** and **expelling**

expend »*verb* (**expends, expending, expended**) spend or use up a resource.

expendable »*adjective* ❶ suitable to be used once only. ❷ able to be sacrificed because unimportant when compared to an overall purpose.
expendability

expended

expending

expenditure »*noun* ❶ the action of spending money. ❷ the amount of money spent.

> ✅ **dit** not **dat**: **expenditure**

expends

expense

> ✅ the ending is **ense**, not **ence**: **expense**

expensive
expensively
expensiveness

experience (verb: **experiences, experiencing, experienced**)
experienced

experiential »*adjective* having to do with experience and observation: *experiential learning.*

experiment (verb: **experiments, experimenting, experimented**)
experimental
experimentally
experimentation
experimenter

expert
expertly

expertise »*noun* great skill or knowledge in a particular field.
– SAY ek-sper-**teez**

expertly

expiate »*verb* (**expiates, expiating, expiated**) do something to show that you are sorry for having done something wrong.
– SAY **ek**-spi-ayt
expiation

expire »*verb* (**expires, expiring, expired**)
❶ (of a document or agreement) cease to be valid. ❷ (of a period of time) come to an end. ❸ (of a person) die. ❹ breath out air from the lungs.

expiry »*noun* the end of the period for which something is valid.
– SAY ek-**spy**-ri

explain (verb: explains, explaining, explained)
explainable
explainer

explanation

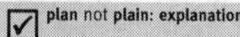
✓ **plan** not **plain**: ex**plan**ation

explanatory »*adjective* giving the reason for something, or making something clear.

expletive »*noun* a swear word.

explicable »*adjective* able to be explained.
– SAY ik-**splik**-uh-b'l

explicate »*verb* (explicates, explicating, explicated) ❶ analyse and develop an idea in detail. ❷ analyse a literary work in order to reveal its meaning.
explication

explicit »*adjective* ❶ clear, detailed, and easy to understand. ❷ showing or describing sexual activity openly and clearly.
– SAY ek-**spli**-sit
explicitly
explicitness

explode (verb: explodes, exploding, exploded)

exploit »*verb* (exploits, exploiting, exploited) ❶ make good use of a resource. ❷ make use of someone unfairly.
»*noun* a daring act.
exploitable
exploitation
exploitative
exploiter

explore (verb: explores, exploring, explored)
exploration
exploratory
explorer

explosion

✓ **s** not **t**: explo**s**ion

explosive
explosively
explosiveness

exponent »*noun* ❶ a promoter of an idea or theory. ❷ a person who does a particular thing skilfully. ❸ (in mathematics) a raised figure beside a number indicating how many times that number is to be multiplied by itself (e.g. 3 in $2^3 = 2 \times 2 \times 2$).

exponential »*adjective* ❶ (of an increase) becoming more and more rapid. ❷ having to do with a mathematical exponent.
– SAY eks-puh-**nen**-sh'l
exponentially

export »*verb* (exports, exporting, exported) ❶ send goods or services to another country for sale. ❷ introduce an idea or custom to another country.
»*noun* ❶ the exporting of goods or services. ❷ an exported item.
exportation
exporter

expose¹ (verb: exposes, exposing, exposed) [reveal]
exposer

expose² »*noun* a report in the news revealing shocking information about someone.
– SAY ek-**spoh**-zay

✓ often written with an acute accent on the final **e**: exposé (as in the original French)

exposed

exposer

exposes

exposing

exposition »*noun* ❶ a careful setting out of the facts or ideas involved in something. ❷ an exhibition. ❸ (in music) the part of a movement in which the principal themes are first presented.

expositor »*noun* a person or thing that explains complicated ideas or theories.
expository

expostulate »*verb* (expostulates, expostulating, expostulated) express strong disapproval or disagreement.
expostulation

exposure

expound »*verb* (expounds, expounding, expounded) present and explain a theory or idea systematically.

express (plural expresses; verb: expresses, expressing, expressed)
expressible

expression
expressionless

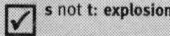
✓ remember the double **s** in expression, expressive, and related words

expressionism »*noun* a style in art, music, or drama in which the artist or writer shows the inner world of emotion rather than external reality.
expressionist

expressionless

expressive »*adjective* clearly showing thoughts or feelings.
expressively
expressiveness

expropriate »*verb* (**expropriates, expropriating, expropriated**) take property from its owner with official approval.
– say eks-**proh**-pri-ayt
expropriation

expulsion »*noun* the action of expelling.

expunge »*verb* (**expunges, expunging, expunged**) remove something completely.

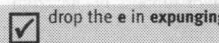 drop the **e** in **expunging**

expurgate »*verb* (**expurgates, expurgating, expurgated**) remove unsuitable material from a text.
– say eks-per-gayt
expurgation
expurgator

exquisite »*adjective* ❶ of great beauty and delicacy. ❷ highly refined: *exquisite taste*. ❸ intensely felt: *the most exquisite kind of agony*.
exquisitely

extant »*adjective* still in existence.

extemporaneous »*adjective* = **EXTEMPORARY**.
– say ek-stem-puh-**ray**-ni-uhss
extemporaneously

extemporary »*adjective* spoken or done without preparation.
– say ek-**stem**-puh-ruh-ri

extempore »*adjective & adverb* spoken or done without preparation: *extempore public speaking*.
– say ek-**stem**-puh-ri

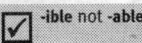 the ending is **ore** not **ory: extempore** is from the Latin phrase *ex tempore* 'on the spur of the moment'

extemporize »*verb* (**extemporizes, extemporizing, extemporized**) make something up as you go along.
– say ek-**stem**-puh-ryz
extemporization

✓ many people prefer the alternative spellings **extemporise, extemporises,** etc.,: both **s** and **z** spellings are correct

extend (verb: **extends, extending, extended**)
extendable
extender

extensible »*adjective* able to be extended.
extensibility

✓ **-ible** not **-able: extensible**

extension

extensive »*adjective* ❶ covering a large area. ❷ large in amount or scale.
extensively

extent

extenuating »*adjective* showing reasons why an offence should be treated less seriously: *extenuating circumstances*.
– say ek-**sten**-yoo-ay-ting
extenuation

exterior »*adjective* having to do with the outside of something.
» *noun* the outer surface or structure of something.

exterminate »*verb* (**exterminates, exterminating, exterminated**) destroy something completely.
extermination
exterminator

external »*adjective* ❶ having to do with the outside of something. ❷ coming from outside an organization or situation. ❸ having to do with another country or institution: *external affairs*.
» *noun* (**externals**) the outward aspects of something.
externally

externalize »*verb* (**externalizes, externalizing, externalized**) express a thought or feeling in words or actions.
externalization

✓ many people prefer the alternative spellings **externalise, externalises,** etc.: both **s** and **z** spellings are correct

externally

extinct »*adjective* ❶ no longer in existence. ❷ (of a volcano) not having erupted in recorded history.

extinction

extinguish (verb: **extinguishes, extinguishing, extinguished**)
extinguisher

extirpate »*verb* (**extirpates, extirpating, extirpated**) search out and destroy something completely.
– say ek-**ster**-payt
extirpation

extol »*verb* (**extols, extolling, extolled**) praise someone or something enthusiastically.

✓ single **l** in **extol** and **extols,** but remember to double it in **extolled** and **extolling**

extort »*verb* (**extorts, extorting, extorted**) obtain something by force, threats, or other unfair means.

extortion
extortionist

☑ tion not **sion** or **cion**: extortion

extortionate »*adjective* (of a price) much too high.
extortionately

extortionist

extorts

extra

extract (verb: **extracts**, **extracting**, **extracted**)
extraction

extractor

☑ the ending is **-or**, not **-er**: extractor

extracts

extra-curricular »*adjective* (of an activity at a school or college) done in addition to the normal curriculum.

extradite »*verb* (**extradites**, **extraditing**, **extradited**) hand over a person accused or convicted of committing a crime in a foreign country to the legal authority of that country.
– SAY ek-**struh**-dyt
extraditable
extradition

extramarital »*adjective* occurring outside marriage.
– SAY eks-truh-**ma**-ri-t'l
extramaritally

extramural »*adjective* (of a course of study) for people who are not full-time members of an educational establishment.
– SAY eks-truh-**myoor**-uhl

extraneous »*adjective* ❶ unrelated to the subject being dealt with. ❷ of external origin: *extraneous noise.*
– SAY ek-**stray**-ni-uhss
extraneously

☑ no **i** in extraneous, anywhere

extraordinaire »*adjective* outstanding in a particular capacity: *a gardener extraordinaire.*
– SAY ek-struh-or-di-**nair**

☑ remember the final **e**, as in French: extraordinaire

extraordinary
extraordinarily

☑ remember to keep the **a** of extra: extraordinary

extrapolate »*verb* (**extrapolates**, **extrapolating**, **extrapolated**) use a fact or conclusion that is valid for one situation and apply it to a larger or different one.

– SAY ek-**strap**-uh-layt
extrapolation

extrasensory perception »*noun* the supposed ability to perceive things by means other than the known senses, e.g. by telepathy.
– SAY eks-truh-**sen**-suh-ri

☑ the ending is **ory** not **ary**: extrasensory

extraterrestrial »*adjective* coming from beyond the earth.
» *noun* a fictional or supposed being from outer space.

extravagant »*adjective* ❶ spending or using more than is necessary or more than you can afford. ❷ costing a great deal. ❸ exceeding what is reasonable.
extravagance
extravagantly

extravaganza »*noun* an elaborate and spectacular entertainment.
– SAY ek-stra-vuh-**gan**-zuh

extreme
extremely

extremist »*noun* a person who holds extreme political or religious views.
extremism

extremity »*noun* (plural **extremities**) ❶ the furthest point or limit. ❷ (**extremities**) a person's hands and feet. ❸ extreme hardship.

☑ plural: drop the **y** and add **ies**: extremities

extricate »*verb* (**extricates**, **extricating**, **extricated**) ❶ free someone from a difficult situation. ❷ free something that is trapped.
extrication

extrinsic »*adjective* coming or operating from outside.
– SAY eks-**trin**-sik
extrinsically

extrovert »*noun* an outgoing, socially confident person.
» *adjective* having to do with an extrovert: *his extrovert personality.*
extroverted

☑ extro not **extra**: extrovert

extrude »*verb* (**extrudes**, **extruding**, **extruded**) thrust or force something out.
extrusion

exuberant »*adjective* ❶ lively and cheerful. ❷ growing thickly: *exuberant foliage.*

– SAY ig-**zyoo**-buh-ruhnt
exuberance
exuberantly

exude »*verb* (**exudes, exuding, exuded**)
❶ discharge or be discharged slowly and steadily. ❷ display an emotion or quality strongly and openly.

exult »*verb* (**exults, exulting, exulted**) show or feel triumphant joy.
exultant
exultantly
exultation

eye (verb: **eyes, eyeing** or **eying, eyed**)
[organ of sight]

> ✓ the present participle of the verb **eye** can be either **eyeing** or **eying**

eyeball
eyebrow
eye-catching
eyed
eyeful

> ✓ -ful not -full: **eyeful**

eyeglass »*noun* (plural **eyeglasses**) a single lens for correcting defective eyesight.

eyeing see the note at EYE.
eyelash

eyelet »*noun* a small round hole made in leather or cloth for threading a lace or cord through, or the metal ring strengthening it.

eyelid

eyeliner »*noun* a cosmetic applied as a line round the eyes.

eye-opener »*noun* a revealing event or situation.

eyepiece »*noun* the lens that is closest to the eye in a microscope or other optical instrument.

eyes
eyeshadow
eyesight

eyesore »*noun* a thing that is very ugly.

eye teeth »*plural noun* the canine teeth.

eyewash

eyewitness »*noun* (plural **eyewitnesses**) a person who has seen something happen.

eying see the note at EYE.

eyrie »*noun* a large nest of an eagle or other bird of prey.
– SAY **eer**-i or **I**-ri

> ℹ do not confuse **eyrie** with **eerie**, which means 'strange and frightening'

Ff

fable »*noun* ❶ a short story which contains a message about doing right and wrong. ❷ a supernatural story containing elements of myth and legend.

fabled »*adjective* famous; mythical.

fabric

fabricate »*verb* (**fabricates, fabricating, fabricated**) construct or manufacture.
fabrication
fabricator

fabulous
fabulously
fabulousness

facade »*noun* ❶ the face of a building. ❷ a deceptive outward appearance.
– SAY fuh-**sahd**

> ✓ can also be written **façade**, with a cedilla on the **c** (as in the original French)

face (verb: **faces, facing, faced**)

facecloth

faceless
facelessness

facelift

faces

face-saving

facet »*noun* ❶ one side of something with many sides, especially of a cut gemstone. ❷ a particular aspect of something: *the many facets of this process.*
– SAY **fa**-sit
faceted

✓ one t in faceted

facetious »*adjective* treating serious issues with inappropriate humour.
– SAY fuh-**see**-shuhss
facetiously
facetiousness

✓ spell with a t even though the pronunciation is *sh*: facetious

facia another way of spelling FASCIA.

facial »*adjective* having to do with the face.
» *noun* a beauty treatment for the face.
– SAY **fay**-sh'l
facially

facile »*adjective* simplistic and superficial: *a facile remark*.
– SAY **fa**-syl
facilely
facileness

facilitate »*verb* (facilitates, facilitating, facilitated) make something easy or easier.
– SAY fuh-**sil**-i-tayt
facilitation
facilitator

✓ one c, one l: facilitate

facility (plural facilities)

✓ one c, one l: facility
plural: drop the y and add ies: facilities

facing

facsimile »*noun* ❶ an exact copy of written or printed material. ❷ a fax.
– SAY fak-**sim**-i-li

✓ spelled with a c not an x: facsimile

fact

faction »*noun* a small group within a larger one that disagrees with some of its beliefs.
factional

factious »*adjective* having to do with opposition or disagreement.
– SAY **fak**-shuhss

factitious »*adjective* artificially created.
– SAY fak-**ti**-shuhss

factor »*noun* ❶ a circumstance, fact, or influence that contributes to a result. ❷ (in mathematics) a number or quantity that when multiplied with another produces a given number or expression.
» *verb* (factors, factoring, factored) (factor in or out) include (or exclude) something as relevant when making a decision.

factorial »*noun* (in mathematics) the product of a number and all those numbers below it, down to 1.

ℹ for example, **factorial 4**, written **4!**, is $4 \times 3 \times 2 \times 1$ (equal to 24)

factories

factoring

factorize »*verb* (factorizes, factorizing, factorized) (in mathematics) break a quantity down into factors.
factorization

✓ many people prefer the alternative spellings **factorise, factorises**, etc., and **factorisation**: both s and z spellings are correct

factors

factory (plural factories)

✓ plural: drop the y and add ies: factories

factotum »*noun* (plural factotums) a person employed to do all kinds of work.
– SAY fak-**toh**-tuhm

✓ watch out for words ending in **um** derived from Latin: they often have plurals ending in **a**: addend*um*/addend*a*; substrat*um*/substrat*a*. This is not the case with **factotum**, which is derived from Latin *fac!* 'do!' + *totum* 'the whole thing', and has a regular plural ending in s: factotums.

factual
factually

faculty »*noun* (plural faculties) ❶ a basic mental or physical power. ❷ a talent. ❸ a department or group of related departments in a university. ❹ (in American English) the teaching or research staff of a university or college.

✓ plural: drop the y and add ies: faculties

fad
faddish

faddy (adjective: faddier, faddiest)
faddiness

fade (verb: fades, fading, faded)

faeces »*plural noun* waste matter remaining after food has been digested, discharged from the bowels.
– SAY **fee**-seez

✓ scientists often use the American spelling with just e rather than **ae**: feces (this pattern is followed in other British and American spellings, e.g. an*ae*mia/an*e*mia)

Faeroese another way of spelling FAROESE.

faff (verb: faffs, faffing, faffed)

fag (verb: fags, fagging, fagged)

faggot »*noun* ❶ (in British English) a ball of seasoned chopped liver which is baked or fried. **❷** a bundle of sticks bound together as fuel. **❸** (used in an insulting way in American English) a homosexual man.

> ☑ double g: **faggot**

fags

Fahrenheit »*noun* a scale of temperature on which water freezes at 32 degrees and boils at 212 degrees.
– **SAY** fa-ruhn-hyt

> ☑ remember the first **h**, and the **e** comes before the **i**: the scale was named after the German physicist Gabriel Daniel *Fahrenheit*

fail (verb: **fails, failing, failed**)
failing

fail-safe

failure

fain (an old word) »*adjective* **❶** pleased or willing: *the traveller was fain to proceed.* **❷** obliged by the situation.
»*adverb* gladly: *I would fain get a little rest.*

> ⓘ do not confuse **fain** with **feign**, which means 'pretend'

faint (adjective: **fainter, faintest**; verb: **faints, fainting, fainted**) [only just visible or perceptible; very slight; lose consciousness]
faintly
faintness

> ⓘ do not confuse **faint** with **feint**, which means 'mock attack' or 'make a deceptive movement'

faint-hearted

fainting

faintly

faintness

faints

fair (adjective: **fairer, fairest**) [treating people equally or justly; light coloured; a festival or carnival]
fairly
fairness

> ⓘ do not confuse **fair** (*that's not fair* | *fair-haired* | *all the fun of the fair*) with **fare**, which means 'money paid by passengers' (*pay the fare*), 'range of food offered' (*traditional English fare*), or 'make progress' (*fare thee well*)

fairground

fairies

fairing »*noun* an external structure added to increase streamlining on a vehicle, boat, or aircraft.

Fair Isle »*noun* a traditional multicoloured geometric design used in knitwear.

> ⓘ from *Fair Isle* in the Shetlands

fairly

fairness

fairway »*noun* **❶** the part of a golf course between a tee and a green. **❷** a channel in a river or harbour which can be used by shipping.

fair-weather friend

fairy »*noun* (plural **fairies**)

> ☑ plural: drop the **y** and add **ies: fairies**

fairyland

fairy ring »*noun* a ring of dark grass caused by fungi, once believed to have been made by fairies dancing.

fairy tale

> ☑ add a hyphen if you use this word as an adjective, as in *a fairy-tale romance*

fait accompli »*noun* a thing that has been done or decided and cannot now be altered.
– **SAY** fayt uh-**kom**-pli

> ⓘ **fait accompli** is a French phrase meaning 'accomplished fact'

faith

faithful

faithfully
faithfulness

> ⓘ you use **yours faithfully** to end a formal letter in which you do not address the recipient by their personal name but with a formula such as 'Dear Sir'

> ☑ **-ful** not **-full: faithful**

faithless

faithlessly
faithlessness

fajitas »*plural noun* a Mexican dish of strips of spiced meat with vegetables and cheese, wrapped in a tortilla.
– **SAY** fuh-**hee**-tuhz

> ☑ spelled **j** but pronounced **h: fajitas** (a word of Spanish origin)

fake (verb: **fakes, faking, faked**)
faker
fakery

fakir »*noun* a Muslim or Hindu holy man who lives by begging.
– **SAY** fay-keer or fa-keer

falafel »*noun* a Middle Eastern dish of mashed chickpeas with spices, made into balls and deep-fried.
– SAY fuh-**laff**-uhl

 an Arabic word, often also spelled **felafel** in English; both **falafel** and **felafel** are correct

falcon

falconry »*noun* the keeping and training of birds of prey, especially for hunting.
falconer

fall (verb: **falls**, **falling**, **fell**; past participle **fallen**)
faller

fallacies

fallacious »*adjective* based on a fallacy; misleading.
– SAY fuh-**lay**-shuhss

 double l: **fallacious**

fallacy »*noun* (plural **fallacies**) ❶ a mistaken belief. ❷ a false or misleading argument.
– SAY **fal**-luh-si

fallback

fallen past participle of **FALL**.

faller

fall guy »*noun* a person who is blamed for something that is not their fault.

fallible »*adjective* capable of making mistakes or being wrong.
– SAY **fal**-li-b'l
fallibility
fallibly

 double l, and **-ible** not **-able**: **fallible**

falling

falling star »*noun* a meteor or shooting star.

fall-off »*noun* a decrease.

Fallopian tubes »*noun* the pair of tubes along which eggs travel from the ovaries to the uterus of a female mammal.
– SAY fuh-**loh**-pi-uhn

 capital F, double l: **Fallopian**, after the Italian anatomist Gabriello *Fallopio*

fallout »*noun* ❶ radioactive particles spread over a wide area after a nuclear explosion. ❷ the unfavourable side effects of a situation.

fallow »*adjective* ❶ (of farmland) ploughed and harrowed but left for a period without being sown. ❷ (of a period of time) when very little is done or achieved: *a fallow period.*
fallowness

falls

false
falsely
falseness
falsity

falsehood »*noun* ❶ a statement that is not true. ❷ the condition of being false.

falsely

falseness

false pretences »*noun* behaviour that is intended to deceive.

falsetto »*noun* (plural **falsettos**) a high-pitched singing voice above a person's natural range, used by male singers.
– SAY fawl-**set**-toh or fol-**set**-toh

 the plural of **falsetto**, an Italian word, has **os** not **oes**: **falsettos**

falsify »*verb* (**falsifies**, **falsifying**, **falsified**) alter something so as to mislead: *they had falsified evidence.*
falsification

falsity

falter »*verb* (**falters**, **faltering**, **faltered**) ❶ lose strength or momentum. ❷ move or speak hesitantly.

fame

famed »*adjective* famous; well known.

familial »*adjective* having to do with a family.
– SAY fuh-**mil**-i-uhl

familiar
familiarity
familiarly

familiarize »*verb* (**familiarizes**, **familiarizing**, **familiarized**) ❶ (**familiarize with**) give someone knowledge of something. ❷ make something easier to understand.
familiarization

 many people prefer the alternative spellings **familiarise**, **familiarises**, etc., and **familiarisation**: both **s** and **z** spellings are correct

familiarly

family (plural **families**)

 plural: drop the **y** and add **ies**: **families**

family tree »*noun* a diagram showing the relationship between people in a family.

famine »*noun* a period when food is very scarce.

famished »*adjective* (in informal English) very hungry.

famous
 famously

fan (verb: **fans, fanning, fanned**)

 double the **n** in **fanned** and **fanning**

fanatic »*noun* a person who is too enthusiastic about something.
 fanatical
 fanatically
 fanaticism

fan belt »*noun* a belt driving the fan that cools the radiator of a motor vehicle.

fanciable

fancier

fanciful »*adjective* ❶ existing only in the imagination. ❷ very unusual or creative: *lavish and fanciful costumes.*
 fancifully

 -ful not -full: fanciful

fancy (plural **fancies**; adjective: **fancier, fanciest**; verb: **fancies, fancying, fancied**)
 fanciable
 fancier

fancy-free »*adjective* not in love.

fancying

fandango »*noun* (plural **fandangoes** or **fandangos**) a lively Spanish dance for two people.

 the plural of **fandango** can have **oes** or **os: fandangoes** or **fandangos**

fanfare »*noun* a short tune played on brass instruments to announce someone or something.

fang »*noun* ❶ a canine tooth of a dog or wolf. ❷ a tooth with which a snake injects poison.

fanlight »*noun* a small semicircular window over a door or another window.

fanned

fannies

fanning

fanny (plural **fannies**)

fans

fantasia »*noun* ❶ a musical composition that does not follow a conventional form. ❷ a musical composition based on several familiar tunes.
 – **say** fan-**tay**-zi-uh or fan-tuh-**zee**-uh

fantasize »*verb* (**fantasizes, fantasizing, fantasized**) daydream about something that you want to happen: *he fantasized about emigrating.*
 fantasist

✓ many people prefer the alternative spellings **fantasise, fantasises**, etc.: both **s** and **z** spellings are correct

fantastic
 fantastical
 fantastically

fantasy »*noun* (plural **fantasies**) ❶ the imagining of things that do not exist in reality. ❷ a daydream about something that you want to happen. ❸ a type of fiction that involves magic and adventure.

✓ you sometimes come across the old spelling **phantasy**, which is similar to the original Greek form
plural: drop the **y** and add **ies: fantasies**

fanzine »*noun* a magazine for fans of a particular performer or interest.

FAQ »*abbreviation* (in computing) frequently asked questions.

far (adverb & adjective: **further, furthest** or **farther, farthest**)

ℹ for an explanation of the difference between **farther** and **further**, see the note at **FURTHER**

farad »*noun* the basic unit of electrical capacitance.
 – **say** fa-rad

faraway »*adjective* ❶ remote or distant. ❷ lost in thought; dreamy: *a faraway look.*

farce »*noun* ❶ a comedy based on situations which are ridiculous and improbable. ❷ an absurd event.

farcical »*adjective* absurd or ridiculous.

fare (verb: **fares, faring, fared**) [money paid by passengers; range of food offered; make progress]

ℹ do not confuse **fare** (*pay the fare | traditional English fare | fare thee well*) with **fair**, which means 'treating people equally or justly' (*that's not fair*), 'light coloured' (*fair-haired*), or 'festival or carnival' (*all the fun of the fair*)

Far East »*noun* China, Japan, and other countries of east Asia.
 Far Eastern

fares

farewell

far-fetched »*adjective* exaggerated or unlikely: *a far-fetched plot.*

far-flung »*adjective* distant or remote.

faring present participle of **FARE**.

farm (verb: **farms, farming, farmed**)
 farmer

farmhand

f

farmhouse

farming

farms

farmstead »*noun* a farm and its buildings.

farmyard

Faroese (plural **Faroese**) [of the Faroe Islands]
– SAY fair-oh-**eez**

> ✓ **Faroese** can also be spelled **Faeroese**: both forms are correct

farrago »*noun* (plural **farragos**) a confused mixture.
– SAY fuh-**rah**-goh or fuh-**ray**-goh

> ✓ double **r**: **farrago**
> the plural of **farrago** has **os** not **oes**: **farragos**

far-reaching

farrier »*noun* a person who shoes horses.
farriery

farrow »*noun* a litter of pigs.
»*verb* (**farrows, farrowing, farrowed**) (of a sow) give birth to piglets.

far-seeing

Farsi »*noun* the modern form of the Persian language.
– SAY far-**see**

far-sighted

fart (verb: **farts, farting, farted**)

farther [more far]

> ℹ️ for an explanation of the difference between **farther** and **further**, see the note at **FURTHER**

farthermost [most far]

farthest [most far]

farthing »*noun* a former British coin worth a quarter of an old penny.

farting

farts

fascia »*noun* ❶ a board covering the ends of rafters or other fittings. ❷ a signboard on a shopfront. ❸ the dashboard of a motor vehicle.
– SAY **fay**-shuh

> ✓ **fascia**, which comes from the Latin word *fascia* 'band, door frame', is sometimes spelled **facia**

fascinate »*verb* (**fascinates, fascinating, fascinated**) interest or charm someone greatly.
fascinating
fascinatingly
fascination

fascism »*noun* ❶ a right-wing system of government characterized by extreme nationalistic beliefs. ❷ an attitude which is extremely intolerant or right-wing.
– SAY **fash**-i-z'm
fascist
fascistic

> ✓ remember, there is an **s** before the **c** in **fascism** and **fascist**

fashion (verb: **fashions, fashioning, fashioned**)

fashionable
fashionably

fashioned

fashioning

fashions

fast[1] (adjective: **faster, fastest**) [moving quickly; fixed]

fast[2] (verb: **fasts, fasting, fasted**) [go without food]

fasten (verb: **fastens, fastening, fastened**)
fastener
fastening

faster

fastest

fastidious »*adjective* ❶ paying a lot of attention to detail. ❷ very concerned about cleanliness.
– SAY fa-**stid**-i-uhss
fastidiously
fastidiousness

fasting

fastness »*noun* (plural **fastnesses**) ❶ a place that is secure and well protected. ❷ the ability of a dye to keep its colour.

fasts

fast-track »*verb* (**fast-tracks, fast-tracking, fast-tracked**) speed up the development or progress of something.

fat (adjective: **fatter, fattest**)
fatness
fattish

> ✓ double the **t** in **fatter, fattest,** and **fattish**

fatal »*adjective* ❶ causing death. ❷ leading to failure or disaster.
fatally

fatalism »*noun* the belief that all events are decided in advance by a supernatural power.
fatalist
fatalistic

fatality »*noun* (plural **fatalities**) a death occurring in a war, or caused by an accident or disease.

> ✓ plural: drop the **y** and add **ies**: **fatalities**

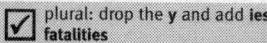

fate »*noun* ❶ a supernatural power believed to control all events. ❷ the things that will inevitably happen to someone.
» *verb* (**be fated**) be destined to happen in a particular way: *they were fated to meet up again.*

fateful »*adjective* having important, often unpleasant, consequences.
fatefully

 -ful not **-full: fateful**

father (verb: **fathers, fathering, fathered**) [male parent]
fatherhood
fatherless

Father Christmas

fathered

fatherhood

fathering

father-in-law (plural **fathers-in-law**)

 make the plural by adding **s** after **father** not **law: fathers-in-law**

fatherland »*noun* a person's native country.

fatherless

fatherly »*adjective* protective and affectionate.

fathers

Father's Day

fathom »*noun* a length of six feet (1.8 metres), used in measuring the depth of water.
» *verb* (**fathoms, fathoming, fathomed**) understand after much thought: *I can't fathom him out.*
fathomless

 keep a single **m** in **fathomed** and **fathoming**

fatigue »*noun* ❶ extreme tiredness. ❷ weakness in metals caused by repeated stress. ❸ (**fatigues**) loose-fitting clothing of a sort worn by soldiers.
» *verb* (**fatigues, fatiguing, fatigued**) make someone extremely tired.

 remember, there is a **u** in **fatigue**

fatten (verb: **fattens, fattening, fattened**)

fatter

fattest

fattier

fatties

fattiest

fattish

fatty (adjective: **fattier, fattiest**; plural **fatties**)

fatty acid »*noun* (in chemistry) an organic acid whose molecule contains a hydrocarbon chain.

fatuous »*adjective* silly and pointless.
fatuity
fatuously

fatwa »*noun* an authoritative ruling on a point of Islamic law.
– **SAY** fat-wah

 no **h** at the end: **fatwa**

faucet »*noun* (mainly in American English) a tap.
– **SAY** faw-sit

fault (verb: **faults, faulting, faulted**)
faultless
faultlessly
faulty

faun »*noun* (in Roman mythology) a god of woods and fields, with a human body and a goat's horns, ears, legs, and tail.

ⓘ on the difference between a **faun** and a **fawn**, see the note at **FAWN**[1]

fauna »*noun* the animals of a particular region or period (as opposed to the *flora* or plants).
– **SAY** faw-nuh
faunal

Faustian »*adjective* (of an agreement) offering great advantages but promising eventual problems.
– **SAY** fowst-i-uhn

ⓘ named after the 16th-century German astronomer and necromancer Johann *Faust*, reputed to have sold his soul to the Devil

faux pas »*noun* (plural **faux pas**) a mistake which causes embarrassment in a social situation.
– **SAY** foh **pah** [singular and plural]

ⓘ a French phrase meaning 'false step'

favor etc. American spelling of **FAVOUR** etc.

favour (verb: **favours, favouring, favoured**)

 -our not **-or: favour** (the spelling **favor** is American, as are **favorite** and **favorable**)

favourable
favourably

favoured

favouring

favourite

favouritism »*noun* the unfair favouring of one person or group.

favours

fawn¹ »*noun* ❶ a young deer. ❷ a light brown colour.

> ℹ️ do not confuse **fawn** with **faun**: a **fawn** is a young deer, or a light brown colour, whereas a **faun** is a Roman god that is part man, part goat

fawn² »*verb* (**fawns, fawning, fawned**) try to gain someone's approval by flattering them: *people fawn over you when you're famous.*

fax »*noun* (plural **faxes**) ❶ an exact copy of a document which has been scanned and transmitted electronically. ❷ a machine for transmitting and receiving such documents.
»*verb* (**faxes, faxing, faxed**) send a document by fax.

faze »*verb* (**fazes, fazing, fazed**) disturb or disconcert someone.

FBI »*abbreviation* (in the US) Federal Bureau of Investigation.

FE »*abbreviation* further education.

fealty »*noun* (a historical term) the loyalty sworn to a feudal lord by his tenant.
– **say** fee-uhl-ti

fear (verb: **fears, fearing, feared**)
fearful
   fearfully

> ✅ -ful not -full: **fearful**

fearing
fearless
   fearlessly
fears
fearsome »*adjective* frightening.
   fearsomely
feasible »*adjective* ❶ able to be done easily. ❷ (in informal English) likely; probable.
   feasibility
   feasibly

> ℹ️ in formal writing do not use **feasible** to mean 'likely' or 'probable'

feast (verb: **feasts, feasting, feasted**)

feat »*noun* an achievement requiring great courage, skill, or strength.

feather (verb: **feathers, feathering, feathered**)
   feathery

feather-bed »*verb* (**feather-beds, feather-bedding, feather-bedded**) provide with very favourable conditions.

feathered
feathering
feathers
featherweight »*noun* a weight in boxing coming between bantamweight and lightweight.
feathery
feature (verb: **features, featuring, featured**)
   featureless
febrile »*adjective* ❶ having the symptoms of a fever. ❷ overactive and excitable: *her febrile imagination.*
– **say** fee-bryl

February

> ✅ although many people don't pronounce it, there is an r straight after the b in **February**

feces American spelling of **faeces**.

feckless »*adjective* ❶ having little determination or purpose. ❷ irresponsible.
   fecklessly
   fecklessness

fecund »*adjective* highly fertile; able to produce offspring.
– **say** fek-uhnd or fee-kuhnd
   fecundity

fed past and past participle of **feed**.

federal »*adjective* ❶ having a system of government in which several states unite under a central authority but keep control of their internal affairs. ❷ having to do with the central government of a federation.
   federalism
   federalist
   federally

federate »*verb* (**federates, federating, federated**) join together as a federation.

federation »*noun* ❶ a group of states united under a central authority in which individual states keep control of their internal affairs. ❷ a group organized like a federation.

fedora »*noun* a soft felt hat with a curled brim and the crown creased lengthways.
– **say** fi-dor-uh

fee

feeble (adjective: **feebler, feeblest**)
   feebleness
   feebly

feed (verb: **feeds, feeding, fed**)
   feeder

feedback »*noun* ❶ comments made in response to something you have done. ❷ the return of part of the output of an amplifier to its input, causing a whistling sound.

feeder

feeding

feeds

feel (verb: **feels**, **feeling**, **felt**)
  feeler

feel-good »*adjective* causing a feeling of happiness and well-being.

feeling
  feelingly

feels

feet plural of FOOT.

feign »*verb* (**feigns**, **feigning**, **feigned**) pretend to feel or have: *she feigned nervousness.*

> **i** do not confuse **feign** with **fain**, which is an old word meaning 'pleased', 'willing', or 'gladly'

feint »*noun* a movement made to deceive an opponent, especially in boxing or fencing.
» *verb* (**feints**, **feinting**, **feinted**) make a feint.
» *adjective* (of paper) printed with faint lines as a guide for handwriting.
– SAY faynt

> **i** do not confuse **feint** with **faint**, which means 'only just visible or perceptible', 'very slight', or 'lose consciousness'

feisty »*adjective* (**feistier**, **feistiest**) (in informal English) spirited and exuberant.
– SAY fy-sti
  feistiness

felafel another way of spelling FALAFEL.

feldspar »*noun* a pale mineral found in many kinds of rock.

> ✓ can also be spelled without a **d**: both **feldspar** and **felspar** are correct

felicitations »*plural noun* congratulations.

felicities

felicitous »*adjective* well chosen or appropriate.
– SAY fuh-li-si-tuhss
  felicitously

felicity »*noun* (plural **felicities**) ❶ great happiness. ❷ the ability to express yourself in an appropriate way. ❸ a pleasing feature of a work of literature or art.

feline »*adjective* having to do with a cat or cats.
» *noun* a cat or other animal of the cat family.
– SAY fee-lyn

fell[1] past of FALL.

fell[2] »*verb* (**fells**, **felling**, **felled**) ❶ cut down a tree. ❷ knock down.

fell[3] »*noun* a hill or stretch of high moorland in northern England.

fellatio »*noun* oral stimulation of a man's penis.
– SAY fe-lay-shi-oh

felled

felling

fellow
  fellowship

fells

felon »*noun* a person who has committed a felony.
– SAY fe-luhn

felonious »*adjective* having to do with crime.
– SAY fi-loh-ni-uhss
  feloniously

felony »*noun* (plural **felonies**) (in the US) a serious crime.

> ✓ plural: drop the **y** and add **ies**: **felonies**

felspar another way of spelling FELDSPAR.

felt[1] »*noun* cloth made from wool that has been rolled and pressed.

felt[2] past and past participle of FEEL.

felt-tipped pen

felt-tip pen

female
  femaleness

feminine
  femininity

feminise another way of spelling FEMINIZE.

feminism »*noun* a movement or theory that supports women's rights on the grounds of equality of the sexes.
  feminist

feminize »*verb* (**feminizes**, **feminizing**, **feminized**) make more feminine or female.
  feminization

> ✓ many people prefer the alternative spellings **feminise**, **feminises**, etc., and **feminisation**: both **s** and **z** spellings are correct

femme fatale »*noun* (plural **femmes fatales**) an attractive and seductive woman.
– SAY fam fuh-tahl [singular and plural]

> ✓ make the plural by adding **s** after **femme** and after **fatale**: **femmes fatales** **femme fatale** means 'disastrous woman' in French

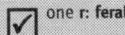

femur »*noun* (plural **femurs** or **femora**) the bone of the thigh.
– say fee-mer [singular], fem-uh-ruh [plural]
femoral

> ✓ the plural of **femur** can be either **femora** (as in Latin) or **femurs**: both are correct

fen »*noun* a low and marshy or frequently flooded area of land.

fence (verb: **fences, fencing, fenced**)
fencer

fencing

fend »*verb* (**fends, fending, fended**) ❶ (**fend for yourself**) look after and provide for yourself. ❷ (**fend off**) defend yourself from.

fender »*noun* ❶ a low frame around a fireplace to keep in falling coals. ❷ a cushioning device hung over a ship's side to protect it against impact. ❸ (in American English) the mudguard or area around the wheel well of a vehicle.

fending

fends

feng shui »*noun* an ancient Chinese system of designing buildings and positioning objects inside buildings to ensure a favourable flow of energy.
– say feng **shoo**-i or fung **shway**

fennel »*noun* a plant, the leaves and seeds of which are used as a herb, and the base of which is eaten as a vegetable.
– say fen-n'l

> ✓ double **n**: **fennel**

fenugreek »*noun* a plant with aromatic seeds that are used as a spice.
– say fen-yuu-greek

feral »*adjective* ❶ (of an animal or plant) wild, especially after having been domesticated. ❷ savage or fierce.
– say fe-ruhl or feer-uhl

> ✓ one **r**: **feral**

ferment »*verb* (**ferments, fermenting, fermented**) ❶ break down chemically through the action of yeast or bacteria. ❷ stir up disorder.
»*noun* social unrest or disorder.

fermentation »*noun* the chemical breakdown of a substance by bacteria, yeasts, or other micro-organisms, such as when sugar is converted into alcohol.

fermented

fermenting

ferments

fern »*noun* a flowerless plant which has feathery or leafy fronds.
ferny

ferocious »*adjective* savagely fierce, cruel, or violent.
– say fuh-**roh**-shuss
ferociously

ferocity »*noun* the state of being ferocious.
– say fuh-**ross**-i-ti

ferret »*noun* a small fierce animal with a long thin body, used for catching rabbits.
»*verb* (**ferrets, ferreting, ferreted**)
❶ (**ferreting**) hunting with ferrets.
❷ search for something in a place or container. ❸ (**ferret out**) discover something by searching thoroughly.
– say ferr-it
ferrety

> ✓ do not double the **t** in **ferreting, ferreted,** and **ferrety**

ferried

ferries

Ferris wheel »*noun* a fairground ride consisting of a giant upright revolving wheel with passenger cars hanging from its outer edge.

> ℹ named after the American engineer George W. G. *Ferris*

ferrous »*adjective* (of metals) containing iron.
– say ferr-uhss

ferrule »*noun* a metal ring or cap which strengthens the end of a handle, stick, or tube.

ferry (plural **ferries**; verb: **ferries, ferrying, ferried**)

> ✓ plural: drop the **y** and add **ies**: **ferries**

ferryman (plural **ferrymen**)

fertile »*adjective* ❶ (of soil or land) producing abundant vegetation or crops. ❷ (of a person, animal, or plant) able to conceive young or produce seed. ❸ producing a lot of new ideas: *a fertile debate.*
fertility

fertilise another way of spelling **FERTILIZE**.

fertiliser another way of spelling **FERTILIZER**.

fertilize »*verb* (**fertilizes, fertilizing, fertilized**) ❶ introduce sperm or pollen into an egg, female animal, or plant, so that a new individual develops. ❷ add fertilizer to soil.
fertilization

✓ many people prefer the alternative spellings **fertilise, fertilises**, etc., and **fertilisation**: both **s** and **z** spellings are correct

fertilizer »*noun* a substance added to soil to make it more fertile.

✓ **fertilizer** can also be spelled **fertiliser**: both spellings are correct

fervent »*adjective* intensely passionate.
– say fer-vuhnt
fervently

✓ -**vent** not -**vant**: **fervent**

fervid »*adjective* fervent.
fervidly

fervour »*noun* intense and passionate feeling.

✓ -**our** not -**or**: **fervour** (the spelling without the **u** is American)

festal »*adjective* relating to a festival.

fester »*verb* (**festers, festering, festered**)
❶ (of a wound or sore) become septic.
❷ become rotten. ❸ become worse: *tensions began to fester between Rose and Nick.*

festival

festive »*adjective* relating to or suitable for a festival: *the festive season.*
festively

festivity »*noun* (plural **festivities**) ❶ joyful celebration. ❷ (**festivities**) activities or events celebrating a special occasion.

✓ plural: drop the **y** and add **ies**: **festivities**

festoon »*noun* a decorative chain of flowers, leaves, or ribbons, hung in a curve.
»*verb* (**festoons, festooning, festooned**) decorate with festoons or other decorations.
– say fess-**toon**

feta »*noun* a white salty Greek cheese made from the milk of ewes or goats.
– say fet-uh

fetal »*adjective* relating to a fetus.
– say fee-t'l

fetch (verb: **fetches, fetching, fetched**)

fete »*noun* an outdoor event held to raise funds for charity, involving entertainment and the sale of goods.
»*verb* (**fetes, feting, feted**) honour or entertain someone lavishly.
– say fayt

✓ **fete** can also be spelled **fête**, with a circumflex accent above the **e** (as in the original French)

fetid »*adjective* smelling very unpleasant.
– say fe-tid or fee-tid

✓ **fetid** can also be spelled **foetid**, with an **o** before the **e**: both spellings are correct

feting

fetish »*noun* ❶ an object worshipped for its supposed magical powers. ❷ a form of sexual desire in which satisfaction is focused abnormally on an object, part of the body, etc. ❸ something to which a person is obsessively devoted: *he had a fetish about purity.*
fetishism
fetishist
fetishistic

fetlock »*noun* a joint of a horse's leg between the knee and the hoof.

fetor »*noun* a strong, foul smell.
– say fee-ter

fetter »*noun* ❶ a chain or shackle placed around a prisoner's ankles. ❷ (**fetters**) restraints or controls.
»*verb* (**fetters, fettering, fettered**) ❶ restrain someone with fetters. ❷ (**be fettered**) be restricted.

fettle »*noun* condition: *the aircraft is in fine fettle.*

fettuccine »*plural noun* pasta made in ribbons.
– say fet-tuh-**chee**-ni

✓ double **t**, double **c**: **fettuccine** is an Italian word meaning 'little ribbons'

fetus »*noun* (plural **fetuses**) an unborn offspring of a mammal, in particular an unborn human more than eight weeks after conception.
– say fee-tuhss

✓ **fetus** can also be spelled **foetus**, with an **o** before the **e**, but **fetus** is the more common form of the two, and the one used by scientists

feud »*noun* a long-lasting and bitter dispute.
»*verb* (**feuds, feuding, feuded**) take part in a feud.

feudal »*adjective* having to do with feudalism.

feudalism »*noun* the main social system in medieval Europe, in which people worked and fought for a nobleman in return for land.

feuded

feuding

feuds

fever
> feverish
> feverishly

fevered »*adjective* ❶ affected with fever. ❷ nervously excited or agitated: *my fevered imagination.*

feverfew »*noun* a plant with daisy-like flowers, used as a herbal remedy for headaches.

fever pitch »*noun* a state of extreme excitement.

few (adjective: **fewer, fewest**)

> [i] use **fewer** with plural nouns, as in *eat fewer cakes* or *there are fewer people here today*. Use **less** with nouns referring to things that cannot be counted, as in *there is less blossom on this tree*. It is wrong to use **less** with a plural noun (*less people, less cakes*).

fey »*adjective* ❶ unworldly and vague. ❷ able to see into the future.

fez »*noun* (plural **fezzes**) a conical red hat with a flat top, worn by men in some Muslim countries.

> [✓] plural: double the **z** and add **es**: **fezzes**

fiance »*noun* a man to whom you are engaged to be married.
– SAY fi-**on**-say

> [✓] **fiance** can also be spelled **fiancé**, with an acute accent above the **e** (as in the original French)

fiancee »*noun* a woman to whom you are engaged to be married.
– SAY fi-**on**-say

> [✓] **fiancee** can also be spelled **fiancée**, with an acute accent above the first **e** (as in the original French)

fiasco »*noun* (plural **fiascos**) a ridiculous or humiliating failure.
– SAY fi-**ass**-koh

> [✓] the plural of **fiasco**, an Italian word, has **os** not **oes**: **fiascos**

fiat »*noun* an official order or authorization.
– SAY **fy**-at

> [i] **fiat** means 'let it be done' in Latin

fib (verb: **fibs, fibbing, fibbed**)
> **fibber**

> [✓] double the **b** in **fibbing, fibbed**, and **fibber**

fiber American spelling of **FIBRE**.

fibre »*noun* ❶ a strand from which a plant or animal tissue, mineral substance, or textile is formed. ❷ a substance formed of fibres. ❸ the part of some foods, that is difficult to digest and which helps food to pass through the body. ❹ strength of character: *he's lacking in moral fibre.*

> [✓] **bre** not **ber**: **fibre** (the spelling **fiber**, by itself and in related words, is American)

fibreboard »*noun* a building material made of compressed wood fibres.

fibreglass »*noun* ❶ a reinforced plastic material containing glass fibres. ❷ a textile fabric made from woven glass fibres.

fibre optics »*noun* the use of thin flexible transparent fibres to transmit light signals, used for telecommunications or for internal inspection of the body.
> **fibre-optic**

fibril »*noun* a small or slender fibre.
– SAY **fy**-bril

fibrillate »*verb* (of a muscle, especially in the heart) suffer uncoordinated contraction of its individual fibres.
– SAY **fyb**-ri-layt or **fib**-ri-layt
> **fibrillation**

fibroid »*adjective* relating to fibres or fibrous tissue.
» *noun* a non-cancerous tumour of fibrous tissues, developing in the womb.

fibrosis »*noun* the thickening and scarring of connective tissue, as a result of injury.
– SAY fy-**broh**-siss

fibrous »*adjective* having to do with or made of fibres.

fibs

fibula »*noun* (plural **fibulae** or **fibulas**) the outer of the two bones between the knee and the ankle, parallel with the tibia.
– SAY **fib**-yuu-luh [singular], **fib**-yuu-lee [plural]

> [✓] make the plural by adding **e** (like the original Latin) or **s**: **fibulae** or **fibulas**

fickle »*adjective* changeable in your loyalties.
> **fickleness**

fiction

fictional

fictionalize »*verb* (**fictionalizes, fictionalizing, fictionalized**) make into a fictional story.

> [✓] many people prefer the alternative spellings **fictionalise, fictionalises**, etc.: both **s** and **z** spellings are correct

fictitious »*adjective* imaginary or invented; not real.

– **say** fik-**tish**-uhss

 tious not **cious: fictitious**

fiddle (verb: **fiddles, fiddling, fiddled**)
   fiddler

fiddlesticks

fiddling

fiddly

fidelity »*noun* ❶ continuing faithfulness to a person, cause, or belief. ❷ the degree of exactness with which something is copied or reproduced.
– **say** fi-**del**-i-ti

fidget (verb: **fidgets, fidgeting, fidgeted**)
   fidgety

 do not double the **t** in **fidgeting, fidgeted,** and **fidgety**

fief »*noun* ❶ (a historical term) an estate of land held under the feudal system. ❷ a person's area of operation or control.
– **say** feef
   fiefdom

the usual rule is **i** before **e**, except after **c: fief**

field (verb: **fields, fielding, fielded**)
   fielder

field events »*plural noun* athletic sports other than races, such as throwing and jumping events.

fieldfare »*noun* a large thrush with a grey head.

fielding

field marshal »*noun* the highest rank of officer in the British army.

field officer »*noun* a major, lieutenant colonel, or colonel.

fields

field sports »*plural noun* the sports of hunting, shooting, and fishing.

field test »*noun* a test carried out in the place where a product is to be used.

field trial »*noun* a field test.

fieldwork »*noun* practical work conducted by a researcher in the field.

fiend »*noun* ❶ an evil spirit. ❷ a very wicked or cruel person. ❸ (in informal English) an enthusiast: *an exercise fiend.*
– **say** feend

the usual rule is **i** before **e**, except after **c: fiend**

fiendish »*adjective* ❶ extremely cruel or unpleasant. ❷ extremely difficult.
   fiendishly

fierce
   fiercely
   fierceness

the usual rule is **i** before **e**, except after **c: fierce**

fiery »*adjective* (**fierier, fieriest**)
❶ consisting of or resembling fire. ❷ quick-tempered or passionate.
   fierily

ier not **ire: fiery**

fiesta »*noun* (in Spanish-speaking countries) a religious festival.
– **say** fi-**ess**-tuh

FIFA »*abbreviation* Fédération Internationale de Football Association, the international governing body of soccer.
– **say** fee-fuh

fife »*noun* a small flute used in military bands.

fifteen
   fifteenth

fifth
   fifthly

fifth column »*noun* a group within a country at war who are working for its enemies.
   fifth columnist

from a general in the Spanish Civil War, who while leading four columns of troops towards Madrid, said that he had a fifth column inside the city

fifthly

fifty (plural **fifties**)
   fiftieth

plural: drop the **y** and add **ies: fifties**

fifty-fifty »*adjective & adverb* with equal shares or chances.

fig »*noun* a soft sweet pear-shaped fruit with many small seeds.

fight (verb: **fights, fighting, fought**)
   fighter

fightback

fighter

fighting

fights

figment »*noun* a thing that exists only in the imagination.
– **say** fig-**muhnt**

figuration »*noun* ❶ ornamentation using designs. ❷ (in music) use of elaborate counterpoint.

figurative »*adjective* ❶ not using words literally; metaphorical. ❷ (of art)

representing people or things as they appear in real life.
figuratively

figure (verb: **figures, figuring, figured**)

figurehead *»noun* ❶ a carved bust or full-length figure at the prow of an old-fashioned sailing ship. ❷ a leader without real power.

figure of speech *»noun* a word or phrase used in a non-literal sense to add interest to speech or writing.

figures

figure skating *»noun* the sport of skating in set patterns.

figurine *»noun* a small statue of a human form.
– SAY fi-guh-**reen**

figuring

Fijian

filament *»noun* ❶ a slender thread-like object. ❷ a metal wire in an electric light bulb, which glows white-hot when an electric current is passed through it.
– SAY fil-uh-**muhnt**
filamentary
filamentous

 one l, one m: **filament**

filbert *»noun* a cultivated hazelnut.

filch *»verb* (**filches, filching, filched**) (in informal English) steal.

file (verb: **files, filing, filed**)

filial *»adjective* having to do with a son or daughter.
– SAY fil-i-uhl

filibuster *»noun* prolonged speaking which obstructs progress in a law-making assembly.
»verb (**filibusters, filibustering, filibustered**) obstruct legislation with a filibuster.

 fili- not filly-: **filibuster**

filigree *»noun* delicate ornamental work of fine gold, silver, or copper wire.
– SAY fil-i-**gree**
filigreed

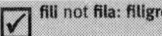 fili not fila: **filigree**

filing

filings *»plural noun* small particles rubbed off by a file.

Filipina *»noun* (plural **Filipinas**) a woman or girl from the Philippines.

Filipino *»noun* (plural **Filipinos**) ❶ a person from the Philippines. ❷ the national language of the Philippines.
» adjective relating to the Philippines or to Filipinos.
– SAY fi-li-pee-noh

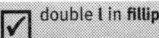 the plural of **Filipino**, a Spanish word, has **os** not **oes**: **Filipinos**

fill (verb: **fills, filling, filled**)

filler

fillet *»noun* ❶ a boneless piece of meat from near the loins or the ribs of an animal. ❷ a boned side of a fish. ❸ a band or ribbon binding the hair.
» verb (**fillets, filleting, filleted**) remove the bones from a fish.

✓ do not double the t in **filleting** and **filleted**

fillies
filling

fillip *»noun* a stimulus or boost.
– SAY fil-lip

✓ double l in **fillip**

fills

filly *»noun* (plural **fillies**) ❶ a young female horse. ❷ (mainly used in a humorous way) a lively girl or young woman.

film (verb: **films, filming, filmed**)

filmstrip

filmy *»adjective* (**filmier, filmiest**) ❶ thin and almost transparent. ❷ covered with a thin film.

filo *»noun* a kind of Greek flaky pastry in the form of very thin sheets.
– SAY fee-loh

✓ **filo** can also be spelled **phyllo** (as in Greek *phullo* 'leaf'): both spellings are correct

filter (verb: **filters, filtering, filtered**)

filth

filthy (adjective: **filthier, filthiest**)

filtrate *»noun* a liquid which has passed through a filter.
– SAY fil-trayt

filtration *»noun* the action of passing something through a filter.
– SAY fil-tray-sh'n

fin

final
finality
finally

finale *»noun* the last part of a piece of music, an entertainment, or a public event.

– say fi-**nah**-li

 an Italian word, **finale** has an **le** ending

finalise another way of spelling **FINALIZE**.

finalist

finality

finalize (verb: **finalizes, finalizing, finalized**)
finalization

 many people prefer the alternative spellings **finalise, finalises,** etc.: both **s** and **z** spellings are correct

finally

finance (verb: **finances, financing, financed**)

financial
financially

financial year »*noun* a year as reckoned for taxing or accounting purposes (in Britain reckoned from 6 April).

financier »*noun* a person who manages the finances of governments or other large organizations.
– say fy-**nan**-si-er or fi-**nan**-si-er

 i before **e**, even though it is after **c**: **financier** does not follow the usual rule

financing

finch

find (verb: **finds, finding, found**)
finder

fine (adjective: **finer, finest**; verb: **fines, fining, fined**)
finely
fineness

fine art »*noun* art intended to appeal to the sense of beauty, such as painting or sculpture.

fined

finely

fineness

finer

finery »*noun* showy clothes or decoration.
– say fy-**nuh**-ri

fines

finesse »*noun* ❶ elegant or delicate skill. ❷ subtle skill in handling people or situations.
»*verb* (**finesses, finessing, finessed**) do something in a skilful and delicate manner.
– say fi-**ness**

 one **n**, two **s**'s, and **e** at the end: **finesse** is a French word

finest

fine-tooth comb

 it is not *a fine toothcomb* (as if you combed your teeth), but a **fine-tooth comb** (or **fine-toothed comb**), i.e. one with narrow, closely-spaced teeth

fine-tune »*verb* (**fine-tunes, fine-tuning, fine-tuned**) make small adjustments to something so as to improve performance.

finger (verb: **fingers, fingering, fingered**)

fingerboard »*noun* a flat strip on the neck of a stringed instrument, against which you press the strings in order to vary the pitch.

fingered

fingering

fingerless

fingernail

fingerprint (verb: **fingerprints, fingerprinting, fingerprinted**)

fingers

fingertip

finial »*noun* an ornamental top or end of a roof or object.
– say **fin**-i-uhl

finicky »*adjective* ❶ fussy. ❷ excessively detailed or elaborate.

 one **n**: **finicky**

fining

finish (verb: **finishes, finishing, finished**)
finisher

finishing school »*noun* a private college where girls are taught how to behave correctly in fashionable society.

finite »*adjective* limited in size or extent.
– say **fy**-nyt
finitely
finiteness

 one **n**: **finite**

Finn »*noun* a person from Finland.
Finnish [of Finland]

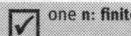 double **n**: **Finnish**

fiord another way of spelling **FJORD**.

fir »*noun* an evergreen coniferous tree with upright cones and needle-shaped leaves.

fire (verb: **fires, firing, fired**)

firearm »*noun* a rifle, pistol, or other portable gun.

fireball »*noun* ❶ a large bright meteor. ❷ an energetic or hot-tempered person.

firebomb (verb: **firebombs, firebombing, firebombed**)

firebrand »*noun* a person who passionately supports a particular cause and often stirs up unrest.

firebreak »*noun* a strip of open space in a forest to stop a fire from spreading.

firecracker »*noun* a firework that makes a loud bang.

fired

fire-eater

firefight
  firefighter
  firefighting

firefly »*noun* (plural **fireflies**) a kind of beetle which glows in the dark.

fireguard »*noun* a protective screen or grid placed in front of an open fire.

firelighter

fireman (plural **firemen**)

fireplace

firepower

fireproof

fires

fireside

firestorm »*noun* a very fierce fire, fanned by strong currents of air drawn in from the surrounding area.

firetrap »*noun* a building without enough fire exits in case of fire.

firewall »*noun* a part of a computer system or network that blocks unauthorized access to a network while allowing outward communication.

firewood

firework

firing

firing line »*noun* ❶ the front line of troops in a battle. ❷ a position where you are likely to be criticized.

firing squad »*noun* a group of soldiers ordered to shoot a condemned person.

firm (verb: **firms, firming, firmed**)
  firmly
  firmness

firmament »*noun* (a poetic term) the heavens; the sky.

> ✓ ent not ant: firm**ament**

firmed

firming

firmly

firmness

firms

first

first aid

firstborn »*noun* the first child to be born to someone.

first-class

first-degree »*adjective* (of burns) causing only reddening of the skin.

first-hand »*adjective & adverb* from the original source or personal experience; direct.

first lady »*noun* the wife of the President of the United States.

firstly

first mate »*noun* the officer second in command to the master of a merchant ship.

first name see the note at **CHRISTIAN NAME**.

first officer »*noun* ❶ the first mate on a merchant ship. ❷ the second in command to the captain on an aircraft.

first person »*noun* the form of a pronoun or verb used to refer to yourself, or to a group including yourself.

first-rate »*adjective* excellent.

firth »*noun* a narrow channel of the sea that runs inland, especially in Scotland.

fiscal »*adjective* relating to the income received by a government, especially as raised through taxes.
– **SAY** fiss-k'l
  fiscally

> ✓ there is no **k: fiscal**

fish (plural **fish** or **fishes**; verb: **fishes, fishing, fished**)

> ℹ️ when referring to more than one fish, the normal plural is **fish**, as in *he caught two fish*. When you want to talk about different kinds of fish, however, you should use **fishes**: *freshwater fishes of the British Isles*.

fisheries

fisherman (plural **fishermen**)

fishery »*noun* (plural **fisheries**) a place where fish are reared for food, or caught in numbers.

fishes

fisheye lens »*noun* a very wide-angle lens which gives a curved image.

fishier [more fishy]

fishiest

fishing

fish kettle »*noun* an oval pan for boiling fish.

fishmonger »*noun* a person who sells fish for food.

fishnet »*noun* an open mesh fabric resembling a fishing net.

fishtail »*noun* an object which is forked like a fish's tail.
» *verb* (**fishtails, fishtailing, fishtailed**) travel with a side-to-side motion.

fishwife »*noun* (plural **fishwives**) a woman with a loud, coarse voice.

fishy (adjective: **fishier, fishiest**)

fissile »*adjective* ❶ able to undergo nuclear fission. ❷ (of rock) easily split.
– SAY fiss-yl

fission »*noun* ❶ the action of splitting into two or more parts. ❷ a reaction in which an atomic nucleus splits in two, releasing a great deal of energy. ❸ (in biology) reproduction by means of a cell dividing into two or more new cells.
– SAY fi-sh'n

fissure »*noun* a long, narrow crack.
– SAY fi-sher

fist (verb: **fists, fisting, fisted**)
fistful

fisticuffs »*plural noun* fighting with the fists.

fisting

fists

fit (adjective: **fitter, fittest**; verb: **fits, fitting, fitted**)
fitness

✓ double the t to spell **fitter, fittest, fitting,** and **fitted**

fitful »*adjective* occurring or working irregularly.
fitfully

✓ -ful not -full: **fitful**

fitment »*noun* a fixed item of furniture or piece of equipment.

fitness

fits

fitted

fitter

fittest

fitting
fittingly

five
fivefold

fiver

fix (verb: **fixes, fixing, fixed**)
fixer

fixate »*verb* (**fixates, fixating, fixated**) (**fixate on** or **be fixated on**) be obsessed with.
– SAY fik-sayt

fixation »*noun* an excessive interest in someone or something; an obsession.

fixative »*noun* a substance used to fix or protect something.
– SAY fik-suh-tiv

fixed

fixer

fixes

fixing

fixity »*noun* the state of being unchanging or permanent.

fixture

fizz (verb: **fizzes, fizzing, fizzed**)

fizzier

fizziest

fizziness

fizzing

fizzle (verb: **fizzles, fizzling, fizzled**)

fizzy (adjective: **fizzier, fizziest**)
fizziness

fjord »*noun* a long, narrow inlet of the sea between high cliffs, especially in Norway.
– SAY fyord or fee-ord

✓ **fjord** (a Norwegian word) can also be spelled **fiord**: both spellings are correct

flab

flabbergast (verb: **flabbergasts, flabbergasting, flabbergasted**)

flabby (adjective: **flabbier, flabbiest**)
flabbiness

flaccid »*adjective* soft and limp.
– SAY flass-id or flak-sid
flaccidity

✓ note the double c: **flaccid**

flack another way of spelling **FLAK**.

flag (verb: **flags, flagging, flagged**)

flagellate »*verb* (**flagellates, flagellating, flagellated**) whip someone as a form of religious punishment or for sexual pleasure.
– SAY fla-juh-layt
flagellation

✓ single g but double l: **flagellate**

flageolet »*noun* a very small flute-like instrument resembling a recorder.
– SAY fla-juh-lay or fla-juh-**let**

flagged

flagging

flagon »*noun* a large bottle or jug for wine, cider, or beer.
– SAY fla-guhn

☑ there is only one **g**: **flagon**

flagpole

flagrant »*adjective* very obvious and unashamed.
– **SAY** flay-gruhnt
flagrantly

ℹ️ do not confuse **flagrant** with **fragrant**, which means 'having a pleasant smell'

flags

flagship

flagstone »*noun* a flat stone slab used for paving.

flail »*noun* a tool or machine that is swung to separate grains of wheat from the husks.
» *verb* (**flails, flailing, flailed**) ❶ swing something wildly. ❷ (**flail around** or **about**) move around in an uncontrolled way.

flair »*noun* ❶ a natural ability or talent. ❷ stylishness.

ℹ️ do not confuse **flair** with **flare**, which means 'a burst of flame or light'

flak »*noun* ❶ anti-aircraft fire. ❷ strong criticism.

☑ **flak** (a German word, short for *Fliegerabwehrkanone* 'aviator-defence gun') can also be spelled **flack**: both spellings are correct

flake (verb: **flakes, flaking, flaked**)

flakier

flakiest

flakiness

flaking

flak jacket »*noun* a sleeveless jacket reinforced with metal, worn as protection against bullets and shrapnel.

flaky (adjective: **flakier, flakiest**)
flakiness

☑ **ky** not **key**: **flaky**

flambe »*verb* (**flambes, flambeing, flambeed**) cover food with spirits and set it alight briefly.
– **SAY** flom-bay

☑ **flambe** can also be spelled **flambé**, with an acute accent on the **e** (as in the original French)

flamboyant
flamboyance
flamboyantly

☑ **ant** not **ent**: **flamboyant**

flame (verb: **flames, flaming, flamed**)

flamenco »*noun* a lively style of Spanish guitar music accompanied by singing and dancing.

☑ there is no **k**: **flamenco**

flameproof

flames

flame-thrower

flaming

flamingo »*noun* (plural **flamingos** or **flamingoes**) a wading bird with mainly pink or scarlet plumage and a long neck and legs.

☑ the plural of **flamingo** can have **os** or **oes**: **flamingos** or **flamingoes**

flammable »*adjective* easily set on fire.
– **SAY** flam-muh-b'l
flammability

ℹ️ the words **flammable** and **inflammable** both mean 'easily set on fire'. However, it is safer to use **flammable**, as the *in-* in **inflammable** can suggest that the word means 'non-flammable'.

flan

flange »*noun* a projecting flat rim for strengthening an object or attaching it to something.
flanged

flank (verb: **flanks, flanking, flanked**)

flanker »*noun* (in rugby) a wing forward.

flanking

flanks

flannel (verb: **flannels, flannelling, flannelled**)

☑ double the **l** to spell **flannelling** and **flannelled**

flannelette »*noun* a cotton fabric resembling flannel.

☑ **ette** not **et**: **flannelette**

flannelled

flannelling

flannels

flap (verb: **flaps, flapping, flapped**)
flappy

☑ double the **p** to spell **flapping** and **flapped**

flapjack »*noun* ❶ (in British English) a soft biscuit made from oats and butter. ❷ (in American English) a pancake.

flapped

flapper »*noun* (in informal English) a fashionable and unconventional young woman of the 1920s.

flapping

flappy

flaps

flare (verb: **flares, flaring, flared**) [sudden burst of flame; burn suddenly]

> ℹ️ do not confuse **flare** with **flair**, which means 'natural ability'

flash (verb: **flashes, flashing, flashed**)

flashback

flashbulb

flashed

flashes

flash flood »*noun* a sudden local flood resulting from very heavy rainfall.

flashgun

flashier [more flashy]

flashiest

flashily

flashiness

flashing »*noun* a strip of metal used to seal the junction of a roof with another surface.

flashlight

flashover »*noun* ❶ a high-voltage electric short circuit. ❷ the very rapid spread of a fire through the air.

flashpoint

flashy (adjective: **flashier, flashiest**)
flashily
flashiness

flask

flat (adjective: **flatter, flattest**)
flatly
flatness
flattish

flatbed »*noun* ❶ a vehicle with a flat load-carrying area. ❷ (in computing) a scanner, plotter, or other device which keeps paper flat during use.

flatfish

flat-footed

flatly

flatmate

flatness

flat race »*noun* a horse race over a course with no jumps.

flatten (verb: **flattens, flattening, flattened**)

flatter (verb: **flatters, flattering, flattered**)
flatterer

flattery (plural **flatteries**)

flattest

flattish

flatulent »*adjective* suffering from a build-up of gas in the intestines or stomach.
– SAY flat-yuu-luhnt
flatulence

> ✓ ent not ant: **flatulent**

flatworm »*noun* a type of worm, such as a tapeworm, with a simple flattened body.

flaunt »*verb* (**flaunts, flaunting, flaunted**) display proudly or obviously.

> ℹ️ do not confuse **flaunt** with **flout**, which means 'ignore a rule'

flautist »*noun* a flute player.
– SAY flaw-tist

> ✓ flau not flu: **flautist** (the spelling **flutist** is American)

flavor etc. American spelling of **FLAVOUR** etc.

flavour (verb: **flavours, flavouring, flavoured**)
flavouring
flavourless
flavoursome

> ✓ -our not -or: **flavour** (the spelling **flavor** is American)

flaw »*noun* ❶ a mark or fault that spoils something. ❷ a weakness or mistake.
flawed
flawless
flawlessly

flax »*noun* a blue-flowered plant that is grown for its seed (linseed) and for its stalks, from which thread is made.

flaxen »*adjective* (a poetic term) (of hair) pale yellow.

flay »*verb* (**flays, flaying, flayed**) ❶ strip the skin from a body. ❷ whip or beat very harshly.

flea [insect]

> ℹ️ do not confuse **flea** with **flee** meaning 'run away'

flea market »*noun* a street market selling second-hand goods.

fleck (verb: **flecks, flecking, flecked**)

fled past and past participle of **FLEE**.

fledged »*adjective* (of a young bird) having developed wing feathers that are large enough for it to fly.

fledgling »*noun* a young bird that has just learned to fly.

> ✓ **fledgling** can also be spelled **fledgeling**: both spellings are correct

flee (verb: **flees, fleeing, fled**) [run away]

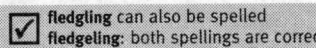

| i | do not confuse **flee** with **flea**, which means 'a jumping insect' |

fleece »*noun* ❶ the wool coat of a sheep. ❷ a soft, warm fabric with a pile.
» *verb* (**fleeces, fleecing, fleeced**) (in informal English) swindle someone.
fleeced
fleecy

fleeing

flees

fleet[1] [group of ships]

fleet[2] »*adjective* (**fleeter, fleetest**) fast and nimble.

fleeting
fleetingly

Flemish »*noun* ❶ (**the Flemish**) the people of Flanders, a region divided between Belgium, France, and the Netherlands. ❷ the Dutch language as spoken in Flanders.
» *adjective* relating to Flanders or the Flemish.

flesh (verb: **fleshes, fleshing, fleshed**)

fleshier

fleshiest

fleshiness

fleshing

fleshly »*adjective* relating to the body and its needs.

fleshpots »*plural noun* (mainly used in a humorous way) places with a lot of nightlife and lively entertainment.

fleshy (adjective: **fleshier, fleshiest**)
fleshiness

fleur-de-lis »*noun* (plural **fleurs-de-lis**) a design showing a lily made up of three petals bound together at the bottom.
– **SAY** fler-duh-**lee** [singular and plural]

| ✓ | from a French phrase meaning 'flower of the lily': the plural of **fleur-de-lis** adds an **s** to **fleur**: **fleurs-de-lis**. **Fleur-de-lis** can also be spelled **fleur-de-lys**: both spellings are correct. |

flew past of **FLY**.

flex »*verb* (**flexes, flexing, flexed**) ❶ bend a limb or joint. ❷ tighten a muscle. ❸ warp or bend and then return to shape.
» *noun* a cable for carrying electric current to an appliance.

flexible
flexibility
flexibly

| ✓ | **-ible** not **-able**: **flexible** |

flexing

flexion »*noun* the action of bending or the state of being bent.
– **SAY** flek-sh'n

flexitime »*noun* a system that lets you vary your working hours.

flibbertigibbet »*noun* a person who is not interested in serious things.

flick (verb: **flicks, flicking, flicked**)

flicker (verb: **flickers, flickering, flickered**)

flicking

flick knife »*noun* a knife with a blade that springs out from the handle when you press a button.

flicks

flier another way of spelling **FLYER**.

flight

flight deck »*noun* ❶ the cockpit of a large aircraft. ❷ the deck of an aircraft carrier.

flightier

flightiest

flightiness

flightless »*adjective* (of a bird or insect) naturally unable to fly.

flighty »*adjective* (**flightier, flightiest**) unreliable and uninterested in serious things.
flightiness

flimflam »*noun* insincere and unconvincing talk.

flimsy (adjective: **flimsier, flimsiest**)
flimsily
flimsiness

flinch (verb: **flinches, flinching, flinched**)

fling (verb: **flings, flinging, flung**)

flint »*noun* ❶ a hard grey rock. ❷ a piece of flint or a metal alloy, used to produce a spark in a cigarette lighter.

flintily

flintiness

flintlock »*noun* an old-fashioned type of gun fired by a spark from a flint.

flinty »*adjective* ❶ having to do with or like flint. ❷ grim and hard.
flintily
flintiness

flip (verb: **flips, flipping, flipped**)

| ✓ | double the **p** to spell **flipping** and **flipped** |

flip-flop

flippant »*adjective* not properly serious or respectful.
flippancy
flippantly

☑ **ant** not **ent: flippant**

flipped
flipper
flipping
flips
flip side »*noun* ❶ the B-side of a pop single. ❷ the reverse or unwelcome aspect of a situation.
flirt (verb: **flirts, flirting, flirted**)
flirtation
flirty

☑ **flirt** is spelled with an **i**, not an **e**, in the middle

flirtatious »*adjective* liking to flirt.

☑ **tious** not **cious: flirtatious**

flirted
flirting
flirts
flirty
flit (verb: **flits, flitting, flitted**)
flitter »*verb* (**flitters, flittering, flittered**) move quickly here and there.
flitting
float (verb: **floats, floating, floated**)
floater
floating voter »*noun* a person who does not vote for the same political party all the time.
floats
floaty »*adjective* (of a garment or fabric) light and flimsy.
flocculent »*adjective* looking like tufts of wool.
– SAY flok-kyuu-luhnt
flock[1] (verb: **flocks, flocking, flocked**) [group of animals; gather]
flock[2] »*noun* ❶ a soft material for stuffing cushions and quilts. ❷ powdered wool or cloth, used to give a raised pattern on wallpaper.
flocked
flocking
flocks
floe »*noun* a sheet of floating ice.

ℹ do not confuse **floe** with **flow**, which means 'move in a stream'

flog »*verb* (**flogs, flogging, flogged**)
flogger
flood (verb: **floods, flooding, flooded**)
floodgate

floodlight (verb: **floodlights, floodlighting, floodlit**)
flood plain »*noun* a low-lying area next to a river that is regularly flooded.
floods
floor (verb: **floors, flooring, floored**) [the lower surface of a room]
floorboard
floored
flooring
floors
floozy »*noun* (plural **floozies**) (in informal English) an immoral or sexually provocative girl or woman.

☑ **floozy** can also be spelled **floozie**

flop (verb: **flops, flopping, flopped**)

☑ double the **p** to spell **flopping** and **flopped**

floppy (plural **floppies**)
floppily
floppiness

☑ plural: drop the **y** and add **ies: floppies**

flora »*noun* ❶ the plants of a particular region or period (as opposed to the *fauna* or animals). ❷ the bacteria found naturally in the intestines.
floral
Florentine »*adjective* relating to the city of Florence in Italy.
» *noun* a person from Florence.
– SAY flo-ruhn-tyn
floret »*noun* ❶ one of the small flowers making up a composite flower head. ❷ one of the flowering stems making up a head of cauliflower or broccoli.
floribunda »*noun* a plant, especially a rose, with dense clusters of flowers.

ℹ **floribunda** is a Latin word meaning 'freely flowering'

florid »*adjective* ❶ having a red or flushed complexion. ❷ over-elaborate or ornate.
florin »*noun* a former British coin worth two shillings.
florist
floristry
floss »*noun* ❶ untwisted silk thread used in embroidery. ❷ a soft thread used to clean between the teeth.
» *verb* (**flosses, flossing, flossed**) clean between your teeth with dental floss.
flossy
flotation »*noun* ❶ the action of floating. ❷ the process of offering a company's

f

shares for sale on the stock market for the first time.
– say floh-**tay**-sh'n

 flot- not float-: **flotation**

flotilla »*noun* a small fleet of ships or boats.
– say fluh-**til**-luh

 one t, two **l**'s: **flotilla** is a Spanish word

flotsam »*noun* wreckage found floating on the sea.
– say flot-suhm

flounce[1] »*verb* (**flounces, flouncing, flounced**) move in a way that emphasizes anger or impatience.
» *noun* an exaggerated action expressing annoyance or impatience.

flounce[2] »*noun* a wide strip of material gathered and sewn to a skirt or dress.
flouncy

flounder[1] »*verb* (**flounders, floundering, floundered**) ❶ stagger clumsily in mud or water. ❷ have trouble doing or understanding something.

ℹ️ do not confuse **flounder** with **founder**, meaning 'fail or come to nothing'

flounder[2] »*noun* a small flatfish of shallow coastal waters.

flour (verb: **flours, flouring, floured**)
floury

flourish »*verb* (**flourishes, flourishing, flourished**) ❶ grow or develop in a healthy or vigorous way. ❷ be successful. ❸ wave something about in a noticeable way.
» *noun* ❶ a bold or unrestrained gesture. ❷ an ornamental flowing curve in handwriting. ❸ a fanfare played by brass instruments.

flours

floury

flout »*verb* (**flouts, flouting, flouted**) openly fail to follow a rule, law, or custom.
– say flowt

ℹ️ do not confuse **flout** with **flaunt**, which means 'display proudly or obviously'

flow (verb: **flows, flowing, flowed**) [move steadily in a stream; a steady stream]

ℹ️ do not confuse **flow** with **floe**, which means 'a sheet of floating ice'

flow chart »*noun* a diagram showing the sequence of stages that makes up a complex process.

flow diagram »*noun* a flow chart.

flowed

flower (verb: **flowers, flowering, flowered**) [part of plant; produce flowers]
flowerless

floweriness

flowerless

flowerpot

flowers

flowery »*adjective* ❶ full of, decorated with, or like flowers. ❷ (of speech or writing) elaborate.

flowing

flown

flows

flu »*noun* influenza.

fluctuate »*verb* (**fluctuates, fluctuating, fluctuated**) rise and fall irregularly in number or amount.
fluctuation

flue »*noun* ❶ a passage in a chimney for smoke and waste gases. ❷ a pipe or passage for conveying heat.
– say floo

✓ don't forget the **e** on the end: **flue**

fluent »*adjective* ❶ speaking or writing in a clear and natural way. ❷ (of a language) used easily and accurately. ❸ smoothly graceful and easy: *a runner in fluent motion.*
– say floo-uhnt
fluency
fluently

fluff (verb: **fluffs, fluffing, fluffed**)

fluffy (adjective: **fluffier, fluffiest**)
fluffily
fluffiness

flugelhorn »*noun* a brass musical instrument like a cornet but with a mellower tone.
– say floo-g'l-horn

✓ **gel** not **gle**: **flugelhorn** is a German word

fluid »*noun* a substance, such as a liquid or gas, that has no fixed shape and gives way easily to outside pressure.
» *adjective* ❶ able to flow easily. ❷ not stable. ❸ graceful.
fluidity
fluidly

fluid ounce »*noun* (in the UK) one twentieth of a pint (approximately 0.028 litre).

fluke »*noun* ❶ a lucky chance occurrence. ❷ one of the lobes of a whale's tail. ❸ a triangular plate on the arm of an anchor. ❹ a parasitic flatworm.

» *verb* (**flukes, fluking, fluked**) achieve something by luck rather than skill.

fluky

✓ fluky can also be spelled **flukey**

flume »*noun* ❶ an artificial channel carrying water. ❷ a water slide at a swimming pool or amusement park.

flummery »*noun* empty talk or compliments.

flummox »*verb* (**flummoxes, flummoxing, flummoxed**) (in informal English) completely baffle someone.

✓ double m, and **x** not **cks** at the end: **flummox**

flung past and past participle of FLING.

flunk »*verb* (**flunks, flunking, flunked**) (in informal English) fail an examination.

flunkey »*noun* (plural **flunkeys**) ❶ a uniformed manservant or footman. ❷ a person who performs menial tasks.

✓ flunkey can also be spelled **flunky** (plural **flunkies**)

flunkies

flunking

flunks

flunky another way of spelling FLUNKEY.

fluoresce »*verb* (**fluoresces, fluorescing, fluoresced**) shine or glow brightly due to fluorescence.
– SAY floo-uh-**ress**

fluorescence »*noun* ❶ light emitted by a substance when it is exposed to radiation such as ultraviolet light or X-rays. ❷ the property of emitting light in this way.

✓ be careful that the beginning of **fluorescence, fluorescent**, etc. is **fluor**- not **flour**-

fluorescent »*adjective* ❶ having or showing fluorescence. ❷ (of lighting) based on fluorescence from a substance lit by ultraviolet light. ❸ vividly colourful.

fluoridate »*verb* (**fluoridates, fluoridating, fluoridated**) add traces of fluorides to something.
– SAY floo-uh-ri-dayt or flor-i-dayt
fluoridation

fluoride »*noun* ❶ a compound of fluorine with another element or group. ❷ a fluorine-containing salt added to water supplies or toothpaste to reduce tooth decay.
– SAY floo-uh-ryd

✓ **fluor**-, not **flour**-, in **fluoride, fluorspar**, etc.

fluorine »*noun* a poisonous and extremely reactive pale yellow gas.
– SAY floo-uh-reen

fluorite »*noun* a mineral form of calcium fluoride.

fluorspar »*noun* = FLUORITE.
– SAY floo-uh-spar

flurry »*noun* (plural **flurries**) ❶ a small swirling mass of snow, leaves, etc. moved by a sudden gust of wind. ❷ a sudden short spell of commotion or excitement. ❸ a number of things arriving suddenly and at the same time.
» *verb* (**flurries, flurrying, flurried**) move in an agitated or excited way.

✓ plural: drop the **y** and add **ies**: **flurries**

flush (verb: **flushes, flushing, flushed**)

fluster »*verb* (**flusters, flustering, flustered**) make someone agitated or confused.
» *noun* a flustered state.

flute »*noun* ❶ a high-pitched wind instrument consisting of a tube with holes along it. ❷ a tall, narrow wine glass.
» *verb* (**flutes, fluting, fluted**) speak in a tuneful way.
fluty

flutist American spelling of FLAUTIST.

flutter (verb: **flutters, fluttering, fluttered**)
fluttery

✓ two **t**'s, one r: **flutter**

fluty

fluvial »*adjective* having to do with a river.
– SAY floo-vi-uhl

flux »*noun* (plural **fluxes**) ❶ continuous change. ❷ the action or an instance of flowing. ❸ an abnormal discharge of matter from or within the body.

fly (plural **flies**; verb: **flies, flying, flew**; past participle **flown**)

✓ plural: drop the **y** and add **ies**: **flies**

flyaway »*adjective* (of hair) fine and difficult to control.

fly-by-night »*adjective* unreliable or untrustworthy.

flycatcher »*noun* a perching bird that catches flying insects.

flyer

✓ flyer can also be spelled **flier**: both spellings are correct

fly-fishing

flying

flying fish »*noun* a fish of warm seas which leaps out of the water and uses its wing-like fins to glide for some distance.

flying saucer »*noun* a disc-shaped flying craft supposedly piloted by aliens.

flying squad »*noun* a division of a police force which is capable of reaching an incident quickly.

flyleaf »*noun* (plural **flyleaves**) a blank page at the beginning or end of a book.

flyover »*noun* a bridge carrying one road or railway line over another.

flypaper »*noun* sticky, poison-treated strips of paper that are hung indoors to catch and kill flies.

fly-past »*noun* a ceremonial flight of aircraft past a person or a place.

fly-post »*verb* (**fly-posts, fly-posting, fly-posted**) put up advertising posters in places where they are not permitted.

flysheet »*noun* a fabric cover over a tent, to keep the rain out.

flyweight »*noun* a weight in boxing and other sports coming between light flyweight and bantamweight.

flywheel »*noun* a heavy revolving wheel in a machine which is used to increase the machine's momentum and thereby make it more stable or provide it with a reserve of available power.

FM »*abbreviation* frequency modulation.

foal »*noun* a young horse or related animal. »*verb* (**foals, foaling, foaled**) (of a mare) give birth to a foal.

foam (verb: **foams, foaming, foamed**)
foamy

fob[1] »*noun* ❶ a chain attached to a watch for carrying in a waistcoat or waistband pocket. ❷ a small pocket for carrying a watch. ❸ a tab on a key ring.

fob[2] »*verb* (**fobs, fobbing, fobbed**) ❶ (**fob off**) try to deceive someone into accepting excuses or something inferior. ❷ (**fob off on**) give something inferior to someone.

> ✓ double the **b** in **fobbing** and **fobbed**

focaccia »*noun* a type of Italian bread made with olive oil and flavoured with herbs.
– SAY fuh-**kach**-uh

> ✓ one **c** before the **a** and two after it: **focaccia**

focal »*adjective* relating to a focus.
– SAY **foh**-k'l

focal length »*noun* the distance between the centre of a lens or curved mirror and its focus.

focal point »*noun* ❶ the point at which rays or waves from a lens or mirror meet, or the point from which rays or waves going in different directions appear to come. ❷ the centre of interest or activity.

foci plural of FOCUS.

fo'c'sle another way of spelling FORECASTLE.

focus (plural **focuses** or **foci**; verb: **focuses, focusing, focused**)
focuser

> ✓ make the plural by adding **es** or by changing the **us** ending to **i** (like the original Latin): **focuses** or **foci** (SAY foh-sI). Do not double the **s** in **focusing** and **focused**.

focus group »*noun* a group of people assembled to assess a new product, political campaign, television series, etc.

focusing

fodder »*noun* ❶ food for cattle and other livestock. ❷ a person or thing regarded only as material to satisfy a need: *young people ending up as factory fodder*.

foe »*noun* an enemy or opponent.

foetid another way of spelling FETID.

foetus see the note at FETUS.
foetal

fog (verb: **fogs, fogging, fogged**)

fogey »*noun* (plural **fogeys**) a very old-fashioned or conservative person.
– SAY **foh**-gi

> ✓ **fogey** can also be spelled **fogy** (plural **fogies**)

fogged

foggier

foggiest

fogging

foggy (adjective: **foggier, foggiest**)

foghorn

fogies

fogs

fogy another way of spelling FOGEY.

foible »*noun* a minor weakness or eccentricity.
– SAY **foy**-b'l

foie gras »*noun* = PATE DE FOIE GRAS.
– SAY fwah **grah**

foil[1] »*verb* (**foils, foiling, foiled**) prevent the success of a plan or undertaking.

foil[2] »*noun* ❶ metal in the form of a thin flexible sheet. ❷ a person or thing that contrasts with and so enhances the qualities of another.

foil³ »*noun* a light, blunt-edged fencing sword with a button on its point.

foist »*verb* (**foists, foisting, foisted**) (**foist on**) impose an unwelcome person or thing on.
– SAY foysst

fold¹ (verb: **folds, folding, folded**) [bend something over on itself]
foldable

fold² »*noun* ❶ a pen or enclosure for livestock. ❷ (**the fold**) a group or community with shared aims and values.

folder

folding

folds

foliage »*noun* the leaves of plants.
– SAY foh-li-ij

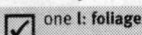 one l: **foliage**

foliate »*verb* (**foliates, foliating, foliated**) decorate with leaves or a leaf-like pattern.
– SAY foh-li-ayt

folic acid »*noun* a vitamin of the B complex found especially in leafy green vegetables, liver, and kidney.

folio »*noun* (plural **folios**) ❶ a sheet of paper folded once to form two leaves (four pages) of a book. ❷ a book made up of such sheets. ❸ an individual leaf of paper numbered on the front side only. ❹ the page number in a printed book.
– SAY foh-li-oh

✓ the plural of **folio** has **os** not **oes**: **folios**

folk

folklore »*noun* the traditional beliefs, stories, and customs of a community, passed on by word of mouth.

folksy »*adjective* (**folksier, folksiest**) traditional and homely.
folksiness

folk tale »*noun* a traditional story originally passed on by word of mouth.

follicle »*noun* a small cavity or pouch in the body.
– SAY fol-li-k'l
follicular

✓ double l, and le not al at the end: **follicle**

follies

follow (verb: **follows, following, followed**)

follower

following

follow-my-leader

follows

follow-through

follow-up

folly »*noun* (plural **follies**) ❶ foolishness. ❷ a foolish act or idea. ❸ an ornamental building with no practical purpose.

foment »*verb* (**foments, fomenting, fomented**) stir up revolution or conflict.
– SAY foh-**ment**

fond (adjective: **fonder, fondest**)
fondly
fondness

fondant »*noun* a thick paste made of sugar and water, used in making sweets and icing cakes.
– SAY fon-duhnt

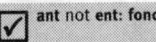 **ant** not **ent**: **fondant**

fonder

fondest

fondle (verb: **fondles, fondling, fondled**)

fondly

fondness

fondue »*noun* a dish in which you dip small pieces of food into melted cheese or a hot sauce.
– SAY fon-dyoo

✓ **ue** not **oo**: **fondue** is a French word meaning 'melted'

font¹ »*noun* a large stone bowl in a church for the water used in baptism.

font² »*noun* a set of type of a particular size and design.

✓ in this sense, **font** can also be written **fount**: both are correct

fontanelle »*noun* a soft area between the bones of the skull in a baby or fetus.
– SAY fon-tuh-**nel**

✓ **lle** at the end: **fontanelle** (the spelling **fontanel** is American)

food

food chain »*noun* a series of living things, each of which depend on the next as a source of food.

foodstuff

fool (verb: **fools, fooling, fooled**)
foolery

foolhardy »*adjective* recklessly bold or rash.
foolhardily
foolhardiness

fooling

foolish
foolishly
foolishness

foolproof

fools

foolscap »*noun* a size of paper, about 330 × 200 (or 400) mm.

> ☑ **fool-** not **full-: foolscap**

fool's gold »*noun* pyrite, a brassy yellow mineral that can be mistaken for gold.

fool's paradise »*noun* a state of happiness based on not knowing about or ignoring possible trouble.

foot (plural **feet**; verb: **foots, footing, footed**)
footless

footage »*noun* ❶ a length of film made for cinema or television. ❷ size or length measured in feet.

foot-and-mouth disease »*noun* a disease caused by a virus in cattle and sheep, causing ulcers on the hoofs and around the mouth.

football
footballer
footballing

footbrake

footbridge

footed

footer »*noun* ❶ a person or thing of a specified number of feet in length or height: *a six-footer*. ❷ a line of text appearing at the foot of each page of a book or document.
– **SAY** fuut-er

footfall »*noun* ❶ the sound of a footstep or footsteps. ❷ the number of people entering a shopping area in a given time.

foothill »*noun* a low hill at the base of a mountain or mountain range.

foothold »*noun* ❶ a place where you put a foot down securely while climbing. ❷ a secure position from which to make further progress.

footing »*noun* ❶ (**your footing**) a secure grip with your feet. ❷ the basis on which something is established or operates.

footless

footlights »*plural noun* a row of spotlights along the front of a stage at the level of the actors' feet.

footling »*adjective* unimportant and irritating.
– **SAY** foot-ling

footloose »*adjective* free to do as you please.

footman »*noun* (plural **footmen**) a uniformed servant who lets in visitors and waits at table.

footmark

footmen

footnote

footpath

footplate »*noun* the platform for the driver or crew in the cab of a train.

footprint

foots

footsie »*noun* (**play footsie**) (in informal English) playfully touch someone's feet with your own to express romantic interest.

footsore »*adjective* having sore feet from much walking.

footstep

footstool

footwear

footwork

fop »*noun* a man who is too concerned with his clothes and appearance.
foppish

for

fora plural of **FORUM**.

forage »*verb* (**forages, foraging, foraged**) ❶ search for food. ❷ obtain food by searching.
»*noun* ❶ food for horses and cattle. ❷ an act of foraging.
– **SAY** fo-rij
forager

foray »*noun* ❶ a sudden attack or move into enemy territory. ❷ a brief but spirited attempt to become involved in a new activity.
– **SAY** fo-ray

forbad past of **FORBID**.

forbade past of **FORBID**.

forbear[1] »*verb* (**forbears, forbearing, forbore**; past participle **forborne**) stop yourself from doing something.
– **SAY** for-**bair**

> ☑ **for-** not **fore-: forbear**
> do not confuse with **forebear** meaning 'an ancestor' (sometimes also spelled **forebear**)

forbear[2] another way of spelling **FOREBEAR**.

forbearance »*noun* patient self-control.

> ☑ **for-** not **fore-: forbearance**

forbearing »*adjective* patient and self-controlled.

forbears

forbid (verb: **forbids, forbidding, forbade** or **forbad**; past participle **forbidden**)

 double the **d** in **forbidding** and **forbidden**

forbidding »*adjective* appearing unfriendly or threatening.
forbiddingly

forbids

forbore past of FORBEAR[1].

forborne past participle of FORBEAR[1].

force (verb: **forces, forcing, forced**)

force-feed (verb: **force-feeds, force-feeding, force-fed**)

forceful
forcefully
forcefulness

 -ful not **-full: forceful**

forcemeat »*noun* a mixture of chopped and seasoned meat or vegetables used as a stuffing or garnish.

forceps »*plural noun* ❶ a pair of pincers used in surgery or in a laboratory. ❷ a large instrument of such a type with broad blades, used to help in the delivery of a baby.
– SAY for-seps

forces

forcible »*adjective* done by force.
forcibly

 -ible not **-able: forcible**

forcing

ford »*noun* a shallow place in a river or stream where it can be crossed.
»*verb* (**fords, fording, forded**) cross a river or stream at a ford.
fordable

fore »*adjective* found or placed in front.
»*noun* the front part of something.
»*exclamation* called out as a warning to people in the path of a golf ball.

forearm[1] [part of arm]

forearm[2] »*verb* (**be forearmed**) be prepared in advance for danger or attack.
– SAY for-**arm**

forebear »*noun* an ancestor.

 forebear can also be spelled **forbear**, but avoid confusion with **forbear** meaning 'stop yourself from doing something'

forebode »*verb* (**forebodes, foreboding, foreboded**) be an advance warning of something bad.

 fore- not **for-: forebode**

foreboding »*noun* a feeling that something bad will happen.

forecast (verb: **forecasts, forecasting, forecast** or **forecasted**)
forecaster

forecastle »*noun* the forward part of a ship below the deck, traditionally used as the crew's living quarters.
– SAY fohk-s'l

 forecastle can also be spelled **fo'c's'le**: both spellings are correct

forecasts

foreclose »*verb* (**forecloses, foreclosing, foreclosed**) ❶ take possession of a property because someone has failed to keep up their mortgage payments. ❷ rule out or prevent a course of action.
foreclosure

forecourt »*noun* an open area in front of a large building or petrol station.

forefather »*noun* an ancestor.

forefeet

forefinger

forefoot »*noun* (plural **forefeet**) one of the two front feet of a four-footed animal.

forefront »*noun* the leading position.

forego[1] another way of spelling FORGO.

forego[2] »*verb* (**foregoes, foregoing, forewent**; past participle **foregone**) (an old word) come before in place or time.

 do not confuse **forego** meaning 'come before in place or time' with **forgo** which means 'go without something you want'

foregoing »*adjective* previously mentioned.

foregone

foreground

forehand »*noun* (in racket sports) a stroke played with the palm of the hand facing in the direction of the stroke.

forehead

foreign
foreignness

 e before **i: foreign** does not follow the usual rule

foreign body »*noun* a piece of unwanted matter that has entered the body from outside.

foreigner

foreign exchange »*noun* the currency of other countries.

foreignness

foreknowledge »*noun* awareness of something before it happens or exists.

foreland »*noun* ❶ an area of land in front of a particular feature. ❷ a piece of land that projects into the sea.

foreleg

forelock »*noun* a lock of hair growing just above the forehead.

foreman »*noun* (plural **foremen**) ❶ a worker who supervises other workers. ❷ (in a law court) a person who is head of a jury and speaks on its behalf.

foremast »*noun* the mast of a ship nearest the bow.

foremen

foremost

foremother »*noun* a female ancestor.

forename see the note at **CHRISTIAN NAME**.

forensic »*adjective* ❶ having to do with the use of scientific methods in the investigation of crime. ❷ having to do with courts of law.
– **SAY** fuh-**ren**-sik
  forensically

✓ one r: **forensic**

foreplay »*noun* sexual activity that occurs before intercourse.

forerunner »*noun* a person or thing which comes before and influences someone or something else.

foresail »*noun* the main sail on a foremast.

foresee (verb: **foresees, foreseeing, foresaw**; past participle **foreseen**)
  foreseeable

foreshadow »*verb* (**foreshadows, foreshadowing, foreshadowed**) be a warning or indication of a future event.

foreshore »*noun* the part of a shore between high- and low-water marks, or between the water and land that has been cultivated or built on.

foreshorten »*verb* (**foreshortens, foreshortening, foreshortened**) ❶ portray an object or view as closer or shallower than it really is. ❷ reduce something in time or scale.

foresight »*noun* the ability to predict and prepare for future events and needs.

foreskin »*noun* the roll of skin covering the end of the penis.

forest
  forested

✓ one r: **forest**

forestall »*verb* (**forestalls, forestalling, forestalled**) prevent or delay something by taking action in advance.
– **SAY** for-**stawl**

✓ fore- not for-: **forestall**

forested

forester »*noun* a person in charge of a forest or skilled in forestry.

forestry »*noun* the science or practice of planting and taking care of forests.

foretaste »*noun* a sample of something that lies ahead.

foretell »*verb* (**foretells, foretelling, foretold**) predict.
  foreteller

✓ fore- not for-: **foretell**

forethought »*noun* careful consideration of what will be necessary or may happen in the future.

foretold past and past participle of **FORETELL**.

forever

forewarn (verb: **forewarns, forewarning, forewarned**)

forewent another way of spelling **FORWENT**.

forewoman (plural **forewomen**)

foreword »*noun* a short introduction to a book.

✓ fore- not for-, and -word not -ward: **foreword** (not the same word as **forward**)

forfeit »*verb* (**forfeits, forfeiting, forfeited**) be deprived of something as a penalty for doing wrong.
»*noun* a penalty for doing wrong.
»*adjective* lost or given up as a forfeit.
– **SAY** for-fit
  forfeiture

✓ e before i: **forfeit** does not follow the usual rule

forgave past of **FORGIVE**.

forge[1] »*verb* (**forges, forging, forged**) ❶ shape a metal object by heating and hammering it. ❷ create something through effort: *forge a close relationship.* ❸ produce a copy of a banknote, signature, etc. to deceive people.
»*noun* ❶ a blacksmith's workshop. ❷ a furnace for melting or refining metal.
  forger

forge[2] »*verb* (**forges, forging, forged**) ❶ move forward gradually or steadily. ❷ (**forge ahead**) make progress.

forgery (plural **forgeries**)

> ✓ plural: drop the **y** and add **ies**: **forgeries**

forges

forget (verb: **forgets**, **forgetting**, **forgot**; past participle **forgotten** or **forgot**)
forgettable

> ✓ double the **t** in **forgetting**, **forgotten**, and **forgettable**

forgetful
forgetfully
forgetfulness

> ✓ **-ful** not **-full**: **forgetful**

forget-me-not »*noun* a plant with light blue flowers.

forgets

forgettable

forgetting

forging

forgive (verb: **forgives**, **forgiving**, **forgave**; past participle **forgiven**)
forgivable
forgiving

forgiveness

forgiving

forgo »*verb* (**forgoes**, **forgoing**, **forwent**; past participle **forgone**) go without something you want.

> ✓ **forgo** can also be spelled **forego**, but use the spelling **forgo** to avoid confusion with **forego** meaning 'go before'

forgot past of **FORGET**.

forgotten past participle of **FORGET**.

fork (verb: **forks**, **forking**, **forked**)
forked

forklift truck

forks

forlorn »*adjective* ❶ pitifully sad and lonely. ❷ unlikely to succeed: *a forlorn attempt to escape.*
forlornly

form (verb: **forms**, **forming**, **formed**)
formless

formal »*adjective* ❶ suitable for official or important occasions. ❷ officially recognized. ❸ arranged in a precise or regular way.
formally

formaldehyde »*noun* a strong-smelling gas dissolved in water and used as a preservative and disinfectant.
– say for-**mal**-di-hyd

> ✓ **-hyde** not **-hide**: **formaldehyde**

formalin »*noun* a solution of formaldehyde in water.
– say for-muh-lin

formalise another way of spelling **FORMALIZE**.

formality

> ✓ plural: drop the **y** and add **ies**: **formalities**

formalize »*verb* (**formalizes**, **formalizing**, **formalized**) ❶ make an arrangement official. ❷ give something a definite shape or structure.

> ✓ many people prefer the alternative spellings **formalise**, **formalises**, etc.: both **s** and **z** spellings are correct

formally [in a formal manner]

format »*noun* ❶ the way in which something is arranged or presented. ❷ the shape, size, and presentation of a book, document, etc.
» *verb* (**formats**, **formatting**, **formatted**) give something a particular format.

> ✓ double the **t** when spelling **formatting** and **formatted**

formation

formative »*adjective* having a strong influence in the way something is formed.

formats

formatted

formatting

formed

former[1] »*adjective* ❶ having previously been the specified thing. ❷ in the past. ❸ (**the former**) referring to the first of two things mentioned.

former[2] »*noun* ❶ a person or thing that forms something. ❷ (in British English) a person in a particular school year: *a fifth-former.*

formerly [in the past]

Formica »*noun* (trademark) a hard, strong plastic material used for worktops, cupboard doors, etc.
– say for-**my**-kuh

formic acid »*noun* an acid present in the fluid discharged by some ants.

formidable »*adjective* frightening or intimidating through being very large, powerful, or capable.
– say for-mi-duh-b'l or for-**mid**-uh-b'l
formidably

forming

formless

forms
formula (plural **formulae** or **formulas**)

> ☑ the plural of **formula** is **formulae** (SAY for-myuu-lee), like the original Latin, in mathematical and chemical senses, but **formulas** in other senses

formulaic »*adjective* ❶ containing a set form of words. ❷ made by closely following a rule or style.
– SAY for-myuu-**lay**-ik

formulas
formulate »*verb* (**formulates**, **formulating**, **formulated**) ❶ create or prepare something methodically. ❷ express an idea clearly or briefly.
– SAY for-myuu-layt
formulation
formulator

fornicate »*verb* (**fornicates**, **fornicating**, **fornicated**) (used in a disapproving way) have sex with someone you are not married to.
fornication
fornicator

forsake »*verb* (**forsakes**, **forsaking**, **forsook**; past participle **forsaken**) ❶ abandon. ❷ give up.

forsooth »*adverb* (an old word) indeed.

forswear »*verb* (**forswears**, **forswearing**, **forswore**; past participle **forsworn**) ❶ agree to give up or do without something. ❷ (**forswear yourself** or **be forsworn**) lie after swearing to tell the truth.

forsythia »*noun* a shrub with bright yellow flowers.
– SAY for-**sy**-thi-uh

fort »*noun* a building constructed to defend a place against attack.

forte »*noun* a thing for which someone has a particular talent.
» *adverb & adjective* (in music) loud or loudly.
– SAY **for**-tay

forth [out from a starting point and forwards]

> ☑ do not confuse **forth** with **fourth**, which means 'number four in a series'

forthcoming »*adjective* ❶ about to happen or appear. ❷ made available when required: *help was not forthcoming.* ❸ willing to reveal information.

forthright »*adjective* direct and outspoken.
forthrightly
forthrightness

forthwith »*adverb* without delay.

forties

fortify (verb: **fortifies**, **fortifying**, **fortified**)
fortification

fortissimo »*adverb & adjective* (in music) very loud or loudly.
– SAY for-**tiss**-i-moh

> ☑ double **s** but single **m**: **fortissimo**

fortitude »*noun* courage and strength when facing pain or trouble.

fortnight
fortnightly
fortress (plural **fortresses**)

fortuitous »*adjective* happening by chance.
– SAY for-**tyoo**-i-tuhss
fortuitously
fortuitousness

> ℹ strictly speaking, you should use **fortuitous** to mean 'happening by chance' (whether good or bad), and **fortunate** to mean 'happening by good fortune'

fortunate
fortunately
fortune
fortune-teller
fortune-telling

forty (plural **forties**)
fortieth

> ☑ **for-** not **four-**: **forty**
> plural: drop the **y** and add **ies**: **forties**

forum »*noun* (plural **forums** or **fora**) ❶ a meeting or opportunity for an exchanging views. ❷ (in ancient Roman cities) a square or marketplace used for public business.

> ☑ the plural can be either **fora** (like the original Latin) or **forums**

forward (verb: **forwards**, **forwarding**, **forwarded**)
forwarder
forwardly
forwards

forwent past of **FORGO**.

fossil »*noun* ❶ the remains of a prehistoric plant or animal that have become hardened into rock. ❷ (mainly used in a humorous way) a very out-of-date person or thing.

> ☑ note that it is **il** at the end: **fossil**

fossil fuel »*noun* a fuel such as coal or gas, that is formed from the remains of animals and plants.

fossilize »*verb* (**fossilizes**, **fossilizing**, **fossilized**) preserve an animal or plant so

that it becomes a fossil.
fossilization

✓ many people prefer the alternative spellings **fossilise, fossilises**, etc., and **fossilisation**: both **s** and **z** spellings are correct

foster »*verb* (**fosters, fostering, fostered**) ❶ encourage the development of something. ❷ bring up a child that is not your own by birth.
fosterer

fought past and past participle of **FIGHT**.

foul (verb: **fouls, fouling, fouled**) [disgusting, make foul]
foully
foulness

ℹ do not confuse **foul** with **fowl**, which means 'a domesticated bird'

foul-mouthed »*adjective* using bad language.

foulness

fouls

found[1] past and past participle of **FIND**.

found[2] »*verb* (**founds, founding, founded**) ❶ establish an institution or organization. ❷ (**be founded on**) be based on a particular concept.

found[3] »*verb* (**founds, founding, founded**) melt and mould metal to make an object.

foundation
foundational

foundation stone »*noun* a stone laid to celebrate the founding of a building.

founded

founder[1] »*noun* a person who founds an institution or settlement.

founder[2] »*verb* (**founders, foundering, foundered**) ❶ (of a ship) fill with water and sink. ❷ (of a plan or undertaking) fail or break down.

ℹ do not confuse **founder** with **flounder**, which means 'struggle; be in a state of confusion'

founding

founding father »*noun* ❶ a founder. ❷ (**Founding Father**) a member of the group of men that drew up the constitution of the United States in 1787.

foundling »*noun* a young child that has been abandoned by its parents and is discovered and cared for by others.

foundry »*noun* (plural **foundries**) a workshop or factory for casting metal.

founds

fount[1] »*noun* ❶ a source of a desirable quality. ❷ (a poetic term) a spring or fountain.

fount[2] »*noun* = **FONT**[2].

fountain

✓ **tain** not **tin**: foun**tain**

fountainhead »*noun* an original source of something.

four
fourfold

four-poster »*noun* a bed with a post at each corner holding up a canopy.

foursome »*noun* a group of four people.

fourteen
fourteenth

fourth [number four in a series]
fourthly

✓ do not confuse **fourth** with **forth**, which means 'out from a starting point and forwards'

four-wheel drive »*noun* a system which provides power directly to all four wheels of a vehicle.

fowl »*noun* (plural **fowl** or **fowls**) ❶ a domesticated bird kept for its eggs or meat. ❷ birds as a group.

ℹ do not confuse **fowl** with **foul**, which means 'disgusting'

fox (plural **foxes**; verb: **foxes, foxing, foxed**)

foxglove »*noun* a tall plant with erect spikes of flowers shaped like the fingers of gloves.

foxhole »*noun* a hole in the ground used by troops as a shelter against the enemy or as a place to fire from.

foxhound »*noun* a dog trained to hunt foxes in packs.

fox-hunting

foxier

foxiest

foxily

foxiness

foxing

foxtrot »*noun* a ballroom dance which involves switching between slow and quick steps.
» *verb* (**foxtrots, foxtrotting, foxtrotted**) dance the foxtrot.

✓ double the **t** to spell **foxtrotting** and **foxtrotted**

foxy »*adjective* (**foxier, foxiest**) ❶ like a fox. ❷ (in informal English) crafty or sly. ❸ (in informal English) sexually attractive.

f

foxily
foxiness

foyer »*noun* a large entrance hall in a hotel or theatre.
– SAY foy-ay

> ✓ note the **er** ending: **foyer** is a French word

fracas »*noun* (plural **fracas**) a noisy disturbance or quarrel.
– SAY fra-kah [singular], fra-kah or fra-kahz [plural]

> ℹ **fracas** is a French word and the final **s** of the singular **fracas** is not pronounced

fractal »*noun* a curve or geometrical figure, each part of which has the same statistical character as the whole.
» *adjective* relating to or of the nature of a fractal or fractals.
– SAY frak-t'l

fraction »*noun* ❶ a number that is not a whole number (e.g. ½, 0.5). ❷ a very small part or amount.

fractional »*adjective* ❶ having to do with a fraction. ❷ very small in amount.
fractionally

fractious »*adjective* ❶ bad-tempered. ❷ difficult to control.
– SAY frak-shuhss
fractiously
fractiousness

> ✓ **tious** not **cious**: **fractious**

fracture (verb: **fractures, fracturing, fractured**)

fragile
fragility

fragment (verb: **fragments, fragmenting, fragmented**)
fragmentary
fragmentation

> ✓ **ent** not **ant**: **fragment**

fragrance
fragranced

> ✓ **ance** not **ence**: **fragrance**

fragrant [having a pleasant smell]
fragrantly

> ℹ do not confuse **fragrant** with **flagrant**, which means 'very obvious and unashamed'

frail (adjective: **frailer, frailest**)
frailly
frailness

frailty (plural **frailties**)

frame (verb: **frames, framing, framed**)
frameless
framer

framework

franc »*noun* the basic unit of money of France, Belgium, and several other countries.

> ℹ do not confuse **franc** with **frank**, which means 'honest' or 'an official mark on a letter'

franchise »*noun* ❶ a licence allowing a person or company to use or sell certain products. ❷ a business that has been given a franchise. ❸ the right to vote in elections.
» *verb* (**franchises, franchising, franchised**) ❶ grant someone or something a franchise. ❷ grant a franchise for goods or a service.
franchisee

> ✓ **franchise** cannot be spelled with an **ize** ending

Franciscan »*noun* a monk or nun of a Christian religious order following the rule of St Francis of Assisi.
» *adjective* having to do with St Francis or the Franciscans.
– SAY fran-**siss**-kuhn

franglais »*noun* a blend of French and English.
– SAY frong-glay

frank[1] »*adjective* ❶ honest and direct. ❷ open or undisguised.
frankly
frankness

> ℹ do not confuse **frank** with **franc** referring to French currency

frank[2] »*verb* (**franks, franking, franked**) stamp an official mark on a letter or parcel to indicate that postage has been paid or does not need to be paid.
» *noun* a franking mark on a letter or parcel.

Frankenstein »*noun* a thing that terrifies or destroys the person who made it.
– SAY **frang**-kuhn-styn

> ℹ the name **Frankenstein** comes from a novel by Mary Shelley: in the original story **Frankenstein** is the name of the scientist who creates the monster, not the monster itself (which does not have a name)

frankfurter »*noun* a seasoned smoked sausage made of beef and pork.

frankincense »*noun* a kind of sweet-smelling gum that is burnt as incense.
– SAY **frang**-kin-senss

✓ **-cense** not **-sense**: **frankincense**

franking
frankly
frankness
franks
frantic
  frantically

✓ there is no **k**: **frantic**

frappe »*adjective* (of a drink) iced or chilled.
– SAY **frap**-pay

✓ **frappe** can also be written **frappé**, with an acute accent on the **e** (as in the original French)

fraternal »*adjective* ❶ brotherly. ❷ having to do with a fraternity.
– SAY fruh-**ter**-n'l
  fraternally

fraternise another way of spelling
  FRATERNIZE.

fraternity »*noun* (plural **fraternities**) ❶ a group of people sharing a common profession or interests. ❷ (in American English) a male students' society in a university or college. ❸ friendship and mutual support within a group.
– SAY fruh-**ter**-ni-ti

fraternize »*verb* (**fraternizes, fraternizing, fraternized**) be on friendly terms.
– SAY **frat**-er-nyz
  fraternization

✓ many people prefer the alternative spellings **fraternise, fraternises**, etc., and **fraternisation**: both **s** and **z** spellings are correct

fratricide »*noun* ❶ the killing by someone of their brother or sister. ❷ the accidental killing of your own forces in war.
– SAY **frat**-ri-syd

fraud »*noun* ❶ the crime of deceiving someone to gain money or goods. ❷ a person who deceives others by claiming to be something they are not.
  fraudster

fraudulent »*adjective* ❶ involving fraud. ❷ deceitful or dishonest.
– SAY **fraw**-dyuu-luhnt
  fraudulence
  fraudulently

✓ **ent** not **ant**: **fraudulent**

fraught »*adjective* ❶ (**fraught with**) filled with something undesirable. ❷ causing or feeling anxiety or stress.

– SAY frawt
fray (verb: **frays, fraying, frayed**)
frazzled
freak (verb: **freaks, freaking, freaked**)
  freakish
freaky (adjective: **freakier, freakiest**)
  freakier
  freakiness
freckle
  freckled
  freckly
free (adjective: **freer, freest**; verb: **frees, freeing, freed**)

✓ note that there are two **e**'s in **freeing**

freebie »*noun* (in informal English) a thing given free of charge.

freeboard »*noun* the height of a ship's side between the waterline and the deck.

freebooter »*noun* a person who behaves in a lawless way for their own gain.

freeborn »*adjective* not born in slavery.

Free Church »*noun* a Christian Church which has separated from an established Church.

freed
freedom

free enterprise »*noun* a system in which private businesses compete with each other.

free fall »*noun* unrestricted downward movement under the force of gravity.

free-for-all

free-form »*adjective* not in a regular or formal structure.

freehand »*adjective & adverb* drawn by hand without a ruler or other aid.

freehold »*noun* permanent possession of land or property with the freedom to sell it whenever you wish.
  freeholder

free house »*noun* a public house not controlled by a brewery.

freeing

freelance »*adjective* self-employed and working for different companies on particular assignments.
»*verb* (**freelances, freelancing, freelanced**) earn your living as a freelance.
  freelancer

freeload »*verb* (**freeloads, freeloading, freeloaded**) (in informal English) take advantage of other people's generosity without giving anything in return.
  freeloader

freely

freeman »*noun* (plural **freemen**) ❶ a person who has been given the freedom of a city. ❷ (a historical term) a person who is not a slave or serf.

free market »*noun* an economic system in which prices are determined by unrestricted competition between privately owned businesses.

Freemason »*noun* a member of an international organization whose members help each other and hold secret ceremonies.
Freemasonry

freemen

freer [more free]

free-range »*adjective* referring to farming in which animals are kept in natural conditions where they can move around freely.

frees

freesia »*noun* a small plant with fragrant, colourful flowers.
– SAY free-zi-uh

> ✓ sia not zia: freesia

freest [most free]
free-standing

freestyle »*adjective* (of a contest or sport) having few restrictions on the technique that competitors use.

freethinker »*noun* a person who questions or rejects accepted opinions.

free trade »*noun* unrestricted international trade without taxes or regulations on imports and exports.

free verse »*noun* poetry that does not rhyme or have a regular rhythm.

freeway »*noun* (in American English) a dual-carriageway main road.

freewheel »*verb* (**freewheels, freewheeling, freewheeled**) ride a bicycle without using the pedals.

free will »*noun* the power to act according to your own wishes.

freeze (verb: **freezes, freezing, froze**; past participle **frozen**)

freeze-dry »*verb* (**freeze-dries, freeze-drying, freeze-dried**) preserve something by rapidly freezing it and then drying it in a vacuum.

freeze-frame »*noun* the facility of stopping a film or videotape to obtain a single motionless image.

freezer

freezes
freezing

freight »*noun* goods transported by truck, train, ship, or aircraft.
» *verb* (**freights, freighting, freighted**) transport goods by truck, train, etc.
– SAY frayt

> ✓ e before i: freight does not follow the usual rule

freighter »*noun* a large ship or aircraft designed to carry freight.

freighting
freights
French

French horn »*noun* a brass instrument with a coiled tube and a wide opening at the end.

Frenchman (plural **Frenchmen**)

French polish »*noun* a kind of polish used on wood to give it a very glossy finish.

Frenchwoman (plural **Frenchwomen**)

frenetic »*adjective* fast and energetic in a rather wild and uncontrolled way.
– SAY fruh-net-ik
frenetically

> ✓ there is no k: frenetic

frenzy (plural **frenzies**)
frenzied
frenziedly

> ✓ plural: drop the y and add ies: frenzies

frequency (plural **frequencies**)

> ✓ ency not ancy: frequency
> plural: drop the y and add ies: frequencies

frequency modulation »*noun* the varying of the frequency of a sound wave, used as a means of broadcasting a radio signal.

frequent (verb: **frequents, frequenting, frequented**)
frequenter
frequently

fresco »*noun* (plural **frescoes** or **frescos**) a painting that is done on wet plaster on a wall or ceiling.
– SAY fress-koh
frescoed

> ✓ the plural of fresco, an Italian word, can either have oes or os: frescoes or frescos

fresh
freshly
freshness

freshen (verb: **freshens, freshening, freshened**)

fresher »*noun* a first-year student at college or university.

freshly

freshness

freshwater

fret[1] (verb: **frets, fretting, fretted**) [worry]

fret[2] »*noun* **❶** an ornamental design of vertical and horizontal lines. **❷** one of the ridges on the neck of guitars and similar instruments, used for fixing the positions of the fingers.

fretful

   fretfully

   fretfulness

 -ful not **-full: fretful**

frets

fretsaw »*noun* a saw with a narrow blade for cutting designs in thin wood or metal.

fretted

fretting

fretwork »*noun* ornamental design in wood.

Freudian »*adjective* **❶** having to do with the Austrian psychotherapist Sigmund Freud and his methods of psychoanalysis. **❷** betraying unconscious thoughts: *a Freudian slip.*
− SAY froy-di-uhn

friable »*adjective* easily crumbled.
− SAY fry-uh-b'l

friar »*noun* a member of certain religious orders of men.

 ar not **er: friar**

friary »*noun* (plural **friaries**) a building or community occupied by friars.

fricassee »*noun* a dish of stewed or fried pieces of meat served in a thick white sauce.
− SAY fri-kuh-say or fri-kuh-see
   fricasseed

 **fricassee** can also be spelled **fricassée**, with an acute accent on the **e** (as in the original French)

friction »*noun* **❶** the resistance that one surface or object encounters when moving over another. **❷** the action of one surface or object rubbing against another. **❸** conflict or disagreement.

   frictional

   frictionless

Friday

fridge

fridge-freezer

fried past and past participle of FRY[1].

friend

   friendless

   friendship

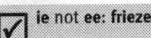 the usual rule is **I** before **e**, except after **c: friend**

friendly (adjective: **friendlier, friendliest**; plural **friendlies**)

   friendliness

friendly society »*noun* (in the UK) an association owned by its members providing sickness benefits, life assurance, and pensions.

friendship

fries

Friesian »*noun* an animal of a black-and-white breed of dairy cattle.
− SAY free-zh'n

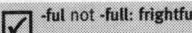 **Fries** not **Fris** or **Frees: Friesian**

frieze »*noun* a broad horizontal band of sculpted or painted decoration.
− SAY freez

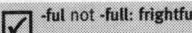 **ie** not **ee: frieze**

frigate »*noun* a warship with mixed weapons and equipment.
− SAY fri-guht

fright

frighten (verb: **frightens, frightening, frightened**)

   frightened

   frightener

frightening

   frighteningly

frightens

frightful

   frightfully

 -ful not **-full: frightful**

frigid »*adjective* **❶** very cold. **❷** (of a woman) unable to be sexually aroused.
− SAY fri-jid
   frigidity
   frigidly

frill

   frilled

   frilly

fringe (verb: **fringes, fringing, fringed**)

fringe benefit »*noun* a benefit received from your employer which is additional to your wages or salary.

fringed

fringes

fringing

frippery »*noun* (plural **fripperies**) ❶ showy or unnecessary ornament. ❷ a frivolous thing.

frisbee »*noun* (trademark) a plastic disc that you skim through the air as an outdoor game.

 bee not by: **frisbee**

frisk »*verb* (**frisks**, **frisking**, **frisked**) ❶ pass your hands over someone in a search for hidden weapons or drugs. ❷ skip or move playfully.

frisky »*adjective* (**friskier**, **friskiest**) playful and full of energy.
friskily
friskiness

frisson »*noun* a thrill.
– SAY free-son or fri-son

 double s: **frisson** (a French word)

fritillary »*noun* ❶ a plant with hanging bell-like flowers. ❷ a butterfly with orange-brown wings chequered with black.
– SAY fri-til-luh-ri

 one t, two l's: **fritillary**

fritter[1] »*verb* (**fritters**, **frittering**, **frittered**) (**fritter away**) waste time, money, or energy on unimportant matters.

fritter[2] »*noun* a piece of food that is coated in batter and deep-fried.

frivolous »*adjective* ❶ not having any serious purpose or value. ❷ (of a person) carefree and not serious.
frivolity
frivolously

frizz (verb: **frizzes**, **frizzing**, **frizzed**)

frizzy (adjective: **frizzier**, **frizziest**)
frizziness

fro see TO AND FRO.

frock

frock coat »*noun* a man's double-breasted, long-skirted coat.

frog
froggy

frogman »*noun* (plural **frogmen**) a diver equipped with a rubber suit, flippers, and breathing equipment.

frogmarch »*verb* (**frogmarches**, **frogmarching**, **frogmarched**) force someone to walk forward by pinning their arms from behind.

frogmen

frogspawn

frolic »*verb* (**frolics**, **frolicking**, **frolicked**) play or move about in a cheerful and lively way.
» *noun* a playful action or movement.

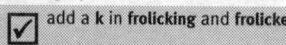 add a **k** in **frolicking** and **frolicked**

frolicsome »*adjective* lively and playful.

 no k: **frolicsome**

from

fromage frais »*noun* a type of smooth soft fresh cheese.
– SAY from-ah*zh* fray

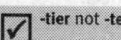 **fromage frais** is French for 'fresh cheese'

frond »*noun* the leaf of a palm, fern, or similar plant.

front (verb: **fronts**, **fronting**, **fronted**)

frontage »*noun* ❶ the front of a building. ❷ a strip of land next to a street or waterway.

frontal »*adjective* having to do with the front.
frontally

front bench »*noun* (in the UK) the foremost seats in the House of Commons, occupied by the members of the cabinet and shadow cabinet.
frontbencher

fronted

front-end »*adjective* having to do with the front.

frontier »*noun* ❶ a border separating two countries. ❷ the furthest part of land which has been settled. ❸ the limit of what is known or achieved in a particular area.

 -tier not -teir: **frontier**

frontiersman »*noun* (plural **frontiersmen**) a man living in the region of a frontier.

frontierswoman (plural **frontierswomen**)

fronting

frontispiece »*noun* an illustration facing the title page of a book.
– SAY frun-tiss-peess

front line »*noun* the part of an army that is closest to the enemy.

frontman (plural **frontmen**)

front-runner »*noun* the contestant that is leading in a competition.

fronts

frost (verb: frosts, frosting, frosted)

frostbite »*noun* injury to parts of the body caused by exposure to extreme cold.

frosted »*adjective* ❶ covered with frost. ❷ (of glass) having a semi-transparent textured surface.

frostier

frostiest

frostily

frostiness

frosting

frosts

frosty (adjective: frostier, frostiest)
frostily
frostiness

froth (verb: froths, frothing, frothed)
frothy

frown (verb: frowns, frowning, frowned)

frowsty »*adjective* having a stale, warm, and stuffy atmosphere.

frowzy »*adjective* scruffy or neglected in appearance.
– SAY frow-zi

> ☑ frowzy can also be spelled **frowsy**: both spellings are correct

froze past of FREEZE.

frozen past participle of FREEZE.

fructose »*noun* a simple sugar found chiefly in honey and fruit.
– SAY fruk-tohz

frugal »*adjective* sparing with money or food.
– SAY froo-g'l
frugality
frugally

fruit (verb: fruits, fruiting, fruited)

fruitcake

fruited

fruiterer »*noun* a person who sells fruit.

> ☑ repeat the **er: fruiterer**

fruitful »*adjective* ❶ producing a lot of fruit. ❷ producing good results.
fruitfully
fruitfulness

> ☑ **-ful** not **-full: fruitful**

fruitier

fruitiest

fruitiness

fruiting

fruition »*noun* the fulfilment of a plan or project.

– SAY fruu-i-sh'n

fruitless »*adjective* ❶ failing to achieve the desired results. ❷ not producing fruit.
fruitlessly

fruits

fruity »*adjective* (fruitier, fruitiest) ❶ having to do with fruit. ❷ (of a voice) mellow, deep, and rich. ❸ (in informal English) sexually suggestive.
fruitiness

frump »*noun* an unattractive woman who wears dowdy old-fashioned clothes.
frumpy

frustrate (verb: frustrates, frustrating, frustrated)
frustrating
frustration

fry[1] (verb: fries, frying, fried) [cook in hot oil]

fry[2] »*plural noun* young fish.

fryer

frying

frypan

fry-up

FTSE index »*noun* a figure (published by the *Financial Times*) indicating the relative prices of shares on the London Stock Exchange.

> ℹ short for *Financial Times Stock Exchange*, the **FTSE index** is also known as the **FT index**

fuchsia »*noun* ❶ an ornamental shrub with drooping tubular flowers. ❷ a vivid purplish-red colour.
– SAY fyoo-shuh

> ☑ **chs** not **sh: fuchsia** is named after the German botanist Leonhard *Fuchs*

fuck (verb: fucks, fucking, fucked)
fucker

fuddled »*adjective* confused or dazed.

fuddy-duddy (plural fuddy-duddies)

fudge »*noun* ❶ a soft sweet made from sugar, butter, and milk or cream. ❷ an attempt to present an issue in a vague way.
» *verb* (fudges, fudging, fudged) ❶ present something in a vague way. ❷ manipulate facts or figures so as to present a desired picture.

fuel (verb: fuels, fuelling, fuelled)

> ☑ double the **l** in **fuelling** and **fuelled** (the spellings with a single **l** are American)

fuel cell »*noun* a cell producing an electric current direct from a chemical reaction.

fuel injection »*noun* the direct introduction of fuel into the cylinders of an internal-combustion engine.
   fuel-injected

fuelled

fuelling

fuels

fug »*noun* (in informal English) a warm, stuffy atmosphere.

fugal »*adjective* (in music) relating to a fugue.

fugitive »*noun* a person who has escaped from captivity or is in hiding.
» *adjective* quick to disappear: *a fugitive memory.*
– SAY fyoo-ji-tiv

fugue »*noun* a piece of music in which a short melody or phrase is introduced by one part and successively taken up by others.
– SAY fyoog

Fuhrer »*noun* the title assumed by Hitler as leader of Germany.
– SAY fyoo-uh-ruh

> ✓ **Fuhrer** can also be spelled **Führer**, with an umlaut accent above the **u** (as in the original German)

fulcrum »*noun* (plural **fulcra** or **fulcrums**) the point on which a lever turns or is supported.

> ✓ the plural can be either **fulcra** (like the original Latin) or **fulcrums**

fulfil (verb: **fulfils, fulfilling, fulfilled**)
   fulfilment

> ✓ there is no double l in **fulfil, fulfils,** and **fulfilment** (the spelling of these words with **ill** is American)

full[1] (adjective: **fuller, fullest**) [holding as much as possible]

full[2] »*verb* (**fulls, fulling, fulled**) clean, shrink, and thicken cloth using heat, pressure, and moisture.

fullback »*noun* a player in a defensive position near the goal in a game such as soccer.

full-blooded

full-blown »*adjective* fully developed.

full board »*noun* the providing of accommodation and all meals at a hotel or guest house.

full-bodied »*adjective* rich and satisfying in flavour or sound.

fulled

fuller[1] »*noun* a person whose occupation is fulling cloth.

fuller[2] [more full]

fullest

full-frontal

full house »*noun* ❶ a theatre or meeting that is filled to capacity. ❷ a poker hand with three of a kind and a pair. ❸ a winning card at bingo.

fulling

fullness

> ✓ **fullness** can also be spelled **fulness**: both spellings are correct

fulls

full-scale

full stop »*noun* a punctuation mark (.) used at the end of a sentence or an abbreviation.

full-time
   full-timer

fully

fulmar »*noun* a grey and white northern seabird.
– SAY fuul-mer

fulminate »*verb* (**fulminates, fulminating, fulminated**) protest strongly.
– SAY fuul-mi-nayt or ful-mi-nayt
   fulmination

fulness another way of spelling FULLNESS.

fulsome »*adjective* ❶ excessively flattering. ❷ of large size or quantity; generous: *fulsome details.*
   fulsomely

> ℹ take care when using **fulsome**, because its meaning can be unclear. An expression like *fulsome praise* can mean two things: to some it means 'generous praise', but to others 'flattering or insincere praise'.

> ✓ only one l in **fulsome**

fumarole »*noun* an opening in or near a volcano, through which hot sulphurous gases emerge.
– SAY fyoo-muh-rohl

> ✓ **fumar** not **fumer**: **fumarole**

fumble (verb: **fumbles, fumbling, fumbled**)

fume (verb: **fumes, fuming, fumed**)

fumigate »*verb* (**fumigates, fumigating, fumigated**) disinfect something with the fumes of certain chemicals.
– SAY fyoo-mi-gayt
   fumigation

> ✓ one m, one g: **fumigate**

fuming

fun

function (verb: **functions, functioning, functioned**)
  functionless

functional »*adjective* ❶ having to do with a function. ❷ designed to be practical and useful. ❸ working or operating.
  functionality
  functionally

functionary »*noun* (plural **functionaries**) an official.

functioned

functioning

functionless

functions

fund (verb: **funds, funding, funded**)
  funding

fundamental »*adjective* of basic importance.
  » *noun* a basic rule or principle.
  fundamentally

fundamentalism »*noun* ❶ a form of Protestant Christianity which promotes the belief that the Bible is literally true. ❷ the strict following of the writings or basic teachings of any religion or system of thought.
  fundamentalist

fundamentally

funded

funding

fund-raiser
  fund-raising

funds

funeral

funeral director »*noun* an undertaker.

funeral parlour »*noun* a place where dead people are prepared for burial or cremation.

funerary »*adjective* having to do with a funeral or the remembrance of the dead.
  – SAY fyoo-nuh-ruh-ri

funereal »*adjective* having the solemn character appropriate to a funeral.
  – SAY fyoo-**neer**-i-uhl
  funereally

funfair

fungal

fungi plural of **FUNGUS**.

fungicide »*noun* a chemical that destroys fungus.
  – SAY fun-ji-syd or fung-gi-syd
  fungicidal

fungus »*noun* (plural **fungi**) an organism, such as a mould or mushroom, that grows

on plants or decaying vegetable matter and reproduces by spores.
  – SAY fung-guhss [singular], fung-gI [plural]
  fungal

✓ make the plural by changing the **us** ending to **i** (like the original Latin): **fungi**

funicular »*adjective* (of a railway on a steep slope) operated by a cable attached to cars which balance each other while one goes up and the other down.

funk[1] (in informal English) »*noun* a state of panic or depression.
  » *verb* (**funks, funking, funked**) avoid doing something out of fear.

funk[2] »*noun* a style of popular dance music of US black origin, having a strong rhythm.

funky (adjective: **funkier, funkiest**)
  funkily
  funkiness

funnel (verb: **funnels, funnelling, funnelled**)

✓ double the l in **funnelling** and **funnelled** (the spellings with a single l are American)

funny (adjective: **funnier, funniest**)
  funnily

✓ drop the y and add **ier** or **iest** to spell **funnier** or **funniest**

fur (verb: **furs, furring, furred**)

✓ double the r in **furring** and **furred**

furbelow »*noun* ❶ a flounce on a skirt or petticoat. ❷ (**furbelows**) showy trimmings.

furies

furious
  furiously

furl »*verb* (**furls, furling, furled**) roll or fold up neatly and securely.

furlong »*noun* an eighth of a mile, 220 yards.

furlough »*noun* permission to leave your duties or job for a period of time.
  – SAY fer-loh

furls

furnace »*noun* ❶ an enclosed chamber for heating material to very high temperatures. ❷ a very hot place.

furnish (verb: **furnishes, furnishing, furnished**)

furnishings

furniture

furore »*noun* an outbreak of public anger or excitement.

f

– SAY fyoo-**ror**-i

✓ don't forget the **e** at the end: **furore** (the spelling **furor** is American)

furred

furrier[1] »*noun* a person who prepares or deals in furs.
– SAY **furr**-i-er

furrier[2] [more furry]

furriest

furriness

furring

furrow »*noun* ❶ a long, narrow trench made in the ground by a plough. ❷ a rut or groove. ❸ a deep wrinkle on a person's face.
» *verb* (**furrows**, **furrowing**, **furrowed**) ❶ make a furrow in. ❷ mark or be marked with furrows.

furry (adjective: **furrier**, **furriest**)
furriness

furs

further (verb: **furthers**, **furthering**, **furthered**)

ℹ when should you use **further** and when is it better to say **farther**? When talking about distance, you can use either: *she moved further down the train* and *she moved farther down the train* are both correct. However, you should use **further** when you mean 'in addition to what has already been done' (*I won't trouble you any further*) or when you mean 'additional' (*phone for further information*). As a verb, only **further** can be used (*he was trying to further his career*).

furtherance »*noun* the advancement of a plan or interest.

✓ **ance** not **ence**: **furtherance**

furthered

furthering

furthermore

furthers

furthest

✓ **farthest** can also be used to mean **furthest**: both are correct

furtive »*adjective* trying to avoid being noticed in a secretive or guilty way.
furtively
furtiveness

fury »*noun* (plural **furies**) ❶ extreme anger. ❷ extreme strength or violence: *the fury of a gathering storm*. ❸ (**Furies**) (in Greek mythology) three goddesses who punished people for their crimes.

✓ plural: drop the **y** and add **ies**: **furies**

furze »*noun* = GORSE.

fuse[1] »*verb* (**fuses**, **fusing**, **fused**) ❶ join or combine to form a whole. ❷ melt something so it joins with something else. ❸ (of an electrical appliance) stop working when a fuse melts. ❹ fit a circuit or electrical appliance with a fuse.
» *noun* a safety device consisting of a strip of wire that melts and breaks an electric circuit if the current goes beyond a safe level.

fuse[2] »*noun* ❶ a length of material which is lit to explode a bomb or firework. ❷ a device in a bomb that controls the timing of the explosion.
» *verb* (**fuses**, **fusing**, **fused**) fit a fuse to a bomb.

✓ **s** not **z**: **fuse** (the spelling **fuze** is American)

fuselage »*noun* the main body of an aircraft.
– SAY **fyoo**-zuh-lah*zh* or **fyoo**-zuh-lij

✓ **sel** not **sil**: **fuselage**

fusible »*adjective* able to be melted easily.

✓ **-ible** not **-able**: **fusible**

fusil »*noun* (a historical term) a light musket.
– SAY **fyoo**-zil

fusilier »*noun* (**Fusilier**) a member of any of several British regiments formerly armed with fusils.
– SAY fyoo-zi-**leer**

✓ one **s**, one **l**: **fusilier**

fusillade »*noun* a series of shots fired at the same time or quickly one after the other.
– SAY fyoo-zi-**layd**

✓ one **s**, two **l**'s: **fusillade**

fusilli »*plural noun* pasta pieces in the form of short spirals.
– SAY fyuu-**zee**-li

✓ one **s**, two **l**'s: **fusilli** is an Italian word meaning 'little spindles'

fusion »*noun* ❶ the joining of two or more things together to form a whole. ❷ a reaction in which the nuclei of atoms fuse to form a heavier nucleus, releasing a great deal of energy.

fuss (plural **fusses**; verb: **fusses**, **fussing**, **fussed**)

fussier

fussiest

fussily

fussiness

fusspot »*noun* (in informal English) a fussy person.

fussy (adjective: **fussier**, **fussiest**)
fussily
fussiness

fustian »*noun* a thick, hard-wearing cloth woven with parallel diagonal lines.
– SAY **fuss**-ti-uhn

fusty »*adjective* (**fustier**, **fustiest**)
❶ smelling stale or damp. ❷ old-fashioned.
fustiness

futile »*adjective* pointless.
futilely
futility

futon »*noun* a Japanese padded mattress that can be rolled up.
– SAY **foo**-ton

future

Futurism »*noun* an early 20th-century artistic movement which rejected traditional forms and embraced modern technology.
Futurist

futuristic »*adjective* ❶ having or involving very modern technology or design. ❷ (of a film or book) set in the future.

futurity »*noun* (plural **futurities**) ❶ the future time. ❷ a future event.
– SAY fyoo-**tyoor**-i-ti

fuze American spelling of FUSE².

fuzz

fuzzy (adjective: **fuzzier**, **fuzziest**)
fuzzily
fuzziness

fuzzy logic »*noun* a form of mathematical logic in which things can have fractional values rather than being simply true or false.

Gg

gab (verb: **gabs**, **gabbing**, **gabbed**)

> ☑ double the **b** in **gabbing** and **gabbed**

gabardine another way of spelling GABERDINE.

gabbed

gabbing

gabble (verb: **gabbles**, **gabbling**, **gabbled**)
gabbler

gaberdine »*noun* ❶ a smooth, hard-wearing worsted or cotton cloth. ❷ a raincoat made of gaberdine.
– SAY ga-ber-**deen**

> ☑ **gaberdine** can also be spelled **gabardine**: both spellings are correct

gable »*noun* the triangular upper part of a wall at the end of a ridged roof.

Gabonese (plural **Gabonese**) [of Gabon]
– SAY ga-buh-**neez**

gabs

gad »*verb* (**gads**, **gadding**, **gadded**) (**gad about** or **around**) (in informal English) go around from one place to another in search of pleasure.

> ☑ double the **d** in **gadding** and **gadded**

gadfly »*noun* (plural **gadflies**) ❶ a fly that bites livestock. ❷ an annoying or provoking person.

gadget
gadgetry

gadolinium »*noun* a soft silvery-white metallic chemical element.

gads

Gael »*noun* a Gaelic-speaking person.
– SAY gayl

Gaelic »*noun* ❶ (also **Scottish Gaelic**) a Celtic language spoken in western Scotland. ❷ (also **Irish Gaelic**) Irish, the Celtic language of Ireland.
»*adjective* having to do with these languages and their speakers.
– SAY **gay**-lik or **gal**-lik

gaff »*noun* ❶ a stick with a hook for landing large fish. ❷ (**blow the gaff**) (in informal English) reveal a plot or secret.

g

❸ (in informal English) a person's house, flat, or shop.

» *verb* (**gaffs**, **gaffing**, **gaffed**) hook a fish with a gaff.

gaffe »*noun* an embarrassing blunder.
– SAY gaf

> ✓ remember the **e**: **gaffe** (a French word)

gaffed

gaffer

gaffing

gaffs

gag (verb: **gags**, **gagging**, **gagged**)

gaga »*adjective* (in informal English) rambling in speech or thought, especially as a result of old age.

gage American spelling of GAUGE.

gagged

gagging

gaggle »*noun* ❶ a flock of geese. ❷ (in informal English) a disorderly group of people.

gags

Gaia »*noun* the earth, considered to act as a huge self-regulating organism.
– SAY gy-uh
 Gaian

> ℹ️ named after the Greek earth goddess *Gaia*. The Gaia hypothesis was proposed by the English scientist James Lovelock.

gaiety

> ✓ note the spelling **aie**: **gaiety** (the spelling **gayety** is American)

gaily

gain (verb: **gains**, **gaining**, **gained**)

gainful »*adjective* (of employment) paid; profitable.
 gainfully

> ✓ **-ful** not **-full**: **gainful**

gaining

gains

gainsay »*verb* (**gainsays**, **gainsaying**, **gainsaid**) deny or contradict.
 gainsayer

gait »*noun* a way of walking.

> ℹ️ do not confuse **gait** with **gate**, which means 'a hinged barrier'

gaiter »*noun* a covering of cloth or leather for the ankle and lower leg.

gal »*noun* (in informal English) a girl or young woman.

gala »*noun* ❶ a celebration or special entertainment. ❷ (in British English) a special sports event, especially a swimming competition.
– SAY gah-luh or gay-luh

galactic »*adjective* relating to a galaxy.
– SAY guh-**lak**-tik

galaxy »*noun* (plural **galaxies**) ❶ a large system of stars. ❷ (**the Galaxy**) the system of stars that includes the sun and the earth; the Milky Way.

> ✓ plural: drop the **y** and add **ies**: **galaxies**

gale »*noun* ❶ a very strong wind. ❷ an outburst of laughter.

gall »*noun* ❶ bold and impudent behaviour. ❷ bitterness or cruelty. ❸ annoyance; irritation. ❹ a sore on the skin made by rubbing. ❺ an abnormal growth on plants and trees.

» *verb* (**galls**, **galling**, **galled**) annoy; irritate.

gallant »*adjective* ❶ brave; heroic. ❷ (of a man) polite and charming to women.

» *noun* a man who is polite and charming to women.
– SAY gal-luhnt [brave], guh-**lant** [polite and charming]
 gallantly

> ✓ **ant** not **ent**: **gallant**

gallantry (plural **gallantries**)

gall bladder »*noun* a small sac-shaped organ beneath the liver, in which bile is stored.

galled

galleon »*noun* (a historical term) a large sailing ship with three or more decks and masts.

gallery (plural **galleries**)

> ✓ **ery** not **ary**: **gallery**
> plural: drop the **y** and add **ies**: **galleries**

galley »*noun* (plural **galleys**) ❶ (a historical term) a low, flat ship with one or more sails and up to three banks of oars. ❷ a narrow kitchen in a ship or aircraft.

Gallic »*adjective* having to do with France or the French.
– SAY gal-lik

> ✓ there is no **k**: **Gallic**

gallimaufry »*noun* a jumble or varied mixture.
– SAY gal-li-**maw**-fri

galling

gallium »*noun* a soft, silvery-white metallic chemical element.
– SAY gal-li-uhm

gallivant »*verb* (**gallivants, gallivanting, gallivanted**) (in informal English) go from place to place seeking pleasure and entertainment.
– SAY gal-li-vant

> ✓ double l: **gallivant**

gallon »*noun* a unit of volume for liquid measure equal to eight pints (in Britain, 4.55 litres).

gallop (verb: **gallops, galloping, galloped**) **galloper**

> ✓ do not double the p to spell **galloping** and **galloped**

gallows »*plural noun* ❶ a structure used for hanging a person. ❷ (**the gallows**) execution by hanging.

gallows humour »*noun* grim humour in a desperate or hopeless situation.

galls

gallstone »*noun* a hard mass of crystals formed in the gall bladder or bile ducts in some medical conditions, causing pain and obstruction.

galore »*adjective* in abundance: *there were prizes galore.*

galoshes »*plural noun* rubber shoes worn over normal shoes in wet weather.
– SAY guh-**losh**-iz

galvanic »*adjective* relating to electric currents produced by chemical action.
– SAY gal-**van**-ik

galvanize »*verb* (**galvanizes, galvanizing, galvanized**) ❶ shock or excite someone into doing something. ❷ (**galvanized**) (of iron or steel) coated with a protective layer of zinc.
– SAY gal-vuh-nyz

> ✓ many people prefer the alternative spellings **galvanise, galvanises**, etc.: both **s** and **z** spellings are correct

Gambian [of the Gambia]

gambit »*noun* something that somebody says or does that is meant to give them an advantage.

gamble (verb: **gambles, gambling, gambled**) [play games of chance, a risk] **gambler**

> ℹ do not confuse **gamble** with **gambol**, which means 'run about playfully'

gambol »*verb* (**gambols, gambolling, gambolled**) run or jump about playfully.

> ℹ do not confuse **gambol** with **gamble** meaning 'play games of chance'

> ✓ double the l to spell **gambolling** and **gambolled** (the spelling with a single l is American)

game (verb: **games, gaming, gamed**)
gamely
gameness
gamer

gamekeeper

gamely

gameness

gamer

games

gamesmanship »*noun* the ability to win games by making your opponent feel less confident.

gamete »*noun* (in biology) a cell which is able to unite with another of the opposite sex in sexual reproduction to form a zygote.
– SAY gam-eet

gamey another way of spelling GAMY.

gamier [more gamy]

gamiest

gamine »*noun* a girl with a mischievous, boyish charm.
»*adjective* characteristic of a gamine.
– SAY ga-**meen**

gaming

gamma »*noun* the third letter of the Greek alphabet (Γ, γ).

gamma rays »*plural noun* electromagnetic radiation of shorter wavelength than X-rays.

gammon »*noun* ❶ ham which has been cured like bacon. ❷ the bottom piece of a side of bacon, including a hind leg.

gammy »*adjective* (in informal English) (of a leg) unable to be used normally because of injury or pain.

gamut »*noun* the complete range or scope of something.
– SAY gam-uht

gamy »*adjective* (**gamier, gamiest**) (of meat) having the strong flavour or smell of game when it is high.
gaminess

> ✓ **gamy** can also be spelled with an **e**: **gamey**

gander »*noun* a male goose.

gang (verb: **gangs, ganging, ganged**)

gangland

ganglia plural of GANGLION.

gangling »*adjective* (of a person) tall, thin, and awkward.

ganglion »*noun* (plural **ganglia** or **ganglions**) ❶ a mass of nerve cells. ❷ swelling in a tendon.
– sᴀʏ gang-gli-uhn

> ☑ the plural can be either **ganglia** (like the original Greek) or **ganglions**

gangly »*adjective* = ɢᴀɴɢʟɪɴɢ.

gangplank

gangrene »*noun* the death of body tissue, caused by an obstructed blood supply or by infection.
– sᴀʏ gang-green
gangrenous

> ☑ -grene not -green: gangrene

gangs

gangster
gangsterism

gangway

ganja »*noun* cannabis.
– sᴀʏ gan-juh

gannet »*noun* a large seabird with mainly white plumage.

> ☑ double n and single t: gannet

gantry »*noun* (plural **gantries**) a bridge-like structure that supports a crane, railway signals, or a spacecraft before it is launched.

gaol another of way of spelling ᴊᴀɪʟ.

gap
gappy

gape (verb: **gapes, gaping, gaped**)

gappy

gap year »*noun* a period taken by a student as a break from education between leaving school and starting a university or college course.

garage (verb: **garages, garaging, garaged**)

garam masala »*noun* a spice mixture used in Indian cookery.
– sᴀʏ ga-ruhm muh-**sah**-luh

garb »*noun* unusual or distinctive clothes.
» *verb* (**be garbed**) be dressed in distinctive clothes.

garbage

garbed

garble (verb: **garbles, garbling, garbled**)

Garda »*noun* the state police force of the Irish Republic.
– sᴀʏ gar-duh

garden (verb: **gardens, gardening, gardened**)

gardener

> ☑ remember, one n and two e's in gardener

gardenia »*noun* a tree or shrub with large white or yellow flowers.
– sᴀʏ gar-**dee**-ni-uh

> ☑ e not ee: gardenia

gardening

gardens

gargantuan »*adjective* enormous.
– sᴀʏ gar-gan-tyuu-uhn

gargle (verb: **gargles, gargling, gargled**)

gargoyle »*noun* a spout in the form of an ugly person or animal that carries water away from the roof of a building.
– sᴀʏ gar-goyl

> ☑ oyle not oil: gargoyle

garish »*adjective* unpleasantly bright and showy.
– sᴀʏ gair-ish
garishly

garland »*noun* a wreath of flowers and leaves, worn on the head or hung as a decoration.
» *verb* (**garlands, garlanding, garlanded**) crown someone or something with a garland.

garlic »*noun* a plant of the onion family with a strong taste and smell, used to give flavour to food.
garlicky

> ☑ there is no k in garlic, but add one in garlicky

garment

garner »*verb* (**garners, garnering, garnered**) gather or collect something.

> ☑ do not double the final r to spell garnering or garnered

garnet »*noun* a red semi-precious stone.

garnish »*verb* (**garnishes, garnishing, garnished**) use an ingredient as decoration for a dish of food.
» *noun* an ingredient used in this way.

garret »*noun* a room in the roof of a house.

> ☑ only one t in garret

garrison »*noun* a body of troops stationed in a fortress or town to defend it.
» *verb* (**garrisons, garrisoning, garrisoned**) provide a place with a garrison.

✓ double r but single s: **garrison**
do not double the **n** in **garrisoned** and **garrisoning**

garrotte »*verb* (**garrottes, garrotting, garrotted**) kill someone by strangling them.
» *noun* a wire or cord used for strangling someone.
– SAY guh-**rot**

✓ double r and double t: **garrotte, garrotted**, etc. (spellings with a single **t** are American)

garrulous »*adjective* extremely talkative.
– SAY ga-ruh-luhss
garrulity
garrulously
garrulousness

garter »*noun* a band worn around the leg to keep up a stocking or sock.
gartered

gas (plural **gases**; verb: **gases, gassing, gassed**)

✓ do not double the **s** to make the plural: **gases**. The spelling **gasses**, which is mainly American, is often seen and is becoming more accepted.

gasbag

gaseous »*adjective* relating to or like a gas.
– SAY gass-i-uhss
gaseousness

gases

gash (verb: **gashes, gashing, gashed**)

gasket »*noun* a sheet or ring of rubber that seals the join between two surfaces in an engine or other device.

gaslight
gaslit

gasoline »*noun* (in American English) = PETROL.

gasometer »*noun* a large tank in which gas is stored before it is distributed.
– SAY gass-**om**-i-ter

✓ -meter not -metre: **gasometer**

gasp (verb: **gasps, gasping, gasped**)

gassed

gasses see the note at GAS.

gassier

gassiest

gassiness

gassing

gassy (adjective: **gassier, gassiest**)
gassiness

gastric »*adjective* having to do with the stomach.

✓ there is no **k**: **gastric**

gastric flu »*noun* a short-lived illness affecting the stomach.

gastric juice »*noun* acid produced by the stomach to help digest food.

gastro-enteritis »*noun* inflammation of the stomach and intestines.

gastronomy »*noun* the practice or art of cooking and eating good food.
– SAY gass-**tron**-uh-mi
gastronomic

gastropod »*noun* one of a group of molluscs which includes snails and slugs.
– SAY gass-truh-pod

✓ gastro not gastero: **gastropod**

gas turbine »*noun* a turbine driven by the hot gases produced by burning fuel (as in a jet engine).

gasworks

gate [hinged barrier]

ℹ do not confuse **gate** with **gait**, which means 'a way of walking'

gateau »*noun* (plural **gateaus** or **gateaux**) a rich cake.
– SAY gat-oh [singular], gat-ohz [plural]

✓ the plural of **gateau** can add either an **s** or an **x**: **gateaus** or **gateaux** (it is a French word)

gatecrash »*verb* (**gatecrashes, gatecrashing, gatecrashed**) enter a party without being invited.
gatecrasher

gatefold »*noun* an oversized page in a book or magazine, intended to be opened out for reading.

gatehouse

gatekeeper

gateleg table »*noun* a table with hinged legs that swing out from the centre to support folding leaves.

gatepost

gateway

gather (verb: **gathers, gathering, gathered**)
gatherer

gathering

gathers

gauche »*adjective* socially awkward or unsophisticated.
– SAY gohsh
gauchely
gaucheness

gaucho »*noun* (plural **gauchos**) a cowboy from the plains of South America.

g

– **SAY** gow-choh

> ✓ the plural of **gaucho** has **os** not **oes**: **gauchos**

gaudy »*adjective* (**gaudier**, **gaudiest**) very bright or showy in a tasteless way.
gaudily
gaudiness

gauge »*noun* **❶** an instrument for measuring the amount or level of something. **❷** the thickness or size of a wire, tube, bullet, etc. **❸** the distance between the rails of a railway track.
» *verb* (**gauges**, **gauging**, **gauged**)
❶ estimate or measure something.
❷ judge a situation or mood.

> ✓ note the **au** in the middle: **gauge** (the spelling **gage** is American)

gaunt »*adjective* **❶** (of a person) looking thin and exhausted. **❷** (of a place) grim or desolate.
gauntly
gauntness

gauntlet »*noun* **❶** a stout glove with a long loose wrist. **❷** a glove worn as part of medieval armour. **❸** (**run the gauntlet**) go through an intimidating crowd or experience in order to achieve something.

gauze »*noun* **❶** a thin transparent fabric. **❷** thin cloth used for cleaning and protecting wounds. **❸** a fine wire mesh.
– **SAY** gawz
gauzy

gave past of **GIVE**.

gavel »*noun* a small hammer struck by a judge or auctioneer in order to get people's attention.
– **SAY** ga-v'l

> ✓ **el** not **al**: **gavel**

gavotte »*noun* a French dance, popular in the 18th century.
– **SAY** guh-vot

gawk »*verb* (**gawks**, **gawking**, **gawked**) stare in a stupid or rude way.

gawky (adjective: **gawkier**, **gawkiest**)
gawkily
gawkiness

gawp (verb: **gawps**, **gawping**, **gawped**)

gay (adjective: **gayer**, **gayest**)
gayness

> **ⓘ** **gay** is now a standard term for 'homosexual'. Therefore, it is now very difficult to use **gay** in its earlier meanings: 'carefree' or 'bright and showy'

gayety American spelling of **GAIETY**.

gayness

gaze (verb: **gazes**, **gazing**, **gazed**)
gazer

gazebo »*noun* (plural **gazebos** or **gazeboes**) a summer house offering a wide view of the surrounding area.
– **SAY** guh-zee-boh

> ✓ the plural of **gazebo** can have **os** or **oes**: **gazebos** or **gazeboes**

gazed

gazelle »*noun* a small antelope.

> ✓ **lle** at the end: **gazelle**

gazer

gazes

gazette »*noun* a journal or newspaper.

> ✓ **tte** at the end: **gazette**

gazetteer »*noun* an alphabetical list or dictionary of places.
– **SAY** ga-zuht-**teer**

gazing

gazpacho »*noun* (plural **gazpachos**) a cold Spanish soup made from tomatoes and peppers.
– **SAY** guhs-**pach**-oh

> ✓ the plural of **gazpacho** has **os** not **oes**: **gazpachos**

gazump »*verb* (**gazumps**, **gazumping**, **gazumped**) (in informal English) offer or accept a higher price for a house after a lower offer has already been accepted.
– **SAY** guh-**zump**
gazumper

GBH »*abbreviation* grievous bodily harm.

GCE »*abbreviation* General Certificate of Education.

GCSE »*abbreviation* General Certificate of Secondary Education.

GDP »*abbreviation* gross domestic product.

gear (verb: **gears**, **gearing**, **geared**)

gearbox

geared

gearing

gears

gearstick

gearwheel »*noun* **❶** a toothed wheel in a set of gears. **❷** (on a bicycle) a cogwheel driven directly by the chain.

gecko »*noun* (plural **geckos** or **geckoes**) a lizard with sticky pads on the feet.
– **SAY** gek-koh

> ✓ the plural of **gecko** can have **os** or **oes**: **geckos** or **geckoes**

geek »*noun* (in informal English) ❶ an awkward or unfashionable person. ❷ a person who is obsessed with something: *a computer geek*.
geeky

geese plural of GOOSE.

geezer »*noun* (in informal English) a man.

Geiger counter »*noun* a device for measuring radioactivity.
– SAY gy-ger

 named after the German physicist Hans *Geiger*

geisha »*noun* (plural **geisha** or **geishas**) a Japanese hostess trained to entertain men with conversation, dance, and song.
– SAY gay-shuh

gel »*noun* a jelly-like substance used on hair or skin.
» *verb* (**gels**, **gelling**, **gelled**) ❶ smooth your hair with gel. ❷ another way of spelling JELL.
– SAY jel

gelatin »*noun* a clear substance made by boiling animal bones and used to make jelly, glue, and photographic film.
– SAY jel-uh-tin
gelatinous

 gelatin can also be spelled with an **e** on the end: **gelatine** (both spellings are correct)

geld »*verb* (**gelds**, **gelding**, **gelded**) castrate a male animal.

gelding »*noun* a castrated animal, especially a male horse.

gelds

gelignite »*noun* an explosive made from nitroglycerine.
– SAY jel-ig-nyt

gelled

gelling

gels

gem

Gemini »*noun* a constellation and a sign of the zodiac (the Twins, 21 May–20 June).

gemstone

gendarme »*noun* a police officer in French-speaking countries.
– SAY zhon-darm

 note the final **e**: **gendarme**

gender »*noun* ❶ the state of being male or female. ❷ the members of one or other sex. ❸ one of the grammatical classes into which nouns and pronouns are divided in some languages.
gendered

 gender usually refers to cultural or social differences, whereas **sex** usually refers to biological differences

gene »*noun* a distinct sequence of DNA forming part of a chromosome, by which offspring inherit characteristics from a parent.

genealogy »*noun* (plural **genealogies**) ❶ a line of descent traced from an ancestor. ❷ the study of lines of descent.
– SAY jee-ni-**al**-uh-ji
genealogist

gene pool »*noun* the stock of different genes in a group within which breeding takes place.

genera plural of GENUS.

general

generalise another way of spelling GENERALIZE.

generalist »*noun* a person competent in several different fields or activities.

generality »*noun* (plural **generalities**) ❶ a general statement rather than one that is specific or detailed. ❷ the quality or state of being general. ❸ (**the generality**) the majority.

generalize (verb: **generalizes**, **generalizing**, **generalized**)
generalization

 many people prefer the alternative spellings **generalise**, **generalises**, etc., and **generalisation**: both **s** and **z** spellings are correct

generally

general practitioner »*noun* a doctor who treats patients in a community rather than at a hospital.

generate (verb: **generates**, **generating**, **generated**)

generation

generation gap »*noun* a difference in attitudes between people of different generations.

generator »*noun* ❶ a person or thing that generates. ❷ a machine for producing electricity.

 -or not -er: **generator**

generic »*adjective* ❶ referring to a class or group of things. ❷ (of goods) having no brand name. ❸ (in biology) relating to a genus.
– SAY ji-**ne**-rik
generically

 there is no **k** in **generic**

g

generous
generosity
generously

 drop the **u** when spelling **generosity**

genesis »*noun* ❶ the origin or development of something. ❷ (**Genesis**) the first book of the Bible, which includes the story of the creation of the world.
– SAY jen-i-siss

 one single **n**, two single **s**'s: **genesis**

gene therapy »*noun* the introduction of normal genes into cells in order to correct genetic disorders.

genetic »*adjective* ❶ relating to genes or heredity. ❷ relating to genetics.
genetical
genetically

genetically modified »*adjective* (of an organism) containing genetic material that has been artificially altered so as to produce a desired characteristic.

genetic code »*noun* the means by which DNA and RNA molecules carry genetic information.

genetic engineering »*noun* the changing of the characteristics of an organism by altering its genetic material.

genetic fingerprinting »*noun* the analysis of DNA from samples of body tissues or fluids in order to identify individuals.

geneticist

genetic profiling »*noun* = GENETIC FINGERPRINTING.

genetics »*plural noun* the study of the way characteristics are passed from one generation of animals or plants to another.
geneticist

genial »*adjective* friendly and cheerful.
– SAY jee-ni-uhl
geniality
genially

genie »*noun* (plural **genii** or **genies**) (in Arabian folklore) a spirit.
– SAY jee-ni [singular], jee-ni-I or jee-niz [plural]

 make the plural by adding **s**, or by changing the **e** ending and adding **i**: **genies** or **genii**. The plural **genii** comes from its Latin equivalent *genius*.

genital

genitalia »*plural noun* the genitals.
– SAY jen-i-tay-li-uh

genitals

genitive »*adjective* the form of a noun, pronoun, or adjective used to show possession.
– SAY jen-i-tiv

genius (plural **geniuses**)

 make the plural by adding **es**: **geniuses**

genocide »*noun* the deliberate killing of a very large number of people from a particular ethnic group or nation.
– SAY jen-uh-syd
genocidal

genome »*noun* (in biology) ❶ the full set of the chromosomes of an organism. ❷ the complete set of genetic material of an organism.
– SAY jee-nohm

genotype »*noun* (in biology) the genetic make-up of an individual organism.
– SAY jen-uh-typ or jee-nuh-typ

genre »*noun* a style or category of art or literature.
– SAY zhon-ruh or jon-ruh

gent

genteel »*adjective* affectedly polite and refined.
genteelly

 eel not **ile**: **genteel**

gentian »*noun* a plant with violet or blue trumpet-shaped flowers.
– SAY jen-sh'n

Gentile »*adjective* not Jewish.
»*noun* a person who is not Jewish.
– SAY jen-tyl

gentility »*noun* polite and refined behaviour.

gentle (adjective: **gentler**, **gentlest**)
gentleness
gently

gentlefolk »*plural noun* (an old word) people of noble birth or good social position.

gentleman (plural **gentlemen**)
gentlemanly

gentleman's agreement »*noun* an arrangement which is based on trust rather than being legally binding.

gentlemen

gentleness

gentler

gentlest

gently

gentrify »*verb* (**gentrifies**, **gentrifying**, **gentrified**) renovate a house or district so

that it follows middle-class taste.
gentrification

gentry »*noun* the people of the class next below the nobility.

genuflect »*verb* (**genuflects, genuflecting, genuflected**) briefly bend one knee to the ground in worship or as a sign of respect.
– SAY jen-yuu-flekt
genuflection

> ✓ there is no **x** in **genuflects** or **genuflection**

genuine
genuinely
genuineness

genus »*noun* (plural **genera**) ❶ a category in scientific classification that ranks above species and below family. ❷ a class of things which have common characteristics.
– SAY jee-nuhss [singular], jen-uh-ruh [plural]

> ✓ the plural of **genus**, a Latin word, is **genera**

geodesic »*adjective* relating to a method of construction based on straight lines between points on a curved surface.
– SAY jee-oh-**dess**-ik or jee-oh-**dee**-sik

geographer

geographical
geographic
geographically

geography
geographer

geology »*noun* ❶ the science which deals with the physical structure and substance of the earth. ❷ the geological features of a district.
geological
geologically
geologist

geometric »*adjective* ❶ relating to geometry. ❷ (of a design) decorated with regular lines and shapes.
– SAY ji-uh-**met**-rik
geometrical
geometrically

geometry »*noun* (plural **geometries**) ❶ the branch of mathematics concerned with the properties and relations of points, lines, surfaces, and solids. ❷ the shape and relative arrangement of the parts of something.
– SAY ji-**om**-uh-tri

geopolitics »*plural noun* politics, especially international relations, as influenced by geographical factors.
geopolitical

Geordie »*noun* (in informal English) a person from Tyneside.

georgette »*noun* a thin silk or crepe dress material.
– SAY jor-**jet**

> ✓ double **t** and **e** at the end: **georgette** was named after the French dressmaker *Georgette* de la Plante

Georgian

geothermal »*adjective* relating to or produced by the internal heat of the earth.

geranium »*noun* a garden plant with red, white, or pink flowers.

> ✓ one **r**, one **n**: **geranium** unlike many words which end in **um**, the plural of **geranium** is simply **geraniums**

gerbera »*noun* a tropical plant with large brightly coloured flowers.
– SAY **jer**-buh-ruh

gerbil

geriatric »*adjective* relating to old people. »*noun* an old person, especially one receiving special care.
– SAY je-ri-**at**-rik

geriatrics »*plural noun* the branch of medicine or social science concerned with the health and care of old people.
geriatrician

germ

German

germane »*adjective* relevant to a subject under consideration.
– SAY jer-**mayn**

> ✓ -mane not -main: **germane**

Germanic »*adjective* ❶ referring to the language family that includes English, German, Dutch, and the Scandinavian languages. ❷ referring to the peoples of ancient northern and western Europe speaking such languages. ❸ characteristic of Germans or Germany. »*noun* ❶ the Germanic languages as a group. ❷ the ancient language from which these developed.

germanium »*noun* a grey crystalline element with semiconducting properties, resembling silicon.
– SAY jer-**may**-ni-uhm

German measles »*plural noun* = RUBELLA.

German shepherd »*noun* a large breed of dog often used as guard dogs; an Alsatian.

germicidal »*adjective* harmful to germs.

germinal »*adjective* ❶ relating to a gamete or embryo. ❷ in the earliest stage of development.

g

germinate »*verb* (**germinates**, **germinating**, **germinated**) (of a seed or spore) begin to grow and put out shoots after a period of being dormant.
germination

gerontology »*noun* the scientific study of old age and old people.
– SAY je-ruhn-**tol**-uh-ji

gerrymander »*verb* (**gerrymanders**, **gerrymandering**, **gerrymandered**) alter the boundaries of an electoral constituency so as to favour one party.

> **i** the word **gerrymander** was formed from the name of Governor Elbridge *Gerry* of Massachusetts, and the word *salamander*, because of the similarity between a salamander and the shape of a voting district created when he was in office

> ✓ do not double the final **r** when spelling **gerrymandering** and **gerrymandered**

gerund »*noun* a verb form which functions as a noun, in English ending in -*ing* (e.g. *asking* in *do you mind my asking you?*).
– SAY je-ruhnd

gesso »*noun* a hard compound of plaster of Paris or whiting in glue, used in sculpture.
– SAY **jess**-oh

gestalt »*noun* (mainly in psychology) an organized whole that is seen as more than the sum of its parts.
– SAY guh-**shtahlt** or guh-**stahlt**

> **i** **gestalt** is a German word meaning 'form, shape'

Gestapo »*noun* the German secret police under Nazi rule.
– SAY ge-**stah**-poh

gestate »*verb* (**gestates**, **gestating**, **gestated**) ❶ carry a fetus in the womb from conception to birth. ❷ (of a fetus) develop in the womb.
– SAY **jess**-tayt

gestation »*noun* ❶ the process of carrying or the state of being carried in the womb between conception and birth. ❷ the development of a plan or idea over a period of time.
– SAY jess-**tay**-sh'n

gesticulate »*verb* (**gesticulates**, **gesticulating**, **gesticulated**) make dramatic gestures instead of speaking or in order to emphasize what you are saying.
– SAY jess-**tik**-yuu-layt
gesticulation

gesture (verb: **gestures**, **gesturing**, **gestured**)
gestural

get (verb: **gets**, **getting**, **got** or (in American English) **gotten**)

> **i** even though it is such a common word, **get** still has a rather informal feel. In writing or formal speech, try to use another word, e.g. *receive*, *catch*, *experience*, *suffer*, etc.

> ✓ double the **t** in **getting**

getaway

gets

getting

get-together

get-up »*noun* (in informal English) an outfit, especially an unusual one.

gewgaw »*noun* a showy thing, especially one that is worthless.
– SAY **gyoo**-gor

geyser »*noun* a hot spring that sometimes sends a column of water and steam into the air.
– SAY **gee**-zer or **gy**-zer

> ✓ **gey** not **gui** or **gee**: **geyser** comes from the name of a particular spring in Iceland

Ghanaian [of Ghana]
– SAY gah-**nay**-uhn

ghastly (adjective: **ghastlier**, **ghastliest**)
ghastliness

> ✓ don't forget the **h**: **ghastly**

gherkin »*noun* a small pickled cucumber.
– SAY **ger**-kin

> ✓ **er** not **ur**, and don't forget the **h**: **gherkin**

ghetto »*noun* (plural **ghettos** or **ghettoes**) ❶ a part of a city occupied by a minority group. ❷ (a historical term) the Jewish area in a city.
– SAY **get**-toh

> ✓ don't forget the **h** or the double **t**: **ghetto**. The plural can have **os** or **oes**: **ghettos** or **ghettoes**.

ghettoize »*verb* (**ghettoizes**, **ghettoizing**, **ghettoized**) restrict people to an isolated or segregated place or situation.
ghettoization

> ✓ many people prefer the alternative spellings **ghettoise**, **ghettoises**, etc., and **ghettoisation**: both **s** and **z** spellings are correct

ghillie another way of spelling GILLIE.

ghost

ghosting »*noun* the appearance of a secondary image on a television or other display screen.

ghostly (adjective: **ghostlier, ghostliest**)

ghost town »*noun* a town with few or no remaining inhabitants.

ghost writer »*noun* a person employed to write material for another person, who is the named author.

ghoul »*noun* ❶ an evil spirit or phantom. ❷ a person with an unhealthy interest in death or disaster.
– SAY gool
ghoulish
ghoulishly
ghoulishness

☑ don't forget the **h**: **ghoul**

GI »*noun* (plural **GIs**) a private soldier in the US army.

ℹ short for *government issue* or *general issue* (referring to military equipment)

giant

giantess (plural **giantesses**)

giant-killer
giant-killing

gibber (verb: **gibbers, gibbering, gibbered**)

gibberish

gibbers

gibbet »*noun* (a historical term) ❶ a gallows. ❷ an upright post with an arm on which the bodies of executed criminals were left hanging.
– SAY jib-bit

gibbon »*noun* a small ape with long, powerful arms, native to SE Asia.

gibbous »*adjective* (of the moon) having the part lit up bigger than a semicircle and less than a circle.
– SAY gib-buhss

giblets »*plural noun* the liver, heart, gizzard, and neck of a chicken or other fowl.
– SAY jib-lits

giddy »*adjective* (**giddier, giddiest**) ❶ having the feeling that everything is moving and you are going to fall. ❷ excitable and frivolous.
giddiness

giddy-up

gift (verb: **gifts, gifting, gifted**)

gift-wrap (verb: **gift-wraps, gift-wrapping, gift-wrapped**)

☑ double the **p** in **gift-wrapping** and **gift-wrapped**

gig[1] »*noun* (mainly a historical term) a light two-wheeled carriage pulled by one horse.
– SAY gig or jig

gig[2] »*noun* a live performance by a musician or other performer.
– SAY gig

gigabyte »*noun* (in computing) a unit of information equal to one thousand million bytes.
– SAY gig-uh-byt or jig-uh-byt

☑ **-byte** not **-bite**: **gigabyte**

gigantic

giggle (verb: **giggles, giggling, giggled**)
giggly

gigolo »*noun* (plural **gigolos**) a young man paid by an older woman to be her escort or lover.
– SAY jig-uh-loh

☑ the plural of **gigolo** (a French word) has **os** not **oes**: **gigolos**

gild »*verb* (**gilds, gilding, gilded**) ❶ cover something thinly with gold. ❷ (**gilded**) wealthy and privileged: *gilded youth.*
gilding

gilet »*noun* a light sleeveless padded jacket.
– SAY zhi-lay [singular and plural]

☑ **et** at the end: **gilet** is a French word meaning 'waistcoat'

gill[1] »*noun* ❶ the organ used for breathing in fishes and some amphibians. ❷ the plates on the underside of mushrooms and many toadstools.
– SAY gil

gill[2] »*noun* a unit of liquid measure, equal to a quarter of a pint.
– SAY jil

gillie »*noun* (in Scotland) an attendant on a hunting or fishing expedition.
– SAY gil-li

☑ **gillie** can also be spelled **ghillie**, with an **h** after the **g**

gillyflower »*noun* a fragrant flower such as the wallflower or white stock.
– SAY jil-li-flow-er

☑ **gillyflower** can also be spelled **gilliflower**: both spellings are correct

gilt »*adjective* covered thinly with gold leaf or gold paint.
»*noun* gold leaf or gold paint applied in a thin layer to a surface.

i do not confuse **gilt** with **guilt**, which means 'the fact of having done something wrong'

gilt-edged »*adjective* (of investments) safe and reliable.

gimcrack »*adjective* showy but flimsy or poorly made.
» *noun* a cheap and showy ornament.
– SAY jim-krak

gimlet »*noun* a T-shaped tool with a screw-tip for boring holes.
– SAY gim-lit

gimmick »*noun* a trick or device intended to attract attention rather than fulfil a useful purpose.
gimmickry
gimmicky

✓ double **m**: **gimmick**

gin »*noun* **❶** a clear alcoholic spirit flavoured with juniper berries. **❷** a machine for separating cotton from its seeds. **❸** a machine for raising and moving heavy weights. **❹** a trap for catching small game.

ginger »*noun* **❶** a hot, fragrant spice made from the stem of a SE Asian plant. **❷** a light reddish-yellow colour.
» *verb* (gingers, gingering, gingered) (ginger up) make something more active or exciting.

gingerbread

gingered

gingering

gingerly »*adverb* in a careful or cautious manner.

gingers

gingham »*noun* lightweight cotton cloth with a checked pattern.
– SAY ging-uhm

✓ don't forget the **h**: **gingham**

gingivitis »*noun* inflammation of the gums.
– SAY jin-ji-vy-tiss

ginkgo »*noun* (plural ginkgos or ginkgoes) a Chinese tree with fan-shaped leaves and yellow flowers.
– SAY ging-koh

✓ be careful with the spelling of **ginkgo**, which comes from Chinese: the **k** comes before the second **g**
the plural can have either **os** or **oes**: ginkgos or ginkgoes

ginormous »*adjective* (in informal English) extremely large.

ginseng »*noun* the tuber of an east Asian and North American plant, supposed to have medicinal properties.
– SAY jin-seng

gip another way of spelling GYP.

gipsy another way of spelling GYPSY.

giraffe

✓ one r, two f's: **giraffe**

gird »*verb* (girds, girding, girded; past participle girded or girt) **❶** encircle or secure something with a belt or band. **❷** (gird your loins) prepare and strengthen yourself for what is to come.

girder »*noun* a large iron or steel beam used in building bridges and large buildings.

girding

girdle »*noun* **❶** a belt or cord worn round the waist. **❷** a woman's elasticated corset extending from waist to thigh.
» *verb* (girdles, girdling, girdled) encircle the body with a girdle or belt.

girds

girl
girlhood

girlfriend

Girl Guide

girlhood

girlish
girlishly
girlishness

girn another way of spelling GURN.

giro »*noun* (plural giros) **❶** a system in which money is transferred electronically, involving banks, post offices, and public utilities. **❷** a cheque or payment by giro.

✓ the plural of **giro**, an Italian word, has **os** not **oes**: **giros**

girt past participle of GIRD.

girth »*noun* **❶** the measurement around the middle of something. **❷** a band attached to a saddle and fastened around a horse's belly.

gist »*noun* the general meaning of a speech or text.
– SAY jist

git

give (verb: gives, giving, gave; past participle given)
giver

giveaway

given

given name see the note at CHRISTIAN NAME.

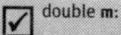

giver
gives
giving

gizmo »*noun* (plural **gizmos**) (in informal English) a gadget, especially one you cannot name.

> ✓ the plural of **gizmo** has **os** not **oes**: **gizmos**

gizzard »*noun* **❶** a muscular part of a bird's stomach for grinding food. **❷** a muscular stomach of some fish, insects, and other invertebrates.

> ✓ double **z**, and **ard** not **erd**: **gizzard**

glace »*adjective* (of fruit) having a glossy appearance due to being preserved in sugar.
– **SAY** gla-say

> ✓ **glace** can also be spelled **glacé**, with an acute accent above the **e** (as in the original French)

glacial »*adjective* **❶** relating to ice, especially in the form of glaciers. **❷** extremely cold or unfriendly.

glaciation »*noun* (in geology) the state or result of being covered by glaciers.

glacier »*noun* a slowly moving mass of ice formed by the accumulation of snow on mountains or near the poles.
– **SAY** gla-si-er or glay-si-er

glad (adjective: **gladder**, **gladdest**)
gladly
gladness

> ✓ double the **d** in **gladder** and **gladdest**, but not in **gladly** and **gladness**

gladden (verb: **gladdens**, **gladdening**, **gladdened**)

> ✓ two **d**'s, one **n**: **gladden**

gladder
gladdest

glade »*noun* an open space in a wood or forest.

gladiator »*noun* (in ancient Rome) a man trained to fight with weapons against other men or wild animals in an arena.
gladiatorial

> ✓ **-or** not **-er**: **gladiator**

gladiolus »*noun* (plural **gladioli** or **gladioluses**) a plant with sword-shaped leaves and spikes of brightly coloured flowers.
– **SAY** glad-i-**oh**-luhss [singular], glad-i-**oh**-ll or glad-i-**oh**-luhss-iz [plural]

> ✓ make the plural by changing the **us** ending to **i** (like the original Latin) or by adding **es**: **gladioli** or **gladioluses**

gladly
gladness

glamorize »*verb* (**glamorizes**, **glamorizing**, **glamorized**) make something seem glamorous or desirable, especially falsely so.
glamorization

> ✓ there is no **u** in **glamorize** many people prefer the alternative spellings **glamorise**, **glamorises**, etc.: both **s** and **z** spellings are correct

glamorous
glamorously

> ✓ **mor** not **mour**: **glamorous**

glamour »*noun* an attractive and exciting quality.

> ✓ **-our** not **-or**: **glamour** (the spelling **glamor** is American)

glance »*verb* (**glances**, **glancing**, **glanced**) **❶** take a brief or hurried look. **❷** (**glance off**) hit something at an angle and bounce off obliquely.
» *noun* a brief or hurried look.
glancing

gland »*noun* **❶** an organ of the body which secretes particular chemical substances. **❷** a lymph node.

glandular »*adjective* relating to or affecting a gland or glands.

glandular fever »*noun* an infectious disease characterized by swelling of the lymph glands and prolonged fatigue.

glare (verb: **glares**, **glaring**, **glared**)

glaring »*adjective* extremely obvious.
glaringly

glasnost »*noun* (in the former Soviet Union) the policy or practice of more open government.
– **SAY** glaz-nosst

glass (plural **glasses**; verb: **glasses**, **glassing**, **glassed**)
glassful

glass-blowing »*noun* the craft of making glassware by blowing semi-liquid glass through a long tube.

glass ceiling »*noun* an imaginary barrier to progress in a profession, especially affecting women and members of minorities.

glassed
glasses

g

glass fibre »*noun* a strong material containing glass filaments.

glassful

 -ful not -full: **glassful**

glasshouse »*noun* a greenhouse.

glassier [more glassy]

glassiest

glassing

glasspaper »*noun* paper covered with powdered glass, used for smoothing and polishing.

glassware

glass wool »*noun* glass in the form of fine fibres used for packing and insulation.

glassy (adjective: **glassier, glassiest**)

Glaswegian »*noun* a person from Glasgow.
» *adjective* relating to Glasgow.
– **say** glaz-**wee**-j'n

glaucoma »*noun* a condition of increased pressure within the eyeball, causing gradual loss of sight.
– **say** glaw-**koh**-muh

glaze »*verb* (**glazes, glazing, glazed**) ❶ fit panes of glass into a structure. ❷ enclose or cover something with glass. ❸ cover with a glaze. ❹ lose brightness and animation: *her eyes glazed over.*
» *noun* ❶ a glass-like coating for pottery. ❷ a thin topcoat of clear paint. ❸ a liquid used to form a shiny coating on food.

glazier »*noun* a person whose trade is fitting glass into windows and doors.
– **say** glay-zi-er

glazing

gleam (verb: **gleams, gleaming, gleamed**)

glean »*verb* (**gleans, gleaning, gleaned**) ❶ collect information gradually from various sources. ❷ (a historical term) gather leftover grain after a harvest.

gleanings »*plural noun* things gathered from various sources.

gleans

glebe »*noun* (a historical term) a piece of land serving as part of a clergyman's benefice and providing income.
– **say** gleeb

glee

gleeful
  gleefully

 -ful not -full: **gleeful**

glen »*noun* a narrow valley, especially in Scotland or Ireland.

glib »*adjective* (**glibber, glibbest**) able to express yourself well, but not meaning what you say.
glibly
glibness

 double the **b** in **glibber** and **glibbest**, but not in **glibly** and **glibness**

glide (verb: **glides, gliding, glided**)

glider »*noun* a light aircraft designed to fly without using an engine.

glides

gliding

glimmer (verb: **glimmers, glimmering, glimmered**)

glimpse (verb: **glimpses, glimpsing, glimpsed**)

 don't forget the **p**: **glimpse**

glint (verb: **glints, glinting, glinted**)

glisten (verb: **glistens, glistening, glistened**)

glitch »*noun* (in informal English) ❶ a sudden fault or irregularity of equipment. ❷ an unexpected setback in a plan.

glitter (verb: **glitters, glittering, glittered**)

glitterati »*plural noun* (in informal English) fashionable people involved in show business or other glamorous activity.
– **say** glit-tuh-**rah**-ti

glittered

glittering

glitters

glittery

glitz »*noun* (in informal English) showy but superficial display.

glitzy (adjective: **glitzier, glitziest**)

gloaming »*noun* (**the gloaming**) twilight; dusk.

gloat »*verb* (**gloats, gloating, gloated**) be smug or pleased about your own success or another's misfortune.
» *noun* an act of gloating.
gloater
gloating

glob

global
  globally

globalize »*verb* (**globalizes, globalizing, globalized**) organize business, culture, etc. on a worldwide scale.
globalization

 many people prefer the alternative spellings **globalise, globalises,** etc., and **globalisation**: both **s** and **z** spellings are correct

globally

global warming »*noun* the gradual increase in the overall temperature of the earth's atmosphere due to increased levels of carbon dioxide and other pollutants.

globe

globetrotter
globetrotting

globular »*adjective* ❶ globe-shaped; spherical. ❷ composed of globules.

 ar not er: **globular**

globule »*noun* a small round particle of a substance; a drop.

glockenspiel »*noun* a musical instrument containing metal pieces which you strike with small hammers.
– **SAY** glok-uhn-speel or glok-uhn-shpeel

i **glockenspiel** is a German word meaning 'bell play'

gloom

gloomy (adjective: **gloomier**, **gloomiest**)
gloomily
gloominess

gloop
gloopy

glorify »*verb* (**glorifies**, **glorifying**, **glorified**) ❶ describe or represent something as admirable. ❷ (**glorified**) made to appear more important or special than is really the case: *a glorified courier*. ❸ praise and worship God.
glorification

glorious
gloriously

glory (plural **glories**; verb: **glories**, **glorying**, **gloried**)

☑ plural: drop the **y** and add **ies**: **glories**

gloss[1] »*noun* (plural **glosses**) ❶ the shine on a smooth surface. ❷ a type of paint which dries to a bright shiny surface. ❸ an attractive appearance that hides something less attractive.
»*verb* (**glosses**, **glossing**, **glossed**) ❶ give something a glossy appearance. ❷ (**gloss over**) try to conceal something by mentioning it only briefly.

gloss[2] »*noun* (plural **glosses**) a translation or explanation of a word, phrase, or passage.
»*verb* (**glosses**, **glossing**, **glossed**) provide a gloss for a word, phrase, or passage.

glossary »*noun* (plural **glossaries**) an alphabetical list of words relating to a specific subject or text, with explanations.

glossed

glosses

glossier

glossiest

glossiness

glossing

glossy (adjective: **glossier**, **glossiest**)
glossiness

glottal »*adjective* of or produced by the glottis.

glottal stop »*noun* a speech sound made by opening and shutting the glottis, commonly used instead of a properly sounded *t* (e.g. in pronouncing *Saturday* as *Sa-er-day*).

glottis »*noun* the part of the larynx made up of the vocal cords and the slit-like opening between them.
– **SAY** glot-tiss

glove

glovebox

glow (verb: **glows**, **glowing**, **glowed**)

glower »*verb* (**glowers**, **glowering**, **glowered**) have an angry or sullen look on your face.
»*noun* an angry or sullen look.
– **SAY** *rhymes with* power

glowing

glows

glow-worm »*noun* a beetle, the female of which sends out light to attract males.

gloxinia »*noun* a tropical plant with large, bell-shaped flowers.
– **SAY** glok-**sin**-i-uh

glucose »*noun* a simple sugar which is an important energy source in living organisms.
– **SAY** gloo-kohz

glue (verb: **glues**, **gluing** or **glueing**, **glued**)
gluey

☑ **gluing** and **glueing** are both correct

glue ear »*noun* blocking of the Eustachian tube by mucus, occurring especially in children and causing impaired hearing.

glueing

glues

glue-sniffing

gluey

glug (verb: **glugs**, **glugging**, **glugged**)

gluing

glum (adjective: **glummer**, **glummest**)
glumly

double the **m** in **glummer** and **glummest**, but not in **glumly**

glut »*noun* an excessively large supply.
» *verb* (**gluts, glutting, glutted**) supply or fill something to excess.

 double the **t** in **glutting** and **glutted**

glutamate »*noun* a salt or ester of an amino acid which is a constituent of many proteins.

gluten »*noun* a protein present in cereal grains, which is responsible for the elastic texture of dough.
– SAY gloo-tuhn

gluteus muscles »*plural noun* the muscles in the buttocks which move the thighs.
– SAY gloo-ti-uhss

glutinous »*adjective* like glue in texture; sticky.
– SAY gloo-ti-nuhss

gluts

glutted

glutting

glutton »*noun* ❶ an extremely greedy eater. ❷ a person with a great eagerness or capacity for something.
gluttonous

 double **t**: **glutton**

gluttony »*noun* the habit of eating too much.

glycerine »*noun* = GLYCEROL.
– SAY gli-suh-reen

 don't forget the **e** on the end : **glycerine** (the spelling **glycerin** is American)

glycerol »*noun* a liquid formed as a by-product in soap manufacture, used as a softening agent and laxative.
– SAY gli-suh-rol

GM »*abbreviation* genetically modified.

GMT »*abbreviation* Greenwich Mean Time.

gnarled »*adjective* knobbly, rough, and twisted.

gnarly »*adjective* (**gnarlier, gnarliest**) gnarled.

gnash »*verb* (**gnashes, gnashing, gnashed**) grind your teeth together, especially as a sign of anger.
– SAY nash
gnasher

gnat »*noun* a small two-winged fly resembling a mosquito.

gnaw (verb: **gnaws, gnawing, gnawed**)

gnocchi »*plural noun* small dumplings made from potato, semolina, or flour.
– SAY nyok-ki

 double **c** and **h** before the **i**: **gnocchi** is an Italian word

gnome

gnomic »*adjective* expressed in a short, clever way, but difficult to understand.
– SAY noh-mik

GNP »*abbreviation* gross national product.

gnu »*noun* a large African antelope with a long head and a beard and mane.
– SAY noo

GNVQ »*abbreviation* General National Vocational Qualification.

go (verb: **goes, going, went**; past participle **gone**)

goad »*noun* ❶ a spiked stick used for driving cattle. ❷ a thing that stimulates someone into action.
» *verb* (**goads, goading, goaded**) ❶ provoke someone to action. ❷ urge on an animal with a goad.

go-ahead

goal

goalie

goalkeeper

goalless

goalpost

goat

goatee »*noun* a small pointed beard like that of a goat.
– SAY goh-tee

goatherd »*noun* a person who looks after goats.

gob (verb: **gobs, gobbing, gobbed**)

 double the **b** in **gobbing** and **gobbed**

gobbet »*noun* a piece of flesh, food, or other matter.

 double **b** and **-et** not **-it** at the end: **gobbet**

gobbing

gobble (verb: **gobbles, gobbling, gobbled**)

gobbledegook »*noun* pompous or unintelligible language.

 gobbledegook can also be spelled **gobbledygook**

gobbler

gobbles

gobbling

go-between

gobies plural of GOBY.

goblet »*noun* ❶ a drinking glass with a foot and a stem. ❷ a container forming part of a liquidizer.

goblin

gobs

gobsmacked »*adjective* (in informal English) utterly astonished.

gobstopper »*noun* a hard round sweet.

goby »*noun* (plural **gobies**) a small sea fish, typically with a sucker on the underside.
– SAY goh-bi

go-cart another way of spelling GO-KART.

god
  godlike

> ☑ use a capital **G** when referring to the supreme deity of Christianity and other monotheistic religions

godchild (plural **godchildren**)

god-daughter

goddess (plural **goddesses**)

> ☑ double **d**, double **s**: **goddess**

godetia »*noun* a North American plant with showy lilac to red flowers.
– SAY goh-**dee**-shuh

godfather

God-fearing

godforsaken »*adjective* lacking any merit or attraction.

godhead »*noun* ❶ (**the Godhead**) God. ❷ divine nature.

godless »*adjective* ❶ not believing in a god or God. ❷ wicked.
  godlessness

godlike

godly »*adjective* very religious.
  godliness

godmother

godparent »*noun* a person who presents a child at baptism and promises to be responsible for their religious education.

godsend »*noun* something very helpful or welcome at a particular time.

godson

godwit »*noun* a large, long-legged wading bird with a long bill.

goer

goes

gofer »*noun* (mainly in American English) a person who runs errands; a dogsbody.
– SAY goh-fer

> ☑ do not confuse **gofer** with **gopher**, referring to a burrowing rodent

go-getter »*noun* an energetic and very enterprising person.
  go-getting

goggle (verb: **goggles**, **goggling**, **goggled**)

goggles

goggling

go-go dancer

going

going concern »*noun* a thriving business.

going-over

goings-on

goitre »*noun* a swelling of the neck resulting from enlargement of the thyroid gland.
– SAY goy-ter

> ☑ **tre** not **ter**: **goitre** (**goiter** is the American spelling)

go-kart

> ☑ **go-kart** can also be spelled **go-cart**: both spellings are correct

gold

goldcrest »*noun* a very small warbler with a yellow or orange crest.

gold-digger »*noun* a woman who forms relationships with men purely for financial gain.

golden

golden age »*noun* ❶ an extremely happy, often imaginary past time of peace and prosperity. ❷ the period when a specified art or activity is at its peak: *the golden age of cinema.*

golden goose »*noun* a continuing source of wealth or profit that may be exhausted if it is not used carefully.

golden handshake »*noun* a payment given to someone who is made redundant or retires early.

golden jubilee »*noun* the fiftieth anniversary of an important event.

golden mean »*noun* the ideal middle position between two extremes.

goldenrod »*noun* a plant with tall spikes of bright yellow flowers.

golden wedding »*noun* the fiftieth anniversary of a wedding.

goldfield »*noun* a district in which gold is found as a mineral.

goldfinch »*noun* a brightly coloured finch with a yellow patch on each wing.

goldfish

gold leaf »*noun* gold beaten into a very thin sheet, used in gilding.

gold rush »*noun* a rapid movement of people to a newly discovered goldfield.

goldsmith »*noun* a person who makes gold articles.

golf
golfer
golfing

golliwog »*noun* a soft doll with a black face and fuzzy hair.

> ☑ **golli-** not **golly-: golliwog**

gonad »*noun* a bodily organ that produces gametes; a testis or ovary.
– SAY goh-nad

gondola »*noun* a flat-bottomed boat used on Venetian canals, worked by one oar at the stern.
– SAY gon-duh-luh

gondolier »*noun* a person who propels and steers a gondola.
– SAY gon-duh-leer

> ☑ **ier** not **er: gondolier**

gone

goner »*noun* (in informal English) a person or thing that cannot be saved.
– SAY gon-er

gong

gonorrhoea »*noun* a sexually transmitted disease caused by bacteria, often involving a discharge of pus from the urethra or vagina.
– SAY gon-uh-ree-uh

> ☑ single **n**, double **r**, and **hoea** at the end: **gonorrhoea** (the spelling **gonorrhea** is American)

goo

good (adjective: **better**, **best**)

goodbye

good-for-nothing

Good Friday »*noun* the Friday before Easter Sunday, on which Christians commemorate the Crucifixion of Jesus.

good-humoured

goodie another way of spelling **GOODY**.

goodies

goodish

good-looking

goodly »*adjective* quite large in size or quantity.

goodness

goods and chattels »*plural noun* all kinds of personal possessions.

good-tempered

goodwill

goody (plural **goodies**)

> ☑ **goody** can also be spelled **goodie**

goody-goody »*noun* (in informal English) a smug person who behaves well in order to impress others.

gooey
gooeyness

goof (verb: **goofs**, **goofing**, **goofed**)

goofy (adjective: **goofier**, **goofiest**)
goofily
goofiness

googly »*noun* (plural **googlies**) (in cricket) an off break bowled with an apparent leg-break action.

goolies [testicles]

goon »*noun* (in informal English) ❶ a foolish or eccentric person. ❷ a thug.

goosander »*noun* a large diving duck, the male of which has a dark green head and whitish underparts.
– SAY goo-san-der

goose (plural **geese**)

gooseberry (plural **gooseberries**)

> ☑ plural: drop the **y** and add **ies**: **gooseberries**

gooseflesh

goose pimples

goose step »*noun* a military marching step in which the legs are kept straight.
»*verb* (**goose-steps**, **goose-stepping**, **goose-stepped**) march with such a step.

> ☑ add a hyphen when using **goose-step** as a verb

gopher »*noun* a burrowing American rodent with pouches on its cheeks.
– SAY goh-fer

> ☑ **ph** not **f: gopher** (**gofer** is an informal American term meaning 'dogsbody')

Gordian knot »*noun* (**cut the Gordian knot**) solve a difficult problem in a forceful or direct way.
– SAY gor-di-uhn

> ⓘ from the legendary knot tied by King *Gordius* and cut through by Alexander the Great in response to the prophecy that whoever untied it would rule Asia

gore »*noun* ❶ blood that has been shed. ❷ a triangular piece of material used in making a garment, sail, or umbrella.
»*verb* (**gores**, **goring**, **gored**) (of an animal such as a bull) pierce or stab with a horn or tusk.

gorge »*noun* a narrow valley or ravine.

» *verb* (**gorges**, **gorging**, **gorged**) eat a large amount greedily.

gorgeous
  gorgeously
  gorgeousness

gorges

gorging

gorgon »*noun* ❶ (in Greek mythology) one of three sisters with snakes for hair, who had the power to turn anyone who looked at them to stone. ❷ a frightening or repulsive woman.
– SAY gor-guhn

Gorgonzola »*noun* a strong-flavoured Italian cheese with bluish-green veins.
– SAY gor-guhn-**zoh**-luh

gorier

goriest

gorilla [large ape]

 one r, two **l**'s: **gorilla** (and not to be confused with **guerrilla**)

goring

gormless »*adjective* stupid or slow-witted.
  gormlessly
  gormlessness

gorse »*noun* a yellow-flowered shrub with thin prickly leaves.

gory »*adjective* (**gorier**, **goriest**) ❶ involving violence and bloodshed. ❷ covered in blood.

gosh

goshawk »*noun* a short-winged hawk resembling a large sparrowhawk.
– SAY goss-hawk

gosling »*noun* a young goose.

 gos not goos: **gosling**

gospel
  gospeller

gossamer »*noun* a fine substance consisting of cobwebs spun by small spiders.
» *adjective* very fine and flimsy.

 two s's, one m: **gossamer**

gossip (verb: **gossips**, **gossiping**, **gossiped**)
  gossiper
  gossipy

 do not double the p in **gossiping**, **gossiped**, **gossiper**, and **gossipy**

got past and past participle of GET.

Goth »*noun* ❶ a member of a Germanic people that invaded the Roman Empire between the 3rd and 5th centuries. ❷ (**goth**) a style of rock music typically having mystical lyrics. ❸ a member of a subculture favouring black clothing and goth music.

Gothic »*adjective* ❶ having to do with the ancient Goths. ❷ of the style of architecture common in western Europe in the 12th–16th centuries. ❸ very gloomy or horrifying.
» *noun* ❶ the language of the Goths. ❷ Gothic architecture.

 no k: **Gothic**

gotten American past participle of GET.

gouache »*noun* ❶ a method of painting using opaque pigments ground in water and thickened with a glue-like substance. ❷ paint of this kind.
– SAY goo-**ash** or gwash

gouge »*verb* (**gouges**, **gouging**, **gouged**) ❶ make a rough hole in a surface. ❷ (**gouge out**) cut or force something out roughly.
» *noun* ❶ a chisel with a concave blade. ❷ a hole or groove made by gouging.

goulash »*noun* a rich Hungarian stew of meat and vegetables.
– SAY goo-lash

gourd »*noun* ❶ the large hard-skinned fruit of a climbing or trailing plant. ❷ a container made from the hollowed skin of a gourd.

gourmand »*noun* ❶ a person who enjoys eating and sometimes eats too much. ❷ a person who is knowledgeable about good food.
– SAY goor-muhnd or gor-muhnd

the words **gourmand** and **gourmet** do not mean exactly the same thing: while both can be used to mean 'a person who is knowledgeable about good food', **gourmand** more usually means 'a person who enjoys eating and sometimes eats too much'

gourmet »*noun* a person who is knowledgeable about good food.
» *adjective* suitable for a gourmet: *a gourmet meal.*
– SAY goor-may

 et at the end: **gourmet** is a French word

gout »*noun* a disease causing the joints to swell and become painful.
– SAY gowt
  gouty

govern (verb: **governs**, **governing**, **governed**)
  governable

g

governance »*noun* the action or manner of governing.

☑ ance not ence: **governance**

governed

governess »*noun* (plural **governesses**) a woman employed to teach children in a private household.

governing

government
governmental

☑ don't forget the **n** before the **m**: **government**

governor
governorship

☑ -or not -er: **governor**

Governor General »*noun* (plural **Governors General**) the chief representative of the British king or queen in a Commonwealth country of which that king or queen is head of state.

governorship

governs

gown

GP »*abbreviation* general practitioner.

grab (verb: **grabs, grabbing, grabbed**)

☑ double the **b** in **grabbing** and **grabbed**

grace (verb: **graces, gracing, graced**)

graceful
gracefully
gracefulness

☑ -ful not -full: **graceful**

graceless
gracelessly
gracelessness

grace note »*noun* (in music) an extra note which is not essential to the harmony or melody.

graces

gracing

gracious
graciously
graciousness

gradation »*noun* ❶ a scale of gradual changes from one thing to another. ❷ a stage in a such a scale.

grade (verb: **grades, grading, graded**)

gradient »*noun* ❶ a sloping part of a road or railway. ❷ the degree to which something slopes.
– SAY gray-di-uhnt

☑ ent not ant: **gradient**

grading

gradual
gradualism
gradually
gradualness

graduate (verb: **graduates, graduating, graduated**)
graduation

Graeco-Roman »*adjective* Greek and Roman.
– SAY gree-koh-**roh**-muhn

☑ ae not e: **Graeco-Roman** (the spelling with **Greco-** is American)

graffiti »*noun* unauthorized writing or drawings on a surface in a public place.
– SAY gruh-**fee**-ti

☑ two **f**'s, one **t**: **graffiti** is an Italian word
in Italian the word **graffiti** is a plural noun (the singular is *graffito*), but in English it is generally treated as a singular, similar to a word like **writing**

graft »*noun* ❶ a shoot from one plant inserted into another to form a new growth. ❷ a piece of bodily tissue that is transplanted surgically to replace damaged tissue. ❸ hard work. ❹ bribery and other corrupt measures used to gain advantage in politics or business.
» *verb* (**grafts, grafting, grafted**) ❶ insert or transplant tissue as a graft. ❷ add something to something else, especially inappropriately. ❸ work hard.
grafter

Grail »*noun* (in medieval legend) the cup or platter used by Jesus at the Last Supper.

grain

grainy »*adjective* (**grainier, grainiest**) ❶ resembling or consisting of grains. ❷ (of a photograph) showing visible particles of emulsion. ❸ (of wood) having prominent grain.

gram »*noun* a basic unit of mass in the metric system.

☑ only one **m**: **gram** (the spelling **gramme** is old-fashioned)

grammar »*noun* ❶ the whole system and structure of a language. ❷ knowledge and use of the rules or principles of grammar. ❸ a book on grammar.

☑ ar not er: **grammar**

grammarian »*noun* a person who studies and writes about grammar.

– **SAY** gruh-**mair**-i-uhn

grammar school »*noun* (in the UK) a state secondary school to which pupils are admitted on the basis of ability.

grammatical »*adjective* **❶** having to do with grammar. **❷** following the rules of grammar.
– **SAY** gruh-**mat**-i-k'l
grammatically

> ✓ two m's, one t: **grammatical**

gramme see the note at **GRAM**.

gramophone »*noun* (old-fashioned) a record player.

grampa »*noun* (in informal English) grandfather.

grampus »*noun* (plural **grampuses**) a killer whale or other dolphin-like sea animal.
– **SAY** gram-puhss

gran

granary »*noun* (plural **granaries**) a storehouse for grain.

grand
  grandly
  grandness

grandad

> ✓ **grandad** can also be spelled with a double d: **granddad** (both spellings are correct)

grandchild (plural **grandchildren**)

granddaughter

> ✓ note the double d: **granddaughter**

grande dame »*noun* an influential woman.
– **SAY** grond **dam**

> ℹ from a French phrase meaning 'grand lady'

grandee »*noun* a person of high status and social rank.
– **SAY** gran-**dee**

grandeur »*noun* **❶** the quality of being great and impressive. **❷** high status and social rank.
– **SAY** gran-**dyer**

grandfather

grandiloquent »*adjective* pompous in style and using long and fancy words.
– **SAY** gran-**dil**-uh-kwuhnt
  grandiloquence
  grandiloquently

> ✓ ent not ant: **grandiloquent**

grandiose »*adjective* (of a plan or building) very large and ambitious and intended to impress.
– **SAY** gran-di-ohss
  grandiosely

> ✓ the ending is **iose** not **oise**: **grandiose**

grandly

grandma

grand mal »*noun* a serious form of epilepsy which can cause lengthy periods of unconsciousness.
– **SAY** gron **mal**

> ℹ from a French phrase which means 'great sickness'

grand master »*noun* a chess player of the highest class.

> ✓ **grand master** can also be written as one word: **grandmaster** (both are correct)

grandmother

grandness

grandpa

grandparent

grand piano »*noun* a large piano which has the body, strings, and soundboard arranged horizontally.

Grand Prix »*noun* (plural **Grands Prix**) a race forming part of a motor-racing or motorcycling world championship.
– **SAY** gron **pree** [singular and plural]

> ✓ the plural of **Grand Prix** adds an s to **Grand**: **Grands Prix** (it is from a French phrase meaning 'great prize')

grand slam »*noun* the winning of each of a group of major sports championships or matches in the same year.

grandson

grandstand »*noun* the main stand at a racecourse or sports ground.

grange »*noun* a country house with farm buildings attached.

granite »*noun* a very hard rock made up of quartz, mica, and feldspar.
– **SAY** gran-it

> ✓ remember the final e: **granite**

granny (plural **grannies**)

> ✓ **granny** can also be spelled **grannie**: both are correct

granny knot »*noun* a reef knot with the ends crossed the wrong way and therefore liable to slip.

grant (verb: **grants**, **granting**, **granted**)

grant-maintained »*adjective* (of a school) funded by central government and self-governing.

grants

gran turismo »*noun* (plural **gran turismos**) a high-performance model of car.
– SAY gran tuu-**riz**-moh

> ℹ from an Italian phrase meaning 'great touring'

granular »*adjective* ❶ resembling or consisting of granules. ❷ having a roughened surface or structure.
granularity

> ✓ ar not er: **granular**

granulated »*adjective* in the form of granules.
granulation

granule »*noun* a small compact particle of a substance.
– SAY gran-yool

grape

grapefruit (plural **grapefruit**)

grapeshot »*noun* (a historical term) ammunition consisting of a number of small iron balls fired together from a cannon.

grapevine

graph »*noun* a diagram showing how two or more sets of numbers relate to each other.

graphic »*adjective* ❶ relating to the use of lettering, lines, colours, and symbols as visual elements in a design. ❷ giving vivid detail. ❸ of or in the form of a graph.
» *noun* a design or visual image.
graphically

graphic design »*noun* the design of books, posters, and other printed materials.

graphics

graphite »*noun* a grey form of carbon used as a solid lubricant and as pencil lead.

graphology »*noun* the study of handwriting as a guide to types of personality.
graphologist

grapnel »*noun* a grappling hook.
– SAY grap-nuhl

> ✓ single **l** at the end: **grapnel**

grappa »*noun* a brandy made from grapes after they have been pressed in winemaking.

grapple (verb: **grapples, grappling, grappled**)

grappling hook »*noun* a device with iron claws, used for dragging or grasping.

grappling iron »*noun* = GRAPPLING HOOK.

grasp (verb: **grasps, grasping, grasped**)

grasping »*adjective* greedy.

grasps

grass (plural **grasses**; verb: **grasses, grassing, grassed**)

grasshopper

grassier [more grassy]

grassiest

grassing

grassland

grass roots »*plural noun* the ordinary people in an organization or society, rather than the leaders.

grassy (adjective: **grassier, grassiest**)

grate »*verb* (**grates, grating, grated**) shred food.
» *noun* a metal frame in a fireplace in which the coals or wood are placed.

> ℹ do not confuse **grate** with **great**, meaning 'more than the average'

grateful
gratefully

> ✓ **grate-** not **great-**, and **-ful** not **-full**: **grateful**

grater

gratify »*verb* (**gratifies, gratifying, gratified**) ❶ give someone pleasure or satisfaction. ❷ indulge or satisfy a desire.
gratification
gratifying
gratifyingly

gratin »*noun* a dish with a browned crust of bread crumbs or melted cheese.
– SAY gra-tan

grating[1] »*adjective* ❶ sounding harsh and unpleasant. ❷ irritating.
gratingly

grating[2] »*noun* a framework of parallel or crossed bars that cover an opening.

gratis »*adverb & adjective* free of charge.
– SAY grah-tiss

> ✓ single **s** at the end: **gratis**. It comes from a Latin word meaning 'as a kindness'.

gratitude

gratuities

gratuitous »*adjective* having no justifiable reason or purpose.
– SAY gruh-**tyoo**-i-tuhss
gratuitously
gratuitousness

gratuity »*noun* (plural **gratuities**) a small financial reward; a tip.
- SAY gruh-**tyoo**-i-ti

grave (adjective: **graver**, **gravest**)
 gravely
 graveness

grave accent »*noun* a mark (`) placed over a vowel in some languages to indicate a change in its sound quality.
- SAY grahv

gravel

gravelly »*adjective* ❶ resembling or containing gravel. ❷ (of a voice) deep and rough.

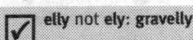 **elly** not **ely**: **gravelly**

gravely [in a grave manner]

graveness

graven image »*noun* a carved figure of a god used as an idol.

graver[1] »*noun* an engraving tool.

graver[2] [more grave]

gravest

gravestone

graveyard

gravies

gravitas »*noun* a serious and dignified manner.
- SAY gra-vi-tass

gravitate »*verb* (**gravitates**, **gravitating**, **gravitated**) be drawn towards a place, person, or thing.
- SAY gra-vi-tayt

gravitation »*noun* movement towards a centre of gravity.
 gravitational

gravity »*noun* ❶ the force that attracts a body towards the centre of the earth, or towards any other physical body having mass. ❷ extreme importance or seriousness. ❸ a solemn manner.

gravy (plural **gravies**)

gravy train »*noun* a situation in which someone can easily make a lot of money.

gray American spelling of **GREY**.

grayling »*noun* a silvery-grey freshwater fish.

graze (verb: **grazes**, **grazing**, **grazed**)

grazing »*noun* grassland suitable for animals to graze.

grease (verb: **greases**, **greasing**, **greased**)

greasepaint »*noun* a waxy substance used as make-up by actors.

greaseproof »*adjective* not allowing grease to pass through it.

greases

greasier

greasiest

greasily

greasiness

greasing

greasy (adjective: **greasier**, **greasiest**)
 greasily
 greasiness

great (adjective: **greater**, **greatest**) [large; more than the average]
 greatly
 greatness

ℹ️ do not confuse **great** with **grate**, which means either 'shred food' or 'a metal frame in a fireplace'

great-aunt

great circle »*noun* a circle on the surface of a sphere which lies in a plane passing through the sphere's centre.

greatcoat »*noun* a long heavy overcoat.

Great Dane »*noun* a very large dog with short hair.

greatly

great-nephew

greatness

great-niece

great-uncle

Great War »*noun* the First World War.

greave »*noun* (a historical term) a piece of armour for the shin.

ℹ️ do not confuse **greave** with **grieve**, which means 'suffer grief'

grebe »*noun* a diving bird with a long neck.
- SAY greeb

Grecian »*adjective* relating to ancient Greece.
- SAY gree-sh'n

✓ **Grec** not **Greec**: **Grecian**

Greco-Roman American spelling of **GRAECO-ROMAN**.

greed

greedy (adjective: **greedier**, **greediest**)
 greedily
 greediness

Greek

green (adjective: **greener**, **greenest**; verb: **greens**, **greening**, **greened**)
 greenish
 greenness

green belt »*noun* an area of open land around a city, on which building is restricted.

green card »*noun* a permit allowing a foreigner to live and work permanently in the US.

greened

greener

greenery

greenest

green-eyed monster »*noun* (mainly used in a humorous way) jealousy.

greenfield »*adjective* (of a site) previously undeveloped.

greenfinch »*noun* a large finch with green and yellow plumage.

green fingers »*plural noun* natural ability in growing plants.

greenfly »*noun* (plural **greenfly**) a green aphid.

greengage »*noun* a sweet greenish fruit resembling a small plum.

 -gage not **-gauge**: greengage

greengrocer

greenhorn »*noun* an inexperienced or naive person.

greenhouse

greenhouse effect »*noun* the tendency of atmospheric temperature to rise because certain gases absorb infrared radiation from the earth.

greenhouse gas »*noun* a gas that contributes to the greenhouse effect by absorbing infrared radiation.

greening

greenish

Greenlander »*noun* a person from Greenland.

green light »*noun* ❶ a green traffic light indicating that you can go. ❷ permission to go ahead with a project.

greenness

green room »*noun* a room in a theatre or studio in which performers can relax when they are not performing.

greens

greenstick fracture »*noun* a fracture of the bone in which one side of the bone is broken and the other only bent.

greensward »*noun* (an old word) grass-covered ground.
– **SAY** green-sword

Greenwich Mean Time »*noun* the time measured at the meridian of zero longitude which passes through Greenwich in London, used as the standard time in a zone that includes the British Isles.

 Green- not **Gren-**: Greenwich Mean Time

greenwood »*noun* (an old word) a wood or forest in leaf.

greet (verb: **greets**, **greeting**, **greeted**)

greeting

greets

gregarious »*adjective* ❶ enjoying being with people; sociable. ❷ (of animals) living in flocks or colonies.
– **SAY** gri-**gair**-i-uhss
gregariously
gregariousness

Gregorian chant »*noun* medieval church music for voices.
– **SAY** gri-**gor**-i-uhn

i named after St *Gregory* the Great

gremlin »*noun* a mischievous sprite regarded as responsible for unexplained mechanical or electrical faults.

grenade »*noun* a small bomb, especially one thrown by hand.
– **SAY** gruh-**nayd**

Grenadian [of Grenada in the Caribbean]
– **SAY** gri-**nay**-di-uhn

grenadier »*noun* ❶ (a historical term) a soldier armed with grenades. ❷ (**Grenadiers**(or **Grenadier Guards**) the first regiment of the royal household infantry.
– **SAY** gren-uh-**deer**

 ier not **eer**: grenadier

grew past of **GROW**.

grey (adjective: **greyer**, **greyest**; verb: **greys**, **greying**, **greyed**)
greyish
greyness

 e in the middle, not **a**: grey (the spelling **gray** is American)

grey area »*noun* a subject, situation, or area of activity that does not easily fit into existing categories.

greyed

greyer

greyest

greyhound

greying

g

greyish

greylag »*noun* a large goose with mainly grey plumage.

greyness

greys

grid

griddle »*noun* a circular iron plate that is heated and used for cooking food.
» *verb* (**griddles, griddling, griddled**) cook food on a griddle.

gridiron »*noun* ❶ a frame of parallel metal bars used for grilling meat or fish over an open fire. ❷ a grid pattern. ❸ a field for American football, marked with regularly spaced parallel lines.
– **say** grid-I-uhn

gridlock »*noun* a traffic jam affecting a whole network of streets.
gridlocked

grief

> ✓ the usual rule is **i** before **e** except after **c**: **grief**

grievance »*noun* a cause for complaint.

> ✓ **ance** not **ence**: **grievance**

grieve (verb: **grieves, grieving, grieved**) [suffer grief]

> ✓ **ie** not **ea**: **grieve** (a **greave** is a piece of armour)

grievous »*adjective* (of something bad) very severe or serious.
grievously

> ✓ **vous** not **vious**: **grievous**

grievous bodily harm »*noun* (in law) serious physical injury deliberately inflicted on someone.

grievously

griffin »*noun* a mythical creature with the head and wings of an eagle and the body of a lion.

> ✓ **griffin** can also be spelled **gryphon**: both spellings are correct

griffon »*noun* ❶ a small terrier-like dog. ❷ a large vulture with pale brown plumage.

grill (verb: **grills, grilling, grilled**)

grille »*noun* a framework of metal bars or wires.

> ✓ **grille** can also be spelled without the final **e**: **grill** (both spellings are correct)

grilled

grilling

grills

grim (adjective: **grimmer, grimmest**)
grimly
grimness

> ✓ double the **m** to spell **grimmer** and **grimmest**

grimace »*noun* a twisted expression on a person's face, expressing disgust, pain, or wry amusement.
» *verb* (**grimaces, grimacing, grimaced**) make a grimace.
– **say** gri-mayss or gri-muhss

grime

grimier

grimiest

grimily

griminess

grimly

grimmer

grimmest

grimness

grimy (adjective: **grimier, grimiest**)
grimily
griminess

> ✓ **my** not **mey**: **grimy**

grin (verb: **grins, grinning, grinned**)

> ✓ double the **n** to spell **grinning** or **grinned**

grind (verb: **grinds, grinding, ground**; past participle **ground**)
grinding
grindingly

grindstone »*noun* ❶ a revolving disc of abrasive material used for sharpening or polishing metal objects. ❷ a millstone.

gringo »*noun* (plural **gringos**) (in informal English) (in Latin America) a white English-speaking person.

> ✓ the plural of **gringo** has **os** not **oes**: **gringos**. It is a Spanish word meaning 'foreign'.

grinned

grinning

grins

grip (verb: **grips, gripping, gripped**)
gripper
gripping

> ✓ double the **p** to spell **gripping** and **gripped**

gripe »*verb* (**gripes, griping, griped**)
❶ grumble. ❷ give someone a pain in the stomach or intestines.

g

» **noun ❶** a trivial complaint. **❷** pain in the stomach or intestines.

gripped

gripper

gripping

grips

grisly »*adjective* (grislier, grisliest) causing horror or revulsion.
– SAY griz-li
grisliness

> **i** do not confuse **grisly** with **grizzly**, as in *grizzly bear*: **grizzly** refers to the bear's white-tipped fur

grist »*noun* corn that is ground to make flour.

gristle »*noun* tough inedible cartilage in meat.
gristly

grit (verb: grits, gritting, gritted)

> ✓ double the **t** to spell **gritting** and **gritted**

gritty (adjective: grittier, grittiest)
grittily
grittiness

grizzle »*verb* (grizzles, grizzling, grizzled) (of a child) cry or whimper fretfully.

grizzled »*adjective* having grey or grey-streaked hair.

grizzles

grizzling

grizzly bear »*noun* a large variety of brown bear often having white-tipped fur.

> **i** do not confuse **grizzly** with **grisly**, which means 'causing horror or revulsion'

> ✓ **ly** not **ley**: grizzly

groan (verb: groans, groaning, groaned)
groaner

groat »*noun* (a historical term) an English silver coin worth four old pence.

grocer

grocery (plural groceries)

> ✓ plural: drop the **y** and add **ies**: groceries

grog »*noun* spirits mixed with water.

groggy (adjective: groggier, groggiest)
groggily
grogginess

groin[1] »*noun* the area between the stomach and the thigh.

groin[2] American spelling of GROYNE.

grommet »*noun* **❶** a protective ring in a hole that a rope or cable passes through.

❷ a tube fitted in the eardrum to drain fluid from the middle ear.

groom »*verb* (grooms, grooming, groomed) **❶** brush and clean the coat of a horse or dog. **❷** give someone or something a neat and tidy appearance. **❸** train someone for a particular purpose or activity.
» **noun ❶** a person employed to take care of horses. **❷** a bridegroom.

groove (verb: grooves, grooving, grooved)
grooved

groovy (adjective: groovier, grooviest)
groovily
grooviness

> ✓ **vy** not **vey**: groovy

grope (verb: gropes, groping, groped)
groper

grosgrain »*noun* a heavy ribbed fabric of silk or rayon.
– SAY groh-grayn

gross (adjective: grosser, grossest; verb: grosses, grossing, grossed)
grossly
grossness

gross domestic product »*noun* the total value of goods produced and services provided within a country during one year.

grossed

grosser [more gross]

grosses

grossest

grossing

grossly

gross national product »*noun* the total value of goods produced and services provided by a country during one year, equal to the gross domestic product plus the net income from foreign investments.

grossness

grotesque »*adjective* **❶** ugly or distorted in a way that is funny or frightening. **❷** shocking.
» **noun** a grotesque figure or image.
– SAY groh-tesk
grotesquely
grotesqueness

grotesquerie »*noun* (plural grotesqueries) grotesque quality or things.
– SAY groh-tesk-uh-ri

> ✓ **ie** not **y**: grotesquerie

grotto »*noun* (plural grottoes or grottos) a small picturesque cave, or a construction imitating one.

☑ the plural of **grotto** can have either **os** or **oes**: **grottos** or **grottoes**

grotty (adjective: **grottier**, **grottiest**)
grottiness

grouch »*noun* ❶ a person who is often grumpy. ❷ a complaint or grumble.

grouchy »*adjective* (**grouchier**, **grouchiest**) irritable and bad-tempered.
grouchily
grouchiness

ground (verb: **grounds**, **grounding**, **grounded**)

ground-breaking

grounded

groundhog »*noun* (in American English) = WOODCHUCK.

grounding »*noun* basic training or instruction in a subject.

groundless

groundling »*noun* a spectator or reader considered to have poor taste.

groundnut »*noun* = PEANUT.

ground rule »*noun* a basic principle which governs an action or procedure.

grounds

groundsel »*noun* a plant with small yellow flowers.
– SAY grownd-s'l

☑ remember the **d**, and only one **l**: **groundsel**

groundsheet

groundsman »*noun* (plural **groundsmen**) a person who maintains a sports ground or the grounds of a large building.

ground squirrel »*noun* a squirrel of a group including the chipmunk, living in burrows.

groundswell »*noun* ❶ a large swell in the sea. ❷ a build-up of opinion in a large section of the population.

groundwater »*noun* water held underground in the soil or in rock.

groundwork

group (verb: **groups**, **grouping**, **grouped**)

group captain »*noun* a rank of officer in the RAF, above wing commander and below air commodore.

groupie »*noun* a young woman who follows a pop group or celebrity around.

grouping

groups

grouse[1] »*noun* (plural **grouse**) a game bird with a plump body and feathered legs.

grouse[2] »*verb* (**grouses**, **grousing**, **groused**) complain pettily; grumble.
» *noun* a grumble or complaint.

grout »*noun* a mortar or paste for filling the gaps between tiles.
» *verb* (**grouts**, **grouting**, **grouted**) fill in gaps between tiles with grout.
– SAY growt

grove »*noun* a small wood, orchard, or group of trees.

grovel »*verb* (**grovels**, **grovelling**, **grovelled**) ❶ crouch or crawl on the ground. ❷ be very humble to someone to make them forgive you or treat you favourably.
groveller

☑ double the **l** in **grovelling**, **grovelled**, and **groveller** (the spellings **groveling**, **groveled**, and **groveler** are American)

grow (verb: **grows**, **growing**, **grew**; past participle **grown**)
grower

growbag »*noun* a bag containing potting compost, in which plants such as tomatoes can be grown.

grower

growing

growl (verb: **growls**, **growling**, **growled**)
growler

grown

grown-up

grows

growth

growth industry »*noun* an industry that is developing particularly quickly.

groyne »*noun* a low wall built out into the sea from a beach to prevent erosion and drifting.

☑ **oyne** not **oin**: **groyne** (the spelling **groin** is American)

grub »*noun* ❶ the larva of an insect. ❷ (in informal English) food.
» *verb* (**grubs**, **grubbing**, **grubbed**) ❶ dig shallowly in soil. ❷ search or work clumsily and unmethodically.

☑ double the **b** in **grubbing** and **grubbed**

grubby (adjective: **grubbier**, **grubbiest**)
grubbily
grubbiness

grudge (verb: **grudges**, **grudging**, **grudged**)

grudging
grudgingly

gruel »*noun* a thin liquid food of oatmeal or other meal boiled in milk or water.

g

gruelling »*adjective* extremely tiring and demanding.
gruellingly

> ✅ double **l**: gruelling (the spelling **grueling** is American)

gruesome »*adjective* ❶ causing disgust or horror. ❷ extremely unpleasant.
gruesomely
gruesomeness

gruff (adjective: **gruffer, gruffest**)
gruffly
gruffness

grumble (verb: **grumbles, grumbling, grumbled**)
grumbler

grump

grumpy (adjective: **grumpier, grumpiest**)
grumpily
grumpiness

grunge »*noun* ❶ (in American English) grime; dirt. ❷ a style of rock music with a loud and harsh guitar sound and lazy vocal delivery.
grungy

grunt (verb: **grunts, grunting, grunted**)
grunter

Gruyere »*noun* a tangy Swiss cheese.
– **say** groo-yair

> ✅ Gruyere can also be spelled **Gruyère**, with a grave accent above the **e**: it is named after *Gruyère*, a district in Switzerland

gryphon another way of spelling **GRIFFIN**.

G-string »*noun* a skimpy undergarment covering the genitals, consisting of a narrow strip of cloth attached to a waistband.

guacamole »*noun* a dish of mashed avocado.
– **say** gwa-kuh-**moh**-lay

> ✅ -mole not -moli or -moly: guacamole

guano »*noun* the excrement of seabirds, used as a fertilizer.
– **say** gwah-noh

guarantee (verb: **guarantees, guaranteeing, guaranteed**)

> ✅ gua not gau: guarantee

guarantor »*noun* a person or organization that gives or acts as a guarantee.
– **say** ga-ruhn-**tor**

guard (verb: **guards, guarding, guarded**)

> ✅ gua not gau: guard

guarded »*adjective* cautious and having possible reservations.
guardedly

guardhouse »*noun* a building used to house a military guard or to detain military prisoners.

guardian
guardianship

guarding

guardroom »*noun* a guardhouse.

guards

guardsman (plural **guardsmen**)

Guatemalan

guava »*noun* a tropical fruit with pink juicy flesh.
– **say** gwah-vuh

gubbins »*plural noun* (in informal English) ❶ miscellaneous items. ❷ a gadget.

gubernatorial »*adjective* having to do with a governor of a US state.
– **say** goo-ber-nuh-**tor**-i-uhl

gudgeon »*noun* ❶ a small freshwater fish often used as bait by anglers. ❷ a pivot or spindle on which something swings or rotates. ❸ the tubular part of a hinge into which the pin fits.
– **say** guj-uhn

> ✅ don't forget the **d**: gudgeon

guelder rose »*noun* a shrub with creamy-white flowers followed by semi-transparent red berries.
– **say** gel-der

Guernsey »*noun* (plural **Guernseys**) a breed of dairy cattle from Guernsey in the Channel Islands.
– **say** gern-zi

guerrilla »*noun* a member of a small independent group fighting against the government or regular forces.
– **say** guh-**ril**-luh

> ✅ guerrilla (not to be confused with **gorilla**) can also be spelled **guerilla**, with only one **r**: both spellings are correct. **Guerrilla** is a Spanish word meaning 'little war'.

guess (plural **guesses**; verb: **guesses, guessing, guessed**)
guesser

guesstimate (in informal English) »*noun* an estimate based on a mixture of guesswork and calculation.
– **say** gess-ti-muht

> ✅ guesstimate can also be spelled **guestimate**: both spellings are correct

guesswork

guest

guff

guffaw (verb: **guffaws**, **guffawing**, **guffawed**)

guidance

> ✓ ance not ence: guidance

guide (verb: **guides**, **guiding**, **guided**)

guidebook

guided

guideline

guides

guiding

guild »*noun* ❶ a medieval association of craftsmen or merchants. ❷ an association of people for a common purpose.

guilder »*noun* (plural **guilder** or **guilders**) the basic unit of money of the Netherlands.
– SAY gil-der

guildhall »*noun* ❶ the meeting place of a guild or corporation. ❷ a town hall.

guile »*noun* sly or cunning intelligence.
– SAY gyl
guileful

guileless »*adjective* very honest and sincere.
guilelessly

guillemot »*noun* an auk (seabird) with a narrow pointed bill.
– SAY gil-li-mot

> ✓ guille not gilli: guillemot

guillotine »*noun* ❶ a machine with a heavy blade, used for beheading people. ❷ a device with a descending or sliding blade used for cutting paper or sheet metal.
»*verb* (**guillotines**, **guillotining**, **guillotined**) behead someone with a guillotine.
– SAY gil-luh-teen

> ✓ two l's, one t: guillotine

guilt [remorse]

> ✓ don't forget the u: guilt

guiltier

guiltiest

guiltily

guiltless

guilty (adjective: **guiltier**, **guiltiest**)
guiltily

guinea »*noun* ❶ the sum of £1.05 (21 shillings in pre-decimal currency), used mainly for determining professional fees

and auction prices. ❷ a former British gold coin with a value of 21 shillings.
– SAY gi-ni

> ✓ ea at the end: guinea

guineafowl »*noun* (plural **guineafowl**) a large African game bird with slate-coloured, white-spotted plumage.

Guinean

guinea pig

guipure »*noun* heavy lace consisting of embroidered motifs held together by large connecting stitches.
– SAY gi-pyoor

guise »*noun* an external form, appearance, or manner: *in the guise of an inspector.*
– SAY gyz

> ✓ se not ze: guise

guitar
guitarist

Gulag »*noun* the system of harsh labour camps in the former Soviet Union.
– SAY goo-lag

gulf »*noun* ❶ a deep inlet of the sea almost surrounded by land, with a narrow mouth. ❷ a deep ravine. ❸ a large difference between two people, concepts, or situations.

gull »*noun* ❶ a long-winged seabird having white plumage with a grey or black back. ❷ a person who is fooled or deceived.
»*verb* (**gulls**, **gulling**, **gulled**) fool or deceive someone.

gullet »*noun* the passage by which food passes from the mouth to the stomach.

> ✓ -et not -it: gullet

gullible »*adjective* easily believing what people tell you.
gullibility
gullibly

> ✓ double l, and -ible not -able: gullible

gullies

gulling

gulls

gully »*noun* (plural **gullies**) ❶ a ravine or deep channel caused by the action of running water. ❷ a gutter or drain.

> ✓ the ending is y, not ey: gully

gulp (verb: **gulps**, **gulping**, **gulped**)
gulper

gum (verb: **gums**, **gumming**, **gummed**)

☑ double the **m** in **gumming** and **gummed**

gum arabic »*noun* a gum produced by some kinds of acacia and used as glue and in incense.

gumboil »*noun* a small swelling formed on the gum at the root of a tooth.

gumboot »*noun* a wellington boot.

gumdrop »*noun* a firm, jelly-like sweet.

gummed

gumminess

gumming

gummy »*adjective* ❶ sticky. ❷ toothless. **gumminess**

gumption »*noun* initiative and resourcefulness.

☑ don't forget the **p**: **gumption**

gums

gumshield

gun (verb: **guns**, **gunning**, **gunned**)

☑ double the **n** in **gunning** and **gunned**

gunboat »*noun* a small ship armed with guns.

gun dog »*noun* a dog trained to collect game that has been shot.

gunfire

gunge

gung-ho »*adjective* unthinkingly enthusiastic and eager, especially about taking part in fighting.
– SAY gung-**hoh**

ℹ️ **gung-ho** comes from a word meaning 'work together' in Chinese

gunk

gunman (plural **gunmen**)

gunmetal »*noun* ❶ a grey corrosion-resistant form of bronze containing zinc. ❷ a dull bluish-grey colour.

gunned

gunnel another way of spelling GUNWALE.

gunner

gunnery

gunning

gunplay

gunpoint

gunpowder

gunrunner »*noun* a person who illegally sells or imports guns.
gunrunning

guns

gunship »*noun* a heavily armed helicopter.

gunsight »*noun* a device on a gun enabling it to be aimed accurately.

gunslinger »*noun* a man who carries a gun.

gunsmith »*noun* a person who makes and sells small firearms.

gunwale »*noun* the upper edge or planking of the side of a boat.
– SAY gun-n'l

☑ **gunwale** can also be spelled **gunnel**: both spellings are correct

guppy »*noun* (plural **guppies**) a small freshwater fish native to tropical America.
– SAY gup-pi

gurdwara »*noun* a Sikh place of worship.
– SAY goor-**dwah**-ruh

gurgle (verb: **gurgles**, **gurgling**, **gurgled**)

Gurkha »*noun* ❶ a member of a people of Nepal noted for their ability as soldiers. ❷ a member of a regiment in the British army established for recruits from Nepal.
– SAY ger-kuh

☑ **kha** not **kah**: **Gurkha**

gurn »*verb* (**gurns**, **gurning**, **gurned**) pull a grotesque face.
– SAY gern

☑ **gurn** can also be spelled **girn**: both spellings are correct

gurnard »*noun* a small fish with three finger-like bony parts to its fins.
– SAY ger-nerd

gurned

gurning

gurns

guru »*noun* ❶ a Hindu spiritual teacher. ❷ one of the ten first leaders of the Sikh religion. ❸ an influential teacher or popular expert.
– SAY guu-roo

gush (verb: **gushes**, **gushing**, **gushed**)
gushing

gushy »*adjective* (**gushier**, **gushiest**) expressing approval in an overenthusiastic way.

gusset »*noun* a piece of material sewn into a garment to strengthen or enlarge a part of it.

☑ **-et** not **-it**: **gusset**

gust (verb: **gusts**, **gusting**, **gusted**)
gustily
gusto »*noun* enjoyment or vigour.

gusts
gusty
　gustily
gut (verb: **guts, gutting, gutted**)

> ✓ double the t in **gutting** and **gutted**

gutless »*adjective* lacking courage or determination.

guts

gutsy »*adjective* (**gutsier, gutsiest**) courageous and determined.
　gutsiness

gutted

gutter »*noun* a shallow trough or channel for carrying off rainwater.
» *verb* (**gutters, guttering, guttered**) (of a flame) flicker and burn unsteadily.
　guttering

guttersnipe »*noun* a street urchin.

gutting

guttural »*adjective* ❶ (of a speech sound) produced in the throat. ❷ (of speech) characterized by guttural sounds.
– **say** gut-tuh-ruhl
　gutturally

> ✓ tur not ter: **guttural**

guy[1] »*noun* (in informal English) a man.
» *verb* (**guys, guying, guyed**) ridicule.

guy[2] »*noun* a rope or line fixed to the ground to secure a tent.

Guyanese (plural **Guyanese**) [of Guyana]

guyed

Guy Fawkes Night

guying

guys

guzzle (verb: **guzzles, guzzling, guzzled**)

gybe »*verb* (**gybes, gybing, gybed**) change the course of a sailing boat by swinging the sail across a following wind.
» *noun* an act of gybing.
– **say** jyb

> ✓ gy not ji: **gybe** (the spelling **jibe** is American)

gym

gymkhana »*noun* an event consisting of a series of competitions on horseback.
– **say** jim-**kah**-nuh

> ✓ don't forget the h: **gymkhana**

gymnasium (plural **gymnasiums** or **gymnasia**)

> ✓ the plural can be either **gymnasia** (like the original Latin) or **gymnasiums**

gymnast
gymnastics
　gymnastic
gymslip

gynaecology »*noun* the branch of medicine concerned with conditions and diseases specific to women and girls.
– **say** gy-ni-**kol**-uh-ji
　gynaecological
　gynaecologist

> ✓ naec not nec: **gynaecology** (the spelling **gynecology** is American)

gyp »*noun* (in informal English) pain or discomfort.
– **say** jip

> ✓ gyp can also be spelled **gip**: both spellings are correct

gypsies

gypsophila »*noun* a garden plant with small pink or white flowers.
– **say** jip-**soff**-i-luh

> ✓ ila not lia: **gypsophila**

gypsum »*noun* a soft white or grey mineral used to make plaster of Paris and in the building industry.
– **say** jip-suhm

gypsy (plural **gypsies**)

> ✓ gypsy can also be spelled **gipsy**, with an i instead of a y
> plural: drop the y and add **ies**: **gypsies**

gyrate »*verb* (**gyrates, gyrating, gyrated**) ❶ move in a circle or spiral. ❷ dance in a wild manner.
– **say** jy-**rayt**
　gyration
　gyratory

gyrocompass »*noun* (plural **gyrocompasses**) a compass in which the direction of true north is maintained by a gyroscope.

gyroscope »*noun* a device, used to provide stability or maintain a fixed direction, consisting of a wheel or disc spinning rapidly about an axis which is itself free to alter in direction.
　gyroscopic

g

Hh

habeas corpus »*noun* a written order that an arrested person be brought before a judge or into court, to decide whether or not their detention is lawful.
– **SAY** hay-bi-uhss **kor**-puhss

> ✓ **habeas corpus** means 'you shall have the body (in court)' in Latin

haberdasher »*noun* ❶ a dealer in dressmaking and sewing goods. ❷ (in American English) a dealer in men's clothing.
– **SAY** **hab**-er-dash-er
   haberdashery

habiliment »*noun* (an old word) clothing.
– **SAY** huh-**bil**-i-muhnt

habit

habitable »*adjective* suitable to live in.
   habitability

habitat »*noun* the natural home or environment of an animal or plant.

habitation »*noun* ❶ the state of living somewhere. ❷ a house or home.

habit-forming

habitual »*adjective* ❶ done constantly or as a habit. ❷ usual: *his habitual dress.*
– **SAY** huh-**bit**-yuu-uhl
   habitually

habituate »*verb* (**habituates, habituating, habituated**) make or become accustomed to something.
   habituation

habitue »*noun* a resident of or frequent visitor to a place.
– **SAY** huh-**bit**-yuu-ay

> ✓ **habitue** can also be spelled **habitué**, with an acute accent on the **e** (as in the original French)

hachures »*plural noun* parallel lines used on maps to shade in hills.
– **SAY** ha-**shyoorz**

hacienda »*noun* (in Spanish-speaking countries) a large estate with a house.
– **SAY** ha-si-**en**-duh

hack (verb: **hacks, hacking, hacked**)

hacker »*noun* a person who uses computers to gain unauthorized access to data.

hackles »*plural noun* hairs along an animal's back which rise when it is angry or alarmed.

hackney »*noun* (plural **hackneys**) ❶ a light horse with a high-stepping trot. ❷ a horse-drawn vehicle kept for hire.

hackney carriage »*noun* (in British English) an official term for a taxi.

hackneyed »*adjective* (of a phrase or idea) unoriginal and dull.

> ✓ **neyed** not **nied: hackneyed**

hacks

hacksaw »*noun* a saw with a narrow blade set in a frame.

had past and past participle of **HAVE**.

haddock (plural **haddock**)

> ✓ double **d: haddock**

Hades »*noun* (in Greek mythology) the underworld.
– **SAY** **hay**-deez

hadn't [had not]

> ✓ be careful to put the apostrophe where a letter has been left out, that is between the **n** and **t** of **not: hadn't**

haematite »*noun* a reddish-black mineral consisting of ferric oxide.
– **SAY** **hee**-muh-tyt

> ✓ **hae** not **he: haematite** (the spelling **hematite** is American)

haematology »*noun* the scientific study of the blood.
– **SAY** hee-muh-**tol**-uh-ji
   haematologist

> ✓ in **haematology**, and in other words related to the blood such as **haemoglobin** and **haemophilia**, the British spelling is **hae** while the American spelling begins **he** (**hematology, hemoglobin**, etc.)

h

haemoglobin »*noun* a red protein responsible for transporting oxygen in the blood.
– SAY hee-muh-**gloh**-bin

haemophilia »*noun* a medical condition in which the ability of the blood to clot is reduced, causing severe bleeding from even a slight injury.
– SAY hee-muh-**fi**-li-uh

haemophiliac »*noun* a person suffering from haemophilia.

haemorrhage »*noun* ❶ an escape of blood from a burst blood vessel. ❷ a damaging loss of something valuable.
» *verb* (**haemorrhages, haemorrhaging, haemorrhaged**) ❶ suffer a haemorrhage. ❷ use or spend in large amounts, seemingly uncontrollably: *the business was haemorrhaging cash.*
– SAY **hem**-uh-rij

> ✓ note the double **r** and **h** in the middle of both **haemorrhage** and **haemorrhoid**, and don't forget the **hae** at the beginning (the spellings with **he** are American)

haemorrhoid »*noun* a swollen vein in the region of the anus.
– SAY **hem**-uh-royd

hafnium »*noun* a hard silver-grey metal resembling zirconium.
– SAY **haf**-ni-uhm

haft »*noun* the handle of a knife, axe, or spear.

hag

haggard »*adjective* looking exhausted and unwell.

> ✓ double **g**: **haggard**

haggis »*noun* (plural **haggis**) a Scottish dish consisting of seasoned sheep's or calf's offal mixed with suet and oatmeal.

haggle »*verb* (**haggles, haggling, haggled**) bargain persistently over a price.
haggler

hagiography »*noun* ❶ the writing of the lives of saints. ❷ a biography idealizing its subject.
– SAY ha-gi-**og**-ruh-fi
hagiographer

hag-ridden »*adjective* suffering from nightmares or anxieties.

ha-ha »*noun* a ditch with a wall below ground level, forming a boundary to a park or garden without interrupting the view.

haiku »*noun* (plural **haiku** or **haikus**) a Japanese poem of seventeen syllables.
– SAY hy-koo

hail¹ »*noun* ❶ pellets of frozen rain falling in showers. ❷ a large number of things hurled forcefully through the air.

hail² »*verb* (**hails, hailing, hailed**) ❶ call out to someone to attract attention. ❷ describe someone enthusiastically as: *he has been hailed as the new James Dean.* ❸ (**hail from**) have your home or origins in.

> ℹ do not confuse **hail** with **hale**, which means 'strong and healthy'

Hail Mary »*noun* (plural **Hail Marys**) a prayer to the Virgin Mary, used chiefly by Roman Catholics.

> ✓ make the plural simply by adding **s**: **Hail Marys**

hails

hailstone »*noun* a pellet of hail.

hair [thread-like strands that grow out of the skin]

> ℹ do not confuse **hair** with **hare**, which is a fast-running animal

hairband

hairbrush

haircut

hairdo (plural **hairdos**)

hairdresser
hairdressing

hairdryer

> ✓ **hairdryer** can also be spelled **hairdrier**: both spellings are correct

hairgrip

hairier

hairiest

hairiness

hairline

hairnet

hairpiece

hairpin

hairpin bend »*noun* a sharp U-shaped bend in a road.

hair-raising »*adjective* very frightening.

hair shirt »*noun* a shirt made of stiff cloth woven from horsehair, formerly worn as a way of punishing yourself.

hairslide

hair-splitting »*noun* the making of overly fine distinctions.

hairspray

hairspring »*noun* a flat coiled spring that regulates the movement of the balance wheel in a watch.

h

hairstyle
hairstyling
hairstylist

hair trigger »*noun* a firearm trigger set for release at the slightest pressure.

hairy (adjective: hairier, hairiest)
hairiness

> ✓ drop the y and add ier or iest to spell **hairier** or **hairiest**

Haitian [of Haiti]
– SAY hay-sh'n

hajj »*noun* the pilgrimage to Mecca which all Muslims are expected to make at least once.

> ✓ hajj can also be spelled haj: both spellings are correct

haka »*noun* a ceremonial Maori war dance.
– SAY hah-kuh

hake »*noun* a long, edible sea fish with strong teeth.

halal »*adjective* (of meat) prepared according to Muslim law.
– SAY huh-**lahl**

halberd »*noun* (a historical term) a combined spear and battleaxe.
– SAY hal-berd
halberdier

> ✓ -berd not -bard: halberd

halcyon »*adjective* (of a past time) extremely happy and peaceful.
– SAY hal-si-uhn

> ✓ cyon not cion: halcyon

hale »*adjective* (of an old person) strong and healthy.
haleness

> ✓ do not confuse hale with hail, which means 'call out to someone to attract attention' and 'pellets of frozen rain'

half (plural halves)

half-and-half

halfback »*noun* a player in a ball game whose position is between the forwards and fullbacks.

half-baked »*adjective* poorly planned or considered.

half board »*noun* the providing of bed, breakfast, and one main meal at a hotel or guest house.

half-brother

half-century (plural half-centuries)

half-crown »*noun* a former British coin equal to two shillings and sixpence (12½p).

half-dozen

half-hardy »*adjective* (of a plant) able to grow outdoors except in severe frost.

half-hearted
half-heartedly
half-heartedness

half hitch »*noun* a knot formed by passing the end of a rope round itself and then through the loop created.

half-hour
half-hourly

half-life »*noun* the time taken for the radioactivity of substance to fall to half its original value.

half-light

half-moon

half nelson »*noun* a wrestling hold in which one arm is passed under the opponent's arm from behind and the hand is applied to the neck.

halfpenny »*noun* (plural **halfpennies** or **halfpence**) a former British coin equal to half a penny.
– SAY hayp-ni [singular], hayp-neez or hay-puhnss [plural]

> ℹ the plural **halfpennies** is used to refer to separate coins, and the alternative plural **halfpence** is used when referring to a sum of money

> ✓ halfpenny can also be spelled ha'penny: both spellings are correct

halfpennyworth »*noun* as much as could be bought for a halfpenny.
– SAY hay-puhth or hayp-ni-wuhth

> ✓ halfpennyworth can also be spelled ha'p'orth: both spellings are correct

half-sister

half-term

half-timbered »*adjective* having walls with a timber frame and a brick or plaster filling.

half-time

half-truth

half-volley »*noun* (in sport) a strike of the ball immediately after it bounces.

halfway

halfwit »*noun* a stupid person.
half-witted

half-yearly

halibut »*noun* (plural halibut) a large marine flatfish which is used for food.
– SAY ha-li-buht

halitosis »*noun* unpleasant-smelling breath.
– SAY ha-li-toh-siss

✓ sis not **siss**: **halitosis**

hall

hallelujah »*exclamation* God be praised.
– SAY hal-li-**loo**-yuh

✓ **hallelujah** can also be written **alleluia**: both spellings are correct

hallmark »*noun* ❶ an official mark stamped on articles of gold, silver, or platinum to certify that they are pure. ❷ a distinctive feature: *the hallmark of fine champagnes.*
» *verb* (**hallmarks**, **hallmarking**, **hallmarked**) stamp something with a hallmark.

hallowed »*adjective* ❶ made holy. ❷ greatly honoured and respected.
– SAY **hal**-loh

Halloween »*noun* the night of 31 October, the eve of All Saints' Day.

✓ **Halloween** can also be spelled **Hallowe'en**: both are correct

hallucinate »*verb* (**hallucinates**, **hallucinating**, **hallucinated**) see something which is not actually there.
– SAY huh-**loo**-si-nayt
hallucination
hallucinatory

hallucinogen »*noun* a drug causing hallucinations.
– SAY huh-**loo**-si-nuh-juhn
hallucinogenic

✓ gen not **gin**: **hallucinogen**

hallway

halo »*noun* (plural **haloes** or **halos**) ❶ (in a painting) a circle of light surrounding the head of a holy person. ❷ a circle of light round the sun or moon.
– SAY **hay**-loh
haloed

✓ the plural of **halo** can have **oes** or **os**: **haloes** or **halos**

halogen »*noun* one of the group of elements including fluorine, chlorine, bromine, iodine, and astatine.
» *adjective* using a filament surrounded by halogen vapour: *a halogen bulb.*
– SAY **hal**-uh-juhn

halon »*noun* one of a group of compounds of carbon with halogens, used in fire extinguishers.
– SAY **hay**-lon

halt¹ (verb: **halts**, **halting**, **halted**) [stop]

halt² »*adjective* (an old word) lame.

halter »*noun* ❶ a rope or strap placed around the head of an animal and used to lead or tie it to something. ❷ a strap passing behind the neck by which the bodice of a sleeveless dress or top is held in place.

halter neck »*noun* a style of neckline using a halter.

halting »*adjective* slow and hesitant.
haltingly

halts

halve (verb: **halves**, **halving**, **halved**)

halves

halving

halyard »*noun* a rope used for raising and lowering a sail or flag on a ship.
– SAY **hal**-yerd

✓ haly not **halli**: **halyard**

ham¹ [meat]

ham² »*noun* ❶ an actor who overacts, or piece of overacting. ❷ an amateur radio operator.
» *verb* (**hams**, **hamming**, **hammed**) overact.

✓ double the **m** to spell **hamming** and **hammed**

hamburger

ham-fisted

hamlet »*noun* a small village.

hammed

hammer (verb: **hammers**, **hammering**, **hammered**)

hammer drill »*noun* a power drill that delivers a rapid succession of blows.

hammered

hammerhead »*noun* a shark with flattened blade-like extensions on either side of the head.

hammering

hammers

hammer toe »*noun* a toe that is bent permanently downwards.

hammier [more hammy]

hammiest

hamming

hammock

✓ note the double **m**: **hammock**

hammy »*adjective* (**hammier**, **hammiest**) (of acting or an actor) exaggerated.

hamper¹ »*noun* ❶ a basket used for food and other items needed on a picnic. ❷ (in British English) a box containing food and drink for a special occasion.

hamper[2] **»verb** (**hampers, hampering, hampered**) slow something or someone down.

hams

hamster

> ☑ there is no **p**: **hamster**

hamstring **»noun** one of five tendons at the back of a person's knee.
» verb (**hamstrings, hamstringing, hamstrung**) ❶ cripple someone by cutting their hamstrings. ❷ severely restrict someone or something.

hand (verb: **hands, handing, handed**)

handbag

handball

handbill **»noun** a small printed advertisement or other notice that someone hands out.

handbook

handbrake

handcrafted **»adjective** made skilfully by hand.

handcuff (verb: **handcuffs, handcuffing, handcuffed**)

handed

handful

> ☑ **-ful** not **-full**: **handful**

handgun

handhold

handicap **»noun** ❶ a thing that makes it difficult for someone to do something. ❷ (old-fashioned) a permanent physical or mental disability. ❸ a disadvantage given to a leading competitor in a sport in order to make the chances more equal. ❹ the extra weight given as a handicap to a racehorse. ❺ the number of strokes by which a golfer normally exceeds par for a course.
» verb (**handicaps, handicapping, handicapped**) make it difficult for someone to do something.

handicapped

> ℹ although **handicapped** used to be the accepted way of talking about people with physical and mental disabilities, it is now better to say **disabled**

handicapping

handicaps

handicraft **»noun** ❶ the skilled making of decorative objects by hand. ❷ an object made in this way.

> ☑ note that it is **i** not **y** in the middle: **handicraft**

handier

handiest

handily

handiness

handing

handiwork **»noun** ❶ (your handiwork) something that you have made or done. ❷ the making of things by hand.

> ☑ note that it is **i** not **y** in the middle: **handiwork**

handkerchief (plural **handkerchiefs** or **handkerchieves**)

> ☑ do not forget the **d**: **handkerchief**. The plural of **handkerchief** can either add an **s**: **handkerchiefs**, or drop the **f** and add **ves**: **handkerchieves** (both are correct).

handle (verb: **handles, handling, handled**)
  handled
  handler
  handling

handlebar

handled

handler

handles

handling

handmade

handmaid **»noun** (an old word) a female servant.

handmaiden **»noun** (an old word) = **HANDMAID**.

hand-me-down

handout

handover

hand-pick (verb: **hand-picks, hand-picking, hand-picked**)

handprint

hands

handset

handshake

handsome (adjective: **handsomer, handsomest**) [good-looking]
  handsomely
  handsomeness

> ☑ do not forget the **d**: **handsome** (a **hansom** is a horse-drawn cab)

handspring **»noun** a jump through the air on to your hands followed by another on to your feet.

handstand

handwriting

handwritten

handy (adjective: **handier**, **handiest**)
handily
handiness

handyman (plural **handymen**)

hang (verb: **hangs**, **hanging**, **hung** or **hanged**)

> ℹ️ **hang** has two past tense and past participle forms: **hanged** and **hung**. You should use **hung** in general situations, as in *they hung out the washing*, while **hanged** should only be used when talking about executing someone by hanging, as in *the prisoner was hanged*.

hangar »*noun* a large building used for housing aircraft.
– ꜱᴀʏ hang-er

> ☑️ **ar** not **er**: **hangar**

hangdog »*adjective* having a sad or guilty appearance.

hanged

hanger [person or thing that hangs something]

> ℹ️ do not confuse **hanger** with **hangar**, which means 'a building for housing aircraft'

hanger-on »*noun* (plural **hangers-on**) a person who tries to be friendly with some who is rich or famous or more important.

> ☑️ the plural of **hanger-on** adds an **s** to **hanger**: **hangers-on**

hang-glider »*noun* a glider consisting of a frame with fabric stretched over it, from which the pilot is suspended in a harness.
hang-gliding

hanging

hangman (plural **hangmen**)

hangnail »*noun* a piece of torn skin at the root of a fingernail.

hangover

hangs

hang-up »*noun* an emotional problem caused by worry or embarrassment about something.

hank »*noun* a coil or length of wool, hair, or other material.

hanker »*verb* (**hankers**, **hankering**, **hankered**) (**hanker after** or **for** or **to do**) feel a strong desire for something or to do something.

hanky (plural **hankies**)

> ☑️ **hanky** can also be spelled **hankie**: both spellings are correct

hanky-panky

Hanoverian »*adjective* relating to the royal house of Hanover, who ruled as kings and queens in Britain from 1714 to 1901.
– ꜱᴀʏ han-uh-**veer**-i-uhn

Hansard »*noun* the official record of debates in the British, Canadian, Australian, or New Zealand parliament.

> ℹ️ note the capital **H**: **Hansard** is named after the English printer Thomas C. **Hansard**

hansom »*noun* (a historical term) a two-wheeled horse-drawn cab for two passengers, with the driver seated behind.

> ☑️ do not confuse the spelling of **hansom** with **handsome**, which means 'good-looking'

Hanukkah »*noun* a Jewish festival of lights held in December, in memory of the rededication of the Jewish Temple in Jerusalem.
– ꜱᴀʏ han-uu-kuh or **khan**-uu-kuh

> ☑️ **Hanukkah** can also be spelled **Chanukkah**: both spellings are correct

ha'penny another way of spelling
HALFPENNY.

haphazard
haphazardly

> ☑️ **ard** not **erd**: **haphazard**

hapless »*adjective* unlucky.
haplessly

ha'p'orth another way of spelling
HALFPENNYWORTH.

happen (verb: **happens**, **happening**, **happened**)

> ☑️ double **p**, single **n**: **happen**, **happened**, **happening**

happening

happens

happy (adjective: **happier**, **happiest**)
happily
happiness

> ☑️ drop the **y** and add **ier** or **iest** to spell **happier** or **happiest**

happy-go-lucky

happy hour »*noun* a period of the day when drinks are sold at reduced prices in a bar.

hara-kiri »*noun* a former Japanese method of ritual suicide in which a person cuts open their stomach with a sword.
– ꜱᴀʏ ha-ruh-**ki**-ri

> ℹ️ **hara-kiri** is a Japanese term which means 'belly-cutting'

h

harangue »*verb* (harangues, haranguing, harangued) use loud and aggressive language in criticizing someone or trying to persuade them to do something.
» *noun* something said in a loud and aggressive way.
– SAY huh-**rang**

> ✓ remember the **ue** on the end, but drop the **e** to spell **haranguing**

harass »*verb* (harasses, harassing, harassed) ❶ subject someone to constant interference or bullying. ❷ make repeated small-scale attacks on an enemy in order to wear down their resistance.
– SAY ha-ruhss or huh-**rass**
harasser
harassment

> ✓ single **r** and double **s**: harass

harbinger »*noun* a person or thing that announces or signals the approach of something.
– SAY har-bin-jer

harbour (verb: harbours, harbouring, harboured)

> ✓ do not forget the **u**: harbour (the spelling harbor is American)

hard (adjective: harder, hardest)
hardness

hardback

hardbitten »*adjective* tough and cynical.

hardboard »*noun* stiff board made of compressed wood pulp.

hard-boiled

hard cash »*noun* coins and banknotes as opposed to other forms of payment.

hard copy »*noun* a printed version on paper of data held in a computer.

hard core

> ✓ add a hyphen if you use **hard core** as an adjective, as in *hard-core supporters*

hardcover »*noun* = HARDBACK.

hard disk »*noun* (in computing) a rigid magnetic disk on which a large amount of data can be stored.

harden (verb: hardens, hardening, hardened)
hardened

harder

hardest

hard-headed »*adjective* tough and realistic.
hard-headedly
hard-headedness

hard-hearted
hard-heartedly
hard-heartedness

hard labour »*noun* heavy manual work as a punishment.

hard line »*noun* a strict policy or attitude.
» *adjective* (hard-line) very strict.
hardliner

> ✓ add a hyphen if you use this word as an adjective, as in *a hard-line activist*

hardly

> ⓘ avoid using **hardly** in a negative construction, such as *I can't hardly wait*; the correct construction is *I can hardly wait*

hardness

hard-nosed

hard palate »*noun* the bony front part of the roof of the mouth.

hard-pressed »*adjective* in difficulties or under pressure.

hard sell »*noun* a policy or technique of aggressive selling or advertising.

hardship

hard shoulder »*noun* a strip of ground with a hard surface alongside a motorway for use in an emergency.

hardware »*noun* ❶ tools and other items used in the home and in activities such as gardening. ❷ the machines, wiring, and other physical parts of a computer. ❸ heavy military equipment such as tanks and missiles.

hardwood

hardy (adjective: hardier, hardiest)
hardily
hardiness

hare (verb: hares, haring, hared) [fast-running animal; run quickly]

> ⓘ do not confuse **hare** with **hair**, which is what grows out of your head

harebell »*noun* a plant with pale blue bell-shaped flowers.

hare-brained »*adjective* foolish; ill-judged.

Hare Krishna »*noun* a member of a religious sect based on the worship of the Hindu god Krishna.
– SAY ha-ri **krish**-nuh

harelip

> ⓘ avoid using the word **harelip**, as it may cause offence; use **cleft lip** instead

harem »*noun* ❶ the separate part of a Muslim household reserved for women. ❷ the women living in this area.

– **say** hah-**reem** or hah-**reem**

✓ rem not reem: harem

haricot »*noun* a round white bean which is dried and used as a vegetable.
– **say** ha-ri-koh

✓ haricot is a French word, ending in a silent **t**

hark »*verb* (**harks, harking, harked**) ❶ listen. ❷ (**hark at**) used to draw attention to a foolish or arrogant remark: *hark at you.* ❸ (**hark back**) recall an earlier period.

harken another way of spelling **HEARKEN**.

harking

harks

harlequin »*noun* (in traditional pantomime) a character who wears a mask and a diamond-patterned costume. »*adjective* in varied colours.
– **say** har-li-kwin

harlot »*noun* (an old word) a prostitute, or a woman who has many brief sexual relationships.

✓ single t: harlot

harm (verb: **harms, harming, harmed**)

harmful
harmfully
harmfulness

✓ -ful not -full: harmful

harming

harmless
harmlessly
harmlessness

harmonic »*adjective* relating to or characterized by harmony.
– **say** har-**mon**-ik
harmonically

harmonica »*noun* a small rectangular wind instrument with a row of metal reeds capable of producing different notes.

harmonically

harmonies

harmonious »*adjective* ❶ tuneful. ❷ arranged in a pleasing way so that each part goes well with the others. ❸ free from conflict.
harmoniously
harmoniousness

harmonise another way of spelling **HARMONIZE**.

harmonium »*noun* a keyboard instrument in which the notes are produced by air driven through metal reeds by foot-operated bellows.

harmonize »*verb* (**harmonizes, harmonizing, harmonized**) ❶ (in music) add notes to a melody to produce harmony. ❷ make or be harmonious.
harmonization

✓ many people prefer the alternative spellings **harmonise, harmonises**, etc., and **harmonisation**: both **s** and **z** spellings are correct

harmony »*noun* (plural **harmonies**) ❶ the combination of musical notes sounded at the same time to produce chords with a pleasing effect. ❷ a pleasing quality when things are arranged well together. ❸ agreement.

✓ plural: drop the **y** and add **ies**: harmonies

harms

harness »*noun* (plural **harnesses**) ❶ a set of straps by which a horse or other animal is fastened to a cart, plough, etc. and is controlled by its driver. ❷ a similar arrangement of straps used for attaching someone's body to something or for restraining a young child.
»*verb* (**harnesses, harnessing, harnessed**) ❶ fit a person or animal with a harness. ❷ control and make use of resources.

✓ there is one **n** but a double **s**: harness

harp »*noun* a musical instrument consisting of a frame supporting a series of strings of different lengths, played by plucking with the fingers.
»*verb* (**harps, harping, harped**) (**harp on**) keep talking about something in a boring way.
harpist

harpies plural of **HARPY**.

harping

harpist

harpoon »*noun* a barbed spear-like missile used for catching whales and other large sea creatures.
»*verb* (**harpoons, harpooning, harpooned**) spear something with a harpoon.

harps

harpsichord »*noun* a keyboard instrument with horizontal strings plucked by points operated by pressing the keys.
harpsichordist

✓ psi not pis, and -chord not -cord: harpsichord

harpy »*noun* (plural **harpies**) ❶ (in Greek and Roman mythology) a cruel creature

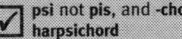

with a woman's head and body and a bird's wings and claws. ❷ a greedy or cruel woman.

harridan »*noun* a bossy or aggressive old woman.

 -an not -en: harridan

harried

harrier

harries

harrow »*noun* an implement consisting of a heavy frame set with teeth which is dragged over ploughed land to break up or spread the soil.
» *verb* (**harrows, harrowing, harrowed**) draw a harrow over ground.

harrowing »*adjective* very distressing.

harrows

harry »*verb* (**harries, harrying, harried**) ❶ carry out repeated attacks on an enemy. ❷ persistently harass someone.

harsh (adjective: **harsher, harshest**)
harshly
harshness

hart »*noun* an adult male deer.

hartebeest »*noun* a large African antelope with a long head and sloping back, related to the gnus.
– SAY **har**-ti-beest

 -beest not -beast: hartebeest

harum-scarum »*adjective* reckless.

harvest »*noun* ❶ the process or period of gathering in crops. ❷ the season's yield or crop.
» *verb* (**harvests, harvesting, harvested**) gather in a crop.
harvester

harvest mouse »*noun* a small mouse with a tail which it can use for grasping.

harvests

has present of **HAVE** [as in *he has*].

has-been »*noun* a person or thing that is old-fashioned or no longer significant.

hash »*noun* ❶ a dish of chopped cooked meat reheated with potatoes. ❷ a jumble. ❸ hashish. ❹ the symbol #.

hash browns »*plural noun* a dish of chopped and fried cooked potatoes.

hashish »*noun* cannabis.

haslet »*noun* a cold meat consisting of chopped and compressed pork offal.
– SAY **haz**-lit or **hayz**-lit

hasn't [has not]

 be careful to put the apostrophe where the letter has been left out, that is between the **n** and **t** of not: hasn't

hasp »*noun* a hinged metal plate that forms part of a fastening and is fitted over a metal loop and secured by a pin or padlock.

hassle (verb: **hassles, hassling, hassled**)

 ss not st: hassle

hassock »*noun* a cushion for kneeling on in church.

haste [speed or urgency of action]

hasten (verb: **hastens, hastening, hastened**)

hasty (adjective: **hastier, hastiest**)
hastily
hastiness

hat
hatful
hatless
hatted

hatband

hatch[1] [small opening allowing access]

hatch[2] (verb: **hatches, hatching, hatched**) [come out of an egg]

hatch[3] »*verb* (**hatches, hatching, hatched**) (in drawing) shade an area with closely drawn parallel lines.
hatching

hatchback »*noun* a car with a door across the full width and height at the back end for easy loading.

hatched

hatches

hatchet »*noun* a small axe with a short handle.

 there is only one **t** at the end: hatchet

hatchet-faced »*adjective* sharp-featured and grim-looking.

hatchet man »*noun* ❶ a person employed to carry out unpleasant tasks. ❷ a harsh critic.

hatching

hatchling »*noun* a newly hatched young animal.

hatchway »*noun* an opening or hatch, especially in a ship's deck.

hate (verb: **hates, hating, hated**)
hater

hateful
hatefully
hatefulness

 -ful not -full: hateful

hater

hates

hatful

> ✓ -ful not -full: **hatful**

hating

hatless

hatpin

hatred »*noun* very strong hate.

hatted

hatter

hat-trick »*noun* three successes of the same kind.

hauberk »*noun* (a historical term) a full-length coat of mail.
– SAY haw-berk

haughty »*adjective* (**haughtier, haughtiest**) arrogant and contemptuous of others.
haughtily
haughtiness

haul (verb: **hauls, hauling, hauled**)

haulage »*noun* the commercial transport of goods.

hauled

haulier »*noun* a person or company employed in the commercial transport of goods by road.

hauling

haulm »*noun* a plant stalk.
– SAY hawm

hauls

haunch »*noun* ❶ a person or animal's buttock and thigh. ❷ the leg and loin of an animal, as food.

haunt (verb: **haunts, haunting, haunted**)
haunted
haunter

haunting
hauntingly

haunts

haute couture »*noun* the designing and making of high-quality clothes by leading fashion houses.
– SAY oht kuu-**tyoor**

> ℹ from a French phrase meaning 'high dressmaking'

haute cuisine »*noun* high-quality cooking in the traditional French style.
– SAY oht kwi-**zeen**

> ℹ from a French phrase meaning 'high cookery'

hauteur »*noun* proud haughtiness of manner.
– SAY oh-**ter**

> ✓ note the **eur** at the end: **hauteur** is a French word

have (verb: **has, having, had**)

haven »*noun* ❶ a place of safety. ❷ a harbour or small port.

haven't [have not]

> ✓ be careful to put the apostrophe where a letter has been left out, that is between the **n** and **t** of **not**: **haven't**

haver »*verb* (**havers, havering, havered**) be indecisive; dither.
– SAY hay-ver

haversack »*noun* a small, sturdy bag carried on the back or over the shoulder.

having

havoc »*noun* ❶ widespread destruction. ❷ great confusion or disorder.

> ✓ no k at the end of **havoc**

haw »*noun* the red fruit of the hawthorn.

Hawaiian

> ✓ remember, **Hawaii** and **Hawaiian** have a double i

hawk[1] »*noun* ❶ a fast-flying bird of prey with a long tail. ❷ a person who favours an aggressive policy (the opposite of *dove*).
»*verb* (**hawks, hawking, hawked**) ❶ (of a bird or other flying creature) hunt prey. ❷ hunt game with a trained hawk.
hawkish

hawk[2] »*verb* (**hawks, hawking, hawked**) ❶ offer goods for sale in the street. ❷ clear the throat noisily.
hawker

hawk-eyed

hawking

hawkish

hawks

hawser »*noun* a thick rope for mooring or towing a ship.
– SAY haw-zer

hawthorn »*noun* a thorny shrub or tree with white, pink, or red blossom and small dark red fruits.

hay [mown and dried grass]

hay fever »*noun* an allergy to pollen or dust, causing sneezing and watery eyes.

hayloft

haymaker

hayrick

haystack

haywire »*adjective* (**go haywire**) go out of control.

hazard »*noun* ❶ a danger. ❷ an obstacle, such as a bunker, on a golf course.
» *verb* (**hazards, hazarding, hazarded**) ❶ put something at risk. ❷ dare to say.

 only a single **z** in **hazard**

hazardous »*adjective* dangerous.
hazardously

hazards

haze »*noun* ❶ a thin mist caused by fine particles of dust, pollutants, etc. ❷ a state of mental confusion: *an alcoholic haze.*

hazel »*noun* ❶ a shrub or small tree bearing catkins in spring and nuts in autumn. ❷ a rich reddish-brown colour.

hazelnut

 el not le: **hazelnut**

hazy »*adjective* (**hazier, haziest**) ❶ covered by a haze. ❷ vague or unclear: *hazy memories.*
hazily
haziness

H-bomb

he

ℹ️ **he** used to be used to talk about both males and females when a person's sex was not specified: *every child needs to know that he is loved.* This is now often thought of as outdated and sexist. Instead, you could use **he or she**, but this can be awkward. An alternative is to use **they**: *every child needs to know that they are loved.*

head (verb: **heads, heading, headed**)
headless

headache

headband

headboard

headbutt (verb: **headbutts, headbutting, headbutted**)

headcount »*noun* a count of the number of people present.

headdress (plural **headdresses**)

✓ remember, there are two **d**'s in **headdress**

headed

header

headgear

headhunt »*verb* (**headhunts, headhunting, headhunted**) ❶ (**headhunting**) (among some peoples) collecting the heads of dead enemies as trophies. ❷ find someone who is suitable for a vacant post and

persuade them to leave their current job.
headhunter

headier

headiest

headily

heading

headlamp

headland »*noun* a narrow piece of land that sticks out into the sea.

headless

headlight

headline »*noun* ❶ a heading at the top of a newspaper or magazine article. ❷ (**the headlines**) a summary of the most important items of news.
» *verb* (**headlines, headlining, headlined**) ❶ give an article a headline. ❷ appear as the star performer at a concert.
headliner

headlock »*noun* a method of restraining someone by holding an arm firmly around their head.

headlong »*adverb & adjective* ❶ with the head first. ❷ in a rush.

headman »*noun* (plural **headmen**) the leader of a tribe.

headmaster

headmen

headmistress (plural **headmistresses**)

head-on

headphones

headquarters

headrest

headroom »*noun* the space between the top of a vehicle or a person's head and the ceiling or other structure above.

heads

headscarf (plural **headscarves**)

headset »*noun* a set of headphones with a microphone attached.

headship »*noun* the position of leader, or of head teacher.

headstone »*noun* a stone slab set up at the head of a grave.

headstrong »*adjective* very independent and determined to have your own way.

headwater »*noun* a stream of a river close to its source.

headway »*noun* forward progress.

headwind »*noun* a wind blowing from directly in front.

heady »*adjective* (**headier, headiest**) ❶ (of alcohol) strong. ❷ having a strong or

355

exciting effect: *a heady, exotic perfume.*
headily

heal (verb: **heals**, **healing**, **healed**) [make healthy]
healer

 do not confuse **heal**, meaning 'make healthy' or 'put right', with **heel**, meaning 'back part of the foot' or 'lean over'

health

health farm »*noun* a place where people try to become healthier through dieting, exercise, and treatment.

healthful »*adjective* having or helping towards good health.
healthfully

☑ -ful not -full: **healthful**

healthy (adjective: **healthier**, **healthiest**)
healthily
healthiness

heap (verb: **heaps**, **heaping**, **heaped**)

hear (verb: **hears**, **hearing**, **heard**) [perceive sound]
hearer
hearing

hearken »*verb* (**hearkens**, **hearkening**, **hearkened**) (an old word) listen.
– SAY har-k'n

☑ **hearken** can also be spelled **harken**

hears

hearsay »*noun* information received from other people which is possibly unreliable.

hearse »*noun* a vehicle for conveying the coffin to a funeral.
– SAY herss

☑ remember, there's an **a** in **hearse**

heart [organ that pumps blood]

heartache

heartbeat

heartbreak »*noun* extreme distress.
heartbreaker
heartbreaking
heartbroken

heartburn »*noun* a form of indigestion felt as a burning sensation in the chest.

hearten »*verb* (**heartens**, **heartening**, **heartened**) make someone more cheerful or confident.
heartening

heartfelt »*adjective* deeply and strongly felt.

hearth »*noun* the floor or surround of a fireplace.
– SAY harth

hearthrug

heartier

heartiest

heartily

heartiness

heartland »*noun* the central or most important part of a country or area.

heartless »*adjective* unfeeling or inconsiderate.
heartlessly
heartlessness

heart-rending

heart-searching

heart-throb »*noun* a very good-looking famous man.

heart-to-heart

heart-warming

heartwood »*noun* the dense inner part of a tree trunk, where the hardest wood is to be found.

hearty (adjective: **heartier**, **heartiest**)
heartily
heartiness

heat (verb: **heats**, **heating**, **heated**)
heated
heatedly
heater

heath »*noun* ❶ an area of open uncultivated land covered with heather, gorse, etc. ❷ a shrub with small pink or purple bell-shaped flowers, found on heaths and moors.

heathen »*noun* a person who does not belong to a widely held religion, as seen by those who do.
» *adjective* having to do with heathens.
heathenism

heather »*noun* a shrub with small purple flowers, found on moors and heaths.
heathery

Heath Robinson »*adjective* ridiculously over-complicated in design or construction.

 named after the English cartoonist William *Heath Robinson*

heating

heats

heat-seeking »*adjective* (of a missile) able to detect and home in on heat sent out by a target.

heatstroke »*noun* a feverish condition caused by being exposed to very high temperatures.

heatwave »*noun* a period of abnormally hot weather.

heave (verb: **heaves**, **heaving**, **heaved** or **hove**)

> ℹ️ the past tense **hove** is chiefly used with the nautical meaning 'come to a stop' or 'come in sight', as in *the ship hove to and dropped anchor*

heave-ho

heaven

heavenly

heaven-sent

heavenward

heavenwards

heavier

heavies

heaviest

heavily

heaviness

heaving

heavy (adjective: **heavier**, **heaviest**; plural **heavies**)
heavily
heaviness

heavy-duty

heavy-handed »*adjective* clumsy, insensitive, or overly forceful.

heavy metal »*noun* a type of very loud, forceful rock music.

heavyweight

hebdomadal »*adjective* meeting weekly.
– say heb-**dom**-uh-d'l

hebe »*noun* an evergreen flowering shrub with spikes of mauve, pink, or white flowers, native to New Zealand.
– say **hee**-bi

Hebraic »*adjective* having to do with the Hebrew language or people.
– say hi-**bray**-ik

Hebrew

Hebridean [of the Hebrides]

heck

heckle »*verb* (**heckles**, **heckling**, **heckled**) interrupt a public speaker with comments or abuse.
heckler

hectare »*noun* a unit of land area equal to 10,000 square metres (2.471 acres).
– say hek-**tair**

hectic »*adjective* full of frantic activity.
hectically

hectolitre »*noun* a volume of 100 litres.

hector »*verb* (**hectors**, **hectoring**, **hectored**) talk to someone in a bullying way.

he'd [he had; he would]

hedge »*noun* a fence formed by closely growing bushes or shrubs.
» *verb* (**hedges**, **hedging**, **hedged**)
❶ surround with a hedge. ❷ avoid making a definite statement or decision.

hedgehog

hedgerow »*noun* a hedge of wild shrubs and trees bordering a field.

hedges

hedging

hedonism »*noun* the pursuit of pleasure.
– say hee-duh-**ni**-z'm or hed-uh-**ni**-z'm
hedonist
hedonistic

heebie-jeebies »*plural noun* (in informal English) a state of nervous fear or anxiety.

heed (verb: **heeds**, **heeding**, **heeded**)
heedful

heedless »*adjective* showing a reckless lack of care or attention.
heedlessly

heeds

heel[1] (verb: **heels**, **heeling**, **heeled**) [back part of the foot]
heelless

> ℹ️ do not confuse **heel**, meaning 'back part of the foot' or 'lean over', with **heal**, meaning 'make healthy' or 'put right'

heel[2] »*verb* (**heels**, **heeling**, **heeled**) (of a ship) lean over to one side.

hefty »*adjective* (**heftier**, **heftiest**) ❶ large, heavy, and powerful. ❷ (of a number or amount) considerable.

hegemony »*noun* leadership or dominance.
– say hi-**jem**-uh-ni or hi-**gem**-uh-ni

heifer »*noun* a young cow that has borne no more than one calf.
– say **hef**-fer

> ✅ do not forget there is an **i** in **heifer**

height

> ✅ **ei** not **i**: **height**, **heighten** (exceptions to the rule **i** before **e** except after **c**)

heighten (verb: **heightens**, **heightening**, **heightened**)

heinous »*adjective* utterly wicked.
– say **hay**-nuhss or **hee**-nuhss
heinously
heinousness

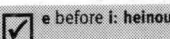
✓ e before i: **heinous**

heir »*noun* ❶ a person who will inherit the property or rank of another when that person dies. ❷ a person who continues the work of someone who has come before them.
– SAY air

✓ **heir** and the family of words derived from it are exceptions to the rule **i** before **e** except after **c**

heir apparent »*noun* (plural **heirs apparent**) ❶ an heir whose claim cannot be set aside by the birth of another heir. ❷ a person who is most likely to succeed to the place of another.

heiress »*noun* (plural **heiresses**) a female heir.

heirloom »*noun* a valuable object that has belonged to a family for several generations.

heir presumptive »*noun* (plural **heirs presumptive**) an heir whose claim may be set aside by the birth of another heir.

heist »*noun* (mainly in American English) a robbery.
– SAY hyst

held past and past participle of **HOLD**.

helical »*adjective* in the shape of a helix.
– SAY he-li-k'l or hee-li-k'l
helically

helices plural of **HELIX**.

helicopter

heliograph »*noun* a device which reflects sunlight in flashes from a movable mirror, used to send signals.

heliotrope »*noun* a plant with fragrant purple or blue flowers.

helipad »*noun* a landing and take-off area for helicopters.

heliport »*noun* an airport or landing place for helicopters.

helium »*noun* a light colourless gas that does not burn.
– SAY hee-li-uhm

helix »*noun* (plural **helices**) an object in the shape of a spiral.
– SAY hee-liks [singular], hee-li-seez [plural]

✓ for the plural, change the **ix** ending to **ices**: **helices**

hell

he'll [he will; he shall]

hell-bent »*adjective* determined to achieve something at all costs.

hellebore »*noun* a poisonous winter-flowering plant with large white, green, or purplish flowers.
– SAY hel-li-bor

Hellenic »*adjective* Greek.
– SAY hel-**len**-ik

Hellenism »*noun* ❶ the national character or culture of Greece. ❷ the study or imitation of ancient Greek culture.

hellfire

hellhole

hellish

hello

hellraiser »*noun* a person who causes trouble by drunken or outrageous behaviour.

helm »*noun* ❶ a tiller or wheel for steering a ship or boat. ❷ (**the helm**) a position of leadership.

helmet
helmeted

helmsman (plural **helmsmen**)

help (verb: **helps**, **helping**, **helped**)
helper

helpful
helpfully
helpfulness

✓ **-ful** not **-full**: **helpful**

helping

helpless
helplessly
helplessness

helpline »*noun* a telephone service providing help with problems.

helpmate »*noun* a helpful companion.

helpmeet »*noun* = **HELPMATE**.

helps

helter-skelter

hem »*noun* the edge of a piece of cloth or clothing which has been turned under and sewn.
» *verb* (**hems**, **hemming**, **hemmed**) ❶ give something a hem. ❷ (**hem in**) surround and restrict the movement of something.

he-man »*noun* (in informal English) a very well-built, masculine man.

hematite etc. American spelling of **HAEMATITE** etc.

he-men

hemiplegia »*noun* paralysis of one side of the body.
– SAY hem-i-**plee**-juh
hemiplegic

h

hemisphere »*noun* ❶ a half of a sphere. ❷ a half of the earth.
hemispherical

hemline »*noun* the level of the lower edge of a skirt or coat.

hemlock »*noun* a highly poisonous plant with small white flowers.

hemmed

hemming

hemoglobin etc. American spelling of HAEMOGLOBIN etc.

hemorrhage etc. American spelling of HAEMORRHAGE etc.

hemp »*noun* ❶ the cannabis plant, the fibre of which is used to make rope, fabrics, etc. ❷ the drug cannabis.

hems

hen

hence »*adverb* ❶ for this reason. ❷ from now.

henceforth »*adverb* from this time on.

henceforward »*adverb* = HENCEFORTH.

henchman »*noun* (plural **henchmen**) (used in a disapproving way) a faithful follower.

henna »*noun* a reddish-brown dye made from the powdered leaves of a tropical shrub.
hennaed

henpecked »*adjective* (of a man) continually criticized and ordered about by his wife.

hepatic »*adjective* having to do with the liver.
– SAY hi-**pat**-ik

hepatitis »*noun* a serious disease of the liver, mainly transmitted by viruses.
– SAY hep-uh-**ty**-tiss

heptagon »*noun* a shape with seven straight sides and angles.
heptagonal

heptathlon »*noun* an athletic contest for women in which each competitor takes part in the same seven events.
– SAY hep-**tath**-luhn
heptathlete

her

herald »*noun* ❶ (a historical term) a person who carried official messages and supervised tournaments. ❷ a sign that something is about to happen. ❸ (in the UK) an official who oversees state ceremonies, orders of rank, and coats of arms.
»*verb* (**heralds**, **heralding**, **heralded**) ❶ be a sign that something is about to happen or

arrive. ❷ announce or describe publicly and approvingly.

heraldic »*adjective* having to do with heraldry.
– SAY hi-**ral**-dik

heralding

heraldry »*noun* the system by which coats of arms are organized and controlled.

heralds

herb

herbaceous »*adjective* (of plants) which do not have woody stems, dying down after flowering.
– SAY her-**bay**-shuhss

herbage »*noun* herbaceous plants.

herbal »*adjective* relating to or made from herbs.

herbalism »*noun* the use of plants in medicine and cookery.
herbalist

herbarium »*noun* (plural **herbaria**) an ordered collection of dried plants.
– SAY her-**bair**-i-uhm [singular], her-**bair**-i-uh [plural]

> ✓ like many other words ending in **um** derived from Latin, **herbarium** has a plural ending in **a**: **herbaria**

herbicide »*noun* a substance used to destroy unwanted plants.

herbivore »*noun* an animal that feeds on plants.
herbivorous

Herculean »*adjective* requiring great strength or effort.
– SAY her-kyuu-**lee**-uhn or her-**kyoo**-li-uhn

> ✓ capital **H**, and the ending is **ean** not **ian**: **Herculean** (named after the mythical Roman and Greek hero *Hercules*)

herd »*noun* ❶ a large group of animals that live or are kept together. ❷ (used in a disapproving way) a large group of people.
»*verb* (**herds**, **herding**, **herded**) make animals or people move in a large group.

herdsman (plural **herdsmen**)

here [in, at, or to this place]

hereabouts

> ✓ keep both **e**'s of here in **hereabouts**. The **s** can be left off: **hereabout** is also correct.

hereafter »*adverb* from now on or at some time in the future.
»*noun* (**the hereafter**) life after death.

> ✓ here- not her-: **hereafter**

hereby »*adverb* as a result of this.

hereditary »*adjective* ❶ passed on by parents to their children or young. ❷ having to do with the inheriting of something.
– sᴀʏ hi-**red**-i-tuh-ri

heredity »*noun* ❶ the passing on of characteristics from one generation to another. ❷ the inheriting of a title, office, etc.
– sᴀʏ hi-**red**-i-ti

herein »*adverb* in this document, book, or matter.

hereof »*adverb* of this document.

heresy »*noun* (plural **heresies**) ❶ belief which goes against traditional religious teachings. ❷ opinion greatly at odds with what is generally accepted.
– sᴀʏ **he**-ri-si

heretic »*noun* a person believing in or practising heresy.
– sᴀʏ **he**-ri-tik
heretical sᴀʏ he-**ret**-i-k'l
heretically

hereto »*adverb* to this matter or document.

heretofore »*adverb* before now.

hereupon »*adverb* after or as a result of this.

herewith »*adverb* with this letter.

heritable »*adjective* able to be inherited.
heritability

heritage »*noun* ❶ property that is or may be inherited. ❷ valued things such as historic buildings that have been passed down from previous generations.

 tage not tidge: **heritage**

hermaphrodite »*noun* ❶ a person or animal having both male and female sex organs. ❷ a plant having stamens and pistils in the same flower.
– sᴀʏ her-**maf**-ruh-dyt

hermetic »*adjective* (of a seal or closure) complete and airtight.
– sᴀʏ her-**met**-ik
hermetically

hermit »*noun* a person living completely alone, especially for religious reasons.

hermitage »*noun* the home of a hermit.

hernia »*noun* (plural **hernias** or **herniae**) a condition in which part of an organ protrudes through the wall of the cavity containing it.
– sᴀʏ **her**-ni-uh [singular], **her**-ni-ee [plural]

 make the plural by adding **s** or by adding **e** (like the original Latin): **hernias** and **herniae**

hero (plural **heroes**)

 the plural of **hero** has **oes** not **os**: **heroes**

heroic
heroically

heroin »*noun* a highly addictive painkilling drug.

 do not confuse the spellings of the drug **heroin**, with no **e** at the end, and **heroine**, a female hero

heroine [a female hero]

heroism

heron »*noun* a large fish-eating bird with long legs, a long neck, and a long pointed bill.

hero worship »*noun* excessive admiration for someone.
» *verb* (**hero-worships**, **hero-worshipping**, **hero-worshipped**) admire someone excessively.

 remember the hyphen when using the verb form: **hero-worship** double the **p** in **hero-worshipping** and **hero-worshipped**

herpes »*noun* a disease caused by a virus, affecting the skin or the nervous system.
– sᴀʏ **her**-peez

herpetology »*noun* the study of reptiles and amphibians.
– sᴀʏ her-pi-**tol**-uh-ji
herpetological
herpetologist

herring

herringbone »*noun* a zigzag pattern consisting of columns of short parallel lines, with all the lines in one column sloping one way and all the lines in the next column sloping the other way.

hers

 no apostrophe: **hers**

herself

hertz »*noun* (plural **hertz**) the basic unit of frequency, equal to one cycle per second.

he's [he is; he has]

hesitant »*adjective* slow to act or speak through being indecisive or reluctant.
hesitancy
hesitantly

 ant not ent: **hesitant**

hesitate (verb: **hesitates**, **hesitating**, **hesitated**)
hesitation

hessian »*noun* a strong, coarse fabric made from hemp or jute.

 double s: hessian

heterodox »*adjective* not following traditional standards or beliefs.
– SAY het-uh-ruh-doks
heterodoxy

heterogeneous »*adjective* varied: *a heterogeneous collection.*
– SAY het-uh-ruh-**jee**-ni-uhss
heterogeneity

 the ending is **eous**, with an *e*, not **ous: heterogeneous**

heterosexual »*adjective* sexually attracted to the opposite sex.
» *noun* a heterosexual person.
heterosexuality
heterosexually

het up »*adjective* (in informal English) angry and agitated.

heuristic »*adjective* allowing a person to discover or learn something for themselves.
– SAY hyuu-uh-**riss**-tik

hew »*verb* (**hews**, **hewing**, **hewed**, past participle **hewn** or **hewed**) ❶ chop or cut wood, coal, etc. with an axe or other tool. ❷ shape something by hewing a hard material.
– SAY hyoo
hewer

i do not confuse **hew** with **hue**, which means 'a colour or shade'

hexagon »*noun* a shape with six straight sides and angles.
– SAY **hek**-suh-guhn
hexagonal

hexagram »*noun* a six-pointed star formed by two intersecting equilateral triangles.

 -gram not -gramme: hexagram

hexameter »*noun* a line of verse made up of six metrical feet.
– SAY hek-**sam**-i-ter

 -meter not -metre: hexameter

hey [exclamation]

heyday »*noun* (**your heyday**) the period of your greatest success, activity, or energy.

HGV »*abbreviation* heavy goods vehicle.

hi [greeting]

hiatus »*noun* (plural **hiatuses**) a pause or gap in a series or sequence.
– SAY hy-**ay**-tuhss

 make the plural by adding **es: hiatuses**

hibernate »*verb* (**hibernates**, **hibernating**, **hibernated**) (of an animal) spend the winter in a state like deep sleep.
hibernation

Hibernian »*adjective* Irish.
» *noun* an Irish person.
– SAY hy-**ber**-ni-uhn

hibiscus »*noun* a plant with large brightly coloured flowers.
– SAY hi-**biss**-kuhss

hiccup (verb: **hiccups**, **hiccuping**, **hiccuped**)

 hiccup can also be spelled **hiccough**: both spellings are correct

hick »*noun* an unsophisticated person from the country.

hickory »*noun* a tree with tough, heavy wood and edible nuts.

hid past of HIDE¹.

hidden past participle of HIDE¹.

hidden agenda »*noun* a secret motive or plan.

hide¹ (verb: **hides**, **hiding**, **hid**; past participle **hidden**) [put or keep out of sight]

hide² »*noun* the skin of an animal.

hide-and-seek

hideaway

hidebound »*adjective* unwilling or unable to change because of tradition or convention.

hideous
hideously
hideousness

 eous not ious: hideous

hideout

hides

hidey-hole

hiding »*noun* ❶ a physical beating. ❷ a severe defeat.

hierarchy »*noun* (plural **hierarchies**) ❶ a system in which people are ranked one above the other according to status or authority. ❷ a classification of things according to their relative importance.
– SAY hy-uh-**rah**-ki
hierarchical

 ie not ei, and remember the second r: hierarchy

hieroglyph »*noun* a picture of an object representing a word, syllable, or sound, as found in ancient Egyptian and certain other writing systems.

– **SAY** hy-ruh-glif

hieroglyphics »*noun* writing consisting of hieroglyphs.
hieroglyphic

> ✓ **hier-** not **heir-** or **hir-: hieroglyphics**

hifalutin another way of spelling **HIGHFALUTIN**.

hi-fi »*adjective* having to do with high fidelity sound.
» *noun* (plural **hi-fis**) a set of equipment for reproducing high-fidelity sound.

higgledy-piggledy »*adverb & adjective* in confusion or disorder.

high (adjective: **higher, highest**)

highbrow »*adjective* intellectual or refined in taste.

High Church »*noun* a tradition within the Anglican Church which gives an important place to ritual and the authority of bishops and priests.

high commission »*noun* an embassy of one Commonwealth country in another.
high commissioner

high court »*noun* a supreme court of justice.

Higher »*noun* (in Scotland) the more advanced of the two main levels of the Scottish Certificate of Education (the other being *ordinary grade*).

higher

higher education »*noun* education to degree level or equivalent, provided at universities, colleges, or polytechnics.

highest

highest common factor »*noun* the highest number that can be divided exactly into each of two or more numbers.

highfalutin »*adjective* affectedly grand or self-important.
– **SAY** hy-fuh-**loo**-tin

> ✓ **highfalutin** can also be spelled **hifalutin**

high fidelity »*noun* the reproduction of sound with little distortion.

high five »*noun* a gesture of celebration or greeting in which two people slap each other's palms with their arms raised.

high-flier another way of spelling **HIGH-FLYER**.

high-flown »*adjective* grand-sounding.

high-flyer »*noun* a very successful person.

> ✓ **high-flyer** can also be spelled **high-flier**: both spellings are correct

high-handed »*adjective* using authority without considering the feelings of others.
high-handedly

high-impact »*adjective* ❶ (of a material) able to withstand great impact without breaking. ❷ (of exercises) placing a great deal of stress on the body.

high jinks »*plural noun* high-spirited fun.

highland »*noun* (also **highlands**) ❶ an area of high or mountainous land. ❷ (**the Highlands**) the mountainous northern part of Scotland.
highlander

high-level

highlight (verb: **highlights, highlighting, highlighted**)

highlighter

highly

highly strung »*adjective* very nervous and easily upset.

high-minded »*adjective* having strong moral principles.

highness

high-octane »*adjective* ❶ (of petrol) having a high octane number and therefore allowing an engine to run smoothly. ❷ powerful or dynamic: *high-octane charm.*

high-powered

high-rise »*adjective* (of a building) having many storeys.

high roller »*noun* a person who gambles or spends large sums of money.

high seas »*plural noun* (**the high seas**) the areas of the sea that are not under the control of any one country.

high-spirited

high street

> ✓ when using **high street** as an adjective, add a hyphen, as in *high-street fashion*

high tea »*noun* a meal eaten in the late afternoon or early evening.

high-tech

> ✓ **high-tech** can also be spelled **hi-tech**: both are correct

high-tensile »*adjective* (of metal) very strong under tension.

high treason »*noun* the crime of betraying your country.

highway

highwayman »*noun* (plural **highwaymen**) (a historical term) a man who held up and robbed travellers.

h

hijack »*verb* (hijacks, hijacking, hijacked) ❶ illegally seize control of an aircraft, ship, etc. while it is travelling somewhere. ❷ take over something and use it for a different purpose.
» *noun* an instance of hijacking.
hijacker

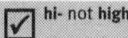 hi- not high-: hijack

hike (verb: hikes, hiking, hiked)
hiker

hilarious
hilariously
hilarity

 -lar- not -lair-: hilarious

hill

hillbilly »*noun* (plural hillbillies) (in American English) an unsophisticated country person.

hillier [more hilly]

hilliest

hillock »*noun* a small hill or mound.

hillwalking

hilly (adjective: hillier, hilliest)

hilt »*noun* the handle of a sword, dagger, or knife.

him

Himalayan »*adjective* having to do with the Himalayas, a mountain system in southern Asia.

himself

hind[1] »*adjective* situated at the back.

hind[2] »*noun* a female deer.

hinder[1] »*verb* (hinders, hindering, hindered) delay or obstruct.
– say hin-der

hinder[2] »*adjective* situated at or towards the back.
– say hyn-der

Hindi »*noun* a language of northern India derived from Sanskrit.
– say hin-di

hindmost »*adjective* furthest back.

hindquarters »*plural noun* the hind legs and adjoining parts of a four-legged animal.

hindrance »*noun* a thing that hinders.
– say hin-druhnss

✓ rance not rence: hindrance

hindsight »*noun* understanding of a situation or event after it has happened.

Hindu »*noun* (plural Hindus) a follower of Hinduism.
» *adjective* relating to Hinduism.

Hinduism »*noun* a major religion of the Indian subcontinent, which includes belief in reincarnation and the worship of a large number of gods and goddesses.

Hindustani »*noun* a group of languages and dialects spoken in NW India, principally Hindi and Urdu.
– say hin-duu-stah-ni

hinge (verb: hinges, hingeing or hinging, hinged)

✓ the spellings hingeing and hinging, with and without the e, are both correct

hint (verb: hints, hinting, hinted)

hinterland »*noun* ❶ the remote areas of a country, away from the coast and major rivers. ❷ the area around or beyond a major town or port.
– say hin-ter-land

hinting

hints

hip[1] [projection on each side of the body]

hip[2] »*noun* the fruit of a rose.

hip[3] »*adjective* (hipper, hippest) (in informal English) fashionable.
hipness

hip bath »*noun* a bath shaped to sit rather than lie down in.

hip flask »*noun* a small flask for spirits, carried in a hip pocket.

hip hop »*noun* a style of popular music featuring rap with an electronic backing.

hipness

hipper

hippest

hippie another way of spelling HIPPY[1].

hippies

hippo (plural hippo or hippos)

✓ the plural of hippo can be the same, or has os (not oes): hippo or hippos

Hippocratic oath »*noun* an oath (formerly taken by those beginning medical practice) to observe a code of professional behaviour.
– say hip-puh-krat-ik

ℹ named after *Hippocrates*, an ancient Greek physician

hippodrome »*noun* ❶ a theatre or concert hall. ❷ (in ancient Greece or Rome) a course for chariot or horse races.
– say hip-puh-drohm

hippopotamus (plural **hippopotamuses** or **hippopotami**)

> ☑ double **p** before the first **o** and one **p** after it: **hippopotamus**
> make the plural by adding **es** or by changing the **us** ending to **i** (as in Latin): **hippopotamuses** or **hippopotami**

hippy[1] **»noun** (plural **hippies**) a young person who supported peace and free love and dressed unconventionally.

> ☑ in this sense, **hippy** can also be spelled **hippie**

hippy[2] **»adjective** (of a woman) having large hips.

hipster **»adjective** (of a garment) having the waistline at the hips rather than the waist.

» noun (**hipsters**) trousers with such a waistline.

hire (verb: **hires**, **hiring**, **hired**)
hirer

hireling **»noun** a person who is hired to do menial or unpleasant work.

hire purchase **»noun** a system by which someone pays for a thing in regular instalments while having the use of it.

hirer

hires

hiring

hirsute **»adjective** hairy.
– SAY her-syoot
hirsuteness

his

Hispanic **»adjective** having to do with Spain or the Spanish-speaking countries of Central and South America.
» noun a Spanish-speaking person living in the US.
– SAY hi-**span**-ik

hiss (plural **hisses**; verb: **hisses**, **hissing**, **hissed**)

histamine **»noun** a substance which is released within the body in response to an injury or allergy.
– SAY **hiss**-tuh-meen

historian

historic [famous or important in history]

historical [having to do with history; belonging to or set in the past]
historically

> ℹ️ **historic** generally means 'famous or important in history', as in *a historic battle*, whereas **historical** means 'having to do with history' and 'belonging to or set in the past' (*a historical novel*; *of purely historical interest*)

histories

historiography **»noun** ❶ the study of the writing of history and of written histories. ❷ the writing of history.
– SAY hi-sto-ri-**og**-ruh-fi
historiographical

history (plural **histories**)

> ☑ plural: drop the **y** and add **ies**: **histories**

histrionic **»adjective** excessively dramatic.
– SAY hiss-tri-**on**-ik

histrionics **»noun** dramatized behaviour intended to attract attention.

hit (verb: **hits**, **hitting**, **hit**)
hitter

> ☑ double the **t** in **hitting**

hitch (verb: **hitches**, **hitching**, **hitched**)

hitcher **»noun** a hitch-hiker.

hitches

hitch-hike (verb: **hitch-hikes**, **hitch-hiking**, **hitch-hiked**)
hitch-hiker

hitching

hither **»adverb** to or towards this place.

hitherto **»adverb** until this point in time.

hit list **»noun** a list of people to be killed for criminal or political reasons.

hit man **»noun** (plural **hit men**) a person paid to kill someone.

hits

hitter

hitting

HIV **»abbreviation** human immunodeficiency virus (the virus causing Aids).

hive

hives **»plural noun** a rash of round, red, itchy weals on the skin, caused by an allergy.

HIV-positive

HMS **»abbreviation** Her or His Majesty's Ship.

HNC **»abbreviation** (in the UK) Higher National Certificate.

HND **»abbreviation** (in the UK) Higher National Diploma.

hoard [a store of something valuable; collect and store something over time]
hoarder

> ℹ️ do not confuse **hoard** with **horde**, which means 'a large group of people'

h

hoarding »*noun* ❶ a large board used to display advertisements. ❷ a temporary board fence around a building site.

hoards

hoar frost »*noun* a greyish-white feathery deposit of frost.

hoarier

hoariest

hoarse »*adjective* (**hoarser, hoarsest**) (of a voice) rough and harsh.
hoarsely
hoarseness

hoary »*adjective* (**hoarier, hoariest**) ❶ having grey hair. ❷ old and unoriginal: *a hoary old adage.*

hoax »*noun* (plural **hoaxes**) a humorous or cruel deception.
» *verb* (**hoaxes, hoaxing, hoaxed**) deceive someone with a hoax.
hoaxer

hob

hobbies

hobble (verb: **hobbles, hobbling, hobbled**)

hobby (plural **hobbies**)
hobbyist

> ✓ plural: drop the **y** and add **ies**: **hobbies**

hobby horse »*noun* ❶ a child's toy consisting of a stick with a model of a horse's head at one end. ❷ a rocking horse. ❸ a person's favourite topic of conversation.

hobbyist

hobgoblin »*noun* a mischievous imp.

hobnail »*noun* a short heavy-headed nail used to strengthen the soles of boots.
hobnailed

hobnob »*verb* (**hobnobs, hobnobbing, hobnobbed**) spend time socially with rich or important people.

> ✓ double the second **b** in **hobnobbing** and **hobnobbed**

hobo »*noun* (plural **hoboes** or **hobos**) (in American English) a homeless person.

> ✓ the plural of **hobo** can have **oes** or **os**: **hoboes** or **hobos**

Hobson's choice »*noun* a choice of taking what is offered or nothing at all.

> ℹ named after Thomas *Hobson*, who hired out horses, making the customer take the one nearest the door or none at all

hock[1] »*noun* the joint in the back leg of a four-legged animal, between the knee and the fetlock.

hock[2] »*noun* a dry white wine from the German Rhineland.

hock[3] »*verb* (**hocks, hocking, hocked**) (in informal English) pawn an object.

hockey

hocking

hocks

hocus-pocus »*noun* meaningless talk used to deceive someone.

hod »*noun* ❶ a builder's V-shaped open trough attached to a short pole, used for carrying bricks. ❷ a metal container for storing coal.

Hodgkin's disease »*noun* a cancerous disease causing enlargement of the lymph nodes, liver, and spleen.

> ℹ named after the English physician Thomas *Hodgkin*

hoe »*noun* a long-handled gardening tool with a thin metal blade.
» *verb* (**hoes, hoeing, hoed**) use a hoe to turn earth or cut through weeds.

> ✓ do not drop the **e** when spelling **hoeing**

hoedown »*noun* (in American English) a lively folk dance.

hoeing

hoes

hog (verb: **hogs, hogging, hogged**)

Hogmanay »*noun* (in Scotland) New Year's Eve.

hogs

hogshead »*noun* ❶ a large cask. ❷ a measure of liquid volume equal to 52.5 imperial gallons (238.7 litres) for wine or 54 imperial gallons (245.5 litres) for beer.

hogwash

hogweed »*noun* a large white-flowered weed, formerly used for feeding pigs.

hoick »*verb* (**hoicks, hoicking, hoicked**) lift or pull something with a jerk.
» *noun* a jerky pull.

hoi polloi »*plural noun* (used in a disapproving way) the common people.
– **SAY** hoy puh-**loy**

> ℹ **hoi polloi** is a Greek phrase meaning 'the many'

hoist »*verb* (**hoists, hoisting, hoisted**) ❶ raise something using ropes and pulleys. ❷ haul or lift up something.
» *noun* ❶ an act of hoisting. ❷ an apparatus for hoisting.

hoity-toity »*adjective* snobbish.

hokey-cokey »*noun* a group song and dance performed in a circle, involving the shaking of each limb in turn.

hokum »*noun* ❶ nonsense. ❷ overused or sentimental material in a film, book, etc.
– SAY hoh-kuhm

hold (verb: **holds**, **holding**, **held**)
  holder

holdall

holding

holding company »*noun* a company created to buy shares in other companies, which it then controls.

holds

hold-up

hole (verb: **holes**, **holing**, **holed**)

holey [having holes]

holiday (verb: **holidays**, **holidaying**, **holidayed**)

holidaymaker

holidays

holier

holier-than-thou »*adjective* offensively certain that you are morally superior.

holiest

holiness

> ✓ note that it is **i** not **y** in the middle: **holiness**

holing

holistic »*noun* treating the whole person rather than just the symptoms of a disease.
– SAY hoh-**liss**-tik or ho-**liss**-tik

hollandaise sauce »*noun* a creamy sauce made of butter, egg yolks, and vinegar.
– SAY hol-uhn-dayz or hol-uhn-**dayz**

holler (verb: **hollers**, **hollering**, **hollered**) [shout]

hollies

hollow (verb: **hollows**, **hollowing**, **hollowed**) [empty inside]
  hollowly
  hollowness

holly (plural: **hollies**) [plant with prickly leaves]

hollyhock »*noun* a tall plant with large showy flowers.

holmium »*noun* a soft silvery-white metallic element.
– SAY hohl-mi-uhm

holm oak »*noun* an evergreen oak with dark green glossy leaves.

holocaust »*noun* ❶ destruction or slaughter on a very large scale. ❷ (the Holocaust) the mass murder of Jews under the German Nazi regime in World War II.
– SAY hol-uh-kawst

Holocene »*adjective* relating to the geological period from about 10,000 years ago to the present.
– SAY hol-uh-seen

hologram »*noun* a picture that looks three-dimensional when it is lit up.
– SAY hol-uh-gram
  holographic

> ✓ -gram not -gramme: hologram

hols »*plural noun* (in informal English) holidays.

holster »*noun* a holder for carrying a handgun.
– SAY hohl-ster

holy (adjective: **holier**, **holiest**) [dedicated to God]
  holiness

> ✓ drop the **y** and add **ier** and **iest** to spell **holier** or **holiest**

holy day »*noun* a religious festival.

Holy Ghost »*noun* = HOLY SPIRIT.

holy of holies »*noun* ❶ (a historical term) the inner chamber of the sanctuary in the Jewish Temple in Jerusalem. ❷ a place seen as most sacred.

holy orders »*plural noun* the rank of an ordained minister of the church.

Holy Roman Empire »*noun* the western part of the Roman empire, as revived by Charlemagne in 800.

Holy Spirit »*noun* (in Christianity) God as spiritually active in the world.

Holy Week »*noun* the week before Easter.

homage »*noun* honour shown to someone in public.
– SAY hom-ij

> ✓ single **m**: homage (in the arts, the French word *hommage* is sometimes used)

homburg »*noun* a man's felt hat with a narrow curled brim.
– SAY hom-berg

> ✓ burg not berg: homburg is named after the German town of *Homburg*

home (verb: **homes**, **homing**, **homed**)

homecoming

homed

home economics »*noun* the study of cookery and household management.

home-grown

Home Guard »*noun* the British volunteer force organized in 1940 to defend the UK against invasion.

home help »*noun* a person employed to help someone with household work.

homeland

homeless
homelessness

homely »*adjective* (**homelier**, **homeliest**) ❶ (in British English) simple but comfortable. ❷ unsophisticated. ❸ (in American English) (of a person) unattractive.
homeliness

home-made

homemaker

Home Office »*noun* the British government department dealing with law and order, immigration, etc. in England and Wales.

homeopathy »*noun* a form of complementary medicine which treats diseases by tiny doses of natural substances that would normally produce symptoms of the disease.
– SAY hoh-mi-**op**-uh-thi
homeopath
homeopathic

> ✓ **homeopathy** can also be spelled **homoeopathy**: both spellings are correct

home page »*noun* the main page of an individual's or organization's Internet site.

home run »*noun* (in baseball) a hit that allows the batter to make a run around all the bases.

homes

Home Secretary »*noun* (plural **Home Secretaries**) (in the UK) the Secretary of State in charge of the Home Office.

homesick
homesickness

homespun »*adjective* simple and unsophisticated.

homestead »*noun* a house with surrounding land and outbuildings.
homesteader

> ✓ **stead** not **sted**: home**stead**

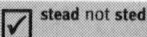

home truth »*noun* an unpleasant fact about yourself that someone else tells you.

homeward

homewards

homework

homey »*adjective* ❶ comfortable and cosy. ❷ unsophisticated.

homicide »*noun* murder.
– SAY hom-i-syd
homicidal

homiletic »*adjective* having to do with or like a homily.
– SAY hom-i-**let**-ik

homily »*noun* (plural **homilies**) ❶ a talk on a religious subject. ❷ a dull talk on a moral issue.
– SAY hom-i-li

homing

hominid »*noun* a member of the family of primates which includes humans and their prehistoric ancestors.
– SAY hom-i-nid

homoeopathy another way of spelling HOMEOPATHY.

homoerotic »*adjective* relating to sexual desire centred on a person of the same sex.
– SAY hoh-moh-i-**rot**-ik
homoeroticism

homogeneous »*adjective* ❶ alike. ❷ made up of parts all of the same kind.
– SAY hom-uh-**jee**-ni-uhss
homogeneity

> ✓ **eous**, with an **e**, not **ous**: homogen**eous**

homogenize »*verb* (**homogenizes**, **homogenizing**, **homogenized**) ❶ treat milk so that the cream is mixed in. ❷ make a group of things alike.

> ✓ many people prefer the alternative spellings **homogenise**, **homogenises**, etc.: both **s** and **z** spellings are correct

homograph »*noun* one of two or more words having the same spelling but different meanings and origins.

homonym »*noun* a word that has the same spelling or pronunciation as another but a different meaning and origin.
– SAY hom-uh-nim

homophobia »*noun* extreme hatred or fear of homosexuality and homosexuals.
homophobe
homophobic

homophone »*noun* one of two or more words having the same pronunciation but different meanings, origins, or spelling (e.g. *new* and *knew*).

Homo sapiens »*noun* the species to which modern humans belong.
– SAY hoh-moh sap-i-enz

homosexual »*adjective* sexually attracted to people of your own sex.

» *noun* a homosexual person.
homosexuality
homosexually

honcho »*noun* (plural **honchos**) (in informal
English) a leader.
– SAY hon-choh

✓ the plural of **honcho**, a Japanese
word, has **os** not **oes**: **honchos**

Honduran [of Honduras]

hone »*verb* (hones, honing, honed)
❶ sharpen a tool with a stone. ❷ make
something sharper or more efficient.

honest

honestly

honesty

honey (plural **honeys**)

✓ the plural of **honey** simply adds an **s**:
honeys

honeybee

honeycomb »*noun* a structure of six-sided
wax compartments made by bees to store
honey and eggs.

honeydew »*noun* a sweet, sticky substance
produced by small insects feeding on the
sap of plants.

honeyed

honeymoon
honeymooner
honeymooning

honeypot

honeysuckle »*noun* a climbing shrub with
sweet-smelling yellow and pink flowers.

honing

honk (verb: **honks, honking, honked**)

honky-tonk »*noun* ❶ a cheap bar or club.
❷ ragtime piano music.

honor American spelling of **HONOUR**.

honorable American spelling of
HONOURABLE.

honorarium »*noun* (plural **honorariums** or
honoraria) a voluntary payment for
professional services which are offered
without charge.
– SAY on-uh-**rair**-i-uhm [singular], on-uh-
rair-i-uh [plural]

✓ the plural can be either **honoraria**
(like the original Latin) or
honorariums

honorary »*noun* ❶ (of a title or position)
given as an honour. ❷ (of a position or
the person who holds it) unpaid.

✓ honor- not honour-: **honorary**

honorific »*adjective* given as a mark of
respect.

✓ note there is no **u**: **honorific**

honour (verb: **honours, honouring,
honoured**)

✓ -our not -or: **honour** (the spelling
honor is American)

honourable »*adjective* ❶ deserving
honour. ❷ (**Honourable**) a title given to
MPs, nobles, and certain high officials.
honourably

✓ -our- not -or-: **honourable** (the spelling
honorable is American)

honoured

honouring

honours

hooch »*noun* (in informal English) alcoholic
drink.

✓ **hooch** can also be spelled with a **t**:
hootch (both spellings are correct)

hood (verb: **hoods, hooding, hooded**)
hooded

hoodlum »*noun* a gangster or violent
criminal.

hoodoo »*noun* ❶ voodoo. ❷ a run or cause
of bad luck.

hoodwink »*verb* (hoodwinks, hoodwinking,
hoodwinked) deceive or trick someone.

hoof (plural **hoofs** or **hooves**)
hoofed

✓ the plural of **hoof** can either add **s**:
hoofs, or drop the **f** and add **ves**:
hooves (both are correct)

hook (verb: **hooks, hooking, hooked**)

hookah »*noun* a kind of tobacco pipe used
in eastern countries, in which the smoke is
drawn through water to cool it.
– SAY huuk-uh

hooked

hooker »*noun* ❶ (in rugby) the player in the
middle of the front row of the scrum.
❷ (in informal English) a prostitute.

hooking

hooks

hookworm »*noun* a worm which can infest
the intestines of people and animals.

hooligan
hooliganism

✓ gan not gen: **hooligan**

hoop
hooped

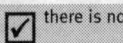

hoopla »*noun* ❶ a game in which rings are thrown in an attempt to encircle a prize. ❷ unnecessary fuss.

✓ there is no **h** at the end of **hoopla**

hoopoe »*noun* a pink bird with a long downcurved bill and black-and-white wings and tail.

hooray

hoot (verb: **hoots, hooting, hooted**)

hootch another way of spelling **HOOCH**.

hooted

hooter

hooting

hoots

hoover »*noun* (trademark) a vacuum cleaner.
» *verb* (**hoovers, hoovering, hoovered**) clean with a vacuum cleaner.

hooves plural of **HOOF**.

hop (verb: **hops, hopping, hopped**) [jump on one leg]

✓ double the **p** when spelling **hopping** and **hopped**

hope (verb: **hopes, hoping, hoped**)

hopeful
hopefulness

✓ -ful not -full: **hopeful**

hopefully

ℹ the standard meaning of **hopefully** is 'in a hopeful manner', as in *she looked up hopefully*. Some people think that the modern use of **hopefully** to mean 'it is to be hoped that', as in *hopefully, we will get a result tomorrow*, is incorrect, and you should be careful about using **hopefully** in formal speech or writing.

hopeless
hopelessly
hopelessness

hopes

hoping

hopped

hopper »*noun* a container that tapers downwards and empties its contents at the bottom.

hopping

hops »*noun* the dried flowers of a climbing plant, used to give beer a bitter flavour.

hopscotch »*noun* a children's game in which they hop over squares marked on the ground.

horde »*noun* a large group of people.

ℹ do not confuse **horde** with **hoard**, which means 'a store of things'

horizon »*noun* ❶ the line at which the earth's surface and the sky appear to meet. ❷ (**horizons**) the limit of a person's understanding, experience, or interest.

horizontal »*adjective* parallel to the ground.
» *noun* a horizontal line or surface.
horizontally

hormone »*noun* a substance produced in the body that stimulates cells or tissues to action.
hormonal

hormone replacement therapy »*noun* treatment with certain hormones to make symptoms of the menopause or osteoporosis less severe.

horn
horned

hornbeam »*noun* a tree with hard pale wood.

horned

hornet »*noun* a kind of large wasp.

✓ single **t** at the end: **hornet**

hornier

horniest

hornpipe »*noun* a lively solo dance traditionally performed by sailors.

horn-rimmed »*adjective* (of glasses) having rims made of horn or a similar substance.

horny »*adjective* (**hornier, horniest**) ❶ made of or like horn. ❷ hard and rough. ❸ (in informal English) sexually aroused or arousing.

horology »*noun* ❶ the study and measurement of time. ❷ the art of making clocks and watches.
– **say** ho-**rol**-uh-ji

horoscope »*noun* a forecast of a person's future based on the positions of the stars and planets at the time of their birth.

✓ horo- not horror-: **horoscope**

horrendous
horrendously

horrible
horribly

horrid
horridly
horridness

horrific
horrifically

horrify (verb: **horrifies, horrifying, horrified**)
horrified
horrifying
horrifyingly

horror

hors d'oeuvre »*noun* (plural **hors d'oeuvre** or **hors d'oeuvres**) a small savoury first course of a meal.
– SAY or **derv** [singular], or **derv** or or **dervz** [plural]

> ℹ from a French phrase which means 'outside the work'

horse (verb: **horses, horsing, horsed**)

horseback

horsebox (plural **horseboxes**)

horse chestnut »*noun* ❶ a large tree that produces nuts (conkers) in a spiny case. ❷ a conker.

horsed

horseflesh

horsefly »*noun* (plural **horseflies**) a large fly that bites horses and other large mammals.

horsehair

horseman (plural **horsemen**)
horsemanship

horseplay »*noun* rough, high-spirited play.

horsepower »*noun* (plural **horsepower**) a unit of power equal to 550 foot-pounds per second (about 750 watts).

> ☑ the plural of **horsepower** is the same: **horsepower**

horseradish »*noun* a plant with strong-tasting roots which are made into a sauce.

horses

horseshoe

horsewhip (verb: **horsewhips, horsewhipping, horsewhipped**)

> ☑ double the p to spell **horsewhipping** and **horsewhipped**

horsewoman (plural **horsewomen**)

horsey

> ☑ **horsey** can also be spelled without the e: **horsy**

horsing

hortatory »*adjective* strongly urging someone to do something.
– SAY hor-tuh-tuh-ri

horticulture »*noun* the cultivation and care of gardens.
horticultural
horticulturist

hosanna »*noun & exclamation* a cry of praise or joy used in the Bible.

> ☑ **hosanna** can also be spelled with an h at the end: **hosannah** (both spellings are correct)

hose (verb: **hoses, hosing, hosed**)

hoses

hosiery »*noun* stockings, socks, and tights.
– SAY hoh-zi-uh-ri

hosing

hospice »*noun* a home for people who are terminally ill.

hospitable
– SAY hoss-pit-uh-b'l
hospitably

> ☑ -able not -ible: **hospitable**

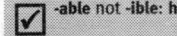

hospital

hospitalise another way of spelling **HOSPITALIZE**.

hospitality

hospitalize »*verb* (**hospitalizes, hospitalizing, hospitalized**) admit someone to hospital for treatment.
hospitalization

> ☑ many people prefer the alternative spellings **hospitalise, hospitalises**, etc., and **hospitalisation**: both s and z spellings are correct

host[1] (verb: **hosts, hosting, hosted**) [person who entertains guests; entertain guests]

host[2] »*noun* (**a host** or **hosts of**) a large number of.

host[3] »*noun* (**the Host**) the bread used in the Christian ceremony of the Eucharist.

hostage

hostel »*noun* a place which provides cheap food and lodging for a particular group of people.
hostelling

hostelry »*noun* (plural **hostelries**) (an old word) an inn or pub.

hostess (plural **hostesses**)

hostile

hostility »*noun* (plural **hostilities**)
❶ aggressively unfriendly behaviour.
❷ (**hostilities**) acts of warfare.
– SAY hoss-til-i-ti

> ☑ plural: drop the y and add ies: **hostilities**

hot (adjective: **hotter, hottest**; verb: **hots, hotting, hotted**)
hotly
hotness

> ☑ double the t to spell **hotter, hottest, hotting**, and **hotted**

hotbed »*noun* a place where a lot of a particular activity is happening: *a hotbed of crime.*

hot-blooded »*adjective* passionate.

hotchpotch »*noun* a confused mixture.

hot cross bun

hot dog

hotel

hotelier »*noun* a person who owns or manages a hotel.
– sᴀʏ hoh-tel-i-er

hotfoot »*adverb* in eager haste.
» *verb* (hotfoots, hotfooting, hotfooted) (hotfoot it) hurry eagerly.

> ✔ do not double the **t** to spell **hotfooting** and **hotfooted**

hothead »*noun* an impetuous or quick-tempered person.
hot-headed

hothouse »*noun* ❶ a heated greenhouse. ❷ an environment that encourages rapid growth.

hotline »*noun* a direct telephone line set up for a specific purpose.

hotly

hotness

hot pants »*plural noun* women's tight, brief shorts.

hotplate

hotpot »*noun* a casserole of meat and vegetables with a covering layer of sliced potato.

hot rod »*noun* a car specially adapted to be fast.

hots

hotshot »*noun* (in informal English) an important or very skilled person.

hotted

hot-tempered

Hottentot »*noun & adjective* formerly used to refer to the Khoikhoi peoples of South Africa and Namibia.

> ℹ the word **Hottentot** is now regarded as offensive

hotter

hottest

hotting

hot-water bottle

hot-wire »*verb* (hot-wires, hot-wiring, hot-wired) start a vehicle without using the ignition switch.

Houdini »*noun* (plural **Houdinis**) a person skilled at escaping from desperate situations.

> ✔ capital **H**: **Houdini** (named after the American magician and escape artist Harry *Houdini*)

houmous another way of spelling **hummus**.

hound (verb: **hounds, hounding, hounded**)

hour

hourglass »*noun* (plural **hourglasses**) a device with two connected glass bulbs containing sand that takes an hour to fall from the upper to the lower bulb.
» *adjective* shaped like an hourglass.

hourly

house (verb: **houses, housing, housed**)

house arrest »*noun* the state of being kept as a prisoner in your own house.

houseboat

housebound »*adjective* unable to leave your house.

housebreaking »*noun* the action of breaking into a building to commit a crime.
housebreaker

housecoat

housed

housefly (plural **houseflies**)

household
householder

house husband »*noun* a man whose main occupation is caring for his family and looking after the home.

housekeeper
housekeeping

housemaid

housemaid's knee »*noun* swelling of the fluid-filled cavity covering the kneecap.

house martin »*noun* a black-and-white bird which nests on buildings.

housemaster »*noun* a teacher in charge of a house at a boarding school.

housemistress (plural **housemistresses**)

House of Commons »*noun* the chamber of the UK Parliament whose members are elected.

House of Lords »*noun* the chamber of UK Parliament whose members are peers and bishops.

House of Representatives »*noun* the lower house of the US Congress.

house-proud

houseroom

houses

Houses of Parliament »*plural noun* the Houses of Lords and Commons in the UK regarded together.

house-train »*verb* (house-trains, house-training, house-trained) train a pet to urinate and defecate outside the house.

house-warming »*noun* a party held to celebrate moving into a new home.

housewife (plural housewives)
housewifely
housewifery

housework

housing

hove past tense of HEAVE.

hovel »*noun* a small dirty or run-down dwelling.

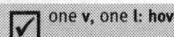 one **v**, one **l**: hovel

hover (verb: hovers, hovering, hovered)

hovercraft »*noun* (plural hovercraft) a vehicle that travels over land or water on a cushion of air.

hovered

hovering

hovers

how

howdah »*noun* a seat for riding on the back of an elephant.
– SAY how-duh

however

howitzer »*noun* a short gun for firing shells at a high angle.
– SAY how-it-ser

howl (verb: howls, howling, howled)

howler »*noun* a stupid mistake.

howling

howls

hoyden »*noun* (old-fashioned) a girl who behaves in a high-spirited or wild way.
hoydenish

HQ »*abbreviation* headquarters.

HRH »*abbreviation* Her (or His) Royal Highness.

HRT »*abbreviation* hormone replacement therapy.

hub »*noun* ❶ the central part of a wheel, rotating on or with the axle. ❷ the centre of an activity or region.

hubbies

hubbub »*noun* ❶ a loud confused noise caused by a crowd. ❷ a busy, noisy situation.

 two **b**'s in the middle, one at the end: hubbub

hubby (plural hubbies)

hubcap

hubris »*noun* excessive pride or self-confidence.
– SAY hyoo-briss
hubristic

huckster »*noun* a person who sells small items, either door-to-door or from a stall.

huddle (verb: huddles, huddling, huddled)

hue »*noun* ❶ a colour or shade. ❷ a particular aspect of something: *men of all political hues.*

ℹ️ do not confuse **hue** with **hew**, which means 'chop or cut wood'

hue and cry »*noun* a strong public outcry.

huff (verb: huffs, huffing, huffed)

huffy
huffily

hug (verb: hugs, hugging, hugged)

huge (adjective: huger, hugest)
hugely
hugeness

hugged

hugger-mugger »*adjective* confused or disorderly.
» *noun* ❶ confusion. ❷ secrecy.

hugging

hugs

Huguenot »*noun* a French Protestant of the 16th–17th centuries.
– SAY hyoo-guh-noh

hula »*noun* a dance performed by Hawaiian women, in which the dancers sway their hips.
– SAY hoo-luh

hula hoop

hulk »*noun* ❶ an old ship stripped of fittings and permanently moored. ❷ a large or clumsy person or thing.

hulking »*adjective* very large or clumsy.

hull[1] »*noun* the main body of a ship.

hull[2] »*noun* ❶ the outer covering of a fruit or seed. ❷ the cluster of leaves and stalk on a strawberry or raspberry.
» *verb* (hulls, hulling, hulled) remove the hulls from a fruit or seed.

hullabaloo »*noun* (in informal English) an uproar.

hulled

hulling

hulls

hum (verb: hums, humming, hummed)
hummable
hummer

 double the **m** in **humming**, **hummed**, and **hummable**

h

human
  humanly
  humanness

humane »*adjective* showing concern and kindness towards others.
– SAY hyuu-**mayn**
  humanely

humanise another way of spelling HUMANIZE.

humanism »*noun* ❶ a system of thought that stresses people's ability to use their reason and intelligence to live their lives, rather than relying on religious belief. ❷ a Renaissance cultural movement which revived interest in ancient Greek and Roman thought.
  humanist
  humanistic

humanitarian »*adjective* concerned with human welfare.
» *noun* a humanitarian person.
– SAY hyuu-man-i-**tair**-i-uhn
  humanitarianism

humanities »*noun* studies concerned with human culture, such as literature or history.

humanity »*noun* ❶ human beings as a whole. ❷ the condition of being human. ❸ sympathy and kindness towards others.

humanize »*verb* (humanizes, humanizing, humanized) make something more pleasant or suitable for people.
  humanization

> many people prefer the alternative spellings **humanise, humanises,** etc.: both **s** and **z** spellings are correct

humankind

humanly

humanness

humanoid »*adjective* like a human in appearance or character.
» *noun* a humanoid being.

humble »*adjective* (humbler, humblest) ❶ having a modest or low opinion of your own importance. ❷ of low rank. ❸ not large, important, or elaborate.
» *verb* (humbles, humbling, humbled) make someone seem less dignified or important.
  humbly

humbug »*noun* ❶ false or misleading talk or behaviour. ❷ a person who is not sincere or honest. ❸ a boiled peppermint sweet.

humdinger »*noun* (in informal English) an outstanding person or thing.

humdrum »*adjective* lacking excitement or variety; dull.

humerus »*noun* (plural **humeri**) the bone of the upper arm, between the shoulder and the elbow.
– SAY hyoo-muh-ruhss [singular], hyoo-muh-rI [plural]
  humeral

> ✓ make the plural by changing the **us** ending to **i** (like the original Latin): **humeri**

humid »*adjective* (of the air or weather) damp and warm.
– SAY hyoo-mid

> ✓ single **m**: **humid**

humidify »*verb* (humidifies, humidifying, humidified) increase the level of moisture in air.
  humidification
  humidifier

humidity »*noun* ❶ the state of being humid. ❷ the amount of moisture in the air.

humiliate (verb: humiliates, humiliating, humiliated)
  humiliation

> ✓ one **m**, one **l**: **humiliate**

humility »*noun* the quality of being humble.

hummable

hummed

humming

hummingbird »*noun* a small American bird able to hover by beating its wings extremely fast.

hummock »*noun* a small hill or mound.
  hummocky

hummus »*noun* a thick Middle Eastern dip made from ground chickpeas and sesame seeds.
– SAY huu-muhss or hoo-muhss

> ✓ an Arabic word, often also spelled **houmous**; both **hummus** and **houmous** are correct

humongous

> ✓ **humongous** can also be spelled **humungous**

humor American spelling of HUMOUR.

humorist »*noun* a writer or speaker who is noted for being amusing.

> **mor** not **mour**: **humorist**

humorous
  humorously

-or not **-our**: **humorous**

humour (verb: **humours**, **humouring**, **humoured**)
humourless

✓ **mour** not **mor**: **humour** (the spelling **humor** is American). However, two other words derived from **humour**, **humorist** and **humorous**, drop the u from the middle.

hump (verb: **humps**, **humping**, **humped**)
humpy

humpback
humpbacked

humped

humping

humps

humpy

hums

humungous another way of spelling **HUMONGOUS**.

humus »*noun* a substance found in soil, formed from dead leaves and other plant material.
– SAY hyoo-muhss

✓ only one **m**, and the ending is **us** not **ous**: **humus** (**hummus** is a Middle Eastern dip)

Hun »*noun* ❶ a member of a people from Asia who invaded Europe in the 4th–5th centuries. ❷ (used in an insulting way) a German.

hunch (verb: **hunches**, **hunching**, **hunched**)

hunchback

hunched

hunches

hunching

hundred
hundredfold
hundredth

hundredweight »*noun* (plural **hundredweight** or **hundredweights**) ❶ a unit of weight equal to 112 lb (about 50.8 kg). ❷ (in American English) a unit of weight equal to 100 lb (about 45.4 kg).

hung see the note at HANG.

Hungarian

hunger (verb: **hungers**, **hungering**, **hungered**)

hung-over

hungry (adjective: **hungrier**, **hungriest**)
hungrily

✓ drop the **y** and add **ier** or **iest** to spell **hungrier** or **hungriest**

hunk

hunker »*verb* (**hunkers**, **hunkering**, **hunkered**) squat or crouch down low.

hunkers »*plural noun* (in informal English) haunches.

hunky (adjective: **hunkier**, **hunkiest**)

hunky-dory »*adjective* (in informal English) excellent.

hunt (verb: **hunts**, **hunting**, **hunted**)

hunter

hunting

huntress »*noun* (plural **huntresses**) a female hunter.

hunts

huntsman »*noun* (plural **huntsmen**) ❶ a person who hunts. ❷ a person in charge of hounds during a fox hunt.

hurdle (verb: **hurdles**, **hurdling**, **hurdled**)
hurdler

hurdy-gurdy »*noun* (plural **hurdy-gurdies**) a musical instrument with a droning sound played by turning a handle, with keys worked by the other hand.
– SAY her-di-ger-di

hurl (verb: **hurls**, **hurling**, **hurled**)
hurler

hurley »*noun* = HURLING.

hurling »*noun* an Irish game resembling hockey.

hurls

hurly-burly »*noun* busy and noisy activity.

hurrah

✓ **hurrah** can also be spelled **hooray** or **hurray**: all three spellings are correct

hurricane

✓ double **r**: **hurricane**

hurricane lamp »*noun* an oil lamp in which the flame is protected from the wind by a glass tube.

hurry (verb: **hurries**, **hurrying**, **hurried**)
hurried
hurriedly

hurt (verb: **hurts**, **hurting**, **hurt**)

hurtful
hurtfully

✓ **-ful** not **-full**: **hurtful**

hurting

hurtle »*verb* (**hurtles**, **hurtling**, **hurtled**) move at great speed.

hurts

husband »*noun* a married man in relation to his wife.

h

» **verb** (**husbands**, **husbanding**, **husbanded**) use resources carefully and without wasting them.
husbandly

husbandry »**noun** ❶ farming. ❷ careful management of resources.

husbands

hush (verb: **hushes**, **hushing**, **hushed**)

hushing

husk »**noun** the dry outer covering of some fruits or seeds.
» **verb** (**husks**, **husking**, **husked**) remove the husk from fruits or seeds.

husky[1] (adjective: **huskier**, **huskiest**) [low-pitched and hoarse]
huskily
huskiness

husky[2] »**noun** (plural **huskies**) a powerful dog of a breed used in the Arctic for pulling sledges.

hussar »**noun** (a historical term) (now only in titles) a soldier in a light cavalry regiment.
– SAY huu-**zar**

hussy »**noun** (plural **hussies**) (mainly used in a humorous way) a girl or woman who behaves in an immoral or cheeky way.

hustings »**noun** the political meetings and speeches that take place before an election.

hustle »**verb** (**hustles**, **hustling**, **hustled**) ❶ push or move someone roughly. ❷ (**hustle into**) make someone act quickly and without giving them time to think about it. ❸ obtain something dishonestly or by forceful action.
» **noun** busy movement and activity.
hustler

hut

hutch

hyacinth »**noun** a plant with sweet-smelling bell-shaped flowers.
– SAY **hy**-uh-sinth

hyaena another way of spelling HYENA.

hybrid »**noun** ❶ the offspring of two plants or animals of different species or varieties. ❷ a thing made by combining two different elements.

hybridize »**verb** (**hybridizes**, **hybridizing**, **hybridized**) breed individuals of two different species or varieties to produce hybrids.
hybridization

> ✓ many people prefer the alternative spellings **hybridise**, **hybridises**, etc., and **hybridisation**: both **s** and **z** spellings are correct

hydra »**noun** a minute freshwater invertebrate animal with a tubular body and tentacles around the mouth.

hydrangea »**noun** a shrub with white, blue, or pink flowers growing in clusters.
– SAY hy-**drayn**-juh

hydrant »**noun** a water pipe with a nozzle to which a fire hose can be attached.
– SAY hy-**druhnt**

> ✓ **ant** not **ent**: hydr**ant**

hydrate »**noun** a compound in which water molecules are chemically bound to another compound or an element.
» **verb** (**hydrates**, **hydrating**, **hydrated**) cause something to absorb or combine with water.
– SAY hy-drayt [noun], hy-**drayt** [verb]
hydration

hydraulic »**adjective** relating to or operated by a liquid moving in a confined space under pressure.
– SAY hy-**dro**-lik
hydraulically

hydraulics »**noun** the branch of science concerned with the use of liquids moving under pressure to provide mechanical force.

hydro »**noun** (plural **hydros**) a hotel or health farm providing hydropathic and other treatment.

> ✓ the plural of **hydro** has **os** not **oes**: hydr**os**

hydrocarbon »**noun** one of the many compounds of hydrogen and carbon.

hydrocephalus »**noun** a condition in which fluid collects in the brain.
– SAY hy-druh-**sef**-uh-luhss or hy-druh-**kef**-uh-luhss

hydrochloric acid »**noun** a corrosive acid containing hydrogen and chlorine.

hydrodynamics »**noun** the branch of science concerned with the forces acting on or generated by liquids.
hydrodynamic

hydroelectric »**adjective** having to do with the use of flowing water to generate electricity.
hydroelectricity

hydrofoil »**noun** ❶ a boat fitted with structures (known as foils) which lift the hull clear of the water at speed. ❷ one of the foils of such a craft.

hydrogen »**noun** a highly flammable gas which is the lightest of the chemical elements.
– SAY **hy**-druh-juhn

hydrogenated »*adjective* combined with hydrogen.
– say hy-**droj**-uh-nay-tid
hydrogenation

hydrogen bomb »*noun* a nuclear bomb whose destructive power comes from the fusion of hydrogen nuclei.

hydrography »*noun* the science of charting seas, lakes, and rivers.
hydrographer
hydrographic

hydrology »*noun* the branch of science concerned with the properties and distribution of water on the earth's surface.
hydrological
hydrologist

hydrolysis »*noun* the chemical breakdown of a compound due to reaction with water.
– say hy-**drol**-i-siss

hydrometer »*noun* an instrument for measuring the density of liquids.
– say hy-**drom**-i-ter

hydropathy »*noun* the treatment of illness through the use of water, either internally or by external means such as steam baths.
– say hy-**drop**-uh-thi
hydropathic

hydrophobia »*noun* ❶ extreme fear of water, especially as a symptom of rabies. ❷ rabies.

hydrophobic »*adjective* ❶ repelling or failing to mix with water. ❷ having to do with hydrophobia.

hydroplane »*noun* a light, fast motor boat designed to skim over the surface of water.

hydroponics »*noun* the growing of plants in sand, gravel, or liquid, with added nutrients but without soil.
– say hy-druh-**pon**-iks
hydroponic

hydrotherapy »*noun* the use of exercises in a pool to treat conditions such as arthritis.
hydrotherapist

hydrothermal »*adjective* relating to the action of heated water in the earth's crust.

hydrous »*adjective* containing water.

hydroxide »*noun* a compound containing OH negative ions together with a metallic element.

hyena »*noun* a doglike African mammal.

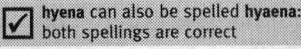
hyena can also be spelled **hyaena**: both spellings are correct

hygiene

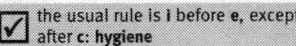
the usual rule is **i** before **e**, except after **c**: **hygiene**

hygienic
hygienically

hygienist »*noun* an expert in hygiene.

hygrometer »*noun* an instrument for measuring humidity.
– say hy-**grom**-i-ter

hymen »*noun* a membrane which partially closes the opening of the vagina and is usually broken when a woman or girl first has sex.
– say hy-muhn

hymn »*noun* a religious song of praise, especially a Christian one.
»*verb* (**hymns**, **hymning**, **hymned**) praise or celebrate something.

don't forget the **n** at the end: **hymn**

hymnal »*noun* a book of hymns.
– say him-nuhl

hymned

hymning

hymnody »*noun* the singing or composition of hymns.
– say **him**-nuh-di

hymns

hype »*noun* publicity or promotion that is excessive or that exaggerates how good something is.
»*verb* (**hypes**, **hyping**, **hyped**) ❶ promote or publicize something in an excessive or exaggerated way. ❷ (**be hyped up**) be very excited or tense.

hyper »*adjective* (in informal English) full of nervous energy.

hyperactive »*adjective* abnormally or extremely active.
hyperactivity

hyperbola »*noun* (plural **hyperbolas** or **hyperbolae**) a symmetrical curve formed when a cone is cut by a plane nearly parallel to the cone's axis.
– say hy-**per**-buh-luh [singular], hy-**per**-buh-li [plural]

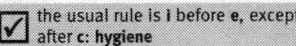
make the plural either by adding **s** or by adding **e** (as in Latin): **hyperbolas** or **hyperbolae**

hyperbole »*noun* exaggerated statements that are not meant to be taken in the strict sense of the words.
– say hy-**per**-buh-li

hyperbolic »*adjective* ❶ (of language) deliberately exaggerated. ❷ relating to a hyperbola.
– say hy-per-**bol**-ik

hypercritical »*adjective* excessively critical.

☑ do not confuse **hypercritical** with **hypocritical**, which means 'showing hypocrisy'

hyperinflation »*noun* inflation of prices or wages occurring at a very high rate.

hyperlink »*noun* (in computing) a link from a hypertext document to another location.

hypermarket »*noun* a very large supermarket.

hypermedia »*noun* (in computing) an extension to hypertext providing multimedia facilities, such as sound and video.

hypersensitive »*adjective* excessively sensitive.
hypersensitivity

hypersonic »*adjective* ❶ relating to speeds of more than five times the speed of sound. ❷ relating to sound frequencies above about a thousand million hertz.

hypertension »*noun* abnormally high blood pressure.
hypertensive

ℹ️ **hypertension**, or 'high blood pressure', and **hypotension**, or 'low blood pressure', are one of a number of pairs of words which look and sound quite similar but have opposite meanings. The prefix **hyper-** (from Greek *huper*) means 'over, above', whereas **hypo-** (from Greek *hupo*) means 'under, below'.

hypertext »*noun* (in computing) a software system allowing users to move quickly between related documents or sections of text.

hypertrophy »*noun* abnormal enlargement of an organ or tissue resulting from an increase in size of its cells.
– SAY hy-**per**-truh-fi
hypertrophied

hyperventilate »*verb* (**hyperventilates, hyperventilating, hyperventilated**) breathe at an abnormally rapid rate.
hyperventilation

hypes

hyphen »*noun* the sign (-) used to join words together or to divide a word into parts between one line and the next.
– SAY hy-**fuhn**

hyphenate »*verb* (**hyphenates, hyphenating, hyphenated**) write or separate words with a hyphen.
hyphenation

hyping

hypnosis »*noun* the practice of causing a person to enter a state of consciousness in which they respond very readily to suggestions or commands.

☑ no double **s**: **hypnosis**

hypnotherapy »*noun* the use of hypnosis to treat physical or mental problems.
hypnotherapist

hypnotic »*adjective* ❶ having to do with hypnosis. ❷ causing a very relaxed or drowsy state. ❸ (of a drug) producing sleep.
hypnotically

hypnotise another way of spelling HYPNOTIZE.

hypnotism »*noun* the study or practice of hypnosis.
hypnotist

hypnotize »*verb* (**hypnotizes, hypnotizing, hypnotized**) produce a state of hypnosis in someone.

☑ many people prefer the alternative spellings **hypnotise, hypnotises**, etc.: both **s** and **z** spellings are correct

hypoallergenic »*adjective* unlikely to cause an allergic reaction.

hypochondria »*noun* constant and excessive anxiety about your health.
– SAY hy-puh-**kon**-dri-uh

☑ **chon** not **con**: **hypochondria**

hypochondriac »*noun* a person who is excessively anxious about their health.

hypocrisy »*noun* behaviour in which a person pretends to have higher standards or beliefs than they really have.
– SAY hi-**pok**-ruh-si

☑ **isy** not **icy**: **hypocrisy**

hypocrite »*noun* a person who pretends to have higher standards or beliefs than they really have.
hypocritical

☑ **hypo** not **hyper**, and don't forget the **e** at the end: **hypocrite**

hypodermic »*adjective* (of a needle or syringe) used to inject a drug or other substance beneath the skin.
»*noun* a hypodermic syringe or injection.

hypotension »*noun* abnormally low blood pressure.
hypotensive

ℹ️ on the difference between **hyper-** and **hypo-** words, see the note at
HYPERTENSION

hypotenuse »*noun* the longest side of a right-angled triangle, opposite the right angle.
– sᴀʏ hy-**pot**-uh-nyooz

☑ one **t**, one **n**: **hypotenuse**

hypothermia »*noun* the condition of having an abnormally low body temperature.
– sᴀʏ hy-puh-**ther**-mi-uh

☑ **hypo-** not **hyper- hypothermia** (**hyperthermia** refers to abnormally high temperature: see the note at **HYPERTENSION**)

hypothesis »*noun* (plural **hypotheses**) an idea that has not yet been proved to be true or correct.
– sᴀʏ hy-**poth**-i-siss [singular], hy-**poth**-i-seez [plural]

☑ make the plural by changing the **-is** ending to **-es** (as in Latin): **hypotheses**

hypothesize »*verb* (**hypothesizes**, **hypothesizing**, **hypothesized**) put something forward as a hypothesis.

☑ many people prefer the alternative spellings **hypothesise**, **hypothesises**, etc.: both **s** and **z** spellings are correct

hypothetical »*adjective* based on or having to do with an imagined or possible situation rather than fact.
– sᴀʏ hy-puh-**thet**-i-k'l
hypothetically

hyrax »*noun* a small plant-eating mammal with a short tail, found in Africa and Arabia.
– sᴀʏ hy-raks

hyssop »*noun* a bushy plant whose bitter minty leaves are used in cookery and herbal medicine.
– sᴀʏ **hiss**-uhp

☑ two **s**'s, one **p**: **hyssop**

hysterectomy »*noun* (plural **hysterectomies**) a surgical operation to remove all or part of the womb.
– sᴀʏ hiss-tuh-**rek**-tuh-mi

hysteria »*noun* ❶ a mental disorder which causes extreme and unpredictable emotions and attention-seeking behaviour in sufferers. ❷ extreme or uncontrollable emotion or excitement.

hysteric »*noun* a person suffering from hysteria.

hysterical »*adjective* ❶ having to do with hysteria. ❷ wildly uncontrolled. ❸ very funny.
hysterically

hysterics »*noun* ❶ wildly emotional behaviour. ❷ uncontrollable laughter.

Ii

iambic »*adjective* (of rhythm in poetry) having one unstressed syllable followed by one stressed syllable.
– sᴀʏ I-**am**-bik

Iberian »*adjective* relating to the peninsula that consists of modern Spain and Portugal.
»*noun* a person from Spain or Portugal.
– sᴀʏ I-**beer**-i-uhn

ibex »*noun* (plural **ibex** or **ibexes**) a wild mountain goat with long, thick ridged horns.
– sᴀʏ I-beks

ibid. »*adverb* in the same book as something that has just been referred to.
– sᴀʏ **ib**-id

ℹ **ibid.** is short for the Latin word *ibidem*, meaning 'in the same place'

ibis »*noun* (plural **ibis** or **ibises**) a large wading bird with a long curved bill.
– sᴀʏ I-biss

ibuprofen »*noun* a medicine used to relieve pain and to reduce inflammation.
– sᴀʏ I-byoo-**proh**-fen

ice (verb: **ices**, **icing**, **iced**)

☑ drop the **e** to spell **icing**

ice age »*noun* a period of time when ice sheets covered much of the earth's surface.

iceberg

✓ berg not burg: iceberg

icebox

ice-breaker »*noun* a ship designed for breaking a channel through ice.

ice cap »*noun* a large area that is permanently covered with ice, especially at the North and South Poles.

ice cream

iced »*adjective* ❶ cooled or mixed with ice: *iced water*. ❷ decorated with icing.

ice hockey

Icelander

Icelandic

ices

ice skate (verb: **ice-skates, ice-skating, ice-skated**)
ice skater
ice skating

✓ add a hyphen if you use this as a verb: **ice-skate, ice-skates,** etc.

ichneumon »*noun* a small wasp which lays its eggs in or on the larvae of other insects.
– SAY ik-**nyoo**-muhn

ichthyology »*noun* the study of fishes.
– SAY ik-thi-**ol**-uh-ji
ichthyologist

ichthyosaur »*noun* a fossil reptile that lived in the sea, with a dolphin-like body.
– SAY ik-thi-uh-sor

icicle »*noun* a hanging piece of ice formed when dripping water freezes.

icier

iciest

icily

iciness

icing

icon »*noun* ❶ (in the Orthodox Church) a painting of a holy person which is itself regarded as holy. ❷ a person or thing that is seen as a symbol of something. ❸ (in computing) a symbol on a computer screen that represents a program.
– SAY I-kon
iconic

✓ when used to mean 'a painting of a holy person', **icon** is sometimes spelled **ikon**, with a **k** as in Greek

iconify »*verb* (**iconifies, iconifying, iconified**) (in computing) reduce a window on a computer screen to an icon.
– SAY I-**kon**-i-fI

iconoclast »*noun* a person who attacks popular beliefs or established values and practices.
– SAY I-kon-uh-klast
iconoclasm
iconoclastic

iconography »*noun* ❶ the use or study of pictures or symbols in visual arts. ❷ the pictures or symbols associated with a person or movement.
– SAY I-kuh-**nog**-ruh-fi
iconographer
iconographic

icosahedron »*noun* (plural **icosahedra** or **icosahedrons**) a three-dimensional shape with twenty plane faces.
– SAY I-koss-uh-**hee**-druhn

✓ the plural can be either **icosahedra** (like the original Greek) or **icosahedrons**

icy (adjective: **icier, iciest**)
icily
iciness

✓ drop the **y** and add **ier** and **iest** to spell **icier** or **iciest**

ID »*abbreviation* identification or identity.

I'd [I had; I should; I would]

id »*noun* the part of the mind that consists of a person's unconscious instincts and feelings.

idea

ideal
ideally

idealise another way of spelling **IDEALIZE**.

idealism »*noun* ❶ the belief that things can be made ideal, even when this is unrealistic. ❷ the representation of things as better than they really are.
idealist
idealistic
idealistically

idealize »*verb* (**idealizes, idealizing, idealized**) represent something as better than it really is.
idealization

✓ many people prefer the alternative spellings **idealise, idealises,** etc., and **idealisation**: both **s** and **z** spellings are correct

ideally

idee fixe »*noun* (plural **idees fixes**) an obsession.
– SAY ee-day **feeks** [singular and plural]

✓ **idee fixe** can also be spelled **idée fixe**, with an acute accent on the first **e** (it is from a French phrase which means 'fixed idea')

identical
  identically

identifiable

identifiably

identification

identify (verb: **identifies, identifying, identified**)
  identifiable
  identifiably
  identifier

identikit »*noun* (trademark) a picture of a person wanted by the police, put together from a set of typical facial features.

identity (plural **identities**)

> ✓ plural: drop the **y** and add **ies**: **identities**

ideogram »*noun* a symbol used in a writing system to represent the idea of a thing rather than the sounds used to say it (e.g. a numeral).
– **say** id-i-uh-gram

ideograph »*noun* = IDEOGRAM.

ideological

ideologically

ideologies

ideologue »*noun* a person who follows an ideology in a strict and inflexible way.
– **say** I-di-uh-log

ideology »*noun* (plural **ideologies**) ❶ a system of ideas and principles that an economic or political theory is based on. ❷ the set of beliefs held by a particular group.
– **say** I-di-**ol**-uh-ji or i-di-**ol**-uh-ji
  ideological
  ideologically

> ✓ plural: drop the **y** and add **ies**: **ideologies**

idiocy »*noun* (plural **idiocies**) extremely stupid behaviour.
– **say** id-i-uh-si

> ✓ plural: drop the **y** and add **ies**: **idiocies**

idiom »*noun* ❶ a group of words whose overall meaning is different from the meanings of the individual words (e.g. *over the moon*). ❷ a form of language used by particular people. ❸ a style of music or art.
– **say** id-i-uhm

idiomatic »*adjective* using expressions that are natural to a native speaker of a language.
  idiomatically

idiosyncrasy »*noun* (plural **idiosyncrasies**) ❶ a person's particular way of behaving or

thinking. ❷ a distinctive or peculiar feature of a thing.
– **say** id-i-oh-**sing**-kruh-si

> ✓ **asy** not **acy**: **idiosyncrasy**

idiosyncratic »*adjective* having to do with idiosyncrasy; individual.
– **say** id-i-oh-sing-**krat**-ik
  idiosyncratically

idiot

idiotic
  idiotically

idle (adjective: **idler, idlest**; verb: **idles, idling, idled**) [not active; not working]
  idleness
  idler
  idly

idol »*noun* ❶ a statue or picture of a god that is worshipped. ❷ a person who is greatly admired.

idolatry »*noun* worship of idols.
– **say** I-**dol**-uh-tri
  idolater
  idolatrous

idolize »*verb* (**idolizes, idolizing, idolized**) admire or love someone greatly or excessively.

> ✓ many people prefer the alternative spellings **idolise, idolises**, etc.: both **s** and **z** spellings are correct

idyll »*noun* ❶ a very happy or peaceful time or situation. ❷ a short piece of writing describing a peaceful scene of country life.
– **say** i-dil

> ✓ note the double **l**: **idyll**

idyllic »*adjective* very happy, peaceful, or beautiful.
– **say** i-**dil**-ik
  idyllically

i.e. »*abbreviation* that is to say.

> ℹ **i.e.** is short for the Latin phrase *id est*, which means 'that is'

if

iffy (adjective: **iffier, iffiest**)

igloo »*noun* a dome-shaped Eskimo house built from blocks of solid snow.

igneous »*adjective* (of rock) formed when molten rock has solidified.
– **say** ig-ni-uhss

ignite »*verb* (**ignites, igniting, ignited**) ❶ catch fire or set something on fire. ❷ provoke someone or something.
  igniter

☑ -nite not -night: ignite

ignition »*noun* ❶ the action of igniting. ❷ the mechanism in a vehicle that ignites the fuel to start the engine.

ignoble »*adjective* not good or honest; dishonourable.
ignobly

ignominious »*adjective* deserving or causing public disgrace or shame.
– SAY ig-nuh-**min**-i-uhss
ignominiously

ignominy »*noun* public shame or disgrace.
– SAY ig-nuh-mi-ni

ignoramus »*noun* (plural **ignoramuses**) an ignorant or stupid person.
– SAY ig-nuh-**ray**-muhss

☑ the plural of **ignoramus** adds **es**: ignoramuses

ignorance

☑ ance not ence: ignorance

ignorant
ignorantly

☑ ant not ent: ignorant

ignore (verb: **ignores, ignoring, ignored**)

iguana »*noun* a large tropical American lizard with a spiny crest along the back.
– SAY i-**gwah**-nuh

ikon another way of spelling ICON.

ileum »*noun* (plural **ilea**) the third and lowest part of the small intestine.
– SAY il-i-uhm [singular], il-i-uh [plural]

☑ like many other words ending in **um** derived from Latin, **ileum** has a plural ending in **a**: **ilea**

iliac »*adjective* relating to the ilium or the nearby regions of the lower body.
– SAY il-i-ak

ilium »*noun* (plural **ilia**) the large broad bone forming the upper part of each half of the pelvis.
– SAY il-i-uhm [singular], il-i-uh [plural]

☑ like many other words ending in **um** derived from Latin, **ilium** has a plural ending in **a**: **ilia**

ilk »*noun* a type: *fascists, racists, and others of that ilk.*

I'll [I shall; I will]

ill

ill-advised

ill-bred »*adjective* badly brought up or rude.

ill-disposed »*adjective* unfriendly or unsympathetic.

illegal »*adjective* against the law.
illegality
illegally

illegible »*adjective* not clear enough to be read.
– SAY il-**lej**-i-b'l
illegibility
illegibly

☑ there is no **d** in **illegible**
-ible not -able: illegible

illegitimate »*adjective* ❶ not allowed by law or rules. ❷ (of a child) born of parents not married to each other.
– SAY il-li-**jit**-i-muht
illegitimacy
illegitimately

☑ ate not ite: illegitimate

ill-fated

ill-favoured »*adjective* unattractive.

ill-gotten

illiberal »*adjective* not allowing freedom of thought or behaviour.

illicit »*adjective* forbidden by law, rules, or accepted standards.
– SAY il-**li**-sit
illicitly

ⓘ do not confuse **illicit** with **elicit** meaning 'draw out a response'

illimitable »*adjective* limitless.

illiterate »*adjective* ❶ unable to read or write. ❷ not knowing very much about a particular subject.
illiteracy
illiterately

☑ double **l**, single **t**: illiterate

illness

illogical »*adjective* not sensible or based on sound reasoning.
illogicality
illogically

ill-starred »*adjective* unlucky.

ill-tempered

ill-treat (verb: **ill-treats, ill-treating, ill-treated**)

illuminate »*verb* (**illuminates, illuminating, illuminated**) ❶ light up. ❷ help to explain or make clear: *he illuminates science for the interested reader.* ❸ decorate a manuscript with gold, silver, or coloured designs.
– SAY il-**loo**-mi-nayt
illuminator

illumination »*noun* ❶ lighting or light.
❷ (**illuminations**) lights used in decorating
a building for a special occasion.
❸ understanding.

illuminator

illumine »*verb* (**illumines, illumining,
illumined**) (an old word) light up;
illuminate.

illusion »*noun* ❶ a false idea or belief. ❷ a
thing that seems to be something that it is
not or seems to exist but does not.
– SAY il-**lyoo**-zh'n

> ℹ️ do not confuse **illusion** with **allusion**,
> which means 'an indirect reference
> to something'

illusionist »*noun* a magician or conjuror.

illusive »*adjective* = ILLUSORY.

illusory »*adjective* not real, although
seeming to be.
– SAY il-**loo**-suh-ri

illustrate »*verb* (**illustrates, illustrating,
illustrated**) ❶ provide a book or magazine
with pictures. ❷ make something clear by
using examples, charts, etc. ❸ act as an
example of something.
illustrator

illustration

illustrative »*adjective* acting as an example
or explanation.

illustrator

illustrious »*adjective* famous and admired
for what you have achieved.
– SAY il-**luss**-tri-uhss
illustriousness

I'm [I am]

image (verb: **images, imaging, imaged**)

imager »*noun* an electronic device which
records images.

imagery »*noun* ❶ language that produces
images in the mind;a simile or metaphor.
❷ pictures as a whole.

images
imaginable
imaginary

> ✓ ary not ery: **imaginary**

imagination
imaginative
  imaginatively
  imaginativeness
imagine (verb: **imagines, imagining,
imagined**)
imaging
imagining

imam »*noun* the person who leads prayers
in a mosque.
– SAY i-**mahm**

imbalance »*noun* a lack of proportion or
balance.

> ✓ im- not in-: **imbalance**

imbecile »*noun* a stupid person.
– SAY im-bi-seel
  imbecilic
  imbecility

imbed mainly American spelling of EMBED.

imbibe »*verb* (**imbibes, imbibing, imbibed**)
❶ drink alcohol. ❷ absorb ideas or
knowledge.
– SAY im-**byb**
  imbiber

imbroglio »*noun* (plural **imbroglios**) a very
confused or complicated situation.
– SAY im-**broh**-li-oh

> ✓ the plural of **imbroglio**, an Italian
> word, has **os** not **oes**: **imbroglios**

imbue »*verb* (**imbues, imbuing, imbued**) fill
someone or something with a feeling or
quality.
– SAY im-**byoo**

> ✓ drop the **e** to spell **imbuing**

IMF »*abbreviation* International Monetary
Fund.

imitate »*verb* (**imitates, imitating, imitated**)
❶ follow as a model; copy. ❷ copy the
way that a person speaks or behaves in
order to amuse people.
imitator

> ✓ im not imm: **imitate**

imitation

imitative »*adjective* imitating or copying
something.
– SAY im-i-**tuh**-tiv

imitator

immaculate
  immaculately

Immaculate Conception »*noun* (in the
Roman Catholic Church) the doctrine that
the Virgin Mary was free from sin from
the moment she was conceived by her
mother.

> ℹ️ the doctrine of the **Immaculate
> Conception** is not the same as that of
> the **Virgin Birth**, which is that Mary
> conceived a child even though she was a
> virgin

immaculately

immanent »*adjective* ❶ present within; inherent. ❷ (of God) permanently present throughout the universe.
– SAY im-muh-nuhnt
immanence

> ⓘ do not confuse **immanent** with **imminent**, which means 'about to happen'

immaterial »*adjective* ❶ unimportant under the circumstances. ❷ spiritual rather than physical.

immature »*adjective* ❶ not fully developed. ❷ behaving in a way that is typical of someone younger.
immaturely
immaturity

immeasurable »*adjective* too large or extreme to measure.
immeasurably

immediacy

immediate
immediately

immemorial »*adjective* existing for longer than people can remember: *from time immemorial.*

immense
immensely
immensity

immerse »*verb* (immerses, immersing, immersed) ❶ dip or cover something completely in a liquid. ❷ (immerse oneself or be immersed) involve yourself deeply in an activity.

immersion »*noun* ❶ the action of immersing. ❷ deep involvement in an activity.

immersion heater »*noun* an electric device in a water tank which heats water for a house.

immigrant »*noun* a person who comes to live permanently in a foreign country.

> ⓘ an **immigrant**, who comes into the country, is the opposite of an **emigrant**, who leaves it

> ✓ ant not ent: immigrant

immigrate »*verb* (immigrates, immigrating, immigrated) come to live permanently in a foreign country.
immigration

imminent »*adjective* about to happen.
imminence
imminently

> ⓘ do not confuse **imminent** with **immanent**, which means 'present within or throughout'

> ✓ ent not ant: imminent

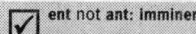

immiscible »*adjective* (of liquids) not able to be mixed together.
– SAY im-miss-i-b'l

immobile »*adjective* ❶ not moving. ❷ not able to move.
immobility

immobilize »*verb* (immobilizes, immobilizing, immobilized) prevent something from moving or operating as normal.
immobilization
immobilizer

> ✓ many people prefer the alternative spellings **immobilise, immobilises,** etc., and **immobilisation** and **immobiliser**: both s and z spellings are correct

immoderate »*adjective* not sensible or controlled; excessive.
immoderately

immodest »*adjective* not humble or decent.
immodestly
immodesty

immolate »*verb* (immolates, immolating, immolated) kill or sacrifice someone by burning them.
– SAY im-muh-layt
immolation

immoral »*adjective* not following accepted standards of morality.
immorality
immorally

> ⓘ do not confuse **immoral** with **amoral**, which means 'not concerned with morality'

immortal »*adjective* ❶ living forever. ❷ deserving to be remembered forever.
» *noun* ❶ an immortal god. ❷ a person who will be famous for a very long time.
immortality

immortalize »*verb* (immortalizes, immortalizing, immortalized) make someone or something immortal.

> ✓ many people prefer the alternative spellings **immortalise, immortalises,** etc.: both s and z spellings are correct

immovable »*adjective* ❶ not able to be moved. ❷ unable to be changed or persuaded.
immovably

> ✓ there is no e after the v: immovable

immune »*adjective* ❶ having a natural ability to resist a particular infection.

❷ not affected by something. ❸ exempt or protected from something.

immunise another way of spelling IMMUNIZE.

immunity »*noun* ❶ the body's ability to resist a particular infection. ❷ the state of being free from a duty or punishment.

immunize »*verb* (**immunizes, immunizing, immunized**) make someone immune to infection.
immunization

> ✓ many people prefer the alternative spellings **immunise, immunises,** etc., and **immunisation:** both **s** and **z** spellings are correct

immunodeficiency »*noun* failure of the body's ability to resist infection.

immunology »*noun* the branch of medicine and biology concerned with immunity to infection.
immunological
immunologist

immunotherapy »*noun* the prevention or treatment of disease with substances that stimulate the body's immune system.

immure »*verb* (**immures, immuring, immured**) confine or imprison someone.
– SAY im-**myoor**
immurement

immutable »*adjective* unchanging or unchangeable.
– SAY im-**myoo**-tuh-b'l
immutably

imp »*noun* ❶ a small, mischievous devil or sprite. ❷ a mischievous child.

impact (verb: **impacts, impacting, impacted**)

impair »*verb* (**impairs, impairing, impaired**) weaken or damage something.
impaired
impairment

> ✓ **-pair** not **-pare: impair**

impala »*noun* (plural **impala**) an antelope of southern and East Africa.
– SAY im-**pah**-luh

impale »*verb* (**impales, impaling, impaled**) pierce something with a sharp instrument.
impalement

impalpable »*adjective* ❶ unable to be felt by touch. ❷ not easily understood.
impalpably

impart »*verb* (**imparts, imparting, imparted**) ❶ communicate information. ❷ give a particular quality to: *the trees impart a certain grandeur to the scene.*
imparter

impartial »*adjective* not favouring one person or thing more than another.
impartiality
impartially

impassable »*adjective* impossible to travel along or over.

impasse »*noun* a situation in which no progress is possible.
– SAY im-**pahss** or am-**pahss**

> ✓ remember the **e** at the end: **impasse.** It is a French word, often pronounced in the French way **am**-pahss.

impassioned »*adjective* filled with or showing great emotion.

impassive »*adjective* not feeling or showing emotion.
impassively
impassiveness
impassivity

impasto »*noun* the technique of laying on paint thickly so that it stands out from the surface of a painting.
– SAY im-**pass**-toh

impatient
impatience
impatiently

impeach »*verb* (**impeaches, impeaching, impeached**) charge the holder of a public office with a serious crime.
impeachment

impeccable »*adjective* without faults or mistakes.
– SAY im-**pek**-kuh-b'l
impeccably

> ✓ double **c: impeccable**

impecunious »*adjective* having little or no money.
– SAY im-pi-**kyoo**-ni-uhss
impecuniousness

impedance »*noun* the total resistance of an electric circuit to the flow of alternating current.
– SAY im-**pee**-duhnss

impede »*verb* (**impedes, impeding, impeded**) delay or block the progress of something.

impediment »*noun* something that delays or blocks the progress of something.

impedimenta »*plural noun* equipment for an activity or expedition, seen as impeding progress.
– SAY im-ped-i-**men**-tuh

impeding

impel »*verb* (**impels, impelling, impelled**) force someone to do something.

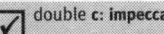

– say im-**pel**
impeller

 double the **l** to spell **impelling**, **impelled**, and **impeller**

impending »*adjective* about to happen.

impenetrable »*adjective* ❶ impossible to get through or into. ❷ impossible to understand.
– say im-**pen**-i-truh-b'l
impenetrably

impenitent »*adjective* not feeling shame or regret.

imperative »*adjective* ❶ of vital importance. ❷ giving a command. ❸ (in grammar) (of a verb) expressing a command, as in *come here!*
»*noun* an essential or urgent thing.
– say im-**pe**-ruh-tiv

imperceptible »*adjective* too slight or gradual to be seen or felt.
imperceptibly

 -**ible** not -**able**: **imperceptible**

imperfect »*adjective* ❶ faulty or incomplete. ❷ (in grammar) (of a verb) referring to a past action that is not yet not completed.
imperfection
imperfectly

imperial »*adjective* ❶ relating to an empire or an emperor. ❷ (of weights and measures) conforming to the system used in the UK before the metric system.

imperialism »*noun* a system in which one country influences other countries, by defeating them in war, forming colonies, etc.
imperialist

imperil »*verb* (**imperils**, **imperilling**, **imperilled**) put someone into danger.

 double the **l** to spell **imperilling** and **imperilled** (the spellings **imperiling** and **imperiled** are American)

imperious »*adjective* expecting to be obeyed.
– say im-**peer**-i-uhss
imperiously
imperiousness

imperishable »*adjective* lasting forever.
imperishably

impermanent »*adjective* not permanent.
impermanence

 ent not **ant**: **impermanent**

impermeable »*adjective* not allowing liquid or gas to pass through.

– say im-**per**-mi-uh-b'l
impermeability

 mea not **mia**: **impermeable**

impersonal »*adjective* ❶ not influenced by or involving personal feelings. ❷ lacking human feelings or atmosphere. ❸ (of a verb) used only with *it* as a subject (as in *it is snowing*).
impersonality
impersonally

impersonal pronoun »*noun* the pronoun *it* when not referring to a thing, as in *it was snowing*.

impersonate »*verb* (**impersonates**, **impersonating**, **impersonated**) pretend to be another person in order to entertain or deceive people.
impersonation
impersonator

impertinent »*adjective* not showing proper respect.
impertinence
impertinently

imperturbable »*adjective* unable to be upset or excited.
– say im-per-**ter**-buh-b'l
imperturbability
imperturbably

impervious »*adjective* ❶ not allowing a liquid or gas to pass through. ❷ (**impervious to**) unable to be affected by something.
– say im-**per**-vi-uhss
imperviously
imperviousness

impetigo »*noun* a contagious skin infection forming spots and yellow sores.
– say im-pi-**ty**-goh

impetuous »*adjective* acting or done quickly and without thinking or being careful.
impetuously
impetuousness

impetus »*noun* ❶ the force or energy with which something moves. ❷ the force that makes something happen or happen more quickly: *the impetus for change*.

impiety »*noun* lack of religious respect.
– say im-**py**-i-ti

impinge »*verb* (**impinges**, **impinging**, **impinged**) have an effect or impact on something.
impingement

impious »*adjective* not showing respect or reverence.
– say **im**-pi-uhss or im-**py**-uhss

implacable »*adjective* ❶ unwilling to stop being hostile towards someone or something. ❷ unstoppable.
– say im-**plak**-uh-b'l
  implacability
  implacably

implant »*verb* (**implants, implanting, implanted**) ❶ insert tissue or an artificial object into someone's body, by means of a surgical operation. ❷ fix an idea firmly into someone's mind.
» *noun* a thing that is implanted.
  implantation

implausible »*adjective* not seeming reasonable or probable.
  implausibility
  implausibly

implement »*noun* a tool, utensil, or instrument that is used for a particular purpose.
» *verb* (**implements, implementing, implemented**) put something into effect.
  implementation

> ☑ **imple** not **impli**: **implement**

implicate »*verb* (**implicates, implicating, implicated**) ❶ show that someone is involved in a crime. ❷ (**be implicated in**) be partly responsible for.

implication »*noun* ❶ the conclusion that can be drawn from something, despite not being directly stated. ❷ a possible effect. ❸ not doubted or questioned.

implicit »*adjective* ❶ suggested without being directly expressed. ❷ (**implicit in**) forming part of something, though not directly expressed. ❸ not doubted or questioned: *an implicit faith in God.*
– say im-**pliss**-it
  implicitly

implied

implies

implode »*verb* (**implodes, imploding, imploded**) collapse or make something collapse violently inwards.
– say im-**plohd**
  implosion

implore »*verb* (**implores, imploring, implored**) beg earnestly or desperately.

implosion

imply »*verb* (**implies, implying, implied**) ❶ suggest rather than state directly. ❷ suggest as a possible effect.

> ℹ do not confuse **imply** and **infer**. If a speaker or writer **implies** something, as in *he implied that the General was a traitor*, it means that the person is suggesting something though not saying it

directly. If you **infer** something from what has been said, as in *we inferred from his words that the General was a traitor*, this means that you come to the conclusion that this is what they really mean.

impolite
  impolitely
  impoliteness

impolitic »*adjective* not expedient or sensible.

imponderable »*adjective* difficult or impossible to assess.
» *noun* an imponderable part of something.

import »*verb* (**imports, importing, imported**) ❶ bring goods or services into a country from abroad. ❷ transfer computer data into a file or document.
» *noun* ❶ an imported article or service. ❷ the action of importing. ❸ the implied meaning of something. ❹ importance.
  importation
  importer

important
  importance
  importantly

> ☑ **ant** not **ent**: **important**

importation

imported

importer

importing

imports

importunate »*adjective* very persistent.
– say im-**por**-tyuu-nuht

importune »*verb* (**importunes, importuning, importuned**) ask someone persistently for something.
– say im-por-**tyoon**

impose »*verb* (**imposes, imposing, imposed**) ❶ force something to be accepted. ❷ (often **impose on**) take unfair advantage of someone.

imposing »*adjective* grand and impressive.
  imposingly

imposition »*noun* ❶ the action of imposing something. ❷ something imposed and felt to be unfair.

impossibility (plural **impossibilities**)

> ☑ plural: drop the **y** and add **ies**: **impossibilities**

impossible
  impossibly

impostor »*noun* a person who pretends to be someone else in order to deceive or cheat others.

impostor can also be spelled with an er: **imposter** (both spellings are correct)

imposture »*noun* an act of pretending to be someone else in order to deceive.

impotent »*adjective* **❶** helpless or powerless. **❷** (of a man) unable to achieve an erection.
– say im-puh-tuhnt
impotence
impotently

impound »*verb* (**impounds, impounding, impounded**) **❶** officially seize something. **❷** shut up domestic animals in an enclosure.

impoverish »*verb* (**impoverishes, impoverishing, impoverished**) **❶** make someone poor. **❷** make worse in quality: *grazing impoverished the land*.
impoverishment

impracticable »*adjective* not able to be done.
impracticability

i **impracticable** and **impractical** do not mean exactly the same thing. **Impracticable** means 'impossible to carry out' and is normally used of a specific procedure or course of action; **impractical** is used in more general senses, often to mean simply 'unrealistic' or 'not sensible'

impractical »*adjective* not sensible or realistic.
impracticality
impractically

imprecation »*noun* a spoken curse.

imprecise
imprecisely
imprecision

impregnable »*adjective* **❶** unable to be captured or broken into. **❷** unable to be defeated.
impregnability
impregnably

impregnate »*verb* (**impregnates, impregnating, impregnated**) **❶** soak something with a substance. **❷** fill someone or something with a feeling or quality. **❸** make a woman or female animal pregnant.
impregnation

impresario »*noun* (plural **impresarios**) a person who organizes plays, concerts, or operas.
– say im-pri-sah-ri-oh

☑ -pres- not -press-: **impresario** the plural of **impresario**, an Italian word, has os not oes: **impresarios**

impress (verb: **impresses, impressing, impressed**)

impression

☑ double s: **impression**

impressionable »*adjective* easily influenced.

Impressionism »*noun* a style of painting concerned with showing the visual impression of a particular moment, especially the shifting effects of light.
Impressionist

impressionist »*noun* an entertainer who impersonates famous people.

impressionistic »*adjective* based on personal impressions.

impressive
impressively
impressiveness

 double s: **impressive**

imprimatur »*noun* **❶** the authority or approval of somebody. **❷** an official licence issued by the Roman Catholic Church to print a religious book.
– say im-pri-mah-ter or im-pri-may-ter

i **imprimatur** means 'let it be printed' in Latin

imprint (verb: **imprints, imprinting, imprinted**)

imprison (verb: **imprisons, imprisoning, imprisoned**)
imprisonment

improbable
improbability
improbably

impromptu »*adjective & adverb* done without being planned or rehearsed.
– say im-promp-tyoo

improper
improperly

improper fraction »*noun* a fraction in which the numerator is greater than the denominator, such as ⁵⁄₄.

improperly

impropriety »*noun* (plural **improprieties**) improper behaviour.
– say im-pruh-pry-uh-ti

improve (verb: **improves, improving, improved**)
improver

improvement

improver

improves

improvident »*adjective* not thinking about or preparing for the future.

improving

improvise »*verb* (**improvises, improvising, improvised**) ❶ invent and perform music, drama, or poetry on the spur of the moment. ❷ make something from whatever is available.
improvisation
improvisatory
improviser

> ☑ unlike most verbs ending in **ise**, **improvise** cannot be spelled with an **ize** ending

imprudent »*adjective* not sensible or careful.
imprudently

impudent »*adjective* not showing proper respect for another person; cheeky.
– SAY im-pyuu-duhnt
impudence
impudently

impugn »*verb* (**impugns, impugning, impugned**) express doubts about the truth or honesty of something.
– SAY im-**pyoon**

> ☑ **pugn** not **pune**: impugn

impulse

impulsion »*noun* ❶ an urge to do something. ❷ a driving force.

impulsive »*adjective* acting or done without thinking ahead.
impulsively
impulsiveness

impunity »*noun* freedom from being punished or harmed.
– SAY im-**pyoo**-ni-ti

impure

impurity (plural **impurities**)

> ☑ plural: drop the **y** and add **ies**: **impurities**

impute »*verb* (**imputes, imputing, imputed**) believe that something has been done or caused by someone or something: *madness among the troops was imputed to shell shock*.
imputation

in

inability

in absentia »*adverb* while not present.
– SAY in ab-sen-ti-uh or in ab-**sen**-shi-uh

> ℹ️ **in absentia** means 'in absence' in Latin

inaccessible
inaccessibility

> ☑ **-ible** not **-able**: inaccessible

inaccurate
inaccuracy
inaccurately

inaction

inactive
inactivity

inadequacy (plural **inadequacies**)

> ☑ plural: drop the **y** and add **ies**: **inadequacies**

inadequate
inadequately

inadmissible »*adjective* (of evidence in court) not accepted as valid.
inadmissibility

> ☑ **-ible** not **-able**: inadmissible

inadvertent »*adjective* not deliberate; unintentional.
inadvertently

> ☑ **ent** not **ant**: inadvertent

inadvisable
inadvisability

> ☑ **vis** not **viz**: inadvisable

inalienable »*adjective* unable to be taken away or given away.

inamorata »*noun* (plural **inamoratas**) a person's female lover.

inamorato »*noun* (plural **inamoratos**) a person's lover.
– SAY i-nam-uh-**rah**-toh

> ☑ the plural of **inamorato**, an Italian word, has **os** not **oes**: inamoratos

inane »*adjective* lacking sense; silly.
inanely

inanimate »*adjective* ❶ not alive. ❷ showing no sign of life.

inanity »*noun* (plural **inanities**) silliness.

inapplicable »*adjective* not relevant or appropriate.
inapplicability

inappropriate
inappropriately
inappropriateness

inarticulate »*adjective* ❶ unable to express your ideas clearly. ❷ not expressed in words.
inarticulacy
inarticulately

inasmuch

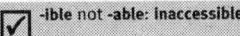

inattentive
inattention
inattentively

inaudible »*adjective* unable to be heard.
inaudibility
inaudibly

inaugural »*adjective* marking the beginning of an organization or period of office.
– SAY in-aw-gyuu-ruhl

inaugurate »*verb* (**inaugurates, inaugurating, inaugurated**) ❶ begin or introduce a system or project. ❷ establish someone in office with a special ceremony. ❸ mark the opening or introduction of a building, service, etc. with a ceremony.
– SAY in-aw-gyuu-rayt
inauguration

inauspicious »*adjective* not likely to lead to success.
inauspiciously

inauthentic »*noun* not genuine or sincere.

inboard »*adverb & adjective* within or towards the centre of a ship, aircraft, or vehicle.

inborn »*adjective* existing from birth.

inbound »*adjective & adverb* travelling back to an original point of departure.

inbred »*adjective* ❶ produced by breeding from closely related individuals. ❷ existing from birth; inborn.

inbreeding »*noun* breeding from closely related people or animals.

inbuilt »*adjective* present as an original or vital part.

Inca »*noun* a member of a South American Indian people living in the central Andes before the Spanish conquest in the early 1530s.

incalculable »*adjective* ❶ too great to be calculated or estimated. ❷ not able to be calculated or estimated.
incalculably

in camera »*adverb* taking place in the private rooms of a judge, without the press and public being present.

 in camera is a Latin phrase which means 'in the chamber'

incandescent »*adjective* ❶ glowing as a result of being heated. ❷ (of an electric light) containing a filament which glows white-hot when heated by an electric current.
– SAY in-kan-dess-uhnt
incandescence

 scent not **sent**: incandescent

incantation »*noun* words said as a magic spell or charm.
incantatory

incapable
incapability

incapacitate »*verb* (**incapacitates, incapacitating, incapacitated**) prevent someone from functioning in a normal way.
– SAY in-kuh-pa-si-tayt
incapacitation

incapacity »*noun* physical or mental inability to do something.

incarcerate »*verb* (**incarcerates, incarcerating, incarcerated**) imprison someone.
– SAY in-kah-suh-rayt
incarceration

incarnate »*adjective* ❶ (of a god or spirit) in human form. ❷ in physical form: *she was beauty incarnate.*
» *verb* (**incarnates, incarnating, incarnated**) be the living embodiment of a quality.
– SAY in-kaar-nuht [adjective], in-kaar-nayt [verb]

incarnation »*noun* ❶ a living embodiment of a god, spirit, or quality. ❷ (**the Incarnation**) (in Christian belief) the embodiment of God the Son in human flesh as Jesus Christ.

incautious

incendiary »*adjective* ❶ (of a bomb or other device) designed to cause fires. ❷ tending to stir up conflict.
» *noun* (plural **incendiaries**) an incendiary bomb.
– SAY in-sen-di-uh-ri

incense[1] »*noun* a substance that is burned for the sweet smell it produces.
– SAY in-senss

 -cense not **-sence** or **-sense**: incense

incense[2] »*verb* (**incenses, incensing, incensed**) make someone very angry.
– SAY in-senss

incentive »*noun* a thing that influences or encourages someone to do something.

inception »*noun* the beginning of an organization or activity.

incessant »*adjective* never stopping.
incessantly

 double **s**, and **ant** not **ent**: incessant

incest »*noun* sex between people who are too closely related to marry each other.

incestuous »*adjective* ❶ involving incest.
❷ excessively close and wishing to keep
out outside influence.
– SAY in-**sess**-tyoo-uhss

inch »*noun* a unit of length equal to one
twelfth of a foot (2.54 cm).
» *verb* (**inches, inching, inched**) move along
slowly and carefully.

inchoate »*adjective* just begun and so not
fully formed or developed.
– SAY in-**koh**-uht or **in**-koh-uht

incidence »*noun* ❶ the occurrence, rate, or
frequency of something. ❷ (in physics) the
meeting of a line or ray with a surface.

incident »*noun* ❶ an event. ❷ a violent
event, such as an attack.
» *adjective* ❶ (**incident to**) resulting from.
❷ (of light or other radiation) falling on a
surface.

> ✓ **ent** not **ant: incident**

incidental »*adjective* ❶ occurring in
connection with or as a result of
something else. ❷ occurring as a minor
result of something.

incidentally

> ✓ note that it is **-ally** on the end:
> **incidentally**

incinerate »*verb* (**incinerates, incinerating,
incinerated**) destroy something by burning
it.
– SAY in-**sin**-uh-rayt
incineration

incinerator »*noun* a device for incinerating
rubbish.

> ✓ **-or** not **-er: incinerator**

incipient »*adjective* beginning to happen
or develop.
– SAY in-**sip**-i-uhnt
incipiently

incise »*verb* (**incises, incising, incised**)
❶ make a cut or cuts in a surface. ❷ cut a
mark into a surface.

> ✓ **incise** cannot be spelled with an **ize**
> ending

incision »*noun* ❶ a cut made as part of a
surgical operation. ❷ the action of cutting
into something.

incisive »*adjective* ❶ showing clear
thought and good understanding. ❷ quick
and direct.
incisively
incisiveness

incisor »*noun* a narrow-edged tooth at the
front of the mouth.

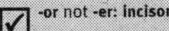

> ✓ **-or** not **-er: incisor**

incite »*verb* (**incites, inciting, incited**) ❶ stir
up violent or unlawful behaviour. ❷ urge
someone to act in a violent or unlawful
way.
incitement
inciter

incivility »*noun* rude speech or behaviour.

inclement »*adjective* (of the weather)
unpleasantly cold or wet.
– SAY in-**klem**-uhnt
inclemency

inclination »*noun* ❶ a natural tendency to
act or feel in a particular way.
❷ (**inclination for** or **to** or **towards**) an
interest in or liking for. ❸ a slope or slant.
❹ the angle at which a straight line or
plane slopes away from another.

incline »*verb* (**inclines, inclining, inclined**)
❶ be willing or tend to do or think.
❷ have a particular tendency or talent.
❸ lean or bend.
» *noun* a slope.

inclose see the note at ENCLOSE.

inclosure see the note at ENCLOSE.

include (verb: **includes, including, included**)

including

inclusion

inclusive »*adjective* ❶ including
everything expected or required.
❷ between the limits stated: *the ages of 55
to 59 inclusive.*
inclusively
inclusiveness

incognito »*adjective & adverb* having your
true identity concealed.
– SAY in-kog-**nee**-toh

> ℹ **incognito** is an Italian word meaning
> 'unknown'

incoherent »*adjective* ❶ hard to
understand; unclear. ❷ not logical or
well-organized.
incoherence
incoherently

> ✓ **ent** not **ant: incoherent**

incombustible »*adjective* that does not
burn.

> ✓ **-ible** not **-able: incombustible**

income

incomer »*noun* a person who has come to
live in an area in which they have not
grown up.

incoming

incommensurable »*adjective* not able to be judged or measured by the same standards.
– SAY in-kuh-**men**-shuh-ruh-b'l
incommensurability

incommensurate »*adjective* (incommensurate with) not in keeping or in proportion with.
– SAY in-kuh-**men**-shuh-ruht

incommode »*verb* (incommodes, incommoding, incommoded) cause someone inconvenience.

 double m: **incommode**

incommunicado »*adjective & adverb* not allowed to communicate with other people.
– SAY in-kuh-myoo-ni-**kah**-doh

 double m, single n: **incommunicado** (from Spanish)

incomparable
incomparably

incompatible »*adjective* ❶ (of two things) not able to exist or be used together. ❷ (of two people) unable to live or work together without disagreeing.
incompatibility

 -ible not -able: **incompatible**

incompetent »*adjective* not skilful enough to do something successfully.
incompetence
incompetently

incomplete
incompletely
incompleteness

incomprehensible »*adjective* not able to be understood.
incomprehensibility
incomprehensibly
incomprehension

 -ible not -able: **incomprehensible**

inconceivable »*adjective* not capable of being imagined or grasped mentally.
inconceivably

 inconceivable follows the usual rule: i before e except after c

inconclusive »*adjective* not leading to a firm conclusion.
inconclusively
inconclusiveness

incongruity »*noun* (plural incongruities) lack of consistency amongst the parts or qualities of something.

incongruous »*adjective* out of place.

– SAY in-**kong**-groo-uhss
incongruously

inconsequential »*adjective* not important.

 don't forget the u after the q: **inconsequential**

inconsiderable »*adjective* small in size or amount.

inconsiderate »*adjective* thoughtlessly causing hurt or trouble to others.
inconsiderately

inconsistent
inconsistency
inconsistently

inconsolable »*adjective* not able to be comforted.
inconsolably

inconspicuous »*adjective* not noticeable.
inconspicuously

inconstant

incontestable »*adjective* not able to be disputed.
incontestably

incontinent »*adjective* ❶ unable to control your bladder or bowels. ❷ lacking control.
incontinence

incontrovertible »*adjective* not able to be denied or disputed.
incontrovertibly

 -ible not -able: **incontrovertible**

inconvenience (verb: inconveniences, inconveniencing, inconvenienced)
inconvenient
inconveniently

incorporate »*verb* (incorporates, incorporating, incorporated) include something as part of a whole.
incorporation

incorporated »*adjective* (of a company) formed into a legal corporation.

incorporates

incorporating

incorporation

incorporeal »*adjective* without a physical body or form.
– SAY in-kor-**por**-i-uhl

incorrect
incorrectly
incorrectness

incorrigible »*adjective* having bad habits that cannot be changed.
incorrigibly

 -ible not -able: **incorrigible**

391

incorruptible »*adjective* ❶ too honest to be corrupted by taking bribes. ❷ not prone to death or decay.
incorruptibly

> ☑ -**ible** not -**able**: **incorruptible**

increase (verb: **increases, increasing, increased**)

increasingly

incredible [impossible or hard to believe]
incredibly

incredulity »*noun* the state of being unwilling or unable to believe something.
– **SAY** in-kri-**dyoo**-li-ti

incredulous »*adjective* unwilling or unable to believe something.
incredulously

> ℹ️ do not confuse **incredulous** and **incredible**: something that cannot be believed is **incredible**, while someone who cannot believe it is **incredulous**

increment »*noun* an increase in a number or an amount.
incremental
incrementally

incriminate »*verb* (**incriminates, incriminating, incriminated**) make someone appear guilty of a crime or wrongdoing.
incrimination

incrust see the note at **ENCRUST**.

incubate »*verb* (**incubates, incubating, incubated**) ❶ (of a bird) sit on eggs to keep them warm so that they hatch. ❷ keep bacteria or cells at a suitable temperature so that they develop. ❸ (of an infectious disease) develop slowly without obvious signs.
incubation

incubator »*noun* ❶ an apparatus used to hatch eggs or grow micro-organisms. ❷ a heated enclosed apparatus in which premature babies can be cared for.

> ☑ -**or** not -**er**: **incubator**

incubus »*noun* (plural **incubi**) a male demon believed to have sex with sleeping women.
– **SAY** ing-kyuu-buhss [singular], ing-kyuu-bI [plural]

> ☑ make the plural by changing the **us** ending to **i** (as in Latin): **incubi**

inculcate »*verb* (**inculcates, inculcating, inculcated**) fix an idea or habit in someone's mind by repetition.
– **SAY** in-kul-kayt
inculcation

incumbency »*noun* (plural **incumbencies**) the period during which a person is in office.

incumbent »*adjective* ❶ (**incumbent on** or **upon**) necessary for someone as a duty. ❷ currently holding an official position.
» *noun* the holder of an official position.
– **SAY** in-**kum**-buhnt

> ☑ **ent** not **ant**: **incumbent**

incur »*verb* (**incurs, incurring, incurred**) bring something unwelcome upon yourself.

> ☑ one **r** in **incur** and **incurs**, two in **incurring** and **incurred**

incurable
incurably

incurious »*adjective* not eager to know something.

incurred

incurring

incurs

incursion »*noun* a sudden or brief invasion or attack.

indebted »*adjective* owing money or gratitude.
indebtedness

> ☑ don't forget the **b**: **indebted**

indecent
indecency
indecently

indecipherable »*adjective* not able to be read or understood.
– **SAY** in-di-**sy**-fuh-ruh-b'l

indecisive
indecision
indecisively
indecisiveness

indeed

indefatigable »*adjective* never tiring or stopping.
– **SAY** in-di-**fat**-i-guh-b'l
indefatigably

indefensible »*adjective* not able to be justified or defended.
indefensibly

> ☑ -**ible** not -**able**: **indefensible**

indefinable »*adjective* not able to be defined or described exactly.
indefinably

indefinite »*adjective* ❶ not clearly stated, seen, or heard. ❷ lasting for an unknown

or unstated length of time.
indefinitely

 ite not ate: indefinite

indefinite article »*noun* the word *a* or *an*.
indefinitely

indelible »*adjective* ❶ (of ink or a mark) unable to be removed. ❷ unable to be forgotten.
– SAY in-**del**-i-b'l
indelibly

 -ible not -able: indelible

indelicate »*adjective* ❶ lacking sensitive understanding; tactless. ❷ slightly indecent.
indelicacy
indelicately

indemnify »*verb* (**indemnifies**, **indemnifying**, **indemnified**) ❶ pay money to someone for harm or loss they have suffered. ❷ protect or insure someone against legal responsibility for their actions.
– SAY in-**dem**-ni-fI
indemnification

indemnity »*noun* (plural **indemnities**) ❶ insurance against or exemption from legal responsibility for your actions. ❷ a sum of money paid to compensate someone for damage or loss.
– SAY in-**dem**-ni-ti

indent »*verb* (**indents**, **indenting**, **indented**) ❶ form hollows, dents, or notches in something. ❷ begin a line of writing further from the margin than the other lines. ❸ make a written order for something.
»*noun* ❶ an official order for goods. ❷ a hollow or notch.

indentation »*noun* ❶ the action of indenting. ❷ a hollow or notch.
indented
indenting
indents

indenture »*noun* a formal agreement or contract, such as one binding an apprentice to work for a master.
independence
independent
independently

 ent not ant: independent

in-depth
indescribable
indescribably

indestructible
indestructibility

 -ible not -able: indestructible

indeterminate »*adjective* not exactly known or defined.
– SAY in-di-**ter**-mi-nuht

index (plural **indexes** or **indices**; verb: **indexes**, **indexing**, **indexed**)
indexation
indexer

 the plural of **index** is usually **indexes**, but **indices** is also used in subjects such as science and medicine

index finger »*noun* the forefinger.
indexing
index-linked »*adjective* (of wages, pensions, etc.) adjusted according to rises or falls in the retail price index.
Indian

 do not use **Indian** (by itself) or **Red Indian** to talk about American native peoples, as these terms are now outdated; use **American Indian** instead

Indian summer »*noun* a period of dry, warm weather in late autumn.

indicate (verb: **indicates**, **indicating**, **indicated**)
indication

indicative »*adjective* ❶ acting as a sign of something. ❷ (of a form of a verb) expressing a simple statement of fact (e.g. *she left*).
– SAY in-**dik**-uh-tiv

indicator

 -or not -er: indicator

indices plural of INDEX.

indict »*verb* (**indicts**, **indicting**, **indicted**) formally accuse or charge someone with a serious crime.
– SAY in-**dyt**
indictable

 dict not dite: indict

indictment »*noun* ❶ a formal charge or accusation of a serious crime. ❷ an indication that something is bad and deserves to be condemned.
– SAY in-**dyt**-muhnt

indicts

indie [independent]

indifferent »*adjective* ❶ having no interest in or sympathy with something. ❷ not very good.

indifference
indifferently

indigenous »*adjective* originating or occurring naturally in a place; native.
– SAY in-**dij**-i-nuhss

 ☑ **gen** not **gin**: **indigenous**

indigent »*adjective* poor; needy.
– SAY **in**-di-juhnt

indigestible
indigestibility

 ☑ **-ible** not **-able**: **indigestible**

indigestion

indignant »*adjective* feeling or showing indignation.
indignantly

 ☑ **ant** not **ent**: **indignant**

indignation »*noun* annoyance caused by what is seen as unfair treatment.

indignity »*noun* (plural **indignities**) treatment that causes you to feel ashamed or embarrassed.

 ☑ plural: drop the **y** and add **ies**: **indignities**

indigo »*noun* a dark blue colour or dye.
– SAY **in**-di-goh

indirect
indirectly
indirectness

indirect speech »*noun* = REPORTED SPEECH.

indiscipline »*noun* lack of discipline.
indisciplined

 ☑ don't forget the **c**: **indiscipline**

indiscreet »*adjective* too ready to reveal things that should remain secret or private.
indiscreetly

 ☑ **creet** not **crete**: **indiscreet**

indiscretion »*noun* ❶ indiscreet behaviour. ❷ an indiscreet act or remark.

indiscriminate »*adjective* done or acting without careful judgement.
– SAY in-diss-**krim**-i-nuht
indiscriminately

indispensable »*adjective* absolutely necessary.
indispensability

 ☑ **-able** not **-ible**: **indispensable**

indisposed »*adjective* ❶ slightly unwell. ❷ unwilling.

indisposition »*noun* ❶ a slight illness. ❷ unwillingness.

indisputable »*adjective* unable to be challenged or denied.
indisputably

indissoluble »*adjective* unable to be destroyed; lasting.
– SAY in-dis-**sol**-yuu-b'l

 ☑ double **s**: **indissoluble**

indistinct »*adjective* not clear or sharply defined.
indistinctly

indistinguishable
indistinguishably

indium »*noun* a soft, silvery-white metallic chemical element, used in some alloys and semiconductor devices.
– SAY **in**-di-uhm

individual
individually

individualise another way of spelling INDIVIDUALIZE.

individualism »*noun* ❶ the quality of being independent and original. ❷ the belief that individual people should have freedom of action rather than be controlled by the state.
individualist
individualistic

individuality

individualize »*verb* (**individualizes**, **individualizing**, **individualized**) make something different to suit the needs of an individual person.

 ☑ many people prefer the alternative spellings **individualise**, **individualises**, etc.: both **s** and **z** spellings are correct

individually

indivisible »*adjective* ❶ unable to be divided or separated. ❷ (of a number) unable to be divided by another number exactly without leaving a remainder.
indivisibility

☑ **-ible** not **-able**: **indivisible**

indoctrinate »*verb* (**indoctrinates**, **indoctrinating**, **indoctrinated**) make someone accept a set of beliefs without considering any alternatives.
indoctrination

Indo-European »*adjective* relating to the family of languages spoken over most of Europe and Asia as far as northern India.

indolent »*adjective* lazy.
– say in-duh-luhnt
indolence
indolently

indomitable »*adjective* impossible to
defeat or subdue.
– say in-**dom**-i-tuh-b'l
indomitably

Indonesian

indoor

indoors

indubitable »*adjective* impossible to
doubt; unquestionable.
– say in-**dyoo**-bi-tuh-b'l
indubitably

induce »*verb* (**induces, inducing, induced**)
❶ persuade or influence someone to do
something. ❷ bring about or cause
something. ❸ bring on labour in
childbirth by drugs or other artificial
means.
inducer
inducible

induced

inducement »*noun* ❶ a thing that
persuades someone to do something. ❷ a
bribe.

inducer

induces

inducible

inducing

induct »*verb* (**inducts, inducting, inducted**)
introduce someone formally to a post or
organization.

inductance »*noun* (in physics) the property
of an electric conductor or circuit that
causes an electromotive force to be
generated by a change in the current
flowing.

 ance not ence: **inductance**

inducted

inducting

induction »*noun* ❶ the action of
introducing someone to a post or
organization. ❷ the action of inducing
something. ❸ a method of reasoning in
which a general rule or conclusion is
drawn from particular facts or examples.
❹ the production of an electric or
magnetic state in an object by bringing an
electrified or magnetized object close to
but not touching it. ❺ the drawing of the
fuel mixture into the cylinders of an
internal-combustion engine.

inductive »*adjective* ❶ using induction to
draw general conclusions from particular
instances. ❷ relating to electric or
magnetic induction.
inductively

inductor »*noun* a component of an
electrical circuit which possesses
inductance.

 -or not -er: **inductor**

inducts

indulge (verb: **indulges, indulging,
indulged**)

indulgence

indulgent »*adjective* readily allowing
someone to do or have whatever they
want or overlooking their faults.
indulgently

 ent not ant: **indulgent**

indulges

indulging

industrial
industrially

industrialise another way of spelling
INDUSTRIALIZE.

industrialism »*noun* a social system in
which industry forms the basis of the
economy.

industrialist »*noun* a person who owns or
controls an industrial business.

industrialize »*verb* (**industrializes,
industrializing, industrialized**) develop
industries in a country or region on a wide
scale.
industrialization

 many people prefer the alternative
spellings **industrialise, industrialises,**
etc., and **industrialisation**: both **s** and **z**
spellings are correct

industrially

industries

industrious »*adjective* hard-working.
industriously

industry »*noun* (plural **industries**) ❶ the
manufacture of goods in factories. ❷ a
branch of economic or commercial
activity. ❸ hard work.

 plural: drop the **y** and add **ies**:
industries

inebriate »*verb* (**inebriates, inebriating,
inebriated**) make someone drunk.
– say i-**nee**-bri-ayt
inebriation

inedible »*adjective* not fit for eating.
inedibility

ineducable »*adjective* considered incapable of being educated.
– SAY in-**ed**-yuu-kuh-b'l

ineffable »*adjective* too great or extreme to be expressed in words.
– SAY in-**ef**-fuh-b'l
ineffably

ineffective [not achieving what you want]
ineffectively
ineffectiveness

> ℹ️ **ineffective** and **ineffectual** do not mean exactly the same thing: **ineffective** means 'not having the effect that you want', whereas **ineffectual** also means 'not forceful enough to achieve what is wanted'

ineffectual »*adjective* ❶ not producing any or the desired effect. ❷ lacking the required forcefulness in a role or situation.
ineffectually

inefficient »*adjective* failing to make the best use of time or resources.
inefficiency
inefficiently

inelegant
inelegance
inelegantly

ineligible »*adjective* not eligible for a post or benefit.
ineligibility

> ☑️ -ible not -able: **ineligible**

ineluctable »*adjective* unable to be resisted or avoided; inescapable.
– SAY in-i-**luk**-tuh-b'l

inept »*adjective* lacking skill.
ineptitude
ineptly

inequality (plural **inequalities**)

> ☑️ plural: drop the **y** and add **ies**: **inequalities**

inequitable »*adjective* unfair; unjust.
inequitably

inequity »*noun* (plural **inequities**) lack of fairness or justice.

ineradicable »*adjective* unable to be destroyed or removed.
– SAY in-i-**rad**-i-kuh-b'l

inert »*adjective* ❶ lacking the ability or strength to move or act. ❷ not reacting chemically: *an inert gas.*
inertly
inertness

inertia »*noun* ❶ a tendency to do nothing or to remain unchanged. ❷ (in physics) a property of matter by which it remains in a state of rest or, if in motion, continues moving in a straight line, unless changed by an external force.
– SAY i-**ner**-shuh

inertly

inertness

inescapable
inescapably

inessential

inestimable »*adjective* too great to be measured.
inestimably

inevitable »*adjective* certain to happen; unavoidable.
inevitability
inevitably

inexact
inexactly

inexcusable
inexcusably

inexhaustible »*adjective* (of a supply) never ending because available in unlimited quantities.

> ☑️ -ible not -able: **inexhaustible**

inexorable »*adjective* ❶ impossible to stop or prevent. ❷ unable to be persuaded.
– SAY in-**ek**-suh-ruh-b'l
inexorability
inexorably

inexpensive
inexpensively

inexperience
inexperienced

inexpert
inexpertly

inexplicable »*adjective* unable to be explained.
– SAY in-ik-**splik**-uh-b'l or in-**ek**-spli-kuh-b'l
inexplicably

in extremis »*adverb* ❶ in an extremely difficult situation. ❷ at the point of death.
– SAY in ek-**stree**-miss

> ℹ️ a Latin phrase literally meaning 'at the outer limits'

inextricable »*adjective* impossible to untangle or separate.
– SAY in-**ek**-stri-kuh-b'l or in-ik-**strik**-uh-b'l
inextricably

infallible »*adjective* incapable of making mistakes or being wrong.

– **SAY** in-**fal**-li-b'l
infallibility
infallibly

infamous »*adjective* ❶ well known for some bad quality or deed. ❷ morally bad.
– **SAY** in-**fuh**-muhss
infamously
infamy

infancy

infant

infanticide »*noun* the killing of an infant.

infantile

infantry »*noun* soldiers who fight on foot.

infantryman (plural **infantrymen**)

infatuated »*adjective* having an intense passion for someone or something.
infatuation

infect »*verb* (**infects**, **infecting**, **infected**) ❶ pass to a person, animal, or plant a germ that causes disease. ❷ contaminate with something harmful. ❸ make someone share a particular feeling.
infection
infective

infectious »*adjective* ❶ (of a disease or germ) able to be passed on through the environment. ❷ liable to spread infection. ❸ likely to spread to or influence others.

infective

infects

infer »*verb* (**infers**, **inferring**, **inferred**) work something out from the information you have available.

> ℹ️ for an explanation of the difference between **imply** and **infer**, see the note at **IMPLY**

> ✅ double the **r** in **inferred** and **inferring**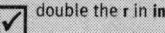

inference »*noun* ❶ a conclusion that you draw when you work something out from the information available to you. ❷ the process of working something out in this way.
– **SAY** in-**fuh**-ruhnss

> ✅ the ending is **ence** not **ance**: **inference**

inferior »*adjective* lower in quality or status (the opposite of *superior*).
» *noun* a person who is lower in status than someone else, or who is not as good at doing something.
inferiority

infernal »*adjective* ❶ having to do with hell or the underworld. ❷ (in informal English) terrible: *an infernal nuisance.*
infernally

inferno »*noun* (plural **infernos**) a large uncontrollable fire.

> ✅ the plural of **inferno**, an Italian word, has **os** not **oes**: **infernos**

inferred

inferring

infers

infertile
infertility

infest »*verb* (**infests**, **infesting**, **infested**) (especially of insects or rats) be present in large numbers so as to cause damage or disease.
infestation

infidel »*noun* (mainly a historical term) a person who has no religion or whose religion is not that of the majority.
– **SAY** in-**fi**-duhl

infidelity »*noun* (plural **infidelities**) the action or state of not being faithful to your partner.

infighting »*noun* conflict within a group or organization.

infiltrate »*verb* (**infiltrates**, **infiltrating**, **infiltrated**) ❶ enter or gain access to an organization or place secretly and gradually. ❷ filter into a place.
infiltration
infiltrator

infinite »*adjective* ❶ having no limits and impossible to measure. ❷ very great in amount or degree: *with infinite care.*
infinitely

infinitesimal »*adjective* extremely small.
– **SAY** in-fi-ni-**tess**-i-muhl
infinitesimally

infinities

infinitive »*noun* the basic uninflected form of a verb, normally occurring in English with the word *to* (as in *to see, to ask*).
– **SAY** in-**fin**-i-tiv

infinity »*noun* (plural **infinities**) ❶ the state or quality of being infinite. ❷ a very great number or amount. ❸ (in mathematics) a number greater than any quantity or countable number (written ∞).

infirm »*adjective* physically weak.

infirmary »*noun* (plural **infirmaries**) a place where sick people are cared for.

> ✅ plural: drop the **y** and add **ies**: **infirmaries**

infirmity »*noun* (plural **infirmities**) physical or mental weakness.

> ✅ plural: drop the **y** and add **ies**: **infirmities**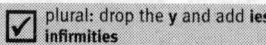

in flagrante delicto »*adverb* in the very act of wrongdoing.
– **say** in fluh-gran-tay di-**lik**-toh

> **i** **in flagrante delicto** is a Latin phrase literally meaning 'in flaming crime'

inflame »*verb* (**inflames, inflaming, inflamed**) **①** make someone feel something passionately. **②** make a difficult situation worse. **③** cause inflammation in a part of the body.

inflammable »*adjective* easily set on fire.
inflammability

> **i** the words **inflammable** and **flammable** both mean 'easily set on fire'. However, it is safer to use **flammable**, as the *in-* in **inflammable** can suggest that the word means 'non-flammable'.

inflammation »*noun* a condition in which an area of the skin is red, swollen, and hot.

> ✓ double m in **inflammation** and **inflammatory**

inflammatory »*adjective* **①** making people feel worked up and angry. **②** relating to or causing inflammation.

inflatable

inflate »*verb* (**inflates, inflating, inflated**) **①** expand something by filling it with air or gas. **②** increase something by a large amount. **③** increase price levels in an economy. **④** exaggerate: *you have a very inflated opinion of your worth.*

inflation »*noun* **①** the action of inflating or the condition of being inflated. **②** increase in the general level of prices in an economy.
inflationary

inflect »*verb* (**inflects, inflecting, inflected**) **①** (of a word) change by inflection. **②** vary the tone or pitch of the voice.

inflection »*noun* **①** a change in the form of a word to show a grammatical function or a quality such as tense, person, or number. **②** a variation in tone or pitch of the voice. **③** a change of curvature from convex to concave.

> ✓ -**flect**- not -**flex**-: **inflection**

inflects

inflexible »*adjective* **①** not able to be altered or adapted. **②** unwilling to change or compromise. **③** not able to be bent.
inflexibility
inflexibly

> ✓ -**ible** not -**able**: **inflexible**

inflict »*verb* (**inflicts, inflicting, inflicted**) (**inflict on**) **①** cause someone to feel something unpleasant or painful. **②** impose something unwelcome on someone.
infliction

> **i** do not confuse **inflict** with **afflict**, which means 'cause pain or suffering to', as in *his younger child was afflicted with a skin disease*

influence (verb: **influences, influencing, influenced**)

influential »*adjective* having great influence.
influentially

influenza »*noun* a highly contagious infection spread by a virus and causing fever, severe aching, and catarrh.

influx »*noun* (plural **influxes**) the arrival or entry of large numbers of people or things.

infomercial »*noun* an advertising film which promotes a product in an informative and supposedly objective style.

inform (verb: **informs, informing, informed**)

informal »*adjective* **①** relaxed, friendly, or unofficial. **②** (of clothes) suitable for everyday wear; casual. **③** referring to the language of everyday speech and writing, rather than that used in official situations.
informality
informally

informant »*noun* a person who gives information to another.

information

information technology »*noun* the study or use of computers and telecommunications for storing, retrieving, and sending information.

informative »*adjective* providing useful information.
informatively
informativeness

informed

informer

informing

informs

infraction »*noun* a breaking of a law or agreement.

infra dig »*adjective* beneath your dignity.
– **say** in-fruh dig

> **i** from the Latin phrase *infra dignitatem*, literally 'beneath dignity'

infrared »*noun* invisible electromagnetic radiation having a wavelength just greater than that of red light.
» *adjective* relating to such radiation.

infrastructure »*noun* the basic physical and organizational structures (e.g. buildings, roads, power supplies) needed for the operation of a society or enterprise.

> ✓ infra- not infer-: infrastructure

infrequent
infrequency
infrequently

infringe »*verb* (infringes, infringing, infringed) ❶ break a law, rule, or agreement. ❷ gradually intrude on a right or privilege.
infringement

infuriate »*verb* (infuriates, infuriating, infuriated) make someone irritated or angry.
– SAY in-**fyoor**-i-ayt
infuriating
infuriatingly

infuse »*verb* (infuses, infusing, infused) ❶ spread throughout something. ❷ soak tea, herbs, etc. to extract the flavour or healing properties.
infuser

infusion »*noun* ❶ a drink or extract prepared by infusing. ❷ the action of infusing.

ingenious »*adjective* clever, original, and inventive.
– SAY in-**jee**-ni-uhss
ingeniously

> ℹ️ do not confuse ingenious with ingenuous, which means 'innocent and unsuspecting'

ingenue »*noun* an innocent or naive young woman.
– SAY an-*zh*uh-nyoo

> ✓ ingenue can also be spelled ingénue, with an acute accent above the first e (as in the original French)

ingenuity »*noun* the quality of being ingenious.
– SAY in-ji-**nyoo**-i-ti

ingenuous »*adjective* innocent and unsuspecting.
– SAY in-**jen**-nyoo-uhss
ingenuously

> ℹ️ do not confuse ingenuous with ingenious, which means 'clever, original, and inventive'

ingest »*verb* (ingests, ingesting, ingested) take food or drink into the body by swallowing or absorbing it.
ingestion

inglenook »*noun* a space on either side of a large fireplace.

inglorious
ingloriously

ingoing »*adjective* going towards or into.

ingot »*noun* a rectangular block of steel, gold, or other metal.

> ✓ one g, one t: ingot

ingrain »*verb* (ingrains, ingraining, ingrained) firmly fix or establish a habit, belief, or attitude in a person.

> ✓ ingrain can also be spelled engrain

ingrained »*adjective* ❶ firmly established. ❷ (of dirt) deeply embedded.

> ✓ ingrained can also be spelled engrained

ingraining

ingrains

ingrate »*noun* an ungrateful person.
– SAY in-grayt

ingratiate »*verb* (ingratiates, ingratiating, ingratiated) (ingratiate yourself) do things in order to make someone like you.
– SAY in-**gray**-shi-ayt

ingratitude »*noun* a lack of appropriate gratitude.

ingredient »*noun* ❶ one of the substances that are combined to make a particular dish. ❷ a component part or element.

> ✓ ient not iant: ingredient

ingress »*noun* (plural ingresses) ❶ the action of entering. ❷ a place or means of access.
– SAY in-gress

ingrown »*adjective* (of a toenail) having grown into the flesh.
ingrowing

inhabit »*verb* (inhabits, inhabiting, inhabited) live in or occupy a place.
inhabitable

> ✓ do not double the t in inhabiting and inhabited

inhabitant »*noun* a person or animal that lives in or occupies a place.

inhabited

inhabiting

inhabits

inhalant »*noun* a medicine that is inhaled.

inhale »*verb* (**inhales, inhaling, inhaled**) breathe in air, gas, smoke, etc.
– SAY in-**hayl**
inhalation

inhaler »*noun* a portable device used for inhaling a drug.

inhales

inhaling

inhere »*verb* (**inheres, inhering, inhered**) (**inhere in**) exist in something as an essential or permanent part.

inherent »*adjective* existing in something as a permanent or essential quality.
– SAY in-**herr**-uhnt or in-**heer**-uhnt
inherently

 her not **heer**: in**her**ent

inheres

inhering

inherit »*verb* (**inherits, inheriting, inherited**) ❶ receive money, property, or a title from someone when they die. ❷ have a quality or characteristic passed on to you from your parents or ancestors. ❸ receive or be left with a situation or object from a former owner.
inheritor

 do not double the **t** in in**heriting** and in**herited**

inheritance »*noun* ❶ a thing that is inherited. ❷ the action of inheriting.

 ance not **ence**: inherit**ance**

inherited

inheriting

inheritor

inherits

inhibit »*verb* (**inhibits, inhibiting, inhibited**) ❶ prevent or slow down a process. ❷ make someone unable to act in a relaxed and natural way.
inhibited
inhibitor

 do not double the **t** in in**hibiting** and in**hibited**

inhibition »*noun* ❶ the action of inhibiting. ❷ a feeling that makes one unable to act in a relaxed and natural way.

inhibitor

inhibits

inhospitable »*adjective* ❶ (of an environment) harsh and difficult to live in.

❷ unwelcoming.
inhospitably

in-house »*adjective & adverb* within an organization.

inhuman »*adjective* ❶ lacking positive human qualities; cruel and barbaric. ❷ not human in nature or character.
inhumanly

inhumane »*adjective* without pity for misery or suffering; cruel.
inhumanely

inhumanity »*noun* (plural **inhumanities**) cruel and brutal behaviour.

inhumanly

inimical »*adjective* tending to obstruct or harm; hostile.
– SAY i-**nim**-i-k'l

inimitable »*adjective* impossible to imitate; unique.
– SAY i-**nim**-i-tuh-b'l
inimitably

iniquity »*noun* (plural **iniquities**) the quality of being unjust or wrong.
– SAY i-**ni**-kwi-ti
iniquitous

 plural: drop the **y** and add **ies**: iniquit**ies**

initial »*adjective* existing or occurring at the beginning.
»*noun* the first letter of a name or word.
»*verb* (**initials, initialling, initialled**) mark something with your initials as a sign of approval or agreement.
initially

 double the **l** in in**itialling** and in**itialled** (the spellings **initialing** and **initialed** are American)

initialled

initialling

initially

initials

initiate »*verb* (**initiates, initiating, initiated**) ❶ cause a process or action to begin. ❷ admit someone into a society or group with formal ceremony. ❸ (**initiate into**) introduce someone to a new activity or skill.
– SAY i-**ni**-shi-ayt
initiation

initiative »*noun* ❶ the ability to act independently and with a fresh approach. ❷ the power or opportunity to act before others do. ❸ a fresh approach to a problem.

inject (verb: **injects, injecting, injected**)
injector

injection

injector

injects

in-joke

injudicious »*adjective* showing poor judgement; unwise.
injudiciously

injunction »*noun* ❶ an order by a court of law stating that someone must or must not do something. ❷ a strong warning.

injure (verb: **injures, injuring, injured**)

injurious »*adjective* causing or likely to cause injury.
– **say** in-**joor**-i-uhss

injury (plural **injuries**)

> ☑ plural: drop the **y** and add **ies**: **injuries**

injustice

ink (verb: **inks, inking, inked**)

inkier

inkiest

inking

ink-jet printer »*noun* a printer in which the characters are formed by tiny jets of ink.

inkling »*noun* a slight suspicion; a hint.

inks

inkstand »*noun* a stand for ink bottles, pens, and other stationery items.

inkwell »*noun* a container for ink that fits into a hole in a desk.

inky (adjective: **inkier, inkiest**)

inlaid past and past participle of **INLAY**.

inland

inland revenue »*noun* (in the UK) the government department responsible for collecting income tax and some other taxes.

in-law

inlay »*verb* (**inlays, inlaying, inlaid**) fix pieces of a different material into a surface as a form of decoration.
» *noun* ❶ inlaid decoration. ❷ a material or substance used for inlaying.

inlet »*noun* ❶ a small arm of the sea, a lake, or a river. ❷ a place or means of entry.

in-line skate »*noun* a type of roller skate in which the wheels are fixed in a single line along the sole.

in loco parentis »*adverb & adjective* in the place of a parent.
– **say** in loh-koh puh-**ren**-tiss

> ℹ **in loco parentis** is a Latin phrase

inlying »*adjective* within or near a centre.
– **say** in-ly-ing

inmate »*noun* a person who lives in an institution such as a prison or hospital.

in memoriam »*preposition* in memory of a dead person.
– **say** in mi-**mor**-i-am

> ☑ the ending is **iam** not **ium**: **in memoriam** is a Latin phrase

inmost

inn

innards »*plural noun* ❶ internal organs. ❷ the internal workings of a device or machine.

innate »*adjective* inborn; natural.
– **say** in-**nayt**
innately

> ☑ double **n**: **innate**

inner

inner ear »*noun* the parts of the ear embedded in the bones of the skull, consisting of the semicircular canals and cochlea.

innermost

innings »*noun* (plural **innings**) one of the divisions of a game of cricket during which one side has a turn at batting.

innkeeper

innocent
innocence
innocently

innocuous »*adjective* not harmful or offensive.
– **say** in-**nok**-yoo-uhss
innocuously

Inn of Court »*noun* (in the UK) each of the four legal societies having the exclusive right of admitting people to the English bar.

innovate »*verb* (**innovates, innovating, innovated**) introduce new methods, ideas, or products.
– **say** in-nuh-vayt
innovator

> ☑ two **n**'s, one **v**: **innovate**

innovation »*noun* ❶ the action of innovating. ❷ a new method, idea, or product.

> double **n** at the beginning: **innovation**

innovative »*adjective* ❶ featuring new methods; original. ❷ (of a person) original and creative in thinking.
– **say** in-nuh-vuh-tiv

innovator

innuendo »*noun* (plural **innuendoes** or **innuendos**) a remark which makes an indirect reference to something.
– **say** in-yuu-**en**-doh

 inn- not **in-**: innuendo is a Latin word meaning 'by pointing to'. Spell the plural with **oes** or **os**: **innuendoes** or **innuendos**.

innumerable »*adjective* too many to be counted.

innumerate »*adjective* without a basic knowledge of mathematics and arithmetic.

inoculate »*verb* (**inoculates**, **inoculating**, **inoculated**) = VACCINATE.
– **say** i-**nok**-yuu-layt
inoculation

 one **n**, one **c**: **inoculate**

inoffensive
inoffensively
inoffensiveness

inoperable »*adjective* ❶ (of an illness) not able to be cured by a medical operation. ❷ not able to be used or operated.

inoperative »*adjective* not working or taking effect.

inopportune »*adjective* occurring at an inconvenient time.
inopportunely
inopportuneness

inordinate »*adjective* unusually large; excessive.
– **say** in-**or**-di-nuht
inordinately

inorganic »*adjective* ❶ not coming from a living organism. ❷ (in chemistry) referring to compounds which do not contain carbon.

inpatient »*noun* a patient who is staying day and night in a hospital while receiving treatment.

input »*noun* ❶ what is put or taken in by a system or process. ❷ a person's contribution. ❸ the action of putting data into a computer. ❹ a place or device from which energy or information enters a computer or other machine.
» *verb* (**inputs**, **inputting**, **input**) put data into a computer.

 double the **t** in **inputting**

inquest »*noun* ❶ an official inquiry to gather the facts relating to an incident. ❷ an inquiry by a coroner's court into the cause of a death.

inquire (verb: **inquires**, **inquiring**, **inquired**)
inquirer

ℹ traditionally, in British English, **inquire** means 'make a formal investigation', while **enquire** is used to mean simply 'ask'

inquiry (plural **inquiries**)

 plural: drop the **y** and add **ies**: **inquiries**

inquisition »*noun* ❶ a long period of intensive questioning or investigation. ❷ the verdict of a coroner's jury. ❸ (**Inquisition**) (a historical term) a tribunal established by the Pope in certain countries for the suppression of heresy.

inquisitive »*adjective* ❶ eager to find things out. ❷ prying.
inquisitively
inquisitiveness

inquisitor »*noun* a person conducting an inquisition.
– **say** in-**kwiz**-i-ter
inquisitorial

 -or not **-er**: **inquisitor**

inroad

inrush
inrushing

insane »*adjective* ❶ seriously mentally ill. ❷ extremely foolish; irrational.
insanely
insanity

insanitary »*adjective* so dirty as to be a danger to health.

insatiable »*adjective* impossible to satisfy.
– **say** in-**say**-shuh-b'l
insatiably

inscribe »*verb* (**inscribes**, **inscribing**, **inscribed**) ❶ write or carve words or symbols on a surface. ❷ write a dedication to someone in a book.

inscription »*noun* words or symbols inscribed on a monument, in a book, etc.

inscrutable »*adjective* impossible to understand or interpret.
– **say** in-**skroo**-tuh-b'l
inscrutability
inscrutably

insect

insecticide »*noun* a substance used for killing insects.

insectivore »*noun* an animal that feeds on insects.
– SAY in-**sek**-ti-vor
insectivorous SAY in-sek-**tiv**-uh-ruhss

insecure
insecurely
insecurity

inseminate »*verb* (**inseminates, inseminating, inseminated**) introduce semen into a woman or a female animal.
– SAY in-**sem**-i-nayt
insemination

insensate »*adjective* ❶ lacking physical sensation. ❷ lacking sympathy; unfeeling.

insensible »*adjective* ❶ unconscious. ❷ numb; without feeling.
insensibility
insensibly

> ☑ **-ible** not **-able**: **insensible**

insensitive
insensitively
insensitivity

inseparable
inseparably

insert (verb: **inserts, inserting, inserted**)

insertion

inserts

in-service »*adjective* (of training) intended to take place during the course of employment.

inset »*noun* ❶ a thing inserted. ❷ a small picture or map inserted within the border of a larger one.
»*verb* (**insets, insetting, inset**) put something in as an inset.

> ☑ double the **t** in **insetting**

inshore »*adjective* at sea but close to the shore.
»*adverb* towards or closer to the shore.

inside

insider

insidious »*adjective* proceeding in a gradual and harmful way.
– SAY in-**sid**-i-uhss
insidiously
insidiousness

insight »*noun* ❶ the ability to understand the truth about someone or something. ❷ an understanding of this kind.
insightful

insignia »*noun* (plural **insignia**) a badge or symbol indicating a person's rank, position, or membership of an organization.

> ℹ in Latin **insignia** is a plural noun, but in English it is treated as singular, with the plural also **insignia**

insignificant
insignificance
insignificantly

insincere
insincerely
insincerity

> ☑ **cere** not **sere**: **insincere**

insinuate »*verb* (**insinuates, insinuating, insinuated**) ❶ suggest something bad in an indirect and unpleasant way. ❷ (**insinuate yourself into**) move yourself gradually into a favourable position.
– SAY in-**sin**-yuu-ayt

insinuation »*noun* an unpleasant hint or suggestion.

insipid »*adjective* ❶ lacking flavour. ❷ lacking liveliness or interest.
– SAY in-**si**-pid
insipidly
insipidness

> ☑ only one **p**: **insipid**

insist (verb: **insists, insisting, insisted**)

insistent
insistence
insistently

> ☑ **ent** not **ant**: **insistent**

insisting

insists

in situ »*adverb & adjective* in the original or appropriate position.
– SAY in **sit**-yoo

> ℹ **in situ** is a Latin phrase

insofar

insole »*noun* ❶ a removable sole worn inside a shoe. ❷ the fixed inner sole of a boot or shoe.

insolent »*adjective* rude and disrespectful.
insolence
insolently

insoluble »*adjective* ❶ impossible to solve. ❷ (of a substance) unable to be dissolved.
insolubility

insolvent »*adjective* not having enough money to pay your debts.
insolvency

insomnia »*noun* the condition of being unable to sleep.
insomniac

insomuch

insouciant »*adjective* casually unconcerned.
– say in-**soo**-si-uhnt
insouciance
insouciantly

inspect (verb: inspects, inspecting, inspected)
inspection

inspector
inspectorate

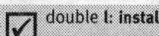 -or not -er: inspector

inspects

inspiration »*noun* ❶ the process of being inspired. ❷ a person or thing that inspires. ❸ a sudden clever idea.
inspirational

inspire »*verb* (inspires, inspiring, inspired) ❶ fill someone with the urge or ability to do or feel something. ❷ create a feeling in a person. ❸ give rise to something.
inspiring

inspired »*adjective* showing inspiration.

inspires

inspiring

instability (plural instabilities)

install »*verb* (installs, installing, installed) ❶ place or fix equipment in position ready for use. ❷ establish someone in a new place, condition, or role.

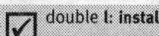 double l: install

installation »*noun* ❶ the action of installing. ❷ a large piece of equipment installed for use. ❸ a military or industrial establishment. ❹ an art exhibit constructed within a gallery.

installed

installing

installs

instalment »*noun* ❶ a sum of money due as one of several payments made over a period of time. ❷ one of several parts of something published or broadcast at intervals.

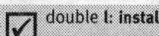 only one l: instalment (the spelling installment is American)

instance (verb: instances, instancing, instanced)

instant
instantly

instantaneous »*adjective* happening or done instantly.
– say in-stuhn-**tay**-ni-uhss
instantaneously

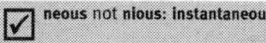 neous not nious: instantaneous

instantly

instead

instep »*noun* the part of a person's foot between the ball and the ankle.

instigate »*verb* (instigates, instigating, instigated) ❶ make something happen or come about. ❷ (instigate to or to do) encourage someone to do.
– say **in**-sti-gayt
instigation
instigator

instil »*verb* (instils, instilling, instilled) gradually but firmly establish an idea or attitude in someone's mind.
– say in-**stil**

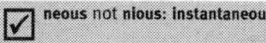 one l in instil and instils, two in instilling and instilled (the spellings instill and instills are American)

instinct »*noun* ❶ an inborn tendency to behave in a certain way. ❷ a natural ability or skill.
instinctual

instinctive »*adjective* based on instinct rather than thought or training.
instinctively

instinctual

institute »*noun* an organization for the promotion of science, education, etc.
»*verb* (institutes, instituting, instituted) ❶ begin or establish something. ❷ appoint someone to a position.

institution »*noun* ❶ an important organization or public body, such as a university or Church. ❷ an organization providing residential care for people with special needs. ❸ an established law or custom.

institutional »*adjective* having to do with or typical of an institution.
institutionally

institutionalize »*verb* (institutionalizes, institutionalizing, institutionalized) ❶ establish something as a usual thing in an organization or culture. ❷ place someone in a residential institution. ❸ (be or become institutionalized) suffer the ill effects of living for a long time in a residential institution.

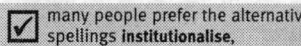 many people prefer the alternative spellings institutionalise,

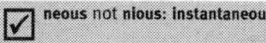

institutionalises, etc.: both **s** and **z**
spellings are correct

institutionally

instruct (verb: **instructs**, **instructing**,
instructed)

instruction

instructive »*adjective* useful and
informative.

instructor

 -or not -er: **instructor**

instructress (plural **instructresses**)

instructs

instrument

instrumental »*adjective* ❶ acting as a
means of achieving something. ❷ (of
music) performed on instruments.
» *noun* a piece of music performed by
instruments, with no vocals.
instrumentally

instrumentalist »*noun* a player of a
musical instrument.

instrumentation »*noun* ❶ the instruments
used in a piece of music. ❷ the
arrangement of a piece of music for
particular instruments.

insubordinate »*adjective* disobedient.
insubordination

insubstantial »*adjective* lacking strength
and solidity.
insubstantially

insufferable »*adjective* ❶ too extreme to
bear; intolerable. ❷ unbearably arrogant
or conceited.
insufferably

insufficient
insufficiency
insufficiently

insular »*adjective* ❶ isolated from outside
influences, and often narrow-minded as a
result. ❷ relating to or from an island.
insularity

 lar not **ler**: **insular**

insulate »*verb* (**insulates**, **insulating**,
insulated) ❶ place material between one
thing and another to prevent loss of heat
or intrusion of sound. ❷ cover something
with non-conducting material to prevent
electricity passing through it. ❸ protect
someone from something unpleasant.
insulator

insulation »*noun* ❶ the action of
insulating. ❷ material used to insulate
something.

insulator

insulin »*noun* a hormone produced in the
pancreas, which regulates glucose levels
in the blood, and the lack of which causes
diabetes.
– **say** in-**syuu**-lin

insult (verb: **insults**, **insulting**, **insulted**)

insuperable »*adjective* impossible to
overcome.
– **say** in-**syoo**-puh-ruh-b'l

insupportable
insupportably

insurable

insurance »*noun* ❶ the action of insuring.
❷ money paid to insure against something
or by an insurance company in the event
of damage, injury, etc. ❸ a thing
providing protection against a possible
event.

 on the difference between **insurance**
and **assurance**, see the note at
ASSURANCE

 ance not **ence**: **insurance**

insure »*verb* (**insures**, **insuring**, **insured**)
❶ arrange for financial compensation
should something be lost or damaged or
should someone be hurt or killed, in
exchange for regular payments to a
company. ❷ secure the payment of a sum
in this way. ❸ (**insure against**) protect
someone against a possible eventuality.
❹ = **ensure**.
insurable
insurer

 insure and **ensure** mean the same
thing in the general sense 'make
certain that something will occur or be so',
but only **insure** is used to refer to the
arranging of compensation in the event of
loss or damage

insurgency »*noun* (plural **insurgencies**) a
rising or revolt.

insurgent »*adjective* fighting against a
system or an authority.
» *noun* a rebel or revolutionary.
– **say** in-**ser**-juhnt

insuring

insurmountable »*adjective* too great to be
overcome.
– **say** in-ser-**mown**-tuh-b'l

insurrection »*noun* a violent uprising
against authority.
– **say** in-suh-**rek**-sh'n

 double r: **insurrection**

intact

intaglio »*noun* (plural **intaglios**) an incised or engraved design.
– SAY in-ta-li-oh

 the plural of **intaglio**, an Italian word, has **os** not **oes**: **intaglios**

intake

intangible »*adjective* ❶ not solid or real and therefore unable to be touched. ❷ vague and abstract.
» *noun* an intangible thing.
intangibility
intangibly

-**ible** not -**able**: **intangible**

integer »*noun* a whole number.
– SAY in-ti-jer

integral »*adjective* ❶ necessary to make a whole complete; fundamental. ❷ included as part of a whole.
» *noun* (in mathematics) a function of which a given function is the derivative, and which may express the area under the curve of a graph of the function.
– SAY in-ti-gruhl or in-**teg**-ruhl [adjective], **in**-ti-gruhl [noun]
integrally

integrate »*verb* (integrates, integrating, integrated) ❶ combine with something or be combined to form a whole. ❷ make someone accepted as part of a group.
– SAY in-ti-grayt

integrated circuit »*noun* an electronic circuit on a small piece of semiconducting material, performing the same function as a larger circuit of separate components.

integrates
integrating

integration »*noun* ❶ the action of integrating. ❷ the mixing of peoples or groups previously kept apart.

integrity »*noun* ❶ the quality of being honest, fair, and good. ❷ the state of being whole or unified. ❸ soundness of construction.
– SAY in-**teg**-ri-ti

intellect »*noun* the power of using your mind to reason and understand.

intellectual »*adjective* ❶ relating or appealing to the intellect. ❷ having a highly developed intellect.
» *noun* a person with a highly developed intellect.
intellectually

intellectual property »*noun* intangible property that is the result of creativity, e.g. patents or copyrights.

intelligence

intelligence quotient »*noun* a number representing a person's reasoning ability, 100 being average.

intelligent
intelligently

ent not **ant**: **intelligent**

intelligentsia »*noun* intellectuals or highly educated people.
– SAY in-tel-li-**jent**-si-uh

don't forget the **t**: **intelligentsia**

intelligible »*adjective* able to be understood.
– SAY in-**tel**-li-ji-b'l
intelligibility
intelligibly

-**ible** not -**able**: **intelligible**

intemperate »*adjective* lacking self-control.
intemperately

intend (verb: intends, intending, intended)

intense »*adjective* (intenser, intensest) ❶ of extreme force, degree, or strength. ❷ extremely earnest or serious.
intensely

 intense and **intensive** are similar in meaning, but they are used differently: **intense** is used to show how someone feels about something, as in *the course was intense*, while **intensive** describes something factually, as in *an intensive course* (a course designed to cover a lot of ground in a short time)

intensify »*verb* (intensifies, intensifying, intensified) make something or become more intense.
intensification
intensifier

intensity »*noun* (plural intensities) the quality of being intense.

intensive »*adjective* ❶ very thorough or vigorous. ❷ (of agriculture) aiming to achieve the highest possible yields within a limited area. ❸ concentrating on or making much use of something: *labour-intensive methods*.
intensively

on the difference between **intensive** and **intense**, see the note at **INTENSE**

intent »*noun* intention or purpose.
» *adjective* ❶ (intent on) determined to do. ❷ (intent on) attentively occupied with. ❸ showing earnest and eager attention.

intention

intentional
intentionally

intentioned

intently

inter »*verb* (inters, interring, interred) place a dead body in a grave or tomb.
– say in-ter

 do not confuse **inter** and **intern**: someone who is **interred** is buried, while someone who is **interned** is imprisoned

✓ double the r in **interring** and **interred**

interact »*verb* (interacts, interacting, interacted) (of two people or things) act so as to affect each other.
interaction

interactive »*adjective* ❶ influencing each other. ❷ (of a computer or other electronic device) allowing a two-way flow of information between it and a user.
interactively

interacts

inter alia »*adverb* among other things.
– say in-ter ay-li-uh

 inter alia is a Latin phrase

interbreed »*verb* (interbreeds, interbreeding, interbred) breed an animal with an animal of a different race or species.

intercede »*verb* (intercedes, interceding, interceded) intervene on behalf of another.

✓ **cede** not **sede**: inter**cede**

intercept »*verb* (intercepts, intercepting, intercepted) obstruct and prevent someone or something from continuing to a destination.
» *noun* ❶ an act of intercepting. ❷ (in mathematics) the point at which a line cuts the axis of a graph.
– say in-ter-sept [verb], in-ter-sept [noun]
interception
interceptor

✓ **cept** not **sept**: inter**cept**

intercession »*noun* ❶ the action of interceding. ❷ the saying of a prayer on behalf of another person.
intercessor

interchange (verb: interchanges, interchanging, interchanged)

interchangeable
interchangeability
interchangeably

intercity »*adjective* existing or travelling between cities.

intercom »*noun* an electrical device allowing one-way or two-way communication.

intercommunication

interconnect »*verb* (interconnects, interconnecting, interconnected) connect two things with each other.
interconnected
interconnection

intercontinental »*adjective* relating to or travelling between continents.

intercourse

intercut »*verb* (intercuts, intercutting, intercut) alternate scenes with contrasting scenes in a film.

✓ double the t in **intercutting**

interdenominational »*adjective* relating to more than one religious denomination.

interdepartmental »*adjective* relating to more than one department.

interdependent »*adjective* dependent on each other.
interdependence

interdisciplinary »*adjective* relating to more than one branch of knowledge.

interest (verb: interests, interesting, interested)
interested

interesting
interestingly

interests

interface »*noun* ❶ a point where two things meet and interact. ❷ a device or program enabling a user to communicate with a computer, or for connecting two items of hardware or software.
» *verb* (interfaces, interfacing, interfaced) (interface with) ❶ interact with something. ❷ (in computing) connect with something by an interface.

interfaith »*adjective* relating to or between different religions.

interfere (verb: interferes, interfering, interfered)
interfering

interference

interferes

interfering

intergalactic »*adjective* relating to or situated between galaxies.

407

407

intergovernmental » intern

intergovernmental »*adjective* relating to or conducted between governments.

interim »*noun* the time between two events.
» *adjective* lasting for a short time; provisional.
– SAY in-tuh-rim

one r, one m: **interim**

interior »*adjective* ❶ having to do with the inside of something. ❷ remote from the coast or frontier; inland.
» *noun* ❶ the interior part. ❷ the internal affairs of a country.

interject »*verb* (**interjects, interjecting, interjected**) say something suddenly as an interruption.
– SAY in-ter-**jekt**

interjection »*noun* an exclamation (e.g. *ah!*).

interlace »*verb* (**interlaces, interlacing, interlaced**) weave two things together.

interleave »*verb* (**interleaves, interleaving, interleaved**) ❶ insert blank leaves between the pages of a book. ❷ place something between the layers of something else.

interlink »*verb* (**interlinks, interlinking, interlinked**) join or connect things together.

interlock »*verb* (**interlocks, interlocking, interlocked**) (of two parts) engage with each other by overlapping or fitting together.
» *noun* a fabric with closely interlocking stitches allowing it to stretch.

interlocutor »*noun* a person who takes part in a conversation.
– SAY in-ter-**lok**-yuu-ter

-or not -er at the end: **interlocutor**

interlocutory »*adjective* relating to dialogue.
– SAY in-ter-**lok**-yuu-tuh-ri

interloper »*noun* a person who interferes in another's affairs; an intruder.

interlude »*noun* ❶ a period of time that contrasts with what goes before and after. ❷ a pause between the acts of a play. ❸ a piece of music played between other pieces or between the verses of a hymn.

intermarry »*verb* (**intermarries, intermarrying, intermarried**) (of people of different races, castes, or religions) become connected by marriage.
intermarriage

intermediary »*noun* (plural **intermediaries**) a person who tries to settle a dispute between others.
» *adjective* in the role of an intermediary.
– SAY in-ter-**mee**-di-uh-ri

plural: drop the **y** and add **ies**: **intermediaries**

intermediate »*adjective* ❶ coming between two things in time, place, character, etc. ❷ having more than basic knowledge or skills but not yet advanced.
» *noun* an intermediate person or thing.
– SAY in-ter-**mee**-di-uht

interment »*noun* the burial of a dead body in a grave or tomb.
– SAY in-ter-muhnt

only one r: **interment** (and not to be confused with **internment**)

intermezzo »*noun* (plural **intermezzi** or **intermezzos**) a short connecting instrumental movement between parts of an opera or other musical work, or between the acts of a play.
– SAY in-ter-**met**-soh [singular], in-ter-**met**-si [plural]

make the plural by adding **s** or, as in the original Italian, by changing the **o** ending to **i**: **intermezzos** or **intermezzi**

interminable »*adjective* endless.
interminably

intermingle »*verb* (**intermingles, intermingling, intermingled**) mix or mingle two or more things together.

intermission »*noun* ❶ a pause or break. ❷ an interval between parts of a play or film.

intermittent »*adjective* happening at irregular intervals.
intermittently

double t then **ent** not **ant** at the end: **intermittent**

intermix »*verb* (**intermixes, intermixing, intermixed**) mix two or more things together.

intern »*verb* (**interns, interning, interned**) confine someone as a prisoner.
» *noun* (in American English) ❶ a recent medical graduate receiving supervised training in a hospital. ❷ a student or trainee who does a job to gain work experience or for a qualification.
– SAY in-**tern** [verb], **in**-tern [noun]
internment
internship

do not confuse **intern** and **inter**: someone who is **interned** is a prisoner, while someone who is **interred** is a corpse

internal »*adjective* ❶ having to do with the inside of something. ❷ relating to affairs and activities within a country or organization. ❸ in your mind or soul.
internally

internal-combustion engine »*noun* an engine in which power is generated by the expansion of hot gases from the burning of fuel with air inside the engine.

internalize »*verb* (**internalizes, internalizing, internalized**) make a belief or attitude part of your behaviour or thinking.
internalization

✓ many people prefer the alternative spellings **internalise, internalises**, etc., and **internalisation**: both **s** and **z** spellings are correct

internally
international
internationally

International Date Line »*noun* an imaginary North–South line through the Pacific Ocean, to the east of which the date is a day earlier than it is to the west.

internationalise another way of spelling **INTERNATIONALIZE**.

internationalism »*noun* belief in cooperation and understanding between nations.
internationalist

internationalize »*verb* (**internationalizes, internationalizing, internationalized**) make something international.
internationalization

✓ many people prefer the alternative spellings **internationalise, internationalises**, etc., and **internationalisation**: both **s** and **z** spellings are correct

internationally

internecine »*adjective* (of conflict) taking place between members of a group.
– say in-ter-**nee**-syn

interned

internee »*noun* a prisoner.

Internet »*noun* an international information network linking computers.

interning
internment

ℹ️ **internment** means 'confinement as a prisoner' and should not be confused with **interment** meaning 'burial'

interns

internship

interpersonal »*adjective* relating to relationships between people.

interplanetary »*adjective* situated or travelling between planets.

✓ **ary** not **ery**: interplanetary

interplay »*noun* the way in which things interact.

Interpol »*noun* an international organization that coordinates investigations made by the police forces of member countries into international crimes.

interpolate »*verb* (**interpolates, interpolating, interpolated**) ❶ insert something different or additional. ❷ add a remark to a conversation. ❸ (in mathematics) insert an intermediate term into a series by estimating or calculating it from surrounding known values.
– say in-ter-puh-layt
interpolation

interpose »*verb* (**interposes, interposing, interposed**) ❶ insert something between one thing and another. ❷ intervene between parties.

interpret (verb: **interprets, interpreting, interpreted**)
interpretable
interpretative
interpretive

✓ do not double the **t** in **interpreting** and **interpreted**

interpretation

✓ **pret** not **pet**: interpretation

interpretative
interpreter
interpretive

interracial »*adjective* existing between or involving different races.

interred

interregnum »*noun* (plural **interregnums** or **interregna**) a period between regimes when normal government is suspended.
– say in-ter-**reg**-nuhm

✓ the plural can be either **interregna** (like the original Latin) or **interregnums**

interrelate »*verb* (**interrelates, interrelating, interrelated**) (of two people or things) relate or connect to one other.
interrelation

interring

interrogate »*verb* (interrogates, interrogating, interrogated) ask someone questions in a thorough or aggressive manner.
interrogation
interrogator

 two r's, one g: **interrogate**

interrogative »*adjective* in the form of a question or used in questions.
» *noun* a word used in questions, e.g. *how* or *what*.
– SAY in-ter-**rog**-uh-tiv

interrogator

interrogatory »*adjective* questioning.
– SAY in-ter-**rog**-uh-tuh-ri

interrupt (verb: interrupts, interrupting, interrupted)
interrupter
interruption

 double r: **interrupt**

inters

intersect »*verb* (intersects, intersecting, intersected) ❶ divide something by passing or lying across it. ❷ (of lines, roads, etc.) cross or cut each other.

intersection »*noun* a point at which two roads, lines, etc. intersect.

intersects

intersperse »*verb* (intersperses, interspersing, interspersed) scatter or place something among or between other things.

interstate »*adjective* existing or carried on between states.
» *noun* one of a system of motorways running between US states.

interstellar »*adjective* occurring or situated between stars.

interstice »*noun* a small intervening space.
– SAY in-ter-stiss
interstitial

intertwine »*verb* (intertwines, intertwining, intertwined) twist or twine two things together.

interval

intervene »*verb* (intervenes, intervening, intervened) come between two people or things so as to prevent or alter the result or course of events.
» *adjective* (intervening) occur or be between or among.

intervention »*noun* ❶ the action of intervening. ❷ interference by a state in another's affairs.

interventionist »*adjective* favouring intervention.
interventionism

interview (verb: interviews, interviewing, interviewed)
interviewee
interviewer

interwar »*adjective* existing in the period between two wars.

interweave »*verb* (interweaves, interweaving, interwove; past participle interwoven) weave two or more fibres or strands together.

intestate »*adjective* not having made a will before you die.
– SAY in-**tess**-tayt
intestacy

intestine »*noun* the long tubular organ leading from the end of the stomach to the anus.
intestinal

intestines »*plural noun* = INTESTINE.

intimacy »*noun* (plural intimacies) ❶ close familiarity or friendship. ❷ an intimate act or remark.

intimate[1] [close and friendly; private and personal]
– SAY in-ti-muht
intimately

intimate[2] »*verb* (intimates, intimating, intimated) say or suggest that something is the case: *he has intimated his decision to retire.*
– SAY in-ti-mayt
intimation

intimidate »*verb* (intimidates, intimidating, intimidated) frighten someone into doing something.
intimidation
intimidatory

into

intolerable »*adjective* unable to be endured.
intolerably

intolerant »*adjective* not willing to accept ideas or ways of behaving that are different to your own.
intolerance
intolerantly

 ant not ent: **intolerant**

intonation »*noun* ❶ the rise and fall of the voice in speaking. ❷ the action of intoning.

intone »*verb* (intones, intoning, intoned) say or recite something with little rise and fall of the pitch of the voice.

– SAY in-**tohn**

intoxicate »*verb* (intoxicates, intoxicating, intoxicated) ❶ (of alcoholic drink or a drug) cause someone to lose control of themselves. ❷ excite or exhilarate someone.
intoxication

intractable »*adjective* ❶ hard to solve or deal with. ❷ stubborn.
– SAY in-**trak**-tuh-b'l
intractability
intractably

intramural »*adjective* forming part of normal university or college studies.
– SAY in-truh-**myoor**-uhl

Intranet »*noun* a computer network for use within an organization, created with Internet software.
– SAY **in**-truh-net

intransigent »*adjective* refusing to change your views or behaviour.
– SAY in-**tran**-zi-juhnt
intransigence
intransigently

intransitive »*adjective* (of a verb) not taking a direct object, e.g. *look* in *look at the sky*, as opposed to *transitive*.
– SAY in-**tran**-zi-tiv

intrauterine »*adjective* within the womb.
– SAY in-truh-**yoo**-tuh-ryn

intrauterine device »*noun* a contraceptive device in the form of a coil, fitted inside the womb.

intravenous »*adjective* within or into a vein or veins.
– SAY in-truh-**vee**-nuhss
intravenously

 -ven- not -vein-: intravenous

intrepid »*adjective* fearless; adventurous.
– SAY in-**tre**-pid
intrepidity
intrepidly

intricacy »*noun* (plural intricacies) ❶ the quality of being intricate. ❷ (intricacies) details.
– SAY **in**-tri-kuh-si

 plural: drop the y and add ies: intricacies

intricate »*adjective* very complicated or detailed.
intricately

intrigue »*verb* (intrigues, intriguing, intrigued) ❶ arouse great curiosity in someone. ❷ plot something illegal or harmful.

» *noun* ❶ the plotting of something illegal or harmful. ❷ a secret love affair.
– SAY in-**treeg** [verb], **in**-treeg [noun]
intriguer
intriguing

 gue not ge: intrigue

intrinsic »*adjective* belonging to the basic nature of someone or something; essential.
– SAY in-**trin**-sik
intrinsically

introduce (verb: introduces, introducing, introduced)

introduction

introductory

introspection »*noun* the examination of your own thoughts or feelings.
introspective
introspectively

introvert »*noun* a shy, quiet person who is mainly concerned with their own thoughts and feelings.
» *adjective* having to do with an introvert.
introversion
introverted

 intro not intra: introvert

intrude (verb: intrudes, intruding, intruded)
intruder

intrusion »*noun* ❶ the action of intruding. ❷ a thing that intrudes.

intrusive »*adjective* intruding or tending to intrude.
intrusively
intrusiveness

intuit »*verb* (intuits, intuiting, intuited) understand or work something out by intuition.
– SAY in-**tyoo**-it

intuition »*noun* the ability to understand or know something immediately, without conscious reasoning.

intuitive »*adjective* having to do with intuition.
intuitively
intuitiveness

intuits

Inuit »*noun* ❶ (plural Inuit or Inuits) a member of a people of northern Canada and parts of Greenland and Alaska. ❷ the language of this people.
– SAY **in**-yuu-it or **in**-uu-it

 on the terms **Inuit** and **Eskimo**, see the note at **ESKIMO**

inundate »*verb* (inundates, inundating, inundated) ❶ flood a place. ❷ overwhelm someone with things to be dealt with.
– sᴀʏ in-uhn-dayt
inundation

 inun not **innun**: inundate

inure »*verb* (inures, inuring, inured) make someone used to something unpleasant.
– sᴀʏ i-nyoor

invade (verb: invades, invading, invaded) invader

invalid[1] »*noun* a person made weak or disabled by illness or injury.
»*verb* (invalids, invaliding, invalided) remove a person from active service in the armed forces because of injury or illness.
– sᴀʏ in-vuh-lid

invalid[2] »*adjective* ❶ not recognized in law. ❷ not true because based on incorrect information or unsound reasoning.
– sᴀʏ in-val-id

invalidate »*verb* (invalidates, invalidating, invalidated) make something invalid.
invalidation

invalided

invaliding

invalidity »*noun* ❶ the condition of being an invalid. ❷ the fact of being invalid.

invalids

invaluable »*adjective* extremely useful.
invaluably

invariable »*adjective* ❶ never changing. ❷ (in mathematics) (of a quantity) constant.
invariably

invasion

invasive »*adjective* ❶ tending to invade or intrude. ❷ (of medical procedures) involving the introduction of instruments or other objects into the body.

invective »*noun* strongly abusive or critical language.

inveigh »*verb* (inveighs, inveighing, inveighed) (inveigh against) speak or write about someone or something with great hostility.
– sᴀʏ in-vay

 veigh not **vey**: inveigh

inveigle »*verb* (inveigles, inveigling, inveigled) (inveigle someone into) persuade someone to do something by deceiving or flattering them.
– sᴀʏ in-vay-g'l

 veig not **veg**: inveigle

invent (verb: invents, inventing, invented) inventor

invention

inventive »*adjective* having or showing creativity or original thought.
inventively
inventiveness

inventor

 -or not **-er**: inventor

inventory »*noun* (plural inventories) ❶ a complete list of items. ❷ a quantity of goods in stock.
– sᴀʏ in-vuhn-tuh-ri

 plural: drop the **y** and add **ies**: inventories

invents

inverse »*adjective* opposite in position, direction, order, or effect.
»*noun* ❶ a thing that is the opposite or reverse of another. ❷ (in mathematics) a reciprocal quantity.
inversely

inverse proportion »*noun* a relation between two quantities such that one increases in proportion as the other decreases.

inversion »*noun* the action of inverting.

invert »*verb* (inverts, inverting, inverted) put something upside down or in the opposite position, order, or arrangement.

invertebrate »*noun* an animal having no backbone, such as an insect, mollusc, etc.
»*adjective* relating to such animals.
– sᴀʏ in-ver-ti-bruht

teb not **tib** or **tab**: invertebrate

inverted

inverted comma »*noun* a quotation mark.

inverting

inverts

invest (verb: invests, investing, invested) investor

investigate (verb: investigates, investigating, investigated)
investigation
investigator

investigative »*adjective* ❶ having to do with investigating. ❷ (of journalism or a journalist) investigating and seeking to expose dishonesty or injustice.
– sᴀʏ in-vess-ti-guh-tiv

investigator

-or not **-er: investigator**

investing

investiture »*noun* ❶ the action of formally investing a person with honours or rank. ❷ a ceremony at which this takes place.
– SAY in-**vess**-ti-cher

investment

investor

 -or not **-er: investor**

invests

inveterate »*adjective* ❶ having a long-standing and firmly established habit. ❷ (of a feeling or habit) firmly established.
– SAY in-**vet**-uh-ruht

invidious »*adjective* unacceptable, unfair, and likely to arouse resentment or anger in others.
– SAY in-**vid**-i-uhss
invidiously

invigilate »*verb* (invigilates, invigilating, invigilated) supervise candidates during an examination.
– SAY in-**vij**-i-layt
invigilation
invigilator

 -vigil- (not **-vidul-**) in the middle, with one g and one l: **invigilate**

invigorate »*verb* (invigorates, invigorating, invigorated) give someone strength or energy.
– SAY in-**vig**-uh-rayt
invigorating
invigoration

 one g, one r, and no u: **invigorate**

invincible »*adjective* too powerful to be defeated or overcome.
– SAY in-**vin**-si-b'l
invincibility
invincibly

 -ible not **-able: invincible**

inviolable »*adjective* never to be attacked or dishonoured.
– SAY in-**vy**-uh-luh-b'l
inviolability

inviolate »*adjective* free from injury or violation.
– SAY in-**vy**-uh-luht

invisible

 -ible not **-able: invisible**

invitation

invite (verb: invites, inviting, invited)
invitee

inviting »*adjective* tempting or attractive.
invitingly

in vitro »*adjective & adverb* (of biological processes) taking place in a test tube or elsewhere outside a living organism.
– SAY in **vee**-troh

 in vitro is Latin for 'in glass'. The opposite is **in vivo** (SAY in **vee**-voh), meaning 'in a living organism'.

invocation »*noun* ❶ the action of invoking. ❷ an appeal to a god or spirit.
– SAY in-vuh-**kay**-sh'n

invoice »*noun* a list of goods or services provided, with a statement of the payment that is due.
»*verb* (invoices, invoicing, invoiced) send an invoice to someone.

invoke »*verb* (invokes, invoking, invoked) ❶ appeal to someone or something as an authority or in support of an argument. ❷ call on a god or spirit. ❸ call earnestly for something.
– SAY in-**vohk**

involuntary
involuntarily

tary not **try: involuntary**

involve (verb: involves, involving, involved)
involvement

involved »*adjective* ❶ connected. ❷ difficult to comprehend; complicated.

involvement

involves

involving

invulnerable »*adjective* impossible to harm or damage.
invulnerability

inward
inwardly

inward-looking

inwardly

inwards

in-your-face »*adjective* blatantly aggressive or provocative.

iodide »*noun* a compound of iodine with another element or group.
– SAY **I**-uh-dyd

iodine »*noun* ❶ a black, non-metallic chemical element of the halogen group. ❷ an antiseptic solution of iodine in alcohol.
– SAY **I**-uh-deen

ion »*noun* an atom or molecule with a net electric charge through loss or gain of electrons.
– **SAY** I-uhn
ionic

Ionic »*adjective* relating to a style of classical architecture distinguished by columns with scrolls at the top.
– **SAY** I-on-ik

ionize »*verb* (ionizes, ionizing, ionized) convert an atom, molecule, or substance into an ion or ions.
– **SAY** I-uh-nyz
ionization

> ✓ many people prefer the alternative spellings **ionise, ionises,** etc., **ionisation,** and **ioniser:** both **s** and **z** spellings are correct

ionizer »*noun* a device which produces ions, especially one used to improve the quality of the air in a room.

ionosphere »*noun* the layer of the atmosphere above the mesosphere.
– **SAY** I-on-uh-sfeer

iota »*noun* ❶ the ninth letter of the Greek alphabet (I, ι). ❷ an extremely small amount.
– **SAY** I-oh-tuh

IOU »*noun* a signed document acknowledging a debt.

> ℹ from *I owe you*

ipso facto »*adverb* by that very fact or act.
– **SAY** ip-soh fak-toh

> ℹ **ipso facto** is a Latin phrase

IQ »*abbreviation* intelligence quotient.

IRA »*abbreviation* Irish Republican Army.

Iranian

Iraqi (plural **Iraqis**)

irascible »*adjective* hot-tempered; irritable.
– **SAY** i-rass-i-b'l
irascibility

> ✓ **sc** in the middle, and **-ible** not **-able** at the end: **irascible**

irate »*adjective* extremely angry.
– **SAY** I-rayt
irately

> ✓ only one **r: irate**

ire »*noun* anger.

iridescent »*adjective* showing bright colours that seem to change when seen from different angles.
– **SAY** i-ri-dess-uhnt
iridescence

> ✓ just one **r** and do not forget the **c:** iridescent

iridium »*noun* a hard, dense silvery-white metallic element.
– **SAY** i-rid-i-uhm

iris »*noun* (plural **irises**) ❶ the round coloured part of the eye, with the pupil in the centre. ❷ a plant with sword-shaped leaves and purple, yellow, or white flowers.

Irish
Irishness

Irish coffee »*noun* coffee mixed with a dash of Irish whisky.

Irishman (plural **Irishmen**)

Irishness

Irish stew »*noun* a stew made with mutton, potatoes, and onions.

Irishwoman (plural **Irishwomen**)

irk »*verb* (irks, irking, irked) irritate someone.
irksome

iron (verb: irons, ironing, ironed)

Iron Age »*noun* a period that came after the Bronze Age when weapons and tools came to be made of iron.

Iron Curtain »*noun* (the Iron Curtain) an imaginary barrier separating the former Soviet bloc and the West before communism in eastern Europe ended.

ironed

ironic »*adjective* ❶ the use of words that say the opposite of what you really mean in order to make a point. ❷ the strange or amusing aspect of a situation that is the opposite to one you had expected.
– **SAY** I-ron-ik
ironical
ironically

ironies

ironing

ironmonger »*noun* a person who sells tools and other hardware.
ironmongery

irons

ironworks

irony »*noun* (plural **ironies**) ❶ the use of words that say the opposite of what you really mean in order to make a point. ❷ the strange or amusing aspect of a situation that is opposite to one you had expected.
– **SAY** I-ruh-ni

> ℹ **irony** and **sarcasm** do not mean exactly the same thing: **irony** is generally used in a gentle or humorous

way, whereas **sarcasm** tends to be used to mock someone or show contempt

> ☑ plural: drop the **y** and add **ies: ironies**

irradiate »*verb* (**irradiates, irradiating, irradiated**) ❶ expose someone to radiation. ❷ shine light on something.
irradiation

irrational »*adjective* not logical or reasonable.
irrationality
irrationally

irreconcilable »*adjective* ❶ incompatible. ❷ not able to be settled: *irreconcilable differences.*
irreconcilably

irrecoverable »*adjective* not able to be recovered or remedied.
irrecoverably

irredeemable »*adjective* not able to be saved, improved, or corrected.
irredeemably

irredentist »*noun* a person who argues for the restoration to their country of any territory that formerly belonged to it.
– **say** ir-ri-**den**-tist

irreducible »*adjective* not able to be reduced or simplified.
irreducibly

irrefutable »*adjective* impossible to deny or disprove.
– **say** ir-**ref**-yuu-tuh-b'l or ir-ri-**fyoo**-tuh-b'l
irrefutably

irregular
irregularly

> ☑ **ar** not **er: irregular**

irregularity (plural **irregularities**)

> ☑ plural: drop the **y** and add **ies: irregularities**

irregularly
irrelevant
irrelevance
irrelevantly

> ☑ **ant** not **ent: irrelevant**

irreligious »*adjective* indifferent or hostile to religion.

irremediable »*adjective* impossible to remedy.
– **say** ir-ri-**mee**-di-uh-b'l

irreparable »*adjective* impossible to put right or repair.
– **say** ir-**rep**-uh-ruh-b'l
irreparably

> ☑ **par** not **pair: irreparable**

irreplaceable »*adjective* impossible to replace if lost or damaged.
irreplaceably

irrepressible »*adjective* not able to be restrained.
irrepressibly

irreproachable »*adjective* blameless and impossible to criticize.

irresistible »*adjective* too tempting or powerful to be resisted.
irresistibly

> ☑ **-ible** not **-able: irresistible**

irresolute »*adjective* uncertain.
irresolutely

irrespective »*adjective* (**irrespective of**) regardless of.
irrespectively

irresponsible
irresponsibility
irresponsibly

irretrievable »*adjective* not able to be brought back or made right.
irretrievably

irreverent »*adjective* disrespectful.
irreverence
irreverently

irreversible »*adjective* impossible to be reversed or altered.
irreversibility
irreversibly

irrevocable »*adjective* not able to be changed, reversed, or recovered.
– **say** ir-**rev**-uh-kuh-b'l
irrevocably

irrigate »*verb* (**irrigates, irrigating, irrigated**) supply water to land or crops through channels.
irrigation

irritable
irritability
irritableness
irritably

> ☑ **-able** not **-ible: irritable**

irritant »*noun* ❶ a substance that irritates the skin or a part of the body. ❷ a source of continual annoyance.

> ☑ **ant** not **ent: irritant**

irritate (verb: **irritates, irritating, irritated**)
irritating
irritatingly
irritation

irrupt »*verb* (irrupts, irrupting, irrupted) enter forcibly or suddenly.
– **say** ir-**rupt**
irruption

> ℹ do not confuse **irrupt** with **erupt**, which means 'break out suddenly'

is

ISA »*abbreviation* individual savings account.

isinglass »*noun* a kind of gelatin obtained from fish.
– **say** I-zing-glahs

Islam »*noun* ❶ the religion of the Muslims, regarded by them to have been revealed through Muhammad as the Prophet of Allah. ❷ the Muslim world.
– **say** iz-lahm

Islamic »*adjective* relating to Islam.
– **say** iz-**lam**-ik

island
islander

isle »*noun* an island.

islet »*noun* a small island.
– **say** I-lit

isn't [is not]

> ✓ be careful to put the apostrophe where a letter has been left out, that is between the **n** and **t** of **not**: **isn't**

isobar »*noun* a line on a map that connects points having the same atmospheric pressure.
– **say** I-soh-bar

isolate (verb: isolates, isolating, isolated)
isolated

> ✓ **is**- not **iss**-: **isolate**

isolation

isolationism »*noun* a policy of remaining apart from the political affairs of other countries.
isolationist

isomer »*noun* (in chemistry) one of two or more compounds with the same formula but a different arrangement of atoms and different properties.
– **say** I-suh-mer

isometric »*adjective* having equal dimensions.

isosceles »*adjective* (of a triangle) having two sides of equal length.
– **say** I-**soss**-i-leez

> ✓ do not forget the **c** in the middle: **isosceles**

isotherm »*noun* a line on a map that connects points having the same temperature.
– **say** I-soh-therm
isothermal

isotonic »*adjective* (of liquid) containing essential salts and minerals in the same concentration as in the body.
– **say** I-soh-**ton**-ik

isotope »*noun* (in physics) one of two or more forms of the same element that contain equal numbers of protons but different numbers of neutrons in their nuclei.
– **say** I-suh-tohp
isotopic

ISP »*abbreviation* Internet service provider.

Israeli (plural Israelis)

> ℹ do not confuse **Israeli** with **Israelite**: an **Israeli** is a person from the modern state of Israel but an **Israelite** was a member of the ancient Hebrew nation

> ✓ the plural of **Israeli** has **is** not **ies** at the end: **Israelis**

Israelite

issue (verb: issues, issuing, issued)

isthmus »*noun* (plural isthmuses) a narrow strip of land with sea on either side, linking two larger areas of land.
– **say** isth-muhss or ist-muhss

> ✓ do not forget the **h** in the middle: **isthmus**

IT »*abbreviation* information technology.

it

Italian

Italianate »*adjective* Italian in character or appearance.

italic »*adjective* (of a typeface) sloping to the right, used especially for emphasis and in foreign words.
»*noun* an italic typeface or letter.
– **say** i-**tal**-ik

italicize »*verb* (italicizes, italicizing, italicized) print text in italics.

> ✓ many people prefer the alternative spellings **italicise**, **italicises**, etc.: both **s** and **z** spellings are correct

itch (verb: itches, itching, itched)

itchy (adjective: itchier, itchiest)
itchiness

it'd [it had; it would]

item

itemize »*verb* (itemizes, itemizing, itemized) present a quantity as a list of individual items or parts.

 many people prefer the alternative spellings **itemise**, **itemises**, etc.: both **s** and **z** spellings are correct

iterate »*verb* (**iterates, iterating, iterated**) do or say something repeatedly.
– SAY **it**-uh-rayt
iteration

itinerant »*adjective* travelling from place to place.
» *noun* an itinerant person.
– SAY I-**tin**-uh-ruhnt

itinerary »*noun* (plural **itineraries**) a planned route or journey.
– SAY I-**tin**-uh-ruh-ri

 note that the ending is **-erary**, not **-ery**: **itinerary**
plural: drop the **y** and add **ies**: **itineraries**

it'll [it shall; it will]

its [belonging to a thing or person]

[i] do not confuse **its** meaning 'belonging to a thing, or to a child or animal whose sex is not specified' (as in *turn the camera on its side*) with the form **it's** (short for either **it is** or **it has**, as in *it's my fault*; *it's hot today*)

it's [it is; it has]

itself

itsy-bitsy

IUD »*abbreviation* intrauterine device.

I've [I have]

IVF »*abbreviation* in vitro fertilization.

ivies

Ivorian [of the Ivory Coast]

ivory »*noun* (plural **ivories**) ❶ the hard creamy-white substance of which elephants' or walruses' tusks are made. ❷ the creamy-white colour of ivory. ❸ (**the ivories**) the keys of a piano.

[✓] plural: drop the **y** and add **ies**: **ivories**

ivory tower »*noun* a situation in which someone leads a privileged life and does not have to face normal difficulties.

ivy »*noun* (plural **ivies**) an evergreen climbing plant, typically with five-pointed leaves.

Ivy League »*noun* a group of long-established universities in the eastern US.

Jj

jab (verb: **jabs, jabbing, jabbed**)

[✓] double the **b** to spell **jabbing** and **jabbed**

jabber (verb: **jabbers, jabbering, jabbered**)

jabbing

jabot »*noun* a ruffle on the front of a shirt or blouse.
– SAY **zha**-boh

[✓] note the **ot** ending: **jabot** is a French word, and the **t** is silent

jabs

jacaranda »*noun* a tropical American tree which has blue trumpet-shaped flowers and fragrant wood.
– SAY ja-kuh-**ran**-duh

jack (verb: **jacks, jacking, jacked**)

jackal »*noun* a wild dog that often hunts or scavenges in packs.
– SAY ja-kuhl

 al not **all**: **jackal**

jackass »*noun* (plural **jackasses**) ❶ a stupid person. ❷ a male ass or donkey.

jackboot »*noun* a leather military boot reaching to the knee.

jackdaw »*noun* a small grey-headed crow, noted for its inquisitiveness.

jacked

jacket

Jack Frost »*noun* a figure representing frost.

jackhammer »*noun* a portable pneumatic hammer or drill.

jacking

jack-in-the-box (plural **jack-in-the-boxes**)

jackknife »*noun* (plural **jackknives**) ❶ a large knife with a folding blade. ❷ a dive in which the body is bent at the waist and then straightened.

» verb (**jackknifes, jackknifing, jackknifed**) ❶ move your body into a bent or doubled-up position. ❷ (of an articulated vehicle) bend into a V-shape in an uncontrolled skidding movement.

jack-o'-lantern »*noun* a lantern made from a hollowed-out pumpkin or turnip in which holes are cut to resemble a face.

jack plug »*noun* a plug consisting of a single shaft used to make a connection which transmits a signal.

jackpot

jackrabbit »*noun* a North American prairie hare.

Jack Russell »*noun* a small terrier with short legs.

jacks

Jacobean »*adjective* having to do with the reign of James I of England (1603–1625).
– say jak-uh-**bee**-uhn

> **ean** not **ian**: Jacob**ean**

Jacobin »*noun* ❶ (a historical term) a member of a radical democratic club formed in Paris in 1789. ❷ an extreme political radical.
– say **jak**-uh-bin
Jacobinism

Jacobite »*noun* a supporter of the deposed James II and his descendants in their claim to the British throne.
– say **jak**-uh-byt

jacquard »*noun* ❶ a loom used for the weaving of patterned and brocaded fabrics. ❷ a fabric made on a jacquard loom.
– say ja-**kard** or ja-**kuhd**

jacuzzi »*noun* (plural **jacuzzis**) (trademark) a large, wide bath having jets of water to massage the body.
– say juh-**koo**-zi

> ℹ️ named after the Italian-born American inventor Candido *Jacuzzi*

> single **c** but double **z**: ja**cuzzi**

jade »*noun* a hard bluish-green precious stone.

jaded »*adjective* tired out or lacking enthusiasm after having had too much of something.

jag »*verb* (**jags, jagging, jagged**) stab, pierce, or prick something.
»*noun* a sharp projection.

jagged
jaggedly
jaggedness

jagging

jags

jaguar »*noun* a large cat with a yellowish-brown coat with black spots, found mainly in Central and South America.
– say **jag**-yuu-er

jail (verb: **jails, jailing, jailed**)
jailer

> ✓ **jail** can also be spelled **gaol**: both spellings are correct

jailbait »*noun* (in informal English) a sexually attractive young woman who is too young to have sex legally.

jailbird »*noun* (in informal English) a person who is or has often been in prison.

jailbreak
jailed
jailer
jailhouse
jailing
jails

Jain »*noun* a member of an Indian religion founded in the 6th century BC, characterized by non-violence and self-discipline.
– say jayn
Jainism

jalapeno »*noun* (plural **jalapenos**) a very hot green chilli pepper.
– say hal-uh-**pay**-nyoh

> ✓ **jalapeno** can also be spelled **jalapeño**, with a tilde over the **n** (as in the original Spanish)
> the plural of **jalapeno** has **os** not **oes**: jalapen**os**

jalopy »*noun* (plural **jalopies**) (in informal English) an old car in a very poor condition.
– say juh-**lop**-i

jalousie »*noun* a blind or shutter made of a row of angled slats.
– say **zha**-loo-zee

jam (verb: **jams, jamming, jammed**)

> ✓ double the **m** to spell **jamming** and **jammed**

Jamaican [of Jamaica]

jamb »*noun* a side post of a doorway, window, or fireplace.
– say jam

jamboree »*noun* a lavish or noisy celebration or party.
– say jam-buh-**ree**

jammed
jamming
jammy

jam-packed

jams

jangle (verb: **jangles, jangling, jangled**)
jangly

janitor »*noun* a caretaker of a building.
– say jan-i-ter

> ✓ -or not -er: **janitor**

January

japan »*noun* a black glossy varnish of a type that originally came from Japan.
» *verb* (**japans, japanning, japanned**) cover a surface with japan.

> ✓ double the **n** to spell **japanning** and **japanned**

Japanese (plural **Japanese**)

japanned

japanning

japans

jape »*noun* a practical joke.

japonica »*noun* an Asian shrub with bright red flowers and edible fruits.
– say juh-pon-i-kuh

jar (verb: **jars, jarring, jarred**)

> ✓ double the **r** to spell **jarring** and **jarred**

jardiniere »*noun* an ornamental pot or stand for displaying plants.
– say *zh*ah-din-yair

> ✓ **jardiniere** can also be spelled **jardinière**, with a grave accent on the first **e** (as in the original French)

jargon »*noun* words or expressions used by a particular group that are difficult for others to understand.

jarred

jarring

jars

jasmine »*noun* a shrub or climbing plant with fragrant flowers.

jasper »*noun* a reddish-brown variety of quartz.

jaundice »*noun* ❶ a condition in which someone's skin takes on a yellow colour, due to a bile disorder. ❷ bitterness or resentment.
– say jawn-diss
jaundiced

jaunt »*noun* a short trip taken for pleasure.

jaunty »*adjective* (**jauntier, jauntiest**) having a lively and self-confident manner.
jauntily
jauntiness

javelin »*noun* a long spear thrown in a competitive sport or as a weapon.

jaw (verb: **jaws, jawing, jawed**)

jawbone

jaw-dropping

jawed

jawing

jawless

jaws

jay »*noun* a noisy bird of the crow family with boldly patterned plumage.

jaywalk »*verb* (**jaywalks, jaywalking, jaywalked**) walk in or across a road without regard for approaching traffic.
jaywalker

jazz (verb: **jazzes, jazzing, jazzed**)

jazzy »*adjective* (**jazzier, jazziest**) ❶ of or in the style of jazz. ❷ bright, colourful, and showy.

jealous
jealously
jealousy

jeans

jeep »*noun* (trademark) a sturdy motor vehicle with four-wheel drive.

jeer (verb: **jeers, jeering, jeered**)

Jehovah »*noun* a form of the Hebrew name of God used in some translations of the Bible.
– say ji-hoh-vuh

> ✓ note the **h** at the end: **Jehovah**

Jehovah's Witnesses »*plural noun* a Christian sect that denies many traditional Christian doctrines and preaches the Second Coming.

jejune »*adjective* ❶ naive and simplistic. ❷ (of ideas or writings) dull.
– say ji-joon

Jekyll and Hyde »*noun* a person displaying alternately good and evil personalities.
– say je-kuhl

> ℹ from Robert Louis Stevenson's story *The Strange Case of Dr Jekyll and Mr Hyde*

jell »*verb* (**jells, jelling, jelled**) ❶ (of jelly or a similar substance) set or become firmer. ❷ take definite form or begin to work well.

> ✓ **jell** can also be spelled **gel**: both spellings are correct

jelly (plural **jellies**; verb: **jellies, jellying, jellied**)

jellyfish »*noun* a marine animal with a soft jelly-like body that has stinging tentacles around the edge.

jemmy »*noun* (plural **jemmies**) a short crowbar.
» *verb* (**jemmies, jemmying, jemmied**) force open a window or door with a jemmy.

je ne sais quoi »*noun* a quality that cannot be easily identified.
– SAY *zh*uh nuh say **kwah**

> i from a French phrase meaning 'I do not know what'

jenny »*noun* (plural **jennies**) a female donkey or ass.

jeopardize »*verb* (**jeopardizes, jeopardizing, jeopardized**) risk harming or destroying something.
– SAY **jep**-er-dyz

> ✓ many people prefer the alternative spellings **jeopardise, jeopardises**, etc.: both **s** and **z** spellings are correct
> **jeop** not **jep: jeopardize**

jeopardy »*noun* danger of loss, harm, or failure.
– SAY **jep**-er-di

jerboa »*noun* a rodent with very long hind legs that lives in the desert.
– SAY jer-**boh**-uh or **jer**-boh-uh

jeremiad »*noun* a long list of your troubles.
– SAY je-ri-**my**-ad

> i referring to the Lamentations of Jeremiah in the Old Testament

jerk (verb: **jerks, jerking, jerked**)

jerkier

jerkiest

jerkily

jerkin »*noun* a sleeveless jacket.

jerkiness

jerking

jerks

jerky (adjective: **jerkier, jerkiest**)
jerkily
jerkiness

jeroboam »*noun* a wine bottle with a capacity four times larger than that of an ordinary bottle.
– SAY jer-uh-**boh**-uhm

> i named after *Jeroboam*, a king of Israel in the Bible

Jerry »*noun* (plural **Jerries**) (old-fashioned) a German or Germans collectively.

jerry-built »*adjective* badly or hastily built.

jerrycan »*noun* a large flat-sided metal container for storing or carrying liquids.

jersey (plural **jerseys**)

> ✓ the plural of **jersey** simply adds an **s**: **jerseys**

Jerusalem artichoke »*noun* a knobbly root vegetable with white flesh.

jest »*noun* a joke.
» *verb* (**jests, jesting, jested**) speak or act in a joking manner.

jester »*noun* (a historical term) a man who entertained the king and queen and others in a medieval court by telling jokes.

jesting

jests

Jesuit »*noun* a member of the Society of Jesus, a Roman Catholic order of priests.
– SAY **jez**-yuu-it

Jesuitical »*adjective* having to do with the Jesuits.

Jesus

jet[1] (verb: **jets, jetting, jetted**) [spurt out; a rapid stream of liquid]

> ✓ double the **t** when spelling **jetting** and **jetted**

jet[2] »*noun* ❶ a hard black semi-precious mineral. ❷ a glossy black colour.

jete »*noun* (in ballet) a spring from one foot to the other, with the following leg extended backwards while in the air.
– SAY *zh*e-tay or *zh*uh-**tay**

> ✓ **jete** can also be spelled **jeté**, with an acute accent on the second **e** (as in the original French)

jet engine »*noun* an engine which drives an aircraft forward by sending out behind it a high-speed jet of gas obtained by burning fuel in air.

jet lag »*noun* extreme tiredness felt after a long flight across different time zones.
jet-lagged

jets

jetsam »*noun* unwanted material thrown overboard from a ship and washed ashore.
– SAY **jet**-suhm

jet set »*noun* (**the jet set**) wealthy people who frequently travel abroad for pleasure.
jet-setter
jet-setting

jet ski »*noun* (plural **jet skis**) (trademark) a small jet-propelled vehicle which skims across the surface of water, ridden in a similar way to a motorcycle.
jet-skiing

jet stream »*noun* one of several very strong, narrow air currents encircling the globe several miles above the earth.

jetted

jetties

jetting

jettison »*verb* (**jettisons, jettisoning, jettisoned**) ❶ throw or drop something from an aircraft or ship. ❷ abandon or discard something.
– say jet-i-suhn or jet-i-zuhn

jetty »*noun* (plural **jetties**) a landing stage or small pier where boats can be moored.

Jew

jewel
  jewelled

> ✓ double the **l** to spell **jewelled** (the spelling **jeweled** is American)

jeweller

> ✓ double **l**: **jeweller** (the spelling **jeweler** is American)

jewellery

> ✓ double the **l** and do not forget the **e** after the **ll**: **jewellery** (the spelling **jewelry** is American)

Jewess »*noun* (plural **Jewesses**) a Jewish woman or girl.

> ℹ **Jewess** is often regarded as an offensive term

Jewish
  Jewishness

Jewry »*noun* Jews as a group.

Jew's harp »*noun* a small musical instrument like a U-shaped harp, held between the teeth and struck with a finger.

Jezebel »*noun* an immoral woman.
– say jez-uh-bel

jib¹ »*noun* ❶ (in sailing) a triangular sail in front of the mast. ❷ the projecting arm of a crane.

jib² »*verb* (**jibs, jibbing, jibbed**) (**jib at**) ❶ be unwilling to do or accept something. ❷ (of a horse) stop and refuse to go on.

> ✓ double the **b** to spell **jibbing** and **jibbed**

jibe¹ »*noun* an insulting remark.
» *verb* (**jibes, jibing, jibed**) make jibes.

jibe² American spelling of **GYBE**.

jiffy »*noun* (in informal English) a moment.

jig »*noun* ❶ a lively leaping dance. ❷ a device that holds something firmly and guides the tools working on it.
» *verb* (**jigs, jigging, jigged**) ❶ dance a jig. ❷ move up and down with a quick jerky motion.

jigger »*verb* (**jiggers, jiggering, jiggered**) (in informal English) ❶ tamper with something. ❷ (**jiggered**) broken or exhausted.

jiggery-pokery

jigging

jiggle (verb: **jiggles, jiggling, jiggled**)
  jiggly

jigs

jigsaw

jihad »*noun* a holy war undertaken by Muslims against unbelievers.
– say ji-hahd or ji-had

jilt »*verb* (**jilts, jilting, jilted**) abruptly break off a relationship with a lover.

jingle (verb: **jingles, jingling, jingled**)
  jingly

jingoism »*noun* excessive support for your country.
  jingoist
  jingoistic

jink »*verb* (**jinks, jinking, jinked**) change direction suddenly and nimbly.
» *noun* a sudden quick change of direction.

jinx »*noun* (plural **jinxes**) a person or thing that brings bad luck.
» *verb* (**jinxes, jinxing, jinxed**) bring someone bad luck.

jitterbug »*noun* a fast dance performed to swing music, popular in the 1940s.

jitters »*noun* (**the jitters**) a feeling of extreme nervousness.
  jittery

jiu-jitsu another way of spelling **JU-JITSU**.

jive »*noun* a lively dance popular in the 1940s and 1950s, performed to swing music or rock and roll.
» *verb* (**jives, jiving, jived**) dance the jive.

job (verb: **jobs, jobbing, jobbed**)

> ✓ double the **b** to spell **jobbing** and **jobbed**

jobcentre

jobless
  joblessness

job lot »*noun* a batch of articles sold or bought at one time.

jobs

job-share (verb: **job-shares, job-sharing, job-shared**)

jobsworth »*noun* an official who mindlessly upholds petty rules.

Jock »*noun* (in informal English) a Scotsman.

jockey »*noun* (plural **jockeys**) a professional rider in horse races.

» *verb* (jockeys, jockeying, jockeyed) struggle to gain or achieve something.

> ☑ the plural of **jockey** simply adds an **s**: **jockeys**

jockstrap *»noun* a support or protection for the male genitals.

jocose *»adjective* playful or humorous.
– **say** juh-**kohss**
jocosely
jocoseness

jocular *»adjective* humorous.
– **say** jok-yuu-ler
jocularity
jocularly

jocund *»adjective* cheerful and light-hearted.
– **say** jo-kuhnd or joh-kuhnd

jodhpurs *»plural noun* trousers worn for horse riding that are close-fitting below the knee and have strengthened patches on the inside of the leg.
– **say** jod-perz

> ☑ note the **h** in the middle: **jodhpurs** are named after the Indian city of *Jodhpur*

joey *»noun* (plural joeys) (in Australian English) a young kangaroo, wallaby, or possum.

> ☑ the plural of **joey** simply adds an **s**: **joeys**

jog (verb: jogs, jogging, jogged)
jogged
jogger
jogging
joggle (verb: joggles, joggling, joggled)
jogs

john *»noun* (in informal American English) a toilet.

John Bull *»noun* a character representing England or the typical Englishman.

johnny (plural johnnies)

> ☑ remember the double **n**: **johnny**. It can also be spelled with an **ie** ending: **johnnie**.

joie de vivre *»noun* lively and cheerful enjoyment of life.
– **say** zhwah duh vee-vruh

> ℹ from a French phrase which means 'joy of living'

join (verb: joins, joining, joined)

joiner *»noun* ❶ a person who puts together the wooden parts of a building. ❷ a person who readily joins groups.

joinery *»noun* ❶ the wooden parts of a building as a group. ❷ the work of a joiner.

joining
joins
joint
jointed
jointly

joist *»noun* a length of timber or steel supporting part of the structure of a building.

> ☑ spelled with an **i**, not **y**: **joist**

jojoba *»noun* an oil extracted from the seeds of a North American shrub.
– **say** huh-**hoh**-buh or hoh-**hoh**-buh

> ☑ note that this word is spelled with **j**'s not **h**'s: **jojoba** is a Spanish word

joke (verb: jokes, joking, joked)
jokey
joker
jokes
jokey
joking
jollied
jollier
jollies
jolliest

jollification *»noun* merrymaking.

jollily
jolliness

jollity *»noun* ❶ lively and cheerful activity. ❷ the quality of being jolly.

jolly (adjective: jollier, jolliest; verb: jollies, jollying, jollied)
jollily
jolliness

Jolly Roger *»noun* a pirate's flag with a white skull and crossbones on a black background.

jolt (verb: jolts, jolting, jolted)

Jordanian [of Jordan]

josh *»verb* (joshes, joshing, joshed) tease someone playfully.

joss stick *»noun* a thin stick of a sweet-smelling substance, burnt as incense.

jostle (verb: jostles, jostling, jostled)

jot (verb: jots, jotting, jotted)

> ☑ double the **t** to spell **jotting** and **jotted**

jotter
jotting

joule *»noun* (in physics) a basic unit of energy or work.
– **say** jool

journal »*noun* ❶ a newspaper or magazine dealing with a particular subject. ❷ a diary or daily record.

journalese »*noun* a writing style containing many cliches, said to be used by some journalists.

journalism

journalist
journalistic

journey (plural **journeys**; verb: **journeys, journeying, journeyed**)

> ✓ the plural of **journey** simply adds an s: **journeys**

journeying

journeyman »*noun* (plural **journeymen**) ❶ a skilled worker who is employed by another. ❷ a worker who is reliable but not outstanding.

journeys

joust »*verb* (**jousts, jousting, jousted**) ❶ (of medieval knights) fight each other with lances while on horseback. ❷ compete for superiority.
»*noun* a jousting contest.
jouster

Jove »*noun* (**by Jove**) (old-fashioned) used for emphasis or to indicate surprise.

> ℹ **Jove** is another name for the Roman god Jupiter

jovial »*adjective* cheerful and friendly.
– say joh-vi-uhl
joviality
jovially

jowl »*noun* ❶ the lower part of a cheek. ❷ the loose skin at the throat of cattle or hanging from the head or neck of birds.
jowly

joy

joyful
joyfully
joyfulness

> ✓ -ful not -full: **joyful**

joyless

joyous
joyously
joyousness

joypad »*noun* a device for a computer games console which uses buttons to control an image on the screen.

joyride »*noun* (in informal English) ❶ a fast ride in a stolen vehicle. ❷ a ride for enjoyment.
joyrider
joyriding

joystick »*noun* ❶ the control column of an aircraft. ❷ a lever for controlling the movement of an image on a computer screen.

JP »*abbreviation* Justice of the Peace.

jubilant »*adjective* happy and triumphant.
jubilantly

jubilation »*noun* a feeling of great happiness and triumph.

jubilee »*noun* a special anniversary.

Judaic »*adjective* having to do with Judaism or the Jews of ancient Israel.
– say joo-day-ik

Judaism »*noun* ❶ the religion of the Jews, based on the Old Testament and the Talmud. ❷ Jews as a group.
– say joo-day-i-z'm

Judas »*noun* (plural **Judases**) a person who betrays a friend.

> ℹ from the name *Judas* Iscariot, the disciple who betrayed Christ

judder (verb: **judders, juddering, juddered**)
juddery

judge (verb: **judges, judging, judged**)

judgement

> ✓ in British English **judgement** is usually spelled with an **e** after the **g**: **judgement**; the spelling **judgment** is usual in legal contexts and in American English

judgemental »*adjective* ❶ having to do with the use of judgement. ❷ being too critical of others.
judgementally

> ✓ **judgemental** can also be spelled without its first **e**: **judgmental**

Judgement Day »*noun* the time of the Last Judgement.

judges

judging

judgment another way of spelling JUDGEMENT.

judgmental another way of spelling JUDGEMENTAL.

judicature »*noun* ❶ the organization and putting into practice of justice. ❷ (**the judicature**) judges as a group.
– say joo-dik-uh-cher

judicial »*adjective* having to do with a law court or judge.
– say joo-di-sh'l
judicially

judiciary »*noun* (plural **judiciaries**) (**the judiciary**) judges as a group.
– say joo-di-shuh-ri

judicious »*adjective* having or done with good judgement.
– SAY joo-**di**-shuhss
judiciously
judiciousness

judo »*noun* a sport of unarmed combat, in which you use particular holds and leverage to unbalance your opponent.

> ℹ️ judo means 'gentle way' in Japanese

jug

juggernaut »*noun* a large heavy vehicle.
– SAY **jug**-ger-nawt

> ☑️ -naut not -nought: juggernaut

juggle (verb: juggles, juggling, juggled)
juggler

jugular »*adjective* having to do with the neck or throat.
– SAY **jug**-yuu-ler

> ☑️ ar not er: jugular

jugular vein »*noun* one of several large veins in the neck, carrying blood from the head.

juice (verb: juices, juicing, juiced)
juicer
juices
juicier
juiciest
juicily
juiciness
juicing
juicy (adjective: juicier, juiciest)
juicily
juiciness

ju-jitsu »*noun* a Japanese system of unarmed combat.
– SAY joo **jit**-soo

> ℹ️ from a Japanese phrase which means 'gentle skill'

> ☑️ ju-jitsu can also be spelled jiu-jitsu: both spellings are correct

jukebox (plural jukeboxes)

julep »*noun* a sweet drink made from sugar syrup.
– SAY **joo**-lep

julienne »*noun* a portion of food cut into short, thin strips.
– SAY joo-li-**en**

> ☑️ note the nne ending: julienne is a French word

July

jumble (verb: jumbles, jumbling, jumbled)

jumbo »*noun* (plural jumbos) a very large person or thing.
» *adjective* very large.

> ☑️ the plural of jumbo has os not oes: jumbos

jumbo jet »*noun* a very large airliner carrying several hundred passengers.

jump (verb: jumps, jumping, jumped)
jumper
jumpier
jumpiest
jumpily
jumpiness
jumping

jump jet »*noun* a jet aircraft that can take off and land without a runway.

jump lead »*noun* one of a pair of cables for recharging a battery in a motor vehicle by connecting it to the battery in another.

jumps

jump-start »*verb* (jump-starts, jump-starting, jump-started) start a vehicle with jump leads or by a sudden release of the clutch while it is being pushed.
» *noun* an act of jump-starting a car.

jumpsuit »*noun* a one-piece garment incorporating trousers and a sleeved top.

jumpy (adjective: jumpier, jumpiest)
jumpily
jumpiness

junction »*noun* ❶ a point where things meet or are joined. ❷ a place where roads or railway lines meet.

juncture »*noun* ❶ a particular point in time. ❷ a place where things join.

June

jungle

junior

juniper »*noun* an evergreen shrub with sweet-smelling berry-like cones.
– SAY **joo**-ni-per

junk (verb: junks, junking, junked)

junket »*noun* ❶ a dish of sweetened curds of milk. ❷ an extravagant trip or party.
– SAY **jung**-kit

junkie »*noun* (in informal English) a drug addict.

> ☑️ junkie can also be spelled junky

junking
junks
junky another way of spelling JUNKIE.
junkyard

j

junta »*noun* a group ruling a country after taking power by force.
– say **jun**-tuh or **huun**-tuh

> ℹ️ junta can be pronounced with a **h** sound: it is a Spanish word

Jupiter

Jurassic »*adjective* relating to the geological period from about 208 to 146 million years ago.
– say juu-**rass**-ik

jurisdiction »*noun* ❶ the official power to make legal decisions. ❷ the area over which the legal authority of a court or other institution extends.
– say joo-riss-**dik**-sh'n
jurisdictional

jurisprudence »*noun* ❶ the study of the philosophy and theory of law. ❷ a legal system.
– say joo-riss-**proo**-duhnss

jurist »*noun* an expert in law.
– say **joor**-ist

> ℹ️ do not confuse a **jurist** with a **juror**, who is a member of a jury

juror »*noun* a member of a jury.

> ✓ **-or** not **-er: juror**

jury »*noun* (plural **juries**) ❶ a group of people who are required to attend a legal case and make a verdict based on the evidence presented. ❷ a body of people judging a competition.

> ✓ plural: drop the **y** and add **ies: juries**

jury-rigged »*adjective* makeshift or improvised.

just
justly
justness

justice

Justice of the Peace »*noun* (in the UK) a non-professional magistrate appointed to hear minor cases in a town or county.

justifiable »*adjective* able to be shown to be right or reasonable.
justifiably

justify (verb: **justifies, justifying, justified**)
justification

justly

justness

jut (verb: **juts, jutting, jutted**)

> ✓ double the **t** to spell **jutting** and **jutted**

jute »*noun* rough fibre made from the stems of a tropical plant, used for making rope or woven into sacking.

juts

jutted

jutting

juvenile »*adjective* ❶ having to do with young people, birds, or animals. ❷ childish.
»*noun* ❶ a young person, bird, or animal. ❷ a person below the age at which they have adult status in law (18 in most countries).
– say **joo**-vuh-nyl

juvenile delinquent »*noun* a young person who regularly commits crimes.

juvenilia »*plural noun* works produced by an author or artist when they were young.
– say joo-vuh-**nil**-i-uh

juxtapose »*verb* (**juxtaposes, juxtaposing, juxtaposed**) place two things close together.
– say juk-stuh-**pohz**
juxtaposition

Kk

Kabbalah »*noun* the ancient Jewish tradition of mystical interpretation of the Bible.
– say kuh-**bah**-luh
Kabbalistic

> ✓ Kabbalah can also be spelled without the **h: Kabbala**

kabob American spelling of **KEBAB**.

kaftan »*noun* ❶ a man's long belted tunic, worn in the Near East. ❷ a woman's long loose dress. ❸ a loose shirt or top.
– say **kaf**-tan

> ✓ kaftan can also be spelled **caftan**: both spellings are correct

Kaiser »*noun* (a historical term) the German Emperor, the Emperor of Austria, or the head of the Holy Roman Empire.
– **SAY** ky-zer

Kalashnikov »*noun* a type of rifle or sub-machine gun made in Russia.
– **SAY** kuh-**lash**-ni-kof

kale »*noun* a type of cabbage producing erect stems with large leaves and no compact head.

kaleidoscope »*noun* ❶ a tube containing mirrors and pieces of coloured glass or paper, whose reflections produce changing patterns when the tube is turned. ❷ a constantly changing pattern.
– **SAY** kuh-**ly**-duh-skohp
kaleidoscopic

> ✓ remember the **e** in **leid: kaleidoscope**

Kama Sutra »*noun* an ancient Indian text on the art of love and sexual technique.
– **SAY** kah-muh **soo**-truh

kamikaze »*noun* (in the Second World War) a Japanese aircraft loaded with explosives and deliberately crashed on to an enemy target, in a mission carried out by the pilot as an act of suicide.
» *adjective* potentially causing death or harm to yourself.
– **SAY** ka-mi-**kah**-zi

> ℹ from a Japanese word which means 'divine wind'

kangaroo

> ✓ **gar** not **ger: kangaroo**

kangaroo court »*noun* a court set up unofficially and without the use of proper evidence or procedures, with the aim of finding someone guilty.

kaolin »*noun* a fine soft white clay, used for making china and in medicine.
– **SAY** kay-uh-lin

kapok »*noun* a substance resembling cotton wool which grows around the seeds of a tropical tree, used as padding.
– **SAY** kay-pok

kappa »*noun* the tenth letter of the Greek alphabet (**K**, **κ**).

kaput »*adjective* (in informal English) broken and useless.
– **SAY** kuh-**puut**

karaoke »*noun* a form of entertainment in which people sing popular songs over pre-recorded backing tracks.
– **SAY** ka-ri-**oh**-ki

> ℹ **karaoke** means 'empty orchestra' in Japanese

> ✓ there is no **i** in **karaoke**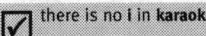

karate »*noun* an oriental system of unarmed combat using the hands and feet to deliver and block blows.
– **SAY** kuh-**rah**-ti

> ℹ **karate** means 'empty hand' in Japanese

karma »*noun* (in Hinduism and Buddhism) the sum of a person's actions in this and previous lives, seen as affecting their fate.
– **SAY** kar-muh
karmic

kart »*noun* a small unsprung racing-car with the engine at the back.
karting

kasbah »*noun* a North African citadel and the old, narrow streets that surround it.
– **SAY** kaz-bah

> ✓ an Arabic word, **kasbah** can also be spelled **casbah**

kayak »*noun* a canoe made of a light frame with a watertight covering.
» *verb* (**kayaks, kayaking, kayaked**) travel in a kayak.
– **SAY** ky-ak

> ✓ **kay** not **ky: kayak** (an Inuit word)

Kazakh [of Kazakhstan]
– **SAY** kuh-**zak** or **ka**-zak

kazoo »*noun* a simple musical instrument consisting of a pipe with a hole in it, over which is a membrane that vibrates and buzzes when the player hums into it.
– **SAY** kuh-**zoo**

kebab »*noun* a dish of pieces of meat, fish, or vegetables roasted or grilled on a skewer or spit.
– **SAY** ki-**bab**

> ✓ **ke** not **ka**, and **bab** not **bob: kebab** (the spelling **kabob** is American)

kedge »*noun* a small anchor with a rope attached to it, used to move a boat by hauling on the rope.

kedgeree »*noun* a dish of smoked fish, rice, and hard-boiled eggs.
– **SAY** kej-uh-ree

> ✓ **ree** not **rie: kedgeree**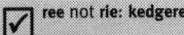

keel »*noun* a structure running along the length of the base of a ship, often extended downwards to increase stability.
» *verb* (**keels, keeling, keeled**) (**keel over**)
❶ (of a boat or ship) turn over on its side.
❷ fall over.

keelhaul »*verb* (**keelhauls, keelhauling, keelhauled**) (mainly used in a humorous way) punish someone severely.

> ℹ from a former punishment in which a person was dragged through the water under a boat

keeling

keels

keelson »*noun* a structure running the length of a ship, that fastens the timbers of the floor to the keel.
– *say* keel-suhn

> ☑ **keelson** can also be spelled with a single **e: kelson**

keen[1] (adjective: **keener, keenest**) [eager and enthusiastic]
keenly
keenness

keen[2] »*verb* (**keens, keening, keened**) ❶ wail in grief for a dead person. ❷ make an eerie wailing sound.

keep (verb: **keeps, keeping, kept**)

keeper

keep-fit

keeping

keeps

keepsake »*noun* a small item kept in memory of the person who gave it or originally owned it.

keg »*noun* a small barrel.

kelim another way of spelling **KILIM**.

kelp »*noun* a very large brown seaweed.

kelpie »*noun* a water spirit of Scottish folklore, usually taking the form of a horse.
– *say* kel-pi

kelson another way of spelling **KEELSON**.

kelvin »*noun* (in physics) the basic unit of temperature, equal to the degree Celsius.

> ℹ named after the British physicist Lord Kelvin

Kelvin scale »*noun* the scale of temperature with absolute zero as zero and the freezing point of water as 273.15 kelvins.

ken »*noun* (**your ken**) your range of knowledge or sight.

kendo »*noun* a Japanese form of fencing with two-handed bamboo swords.
– *say* ken-doh

> ℹ **kendo** means 'sword way' in Japanese

kennel

Kenyan

kept past and past participle of **KEEP**.

keratin »*noun* a protein forming the basis of hair, feathers, hoofs, claws, and horns.
– *say* ke-ruh-tin

kerb [stone edging to a pavement]

> ☑ do not confuse **kerb** with **curb**, which means 'something that limits or restrains something' (the use of the spelling **curb** to mean **kerb** is American)

kerb-crawling »*noun* driving slowly along the edge of the road in search of a prostitute.
kerb-crawler

kerbstone

kerchief »*noun* (plural **kerchiefs**) ❶ a piece of fabric used to cover the head. ❷ a handkerchief.

kerfuffle »*noun* (in informal English) a commotion or fuss.
– *say* ker-fuf-fuhl

kernel »*noun* ❶ a softer part of a nut, seed, or fruit stone contained within its hard shell. ❷ the seed and hard husk of a cereal. ❸ the central part of something.

> ☑ e**l** not a**l**: kern**el**

kerosene »*noun* a light fuel oil distilled from petroleum; paraffin oil.
– *say* ke-ruh-seen

> ☑ **kerosene** can also be spelled **kerosine**: both spellings are correct

kestrel »*noun* a small falcon that hunts by hovering with rapidly beating wings.

ketch »*noun* a small sailing boat with two masts.

ketchup

ketone »*noun* one of a class of organic compounds including acetone.
– *say* kee-tohn

kettle

kettledrum »*noun* a large drum shaped like a bowl, with adjustable pitch.

key (plural **keys**; verb: **keys, keying, keyed**)

keyboard (verb: **keyboards, keyboarding, keyboarded**)
keyboarder

keyed

key grip »*noun* the person in a film crew who is in charge of the camera equipment.

keyhole

keyhole surgery »*noun* surgery carried out through a very small cut made in the affected area.

keying

k

keynote *»noun* ❶ a central theme. ❷ the musical note on which a key is based. *» adjective* (of a speech) setting out the central theme of a conference.

keypad

keypunch *»noun* a device for transferring data by means of punched holes on a series of cards or paper tape.

keys

key signature *»noun* (in music) a combination of sharps or flats after the clef at the beginning of each stave, indicating the key of a composition.

keystone *»noun* ❶ a central stone at the top of an arch, locking the whole together. ❷ the central part of a policy or system.

keystroke *»noun* a single depression of a key on a keyboard.

keyword *»noun* ❶ a word or concept of great significance. ❷ a significant word mentioned in an index. ❸ a word used in a computer system to indicate the content of a document.

khaki *»noun* (plural **khakis**) ❶ a cotton or wool fabric of a dull brownish-yellow colour. ❷ a dull brownish-yellow colour.
– SAY kah-ki

> ☑ **kha** not **kah**: **khaki**. The plural has **is** not **ies**: **khakis**.

khan *»noun* a title given to rulers and officials in central Asia, Afghanistan, and certain other Muslim countries.
– SAY kahn

khazi *»noun* (plural **khazies**) (in informal English) a toilet.
– SAY kah-zi

kibble *»verb* (**kibbles**, **kibbling**, **kibbled**) grind or chop beans, grain, etc. coarsely.

kibbutz *»noun* (plural **kibbutzim**) a farming settlement in Israel in which work is shared between its members.
– SAY kib-**buuts** [singular], kib-**buuts**-im [plural]

> ℹ **kibbutz** is a modern Hebrew word meaning 'gathering'

kibitzer *»noun* a person who looks on and offers unwelcome advice, especially at a card game.
– SAY kib-it-ser
kibitzing

> ☑ only one **b** in **kibitzer** (a Yiddish word)

kibosh *»noun* (**put the kibosh on**) (in informal English) firmly put an end to.
– SAY ky-bosh

> ☑ **kibosh** can also be spelled **kybosh**: both spellings are correct

kick (verb: **kicks**, **kicking**, **kicked**)
kicker

kickes

kickback *»noun* ❶ a sudden forceful springing back. ❷ an underhand payment made to someone who has helped to arrange a business or political deal.

kick-boxing *»noun* a form of martial art which combines boxing with kicking with bare feet.

kicked

kicker

kicking

kick-off

kicks

kickstand *»noun* a metal rod attached to a bicycle or motorcycle that may be kicked upright to support the vehicle when it is not being ridden.

kick-start *»verb* (**kick-starts**, **kick-starting**, **kick-started**) ❶ start an engine on a motorcycle with a downward thrust of a pedal. ❷ stimulate a process.
» noun ❶ an act of kick-starting. ❷ a device to kick-start an engine.

kid (verb: **kids**, **kidding**, **kidded**)

> ☑ double the **d** in **kidding** and **kidded**

kiddie (plural **kiddies**)

> ☑ **kiddie** can also be spelled **kiddy**

kidding

kiddy another way of spelling **KIDDIE**.

kidnap (verb: **kidnaps**, **kidnapping**, **kidnapped**)
kidnapper

> ☑ double the **p** in **kidnapping** and **kidnapped** (the spellings **kidnaping** and **kidnaped** are American)

kidney (plural **kidneys**)

kidney bean *»noun* a dark red kidney-shaped bean.

kidneys

kidology *»noun* (in informal English) the practice of deliberately deceiving or teasing someone.

kids

kilim *»noun* a carpet or rug woven without a pile, made in Turkey, Kurdistan, and neighbouring areas.
– SAY ki-**leem** or **kee**-lim

k

kilim can also be spelled **kelim**: both spellings are correct

kill (verb: **kills, killing, killed**)

killer

killer whale »*noun* a large toothed whale with black-and-white markings and a prominent fin on its back.

killing

killjoy »*noun* a person who spoils the enjoyment of others by behaving very seriously.

kills

kiln »*noun* an oven for baking or drying things.

kilo »*noun* (plural **kilos**) a kilogram.

 the plural of **kilo** has **os** not **oes**: **kilos**

kilobyte »*noun* (in computing) a unit of memory or data equal to 1,000 bytes.

kilogram »*noun* a unit of mass in the metric system, equal to 1,000 grams.

✓ **-gram** not **-gramme**: **kilogram**

kilohertz »*noun* a unit of frequency equal to 1,000 hertz.

kilojoule »*noun* a unit of energy equal to 1,000 joules.

kilolitre »*noun* a volume of 1,000 litres (equivalent to 220 imperial gallons).

✓ **re** not **er**: **kilolitre** (the spelling **kiloliter** is American)

kilometre »*noun* a metric unit of distance equal to 1,000 metres (approximately 0.62 miles).
– say **kil**-uh-mee-ter or ki-**lom**-i-ter
kilometric

✓ **re** not **er**: **kilometre** (the spelling **kilometer** is American)

kiloton »*noun* a unit of explosive power equivalent to 1,000 tons (or tonnes) of TNT.

 kiloton may be spelled **kilotonne** with metric tons

kilovolt »*noun* 1,000 volts.

kilowatt »*noun* 1,000 watts.

kilowatt-hour »*noun* a measure of electrical energy equivalent to one kilowatt operating for one hour.

kilt
kilted

kilter »*noun* (**out of kilter**) out of balance.

kimono »*noun* (plural **kimonos**) a long, loose Japanese robe having wide sleeves and tied with a sash.
– say ki-**moh**-noh

 one m, one n: **kimono** the plural of **kimono** has **os** not **oes**: **kimonos**

kin »*noun* your family and relations.

kind[1] [class or type]

 when using **kind** to refer to a plural noun, it is wrong to say *these kind* as in *these kind of questions are not relevant*: you should use **kinds** instead, as in *these kinds of questions are not relevant*

kind[2] (adjective: **kinder, kindest**) [considerate and generous]

kindergarten »*noun* a nursery school.
– say **kin**-der-gar-tuhn

ℹ **kindergarten** is a German word meaning 'children's garden'

kindest

kindle »*verb* (**kindles, kindling, kindled**)
❶ light a flame. ❷ arouse an emotion.
– say **kin**-d'l

kindling »*noun* small sticks used for lighting fires.

kindly (adjective: **kindlier, kindliest**)
kindliness

kindness (plural **kindnesses**)

kindred »*noun* ❶ your family and relations. ❷ relationship by blood.
»*adjective* similar in kind.
– say **kin**-drid

kindred spirit »*noun* a person whose interests or attitudes are similar to your own.

kinematics »*plural noun* the branch of mechanics concerned with the motion of objects without reference to the forces which cause the motion.
– say kin-i-**mat**-iks
kinematic

kinesis »*noun* (plural **kineses**) movement.
– say ki-**nee**-siss [singular], ki-**nee**-seez [plural]

✓ make the plural by changing the **-is** ending to **-es** (like the original Greek): **kineses**

kinetic »*adjective* relating to or resulting from motion.
– say ki-**net**-ik
kinetically

kinfolk »*plural noun* = KINSFOLK.

king
kingly
kingship

kingdom

kingfisher »*noun* a colourful bird with a large head and long sharp beak which dives to catch fish in streams and rivers.

kingly

kingmaker »*noun* a person who brings leaders to power by using their political influence.

kingpin »*noun* ❶ a large bolt in a central position. ❷ a vertical bolt used as a pivot. ❸ a person or thing that is essential to the success of an organization or operation.

kingship

king-size

king-sized

kink »*noun* ❶ a sharp twist in something long and narrow. ❷ a flaw or difficulty in a plan or operation. ❸ a peculiar habit or characteristic.
» *verb* (**kinks, kinking, kinked**) form a kink.

kinky »*adjective* (**kinkier, kinkiest**) ❶ having kinks or twists. ❷ having to do with unusual sexual behaviour.

kinsfolk »*plural noun* a person's blood relations, seen as a group.

kinship »*noun* ❶ blood relationship. ❷ a sharing of characteristics or origins.

kinsman »*noun* (plural **kinsmen**) one of a person's blood relations.

kinswoman (plural **kinswomen**)

kiosk »*noun* ❶ a small open-fronted hut from which newspapers, refreshments, tickets, etc. are sold. ❷ a public telephone booth.
– SAY kee-ossk

kip (in informal English) »*noun* a sleep.
» *verb* (**kips, kipping, kipped**) sleep.

> ☑ double the **p** in **kipping** and **kipped**

kipper »*noun* a herring that has been split open, salted, and dried or smoked.

kipper tie »*noun* a very wide tie.

kipping

kips

kirby grip »*noun* a hairgrip consisting of a thin folded and sprung metal strip.

> ☑ **kirby grip** can also be spelled **Kirbigrip** and is a trademark when spelled like this

Kirghiz another way of spelling **KYRGYZ**.

kirk »*noun* (in Scottish English) ❶ a church. ❷ (**the Kirk(** or **the Kirk of Scotland**) the Church of Scotland.

Kirk session »*noun* the lowest court in the Church of Scotland.

kirsch »*noun* brandy distilled from the fermented juice of cherries.
– SAY ki-uhsh

kismet »*noun* fate.

> ℹ️ **kismet** is an Arabic word meaning 'division, lot'

kiss (verb: **kisses, kissing, kissed**)
kissable

kiss curl »*noun* a small curl of hair on the forehead, at the nape of the neck, or in front of the ear.

kissed

kisser

kisses

kissing

kissogram »*noun* a novelty greeting delivered by a man or woman who accompanies it with a kiss.

kit[1] »*noun* a set of articles or equipment for a specific purpose.
» *verb* (**kits, kitting, kitted**) (**kit out**) provide someone with appropriate clothing or equipment.

> ☑ double the **t** in **kitting** and **kitted**

kit[2] »*noun* the young of certain animals, e.g. the beaver, ferret, and mink.

kitbag »*noun* a long, cylindrical canvas bag for carrying a soldier's possessions.

kitchen

kitchenette »*noun* a small kitchen or part of a room equipped as a kitchen.

kitchen-sink »*adjective* (of drama) realistic in dealing with drab or sordid subjects.

kitchenware

kite

Kitemark »*noun* (trademark) (in the UK) an official kite-shaped mark on goods approved by the British Standards Institution.

kith »*noun* (**kith and kin**) your relations.

kits

kitsch »*noun* art, objects, or design that is tastelessly garish or sentimental.
kitschy

> ☑ remember the **s** in the middle: **kitsch** is a German word

kitten

kittenish »*adjective* playful, lively, or flirtatious.

kitties

kitting

k

kittiwake »*noun* a small gull that nests on sea cliffs and has a loud call that sounds like its name.

kitty »*noun* (plural **kitties**) ❶ a fund of money for use by a number of people. ❷ a pool of money in some card games.

kiwi »*noun* (plural **kiwis**) ❶ a tailless New Zealand bird that cannot fly. ❷ (in informal English) a New Zealander.

✓ the plural has **is not ies: kiwis**

kiwi fruit »*noun* (plural **kiwi fruit**) the fruit of an Asian climbing plant, with a thin hairy skin, green flesh, and black seeds.

kiwis

klaxon »*noun* (trademark) a vehicle horn or warning hooter.
– SAY klak-suhn

✓ **klax** not **klacks: klaxon**

Kleenex »*noun* (plural **Kleenex** or **Kleenexes**) (trademark) a paper tissue.

kleptomania »*noun* a recurring urge to steal.
– SAY klep-tuh-**may**-ni-uh
kleptomaniac

knack

knackered

knacker's yard »*noun* a place where old or injured animals are slaughtered.

knapsack »*noun* a soldier's or hiker's bag with shoulder straps, carried on the back.

✓ **knap** not **nap: knapsack**

knapweed »*noun* a plant with purple thistle-like flower heads.

knave »*noun* ❶ (an old word) a dishonest man. ❷ (in cards) a jack.
knavery
knavish

knead »*verb* (**kneads, kneading, kneaded**) ❶ work dough or clay with the hands. ❷ massage something as if kneading it.

knee (verb: **knees, kneeing, kneed**)

kneecap »*noun* the outward-curving bone in front of the knee joint.
» *verb* (**kneecaps, kneecapping, kneecapped**) shoot someone in the knee or leg as a punishment.

✓ double the **p** in **kneecapping** and **kneecapped**

kneed

knee-high

kneeing

knee-jerk »*noun* an involuntary kick caused by a blow on the tendon just below the knee.
» *adjective* automatic and unthinking: *a kneejerk reaction.*

kneel (verb: **kneels, kneeling, knelt** or **kneeled**)
kneeler

knees

knees-up

knell »*noun* the sound of a bell rung solemnly.
– SAY nel

knelt past and past participle of **KNEEL**.

knew past of **KNOW**.

knickerbockers »*plural noun* loose-fitting breeches gathered at the knee or calf.

knickers

knick-knack »*noun* a small worthless object.

✓ **knick-knack** can also be spelled **nick-nack**

knife (plural **knives**; verb: **knifes, knifing, knifed**)

knife-edge »*noun* a very tense or dangerous situation.

knifes

knifing

knight »*noun* ❶ (in the Middle Ages) a man of noble rank with a duty to fight for his king. ❷ (in the UK) a man awarded a title by the King or Queen and entitled to use 'Sir' in front of his name. ❸ a chess piece that moves by jumping to the opposite corner of a rectangle two squares by three.
» *verb* (**knights, knighting, knighted**) give a man the title of knight.
knighthood
knightly

knight errant »*noun* a medieval knight who wandered in search of adventure.

knighthood

knighting

knightly

knights

knit (verb: **knits, knitting, knitted** or **knit**)
knitter
knitting

✓ double the **t** in **knitting, knitted**, and **knitter**

knitwear

knives

k

knob
  knobbed
  knobby

knobble »*noun* a small lump on something.
  knobbly

knock (verb: **knocks, knocking, knocked**)

knockabout »*adjective* (of comedy) rough and slapstick.

knock-back »*noun* (in informal English) a refusal or setback.

knock-down »*adjective* (of a price) very low.

knocked

knocker

knocking

knock-kneed

knock-off »*noun* (in informal English) a copy or imitation.

knock-on effect

knockout

knocks

knock-up »*noun* (in racket sports) a period of practice play before a game.

knoll »*noun* a small hill or mound.
– say nol

 double l: **knoll**

knot (verb: **knots, knotting, knotted**)

 double the t in **knotting** and **knotted**

knothole »*noun* a hole in a piece of wood where a knot has fallen out.

knots

knotted

knottier

knottiest

knotting

knotty (adjective: **knottier, knottiest**)

know (verb: **knows, knowing, knew**; past participle **known**)
  knowable

know-all

know-how

knowing
  knowingly
  knowingness

know-it-all

knowledge

 don't forget the **d**: **knowledge**

knowledgeable »*adjective* intelligent and well informed.
  knowledgeably

 knowledgeable can also be spelled **knowledgable**

known

knows

knuckle (verb: **knuckles, knuckling, knuckled**)

knuckleduster »*noun* a metal guard worn over the knuckles in fighting to increase the effect of blows.

knuckles

knuckling

knurl »*noun* a small projecting knob or ridge.
– say rhymes with curl
  knurled

KO »*noun* a knockout in a boxing match.
» *verb* (**KO's, KO'ing, KO'd**) knock someone out in a boxing match.

koala »*noun* a bear-like tree-dwelling Australian animal that has thick grey fur and feeds on eucalyptus leaves.
– say koh-**ah**-luh

 the term **koala bear** is strictly incorrect as koalas are completely unrelated to bears

kohl »*noun* a black powder used as eye make-up.

kohlrabi »*noun* (plural **kohlrabies**) a variety of cabbage with an edible turnip-like stem.
– say kohl-**rah**-bi

 the plural has **ies** not **is**: **kohlrabies**

koi »*noun* (plural **koi**) a large common Japanese carp.
– say koy

Komodo dragon »*noun* a very large lizard found on Komodo and some other Indonesian islands.

kook »*noun* (in American English) a mad or unconventional person.
  kooky

kookaburra »*noun* a noisy Australasian kingfisher that feeds on reptiles and birds.
– say **kuu**-kuh-bur-ruh

 double r: **kookaburra**

kooky

kop »*noun* a high bank of terracing at a soccer ground.

k

kopek »*noun* a unit of money of Russia and some other countries of the former USSR, equal to one hundredth of a rouble.
– SAY koh-pek or ko-pek

> ✓ **kopek** can also be spelled **copeck** or **kopeck**: all three spellings are correct

Koran »*noun* the sacred book of Islam, believed to be the word of God as told to Muhammad and written down in Arabic.
– SAY ko-**rahn**

> ✓ **Koran**, an Arabic word meaning 'recitation', can also be spelled **Quran** or **Qur'an**: all three spellings are correct

Korean

korma »*noun* a mild Indian curry of meat or fish marinated in yogurt or curds.
– SAY kor-muh

kosher »*adjective* ❶ (of food) prepared according to the requirements of Jewish law. ❷ (in informal English) genuine and legitimate.
– SAY koh-sher

> 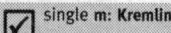 **kosher** is a Hebrew word meaning 'proper'

Kosovar »*noun* a person from Kosovo, a province of Serbia whose population is largely of Albanian descent.
– SAY koss-uh-var
Kosovan

kowtow »*verb* (**kowtows, kowtowing, kowtowed**) ❶ (a historical term) kneel and touch the ground with the forehead in submission as part of Chinese custom. ❷ be too meek and obedient towards someone.
– SAY kow-**tow**

kraal (in South African English) »*noun* ❶ a traditional African village of huts. ❷ an enclosure for sheep and cattle.
– SAY krahl

Kraut »*noun* (used in an insulting way) a German.
– SAY krowt

Kremlin »*noun* the citadel in Moscow, housing the Russian government.

> ✓ single m: **Kremlin**

krill »*plural noun* small shrimp-like crustaceans which are the main food of baleen whales.

krona »*noun* ❶ (plural **kronor**) the basic unit of money of Sweden. ❷ (plural **kronur**) the basic unit of money of Iceland.
– SAY kroh-nuh [singular and plural]

krone »*noun* (plural **kroner**) the basic unit of money of Denmark and Norway.
– SAY kroh-nuh [singular and plural]

krugerrand »*noun* a South African gold coin with a portrait of President Kruger on it.
– SAY kroo-ger-rand

krypton »*noun* a colourless, odourless, gaseous chemical element, present in small amounts in the air and used in some kinds of electric light.
– SAY krip-ton

kudos »*noun* praise and honour.
– SAY kyoo-doss

> ℹ although it ends in **s**, the word **kudos**, meaning 'praise' is not a plural word. This means that there is no singular form **kudo** and that use of it as a plural, as in *he received many kudos for his work*, is wrong.

kudu »*noun* (plural **kudu** or **kudus**) a striped African antelope, the male of which has long spirally curved horns.

Ku Klux Klan »*noun* a secret organization of white people in the US who are violently opposed to black people.
– SAY koo kluks **klan**

kumquat »*noun* a small orange-like fruit.
– SAY kum-kwot

kung fu »*noun* a Chinese martial art resembling karate.

> ℹ **kung fu** is a Chinese term, and comes from the words for 'merit' and 'master'

Kurd »*noun* a member of an Islamic people living in Kurdistan, a region in the Middle East.
Kurdish

Kuwaiti (plural **Kuwaitis**)
– SAY kuu-**way**-ti

kwashiorkor »*noun* malnutrition caused by protein deficiency, affecting young children in the tropics.
– SAY kwa-shi-**or**-kor

> ✓ the ending is **orkor**, not **okor**: **kwashiorkor** (a Ghanaian word)

kybosh another way of spelling **KIBOSH**.

kyle »*noun* (in Scottish English) a narrow sea channel.

Kyrgyz (plural **Kyrgyz**) [of Kyrgyzstan]
– SAY ker-giz

> 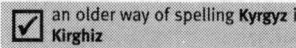 an older way of spelling **Kyrgyz** is **Kirghiz**

Ll

lab

label (verb: **labels, labelling, labelled**)

> ✓ **el** not **le**: la**bel**
> double the final **l** in **labelling** and
> **labelled** (the spellings **labeling** and **labeled**
> are American)

labia »*plural noun* the inner and outer folds
of the vulva.
– SAY **lay**-bi-uh

> ℹ **labia** is the plural of the Latin
> singular **labium** 'lip'

labial »*adjective* relating to the lips or the
labia.

labor etc. American spelling of **LABOUR** etc.

laboratory (plural **laboratories**)

> ✓ plural: drop the **y** and add **ies**:
> **laboratories**

laborious »*adjective* ❶ requiring much
time and effort. ❷ showing obvious signs
of effort: *a slow, laborious speech.*
laboriously

labour (verb: **labours, labouring, laboured**)
labourer

> ✓ **-our** not **-or**: la**bour** (the spelling **labor**,
> by itself and in related words, is
> American)

labour-intensive »*adjective* needing a
large workforce or a large amount of work
in relation to what is produced.

Labour Party »*noun* a British political
party formed to represent the interests of
ordinary working people.

labours

labour-saving

Labrador »*noun* a breed of retriever with a
black or yellow coat, used as a gun dog or
guide dog.

laburnum »*noun* a small tree with hanging
clusters of yellow flowers followed by
pods of poisonous seeds.
– SAY luh-**ber**-nuhm

labyrinth »*noun* ❶ a complicated irregular
network of passages. ❷ a complex and
confusing arrangement. ❸ a complex

structure in the inner ear which contains
the organs of hearing and balance.
– SAY **lab**-uh-rinth
labyrinthine

> ✓ don't forget the **y**: la**by**rinth (from a
> Greek word referring originally to the
> maze built to house the Minotaur)

lac »*noun* a substance secreted by an insect
and used to make varnish, shellac, etc.

lace (verb: **laces, lacing, laced**)

lacerate »*verb* (**lacerates, lacerating,
lacerated**) tear or deeply cut the flesh or
skin.
– SAY **lass**-uh-rayt
laceration

laces

lachrymal »*adjective* connected with
weeping or tears.
– SAY **lak**-ri-muhl

> ✓ **lachrymal** can also be spelled
> **lacrimal**: both spellings are correct

lachrymose »*adjective* ❶ tearful. ❷ sad: *a
lachrymose children's classic.*
– SAY **lak**-ri-mohss

lacier

laciest

lacing

lack (verb: **lacks, lacking, lacked**)

lackadaisical »*adjective* lacking
enthusiasm and thoroughness.
– SAY lak-uh-**day**-zi-k'l
lackadaisically

lacked

lackey »*noun* (plural **lackeys**) ❶ a servant.
❷ a person who is too willing to serve or
obey others.

> ✓ the plural has **eys** not **ies**: **lackeys**

lacking

lacklustre »*adjective* ❶ lacking in energy,
force, or inspiration. ❷ (of the hair or
eyes) not shining.

> ✓ **tre** not **ter**: lacklus**tre** (the spelling
> **lackluster** is American)

lacks

laconic »*adjective* using very few words.
– SAY luh-**kon**-ik
laconically

lacquer »*noun* ❶ a varnish made of shellac, the sap of an East Asian tree, or of chemically-produced substances. ❷ decorative wooden goods coated with lacquer. ❸ a chemical substance sprayed on hair to keep it in place.
» *verb* (**lacquers, lacquering, lacquered**) coat something with lacquer.
– SAY lak-ker

lacrimal another way of spelling LACHRYMAL.

lacrosse »*noun* a team game (first played by American Indians) in which a ball is thrown, carried, and caught with a long-handled stick having a net at one end.
– SAY luh-**kross**

> don't forget the e at the end: **lacrosse** comes from French *le jeu de la crosse* 'the game of the hooked stick'

lactate »*verb* (**lactates, lactating, lactated**) (of a female mammal) produce milk.
lactation

lacteal »*adjective* conveying milk or milky fluid.
– SAY lak-ti-uhl

lactic »*adjective* relating to or obtained from milk.

lactic acid »*noun* an acid present in sour milk, and produced in the muscles during strenuous exercise.

lactose »*noun* a sugar present in milk.
– SAY lak-tohz

lacto-vegetarian »*noun* a person who eats only dairy products and vegetables.

lacuna »*noun* (plural **lacunae** or **lacunas**) ❶ a gap or missing portion. ❷ a cavity or sunken area in bone.
– SAY luh-**kyoo**-nuh [singular], luh-**kyoo**-nee [plural]

> the plural can be spelled either with an e (as in Latin) or with an s: **lacunae** or **lacunas**

lacy (adjective: **lacier, laciest**)

> drop the y and add ier or iest to spell **lacier** or **laciest**

lad

ladder (verb: **ladders, laddering, laddered**)

laddie

laddish
laddishness

laden »*adjective* heavily loaded or weighed down.

la-di-da »*adjective* affected or snobbish.

> **la-di-da** can also be spelled **lah-di-dah**: both spellings are correct

ladies

ladies' man

ladle (verb: **ladles, ladling, ladled**)
ladleful

> **dle** not **del**: **ladle**

lady (plural **ladies**)

> plural: drop the y and add ies: **ladies**

ladybird

Lady Day »*noun* the Christian feast of the Annunciation, 25 March.

lady-in-waiting »*noun* (plural **ladies-in-waiting**) a woman who accompanies and looks after a queen or princess.

ladykiller »*noun* a charming man who regularly seduces women.

ladylike

ladyship »*noun* (**Her** or **Your Ladyship**) a respectful way of referring to or addressing a Lady.

lag »*verb* (**lags, lagging, lagged**) ❶ fall behind. ❷ cover a boiler, pipes, etc. with material designed to prevent heat loss.
» *noun* ❶ a period of time between two events. ❷ (in informal English) a person who has been frequently convicted and sent to prison.

lager

laggard »*noun* a person who falls behind others.
» *adjective* slower than desired or expected.

> double g and ard not erd: **laggard**

lagged

lagging »*noun* material providing protection against heat loss for a boiler, pipes, etc.

lagoon »*noun* a stretch of salt water separated from the sea by a low sandbank or coral reef.

> one g, two o's: **lagoon**

lags

lah-di-dah another way of spelling LA-DI-DA.

laid

laid-back »*adjective* relaxed and easy-going.

lain past participle of LIE¹.

lair »*noun* ❶ a wild animal's resting place. ❷ a person's hiding place or den.

laird »*noun* (in Scotland) a person who owns a large estate.

laissez-faire »*noun* a policy of leaving things to take their own course, without interfering.
– say less-ay-**fair**

> ℹ **laissez-faire** means 'allow to do' in French

laity »*noun* the people who are not priests or ministers of the Church.
– say lay-i-ti

lake

lam »*verb* (**lams, lamming, lammed**) hit something hard or repeatedly.

> ✓ double the **m** in **lamming** and **lammed**

lama »*noun* ❶ a title given as a mark of respect to a spiritual leader in Tibetan Buddhism. ❷ a Tibetan or Mongolian Buddhist monk.
– say **lah**-muh

> ℹ **lama** is Tibetan for 'superior one', and it is not to be confused with the South American animal, the **llama**

lamb (verb: **lambs, lambing, lambed**) [young sheep]

lambada »*noun* a fast Brazilian dance which couples perform in close physical contact.
– say lam-**bah**-duh

lambaste »*verb* (**lambastes, lambasting, lambasted**) criticize someone harshly.
– say lam-**baysst** or lam-**bast**

> ✓ **lambaste** can also be spelled **lambast**: both spellings are correct

lambda »*noun* the eleventh letter of the Greek alphabet (Λ, λ).
– say **lam**-duh

lambed

lambent »*adjective* lit up or flickering with a soft glow.
– say **lam**-buhnt

lambing [giving birth to lambs]

lambs

lambswool

lame[1] [walking with difficulty due to injury of the leg or foot]
  lamely
  lameness

lame[2] »*noun* fabric with interwoven gold or silver threads.
– say **lah**-may

> ✓ the name of the fabric **lame** can also be spelled **lamé**, with an acute accent (as in the original French)

lame duck »*noun* ❶ an unsuccessful person or thing. ❷ (in American English) an official in the final period of office, after the election of a successor.

lamely

lameness

lament »*noun* ❶ a passionate expression of grief. ❷ a song, piece of music, or poem expressing grief or regret.
»*verb* (**laments, lamenting, lamented**) ❶ mourn a person's death. ❷ (**lamented** or **late lamented**) a way of referring to a dead person. ❸ express regret or disappointment about something.
– say luh-**ment**
  lamentation

lamentable »*adjective* very bad or regrettable.
– say la-muhn-tuh-b'l
  lamentably

lamentation

lamented

lamenting

laments

lamina »*noun* (plural **laminae**) a thin layer, plate, or scale of rock, tissue, or other material.
– say **lam**-i-nuh [singular], **lam**-i-nee [plural]
  laminar

> ✓ make the plural by adding an **e** (like the original Latin): **laminae**

laminate »*verb* (**laminates, laminating, laminated**) ❶ cover a flat surface with a layer of protective material. ❷ make something by placing layer on layer. ❸ split something into layers or leaves. ❹ beat or roll metal into thin plates.
»*noun* a laminated structure or material.
  lamination
  laminator

> ✓ one **m**, one **n**: **laminate**

Lammas »*noun* the first day of August, formerly observed as harvest festival.
– say **lam**-muhss

lammed

lamming [hitting hard]

lamp

lampblack »*noun* a black pigment made from soot.

lamplight
  lamplit

lampoon »*verb* (**lampoons, lampooning, lampooned**) publicly mock or ridicule someone.

» *noun* a mocking attack.

lamprey »*noun* (plural **lampreys**) an eel-like jawless fish that has a sucker mouth with horny teeth.
– SAY lam-pri

 rey not ry: lamprey

lampshade

lams

Lancastrian »*noun* **❶** a person from Lancashire or Lancaster. **❷** a follower of the House of Lancaster in the Wars of the Roses.
» *adjective* relating to Lancashire or Lancaster, or the House of Lancaster.

 trian not trien: Lancastrian

lance »*noun* **❶** a long weapon with a wooden shaft and a pointed steel head, formerly used by a horseman in charging. **❷** a metal pipe supplying a jet of oxygen to a furnace or to make a very hot flame for cutting.
» *verb* (**lances, lancing, lanced**) **❶** prick or cut open a boil or wound with a sharp instrument. **❷** pierce something with or as if with a lance.

lance corporal »*noun* a rank of non-commissioned officer in the British army, above private and below corporal.

lanced

lanceolate »*adjective* having a narrow oval shape tapering to a point at each end.
– SAY lahn-si-uh-luht

lancer »*noun* a soldier of a cavalry regiment armed or formerly armed with lances.

lances

lancet »*noun* a small, broad two-edged knife with a sharp point, used in surgery.
– SAY lahn-sit

lancing

land (verb: **lands, landing, landed**)
landless

land agent »*noun* **❶** a person employed to manage an estate on behalf of its owners. **❷** a person who deals with the sale of land.

landau »*noun* an enclosed horse-drawn carriage.
– SAY lan-dor or lan-dow

landed »*adjective* owning a lot of land.

landfall »*noun* arrival on land after a sea or air journey.

landfill »*noun* **❶** the disposal of rubbish by burying it. **❷** rubbish that is buried.

landform »a natural feature of the earth's surface.

landing

landlady (plural **landladies**)

 plural: drop the **y** and add **ies**: landladies

landless

landline »*noun* a conventional telecommunications connection by cable laid across land.

landlocked »*adjective* surrounded by land.

landlord

landlubber »*noun* a person unfamiliar with the sea or sailing.

landmark

landmine

landowner
landowning

lands

landscape »*noun* **❶** all the visible features of an area of land. **❷** a picture of an area of countryside.
» *verb* (**landscapes, landscaping, landscaped**) improve the appearance of land by changing its contours, planting trees and shrubs, etc.

landslide

landslip

landward

landwards

lane

language

 remember the **u**: language

languid »*adjective* **❶** reluctant to exert yourself physically. **❷** weak or faint.
– SAY lang-gwid
languidly

languish »*verb* (**languishes, languishing, languished**) **❶** become weak or faint. **❷** be kept in an unpleasant place or situation: *he was languishing in jail.*

languor »*noun* tiredness or inactivity, especially when pleasurable.
– SAY lang-ger
languorous
languorously

 -uor not -or: languor

lank »*adjective* **❶** (of hair) long, limp, and straight. **❷** lanky.

lanky (adjective: **lankier, lankiest**)
lankiness

lanolin »*noun* a fatty substance from sheep's wool, used in skin cream.

lantern

lantern-jawed »having long, thin jaws.

lanthanum »*noun* a silvery-white rare-earth metallic chemical element.
– SAY lan-thu-nuhm

lanyard »*noun* ❶ a rope used on a ship, e.g. to raise and lower sails. ❷ a cord around the neck or shoulder for holding a whistle or similar object.
– SAY lan-yerd

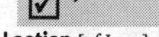 ✓ -yard not -iard: lanyard

Laotian [of Laos]
– SAY low-shuhn

lap (verb: **laps, lapping, lapped**)

 ✓ double the p to spell **lapping** and **lapped**

laparoscopy »*noun* (plural **laparoscopies**) an operation to make an opening into a person's abdomen to view the organs with a fibre-optic device or perform small-scale surgery.
– SAY lap-uh-**ros**-kuh-pi

lapdog »*noun* ❶ a small pampered pet dog. ❷ a person who is completely under the influence of another.

lapel »*noun* the part on each side of a coat or jacket which is folded back against the front opening.

✓ single p, single l: **lapel**

lapidary »*adjective* ❶ relating to the engraving, cutting, or polishing of gems. ❷ (of language) elegant and concise.
– SAY la-pi-duh-ri

lapis lazuli »*noun* ❶ a bright blue rock used in jewellery. ❷ ultramarine.
– SAY lap-iss **laz**-yuu-lI

Lapp »*noun* ❶ a member of a people of the extreme north of Scandinavia. ❷ the language of this people.

ℹ although the term **Lapp** is still very common, the people themselves prefer to be called **Sami**

lapped

lappet »*noun* ❶ a fold or hanging piece of flesh in some animals. ❷ a loose or overlapping part of a garment.
– SAY lap-pit

lapping

laps

lapse (verb: **lapses, lapsing, lapsed**)

laptop »*noun* a portable computer.

lapwing »*noun* a black-and-white bird with a crest on the head.

larboard »*noun* (an old word) the port side of a ship.

larceny »*noun* (plural **larcenies**) theft of personal property.
– SAY **lar**-suh-ni
larcenist
larcenous

ℹ the term **larceny** was replaced as an official crime in English law by theft in 1968

larch »*noun* a coniferous tree with hard wood and bright green needles that fall in winter.

lard (verb: **lards, larding, larded**)

larder

larding

lards

lardy

large (adjective: **larger, largest**)
largely
largeness
largish

large-scale

largesse »*noun* ❶ generosity. ❷ money or gifts given generously.
– SAY lar-**zhess** or lar-**jess**

✓ **largesse** can also be spelled without the final **e**: **largess** (both spellings are correct)

largest

largish

largo »*adverb & adjective* (in music) in a slow tempo and dignified in style.
– SAY **lar**-goh

lariat »*noun* a rope used as a lasso or for tethering animals.
– SAY la-ri-uht

✓ single t at the end: **lariat**

lark »*noun* ❶ a brown bird that sings while flying. ❷ an amusing adventure or escapade. ❸ (in British English) a foolish or trivial activity: *he's serious about this music lark.*
» *verb* (**larks, larking, larked**) behave in a playful and mischievous way.

larkspur »*noun* a plant with spiked flowers.

larva »*noun* (plural **larvae**) an immature form of an insect that looks very different from the adult creature, e.g. a caterpillar.
– SAY **lar**-vuh [singular], **lar**-vee [plural]
larval

☑️ not to be confused with **lava**, which is molten rock
make the plural by adding e (like the original Latin): **larvae**

larynges plural of **LARYNX**.

laryngitis »*noun* inflammation of the larynx.
– SAY la-rin-**jy**-tiss

larynx »*noun* (plural **larynxes** or **larynges**) the area at the top of the throat forming an air passage to the lungs and containing the vocal cords.
– SAY la-**ringks** [singular], luh-**rin**-jeez [plural]

ℹ️ the correct Greek plural is **larynges**

lasagne »*noun* ❶ pasta in the form of sheets. ❷ an Italian dish consisting of layers of lasagne baked with meat or vegetables and a cheese sauce.
– SAY luh-**zan**-yuh

lascivious »*adjective* feeling or showing an open or offensive sexual desire.
– SAY luh-**siv**-i-uhss
lasciviously
lasciviousness

☑️ lasc- not lass-: **lascivious**

laser »*noun* a device that produces an intense narrow beam of light.

☑️ s not z, and er not ar: **laser** (an acronym for *light amplification by stimulated emission of radiation*)

laserdisc »*noun* a disc resembling a large compact disc, used for high-quality video and multimedia.

laser printer »*noun* a computer printer in which a laser is used to form a pattern on a light-sensitive drum, which attracts toner.

lash (verb: **lashes, lashing, lashed**)
lashing

lass (plural **lasses**)

Lassa fever »*noun* an often fatal disease passed on by a virus and occurring chiefly in West Africa.
– SAY lass-uh

ℹ️ **Lassa fever** is named after a village in Nigeria

lassie

lassitude »*noun* weariness; lack of energy.

lasso »*noun* (plural **lassos** or **lassoes**) a rope with a noose at one end, used for catching cattle.
» *verb* (**lassoes, lassoing, lassoed**) catch an animal with a lasso.

– SAY luh-**soo** or lass-**oh**

☑️ despite the pronunciation, **lasso** is correctly spelled with one **o** at the end, not two
the plural of **lasso** can have either **os** or **es**: **lassos** or **lassoes**

last[1] (plural **last**) [coming after all others; the last person or thing]

last[2] (verb: **lasts, lasting, lasted**) [continue]

last[3] »*noun* a block used by a shoemaker for shaping or repairing a shoes.

last-ditch

lasted

lasting
lastingly

lastly

last post »*noun* (in the British armed forces) a bugle call giving notice of the hour of retiring at night, played also at military funerals and acts of remembrance.

last rites »*plural noun* Christian rites given to a person who is about to die.

lasts

latch (verb: **latches, latching, latched**)

latchkey »*noun* a key of an outer door of a house.

late (adjective: **later, latest**)

latecomer

lateen sail »*noun* a triangular sail set at an angle of 45° to the mast.
– SAY la-**teen**

lately

latent »*adjective* existing but not yet developed, showing, or active: *her latent talent.*
latency
latently

latent heat »*noun* the heat needed to change a solid into a liquid or vapour, or a liquid into a vapour, without change of temperature.

later

lateral »*adjective* of, at, towards, or from the side or sides.
– SAY **lat**-uh-ruhl
laterally

lateral thinking »*noun* the solving of a problem by thinking of new ways to approach it.

latest

latex »*noun* ❶ a milky fluid in some plants, which thickens when exposed to the air. ❷ a synthetic product resembling this, used to make paints, coatings, etc.

- **say** lay-teks

lath »*noun* (plural **laths**) a thin, flat strip of wood.

lathe »*noun* a machine that shapes pieces of wood or metal by turning them against a cutting tool.
- **say** *rhymes with* bathe

lather »*noun* **❶** a frothy mass of bubbles produced by soap when mixed with water. **❷** heavy sweat visible on a horse's coat as a white foam.
» *verb* (**lathers, lathering, lathered**) **❶** cover with or form a lather. **❷** cover or spread generously with a substance.

Latin

Latina »*noun* (plural **Latinas**) a female Latin American inhabitant of the United States.
- **say** luh-tee-nuh

Latin American »*adjective* relating to the parts of the American continent where Spanish or Portuguese are spoken.
» *noun* a person from this region.

Latinate »*adjective* (of language) having the character of Latin.
- **say** lat-i-nayt

Latino »*noun* (plural **Latinos**) a Latin American inhabitant of the United States.
- **say** luh-tee-noh

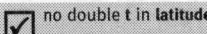 the plural of **Latino** has **os** not **oes**: **Latinos**

latitude »*noun* **❶** the distance of a place north or south of the equator. **❷** (**latitudes**) regions a particular distance from the equator: *northern latitudes*. **❸** scope for freedom of action or thought.
- **say** la-ti-tyood

✓ no double **t** in **latitude**

latrine »*noun* a toilet in a camp or barracks.
- **say** luh-**treen**

latte »*noun* a drink of frothy steamed milk to which a shot of espresso coffee is added.
- **say** lah-tay

latter »*adjective* **❶** nearer to the end than to the beginning. **❷** recent. **❸** (**the latter**) referring to the second or second-mentioned of two people or things.

latter-day »*adjective* modern or contemporary: *a latter-day Noah*.

Latter-Day Saints »*plural noun* the Mormons' name for themselves.

latterly »*adverb* **❶** recently. **❷** in the later stages of a period of time.

lattice »*noun* a structure or pattern of strips crossing each other with square or diamond-shaped spaces left between.
latticed
latticework

Latvian

laud »*verb* (**lauds, lauding, lauded**) praise someone highly.
- **say** lawd

laudable »*adjective* deserving praise and commendation.
laudably

laudanum »*noun* a liquid containing opium, formerly used as a painkiller.
- **say** law-duh-nuhm

laudatory »*adjective* expressing praise and commendation.
- **say** law-duh-tuh-ri

lauded

lauding

lauds

laugh (verb: **laughs, laughing, laughed**)

laughable
laughably

✓ **-able** not **-ible: laughable**

laughed

laughing

laughs

laughter

launch (verb: **launches, launching, launched**)
launcher

launder (verb: **launders, laundering, laundered**)

launderette

✓ **launderette** can also be spelled without the **e** between the **d** and **r: laundrette**

laundering

launders

laundress (plural **laundresses**)

laundrette another way of spelling **LAUNDERETTE**.

laundromat »*noun* (trademark in the US) a launderette.

laundry (plural **laundries**)

✓ plural: drop the **y** and add **ies: laundries**

laureate »*noun* **❶** a person given an award for outstanding creative or intellectual achievement. **❷** a poet laureate.
- **say** lo-ri-uht

 remember the **e** at the end of **laureate**

laurel »*noun* ❶ an evergreen shrub or small tree with dark green glossy leaves. ❷ (**laurels**) a crown of bay leaves awarded as a mark of honour in classical times. ❸ (**laurels**) honour or praise.

> ✓ **el** not **ell: laurel**

lava »*noun* hot molten rock that erupts from a volcano, or solid rock formed when this cools.

> ✓ no **r** in **lava** (not to be confused with a **larva** or caterpillar)

lavatorial »*adjective* (of conversation or humour) characterized by reference to lavatories and bodily functions.

lavatory (plural **lavatories**)

> ✓ plural: drop the **y** and add **ies: lavatories**

lavender »*noun* ❶ a small strong-smelling shrub with bluish-purple flowers. ❷ a pale bluish-purple colour.

> ✓ end **and er: lavender** (only one **a**)

lavish »*adjective* ❶ very rich, elaborate, or luxurious. ❷ giving or given in great amounts.
»*verb* (**lavishes, lavishing, lavished**) (**lavish on**) give something in abundant or extravagant quantities.
lavishly

law

law-abiding »*adjective* obeying the laws of society.

lawbreaker

lawful »*adjective* allowed by or obeying law or rules.
lawfully
lawfulness

> ℹ what is the difference between **lawful** and **legal**? **Lawful** refers to the law but also to the rules applying to an activity, whereas **legal** refers only to law: thus there might be some debate as to whether a goal scored in soccer is **lawful**, but not whether it is **legal**.

> ✓ -**ful** not -**full: lawful**

lawless
lawlessly
lawlessness

law lord »*noun* (in the UK) a member of the House of Lords qualified to perform its legal work.

lawmaker

lawn[1] [area of mown grass]

lawn[2] »*noun* a fine linen or cotton fabric.

lawnmower

lawsuit »*noun* a claim brought to a law court to be decided.

lawyer

lax »*adjective* (**laxer, laxest**) ❶ not sufficiently strict, severe, or careful. ❷ (of limbs or muscles) relaxed.
laxity
laxness

laxative »*adjective* tending to make someone empty their bowels.
»*noun* a laxative drug or medicine.

laxer

laxest

laxity

laxness

lay[1] (verb: **lays, laying, laid**) [put something down]

> ℹ make sure that you use the words **lay** and **lie** correctly. **Lay** generally means 'put something down', as in *they are going to lay the carpet*, whereas **lie** broadly means 'be in a horizontal position to rest', as in *why don't you lie down?* The past tense and past participle of **lay** is **laid**, as in *they laid the carpet*; the past tense of **lie** is **lay** (*he lay on the floor*) and the past participle is **lain** (*she had lain awake for hours*).

lay[2] »*adjective* ❶ not having an official position in the church. ❷ not having professional qualifications or expert knowledge.

lay[3] past of **LIE**[1].

layabout

lay-by »*noun* (plural **lay-bys**) an area at the side of a road where vehicles may stop.

> ✓ the plural of **lay-by** simply adds an **s: lay-bys**

layer (verb: **layers, layering, layered**)

layette »*noun* a set of clothing and bedclothes for a new baby.

laying

layman »*noun* (plural **laymen**) ❶ a member of a Church who is not a priest or minister. ❷ a person without professional or specialized knowledge.

lay-off »*noun* a temporary break from an activity.

layout

layperson »*noun* = LAYMAN.

lays

laze (verb: **lazes, lazing, lazed**)

lazy (adjective: **lazier**, **laziest**)
 lazily
 laziness
lazybones (plural **lazybones**)
lea »*noun* an open area of grassy land.

> ℹ️ do not confuse **lea** with **lee**, which means 'shelter from wind or weather given by an object'

leach »*verb* (**leaches**, **leaching**, **leached**) remove a substance from soil by the action of water passing through it.

> ✅ **ea** in the middle: **leach** (a **leech** is a bloodsucking creature)

lead¹ (verb: **leads**, **leading**, **led**) [cause a person to go with you]

> ℹ️ remember that the past tense and participle of the verb **lead** is **led**, without an **a**, as in *the captain led from the front* and *she has led a sheltered life*. Do not confuse this with the metal **lead**.

lead² »*noun* ❶ a heavy bluish-grey metallic element. ❷ the part of a pencil that makes a mark.
leaded »*adjective* ❶ framed, covered, or weighted with lead. ❷ (of petrol) containing lead.
leaden »*adjective* ❶ dull, heavy, or slow. ❷ dull grey in colour of lead.
 leadenly
leader
 leaderless
 leadership
leading
leads
lead-up
leaf (plural **leaves**; verb: **leafs**, **leafing**, **leafed**)

> ✅ note that the noun drops the **f** and adds **ves** to form the plural, but the verb keeps the **f** in inflections: **leafs**, **leafing**, etc.

leafier
leafiest
leafiness
leafing
leaflet (verb: **leaflets**, **leafleting**, **leafleted**)

> ✅ do not double the **t** to spell **leafleting** and **leafleted**

leafs
leafy (adjective: **leafier**, **leafiest**)
 leafiness
league »*noun* ❶ a collection of people, countries, or groups that combine for a particular purpose. ❷ a group of sports clubs which play each other over a period for a championship. ❸ a class of quality or excellence. ❹ a former measure of distance, of about three miles.
leak (verb: **leaks**, **leaking**, **leaked**) [allow contents to escape through a hole or crack]
 leakage
 leaky
lean¹ (verb: **leans**, **leaning**, **leaned** or **leant**) [be in or move into a sloping position]
lean² »*adjective* (**leaner**, **leanest**) ❶ (of a person) having little fat; thin. ❷ (of meat) containing little fat. ❸ difficult and unproductive.
 » *noun* the lean part of meat.
 leanness
lean-to »*noun* (plural **lean-tos**) a small building sharing a wall with a larger building.
leap (verb: **leaps**, **leaping**, **leaped** or **leapt**)
leapfrog (verb: **leapfrogs**, **leapfrogging**, **leapfrogged**)
leaping
leaps
leapt
leap year »*noun* a year with 366 days, occurring every four years.
learn (verb: **learns**, **learning**, **learned** or **learnt**)
 learner

> ✅ remember the **a** in **learn** and related words like **learner**

learned »*adjective* having gained a lot of knowledge by studying.
 – SAY ler-nid
 learnedly
 learnedness
learner
learning
learning curve »*noun* the rate of a person's progress in gaining experience or new skills.
learns
learnt
lease »*noun* an agreement by which one person uses the land, property, etc. of another for a specified time in return for payment.
 »*verb* (**leases**, **leasing**, **leased**) let or rent something on lease.
leasehold »*noun* the holding of property by lease.
 leaseholder
leash »*noun* a dog's lead.
leasing

least

leastways »*adverb* (in informal English) at least.

leather

leathery »*adjective* having a tough, hard texture like leather.

leave (verb: **leaves, leaving, left**)
leaver

leaven »*noun* a substance added to dough to make it ferment and rise.
» *verb* (**leavens, leavening, leavened**)
❶ cause dough or bread to ferment and rise by adding leaven. ❷ improve: *the debate was leavened by humour.*
– SAY lev-uhn

leaver

leaves

leave-taking

leaving

leavings »*plural noun* things that have been left as worthless.

Lebanese (plural **Lebanese**)

lecher »*noun* a lecherous man.
lechery

lecherous »*adjective* showing excessive or offensive sexual desire.
lecherously
lecherousness

> ✓ there is no t in **lecherous**

lechery

lectern »*noun* a tall stand with a sloping top from which a speaker can read while standing up.
– SAY lek-tern

lecture (verb: **lectures, lecturing, lectured**)
lecturer
lectureship

led past and past participle of **LEAD**[1].

ledge

ledger »*noun* ❶ a book or other collection of financial accounts. ❷ a weight on a fishing line.

> ✓ remember, there is a **d** in **ledger**

lee »*noun* ❶ shelter from wind or weather given by an object. ❷ (also **lee side**) the sheltered side; the side away from the wind.

> ℹ do not confuse **lee** with **lea**, which means 'open area of grassy land'

leech »*noun* ❶ a worm that sucks the blood of animals or people. ❷ a person who makes profit from or lives off others.

» *verb* (**leeches, leeching, leeched**) (**leech on** or **off**) habitually exploit or rely on someone.

> ℹ do not confuse **leech** with **leach**, which means 'remove a substance from soil by the action of water'

leek [vegetable]

leer »*verb* (**leers, leering, leered**) look or gaze at someone in a lustful or unpleasant way.
» *noun* a lustful or unpleasant look.

leery »*adjective* (**leerier, leeriest**) cautious or wary.
leeriness

lees »*plural noun* the sediment of wine in the barrel; dregs.

leeward »*adjective & adverb* on or towards the side sheltered from the wind and towards which the wind is blowing.
– SAY lee-werd or loo-erd

leeway »*noun* the amount of freedom to move or act that is available.

left[1] [opposite of *right*]

left[2] past and past participle of **LEAVE**.

left-field »*adjective* (in American English) unconventional or experimental.

left-handed

left-hander

leftie another way of spelling **LEFTY**.

lefties

leftism »*noun* left-wing political views or policies.
leftist

left luggage »*noun* luggage left in temporary storage at a railway station, bus station, or airport.

leftmost

leftover

leftward

leftwards

left wing »*noun* ❶ the radical, reforming, or socialist section of a political party or system. ❷ the left side of a sports team on the field or of an army.
left-winger

> ✓ when using **left wing** as an adjective, add a hyphen, as in *left-wing activists*

lefty »*noun* (plural **lefties**) (in informal English) ❶ a left-wing person. ❷ a left-handed person.

> ✓ **lefty** can also be spelled **leftie**

leg (verb: **legs, legging, legged**)

legacy »*noun* (plural **legacies**) **①** an amount of money or property left to someone in a will. **②** something handed down by a predecessor.

> ✓ plural: drop the **y** and add **ies**: **legacies**

legal »*adjective* **①** having to do with or required by the law. **②** permitted by law.
legally

> ℹ on the difference between **legal** and **lawful**, see the note at **LAWFUL**

legal aid »*noun* payment from public funds given to people who cannot afford to pay for legal advice.

legalese »*noun* the formal and technical language of legal documents.
– SAY lee-guh-leez

legalise another way of spelling **LEGALIZE**.

legality »*noun* (plural **legalities**) **①** the quality or state of being legal. **②** (**legalities**) obligations imposed by law.

legalize »*verb* (**legalizes**, **legalizing**, **legalized**) make something legal.
legalization

> ✓ many people prefer the alternative spellings **legalise**, **legalises**, etc., and **legalisation**: both **s** and **z** spellings are correct

legally

legal tender »*noun* coins or banknotes that must be accepted if offered in payment.

legate »*noun* a representative of the Pope.
– SAY le-guht

legation »*noun* **①** a diplomat below the rank of ambassador, and their staff. **②** the official residence of a diplomat.
– SAY li-gay-sh'n

legato »*adverb & adjective* (in music) in a smooth, flowing manner.
– SAY li-gah-toh

legend

legendary »*adjective* **①** having to do with legends. **②** remarkable enough to be famous.

> ✓ **dary** not **dry**: **legendary**

legerdemain »*noun* **①** skilful use of your hands when performing conjuring tricks. **②** deception; trickery.
– SAY le-jer-di-**mayn**

legged

leggier

leggiest

legging

leggy »*adjective* (**leggier**, **leggiest**) **①** long-legged. **②** (of a plant) having a long and straggly stem or stems.

legible »*adjective* (of handwriting or print) clear enough to read.
legibility
legibly

> ✓ there is no **d**, and the ending is **-ible** not **-able**: **legible**

legion »*noun* **①** a division of 3,000–6,000 men in the ancient Roman army. **②** (**a legion** or **legions of**) a vast number of people or things.
» *adjective* great in number.

legionary »*noun* (plural **legionaries**) a soldier in an ancient Roman legion.
» *adjective* having to do with an ancient Roman legion.

legionnaire »*noun* a member of the French Foreign legion, or of an association of former servicemen and servicewomen.
– SAY lee-juh-**nair**

> ✓ double **n**, and an **e** at the end: **legionnaire** is a French word

legionnaires' disease »*noun* a form of pneumonia spread chiefly in water droplets through air conditioning systems.

> ℹ so called because of an outbreak at an American Legion meeting in 1976

leg iron »*noun* a metal band or chain placed around a prisoner's ankle as a restraint.

legislate »*verb* (**legislates**, **legislating**, **legislated**) **①** make or enact laws. **②** (**legislate for** or **against**) prepare for a situation or event.
– SAY lej-iss-layt

> ✓ **leg** not **ledg**: **legislate**

legislation »*noun* laws as a whole.

legislative »*adjective* **①** having the power to make laws. **②** relating to laws or a legislature.
– SAY lej-iss-luh-tiv

legislator »*noun* a person who makes laws.

> ✓ **-or** not **-er**: **legislator**

legislature »*noun* the legislative body of a state.
– SAY lej-iss-luh-cher

legitimate »*adjective* **①** allowed by the law or to rules. **②** able to be defended with reasoning. **③** (of a child) born of parents lawfully married to each other.

» verb (**legitimates**, **legitimating**, **legitimated**) make something legitimate.
– SAY li-**jit**-i-muht [adjective], li-**jit**-i-mayt [verb]
legitimacy
legitimately
legitimation

✓ leg not lig, and ate not ite: **legitimate**

legitimize **»verb** (**legitimizes**, **legitimizing**, **legitimized**) make something legitimate.
– SAY li-**jit**-i-myz

✓ many people prefer the alternative spellings **legitimise**, **legitimises**, etc.: both s and z spellings are correct

legless

legroom

legs

legume **»noun** ❶ a plant with seeds in pods, such as a pea. ❷ a seed, pod, or other part of such a plant, used as food.
– SAY **leg**-yoom

leguminous **»adjective** relating to plants that bear their seeds in pods, such as the pea.
– SAY li-**gyoo**-mi-nuhss

legwork **»noun** work that involves tiring or tedious movement from place to place.

lei **»noun** a Polynesian garland of flowers.
– SAY lay

Leicester **»noun** a mild, firm orange-coloured cheese originally made in Leicestershire.

leisure
leisured
leisurely

✓ leis not les: **leisure**

leisurewear

leitmotif **»noun** a frequently repeated theme in a musical or literary composition.
– SAY **lyt**-moh-teef

✓ a German word meaning 'leading motif', **leitmotif** can also be spelled **leitmotiv**: both spellings are correct

lemming **»noun** a short-tailed Arctic rodent, which periodically migrates in large numbers in search of food.

lemon

✓ only one m: **lemon**

lemonade

lemon grass **»noun** a tropical grass which yields an oil that smells of lemon, used in

Asian cooking and in perfumery and medicine.

lemur **»noun** a tree-dwelling primate with a pointed snout, found only in Madagascar.
– SAY **lee**-mer

lend (verb: **lends**, **lending**, **lent**)
lender

length

lengthen (verb: **lengthens**, **lengthening**, **lengthened**)

lengthier

lengthiest

lengthways

lengthwise

lengthy (adjective: **lengthier**, **lengthiest**)

✓ drop the y and add ier or iest to spell **lengthier** or **lengthiest**

lenient **»adjective** not strict; merciful.
– SAY **lee**-ni-uhnt
leniency
leniently

✓ ent not ant: **lenient**

lens **»noun** (plural **lenses**) ❶ a piece of transparent curved material that concentrates or spreads out light rays. ❷ the light-gathering device of a camera. ❸ the transparent part of the eye that focuses light on to the retina.
– SAY lenz

Lent **»noun** (in the Christian Church) the period immediately before Easter, which is devoted to fasting and penitence.

lent past and past participle of **LEND**.

Lenten **»adjective** having to do with Lent.

lentil **»noun** a pulse which is dried and then soaked and cooked prior to eating.

lento **»adverb & adjective** (in music) slow or slowly.

Leo **»noun** a constellation and sign of the zodiac (the Lion, 23 July–22 August).

leonine **»adjective** having to do with or resembling a lion or lions.
– SAY **lee**-uh-nyn

leopard

leotard

leper **»noun** ❶ a person suffering from leprosy. ❷ a person who is shunned by others: *a social leper.*

Lepidoptera **»plural noun** butterflies and moths collectively.
– SAY lep-i-**dop**-tuh-ruh

leprechaun **»noun** (in Irish folklore) a small, mischievous sprite.
– SAY **lep**-ruh-kawn

leprosy »*noun* a contagious disease that causes discoloration and lumps on the skin and, in severe cases, disfigurement and deformities.

leprous »*adjective* referring to or suffering from leprosy.

lesbian »*noun* a homosexual woman.
» *adjective* referring to lesbians or lesbianism.
  lesbianism

> ✓ **les** not **lez**: **lesbian** (from the name of the Greek island of *Lesbos*, home of the poet Sappho who is associated with lesbianism)

lese-majeste »*noun* the action of insulting or demeaning a monarch.
– **say** leez ma-jiss-ti

> ✓ **lese-majeste** can also be written **lèse-majesté**, with acute and grave accents (as in French). It comes from Latin, meaning 'injured sovereignty', and is sometimes written **lese-majesty**.

lesion »*noun* an area of skin or part of the body which has suffered damage.
– **say** lee-*zh*uhn

less

> ℹ️ for an explanation of the difference between **less** and **fewer**, see the note at **FEW**

lessee »*noun* a person who holds the lease of a property.

lessen (verb: **lessens, lessening, lessened**) [make or become less]

lesser

lesson [period of learning or teaching]

lessor »*noun* a person who leases or lets a property to another.

> ✓ **-or** not **-er**: **lessor**

lest »*conjunction* ❶ with the intention of preventing; to avoid the risk of. ❷ because of the possibility of.

let (verb: **lets, letting, let**) [allow]

> ✓ double the **t** in **letting**

let-down

lethal »*adjective* ❶ enough to cause death. ❷ very harmful or destructive.
– **say** lee-th'l
  lethally

lethargy »*noun* a lack of energy and enthusiasm.
– **say** leth-er-ji
  lethargic
  lethargically

let-off

lets [as in *she lets the cat out*]

let's [let us, as in *let's have a drink*]

letter

letter box »*noun* ❶ a slot in a door through which mail is delivered. ❷ **(letterbox)** a format for presenting widescreen films on a standard television screen, in which the image fills the width but not the height of the screen.

lettered »(an old word) able to read and write.

letterhead »*noun* a printed heading on stationery.

lettering

letting

lettuce

> ✓ **uce** not **ice**: **lettuce**

let-up

leukaemia »*noun* a serious disease in which increased numbers of immature or abnormal white cells are produced, stopping the production of normal blood cells.
– **say** loo-kee-mi-uh

> ✓ as with other words derived from the Greek word *haima* 'blood' (such as **haemorrhage**), **leukaemia** is spelled with **aem** not **eam** or **em**. The spelling **leukemia** is American.

levee[1] »*noun* a formal reception of visitors or guests.
– **say** lev-i or lev-ay

levee[2] »*noun* ❶ an embankment built to prevent the overflow of a river. ❷ a ridge of sediment deposited naturally alongside a river.
– **say** lev-i or li-vee

level (verb: **levels, levelling, levelled**)

> ✓ double the final **l** in **levelling** and **levelled** (the spellings **leveling** and **leveled** are American)

level-headed
  level-headedness

levelled

levelling

levels

lever »*noun* ❶ a bar resting on a pivot, used to move a load with one end when pressure is applied to the other. ❷ an arm or handle that is moved to operate a mechanism.

» *verb* (**levers**, **levering**, **levered**) **❶** lift or move something with a lever. **❷** move something with effort.

leverage »*noun* **❶** the exertion of force by means of a lever. **❷** the power to influence: *political leverage.*

levered

leveret »*noun* a young hare in its first year.
– SAY lev-uh-rit

levering

levers

leviathan »*noun* **❶** (in biblical use) a sea monster. **❷** a very large or powerful thing.
– SAY li-vy-uh-thuhn

levied

levies

levitate »*verb* (**levitates**, **levitating**, **levitated**) rise or cause something to rise and hover in the air.
– SAY lev-i-tayt
levitation

 only one **v**: **levitate**

levity »*noun* the treatment of a serious matter with humour or lack of respect.

levy »*noun* (plural **levies**) **❶** the imposing of a tax, fee, fine, or subscription. **❷** a sum of money raised by a levy.
» *verb* (**levies**, **levying**, **levied**) impose or seize something as a levy.

lewd »*adjective* crude and offensive in a sexual way.
lewdly
lewdness

lexical »*adjective* **❶** relating to the words of a language. **❷** relating to a lexicon or dictionary.
lexically

lexicography »*noun* the practice of writing dictionaries.
– SAY leks-i-kog-ruh-fi
lexicographer

lexicon »*noun* **❶** the vocabulary of a person, language, or branch of knowledge. **❷** a dictionary.

ley »*noun* a piece of land where grass is grown temporarily.
– SAY rhymes with pay

ley line »*noun* a supposed straight line connecting three or more ancient sites, associated by some people with lines of energy.
– SAY rhymes with pay or pea

LGV »*abbreviation* large goods vehicle.

liability »*noun* (plural **liabilities**) **❶** the state of being liable. **❷** a sum of money

that is owed. **❸** a person or thing likely to cause you embarrassment or trouble.

 plural: drop the **y** and add **ies**: **liabilities**

liable »*adjective* **❶** responsible by law. **❷** (**liable to**) able to be punished by law for something. **❸** (**liable to do**) likely to do something. **❹** (**liable to**) likely to experience something undesirable.

liaise »*verb* (**liaises**, **liaising**, **liaised**) **❶** cooperate on a matter of shared concern. **❷** (**liaise between**) act as a link to assist communication between two or more people or groups.
– SAY li-ayz

two **i**'s: **liaise**

liaison »*noun* **❶** communication or cooperation between people or organizations. **❷** a sexual relationship.

many people forget the second **i** of **liaison** (a French word)

liana »*noun* a woody climbing plant that hangs from trees.
– SAY li-ah-nuh

liane »*noun* = LIANA.

liar

ar not **er**: **liar**

libation »*noun* **❶** a drink poured out as an offering to a god. **❷** (mainly used in a humorous way) an alcoholic drink.
– SAY ly-bay-sh'n

libel »*noun* the publication of a false statement that is damaging to a person's reputation.
» *verb* (**libels**, **libelling**, **libelled**) publish a false statement about someone.
libellous

double the **l** in **libelling** and **libelled** (the spellings **libeling** and **libeled** are American)

liberal »*adjective* **❶** respectful and accepting of behaviour or opinions different from your own. **❷** (of a society, law, etc.) favourable to individual rights and freedoms. **❸** (in politics) supporting the freedom of individuals and favouring moderate political reform. **❹** (**Liberal**) of the Liberal Democrat party. **❺** not strictly literal or exact. **❻** generous in applying or adding something.
» *noun* a person with liberal views.
liberalism
liberally

use a capital **L** when referring to the Liberal Democrat party (*the Liberal* *leader*), but a small **l** in other cases (*liberal citizenship laws*, *liberal amounts of wine*)

liberalise another way of spelling **LIBERALIZE**.

liberalism

liberalize »*verb* (**liberalizes, liberalizing, liberalized**) remove or loosen restrictions on something.
liberalization

> ✓ many people prefer the alternative spellings **liberalise, liberalises**, etc., and **liberalisation**: both **s** and **z** spellings are correct

liberally

liberate »*verb* (**liberates, liberating, liberated**) ❶ set a person free. ❷ (**liberated**) free from social conventions.
liberation
liberator

Liberian [of Liberia]

libertarian »*noun* a person who believes that the state should not restrict the liberty of individual people.
libertarianism

libertine »*noun* a man who behaves immorally, especially in sexual matters.
– SAY li-ber-teen
libertinism

liberty »*noun* (plural **liberties**) ❶ the state of being free. ❷ a right or privilege. ❸ the power or ability to act as you please. ❹ a rude remark or action.

> ✓ plural: drop the **y** and add **ies**: **liberties**

libidinous »*adjective* having or showing excessive sexual drive.
– SAY li-**bid**-i-nuhss

libido »*noun* (plural **libidos**) sexual desire.
– SAY li-**bee**-doh

> ✓ the plural of **libido** (a Latin word meaning 'lust') has **os** not **oes**: **libidos**

Libra »*noun* a constellation and sign of the zodiac (the Scales or Balance, 23 September–22 October).
– SAY lee-bruh

librarian
librarianship

library (plural **libraries**)

> ✓ don't forget the first **r**: library plural: drop the **y** and add **ies**: **libraries**

libretto »*noun* (plural **libretti** or **librettos**) the words of an opera or other long vocal work.

– SAY li-**bret**-toh [singular], li-**bret**-ti [plural]
librettist

> ✓ the plural can be spelled either with an **i** (as in the original Italian) or **os**: **libretti** or **librettos**

Libyan [of Libya]

lice plural of **LOUSE**.

licence »*noun* ❶ an official permit to own, use, or do something. ❷ a writer's or artist's freedom to alter facts or ignore accepted rules. ❸ freedom to behave without restraint.

> ✓ in British English, **licence** is the spelling for the noun, and **license** for the verb; American English uses the **ense** spelling for both

license »*verb* (**licenses, licensing, licensed**) ❶ grant a licence to someone. ❷ authorize something.
» *noun* American spelling of **LICENCE**.

licensee »*noun* the holder of a licence, especially to sell alcoholic drinks.

licenses

licensing

licentiate »*noun* the holder of a certificate allowing them to practise a particular profession.
– SAY ly-**sen**-shi-uht

licentious »*adjective* unprincipled in sexual matters.
– SAY ly-**sen**-shuhss
licentiously
licentiousness

> ✓ **tious** not **cious**: **licentious**

lichen »*noun* a simple plant consisting of a fungus living in close association with an alga, growing on rocks, walls, and trees.
– SAY **ly**-kuhn or **li**-chuhn

lick (verb: **licks, licking, licked**)

lickety-split

licking

licks

lickspittle »*noun* a person who behaves with excessive obedience to those in power.

licorice American spelling of **LIQUORICE**.

lid
lidded

lido »*noun* (plural **lidos**) a public open-air swimming pool.
– SAY **lee**-doh or **ly**-doh

> ✓ the plural of **lido**, an Italian word, has **os** not **oes**: **lidos**

lie[1] (verb: **lies, lying, lay;** past participle **lain**) [take up a horizontal position]

> ℹ for the correct use of **lay** and **lie**, see the note at **LAY**[1]

lie[2] (verb: **lies, lying, lied**) [intentionally false statement; tell a lie]

Liebfraumilch »*noun* a light white wine from the Rhine valley in Germany.
– SAY leeb-frow-milsh

> ℹ **Liebfraumilch** in German means 'milk of the Dear Lady', i.e. the Virgin Mary, patroness of a convent where it was first made

lied »*noun* (plural **lieder**) a type of German song for solo voice with piano accompaniment.
– SAY leed [singular], lee-der [plural]

lie-down

liege »*noun* (a historical term) ❶ (also **liege lord**) a feudal superior. ❷ a vassal or subject.
– SAY leej

> ☑ the usual rule is **i** before **e**, except after **c**: **liege**

lie-in

lies

lieu »*noun* (**in lieu** or **in lieu of**) instead of.
– SAY lyoo or loo

lieutenant »*noun* ❶ a deputy or substitute acting for a superior. ❷ a rank of officer in the British army or in the navy.
– SAY lef-**ten**-uhnt

> ☑ there is no **f** in **lieutenant**

lieutenant colonel »*noun* a rank of officer in the army and the US air force, above major and below colonel.

lieutenant commander »*noun* a rank of officer in the navy, above lieutenant and below commander.

lieutenant general »*noun* a high rank of officer in the army, above major general and below general.

life (plural **lives**)

life assurance »*noun* = LIFE INSURANCE.

lifebelt

lifeblood »*noun* a vital factor or force.

lifeboat

lifebuoy

life form »*noun* any living thing.

lifeguard

life insurance »*noun* insurance that pays out a sum of money either on the death of the insured person or after a set period.

lifeless

lifelike

lifeline »*noun* ❶ a rope or line thrown to rescue someone in difficulties in water. ❷ a thing which is essential for the continued existence of someone or something.

lifelong

life peer »*noun* (in the UK) a peer whose title cannot be inherited.

lifesaver

life sciences »*plural noun* the sciences concerned with the study of living organisms, including biology, botany, and zoology.

lifespan »*noun* the length of time for which a person or animal lives or a thing functions.

lifestyle

life-support

life-threatening

lifetime

lift (verb: **lifts, lifting, lifted**)
lifter

lift-off

lifts

ligament »*noun* a band of tissue which connects two bones or cartilages or holds together a joint.
– SAY lig-uh-muhnt

> ☑ **ent** not **ant**: **ligament**

ligature »*noun* ❶ a cord used to tie up a bleeding artery. ❷ (in music) a slur or tie.
– SAY lig-uh-cher

light[1] (verb: **lights, lighting, lit;** past participle **lit** or **lighted**) [the form of energy that makes things visible]
lightless

light[2] (adjective: **lighter, lightest**) [of little weight]
lightly
lightness

light[3] »*verb* (**lights, lighting,** past and past participle **lit** or **lighted**) (**light on** or **upon**) discover something by chance.

lighten (verb: **lightens, lightening, lightened**)

lighter[1] »*noun* a device producing a small flame, used to light cigarettes.

lighter[2] »*noun* a barge used to transfer goods to and from ships in harbour.

lightest

light-fingered »*adjective* tending to steal things.

light-headed »*adjective* dizzy and slightly faint.

light-hearted
light-heartedly

lighthouse

lighting

lightless

lightly

lightness

lightning

> ☑ there is no **e** in the middle: **lightning**

lights »*plural noun* the lungs of sheep, pigs, or bullocks as food.

lightweight »*noun* ❶ a weight in boxing and other sports coming between featherweight and welterweight. ❷ a person of little importance: *a political lightweight*.

light year »*noun* the distance that light travels in one year, nearly 6 million million miles.

ligneous »*adjective* consisting of or resembling wood.
– SAY lig-ni-uhss

lignite »*noun* soft brownish coal.

likable another way of spelling LIKEABLE.

like (verb: **likes**, **liking**, **liked**)

> ℹ in writing and formal speech, do not use **like** to mean 'as if', as in *he's behaving like he owns the place*; you should use **as if** or **as though** instead

likeable

> ☑ **likeable** can also be spelled without the **e**: **likable**

liked

likelier

likeliest

likelihood

> ☑ likeli- not likely-: **likelihood**

likely (adjective: **likelier**, **likeliest**)

like-minded

liken (verb: **likens**, **likening**, **likened**)

likeness (plural **likenesses**)

likening

likens

likes

likewise

liking

lilac »*noun* ❶ a shrub or small tree with fragrant violet, pink, or white blossom. ❷ a pale pinkish-violet colour.

> ☑ there is no **k** at the end: **lilac**

lilies

Lilliputian »*adjective* very small or unimportant.
– SAY lil-li-**pyoo**-sh'n

> ☑ double **l** in the middle: **Lilliputian** (from the country of *Lilliput* in Jonathan Swift's *Gulliver's Travels*, inhabited by people six inches tall)

lilo »*noun* (plural **lilos**) an inflatable mattress used as a bed or for floating on water.
– SAY ly-loh

> ☑ lilo can also be spelled **Li-lo** and is a trademark when spelled like this

lilt »*noun* ❶ a characteristic rising and falling of the voice when speaking. ❷ a gentle rhythm in a tune.
» *verb* (**lilts**, **lilting**, **lilted**) speak or sing with a lilt.

lily »*noun* (plural **lilies**) a plant with large trumpet-shaped flowers on a tall, slender stem.

> ☑ plural: drop the **y** and add **ies**: **lilies**

lily-livered »*adjective* cowardly.

lily-white »*adjective* ❶ pure white. ❷ totally innocent or pure.

lima bean »*noun* an edible flat whitish bean.
– SAY lee-muh

> ℹ from *Lima*, the capital of Peru

limb

> ☑ mb not mn: **limb** (**limn** is a poetic word meaning 'paint or describe something')

limber »*adjective* supple; flexible.
» *verb* (**limbers**, **limbering**, **limbered**) (**limber up**) warm up in preparation for exercise or activity.
– SAY *rhymes with* timber

limbo[1] »*noun* ❶ (in some Christian beliefs) the supposed dwelling place of the souls of unbaptized infants, and of good people who died before Jesus. ❷ an uncertain period of waiting.

limbo[2] »*noun* (plural **limbos**) a West Indian dance in which a person bends backwards to pass under a horizontal bar.

lime[1] »*noun* a white alkaline substance used as a building material or fertilizer.

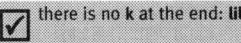

lime² »*noun* ❶ a green citrus fruit similar to a lemon. ❷ a bright light green colour. ❸ a drink made from lime juice.

lime³ »*noun* a deciduous tree with heart-shaped leaves and yellowish blossom.

limeade »*noun* a drink made from lime juice sweetened with sugar.

limelight »*noun* ❶ the focus of public attention. ❷ a strong white light produced by heating lime, formerly used in theatres.

limerick »*noun* a humorous five-line poem with a rhyme scheme *aabba*.

limestone »*noun* a hard rock composed mainly of calcium carbonate.

Limey »*noun* (plural **Limeys**) (in informal American and Australian English) a British person.

limit (verb: **limits, limiting, limited**)
limitless

> ✓ do not double the **t** when spelling **limiting** or **limited**

limitation »*noun* ❶ a restriction. ❷ a fault or failing.

limited

limited company »*noun* a private company whose owners only have legal responsibility for its debts up to specified amounts.

limiting

limitless

limits

limn »*verb* (**limns, limning, limned**) (a poetic term) depict or describe something in painting or words.
– **SAY** lim

limo »*noun* (plural **limos**) (in informal English) a limousine.

> ✓ the plural of **limo** has **os** not **oes**: **limos**

limousine »*noun* a large, luxurious car.

> ℹ the word **limousine** comes from *Limousin*, a region of central France

limp¹ »*verb* (**limps, limping, limped**) ❶ walk with difficulty because of an injured leg or foot. ❷ (of a damaged ship or aircraft) proceed with difficulty.
» *noun* a limping way of walking.

limp² »*adjective* ❶ not stiff or firm. ❷ without energy or will.
limply
limpness

limpet »*noun* a shellfish with a muscular foot for clinging tightly to rocks.

limpid »*adjective* ❶ (of a liquid or the eyes) clear. ❷ (especially of writing or

music) clear or tuneful.
limpidly

limping

limply

limpness

limps

linchpin »*noun* ❶ a pin through the end of an axle keeping a wheel in position. ❷ an extremely important person or thing.

> ✓ **linchpin** can also be spelled **lynchpin**: both spellings are correct

linctus »*noun* thick liquid cough medicine.

linden »*noun* a lime tree.

line (verb: **lines, lining, lined**)

lineage »*noun* ancestry or pedigree.
– **SAY** lin-i-ij

lineal »*adjective* ❶ in a direct line of descent or ancestry. ❷ linear.
– **SAY** lin-i-uhl

lineament »*noun* (a poetic term) a distinctive feature, especially of the face.
– **SAY** lin-i-uh-muhnt

linear »*adjective* ❶ arranged in or extending along a straight line. ❷ consisting of lines or outlines. ❸ involving one dimension only. ❹ progressing from one stage to another in a series of steps.
– **SAY** lin-i-er
linearity
linearly

lined

line drawing »*noun* a drawing based on the use of line rather than shading.

line manager »*noun* a manager to whom an employee is directly responsible.

linen »*noun* ❶ cloth woven from flax. ❷ articles such as sheets or clothes made, or traditionally made, of linen.

line-out »*noun* (in Rugby Union) the forming of parallel lines of players when the ball is thrown in from the touchline.

liner »*noun* ❶ a large passenger ship. ❷ a cosmetic for outlining or emphasizing a facial feature. ❸ a lining of a garment, container, etc.

lines

linesman »*noun* (plural **linesmen**) (in games played on a field or court) an official who assists the referee or umpire in deciding whether the ball is out of play.

line-up

ling¹ »*noun* a long-bodied sea fish.

ling² »*noun* the common heather.

linger (verb: **lingers, lingering, lingered**)
lingering

lingerie »*noun* women's underwear and nightclothes.
– **SAY** lan-*zh*uh-ri

lingo »*noun* (plural **lingos** or **lingoes**) (in informal English) ❶ a foreign language. ❷ the jargon of a particular subject or group.

> ✓ the plural of **lingo** can have **os** or **oes**: **lingos** or **lingoes**

lingua franca »*noun* (plural **lingua francas**) a language used as a common language between speakers whose native languages are different.
– **SAY** ling-gwuh **frang**-kuh

> ⚡ **lingua franca** is from an Italian phrase meaning 'Frankish tongue' (the Franks were an ancient people who once controlled much of Europe)

linguine »*plural noun* small ribbons of pasta.
– **SAY** ling-**gwee**-nay or ling-**gwee**-ni

linguist »*noun* ❶ a person who is good at foreign languages. ❷ a person who studies linguistics.

linguistic »*adjective* relating to language or linguistics.

linguistics »*plural noun* the scientific study of language.

liniment »*noun* an ointment rubbed on the body to relieve pain or bruising.

lining

link (verb: **links, linking, linked**)

linkage »*noun* ❶ the action of linking or the state of being linked. ❷ a system of links.

linked

linking

links

link-up

linnet »*noun* a finch with a reddish breast and forehead.

lino »*noun* (plural **linos**) linoleum.

linoleum »*noun* a shiny floor covering made from a mixture of linseed oil and powdered cork.
– **SAY** li-**noh**-li-uhm

linseed »*noun* the seeds of the flax plant, which produce an oil used in paint and varnish.

lint »*noun* ❶ short, fine fibres which separate from cloth or yarn during processing. ❷ a fabric used for dressing wounds.

lintel »*noun* a horizontal support across the top of a door or window.

> ✓ **el** not **le** or **ell**: **lintel**

lion

lioness (plural **lionesses**)

lion-hearted »*adjective* brave and determined.

lionize »*verb* (**lionizes, lionizing, lionized**) treat someone as a celebrity.

> ✓ many people prefer the alternative spellings **lionise, lionises**, etc.: both **s** and **z** spellings are correct

lip

lipid »*noun* (in chemistry) one of a class of fats that are insoluble in water.
– **SAY** lip-id

liposuction »*noun* a technique in cosmetic surgery for sucking out excess fat from under the skin.
– **SAY** lip-oh-suk-sh'n or ly-poh-suk-sh'n

lip-read »*verb* (**lip-reads, lip-reading, lip-read**) understand speech from watching a speaker's lip movements.
lip-reader

lip salve »*noun* a preparation to prevent or relieve sore or chapped lips.

lipstick

lip-sync »*verb* (**lip-syncs, lip-syncing, lip-synced**) move your lips in time with pre-recorded music or speech.

> ✓ **lip-sync** can also be spelled **lip-synch**: both spellings are correct

liquefy »*verb* (**liquefies, liquefying, liquefied**) make or become liquid.
– **SAY** lik-wi-fl
liquefaction

> ✓ **liquefy** can also be spelled **liquify**: both spellings are correct

liqueur »*noun* a strong, sweet flavoured alcoholic spirit.
– **SAY** li-**kyoor**

> ✓ note the **queu** in the middle: **liqueur** is a French word

liquid
liquidness

liquidate »*verb* (**liquidates, liquidating, liquidated**) ❶ wind up the affairs of a company. ❷ convert assets into cash. ❸ pay off a debt. ❹ (in informal English) kill.
liquidator
liquidation

liquidise another way of spelling **LIQUIDIZE**.

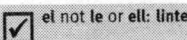

liquidity »*noun* (in finance) ❶ the availability of assets that can easily be converted into cash. ❷ assets that can easily be converted into cash.
– SAY li-kwid-i-ti

liquidize »*verb* (**liquidizes, liquidizing, liquidized**) convert solid food into a liquid or puree.
liquidizer

☑ many people prefer the alternative spellings **liquidise, liquidises,** etc., and **liquidiser:** both **s** and **z** spellings are correct

liquidness

liquify another way of spelling **LIQUEFY**.

liquor »*noun* ❶ alcoholic drink, especially spirits. ❷ liquid that has been produced in cooking.
– SAY lik-er

☑ note that the ending is **quor: liquor**

liquorice »*noun* a black substance made from the juice of a root and used as a sweet and in medicine.
– SAY lik-uh-riss or lik-uh-rish

☑ **quo** not **co,** and **-rice** not **-rish: liquorice** (the spelling **licorice** is American)

lira »*noun* (plural **lire**) the basic unit of money of Italy and Turkey.
– SAY leer-uh [singular] leer-uh or leer-ay [plural]

lisp »*noun* a speech defect in which *s* is pronounced like a *th*.
» *verb* (**lisps, lisping, lisped**) speak with a lisp.

lissom »*adjective* slim, supple, and graceful.

☑ **lissom** can also be spelled with an **e** on the end: **lissome**

list[1] (verb: **lists, listing, listed**) [connected items written down; make a list]

list[2] »*verb* (**lists, listing, listed**) (of a ship) lean over to one side.
» *noun* an instance of listing.

listed »*adjective* (of a building in the UK) officially protected because of its historical importance.

listen (verb: **listens, listening, listened**)
listener

listeria »*noun* a type of bacterium which infects humans and animals through contaminated food.
– SAY li-steer-i-uh

listing

listless »*adjective* lacking energy or enthusiasm.
listlessly
listlessness

list price »*noun* the price of an article as stated by the manufacturer.

lists

lit past and past participle of **LIGHT**[1], **LIGHT**[3].

litany »*noun* (plural **litanies**) ❶ a series of appeals to God used in church services. ❷ a tedious recital.
– SAY li-tuh-ni

☑ plural: drop the **y** and add **ies: litanies**

liter American spelling of **LITRE**.

literacy »*noun* the ability to read and write.

literal »*adjective* ❶ using or interpreting words in their usual or most basic sense. ❷ (of a translation) representing the exact words of the original text. ❸ not exaggerated or distorted.
literalness

literally »*adverb* in a literal way.

 you should be careful how you use **literally,** which strictly means 'with the exact literal meaning of the words used'. If you use it to emphasize words which should not be taken literally, as in *we literally killed ourselves laughing* or *we are literally paid peanuts,* the effect can be unintentionally funny.

literalness

literary »*adjective* ❶ having to do with literature. ❷ (of language) characteristic of literature or formal writing.

☑ **rary** not **ery: literary**

literate »*adjective* ❶ able to read and write. ❷ knowledgeable in a particular field: *computer literate.*
literately

literati »*plural noun* educated people who are interested in literature.
– SAY li-tuh-**rah**-ti

 literati is the plural of Latin *literatus* 'acquainted with letters'

literature »*noun* ❶ written works that are regarded as having artistic merit. ❷ books and printed information on a particular subject.

☑ **liter-** not **litter-: literature**

lithe »*adjective* slim, supple, and graceful.

– **SAY** ly*th*
lithely
litheness

lithium »*noun* a silver-white metallic chemical element.
– **SAY** li-**thi**-uhm

lithograph »*noun* a print made by lithography.
– **SAY** li-**thuh**-grahf or **ly**-thuh-grahf
lithographic

lithography »*noun* printing from a flat metal surface which has been prepared so that ink sticks only where it is required.
– **SAY** li-**thog**-ruh-fi

Lithuanian

litigant »*noun* a person involved in a lawsuit.

litigate »*verb* (**litigates, litigating, litigated**)
❶ go to law; be a party to a lawsuit.
❷ take a dispute to a law court.
– **SAY** **li**-ti-gayt
litigation

litigious »*adjective* tending to go to a law court to settle disputes.
– **SAY** li-**ti**-juhss
litigiously
litigiousness

litmus »*noun* a dye that is red under acid conditions and blue under alkaline conditions.
– **SAY** **lit**-muhss

 mus not **muss**: **litmus**

litmus test »*noun* a reliable test of the quality or truth of something.

litotes »*noun* understatement in which something is communicated by expressing the negative of its opposite (e.g. *I shan't be sorry* for *I shall be glad*).
– **SAY** ly-**toh**-teez

litre »*noun* a metric unit of capacity equal to 1,000 cubic centimetres (about 1.75 pints).

 re not **er**: **litre** (the spelling **liter** is American)

litter (verb: **litters, littering, littered**)

little (adjective: **littler, littlest**; adverb: **less, least**)
littleness

Little Englander »*noun* a person opposed to an international role or policy for Britain.

littleness

little people »*plural noun* fairies or leprechauns.

littler

littlest

littoral »*adjective* relating to the shore of the sea or a lake.
– **SAY** lit-tuh-ruhl

 double **t**, and **-or-** in the middle: **littoral** (**literal** means 'using words in their most basic sense')

liturgical »*adjective* relating to liturgy or public worship.
– **SAY** li-**tur**-ji-k'l
liturgically

liturgy »*noun* (plural **liturgies**) a set form of public worship used in the Christian Church.
– **SAY** **li**-ter-ji

plural: drop the **y** and add **ies**: **liturgies**

livable American spelling of LIVEABLE.

live[1] (verb: **lives, living, lived**) [remain alive]
– **SAY** liv

live[2] [living]
– **SAY** lyv

liveable »*adjective* worth living, or fit to live in.

vea not **va**: **liveable** (the spelling **livable** is American)

lived

lived-in »*adjective* (of a room or building) showing comforting signs of wear and use.

live-in »*adjective* ❶ (of a domestic employee) resident in an employer's house. ❷ living with another in a sexual relationship.

livelier

liveliest

livelihood »*noun* a way of obtaining the things necessary for life.

liveliness

livelong »*adjective* (a poetic term) (of a period of time) entire: *all this livelong day*.
– **SAY** liv-long

lively (adjective: **livelier, liveliest**)
liveliness

drop the **y** and add **ier** or **iest** to spell **livelier** or **liveliest**

liven »*verb* (**livens, livening, livened**) (**liven up**) make or become more lively or interesting.

liver

liveried

liveries

Liverpudlian »*noun* a person from Liverpool.
» *adjective* relating to Liverpool.

liverwort »*noun* a small flowerless green plant.
– SAY li-ver-wert

livery »*noun* (plural **liveries**) ❶ a special uniform worn by a servant or official. ❷ a distinctive design and colour scheme used on the vehicles or products of a company.
liveried

> ☑ plural: drop the **y** and add **ies**: **liveries**

livery company »*noun* one of a number of companies of the City of London descended from the medieval trade guilds.

lives plural of LIFE.

livestock »*noun* farm animals.

live wire »*noun* (in informal English) an energetic and lively person.

livid »*adjective* ❶ furiously angry. ❷ having a dark inflamed appearance.
lividly
lividness

living

living wage »*noun* a wage which is high enough to provide a normal standard of living.

living will »*noun* a written statement which says what a person wishes regarding their medical treatment in circumstances in which they are no longer able to agree to something.

lizard

llama »*noun* a domesticated South American animal related to the camel.
– SAY lah-muh

> ☑ remember the double **l** at the beginning: **llama** (a **lama** is a Tibetan Buddhist leader or monk)

lo »*exclamation* (an old word) used to draw attention to something interesting or surprising.

loach »*noun* a small freshwater fish.

load (verb: **loads, loading, loaded**)
loaded
loader
loading

loadstone another way of spelling LODESTONE.

loaf[1] (plural **loaves**) [quantity of bread]

> ☑ the plural of **loaf** drops the **f** and adds **ves**: **loaves**

loaf[2] »*verb* (**loafs, loafing, loafed**) spend your time idly.
loafer

loam »*noun* a fertile soil of clay and sand.
loamy

loan (verb: **loans, loaning, loaned**) [a sum lent; lend something]

> ℹ do not confuse **loan** with **lone**, which means 'alone'

loath »*adjective* reluctant or unwilling to do something.
– SAY lohth

> ☑ **loath** can also be spelled without the **a**: **loth**. It should not be confused with with **loathe**, which means 'dislike something greatly'.

loathe »*verb* (**loathes, loathing, loathed**) feel hatred or disgust for someone or something.
– SAY loh*th*

loathsome »*adjective* causing hatred or disgust.
loathsomely
loathsomeness

> ☑ **loath-** not **loathe-**: **loathsome**

loaves plural of LOAF[1].

lob »*verb* (**lobs, lobbing, lobbed**) throw or hit something in a high arc.
» *noun* (in soccer or tennis) a ball lobbed over an opponent.

lobby »*noun* (plural **lobbies**) ❶ an open area inside the entrance of a public building. ❷ one of several large halls in the Houses of Parliament in which MPs meet members of the public. ❸ one of two corridors in the Houses of Parliament where MPs vote. ❹ a group of people who try to influence politicians on a particular issue.
» *verb* (**lobbies, lobbying, lobbied**) try to influence a politician on an issue.
lobbyist

lobe »*noun* ❶ a roundish and flattish part that hangs down or projects from something. ❷ one of the sections of the main part of the brain.
lobed

lobelia »*noun* a garden plant with blue or scarlet flowers.
– SAY luh-bee-li-uh

lobotomy »*noun* (plural **lobotomies**) a surgical operation that involves cutting into part of the brain, formerly used to treat mental illness.
– SAY luh-bot-uh-mi

lobs

lobster

local
locally

locale »*noun* a place where a particular activity or event takes place.
– SAY loh-**kahl**

localise another way of spelling **LOCALIZE**.

locality »*noun* (plural **localities**) ❶ an area or neighbourhood. ❷ the position or site of something.

 plural: drop the **y** and add **ies**: **localities**

localize »*verb* (**localizes**, **localizing**, **localized**) restrict something to a particular place.
localization

☑ many people prefer the alternative spellings **localise**, **localises**, etc., and **localisation**: both **s** and **z** spellings are correct

locally

locate (verb: **locates**, **locating**, **located**)
locator

location
locational

locator

loch »*noun* (in Scotland) a lake, or a narrow strip of sea almost surrounded by land.

loci plural of **LOCUS**.

lock (verb: **locks**, **locking**, **locked**)
lockable
locked

locker

locket »*noun* a small ornamental case worn round a person's neck, used to hold a tiny photograph, a lock of hair, etc.

locking

lockjaw »*noun* a form of the disease tetanus in which the jaws become stiff and tightly closed.

lockout »*noun* a situation in which an employer refuses to allow employees to enter their place of work until they agree to certain conditions.

locks

locksmith »*noun* a person who makes and repairs locks.

lock-up »*noun* ❶ a makeshift jail. ❷ a garage or small shop separate from living quarters, that can be locked up.

locomotion »*noun* movement or the ability to move from one place to another.

locomotive »*noun* a powered railway vehicle used for pulling trains.
» *adjective* relating to locomotion.

locum »*noun* a doctor or priest standing in for another who is temporarily away.

– SAY loh-**kuhm**

ℹ from the Latin phrase *locum tenens* 'one holding a place'

locus »*noun* (plural **loci**) ❶ a particular position, point, or place. ❷ (in mathematics) a curve or other figure formed by all the points satisfying a particular condition.
– SAY loh-**kuhss** [singular], loh-**sI** [plural]

☑ the plural of **locus** (a Latin word) drops the **us** and adds **i**: **loci**

locust »*noun* a large tropical grasshopper which migrates in vast swarms.

locution »*noun* ❶ a word or phrase. ❷ a person's particular way of speaking.
– SAY luh-**kyoo**-shuhn

lode »*noun* a vein of metal ore in the earth.
– SAY lohd

lodestar »*noun* a star that is used to guide the course of a ship.

lodestone »*noun* a piece of magnetic iron ore, used as a magnet.

☑ **lodestone** can also be spelled **loadstone**

lodge (verb: **lodges**, **lodging**, **lodged**)

lodger

lodges

lodging

loft (verb: **lofts**, **lofting**, **lofted**)

lofty »*adjective* (**loftier**, **loftiest**) ❶ tall and impressive. ❷ morally good; noble: *lofty ideals*. ❸ proud and superior.
loftily
loftiness

☑ drop the **y** and add **ier** or **iest** to spell **loftier** or **loftiest**

log[1] (verb: **logs**, **logging**, **logged**) [a cut part of a tree; enter facts in a log]
logger

log[2] »*noun* a logarithm.

loganberry »*noun* (plural **loganberries**) an edible red soft fruit, similar to a large raspberry.

logarithm »*noun* one of series of numbers which allows you to make calculations by adding and subtracting rather than multiplying and dividing.
– SAY log-uh-ri-*th*uhm
logarithmic

☑ **-rithm** not **-rhythm**: **logarithm**

logbook

logged

logger

loggerheads »*plural noun* (at loggerheads) in strong disagreement.

loggia »*noun* a gallery with one or more open sides, especially one facing a garden.
– SAY loh-ji-uh

> ☑ note the double **g**: **loggia** is an Italian word

logging

logic »*noun* ❶ the science of reasoning. ❷ clear, sound reasoning. ❸ a set of principles used in preparing a computer or electronic device to perform a task.
logician

logical
logically

logician

logistic »*adjective* relating to logistics.
– SAY luh-**jiss**-tik
logistical
logistically

logistics »*plural noun* the detailed organization of a large and complex exercise.
– SAY luh-**jiss**-tiks

logjam »*noun* a situation that seems unable to be settled; a deadlock.

logo »*noun* (plural **logos**) a design or symbol chosen by an organization to identify its products.
– SAY loh-goh

> ☑ the plural of **logo** has **os** not **oes**: **logos**

logs

loin »*noun* ❶ the part of the between the ribs and the hip bones. ❷ a joint of meat from this part of an animal. ❸ (**loins**) (a poetic term) a person's sexual organs.

loincloth »*noun* a piece of cloth wrapped round the hips, worn by men in some hot countries.

loiter »*verb* (**loiters**, **loitering**, **loitered**) stand around without any obvious purpose.
loiterer

loll »*verb* (**lolls**, **lolling**, **lolled**) ❶ sit, lie, or stand in a lazy, relaxed way. ❷ hang loosely.

lollies

lollipop

> ☑ lolli- not lolly-: **lollypop**

lollop »*verb* (**lollops**, **lolloping**, **lolloped**) move in a series of clumsy bounding steps.

lolly (plural **lollies**)

Londoner

lone [solitary; alone]

> ℹ do not confuse **lone** with **loan**, 'a sum lent; lend something'

lonely (adjective: **lonelier**, **loneliest**)
loneliness

> ☑ drop the **y** and add **ier** or **iest** to spell **lonelier** or **loneliest**

loner »*noun* a person who prefers to be alone.

lonesome »*adjective* lonely.
lonesomeness

long (adjective & adverb: **longer**, **longest**; verb: **longs**, **longing**, **longed**)

longbow »*noun* (a historical term) a large bow used for shooting arrows.

long-distance »*adjective* travelling or operating between distant places.
»*adverb* between distant places.

longed

longer

longest

longevity »*noun* long life.
– SAY lon-jev-i-ti

longhand »*noun* ordinary handwriting (as opposed to shorthand, typing, or printing).

longing
longingly

longish

longitude »*noun* the distance of a place east or west of the Greenwich meridian, measured in degrees.
– SAY long-i-tyood

> ☑ longi not longti or longdi: **longitude**

longitudinal »*adjective* ❶ extending lengthwise. ❷ relating to longitude.
– SAY long-i-**tyoo**-di-n'l
longitudinally

long johns »*plural noun* underpants with closely fitted legs extending to the ankles.

long-life »*adjective* (of food or drink) treated so as to stay fresh for longer than usual.

long-lived

long-playing »*adjective* (of a record) 12 inches (about 30 cm) in diameter and designed to rotate at 33⅓ revolutions per minute.

long-range

longs

longship »*noun* a long, narrow warship with oars and a sail, used by the Vikings.

longshore »*adjective* relating to or moving along the seashore.

long-sighted »*adjective* unable to see things clearly if they are close to the eyes.

long-standing

long-suffering

long wave »*noun* a radio wave of a wavelength above one kilometre (and a frequency below 300 kilohertz).

longways

long-winded

loo

loofah »*noun* a long rough object used to wash yourself with in the bath, consisting of the dried inner parts of a tropical fruit.
– **SAY** loo-fuh

look (verb: **looks, looking, looked**)

lookalike

looked

looker

look-in »*noun* a chance to take part in something.

looking

lookout

looks

loom[1] »*noun* a machine for weaving cloth.

loom[2] »*verb* (**looms, looming, loomed**) ❶ appear as a vague and threatening shape. ❷ (of something bad) seem about to happen.

loony (plural **loonies**; adjective: **loonier, looniest**)

loop (verb: **loops, looping, looped**)
    looper

loophole »*noun* a mistake or piece of vague wording that enables someone to avoid obeying a law or keeping to a contract.

loopier

loopiest

looping

loops

loopy (adjective: **loopier, loopiest**)

loose (verb: **looses, loosing, loosed**) [not tightly fixed in place; unfasten]
    loosely
    looseness

ℹ️ do not confuse the words **loose** and **lose**. As a verb **loose** means 'unfasten or set free' (as in *the hounds have been loosed*), while **lose** means 'no longer have' or 'become unable to find' (as in *she was upset about losing her job*).

loose box »*noun* a stable or stall in which a horse is kept without a tether.

loose cannon »*noun* a person who behaves in an unpredictable and potentially harmful way.

loosed

loose-leaf »*adjective* (of a folder) having sheets of paper that can be added or removed.

loosen (verb: **loosens, loosening, loosened**)

looses

loosing

loot »*noun* ❶ property taken from an enemy in war or stolen by thieves. ❷ (in informal English) money.
»*verb* (**loots, looting, looted**) steal goods from a building during a war or riot.
    looter

lop »*verb* (**lops, lopping, lopped**) ❶ cut off a branch or limb from a tree or body. ❷ (in informal English) reduce by a particular amount.
    lopper

lope »*verb* (**lopes, loping, loped**) run with a long bounding stride.
»*noun* a long bounding stride.

lopped

lopper

lopping

lops

lopsided
    lopsidedly
    lopsidedness

loquacious »*adjective* talkative.
– **SAY** lo-**kway**-shuhss
    loquaciously
    loquaciousness

✅ **cious** not **tious**: loquacious

loquacity »*noun* the quality of being talkative.
– **SAY** lo-**kwass**-i-ti

lord

Lord Chancellor »*noun* the highest judge in the United Kingdom and Speaker of the House of Lords.

Lord Lieutenant »*noun* the representative of the Queen and head of magistrates in each county.

lordly »*adjective* (**lordlier, lordliest**) like a lord; proud or superior.

Lordship »*noun* (**His** or **Your** etc. **Lordship**) a form of address to a judge, bishop, or nobleman.

lore »*noun* a body of traditions and knowledge on a subject.

ℹ️ do not confuse **lore** with **law**, 'the rules that govern the people in a country'

lorgnette »*noun* a pair of glasses held by a long handle at one side.
– SAY lor-**nyet**

✓ note the **ette** ending: **lorgnette** (it is a French word)

lorry (plural **lorries**)

✓ plural: drop the **y** and add **ies**: **lorries**

lose (verb: **loses**, **losing**, **lost**) [no longer have; become unable to find]
– SAY looz
loser

ℹ️ do not confuse **lose** with **loose**: see the note at **LOOSE**

loss (plural **losses**)

loss-leader »*noun* a product sold at a loss to attract customers.

lost past and past participle of **LOSE**.

lot

ℹ️ although **a lot of** and **lots of** are often used in speech, it is better not to use them in formal writing; use **many** or **a large number** instead

✓ **a lot** is two words, not one

loth another way of spelling **LOATH**.

Lothario »*noun* (plural **Lotharios**) a man who behaves selfishly in his sexual relationships.
– SAY luh-**thair**-i-oh or luh-**thah**-ri-oh

lotion »*noun* a creamy liquid put on the skin as a medicine or cosmetic.

lottery »*noun* (plural **lotteries**) ❶ a way of raising money by selling numbered tickets and giving prizes to the holders of numbers drawn at random. ❷ something whose success or outcome is controlled by luck.

lotus »*noun* (plural **lotuses**) ❶ a kind of large water lily. ❷ (in Greek mythology) a fruit that causes dreamy forgetful feelings.

lotus position »*noun* a cross-legged position that people take up when they are meditating, with the feet resting on the thighs.

louche »*adjective* having a bad reputation but still attractive.
– SAY loosh

loud
loudly
loudness

loudhailer

loudly

loudmouth

loudness

loudspeaker

lough »*noun* (in Ireland) a lake, or narrow strip of sea almost surrounded by land.
– SAY lokh

lounge (verb: **lounges**, **lounging**, **lounged**)
lounger

lour »*verb* (**lours**, **louring**, **loured**) ❶ scowl. ❷ (of the sky) look dark and threatening.
– SAY *rhymes with* flour

✓ **lour** can also be spelled **lower**

louse »*noun* ❶ (plural **lice**) a small insect which lives as a parasite on animals or plants. ❷ (plural **louses**) an unpleasant person.
»*verb* (**louses**, **lousing**, **loused**) (**louse up**) spoil something.

lousy (adjective: **lousier**, **lousiest**)
lousily
lousiness

lout »*noun* a rude or aggressive man or boy.
loutish

louvre »*noun* one of a set of slanting slats fixed at intervals in a door, shutter, etc. to allow air or light through.
– SAY **loo**-ver
louvred

✓ **vre** not **ver**: **louvre** (the spelling **louver** is American)

lovable
lovably

✓ **lovable** can also be spelled with an **e** after the **v**: **loveable**

lovage »*noun* a herb used in cookery.
– SAY **luv**-ij

✓ **lov-** not **love-**: **lovage**

love (verb: **loves**, **loving**, **loved**)
loveless

loveable another way of spelling **LOVABLE**.

lovebird »*noun* ❶ a kind of small parrot that shows affection for its mate. ❷ (**lovebirds**) an affectionate couple.

loved

loveless

lovelier

loveliest

loveliness

lovelorn »*adjective* unhappy because you love someone who does not feel the same way about you.

lovely (adjective: **lovelier, loveliest**)
loveliness

 drop the **y** and add **ier** or **iest** to spell **lovelier** or **loveliest**

lover

loves

lovesick

lovey-dovey

loving
lovingly

low[1] (adjective: **lower, lowest**) [not high]
lowness

low[2] »*verb* (**lows, lowing, lowed**) (of a cow) moo.

lowbrow »*adjective* not intellectual or interested in culture.

Low Church »*noun* a tradition within the Church of England that places little emphasis on ritual and the authority of bishops and priests.

low-down (in informal English) »*adjective* unfair or dishonest.
» *noun* (**the low-down**) the important facts about something.

lower[1] (verb: **lowers, lowering, lowered**) [less high]
lowermost

lower[2] another way of spelling **LOUR**.

lower case »*noun* small letters as opposed to capitals.

lowered

lower house »*noun* the larger body of a parliament with two chambers, usually with elected members.

lowering

lowermost

lowers

lowest

lowest common denominator »*noun* (in mathematics) the lowest number that the bottom number of a group of fractions can be divided into exactly.

lowest common multiple »*noun* (in mathematics) the lowest quantity that is a multiple of two or more given quantities.

low-key »*adjective* not elaborate or showy.

lowland »*noun* **❶** low-lying country.
❷ (**the Lowlands**) the part of Scotland lying south and east of the Highlands.

– SAY loh-luhnd
lowlander

low-level

lowlier

lowliest

low life »*noun* dishonest or immoral people or activities.

lowliness

low-loader »*noun* a truck with a low floor and no sides, for heavy loads.

lowly »*adjective* (**lowlier, lowliest**) low in status or importance.
lowliness

 drop the **y** and add **ier** or **iest** to spell **lowlier** or **lowliest**

low-lying

lowness

loyal
loyally

loyalist »*noun* **❶** a person who remains loyal to the established ruler or government. **❷** (**Loyalist**) a person who believes that Northern Ireland should remain part of Great Britain.
loyalism

loyally

loyalty (plural **loyalties**)

plural: drop the **y** and add **ies**: **loyalties**

lozenge »*noun* **❶** a diamond-shaped figure. **❷** a small tablet of medicine that is sucked to soothe a sore throat.
– SAY loz-inj

LP »*abbreviation* long-playing (record).

L-plate

LSD »*noun* a powerful drug that causes hallucinations.

ℹ️ **LSD** stands for *lysergic acid diethylamide*

lubricant »*noun* a substance, e.g. oil or grease, for lubricating part of a machine.

lubricate »*verb* (**lubricates, lubricating, lubricated**) apply oil or grease to machinery so that it moves easily.
– SAY loo-bri-kayt
lubrication
lubricator

lubricious »*adjective* referring to sexual matters in a rude or offensive way; lewd.
– SAY loo-bri-shuhss

lucent »*adjective* (a poetic term) shining.
– SAY loo-suhnt

lucerne »*noun* = **ALFALFA**.
– SAY loo-sern

lucid »*adjective* ❶ easy to understand; clear. ❷ showing an ability to think clearly.
– SAY loo-sid
 lucidity
 lucidly

Lucifer »*noun* the Devil.
– SAY loo-si-fer

luck

luckier

luckiest

luckily

luckless

lucky (adjective: **luckier**, **luckiest**)

> ☑ drop the **y** and add **ier** or **iest** to spell **luckier** or **luckiest**

lucrative »*adjective* making a large profit.
– SAY loo-kruh-tiv
 lucratively

lucre »*noun* (a poetic term) money.
– SAY loo-ker

Luddite »*noun* ❶ a member of any of the early 19th century groups of English workers who destroyed machinery, which they thought was threatening their jobs. ❷ a person opposed to new technology.
– SAY lud-dyt

> ☑ double **d**: **Luddite**. The *Luddites* were probably named after a Ned *Lud* who took part in destroying machines.

ludicrous »*adjective* absurd; ridiculous.
– SAY loo-di-kruhss
 ludicrously
 ludicrousness

ludo »*noun* a board game in which players move counters according to throws of a dice.

luff »*verb* (**luffs**, **luffing**, **luffed**) steer a sailing ship nearer the wind.

lug[1] (verb: **lugs**, **lugging**, **lugged**) [carry or drag]

lug[2] »*noun* ❶ (in informal English) an ear. ❷ a projection on an object by which it may be carried or fixed in place.

luge »*noun* a light toboggan ridden in a sitting or lying position.
– SAY loo*zh*

luggage

lugged

lugger »*noun* a small ship with two or three masts and a four-sided sail on each.

lugging

lugs

lugubrious »*adjective* sad and gloomy.

– SAY luu-**goo**-bri-uhss
 lugubriously
 lugubriousness

lugworm »*noun* a worm living in muddy sand by the sea, used as fishing bait.

lukewarm

lull »*verb* (**lulls**, **lulling**, **lulled**) ❶ make someone relaxed or calm. ❷ make someone feel safe or confident, even if they are at risk of something bad. ❸ calm doubts, fears, etc. by deception.
»*noun* a quiet period between times of activity.

lullaby »*noun* (plural **lullabies**) a soothing song sung to send a child to sleep.

> ☑ plural: drop the **y** and add **ies**: **lullabies**

lulled

lulling

lulls

lumbago »*noun* pain in the lower back.
– SAY lum-**bay**-goh

lumbar »*adjective* relating to the lower back.
– SAY lum-ber

> ☑ **ar** not **er**: **lumbar**

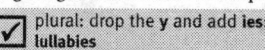

lumber »*noun* ❶ disused articles of furniture that take up space. ❷ timber sawn into rough planks.
»*verb* (**lumbers**, **lumbering**, **lumbered**) ❶ give someone an unwanted responsibility. ❷ move in a slow, heavy, awkward way.

lumberjack »*noun* a person who cuts down trees, cuts them into logs, or transports them.

lumberman »*noun* (plural **lumbermen**) a lumberjack.

lumbers

luminary »*noun* (plural **luminaries**) a person who inspires or influences others.
– SAY loo-mi-nuh-ri

> ☑ plural: drop the **y** and add **ies**: **luminaries**

luminescence »*noun* the production of light by a substance that has not been heated, as in fluorescence.
– SAY loo-mi-**ness**-uhss
 luminescent

luminosity »*noun* the quality of being luminous.

luminous »*adjective* ❶ bright or shining, especially in the dark. ❷ (in physics) relating to visible light.

– sᴀʏ loo-mi-nuhss
  luminously

lump (verb: **lumps**, **lumping**, **lumped**)

lumpectomy »*noun* (plural **lumpectomies**)
a surgical operation in which a lump is
removed from the breast.

lumped

lumpen »*adjective* ❶ lumpy and
misshapen. ❷ stupid or loutish.

lumpier

lumpiest

lumpily

lumpiness

lumping

lumpish »*adjective* ❶ roughly or clumsily
shaped. ❷ stupid and lethargic.

lumps

lumpy (adjective: **lumpier**, **lumpiest**)
  lumpily
  lumpiness

lunacy »*noun* ❶ insanity. ❷ great
stupidity.

lunar »*adjective* having to do with or like
the moon.
– sᴀʏ loo-ner

lunar month »*noun* a month measured
between one new moon and the next
(roughly 29½ days).

lunatic »*noun* ❶ a person who is mentally
ill. ❷ a very foolish person.

> ℹ️ the terms **lunatic** and **lunacy** are not
> used by professionals such as
> doctors or psychiatrists to refer to mental
> illness

lunch (verb: **lunches**, **lunching**, **lunched**)
  luncher

lunch box (plural **lunch boxes**)

luncheon

luncheon meat »*noun* minced cooked
pork mixed with cereal, sold in a tin.

luncher

lunches

lunching

lunchtime

lung
  lungful

lunge (verb: **lunges**, **lunging** or **lungeing**,
lunged)

> ✅ both **lunging** and **lungeing**, with or
> without the **e**, are acceptable

lungful

> ✅ -ful not -full: **lungful**

lupin »*noun* a plant with a tall stem
bearing many small colourful flowers.
– sᴀʏ loo-pin

> ✅ **lupin** can also be spelled **lupine**, with
> an **e** on the end

lupine »*adjective* having to do with a wolf
or wolves.
– sᴀʏ loo-pyn

lurch (verb: **lurches**, **lurching**, **lurched**)

lurcher »*noun* a dog that is a cross between
a greyhound and a retriever, collie, or
sheepdog.

lurches

lurching

lure »*verb* (**lures**, **luring**, **lured**) tempt a
person or animal to do something.
»*noun* ❶ a type of bait used in fishing or
hunting. ❷ the attractive qualities of
something: *the lure of the city*.

lurex »*noun* (trademark) yarn or fabric
containing a glittering metallic thread.
– sᴀʏ lyoo-reks

lurid »*adjective* ❶ unpleasantly bright in
colour. ❷ (of a description) deliberately
containing many shocking details.
– sᴀʏ lyoor-id
  luridly
  luridness

luring

lurk (verb: **lurks**, **lurking**, **lurked**)
  lurker

luscious »*adjective* ❶ having a pleasingly
rich, sweet taste. ❷ (of a woman) sexually
attractive.
  lusciously
  lusciousness

> ✅ **sc** in the middle: **luscious**

lush »*adjective* (**lusher**, **lushest**) ❶ (of
plants) growing thickly and strongly.
❷ rich or luxurious.
  lushly
  lushness

lust (verb: **lusts**, **lusting**, **lusted**)

lustful
  lustfully
  lustfulness

> ✅ -ful not -full: **lustful**

lustier

lustiest

lustily

lustiness

lusting

lustre »*noun* ❶ a soft glow or shine.
❷ prestige or honour.
lustreless

 tre not **ter: lustre** (the spelling **luster** is American)

lustrous »*adjective* having lustre; shining.
lustrously
lustrousness

lusts

lusty »*adjective* (**lustier, lustiest**) healthy and strong; vigorous.
lustily
lustiness

lute »*noun* a stringed instrument having a long neck and a rounded body with a flat front, played by plucking.

lutenist »*noun* a lute player.
– SAY **loo**-tuh-nist

lutetium »*noun* a rare silvery-white metallic chemical element.
– SAY **loo**-**tee**-shi-uhm

Lutheran »*noun* a member of the Lutheran Church, a Protestant Church based on the beliefs of the German theologian Martin Luther.
»*adjective* relating to the teachings of Martin Luther or to the Lutheran Church.
Lutheranism

luvvy »*noun* (plural **luvvies**) (mainly used in a disapproving way) an effusive or affected actor or actress.

 luvvy can also be spelled **luvvie**

Luxembourger »*noun* a person from Luxembourg.
– SAY **luk**-suhm-ber-ger

✓ remember the **o** in **Luxembourger**

luxuriant »*adjective* growing thickly and strongly: *luxuriant vegetation*.
– SAY lug-**zhoor**-i-uhnt
luxuriance
luxuriantly

ⓘ do not confuse **luxuriant** with **luxurious**, which means 'very comfortable, elegant, and expensive'

luxuriate »*verb* (**luxuriates, luxuriating, luxuriated**) (**luxuriate in** or **over**) enjoy something as a luxury.
– SAY lug-**zhoor**-i-ayt

luxuries

luxurious »*adjective* ❶ very comfortable, elegant, and expensive: *a luxurious lifestyle*. ❷ giving pleasure to the senses: *a luxurious scented bath*.

luxuriously
luxuriousness

ⓘ do not confuse **luxurious** with **luxuriant**, which means 'growing thickly and strongly'

luxury (plural **luxuries**)

✓ plural: drop the **y** and add **ies: luxuries**

lychee »*noun* a small rounded fruit with sweet white flesh, a large stone, and thin rough skin.
– SAY **ly**-chee

lychgate »*noun* a roofed gateway to a churchyard.
– SAY **lich**-gayt

Lycra »*noun* (trademark) a synthetic elastic fibre or fabric used for close-fitting clothing.
– SAY **ly**-kruh

lye »*noun* a strongly alkaline solution used for washing or cleansing.

lying[1] present participle of **LIE**[1].

lying[2] present participle of **LIE**[2].

lymph »*noun* a colourless fluid containing white blood cells, which bathes the tissues of the body.
– SAY limf

lymphatic »*adjective* relating to lymph or its production.
– SAY lim-**fat**-ik

lymph gland »*noun* = **LYMPH NODE**.

lymph node »*noun* one of a number of small swellings where lymph is filtered and cells are formed.

lymphoma »*noun* (plural **lymphomas** or **lymphomata**) cancer of the lymph nodes.
– SAY lim-**foh**-muh [singular], lim-**foh**-muh-tuh [plural]

✓ in medicine the Latin or Greek plural **lymphomata** is often used, but the form with **s** is also correct

lynch »*verb* (**lynches, lynching, lynched**) (of a group) kill someone for an alleged crime without a legal trial, especially by hanging.

lynchpin another way of spelling **LINCHPIN**.

lynx »*noun* (plural **lynxes** or **lynx**) a wild cat with a short tail and tufted ears.

lyre »*noun* a stringed instrument like a small U-shaped harp with strings fixed to a crossbar, used in ancient Greece.

lyric »*noun* ❶ (also **lyrics**) the words of a song. ❷ a lyric poem or verse.
»*adjective* (of poetry) expressing the writer's thoughts and emotions.

lyrical »*adjective* ❶ (of literature or music) expressing the writer's emotions in an imaginative and beautiful way. ❷ relating to the words of a popular song.
lyrically

lyricism »*noun* expression of emotion in writing or music in an imaginative and beautiful way.

lyricist »*noun* a person who writes the words to popular songs.

Mm

MA »*abbreviation* Master of Arts.

ma'am »*noun* madam.

mac

macabre »*adjective* disturbing and horrifying because concerned with death and injury.
– SAY muh-**kah**-bruh

macadam »*noun* broken stone used with tar or bitumen for surfacing roads and paths.
– SAY muh-**kad**-uhm

macadamia »*noun* the round edible nut of an Australian tree.
– SAY ma-kuh-**day**-mi-uh

macaque »*noun* a medium-sized monkey with a long face and cheek pouches for holding food.
– SAY muh-**kak**

macaroni »*noun* pasta in the form of narrow tubes.

 one c, one r, one n: macaroni

macaroon »*noun* a light biscuit made with egg white and ground almonds or coconut.

macaw »*noun* a brightly coloured parrot with a long tail, native to Central and South America.
– SAY muh-**kaw**

McCarthyism »*noun* a campaign against suspected communists in American public life carried out under Senator Joseph McCarthy from 1950–4.
McCarthyite

McCoy »*noun* (the real McCoy) the real thing.

mace[1] »*noun* ❶ (a historical term) a heavy club with a spiked metal head. ❷ a ceremonial staff carried by an official such as a mayor as a sign of authority. ❸ (**Mace**) (trademark) a stinging chemical sprayed from an aerosol to disable attackers.

mace[2] »*noun* a spice made from the dried outer covering of the nutmeg.

Macedonian [of Macedonia]
– SAY mass-i-**doh**-ni-uhn

macerate »*verb* (**macerates, macerating, macerated**) soften or break up food by soaking it in a liquid.
– SAY **mass**-uh-rayt
maceration

Mach »*noun* used with a numeral (as **Mach 1, Mach 2,** etc.) to indicate the speed of sound, twice the speed of sound, etc.

> **i** named after the Austrian physicist Ernst *Mach*

machete »*noun* a broad, heavy knife used as a tool or weapon.
– SAY muh-**shet**-i

> ✓ ete not eti: **machete** is a Spanish word

Machiavellian »*adjective* trying to achieve what you want in a cunning and underhand way.
– SAY ma-ki-uh-**vel**-i-uhn

> **i** from the name of the Italian statesman Niccolo *Machiavelli*

machinations »*plural noun* plots and scheming.
– SAY ma-shi-**nay**-shuhnz

machine (verb: **machines, machining, machined**)

machine code »*noun* a computer programming language consisting of instructions which a computer can respond to directly.

machined

machine language »*noun* = MACHINE CODE.

machine-readable »*adjective* in a form that a computer can process.

machinery

> ery not ary: machinery

machines

machine tool »*noun* a fixed powered tool for cutting or shaping metal, wood, etc.

machining

machinist »*noun* a person who operates a machine or who makes machinery.

machismo »*noun* strong or aggressive male pride.
– SAY muh-**kiz**-moh

macho »*adjective* showing aggressive pride in being male.
– SAY ma-**choh**

mackerel

mackintosh »*noun* a full-length waterproof coat.

> ✓ **mackintosh** can also be spelled **macintosh**, and is named after the Scottish inventor Charles *Macintosh*

macrame »*noun* the craft of knotting cord or string in patterns to make decorative articles.
– SAY muh-**krah**-mi

> ✓ **macrame** can also be spelled **macramé**, with an acute accent above the **e** (as in the original French)

macrobiotic »*adjective* (of diet) consisting of organic unprocessed foods, based on Buddhist principles of the balance of yin and yang.
– SAY mak-roh-by-**ot**-ik

macrocosm »*noun* ❶ the whole of a complex structure. ❷ the universe.
– SAY **mak**-roh-ko-z'm

macroeconomics »*noun* the branch of economics concerned with large-scale or general economic factors, such as interest rates.

macron »*noun* a written or printed mark (¯) used to indicate a long vowel in some languages, or a stressed vowel in verse.

macroscopic »*adjective* ❶ large enough to be seen without a microscope. ❷ relating to general analysis.

mad (adjective: **madder**, **maddest**)
madly
madness

Madagascan [of Madagascar]

madam

Madame »*noun* (plural **Mesdames**) a title or form of address for a French-speaking woman.
– SAY muh-**dam** [singular], may-**dam** [plural]

madcap »*adjective* acting without thought; reckless.

mad cow disease »*noun* (in informal English) = BSE.

madden »*verb* (**maddens**, **maddening**, **maddened**) make someone very annoyed.

madder »*noun* a red dye obtained from the roots of a plant.

maddest

made past and past participle of MAKE.

Madeira »*noun* a strong sweet white wine from the island of Madeira.

Madeira cake »*noun* a rich kind of sponge cake.

Mademoiselle »*noun* (plural **Mesdemoiselles**) a title or form of address for an unmarried French-speaking woman.
– SAY ma-duh-mwah-**zel** [singular], may-duh-mwa-**zel** [plural]

made-up

madhouse

madly

madman (plural **madmen**)

madness

Madonna »*noun* (**the Madonna**) the Virgin Mary.

madras »*noun* ❶ a colourful striped or checked cotton fabric. ❷ a hot spiced curry dish.
– SAY muh-**drass**

madrigal »*noun* a 16th- or 17th-century song for several voices without instrumental accompaniment.

maelstrom »*noun* ❶ a powerful whirlpool. ❷ a situation of confusion or upheaval.
– SAY **mayl**-struhm

> ✓ **mael**- not **male**-: **maelstrom** is a Dutch word

maenad »*noun* (in ancient Greece) a female follower of the god Bacchus.
– SAY **mee**-nad

maestro »*noun* (plural **maestri** or **maestros**) a famous and talented man, especially a conductor or classical musician.
– SAY **my**-stroh [singular], **my**-stri [plural]

> ✓ **maestro** is Italian for 'master', and therefore the Italian plural **maestri** is often used, but **maestros** is also correct

Mafia »*noun* ❶ (**the Mafia**) an international criminal organization originating in Sicily. ❷ (**mafia**) a powerful group which secretly influences matters.

Mafioso »*noun* (plural **Mafiosi**) a member of the Mafia.
– SAY ma-fi-**oh**-soh [singular], ma-fi-**oh**-si [plural]

magazine

magenta »*noun* a light mauvish crimson.
– say muh-**jen**-tuh

maggot »*noun* a soft-bodied larva of a fly or other insect, found in decaying matter.

magi plural of **MAGUS**.

magic (verb: **magics, magicking, magicked**)
magical
magically

> ✓ add a **k** to spell **magicking** and **magicked**

magician

magicked

magicking

magics

magisterial »*adjective* ❶ having or showing great authority. ❷ relating to a magistrate.
– say ma-ji-**steer**-i-uhl
magisterially

magistracy »*noun* (plural **magistracies**)
❶ the post of magistrate. ❷ magistrates as a group.
– say **ma**-jiss-truh-si

magistrate »*noun* an official who judges minor cases and holds preliminary hearings.

magma »*noun* very hot liquid or semi-liquid material under the earth's crust, which is erupted as lava or cools to form other igneous rocks.
– say **mag**-muh

magnanimous »*adjective* generous or forgiving towards a rival or enemy.
– say mag-**nan**-i-muhss
magnanimously
magnanimity

magnate »*noun* a wealthy and influential person, especially in business.
– say **mag**-nayt

magnesia »*noun* a compound of magnesium used to reduce stomach acid and as a laxative.
– say mag-**nee**-*zh*uh or mag-**nee**-zi-uh

magnesium »*noun* a silvery-white metallic element which burns with a brilliant white flame.
– say mag-**nee**-zi-uhm

magnet

magnetic
magnetically

magnetise another way of spelling **MAGNETIZE**.

magnetism »*noun* ❶ the property displayed by magnets and produced by the movement of electric charges, which results in objects being attracted or pushed away. ❷ the ability to attract and charm people.

magnetize »*verb* (**magnetizes, magnetizing, magnetized**) make something magnetic.
magnetization

> ✓ many people prefer the alternative spellings **magnetise, magnetises**, etc.: both **s** and **z** spellings are correct

magneto »*noun* (plural **magnetos**) a small electric generator containing a permanent magnet and used to provided high-voltage pulses.
– say mag-**nee**-toh

Magnificat »*noun* the hymn of the Virgin Mary, beginning 'my soul magnifies the Lord', sung as a regular part of a Christian service.
– say mag-**nif**-i-kat

> ℹ️ **magnificat** is Latin for 'magnifies'

magnification »*noun* ❶ the action of magnifying something. ❷ the degree to which something can be magnified.

magnificent
magnificence
magnificently

magnify (verb: **magnifies, magnifying, magnified**)
magnifier

magnitude »*noun* ❶ great size or importance. ❷ size. ❸ the degree of brightness of a star.

magnolia »*noun* a tree or shrub with large white or pale pink flowers.

magnum »*noun* (plural **magnums**) a wine bottle of twice the standard size, normally 1½ litres.

magnum opus »*noun* (plural **magnum opuses** or **magna opera**) a work of art, music, or literature that is the most important that a person has produced.
– say mag-**nuhm oh**-puhss [singular], mag-nuh **op**-uh-ruh [plural]

> ℹ️ **magnum opus** means 'great work' in Latin

magpie

magus »*noun* (plural **magi**) ❶ a priest of ancient Persia. ❷ a sorcerer. ❸ (**the Magi**) the three wise men from the East who brought gifts to the infant Jesus.
– say **may**-guhss [singular], **may**-jI [plural]

> ✓ the plural of **magus** is **magi** (as in Latin)

maharaja »*noun* (a historical term) an Indian prince.

> ✓ maharaja can also be spelled **maharajah**, with an **h** on the end

maharani »*noun* (a historical term) a maharaja's wife or widow.

Maharishi »*noun* a great Hindu wise man or spiritual leader.

mahatma »*noun* a wise or holy Hindu leader.

mah-jong »*noun* a Chinese game played with rectangular pieces called tiles.

> ✓ mah-jong can also be spelled **mah-jongg**, with an extra **g**

mahogany »*noun* ❶ hard reddish-brown wood from a tropical tree. ❷ a rich reddish-brown colour.

maid [female servant]

maiden

maidenhead »*noun* (an old word) a girl's or woman's virginity.

mail[1] (verb: **mails**, **mailing**, **mailed**) [letters and parcels; send something by post]

mail[2] »*noun* (a historical term) armour made of metal rings or plates.
mailed

mailbag

mailbox (plural **mailboxes**)

mailed

mailing

mails

mailshot »*noun* a piece of advertising material sent to a large number of addresses.

maim »*verb* (**maims**, **maiming**, **maimed**) injure someone so that part of their body is permanently damaged.

main [greatest or most important; a chief water or gas pipe or electricity cable]

> ℹ do not confuse **main** with **mane**, the hair on the neck of a horse, lion, etc.

mainframe »*noun* a large high-speed computer, especially one supporting a network of workstations.

mainland »*noun* the main area of land of a country, not including islands and separate territories.

mainly

mainmast

mainspring »*noun* the most important or influential part of something.

mainstay »*noun* a thing on which something else depends or is based on.

mainstream

maintain (verb: **maintains**, **maintaining**, **maintained**)

maintenance »*noun* ❶ the action of maintaining something. ❷ financial support that someone gives to their former husband or wife after divorce.

> ✓ **ten** not **tain**: main**ten**ance

maisonette »*noun* a flat on two storeys of a larger building.

maitre d'hotel »*noun* (plural **maitres d'hotel**) the head waiter of a restaurant.
– sᴀʏ may-truh doh-**tel** [singular and plural]

> ✓ maitre d'hotel can also be written **maître d'hôtel**, with circumflex accents above the **i** and the **o** (as in the original French). The shortened form **maitre d'** (plural **maitre d's**) is sometimes used.

maize »*noun* a cereal plant bearing large grains set in rows on a cob.

majestic »*adjective* impressively grand or beautiful.
majestically

majesty (plural **majesties**)

major (verb: **majors**, **majoring**, **majored**)

major-domo »*noun* (plural **major-domos**) the chief steward of a large household.

majored

major general »*noun* a rank of army officer next above brigadier.

majoring

majority (plural **majorities**)

> ℹ the main meaning of **majority** is 'the greater number' and it should be used with plural nouns: *the majority of cases*. Do not use **majority** with nouns that do not take a plural to mean 'the greatest part', as in *she ate the majority of the meal.*

majors

make (verb: **makes**, **making**, **made**)

make-believe

makeover »*noun* a transformation of someone's appearance with cosmetics, hairstyling, and clothes.

maker

makes

makeshift »*adjective* temporary and improvised.

make-up

makeweight »*noun* ❶ something put on a scale to make up the required weight. ❷ an extra person or thing needed to complete something.

making

malachite »*noun* a bright green mineral that contains copper.
– SAY ma-luh-kyt

maladies

maladjusted »*adjective* (of a person) not able to cope well with normal life.
maladjustment

maladroit »*adjective* clumsy.
– SAY mal-uh-**droyt**

malady »*noun* (plural **maladies**) a disease or illness.

> plural: drop the **y** and add **ies**:
> **maladies**

Malagasy »*noun* (plural **Malagasy** or **Malagasies**) ❶ a person from Madagascar. ❷ the language of Madagascar.
– SAY ma-luh-**gass**-i

malaise »*noun* ❶ a general feeling of illness or low spirits. ❷ a long-standing problem that is difficult to identify.
– SAY ma-**layz**

malapropism »*noun* the mistaken use of a word in place of a similar-sounding one (e.g. 'dance a *flamingo*' instead of *flamenco*).
– SAY mal-uh-prop-i-z'm

> ℹ️ named after Mrs *Malaprop* in Richard Sheridan's play *The Rivals*

malaria »*noun* a disease that causes fever and is transmitted by mosquitoes.
malarial

malarkey »*noun* (in informal English) nonsense.

Malawian [of Malawi]

Malay »*noun* ❶ a member of a people inhabiting Malaysia and Indonesia. ❷ the language of the Malays.

Malaysian

malcontent »*noun* a person who is dissatisfied and rebellious.

Maldivian [of the Maldives]
– SAY mawl-**div**-i-uhn

male [not female]
maleness

malediction »*noun* a curse.
– SAY mal-i-**dik**-sh'n

malefactor »*noun* a criminal or wrongdoer.
– SAY mal-i-**fak**-ter

maleness

malevolent »*adjective* wishing to harm other people.
– SAY muh-**lev**-uh-luhnt
malevolence
malevolently

malformation »*noun* the state of being abnormally shaped or formed.
malformed

malfunction »*verb* (**malfunctions, malfunctioning, malfunctioned**) (of equipment or machinery) fail to function normally.
»*noun* a failure to function normally.

Malian [of Mali]

malice »*noun* the desire to harm someone.

malicious »*adjective* meaning to harm other people.
maliciously

malign »*adjective* harmful or evil.
»*verb* (**maligns, maligning, maligned**) say unpleasant things about someone.
– SAY muh-**lyn**
malignity SAY muh-**lig**-ni-ti

> ✓ **ign** not **ine**: malign

m

malignancy »*noun* (plural **malignancies**) ❶ a cancerous growth. ❷ the quality of being harmful or evil.

malignant »*adjective* ❶ harmful; malevolent. ❷ (of a tumour) growing uncontrollably; cancerous.
– SAY muh-**lig**-nuhnt

maligned

maligning

malignity

maligns

malinger »*verb* (**malingers, malingering, malingered**) pretend to be ill in order to avoid work.
malingerer

mall »*noun* ❶ a large enclosed shopping area. ❷ a sheltered walk or promenade.
– SAY mal or mawl

mallard »*noun* a kind of duck with a dark green head.

malleable »*adjective* ❶ able to be hammered or pressed into shape. ❷ easily influenced.
– SAY **mal**-li-uh-b'l
malleability

mallet »*noun* ❶ a hammer with a large wooden head. ❷ a wooden stick with a head like a hammer, for hitting a croquet or polo ball.

mallow »*noun* a plant with pink or purple flowers.

malnourished »*adjective* suffering from malnutrition.
malnourishment

malnutrition »*noun* the state of not having enough food, or not eating enough of the right food.

malodorous »*adjective* smelling very unpleasant.

> ✓ -odor- not -odour-: malodorous

malpractice »*noun* illegal, corrupt, or careless behaviour by a professional person.

malt »*noun* barley or other grain that has been soaked in water, allowed to sprout, and dried, used for brewing or distilling.
malted
malting

Maltese (plural **Maltese**)

malting

maltreat »*verb* (**maltreats**, **maltreating**, **maltreated**) treat badly or cruelly.
maltreatment

mammal »*noun* a warm-blooded animal that has hair or fur, produces milk, and bears live young.
mammalian

mammary »*adjective* relating to the breasts or the milk-producing organs of other mammals.

mammogram »*noun* an image obtained by mammography.
– SAY mam-muh-gram

mammography »*noun* a technique using X-rays to examine the breasts for tumours.
– SAY mam-**mog**-ruh-fi

Mammon »*noun* wealth regarded as an evil influence or false object of worship.

mammoth »*noun* a large extinct form of elephant with a hairy coat and long curved tusks.
» *adjective* huge; enormous.

man (plural **men**; verb: **mans**, **manning**, **manned**)
manlike

> ℹ️ many people now think that the use of the word **man** to mean 'human beings in general' is outdated or sexist; you could use **human beings, the human race**, or **humankind** instead

manacle »*noun* a metal band fastened around a person's hands or ankles to restrict their movement.
» *verb* (**manacles**, **manacling**, **manacled**) restrict someone with manacles.

manage (verb: **manages**, **managing**, **managed**)
manageable

management

manager
managerial
managership

manageress (plural **manageresses**)

managerial

managership

manages

managing

manana »*adverb* tomorrow, or at some time in the future.
– SAY man-**yah**-nuh

> ✓ **manana** can also be spelled **mañana** with a tilde over the **n** (as in the original Spanish)

manatee »*noun* a sea cow found in the tropical Atlantic Ocean.
– SAY man-uh-tee or man-uh-**tee**

Mancunian »*noun* a person from Manchester.
» *adjective* relating to Manchester.

mandala »*noun* a circular design symbolizing the universe in Hinduism and Buddhism.
– SAY man-duh-luh

mandarin »*noun* ❶ (**Mandarin**) the official form of the Chinese language. ❷ (in the past) a high-ranking Chinese official. ❸ a powerful official. ❹ a small citrus fruit with a loose yellow-orange skin.

mandate »*noun* ❶ an official order or permission to do something. ❷ the authority to carry out a policy that is given by voters to the winner of an election.
» *verb* (**mandates**, **mandating**, **mandated**) give someone authority to do something.

mandatory »*adjective* required by law or rules; compulsory.
– SAY man-duh-tuh-ri

mandible »*noun* ❶ the lower jawbone in mammals or fishes. ❷ either of the upper and lower parts of a bird's beak. ❸ either of the parts of an insect's mouth that crush its food.

mandolin »*noun* a musical instrument with a rounded back and metal strings.

> ✓ no **e** at the end of **mandolin**

mandrel »*noun* ❶ a shaft or spindle in a lathe to which work is fixed while being turned. ❷ a cylindrical rod round which metal or other material is forged or shaped.

mandrill »*noun* a large baboon with a red and blue face.

mane »*noun* ❶ a growth of long hair on the neck of a horse, lion, etc. ❷ a person's long hair.

 do not confuse **mane** with **main**, which means 'greatest or most important'

maneuver American spelling of **MANOEUVRE**.

manful »*adjective* brave or determined.
manfully

✓ -**ful** not -**full**: **manful**

manganese »*noun* a hard grey metallic element used in special steels and magnetic alloys.

mange »*noun* a skin disease of some animals that causes itching and hair loss.
– SAY maynj

mangel-wurzel »*noun* = **MANGOLD**.

manger »*noun* a long trough from which horses or cattle feed.

mangetout »*noun* (plural **mangetout** or **mangetouts**) a variety of pea with an edible pod.
– SAY mon*zh*-too [singular and plural]

i **mangetout** means 'eat all' in French

mangier

mangiest

mangle »*noun* a machine with rollers for squeezing wet laundry to remove the water.
» *verb* (**mangles, mangling, mangled**) destroy or severely damage by tearing or crushing.

mango »*noun* (plural **mangoes** or **mangos**) an oval tropical fruit with yellow flesh.

 the plural of **mango** can have **oes** or **os**: **mangoes** or **mangos**

mangold »*noun* a variety of beet grown as feed for farm animals.

mangos

mangrove »*noun* a tropical tree or shrub found in coastal swamps.

mangy »*adjective* (**mangier, mangiest**)
❶ (of an animal) having mange. ❷ in poor condition; shabby.
– SAY mayn-ji

manhandle (verb: **manhandles, manhandling, manhandled**)

manhole »*noun* a covered opening through which a person can enter a sewer or other underground structure.

manhood

mania »*noun* ❶ mental illness in which a person imagines things and has periods of wild excitement. ❷ an extreme enthusiasm: *he had a mania for cars.*

maniac »*noun* ❶ a person who behaves in an extremely wild or violent way. ❷ (in informal English) a person with an extreme enthusiasm for something.
maniacal

✓ no **k** at the end: **maniac**

manic »*adjective* ❶ having to do with mania. ❷ showing wild excitement and energy.
manically

manic depression »*noun* a mental disorder with alternating periods of happiness and depression.
manic-depressive

manicure »*noun* treatment to improve the appearance of the hands and nails.
» *verb* (**manicures, manicuring, manicured**) give a manicure to.
manicurist

manifest[1] »*adjective* clear and obvious.
» *verb* (**manifests, manifesting, manifested**)
❶ show or display: *Liz manifested signs of depression.* ❷ (of an illness or disorder) become apparent. ❸ (of a ghost) appear.
manifestly

manifest[2] »*noun* ❶ a document listing a ship's contents, cargo, crew, and passengers. ❷ a list of passengers or cargo in an aircraft.

manifestation »*noun* ❶ a sign or evidence of something. ❷ an appearance of a god or spirit in physical form.

manifested

manifesting

manifestly

manifesto »*noun* (plural **manifestos**) a public declaration of the policy and aims of a political party.

✓ the plural of **manifesto** has **os** not **oes**: **manifestos**

manifests

manifold »*adjective* many and various.
» *noun* a pipe with several openings, especially in a car engine.

manikin »*noun* a very small person.

✓ can also be spelled with a double **n**: both **manikin** and **mannikin** are correct. See also **MANNEQUIN**.

Manila »*noun* ❶ (also **Manila hemp**) the fibre of a Philippine plant, used for rope, paper, etc. ❷ strong brown paper.

✓ although it is named after *Manila* in the Philippines, this word can also be spelled with a double **l**: **Manilla**

m

manipulate »*verb* (**manipulates, manipulating, manipulated**) ❶ handle or control skilfully. ❷ control or influence in a clever or underhand way.
manipulable
manipulation
manipulator

manipulative »*adjective* manipulating others in a clever or underhand way.

manipulator

mankind »*noun* human beings as whole.

manlier

manliest

manlike

manly (adjective: **manlier, manliest**)
manliness

man-made

manna »*noun* ❶ (in the Bible) the substance supplied by God as food to the Israelites in the wilderness. ❷ something unexpected and beneficial.

manned »*adjective* having a human crew.

mannequin »*noun* a dummy used to display clothes in a shop window.
– SAY man-ni-kin

> ℹ️ see also MANIKIN

manner

mannered »*adjective* ❶ behaving in a specified way: *well-mannered.* ❷ artificial and affected.

mannerism »*noun* ❶ a distinctive gesture or way of speaking. ❷ (**Mannerism**) a style of 16th-century Italian art in which people or objects were shown in an exaggerated or distorted way.
mannerist

mannerly »*adjective* well-mannered.

mannikin another way of spelling MANIKIN.

manning

mannish

manoeuvrable »*adjective* (of a boat or aircraft) able to be manoeuvred easily.
manoeuvrability

> ✅ **vr** not **ver: manoeuvrable**

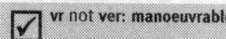

manoeuvre »*noun* ❶ a movement or series of moves requiring skill and care. ❷ a carefully planned scheme. ❸ (**manoeuvres**) a large-scale military exercise.
»*verb* (**manoeuvres, manoeuvring, manoeuvred**) ❶ make a movement or series of moves skilfully and carefully. ❷ guide skilfully or craftily.

> ✅ the standard British spelling has **oeu** in the middle and **re** at the end: **manoeuvre**. In the past the **oe** was usually printed as a ligature (**œ**), but this is old-fashioned. The American spelling is **maneuver**.

man-of-war »*noun* (plural **men-of-war**) (a historical term) an armed sailing ship.

> ✅ you may come across the older spelling **man-o'-war**, with an apostrophe in place of the **f**

manometer »*noun* an instrument for measuring the pressure of fluids.
– SAY muh-**nom**-i-ter

manor »*noun* a large country house with lands.
manorial

man-o'-war another way of spelling MAN-OF-WAR.

manpower »*noun* the number of people working or available for work or service.

manque »*adjective* having never become what you might have been: *an actor manque.*
– SAY mong-kay

> ✅ **manque** can also be written **manqué**, with an acute accent on the **e** (as in the original French)

mans

manse »*noun* the house of a Christian minister in Scotland.

manservant »*noun* a male servant.

mansion »*noun* a large, impressive house.

manslaughter »*noun* the crime of killing a person without meaning to do so.

mantelpiece »*noun* ❶ a structure surrounding a fireplace. ❷ a mantelshelf.

mantelshelf »*noun* a shelf forming the top of a mantelpiece.

mantis »*noun* (plural **mantis** or **mantises**) a large insect that waits motionless for its prey with its forelegs folded like hands in prayer.

> ✅ a fuller name for this insect is **praying mantis**. Remember, it is **praying**, that is 'holding its hands together', not **preying**, 'eating anything that moves'.

mantle »*noun* ❶ a woman's loose sleeveless cloak. ❷ a close covering, such as that of snow. ❸ a cover around a gas jet that produces a glowing light when heated. ❹ a role or responsibility that passes from one person to another. ❺ the region of very hot, dense rock between the earth's crust and its core.

» *verb* (**mantles, mantling, mantled**) (a poetic term) cover as if with a mantle.

mantra **»***noun* (originally in Hinduism and Buddhism) a word or sound repeated to aid concentration when meditating.
– SAY man-truh

manual **»***adjective* ❶ having to do with the hands. ❷ operated by or using the hands.
» *noun* a book giving instructions or information.
manually

manufacture **»***verb* (**manufactures, manufacturing, manufactured**) ❶ make something on a large scale using machinery. ❷ invent evidence or a story.
» *noun* the manufacturing of things.
manufacturer

manure **»***noun* animal dung used for fertilizing land.
» *verb* (**manures, manuring, manured**) spread manure on.

manuscript **»***noun* ❶ a handwritten book, document, or piece of music. ❷ an author's text before printing and publication.

Manx **»***adjective* relating to the Isle of Man.
» *noun* the Celtic language formerly spoken in the Isle of Man.

many

Maoism **»***noun* the communist policies and theories of the former Chinese head of state Mao Zedong (1893–1976).
Maoist

Maori **»***noun* (plural **Maori** or **Maoris**) ❶ a member of the aboriginal people of New Zealand. ❷ the language of this people.
– SAY mow-ri

map (verb: **maps, mapping, mapped**)

✓ double the **p** in **mapping** and **mapped**

maple **»***noun* a tree with five-pointed leaves and winged fruits.

mapped

mapping

maps

mar **»***verb* (**mars, marring, marred**) spoil the appearance or quality of something.

✓ double the **r** in **marring** and **marred**

maraca **»***noun* a container filled with small beans or stones, shaken as a musical instrument.
– SAY muh-**rak**-uh

maraschino cherry **»***noun* a cherry preserved in maraschino, a liqueur made from cherries.

– SAY ma-ruh-**shee**-noh

✓ sch: maraschino (an Italian word for a kind of cherry)

marathon **»***noun* ❶ a long-distance running race, strictly one of 26 miles 385 yards (42.195 km). ❷ a long-lasting and difficult task.

maraud **»***verb* (**marauds, marauding, marauded**) make a raid in search of things to steal.
– SAY muh-**rawd**
marauder

marble (verb: **marbles, marbling, marbled**)

marbling **»***noun* colouring or marking that resembles marble.

March [third month]

march (verb: **marches, marching, marched**)
marcher

Marches **»***plural noun* land on the border between two countries or territories.

marching

marchioness **»***noun* (plural **marchionesses**) ❶ the wife or widow of a marquess. ❷ a woman holding the rank of marquess in her own right.
– SAY mar-shuh-**ness** or mar-shuh-**niss**

Mardi Gras **»***noun* a carnival held in some countries on Shrove Tuesday.
– SAY mar-di **grah**

mare **»***noun* the female of a horse or related animal.

mare's nest **»***noun* ❶ a muddle. ❷ a discovery that turns out to be worthless.

margarine **»***noun* a butter substitute made from vegetable oils or animal fats.

margin **»***noun* ❶ an edge or border. ❷ the blank border on each side of the print on a page. ❸ an amount above or below a given level.

marginal **»***adjective* ❶ relating to or at a margin. ❷ of minor importance. ❸ (of a parliamentary seat) held by a small majority and therefore at risk in an election.
marginality
marginally

marginalia **»***plural noun* notes written or printed in the margin of a book or manuscript.
– SAY mar-ji-**nay**-li-uh

marginalise another way of spelling MARGINALIZE.

marginality

marginalize **»***verb* (**marginalizes, marginalizing, marginalized**) make a

m

person or group become or feel less important or powerful.
marginalization

✓ many people prefer the alternative spellings **marginalise, marginalises,** etc., and **marginalisation**: both **s** and **z** spellings are correct

marginally

marigold »*noun* a plant of the daisy family with yellow or orange flowers.

marijuana »*noun* cannabis.
– SAY ma-ri-**hwah**-nuh

marina »*noun* a purpose-built harbour with moorings for yachts and small boats.

marinade »*noun* a mixture of ingredients in which food is soaked before cooking in order to flavour or soften it.
» *verb* (**marinades, marinading, marinaded**) = MARINATE.

✓ one r, one n: **marinade** while **marinade** can be used in both the noun and verb senses, **marinate** can only be used as a verb

marinate »*verb* (**marinates, marinating, marinated**) soak food in a marinade.

marine »*adjective* ❶ relating to the sea. ❷ relating to shipping or a navy.
» *noun* a member of a body of troops trained to serve on land or sea.

mariner »*noun* a sailor.

marionette »*noun* a puppet worked by strings.

✓ double **t** and an **e** at the end: **marionette** is a French word

marital »*adjective* relating to marriage or the relations between husband and wife.

ℹ do not confuse **marital** with **martial**, which means 'relating to war'

maritime »*adjective* ❶ relating to shipping or other activity taking place at sea. ❷ living or found in or near the sea.

marjoram »*noun* a plant of the mint family, used as a herb in cooking.

mark (verb: **marks, marking, marked**)

marked
  markedly
  markedness

marker

market (verb: **markets, marketing, marketed**)
  marketable

✓ do not double the **t** in **marketing** and **marketed**

marketeer »*noun* a person who sells goods or services in a market.

market garden »*noun* a place where vegetables and fruit are grown for sale.

marketing »*noun* the promoting and selling of products or services.

marketplace

market research »*noun* the gathering of information about consumers' needs, likes, and dislikes.

markets

market value »*noun* the amount for which something can be sold in a competitive market.

marking

marks

marksman »*noun* (plural **marksmen**) a person skilled in shooting.
  marksmanship

mark-up »*noun* ❶ the amount added to the price which goods cost to make, to cover the producer's costs and profit. ❷ (in computing) a set of codes given to different parts of a text.

marl »*noun* ❶ a rock or soil consisting of clay and lime, formerly used as fertilizer. ❷ a type of fabric made with differently coloured threads.

marlin »*noun* a large, edible fish of warm seas, with a pointed snout.

marlinspike »*noun* a pointed metal tool used by sailors to separate strands of rope or wire.

marmalade

✓ **mal** not **mel**: **marmalade**

marmoreal »*adjective* made of or resembling marble.
– SAY mar-**mor**-i-uhl

marmoset »*noun* a small tropical American monkey with a silky coat and a long tail.
– SAY **mar**-muh-zet

marmot »*noun* a heavily built burrowing rodent.
– SAY **mar**-muht

maroon[1] »*noun* ❶ a dark brownish-red colour. ❷ a firework that makes a loud bang, used as a signal.

maroon[2] »*verb* (**be marooned**) be abandoned alone on an island or other inaccessible place.

marque »*noun* a make of car, as distinct from a specific model.

marquee »*noun* a large tent used for social or business events.

marquess »*noun* (plural **marquesses**) a British nobleman ranking above an earl and below a duke.

marquetry »*noun* inlaid work made from small pieces of variously coloured wood, used for the decoration of furniture.
– SAY mar-ki-tri

marquis »*noun* (plural **marquises**) (in some European countries) a nobleman ranking above a count and below a duke.
– SAY mar-kwiss

marquise »*noun* the wife or widow of a marquis, or a woman holding the rank of marquis in her own right.
– SAY mar-keez

marred

marriage

marriageable »*adjective* fit or suitable for marriage.

married

marries

marring

marrow »*noun* ❶ a long vegetable with a thin green skin and white flesh. ❷ a soft fatty substance in the cavities of bones, in which blood cells are produced.

marrowbone »*noun* a bone containing edible marrow.

marry (verb: **marries, marrying, married**)

Mars [planet]

mars [as in *it mars the beauty of the scene*]

marsh
marshy

marshal »*noun* ❶ an officer of the highest rank in the armed forces of some countries. ❷ (in the US) a type of law enforcement officer. ❸ an official responsible for supervising public events.
» *verb* (**marshals, marshalling, marshalled**) ❶ assemble a group of people in order. ❷ bring together facts, information, etc. in an organized way.

> ✓ double the **l** in **marshalling** and **marshalled** (the spellings **marshaling** and **marshaled** are American)

marshland

marshmallow »*noun* ❶ a spongy sweet made from a mixture of sugar, egg white, and gelatin. ❷ (**marsh mallow**) a tall pink-flowered plant whose roots were formerly used to make marshmallow.

marshy

marsupial »*noun* a mammal whose young are born incompletely developed and are carried and suckled in a pouch on the mother's belly.
– SAY mar-soo-pi-uhl

mart »*noun* a trade centre or market.

marten »*noun* a weasel-like forest animal that is hunted for fur in some countries.

> ✓ **-en** not **-in**: **marten** (a **martin** is a bird)

martial »*adjective* having to do with war.

> ℹ do not confuse **martial** with **marital**, which means 'relating to marriage'

martial arts »*plural noun* various sports which originated as forms of self-defence or attack, such as judo, karate, and kung fu.

martial law »*noun* government by the military forces of a country, when ordinary laws do not apply.

Martian »*adjective* relating to the planet Mars.
» *noun* a supposed inhabitant of Mars.

martin »*noun* a small short-tailed swallow.

> ✓ **-in** not **-en**: **martin** (a **marten** is an animal of the weasel family)

martinet »*noun* a person who is very strict and insists on being obeyed.

martingale »*noun* a strap or set of straps running from the noseband or reins to the girth of a horse, used to prevent the horse from raising its head too high.

martyr »*noun* ❶ a person who is killed because of their religious or other beliefs. ❷ a person who exaggerates their difficulties in order to gain sympathy.
» *verb* (**martyrs, martyring, martyred**) make someone a martyr.
martyrdom

> ✓ **tyr** not **ter**: **martyr**

marvel »*verb* (**marvels, marvelling, marvelled**) be filled with wonder.
» *noun* a person or thing that causes a feeling of wonder.

> ✓ double the **l** in **marvelling** and **marvelled** (the spellings **marveling** and **marveled** are American)

marvellous
marvellously

> ✓ double **l**: **marvellous** (the spelling **marvelous** is American)

marvels

Marxism »*noun* the political and economic theories of Karl Marx and Friedrich Engels, which formed the basis for communism.
Marxist

marzipan »*noun* a sweet paste of ground almonds, sugar, and egg whites.

m

☑ zip not sip: **marzipan**

masala »*noun* a mixture of spices ground into a paste or powder and used in Indian cookery.
– SAY muh-**sah**-luh

mascara »*noun* a cosmetic for darkening and thickening the eyelashes.

mascot »*noun* a person, animal, or object that is identified with a person or team and is supposed to bring good luck.

masculine
masculinity

mash (verb: **mashes**, **mashing**, **mashed**)

mask (verb: **masks**, **masking**, **masked**)
masked

masochism »*noun* enjoyment felt in being hurt or humiliated by someone.
– SAY mass-uh-ki-z'm
masochist
masochistic

mason »*noun* ❶ a builder and worker in stone. ❷ (**Mason**) a Freemason.

Masonic »*adjective* relating to Freemasons.

masonry »*noun* stonework.

masque »*noun* a form of dramatic entertainment popular in the 16th and 17th centuries, consisting of dancing and acting performed by masked players.
– SAY mahsk

masquerade »*noun* ❶ a false show. ❷ a ball at which the people attending wear masks.
» *verb* (**masquerades**, **masquerading**, **masqueraded**) ❶ pretend to be someone that you are not. ❷ be disguised as something else: *gossip masquerading as news.*
– SAY mass-kuh-**rayd**

☑ quer not ker: **masquerade**

Mass »*noun* (plural **Masses**) ❶ the Christian service of the Eucharist or Holy Communion. ❷ a musical setting of parts of this service.

mass (plural **masses**; verb: **masses**, **massing**, **massed**) [body of matter with no definite shape; large number of things gathered together; gather into a mass]

massacre »*noun* a brutal slaughter of a large number of people.
» *verb* (**massacres**, **massacring**, **massacred**) brutally kill a large number of people.

☑ cre not cer: **massacre**

massage (verb: **massages**, **massaging**, **massaged**)

massed

masses

masseur »*noun* a person who provides massage professionally.
– SAY ma-**ser**

☑ eur at the end: **masseur** and the feminine form **masseuse** are French words

masseuse »*noun* a woman who provides massage professionally.
– SAY ma-**serz**

massif »*noun* a compact group of mountains.
– SAY ma-**seef**

massing

massive
massively
massiveness

mass-market »*adjective* (of goods) produced in large quantities and appealing to most people.

mass noun »*noun* a noun referring to something which cannot be counted, usually a noun which has no plural form and is not used with *a* or *an*, e.g. *luggage*, *happiness*.

mass-produced

mast¹ »*noun* ❶ a tall upright post on a boat, generally carrying a sail or sails. ❷ any tall upright post.

mast² »*noun* the fruit of forest trees.

mastectomy »*noun* (plural **mastectomies**) an operation to remove a breast.
– SAY ma-**stek**-tuh-mi

master (verb: **masters**, **mastering**, **mastered**)

masterclass »*noun* (plural **masterclasses**) a class given to students by an expert musician.

mastered

masterful »*adjective* ❶ powerful and able to control others. ❷ performed or performing very skilfully.
masterfully

☑ -ful not -full: **masterful**

mastering

masterly »*adjective* performed or performing very skilfully.

ℹ️ **masterly** does not mean the same thing as **masterful**: while both mean 'very skilful', only **masterful** means 'powerful and able to control others'

mastermind »*noun* ❶ a person who is very intelligent. ❷ a person who plans and directs a complex scheme or project.
» *verb* (**masterminds, masterminding, masterminded**) plan and direct a complex scheme or project.

master of ceremonies »*noun* a person in charge of proceedings at a formal event, who introduces the speakers or performers.

masterpiece

masters

mastery »*noun* ❶ complete knowledge or command of a subject or skill. ❷ control or superiority: *man's mastery over nature.*

masthead »*noun* ❶ the highest part of a ship's mast. ❷ the name of a newspaper or magazine printed at the top of the first page.

mastic »*noun* ❶ a gum from the bark of a Mediterranean tree, used in making varnish and chewing gum. ❷ a putty-like waterproof substance used for filling and sealing in building.

masticate »*verb* (**masticates, masticating, masticated**) chew food.
mastication

mastiff »*noun* a dog of a large, strong breed with drooping ears and lips.

mastitis »*noun* inflammation of the mammary gland in the breast or udder.
– say mass-ty-tiss

mastodon »*noun* a large extinct elephant-like mammal.
– say mass-tuh-don

masturbate »*verb* (**masturbates, masturbating, masturbated**) stimulate the genitals with the hand for sexual pleasure.
– say mass-ter-bayt
masturbation
masturbator
masturbatory

mat

matador »*noun* a bullfighter whose task is to kill the bull.
– say ma-tuh-dor

> ℹ️ **matador** is a Spanish word meaning 'killer'

match (verb: **matches, matching, matched**)

matchbox (plural **matchboxes**)

matched

matches

matching

matchless »*adjective* so good that nothing can equal it.

matchmaker »*noun* a person who tries to bring about marriages or relationships between other people.

matchstick

matchwood

mate (verb: **mates, mating, mated**)

matelot »*noun* (in informal English) a sailor.
– say mat-loh

material »*noun* ❶ the matter from which something is or can be made. ❷ items needed for doing or creating something. ❸ cloth.
» *adjective* ❶ having to do with physical objects rather than the mind or spirit. ❷ essential or relevant: *evidence material to the case.*
materially

materialise another way of spelling
MATERIALIZE.

materialism »*noun* the belief that material possessions and physical comfort are more important than spiritual values.
materialist
materialistic

materialize »*verb* (**materialize, materializing, materialized**) ❶ become actual fact. ❷ appear in bodily form.
materialization

> ✅ many people prefer the alternative spellings **materialise, materialises,** etc., and **materialisation**: both **s** and **z** spellings are correct

materially

materiel »*noun* military materials and equipment.
– say muh-tee-ri-el

> ✅ **materiel** can also be written **matériel,** with an acute accent on the **e** (as in the original French)

maternal »*adjective* ❶ having to do with a mother. ❷ related through the mother's side of the family.
maternally

maternity »*noun* the state of being or becoming a mother.

mates

matey
mateyness

> ✅ **mateyness** is sometimes spelled **matiness**: both forms are correct

mathematics
mathematical
mathematically
mathematician

maths

m

matinee »*noun* an afternoon performance in a theatre or cinema.
– SAY **ma**-ti-nay

> ✓ matinee can also be spelled **matinée**, with an acute accent above the **e** (as in the original French)

matiness see the note at MATEY.

mating

matins »*noun* a service of morning prayer.
– SAY **ma**-tinz

matriarch »*noun* ❶ a woman who is the head of a family or tribe. ❷ a powerful older woman.
– SAY **may**-tri-ark
matriarchal
matriarchy

matrices plural of MATRIX.

matricide »*noun* ❶ the killing by someone of their own mother. ❷ a person who kills their mother.
– SAY **ma**-tri-syd or **may**-tri-syd

matriculate »*verb* (**matriculates, matriculating, matriculated**) enrol someone or be enrolled at a college or university.
– SAY muh-**trik**-yuu-layt
matriculation

matrimony »*noun* marriage.
matrimonial

matrix »*noun* (plural **matrices** or **matrixes**) ❶ an environment or material in which something develops. ❷ a mould in which something is cast or shaped. ❸ (in mathematics) a rectangular arrangement of quantities in rows and columns that is manipulated according to particular rules. ❹ a grid-like arrangement of elements.
– SAY **may**-triks [singular], **may**-tri-seez [plural]

> ✓ the plural can either be **matrices** (like the original Latin) or **matrixes**

matron »*noun* ❶ a woman in charge of medical and living arrangements at a boarding school. ❷ a dignified or sedate married woman. ❸ (old-fashioned) a woman in charge of nursing in a hospital.
matronly

matron of honour »*noun* a married woman attending the bride at a wedding.

matt »*adjective* not shiny.

> ✓ matt can also be spelled **matte**, with an **e** on the end

matted

matter (verb: **matters, mattering, mattered**)

matter-of-fact

matters

matting »*noun* material used for mats.

mattock »*noun* a farming tool similar to a pickaxe.

mattress (plural **mattresses**)

> ✓ remember, there is a double **t** in **mattress**

maturation »*noun* the action or process of maturing.
– SAY mat-yuu-**ray**-sh'n

mature »*adjective* ❶ fully grown. ❷ sensible, like an adult. ❸ (of certain foodstuffs or drinks) full-flavoured.
»*verb* (**matures, maturing, matured**) ❶ become mature. ❷ (of an insurance policy) reach the end of its term and hence become payable.
maturely

maturity »*noun* ❶ the state or period of being mature. ❷ the time when an insurance policy matures.

matutinal »*adjective* having to do with the morning.
– SAY ma-**tyuu**-ty-nuhl or muh-**tyoo**-ti-nuhl

maudlin »*adjective* self-pityingly or tearfully sentimental.
– SAY **mawd**-lin

maul »*verb* (**mauls, mauling, mauled**) ❶ wound someone by scratching and tearing them. ❷ treat someone savagely or roughly.

maunder »*verb* (**maunders, maundering, maundered**) move, talk, or act in a rambling way.

Maundy »*noun* specially minted coins given out by the British king or queen at a public ceremony on the Thursday before Easter.

Mauritanian [of Mauritania]

Mauritian [of Mauritius]

mausoleum »*noun* (plural **mausolea** or **mausoleums**) a building housing a tomb or tombs.
– SAY maw-suh-**lee**-uhm [singular], maw-suh-**lee**-uh [plural]

> ✓ the plural can either be **mausolea** (as in Latin) or **mausoleums**

mauve »*noun* a pale purple colour.
mauvish

maverick »*noun* an unconventional or independent-minded person.

maw »*noun* (an old term) the jaws or throat.

mawkish »*adjective* sentimental in a feeble way.
mawkishly
mawkishness

maxi »*noun* (plural **maxis**) a skirt or coat that reaches to the ankle.

maxilla »*noun* (plural **maxillae**) ❶ the bone of the upper jaw. ❷ (in arthropods) each of a pair of chewing mouthparts.
– say mak-**sil**-luh [singular], mak-**sil**-lee [plural]

> ☑ **maxilla** is Latin for 'jaw', and has the Latin **ae** ending in the plural: **maxillae**

maxim »*noun* a short statement expressing a general truth or rule of behaviour.

maximize »*verb* (**maximizes**, **maximizing**, **maximized**) ❶ make something as large or great as possible. ❷ make the best use of something.
maximization

> ☑ many people prefer the alternative spellings **maximise**, **maximises**, etc. and **maximisation**: both **s** and **z** spellings are correct

maximum (plural **maxima** or **maximums**)
maximal

> ☑ the plural can either be **maxima** (as in Latin) or **maximums**

May [fifth month]

may

> ℹ when asking to be allowed to do something, it is better to say **may** (*May we leave now?* rather than *Can we leave now?*). **Can** is mainly used to mean 'be able to', as in the sentence *can he move?* = is he physically able to move?

Maya »*noun* (plural **Maya** or **Mayas**) a member of a Central American people whose civilization died out in about 900 AD.
– say my-uh
Mayan

maybe

May Day »*noun* 1 May, celebrated as a springtime festival or as a day honouring workers.

Mayday »*noun* an international radio distress signal used by ships and aircraft.

> ℹ from French *m'aidez* meaning 'help me'

mayfly »*noun* (plural **mayflies**) an insect with transparent wings which lives for only a very short time.

mayhem »*noun* violent disorder.

mayn't [may not]

> ☑ be careful to put the apostrophe where a letter has been left out, that is between the **n** and **t** of **not**: **mayn't**

mayonnaise

> ☑ double **n**: **mayonnaise** is a French word

mayor »*noun* the elected head of a city or borough council.
mayoral

mayoralty »*noun* (plural **mayoralties**) the period of office of a mayor.
– say **mair**-uhl-ti

mayoress »*noun* (plural **mayoresses**) ❶ the wife of a mayor. ❷ a woman elected as mayor.

maypole »*noun* a decorated pole with long ribbons attached to the top, traditionally used for dancing round on May Day.

maze »*noun* a network of paths and walls or hedges through which a person has to find a way.

mazel tov »*exclamation* (among Jews) congratulations; good luck.
– say ma-zuhl tof

> ℹ **mazel tov** literally means 'good star' in Hebrew

mazurka »*noun* a lively Polish dance.
– say muh-**zer**-kuh

MC »*abbreviation* Master of Ceremonies.

MDF »*abbreviation* medium density fibreboard.

MDMA »*abbreviation* methylenedioxymethamphetamine, the drug Ecstasy.

ME »*abbreviation* myalgic encephalomyelitis, a medical condition causing fever, aching, and severe tiredness.

me

> ℹ it is not correct to use **me** as the subject of a verb, as in *John and me went to the shops*; in this case use **I** instead: *John and I went to the shops*

mea culpa »*noun* said to admit that something is your fault.
– say may-uh **kuul**-puh

> ℹ **mea culpa** means 'by my fault' in Latin

mead »*noun* an alcoholic drink made from honey and water.

meadow

meadowsweet »*noun* a tall plant with creamy-white sweet-smelling flowers.

meagre »*adjective* small in quantity or poor in quality.
meagreness

> ☑ **gre** not **ger**: **meagre** (the spelling **meager** is American)

meal

mealy »*adjective* having to do with meal or flour: *a mealy flavour*.

m

mealy-mouthed »*adjective* reluctant to speak frankly.

mean[1] (verb: **means, meaning, meant**) [intend; signify]

mean[2] (adjective: **meaner, meanest**) [miserly; unkind]
  meanly
  meanness

mean[3] »*noun* ❶ the average value of a set of quantities. ❷ something in the middle of two extremes.
» *adjective* ❶ calculated as a mean. ❷ equally far from two extremes.

meander »*verb* (**meanders, meandering, meandered**) ❶ follow a winding course. ❷ wander in a leisurely way.
» *noun* a bend of a river that curves back on itself.
– **SAY** mi-**an**-der

meaner

meanest

meaning

meaningful
  meaningfully
  meaningfulness

☑ -ful not -full: meaningful

meaningless
  meaninglessly
  meaninglessness

meanly

meanness

☑ double n: meanness

means »*noun* ❶ an agent or method for achieving a result. ❷ money: *a student with limited means.* ❸ wealth: *a man of means.*

means test »*noun* an official investigation of a person's finances to find out whether the person qualifies for welfare benefits from the state.
» *verb* (**means-tests, means-testing, means-tested**) subject someone to or base something on a means test.

☑ when using this term as a verb, remember to add a hyphen: means-test

meant past and past participle of **MEAN**[1].

meantime

meanwhile

measles »*noun* an infectious disease spread by a virus, causing fever and a red rash.

measly »*adjective* (**measlier, measliest**) ridiculously small or few.

measurable
  measurably

measure (verb: **measures, measuring, measured**)
  measurer

measured »*adjective* ❶ slow and regular in rhythm. ❷ carefully considered: *measured prose.*

measureless

measurement

measurer

measures

measuring

meat [animal flesh used as food]

meatball

meaty (adjective: **meatier, meatiest**)
  meatiness

Mecca »*noun* a place which attracts many people of a particular type.

ℹ from the city of *Mecca* in Saudi Arabia, the holiest city for Muslims

mechanic

mechanical
  mechanically

mechanics »*noun* ❶ the branch of study concerned with motion and forces producing motion. ❷ machinery or working parts. ❸ the practical aspects of something: *the mechanics of cello playing.*

mechanise another way of spelling **MECHANIZE**.

mechanism »*noun* ❶ a piece of machinery. ❷ the way in which something works or is brought about.

mechanize »*verb* (**mechanizes, mechanizing, mechanized**) equip something with or cause something to rely on machines or automatic devices.
  mechanization

☑ many people prefer the alternative spellings **mechanise, mechanises**, etc., and **mechanisation**: both **s** and **z** spellings are correct

medal [metal disc awarded for an achievement]

ℹ do not confuse **medal** with **meddle**, which means 'interfere'

medalist American spelling of **MEDALLIST**.

medallion »*noun* ❶ a piece of jewellery in the shape of a medal, worn as a pendant. ❷ a decorative oval or circular painting, panel, or design.

medallist »*noun* a person awarded a medal.

☑ double **l**: **medallist** (the spelling **medalist** is American)

meddle (verb: **meddles, meddling, meddled**) [interfere]
meddler

ℹ️ do not confuse **meddle** with **medal**, which means 'a metal disc given for a special achievement'

meddlesome »*adjective* fond of interfering in other people's affairs.

media »*noun* ❶ television, radio, and newspapers as providers of information. ❷ plural of **MEDIUM**.

ℹ️ the word **media** comes from the Latin plural of **medium**. In the normal sense 'television, radio, and the press as a group', it often behaves as a collective noun (one referring to a group of people or things, such as **staff**), and can be used with either a singular or a plural verb: *the media was informed* or *the media were informed*.

mediaeval another way of spelling **MEDIEVAL**.

medial »*adjective* situated in the middle.
– SAY mee-di-uhl
medially

median »*adjective* ❶ situated in the middle. ❷ referring to the middle term (or average of the middle two terms) of a series of values arranged in order of size. »*noun* ❶ a median value. ❷ (in geometry) a straight line drawn from one of the angles of a triangle to the middle of the opposite side.
– SAY mee-di-uhn

mediate »*verb* (**mediates, mediating, mediated**) try to settle a dispute between two other people or groups.
mediation
mediator

medic »*noun* (in informal English) a doctor or medical student.

medical
medically

medicament »*noun* a medicine.
– SAY mi-dik-uh-muhnt

medicate »*verb* (**medicates, medicating, medicated**) ❶ give someone medicine or a drug. ❷ (**medicated**) containing a medicinal substance.

medication »*noun* ❶ a medicine or drug. ❷ treatment with medicines.

medicinal »*adjective* ❶ having healing properties. ❷ relating to medicines.
medicinally

medicine

medieval »*adjective* relating to the Middle Ages, the period between about 1100 and 1450.
– SAY me-di-ee-v'l

☑ **medieval** can also be spelled with an **ae** in the middle: **mediaeval**

medievalist »*noun* a person who studies medieval history or literature.

mediocre »*adjective* of only average or fairly low quality.
– SAY mee-di-oh-ker

☑ **cre** not **cer**: **mediocre**

mediocrity »*noun* (plural **mediocrities**) ❶ the state of being mediocre. ❷ a person of mediocre ability.
– SAY mee-di-ok-ri-ti

meditate »*verb* (**meditates, meditating, meditated**) ❶ focus your mind and free it of uncontrolled thoughts, as a spiritual exercise or for relaxation. ❷ (**meditate on** or **about**) think carefully about something.

meditation »*noun* ❶ the action or practice of meditating. ❷ a speech or piece of writing giving considered thoughts on a subject.

meditative »*adjective* involving or absorbed in meditation.
meditatively

Mediterranean

☑ one **d**, one **t**, double **r**: **Mediterranean**.

medium (plural **media** or **mediums**)

medium wave »*noun* a radio wave of a frequency between 300 kilohertz and 3 megahertz.

medlar »*noun* a fruit resembling a small brown apple.

medley »*noun* (plural **medleys**) a varied mixture.

meek »*adjective* (**meeker, meekest**) quiet, gentle, and obedient.
meekly
meekness

meerkat »*noun* a small southern African mongoose.

☑ **kat** not **cat**: **meerkat**

meerschaum »*noun* ❶ a soft white clay-like material. ❷ a tobacco pipe with a bowl made from meerschaum.
– SAY meer-shawm or meer-shuhm

☑ note that it is **sch** in the middle: **meerschaum** (it is a German word)

meet (verb: **meets, meeting, met**) [come together with someone]

m

meeting

meets

mega »*adjective* (in informal English) ❶ very large. ❷ excellent.

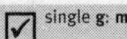
☑ single g: mega

megabyte »*noun* (in computing) a unit of information equal to one million bytes.

megahertz »*noun* (plural **megahertz**) a unit of frequency equal to one million hertz.

megalith »*noun* a large stone that forms a prehistoric monument or part of one.
megalithic

megalomania »*noun* the unfounded belief that you are very powerful and important.
– say me-guh-luh-**may**-ni-uh
megalomaniac

megaphone »*noun* a large cone-shaped device for amplifying the voice so that it can be heard at a distance.

megastar

megaton »*noun* a unit of explosive power, equivalent to one million tons of TNT.

megawatt »*noun* a unit of power equal to one million watts.

melamine »*noun* a hard plastic used to coat the surfaces of tables or worktops.
– say mel-uh-meen

melancholia »*noun* great sadness or depression.
– say me-luhn-**koh**-li-uh

melancholy »*noun* deep and long-lasting sadness.
» *adjective* sad or depressed.
melancholic

melange »*noun* a varied mixture.
– say may-lon*zh*

☑ **melange** can also be spelled **mélange**, with an acute accent over the first **e** (as in the original French)

melanin »*noun* a dark pigment in the hair and skin, responsible for the tanning of skin exposed to sunlight.
– say mel-uh-nin

melanoma »*noun* a form of skin cancer.
– say me-luh-**noh**-muh

meld »*verb* (**melds, melding, melded**) blend.

melee »*noun* ❶ a confused fight or scuffle. ❷ a disorderly mass of people.
– say mel-ay

☑ **melee** can also be spelled **melée**, with an acute accent on the second **e** (as in the original French)

mellifluous »*adjective* pleasingly smooth and musical to hear.

– say mel-**lif**-luu-uhsss
mellifluously
mellifluousness

mellow »*adjective* (**mellower, mellowest**)
❶ pleasantly smooth or soft in sound, taste, or colour. ❷ relaxed and good-humoured.
» *verb* (**mellows, mellowing, mellowed**) make or become mellow.

melodeon »*noun* ❶ a small accordion. ❷ a small organ similar to the harmonium.
– say me-**loh**-di-ihn

melodic »*adjective* ❶ relating to melody.
❷ sounding pleasant.
– say me-**lod**-ik
melodically

melodies

melodious »*adjective* tuneful.
melodiously

melodrama »*noun* ❶ a sensational play with exaggerated characters and exciting events. ❷ behaviour or events resembling melodrama.

☑ melo not mela: melodrama

melodramatic »*adjective* too dramatic and exaggerated.
melodramatically

melody »*noun* (plural **melodies**) ❶ a piece of music with a clear or simple tune.
❷ the main tune in a piece of music.

☑ plural: drop the **y** and add **ies**: **melodies**

melon

☑ only one **l** in **melon**

melt (verb: **melts, melting, melted**)

meltdown »*noun* an accident in a nuclear reactor in which the fuel overheats and melts the reactor core.

melted

melting

melts

member
membership

membrane »*noun* ❶ a skin-like tissue that connects, covers, or lines cells or parts of the body. ❷ a thin skin-like sheet of material.
membraneous
membranous

memento »*noun* (plural **mementos** or **mementoes**) an object kept as a reminder.

☑ mem not mom: memento
the plural of **memento** can have **os** or **oes: mementos** or **mementoes**

memento mori »*noun* (plural **memento mori**) an object kept as a reminder that death is inevitable.
– SAY mi-men-toh **mor**-i

> ℹ️ **memento mori** is a Latin phrase which means 'remember that you have to die'

memo (plural **memos**)

> ✓ the plural of **memo** has **os** not **oes**: **memos**

memoir »*noun* ❶ a historical account or biography written from personal knowledge. ❷ (**memoirs**) an account written by a public figure of their life and experiences.
– SAY **mem**-war

memorabilia »*plural noun* objects kept or collected because of their associations with people or events.
– SAY mem-uh-ruh-**bil**-i-uh

memorable
memorably

memorandum »*noun* (plural **memoranda** or **memorandums**) ❶ a written message. ❷ a note recording something for future use.

> ✓ the plural can be either **memoranda** (like the original Latin) or **memorandums**

memorial »*noun* a stone column or other structure made or built in memory of a person or event.
»*adjective* in memory of someone.

memories

memorize (verb: **memorizes**, **memorizing**, **memorized**)

> ✓ many people prefer the alternative spellings **memorise**, **memorises**, etc.: both **s** and **z** spellings are correct

memory (plural **memories**)

> ✓ plural: drop the **y** and add **ies**: **memories**

men

menace »*noun* ❶ a dangerous or troublesome person or thing. ❷ a threatening quality.
»*verb* (**menaces**, **menacing**, **menaced**) threaten someone.
menacing
menacingly

menage a trois »*noun* an arrangement in which a married couple and the lover of one of them live together.
– SAY may-nah*zh* ah **trwah**

> ✓ **menage a trois** can also be written **ménage à trois**, with an acute and a grave accent: it is a French phrase meaning 'household of three'

menagerie »*noun* a small zoo.
– SAY muh-**naj**-uh-ri

> ✓ note the ending is **erie**: **menagerie** (a French word)

mend (verb: **mends**, **mending**, **mended**)
mender

mendacious »*adjective* untruthful; lying.
– SAY men-**day**-shuss
mendacious
mendacity

mended

mender

mendicant »*adjective* ❶ regularly engaged in begging. ❷ (of a religious order) originally dependent on charitable donations.
»*noun* ❶ a beggar. ❷ a member of a mendicant order.
– SAY **men**-di-kuhnt

mending

mends

menfolk

menhir »*noun* a tall upright prehistoric stone erected as a monument.
– SAY **men**-heer

menial »*adjective* (of work) requiring little skill and lacking status.
»*noun* a person with a menial job.
– SAY **mee**-ni-uhl

meninges »*plural noun* the three membranes that enclose the brain and spinal cord.
– SAY mi-**nin**-jeez

meningitis »*noun* a disease in which the meninges become inflamed owing to infection with a bacterium or virus.
– SAY men-in-**jy**-tiss

> ✓ **itis** not **itus**: **meningitis**

meniscus »*noun* (plural **menisci**) ❶ the curved upper surface of a liquid in a tube. ❷ a thin lens curving outwards on one side and inwards on the other.
– SAY mi-**niss**-kuhss [singular], mi-**niss**-I [plural]

> ✓ the plural of **meniscus** is **menisci** (as in the original Latin)

menopause »*noun* the time when a woman gradually stops having menstrual periods, on average around the age of 50.
menopausal

menorah »*noun* a large branched candlestick used in Jewish worship.
– SAY mi-**nor**-uh

m

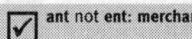

✓ note the **h** at the end: **menorah** (a Hebrew word)

menses »*plural noun* blood discharged from the uterus at menstruation.
– **say** men-seez

menstrual »*adjective* having to do with menstruation.

menstruate »*verb* (**menstruates, menstruating, menstruated**) (of a woman) discharge blood from the lining of the womb each month.
menstruation

mensuration »*noun* ❶ measurement. ❷ the part of geometry concerned with finding lengths, areas, and volumes.
– **say** men-syuu-**ray**-sh'n

menswear

mental »*adjective* ❶ having to do with the mind. ❷ relating to disorders or illnesses of the mind. ❸ (in informal English) crazy.
mentally

ℹ the use of **mental** to mean 'relating to disorders or illnesses of the mind' (as in **mental hospital**) is now regarded as old-fashioned and has largely been replaced by **psychiatric**

mentality »*noun* (plural **mentalities**) a typical way of thinking.

mentally

menthol »*noun* a substance found in peppermint oil, used as a flavouring and in decongestants.
mentholated

mention (verb: **mentions, mentioning, mentioned**)

mentor »*noun* an experienced person who advises you over a period of time.

menu (plural **menus**)

meow another way of spelling **MIAOW**.

MEP »*abbreviation* Member of the European Parliament.

mercantile »*adjective* relating to trade or commerce.
– **say** mer-**kuhn**-tyl

mercenary »*adjective* wanting to do only things that make you money.
» *noun* (plural **mercenaries**) a professional soldier hired to serve in a foreign army.

✓ plural: drop the **y** and add **ies**: **mercenaries**

mercer »*noun* (mainly a historical term) a dealer in textile fabrics.

merchandise »*noun* goods for sale.
» *verb* (**merchandises, merchandising, merchandised**) promote the sale of a product.
merchandiser

✓ many people prefer the alternative spellings **merchandize, merchandizes,** etc. for the verb: both **z** and **s** spellings are correct (but the nouns **merchandise** and **merchandiser** must be spelled with **ise**)

merchant »*noun* a trader who sells goods in large quantities.
» *adjective* (of ships, sailors, or shipping activity) involved with commerce.

✓ **ant** not **ent**: **merchant**

merchantable »*adjective* suitable for sale.

merchant bank »*noun* a bank dealing in commercial loans and investment.

merchant navy »*noun* a country's commercial shipping.

mercies

merciful
mercifully

✓ **-ful** not **-full**: **merciful**

merciless
mercilessly
mercilessness

mercurial »*adjective* ❶ tending to change mood suddenly. ❷ having to do with the element mercury.
– **say** mer-**kyoor**-i-uhl
mercurially

Mercury [planet]

mercury »*noun* a heavy silvery-white liquid metallic element used in some thermometers and barometers.

mercy (plural **mercies**)

✓ plural: drop the **y** and add **ies**: **mercies**

mere[1] »*adjective* ❶ that is nothing more than what is stated or described. ❷ (**the merest**) the smallest or slightest.

mere[2] »*noun* (a poetic term) a lake or pond.

merely »*adverb* only.

meretricious »*adjective* superficially attractive but having no real value.
– **say** me-ri-**tri**-shuhss

merganser »*noun* a fish-eating diving duck with a long, thin jagged bill.
– **say** mer-**gan**-zer

merge »*verb* (**merges, merging, merged**) ❶ combine or be combined into a whole. ❷ blend gradually into something else.

merger »*noun* a merging of two organizations into one.

merges

merging

meridian »*noun* a circle passing at the same longitude through a given place on the earth's surface and the poles.

meringue »*noun* ❶ beaten egg whites and sugar baked until crisp. ❷ a small cake made of meringue.
– SAY muh-**rang**

> 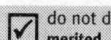 note the **gue** at the end: meringue (a French word)

merino »*noun* (plural **merinos**) a soft wool obtained from breed of sheep with a long, fine fleece.
– SAY muh-**ree**-noh

merit »*noun* ❶ the quality of being good and deserving praise. ❷ a good point or feature.
» *verb* (**merits, meriting, merited**) deserve something.

> 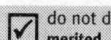 do not double the t in **meriting** and **merited**

meritocracy »*noun* (plural **meritocracies**) a society in which power is held by those people who have the greatest ability.
meritocratic

meritorious »*adjective* deserving reward or praise.

merlin »*noun* a small dark falcon.

mermaid »*noun* a mythical sea creature with a woman's head and body and a fish's tail instead of legs.

merrier

merriest

merrily

merriment »*noun* fun.

> 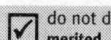 merri- not merry-: merriment

merry (adjective: **merrier, merriest**)
merrily
merriness

> 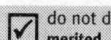 drop the y and add **ier** or **iest** to spell **merrier** or **merriest**

merry-go-round

merrymaking

mesa »*noun* an isolated flat-topped hill with steep sides.
– SAY **may**-ser

Mesdames plural of MADAME.
– SAY may-**dam**

> 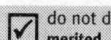 do not forget the s before the d: Mesdames

Mesdemoiselles plural of MADEMOISELLE.
– SAY may-duh-mwah-**zel**

> 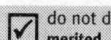 do not forget the s before the d: Mesdemoiselles

mesh »*noun* ❶ material made of a network of wire or thread. ❷ the spacing of the strands of a net. ❸ a complex or constricting situation.
» *verb* (**meshes, meshing, meshed**) ❶ (**mesh with**) be in harmony with. ❷ become entangled or entwined. ❸ (of a gearwheel) lock together with another.

mesmeric »*adjective* hypnotic.
– SAY mez-**me**-rik
mesmerically

mesmerise another way of spelling MESMERIZE.

mesmerism »*noun* (old-fashioned) hypnotism.

> 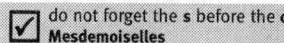 named after the Austrian physician Franz A. *Mesmer*

mesmerize »*verb* (**mesmerizes, mesmerizing, mesmerized**) capture someone's complete attention so that they are engrossed.

> 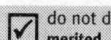 many people prefer the alternative spellings mesmerise, mesmerises, etc.: both s and z spellings are correct

m

meson »*noun* (in physics) a subatomic particle intermediate in mass between an electron and a proton.
– SAY **mee**-zon or **mez**-on

Mesopotamian »*adjective* relating to Mesopotamia, an ancient region of what is now Iraq.
– SAY me-suh-puh-**tay**-mi-uhn

mesosphere »*noun* the region of the earth's atmosphere above the stratosphere and below the thermosphere.

Mesozoic »*adjective* relating to the geological era from about 245 to 65 million years ago.

mesquite »*noun* a spiny American tree producing edible pods.
– SAY me-**skeet**

mess (plural **messes**; verb: **messes, messing, messed**)

message (verb: **messages, messaging, messaged**)

messed

messenger

messes

messiah »*noun* a great leader or saviour.

> 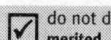 note the h at the end: messiah (a Hebrew word)

messianic »*adjective* ❶ relating to a messiah. ❷ inspired by belief in a messiah.
– SAY mess-i-**an**-ik

messier

messiest

Messieurs plural of MONSIEUR.

messily

messiness

messing

Messrs plural of MR.

> ℹ️ **Messrs** was originally short for *Messieurs*

messy (adjective: **messier**, **messiest**)
messily
messiness

> ✓ drop the **y** and add **ier** or **iest** to spell **messier** or **messiest**

met past and past participle of MEET.

metabolic

metabolise another way of spelling METABOLIZE.

metabolism »*noun* the processes by which food is used for the growth of tissue or the production of energy.
– SAY mi-**tab**-uh-li-z'm
metabolic

metabolize »*verb* (**metabolizes, metabolizing, metabolized**) process or be processed by metabolism.

> ✓ many people prefer the alternative spellings **metabolise, metabolises,** etc.: both **s** and **z** spellings are correct

metal
metalled

metallic »*adjective* ❶ having to do with metal. ❷ (of sound) sharp and ringing.

> ✓ note the double **l**: **metallic**

metallurgy »*noun* the scientific study of metals.
– SAY mi-**tal**-ler-ji or met-uh-**ler**-ji
metallurgical
metallurgist

metalwork

metamorphic »*adjective* (of rock) having been changed by heat or pressure.
metamorphism

metamorphose »*verb* (**metamorphoses, metamorphosing, metamorphosed**)
❶ change completely in form or nature.
❷ (of an insect or amphibian) undergo metamorphosis.
– SAY met-uh-**mor**-fohz

metamorphosis »*noun* (plural **metamorphoses**) ❶ the transformation of an insect or amphibian from an immature form or larva to an adult form in separate stages. ❷ a change in form or nature.

– SAY met-uh-**mor**-fuh-siss [singular], met-uh-**mor**-fuh-seez [plural]

> ✓ make the plural by changing the **-is** ending to **-es** (like the original Greek): metamorphosis

metaphor »*noun* a word or phrase used to represent or stand for something else.
– SAY met-uh-fer

metaphoric »*adjective* = METAPHORICAL.

metaphorical »*adjective* having to do with metaphor.
– SAY met-uh-**forr**-i-k'l
metaphorically

metaphysical »*adjective* ❶ relating to metaphysics. ❷ beyond physical matter.
metaphysically

metaphysics »*noun* the branch of philosophy dealing with the nature of existence, truth, and knowledge.

mete »*verb* (**metes, meting, meted**) (**mete out**) deal out justice, punishment, etc.

meteor »*noun* a small body of matter from outer space that glows as a result of friction with the earth's atmosphere and appears as a shooting star.

> ℹ️ do not confuse a **meteor** with a **meteorite**, which is a piece of rock or metal that has fallen to earth from space

meteoric »*adjective* ❶ relating to meteors or meteorites. ❷ achieving success or promotion rapidly.

meteorite »*noun* a piece of rock or metal that has fallen to the earth from space.

> ℹ️ do not confuse a **meteorite** with a **meteor**, which is a small body of matter from outer space which appears as a shooting star

meteorology »*noun* the study of conditions in the atmosphere, especially for weather forecasting.
– SAY mee-ti-uh-**rol**-uh-ji
meteorological
meteorologist

> ✓ **meteor-** not **meter-**: meteorology

meter[1] »*noun* a device that measures and records the quantity, degree, or rate of something.
»*verb* (**meters, metering, metered**) measure something with a meter.

meter[2] American spelling of METRE[1], METRE[2].

metes

methadone »*noun* a powerful painkiller, used as a substitute for morphine and heroin in treating people who are addicted to those drugs.

– **say** meth-uh-dohn

methane »*noun* a flammable gas which is the main constituent of natural gas.
– **say** mee-thayn or meth-ayn

methanol »*noun* a poisonous flammable alcohol, used to make methylated spirit.

method

method acting »*noun* an acting technique in which an actor tries to identify completely with a character's emotions.

methodical »*adjective* done or doing something in a well organized and systematic way.
methodically

Methodist »*noun* a member of a Christian Protestant group which separated from the Church of England in the 18th-century.
»*adjective* relating to Methodists or Methodism.
Methodism

methodology »*noun* (plural **methodologies**) a system of methods used in a particular field.
methodological

meths »*noun* methylated spirit.

methyl alcohol »*noun* methanol.
– **say** mee-thyl or meth-yl

methylated spirit »*noun* alcohol for use as a solvent or fuel, made unfit for drinking by the addition of methanol and a violet dye.

meticulous »*adjective* very careful and precise.
meticulously
meticulousness

metier »*noun* a trade, profession, or special ability.
– **say** may-ti-ay

> ☑ metier can also be spelled **métier**, with an acute accent on the first **e** (as in the original French)

meting [as in *she began meting out rebukes*]

metonym »*noun* a word or expression used as a substitute for something with which it is closely associated, e.g. *Washington* for the US government.
– **say** met-uh-nim
metonymic
metonymy

metre[1] [unit of length]

> ☑ re not er: **metre** (the spelling **meter** is American)

metre[2] »*noun* the rhythm of a piece of poetry, determined by the number and length of feet in a line.

> ☑ re not er: **metre** (the spelling **meter** is American)

metric »*adjective* relating to or using the metre or the metric system.

metrical »*adjective* ❶ having to do with poetic metre. ❷ having to do with measurement.
metrically

metrical foot »*noun* a group of syllables making up a basic unit of metre in a poem.

metrically

metricate »*verb* (**metricates**, **metricating**, **metricated**) convert a system of measurement to the metric system.
metrication

metric system »*noun* the decimal measuring system based on the metre, litre, and gram as units of length, capacity, and weight or mass.

metric ton »*noun* a unit of weight equal to 1,000 kilograms (2,205 lb).

> ℹ️ also called a **tonne**

metro »*noun* (plural **metros**) an underground railway system in a city.

metronome »*noun* a device that marks time at a selected rate by giving a regular tick, used by musicians.
– **say** met-ruh-nohm
metronomic

metropolis »*noun* (plural **metropolises**) the main city of a country or region.
– **say** mi-trop-uh-liss

metropolitan »*adjective* relating to a metropolis, or to large and densely populated areas.
– **say** me-truh-pol-i-t'n

mettle »*noun* spirit and strength of character.

mew »*verb* (**mews**, **mewing**, **mewed**) (of a cat or gull) make a soft, high-pitched sound like a cry.
»*noun* a mewing noise.

mewl »*verb* (**mewls**, **mewling**, **mewled**) ❶ cry feebly. ❷ mew.

mews »*noun* (plural **mews**) a row of houses or flats converted from stables in a small street or square.

Mexican

meze »*noun* (plural **meze** or **mezes**) (in Turkish, Greek, and Middle Eastern cookery) a selection of hot and cold dishes.
– **say** mez-zay

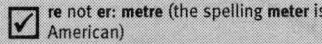

meze can also be spelled with a double z: **mezze**

mezzanine »*noun* a floor extending over only part of the full area of a building, built between two full floors.
– **say** mez-zuh-neen or mets-uh-neen

mezze another way of spelling **MEZE**.

mezzo »*noun* (plural **mezzos**) a female singer with a voice pitched between soprano and contralto.
– **say** met-zoh

mezzo-soprano »*noun* = **MEZZO**.

miaow (verb: **miaows, miaowing, miaowed**)

 miaow can also be spelled **meow**

miasma »*noun* (a poetic term) an unpleasant or unhealthy atmosphere.
– **say** mi-az-muh or my-az-muh

mic »*noun* (in informal English) a microphone.

mica »*noun* a mineral found as tiny shiny scales in rocks.
– **say** my-kuh

mice

Michaelmas »*noun* the day of the Christian festival of St Michael, 29 September.
– **say** mi-k'l-muhss

mickey »*noun* (**take the mickey**) (in informal English) tease or ridicule someone.
mickey-taking

Mickey Finn »*noun* a drink which has been secretly drugged or altered.

micro »*noun* (plural **micros**) a microcomputer or microprocessor.
» *adjective* extremely small.

 the plural of **micro** has **os** not **oes**: **micros**

microbe »*noun* a bacterium; a germ.

microbiology »*noun* the scientific study of living creatures that are so tiny that they can only be seen using a microscope.

microchip »*noun* a miniature electronic circuit made from a tiny wafer of silicon.

microclimate »*noun* the climate of a very small or restricted area.

microcomputer »*noun* a small computer with a microprocessor as its central processor.

microcosm »*noun* a thing that has the features and qualities of something much larger.
– **say** my-kroh-ko-z'm
microcosmic

microelectronics »*noun* the design, manufacture, and use of microchips and minute electric circuits.

microfiche »*noun* a piece of film containing greatly reduced photographs of the pages of a newspaper, book, etc.
– **say** my-kroh-feesh

microfilm »*noun* a length of film containing greatly reduced photographs of a newspaper, book, etc.

microgram »*noun* a mass of one millionth of a gram.

microlight »*noun* a very small, light aircraft for one or two people.

 -light not **-lite**: **microlight**

micrometer »*noun* an instrument which measures small distances or thicknesses.
– **say** my-krom-i-ter

micrometre »*noun* a length of one millionth of a metre.

 a **micrometer** is a measuring instrument and a **micrometre** is a millionth of a metre. In America, the spelling **micrometer** is used for both.

micro-organism »*noun* an organism that is so small that it can only be seen using a microscope.

microphone

microprocessor »*noun* an integrated circuit which can perform the role of a central processing unit of a computer.

micros

microscope

microscopic »*adjective* so small as to be visible only with a microscope.
microscopically

microscopy »*noun* the use of a microscope.
– **say** my-kross-kuh-pi

microsecond »*noun* one millionth of a second.

microsurgery »*noun* surgery performed using very small instruments and a microscope.

microwave »*noun* ❶ an electromagnetic wave with a wavelength in the range 0.001–0.3 m. ❷ an oven that uses microwaves to cook or heat food.
» *verb* (**microwaves, microwaving, microwaved**) cook food in a microwave oven.

mid

Midas touch »*noun* the ability to make a lot of money out of anything you do.

m

ℹ️ from King *Midas*, who in Greek mythology had the power to turn everything he touched into gold

midday

midden »*noun* a dunghill or rubbish heap.

middle

middle-aged

Middle Ages »*plural noun* the period of European history from around 1000 to 1453.

middlebrow »*adjective* in between highbrow and lowbrow.

middle ear »*noun* the air-filled central cavity of the ear, behind the eardrum.

Middle East »*noun* an area of SW Asia and northern Africa, stretching from the Mediterranean to Pakistan.
Middle Eastern

Middle England »*noun* the conservative middle classes in England.

Middle English »*noun* the English language of the period from about 1150 to 1470.

middleman »*noun* (plural **middlemen**) ❶ a person who buys goods from producers and sells them to retailers or consumers. ❷ a person who arranges business or political deals between other people.

middleweight »*noun* a boxing weight coming between welterweight and light heavyweight.

middling »*adjective* average in size, amount, or rank.

midfield
midfielder

midge »*noun* a small two-winged fly, of which many kinds feed on blood.

midget

midi »*noun* (plural **midis**) a woman's calf-length skirt, dress, or coat.
» *adjective* medium-sized.

midland
midlander

midlife

midnight

midriff

midshipman »*noun* (plural **midshipmen**) a low-ranking officer in the Royal Navy.

midships »*adverb & adjective* = AMIDSHIPS.

midst (an old word) »*preposition* in the middle of.
» *noun* the middle point or part.

midstream

midsummer

midterm

midway

midweek

Midwest »*noun* the region of the northern US from Ohio west to the Rocky Mountains.
Midwestern

midwife »*noun* (plural **midwives**) a nurse who is trained to assist women in childbirth.
midwifery

midwinter

midwives

mien »*noun* a person's look or manner.
– SAY meen

☑️ **i** before **e**: **mien** follows the usual rule

miffed

might[1] past of MAY.

might[2] »*noun* great power or strength.

mightier

mightiest

mightily

mightiness

mightn't [might not]

☑️ be careful to put the apostrophe where a letter has been left out, that is between the **n** and **t** of **not**: **mightn't**

mighty (adjective: **mightier**, **mightiest**)
mightily
mightiness

☑️ drop the **y** and add **ier** or **iest** to spell **mightier** or **mightiest**

migraine »*noun* a recurrent throbbing headache, often accompanied by nausea and disturbed vision.
– SAY mee-grayn or my-grayn

☑️ the ending is **-raine**, not **-rain** or **-rane**: **migraine**

migrant »*noun* ❶ an animal that migrates. ❷ a worker who moves from one place to another to find work.
» *adjective* tending to migrate or having migrated.

migrate »*verb* (**migrates**, **migrating**, **migrated**) ❶ (of an animal) move from one place to another according to the seasons. ❷ move to settle in a new area in order to find work.
migration
migratory

mikado »*noun* (a historical term) a title given to the emperor of Japan.
– SAY mi-kah-doh

m

mike »*noun* (in informal English) a microphone.

mil »*noun* one thousandth of an inch.

milch cow »*noun* ❶ a cow kept for milk. ❷ a source of easy profit.
– SAY milsh or milch

mild (adjective: **milder**, **mildest**)
  mildly
  mildness

mildew »*noun* a coating of tiny fungi on plants or damp material such as paper or leather.
  mildewed

mildly

mildness

mile

mileage »*noun* ❶ a number of miles covered. ❷ benefit or advantage: *he got a lot of mileage out of the mix-up.*

> ✓ remember the **e** in the middle: **mileage**

mileometer another way of spelling MILOMETER.

milestone

milieu »*noun* (plural **milieux** or **milieus**) a person's social environment.
– SAY mee-lyer

> ✓ the plural of **milieu** can either be **milieux** (as in the original French) or **milieus**

militant »*adjective* prepared to take aggressive action in support of a political or social cause.
» *noun* a militant person.
  militancy
  militantly

> ✓ ant not ent: **militant**

militarily

militarise another way of spelling MILITARIZE.

militarism »*noun* the belief that a country should possess and readily use strong armed forces.
  militarist
  militaristic

militarize »*verb* (**militarizes**, **militarizing**, **militarized**) ❶ supply a place with soldiers and military equipment. ❷ give a military character to something.

> ✓ many people prefer the alternative spellings **militarise**, **militarises**, etc.: both **s** and **z** spellings are correct

military »*adjective* having to do with soldiers or armed forces.

» *noun* (**the military**) the armed forces of a country.
  militarily

militate »*verb* (**militates**, **militating**, **militated**) (**militate against**) be a powerful factor in preventing something.

> ℹ do not confuse **militate** and **mitigate**: **militate** means 'be a powerful factor in preventing something' (as in *laws that militate against personal freedom*), while **mitigate** means 'make something bad less severe' (as in *drainage schemes helped to mitigate the problem*)

militia »*noun* ❶ a military force made up of civilians, used to supplement a regular army in an emergency. ❷ a rebel force opposing a regular army.
– SAY mi-li-shuh

> ✓ one **l**, one **t**: **militia**

militiaman (plural **militiamen**)

milk (verb: **milks**, **milking**, **milked**)

milkiness

milking

milkmaid

milkman (plural **milkmen**)

milks

milkshake

milksop »*noun* a timid and indecisive person.

milk teeth »*plural noun* temporary teeth in a child or young mammal.

milky
  milkiness

Milky Way »*noun* the galaxy of which our solar system is a part, visible at night as a faint band of light crossing the sky.

mill (verb: **mills**, **milling**, **milled**)

millenarian »*adjective* ❶ having to do with Christian belief in a thousand-year age of blessedness associated with the Second Coming of Jesus. ❷ seeking rapid and radical change.
– SAY mi-li-**nair**-i-uhn

> ✓ single **n**'s in **millenarian** and **millenary**, but not in **millennium** and **millennial**

millenary »*noun* (plural **millenaries**) ❶ a period of a thousand years. ❷ a thousandth anniversary.
» *adjective* consisting of a thousand.
– SAY mi-**len**-uh-ri

millennium »*noun* (plural **millennia** or **millenniums**) ❶ a period of a thousand years. ❷ (**the millennium**) the point at which one period of a thousand years

m

ends and another begins. ❸ an anniversary of a thousand years.
– SAY mi-**len**-i-uhm
millennial

> ✓ two **l**'s, two **n**'s: **millennium**
> the plural of **millennium** can be either **millennia** (as in Latin) or **millenniums**

miller »*noun* a person who owns or works in a grain mill.

millet »*noun* a cereal which bears a large crop of small seeds, used to make flour or alcoholic drinks.

millibar »*noun* a unit of atmospheric pressure equal to 100 pascals.

milligram »*noun* a mass of one thousandth of a gram.

> ✓ **-gram** not **-gramme: milligram**

millilitre »*noun* one thousandth of a litre.

> ✓ **tre** not **ter: millilitre** (the spelling **milliliter** is American)

millimetre »*noun* a length of one thousandth of a metre.

> ✓ **tre** not **ter: millimetre** (the spelling **millimeter** is American)

milliner »*noun* a person who makes or sells women's hats.
millinery

milling

million
millionth

millionaire

> ✓ only one **n: millionaire**

millionairess (plural **millionairesses**)

millionth

millipede »*noun* a small insect-like creature with a long body and lots of legs.

millisecond »*noun* one thousandth of a second.

millpond »*noun* a very still and calm stretch of water.

mills

millstone »*noun* ❶ one of a pair of circular stones used for grinding grain. ❷ a burden of responsibility.

milometer »*noun* an instrument on a vehicle for recording the number of miles travelled.
– SAY my-**lom**-i-ter

> ✓ **milometer** can also be spelled **mileometer**

mime »*noun* ❶ the use of silent gestures and facial expressions to tell a story or show feelings, especially in the theatre.
» *verb* (**mimes, miming, mimed**) ❶ use mime to tell a story or show feelings. ❷ pretend to sing or play an instrument as a recording is being played.

mimesis »*noun* ❶ imitation of the real world in art and literature. ❷ (in biology) mimicry of another animal or plant.
– SAY mi-**mee**-siss or my-**mee**-siss

mimetic »*adjective* having to do with mimesis or mimicry.
– SAY mi-**met**-ik

mimic »*verb* (**mimics, mimicking, mimicked**) ❶ imitate the voice or actions of someone else. ❷ (of an animal or plant) take on the appearance of another in order to hide or for protection.
» *noun* ❶ a person skilled in mimicking. ❷ an animal or plant that mimics.

> ✓ add a **k** in **mimicking** and **mimicked**

mimicry »*noun* ❶ imitation of someone or something. ❷ (in biology) the close external resemblance of an animal or plant to another.

> ✓ there is no **k** in **mimicry**

miming

mimosa »*noun* an acacia tree with delicate fern-like leaves and yellow flowers.
– SAY mi-**moh**-zuh

mimsy »*adjective* rather feeble and prim.

minaret »*noun* a slender tower of a mosque, with a balcony from which Muslims are called to prayer.

> ✓ **et** at the end, not **ette: minaret**

minatory »*adjective* threatening.
– SAY min-uh-**tuh**-ri

mince (verb: **minces, mincing, minced**)

mincemeat »*noun* a mixture of currants, raisins, apples, candied peel, sugar, spices, and suet.

minces

mincing

mind (verb: **minds, minding, minded**)

mind-bending

mind-blowing

mind-boggling

minded

minder

mindful

-ful not **-full**: **mindful**

mind game »*noun* a series of actions planned for its psychological effect on another person.

minding

mindless
  mindlessly
  mindlessness

mind-numbing

minds

mindset »*noun* the established set of attitudes held by someone.

mine¹ [belonging to me]

mine² (verb: **mines**, **mining**, **mined**) [hole or channel dug in the earth; type of bomb; obtain something from a mine]

minefield

miner [person who works in a mine]

mineral »*noun* ❶ a solid inorganic substance occurring naturally, such as copper and silicon. ❷ an inorganic substance needed by the human body for good health, such as calcium and iron. ❸ a substance obtained by mining.

mineralogy »*noun* the scientific study of minerals.
  mineralogical
  mineralogist

mines

mineshaft

minestrone »*noun* an Italian soup containing vegetables and pasta.
– **SAY** mi-ni-**stroh**-ni

rone not **roni**: **minestrone**

minesweeper »*noun* a warship equipped for detecting and removing or destroying explosive mines.

Ming »*adjective* (of Chinese porcelain) made during the Ming dynasty (1368–1644), characterized by elaborate designs and vivid colours.

mingle (verb: **mingles**, **mingling**, **mingled**)

mingy »*adjective* (in informal English) not generous.
– **SAY** min-ji

mini (plural **minis**)

miniature

niat not **nat** in the middle: **miniature**

miniaturise another way of spelling **MINIATURIZE**.

miniaturist »*noun* an artist who paints very small, detailed portraits.

miniaturize (verb: **miniaturizes**, **miniaturizing**, **miniaturized**)
  miniaturization

many people prefer the alternative spellings **miniaturise**, **miniaturises**, etc.: both **s** and **z** spellings are correct

minibar »*noun* a small refrigerator in a hotel room containing various drinks.

minibus

minicab

minicomputer »*noun* a computer of medium power, more than a microcomputer but less than a mainframe.

minidisc »*noun* a disc similar to a small CD, that is able to record sound or data and play it back.

can also be spelled **minidisk**: both **c** and **k** spellings are correct

minim »*noun* a musical note having the time value of two crotchets or half a semibreve, represented by a ring with a stem.

minima plural of **MINIMUM**.

minimal
  minimally

minimalist »*noun* a person who likes or produces art or music using very simple forms and structures.
» *adjective* relating to art or music characterized by very simple forms and structures.
  minimalism

minimally

minimize (verb: **minimizes**, **minimizing**, **minimized**)
  minimization
  minimizer

many people prefer the alternative spellings **minimise**, **minimises**, etc., **minimisation**, and **minimiser**: both **s** and **z** spellings are correct

minimum (plural **minima** or **minimums**)

the plural of **minimum** can either be **minima** (as in Latin) or **minimums**

mining

minion »*noun* an obedient or unimportant follower of a powerful person.

only one **n** in the middle: **minion**

minis plural of **MINI**.

miniseries (plural **miniseries**)

miniskirt

minister »*noun* ❶ a head of a government department. ❷ a diplomatic agent representing a state or king or queen in a foreign country. ❸ a member of the clergy.

» *verb* (ministers, ministering, ministered) (minister to) attend to someone's needs.

ministerial »*adjective* relating to a minister or ministers.

ministering

Minister of State »*noun* (in the UK) a government minister ranking below a Secretary of State.

ministers

Minister without Portfolio »*noun* a government minister who has cabinet status but is not in charge of a specific department of state.

ministrations »*noun* the providing of help or care: *the room was spotless due to the ministrations of the cleaning lady.*

ministry »*noun* (plural ministries) ❶ a government department headed by a minister. ❷ a period of government under one Prime Minister. ❸ the work or office of a minister of religion.

> ☑ try not tery: ministry
> plural: drop the y and add ies: ministries

minivan

miniver »*noun* white fur used for lining or trimming clothes.
– SAY min-i-ver

mink »*noun* a small stoat-like animal farmed for its fur.

minnow »*noun* ❶ a small freshwater fish. ❷ a small or unimportant person.

Minoan »*adjective* relating to a Bronze Age civilization centred on Crete (about 3000–1050 BC).
– SAY mi-**noh**-uhn

minor [not important or serious]

minority (plural minorities)

> ☑ plural: drop the y and add ies: minorities

minster »*noun* a large or important church.

minstrel »*noun* a medieval singer or musician.

> ☑ mins not minis: minstrel

mint¹ [herb]
minty

mint² »*noun* ❶ a place where money is coined. ❷ (a mint) (in informal English) a large sum of money.
» *adjective* as new: *in mint condition.*
» *verb* (mints, minting, minted) ❶ make a coin by stamping metal. ❷ produce something for the first time.

minuet »*noun* a ballroom dance popular in the 18th century.

minus (plural minuses)

minuscule »*adjective* ❶ extremely tiny. ❷ in lower-case letters.
– SAY min-uhss-kyool

> ☑ minus- not minis-: minuscule

minuses

minute¹ [sixty seconds]

minute² [extremely small]
minutely

minute³ »*noun* ❶ (minutes) a written summary of the points discussed at a meeting. ❷ an official written message.
» *verb* (minutes, minuting, minuted) ❶ record the points discussed at a meeting. ❷ send a minute to someone.
– SAY mi-nit

minutiae »*plural noun* small or precise details.
– SAY mi-**nyoo**-shi-ee

> ☑ note the ae ending: minutiae is a Latin word

minuting

minx »*noun* (minxes) a cheeky, cunning, or flirtatious girl or young woman.

Miocene »*adjective* relating to the geological period from about 23.3 to 5.2 million years ago.
– SAY my-oh-seen

miracle

miracle play »*noun* a medieval play based on biblical stories or the lives of the saints.

miraculous
miraculously

mirage »*noun* ❶ an optical illusion caused by atmospheric conditions, especially the appearance of a sheet of water in a desert or on a hot road. ❷ something that appears real or possible but is not in fact so.
– SAY mi-rah*zh* or mi-**rah***zh*

> ☑ only one r: mirage

mire »*noun* ❶ a stretch of swampy or boggy ground. ❷ a difficult situation from which it is hard to escape.
» *verb* (mires, miring, mired) (be mired) ❶ become stuck in or covered with mud. ❷ be in difficulties.

mirror (verb: mirrors, mirroring, mirrored)

mirth »*noun* amusement.
mirthful

miry »*adjective* very muddy or boggy.

m

misadventure »*noun* ❶ (in law) death caused accidentally and not involving negligence or crime. ❷ a mishap.

misalliance »*noun* an unsuitable or unhappy relationship or marriage.

> ☑ ance not ence: misalliance

misanthrope »*noun* a person who dislikes and avoids other people.
– SAY mi-zuhn-throhp
misanthropic
misanthropy

misapprehension »*noun* a mistaken belief.

misappropriate »*verb* (misappropriates, misappropriating, misappropriated) dishonestly or unfairly take something for your own use.
misappropriation

misbegotten »*adjective* not carefully thought out or planned.

misbehave (verb: misbehaves, misbehaving, misbehaved)
misbehaviour

miscalculate (verb: miscalculates, miscalculating, miscalculated)
miscalculation

miscarriage »*noun* the unforced expelling of a fetus from the womb before it is able to survive independently.

miscarriage of justice »*noun* a failure of a court of law to achieve justice.

miscarry »*verb* (miscarries, miscarrying, miscarried) ❶ (of a pregnant woman) have a miscarriage. ❷ (of a plan) fail.

miscast »*verb* (miscasts, miscasting, miscast) give (an actor) an unsuitable role.

miscellaneous »*adjective* ❶ (of items or people) of various types. ❷ (of a collection or group) made up of things of different kinds.

> ☑ misc at the beginning and eous not ious at the end: miscellaneous

miscellany »*noun* (plural miscellanies) a collection of different things.
– SAY mi-sel-luh-ni

mischance »*noun* bad luck.

mischief

mischievous
mischievously
mischievousness

> ☑ the ending is vous not vious: mischievous

miscible »*adjective* (of liquids) capable of being mixed together.

– SAY miss-i-b'l

misconceive »*verb* (misconceives, misconceiving, misconceived) ❶ fail to understand something correctly. ❷ (be misconceived) be badly judged or planned.

> ☑ e before i because it is after c: misconceive follows the usual rule

misconception »*noun* a false or mistaken idea or belief.

misconduct »*noun* unacceptable or improper behaviour.
» verb (misconducts, misconducting, misconducted) (misconduct yourself) behave in an improper manner.

misconstruction »*noun* the action of misconstruing something.

misconstrue »*verb* (misconstrues, misconstruing, misconstrued) interpret something wrongly.

> ☑ rue not rew: misconstrue

miscreant »*noun* a person who behaves badly or unlawfully.
» adjective behaving badly or unlawfully.
– SAY miss-kri-uhnt

> ☑ eant not iant: miscreant

miscue »*verb* (miscues, miscueing or miscuing, miscued) fail to strike the ball properly, especially in snooker.

misdeed

misdemeanour »*noun* ❶ a minor wrongdoing. ❷ (in law) (in the US) an offence seen as less serious than a felony.

> ☑ -our not -or: misdemeanour (the spelling misdemeanor is American)

misdiagnose »*verb* (misdiagnoses, misdiagnosing, misdiagnosed) diagnose something incorrectly.
misdiagnosis

misdial »*verb* (misdials, misdialling, misdialled) dial a telephone number incorrectly.

> ☑ double the l in misdialling and misdialled (the spellings misdialing and misdialed are American)

misdirect »*verb* (misdirects, misdirecting, misdirected) direct or instruct someone wrongly.
misdirection

mise en scene »*noun* ❶ the arrangement of scenery and stage props in a play. ❷ the setting of an event.
– SAY meez on sen

> ☑ mise en scene can also be spelled with a grave accent over the first e in

scene (as in the original French phrase meaning 'putting on stage'): **mise en scène**

miser »*noun* a person who hoards wealth and spends as little as possible.

miserable
miserably

misericord »*noun* a ledge projecting from the underside of a hinged seat in a choir stall, giving support to someone standing when the seat is folded up.
– SAY mi-**zerr**-i-kord

 -**cord** not -**chord**: misericord

miseries

miserly »*adjective* ❶ unwilling to spend money; ungenerous. ❷ (of a quantity) too small.
miserliness

misery (plural **miseries**)

 plural: drop the **y** and add **ies**: miseries

misfire »*verb* (misfires, misfiring, misfired) ❶ (of a gun) fail to fire properly. ❷ (of an internal-combustion engine) fail to ignite the fuel correctly. ❸ fail to produce the intended result.

misfit »*noun* ❶ a person whose behaviour or attitude sets them apart from others. ❷ something that does not fit or fits badly.

 only one **s**: misfit

misfortune

misgivings

misgovern »*verb* (misgoverns, misgoverning, misgoverned) govern unfairly or poorly.

misguided

mishandle (verb: mishandles, mishandling, mishandled)

mishap »*noun* an unlucky accident.

mishear »*verb* (mishears, mishearing, misheard) hear something incorrectly.

mishit »*verb* (mishits, mishitting, mishit) hit or kick a ball badly.

mishmash »*noun* a confused mixture.

misidentify »*verb* (misidentifies, misidentifying, misidentified) identify incorrectly.
misidentification

misinform »*verb* (misinforms, misinforming, misinformed) give someone false or misleading information.
misinformation

misinterpret (verb: misinterprets, misinterpreting, misinterpreted)
misinterpretation

misjudge »*verb* (misjudges, misjudging, misjudged) ❶ form an incorrect opinion of someone. ❷ assess something wrongly: *the horse misjudged the fence.*
misjudgement

mislay »*verb* (mislays, mislaying, mislaid) lose an object by temporarily forgetting where you have left it.

mislead (verb: misleads, misleading, misled)

mismanage (verb: mismanages, mismanaging, mismanaged)
mismanagement

mismatch (verb: mismatches, mismatching, mismatched)

misnomer »*noun* ❶ an inaccurate name. ❷ the wrong use of a name or term.
– SAY miss-**noh**-mer

misogynist »*noun* a man who hates women.
– SAY mi-**soj**-uh-nist
misogynistic

 gyn not **gin**: misogynist

misogyny »*noun* hatred of women.
– SAY mi-**soj**-uh-ni

misplace (verb: misplaces, misplacing, misplaced)

misprint (verb: misprints, misprinting, misprinted)

mispronounce »*verb* (mispronounces, mispronouncing, mispronounced) pronounce something wrongly.
mispronunciation

misquote »*verb* (misquotes, misquoting, misquoted) quote something inaccurately.
misquotation

misread »*verb* (misreads, misreading, misread) read or interpret something wrongly.

misrepresent »*verb* (misrepresents, misrepresenting, misrepresented) give a false or misleading account of something.
misrepresentation

misrule »*noun* ❶ bad government. ❷ disorder.

miss (plural **misses**; verb: misses, missing, missed)

missal »*noun* a book of the texts used in the Catholic Mass.

missed

misses

m

misshapen »*adjective* not having the normal or natural shape.

> note the double s: **misshapen**

missile »*noun* an object or weapon that is thrown or fired at a target.

missing

missing link »*noun* a supposed fossil form that would be intermediate between humans and apes.

mission

missionary »*noun* (plural **missionaries**) a person sent on a religious mission.
» *adjective* having to do with a missionary or religious mission.

> plural: drop the y and add ies: **missionaries**

mission statement »*noun* a summary of the aims and values of an organization.

missis another way of spelling **MISSUS**.

missive »*noun* a letter.

misspell »*verb* (**misspells, misspelling, misspelt** or **misspelled**) spell something wrongly.

> double s: **misspell**

misspend »*verb* (**misspends, misspending, misspent**) spend foolishly.

missus »*noun* (in informal English) a person's wife.

> **missus** can also be spelled **missis**

mist (verb: **mists, misting, misted**)

mistake (verb: **mistakes, mistaking, mistook**; past participle **mistaken**)
mistaken
mistakenly

misted

mister

mistier

mistiest

mistily

mistime »*verb* (**mistimes, mistiming, mistimed**) choose an unsuitable moment to do or say something.

mistiness

misting

mistle thrush »*noun* a large thrush with a harsh call, with a fondness for mistletoe berries.

mistletoe »*noun* an evergreen plant which grows on broadleaf trees and bears white berries in winter.

mistook past of **MISTAKE**.

mistral »*noun* a cold north-westerly wind that blows through southern France, mainly in winter.
– SAY mis-truhl or mi-**strahl**

mistreat »*verb* (**mistreats, mistreating, mistreated**) treat someone badly or unfairly.
mistreatment

mistress (plural **mistresses**)

mistrial »*noun* a trial that is not considered valid because of a mistake in proceedings.

mistrust (verb: **mistrusts, mistrusting, mistrusted**)
mistrustful

mists

misty (adjective: **mistier, mistiest**)
mistily
mistiness

misunderstand (verb: **misunderstands, misunderstanding, misunderstood**)
misunderstanding

misuse »*verb* (**misuses, misusing, misused**)
❶ use something wrongly. ❷ treat someone badly or unfairly.
» *noun* the action of misusing something.

mite »*noun* ❶ a tiny insect-like creature. ❷ a small child or animal. ❸ a very small amount.
» *adverb* (**a mite**) slightly.

miter American spelling of **MITRE**.

mitigate »*verb* (**mitigates, mitigating, mitigated**) make something less severe or serious.
mitigation

> ℹ️ do not confuse **mitigate** and **militate**; **mitigate** means 'make something bad less severe' (as in *drainage schemes helped to mitigate the problem*), while **militate** is used with **against** to mean 'be a powerful factor in preventing' (as in *laws that militate against personal freedom*)

mitochondrion »*noun* (plural **mitochondria**) (in biology) a structure found in large numbers in most cells, in which respiration and energy production occur.
– SAY my-tuh-**kon**-dri-uhn
mitochondrial

> ✓ make the plural by changing the **-on** ending to **-a** (like the original Greek): **mitochondria**

mitre »*noun* ❶ a tall headdress that tapers to a point at front and back, worn by bishops. ❷ a joint made between two pieces of wood cut at an angle in order to form a corner of 90°.

☑ re not er: **mitre** (the spelling **miter** is American)

mitt »*noun* ❶ a mitten. ❷ a glove leaving the fingers and thumb uncovered.

mitten

mix (verb: **mixes, mixing, mixed**; plural **mixes**)

mixed

mixed economy »*noun* an economic system combining private and state enterprise.

mixed marriage »*noun* a marriage between people of different races or religions.

mixed metaphor »*noun* a combination of metaphors that don't make sense when combined (e.g. *this tower of strength will forge ahead*).

mixed-up

mixer

mixes

mixing

mixture

mix-up

mizzen »*noun* the mast aft of a ship's mainmast.

☑ **mizzen** can also be spelled with a single **z**: **mizen**

mnemonic »*noun* a pattern of letters or words used to help remember something. » *adjective* designed to help remember something.
– SAY ni-**mon**-ik

☑ remember that the beginning is **mn**: **mnemonic** (it is from Greek)

moan (verb: **moans, moaning, moaned**)
moaner

moat »*noun* a wide defensive ditch surrounding a castle or town, usually filled with water.

ℹ do not confuse **moat** and **mote**, which means 'a speck'

moated

mob (verb: **mobs, mobbing, mobbed**)

☑ double the **b** to spell **mobbing** and **mobbed**

mobile

mobilise another way of spelling **MOBILIZE**.

mobility »*noun* the quality of being mobile.

mobilize »*verb* (**mobilizes, mobilizing, mobilized**) ❶ organize troops for active service. ❷ organize people or resources for a particular task.
mobilization

☑ many people prefer the alternative spellings **mobilise, mobilises**, etc., and **mobilisation**: both **s** and **z** spellings are correct

Mobius strip »*noun* a surface with one continuous side, formed by joining the ends of a rectangle after twisting one end through 180°.
– SAY mer-bi-uhss

☑ **Mobius** can also be spelled **Möbius**, with an umlaut over the **o** (it is named after the German mathematician August F. *Möbius*)

mobs

mobster »*noun* (in informal English) a gangster.

moccasin »*noun* a soft leather shoe, originally worn by North American Indians.

☑ two **c**'s but one **s**: **moccasin**

mocha »*noun* ❶ a fine-quality coffee. ❷ a drink or flavouring made with this, typically with chocolate added.
– SAY mok-uh

ℹ named after *Mocha*, a port in Yemen

mock (verb: **mocks, mocking, mocked**)

mockery (plural **mockeries**)

mocking

mockingbird »*noun* a long-tailed American songbird, noted for copying the calls of other birds.

mocks

mock-up

MOD »*abbreviation* (in the UK) Ministry of Defence.

modal »*adjective* ❶ relating to mode or form as opposed to substance. ❷ (in grammar) relating to the mood of a verb.

modal verb »*noun* (in grammar) an auxiliary verb expressing necessity or possibility, e.g. *must, shall, will*.

mod cons »*plural noun* modern conveniences, i.e. the amenities and appliances characteristic of a well-equipped modern house.

mode »*noun* ❶ a way in which something occurs or is done. ❷ a style in clothes, art, etc.

model (verb: **models, modelling, modelled**)
modeller

☑ double the **l** to spell **modelling** and **modelled** (the spellings **modeling** and **modeled** are American)

modem »*noun* a device that connects a computer to a telephone line.
– SAY moh-dem

moderate »*adjective* ❶ average in amount, intensity, or degree. ❷ (of a political position) not radical or extreme.
» *noun* a person with moderate views.
» *verb* (**moderates, moderating, moderated**) ❶ make or become less extreme or intense. ❷ check examination papers to ensure that they have been marked consistently.
– SAY mod-uh-ruht [adjective and noun], mod-uh-rayt [verb]
moderately

moderation »*noun* ❶ the avoidance of extremes in your actions or opinions. ❷ the process of moderating something.

moderator »*noun* ❶ a person who helps others to solve a dispute. ❷ a chairman of a debate. ❸ a person who checks examination papers to ensure that they have been marked consistently.

modern
modernity

modernise another way of spelling MODERNIZE.

modernism »*noun* ❶ modern ideas, methods, or styles. ❷ a movement in the arts or religion that aims to break with traditional forms or ideas.
modernist

modernity

modernize »*verb* (**modernizes, modernizing, modernized**) make something modern.
modernization
modernizer

> ✓ many people prefer the alternative spellings **modernise, modernises,** etc., **modernisation** and **moderniser**: both **s** and **z** spellings are correct

modest
modestly

modesty

modicum »*noun* a small quantity of something.
– SAY mod-i-kuhm

modification »*noun* ❶ the action of modifying. ❷ a change made.

modified

modifier »*noun* ❶ a person or thing that modifies. ❷ a word that qualifies the sense of a noun (e.g. *good* and *family* in *a good family house*).

modify »*verb* (**modifies, modifying, modified**) make partial changes to something.

modish »*adjective* fashionable.
– SAY moh-dish
modishly
modishness

modular »*adjective* made up of separate units.

modulate »*verb* (**modulates, modulating, modulated**) ❶ adjust, change, or control something. ❷ vary the strength, tone, or pitch of your voice. ❸ (in music) change from one key to another.
modulation

module »*noun* ❶ one of a set of parts or units that can be used to create a more complex structure. ❷ a unit forming part of a course. ❸ an independent unit of a spacecraft.

modus operandi »*noun* a way of operating or doing something.
– SAY moh-duhss op-uh-ran-di

> ✓ **modus operandi** is a Latin phrase meaning 'way of operating'. It is unusual to need a plural, but if you do it is **modi operandi** (SAY moh-di op-uh-ran-di).

modus vivendi »*noun* ❶ a way of living. ❷ an arrangement allowing conflicting parties to exist peacefully together.
– SAY moh-duhss vi-ven-di

> ✓ **modus vivendi** is a Latin phrase meaning 'way of living'. It is unusual to need a plural, but if you do it is **modi vivendi** (SAY moh-duhss vi-ven-di).

moggie »*noun* (plural **moggies**) (in informal English) a cat.

> ✓ **moggie** can also be spelled with a **y** ending: **moggy**

Mogul »*noun* ❶ a member of the Muslim dynasty of Mongol origin which ruled much of India in the 16th–19th centuries. ❷ (**mogul**) an important or powerful person.
– SAY moh-guhl

> ✓ when referring to the Muslim dynasty, **Mogul** can also be spelled **Moghul** or **Mughal**

mohair »*noun* a fabric made from the hair of the angora goat.

Mohican »*noun* a hair style in which the sides of the head are shaved and a central strip of hair is made to stand up.
– SAY moh-hee-kuhn

moiety »*noun* (plural **moieties**) a half.
– SAY moy-i-ti

moire »*noun* silk fabric treated to give it an appearance like that of rippled water.
– SAY mwar or **mwah**-ray

> ☑ **moire** can also be spelled **moiré**, with an acute accent on the **e** (as in the original French)

moist »*adjective* (**moister, moistest**) slightly wet.
moistly
moistness

moisten (verb: **moistens, moistening, moistened**)

moister

moistest

moistly

moistness

moisture »*noun* tiny droplets of water in the air, on a surface, or in a substance.

moisturize »*verb* (**moisturizes, moisturizing, moisturized**) make something less dry.
moisturizer

> ☑ many people prefer the alternative spellings **moisturise, moisturises**, etc., and **moisturiser**: both **s** and **z** spellings are correct

molar[1] »*noun* a grinding tooth at the back of the mouth.

molar[2] »*adjective* (in chemistry) ❶ of or relating to one mole of a substance. ❷ (of a solution) containing one mole of solute per litre of solvent.

molasses »*noun* ❶ a thick, dark brown liquid obtained from raw sugar. ❷ (in American English) golden syrup.
– SAY muh-**lass**-iz

mold American spelling of **MOULD**.

molder American spelling of **MOULDER**.

Moldovan [of Moldova]

moldy American spelling of **MOULDY**.

mole[1] »*noun* ❶ a small burrowing mammal with dark fur, a long muzzle, and very small eyes. ❷ someone within an organization who secretly passes confidential information to another organization or country.

mole[2] »*noun* a dark blemish on the skin where there is a high concentration of melanin.

mole[3] »*noun* ❶ a large solid structure serving as a pier, breakwater, or causeway. ❷ a harbour formed by a mole.

mole[4] »*noun* (in chemistry) the basic unit of a particular substance which contains as many atoms or molecules as there are atoms in a standard amount of carbon.

molecular »*adjective* relating to or made up of molecules.
– SAY muh-**lek**-yuu-ler

> ☑ **ar** not **er**: **molecular**

molecule »*noun* a group of atoms forming the smallest unit into which a substance can be divided.
– SAY **mol**-i-kyool

molehill »*noun* a small mound of earth thrown up by a burrowing mole.

moleskin »*noun* ❶ the skin of a mole used as fur. ❷ a thick cotton fabric with a soft surface.

molest »*verb* (**molests, molesting, molested**) ❶ pester someone in a hostile way. ❷ assault someone sexually.
molestation
molester

moll »*noun* (in informal English) a gangster's female companion.

mollify »*verb* (**mollifies, mollifying, mollified**) ❶ lessen the anger of someone. ❷ reduce the severity of something.
mollification

mollusc »*noun* an animal without a backbone belonging to a large group including snails, slugs, and mussels, with a soft unsegmented body and often an external shell.
– SAY **mol**-luhsk

> ☑ the ending is **c** not **k**: **mollusc** (the spelling **mollusk** is American)

mollycoddle »*verb* (**mollycoddles, mollycoddling, mollycoddled**) treat someone too indulgently or protectively.

Molotov cocktail »*noun* a crude bomb made up of a bottle of flammable liquid ignited by means of a wick.
– SAY **mol**-uh-tof

> ℹ named after the Soviet statesman Vyacheslav *Molotov*

molt American spelling of **MOULT**.

molten »*adjective* (especially of metal and glass) made liquid by heat.

molto »*adverb* (in music) very.
– SAY **mol**-toh

molybdenum »*noun* a brittle silver-grey metallic element used in some steels and other alloys.
– SAY muh-**lib**-duh-nuhm

mom American spelling of **MUM**.

moment

momentarily »*adverb* ❶ for a very short time. ❷ (in American English) very soon.

momentary

momentous »*adjective* very important.
momentously
momentousness

momentum »*noun* (plural **momenta**) the force gained by a moving object.

✓ like many other words ending in **um** derived from Latin, **momentum** has a plural ending in **a**: **momenta**

mommy (plural **mommies**) American spelling of **MUMMY**[1].

monarch »*noun* a king, queen, or emperor.
monarchies

monarchism »*noun* support for the principle of monarchy.
monarchist

monarchy »*noun* (plural **monarchies**)
❶ government by a monarch. ❷ a state with a monarch.

✓ plural: drop the **y** and add **ies**: **monarchies**

monastery »*noun* (plural **monasteries**) a community of monks living under religious vows.

✓ **tery** not try: **monastery** plural: drop the **y** and add **ies**: **monasteries**

monastic »*adjective* ❶ relating to monks or nuns. ❷ resembling monks or their way of life.
monastically
monasticism

Monday

monetarism »*noun* the theory that inflation is best controlled by limiting the supply of money circulating in an economy.
monetarist

monetary »*adjective* having to do with money.

money (plural **moneys** or **monies**)

ℹ when used to mean 'sums of money', the plural of **money** is either **moneys** or **monies**

moneyed »*adjective* having a lot of money.

money order »*noun* a printed order for payment of a specified amount of money, issued by a bank or post office.

moneys see the note at **MONEY**.

Mongol »*noun* a person from Mongolia.

ℹ do not use **mongol** to refer to a person suffering from **Down's syndrome**. This use is now considered offensive and the term **Down's syndrome** should be used instead.

Mongolian [of Mongolia]

mongoose »*noun* (plural **mongooses**) a small meat-eating mammal with a long body and tail, native to Africa and Asia.

✓ the plural of **mongoose** is **mongooses** (not **mongeese**)

mongrel »*noun* a dog of no definite breed.

monies see the note at **MONEY**.

moniker »*noun* (in informal English) a person's name.
– **say** mon-i-ker

✓ there is no **c**: **moniker**

monitor »*noun* ❶ a person or device that monitors something. ❷ a television used to view a picture from a particular camera or a display from a computer. ❸ a school pupil with special duties. ❹ a large tropical lizard.
» *verb* (**monitors, monitoring, monitored**) keep someone or something under observation.

monk
monkish

monkey (plural **monkeys**; verb: **monkeys, monkeying, monkeyed**)

monkey puzzle »*noun* a coniferous tree with branches covered in spirals of tough spiny leaves.

monkeys

monkey wrench »*noun* a spanner with large adjustable jaws.

monkfish »*noun* an edible sea fish with a long fleshy growth on the snout.

monkish

monkshood »*noun* a poisonous plant with blue or purple flowers.

mono »*noun* monophonic sound.

monochrome »*adjective* (of a photograph or picture) produced in black and white or in varying tones of one colour.
monochromatic

monocle »*noun* a lens worn to improve sight in one eye.

monocular »*adjective* with, for, or using one eye.

monoculture »*noun* the cultivation of a single crop in a particular area.

monogamy »*noun* the state of having only one husband or wife at any one time.
– **say** muh-nog-uh-mi
monogamist
monogamous

monogram »*noun* a motif of two or more interwoven letters, typically a person's initials.
monogrammed

m

499

☑ **-gram** not **-gramme: monogram**

monograph »*noun* a short book on a single subject.

monolingual »*adjective* speaking or expressed in only one language.

monolith »*noun* a large single upright block of stone.

monolithic »*adjective* ❶ formed of a single large block of stone. ❷ very large and impersonal: *a monolithic European superstate.*

monologue »*noun* ❶ a long speech by one actor in a play or film. ❷ a long, boring speech by one person during a conversation.

☑ **logue** not **log: monologue**

monomania »*noun* an obsession with one thing.
– **say** mo-noh-**may**-ni-uh
monomaniac

monomer »*noun* (in chemistry) a molecule that can be linked to other identical molecules to form a polymer.
– **say** mon-uh-**mer**

monophonic »*adjective* (of sound reproduction) using only one channel.

monoplane »*noun* an aircraft with one pair of wings.

monopolize »*verb* (**monopolizes, monopolizing, monopolized**) dominate or take control of someone or something.

☑ many people prefer the alternative spellings **monopolise, monopolises,** etc.: both **s** and **z** spellings are correct

monopoly »*noun* (plural **monopolies**) ❶ the complete control, possession, or use of something by one person or organization. ❷ complete control of trade in particular goods or the supply of a service.
monopolist

☑ plural: drop the **y** and add **ies: monopolies**

monorail »*noun* a railway in which the track consists of a single rail.

monosodium glutamate »*noun* a compound made by the breakdown of vegetable protein and used as to add flavour to food.

monosyllabic »*adjective* ❶ (of a word) having one syllable. ❷ (of a person) saying very little.

monosyllable »*noun* a word of one syllable.

monotheism »*noun* the belief that there is only one god.
– **say** mon-oh-**thee**-i-z'm
monotheist
monotheistic

monotone »*noun* a continuing sound that does not change pitch.

monotonous »*adjective* boring and unchanging.
monotonously
monotony

monoxide

Monsieur »*noun* (plural **Messieurs**) a title or form of address for a French-speaking man, corresponding to *Mr* or *sir*.
– **say** muh-**syer** [singular], mess-**yer** [plural]

☑ to form the plural of **Monsieur,** change **Mon** to **Mes: Messieurs**

Monsignor »*noun* (plural **Monsignori**) the title of a senior Roman Catholic priest.
– **say** mon-**seen**-yer [singular], mon-seen-**yor**-i [plural]

☑ **Monsignor** is an Italian word, and its plural adds an **i: Monsignori**

monsoon »*noun* ❶ a seasonal wind in the Indian subcontinent and SE Asia, bringing rain when blowing from the south-west. ❷ the rainy season accompanying the monsoon.

monster

monstrosity »*noun* (plural **monstrosities**) something that is very large and unattractive.

☑ plural: drop the **y** and add **ies: monstrosities**

monstrous
monstrously
monstrousness

montage »*noun* a picture or film made by putting together pieces from other pictures or films.
– **say** mon-**tahzh**

montane »*adjective* of or inhabiting mountainous country.

Montenegrin »*noun* a person from Montenegro.
» *adjective* relating to Montenegro.
– **say** mon-ti-**nee**-grin

month

monthly

monty »*noun* (**the full monty**) (in informal English) the full amount that is expected or is possible.

monument »*noun* ❶ a statue or structure built in memory of a person or event. ❷ a site of historical importance. ❸ a lasting example of something: *a monument to good taste*.

monumental »*adjective* ❶ very large or impressive. ❷ serving as a monument.
monumentally

moo (verb: **moos, mooing, mooed**; plural **moos**)

mooch »*verb* (**mooches, mooching, mooched**) stand or walk around in a bored way.

mood

moody (adjective: **moodier, moodiest**)
moodily
moodiness

mooed

mooing

moon (verb: **moons, mooning, mooned**)

moonlight »*noun* the light of the moon.
»*verb* (**moonlights, moonlighting, moonlighted**) do a second job without declaring it for tax purposes.
moonlit

moons

moonscape »*noun* a landscape that is rocky and barren like the moon.

moonshine »*noun* ❶ foolish talk or ideas. ❷ (in American English) liquor that is made and sold illegally.

moonstone »*noun* a white semi-precious mineral.

moony »*adjective* dreamy, especially because of being in love.

Moor »*noun* a member of a NW African Muslim people.
Moorish

moor[1] »*noun* a high open area of land that is not cultivated.

moor[2] »*verb* (**moors, mooring, moored**) ❶ fasten a boat to the shore or to an anchor. ❷ (of a boat) be secured somewhere in this way.

moorhen »*noun* a waterbird with black plumage and a red and yellow bill.

mooring »*noun* (also **moorings**) ❶ a place where a boat is moored. ❷ the ropes or cables by which a boat is moored.

Moorish [of the Moors]

moorland

moors

moos

moose »(plural **moose**) (in American English) = **ELK.**

moot »*adjective* uncertain or undecided: *a moot point*.

» *verb* (**moots, mooting, mooted**) put forward a topic for discussion.

mop (verb: **mops, mopping, mopped**)

> ✓ double the p in **mopping** and **mopped**

mope »*verb* (**mopes, moping, moped**) be listless and in low spirits.

moped »*noun* a motorcycle with a small engine.

mopes

moping

mopped

mopping

mops

moraine »*noun* a mass of rocks and sediment carried down and deposited by a glacier.
– SAY muh-**rayn**

moral »*adjective* ❶ concerned with the principles of right and wrong behaviour. ❷ conforming to accepted standards of behaviour. ❸ psychological rather than practical: *moral support*.
» *noun* ❶ a lesson about right or wrong that can be learned from a story or experience. ❷ (**morals**) standards of behaviour, or principles of right and wrong.
morally

morale »*noun* the level of a person's or group's confidence and spirits.

moralise another way of spelling **MORALIZE**.

moralist »*noun* a person who teaches or promotes morality.
moralistic

morality »*noun* (plural **moralities**) ❶ principles concerning the difference between right and wrong. ❷ moral behaviour. ❸ the extent to which an action is right or wrong.

morality play »*noun* a play presenting a moral lesson and having personified qualities as the main characters, popular in the 15th and 16th centuries.

moralize »*verb* (**moralizes, moralizing, moralized**) comment on moral issues, especially disapprovingly.
moralizer

> ✓ many people prefer the alternative spellings **moralise, moralises,** etc., and **moraliser**: both **s** and **z** spellings are correct

morally

moral victory »*noun* a defeat that can be interpreted as a victory in moral terms.

morass »*noun* (plural **morasses**) ❶ an area of muddy or boggy ground. ❷ a complicated situation: *a morass of lies.*
– SAY muh-**rass**

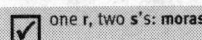 one r, two s's: **morass**

moratorium »*noun* (plural **moratoriums** or **moratoria**) a temporary ban on an activity.
– SAY mo-ruh-**tor**-i-uhm

the plural of **moratorium** can be **moratoria** (as in the original Latin) or **moratoriums**

moray eel »*noun* a predatory eel-like fish of warm seas.

morbid »*adjective* ❶ having an unhealthy interest in unpleasant subjects, especially death and disease. ❷ (in medicine) having to do with disease.
morbidity
morbidly

mordant »*adjective* (especially of humour) sharply sarcastic.
»*noun* a substance that combines with a dye and thereby fixes it in a material.

 ant not ent: **mordant**

more

moreish »*adjective* so pleasant to eat that you want more.

morel »*noun* an edible fungus having a brown oval or pointed cap.
– SAY muh-**rel**

morello »*noun* (plural **morellos**) a kind of sour dark cherry used in cooking.
– SAY muh-**rel**-loh

moreover

don't forget the **e** between the **r** and the **o**: **moreover**

mores »*plural noun* the customs and conventions of a community.
– SAY **mor**-ayz

 mores is a Latin word

morgue »*noun* a mortuary.

moribund »*adjective* ❶ at the point of death. ❷ losing effectiveness and about to end.
– SAY **mo**-ri-bund

Mormon »*noun* a member of the Church of Jesus Christ of Latter-Day Saints.
Mormonism

morn »*noun* (a poetic term) morning.

morning

morning glory »*noun* a climbing plant with trumpet-shaped flowers.

morning star »*noun* the planet Venus, when visible in the east before sunrise.

Moroccan

morocco »*noun* fine flexible leather made (originally in Morocco) from goatskins tanned with sumac.

moron »*noun* a stupid person.
moronic

morose »*adjective* sullen and ill-tempered.
morosely
moroseness

morph »*verb* (**morphs**, **morphing**, **morphed**) (in computer animation) change smoothly and gradually from one image to another.

morphine »*noun* a drug obtained from opium and used in medicine to relieve pain.
– SAY **mor**-feen

morphing

morphology »*noun* the scientific study of forms of living organisms or words.
morphological

morphs

morris dancing »*noun* traditional English folk dancing performed by men wearing costumes with small bells attached and carrying handkerchiefs or sticks.

morrow »*noun* (an old word) the following day.

Morse »*noun* a code in which letters are represented by combinations of long and short light or sound signals.

named after its American inventor Samuel F. B. *Morse*

morsel

mortal »*adjective* ❶ subject to death. ❷ causing death. ❸ (of fear, pain, etc.) very strong. ❹ (of conflict or an enemy) lasting until death. ❺ (in Christian belief) referring to a sin that will deprive the soul of divine grace.
»*noun* a human being.
mortally

mortality »*noun* ❶ the state of being mortal. ❷ death. ❸ (also **mortality rate**) the number of deaths in a particular area or period.

mortally

mortar »*noun* ❶ a mixture of lime with cement, sand, and water, used to hold bricks or stones together. ❷ a cup-shaped container in which substances are crushed with a pestle. ❸ a short cannon for firing shells at high angles.

 ar not er: **mortar**

mortar board »*noun* an academic cap with a flat square top and a tassel.

mortgage »*noun* ❶ a legal agreement by which a bank or building society lends you money, using your house as a security. ❷ an amount of money borrowed or lent under such an agreement.
» *verb* (**mortgages, mortgaging, mortgaged**) give a bank or building society the right to own your house as a security for the money they agree to lend you.

> ✓ don't forget the **t** in the middle, and the **-gage** not **-gauge** ending: **mortgage**

mortgagee »*noun* the lender in a mortgage.

mortgages

mortgaging

mortgagor »*noun* the borrower in a mortgage.

mortice another way of spelling **MORTISE**.

mortician »*noun* an undertaker.

mortify »*verb* (**mortifies, mortifying, mortified**) ❶ cause someone to feel embarrassed or humiliated. ❷ subdue bodily urges by self-denial or discipline.
mortification

mortise »*noun* a hole or recess designed to receive a projection (a tenon) so that the two are held together.
» *verb* (**mortises, mortising, mortised**) ❶ join two parts by a mortise and tenon. ❷ cut a mortise in something.
– **SAY** mor-tiss

> ✓ **mortise** can also be spelled **mortice**: both spellings are correct

mortise lock »*noun* a lock set into the framework of a door in a recess or mortise.

mortises

mortising

mortuary »*noun* (plural **mortuaries**) a room or building in which dead bodies are kept until burial or cremation.
» *adjective* relating to burial or tombs.

> ✓ **tuary** not **tury: mortuary**

mosaic »*noun* a picture or pattern produced by arranging together small coloured pieces of stone, tile, or glass.

mosey (in informal English) »*verb* (**moseys, moseying, moseyed**) walk or move in a leisurely manner.
» *noun* a leisurely walk.

Moslem another way of spelling **MUSLIM**.

mosque »*noun* a Muslim place of worship.

mosquito »*noun* (plural **mosquitoes**) a small fly, some kinds of which transmit diseases through the bite of the female.

> ✓ the plural of **mosquito** has **oes** not **os: mosquitoes**

moss (plural **mosses**)
mossy

most

mostly

MOT »*noun* (in the UK) a compulsory annual test of motor vehicles of more than a specified age.

> ℹ short for *Ministry of Transport*

mote »*noun* a speck.

> ℹ do not confuse **mote** and **moat**, which means 'a wide defensive ditch'

motel »*noun* a roadside hotel for motorists.

motet »*noun* a short piece of sacred choral music.
– **SAY** moh-tet

moth

mothball »*noun* a small ball made from a strong-smelling chemical, placed among stored clothes to deter clothes moths.
» *verb* (**mothballs, mothballing, mothballed**) put a plan or piece of equipment into storage or on hold.

moth-eaten

mother (verb: **mothers, mothering, mothered**)
motherhood
motherless

motherboard »*noun* a printed circuit board containing the main components of a microcomputer.

mothered

motherhood

mothering

Mothering Sunday »*noun* (in the UK) the fourth Sunday in Lent, traditionally a day for honouring your mother.

mother-in-law (plural **mothers-in-law**)

> ✓ plural: the **s** goes after **mother** not **law: mothers-in-law**

motherland »*noun* a person's native country.

motherless

motherly »*adjective* kind and protective.

mother-of-pearl »*noun* a smooth pearly substance lining the shells of oysters and some other molluscs.

mothers

Mother's Day

Mother Superior »*noun* the head of a female religious community.

mother tongue »*noun* a person's native language.

motif »*noun* ❶ a single or repeated image forming a design. ❷ a theme which frequently recurs in an artistic, musical, or literary work.
– SAY moh-teef

motion (verb: **motions, motioning, motioned**)
motionless

motivate »*verb* (**motivates, motivating, motivated**) ❶ provide someone with a motive for doing something. ❷ stimulate someone's interest in or enthusiasm for doing something.
motivator

motivation »*noun* ❶ the reason or reasons behind a person's actions or behaviour. ❷ enthusiasm.
motivational

motivator

motive »*noun* a factor influencing a person to act in a particular way.
» *adjective* producing motion.

motive power »*noun* the energy used to drive machinery.

mot juste »*noun* (plural **mots justes**) (**the mot juste**) the most appropriate word or expression.
– SAY moh *zh*oost [singular and plural]

> ✓ a French term, **mot juste** has **s** after both **mot** and **juste** in the plural: **mots justes**

motley »*adjective* made up of a variety of very different people or things.

motocross »*noun* cross-country racing on motorcycles.

motor (verb: **motors, motoring, motored**)
motorbike
motorboat

motorcade »*noun* a procession of motor vehicles.

motorcycle
 motorcycling
 motorcyclist
motored
motoring
motorised
motorist
motorized

> ✓ the alternative spelling **motorised** is also correct

motor neuron disease »*noun* a progressive disease in which there is degeneration of the nerves supplying the muscles, which waste away.

> ✓ **neuron** rather than **neurone**: see the note at **NEURON**

motors
motorway

motte »*noun* (a historical term) a mound forming the site of a castle or camp.
– SAY mot

mottle »*noun* a mottled marking.

mottled »*adjective* marked with patches of a different colour.

motto »*noun* (plural **mottoes** or **mottos**) a short sentence or phrase expressing a belief or ideal.

> ✓ the plural of **motto** can have **oes** or **os**: **mottoes** or **mottos**

moue »*noun* a pout.
– SAY moo

mould (verb: **moulds, moulding, moulded**)

> ✓ **ould** not **old**: **mould** (the spelling **mold** is American)

moulder »*verb* (**moulders, mouldering, mouldered**) slowly decay.

> ✓ **ould** not **old**: **moulder** (the spelling **molder** is American)

mouldier
mouldiest
moulding
moulds

mouldy (adjective: **mouldier, mouldiest**)

> ✓ **ould** not **old** in the middle: **mouldy** (the spelling **moldy** is American)

moult »*verb* (**moults, moulting, moulted**) shed old feathers, hair, or skin, to make way for a new growth.
» *noun* a period of moulting.

> ✓ **oult** not **olt**: **moult** (the spelling **molt** is American)

mound (verb: **mounds, mounding, mounded**)
mount (verb: **mounts, mounting, mounted**)
mountain

mountaineering »*noun* the sport or activity of climbing mountains.
mountaineer

mountainous »*adjective* ❶ having many mountains. ❷ huge: *mountainous debts*.
mountainside

mountebank »*noun* a swindler.
– SAY mown-ti-bangk

mounted

m

Mountie »*noun* (in informal English) a member of the Royal Canadian Mounted Police.

mounting

mounts

mourn (verb: **mourns, mourning, mourned**) [feel deep sorrow following a death]

mourner

mournful
  mournfully
  mournfulness

 -ful not -full: **mournful**

mourning

mourns

mouse (plural **mice**)

mousetrap

mousey another way of spelling **mousy**.

moussaka »*noun* a Greek dish of minced lamb layered with aubergines and tomatoes and topped with a cheese sauce.
– **say** moo-**sah**-kuh

 two s's, one k: **moussaka**

mousse »*noun* ❶ a light sweet or savoury dish made with cream or egg white and flavoured with fruit, fish, etc. ❷ a light substance used to style the hair.

moustache
  moustached

 mous not **mus**: **moustache** (the spelling **mustache** is American)

mousy »*adjective* ❶ (of hair) of a light brown colour. ❸ timid.

 mousy can also be spelled **mousey**

mouth (verb: **mouths, mouthing, mouthed**)

mouthful

 -ful not -full: **mouthful**

mouthier

mouthiest

mouthing

mouth organ »*noun* a harmonica.

mouthpart

mouthpiece

mouths

mouth-to-mouth

mouthwash

mouth-watering

mouthy »*adjective* (**mouthier, mouthiest**) (in informal English) inclined to talk a lot.

movable

 movable can also be spelled **moveable**, with an **e** in the middle

move (verb: **moves, moving, moved**)
  mover

movement

mover

moves

movie

moving
  movingly

mow (verb: **mows, mowing, mowed**; past participle **mowed** or **mown**)

Mozambican [of Mozambique]

mozzarella »*noun* a firm white Italian cheese made from buffalo's or cow's milk.
– **say** mot-suh-**rel**-luh

 double **z**, single **r**, double **l**: **mozzarella**

MP »*abbreviation* Member of Parliament.

Mr (plural **Messrs**)

Mrs

MS »*abbreviation* ❶ manuscript. ❷ multiple sclerosis.

Ms

MSc »*abbreviation* Master of Science.

MSP »*abbreviation* Member of the Scottish Parliament.

mu »*noun* the twelfth letter of the Greek alphabet (**M, μ**).
– **say** myoo

much
  muchness

muck (verb: **mucks, mucking, mucked**)

muckier

muckiest

mucking

muckraking »*noun* the action of searching out and publicizing scandal.

mucks

mucky (adjective: **muckier, muckiest**)

mucous »*adjective* relating to or covered with mucus.
– **say** myoo-kuhss

mucous membrane »*noun* a tissue that secretes mucus, lining the nose, mouth, and other organs.

mucus »*noun* a slimy substance produced by the mucous membranes and glands of animals for lubrication, protection, etc.
– **say** myoo-kuhss

 the sticky substance is **mucus** not **mucous**: **mucous** is an adjective

m

meaning 'relating to or covered with mucus'

mud

mudbath

muddied

muddier

muddies

muddiest

muddle (verb: muddles, muddling, muddled)
muddled

muddle-headed

muddles

muddling

muddy (adjective: muddier, muddiest; verb: muddies, muddying, muddied)

mudflap

mudflat »*noun* a stretch of muddy land left uncovered at low tide.

mudguard

mud-slinging

muesli »*noun* a mixture of oats, dried fruit, and nuts, eaten with milk at breakfast.
– SAY myooz-li

☑ mues- not muse-: muesli

muezzin »*noun* a man who calls Muslims to prayer.
– SAY moo-ez-zin

muff[1] »*noun* a short tube made of warm material into which the hands are placed for warmth.

muff[2] (in informal English) »*verb* (muffs, muffing, muffed) handle something clumsily.
»*noun* a mistake or failure.

muffin

muffing

muffle (verb: muffles, muffling, muffled)

muffler »*noun* a wrap or scarf worn around the neck and face.

muffles

muffling

muffs

mufti[1] »*noun* (plural muftis) a Muslim legal expert allowed to give rulings on religious matters.

mufti[2] »*noun* civilian clothes when worn by military or police staff.

mug (verb: mugs, mugging, mugged)

☑ double the g in mugged and mugging

mugger

muggier

muggiest

mugginess

mugging

muggins »*noun* (plural muggins or mugginses) (in informal English) a foolish person.

muggy »*adjective* (muggier, muggiest) (of the weather) unpleasantly warm and humid.
mugginess

Mughal another way of spelling MOGUL.

mugs

mugshot »*noun* a photograph of a person's face made for an official purpose.

mulatto »*noun* (plural mulattoes or mulattos) a person with one white and one black parent.
– SAY myoo-lat-toh

☑ one l, two t's: mulatto
the plural of mulatto can have oes or os: mulattoes or mulattos

mulberry (plural mulberries)

mulch »*noun* a mass of leaves, bark, or compost spread around or over a plant for protection or to enrich the soil.
»*verb* (mulches, mulching, mulched) cover something with mulch.

mule »*noun* ❶ the offspring of a male donkey and a female horse. ❷ a slipper or light shoe without a back.

muleteer »*noun* a person who drives mules.
– SAY myoo-li-teer

mulish »*adjective* stubborn.

mull[1] »*verb* (mulls, mulling, mulled) (mull over) think about something at length.

mull[2] »*verb* (mulls, mulling, mulled) warm wine or beer and add sugar and spices to it.

mullah »*noun* a Muslim learned in Islamic theology and sacred law.
– SAY muul-luh

mulled

mullet »*noun* a sea fish that is caught for food.

mulligatawny »*noun* a spicy meat soup originally made in India.
– SAY mu-li-guh-taw-ni

mulling

mullion »*noun* a vertical bar between the panes of glass in a window.
mullioned

mulls

multicolour

m

multicoloured

multicultural »*adjective* relating to or made up of several cultural or ethnic groups.
multiculturalism
multiculturalist

multifaceted »*adjective* having many sides or aspects.

multifarious »*adjective* many and varied.
– SAY mul-ti-fair-i-uhss

multilateral »*adjective* involving three or more participants.

multilingual »*adjective* in or using several languages.

multimedia »*adjective* using more than one means of communicating information.
»*noun* a computer system providing video and audio material as well as text.

multimillion

multimillionaire

multinational »*adjective* involving several countries or nationalities.
»*noun* a company operating in several countries.

multiparty »*adjective* involving several political parties.

multiple »*adjective* ❶ having or involving several different people or things. ❷ (of a disease or injury) affecting several parts of the body.
»*noun* a number that may be divided by another a certain number of times without a remainder.

multiple-choice

multiple sclerosis »*noun* a serious disease of the nervous system that can cause partial paralysis.

multiplex »*adjective* made up of many elements in a complex relationship.
»*noun* a cinema with several separate screens.

multiplication

multiplicity »*noun* (plural **multiplicities**) a large number or variety.

multiplied

multiply[1] (verb: **multiplies**, **multiplying**, **multiplied**) [increase in number or quantity]
multiplier

multiply[2] »*adverb* in different ways or respects.
– SAY mul-ti-pli

multiprocessing »*noun* = MULTITASKING.

multi-purpose

multiracial »*adjective* having to do with people of many races.

multi-storey

multitasking »*noun* (in computing) the carrying out of more than one program or task at the same time.

multitude »*noun* ❶ a large number of people or things. ❷ (**the multitude**) the mass of ordinary people.

multitudinous »*adjective* very numerous.

mum

mumble (verb: **mumbles**, **mumbling**, **mumbled**)

mumbo-jumbo

mummer »*noun* an actor in a traditional English folk play.

mummies

mummify »*verb* (**mummifies**, **mummifying**, **mummified**) (especially in ancient Egypt) preserve a body as a mummy.
mummification

mummy[1] (plural **mummies**) [mother]

mummy[2] »*noun* (plural **mummies**) (especially in ancient Egypt) a body that has been preserved for burial by embalming and wrapping in bandages.

> ✓ plural: drop the **y** and add **ies**: **mummies**

mumps »*plural noun* a disease spread by a virus, causing swelling of the glands at the sides of the face.

munch (verb: **munches**, **munching**, **munched**)

mundane »*adjective* ❶ lacking interest or excitement. ❷ relating to this earthly world rather than a heavenly or spiritual one.
mundanely
mundaneness

municipal »*adjective* relating to a municipality.
municipally

> ✓ the ending is **pal** not **ple**: **municipal**

municipality »*noun* (plural **municipalities**) a town or district that has local government.
– SAY myoo-ni-si-**pal**-i-ti

> ✓ plural: drop the **y** and add **ies**: **municipalities**

munificent »*adjective* very generous.
– SAY myuoo-**nif**-i-suhnt
munificence

munitions »*plural noun* military weapons, ammunition, equipment, and stores.

mural »*noun* a painting executed directly on a wall.

» *adjective* having to do with a wall.

murder (verb: **murders, murdering, murdered**)

murderer

murderess (plural **murderesses**)

murdering

murderous
  murderously
  murderousness

murders

murk *»noun* darkness or fog.

murky (adjective: **murkier, murkiest**)
  murkily
  murkiness

murmur (verb: **murmurs, murmuring, murmured**)

> ✓ do not double the r to spell **murmuring** and **murmured**

Murphy's Law *»noun* a supposed law of nature, to the effect that anything that can go wrong will go wrong.

muscle (verb: **muscles, muscling, muscled**) [body tissue that moves a part of the body]

> ℹ️ do not confuse a **muscle** with a **mussel**, which is a shellfish

> ✓ drop the **e** to spell **muscling**

muscle-bound *»adjective* having over-developed muscles.

muscled

muscleman (plural **musclemen**)

muscles

muscling

muscovado *»noun* unrefined sugar made from sugar cane.
– SAY muss-kuh-**vah**-doh

Muscovite *»noun* a person from Moscow.

muscular
  muscularity
  muscularly

> ✓ ar not er: **muscular**

muscular dystrophy *»noun* an inherited condition in which the muscles gradually become weaker.

muscularity

muscularly

musculature *»noun* the arrangement of muscles in a body or part of a body.

muse[1] *»noun* ❶ (**Muse**) (in Greek and Roman mythology) each of nine goddesses who preside over the arts and sciences. ❷ a woman who is the inspiration for a creative artist.

muse[2] *»verb* (**muses, musing, mused**) ❶ be absorbed in thought. ❷ say something to yourself in a thoughtful manner.

museum

mush (verb: **mushes, mushing, mushed**)

mushier

mushiest

mushily

mushiness

mushing

mushroom (verb: **mushrooms, mushrooming, mushroomed**)

mushy (adjective: **mushier, mushiest**)
  mushily
  mushiness

music

musical
  musicality
  musically

music hall *»noun* ❶ (in the past) a popular form of entertainment involving singing, dancing, and comedy. ❷ a theatre where such entertainment took place.

musician
  musicianship

musicology *»noun* the study of the history and theory of music.

musing

musk *»noun* a strong-smelling substance produced by the male musk deer, used as an ingredient in making perfume.
  musky

musket *»noun* (a historical term) a light gun with a long barrel.

musketeer *»noun* (a historical term) a soldier armed with a musket.

musk ox *»noun* (plural **musk oxen**) a large animal with a thick shaggy coat, native to northern North America and Greenland.

muskrat *»noun* a large North American rodent with a musky smell.

musky

Muslim *»noun* a follower of Islam.
» *adjective* relating to Muslims or Islam.

> ✓ **Muslim** can also be spelled with an **o** and an **e**: **Moslem**

muslin *»noun* lightweight cotton cloth in a plain weave.

musquash *»noun* the fur of the muskrat.
– SAY muss-kwosh

muss »*verb* (musses, mussing, mussed) (in informal English) make something untidy or messy.

mussel »*noun* a small shellfish with a dark brown or purplish-black shell.

> **i** do not confuse a **mussel** with a **muscle**, which is a body tissue

musses

mussing

must [be obliged to]

mustache American spelling of MOUSTACHE.

mustachios »*plural noun* a long or elaborate moustache.
– SAY muh-**stah**-shi-ohz

mustang »*noun* a small wild horse of the south-western US.

mustard

mustard gas »*noun* a liquid whose vapour causes severe irritation and blistering, used in chemical weapons.

muster »*verb* (musters, mustering, mustered) ❶ bring troops together in preparation for battle. ❷ (of people) gather together. ❸ summon up a feeling or attitude.
» *noun* an instance of mustering troops.

mustiness

mustn't [must not]

> ☑ be careful to put the apostrophe where a letter has been left out, that is between the **n** and **t** of **not: mustn't**

musty »*adjective* (mustier, mustiest) having a stale or mouldy smell or taste.
mustiness

mutable »*adjective* able or tending to change.
– SAY **myoo**-tuh-b'l

mutant »*adjective* resulting from or showing the effect of mutation.
» *noun* a mutant form.

mutate »*verb* (mutates, mutating, mutated) undergo mutation.

mutation »*noun* ❶ the process or an instance of changing. ❷ a change in genetic structure which may be passed on to subsequent generations. ❸ a distinct form resulting from such a change.

mute »*adjective* ❶ not speaking. ❷ (old-fashioned) unable to speak. ❸ (of a letter) not pronounced.
» *noun* ❶ (old-fashioned) a person who is unable to speak. ❷ a device used to make the sound of a musical instrument quieter or softer.
» *verb* (mutes, muting, muted) ❶ make the sound of something quieter or softer.

❷ reduce the strength or intensity of something.
mutely
muteness

> **i** do not use the word **mute** to describe a person without the power of speech (as in **deaf mute**), as today it is likely to cause offence

mute swan »*noun* the commonest European swan, having an orange-red bill with a black knob at the base.

mutilate »*verb* (mutilates, mutilating, mutilated) injure or damage something very severely.
mutilation
mutilator

> ☑ one l and one t: **mutilate**

mutineer »*noun* a person who mutinies.

muting

mutinied

mutinies

mutinous »*adjective* rebellious.
mutinously

mutiny »*noun* (plural mutinies) an open rebellion against authority, especially by soldiers or sailors against their officers.
» *verb* (mutinies, mutinying, mutinied) engage in mutiny; rebel.

> ☑ plural: drop the **y** and add **ies**: **mutinies**

mutt »*noun* (in informal English) a dog, especially a mongrel.

mutter (verb: mutters, muttering, muttered)

mutton »*noun* the flesh of mature sheep used as food.

mutual »*adjective* ❶ experienced by two or more people equally: *mutual respect and understanding*. ❷ (of two or more parties) having the same specified relationship to each other. ❸ shared by two or more people: *a mutual friend*
mutually

muzak »*noun* (trademark) recorded light background music played in public places.

muzzier

muzziest

muzzily

muzziness

muzzle »*noun* ❶ the nose and mouth of an animal. ❷ a guard fitted over an animal's muzzle to stop it biting or feeding. ❸ the open end of the barrel of a gun.
» *verb* (muzzles, muzzling, muzzled) ❶ put a muzzle on an animal. ❷ prevent someone expressing their opinions freely.

muzzy »*adjective* (**muzzier**, **muzziest**)
❶ dazed or confused. **❷** blurred or indistinct.
muzzily
muzziness

my

myalgia »*noun* pain in a muscle or group of muscles.
– SAY my-**al**-juh

mycology »*noun* the scientific study of fungi.
– SAY my-**kol**-uh-ji

mycoprotein »*noun* protein obtained from fungi, especially as produced for human consumption.

mynah »*noun* an Asian or Australasian bird, some kinds of which can mimic human speech.

myopia »*noun* short-sightedness.
– SAY my-**oh**-pi-uh

myopic »*adjective* (of a person) short-sighted.
– SAY my-**op**-ik

myriad »*noun* a countless or very great number.
» *adjective* countless.
– SAY **mi**-ri-uhd

myriapod »*noun* a centipede, millipede, or other insect having a long body with numerous leg-bearing segments.
– SAY **mi**-ri-uh-pod

myrrh »*noun* a substance with a sweet smell that is obtained from certain trees and used in perfumes and incense.
– SAY mer

> ✓ note the double r, and the h on the end: **myrrh**

myrtle »*noun* an evergreen shrub with white flowers and purple-black berries.

myself

mysteries

mysterious
mysteriously
mysteriousness

mystery (plural **mysteries**)

> ✓ plural: drop the **y** and add **ies**:
> **mysteries**

mystery play »*noun* a popular medieval play based on biblical stories or the lives of the saints.

mystic »*noun* a person who seeks to know God through prayer and contemplation.
» *adjective* mystical.

mystical »*adjective* **❶** relating to mystics or mysticism. **❷** having a spiritual significance that goes beyond human understanding. **❸** inspiring a sense of spiritual mystery and awe.
mystically

mysticism »*noun* **❶** the belief that knowledge of God can be found through prayer and contemplation. **❷** vague or ill-defined religious or spiritual belief.

mystify »*verb* (**mystifies**, **mystifying**, **mystified**) **❶** confuse or bewilder someone. **❷** make something uncertain or mysterious.
mystification
mystifying

mystique »*noun* an atmosphere of mystery or secrecy that makes something seem impressive or attractive.

myth »*noun* **❶** a traditional story that describes the early history of a people or explains a natural event. **❷** a widely held but false belief. **❸** an imaginary person or thing.

mythical »*adjective* **❶** occurring in or characteristic of myths or folk tales. **❷** imaginary or not real.
mythic
mythically

mythological »*adjective* relating to or found in mythology; mythical.
mythologically

mythology »*noun* (plural **mythologies**) **❶** a collection of myths. **❷** a set of widely held but exaggerated or false beliefs.

myxomatosis »*noun* a highly infectious and usually fatal disease of rabbits.
– SAY mik-suh-muh-**toh**-siss

n

Nn

NAAFI »*abbreviation* Navy, Army, and Air Force Institutes.
– SAY na-fi

naan another way of spelling NAN².

nab (verb: **nabs**, **nabbing**, **nabbed**)

nacho »*noun* (plural **nachos**) a small piece of tortilla topped with melted cheese, peppers, etc.
– SAY na-choh

> the plural of **nacho** has **os** not **oes**: **nachos** (a Mexican Spanish word)

nacre »*noun* mother-of-pearl.
– SAY nay-ker

nadir »*noun* ❶ (in astronomy) the point on the celestial sphere directly opposite the zenith and below an observer. ❷ the lowest or most unsuccessful point.
– SAY nay-deer or na-deer

naevus »*noun* (plural **naevi**) a birthmark or a mole on the skin.
– SAY nee-vuhss [singular], nee-vI [plural]

> note the **ae**: **naevus** (the spelling **nevus** is American)
> the plural of **naevus** (a Latin word) drops the **us** and adds **i**: **naevi**

naff (adjective: **naffer**, **naffest**)
naffness

nag (verb: **nags**, **nagging**, **nagged**)

naiad »*noun* (in classical mythology) a water nymph.
– SAY ny-ad

> note that there are two **a**'s: **naiad**

naif »*noun* a naive person.
– SAY ny-eef

nail (verb: **nails**, **nailing**, **nailed**)

nail-biting

nailed

nailing

nails

naive »*adjective* lacking experience, wisdom, or judgement.
– SAY ny-eev
naively

> **naive** can also be spelled **naïve**, with two dots (a diaeresis) over the **i** to show that the **a** and the **i** are pronounced separately

naivety »*noun* ❶ lack of experience, wisdom, or judgement. ❷ innocence.
– SAY ny-eev-ti

> **naivety** can also be spelled **naiveté** (SAY ny-eev-tay), as in the original French

naked
   nakedly
   nakedness

namby-pamby (plural **namby-pambies**)

name (verb: **names**, **naming**, **named**)

namecheck »*verb* (**namechecks**, **namechecking**, **namechecked**) publicly mention someone's name.

named

name-dropping

nameless

namely

nameplate

names

namesake »*noun* a person or thing with the same name as another.

Namibian

naming

nan¹ [grandmother]

nan² »*noun* a type of soft flat Indian bread.
– SAY nahn

> **nan** can also be spelled with a double **a**: **naan**

nandrolone »*noun* a synthetic hormone with tissue-building properties, used illegally to enhance performance in sport.
– SAY nan-druh-lohn

nanny (plural **nannies**)

> plural: drop the **y** and add **ies**: **nannies**

nanosecond »*noun* one thousand millionth of a second.

> **nano** not **nanno**: **nanosecond** (from the Greek word *nanos* 'dwarf')

nanotechnology »*noun* technology on an atomic or molecular scale.

nap (verb: **naps**, **napping**, **napped**)

napalm »*noun* a highly flammable form of petrol, used in firebombs and flame-throwers.
– SAY nay-pahm

nape »*noun* the back of a person's neck.

naphtha »*noun* a flammable oil extracted from coal, shale, or petroleum.
– SAY naf-thuh

> phth not pth: naphtha

napkin »*noun* a square piece of cloth or paper used at a meal to wipe the fingers or lips and to protect clothes.

Napoleonic

napped

napping

nappy (plural **nappies**)

> plural: drop the **y** and add **ies**: **nappies**

naps

narcissism »*noun* excessive interest in yourself and your physical appearance.
– SAY nar-si-si-z'm
narcissist
narcissistic

> i from the name of *Narcissus*, a beautiful youth in Greek mythology who fell in love with his reflection

narcissus »*noun* (plural **narcissi** or **narcissuses**) a daffodil with a flower that has white or pale outer petals and an orange or yellow centre.
– SAY nar-si-suhss

> the plural can either be **narcissi** (as in Latin), or **narcissuses**

narcotic »*noun* ❶ an addictive drug which affects mood or behaviour. ❷ a drug which causes drowsiness or unconsciousness, or relieves pain.
»*adjective* relating to narcotics.

nark »*noun* (in informal English) a police informer.

narked »*adjective* (in informal English) annoyed.

narrate »*verb* (**narrates**, **narrating**, **narrated**) ❶ give an account of something. ❷ provide a commentary for a film, television programme, etc.
narration
narrator

narrative »*noun* a story.

» *adjective* in the form of a narrative or concerned with narration.

narrator

narrow (adjective: **narrower**, **narrowest**; verb: **narrows**, **narrowing**, **narrowed**)
narrowly
narrowness

narrowboat »*noun* a canal boat less than 7 ft (2.1 metres) wide and steered with a tiller rather than a wheel.

narrowed

narrower

narrowest

narrowing

narrowly

narrow-minded

narrowness

narrows

narwhal »*noun* a small Arctic whale, the male of which has a long twisted tusk.
– SAY nar-wuhl

> note that the ending is **-whal** not **-whale**: narwhal

NASA »*abbreviation* (in the US) National Aeronautics and Space Administration.

nasal »*adjective* relating to the nose.
nasally

nascent »*adjective* just coming into existence and beginning to develop.
– SAY na-suhnt

> **-scent** not **-sent**: nascent

nastier

nastiest

nastily

nastiness

nasturtium »*noun* a trailing garden plant with round leaves and bright orange, yellow, or red flowers.
– SAY nuh-ster-shuhm

> the ending is **ium**, not **ion** or **ian**: nasturtium

nasty (adjective: **nastier**, **nastiest**)
nastily
nastiness

> drop the **y** and add **ier** or **iest** to spell **nastier** or **nastiest**

natal »*adjective* relating to the place or time of a person's birth.
– SAY nay-t'l

nation

national
nationally

national debt »*noun* the total amount of money which a country's government has borrowed.

national grid »*noun* the network of high-voltage power lines between major power stations.

nationalise another way of spelling NATIONALIZE.

nationalism »*noun* ❶ patriotic feeling, often to an excessive degree. ❷ belief in political independence for a particular country.
nationalist
nationalistic

nationality (plural **nationalities**)

> ✓ plural: drop the **y** and add **ies**: **nationalities**

nationalize »*verb* (**nationalizes, nationalizing, nationalized**) put an industry or business under the control of the government.
nationalization

> ✓ many people prefer the alternative spellings **nationalise, nationalises,** etc., and **nationalisation**: both **s** and **z** spellings are correct

nationally

national service »*noun* a period of compulsory service in the armed forces during peacetime.

nationwide

native »*noun* ❶ a person born in a specified place. ❷ a local inhabitant. ❸ an animal or plant that lives or grows naturally in a particular area.
» *adjective* ❶ associated with the place where you were born. ❷ (of a plant or animal) living or growing naturally in a place. ❸ having to do with the original inhabitants of a place. ❹ in a person's character: *native wit*.

> ℹ in phrases such as *a native of Boston* the use of the noun **native** is quite acceptable. But when used as a noun without qualification, as in *this dance is a favourite with the natives,* it has an old-fashioned feel and may cause offence.

Native American »*noun* a member of one of the native peoples of North and South America and the Caribbean Islands.
» *adjective* relating to these peoples.

> ℹ in the US, **Native American** is now the accepted term. In Britain and elsewhere, **American Indian** is more usual.

native speaker »*noun* a person who has spoken a particular language from earliest childhood.

nativity »*noun* (plural **nativities**) ❶ a person's birth. ❷ (**the Nativity**) the birth of Jesus.

NATO »*abbreviation* North Atlantic Treaty Organization.

> ✓ **NATO** can also be written **Nato**

natter (verb: **natters, nattering, nattered**)

natterjack toad »*noun* a small toad with a bright yellow stripe down its back.

natters

natty »*adjective* (**nattier, nattiest**) smart and fashionable.
nattily

natural
naturally
naturalness

natural gas »*noun* gas that is found underground and used as fuel.

natural history »*noun* the scientific study of animals or plants.

naturalise another way of spelling NATURALIZE.

naturalism »*noun* a style in art or literature that shows things as they are in daily life.

naturalist »*noun* a person who studies animals or plants.

> ℹ do not confuse **naturalist** with **naturist**: a **naturist** is a nudist

naturalistic »*adjective* ❶ having to do with real life or nature. ❷ based on the theory of naturalism.

naturalize »*verb* (**naturalizes, naturalizing, naturalized**) ❶ make a foreigner a citizen of a country. ❷ introduce a plant or animal into a region where it is not native.
naturalization

> ✓ many people prefer the alternative spellings **naturalise, naturalises,** etc.: both **s** and **z** spellings are correct

naturally
naturalness

natural selection »*noun* the evolutionary process whereby organisms better adapted to their environment tend to survive and produce more offspring.

nature

naturism »*noun* nudism.
naturist

> ℹ do not confuse **naturism** and **naturist** (a nudist) with **naturalism** and **naturalist**. Naturalism is a style of art or literature, while a **naturalist** studies plants and animals.

naught »*pronoun* (an old word) nothing.

> ☑ au not ou: naught (**nought** means the number zero)

naughty (adjective: **naughtier**, **naughtiest**)
naughtily
naughtiness

nausea »*noun* ❶ a feeling of sickness and wanting to vomit. ❷ disgust or revulsion.
– SAY naw-zi-uh

> ☑ ea not ia: nausea

nauseate »*verb* (**nauseates**, **nauseating**, **nauseated**) make someone feel sick or disgusted.

nauseous »*adjective* ❶ affected with nausea. ❷ causing nausea.

nautical »*adjective* having to do with sailors or navigation.
nautically

nautical mile »*noun* a unit of distance at sea, equal to 1,852 metres (approximately 2,025 yards).

nautilus »*noun* (plural **nautiluses** or **nautili**) a swimming shellfish with a spiral shell.
– SAY naw-ti-luhss [singular], naw-ti-lI [plural]

> ☑ the plural of **nautilus** can be either **nautiluses** or **nautili** (as in Latin)

naval »*adjective* having to do with a navy or navies.

> ☑ al not el: naval (the **navel** is the hollow in a person's belly)

nave »*noun* ❶ the central part of a church. ❷ the hub of a wheel.

navel »*noun* the small hollow in the centre of a person's belly where the umbilical cord was cut off at birth.

> ☑ el not al: navel (**naval** means 'having to do with the navy')

navel-gazing »*noun* absorption in yourself.

navigable »*adjective* wide and deep enough to be used by boats and ships.
navigability

navigate »*verb* (**navigates**, **navigating**, **navigated**) ❶ plan and direct the route of a ship, aircraft, or other form of transport. ❷ guide a boat or vehicle over a specified route. ❸ sail or travel over a stretch of water or land.

navigation »*noun* ❶ the activity of navigating. ❷ the movement of ships.
navigational

navigator »*noun* a person who navigates a ship, aircraft, etc.

> ☑ -or not -er: navigator

navvy »*noun* (plural **navvies**) (mainly a historical term) a labourer employed in building a road or railway.

> ☑ plural: drop the y and add **ies**: **navvies**

navy (plural **navies**)

> ☑ plural: drop the y and add **ies**: **navies**

nay »*adverb* ❶ or rather: *it will take months, nay years.* ❷ (an old word) no.

Nazi »*noun* (plural **Nazis**) (a historical term) a member of the far-right National Socialist German Workers' Party, of which Adolf Hitler was leader.
– SAY naht-si
Nazism

NB »*abbreviation* note well.

> ℹ from Latin *nota bene*

NCO »*abbreviation* non-commissioned officer.

Neanderthal »*noun* ❶ an extinct human living in Europe between about 120,000–35,000 years ago. ❷ a man who is rude or brutish, or who holds very old-fashioned views.
– SAY ni-an-der-tahl

> ℹ the ending is **thal** not **tal**: Neanderthal (named after the region of Germany where remains of such humans were found)

Neapolitan »*noun* a person from the Italian city of Naples.
» *adjective* relating to Naples.
– SAY ni-uh-**pol**-i-tuhn

neap tide »*noun* a tide just after the first or third quarters of the moon when there is least difference between high and low water.

near (adverb, preposition, & adjective: **nearer**, **nearest**; verb: **nears**, **nearing**, **neared**)
nearness

nearby

Near East »*noun* the countries of SW Asia between the Mediterranean and India (including the Middle East).
Near Eastern

neared

nearer

nearest

nearing

nearly

nearness

nears

nearside

near-sighted

neat (adjective: **neater**, **neatest**)
  neatly
  neatness

neaten (verb: **neatens**, **neatening**, **neatened**)

neater

neatest

neath »*preposition* (a poetic term) beneath.

neatly

neatness

nebula »*noun* (plural **nebulae** or **nebulas**) a cloud of gas or dust in outer space.
– SAY neb-yuu-luh [singular], neb-yuu-lee [plural]
  nebular

 the plural of **nebula** can be either **nebulae** (as in the original Latin) or **nebulas**

nebulizer »*noun* a device for producing a fine spray of liquid, used for example for inhaling a medicinal drug.
– SAY neb-yuu-ly-zer

 nebulizer can also be spelled **nebuliser**: both **s** and **z** spellings are correct

nebulous »*adjective* not clearly defined; vague: *nebulous concepts*.
  nebulously

necessarily

necessary

 one **c**, two **s**'s: **necessary**

necessitate »*verb* (**necessitates**, **necessitating**, **necessitated**) ❶ make something necessary. ❷ force someone to do something.

necessity (plural **necessities**)

 plural: drop the **y** and add **ies**: **necessities**

neck (verb: **necks**, **necking**, **necked**)

neckerchief »*noun* a square of cloth worn round the neck.

necking

necklace

necklet »*noun* a close-fitting, rigid ornament worn around the neck.

neckline

necks

necktie

necromancy »*noun* ❶ the practice of trying to communicate with the dead in order to predict the future. ❷ witchcraft or black magic.
– SAY nek-ruh-man-si
  necromancer
  necromantic

necrophilia »*noun* sexual activity with or attraction towards corpses.
– SAY nek-ruh-fil-i-uh
  necrophiliac

necropolis »*noun* (plural **necropolises**) a cemetery.
– SAY ne-krop-uh-liss

necrosis »*noun* (in medicine) the death of most or all of the cells in an organ or tissue.
– SAY ne-kroh-siss
  necrotic

nectar »*noun* ❶ a sugary fluid produced by flowers and made into honey by bees. ❷ (in Greek and Roman mythology) the drink of the gods.

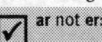 **ar** not **er**: **nectar**

nectarine »*noun* a variety of peach with smooth skin and rich firm flesh.
– SAY nek-tuh-reen

nee »*adjective* born (used in giving a married woman's maiden name): *Mrs Hargreaves, nee Liddell.*
– SAY nay

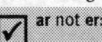 **nee** can also be spelled **née**, with an acute accent above the first **e** (as in the original French)

need (verb: **needs**, **needing**, **needed**)

needful

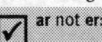 **-ful** not **-full**: **needful**

needier

neediest

neediness

needing

needle (verb: **needles**, **needling**, **needled**)

needlecord »*noun* fine-ribbed corduroy fabric.

needled

needlepoint »*noun* closely stitched embroidery worked over canvas.

needles

needless
  needlessly

needlewoman (plural **needlewomen**)

needlework

needling

needn't [need not]

> ☑ be careful to put the apostrophe where a letter has been left out, that is between the **n** and **t** of **not**: **needn't**

needs

needy (adjective: **needier**, **neediest**)
 neediness

ne'er »*contraction* (a poetic term) never.
– SAY nair

> ☑ be careful to put the apostrophe where a letter has been left out, that is, between the two **e**'s of **never**: **ne'er**

ne'er-do-well »*noun* a person who is lazy or useless.

nefarious »*adjective* wicked or criminal.
– SAY ni-**fair**-i-uhss
 nefariously

negate »*verb* (**negates**, **negating**, **negated**)
 ❶ stop something from having an effect: *alcohol negates the effects of the drug.*
 ❷ deny the existence of something.
– SAY ni-**gayt**

negation »*noun* ❶ the denial of something. ❷ the absence or opposite of something actual or positive: *evil is not merely the negation of goodness.*

negative
 negatively
 negativity

neglect (verb: **neglects**, **neglecting**, **neglected**)

neglectful

> ☑ -ful not -full: **neglectful**

neglecting

neglects

negligee »*noun* a woman's light, flimsy dressing gown.
– SAY neg-li-*zhay*

> ☑ **negligee** can also be spelled **negligée**, with an acute accent (as in the original French)

negligence
 negligent
 negligently

> ☑ ence not ance: **negligence**

negligible »*adjective* so small or unimportant as to be not worth considering.
– SAY neg-li-juh-b'l
 negligibly

> ☑ -ible not -able: **negligible**

negotiable »*adjective* ❶ able to be changed after discussion: *the price was not negotiable.* ❷ (of a cheque etc.) able to be transferred to the legal ownership of another person.

negotiate »*verb* (**negotiates**, **negotiating**, **negotiated**) ❶ try to reach an agreement by discussion. ❷ bring something about by discussion. ❸ find a way over or through an obstacle or difficult path. ❹ transfer a cheque, bill, etc. to the legal ownership of someone else.
 negotiation
 negotiator

Negro »*noun* (plural **Negroes**) a member of a dark-skinned group of peoples that originated in Africa south of the Sahara.

> ☐ do not use the terms **Negro** and **Negress** to refer to black people, as these terms are now thought to be old-fashioned and offensive; use **black** instead

neigh (verb: **neighs**, **neighing**, **neighed**)

neighbour (verb: **neighbours**, **neighbouring**, **neighboured**)
 neighbourly

> ☑ **bour** not **bor**: **neighbour** (the spelling **neighbor**, alone and in related words such as **neighborhood**, is American)

neighbourhood

neighbouring

neighbourly

neighbours

neighed

neighing

neighs

neither

nematode »*noun* a worm of a group with slender, cylindrical, unsegmented bodies.
– SAY nem-uh-tohd

nemesis »*noun* (plural **nemeses**) something that brings about someone's deserved and unavoidable downfall.
– SAY nem-i-siss [singular], nem-i-seez [plural]

> ☑ make the plural by changing the -**is** ending to -**es** (as in the original Greek): **nemeses**

neoclassical »*adjective* relating to the revival of a classical style in the arts.
 neoclassic
 neoclassicism
 neoclassicist

neodymium »*noun* a silvery-white metallic element.
– SAY nee-oh-**dim**-i-uhm

Neolithic »*adjective* relating to the later part of the Stone Age.
– **say** nee-oh-**lith**-ik

neologism »*noun* a new word or expression.
– **say** ni-**ol**-uh-ji-z'm

neon »*noun* an inert gaseous element that glows orange when electricity is passed through it, used in fluorescent lighting.

neonatal »*adjective* relating to newborn children.

neophyte »*noun* ❶ a person who is new to a subject, skill, or belief. ❷ a novice in a religious order, or a newly ordained priest.
– **say** nee-oh-fyt

neoprene »*noun* a synthetic substance resembling rubber.
– **say** nee-oh-preen

Nepalese (plural **Nepalese**)

nephew

nephritis »*noun* inflammation of the kidneys.
– **say** ni-**fry**-tiss

ne plus ultra »*noun* the highest form of something: *the ne plus ultra of editors.*
– **say** nay pluus **uul**-trah

> **i** ne plus ultra is Latin for 'not further beyond'

nepotism »*noun* favouritism shown to relatives or friends, especially by giving them jobs.
– **say** nep-uh-ti-z'm

Neptune

neptunium »*noun* a rare radioactive metallic element.

nerd
nerdy

Nereid »*noun* (in Greek mythology) a sea nymph.
– **say** neer-i-id

> ✓ capital **N**, because they were the daughters of the sea god *Nereus*

nerve (verb: **nerves, nerving, nerved**)

nerve gas »*noun* a poisonous gas which affects the nervous system, causing death or disablement.

nerveless »*adjective* ❶ lacking strength or feeling. ❷ confident.

nerve-racking

> ✓ nerve-racking can also be spelled nerve-wracking

nerves

nerve-wracking another way of spelling **NERVE-RACKING**.

nervier

nerviest

nerving

nervous
nervously
nervousness

nervous system »*noun* the network of nerves which transmits nerve impulses between parts of the body.

nervy (adjective: **nervier, nerviest**)

nest (verb: **nests, nesting, nested**)

nest egg »*noun* a sum of money saved for the future.

nesting

nestle (verb: **nestles, nestling, nestled**)

nestling »*noun* a bird that is too young to leave the nest.

nests

net¹ (verb: **nets, netting, netted**) [open-meshed material of twine or cord; catch with a net]

> ✓ double the **t** in **netting** and **netted**

net² »*adjective* ❶ (of an amount) remaining after tax, discounts, or expenses have been deducted. ❷ (of a weight) not including the packaging. ❸ (of an effect or result) overall.
» *verb* (**nets, netting, netted**) acquire a sum as clear profit.

> ✓ net can also be spelled **nett**, with a double t

netball

nether »*adjective* lower in position.
– **say** ne-*ther*

nethermost

nether regions »*plural noun* ❶ hell. ❷ a person's genitals and bottom.

netherworld »hell.

net profit »*noun* the actual profit after working expenses have been paid.

nets

nett another way of spelling **NET²**.

netted

netting

nettle »*noun* a plant having jagged leaves covered with stinging hairs.
» *verb* (**nettles, nettling, nettled**) annoy someone.

nettlerash »*noun* = **URTICARIA**.

nettles

nettling

network (verb: **networks**, **networking**, **networked**)
networker

neural »*adjective* relating to a nerve or the nervous system.
– SAY nyoor-uhl

neuralgia »*noun* intense pain along a nerve in the head or face.
– SAY nyoo-**ral**-juh
neuralgic

neuritis »*noun* inflammation of a nerve or nerves.
– SAY nyoo-**ry**-tiss

neurology »*noun* the branch of medicine and biology concerned with the nervous system.
neurological
neurologist

neuron »*noun* a cell that transmits nerve impulses.

> ✓ **neuron** is the standard spelling used by scientists; the spelling **neurone** is also used but only by non-scientists

neurosis »*noun* (plural **neuroses**) a mild mental illness in which a person feels depressed or anxious, or behaves in an obsessive way.
– SAY nyoo-**roh**-siss [singular], nyoo-**roh**-seez [plural]

> ✓ make the plural by changing the **-is** ending to **-es** (as in Latin): **neuroses**

neurosurgery »*noun* surgery performed on the nervous system.
neurosurgeon
neurosurgical

neurotic »*adjective* ❶ having to do with neurosis. ❷ excessively sensitive, anxious, or obsessive.
neurotically

neuter »*adjective* ❶ (in grammar) (of a noun) neither masculine or feminine. ❷ (of an animal or plant) having no sexual or reproductive organs.
»*verb* (**neuters**, **neutering**, **neutered**) ❶ operate on an animal so that it cannot produce young. ❷ take away the power of something.

neutral
neutrality
neutrally

neutralize »*verb* (**neutralizes**, **neutralizing**, **neutralized**) ❶ stop something from having an effect. ❷ make something chemically neutral.
neutralization

> ✓ many people prefer the alternative spellings **neutralise**, **neutralises**, etc.,

> and **neutralisation**: both **s** and **z** spellings are correct

neutrally

neutrino »*noun* (plural **neutrinos**) a subatomic particle with a mass close to zero and no electric charge.
– SAY nyoo-**tree**-noh

neutron »*noun* a subatomic particle of about the same mass as a proton but without an electric charge.

never

nevermore

nevertheless

nevus American spelling of **NAEVUS**.

new (adjective: **newer**, **newest**)
newly
newness

New Age »*noun* a broad movement concerned with alternative approaches to traditional Western religion, culture, medicine, etc.

newborn

newcomer

newel »*noun* ❶ the central supporting pillar of a winding staircase. ❷ (also **newel post**) the top or bottom supporting post of a stair rail.
– SAY nyoo-uhl

> ✓ only one **l**: **newel**

newer

newest

newfangled »*adjective* newly developed and unfamiliar.

newly

newly-wed

new moon »*noun* the phase of the moon when it first appears as a slender crescent.

newness

news

newsagent

newscast »*noun* a broadcast news report.
newscaster

newsflash

newsgroup »*noun* a group of Internet users who exchange email on a topic of shared interest.

newsletter

newsman (plural **newsmen**)

newspaper

newspeak »*noun* deliberately misleading and indirect language, used by politicians.

i from George Orwell's novel *Nineteen Eighty-Four*

newsprint

newsreader

newsreel

newsroom

news-stand

newsworthy

newsy »*adjective* (in informal English) full of news.

newt »*noun* a small animal with a slender body and a long tail, that can live in water or on land.

newton »*noun* (in physics) the basic unit of force.

i named after the English scientist Sir Isaac *Newton*

New World »*noun* North and South America.

New Year's Day

New Year's Eve

New Zealander

next

nexus »*noun* (plural **nexuses**) a connection or series of connections.
– **say** nek-suhss

i the correct Latin plural of **nexus** would also be **nexus**, but this is rarely used

NHS »*abbreviation* (in the UK) National Health Service.

nib »*noun* the pointed end part of a pen.

nibble (verb: **nibbles**, **nibbling**, **nibbled**)

Nicam »*noun* a digital television system to provide video signals with high-quality stereo sound.
– **say** ny-kam

i from *near instantaneously companded* (i.e. compressed and expanded) *audio multiplex*

Nicaraguan

nice (adjective: **nicer**, **nicest**)
nicely
niceness

nicety »*noun* (plural **niceties**) **❶** a fine detail or difference. **❷** accuracy.

✓ plural: drop the **y** and add **ies**: **niceties**

niche »*noun* **❶** a shallow recess in a wall, in which an ornament may be displayed. **❷** a position or role to which someone or something is suited. **❸** a particular group at which a marketing campaign is targeted.

– **say** neesh or nich

nick (verb: **nicks**, **nicking**, **nicked**)

nickel »*noun* **❶** a silvery-white metallic element used in alloys. **❷** (in American English) a five-cent coin.

✓ el not le: **nickel**

nicking

nick-nack another way of spelling **KNICK-KNACK**.

nickname (verb: **nicknames**, **nicknaming**, **nicknamed**)

nicks

nicotine »*noun* a poisonous oily liquid found in tobacco.

niece

✓ remember **i** before **e**, except after **c**: **niece** follows the usual rule

niff

nifty (adjective: **niftier**, **niftiest**)
niftily

Nigerian [of Nigeria]

Nigerien [of Niger]
– **say** ny-jeer-i-uhn

niggardly »*adjective* not generous; mean.

✓ double g: **niggardly**

nigger »*noun* a black person.

i the word **nigger** is very offensive, and should not be used

niggle »*verb* (niggles, niggling, niggled) **❶** worry or annoy someone slightly. **❷** criticize someone in a petty way.
»*noun* a minor worry or criticism.
niggly

nigh »*adverb, preposition, & adjective* (an old word) near.

night

nightcap »*noun* **❶** (a historical term) a cap worn in bed. **❷** a hot or alcoholic drink taken at bedtime.

nightclothes

nightclub

nightdress (plural **nightdresses**)

nightfall

nightgown

nightie

nightingale »*noun* a small brownish thrush noted for its tuneful song, often heard at night.

nightjar »*noun* a bird active at night, having grey-brown plumage, large eyes, and a distinctive call.

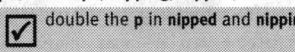
nightlife

nightly

nightmare
  nightmarish

nightshade »*noun* a poisonous plant with black or red berries.

nightshirt

nightspot

nightwatchman (plural **nightwatchmen**)

nihilism »*noun* the belief that nothing has any value, especially religious and moral principles.
– **say** ny-hi-li-z'm
  nihilist
  nihilistic

> ℹ the word **nihilism** is derived from the Latin word *nihil* meaning 'nothing'

nil »*noun* nothing; zero.

nimble (adjective: **nimbler, nimblest**)
  nimbly

nimbus »*noun* (plural **nimbi** or **nimbuses**)
  ❶ a large grey rain cloud. ❷ a luminous cloud or a halo surrounding a supernatural being or saint.
– **say** nim-buhss [singular], nim-bI [plural]

> ✓ the plural of **nimbus** can be either **nimbi** (as in the original Latin) or **nimbuses**

Nimby »*noun* (plural **Nimbys**) (in informal English) a person who objects to unpleasant developments being set up in the area in which they live.
– **say** nim-bi

> ℹ **Nimby** is an acronym from *not in my back yard*

nincompoop

nine
  ninefold

ninepins »*noun* the traditional form of the game of skittles.

nineteen
  nineteenth

ninety (plural **nineties**)
  ninetieth

> ✓ plural: drop the **y** and add **ies**: **nineties**

ninny (plural **ninnies**)

ninth
  ninthly

> ✓ nin- not nine-: **ninth**

niobium »*noun* a silver-grey metallic element.
– **say** ny-oh-bi-uhm

nip (verb: **nips, nipping, nipped**)

> ✓ double the **p** in **nipped** and **nipping**

nipped

nipper

nippier

nippiest

nipping

nipple

nippy (adjective: **nippier, nippiest**)

nips

nirvana »*noun* (in Buddhism) a state of perfect happiness.
– **say** neer-**vah**-nuh

Nissen hut »*noun* a tunnel-shaped hut of corrugated iron with a cement floor.
– **say** niss-uhn

> ℹ named after the British engineer Peter N. *Nissen*

nit »*noun* ❶ the egg of a human head louse. ❷ (in informal English) a stupid person.

nit-picking »*noun* petty criticism.

nitrate »*noun* a salt or ester of nitric acid.
– **say** ny-trayt

nitric acid »*noun* a very corrosive acid.

nitrite »*noun* a salt or ester of nitrous acid.
– **say** ny-tryt

nitrogen »*noun* a gas forming about 78 per cent of the earth's atmosphere.
– **say** ny-truh-juhn

nitrogenous »*adjective* containing nitrogen in chemical combination.
– **say** ny-**tro**-ji-nuhss

nitroglycerine »*noun* an explosive liquid used in dynamite.

> ✓ **nitroglycerine** is also spelled without the final **e**: **nitroglycerin**

nitrous acid »*noun* an unstable, weak acid.

nitrous oxide »*noun* a gas used as an anaesthetic; laughing gas.

nitty-gritty

nitwit

No another way of spelling **NOH**.

no

nob »*noun* (in informal English) an upper-class person.

no-ball »*noun* a ball in cricket that is unlawfully bowled, counting as an extra run to the batting side.

nobble »*verb* (**nobbles, nobbling, nobbled**) (in informal English) ❶ try to influence or

n

thwart something: *an attempt to nobble the jury.* ❷ stop and talk to someone.

Nobel Prize »*noun* one of six international prizes awarded annually for outstanding work in physics, chemistry, physiology or medicine, literature, economics, and the promotion of peace.

> ℹ named after the Swedish chemist and engineer Alfred *Nobel*

nobility »*noun* ❶ the quality of being noble. ❷ the aristocracy.

noble »*adjective* (**nobler, noblest**)
❶ belonging to the aristocracy. ❷ having fine personal qualities that people admire, such as courage and honesty. ❸ magnificent; impressive.
» *noun* a nobleman or noblewoman.
nobly

nobleman (plural **noblemen**)

nobler

noblesse oblige »*noun* the obligation of noble or wealthy people to help those who are less fortunate.
– **SAY** noh-bless oh-bleez*h*

> ℹ from a French phrase meaning 'nobility obliges'

noblest

noblewoman (plural **noblewomen**)

nobly

nobody (plural **nobodies**)

> ✓ plural: drop the **y** and add **ies**: **nobodies**

no-claims bonus »*noun* a reduction in an insurance premium when no claim has been made during an agreed period.

nocturnal »*adjective* done or active at night.
nocturnally

nocturne »*noun* a short piece of music of a dreamy, romantic nature.
– **SAY** nok-tern

nod (verb: **nods, nodding, nodded**)

> ✓ double the **d** in **nodded** and **nodding**

node »*noun* ❶ a point in a network at which lines cross or branch. ❷ the part of a plant stem from which one or more leaves grows. ❸ a small mass of distinct tissue in the body.
nodal

nodule »*noun* a small swelling or lump.
– **SAY** nod-yool
nodular

Noel »*noun* Christmas.

noggin »*noun* ❶ a person's head. ❷ a small quantity of alcoholic drink.

no-go area

Noh »*noun* a type of traditional Japanese drama with dance and song.
– **SAY** noh

> ✓ **Noh** can also be spelled without the final **h**: **No**

no-hoper

noise
noiseless
noiselessly

noisette »*noun* a small round piece of meat.
– **SAY** nwah-zet

> ✓ note the **ette** ending: **noisette** (it is a French word)

noisier

noisiest

noisily

noisiness

noisome »*adjective* having a very unpleasant smell.
– **SAY** noy-suhm

> ℹ note that the meaning of **noisome** has nothing to do with 'noise' (it actually comes from the word *annoy*)

noisy (adjective: **noisier, noisiest**)
noisily
noisiness

> ✓ drop the **y** and add **ier** or **iest** to spell **noisier** or **noisiest**

nomad »*noun* a member of a people that travels from place to place to find fresh pasture for its animals.

nomadic »*adjective* having the life of a nomad; wandering.
nomadically

no-man's-land »*noun* an area between two opposing armies that is not controlled by either.

nom de plume »*noun* (plural **noms de plume**) a name used by a writer instead of their real name; a pen name.
– **SAY** nom duh **ploom** [singular and plural]

> ✓ the plural of **nom de plume** adds an **s** only to **nom**: **noms de plume** (it is a French term which means 'pen name')

nomenclature »*noun* a system of names used in a particular subject.
– **SAY** noh-**men**-kluh-cher

nominal »*adjective* ❶ in name but not in reality. ❷ (of a sum of money) very small, but charged or paid as a sign that

payment is necessary.
nominally

nominate »*verb* (**nominates, nominating, nominated**) ❶ put someone forward as a candidate for a job or award. ❷ arrange a time, date, or place.
nomination
nominator

nominee »*noun* a person who is nominated for a job or award.

nonagenarian »*noun* a person between 90 and 99 years old.
– say non-uh-juh-**nair**-i-uhn

nonagon »*noun* a shape with nine straight sides and angles.
– say non-uh-guhn

nonce »*adjective* (of a word or expression) coined for one occasion.

nonchalant »*adjective* relaxed and unconcerned.
– say non-shuh-luhnt
nonchalance
nonchalantly

 ant not ent: **nonchalant**

non-combatant »*noun* a person who is not engaged in fighting during a war, especially a civilian, army chaplain, or army doctor.

non-commissioned »*adjective* (of a military officer) appointed from the lower ranks rather than holding a commission.

non-committal »*adjective* not showing what you think or which side you are on.
non-committally

 double m, double t: **non-committal**

non compos mentis see COMPOS MENTIS.

non-conductor »*noun* a substance that does not conduct heat or electricity.

nonconformist »*noun* ❶ a person who does not follow accepted ideas or behaviour. ❷ (**Nonconformist**) a member of a Protestant Church which does not follow the beliefs of the established Church of England.
nonconformism
nonconformity

non-contributory »*adjective* (of a pension) funded by regular payments by the employer, not the employee.

nondescript »*adjective* having no special or interesting features.

none

ℹ️ when you use **none** of with a plural noun or pronoun (such as *them* or

us), or a singular noun that refers to a group of people or things, you can use either a singular or plural verb: *none of them is coming tonight* or *none of them are coming tonight*

nonentity »*noun* (plural **nonentities**) an unimportant person or thing.
– say non-**en**-ti-ti

 plural: drop the **y** and add **ies**: **nonentities**

nonetheless

ℹ️ **nonetheless** can also be written as three separate words: **none the less**

non-event

non-existent
non-existence

non-fiction
non-fictional

non-flammable »*adjective* not catching fire easily.

non-intervention »*noun* the policy of not becoming involved in the affairs of other countries.

non-invasive »*adjective* (of medical procedures) not requiring instruments to be put into the body.

non-member

no-no »*noun* (plural **no-nos**) (in informal English) a thing that is not possible or acceptable.

no-nonsense

nonpareil »*adjective* having no match or equal.
» *noun* a person or thing having no match or equal.
– say non-puh-**rayl**

ℹ️ note the unusual **eil** ending: **nonpareil** (a French word)

nonplussed »*adjective* surprised and confused as to how to react.
– say non-**plusst**

non-proliferation »*noun* the prevention of an increase in the number of nuclear weapons that are produced.

nonsense

nonsensical

non sequitur »*noun* a conclusion that does not logically follow from what has just been said.
– say non **sek**-wi-ter

ℹ️ from a Latin phrase meaning 'it does not follow'

non-starter »*noun* ❶ a person or animal that fails to take part in a race. ❷ (in

n

informal English) something that has no chance of succeeding.

non-stick

non-stop

noodles »*plural noun* thin, long strips of pasta.

nook »*noun* a corner or place that is sheltered or hidden from other people.

nooky »*noun* (in informal English) sexual activity or intercourse.

> ✓ nooky can also be spelled **nookie**

noon

noonday »*adjective* taking place or appearing in the middle of the day.

no one

noose »*noun* a loop with a knot which tightens as the rope or wire is pulled, used especially to hang people or trap animals.

nor

Nordic »*adjective* relating to Scandinavia, Finland, and Iceland.

norm »*noun* ❶ the usual or standard thing. ❷ a standard that is required or acceptable.

normal
normality
normally

normalize »*verb* (normalizes, normalizing, normalized) make something normal or become normal.
normalization

> ✓ many people prefer the alternative spellings **normalise, normalises**, etc., and **normalisation**: both **s** and **z** spellings are correct

normally

Norman »*noun* a member of a people of Normandy in northern France who conquered England in 1066.
» *adjective* ❶ relating to the Normans or Normandy. ❷ having to do with the style of Romanesque architecture used in Britain under the Normans.

normative »*adjective* relating to or setting a standard or norm.

Norse »*noun* an ancient or medieval form of Norwegian or a related Scandinavian language.
» *adjective* relating to ancient or medieval Norway or Scandinavia.

Norseman (plural **Norsemen**)

north

North American

northbound

north-east
north-easterly
north-eastern

north-eastward

north-eastwards

northerly

northern

> ✓ remember that the ending is **-ern** not **-en**: northern and northerner

northerner

Northern Lights »*plural noun* the aurora borealis.

north-north-east

north-north-west

North Star »*noun* the Pole Star.

northward

northwards

north-west
north-westerly
north-western

north-westward

north-westwards

Norwegian

> ✓ we not wee: Norwegian

nose (verb: noses, nosing, nosed)

nosebag »*noun* a bag containing fodder, hung from a horse's head.

nosebleed

nosed

nosedive (verb: nosedives, nosediving, nosedived)

nosegay »*noun* a small bunch of flowers.

noses

nosey another way of spelling **NOSY**.

nosh

nosier

nosiest

nosily

nosiness

nosing

nostalgia »*noun* longing for the happy times of the past.
nostalgic
nostalgically

nostril

nostrum »*noun* ❶ a favourite method for improving something. ❷ a medicine that is prepared by an unqualified person and is not effective.

nosy (adjective: **nosier**, **nosiest**)
  nosily
  nosiness

> ✓ **nosy** can also be spelled with an **e**: **nosey**
>
> drop the **y** and add **ier** or **iest** to spell **nosier** or **nosiest**

not

notable
  notably

notary »*noun* (plural **notaries**) a lawyer who is authorized to be a witness when people sign contracts and other documents.

> ℹ the full form of **notary** is **notary public**

notate »*verb* (**notates**, **notating**, **notated**) write music down using notation.

notation »*noun* a system of signs and symbols used in music, mathematics, etc.

notch (verb: **notches**, **notching**, **notched**)

note (verb: **notes**, **noting**, **noted**)

notebook

noted

notepad

notepaper

notes

noteworthy

nothing

nothingness

notice (verb: **notices**, **noticing**, **noticed**)

noticeable
  noticeably

> ✓ remember the **e** in the middle: **noticeable**

noticeboard

noticed

notices

noticing

notifiable »*adjective* (of an infectious disease) that must be reported to the health authorities.

notify »*verb* (**notifies**, **notifying**, **notified**) formally or officially tell someone about something.
  notification

noting

notion »*noun* ❶ an idea or belief. ❷ an understanding: *I had no notion of what she meant.*

notional »*adjective* based on an idea rather than reality.
  notionally

notoriety »*noun* the state of being notorious.
– *SAY* noh-tuh-**ry**-i-ti

> ✓ note the **ety** ending: **notoriety**

notorious »*adjective* famous for something bad.
  notoriously

notwithstanding »*preposition* in spite of.
» *adverb* nevertheless.

nougat »*noun* a sweet made from sugar or honey, nuts, and egg white.
– *SAY* **noo**-gah or **nug**-uht

> ✓ note that the ending is -**at**: **nougat** (it is a French word). Do not confuse **nougat** with **nugget**, which means 'a small lump of precious metal'.

nought [zero]

> ✓ **ou** not **au**: **nought** (**naught** is an old word meaning 'nothing')

noun »*noun* a word (other than a pronoun) that refers to a person, place, or thing, such as *woman*, *France*, or *tree*.

nourish »*verb* (**nourishes**, **nourishing**, **nourished**) ❶ give a person, animal, or plant the food and other substances they need in order to grow and be healthy. ❷ keep a feeling or belief in your mind for a long time.

nourishment »*noun* the food and other substances necessary for life, growth, and good health.

nous »*noun* common sense.
– *SAY* nowss

nouveau riche »*noun* people who have recently become rich and who like to display their wealth in an obvious or tasteless way.
– *SAY* noo-voh **reesh**

> ℹ **nouveau riche** is a French phrase which means 'new rich'

nouvelle cuisine »*noun* a modern style of cookery that emphasizes fresh ingredients and the presentation of the dishes.
– *SAY* noo-voh kwi-**zeen**

> ℹ **nouvelle cuisine** is a French phrase which means 'new cookery'

nova »*noun* (plural **novae** or **novas**) a star that suddenly becomes very bright for a short period.
– *SAY* **noh**-vuh [singular], **noh**-vee [plural]

> ✓ the plural of **nova** can either be **novae** (like the original Latin) or **novas**

novel[1] [book-length story]

novel[2] »*adjective* new in an interesting or unusual way.

n

n

novelise another way of spelling **NOVELIZE**.

novelist

novelize »*verb* (**novelizes, novelizing, novelized**) convert into a novel.
novelization

 many people prefer the alternative spellings **novelise, novelises**, etc., and **novelisation**: both **s** and **z** spellings are correct

novella »*noun* a short novel or long short story.
– SAY nuh-**vel**-luh

novelty »*noun* (plural **novelties**) ❶ the quality of being new and unusual. ❷ a new or unfamiliar thing. ❸ a small toy or ornament.

 plural: drop the **y** and add **ies**: **novelties**

November

novice »*noun* ❶ a person who is new to and lacks experience in a job or situation. ❷ a person who has entered a religious order but has not yet taken their vows.

novitiate »*noun* ❶ the period or state of being a novice. ❷ a novice in a religious order.
– SAY noh-**vi**-shi-uht

 novitiate can also be spelled with a **c** in the middle: **noviciate**

now

nowadays

nowhere

nowt

noxious »*adjective* harmful or very unpleasant.
– SAY **nok**-shuhss

nozzle »*noun* a spout used to control a stream of liquid or gas.

nu »*noun* the thirteenth letter of the Greek alphabet (N, **v**).
– SAY nyoo

nuance »*noun* a very slight difference in meaning, expression, sound, etc.
– SAY **nyoo**-ahnss

nub »*noun* ❶ the central point of a matter. ❷ a small lump.
nubby

nubile »*adjective* (of a girl or young woman) sexually mature and attractive.
– SAY **nyoo**-byl

nuclear »*adjective* ❶ relating to the nucleus of an atom or cell. ❷ using energy released in the fission or fusion of atomic nuclei. ❸ possessing or involving nuclear weapons.

 -clear not **-cular** or **-clier**: **nuclear**

nuclear family »*noun* a couple and their children.

nuclear fuel »*noun* a substance that will undergo nuclear fission and can be used as a source of nuclear energy.

nuclear physics »*noun* the science of atomic nuclei and the way they interact.

nucleated »*adjective* having or formed around a nucleus.
– SAY **nyoo**-kli-ay-tid

nuclei plural of **NUCLEUS**.

nucleic acid »*noun* one of two substances, DNA and RNA, that are present in all living cells.
– SAY nyoo-**klee**-ik or nyoo-**klay**-ik

nucleus »*noun* (plural **nuclei**) ❶ the central and most important part of an object or group. ❷ the positively charged central core of an atom. ❸ (in biology) a structure present in most cells, containing the genetic material.
– SAY **nyoo**-kli-uhss [singular], **nyoo**-kli-I [plural]

 the plural of **nucleus** is **nuclei** (as in Latin)

nude
nudity

nudge (verb: **nudges, nudging, nudged**)

nudist »*noun* a person who goes naked wherever possible.
nudism

nudity

nugatory »*adjective* having no purpose or value.
– SAY **nyoo**-guh-tuh-ri or **noo**-guh-tuh-ri

nugget »*noun* ❶ a small lump of gold or other precious metal found in the earth. ❷ a small but valuable fact.

 do not confuse **nugget** with **nougat**, which is a kind of sweet

nuisance

 nuis not **nus**: **nuisance**

nuke (in informal English) »*noun* a nuclear weapon.
» *verb* (**nukes, nuking, nuked**) attack a place with nuclear weapons.

null »*adjective* ❶ (**null and void**) having no legal force; invalid. ❷ having or associated with the value zero.

nullify »*verb* (**nullifies, nullifying, nullified**) ❶ make something legally invalid. ❷ cancel out the effect of something.
nullification

n

nullity »*noun* (plural **nullities**) ❶ the state of being legally invalid. ❷ a thing of no importance or worth.

numb (verb: **numbs, numbing, numbed**)
numbly
numbness

number (verb: **numbers, numbering, numbered**)
numberless

numbing

numbly

numbness

numbs

numbskull »*noun* (in informal English) a stupid person.

 numbskull can also be spelled numskull, without the **b**

numeracy

numeral »*noun* a symbol or word representing a number.

numerate »*adjective* having a good basic knowledge of arithmetic.
– sᴀʏ nyoo-muh-ruht
numeracy

numeration »*noun* the action of numbering or calculating.

numerator »*noun* (in mathematics) the number above the line in a fraction.

 -or not -er: numerator

numerical »*adjective* having to do with a number or numbers.
numerically

numerology »*noun* the branch of knowledge concerned with the supposed magical power of numbers.
numerological
numerologist

numerous
numerously

numinous »*adjective* having a strong religious or spiritual quality.
– sᴀʏ nyoo-mi-nuhss

numismatic »*adjective* having to do with coins or medals.

numismatics »*noun* the study or collection of coins, banknotes, and medals.
numismatist

numskull another way of spelling
NUMBSKULL.

nun

nuncio »*noun* (plural **nuncios**) (in the Roman Catholic Church) a person who represents the pope in a foreign country.
– sᴀʏ nun-si-oh

 the plural of nuncio has **os** not **oes**: nuncios

nunnery »*noun* (plural **nunneries**) a religious house of nuns.

plural: drop the **y** and add **ies**: nunneries

nuptial »*adjective* having to do with marriage or weddings.
– sᴀʏ nup-sh'l

remember that the ending is **tial** not tual: nuptial

nuptials »*plural noun* a wedding.

nurse (verb: **nurses, nursing, nursed**)

nursemaid »*noun* (old-fashioned) a woman or girl employed to look after a young child or children.

nursery (plural **nurseries**)

plural: drop the **y** and add **ies**: nurseries

nurseryman »*noun* (plural **nurserymen**) a worker in or owner of a plant or tree nursery.

nurses

nursing

nurture »*verb* (**nurtures, nurturing, nurtured**) ❶ encourage the growth or development of a child, plant, etc. ❷ have a hope, belief, or ambition for a long time.
»*noun* the action of nurturing someone or something.

nut (verb: **nuts, nutting, nutted**)
nutty

nutcase

nutcrackers

nuthatch »*noun* a small grey-backed songbird which climbs up and down tree trunks.

nutmeg »*noun* a spice made from the seed of a tropical tree.

nutrient »*noun* a substance that provides nourishment essential for life and growth.
– sᴀʏ nyoo-tri-uhnt

ent not ant: nutrient

nutriment »*noun* nourishment.

nutrition »*noun* ❶ the process of taking in and absorbing nutrients. ❷ the branch of science concerned with this process.
nutritional
nutritionist

nutritious »*adjective* full of nutrients; nourishing.
nutritiously

tious not cious: nutritious

nutritive »*adjective* ❶ having to do with nutrition. ❷ nutritious.

nuts
nutshell
nutted
nutter
nutting
nutty

nuzzle (verb: **nuzzles, nuzzling, nuzzled**)

NVQ »*abbreviation* (in the UK) National Vocational Qualification.

nylon »*noun* ❶ a strong, lightweight, synthetic material which can be made into sheets, fabric, or moulded objects. ❷ (**nylons**) nylon stockings or tights.

nymph »*noun* ❶ (in Greek and Roman mythology) a spirit of nature imagined as a beautiful young woman. ❷ an immature form of an insect such as a dragonfly.

nymphet »*noun* an attractive and sexually mature young girl.

nympho »*noun* (plural **nymphos**) (in informal English) a nymphomaniac.

nymphomania »*noun* uncontrollable sexual desire in a woman.
nymphomaniac

Oo

oaf
oafish

oak
oaky

oak apple »*noun* a growth which forms on oak trees, caused by wasp larvae.

oaken »*adjective* (a poetic term) made of oak.

oakum »*noun* (mainly a historical term) loose fibre obtained by untwisting old rope, used to fill cracks in wooden ships.

oaky

OAP »*abbreviation* old-age pensioner.

oar [pole with a flat blade, used for rowing]

oarsman (plural **oarsmen**)

oarswoman (plural **oarswomen**)

oasis »*noun* (plural **oases**) ❶ a fertile place in a desert where water rises to ground level. ❷ a calm or pleasant area or period in the midst of a hectic or difficult situation.

> ☑ make the plural by changing the **-is** ending to **-es** (as in Latin): **oases**

oast house »*noun* a building containing a kiln for drying hops.

oat
oaty

oatcake

oath »*noun* (plural **oaths**) ❶ a solemn promise to do something or that something is true. ❷ a swear word.

oatmeal »*noun* meal made from ground oats, used in making porridge and oatcakes.

oaty

obbligato »*noun* (plural **obbligatos** or **obbligati**) an instrumental part which forms part of a piece of music and may not be omitted in performance.

> ☑ double **b**: **obbligato** (an Italian word meaning 'obligatory')
> the plural can end with **i** (as in Italian) or **os**

obdurate »*adjective* stubbornly refusing to change your opinion or course of action.
– **SAY** ob-dyuu-ruht
obduracy
obdurately

OBE »*abbreviation* Officer of the Order of the British Empire.

obedient
obedience
obediently

> ☑ **ent** not **ant**: **obedient**

obeisance »*noun* ❶ humble respect: *they paid obeisance to the Prince.* ❷ a gesture expressing this, such as a bow.
– **SAY** oh-**bay**-suhnss
obeisant

> ☑ **obeisance** is an exception to the rule **i** before **e** except after **c**

obelisk »*noun* a four-sided stone pillar that tapers to a point, set up as a monument.

obese »*adjective* very fat.
– SAY oh-**beess**
obesity

obey (verb: **obeys, obeying, obeyed**)

obfuscate »*verb* (**obfuscates, obfuscating, obfuscated**) make something unclear or hard to understand.
– SAY ob-**fuss**-kayt
obfuscation

obituary »*noun* (plural **obituaries**) an announcement that someone has died, published in a newspaper in the form of a brief biography.

> ✓ uary not ury: obit**uary**
> plural: drop the **y** and add **ies**:
> obit**uaries**

object (verb: **objects, objecting, objected**)
objector

objectify »*verb* (**objectifies, objectifying, objectified**) ❶ express something abstract in a physical form. ❷ treat someone as an object rather than a person.
objectification

objecting

objection

objectionable »*adjective* unpleasant or offensive.
objectionably

objective »*adjective* ❶ not influenced by personal feelings or opinions. ❷ having actual existence outside the mind: *a matter of objective fact.* ❸ (in grammar) relating to a case of nouns and pronouns used for the object of a transitive verb or a preposition.
»*noun* a goal or aim.
objectively
objectivity

object lesson »*noun* a clear practical example of a principle or ideal.

objector

objects

objet d'art »*noun* (plural **objets d'art**) a small decorative or artistic object.
– SAY ob-**zhay** dar [singular and plural]

> ℹ objet d'art is French for 'object of art'
> make the plural by adding an **s** after
> objet only: objet**s** d'art

oblate »*adjective* (in geometry) (of a sphere) flattened at the poles.
– SAY ob-**layt**

oblation »*noun* a thing presented or offered to a god.

obligate »*verb* (**obligates, obligating, obligated**) (**be obligated**) be obliged to do something.

obligation »*noun* ❶ something one must do in order to keep to a law or agreement. ❷ the state of being obliged to do something.

obligatory »*adjective* required by a law, rule, or custom; compulsory.
obligatorily

> ✓ tory not try: obliga**tory**

oblige »*verb* (**obliges, obliging, obliged**) ❶ make someone do something by law, necessity, or because it is their duty. ❷ perform a service or favour for someone. ❸ (**be obliged**) be grateful.

obliging »*adjective* willing to do a service or favour; helpful.
obligingly

oblique »*adjective* ❶ at an angle; slanting. ❷ not done in a direct way: *an oblique attack on the President.* ❸ (in geometry) (of a line, plane, etc.) inclined at an angle other than a right angle.
– SAY uh-**bleek**
obliquely
obliquity

> ✓ que not qe: obli**que**

obliterate »*verb* (**obliterates, obliterating, obliterated**) ❶ destroy something completely. ❷ cover something completely.
– SAY uh-**bli**-tuh-rayt
obliteration

oblivion »*noun* ❶ the state of being unaware of what is happening around you. ❷ the state of being forgotten. ❸ the state of being completely destroyed.

oblivious »*adjective* not aware of what is happening around you.
obliviously
obliviousness

oblong

obloquy »*noun* ❶ strong public criticism. ❷ disgrace brought about by strong public criticism.
– SAY ob-luh-kwi

> ✓ quy not qy: oblo**quy**

obnoxious »*adjective* very unpleasant and offensive.
– SAY uhb-**nok**-shuhss
obnoxiously
obnoxiousness

oboe »*noun* a woodwind instrument of treble pitch, played with a double reed.

– **say** oh-boh
oboist

obscene »*adjective* ❶ dealing with sexual matters in an offensive or disgusting way. ❷ (in informal English) (of a payment, pay rise, etc.) unacceptably large.

> ✓ -scene not -sene: obscene

obscenity »*noun* (plural **obscenities**) ❶ the state of being obscene. ❷ an obscene action or word.

> ✓ plural: drop the **y** and add **ies**: obscenities

obscurantism »*noun* the practice of deliberately preventing something from being understood.
– **say** ob-skyuu-**rant**-i-z'm
obscurantist

obscure »*adjective* ❶ not discovered or known about. ❷ not well known. ❸ hard to understand or see.
» *verb* (**obscures, obscuring, obscured**) hide something or make something unclear.
obscurely

obscurity »*noun* (plural **obscurities**) ❶ the state of being unknown or hard to understand. ❷ something that is hard to understand.

obsequies »*plural noun* funeral rites.
– **say** ob-si-kwiz

obsequious »*adjective* too obedient or respectful.
– **say** uhb-**see**-kwi-uhss
obsequiously
obsequiousness

observance »*noun* ❶ behaving in accordance with a law, rule, or ritual. ❷ (**observances**) acts performed for religious or ceremonial reasons.

> ✓ ance not ence: observance

observant

> ✓ ant not ent: observant

observation
observational

observatory »*noun* (plural **observatories**) a building housing a telescope for looking at the stars and planets, or other scientific equipment for observing things.

observe (verb: **observes, observing, observed**)
observable
observer

obsess »*verb* (**obsesses, obsessing, obsessed**) think about someone or something continually and disturbingly.

obsession
obsessional

obsessive »*adjective* thinking continually about someone or something.
obsessively
obsessiveness

obsidian »*noun* a dark glass-like rock, formed when lava solidifies rapidly.
– **say** uhb-**sid**-i-uhn

obsolescent »*adjective* becoming obsolete.
– **say** ob-suh-**less**-uhnt
obsolescence

obsolete »*adjective* no longer produced or used; out of date.

obstacle

obstetric

obstetrician »*noun* a doctor qualified to practise in obstetrics.
– **say** ob-stuh-**tri**-sh'n

obstetrics »*noun* the branch of medicine and surgery concerned with childbirth.
obstetric

> ✓ stet not stret: obstetrics

obstinate »*adjective* ❶ stubbornly refusing to change your mind or what you are doing. ❷ hard to deal with: *an obstinate problem.*
obstinacy
obstinately

obstreperous »*adjective* noisy and difficult to control.
– **say** uhb-**strep**-uh-ruhss
obstreperously
obstreperousness

obstruct (verb: **obstructs, obstructing, obstructed**)

obstruction

obstructive »*adjective* deliberately causing difficulties or delays.

obstructs

obtain (verb: **obtains, obtaining, obtained**)
obtainable

obtrude »*verb* (**obtrudes, obtruding, obtruded**) become noticeable in an unwelcome way.

obtrusive »*adjective* noticeable in an unwelcome way.
obtrusively
obtrusiveness

obtuse »*adjective* ❶ annoyingly slow to understand. ❷ (of an angle) more than 90 and less than 180 degrees. ❸ not sharp or pointed; blunt.

– **SAY** uhb-**tyooss**
  obtusely
  obtuseness

obverse »*noun* ❶ the side of a coin or medal which has the head or main design on it. ❷ the opposite of something.

obviate »*verb* (**obviates**, **obviating**, **obviated**) remove or prevent a need or difficulty.
– **SAY** ob-vi-ayt
  obviation

obvious
  obviously
  obviousness

ocarina »*noun* a small egg-shaped wind instrument with holes for the fingers.
– **SAY** o-kuh-ree-nuh

occasion (verb: **occasions**, **occasioning**, **occasioned**)

> ✓ two **c**'s and one **s**, and **a** not **ai** in the middle: **occasion**

occasional
  occasionally
occasioned
occasioning
occasions

occidental »*adjective* relating to the countries of the West.
– **SAY** ok-si-**den**-tuhl

occiput »*noun* (in anatomy) the back of the head.
– **SAY** ok-si-put
  occipital

occlude »*verb* (**occludes**, **occluding**, **occluded**) close up or block an opening or passage.
– **SAY** uh-**klood**
  occlusion

occult »*noun* (**the occult**) supernatural beliefs, practices, or events.
»*adjective* relating to the occult.
– **SAY** o-**kult** or o-kult
  occultism
  occultist

> ✓ double **c**: **occult**

occupancy »*noun* ❶ the action of occupying a place. ❷ the proportion of accommodation that is occupied.

occupant »*noun* a person who occupies a place or job.

> ✓ **ant** not **ent**: **occupant**

occupation

occupational »*adjective* having to do with a job or profession.

occupational therapy »*noun* the use of particular activities as a method of helping someone recover from illness.

occupy (verb: **occupies**, **occupying**, **occupied**)
  occupier

> ✓ two **c**'s, one **p**: **occupy**

occur (verb: **occurs**, **occurring**, **occurred**)

> ✓ double the **r** in **occurred** and **occurring**

occurrence

> ✓ double **r**: **occurrence**

occurring
occurs
ocean

oceanic »*adjective* relating to the ocean.
– **SAY** oh-si-an-ik or oh-shi-**an**-ik

oceanography »*noun* the branch of science concerned with the study of the sea.
  oceanographer

ocelot »*noun* a medium-sized striped and spotted wild cat, found in South and Central America.
– **SAY** oss-i-lot

ochre »*noun* a type of earth varying from light yellow to brown or red, used as a pigment.
– **SAY** oh-ker

> ✓ **re** not **er**: **ochre** (the spelling **ocher** is American)

o'clock

octagon »*noun* a shape with eight straight sides and eight angles.
  octagonal

> ✓ **octa** not **octo**: **octagon**

octahedron »*noun* (plural **octahedra** or **octahedrons**) a three-dimensional shape with eight plane faces.
– **SAY** ok-tuh-**hee**-druhn
  octahedral

> ✓ the plural of **octahedron** can be **octahedra** (like the original Greek) or **octahedrons**

octane »*noun* a liquid hydrocarbon present in petroleum spirit.

octave »*noun* ❶ a series of eight musical notes occupying the interval between (and including) two notes. ❷ the interval between two such notes.
– **SAY** ok-tiv

octavo »*noun* (plural **octavos**) a size of book page that results from folding each printed sheet into eight leaves (sixteen pages).
– SAY ok-**tah**-voh or ok-**tay**-voh

octet »*noun* ❶ a group of eight musicians. ❷ a musical composition for eight voices or instruments.

October

octogenarian »*noun* a person who is between 80 and 89 years old.
– SAY ok-tuh-ji-**nair**-i-uhn

octopus (plural **octopuses**)

> ℹ️ the standard plural of **octopus** is **octopuses**. However, since the word comes from Greek, the Greek plural **octopodes** is still occasionally used. The plural form **octopi**, formed according to rules for Latin plurals, is incorrect.

octuple »*adjective* ❶ consisting of eight parts or things. ❷ eight times as many or as much.

ocular »*adjective* having to do with the eyes or vision.
– SAY ok-**yuu**-ler

oculist »*noun* a person who specializes in the medical treatment of diseases or defects of the eye.
– SAY ok-**yuu**-list

OD »*verb* (**OD's**, **OD'ing**, **OD'd**) (in informal English) take an overdose of a drug.

odd (adjective: **odder**, **oddest**)
oddly
oddness

oddball »*noun* (in informal English) a strange or eccentric person.

odder

oddest

oddity »*noun* (plural **oddities**) ❶ the quality of being strange. ❷ a strange person or thing.

> ✅ plural: drop the **y** and add **ies**: **oddities**

odd-job man

oddly

oddment »*noun* an item or piece left over from a larger piece or set.

oddness

odds

odds-on »*adjective* ❶ (especially of a horse) with betting odds in favour of winning. ❷ very likely to happen or succeed.

ode »*noun* a poem addressed to a person or thing or celebrating an event.

OD'ing [taking an overdose]

odious »*adjective* very unpleasant; repulsive.
odiously
odiousness

odium »*noun* widespread hatred or disgust.

odor American spelling of **ODOUR**.

odoriferous »*adjective* having an odour.
– SAY oh-duh-**rif**-uh-ruhss

odour »*noun* a particular smell.
odorous
odourless

> ✅ **-dour** not **-dor**: **odour** (the spelling **odor**, except in **odorous**, is American)

OD's [takes an overdose]

odyssey »*noun* (plural **odysseys**) a long eventful journey.
– SAY **od**-i-si

> ℹ️ from the title of a Greek poem describing the adventures of *Odysseus*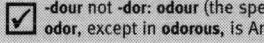

oedema »*noun* an excess of watery fluid in the cavities or tissues of the body.
– SAY i-**dee**-muh

> ✅ **oe** at the beginning: **oedema** (the spelling **edema** is American)

Oedipus complex »*noun* (in the theory of Sigmund Freud) the emotions aroused in a young child by an unconscious sexual desire for the parent of the opposite sex.
– SAY **ee**-di-puhss
Oedipal

> ℹ️ from *Oedipus* in Greek mythology, who unknowingly killed his father and married his mother

o'er »*adverb & preposition* (a poetic term) = **OVER**.

> ✅ be careful to put the apostrophe where a letter has been left out, that is, between the **o** and the **e** of **over**: **o'er**

oesophagus »*noun* (plural **oesophagi** or **oesophaguses**) the muscular tube which connects the throat to the stomach.
– SAY ee-**so**-fuh-guhss [singular], ee-**so**-fuh-jI [plural]

> ✅ **oe** at the beginning: **oesophagus** (the spelling **esophagus** is American) the plural can either be **oesophagi** (as in Latin) or **oesophaguses**

oestrogen »*noun* one of a group of hormones which develop and maintain female characteristics of the body.
– SAY **ee**-struh-juhn or **ess**-truh-juhn

> ✅ **oe** at the beginning: **oestrogen** (the spelling **estrogen** is American)

oestrus »*noun* a recurring period of sexual readiness and fertility in many female mammals.
– **say** ee-struhss or **ess**-truhss

> ✓ **oe** at the beginning: **oestrus** (the spelling **estrus** is American)

oeuvre »*noun* the body of work of an artist, composer, author, etc.
– **say** er-vruh

> ✓ remember the **u** before the **v**: **oeuvre** is a French word, literally meaning 'work'

of

> ℹ️ it is wrong to write the word **of** instead of **have** in phrases such as *I could have told you* (not *I could of told you*)

off

> ℹ️ say **off**, not **off of**, in a sentence such as *the cup fell off the table*; **off of** is not good English and should not be used in writing

offal »*noun* the internal organs of an animal used as food.

offbeat »*adjective* unconventional; unusual.

off-colour »*adjective* slightly unwell.

offcut »*noun* a piece of wood, fabric, etc. that is left behind after cutting a larger piece.

offence

> ✓ **ence** not **ense**: **offence** (the spelling **offense** is American)

offend (verb: **offends, offending, offended**)
offender

offense American spelling of **OFFENCE**.

offensive
offensively

offer (verb: **offers, offering, offered**)
offering

> ✓ do not double the **r** in **offering** and **offered**

offertory »*noun* (plural **offertories**) ❶ the offering of the bread and wine at Holy Communion. ❷ a collection of money made at a Christian church service.
– **say** off-er-tuh-ri

offhand »*adjective* rudely casual or cool in manner.
» *adverb* without previous thought.

office

officer

official »*adjective* ❶ relating to an authority or public organization. ❷ agreed or done by a person or group in a position of authority.
» *noun* a person holding public office or having official duties.
officialdom
officially

> ℹ️ do not confuse **official** with **officious**, which means 'asserting authority or interfering in an overbearing way'

officialese »*noun* formal and wordy language considered to be characteristic of official documents.

officially

officiate »*verb* (**officiates, officiating, officiated**) ❶ act as an official in charge of something. ❷ perform a religious service or ceremony.
– **say** uh-fi-shi-ayt
officiation

> ✓ **c** not **sh** in the middle: **officiate**

officious »*adjective* asserting authority or interfering in an overbearing way.
officiously
officiousness

> ℹ️ do not confuse **officious** with **official**, which refers to an authority or public organization

> ✓ **cious** not **tious**: **officious**

offing »*noun* (**in the offing**) likely to happen or appear soon.

off-key »*adjective & adverb* ❶ (in music) not in the correct key or of the correct pitch. ❷ inappropriate.

off-licence »*noun* (in the UK) a shop selling alcoholic drink to be drunk elsewhere.

off-limits

off-line »*adjective* not connected to a computer.

offload (verb: **offloads, offloading, offloaded**)

off-peak »*adjective & adverb* at a time when demand is less.

off-piste »*adjective & adverb* away from prepared ski runs.

offprint »*noun* a printed copy of an article that originally appeared as part of a larger publication.

off-putting

offset »*verb* (**offsets, offsetting, offset**) cancel out something with an equal and opposite force or effect.

offshoot

offshore »*adjective & adverb* ❶ situated at sea some distance from the shore. ❷ (of the wind) blowing towards the sea from the land. ❸ situated or registered abroad.

offside »*adjective & adverb* (in games such as football) occupying a position on the field where playing the ball is not allowed.
» *noun* the side of a vehicle furthest from the kerb.

offspring

offstage »*adjective & adverb* (in a theatre) not on the stage and so not visible to the audience.

off-white

oft »*adverb* (an old word) often.

often »*adverb* ❶ frequently. ❷ in many instances.

> ℹ the comparative and superlative are usually **more often** and **most often**, not **oftener** and **oftenest**

> ✓ remember the **t** (usually silent) after of-: **often**

ogle »*verb* (**ogles, ogling, ogled**) stare at someone in a lecherous way.

ogre »*noun* ❶ (in folklore) a man-eating giant. ❷ a cruel or terrifying person.

> ✓ re not er: **ogre**

ogress (plural **ogresses**)

oh

ohm »*noun* the basic unit of electrical resistance.

oik »*noun* (in informal English) a rude or unpleasant person.

oil (verb: **oils, oiling, oiled**)

oilcan

oilcloth »*noun* cotton fabric treated with oil to make it waterproof.

oiled

oilfield

oil-fired »*adjective* using oil as fuel.

oilier

oiliest

oiliness

oiling

oil rig »*noun* a structure that stands on the seabed to provide a stable base above water for drilling oil wells.

oils

oilseed »*noun* seed from a cultivated crop that produces oil, especially rape.

oilskin »*noun* ❶ heavy cotton cloth waterproofed with oil. ❷ (**oilskins**) a set of garments made of oilskin.

oily »*adjective* (**oilier, oiliest**) ❶ containing or covered with oil. ❷ resembling oil. ❸ (of a person) unpleasantly smooth and overly flattering.
oiliness

> ✓ drop the **y** and add **ier** or **iest** to spell **oilier** or **oiliest**
> remember that the **y** becomes **i** in **oiliness**

oink [noise of pig]

ointment

OK (verb: **OK's, OK'ing, OK'd**)

> ✓ **OK** can also be spelled **okay** (**okay, okaying, okayed**): both spellings are correct

okapi »*noun* (plural **okapi** or **okapis**) a large plant-eating African mammal with stripes on the hindquarters and upper legs.
– **say** oh-**kah**-pi

okay another way of spelling **OK**.

OK'd

OK'ing

okra »*noun* the long ridged seed pods of a tropical plant, eaten as a vegetable.
– **say** ok-ruh or oh-kruh

OK's

old (adjective: **older, oldest**)
oldish

old-age pensioner

olde »*adjective* old-fashioned in a way that is intended to be attractively quaint.
– **say** ohld or **ohl**-di

> ℹ **olde** is a deliberately old-fashioned spelling of **old**

olden »*adjective* of a former age.

Old English »*noun* the language of the Anglo-Saxons (up to about 1150).

older

oldest

old-fashioned

oldie

oldish

Old Nick »*noun* an informal name for the Devil.

old-time »*adjective* pleasingly traditional or old-fashioned.

old-timer »*noun* (in informal English) a very experienced or long-serving person.

old wives' tale

Old World »*noun* Europe, Asia, and Africa, seen together as the part of the world known before the discovery of the Americas.

ole »*exclamation* bravo!
– **say** oh-**lay**

✓ the **e** is often written with an acute accent, as in the original Spanish: **olé**

oleaginous »*adjective* ❶ oily.
❷ excessively flattering: *oleaginous speeches.*
– SAY oh-li-**aj**-i-nuhss

oleander »*noun* an evergreen shrub with clusters of white, pink, or red flowers.
– SAY oh-li-**an**-der

olfactory »*adjective* relating to the sense of smell.
– SAY ol-**fak**-tuh-ri

✓ ory not ery: **olfactory**

oligarch »*noun* a ruler in an oligarchy.
– SAY **ol**-i-gark

oligarchy »*noun* (plural **oligarchies**) ❶ a small group of people having control of a state. ❷ a state governed by such a group.
oligarchic

✓ plural: drop the **y** and add **ies**: **oligarchies**

Oligocene »*adjective* (in geology) relating to the geological period from about 35.4 to 23.3 million years ago.
– SAY **ol**-i-goh-seen

olive

Olympiad »*noun* ❶ a staging of the Olympic Games. ❷ a period of four years between Olympic Games.
– SAY uh-**lim**-pi-ad

Olympian »*adjective* ❶ having to do with Mount Olympus, traditional home of the Greek gods. ❷ superior and aloof like a god. ❸ relating to the Olympic Games.
»*noun* ❶ one of the twelve Greek gods living on Mount Olympus. ❷ a person who is greatly admired. ❸ a competitor in the Olympic Games.

Olympic

Olympic Games »*plural noun* ❶ a sports festival held every four years in different countries. ❷ an ancient Greek festival with athletic and arts competitions, held every four years.

Omani [of Oman]
– SAY oh-**mah**-ni

ombudsman »*noun* (plural **ombudsmen**) an official who investigates people's complaints against companies or the government.
– SAY **om**-buudz-muhn

ℹ **ombudsman** comes from Swedish, meaning 'legal representative'. The gender-neutral term **ombudsperson** can also be used.

omega »*noun* the last letter of the Greek alphabet (Ω, ω).
– SAY oh-mi-guh

omelette

✓ double **t**, and **e** at the end: **omelette** (the spelling **omelet** is American)

omen

omicron »*noun* the fifteenth letter of the Greek alphabet (O, o).
– SAY oh-**my**-kron

ominous »*adjective* suggesting that something bad is going to happen.
ominously

omissible

✓ one **m**, double **s**: **omissible**

omission

✓ one **m**, double **s**: **omission**

omit (verb: **omits**, **omitting**, **omitted**)

✓ double the **t** in **omitting** and **omitted**

omnibus »*noun* (plural **omnibuses**) ❶ a volume containing several works previously published separately. ❷ a single edition of two or more consecutive programmes previously broadcast separately. ❸ (old-fashioned) a bus.

ℹ **omnibus** is Latin for 'for all'

omnidirectional »*adjective* (in telecommunications) receiving signals from or transmitting in all directions.

omnipotent »*adjective* having unlimited or very great power.
– SAY om-**ni**-puh-tuhnt
omnipotence

omnipresent »*adjective* ❶ present everywhere at the same time.
❷ widespread: *the omnipresent threat of natural disasters.*
omnipresence

omniscient »*adjective* knowing everything.
– SAY om-**ni**-si-uhnt
omniscience

✓ remember the **c** in the middle: **omniscient**

omnivore »*noun* an omnivorous animal.
– SAY **om**-ni-vor

omnivorous »*adjective* feeding on both plants and meat.
– SAY om-**ni**-vuh-ruhss

on

onanism »*noun* masturbation.
– SAY **oh**-nuh-ni-z'm

once

once-over »*noun* (in informal English) a rapid inspection, search, or piece of work.

oncoming »*adjective* moving towards you.

one

one-armed bandit

one-liner »*noun* a short joke or witty remark.

one-man band

oneness »*noun* the state of being whole or in agreement.

one-night stand

one-off

onerous »*adjective* involving a lot of effort and difficulty.
– **SAY** oh-nuh-ruhss or on-uh-ruhss

oneself

one-sided

one-time

one-track mind

one-upmanship »*noun* the technique of gaining an advantage over someone else.

one-way

ongoing

onion

online »*adjective & adverb* controlled by or connected to a computer.

onlooker

only

onomatopoeia »*noun* the use of words that sound like the thing they refer to (e.g. *cuckoo, sizzle*).
– **SAY** on-uh-mat-uh-**pee**-uh
onomatopoeic

> ✓ **oeia** not just **ia** at the end:
> **onomatopoeia**

onrush »*noun* (plural **onrushes**) a surging rush forward.
onrushing

onset

onshore »*adjective & adverb* ❶ situated or occurring on land. ❷ (of the wind) blowing from the sea towards the land.

onside »*adjective & adverb* (in sport) not offside.

onslaught »*noun* ❶ a fierce or destructive attack. ❷ an overwhelmingly large quantity of people or things.

onstage »*adjective & adverb* (in a theatre) on the stage.

onto

> ℹ️ some people regard **onto** written as one word (instead of **on to**) as a mistake (unlike **into**). However, it is useful to distinguish meanings, e.g. between *we drove onto the beach* (i.e. in contact with it) and *we drove on to the beach* (i.e. further in that direction). In American English, **onto** is standard.

ontology »*noun* philosophy concerned with the nature of being.
– **SAY** on-**tol**-uh-ji
ontological

onus »*noun* (plural **onuses**) a responsibility.
– **SAY** oh-nuhss

onward

onwards

onyx »*noun* (plural **onyxes**) a semi-precious stone with layers of different colours.
– **SAY** o-niks or **oh**-niks

oodles »*plural noun* (in informal English) a very great number or amount.

oolite »*noun* limestone consisting of a mass of rounded grains.
– **SAY** oh-uh-lyt

oomph »*noun* (in informal English) excitement, energy, or sexual attractiveness.

oops »*exclamation* (in informal English) used to show awareness of a mistake or minor accident.

ooze (verb: **oozes, oozing, oozed**)
oozy

op »*noun* a surgical operation.

opacity »*noun* the condition of being opaque.
– **SAY** oh-**pa**-si-ti

opal »*noun* a semi-transparent gemstone in which small points of shifting colour can be seen.

opalescent »*adjective* having small points of shifting colour.

> ✓ remember the **c**: **opalescent**

opaque »*adjective* ❶ not able to be seen through. ❷ difficult or impossible to understand.
– **SAY** oh-**payk**

op. cit. »*adverb* in the work already cited.

> ℹ️ from the Latin phrase *opere citato*

open (verb: **opens, opening, opened**)
openly
openness

opencast »*adjective* (of mining) in which coal or ore is extracted from a level near the earth's surface, rather than from shafts.

opened

open-ended »*adjective* having no limit decided in advance.

opener

open-handed »*adjective* generous.

open-heart surgery »*noun* surgery in which the heart is exposed.

opening

open letter »*noun* a letter addressed to a particular person but intended to be published.

openly

open market »*noun* a situation in which companies can trade without restrictions.

open-minded »*adjective* willing to consider new ideas.

openness

> ✓ two **n**'s in **openness**

open-plan »*adjective* having large rooms with few or no dividing walls.

open prison »*noun* a prison with the minimum of restrictions on prisoners' movements and activities.

opens

open season »*noun* the period of the year when restrictions on the killing of certain types of wildlife are lifted.

open-topped

open verdict »*noun* (in law) a verdict that a person's death is suspicious but that the cause is not known.

openwork »*noun* ornamental work in cloth, leather, etc. with regular patterns of openings and holes.

opera[1] [a dramatic work set to music]

opera[2] plural of **opus**.

operable

operate (verb: **operates, operating, operated**)

> ✓ one **p**, one **r**: **operate**

operatic »*adjective* having to do with opera.

operating

operating system »*noun* the low-level software that supports a computer's basic functions.

operating theatre »*noun* a room in which surgical operations are performed.

operation
operational
operationally

> ✓ double the **l** in **operationally**

operations room »*noun* a room from which military or police operations are directed.

operative
operatively

operator

> ✓ **-or** not **-er**: **operator**

operculum »*noun* (plural **opercula**) ❶ a flap of skin protecting a fish's gills. ❷ a plate that closes the opening of a mollusc's shell.
– **say** oh-**per**-kyuu-luhm

> ✓ like many other words ending in **um** derived from Latin, **operculum** has a plural ending in **a**: **opercula**

operetta »*noun* a short opera on a light or humorous theme.

> ✓ one **p**, one **r**, and two **t**'s: **operetta**

ophthalmia »*noun* (in medicine) inflammation of the eye.
– **say** off-**thal**-mi-uh

> ✓ **ph** then **th** in **ophthalmia** and the related words **ophthalmic** and **ophthalmology**

ophthalmic »*adjective* relating to the eye and its diseases.

ophthalmology »*noun* the study and treatment of disorders and diseases of the eye.
– **say** off-thal-**mol**-uh-ji
ophthalmologist

opiate »*noun* a drug containing opium.
– **say** oh-pi-uht

opine »*verb* (**opines, opining, opined**) state as your opinion.

opinion

opinionated

opium »*noun* an addictive drug prepared from the juice of a poppy.

opossum »*noun* ❶ an American marsupial with a tail which it can use for grasping. ❷ (in Australian English) a possum.
– **say** uh-**poss**-uhm

> ✓ one **p**, two **s**'s: **opossum**

opponent

> ✓ double **p**, single **n**: **opponent**

opportune »*adjective* happening or done at an especially convenient or appropriate time.
opportunely

o

☑ double p and -or- not -er- in the middle: **opportune**

opportunist »*noun* a person who takes advantage of opportunities without worrying about whether or not they are right to do so.
» *adjective* taking advantage of immediate opportunities.
opportunism
opportunistic
opportunistically

opportunity (plural **opportunities**)

☑ plural: drop the **y** and add **ies**: **opportunities**

opposable »*adjective* (of the thumb of a primate) capable of facing and touching the other digits on the same hand.

oppose (verb: **opposes**, **opposing**, **opposed**)

☑ double p in **oppose** and related words such as **opposite** and **opposition**

opposite
oppositely

opposition
oppositional

oppress (verb: **oppresses**, **oppressing**, **oppressed**)
oppression
oppressor

☑ double p and double s in **oppress**, **oppressive**, and related words

oppressive
oppressively
oppressiveness

oppressor

opprobrious »*adjective* highly scornful.
– SAY uh-**proh**-bri-uhss

☑ double p and two r's in **opprobrious**

opprobrium »*noun* ❶ harsh criticism or scorn. ❷ public disgrace as a result of shameful behaviour.
– SAY uh-**proh**-bri-uhm

opt (verb: **opts**, **opting**, **opted**)

optic »*adjective* relating to the eye or vision.
» *noun* ❶ a lens or similar part in an optical instrument. ❷ (trademark) a device fastened to the neck of an upside down bottle for measuring out spirits.

optical »*adjective* relating to vision, light, or optics.
optically

optical fibre »*noun* a thin glass fibre through which light can be transmitted.
optically

optician

☑ **cian** not **tian**: **optician**

optics »*noun* the branch of science concerned with vision and the behaviour of light.

optimal »*adjective* best or most favourable.
optimally

optimise another way of spelling **OPTIMIZE**.

optimism »*noun* hopefulness and confidence about the future or the success of something.
optimist
optimistic
optimistically

☑ **opti** not **opto**: **optimism**

optimize »*verb* (**optimizes**, **optimizing**, **optimized**) make the best use of a situation or resource.
optimization

☑ many people prefer the alternative spellings **optimise**, **optimises**, etc., and **optimisation**: both **s** and **z** spellings are correct

optimum »*adjective* most likely to lead to a favourable outcome.
» *noun* (plural **optima** or **optimums**) the most favourable conditions for growth, reproduction, or success.

☑ the plural of **optimum** can be **optima** (like the original Latin) or **optimums**

opting

option

optional »*adjective* available to be chosen but not compulsory.
optionally

optometry »*noun* the occupation of measuring eyesight, prescribing corrective lenses, and detecting eye disease.
optometrist

opts

opulent »*adjective* showily rich and luxurious.
– SAY op-yuu-luhnt
opulence
opulently

☑ one **p**, one **l**: **opulent**

opus »*noun* (plural **opuses** or **opera**) ❶ (in music) a separate composition or set of compositions. ❷ an artistic work.
– SAY oh-**puhss** [singular], op-uh-ruh [plural]

☑ the plural of **opus** (a Latin word meaning 'work') can be **opuses** or the Latin form **opera**

or

oracle »*noun* ❶ (in ancient Greece or Rome) a priest or priestess who acted as a channel for advice or prophecy from the gods. ❷ an authority which is always correct.

oracular »*adjective* ❶ having to do with an oracle. ❷ hard to interpret.
– sᴀʏ o-**rak**-yuu-ler

oral »*adjective* ❶ spoken rather than written. ❷ relating to the mouth. ❸ done or taken by the mouth.
» *noun* a spoken examination.
orally

> ⓘ do not confuse **oral** with **aural**, which means 'having to do with the ear or hearing': both words have the same pronunciation

orange

orangeade

Orangeman »*noun* (plural **Orangemen**) a member of the Orange Order.

Orange Order »*noun* a Protestant political society in Northern Ireland.

> ⓘ named after the Protestant king William of *Orange* (William III of Great Britain and Ireland)

orangery »*noun* (plural **orangeries**) a building like a large conservatory where orange trees are grown.

orang-utan »*noun* a large tree-dwelling ape with long red hair.
– sᴀʏ uh-**rang**-oo-tan

> ✓ **orang-utan** can also be spelled **orang-utang**

orate »*verb* (**orates**, **orating**, **orated**) make a long or pompous speech.

oration »*noun* a formal speech.

orator »*noun* a skilful public speaker.
oratorial

> ✓ -**or** not -**er**: **orator**

oratorical

oratories

oratorio »*noun* (plural **oratorios**) a large-scale musical work on a religious theme for orchestra and voices.
– sᴀʏ o-ruh-**tor**-i-oh

> ✓ the plural of **oratorio** (an Italian word) has **os** not **oes**: **oratorios**

oratory »*noun* (plural **oratories**) ❶ a small chapel for private worship. ❷ formal public speaking. ❸ exaggerated or eloquent language.

– sᴀʏ o-ruh-tri
oratorical

orb »*noun* ❶ a spherical object or shape. ❷ a golden globe with a cross on top, carried by a king or queen.

orbicular »*adjective* circular or spherical.
– sᴀʏ or-**bik**-yuu-ler

orbit »*noun* ❶ the regularly repeated course of a celestial object or spacecraft around a star or planet. ❷ a field of activity or influence.
» *verb* (**orbits**, **orbiting**, **orbited**) move in orbit round a star or planet.
orbiter

> ✓ do not double the **t** in **orbiting** and **orbited**

orbital »*adjective* ❶ relating to an orbit or orbits. ❷ (of a road) passing round the outside of a town.

orbited

orbiter

orbiting

orbits

orchard

orchestra
orchestral
orchestrally

orchestrate »*verb* (**orchestrates**, **orchestrating**, **orchestrated**) ❶ arrange music for performance by an orchestra. ❷ direct a situation to produce a desired effect.
orchestration
orchestrator

orchid »*noun* a plant with bright, unusually shaped flowers.

ordain »*verb* (**ordains**, **ordaining**, **ordained**) ❶ make someone a priest or minister. ❷ officially order something. ❸ (of God or fate) decide something in advance.

ordeal

order (verb: **orders**, **ordering**, **ordered**)

> ✓ do not double the **r** in **ordering** and **ordered**

orderly »*adjective* ❶ neatly and methodically arranged. ❷ well behaved.
» *noun* (plural **orderlies**) ❶ a hospital attendant responsible for various non-medical tasks. ❷ a soldier who carries orders or performs minor tasks for an officer.
orderliness

> ✓ plural: drop the **y** and add **ies**: **orderlies**

order of magnitude »*noun* ❶ a level in a system of ordering things by size or amount, where each level is higher by a factor of ten. ❷ size or quantity.

ordinal »*adjective* relating to order in a series.

ordinal number »*noun* a number defining a thing's position in a series, such as 'first' or 'second'.

ordinance »*noun* ❶ an official order. ❷ a religious rite.

> ℹ️ do not confuse **ordinance** with **ordnance**, which means 'mounted guns' or 'military equipment and stores'

ordinary
    ordinarily
    ordinariness

ordinate »*noun* (in mathematics) a straight line from a point on a graph drawn parallel to the vertical axis and meeting the other; the y-coordinate.
– SAY or-di-nuht

ordination »*noun* the action of ordaining someone as a priest or minister.

ordnance »*noun* ❶ mounted guns. ❷ (in American English) military equipment and stores. ❸ a government department dealing with military stores and materials.
– SAY ord-nuhnss

> ℹ️ do not confuse **ordnance** with **ordinance**, which means 'an official order' or 'a religious rite'

Ordnance Survey »*noun* (in the UK) an official survey organization preparing large-scale detailed maps of the whole country.

Ordovician »*adjective* relating to the geological period from about 510 to 439 million years ago.
– SAY or-duh-**vish**-i-uhn

ordure »*noun* (an old word) dung.
– SAY or-dyuur

ore »*noun* a naturally occurring material from which a metal or valuable mineral can be extracted.

oregano »*noun* a plant with small purple flowers and leaves used as a herb in cookery.
– SAY o-ri-**gah**-noh or uh-**reg**-uh-noh

organ
    organist

organdie »*noun* a fine, semi-transparent, stiff cotton muslin.
– SAY or-guhn-di

> ✅ ie not y at the end: **organdie** (the spelling **organdy** is American)

organic »*adjective* ❶ having to do with living matter. ❷ produced without artificial chemicals such as fertilizers. ❸ (in chemistry) having to do with compounds containing carbon and chiefly or ultimately of biological origin. ❹ having to do with a bodily organ or organs. ❺ (of the parts of a whole) fitting together harmoniously. ❻ (of development or change) continuous or natural.
    organically

organise another way of spelling **ORGANIZE**.

organism »*noun* ❶ an individual animal, plant, or single-celled life form. ❷ a whole made up of parts which are dependent on each other.

organist

organization
    organizational

organize (verb: **organizes, organizing, organized**)
    organizer

> ✅ many people prefer the alternative spellings **organise, organises**, etc., **organiser**, and **organisation**: both **s** and **z** spellings are correct

organza »*noun* a thin, stiff, transparent fabric.
– SAY or-**gan**-zuh

orgasm »*noun* the climax of sexual excitement, experienced as intensely pleasurable sensations centred in the genitals.
» *verb* (**orgasms, orgasming, orgasmed**) have an orgasm.
    orgasmic

orgiastic »*adjective* relating to or like an orgy.
– SAY or-ji-**ass**-tik

orgy »*noun* (plural **orgies**) ❶ a wild party with excessive drinking and much sexual activity. ❷ excessive indulgence in a specified activity: *an orgy of killing*.

> ✅ plural: drop the y and add ies: **orgies**

oriel window »*noun* a window in a large bay built in the upper story of a building.
– SAY **or**-i-uhl

orient »*noun* (**the Orient**) (a poetic term) the countries of the East.
» *verb* (**orients, orienting, oriented**)
❶ position something in relation to the points of a compass or other specified positions. ❷ (**orient yourself**) find your position in relation to unfamiliar surroundings. ❸ tailor something to meet

particular needs: *magazines oriented to students.*
– **SAY** or-i-uhnt [noun], or-i-ent [verb]

oriental »*adjective* having to do with the Far East.
» *noun* a person of Far Eastern descent.

> ℹ️ the term **oriental** is now considered old-fashioned and potentially offensive when used to refer people from the Far East. In America, **Asian** is the standard modern term; in Britain, where **Asian** tends to refer to people from the Indian subcontinent, specific terms such as **Chinese** or **Japanese** are more likely to be used.

orientate »*verb* (orientates, orientating, orientated) = ORIENT.

orientation »*noun* ❶ the action of orienting. ❷ a position in relation to something else. ❸ a person's attitude or natural tendency: *sexual orientation.*

oriented

orienteering »*noun* a competitive sport in which runners have to find their way across rough country with the aid of a map and compass.

orienting

orients

orifice »*noun* an opening in the body.
– **SAY** o-ri-fiss

origami »*noun* the Japanese art of folding paper into decorative shapes and figures.
– **SAY** o-ri-**gah**-mi

origin

original
  originality
  originally

original sin »*noun* (in Christian belief) the tendency to be evil that is thought to be present in all human beings.

originate »*verb* (originates, originating, originated) ❶ have a specified beginning. ❷ create or initiate something.
  origination
  originator

oriole »*noun* a brightly coloured bird with a musical call.
– **SAY** or-i-ohl

> ☑️ do not confuse **oriole** with **aureole**, which means 'a circle of light around the sun or moon'

orison »*noun* (a poetic term) a prayer.
– **SAY** o-ri-zuhn

ormolu »*noun* a gold-coloured alloy of copper, zinc, and tin used in decoration.
– **SAY** or-muh-loo

ornament
  ornamentation

> ☑️ **nam** not **nem**: ornament   **o**

ornamental
  ornamentally

ornamentation

ornate »*adjective* elaborately or highly decorated.
  ornately
  ornateness

ornithology »*noun* the scientific study of birds.
– **SAY** or-ni-**thol**-uh-ji
  ornithological
  ornithologist

orotund »*adjective* ❶ (of the voice) deep and impressive. ❷ (of writing or style) pompous.
– **SAY** o-roh-tund

orphan (verb: orphans, orphaning, orphaned)

> ☑️ do not double the **n** in **orphaning** and **orphaned**

orphanage »*noun* a home which cares for orphans.

> ☑️ **age** not **idge**: orphanage

orphaned

orphaning

orphans

orthodontics »*noun* the treatment of irregularities in the teeth and jaws.
– **SAY** or-thuh-**don**-tiks
  orthodontic
  orthodontist

orthodox »*adjective* ❶ in line with traditional or generally accepted beliefs. ❷ conventional or normal.
  orthodoxly

Orthodox Church »*noun* a branch of the Christian Church in Greece and eastern Europe.

orthodoxies

Orthodox Judaism »*noun* a branch of Judaism which teaches that the requirements of Jewish law and traditional custom must be strictly followed.

orthodoxly

orthodoxy »*noun* (plural orthodoxies) ❶ orthodox beliefs or practice. ❷ an idea which is generally accepted.

orthography »*noun* (plural orthographies) the conventional spelling system of a language.

– **SAY** or-**thog**-ruh-fi
orthographic

orthopaedics »*noun* the branch of
medicine concerned with the correction of
deformities of bones or muscles.
– **SAY** or-thuh-**pee**-diks
orthopaedic

> ✓ **paed** not **ped**: **orthopaedics** (the
> spelling **orthopedics** is American)

orthotics »*noun* the branch of medicine
concerned with the provision and use of
artificial supports or braces.
– **SAY** or-**thot**-iks
orthotic

Orwellian »*adjective* relating to the work
of the British novelist George Orwell,
especially the oppressive totalitarian state
depicted in *Nineteen Eighty-four*.

oryx »*noun* (plural **oryxes**) a large antelope
with long horns, found in arid regions of
Africa and Arabia.
– **SAY** o-riks

Oscar »*noun* (trademark in the US) the
nickname for a gold statuette given as an
Academy award.

oscillate »*verb* (**oscillates**, **oscillating**,
oscillated) ❶ move or swing back and
forth at a regular rate. ❷ waver between
extremes of opinion or emotion.
– **SAY** oss-i-layt
oscillation
oscillator
oscillatory

> ✓ **osc** not **oss**: **oscillate**

oscilloscope »*noun* a device for showing
changes in electrical current as waves on
the screen of a cathode ray tube.

osier »*noun* a small willow with long
flexible shoots used in basketwork.
– **SAY** oh-zi-er

osmium »*noun* a hard, dense silvery-white
metallic element.
– **SAY** oz-mi-uhm

osmoregulation »*noun* (in biology) the
control of water content and salt
concentration in an organism's body.

osmosis »*noun* ❶ a process by which
molecules of a solvent pass through a
semipermeable membrane from a less
concentrated solution into a more
concentrated one. ❷ the gradual
absorbing of ideas.
– **SAY** oz-**moh**-siss
osmotic

osprey »*noun* (plural **ospreys**) a large
black, grey, and white fish-eating bird of
prey.

osseous »*adjective* consisting of or turned
into bone.
– **SAY** oss-i-uhss

ossicle »*noun* a very small bone, especially
in the ear.
– **SAY** oss-i-k'l

ossify »*verb* (**ossifies**, **ossifying**, **ossified**)
❶ turn into bone or bony tissue. ❷ stop
developing: *ossified political institutions*.
– **SAY** oss-i-fl
ossification

ostensible »*adjective* apparently true, but
not necessarily so.
ostensibly

> ✓ **-ible** not **-able**: **ostensible**

ostentation »*noun* showy display which is
intended to impress.

ostentatious »*adjective* showy in a way
which is intended to impress.
– **SAY** oss-ten-**tay**-shuhss
ostentatiously

osteoarthritis »*noun* a condition in which
joint cartilage has decayed, causing pain
and stiffness.

osteopathy »*noun* a system of
complementary medicine involving the
manipulation of the bones and muscles.
– **SAY** oss-ti-**op**-uh-thi
osteopath
osteopathic

osteoporosis »*noun* a medical condition
in which the bones become brittle and
fragile.
– **SAY** oss-ti-oh-puh-**roh**-siss

ostinato »*noun* (plural **ostinatos** or
ostinati) a continually repeated musical
phrase or rhythm.
– **SAY** oss-ti-**nah**-toh [singular], oss-ti-**nah**-ti
[plural]

> ✓ **ostinato** is an Italian word meaning
> 'obstinate', and the plural can be
> formed with an **i** or an **s**

ostler »*noun* (a historical term) a man
employed at an inn to look after
customers' horses.
– **SAY** oss-ler

ostracize »*verb* (**ostracizes**, **ostracizing**,
ostracized) exclude someone from a
society or group.
– **SAY** oss-truh-syz
ostracism

> ✓ many people prefer the alternative
> spellings **ostracise**, **ostracises**, etc.:
> both **s** and **z** spellings are correct

ostrich
other

otherness

otherwise

other-worldly »*adjective* ❶ relating to an imaginary or spiritual world. ❷ having little awareness of the realities of life.

otiose »*adjective* serving no practical purpose.
– sᴀʏ oh-ti-ohss or oh-shi-ohss

otter »*noun* a fish-eating mammal with a long body, dense fur, and webbed feet, living partly in water and partly on land.

Ottoman »*adjective* (a historical term) relating to the Turkish empire ruled by Sultan Osman I and his successors from about 1300 to 1922.
» *noun* (plural **Ottomans**) a Turk of the Ottoman period.

ottoman »*noun* (plural **ottomans**) a low upholstered seat without a back or arms.

ouch

ought

> ℹ️ the correct way of forming negative statements with **ought** is *he ought not to have gone*. Sentences such as *he didn't ought to have gone* and *he hadn't ought to have gone* are sometimes heard but should not be used in writing.

oughtn't [ought not]

> ☑️ be careful to put the apostrophe where a letter has been left out, that is between the **n** and **t** of not: **oughtn't**

Ouija board »*noun* (trademark) a board with letters, numbers, and other signs around its edge, to which a pointer moves, supposedly in answer to questions at a seance.
– sᴀʏ wee-juh

ounce »*noun* ❶ a unit of weight of one sixteenth of a pound avoirdupois (approximately 28 grams). ❷ a very small amount.

our

ours

ourselves

oust »*verb* (**ousts**, **ousting**, **ousted**) drive someone out from a position of power.
– sᴀʏ owsst

out

> ℹ️ you should write **out of** rather than just **out** in sentences such as *he threw it out of the window*

outage »*noun* a period when a power supply or other service is not available.

outback »*noun* the part of Australia that is remote or sparsely populated.

outbid »*verb* (**outbids**, **outbidding**, **outbid**) bid more for something than someone else.

> ☑️ double the **d** in **outbidding**

outboard »*adjective & adverb* ❶ on, towards, or near the outside of a ship or aircraft. ❷ (of a motor) portable and attachable to the outside of the stern of a boat.

outbound »*adjective & adverb* going out or away from a place.

outbreak

outbuilding

outburst

outcast

outclass »*verb* (**outclasses**, **outclassing**, **outclassed**) be far better than someone else.

outcome

outcrop »*noun* a part of a rock formation that is visible on the surface.

outcry (plural **outcries**)

outdated

outdistance »*verb* (**outdistances**, **outdistancing**, **outdistanced**) leave a competitor or pursuer far behind.

outdo (verb: **outdoes**, **outdoing**, **outdid**; past participle **outdone**)

outdoor

outdoors

outer

outermost

outface »*verb* (**outfaces**, **outfacing**, **outfaced**) unsettle or defeat someone by confronting them boldly.

outfall »*noun* the place where a river or drain empties into the sea, a river, or a lake.

outfit (verb: **outfits**, **outfitting**, **outfitted**)

> ☑️ double the **t** in **outfitting** and **outfitted**

outfitter »*noun* (old-fashioned) a shop selling men's clothing.

outfitting

outflank »*verb* (**outflanks**, **outflanking**, **outflanked**) ❶ move round the side of an enemy so as to outmanoeuvre them. ❷ outwit someone.

outflow

outfox »*verb* (**outfoxes**, **outfoxing**, **outfoxed**) defeat someone by being more cunning than them.

o

outgoing »*adjective* ❶ friendly and confident. ❷ leaving an office or position. ❸ going out or away from a place.
» *noun* (**outgoings**) the money that you regularly spend.

outgrow (verb: **outgrows**, **outgrowing**, **outgrew**; past participle **outgrown**)

outgrowth

outgun »*verb* (**outguns**, **outgunning**, **outgunned**) have more or better weapons than someone else.

> ✓ double the **n** in **outgunning** and **outgunned**

outhouse

outing

outlandish »*adjective* bizarre or unfamiliar.
outlandishly

outlast »*verb* (**outlasts**, **outlasting**, **outlasted**) last longer than.

outlaw »*noun* a person who has broken the law and remains at large.
» *verb* (**outlaws**, **outlawing**, **outlawed**) make something illegal.

outlay »*noun* an amount of money spent.

outlet »*noun* ❶ a pipe or hole through which water or gas may escape. ❷ a point from which goods are sold or distributed. ❸ an output socket in an electrical device. ❹ a means of expressing your talents, energy, or emotions. ❺ the mouth of a river.

outlier »*noun* a thing detached from a main body or system.
– SAY owt-ly-er

outline (verb: **outlines**, **outlining**, **outlined**)

outlive (verb: **outlives**, **outliving**, **outlived**)

outlook

outlying »*adjective* situated far from a centre.

outmanoeuvre »*verb* (**outmanoeuvres**, **outmanoeuvring**, **outmanoeuvred**) ❶ evade an opponent by moving faster or more skilfully. ❷ use skill and cunning to gain an advantage over someone.

> ✓ **oeu** in the middle and **re** at the end: **outmanoeuvre**

outmoded »*adjective* old-fashioned.

outnumber (verb: **outnumbers**, **outnumbering**, **outnumbered**)

outpace »*verb* (**outpaces**, **outpacing**, **outpaced**) go faster than someone else.

outpatient »*noun* a patient attending a hospital for treatment without staying overnight.

outperform (verb: **outperforms**, **outperforming**, **outperformed**)

outplay (verb: **outplays**, **outplaying**, **outplayed**)

outpost »*noun* ❶ a small military camp at a distance from the main army. ❷ a remote part of a country or empire.

outpouring

output »*noun* ❶ the amount of something produced. ❷ the process of producing something. ❸ the power, energy, etc. supplied by a device or system. ❹ a place where power or information leaves a system.
» *verb* (**outputs**, **outputting**, **output** or **outputted**) (of a computer) produce data.

> ✓ double the **t** in **outputting** and **outputted**

outrage (verb: **outrages**, **outraging**, **outraged**)

outrageous
outrageously
outrageousness

outran past of OUTRUN.

outrank »*verb* (**outranks**, **outranking**, **outranked**) be of a higher rank or quality than someone else.

outre »*adjective* unusual and rather shocking.
– SAY OO-tray

> ✓ **outre** can also be spelled **outré**, with an acute accent above the **e** (as in the original French word meaning 'exceeded')

outreach »*verb* (**outreaches**, **outreaching**, **outreached**) reach further than someone else.
» *noun* ❶ the extent or length of reaching out. ❷ an organization's involvement with the community.

outrider »*noun* a person in a vehicle or on horseback who escorts or guards another vehicle.

outrigger »*noun* a float fixed parallel to a canoe or small ship in order to help keep it stable.

outright

outrun (verb: **outruns**, **outrunning**, **outran**; past participle **outrun**)

outsell (verb: **outsells**, **outselling**, **outsold**)

outset

outshine (verb: **outshines**, **outshining**, **outshone**)

outside

outsider

outsize

outsized

outskirts »*plural noun* the outer parts of a town or city.

outsmart (verb: **outsmarts**, **outsmarting**, **outsmarted**)

outsold past and past participle of **OUTSELL**.

outsource »*verb* (**outsources**, **outsourcing**, **outsourced**) ❶ obtain goods or a service from an outside supplier. ❷ arrange for work to be done outside a company.

outspoken

outspread

outstanding
   outstandingly

outstay (verb: **outstays**, **outstaying**, **outstayed**)

outstretch (verb: **outstretches**, **outstretching**, **outstretched**)

outstrip »*verb* (**outstrips**, **outstripping**, **outstripped**) ❶ move faster than and overtake someone. ❷ surpass something.

out-take »*noun* a sequence of a film or recording rejected during editing.

outvote (verb: **outvotes**, **outvoting**, **outvoted**)

outward
   outwardly

outwards

outweigh »*verb* (**outweighs**, **outweighing**, **outweighed**) be heavier, greater, or more significant than something else.

outwit »*verb* (**outwits**, **outwitting**, **outwitted**) deceive someone through being cleverer than them.

> double the t in **outwitting** and **outwitted**

ouzo »*noun* a Greek aniseed-flavoured spirit.
– **SAY** oo-zoh

ova plural of **OVUM**.

oval

ovary »*noun* (plural **ovaries**) ❶ a female reproductive organ in which eggs are produced. ❷ the base of the reproductive organ of a flower.
   ovarian

> 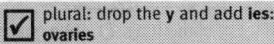 plural: drop the y and add ies: **ovaries**

ovate »*adjective* oval; egg-shaped.
– **SAY** oh-vayt

ovation »*noun* a long, enthusiastic round of applause.

oven

ovenproof

ovenware

over

overachieve »*verb* (**overachieves**, **overachieving**, **overachieved**) do better than expected.
   overachievement
   overachiever

overact »*verb* (**overacts**, **overacting**, **overacted**) act a role in an exaggerated way.

overactive

overall

overalls

overambitious

overanxious

overarch »*verb* (**overarches**, **overarching**, **overarched**) ❶ form an arch over something. ❷ (**overarching**) covering everything: *a single overarching principle*.

overarm

overate past of **OVEREAT**.

overawe »*verb* (**overawes**, **overawing**, **overawed**) impress someone so much that they are silent or nervous.

overbalance (verb: **overbalances**, **overbalancing**, **overbalanced**)

overbearing »*adjective* unpleasantly overpowering.

overbite »*noun* the overlapping of the lower teeth by the upper.

overblown »*adjective* exaggerated or pretentious.

overboard

overbook »*verb* (**overbooks**, **overbooking**, **overbooked**) accept more reservations for a flight or hotel than there is room for.

overburden »*verb* (**overburdens**, **overburdening**, **overburdened**) give someone too much work.

overcame past of **OVERCOME**.

overcast »*adjective* (of the sky or weather) cloudy.

overcautious
   overcaution

overcharge »*verb* (**overcharges**, **overcharging**, **overcharged**) charge too high a price.

overcoat

overcome (verb: **overcomes**, **overcoming**, **overcame**; past participle **overcome**)

overcommit »*verb* (**overcommits**, **overcommitting**, **overcommitted**) (**overcommit yourself**) agree to do more than you are capable of.

O

overcompensate »*verb* (**overcompensates, overcompensating, overcompensated**) do too much when trying to correct a problem.
overcompensation
overcompensatory

overconfident
overconfidence
overconfidently

overcook (verb: **overcooks, overcooking, overcooked**)

overcrowd (verb: **overcrowds, overcrowding, overcrowded**)

overdevelop »*verb* (**overdevelops, overdeveloping, overdeveloped**) develop something too much.

overdo (verb: **overdoes, overdoing, overdid;** past participle **overdone**)

overdose »*noun* an excessive and dangerous dose of a drug.
» *verb* (**overdoses, overdosing, overdosed**) take an overdose.

overdraft »*noun* an arrangement with a bank that lets you take out more money than your account holds.

overdrawn »*adjective* having taken out more money than there is in your bank account.

overdressed »*adjective* dressed too elaborately or formally.

overdrive »*noun* ❶ a mechanism in a motor vehicle providing an extra gear above the usual top gear. ❷ a state of high activity.

overdue

overeager

overeat (verb: **overeats, overeating, overate;** past participle **overeaten**)

overemphasize (verb: **overemphasizes, overemphasizing, overemphasized**)
overemphasis

> ☑ many people prefer the alternative spellings **overemphasise, overemphasises,** etc.: both **s** and **z** spellings are correct

overenthusiasm
overenthusiastic

overestimate (verb: **overestimates, overestimating, overestimated**)
overestimation

overexcite (verb: **overexcites, overexciting, overexcited**)
overexcitement

overexert »*verb* (**overexerts, overexerting, overexerted**) (**overexert yourself**) make too great a mental or physical effort.
overexertion

overexpose (verb: **overexposes, overexposing, overexposed**)
overexposure

overfamiliar »*adjective* ❶ too well known. ❷ informal in a way which is not appropriate.
overfamiliarity

overfill (verb: **overfills, overfilling, overfilled**)

overflow (verb: **overflows, overflowing, overflowed**)

overground

overgrown
overgrowth

overhand

overhang (verb: **overhangs, overhanging, overhung**)

overhaul »*verb* (**overhauls, overhauling, overhauled**) ❶ examine and repair something. ❷ overtake.
» *noun* an act of overhauling.

overhead

overheads »*noun* expenses incurred in running a business or organization.

overhear (verb: **overhears, overhearing, overheard**)

overheat (verb: **overheats, overheating, overheated**)

overindulge »*verb* (**overindulges, overindulging, overindulged**) ❶ have too much of something enjoyable. ❷ give in to the wishes of someone too easily.
overindulgence
overindulgent

overjoyed

overkill »*noun* too much of something.

overlaid past and past participle of OVERLAY.

overlain past participle of OVERLIE.

overland »*adjective & adverb* by land.

overlap (verb: **overlaps, overlapping, overlapped**)

> ☑ double the **p** to spell **overlapping** and **overlapped**

overlay »*verb* (**overlays, overlaying, overlaid**) (often **be overlaid with**) ❶ coat the surface of something. ❷ add a quality, feeling, etc. to something.
» *noun* a covering.

overleaf »*adverb* on the other side of the page.

overlie »*verb* (**overlies, overlying, overlay;** past participle **overlain**) lie on top of something.

overload (verb: **overloads**, **overloading**, **overloaded**)

overlook (verb: **overlooks**, **overlooking**, **overlooked**)

overlord »*noun* a ruler.

overly »*adverb* excessively.

overlying present participle of **OVERLIE**.

overmuch »*adverb, determiner, & pronoun* too much.

overnight

overpaid

overpass »*noun* (plural **overpasses**) a bridge by which a road or railway line passes over another.

overpay (verb: **overpays**, **overpaying**, **overpaid**)
overpayment

overplay »*verb* (**overplays**, **overplaying**, **overplayed**) give too much importance to something.

overpower (verb: **overpowers**, **overpowering**, **overpowered**)
overpowering

overpriced

overprotective

overqualified

overran past of **OVERRUN**.

overrate (verb: **overrates**, **overrating**, **overrated**)
overrated

 note the double r: **overrate**

overreach »*verb* (**overreaches**, **overreaching**, **overreached**) (**overreach yourself**) fail through being too ambitious or trying too hard.

overreact (verb: **overreacts**, **overreacting**, **overreacted**)
overreaction

 note the double r: **overreact**

override (verb: **overrides**, **overriding**, **overrode**; past participle **overridden**)
overriding

overrule (verb: **overrules**, **overruling**, **overruled**)

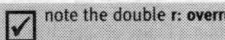 note the double r: **overrule**

overrun (verb: **overruns**, **overrunning**, **overran**; past participle **overrun**)

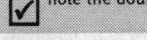 note the double r: **overrun**

oversaw

overseas

oversee »*verb* (**oversees**, **overseeing**, **oversaw**; past participle **overseen**) supervise.
overseer

oversexed »*adjective* having unusually strong sexual desires.

overshadow (verb: **overshadows**, **overshadowing**, **overshadowed**)

overshoes

overshoot »*verb* (**overshoots**, **overshooting**, **overshot**) accidentally go past the place you intended to stop at.

oversight »*noun* an unintentional failure to notice or do something.

oversimplify (verb: **oversimplifies**, **oversimplifying**, **oversimplified**)
oversimplification

oversize

oversized

oversleep (verb: **oversleeps**, **oversleeping**, **overslept**)

overspend (verb: **overspends**, **overspending**, **overspent**)

overspill »*noun* people who move from an overcrowded area to live elsewhere.

overstate »*verb* (**overstates**, **overstating**, **overstated**) state something too strongly; exaggerate.
overstatement

overstay (verb: **overstays**, **overstaying**, **overstayed**)

overstep (verb: **oversteps**, **overstepping**, **overstepped**)

overstretch (verb: **overstretches**, **overstretching**, **overstretched**)

oversubscribed »*adjective* available in quantities that are too small to satisfy demand.

overt »*adjective* done or shown openly.
– **SAY** oh-**vert**
overtly

overtake (verb: **overtakes**, **overtaking**, **overtook**; past participle **overtaken**)

overthrow (verb: **overthrows**, **overthrowing**, **overthrew**; past participle **overthrown**)

overtime

overtly

overtone »*noun* a subtle or secondary quality or implication.

overtook

overture »*noun* ❶ an orchestral piece at the beginning of a musical work. ❷ an orchestral composition in one movement. ❸ (**overtures**) approaches made with the aim of opening negotiations or establishing a relationship.

overturn (verb: **overturns, overturning, overturned**)

overuse (verb: **overuses, overusing, overused**)

overview »*noun* a general review or summary.

overweening »*adjective* showing too much confidence or pride.

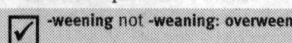
-weening not -weaning: overweening

overweight »*adjective* above a normal, desirable, or permitted weight.

overwhelm (verb: **overwhelms, overwhelming, overwhelmed**)
overwhelming
overwhelmingly

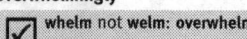
whelm not welm: overwhelm

overwinter »*verb* (**overwinters, overwintering, overwintered**) ❶ spend the winter in a specified place. ❷ (of an insect, plant, etc.) survive through the winter.

overwork (verb: **overworks, overworking, overworked**)

overwrite »*verb* (**overwrites, overwriting, overwrote; past participle overwritten**) ❶ write on top of other writing. ❷ destroy computer data by entering new data in its place.

overwrought »*adjective* ❶ in a state of nervous excitement or anxiety. ❷ too elaborate or complicated.

overzealous »*adjective* excessively enthusiastic or energetic.

ovulate »*verb* (**ovulates, ovulating, ovulated**) (of a woman or female animal) discharge ova (reproductive cells) from the ovary.
– **say** ov-yuu-layt
ovulation

ovum »*noun* (plural **ova**) a female reproductive cell, which can develop into an embryo if fertilized by a male cell.
– **say** oh-vuhm

the plural of **ovum** is **ova** (as in the original Latin word meaning 'egg')

owe (verb: **owes, owing, owed**)

owing

owl
owlet

owlish »*adjective* like an owl.
owlishly

own (verb: **owns, owning, owned**)

owner
ownership

owner-occupier »*noun* a person who owns the house or flat in which they live.

owning

owns

ox (plural **oxen**)

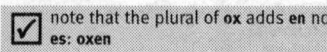
note that the plural of **ox** adds **en** not **es: oxen**

oxbow »*noun* a loop formed by a bend in a river.

Oxbridge »*noun* Oxford and Cambridge universities considered together.

oxen plural of **ox**.

ox-eye daisy »*noun* a daisy which has large white flowers with yellow centres.

oxidation

oxide »*noun* a compound of oxygen with another substance.

oxidise another way of spelling **oxidize**.

oxidization

oxidization can also be spelled oxidisation: both **s** and **z** spellings are correct

oxidize »*verb* (**oxidizes, oxidizing, oxidized**) cause something to combine with oxygen.

many people prefer the alternative spellings **oxidise, oxidises,** etc.: both **s** and **z** spellings are correct

oxtail »*noun* the tail of an ox, used in making soup.

oxyacetylene »*adjective* (of welding or cutting techniques) using a very hot flame produced by mixing acetylene and oxygen.
– **say** ok-si-uh-**set**-i-leen

oxygen »*noun* a colourless, odourless, gas that forms about 20 per cent of the earth's atmosphere.

oxygenate »*verb* (**oxygenates, oxygenating, oxygenated**) supply or treat something with oxygen.
– **say** ok-si-juh-nayt
oxygenated
oxygenation

oxymoron »*noun* a figure of speech in which apparently contradictory terms appear together (e.g. *bittersweet*).
– **say** ok-si-**mor**-on

oyster

oystercatcher »*noun* a wading bird with black or black-and-white plumage and an orange-red bill.

Oz »*noun & adjective* (in informal English) Australia or Australian.

ozone »*noun* a strong-smelling, poisonous form of oxygen.

ozone layer »*noun* a layer in the stratosphere containing a lot of ozone, which protects the earth from the sun's ultraviolet radiation.

Pp

PA »*abbreviation* ❶ personal assistant. ❷ public address.

pace[1] (verb: **paces, pacing, paced**) [a step; walk]

pace[2] »*preposition* with due respect to.
– SAY pah-chay or pay-si

> ℹ️ **pace**, a Latin term meaning 'in peace', is used before the name of someone with whom you are about to disagree, as in *narrative history, pace some theorists, is by no means dead*

paced

pacemaker »*noun* ❶ an artificial device for stimulating and regulating the heart muscle. ❷ a competitor who sets the pace at the beginning of a race or competition.

paces

pacey another way of spelling PACY.

pachyderm »*noun* a very large mammal with thick skin, e.g. an elephant.
– SAY pa-ki-derm

> ✓ pach- not pack-: pachyderm

pacier

paciest

pacific »*adjective* ❶ peaceful. ❷ (Pacific) relating to the Pacific Ocean.

pacification

pacified

pacifier »*noun* ❶ a person or thing that pacifies. ❷ (in American English) a baby's dummy.

pacifies

pacifism »*noun* the belief that disputes should be settled by peaceful means and that violence should never be used.
pacifist

pacify »*verb* (**pacifies, pacifying, pacified**) ❶ make someone less angry or agitated. ❷ make a country peaceful.

pacing

pack (verb: **packs, packing, packed**)
packer

package (verb: **packages, packaging, packaged**)

package holiday »*noun* a holiday organized by a travel agent, the price of which includes arrangements for transport and accommodation.

packager

packages

packaging

pack drill »*noun* a military punishment of marching up and down carrying full equipment.

packed

packer

packet

packhorse »*noun* a horse that is used to carry loads.

pack ice »*noun* a mass of ice floating in the sea.

packing

packs

pact »*noun* a formal agreement between individuals or parties.

pacy »*adjective* (**pacier, paciest**) fast-moving.

> ✓ pacy can also be spelled with an **ey** ending: **pacey**
> drop the **y** and add **ier** or **iest** to spell **pacier** or **paciest**

pad (verb: **pads, padding, padded**)
padded
padding

> ✓ double the **d** to spell **padding** and **padded**

paddle (verb: **paddles, paddling, paddled**)
paddler

paddle steamer »*noun* a boat powered by steam and propelled by large wheels which move the water as they turn.

paddling

paddock »*noun* ❶ a small field or enclosure for horses. ❷ an enclosure next to a racecourse or track where horses or cars are gathered and displayed before a race.

> ☑ note the double **d**: **paddock**

paddy »*noun* (plural **paddies**) a field where rice is grown.

> ☑ plural: drop the **y** and add **ies**: **paddies**

padlock (verb: **padlocks**, **padlocking**, **padlocked**)

padre »*noun* (in informal English) a chaplain in the armed services.
– sᴀʏ **pah**-dray

pads

paean »*noun* a song of praise or triumph.
– sᴀʏ **pee**-uhn

> ☑ **aea** not **ea**: **paean**

paediatrics »*noun* the branch of medicine concerned with children and their diseases.
– sᴀʏ pee-di-**at**-riks
paediatric
paediatrician

> ☑ **paed** not **ped**: **paediatrics** etc. (the spellings **pediatrics**, **pediatrician**, etc. are American)

paedophile »*noun* a person who is sexually attracted to children.
– sᴀʏ **pee**-duh-fyl
paedophilia

> ☑ **paed** not **ped**: **paedophile** (the spelling **pedophile** is American)

paella »*noun* a Spanish dish of rice, chicken, seafood, etc.
– sᴀʏ py-**el**-luh

> ☑ **pae** not **pie**: **paella**

pagan »*noun* a person who holds religious beliefs other than those of the main world religions.
» *adjective* relating to pagans or their beliefs.
paganism

page (verb: **pages**, **paging**, **paged**)

pageant »*noun* an entertainment performed by people in elaborate or historical costumes.
– sᴀʏ **pa**-juhnt

> ☑ note that the ending is **eant**: **pageant**

pageantry »*noun* elaborate display or ceremony.

pageboy »*noun* a boy or young man who works in a hotel or attends a bride at a wedding.

paged

pager »*noun* a small device which bleeps or vibrates to inform you that someone wants to contact you or that it has received a message.

pages

paginate »*verb* (**paginates**, **paginating**, **paginated**) give numbers to the pages of a book, magazine, etc.
– sᴀʏ **pa**-ji-nayt
pagination

paging

pagoda »*noun* a Hindu or Buddhist temple or other sacred building.
– sᴀʏ puh-**goh**-duh

paid past and past participle of **PAY**.

paid-up

pail [bucket]

> ℹ do not confuse **pail** with **pale**, which means 'of a light colour'

pain (verb: **pains**, **paining**, **pained**) [soreness or suffering; suffer pain]

> ℹ do not confuse **pain** with **pane** meaning 'a single sheet of glass'

pained »*adjective* showing or suffering pain.

painful
painfully
painfulness

> ☑ **-ful** not **-full**: **painful**

paining

painkiller
painkilling

painless
painlessly
painlessness

pains

painstaking »*adjective* very careful and thorough.
painstakingly

paint (verb: **paints**, **painting**, **painted**)

paintball »*noun* a combat game in which the players shoot capsules of paint at each other with air guns.

paintbox (plural **paintboxes**)

paintbrush

painted

painter¹ [artist]

painter[2] **»noun** a rope attached to the bow of a boat for tying it to a quay.

painterly **»adjective** ❶ artistic. ❷ (of a painting) using colour, stroke, and texture rather than firm outlines.

painting

paints

paintwork

pair (verb: **pairs**, **pairing**, **paired**) [set of two things]

> ℹ️ do not confuse **pair** with **pare**, which means 'trim something' or **pear**, the fruit

paisley **»noun** an intricate pattern of curved feather-shaped figures.
– **SAY** **payz**-li

> ℹ️ named after the town of *Paisley* in Scotland

pajamas American spelling of **PYJAMAS**.

Pakistani (plural **Pakistanis**)

pal

palace

paladin **»noun** (a historical term) a brave, chivalrous knight.
– **SAY** pa-**luh**-din

Palaeocene **»adjective** relating to the geological period from about 65 to 56.5 million years ago.
– **SAY** pa-li-oh-**seen** or pay-li-oh-**seen**

Palaeolithic **»adjective** relating to the early part of the Stone Age.
– **SAY** pa-li-uh-**lith**-ik or pay-li-uh-**lith**-ik

palaeontology **»noun** the branch of science concerned with fossil animals and plants.
– **SAY** pa-li-on-**tol**-uh-ji or pay-li-on-**tol**-uh-ji
palaeontologist

> ✓ in **palaeontology**, and in other words based on the prefix **palaeo-** 'older, ancient', such as **Palaeocene**, **Palaeolithic**, and **Palaeozoic**, the British spelling has **palaeo** while the American spelling begins **paleo** (**paleontology**, **Paleocene**, etc.)

Palaeozoic **»adjective** relating to the geological period from about 570 to 245 million years ago.
– **SAY** pa-li-uh-**zoh**-ik or pay-li-uh-**zoh**-ik

palanquin **»noun** (in India and the East) a covered vehicle for one passenger, enclosed by curtains and carried on men's shoulders or by animals.
– **SAY** pa-luhn-**keen**

palatable **»adjective** ❶ pleasant to taste. ❷ (of an action or proposal) acceptable.
– **SAY** pa-luh-tuh-**b'l**
palatability

palate **»noun** ❶ the roof of the mouth. ❷ a person's ability to distinguish between different flavours. ❸ a person's taste or liking.

> ℹ️ do not confuse **palate** with **palette**, which refers to an artist's board for mixing colours, or **pallet**, referring to a portable platform or a mattress or bed

palatial **»adjective** spacious or impressive, like a palace.
– **SAY** puh-**lay**-sh'l

palatinate **»noun** (a historical term) a territory under the jurisdiction of a palatine feudal lord.
– **SAY** puh-**lat**-i-nuht

palatine **»adjective** (mainly a historical term) ❶ (of an official or feudal lord) having local authority that elsewhere belongs only to a sovereign. ❷ (of a territory) subject to such authority.
– **SAY** pal-uh-tyn

palaver **»noun** lengthy and boring fuss or discussion.
– **SAY** puh-**lah**-ver

> ✓ **er** not **a** at the end: **palaver**

palazzo **»noun** (plural **palazzos** or **palazzi**) a large, grand building in Italy.
– **SAY** puh-**lat**-soh [singular], puh-**lat**-see [plural]

> ✓ the plural of **palazzo** can be **palazzos** or **palazzi** (as in the original Italian)

pale[1] (adjective: **paler**, **palest**; verb: **pales**, **paling**, **paled**) [of a light shade or colour; become pale]
palely
paleness

> ✓ do not confuse **pale** with **pail**, which means 'a bucket'

pale[2] **»noun** ❶ a wooden stake used with others to form a fence. ❷ a boundary.

palely

paleness

paleontology etc. American spelling of **PALAEONTOLOGY** etc.

paler

pales

palest

Palestinian

palette **»noun** ❶ a thin board on which an artist lays and mixes colours. ❷ the range of colours used by an artist.
– **SAY** pa-lit

> ℹ️ do not confuse **palette** with **palate**, which means 'the roof of the mouth',

p

or **pallet**, referring to a portable platform or a mattress or bed

✓ double **t** and an **e** at the end: **palette** is a French word meaning 'little shovel'

palette knife »*noun* ❶ a thin blade with a handle, for mixing colours or applying or removing paint. ❷ (in British English) a kitchen knife with a long, blunt, round-ended blade.

palimpsest »*noun* ❶ a parchment on which writing has been applied over earlier writing which has been erased. ❷ something used again or altered but still bearing traces of its earlier form: *the house is a palimpsest of the taste of successive owners.*
– SAY pa-limp-sesst

palindrome »*noun* a word or phrase that reads the same backwards as forwards, e.g. *madam.*
– SAY pa-lin-drohm

paling »*noun* ❶ a fence made from stakes. ❷ a stake used in such a fence.
– SAY pay-ling

palisade »*noun* a fence of stakes or iron railings.
– SAY pa-li-sayd

✓ one **l**, one **s**: **palisade**

pall[1] »*noun* ❶ a cloth spread over a coffin, hearse, or tomb. ❷ a dark cloud of smoke, dust, etc. ❸ a general atmosphere of gloom or fear.
– SAY pawl

pall[2] »*verb* (**palls**, **palling**, **palled**) become less appealing through being too familiar.
– SAY pawl

palladium »*noun* a rare silvery-white metallic element resembling platinum.
– SAY puh-lay-di-uhm

pall-bearer »*noun* a person helping to carry or escorting a coffin at a funeral.

palled

pallet »*noun* ❶ a straw mattress or makeshift bed. ❷ a portable platform on which goods can be moved, stacked, and stored.

✓ **et** not **ette** at the end: **pallet** (a **palette** is a board on which an artist mixes paints)

palliasse »*noun* a straw mattress.
– SAY pal-li-ass

palliate »*verb* (**palliates**, **palliating**, **palliated**) ❶ make the symptoms of a disease less severe without curing it. ❷ make something bad less severe.

– SAY pa-li-ayt
palliation

✓ double **i**: **palliate**

palliative »*noun* ❶ a medicine that relieves pain without curing it. ❷ something that makes a problem less severe but does not solve it.
» *adjective* having to do with a palliative.
– SAY pal-li-uh-tiv

pallid »*adjective* ❶ pale, especially because of poor health. ❷ feeble.

palling

pallor »*noun* an unhealthy pale appearance.

✓ **-or** not **-our**: **pallor**

palls

pally »*adjective* (in informal English) having a close, friendly relationship.

palm (verb: **palms**, **palming**, **palmed**)

palmate »*adjective* shaped like a hand with the fingers spread out.
– SAY pal-mayt

palmed

palmetto »*noun* (plural **palmettos**) an American palm with large fan-shaped leaves.
– SAY pal-met-toh

✓ the plural of **palmetto** has **os** not **oes**: **palmettos**

palmier [more palmy]

palmiest

palming

palmistry »*noun* the supposed interpretation of a person's character or prediction of their future by examining their palm.
palmist

palms

Palm Sunday »*noun* the Sunday before Easter.

palmtop »*noun* a computer small and light enough to be held in one hand.

palmy »*adjective* (**palmier**, **palmiest**) comfortable and prosperous: *the palmy days of the 1970s.*

palomino »*noun* (plural **palominos**) a pale golden or tan-coloured horse with a white mane and tail.
– SAY pa-luh-mee-noh

✓ the plural of **palomino** has **os** not **oes**: **palominos**

palpable »*adjective* ❶ able to be touched or felt. ❷ so powerful as to be almost touched or felt: *a palpable sense of loss.*
– SAY pal-puh-b'l
palpably

palpate »*verb* (**palpates, palpating, palpated**) medically examine a part of the body by touch.
– SAY pal-**payt**

palpitate »*verb* (**palpitates, palpitating, palpitated**) ❶ (of the heart) beat rapidly or irregularly. ❷ shake; tremble.
– SAY pal-pi-tayt

palpitation »*noun* ❶ throbbing or trembling. ❷ (**palpitations**) a noticeably rapid, strong, or irregular heartbeat.

palsy »*noun* (plural **palsies**) (old-fashioned) paralysis.
– SAY pawl-zi
palsied

paltry »*adjective* (**paltrier, paltriest**) ❶ (of an amount) very small. ❷ petty; trivial.
paltriness

pampas »*noun* large treeless plains in South America.
– SAY pam-puhss

pampas grass »*noun* a tall South American grass with silky flowering plumes.

pamper (verb: **pampers, pampering, pampered**)

pamphlet »*noun* a small booklet or leaflet containing information about a subject.
» *verb* (**pamphlets, pamphleting, pamphleted**) distribute pamphlets to people.
– SAY pam-flit

pamphleteer »*noun* a writer of pamphlets.
pamphleting
pamphlets

pan (verb: **pans, panning, panned**)

☑ double the n in **panning** and **panned**

panacea »*noun* a solution or remedy for all difficulties or diseases.
– SAY pan-uh-**see**-uh

panache »*noun* impressive confidence of style or manner.
– SAY puh-**nash**

☑ che at the end: **panache** is a French word

panama »*noun* a man's wide-brimmed hat of straw-like material.
Panamanian

panatella »*noun* a long thin cigar.
– SAY pa-nuh-**tel**-luh

☑ one n, two l's: **panatella**

pancake
Pancake Day »*noun* Shrove Tuesday, when pancakes are traditionally eaten.

panchromatic »*adjective* (of black-and-white photographic film) sensitive to all visible colours of the spectrum.

pancreas »*noun* (plural **pancreases**) a large gland behind the stomach which produces digestive enzymes and releases them into the duodenum.
– SAY pang-kri-uhss
pancreatic

☑ eas not eus: **pancreas**

panda
pandemic »*adjective* (of a disease) widespread over a whole country or large part of the world.
» *noun* an outbreak of such a disease.
– SAY pan-**dem**-ik

pandemonium »*noun* uproar or confusion.
– SAY pan-di-**moh**-ni-uhm

☑ dem, not dam or dim: **pandemonium**

pander »*verb* (**panders, pandering, pandered**) (**pander to**) indulge and go along with someone's unreasonable desire or habit.

Pandora's box »*noun* a process that once begun creates many complicated problems.

ℹ from *Pandora* in Greek mythology, who was sent to earth with a box of evils and let them escape

pane [single sheet of glass]

☑ do not confuse the spelling of **pane** with **pain** meaning 'soreness; suffering'

panegyric »*noun* a speech or text in praise of someone or something.
– SAY pa-ni-**ji**-rik

panel
panelled
panelling

☑ only one n and one l: **panel** (but double the l in **panelled** and **panelling**)

panel beater »*noun* a person whose job is to beat out the bodywork of motor vehicles.

panellist »*noun* a member of a panel taking part in a television or radio game or discussion.

☑ double l: **panellist** (the spelling **panelist** is American)

pan-fry »*verb* (**pan-fries, pan-frying, pan-fried**) fry food in a pan in shallow fat.

pang

pangolin »*noun* an insect-eating mammal whose body is covered with horny overlapping scales.
– SAY pang-guh-lin

panic (verb: **panics, panicking, panicked**) **panicky**

☑ add a k when spelling **panicking, panicked**, and **panicky**

panicle »*noun* a loose branching cluster of flowers.
– SAY pan-i-k'l

Panjabi another way of spelling **PUNJABI**.

pannier »*noun* ❶ a bag or box fitted on either side of the rear wheel of a bicycle or motorcycle. ❷ one of a pair of baskets carried by a donkey or similar animal.

☑ double n: **pannier**

panoply »*noun* a complete or impressive collection or display.
– SAY pan-uh-pli

panorama »*noun* ❶ a clear view of a surrounding region. ❷ a complete survey of a subject or sequence of events. **panoramic**

☑ **pano** not **pana**: **panorama**

pan pipes »*plural noun* a musical instrument made from a row of short pipes fixed together.

ℹ️ named after the Greek god of herds and pastures, *Pan*

pansy (plural **pansies**)

☑ plural: drop the **y** and add **ies**: **pansies**

pant (verb: **pants, panting, panted**)

pantaloons »*plural noun* ❶ women's baggy trousers gathered at the ankles. ❷ (a historical term) men's close-fitting breeches fastened below the calf or at the foot.

pantechnicon »*noun* a large van for transporting furniture.
– SAY pan-tek-ni-kuhn

panted

pantheism »*noun* ❶ the belief that God is present in all things. ❷ belief in many or all gods.
– SAY pan-thee-i-z'm **pantheistic**

pantheon »*noun* ❶ all the gods of a people or religion. ❷ an ancient temple dedicated to all the gods. ❸ a collection of particularly famous or important people.
– SAY pan-thi-uhn

☑ **eon** not **ion**: **pantheon**

panther

panties

pantile »*noun* a curved roof tile, fitted to overlap its neighbour.
– SAY pan-tyl

panting

panto »*noun* (plural **pantos**) a pantomime.

☑ the plural of **panto** has **os** not **oes**: **pantos**

pantograph »*noun* ❶ an instrument for copying a drawing on a different scale by a system of hinged and jointed rods. ❷ a framework conveying an electric current to a train or tram from overhead wires.

pantomime »*noun* a theatrical entertainment involving music, topical jokes, and slapstick comedy.

pantry »*noun* (plural **pantries**) a small room or cupboard in which food, crockery, and cutlery are kept.

☑ plural: drop the **y** and add **ies**: **pantries**

pants

pantyhose »*plural noun* (in American English) women's nylon tights.

panzer »*noun* (in the Second World War) a German armoured tank.

ℹ️ **panzer** is a German word meaning 'coat of mail'

pap[1] »*noun* ❶ bland soft or semi-liquid food suitable for babies or invalids. ❷ worthless or trivial reading matter or entertainment.

pap[2] »*noun* (an old word) a woman's breast or nipple.

papa

papacy »*noun* (plural **papacies**) the position or period of office of the pope.
– SAY pay-puh-si

papal »*adjective* relating to the pope or the papacy.
– SAY pay-p'l

paparazzo »*noun* (plural **paparazzi**) a freelance photographer who pursues celebrities to get photographs of them.
– SAY pa-puh-**rat**-soh [singular], pa-puh-**rat**-si [plural]

☑ one r, two z's: **paparazzo** is an Italian word and has the plural **paparazzi**. The word comes from the name of a character in Fellini's film *La Dolce Vita*.

papaw another way of spelling PAWPAW.

papaya »*noun* a tropical fruit like a long melon, with orange flesh and small black seeds.
– SAY puh-**py**-uh

paper (verb: **papers, papering, papered**)

paperback

papered

papering

paperknife (plural **paperknives**)

papers

paper-thin

paper tiger »*noun* a person or thing that appears threatening but is weak or ineffective.

paperweight

paperwork

papier mache »*noun* a mixture of paper and glue that is easily moulded but becomes hard when dry.
– SAY pa-pi-ay **mash**-ay

☑ **papier** (not **paper**) **mache** can also be spelled **papier mâché**, with a circumflex accent above the **a** and an acute accent above the **e** (as in the original French phrase meaning literally 'chewed paper')

papilla »*noun* (plural **papillae**) a small projection on a part of the body or on a plant.
– SAY puh-**pil**-luh [singular], puh-**pil**-lee [plural]

☑ make the plural by adding **e** (as in the original Latin): **papillae**

papilloma »*noun* (plural **papillomas** or **papillomata**) a small wart-like growth.
– SAY pa-pi-**loh**-muh [singular], pa-pi-**loh**-muh-tuh [plural]

☑ in medicine the Latin plural **papillomata** is often used, but the form with **s** is also correct

papist (mainly used in an insulting way) »*noun* a Roman Catholic.
» *adjective* Roman Catholic.
– SAY **pay**-pist
    papism

paprika »*noun* an orange-red powdered spice made from certain varieties of sweet pepper.
– SAY **pap**-ri-kuh or puh-**pree**-kuh

papyrus »*noun* (plural **papyri** or **papyruses**) a material made in ancient Egypt from the stem of a water plant, used for writing or painting on.
– SAY puh-**py**-ruhss [singular], puh-**py**-rI [plural]

☑ the plural of **papyrus** can either be **papyri** (as in Latin) or **papyruses**

par »*noun* the number of golf strokes a first-class player should normally require for a particular hole or course.

ℹ️ **par** is a Latin word meaning 'equal'

parable »*noun* a simple story used to illustrate a moral or spiritual lesson.

parabola »*noun* (plural **parabolas** or **parabolae**) an open plane curve of the kind formed by the intersection of a cone with a plane parallel to its side.
– SAY puh-**rab**-uh-luh [singular], puh-**rab**-uh-lee [plural]

☑ the plural of **parabola** can be either **parabolas** or (as in Latin) **parabolae**

parabolic »*adjective* having to do with or like a parabola.
– SAY pa-ruh-**bol**-ik

paracetamol »*noun* a drug used to relieve pain and reduce fever.
– SAY pa-ruh-**see**-tuh-mol or pa-ruh-**set**-uh-mol

parachute (verb: **parachutes, parachuting, parachuted**)
    parachutist

parade (verb: **parades, parading, paraded**)

paradiddle »*noun* a simple drum roll consisting of four even strokes.
– SAY pa-ruh-di-d'l

paradigm »*noun* ❶ a typical example, pattern, or model of something. ❷ a view of the world which underlies the theories and practice of a scientific subject.
– SAY **pa**-ruh-dym
    paradigmatic SAY pa-ruh-dig-**mat**-ik

☑ -**digm** not -**dime**: **paradigm**

parading

paradise

paradox »*noun* ❶ a statement that sounds absurd or seems to contradict itself but may in fact be true. ❷ a person or thing that combines contradictory qualities.
    paradoxical
    paradoxically

paraffin »*noun* ❶ a flammable waxy solid obtained from petroleum or shale and used for sealing and waterproofing and in candles. ❷ a liquid fuel made in a similar way.

p

✓ one r, two f's, and no e at the end: **paraffin**

paragliding »*noun* a sport in which a person glides through the air by means of a wide parachute after jumping from or being hauled to a height.

paragon »*noun* a person who is excellent, or is the perfect example of a particular quality.

paragraph

Paraguayan

parakeet »*noun* a small parrot with green plumage and a long tail.
– SAY pa-ruh-keet

✓ **parakeet** can also be spelled **parrakeet**, with a double r

paralegal »*noun* a person trained in some legal matters but not fully qualified as a lawyer.

parallax »*noun* the apparent difference in the position of an object when viewed from different positions.
– SAY pa-ruh-laks

parallel »*adjective* ❶ (of lines, planes, or surfaces) side by side and having the same distance continuously between them. ❷ occurring or existing at the same time or in a similar way; corresponding.
»*noun* ❶ a person or thing that is similar to or can be compared to to another. ❷ a similarity or comparison. ❸ (also **parallel of latitude**) one of the imaginary parallel circles of latitude on the earth's surface.
»*verb* (**parallels, paralleling, paralleled**) ❶ run or lie parallel to something. ❷ be similar or corresponding to something.
parallelism

✓ two l's before the e and one l after it: **parallel**

parallelogram »*noun* a shape with four straight sides and opposite sides parallel.
– SAY pa-ruh-**lel**-luh-gram

parallels

Paralympics »*plural noun* an international athletic competition for disabled athletes.
Paralympic

paralyse »*verb* (**paralyses, paralysing, paralysed**) ❶ cause a person or part of the body to become partly or wholly unable to move. ❷ prevent something from functioning normally.

✓ the ending is **yse**, not **ise** or **ize**: **paralyse**. The American spelling is **paralyze**.

paralysis »*noun* (plural **paralyses**) ❶ the loss of the ability to move part or most of the body. ❷ inability to act or function.

– SAY puh-**ral**-i-siss [singular] , puh-**ral**-i-seez [plural]

✓ make the plural by changing the **-is** ending to **-es** (as in Latin): **paralyses**

paralytic »*adjective* ❶ relating to paralysis. ❷ (in informal English) extremely drunk.
paralytically

paralyze American spelling of **PARALYSE**.

paramedic »*noun* a person who is trained to do medical work but is not a fully qualified doctor.
paramedical

parameter »*noun* ❶ something that decides or limits the way in which something is done. ❷ (in mathematics) a quantity which is fixed for the case in question but may vary in other cases.
– SAY puh-**ram**-i-ter

ⓘ do not confuse **parameter** with **perimeter**, which means 'the line at the edge or boundary of something'

paramilitary »*adjective* organized on similar lines to a military force.
»*noun* (plural **paramilitaries**) a member of a paramilitary organization.

✓ plural: drop the y and add **ies**: **paramilitaries**

paramount »*adjective* ❶ more important than anything else. ❷ having supreme power.

paramour »*noun* (an old word) a lover.

paranoia »*noun* ❶ a mental condition which causes sufferers to believe mistakenly that they are being persecuted or are very important. ❷ unjustified suspicion and mistrust of others.
– SAY pa-ruh-**noy**-uh

paranoid »*adjective* having to do with or suffering from paranoia.

paranormal »*adjective* beyond the scope of normal scientific understanding.

parapet »*noun* a low protective wall along the edge of a roof, bridge, or balcony.
– SAY pa-ruh-pit

✓ **pet** not **pit**: parapet

paraphernalia »*noun* miscellaneous equipment needed for a particular activity.
– SAY pa-ruh-fer-**nay**-li-uh

✓ **phern** not **phen**: paraphernalia

paraphrase »*verb* (**paraphrases, paraphrasing, paraphrased**) express the meaning of something using different words.

» *noun* a rewording of a passage.

paraplegia **»***noun* paralysis of the legs and lower body.
– SAY pa-ruh-**plee**-juh
paraplegic

parapsychology **»***noun* the study of mental phenomena which are outside the area of orthodox psychology.

paraquat **»***noun* a poisonous weedkiller.
– SAY pa-ruh-kwot or pa-ruh-kwat

parasailing **»***noun* the sport of gliding through the air wearing an open parachute while being towed by a motor boat.

parascending **»***noun* paragliding or parasailing.

parasite **»***noun* ❶ an organism which lives in or on another organism and benefits at the other's expense. ❷ a person who lives off or exploits others.
parasitism

parasitic **»***adjective* (of an organism) living as a parasite.
parasitically

parasitise another way of spelling
PARASITIZE.

parasitism

parasitize **»***verb* (parasitizes, parasitizing, parasitized) infest or exploit an animal or person as a parasite.
– SAY pa-ruh-sy-tyz or pa-ruh-si-tyz

> ✓ many people prefer the alternative spellings **parasitise, parasitises,** etc.: both **s** and **z** spellings are correct

parasol **»***noun* a light umbrella used to give shade from the sun.

> ✓ one r, one s, one l: **parasol**

paratroops **»***plural noun* troops equipped to be dropped by parachute from aircraft.
paratrooper

parboil **»***verb* (parboils, parboiling, parboiled) partly cook something by boiling.

parcel (verb: parcels, parcelling, parcelled)

> ✓ double the **l** in **parcelling** and **parcelled** (the spellings **parceling** and **parceled** are American)

parch **»***verb* (parches, parching, parched) ❶ make something dry through strong heat. ❷ (parched) extremely thirsty. ❸ roast corn, peas, etc. lightly.

parchment **»***noun* ❶ a stiff material made from the skin of a sheep or goat, formerly used for writing on. ❷ stiff paper treated to resemble parchment.

pardon (verb: pardons, pardoning, pardoned)
pardonable

> ✓ -on not -en: **pardon**

pare **»***verb* (pares, paring, pared) ❶ trim something by cutting away its outer edges. ❷ (pare away or down) reduce or lessen something in a number of small successive stages.

> ℹ do not confuse **pare** with **pair**, which means 'a set of two things', or **pear**, the fruit

parent (verb: parents, parenting, parented)
parental
parenthood

parentage **»***noun* the identity and origins of a person's parents.

parental

parented

parenthesis **»***noun* (plural parentheses)
❶ a word or phrase giving extra information as an aside, indicated in writing by brackets, dashes, or commas. ❷ (parentheses) a pair of round brackets () surrounding such a word or phrase.
– SAY puh-**ren**-thi-siss [singular], puh-**ren**-thi-seez [plural]

> ✓ make the plural by changing the **-is** ending to **-es** (as in Latin): **parentheses**

parenthetic **»***adjective* relating to or inserted as a parenthesis.
– SAY pa-ruhn-**thet**-ik
parenthetical
parenthetically

parenthood

parenting

parents

pares

par excellence **»***adjective* better or more than all others of the same kind: *a designer par excellence.*
– SAY par ek-suh-**lonss**

> ✓ **par excellence** is French for 'by excellence'

pariah **»***noun* ❶ an outcast. ❷ (a historical term) a member of a low caste or of no caste in southern India.
– SAY puh-**ry**-uh

> ✓ don't forget the **h** at the end: **pariah**

paring

parings **»***plural noun* thin strips pared off from something.

parish »*noun* **❶** (in the Christian Church) a district with its own church and clergy. **❷** (in Britain) the smallest unit of local government in rural areas.

parishioner »*noun* a person who lives in a particular Church parish.

parish register »*noun* a book recording christenings, marriages, and burials at a parish church.

Parisian [of Paris; person from Paris]

Parisienne »*noun* a Parisian girl or woman.
– SAY pa-ri-zi-en

parity »*noun* the quality of being equal with or equivalent to something.
– SAY pa-ri-ti

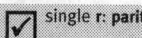 ✓ single r: **parity**

park (verb: **parks, parking, parked**)

parka »*noun* a windproof hooded jacket.

parked

parking

Parkinson's disease »*noun* a progressive disease of the brain and nervous system marked by trembling, stiffness in the muscles, and slow, imprecise movement.

ℹ️ named after the English surgeon James *Parkinson*

parkland

parks

parky »*adjective* (in informal English) chilly.

parlance »*noun* a way of speaking.
– SAY par-luhnss

✓ ance not ence: **parlance**

parley »*noun* (plural **parleys**) a meeting between opponents or enemies to discuss terms for a truce.
» *verb* (**parleys, parleying, parleyed**) hold a parley.
– SAY par-li

parliament »*noun* **❶** (**Parliament**) (in the UK) the highest legislating body, consisting of the king or queen, the House of Lords, and the House of Commons. **❷** a similar body in other countries.
– SAY par-luh-muhnt
parliamentary

✓ lia not la: **parliament**

parliamentarian »*noun* a member of a parliament.

parlour

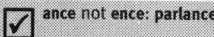 ✓ -our not -or: **parlour** (the spelling parlor is American)

parlous »*adjective* (an old word) dangerously uncertain; precarious.
– SAY par-luhss

Parma ham »*noun* a strongly flavoured Italian ham, eaten uncooked and thinly sliced.

ℹ️ named after the Italian city of *Parma*, which also gives its name to **Parmesan** cheese

Parmesan »*noun* a hard, dry Italian cheese.
– SAY par-mi-zan

parochial »*adjective* **❶** relating to a parish. **❷** having a narrow outlook or range.
– SAY puh-roh-ki-uhl
parochially
parochialism

parody »*noun* (plural **parodies**) a piece of writing, art, or music that deliberately copies the style of someone or something, in order to be funny.
» *verb* (**parodies, parodying, parodied**) produce a parody of something.
– SAY pa-ruh-di
parodist

✓ plural: drop the **y** and add **ies**: **parodies**

parole »*noun* the temporary or permanent release of a prisoner before the end of a sentence, on the condition that they behave well.
» *verb* (**paroles, paroling, paroled**) release a prisoner on parole.

✓ drop the e to spell **paroling**

paroxysm »*noun* a sudden attack of pain, coughing, etc., or a sudden feeling of overwhelming emotion.
– SAY pa-ruhk-si-z'm
paroxysmal

✓ single r, and note the ending is **ysm** not ism: **paroxysm**

parquet »*noun* flooring composed of wooden blocks arranged in a geometric pattern.
– SAY par-ki or par-kay
parquetry

parr »*noun* (plural **parr**) a young salmon or trout.

parrakeet another way of spelling PARAKEET.

parricide »*noun* the killing by someone of their own parent or other near relative.
– SAY pa-ri-syd
parricidal

parried

parries

parrot (verb: **parrots, parroting, parroted**)

> ☑ do not double the **t** to spell **parroting** or **parroted**

parry »*verb* (**parries, parrying, parried**)
❶ ward off a weapon or attack. ❷ say something in order to avoid answering a question directly.
» *noun* (plural **parries**) an act of parrying.

parse »*verb* (**parses, parsing, parsed**) analyse and describe the different parts of a sentence.
– SAY parz
parser

parsec »*noun* a unit of distance in astronomy, equal to about 3.25 light years.

parsimony »*noun* extreme unwillingness to spend money or use resources.
– SAY par-si-muh-ni
parsimonious

parsley »*noun* a herb with crinkly or flat leaves, used in cooking.

parsnip

parson »*noun* (in the Church of England) a parish priest.

parsonage »*noun* a church house provided for a parson.

parson's nose »*noun* a piece of fatty flesh at the tail end of a cooked turkey, goose, etc.

part (verb: **parts, parting, parted**)

partake »*verb* (**partakes, partaking, partook**; past participle **partaken**)
❶ (**partake in**) participate in. ❷ (**partake of**) be characterized by. ❸ (**partake of**) eat or drink.

parted

parterre »*noun* a group of flower beds laid out in a formal pattern.
– SAY par-**tair**

> ☑ note the **rre** ending: **parterre** is a French word

part exchange »*noun* a transaction in which you give something you already own as part of the payment for something new.

partial »*adjective* ❶ not complete or whole. ❷ favouring one side in a dispute. ❸ (**partial to**) liking something.
partiality
partially

participate »*verb* (**participates, participating, participated**) join in something; take part.
participant
participation

participator
participatory

participle »*noun* (in grammar) a word formed from a verb (e.g. *going, gone, being, been*) and used as an adjective or noun (as in *burnt toast*).
– SAY par-**tiss**-i-p'l

particle »*noun* ❶ a tiny portion of matter. ❷ a component of the physical world smaller than an atom, e.g. an electron.

particoloured »*adjective* partly of one colour, partly of another or others.

> ☑ **-coloured** not **-colored** (the spelling **particolored** is American)

particular
particularly

> ☑ **ar** not **er**: particular

particularize »*verb* (**particularizes, particularizing, particularized**) treat something individually or in detail.
particularization

> ☑ many people prefer the alternative spellings **particularise, particularises,** etc., and **particularisation**

particulate »*adjective* relating to or in the form of minute particles.
» *noun* (**particulates**) matter in such a form.
– SAY par-**tik**-yuu-luht

partied

parties

parting

partisan »*noun* ❶ a committed supporter of a party, cause, or person. ❷ a member of an armed group fighting secretly against an occupying force.
» *adjective* prejudiced.
– SAY par-ti-zan
partisanship

> ☑ **s** not **z**: partisan

partition (verb: **partitions, partitioning, partitioned**)

partly

partner (verb: **partners, partnering, partnered**)

partnership

part of speech »*noun* a category in which a word is placed according to its function in grammar, e.g. noun, pronoun, adjective, verb.

partook past of PARTAKE.

partridge »*noun* (plural **partridge** or **partridges**) a game bird with brown feathers and a short tail.

-ridge not **-rige**: **partridge**

parts

part-time

parturient »*adjective* about to give birth; in labour.
– SAY par-**tyoor**-i-uhnt

parturition »*noun* the action of giving birth; childbirth.
– SAY par-tyuu-**rish**-uhn

part-way

party (plural **parties**; verb: **parties, partying, partied**)

 plural: drop the **y** and add **ies**: **parties**

party line »*noun* a policy or policies officially adopted by a political party.

party-pooper

party wall »*noun* a wall between two adjoining buildings or rooms.

parvenu »*noun* (used in an insulting way) a person from a humble background who has recently joined a group of wealthy or famous people.
– SAY par-vuh-noo or par-vuh-nyoo

pascal »*noun* (in physics) the basic unit of pressure.
– SAY pass-kuhl

named after the French scientist Blaise *Pascal*

paschal »*adjective* ❶ relating to Easter. ❷ relating to the Jewish Passover.
– SAY pas-kuhl or pahss-kuhl

pas de deux »*noun* (plural **pas de deux**) a dance for two people.
– SAY pah duh der

pas de deux is a French phrase which means 'step of two'

pashmina »*noun* ❶ fine-quality material made from goat's wool. ❷ a shawl made from this material.
– SAY pash-mee-nuh

paso doble »*noun* (plural **paso dobles**) a fast-paced ballroom dance.
– SAY pa-soh doh-blay

paso doble is a Spanish term which means 'double step'

pass (plural **passes**; verb: **passes, passing, passed**)

passable »*adjective* ❶ acceptable, but not outstanding. ❷ able to be travelled along or on.
passably

 -able not **-ible**: **passable**

passage

passageway

passata »*noun* a thick paste made from sieved tomatoes.
– SAY puh-sah-tuh

passbook »*noun* a book given by a bank or building society to an account holder, recording what has been put into or taken out of the account.

passe »*adjective* no longer fashionable.
– SAY pa-say

 passe can also be written **passé**, with an acute accent on the **e** (it is a French word which means 'gone by')

passed past and past participle of **PASS**.

do not confuse the verbal form **passed** (as in *we have just passed the house*) with **past** (as in *we drove past the house*)

passenger

 er not **ar**: **passenger**

passer-by (plural **passers-by**)

passes

passim »*adverb* (of references) occurring at various places throughout the text.
– SAY pa-sim

passim is a Latin word which means 'everywhere'

passing

passion
passionless

passionate
passionately

passion flower »*noun* a climbing plant with distinctive flowers.

passion fruit »*noun* the edible fruit of some species of passion flower.

passionless

passion play »*noun* a play about the crucifixion of Jesus.

passive »*adjective* ❶ accepting or allowing what happens or what others do, without resistance. ❷ (of verbs) connected with the form of the verb used when the subject is affected by the action of the verb (e.g. *they were killed* as opposed to the active form *he killed them*).
» *noun* a passive form of a verb.
passively
passiveness
passivity

passive resistance »*noun* non-violent opposition to authority.

passive smoking »*noun* the inhaling of smoke from other people's cigarettes.

passivity

pass key »*noun* ❶ a key given only to those who are officially allowed access. ❷ a master key.

Passover »*noun* the major Jewish spring festival, commemorating the liberation of the Israelites from slavery in Egypt.

passport

password

past [gone by in time; time gone by; beyond; so as to pass]

> ℹ️ do not confuse **past** (as in *we drove past the house*) with **passed**, which is the past tense and participle of the verb **pass** (as in *we have just passed the house*)

pasta »*noun* dough formed into various shapes and cooked in boiling water.

paste (verb: **pastes, pasting, pasted**)

pasteboard »*noun* thin board made by pasting together sheets of paper.

pasted

pastel »*noun* ❶ a crayon made of powdered pigments bound with gum or resin. ❷ a picture created using pastels. ❸ a pale shade of a colour.
» *adjective* (of a colour) pale and delicate.

> ℹ️ do not confuse **pastel** with **pastille**, which means 'a small sweet or lozenge'

> ✓ **el** not **le**: past**el**

pastes

pasteurize »*verb* (**pasteurizes, pasteurizing, pasteurized**) destroy the germs in milk by a process of heating and cooling.
– SAY pahss-**tyuu**-ryz
  pasteurization

> ℹ️ named after the French chemist Louis *Pasteur*

> ✓ many people prefer the alternative spellings **pasteurise, pasteurises,** etc., and **pasteurisation**: both **s** and **z** spellings are correct

pastiche »*noun* a piece of writing or work of art produced in a style that imitates that of another work, artist, or period.
– SAY pa-**steesh**

pastie another way of spelling **PASTY**[1].

pastier

pasties

pastiest

pastille »*noun* a small sweet or lozenge.

– SAY **pass**-tuhl or **pass**-til

> ℹ️ do not confuse **pastille** with **pastel**, which means 'a coloured crayon' or 'a pale shade of a colour'

p

pastime

pasting

pastor »*noun* a minister in charge of a Christian church or group.

> ✓ **-or** not **-er**: past**or**

pastoral »*adjective* ❶ relating to the farming or grazing of sheep or cattle. ❷ (of a creative work) showing country life. ❸ relating to the work of a Christian minister in giving personal and spiritual guidance. ❹ relating to a teacher's responsibility for the general well-being of pupils or students.
» *noun* a pastoral poem, picture, or piece of music.
– SAY **pahss**-tuh-ruhl

past participle »*noun* the form of a verb which is used in perfect and passive tenses and sometimes as an adjective, e.g. *looked* in *have you looked?*

pastrami »*noun* highly seasoned smoked beef.
– SAY pa-**strah**-mi

pastry (plural **pastries**)

> ✓ plural: drop the **y** and add **ies**: past**ries**

pasturage »*noun* ❶ land used for pasture. ❷ the pasturing of animals.

pasture »*noun* land covered with grass, suitable for grazing cattle or sheep.
» *verb* (**pastures, pasturing, pastured**) put animals to graze in a pasture.

pasty[1] »*noun* (plural **pasties**) a folded pastry case filled with seasoned meat and vegetables.
– SAY **pass**-ti

> ✓ **pasty** can also be spelled **pastie** plural: drop the **y** and add **ies**: past**ies**

pasty[2] »*adjective* (**pastier, pastiest**) ❶ of or like paste. ❷ (of a person's skin) unhealthily pale.
– SAY **pay**-sti

pat (verb: **pats, patting, patted**)

> ✓ double the **t** in **patted** and **patting**

patch (verb: **patches, patching, patched**)

patchier

patchiest

patchily

patchiness

patching

patchwork

patchy (adjective: **patchier**, **patchiest**)
patchily
patchiness

pate[1] »*noun* (an old word) a person's head.
– SAY payt

pate[2] »*noun* a rich savoury paste made from meat, fish, or other ingredients.
– SAY pa-tay

> ☑ **pate** can also be written **pâté**, with a circumflex on the **a** and an acute accent on the **e** (as in the original French)

pate de foie gras »a pate made from fatted goose liver.
– SAY pa-tay duh fwah **grah**

> ☑ **pate de foie gras** can also be written **pâté de foie gras** (it is a French phrase which means 'pate of fat liver')

patella »*noun* (plural **patellae**) (in anatomy) the kneecap.
– SAY puh-**tel**-luh [singular], puh-**tel**-lee [plural]

> ☑ the plural of **patella** is **patellae** (as in the original Latin)

patent »*noun* a government licence giving the sole right to make, use, or sell an invention for a set period.
» *adjective* ❶ easily recognizable; obvious. ❷ made and marketed under a patent.
» *verb* (**patents**, **patenting**, **patented**) obtain a patent for something.
– SAY pay-t'nt [noun, adjective, and verb] or pa-t'nt [noun and adjective]
patently

> ☑ **ent** not **ant**: pat**ent**

patent leather »*noun* glossy varnished leather.

patent medicine »*noun* a medicine that is made and sold under a patent and available without prescription.

patents

paterfamilias »*noun* the man who is the head of a family or household.
– SAY pay-ter-fuh-**mi**-li-ass

> ℹ it is unusual to need a plural, but if you do it would be **patresfamilias** (SAY pay-treez-fuh-**mi**-li-ass)

paternal »*adjective* ❶ of or like a father. ❷ related through the father.
paternally

paternalism »*noun* the policy of protecting the people you have control over but also of restricting their freedom.

paternalist
paternalistic
paternalistically

paternally

paternity »*noun* ❶ the state of being a father. ❷ descent from a father.

paternity suit »*noun* a court case held to establish the identity of a child's father.

paternoster »*noun* (in the Roman Catholic Church) the Lord's Prayer.
– SAY pa-ter-**noss**-ter

path

path-breaking

pathetic »*adjective* ❶ making you feel pity or sadness. ❷ weak or inadequate.
pathetically

pathfinder

pathname »*noun* (in computing) a description of where an item is to be found in a system of files.

pathogen »*noun* a micro-organism that can cause disease.
– SAY pa-**thuh**-juhn
pathogenic

pathological »*adjective* ❶ of or caused by a disease. ❷ extreme or compulsive: *a pathological liar*.
pathologically

pathology »*noun* ❶ the branch of medicine concerned with the causes and effects of diseases. ❷ the typical behaviour of a disease.
pathologist

pathos »*noun* a quality that makes you feel pity or sadness.
– SAY **pay**-thoss

> ☑ **pa** not **pay**: **pa**thos

pathway

patience »*noun* ❶ the ability to accept delay, trouble, or suffering without becoming angry or upset. ❷ a card game for one player.

patient »*adjective* having or showing patience.
» *noun* a person receiving or registered to receive medical treatment.
patiently

> ☑ **ent** not **ant**: pati**ent**

patina »*noun* ❶ a green or brown film on the surface of old bronze. ❷ a soft glow on wooden furniture produced by age and polishing.
– SAY **pa**-ti-nuh

patio (plural **patios**)

✓ the plural of **patio** (a Spanish word) has **os** not **oes**: **patios**

patisserie »*noun* a shop where pastries and cakes are sold.
– SAY puh-**tiss**-uh-ri or puh-**tee**-suh-ri

✓ single **t**, double **s**, and the ending is **ie**: **patisserie** (a French word)

patois »*noun* (plural **patois**) the local dialect of a region.
– SAY pat-wah [singular], pat-wahz [plural]

patriarch »*noun* ❶ the man who is the head of a family or tribe. ❷ a biblical figure regarded as a father of the human race. ❸ a respected older man.
– SAY **pay**-tri-ark

✓ -**arch** not -**ark**: **patriarch**

patriarchy »*noun* (plural **patriarchies**) a society led or controlled by men.

patrician »*noun* an aristocrat.
»*adjective* relating to or characteristic of aristocrats.
– SAY puh-**tri**-sh'n

patricide »*noun* ❶ the killing by someone of their own father. ❷ a person who kills their father.
– SAY pa-tri-syd

patrimony »*noun* (plural **patrimonies**) property inherited from your father or male ancestor.
– SAY pa-tri-muh-ni

patriot »*noun* a person who strongly supports their country and is prepared to defend it.
patriotic
patriotically
patriotism

patrol (verb: **patrols, patrolling, patrolled**)

✓ double the **l** to spell **patrolling** and **patrolled**

patrolman (plural **patrolmen**)

patron »*noun* ❶ a person who gives financial support to a person or organization. ❷ a regular customer of a restaurant, hotel, etc.

patronage »*noun* ❶ support given by a patron. ❷ the giving of help or a job to someone in return for their support. ❸ custom attracted by a restaurant, hotel, etc.
– SAY pa-truh-nij

patroness (plural **patronesses**)

patronize »*verb* (**patronizes, patronizing, patronized**) ❶ treat someone as if they lack experience or are not very intelligent. ❷ go regularly to a restaurant, hotel, etc.

✓ many people prefer the alternative spellings **patronise, patronises**, etc.: both **s** and **z** spellings are correct

patron saint »*noun* a saint who is believed to protect a particular place or group of people.

pats

patsy »*noun* (plural **patsies**) (in informal English) a person who is taken advantage of.

patted

patter »*verb* (**patters, pattering, pattered**) ❶ make a repeated light tapping sound. ❷ run with quick light steps.
»*noun* ❶ a repeated light tapping sound. ❷ fast continuous talk. ❸ the jargon of a particular group of people.

pattern (verb: **patterns, patterning, patterned**)

✓ remember, the ending is **ern** not **en**: **pattern**

patters

patting

patty »*noun* (plural **patties**) a small pie or pasty.

paucity »*noun* smallness or lack in a supply or quantity.
– SAY **paw**-si-ti

paunch »*noun* an abdomen or stomach that is large and sticks out.
paunchy

pauper »*noun* a very poor person.
pauperism

pause (verb: **pauses, pausing, paused**)

pave (verb: **paves, paving, paved**)
paving

pavement

paves

pavilion »*noun* ❶ a building at a sports ground used for changing and taking refreshments. ❷ a summer house in a park or large garden. ❸ a marquee used at a show or fair. ❹ a temporary display stand at a trade exhibition.

✓ there is only one **l**: **pavilion**

paving

pavlova »*noun* a dessert consisting of a meringue base covered with whipped cream and fruit.
– SAY pav-**loh**-vuh

ℹ️ named after the Russian ballerina Anna *Pavlova*

paw (verb: **paws, pawing, pawed**)

pawn »*noun* **❶** a chess piece of the smallest size and value. **❷** a person used by others for their own purposes.
» *verb* (**pawns, pawning, pawned**) leave an object with a pawnbroker in exchange for borrowing money.

pawnbroker »*noun* a person who is licensed to lend you money at interest in exchange for an object you leave with them and which they can sell if you do not pay the money back.

pawned

pawning

pawns

pawnshop »*noun* a pawnbroker's shop.

pawpaw »*noun* a papaya.
– SAY paw-paw

> ✓ **pawpaw** can also be spelled without the first **w: papaw** (SAY puh-paw)

paws

pay (verb: **pays, paying, paid**)

payable

payback

PAYE »*abbreviation* (in the UK) pay as you earn, a system in which someone's income tax is taken directly from their wages.

payee »*noun* a person to whom money is paid.

paying

payload »*noun* **❶** the part of a vehicle's load which earns revenue; passengers and cargo. **❷** an explosive warhead carried by an aircraft or missile.

paymaster »*noun* **❶** a person who pays you and therefore has control over you. **❷** an official who pays troops or workers.

payment

pay-off

payola »*noun* (in American English) the illegal payment of money to someone in return for their promoting a product in the media.

payout

payphone

payroll »*noun* a list of a company's employees and the amount of money they are to be paid.

pays

payslip

PC »*abbreviation* **❶** personal computer. **❷** police constable. **❸** politically correct; political correctness.

PE »*abbreviation* physical education.

pea

peace [freedom from noise, anxiety, war]

> ✓ do not confuse **peace** with **piece,** which means 'a part of something larger'

peaceable
peacably

peaceful
peacefully
peacefulness

> ✓ -ful not -full: peaceful

peacekeeping
peacekeeper

peacemaker

peacetime

peach

peacock »*noun* a large colourful bird with very long tail feathers that can be fanned out in display.

peahen »*noun* the female of the peacock.

peak (verb: **peaks, peaking, peaked**) [a pointed top; a maximum; reach a highest point]

> ℹ do not confuse **peak** with **peek,** which means 'look secretly', or **pique,** which means 'a feeling of irritation'

peaked »*adjective* (of a cap) having a peak.

peakier

peakiest

peaking

peaks

peaky »*adjective* (**peakier, peakiest**) pale from illness or tiredness.

peal »*noun* **❶** a loud ringing sound of a bell or bells. **❷** a loud sound of thunder or laughter. **❸** a set of bells.
» *verb* (**peals, pealing, pealed**) ring or sound loudly.

> ℹ do not confuse **peal** with **peel,** which means 'remove the skin from something'

peanut

pear [fruit]

> ℹ do not confuse **pear** with **pare,** which means 'trim something', or **pair,** 'a set of two things'

pearl

pearl barley »*noun* barley reduced to small round grains by grinding.

pearlescent »*adjective* having a soft glow resembling that of mother-of-pearl.

> ✓ -scent not -sent: pearlescent

pearly (adjective: **pearlier, pearliest**)

peasant
peasantry

> ✓ a before and after the s: **peasant**

pease pudding »*noun* a dish of split peas boiled with onion and carrot and mashed to a pulp.

pea-shooter »*noun* a toy weapon consisting of a small tube out of which dried peas are blown.

pea-souper »*noun* a very thick yellowish fog.

peat »*noun* partly decomposed vegetable matter formed in boggy ground, dried for use in gardening and as fuel.
peaty

pebble
pebbly

pebble-dash »*noun* mortar with pebbles in it, used as a coating for the outside walls of buildings.

pebbly

pecan »*noun* a smooth pinkish-brown nut obtained from a tree of the southern US.
– **say** pee-kuhn or pi-**kan**

peccadillo »*noun* (plural **peccadilloes** or **peccadillos**) a minor sin or fault.
– **say** pek-kuh-**dil**-loh

> ✓ two **c**'s, two **l**'s: **peccadillo**
> the plural can have **oes** or **os**: **peccadilloes** or **peccadillos**

peccary »*noun* (plural **peccaries**) a piglike mammal found from the south-western US to Paraguay.
– **say** pek-kuh-ri

peck[1] (verb: **pecks, pecking, pecked**) [strike or bite with the beak; kiss lightly]

peck[2] »*noun* a measure of capacity for dry goods, equal to a quarter of a bushel.

pecking order »*noun* a strict order of importance among members of a group.

peckish

pecks

pecs »*plural noun* (in informal English) pectoral muscles.

pectin »*noun* a jelly-like substance present in ripe fruits, used to set jams and jellies.

pectoral »*adjective* having to do with the breast or chest.
– **say** pek-tuh-ruhl

pectoral muscle »*noun* one of four large paired muscles which cover the front of the ribcage.

peculiar »*adjective* ❶ strange or odd. ❷ (**peculiar to**) belonging only to.
peculiarly

> ✓ iar not ier: **peculiar**

p

peculiarity »*noun* (plural **peculiarities**) ❶ an unusual or distinctive feature or habit. ❷ the state of being peculiar.

> ✓ plural: drop the **y** and add **ies**: **peculiarities**

peculiarly

pecuniary »*adjective* having to do with money.
– **say** pi-**kyoo**-ni-uh-ri

pedagogue »*noun* a teacher.
– **say** ped-uh-gog

> ✓ gogue not gog: **pedagogue**

pedagogy »*noun* the profession or theory of teaching.
– **say** ped-uh-go-gi

pedal (verb: **pedals, pedalling, pedalled**) [foot-operated lever; move a bicycle by pressing the pedals]

> **i** do not confuse **pedal** with **peddle**, which means 'sell goods'

> ✓ double the **l** in **pedalling** and **pedalled** (the spellings **pedaling** and **pedaled** are American)

pedalo »*noun* (plural **pedalos** or **pedaloes**) a small pedal-operated pleasure boat.
– **say** ped-uh-loh

> ✓ the plural of **pedalo** can have either **os** or **oes**: **pedalos** or **pedaloes**

pedal pushers »*plural noun* women's calf-length trousers.

pedals

pedant »*noun* a person who is too concerned with minor details or with displaying technical knowledge.
– **say** ped-duhnt
pedantic
pedantically
pedantry

peddle »*verb* (**peddles, peddling, peddled**) ❶ sell goods by going from place to place. ❷ sell an illegal drug or stolen item. ❸ (used in a disapproving way) promote an idea persistently or widely.

> **i** do not confuse **peddle** with **pedal**, which refers to a foot-operated lever for moving a vehicle

peddler another way of spelling PEDLAR.
peddles
peddling

pederasty »*noun* sexual intercourse between a man and a boy.
– SAY ped-uh-rass-ti
    pederast

pedestal »*noun* ❶ the base or support on which a statue or column is mounted. ❷ one of the two supports of a desk or table which has a space for the knees. ❸ the supporting column of a washbasin or toilet pan.

> ✓ **des** not **dis**, and only one **l** at the end: **pedestal**

pedestrian »*noun* a person walking rather than travelling in a vehicle.
» *adjective* dull and boring.

> ✓ **ian** not **ien**: **pedestrian**

pedestrianize »*verb* (**pedestrianizes, pedestrianizing, pedestrianized**) make a street or area accessible only to pedestrians.
    pedestrianization

> ✓ many people prefer the alternative spellings **pedestrianise, pedestrianises**, etc., and **pedestrianisation**: both **s** and **z** spellings are correct

pediatrics American spelling of PAEDIATRICS.

pedicure »*noun* treatment to improve the appearance of the feet and toenails.

pedigree »*noun* ❶ the record of descent of an animal, showing it to be pure-bred. ❷ a person's family background or ancestry. ❸ the history or origin of a person or thing.

pediment »*noun* the triangular upper part of the front of a classical building.

pedlar »*noun* ❶ a travelling trader who sells small goods. ❷ a person who sells illegal drugs or stolen goods. ❸ (used in a disapproving way) a person who spreads or promotes an idea or view.

> ✓ **pedlar** can also be spelled **peddler**

pedometer »*noun* an instrument for estimating the distance travelled on foot by recording the number of steps taken.
– SAY pi-**dom**-i-ter

pedophile American spelling of PAEDOPHILE.

pee (verb: **pees, peeing, peed**)

peek (verb: **peeks, peeking, peeked**) [look quickly or secretly; a quick look]

> ℹ do not confuse **peek** with **peak** meaning 'a pointed top; reach a highest point' or **pique** meaning 'a feeling of irritation'

peekaboo

peeked

peeking

peeks

peel (verb: **peels, peeling, peeled**) [remove the skin from something]
    peeler
    peelings

> ✓ do not confuse **peel** with **peal**, which means 'a loud ringing sound of a bell or bells'

peen »*noun* the rounded or wedge-shaped end of a hammer head opposite the face.

> ✓ **peen** can also be spelled **pein**

peep (verb: **peeps, peeping, peeped**)
    peeper

peephole »*noun* a small hole in a door through which callers may be seen.

peeping

peeping Tom »*noun* a person who likes to spy on people undressing or having sex.

> ℹ the name of a tailor said to have watched Lady Godiva ride naked through Coventry

peeps

peep show »*noun* a form of entertainment in which pictures are viewed through a lens or hole set into a box.

peer[1] »*verb* (**peers, peering, peered**) look at something with difficulty or concentration.

peer[2] »*noun* ❶ a member of the nobility in Britain or Ireland. ❷ a person of the same age, status, or ability as another specified person.

> ℹ do not confuse **peer** with **pier**, referring to a structure built out over water, or a bridge support

peerage »*noun* ❶ the title and rank of peer or peeress. ❷ (**the peerage**) peers as a group.

peered

peeress »*noun* (plural **peeresses**) ❶ a woman holding the rank of a peer in her own right. ❷ the wife or widow of a peer.

peer group »*noun* a group of people of approximately the same age, status, and interests.

peering

peerless »*adjective* better than all others; unrivalled.

peers

pees

peeve »*verb* (**peeves, peeving, peeved**) annoy or irritate someone.
» *noun* a cause of annoyance.

peevish »*adjective* irritable.
peevishly
peevishness

peewit »*noun* the lapwing.

peg (verb: **pegs, pegging, pegged**)

> ✓ double the **g** in **pegged** and **pegging**

pein another way of spelling **PEEN**.

pejorative »*adjective* expressing contempt or disapproval.
– SAY pi-**jo**-ruh-tiv
pejoratively

> ✓ **pej** not **perj**: **pejorative**

Pekinese »*noun* (plural **Pekinese**) a short-legged lapdog with long hair and a snub nose.

pelagic »*adjective* relating to or inhabiting the open sea.
– SAY pi-**la**-jik

pelargonium »*noun* a shrubby plant with red, pink, or white flowers.
– SAY pe-luh-**goh**-ni-uhm

pelican »*noun* a large waterbird with a long bill and a throat pouch.

> ✓ one **l**, one **c**: **pelican**

pelican crossing »*noun* (in the UK) a pedestrian crossing with traffic lights operated by pedestrians.

pelisse »*noun* (a historical term) ❶ a woman's ankle-length cloak with armholes or sleeves. ❷ a fur-lined cloak.
– SAY pi-**leess**

pellagra »*noun* a disease caused by an inadequate diet, in which a person has inflamed skin, diarrhoea, and mental disturbance.
– SAY pel-**lag**-ruh or pel-**lay**-gruh

pellet »*noun* ❶ a small compressed mass of a substance. ❷ a lightweight bullet or piece of small shot.

> ✓ double **l**, single **t**: **pellet**

pell-mell »*adjective & adverb* in a confused or rushed way.

pellucid »*adjective* ❶ transparent or semi-transparent. ❷ easily understood.
– SAY pel-**loo**-sid

> ✓ double **l**: **pellucid**

pelmet »*noun* a narrow border fitted across the top of a door or window to conceal the curtain fittings.

pelota »*noun* a Basque or Spanish ball game played in a walled court with basket-like rackets.
– SAY pi-**loh**-tuh

pelt[1] (verb: **pelts, pelting, pelted**) [hurl missiles at something]

pelt[2] »*noun* the skin of an animal with the fur, wool, or hair still on it.

pelvis »*noun* (plural **pelvises** or **pelves**) the large bony frame at the base of the spine to which the lower limbs are attached.
– SAY pel-**viss** [singular], pel-**veez** [plural]
pelvic

> ✓ the plural of **pelvis** can be **pelvises** or (as in the original Latin) **pelves**

pen (verb: **pens, penning, penned**)

> ✓ double the **n** in **penning** and **penned**

penal »*adjective* ❶ relating to the punishment of offenders under the legal system. ❷ extremely severe: *penal rates of interest.*

penalize »*verb* (**penalizes, penalizing, penalized**) ❶ give someone a penalty or punishment. ❷ (in law) make an action legally punishable. ❸ put someone in an unfavourable position.
penalization

> ✓ many people prefer the alternative spellings **penalise, penalises**, etc., and **penalisation**: both **s** and **z** spellings are correct

penalty (plural **penalties**)

> ✓ plural: drop the **y** and add **ies**: **penalties**

penance »*noun* ❶ an act that a person does, or that is given to them by a priest, for having done wrong. ❷ a sacrament in which a member of the Church confesses sins to a priest and is given formal forgiveness.

> ✓ **ance** not **ence**: **penance**

pence plural of **PENNY** (used for sums of money).

> ℹ avoid using **pence** in the singular to mean 'penny', as in *the chancellor will put one pence on income tax*

penchant »*noun* a strong liking or inclination: *a penchant for champagne.*
– SAY **pon**-shon

> ✓ remember the **t** at the end: **penchant** is a French word meaning 'leaning'

pencil (verb: **pencils**, **pencilling**, **pencilled**)

✓ double the **l** in **pencilling** and **pencilled** (the spellings **penciling** and **penciled** are American)

pendant »*noun* ❶ a piece of jewellery that hangs from a necklace chain. ❷ a light designed to hang from the ceiling.
» *adjective* hanging downwards.

✓ **ant** not **ent**: **pendant**
while both **pendant** and **pendent** can be used to describe something that hangs down, only **pendant** refers to a piece of jewellery or a type of light

pendent »*adjective* hanging down.

pending »*adjective* ❶ waiting to be decided or settled. ❷ about to happen.
» *preposition* awaiting an outcome; until.

pendulous »*adjective* hanging down; drooping.

pendulum »*noun* a weight hung from a fixed point so that it can swing freely, used to regulate the mechanism of a clock.

✓ only one **l**: **pendulum**

penetrate »*verb* (**penetrates**, **penetrating**, **penetrated**) ❶ force a way into or through something. ❷ gain access to an enemy organization or a competitor's market. ❸ understand or gain insight into something. ❹ (**penetrating**) (of a sound) clearly heard through or above other sounds. ❺ (of a man) insert the penis into the vagina or anus of a sexual partner.
penetrable
penetration
penetrative

penfriend

penguin

penicillin »*noun* an antibiotic.

✓ double **l**: **penicillin**

penile »*adjective* having to do with the penis.

peninsula »*noun* a long, narrow piece of land projecting out into a sea or lake.
peninsular

✓ remember, there is no **r** at the end of **peninsula**, but an **r** is added to make the adjective **peninsular** 'of a peninsula'

penis (plural **penises**)

ℹ a Latin plural **penes** (SAY pee-neez) is sometimes used in medical writing

penitent »*adjective* feeling sorrow and regret for having done wrong.
» *noun* a person who repents or submits to penance.

penitence
penitential
penitently

✓ **nit** not **net** in the middle: **penitent**

penitentiary »*noun* (plural **penitentiaries**) (in North America) a prison for people convicted of serious crimes.
– SAY pen-i-ten-shuh-ri

✓ plural: drop the **y** and add **ies**: **penitentiaries**

penknife (plural **penknives**)

pen name »*noun* a name used by a writer instead of their real name.

pennant »*noun* a long, narrow, pointed flag flown on a ship.

✓ double **n**, and **ant** not **ent**: **pennant**

penne »*plural noun* pasta in the form of short wide tubes.
– SAY pen-nay

✓ **penne** is an Italian word meaning 'quills'

penned

pennies

penniless

penning

pennon »*noun* = PENNANT.

penny (plural **pennies** or **pence**)

ℹ use the plural **pennies** when you are referring to separate coins (as in *there were two pennies on the floor*), but **pence** when you are referring to a sum of money (as in *the newspaper cost fifty pence*)

✓ plural: drop the **y** and add **ies**: **pennies**

penny-farthing »*noun* an early type of bicycle with a very large front wheel and a small rear wheel.

penny-pinching »*adjective* unwilling to spend money; miserly.
» *noun* miserliness.
penny-pincher

pennyworth

pen-pusher »*noun* (in informal English) a clerical worker.

pens

pension[1] »*noun* a regular payment made by the state or a company to retired people and to some widows and disabled people.
» *verb* (**pensions**, **pensioning**, **pensioned**) (**pension off**) dismiss someone from employment and pay them a pension.

– **say** pen-sh'n
pensionable
pensioner

pension[2] **»noun** a small hotel in France and other European countries.
– **say** pon-syon

pensive **»adjective** thinking deeply about something.
pensively
pensiveness

penstemon **»noun** a North American plant with snapdragon-like flowers.
– **say** pen-sti-muhn or pen-**stee**-muhn

> ✓ **penstemon** can also be spelled **pentstemon**, with an extra **t**

pentacle **»noun** a pentagram.
– **say** pen-tuh-k'l

pentagon **»noun** ❶ a shape with five straight sides and five angles. ❷ **(the Pentagon)** the headquarters of the US Department of Defense.
pentagonal

pentagram **»noun** a five-pointed star drawn using a continuous line, used as a mystic and magical symbol.

pentameter **»noun** a line of verse consisting of five metrical feet.
– **say** pen-**tam**-i-ter

> ✓ -meter not -metre: **pentameter**

Pentateuch **»noun** the first five books of the Old Testament and Hebrew Scriptures.
– **say** pen-tuh-tyook

pentathlon **»noun** an athletic event comprising five different events for each competitor.
pentathlete

pentatonic **»adjective** (in music) consisting of a scale of five notes.
– **say** pen-tuh-**ton**-ik

Pentecost **»noun** ❶ the Christian festival celebrating the descent of the Holy Spirit on the disciples of Jesus after his Ascension, held on Whit Sunday. ❷ the Jewish festival that takes place fifty days after the second day of Passover.
– **say** pen-ti-kost

> ✓ **Pente** not **Penta**: **Pentecost**

Pentecostal **»adjective** ❶ relating to Pentecost. ❷ relating to a group of Christian Churches that emphasize baptism in the Holy Spirit, evidence of which includes 'speaking in tongues' and healing.

penthouse **»noun** a flat on the top floor of a tall building.

pentstemon another way of spelling **PENSTEMON**.

penultimate **»adjective** last but one.

penumbra **»noun** (plural **penumbrae** or **penumbras**) the partially shaded outer region of the shadow cast by an object.
– **say** pe-**num**-bruh [singular], pe-**num**-bree [plural]

> ✓ the plural of **penumbra** can be **penumbrae** (as in the original Latin) or **penumbras**

penurious **»adjective** extremely poor.
– **say** pi-**nyoor**-i-uhss

penury **»noun** extreme poverty.
– **say** pen-yuu-ri

peon **»noun** an unskilled Spanish-American worker.

peony **»noun** (plural **peonies**) a plant cultivated for its showy flowers.
– **say** pee-uh-ni

> ✓ plural: drop the **y** and add **ies**: **peonies**

people (verb: **peoples, peopling, peopled**)

people carrier **»noun** a motor vehicle with three rows of seats.

peopled

peoples

peopling

PEP **»abbreviation** personal equity plan.

pep (verb: **peps, pepping, pepped**)

> ✓ double the **p** in **pepping** and **pepped**

pepper (verb: **peppers, peppering, peppered**)
peppery

peppercorn

peppered

peppering

peppermint **»noun** ❶ a plant of the mint family which produces aromatic leaves and oil, used as a flavouring in food. ❷ a sweet flavoured with peppermint oil.

pepperoni **»noun** beef and pork sausage seasoned with pepper.
– **say** pep-puh-**roh**-ni

peppers

pepping

peps

pepsin **»noun** the chief digestive enzyme in the stomach.

pep talk »*noun* a talk intended to make someone feel more courageous or enthusiastic.

peptic »*adjective* relating to digestion.

peptic ulcer »*noun* an ulcer in the lining of the stomach or small intestine.

per

peradventure »*adverb* (an old word) perhaps.

perambulate »*verb* (perambulates, perambulating, perambulated) walk or travel from place to place.
– SAY puh-**ram**-byuu-layt
perambulation

perambulator »*noun* = PRAM.

per annum »*adverb* for each year.

> ℹ **per annum** is a Latin phrase meaning 'by year'

per capita »*adverb* & *adjective* for each person.
– SAY per **ka**-pi-tuh

> ℹ **per capita** is a Latin phrase meaning 'by heads'

perceive »*verb* (perceives, perceiving, perceived) ❶ become aware or conscious of something through the senses. ❷ regard something as.

> ☑ remember, **i** before **e** except after **c**: perceive

per cent »*adverb* by a specified amount in or for every hundred.
» *noun* one part in every hundred.

> ☑ **per cent** can also be written as one word: percent

percentage »*noun* ❶ a rate, number, or amount in each hundred. ❷ a proportion or share of a whole.

percentile »*noun* (in statistics) one of 100 equal groups into which a population can be divided.
– SAY per-**sen**-tyl

perceptible »*adjective* able to be perceived.
perceptibly

> ☑ **-ible** not **-able**: perceptible

perception »*noun* ❶ the ability to see, hear, or become aware of something through the senses. ❷ the process of perceiving something. ❸ a way of understanding or interpreting something.

perceptive »*adjective* having good understanding of or insight into people and situations.
perceptively
perceptiveness

perceptual »*adjective* relating to the ability to perceive.
perceptually

perch (verb: perches, perching, perched)

perchance »*adverb* (an old word) by some chance; perhaps.

perched

perches

perching

percipient »*adjective* having good insight or understanding.
– SAY per-**sip**-i-uhnt
percipience
percipiently

> ☑ **cip** not **sip**: percipient

percolate »*verb* (percolates, percolating, percolated) ❶ filter something through a porous surface or substance. ❷ (of information or ideas) spread gradually through a group of people. ❸ prepare coffee in a percolator.
– SAY **per**-kuh-layt
percolation

percolator »*noun* a machine for making coffee, consisting of a pot in which boiling water is circulated through a small chamber that holds the ground beans.

> ☑ **-or** not **-er**: percolator

percussion »*noun* ❶ musical instruments that are played by being struck or shaken. ❷ percussion instruments forming a band or section of an orchestra.
percussionist
percussive

> ☑ double **s**, not **sh**: there is no **cushion** in percussion

perdition »*noun* (in Christian belief) a state of eternal damnation into which a sinful person who has not repented passes after death.
– SAY per-**dish**-uhn

peregrinations »*plural noun* (an old word) travels or wanderings from place to place.
– SAY pe-ri-gri-**nay**-sh'nz

peregrine »*noun* a falcon with a bluish-grey back and wings and pale underparts.
– SAY **pe**-ri-grin

> ☑ remember the **e** at the end: peregrine

peremptory »*adjective* insisting on immediate attention or obedience.
– SAY puh-**remp**-tuh-ri
peremptorily
peremptoriness

perennial »*adjective* ❶ lasting a year or several years. ❷ (of a plant) living for several years. ❸ lasting or doing something for a very long time.
» *noun* a perennial plant.
perennially

✓ one r, two n's: **perennial**

perfect (verb: **perfects, perfecting, perfected**)
perfectible

perfection

perfectionism »*noun* the inability or refusal to be satisfied with something unless it is done perfectly.
perfectionist

perfectly

perfects

perfect tense »*noun* the grammatical tense used to describe a completed action or a state in the past, as in *they have eaten*.

perfidious »*adjective* deceitful and untrustworthy.
– SAY per-**fid**-i-uhss
perfidiously
perfidiousness

perfidy »*noun* deceit; disloyalty.
– SAY **per**-fi-di

perforate »*verb* (**perforates, perforating, perforated**) pierce something and make a hole or holes in it.
– SAY **per**-fuh-rayt
perforation

perforce »*adverb* necessarily; inevitably.

perform (verb: **performs, performing, performed**)
performer

performance

performance art »*noun* an art form that combines visual art with drama.

performed

performer

performing

performing arts »*plural noun* creative activities that are performed in front of an audience, such as drama, music, and dance.

performs

perfume (verb: **perfumes, perfuming, perfumed**)

perfumery »*noun* (plural **perfumeries**) ❶ the making and selling of perfumes. ❷ a shop that sells perfumes.
perfumer

perfumes

perfuming

perfunctory »*adjective* carried out with a minimum of effort or thought.
– SAY per-**fungk**-tuh-ri
perfunctorily

pergola »*noun* an arched structure forming a framework for climbing or trailing plants.
– SAY **per**-guh-luh

perhaps

pericardium »*noun* (plural **pericardia**) the membrane enclosing the heart.
– SAY pe-ri-**kar**-di-uhm

✓ like many words ending in **um** derived from Latin, **pericardium** has a plural ending in **a: pericardia**

pericarp »*noun* the part of a fruit formed from the wall of the ripened ovary.

peridot »*noun* a green semi-precious stone.
– SAY **pe**-ri-dot

perigee »*noun* the point in the orbit of the moon or a satellite at which it is nearest to the earth.
– SAY **pe**-ri-jee

perihelion »*noun* (plural **perihelia**) the point in a planet's orbit at which it is closest to the sun.
– SAY pe-ri-**hee**-li-uhn [singular], pe-ri-**hee**-li-uh [plural]

peril »*noun* a situation of serious and immediate danger.

perilous »*adjective* full of danger or risk.
perilously
perilousness

✓ one r, one l: **perilous**

perimeter »*noun* the continuous line at the boundary or outside edge of something.

✓ -**meter** not -**metre: perimeter**
do not confuse **perimeter** with **parameter**, which usually means 'something that controls or limits the way something is done'

period

periodic »*adjective* appearing or occurring at intervals.
– SAY peer-i-**od**-ik
periodicity

periodical »*adjective* ❶ occurring or appearing at intervals. ❷ (of a magazine or newspaper) published at regular intervals.
» *noun* a periodical magazine or newspaper.
periodically

periodicity

periodic table »*noun* a table of the chemical elements arranged in order of atomic number.

period piece »*noun* an object or work that is set in or characteristic of an earlier historical period.

peripatetic »*adjective* ❶ travelling from place to place. ❷ working or based in a succession of places.
– SAY pe-ri-puh-**tet**-ik
peripatetically

 -patetic not **-pathetic: peripatetic**

peripheral »*adjective* ❶ relating to or situated on the outer limits of something. ❷ of secondary importance. ❸ (of a device) able to be attached to and used with a computer, though not a built-in part of it.
– SAY puh-**rif**-uh-ruhl
peripherally

periphery »*noun* (plural **peripheries**) ❶ the outer limits or edge of an area or object. ❷ the less important part of a subject or group.
– SAY puh-**rif**-uh-ri

 plural: drop the **y** and add **ies: peripheries**

periscope »*noun* a device consisting of a tube attached to a set of mirrors, through which you can see things that are above or behind something else.

perish »*verb* (**perishes, perishing, perished**) ❶ die. ❷ be completely ruined or destroyed. ❸ rot. ❹ (**be perished**) feel very cold.
perisher

perishable »*adjective* (of food) likely to rot quickly.

 -able not **-ible: perishable**

perished

perisher

perishes

perishing »*adjective* extremely cold.
perishingly

peritoneum »*noun* (plural **peritoneums** or **peritonea**) a membrane lining the inside of the abdomen.
– SAY pe-ri-tuh-**nee**-uhm
peritoneal

 the plural of **peritoneum** can be either **peritoneums** or **peritonea** (as in the original Latin)

peritonitis »*noun* inflammation of the peritoneum.

– SAY pe-ri-tuh-**ny**-tiss

periwinkle »*noun* ❶ a plant with flat five-petalled flowers and glossy leaves. ❷ = WINKLE.

perjure »*verb* (**perjures, perjuring, perjured**) (**perjure yourself**) tell a lie in court after swearing to tell the truth; commit perjury.
perjurer

perjury »*noun* the offence of deliberately telling a lie in court after having sworn to tell the truth.
– SAY **per**-juh-ri

perk »*verb* (**perks, perking, perked**) (**perk up**) become or make someone more cheerful or lively.
» *noun* an extra benefit given to an employee in addition to wages.

perky (adjective: **perkier, perkiest**)
perkily
perkiness

perm »*noun* a method of setting the hair in waves or curls and treating it with chemicals so that the style lasts for several months.
» *verb* (**perms, perming, permed**) treat hair in such a way.

 perm is short for **permanent wave**

permafrost »*noun* a thick layer of soil beneath the surface that remains below freezing point throughout the year.

permanent »*adjective* lasting for a long time or forever.
permanence
permanently

 ent not **ant: permanent**

permeable »*adjective* allowing liquids or gases to pass through.
permeability

permeate »*verb* (**permeates, permeating, permeated**) spread throughout something.
permeation

permed

Permian »*adjective* relating to the geological period from about 290 to 245 million years ago.
– SAY **per**-mi-uhn

perming

permissible »*adjective* allowable.

 -ible not **-able: permissible**

permission

 single **m** but double **s: permission**

permissive »*adjective* allowing people a lot of freedom.
permissively
permissiveness

permit (verb: **permits, permitting, permitted**)

> ☑ double the t to spell **permitting** and **permitted**

perms

permutation »*noun* one of several possible ways in which a number of things can be ordered or arranged.

pernicious »*adjective* having a harmful effect.
– say per-**nish**-uhss
perniciously
perniciousness

> ☑ cious not tious: pernicious

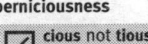

pernickety »*adjective* (in informal English) ❶ fussy. ❷ needing a careful approach.

peroration »*noun* the concluding part of a speech.

peroxide »*noun* a chemical that is used as a bleach or disinfectant.
» *verb* (**peroxides, peroxiding, peroxided**) bleach hair with peroxide.

perpendicular »*adjective* at an angle of 90° to the ground, or to another line or surface.
» *noun* a perpendicular line.
– say per-puhn-**dik**-yuu-ler
perpendicularity
perpendicularly

> ☑ ar not er: perpendicular

perpetrate »*verb* (**perpetrates, perpetrating, perpetrated**) carry out a bad or illegal action.
– say **per**-pi-trayt
perpetration
perpetrator

perpetual »*adjective* ❶ never ending or changing. ❷ so frequent as to seem continual.
– say per-**pet**-yoo-uhl
perpetually

perpetuate »*verb* (**perpetuates, perpetuating, perpetuated**) cause something to continue indefinitely.
perpetuation
perpetuator

perpetuity »*noun* the state of lasting forever.

perplex (verb: **perplexes, perplexing, perplexed**)

perplexity »*noun* (plural **perplexities**) ❶ the state of being puzzled. ❷ a puzzling situation or thing.

perquisite »*noun* a special right or privilege.
– say per-**kwi**-zit

> ⓘ do not confuse **perquisite** with **prerequisite**, which means 'a thing that must happen before something else can happen'

per se »*adverb* in itself or themselves: *it is not these facts per se that are important.*
– say per **say**

> ⓘ per se is a Latin phrase which means 'by itself'

persecute »*verb* (**persecutes, persecuting, persecuted**) ❶ treat someone badly over a long period. ❷ harass someone.
persecution
persecutor

persevere »*verb* (**perseveres, persevering, persevered**) continue doing something in spite of difficulty or lack of success.
perseverance

Persian »*noun* ❶ a person from Persia (now Iran). ❷ the language of ancient Persia or modern Iran. ❸ a breed of domestic cat with long hair and a broad round head.
» *adjective* relating to Persia or Iran.

persiflage »*noun* light mockery or banter.
– say per-si-flah*zh*

persimmon »*noun* a fruit that looks like a large tomato but is very sweet.
– say per-**sim**-muhn

persist »*verb* (**persists, persisting, persisted**) ❶ continue doing something in spite of difficulty or opposition. ❷ continue to exist.
persistent
persistence
persistently

> ☑ ent not ant: persistent

persisting
persists

person (plural **people** or **persons**)

> ⓘ **people** and **persons** are both plurals of **person**, but **people** is the one that is commonly used. **Persons** is used in official or formal contexts, as in *no persons admitted without a pass.*

persona »*noun* (plural **personas** or **personae**) the part of a person's character that is revealed to other people: *her public persona.*

– **say** per-**soh**-nuh [singular], per-**soh**-nee [plural]

☑ the plural of **persona** can be either **personas** or **personae** (as in the original Latin)

personable »*adjective* having a pleasant appearance and manner.
personably

personae plural of **PERSONA**.

personage »*noun* a person (used to express their importance or high status).

personal

personal column »*noun* a section of a newspaper listing private advertisements or messages.

personalise another way of spelling **PERSONALIZE**.

personality (plural **personalities**)

☑ plural: drop the **y** and add **ies**: **personalities**

personalize (verb: **personalizes**, **personalizing**, **personalized**)
personalization

☑ many people prefer the alternative spellings **personalise**, **personalises**, etc.: both **s** and **z** spellings are correct

personally

personal organizer »*noun* a loose-leaf notebook with a diary and address book.

personal pronoun »*noun* a pronoun that shows person, gender, number, and case (such as *I, you, he, she*, etc.)

persona non grata »*noun* an unacceptable or unwelcome person.
– **say** per-soh-nuh nohn **grah**-tuh

☑ it is unusual to need a plural, but if you do it would be **personae non gratae** (**say** per-soh-nee nohn **grah**-tee)

personify »*verb* (**personifies**, **personifying**, **personified**) ❶ give human characteristics to something that is not human. ❷ be an example of a quality or characteristic.
– **say** per-**son**-i-fI
personification

personnel »*plural noun* people employed in an organization.
– **say** per-suh-**nel**

☑ double n, single l: **personnel**

persons

perspective »*noun* ❶ the art of representing things on paper so that they seem to have height, width, depth, and relative distance. ❷ a view. ❸ a particular way of seeing something.

❹ understanding of how important things are in relation to others.

perspex »*noun* (trademark) a tough transparent plastic used as a substitute for glass.

perspicacious »*adjective* quickly gaining insight into things.
– **say** per-spi-**kay**-shuhss
perspicaciously
perspicacity

ℹ️ do not confuse **perspicacious** with **perspicuous**, which means 'clearly expressed and easily understood'

perspicuous »*adjective* ❶ clearly expressed and easily understood. ❷ (of a person) expressing things clearly.
– **say** per-**spik**-yuu-uhss
perspicuity
perspicuously

ℹ️ do not confuse **perspicuous** with **perspicacious**, which means 'quickly gaining an insight into things'

perspiration »*noun* ❶ sweat. ❷ the process of sweating.

perspire »*verb* (**perspires**, **perspiring**, **perspired**) give out sweat through the pores of the skin.

persuade (verb: **persuades**, **persuading**, **persuaded**)
persuadable
persuader

persuasion

persuasive
persuasively
persuasiveness

pert »*adjective* ❶ attractively lively or cheeky. ❷ (of a bodily feature or garment) attractive because neat and jaunty.
pertly
pertness

pertain »*verb* (**pertains**, **pertaining**, **pertained**) be appropriate, related, or relevant to something.

pertinacious »*adjective* persistent.
– **say** per-ti-**nay**-shuhss
pertinaciously
pertinacity

pertinent »*adjective* relevant or appropriate.
pertinence
pertinently

pertly

pertness

perturb »*verb* (**perturbs**, **perturbing**, **perturbed**) make someone anxious or unsettled.

perturbation »*noun* anxiety; uneasiness.
– SAY per-ter-bay-sh'n

peruse »*verb* (**peruses, perusing, perused**)
read or examine something thoroughly or
carefully.
– SAY puh-**rooz**
perusal

> ℹ️ **peruse** is sometimes mistakenly used
> to mean 'read through quickly;
> glance over something'. When used
> correctly it means 'read or examine
> thoroughly or carefully'.

Peruvian

pervade »*verb* (**pervades, pervading,
pervaded**) spread or be present throughout
something.

pervasive »*adjective* spreading widely
through something.
pervasively
pervasiveness

perverse »*adjective* ❶ deliberately
choosing to behave in a way that other
people find unacceptable. ❷ contrary to
what is accepted or expected.
perversely
perverseness

perversion »*noun* ❶ the action of
perverting. ❷ abnormal and unacceptable
sexual behaviour.

perversity »*noun* the state of being
perverse.

pervert »*verb* (**perverts, perverting,
perverted**) ❶ change the form or meaning
of something in a way that distorts what
was first intended. ❷ lead away from
what is right, natural, or acceptable.
» *noun* a person whose sexual behaviour is
abnormal and unacceptable.

perverted »*adjective* sexually abnormal
and unacceptable.
pervertedly

pervious »*adjective* allowing water to pass
through.
– SAY per-vi-uhss

peseta »*noun* the basic unit of money of
Spain.
– SAY puh-say-tuh

pesky (adjective: **peskier, peskiest**)

pessary »*noun* (plural **pessaries**) a small
soluble block inserted into the vagina to
treat infection or as a contraceptive.
– SAY pess-uh-ri

pessimism »*noun* lack of hope or
confidence in the future.
pessimist
pessimistic
pessimistically

pest

pester (verb: **pesters, pestering, pestered**)

pesticide »*noun* a substance for destroying
insects or other pests.

pestilence »*noun* (an old word) a disease
that spreads widely and causes deaths.

pestilent »*adjective* ❶ causing a disease
that spreads widely and from which
people can die. ❷ (in informal English)
annoying.

pestilential »*adjective* ❶ (an old word)
relating to or causing a disease that
spreads widely and causes deaths.
❷ having the nature of a pest.

pestle »*noun* a heavy tool with a rounded
end, used for crushing and grinding
substances in a mortar.
– SAY pess-'l

pesto »*noun* (plural **pestos**) a sauce of
crushed basil leaves, pine nuts, garlic,
Parmesan cheese, and olive oil, served
with pasta.
– SAY pess-toh

> ☑️ the plural of **pesto**, which means
> 'paste' in Italian, has **os** not **oes**:
> **pestos**

pet (verb: **pets, petting, petted**)

> ☑️ double the **t** in **petted** and **petting**

petal

petard »*noun* (a historical term) a small
bomb made of a metal or wooden box
filled with powder.
– SAY pi-**tard**

peter »*verb* (**peters, petering, petered**)
(**peter out**) gradually come to an end.

petersham »*noun* a corded tape used for
stiffening in making dresses and hats.

petiole »*noun* the stalk that joins a leaf to a
stem.
– SAY pee-ti-ohl

petit bourgeois »*adjective* having to do
with the lower middle class, especially in
being conventional and conservative.
» *noun* (plural **petits bourgeois**) a petit
bourgeois person.
– SAY puh-ti **boor**-*zh*wah

> ☑️ the plural (which is pronounced the
> same as the singular) adds an **s** to
> **petit** only: **petits bourgeois** (it is a French
> phrase which means 'little citizen')

petite »*adjective* (of a woman) small and
dainty.

petite bourgeoisie »*noun* the lower
middle class.
– SAY puh-**teet** boor-*zh*wah-**zee**

✓ as **bourgeoisie** ('townsfolk') is a feminine noun in French, the strictly correct form for the adjective here is **petite**, not **petit**

petit four »*noun* (plural **petits fours**) a very small fancy cake, biscuit, or sweet.
– SAY puh-ti **for** [singular], puh-ti **forz** [plural]

✓ the plural adds an **s** to both words: **petits fours** (it is a French term which means 'little oven')

petition »*noun* an appeal or request, especially one signed by a large number of people and presented formally to someone in authority.
» *verb* (**petitions, petitioning, petitioned**) make or present a petition to someone. **petitioner**

petit mal »*noun* a mild form of epilepsy with only very short spells of unconsciousness.
– SAY puh-ti **mal**

✓ from a French phrase which means 'little sickness'

petit point »*noun* embroidery on canvas, using small diagonal stitches.
– SAY puh-ti **poynt** or puh-ti **pwan**

✓ from a French phrase which means 'little stitch'

petits pois »*plural noun* small, fine peas.
– SAY puh-ti **pwah**

ℹ from a French phrase which means 'small peas'

petrel »*noun* a kind of seabird that flies far from land.
– SAY pet-ruhl

✓ **el** not **ol**: **petrel** (**petrol** is the fuel)

Petri dish »*noun* a shallow transparent dish with a flat lid, used in laboratories.
– SAY pet-tri or pee-tri

✓ no **e** at the end: **Petri dish** (it is named after the German scientist Julius R. *Petri*)

petrify »*verb* (**petrifies, petrifying, petrified**) ❶ change organic matter into stone by encrusting or replacing its original substance with a mineral deposit. ❷ paralyse someone with fear.
petrifaction
petrification

petrochemical »*adjective* relating to the chemical properties and processing of petroleum and natural gas.
» *noun* a chemical obtained from petroleum and natural gas.

petrol [fuel]

✓ **ol** not **el**: **petrol** (a **petrel** is a seabird)

petroleum »*noun* oil found in layers of rock and extracted and refined to produce fuels including petrol, paraffin, and diesel oil.

✓ **leum** not **lium**: **petroleum**

petroleum jelly »*noun* a semi-transparent substance obtained from petroleum, used as a lubricant or ointment.

pets

petted

petticoat »*noun* a woman's light undergarment in the form of a skirt or dress.

✓ **petti-** not **petty-**: **petticoat**

pettier

pettiest

pettifogging »*adjective* petty; trivial.

pettily

pettiness

petting

pettish »*adjective* childishly sulky.
pettishly

petty »*adjective* (**pettier, pettiest**) ❶ of little importance. ❷ (of a person's behaviour) small-minded. ❸ minor.
pettily
pettiness

petty cash »*noun* a store of money that is available to spend on small items.

petty officer »*noun* a rank of non-commissioned officer in the navy.

petulant »*adjective* childishly sulky or bad-tempered.
– SAY pet-yuu-luhnt
petulance
petulantly

✓ **ant** not **ent**: **petulant**

petunia »*noun* a plant with white, purple, or red funnel-shaped flowers.
– SAY pi-**tyoo**-ni-uh

pew »*noun* (in a church) a long bench with a back.

pewter »*noun* a metal made by mixing tin with copper and antimony.

pfennig »*noun* a unit of money of Germany, equal to one hundredth of a mark.
– SAY pfen-nig

PG »*abbreviation* (in film classification) parental guidance.

pH »*noun* a figure expressing how acid or alkaline a substance is.

phaeton »*noun* (a historical term) a light, open horse-drawn carriage.
– **say** fay-tuhn

> ℹ from the name of *Phaethon* in Greek mythology, who was allowed to drive the chariot of the sun for a day

phalanger »*noun* a tree-dwelling marsupial native to Australia and New Guinea.
– **say** fuh-**lan**-jer

phalanx »*noun* (plural **phalanxes**) ❶ a group of similar people or things. ❷ a body of troops in close formation.
– **say** fa-langks

phallic »*adjective* relating to or resembling a erect penis.

phallus »*noun* (plural **phalli** or **phalluses**) an erect penis.
– **say** fal-luhss [singular], fal-lI [plural]

> ✓ the plural of **phallus** can be either **phalli** (as in the original Latin) or **phalluses**

phantasm »*noun* (a poetic term) an illusion or figment of the imagination.
– **say** fan-ta-z'm

phantasmagoria »*noun* a sequence of real or imaginary images like that seen in a dream.
– **say** fan-taz-muh-**gor**-i-uh
phantasmagoric
phantasmagorical

phantasy see the note at **FANTASY**.

phantom »*noun* ❶ a ghost. ❷ a figment of the imagination.
» *adjective* not really existing.

pharaoh »*noun* a ruler in ancient Egypt.
– **say** fair-oh
pharaonic

> ✓ note that the ending is **aoh** not **oah**: **pharaoh**

Pharisee »*noun* a member of an ancient Jewish sect who followed religious laws very strictly.
– **say** fa-ri-see

pharmaceutical »*adjective* relating to medicinal drugs.
» *noun* a compound made for use as a medicinal drug.
– **say** far-muh-**syoo**-ti-k'l

pharmacist »*noun* a person who is qualified to prepare and dispense medicinal drugs.

pharmacology »*noun* the branch of medicine concerned with the uses, effects, and action of drugs.
pharmacological
pharmacologist

pharmacy »*noun* (plural **pharmacies**) ❶ a place where medicinal drugs are prepared or sold. ❷ the science or practice of preparing and dispensing medicinal drugs.

> ✓ plural: drop the **y** and add **ies**: **pharmacies**

pharynx »*noun* (plural **pharynges**) the cavity connecting the nose and mouth to the throat.
– **say** fa-ringks [singular], fa-**rin**-jeez [plural]

> ✓ the plural of **pharynx** drops the **x** and adds **ges**: **pharynges**

phase »*noun* ❶ a distinct period or stage in a process of change or development. ❷ one of the aspects of the moon or a planet, according to the amount that it is lit up. ❸ (in physics) the stage that a regularly varying quantity (e.g. an alternating electric current) has reached in relation to zero or another chosen value.
» *verb* (**phases**, **phasing**, **phased**) ❶ carry something out in gradual stages. ❷ (**phase in** or **out**) gradually introduce or withdraw something.

PhD »*abbreviation* Doctor of Philosophy.

> ℹ PhD is an abbreviation of the Latin phrase *philosophiae doctor*

pheasant »*noun* a large long-tailed game bird.

> ✓ **ant** not **ent**: **pheasant**

phenol »*noun* a poisonous white solid obtained from coal tar. Also called **CARBOLIC ACID**.
– **say** fee-nol

phenomena plural of **PHENOMENON**.

phenomenal »*adjective* extraordinary.
phenomenally

phenomenon »*noun* (plural **phenomena**) ❶ a fact or situation that is observed to exist or happen. ❷ a remarkable person or thing.
– **say** fi-**nom**-i-nuhn

> ℹ the word **phenomenon** comes from Greek, and its plural form is **phenomena**. Do not use **phenomena** as if it were a singular form; say *this is a strange phenomenon*, not *this is a strange phenomena*.

pheromone »*noun* a chemical substance released by an animal and causing a response in others of its species.
– SAY fe-ruh-mohn

phi »*noun* the twenty-first letter of the Greek alphabet (Φ, φ).
– SAY fy

phial »*noun* a small cylindrical glass bottle.
– SAY fy-uhl

> **i** do not confuse **phial** with **vial**, which means 'a small container for holding liquid medicines'

philander »*verb* (philanders, philandering, philandered) (of a man) have numerous sexual relationships with women.
– SAY fi-lan-der
philanderer

philanthropic

philanthropically

philanthropist »*noun* a person who gives money to good causes or otherwise seeks to help others.

philanthropy »*noun* the practice of helping people in need, especially by giving money.
philanthropic
philanthropically

philately »*noun* the hobby of collecting postage stamps.
– SAY fi-lat-uh-li
philatelic
philatelist

philharmonic »*adjective* devoted to music (used in the names of orchestras).

philippic »*noun* a bitter verbal attack.
– SAY fi-lip-pik

Philistine »*noun* ❶ a member of a people of ancient Palestine who fought with the Israelites. ❷ (**philistine**) a person who is hostile to or not interested in culture and the arts.
– SAY fil-i-styn
philistinism

> **✓** there is only a single l in **Philistine**

Phillips »*adjective* (trademark) referring to a screw with a cross-shaped slot for turning, or a screwdriver that fits such a screw.

> **i** named after the American manufacturer Henry F. *Phillips*

philology »*noun* the study of the structure and historical development of language and relationships between languages.
philological
philologist

philosopher »*noun* ❶ a person who is engaged in philosophy. ❷ a person who thinks deeply about things.

philosopher's stone »*noun* a mythical substance supposed to change any metal into gold or silver.

philosophical »*adjective* ❶ relating to the study of philosophy. ❷ having a calm attitude when things are difficult.
philosophically

philosophies

philosophize »*verb* (philosophizes, philosophizing, philosophized) think carefully about serious issues.

> **✓** many people prefer the alternative spellings **philosophise, philosophises**, etc.: both **s** and **z** spellings are correct

philosophy »*noun* (plural philosophies) ❶ the study of the fundamental nature of knowledge, reality, and existence. ❷ a particular set or system of beliefs.

> **✓** plural: drop the **y** and add **ies**: philosophies

philtre »*noun* a love potion.
– SAY fil-ter

> **✓** re not er: philtre (the spelling **philter** is American)

phlebitis »*noun* inflammation of the walls of a vein.
– SAY fli-by-tiss

phlegm »*noun* ❶ a mucus in the nose and throat. ❷ (old-fashioned) the ability to remain calm.
– SAY flem

> **✓** note the **g**: phlegm

phlegmatic »*adjective* calm and unemotional.
– SAY fleg-mat-ik
phlegmatically

phloem »*noun* the tissue in plants which conducts food materials downwards from the leaves.
– SAY floh-em

phlox »*noun* a garden plant with clusters of colourful scented flowers.
– SAY floks

> **i** phlox is a Greek word meaning 'flame'

phobia »*noun* a strong irrational fear of something.
phobic

Phoenician »*noun* a member of an ancient people inhabiting Phoenicia in the eastern Mediterranean.

» *adjective* relating to Phoenicia or its people.
– SAY fuh-**nee**-sh'n or fuh-**ni**-sh'n

phoenix »*noun* (in classical mythology) a bird that burned itself on a funeral pyre and was born again from the ashes.
– SAY **fee**-niks

 oe not **eo**: phoenix

phone (verb: **phones**, **phoning**, **phoned**)

phonecard

phoned

phone-in

phones

phonetic »*adjective* ❶ having to do with speech sounds. ❷ (of a system of writing) using symbols that represent sounds.
phonetically

phonetics »*noun* the study of speech sounds.

phoney (adjective: **phonier**, **phoniest**; plural **phoneys**)

 phoney can also be spelled without the **e**: phony

phonic »*adjective* relating to speech sounds.
» *noun* (**phonics**) a method of teaching people to read by correlating sounds with alphabetic symbols.
– SAY **fon**-ik

phonier

phoniest

phoning

phonograph »*noun* ❶ (in British English) an early form of gramophone that could record as well as reproduce sound. ❷ (in American English) a record player.

phonology »*noun* the system of relationships among the basic speech sounds of a language.
– SAY fuh-**nol**-uh-ji
phonological

phony (plural **phonies**) another way of spelling **PHONEY**.

phosphate »*noun* (in chemistry) a salt or ester of phosphoric acid.
– SAY **foss**-fayt

phosphor »*noun* a synthetic fluorescent or phosphorescent substance.
– SAY **foss**-fer

phosphorescence »*noun* a faint light that is given out by a substance with no heat or with such little heat that it cannot be felt.
phosphorescent

scence not **sence**: phosphorescence

phosphoric »*adjective* relating to or containing phosphorus.
– SAY foss-**fo**-rik

phosphorus »*noun* a yellowish waxy solid which can ignite spontaneously and which glows in the dark.
– SAY **foss**-fuh-ruhss
phosphorous

the name of the chemical element is **phosphorus**, ending in **us** not **ous**. **Phosphorous** is an adjective meaning 'relating to or containing phosphorus'.

photo (plural **photos**)

the plural of **photo** has **os** not **oes**: photos

photocall »*noun* a time arranged in advance when people pose for photographers.

photocell »*noun* = **PHOTOELECTRIC CELL**.

photochemistry »*noun* the branch of chemistry concerned with the chemical effects of light.
photochemical

photocopy (plural **photocopies**; verb: **photocopies**, **photocopying**, **photocopied**)
photocopiable
photocopier

 plural: drop the **y** and add **ies**: photocopies

photoelectric »*adjective* involving the production of electricity as a result of the action of light on a surface.

photoelectric cell »*noun* a device using a photoelectric effect to generate current.

photofit »*noun* a picture of a person made up from photographs of parts of other people's faces.

photogenic »*adjective* ❶ looking attractive in photographs. ❷ (in biology) giving off light.
– SAY foh-tuh-**jen**-ik

photograph (verb: **photographs**, **photographing**, **photographed**)
photographer
photographic
photographically

photography

photojournalism »*noun* the use of photographs to report news.
photojournalist

photometer »*noun* an instrument measuring the intensity of light.

– **say** foh-**tom**-i-ter
photometric
photometry

photomontage »*noun* a picture consisting of photographs placed together or overlapping.
– **say** foh-toh-mon-**tah***zh*

photon »*noun* (in physics) a particle representing a quantum of light or other electromagnetic radiation.
– **say** foh-ton

photos

photosensitive »*adjective* responding to light.
photosensitivity

photostat »*noun* (trademark) ❶ a type of machine for making photocopies on special paper. ❷ a copy made by a photostat.

photosynthesis »*noun* the process by which green plants use sunlight to form nutrients from carbon dioxide and water.
photosynthetic

photosynthesize »*verb*
(**photosynthesizes**, **photosynthesizing**, **photosynthesized**) (of a plant) form nutrients by means of photosynthesis.

> ✓ many people prefer the alternative spellings **photosynthesise**, **photosynthesises**, etc.: both **s** and **z** spellings are correct

phototropism »*noun* (in biology) the turning of a plant towards a source of light.
– **say** foh-toh-**troh**-pi-zuhm

phrasal verb »*noun* (in grammar) an idiomatic phrase consisting of a verb and an adverb or preposition, as in *break down* or *see to*.

phrase (verb: **phrases**, **phrasing**, **phrased**)
phrasal

phraseology »*noun* (plural **phraseologies**) a particular form of words used to express an idea.
– **say** fray-zi-**ol**-uh-ji

phrases

phrasing »*noun* division of music into phrases.

phrenology »*noun* (mainly a historical term) the study of the shape and size of a person's skull as a supposed indication of their character and abilities.
– **say** fri-**nol**-uh-ji
phrenologist

phyla plural of **PHYLUM**.

phyllo another way of spelling **FILO**.

phylum »*noun* (plural **phyla**) (in biology) a major division of the animal kingdom.

– **say** fy-luhm [singular], fy-luh [plural]

> ✓ like many other words ending in **um** derived from Latin, **phylum** has a plural ending in **a**: **phyla**

physic »*noun* (an old word) medicinal drugs or medical treatment.

physical
physicality
physically

> ✓ double the **l** in **physically**

physical geography »*noun* the branch of geography concerned with natural features.

physicality
physically

physical sciences »*plural noun* the sciences concerned with the study of inanimate natural objects, including physics, chemistry, and astronomy.

physician »*noun* a person qualified to practise medicine.

physics »*noun* the branch of science concerned with the nature and properties of matter and energy.
physicist

physio »*noun* (plural **physios**) (in informal English) physiotherapy or a physiotherapist.

> ✓ the plural of **physio** has **os** not **oes**: **physios**

physiognomy »*noun* (plural **physiognomies**) a person's face or facial expression.
– **say** fi-zi-**og**-nuh-mi or fi-zi-**on**-uh-mi

physiology »*noun* the scientific study of the way in which living things function.
physiological
physiologist

physios

physiotherapy »*noun* the treatment of disease and injury by massage and exercise.
physiotherapist

physique »*noun* the form, size, and development of a person's body.

pi »*noun* ❶ the sixteenth letter of the Greek alphabet (Π, π). ❷ the ratio of the circumference of a circle to its diameter (approximately 3.14159).
– **say** pI

> ✓ there is no **e** at the end: **pi**

pianissimo »*adverb & adjective* (in music) very soft or softly.

– **say** pi-uh-**niss**-i-moh

piano[1] (plural **pianos**) [a large keyboard instrument]
– **say** pi-**an**-oh
  pianist

> ✓ the plural of **piano** has **os** not **oes**: **pianos**

piano[2] »*adverb & adjective* (in music) soft or softly.
– **say** pi-**ah**-noh

pianoforte »*noun* = **piano**[1].
– **say** pi-an-oh-**for**-tay

> ℹ from Italian *piano e forte* which means 'soft and loud'

pianola »*noun* (trademark) a piano which can be played automatically by means of a roll of perforated paper that controls the movement of the keys.
– **say** pi-uh-**noh**-luh

piazza »*noun* a public square or marketplace, especially in Italy.
– **say** pi-**at**-suh

pic »*noun* (in informal English) a picture, photograph, or film.

picador »*noun* (in bullfighting) a person on horseback who goads the bull with a lance.
– **say** pi-kuh-dor

picaresque »*adjective* relating to fiction dealing with the adventures of a dishonest but appealing hero.
– **say** pi-kuh-**resk**

piccalilli »a pickle of chopped vegetables, mustard, and hot spices.
– **say** pi-kuh-**lil**-li

> ✓ double **c**, single **l**, double **l**: **piccalilli**

piccolo »*noun* (plural **piccolos**) a small flute sounding an octave higher than the ordinary one.

> ✓ the plural of **piccolo**, an Italian word, has **os** not **oes**: **piccolos**

pick (verb: **picks**, **picking**, **picked**)
  picker

pickaxe

picked

picker

picket »*noun* ❶ a person or group of people standing outside a workplace trying to persuade others not to work during a strike. ❷ a pointed wooden stake driven into the ground.
» *verb* (**pickets**, **picketing**, **picketed**) act as a picket outside a workplace.

pickier

pickiest

picking

pickings »*plural noun* ❶ profits or gains. ❷ scraps or leftovers.

pickle (verb: **pickles**, **pickling**, **pickled**)

pick-me-up »*noun* a thing that makes you feel more energetic or cheerful.

pickpocket

picks

pickup »*noun* ❶ a small truck with low sides. ❷ an act of picking up a person or goods.

picky (adjective: **pickier**, **pickiest**)

picnic (verb: **picnics**, **picnicking**, **picnicked**)
  picnicker

> ✓ remember the **k** in **picnicking**, **picnicked**, and **picnicker**

Pict »*noun* a member of an ancient people inhabiting northern Scotland in Roman times.

pictogram »*noun* = **pictograph**.

pictograph »*noun* a small image or picture representing a word or phrase.

pictorial »*adjective* having to do with or expressed in pictures.
  pictorially

picture (verb: **pictures**, **picturing**, **pictured**)

> ✓ there is no **e** in **picturing**

picture-postcard »*adjective* charmingly attractive: *picture-postcard villages*.

picturesque »*adjective* looking attractive in a quaint or charming way.
  picturesquely

piddle »*verb* (**piddles**, **piddling**, **piddled**) (in informal English) ❶ urinate. ❷ (**piddling**) very unimportant or trivial.

pidgin »*noun* a simple form of a language with elements taken from local languages.

pie [baked dish]

> ℹ see the note at **pi**

piebald »*adjective* (of a horse) having irregular patches of two colours.

piece (verb: **pieces**, **piecing**, **pieced**) [part of something larger]

> ℹ do not confuse **piece** with **peace**, which means 'freedom from noise, anxiety, or war'

> ✓ **i** before **e** except after **c**: **piece** there is no **e** after the **c** in **piecing**

piece de resistance »*noun* the most important or impressive part of something.

- **SAY** pyess duh ray-**ziss**-tonss

> ✓ **piece de resistance** can also be written with accents over two of the e's (as in the original French): **pièce de résistance**

piecemeal »*adjective & adverb* done piece by piece over a period of time.

pieces

piecework »*noun* work that is paid for by the amount done and not by the hours worked.

pie chart »*noun* a diagram in which a circle is divided into sections that each represent a proportion of the whole.

piecing

pied »*adjective* having two or more different colours.

pied-a-terre »*noun* (plural **pieds-a-terre**) a small flat or house kept for occasional use.
- **SAY** pyay-dah-**tair** [singular and plural]

> ✓ **pied-a-terre** can also be spelled **pied-à-terre**, with a grave accent on the **a** (as in the original French phrase meaning 'foot to earth')

pie-eyed »*adjective* (in informal English) very drunk.

pier [structure built out over water; bridge support]

> ℹ do not confuse **pier** with **peer**, which means 'member of the nobility' or 'person of equal status', or is used as a verb to mean 'look with concentration'

pierce (verb: **pierces**, **piercing**, **pierced**)
piercer
piercing

piety »*noun* the quality of being deeply religious.
- **SAY** py-uh-ti

piffle

piffling

pig (verb: **pigs**, **pigging**, **pigged**)
piglet

pigeon

> ✓ there is no **d** in **pigeon**

pigeonhole »*noun* ❶ one of a set of small compartments where letters or messages may be left for people. ❷ a category in which someone or something is placed.
» *verb* (**pigeonholes**, **pigeonholing**, **pigeonholed**) place someone or something in a particular category.

pigeon-toed »*adjective* having the toes or feet turned inwards.

pigged

piggery »*noun* (plural **piggeries**) a place where pigs are kept.

> ✓ plural: drop the **y** and add **ies**: **piggeries**

pigging

piggish

piggy

piggyback

pig-headed

piglet

pig iron »*noun* crude iron as first obtained from a smelting furnace.

pigment »*noun* ❶ a natural substance that gives a plant or animal its colour. ❷ a substance used for colouring or painting.
- **SAY** pig-muhnt
pigmentation
pigmented

pigmy another way of spelling **PYGMY**.

pigs

pigskin »*noun* leather made from pig hide.

pigsty »*noun* (plural **pigsties**) ❶ an enclosure for a pig or pigs. ❷ a very dirty or untidy place.

> ✓ plural: drop the **y** and add **ies**: **pigsties**

pigswill »*noun* kitchen refuse and scraps fed to pigs.

pigtail »*noun* a length of hair worn in a plait at the back or on each side of the head.

pike »*noun* a freshwater fish with a long body and sharp teeth.

pikelet »*noun* a thin kind of crumpet.

pikestaff »*noun* (a historical term) the wooden shaft of a pike.

pilaf »*noun* a Middle Eastern or Indian dish of spiced rice and often meat and vegetables.
- **SAY** pi-**laf**

> ✓ **pilaf** (a Turkish word) can also be spelled **pilau** (**SAY** pi-**low**)

pilaster »*noun* a column that projects from a wall.
- **SAY** pi-**lass**-ter

pilau another way of spelling **PILAF**.

pilchard »*noun* a small fish of the herring family.

pile (verb: **piles**, **piling**, **piled**)

piledriver »*noun* a machine for driving piles into the ground.

piles »*plural noun* haemorrhoids.

pile-up »*noun* a crash involving several vehicles.

pilfer »*verb* (**pilfers, pilfering, pilfered**) steal small items of little value.

pilgrim

pilgrimage

piling

pill

pillage »*verb* (**pillages, pillaging, pillaged**) steal from a place roughly and violently.
» *noun* the action of pillaging.

pillar [supporting column]
pillared

> ✓ **ar** not **er**: **pillar** (and not to be confused with **pillow**)

pillbox »*noun* (plural **pillboxes**) ❶ a small round hat. ❷ a small, partly underground, concrete fort.

pillion »*noun* a seat for a passenger behind a motorcyclist.

pillock

pillory »*noun* (plural **pillories**) (in the past) a wooden framework with holes for the head and hands, in which people were locked and left on display as a punishment.
» *verb* (**pillories, pillorying, pilloried**) ❶ put in a pillory. ❷ attack or ridicule someone publicly.

> ✓ plural: drop the **y** and add **ies**: **pillories**

pillow [soft support for lying down]
pillowy

pillowcase

pillowy

pilot (verb: **pilots, piloting, piloted**)

pilot light »*noun* a small gas burner kept alight permanently to light a larger burner when needed.

pilots

pimiento »*noun* (plural **pimientos**) a red sweet pepper.
– SAY pi-**myen**-toh

> ✓ the plural of **pimiento**, a Spanish word, has **os** not **oes**: **pimientos**. It can also be spelled **pimento**, without the **i** in the middle.

pimp »*noun* a man who controls prostitutes and arranges clients for them, taking a percentage of their earnings.
» *verb* (**pimps, pimping, pimped**) act as a pimp.

pimpernel »*noun* a low-growing plant with bright five-petalled flowers.

pimping

pimple
pimpled
pimply

pimps

PIN »*abbreviation* personal identification number.

pin (verb: **pins, pinning, pinned**)

> ✓ double the **n** in **pinning** and **pinned**

pina colada »*noun* a cocktail made with rum, pineapple juice, and coconut.
– SAY pee-nuh kuh-**lah**-duh

> ℹ **pina colada** is Spanish for 'strained pineapple'

pinafore »*noun* a collarless, sleeveless dress worn over a blouse or jumper.

pinball »*noun* a game in which small metal balls are shot across a sloping board and score points by striking targets.

pince-nez »*noun* a pair of eyeglasses with a nose clip instead of earpieces.
– SAY panss-**nay**

> ℹ **pince-nez** is French for 'that pinches the nose'

pincer »*noun* ❶ (**pincers**) a metal tool with blunt inward-curving jaws for gripping and pulling things. ❷ a front claw of a lobster or similar shellfish.

pinch (verb: **pinches, pinching, pinched**)

pinchbeck »*noun* an alloy of copper and zinc resembling gold, used in cheap jewellery.

> ℹ named after the English watchmaker Christopher *Pinchbeck*

pinched

pinches

pinching

pincushion

pine¹ [an evergreen coniferous tree]

pine² »*verb* (**pines, pining, pined**)
❶ become weak. ❷ (**pine for**) miss and long for the return of.

pineal gland »*noun* a small gland at the back of the skull within the brain, secreting a hormone-like substance in some mammals.
– SAY py-**nee**-uhl or **pin**-i-uhl

pineapple

pined

pines

ping (verb: **pings, pinging, pinged**)

ping-pong

pings

pinhead

p

pinhole

pining

pinion »*noun* ❶ the outer part of a bird's wing. ❷ a small cogwheel or spindle that engages with a large cogwheel.
» *verb* (**pinions, pinioning, pinioned**) ❶ tie or hold someone's arms or legs. ❷ cut off the pinion of a bird so that it cannot fly.
– SAY pin-yuhn

pink[1] (adjective: **pinker, pinkest**) [colour]

pink[2] »*noun* a plant with sweet-smelling pink or white flowers.

pink[3] »*verb* (**pinks, pinking, pinked**) cut a scalloped or zigzag edge on fabric.

pinkie »*noun* (in informal English) the little finger.

pinking

pinks

pin money »*noun* a small sum of money for spending on everyday items.

pinna »*noun* (plural **pinnae**) (in anatomy) the external part of the ear.
– SAY pin-nuh [singular], pin-nee [plural]

> ✓ the plural of **pinna**, a Latin word, is **pinnae**

pinnace »*noun* (mainly a historical term) a small boat forming part of the equipment of a larger vessel.
– SAY pin-nis

pinnacle »*noun* ❶ a high pointed piece of rock. ❷ a small pointed turret on a roof. ❸ the most successful point.

pinnae plural of PINNA.

pinnate »*adjective* (chiefly of leaves) having parts arranged on either side like the vanes of a feather.
– SAY pin-nayt

pinned

pinnies

pinning

pinny »*noun* (plural **pinnies**) (in informal English) a pinafore.

pinpoint »*noun* a tiny dot.
» *adjective* absolutely precise.
» *verb* (**pinpoints, pinpointing, pinpointed**) locate exactly.

pinprick

pins

pinstripe »*noun* a very narrow white stripe woven into dark material.
pinstriped

pint »*noun* a unit of volume for liquid or dry measure equal to one eighth of a gallon (in Britain, 0.568 litres).

pintail »*noun* a duck with a long pointed tail.

pintle »*noun* a pin or bolt on which a rudder turns.

pint-sized »*adjective* very small.

pin-tuck »*noun* a very narrow ornamental tuck in a garment.

pin-up

pinwheel »*noun* a small cogwheel with teeth formed by pins set into the rim.

pioneer »*noun* ❶ a person who explores or settles in a new region. ❷ a developer of new ideas or techniques.
» *verb* (**pioneers, pioneering, pioneered**) be the pioneer of a new idea or technique.

pious »*adjective* ❶ religious in a very respectful and serious way. ❷ pretending to be moral and good in order to impress other people. ❸ (of a hope) very much wanted, but unlikely to be achieved.
piously

pip (verb: **pips, pipping, pipped**)

> ✓ double the **p** in **pipped** and **pipping**

pipe (verb: **pipes, piping, piped**)

pipe dream »*noun* a hope or plan that is impossible to achieve.

pipeline

piper

pipes

pipette »*noun* a thin tube used in a laboratory for handling small quantities of liquid, the liquid being drawn into the tube by suction.

> ✓ the ending is **-ette**: **pipette** is French for 'little pipe'

piping

pipistrelle »*noun* a small insect-eating bat.
– SAY pi-pi-**strel** or **pip**-i-strel

pipit »*noun* a brown songbird of open country.

pipped

pippin »*noun* a red and yellow dessert apple.

pipping

pips

pipsqueak »*noun* (used in an insulting way) an unimportant person.

piquant »*adjective* having a pleasantly strong and sharp taste.
– SAY pee-kuhnt or pee-kont
piquancy
piquantly

pique »*noun* resentment arising from hurt pride.
» *verb* (**piques, piquing, piqued**) ❶ stimulate someone's interest. ❷ (**be piqued**) feel hurt or resentful.
– **SAY** peek

piquet »*noun* a type of card game for two players.
– **SAY** pi-**ket** or pi-**kay**

piquing

piracy »*noun* ❶ the attacking and robbing of ships at sea. ❷ the reproduction of a film or recording for profit without permission.

piranha »*noun* a freshwater fish with very sharp teeth that it uses to tear flesh from prey.
– **SAY** pi-**rah**-nuh

> ✓ remember the **h**, which comes after the **n**: **piranha** (a Portuguese word)

pirate »*noun* a person who attacks and robs ships at sea.
» *adjective* taking part in or produced by unauthorized or illegal commercial activity: *pirate recordings*.
» *verb* (**pirates, pirating, pirated**) reproduce a film or recording for profit without permission.
piratical

pirouette »*noun* a movement in ballet involving spinning on one foot.
» *verb* (**pirouettes, pirouetting, pirouetted**) perform a pirouette.
– **SAY** pi-ruu-**et**

> ⓘ **ou** followed by **ette**: **pirouette** is a French word meaning 'spinning top'

piscatorial »*adjective* relating to fishing.
– **SAY** piss-kuh-**tor**-i-uhl

Pisces »*noun* a constellation and sign of the zodiac (the Fish or Fishes, 19 February–20 March).
– **SAY** **py**-seez

> ✓ **sc** in the middle: **Pisces**

piscina »*noun* (plural **piscinas** or **piscinae**) a stone basin in a church, for draining water used in the Mass.
– **SAY** pi-**see**-nuh [singular], pi-**see**-nee [plural]

> ✓ the plural can be either **piscinae** (as in Latin) or **piscinas**

piscine »*adjective* relating to fish.
– **SAY** **pi**-syn

piss (verb: **pisses, pissing, pissed**)
pissed

pistachio »*noun* (plural **pistachios**) a small pale green nut.

– **SAY** pi-**stah**-shi-oh or pi-**sta**-choh

> ✓ the plural of **pistachio** has **os** not **oes**: **pistachios**

piste »*noun* a course or run for skiing.
– **SAY** peesst

pistil »*noun* the female organs of a flower, comprising the stigma, style, and ovary.

pistol [a small gun]

> ✓ **ol** not **il** at the end: **pistol**

piston »*noun* a sliding disc or cylinder fitting closely inside a tube in which it moves up and down as part of an engine or pump.

pit (verb: **pits, pitting, pitted**)

> ✓ double the **t** in **pitting** and **pitted**

pita American spelling of **PITTA**.

pit bull terrier »*noun* a fierce American type of terrier.

pitch (verb: **pitches, pitching, pitched**)

pitch-black

pitchblende »*noun* a mineral found in brown or black pitch-like masses and containing radium.

pitch-dark »*adjective* = **PITCH-BLACK**.

pitched

pitched battle »*noun* a battle in which the time and place are decided beforehand, rather than happening by chance.

pitcher »*noun* ❶ a large jug. ❷ (in baseball) the player who pitches the ball.

pitches

pitchfork »*noun* a farm tool with a long handle and two sharp metal prongs, used for lifting hay.

pitching

piteous »*adjective* deserving or arousing pity.
piteously
piteousness

> ✓ **eous** not **ious**: **piteous**

pitfall »*noun* a hidden danger or difficulty.

pith »*noun* ❶ spongy white tissue lining the rind of citrus fruits. ❷ spongy tissue in the stems and branches of many plants. ❸ the most important part of something.

pithead »*noun* the top of a mineshaft and the area around it.

pithy »*adjective* (**pithier, pithiest**) ❶ (of a fruit or plant) containing much pith. ❷ (of language or style) concise and expressing

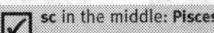

a point clearly and well.
pithily

pitiable »*adjective* ❶ deserving or arousing pity. ❷ deserving contempt: *a pitiable lack of talent.*
pitiably

pitied

pities

pitiful »*adjective* ❶ deserving or arousing pity. ❷ very small or poor.
pitifully
pitifulness

> ☑ -ful not -full: pitiful

pitiless
pitilessly
pitilessness

piton »*noun* a peg or spike driven into a crack to support a climber or a rope.
– SAY pee-ton

pits

pitta »*noun* a type of flat bread which can be split open to hold a filling.

> ☑ pitta can also be spelled pita, but this spelling is most often found in American English

pittance »*noun* a very small or inadequate amount of money.

> ☑ ance not ence: pittance

pitted

pitting

pituitary gland »*noun* a pea-sized gland attached to the base of the brain, important in controlling growth and development.
– SAY pi-tyoo-i-tuh-ri

pity (plural **pities**; verb: **pities**, **pitying**, **pitied**)

> ☑ plural: drop the y and add ies: pities

pivot »*noun* ❶ the central point, pin, or shaft on which a mechanism turns or is balanced. ❷ a person or thing playing a central part in an activity or organization.
» *verb* (**pivots**, **pivoting**, **pivoted**) ❶ turn on or as if on a pivot. ❷ (**pivot on**) depend on.

> ☑ one v, one t: pivot. Do not double the t in pivoting and pivoted.

pivotal »*adjective* ❶ fixed on or as if on a pivot. ❷ of central importance.

pivoted

pivoting

pivots

pixel »*noun* (in electronics) one of the tiny areas of light on a display screen which make up an image.

pixie »*noun* (plural **pixies**) an imaginary being portrayed as a tiny man with pointed ears and a pointed hat.

> ☑ pixie can also be spelled pixy

pizza »*noun* a flat, round base of dough baked with a topping of tomatoes, cheese, and other ingredients.

pizzazz »*noun* (in informal English) a combination of liveliness and style.

> ☑ the usual spelling is pizzazz, although pizaz and pzazz are sometimes found

pizzeria »*noun* a restaurant serving pizzas.
– SAY peet-suh-**ree**-uh

> ☑ pizze- not pizza-: pizzeria (like pizza, an Italian word)

pizzicato »*adverb & adjective* plucking the strings of a stringed instrument with the finger.
– SAY pit-si-**kah**-toh

> ⓘ pizzicato is an Italian word meaning 'pinched'

placard »*noun* a sign for public display, either fixed to a wall or carried during a demonstration.

placate »*verb* (**placates**, **placating**, **placated**) make someone less angry or hostile.
– SAY pluh-**kayt**

place (verb: **places**, **placing**, **placed**)

placebo »*noun* (plural **placebos**) a medicine prescribed in order to reassure the patient rather than for any physical effect.
– SAY pluh-**see**-boh

> ☑ the plural of placebo (Latin for 'I shall please') has os not oes: placebos

placed

placement »*noun* ❶ the action of placing. ❷ a temporary position given to someone in a workplace.

placenta »*noun* (plural **placentae** or **placentas**) an organ in the uterus of a pregnant mammal, nourishing and maintaining the fetus through the umbilical cord.
– SAY pluh-**sen**-tuh [singular], pluh-**sen**-tee [plural]

> ☑ the plural of placenta can be placentae (as in the original Latin) or placentas

places

placid »*adjective* not easily upset or excited.
placidity
placidly

placing

placket »*noun* ❶ an opening in a garment, covering fastenings or for access to a pocket. ❷ a flap of material used to strengthen such an opening.

plagiarize »*verb* (plagiarizes, plagiarizing, plagiarized) take someone else's work or idea and pass it off as your own.
– SAY play-juh-ryz
plagiarism
plagiarist

> ✓ many people prefer the alternative spellings **plagiarise**, **plagiarises**, etc.: both **s** and **z** spellings are correct

plague »*noun* ❶ an infectious disease spread by bacteria and characterized by fever and delirium. ❷ an unusually and unpleasantly large number of insects or animals.
»*verb* (plagues, plaguing, plagued) ❶ cause continual trouble to someone. ❷ pester someone continually.

> ✓ drop the **e** to spell **plaguing**

plaice »*noun* (plural plaice) a brown edible flatfish with orange spots.

> ✓ **ai** not simply **a** in the middle: **plaice**

plaid »*noun* fabric woven in a chequered or tartan design.
– SAY plad

plain (adjective: plainer, plainest) [simple or ordinary, without a pattern; large area of flat land]
plainly
plainness

> ℹ do not confuse **plain** with **plane**, which refers to a completely flat surface, an aeroplane, or a tool used to smooth a wooden surface

plainchant »*noun* = PLAINSONG.

plainer

plainest

plainly

plainness

plain sailing »*noun* smooth and easy progress.

plainsong »*noun* unaccompanied medieval church music sung by a number of voices together.

plaintiff »*noun* a person who brings a case against another in a court of law.

plaintive »*adjective* sounding sad and mournful.
plaintively

plait »*noun* a single length of hair, rope, or other material made up of three or more strands wound together.
»*verb* (plaits, plaiting, plaited) form a material into a plait or plaits.
– SAY plat

> ℹ do not confuse **plait** with **pleat**, which means 'a fold in a cloth item'

plan (verb: plans, planning, planned)
planner

> ✓ double the **n** in **planning**, **planned**, and **planner**

planar »*adjective* (in mathematics) relating to or in the form of a plane.
– SAY play-ner

plane (verb: planes, planing, planed)

> ℹ do not confuse **plane** with **plain**, which means 'simple or ordinary; without a pattern' and 'large area of flat land'; **plane** has various meanings including (as a noun) 'flat surface', 'aeroplane', 'tool for smoothing a surface', and 'kind of tall tree'

planer »*noun* a tool for smoothing a surface.

planes

planet
planetary

planetarium »*noun* (plural planetariums or planetaria) a building in which images of stars, planets, and constellations are projected onto a curved ceiling.
– SAY pla-ni-tair-i-uhm

> ✓ the plural of **planetarium** can be **planetariums** or (as in Latin) **planetaria**

planetary

plangent »*adjective* (of a sound) loud and mournful.
– SAY plan-juhnt

planing

plank
planking

plankton »*noun* tiny organisms living in the sea or fresh water.

> ✓ there is no **c** in **plankton**

planned

planner

planning

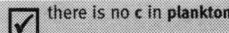

planning permission »*noun* formal permission from local government for building work.

plans

plant (verb: **plants**, **planting**, **planted**)

Plantagenet »*noun* a member of the English royal dynasty which ruled from 1154 until 1485.
– SAY plan-**taj**-uh-nuht

plantain »*noun* ❶ a low-growing plant, with a rosette of leaves and a slender green flower spike. ❷ a type of banana.
– SAY **plan**-tin or **plan**-tayn

plantation »*noun* ❶ a large estate on which crops such as coffee, sugar, and tobacco are grown. ❷ an area in which trees have been planted.

planted

planter »*noun* ❶ a manager or owner of a plantation. ❷ a decorative container in which plants are grown.

planting

plants

plaque »*noun* ❶ an ornamental tablet fixed to a wall to commemorate a person or event. ❷ a sticky deposit on teeth in which bacteria quickly increase in number.

plasma »*noun* ❶ the colourless fluid part of blood, lymph, or milk, in which cells or fat globules are suspended. ❷ (in physics) a gas of positive ions and free electrons with little or no overall electric charge.
– SAY **plaz**-muh

plaster (verb: **plasters**, **plastering**, **plastered**)
plasterer

plasterboard »*noun* board made of plaster set between two sheets of paper, used to line interior walls and ceilings.

plastered

plasterer

plastering

plasters

plastic »*noun* a chemically produced material that can be moulded into shape while soft and then set into a hard or slightly flexible form.
» *adjective* ❶ made of plastic. ❷ easily shaped. ❸ artificial.
plasticity

plasticine »*noun* (trademark) a soft modelling material.

plasticity

plasticky »*adjective* ❶ like plastic. ❷ artificial or of low quality.

plastic surgery »*noun* surgery performed to repair or reconstruct parts of the body damaged as a result of injury or to improve their appearance.

plate (verb: **plates**, **plating**, **plated**)

plateau »*noun* (plural **plateaux** or **plateaus**) ❶ an area of fairly level high ground. ❷ a state of little or no change following a period of activity or progress.
» *verb* (**plateaus**, **plateauing**, **plateaued**) reach a plateau.
– SAY **pla**-toh [singular], **pla**-tohz [plural]

☑ the plural of **plateau** can be **plateaux** (as in the original French) or **plateaus**

plated

platelet »*noun* a small colourless disc-shaped cell fragment without a nucleus, found in large numbers in blood and involved in clotting.

platen »*noun* ❶ a plate in a small printing press which presses the paper against the type. ❷ a cylindrical roller in a typewriter against which the paper is held.
– SAY **pla**-tuhn

plates

platform

plating

platinum »*noun* a precious silvery-white metal.
» *adjective* greyish-white or silvery like platinum.
– SAY **pla**-ti-nuhm

platitude »*noun* a remark that has been used too often to be interesting or thoughtful.
platitudinous

Platonic »*adjective* ❶ having to do with the Greek philosopher Plato or his ideas. ❷ (**platonic**) (of love or friendship) intimate and affectionate but not sexual.
– SAY pluh-**ton**-ik
platonically

platoon »*noun* a subdivision of a company of soldiers.

platter »*noun* a large flat serving dish.

platypus »*noun* (plural **platypuses**) an egg-laying Australian mammal with a duck-like bill and webbed feet with poisonous spurs.
– SAY **pla**-ti-puhss

ℹ the **platypus** is also known as the duck-billed platypus

plaudits »*plural noun* praise.

plausible »*adjective* ❶ seeming reasonable or probable. ❷ skilled at producing persuasive arguments: *a plausible liar.*

plausibility
plausibly

✓ -ible not -able: plausible

play (verb: **plays**, **playing**, **played**)
playable

playback

playboy »*noun* a wealthy man who spends his time seeking pleasure.

played

player

playful
playfully
playfulness

✓ -ful not -full: playful

playground

playgroup

playhouse »*noun* ❶ a theatre. ❷ a toy house for children to play in.

playing

playlist »*noun* a list of songs or pieces of music chosen to be broadcast on a radio station.

playmaker »*noun* a player in a team game who leads attacks or brings teammates into attacking positions.

playmate

play-off »*noun* an extra match played to decide the outcome of a contest.

playpen

plays

playschool

plaything

playwright »*noun* a person who writes plays.

✓ -wright not -write or -right: playwright

plaza »*noun* ❶ an open public space in a built-up area. ❷ (in American English) a shopping centre.

ℹ️ plaza is a Spanish word meaning 'place'

plc »*abbreviation* public limited company.

plea »*noun* ❶ a request made in an urgent and emotional way. ❷ (in law) a formal statement by or on behalf of a person charged with an offence in a law court.

plea-bargaining »*noun* (in law) an arrangement between a prosecutor and a person charged with a crime whereby the latter pleads guilty to a lesser charge in the expectation of a lesser sentence.

plead (verb: **pleads**, **pleading**, **pleaded** or (in American or Scottish English) **pled**)

pleading »*adjective* earnestly appealing: *a pleading look.*
pleadingly

pleads

pleasant
pleasantly
pleasantness

✓ pleas- not ples-: pleasant

pleasantry »*noun* (plural **pleasantries**) ❶ an unimportant remark made as part of a polite conversation. ❷ a mildly amusing joke.

✓ plural: drop the y and add ies: pleasantries

please (verb: **pleases**, **pleasing**, **pleased**)
pleased
pleaser

pleasing
pleasingly

pleasurable
pleasurably

pleasure (verb: **pleasures**, **pleasuring**, **pleasured**)

✓ pleas- not ples-: pleasure

pleat »*noun* a fold in a cloth item, held by stitching the top or side.
»*verb* (**pleats**, **pleating**, **pleated**) fold or form cloth into pleats.

ℹ️ do not confuse **pleat** with **plait**, which means 'a single length of a material made up of three or more strands wound together'

pleb »*noun* (used in an insulting way) a member of the lower social classes.

plebeian »*noun* ❶ (in ancient Rome) a commoner. ❷ a member of the lower social classes.
»*adjective* ❶ relating to the plebeians of ancient Rome. ❷ lower-class or unsophisticated.
– say pli-**bee**-uhn

✓ bei not bi in the middle: plebeian

plebiscite »*noun* the direct vote by everyone entitled to do so on an important public question.
– say **ple**-bi-syt

✓ -scite not -site: plebiscite

plectrum »*noun* (plural **plectrums** or **plectra**) a thin flat piece of plastic or tortoiseshell used to pluck the strings of a guitar or similar musical instrument.

> ✓ the plural of **plectrum** can be **plectrums** or (as in Latin) **plectra**

pled American or Scottish past participle of **PLEAD**.

pledge »*noun* ❶ a solemn promise or undertaking. ❷ something valuable given as a guarantee that a debt will be paid or a promise kept. ❸ (**the pledge**) a solemn undertaking to stop drinking alcohol. ❹ a thing given as a token of love, favour, or loyalty.
» *verb* (**pledges, pledging, pledged**) ❶ solemnly undertake to do or give something. ❷ give something valuable as a guarantee on a loan.

> ✓ **edge** not **ege**: pledge

Pleistocene »*adjective* relating to the geological period from 1.64 million to about 10,000 years ago.
– **SAY** ply-stuh-seen

plenary »*adjective* ❶ full; complete: *plenary powers.* ❷ (of a meeting at a conference or assembly) to be attended by all participants.
» *noun* a plenary meeting.
– **SAY** plee-nuh-ri

plenipotentiary »*noun* (plural **plenipotentiaries**) a person given full power by a government to act on its behalf.
» *adjective* ❶ having full power to take independent action. ❷ (of power) complete.
– **SAY** ple-ni-puh-**ten**-shuh-ri

plenitude »*noun* ❶ a large amount of something. ❷ the condition of being full or complete.

> ✓ **pleni** not **plenti**: plenitude

plenteous »*adjective* (a poetic term) plentiful.

> ✓ **teous** not **tious**: plenteous

plentiful
plentifully

> ✓ **-ful** not **-full**: plentiful

plenty

plenum »*noun* ❶ an assembly of all the members of a group or committee. ❷ (in physics) a space completely filled with matter, or the whole of space seen in such a way.
– **SAY** plee-nuhm

plethora »*noun* an excessive amount of something: *a plethora of complaints.*
– **SAY** ple-thuh-ruh

> i **plethora** is a Latin word meaning 'fullness'

pleura »*noun* (plural **pleurae**) one of a pair of membranes lining the thorax and enveloping the lungs.
– **SAY** ploor-uh [singular], **ploor**-ee [plural]
pleural

> ✓ the plural of **pleura** is **pleurae** (as in Latin)

pleurisy »*noun* inflammation of the pleurae, causing pain during breathing.
– **SAY** ploor-i-si

plexus »*noun* (**plexuses**) ❶ a network of nerves or vessels in the body. ❷ a complex network or web-like structure.

> i the correct Latin plural of **plexus** would also be **plexus**, but this is rarely used

pliable »*adjective* ❶ easily bent. ❷ easily influenced or persuaded.
– **SAY** ply-uh-b'l
pliability

pliant »*adjective* pliable.
pliancy

plie »*noun* a ballet movement in which a dancer bends the knees and straightens them again, having the feet turned right out and heels firmly on the ground.
– **SAY** plee-ay

> ✓ **plie** can also be spelled **pliè**, with an acute accent on the **e** (as in the original French word meaning 'bent')

plied past of **PLY**[2].

pliers »*plural noun* pincers having jaws with flat surfaces, used for gripping small objects or bending wire.
– **SAY** ply-erz

plies

plight[1] »*noun* a dangerous or difficult situation.

plight[2] »*verb* (**plights, plighting, plighted**) (an old word) ❶ solemnly promise faith or loyalty. ❷ (**be plighted to**) be engaged to be married to.

plimsoll »*noun* a light rubber-soled canvas sports shoe.

> ✓ **plimsoll** can also be spelled **plimsole**

Plimsoll line »*noun* a marking on a ship's side showing the limit to which the ship may be legally submerged in the water when loaded with cargo.

> i named after the English politician Samuel *Plimsoll*

plinth »*noun* a heavy block or slab supporting a statue or vase or forming the base of a column.

Pliocene »*adjective* relating to the geological period from about 5.2 to 1.64 million years ago.
– SAY ply-uh-seen

plod (verb: **plods, plodding, plodded**)
plodder

> ☑ double the **d** in **plodding, plodded,** and **plodder**

plonk (verb: **plonks, plonking, plonked**)
plonker
plonking
plonks

plop (verb: **plops, plopping, plopped**)

> ☑ double the **p** in **plopping** and **plopped**

plot (verb: **plots, plotting, plotted**)
plotter

> ☑ double the **t** in **plotting, plotted,** and **plotter**

plough (verb: **ploughs, ploughing, ploughed**)

> ☑ **ough** not **ow**: **plough** (the spelling **plow** is American)

ploughman's lunch »*noun* a meal of bread and cheese with pickle and salad.

ploughs

ploughshare »*noun* the main cutting blade of a plough.

plover »*noun* a short-billed wading bird.
– SAY pluh-ver

plow American way of spelling **PLOUGH**.

ploy »*noun* a cunning act performed to gain an advantage.

pluck (verb: **plucks, plucking, plucked**)

plucky »*adjective* (**pluckier, pluckiest**) determined and brave.
pluckily
pluckiness

plug (verb: **plugs, plugging, plugged**)

> ☑ double the **g** in **plugging** and **plugged**

plughole

plug-in »*noun* (in computing) a module or piece of software which can be added to an existing system to give extra features or functions.

plugs

plum [fruit]

plumage »*noun* a bird's feathers.
– SAY ploo-mij

plumb »*verb* (**plumbs, plumbing, plumbed**) ❶ measure the depth of water. ❷ explore or experience something fully. ❸ test an upright surface to find out if it is vertical. ❹ (**plumb in**) install a bath, washing machine, etc. and connect it to water and drainage pipes.
» *noun* a heavy object attached to a line for finding the depth of water or whether an upright surface is vertical.
» *adverb* exactly: *plumb in the centre.*
» *adjective* vertical.

plumber »*noun* a person who fits and repairs the pipes and fittings of water supply, sanitation, or heating systems.

plumbing

plumb line »*noun* a line with a heavy weight attached to it, used to find the depth of water or to check that something is vertical.

plumbs

plume »*noun* ❶ a long, soft feather or arrangement of feathers. ❷ a long spreading cloud of smoke or vapour.
plumed

plummet »*verb* (**plummets, plummeting, plummeted**) ❶ fall straight down at high speed. ❷ decrease rapidly in value or amount.
» *noun* ❶ a steep and rapid fall or drop. ❷ a plumb line or weight.

> ☑ two **m**'s, one **t**: **plummet**. Do not double the **t** in **plummeting** and **plummeted**.

plummy »*adjective* (**plummier, plummiest**) ❶ like a plum. ❷ (of a person's voice) typical of the English upper classes.

plump (adjective: **plumper, plumpest**; verb: **plumps, plumping, plumped**)
plumpish
plumpness

plumy »*adjective* resembling or decorated with feathers.

plunder »*verb* (**plunders, plundering, plundered**) enter a place by force and steal goods from it.
» *noun* ❶ the action of plundering. ❷ goods obtained by plundering.

plunge (verb: **plunges, plunging, plunged**)
plunger

pluperfect »*adjective* (in grammar) (of a tense) referring to an action completed prior to some past point of time (as in *he had gone by then*).

p

plural »*adjective* ❶ more than one in number. ❷ (in grammar) (of a word or form) referring to more than one.
» *noun* (in grammar) a plural word or form.

pluralise another way of spelling **PLURALIZE**.

pluralism »*noun* ❶ a political system of power-sharing among a number of political parties. ❷ the acceptance within a society of groups that belong to different races or have different political or religious beliefs. ❸ the holding of more than one position in the Church at the same time by one person.
pluralist

plurality »*noun* (plural **pluralities**) ❶ the fact or state of being plural. ❷ a large number of people or things.

pluralize »*verb* (**pluralizes, pluralizing, pluralized**) ❶ make something more numerous. ❷ give a plural form to a word.
pluralization

> ✓ many people prefer the alternative spellings **pluralise, pluralises**, etc., and **pluralisation**: both **s** and **z** spellings are correct

plus (plural **pluses**)

> ✓ do not double the **s** in forming the plural **pluses**

plus fours »*plural noun* men's baggy trousers that are cut short to fit closely below the knee, formerly worn for hunting and golf.

plush »*noun* a fabric with a long, soft nap. » *adjective* (**plusher, plushest**) luxurious.

Pluto

plutocracy »*noun* (plural **plutocracies**) ❶ government by the wealthy. ❷ a society governed by the wealthy.

plutocrat »*noun* a person who is powerful because they are rich.
plutocratic

plutonium »*noun* a radioactive metallic element used as a fuel in nuclear reactors and as an explosive in atomic weapons.
– sᴀʏ ploo-**toh**-ni-uhm

ply[1] »*noun* (plural **plies**) ❶ a thickness or layer of a material. ❷ one of a number of layers or strands of which something is made.

ply[2] »*verb* (**plies, plying, plied**) ❶ work steadily using a tool. ❷ work steadily at your job. ❸ (of a ship or vehicle) travel regularly over a route. ❹ (**ply with**) keep presenting someone with food, drink, or questions.

plywood »*noun* thin strong board consisting of layers of wood glued together.

p.m. »*abbreviation* after noon.

> ℹ from the Latin phrase *post meridiem*

PMT »*abbreviation* premenstrual tension.

pneumatic »*adjective* containing or operated by air or gas under pressure.
– sᴀʏ nyoo-**ma**-tik

> ✓ the beginning is **pneu** (from the Greek **pneuma** 'wind')

pneumonia »*noun* an infection causing inflammation in the lungs.
– sᴀʏ nyoo-**moh**-ni-uh

poach »*verb* (**poaches, poaching, poached**) ❶ cook something by simmering it in a small amount of liquid. ❷ hunt game or catch fish illegally from private or protected areas. ❸ unfairly entice customers, workers, etc. away from someone else.

pock »*noun* a pockmark.
pocked

pocket (verb: **pockets, pocketing, pocketed**)
pocketable

pocketbook

pocketed

pocketing

pockets

pockmark »*noun* ❶ a hollow scar or mark on the skin left by a spot. ❷ a mark or hollow area disfiguring a surface.
» *verb* (**pockmarks, pockmarking, pockmarked**) cover something with pockmarks.

pod[1] »*noun* a long seed-case of a pea, bean, or similar plant.
» *verb* (**pods, podding, podded**) remove peas or beans from their pods before cooking.

> ✓ double the **d** to spell **podding** and **podded**

pod[2] »*noun* a small herd of whales or similar sea mammals.

podgy (adjective: **podgier, podgiest**)
podginess

podium »*noun* (plural **podiums** or **podia**) a small platform on which a person stands to conduct an orchestra or give a speech.
– sᴀʏ **poh**-di-uhm

> ✓ the plural can either be **podiums** or (as in Latin) **podia**

pods

poem

poesy »*noun* (an old word) poetry.

– SAY poh-i-zi

poet

poetess (plural **poetesses**)

poetic

poetical
poetically

poetic justice »*noun* punishment or reward that is deserved.

poetic licence »*noun* freedom to change facts or the normal rules of language to achieve a special effect in writing.

Poet Laureate »*noun* (plural **Poets Laureate**) a poet officially appointed to write poems for important occasions.

> ✓ **Laureate** is actually an adjective, so the plural of **Poet Laureate** adds an **s** to **Poet** only: **Poets Laureate**

poetry

po-faced »*adjective* serious and disapproving.

pogo stick »*noun* a toy for bouncing around on, consisting of a pole on a spring, with a bar to stand on and a handle at the top.

pogrom »*noun* an organized massacre of an ethnic group, originally that of Jews in Russia or eastern Europe.
– SAY pog-rom

> ℹ **pogrom** is a Russian word which means 'devastation'

poignant »*adjective* making you feel sadness or regret.
– SAY poy-nyuhnt
poignancy
poignantly

> ✓ **ant** not **ent**, and do not forget the **g**: **poignant**

poinsettia »*noun* a small shrub with large scarlet bracts, which resemble petals.
– SAY poyn-set-ti-uh

> ℹ named after the American botanist Joel R. *Poinsett*

point (verb: **points, pointing, pointed**)

point-blank

pointed
pointedly

pointer

pointillism »*noun* a way of painting using tiny dots of different colours, which become blended in the viewer's eye.
– SAY pwan-ti-li-z'm
pointillist

pointing »*noun* mortar or cement used to fill the joints of brickwork or tiling.

pointless »*adjective* having little or no sense or purpose.
pointlessly
pointlessness

points

point-to-point »*noun* (plural **point-to-points**) a cross-country race for horses used in hunting.

pointy

poise »*noun* ❶ a graceful way of holding the body. ❷ a calm and confident manner.
» *verb* (**poises, poising, poised**) ❶ be or cause to be balanced or suspended. ❷ (**poised**) calm and confident. ❸ (**be poised to do**) be ready to do something.

poison (verb: **poisons, poisoning, poisoned**)
poisoner

poisoned chalice »*noun* something offered which seems attractive but which is likely to cause problems to the person receiving it.

poisoner

poisoning

poisonous
poisonously

poisons

poke (verb: **pokes, poking, poked**)

poker

poker face »*noun* a blank expression that hides a person's true feelings.

pokes

pokey

pokier

pokiest

poking

poky »*adjective* (**pokier, pokiest**) (of a room or building) uncomfortably small and cramped.

> ✓ **poky** can also be spelled with an **ey** ending: **pokey**

polar »*adjective* ❶ relating to the North or South Poles or the regions around them. ❷ having an electrical or magnetic field. ❸ completely opposite.

> ✓ **ar** not **er**: **polar**

polarise another way of spelling POLARIZE.

polarity »*noun* (plural **polarities**) ❶ the state of having poles or opposites. ❷ the direction of a magnetic or electric field.

polarize »*verb* (**polarizes, polarizing, polarized**) ❶ divide people into two sharply contrasting groups with different opinions. ❷ (in physics) restrict the vibrations of a wave of light to one

direction. ❸ give magnetic or electric polarity to something.
polarization

✓ many people prefer the alternative spellings **polarise**, **polarises**, etc., and **polarisation**: both **s** and **z** spellings are correct

Polaroid »*noun* (trademark) ❶ a material that polarizes the light passing through it, used in sunglasses. ❷ a type of camera that produces a finished print rapidly after each exposure.

polder »*noun* (in the Netherlands) a piece of land reclaimed from the sea or a river.
– SAY **pohl**-der

Pole »*noun* a person from Poland.

pole [long, thin piece of metal or wood; a point at the opposite end to another]

ℹ️ do not confuse **pole** with **poll**, which means 'the process of voting in an election'

poleaxe »*noun* a large axe.
»*verb* (**poleaxes**, **poleaxing**, **poleaxed**) ❶ knock something down with or as if with a poleaxe. ❷ greatly shock or tire someone.

polecat »*noun* ❶ a dark brown weasel-like animal with an unpleasant smell. ❷ (in American English) a skunk.

polemic »*noun* ❶ a speech or piece of writing that argues strongly for or against something. ❷ (also **polemics**) the practice of using fierce argument or discussion.
»*adjective* having to do with fierce discussion.
– SAY puh-**lem**-ik
polemical
polemicist

polenta »*noun* (in Italian cookery) maize flour or a dough made from this, which is boiled and then fried or baked.
– SAY puh-**len**-tuh

pole position »*noun* the most favourable position at the start of a motor race.

Pole Star »*noun* a star located in the part of the sky above the North Pole.

police (verb: **polices**, **policing**, **policed**)
policeman (plural **policemen**)
polices
policewoman (plural **policewomen**)
policies
policing
policy (plural **policies**)

✓ plural: drop the **y** and add **ies**: **policies**

polio »*noun* = POLIOMYELITIS.

poliomyelitis »*noun* a disease that can cause temporary or permanent paralysis.
– SAY poh-li-oh-my-uh-**ly**-tiss

Polish »*noun* the language of Poland.
»*adjective* relating to Poland.
– SAY **poh**-lish

polish (verb: **polishes**, **polishing**, **polished**)
polisher

politburo »*noun* (plural **politburos**) the chief policy-making committee of a communist party.
– SAY po-**lit**-byuu-roh

polite (adjective: **politer**, **politest**)
politely
politeness

politic »*adjective* (of an action) sensible and wise in the circumstances.

political
politically

political correctness »*noun* the avoidance of language or behaviour that could offend certain groups of people.

politically

politically correct »*adjective* showing political correctness.

political prisoner »*noun* a person imprisoned for their political beliefs or actions.

political science »*noun* the study of political activity and behaviour.

politician

politicize »*verb* (**politicizes**, **politicizing**, **politicized**) ❶ make someone interested in politics. ❷ make something a political issue.
politicization

✓ many people prefer the alternative spellings **politicise**, **politicises**, etc., and **politicisation**: both **s** and **z** spellings are correct

politicking »*noun* (used in a disapproving way) political activity.

✓ note the **k**: **politicking**

politics

polity »*noun* (plural **polities**) ❶ a form of government. ❷ a society as a politically organized state.

polka »*noun* a lively dance for couples.

polka dot »*noun* one of a number of round dots evenly spaced to form a pattern.

poll »*noun* ❶ the process of voting in an election. ❷ a record of the number of votes cast.
»*verb* (**polls**, **polling**, **polled**) ❶ record someone's opinion or vote. ❷ (of a

candidate in an election) receive a particular number of votes.
– **say** rhymes with pole or doll

> **i** do not confuse **poll** with **pole**, which means 'a long, thin piece of metal or wood' or 'a point at the opposite end to another'

pollard »*verb* (**pollards**, **pollarding**, **pollarded**) cut off the top and side branches of a tree to encourage new growth.
» *noun* a tree that has been pollarded.
– **say** pol-lerd

polled

pollen »*noun* a powder produced by the male part of a flower, which is carried by bees, the wind, etc. and can fertilize the female part of the same or other flowers.

pollen count »*noun* a measure of the amount of pollen in the air.

pollinate »*verb* (**pollinates**, **pollinating**, **pollinated**) carry pollen to and fertilize a flower or plant.
pollination
pollinator

polling

polls

pollster »*noun* a person who carries out opinion polls.

poll tax »*noun* a tax paid at the same rate by every adult.

pollutant »*noun* a substance that causes pollution.

> ✓ **ant** not **ent**: pollutant

pollute (verb: **pollutes**, **polluting**, **polluted**)
polluter
pollution

polo »*noun* a game similar to hockey, played on horseback with a long-handled mallet.

polonaise »*noun* a slow dance of Polish origin.
– **say** po-luh-**nayz**

> ✓ note that the ending is **aise**: **polonaise** is a French word which means 'Polish'

polo neck »*noun* a collar on a sweater that is high and close-fitting around the neck, and is turned-over.

polo shirt »*noun* a casual short-sleeved shirt with a collar and two or three buttons at the neck.

poltergeist »*noun* a kind of ghost that is said to make loud noises and throw objects around.

– **say** pol-ter-gyst

> ✓ **-geist** not **-ghost**: poltergeist (a German word)

poltroon »*noun* (an old word) a complete coward.
– **say** pol-**troon**

polyandry »*noun* the practice of having more than one husband at the same time.
– **say** po-li-an-dri

polyanthus »*noun* (plural **polyanthus**) a flowering garden plant developed from the wild primrose.
– **say** po-li-**an**-thuhss

polychromatic »*adjective* multicoloured.

polychrome »*adjective* consisting of several colours.

polyester »*noun* a synthetic fibre or resin used to make fabric for clothes.

> ✓ **ter** not **tre**: polyester

polyethylene »*noun* = **POLYTHENE**.
– **say** po-li-**eth**-i-leen

polygamy »*noun* the practice of having more than one wife or husband at the same time.
– **say** puh-**lig**-uh-mi
polygamist
polygamous

> ✓ **lyg** not **lig**: polygamy

polyglot »*adjective* knowing or using several languages.
– **say** po-li-glot

polygon »*noun* a shape with three or more straight sides and angles.
– **say** po-li-guhn
polygonal

polygraph »*noun* a lie detector.

polygyny »*noun* the practice of having more than one wife at the same time.
– **say** puh-**li**-ji-ni

polyhedron »*noun* (plural **polyhedra** or **polyhedrons**) a solid figure with many plane faces.
– **say** po-li-**hee**-druhn
polyhedral

> ✓ the plural of **polyhedron** can be either **polyhedra** (like the original Greek) or **polyhedrons**

polymath »*noun* a person with a wide knowledge of many subjects.
– **say** po-li-math

polymer »*noun* (in chemistry) a substance with a molecular structure formed from many identical small molecules bonded together.

– **say** po-li-mer

polymerize »*verb* (**polymerizes, polymerizing, polymerized**) combine or cause to combine to form a polymer.

> ✓ many people prefer the alternative spellings **polymerise, polymerises,** etc.: both **s** and **z** spellings are correct

polymorphic »*adjective* having several different forms.

polymorphous »*adjective* = **POLYMORPHIC**.

Polynesian

polyp »*noun* ❶ a simple sea creature which remains fixed in the same place, such as coral. ❷ (in medicine) a small lump sticking out from a mucous membrane.
– **say** po-lip

> ✓ **lyp** not **lip**: po**lyp**

polyphony »*noun* the combination of a number of musical parts, each forming an individual melody and harmonizing with each other.
– **say** puh-li-fuh-ni
polyphonic

polystyrene »*noun* a light synthetic material used to protect packaged goods and make containers that keep food or drink hot.
– **say** po-li-**sty**-reen

polysyllabic »*adjective* having more than one syllable.

polytechnic »*noun* (in the past in the UK) a college offering courses at degree level, mainly in technical and vocational subjects.

> ℹ all such colleges now have university status

polytheism »*noun* belief in more than one god.
– **say** po-li-**thee**-i-z'm
polytheist
polytheistic

polythene »*noun* a tough, light, flexible plastic, used for packaging.

polyunsaturated »*adjective* (of fats) having several double and triple bonds between carbon atoms in their molecules (and as a consequence being more easily processed by the body).
polyunsaturates

polyurethane »*noun* a synthetic resin used in paints and varnishes.
– **say** po-li-**yoor**-i-thayn

pomade »*noun* a scented oil or cream for making the hair glossy and smooth.
– **say** puh-**mayd** or puh-**mahd**

pomander »*noun* a ball or perforated container of sweet-smelling substances used to perfume a room or cupboard.
– **say** puh-**man**-der or pom-uhn-der

pomegranate »*noun* a round tropical fruit with a tough orange outer skin and red flesh containing many seeds.
– **say** pom-i-gra-nit

pomelo »*noun* (plural **pomelos**) a large citrus fruit similar to a grapefruit.
– **say** pom-uh-loh

> ✓ the plural of **pomelo** has **os** not **oes**: **pomelos**

Pomeranian »*noun* a small dog with long silky hair.

> ℹ from *Pomerania*, a region of Europe now part of Poland and Germany

pommel »*noun* ❶ the upward curving or projecting front part of a saddle. ❷ a rounded knob on the end of the handle of a sword.
– **say** pum-muhl

pomp »*noun* the special clothes, music, and customs that are part of a grand public ceremony.

pompom »*noun* a small woollen ball attached to a garment for decoration.

> ✓ **pompom** can also be spelled **pompon**

pompous »*adjective* showing in a rather solemn or arrogant way that you have a high opinion of yourself and your own views.
pomposity
pompously

> ✓ **ous** not **os**: pomp**ous** (but not in pompos**i**ty, where the **u** is dropped)

ponce (in informal English) »*noun* ❶ a man who lives off a prostitute's earnings. ❷ (used in an insulting way) an effeminate man.
» *verb* (**ponces, poncing, ponced**) (**ponce about** or **around**) behave in a way that wastes time or looks silly.

poncho »*noun* (plural **ponchos**) a garment made of a thick piece of woollen cloth with a slit in the middle for the head.

> ✓ the plural of **poncho** (a Spanish word from Latin America) has **os** not **oes**: **ponchos**

pond

ponder »*verb* (**ponders, pondering, pondered**) consider something carefully.

ponderous »*adjective* ❶ moving slowly and heavily. ❷ boringly solemn or long-winded.

ponderously
ponderousness
ponders
pondweed
pong
pongy
poniard »*noun* (a historical term) a small, thin dagger.
– SAY pon-yerd
ponies
pontiff »*noun* the Pope.
pontifical »*adjective* having to do with a pope; papal.
– SAY pon-**ti**-fi-k'l
pontificate »*verb* (**pontificates, pontificating, pontificated**) express your opinions in a pompous and overbearing way.
»*noun* (also **Pontificate**) (in the Roman Catholic Church) the office of pope or bishop.
– SAY pon-**ti**-fi-kayt [verb], pon-**ti**-fi-kuht [noun]
ponfication
pontoon »*noun* ❶ a card game in which players try to obtain cards with a value totalling twenty-one. ❷ a flat-bottomed boat or hollow metal container used with others to support a temporary bridge or floating landing stage. ❸ a bridge or landing stage supported by pontoons.
– SAY pon-**toon**
pony (plural **ponies**)

> ☑ plural: drop the **y** and add **ies: ponies**

ponytail
pony-trekking
poo another way of spelling POOH.
pooch »*noun* (in informal English) a dog.
poodle
poof »*noun* (used in an insulting way) an effeminate or homosexual man.
pooh (verb: **poohs, poohing, poohed**)

> ☑ **pooh** can also be spelled without the h: **poo**

pooh-pooh »*verb* (**pooh-poohs, pooh-poohing, pooh-poohed**) dismiss an idea as being not worth considering.
poohs
pool (verb: **pools, pooling, pooled**)

> ☑ do not double the **l** to spell **pooling** and **pooled**

poop »*noun* a raised deck at the rear of a ship.
poor (adjective: **poorer, poorest**)

poorhouse »*noun* a workhouse.
poorly
pootle »*verb* (**pootles, pootling, pootled**) move or travel in a leisurely manner.
pop (verb: **pops, popping, popped**)

> ☑ double the **p** to spell **popping** and **popped**

pop art »*noun* a style of art that uses images taken from popular culture, such as advertisements or films.
popcorn
pope »*noun* (often **the Pope**) the Bishop of Rome as head of the Roman Catholic Church.
popery »*noun* (used in an insulting way) Roman Catholicism.
popgun
popish »*adjective* (used in an insulting way) Roman Catholic.
poplar »*noun* a tall, slender tree with soft wood.

> ☑ **ar** not **er: poplar**

poplin »*noun* a cotton fabric with a finely ribbed surface.
poppadom »*noun* (in Indian cookery) a thin circular piece of spiced bread that is fried until crisp.
– SAY pop-puh-duhm

> ☑ double **p** but single **d: poppadom**. It can also be spelled **poppadum**.

popped
popper »*noun* a press stud.
poppet »*noun* a pretty or charming child.
poppies
popping
poppy (plural **poppies**)

> ☑ plural: drop the **y** and add **ies: poppies**

poppycock »*noun* (in informal English) nonsense.
pops
populace »*noun* the general public.
– SAY pop-yuu-luhss

> ☑ the ending is **ace** not **ous: populace** (**populous** is an adjective meaning 'having a large population')

popular
popularity
popularly
popularise another way of spelling POPULARIZE.
popularity

popularize (verb: **popularizes, popularizing, popularized**)
popularization
popularizer

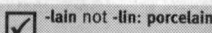 many people prefer the alternative spellings **popularise, popularises**, etc., **popularisation** and **populariser**: both **s** and **z** spellings are correct

popularly

populate »*verb* (**populates, populating, populated**) ❶ live in an area and form its population. ❷ cause people to settle in an area.

population

populism »*noun* politics or other activity carried out with the aim of appealing to or representing ordinary people.
populist

populous »*adjective* having a large population.

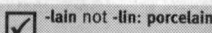 the ending is **ous** not **ace**: **populous** (**populace** is a noun meaning 'the general public')

pop-up

porcelain »*noun* a type of delicate translucent china.
– SAY por-suh-lin

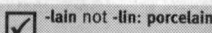 **-lain** not **-lin**: **porcelain**

porch

porcine »*adjective* relating to pigs, or like a pig.
– SAY por-syn

porcupine »*noun* an animal with long protective spines on the body and tail.
– SAY por-kyuu-pyn

pore[1] »*noun* one of many tiny openings in the skin or another surface.

pore[2] »*verb* (**pores, poring, pored**) (**pore over** or **through**) study or read something with close attention.

ℹ️ do not confuse **pore** with **pour**, which means 'flow in a steady stream'

pork

porker »*noun* a young pig raised and fattened for food.

porky (in informal English) »*adjective* fat. »*noun* (plural **porkies**) a lie.

porn »*noun* pornography.

pornography »*noun* commercially produced pictures, writing, or films intended to arouse sexual excitement.
pornographer
pornographic

porous »*adjective* (of a rock or other material) having tiny spaces through which liquid or air can pass.
porosity

porphyry »*noun* a hard, reddish igneous rock containing crystals of feldspar.
– SAY por-fi-ri

porpoise »*noun* a type of small whale with a rounded snout.
– SAY por-puhss or por-poyz

porridge

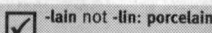 **idge** not **ige** or **age**: **porridge**

port[1] [town with a harbour; a strong sweet red wine; opening or socket]

port[2] »*noun* the side of a ship or aircraft that is on the left when you are facing forward (the opposite of *starboard*).

portable
portability

portage »*noun* ❶ the carrying of a boat or its cargo overland between two waterways. ❷ a place at which this is necessary.
– SAY por-tij

portal »*noun* ❶ a large and impressive doorway or gate. ❷ an Internet site providing a directory of links to other sites.

portcullis »*noun* (plural **portcullises**) a strong, heavy grating that can be lowered to block a gateway to a castle.

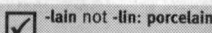 double **l**, single **s**: **portcullis**

portend »*verb* (**portends, portending, portended**) be a sign or warning that something important or unpleasant is likely to happen.

portent »*noun* a sign or warning that something important or unpleasant is likely to happen.

portentous »*adjective* ❶ being a sign that something important is likely to happen. ❷ excessively solemn.
portentously
portentousness

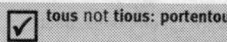 **tous** not **tious**: **portentous**

porter

portfolio »*noun* (plural **portfolios**) ❶ a thin, flat case for carrying drawings, maps, etc. ❷ a set of pieces of creative work collected together to show the range of a person's ability. ❸ a range of investments held by a person or organization. ❹ the area of responsibility of a government minister.

✓ the plural of **portfolio** has **os** not **oes**: **portfolios**

porthole »*noun* a small window on the outside of a ship or aircraft.

portico »*noun* (plural **porticoes** or **porticos**) a roof supported by columns at regular intervals, often forming a porch.
– say por-ti-koh

✓ the plural of **portico** can have **oes** or **os**: **porticoes** or **porticos**

portion (verb: **portions, portioning, portioned**)

portly »*adjective* rather fat.
portliness

portmanteau »*noun* (plural **portmanteaus** or **portmanteaux**) a large travelling bag that opens into two equal parts.
– say port-**man**-toh [singular], port-**man**-tohz [plural]

✓ the plural of **portmanteau** can be **portmanteaux** (as in the original French) or **portmanteaus**

portrait »*noun* ❶ a painting, drawing, or photograph of a person. ❷ a written or filmed description.
portraitist

portraiture »*noun* ❶ the art of making portraits. ❷ portraits as a form of art.

portray (verb: **portrays, portraying, portrayed**)
portrayal

Portuguese (plural **Portuguese**)

✓ **guese** not **gese**: **Portuguese**

pose (verb: **poses, posing, posed**)
poser

poseur »*noun* a person who poses in order to impress; a poser.
– say poh-**zer**

✓ **eur** at the end: **poseur** is a French word

posh (adjective: **posher, poshest**)
poshness

posies

posing

posit »*verb* (**posits, positing, posited**) put something forward as fact or as a basis for argument.
– say po-zit

✓ do not double the **t** in **positing** and **posited**

position (verb: **positions, positioning, positioned**)
positional

positive
positively

positivism »*noun* a system of philosophy that recognizes only things that can be scientifically or logically proved.
positivist

positivity

positron »*noun* (in physics) a subatomic particle with the same mass as an electron and an equal but positive charge.
– say po-zi-tron

posits

posse »*noun* ❶ (a historical term) (in the US) a body of men summoned by a sheriff to enforce the law. ❷ (in informal English) a group of people who are the same in some way.
– say poss-i

✓ **e** not **y** at the end: **posse** is a Latin word meaning 'be able, power'

possess (verb: **possesses, possessing, possessed**)
possessor

✓ remember, there is a double **s** before and after the **e**: **possess**

possession

possessive »*adjective* ❶ demanding someone's total attention and love. ❷ unwilling to share your possessions. ❸ (in grammar) expressing possession (e.g. *theirs, John's*).
possessively
possessiveness

possessive pronoun »*noun* (in grammar) a pronoun showing possession (e.g. *mine*).

possessor

✓ **-or** not **-er**: **possessor**

possibility (plural **possibilities**)

✓ plural: drop the **y** and add **ies**: **possibilities**

possible
possibly

✓ **-ible** not **-able**: **possible**

possum »*noun* ❶ an Australasian marsupial that lives in trees. ❷ (in American English) an opossum.

post (verb: **posts, posting, posted**)

postage

postal

postbox (plural **postboxes**)

postcard

postcode

post-coital »*adjective* occurring or done after sex.

post-date »*verb* (**post-dates, post-dating, post-dated**) ❶ put a date later than the actual one on a cheque or document. ❷ occur at a later date than: *Stonehenge was believed to post-date these structures.*

postdoctoral »*adjective* (of research) done after the completion of a doctorate.

posted

poster

poste restante »*noun* a department in a post office that keeps letters until they are collected by the person they are addressed to.
– **SAY** pohst **ress**-tuhnt

> ℹ **poste restante** means 'mail remaining' in French

posterior »*adjective* at or nearer the rear. »*noun* (mainly used in a humorous way) a person's bottom.

posterity »*noun* all future generations of people.

postern »*noun* (an old word) a back or side entrance.
– **SAY** **poss**-tern or **pohss**-tern

postgraduate »*adjective* relating to study done after completing a first degree. »*noun* a person taking a course of postgraduate study.

post-haste »*adverb* with great speed.

posthumous »*adjective* happening or appearing after the person involved has died.
– **SAY** **poss**-tyuu-muhss
posthumously

> ✓ **thum** not **tum** in the middle: **posthumous**

postilion »*noun* (mainly a historical term) the rider of the leading horse on the left-hand side of a team drawing a coach, when there is no coachman.
– **SAY** po-**stil**-i-uhn

> ✓ **postilion** can also be spelled **postillion**, with a double l

post-Impressionism »*noun* a late 19th-century and early 20th-century style of art in which emphasis was placed on the artist's emotions, as expressed by colour, line, and shape.
post-Impressionist

post-industrial »*adjective* (of an economy or society) no longer relying on heavy industry.

posting

postman (plural **postmen**)

postmark (verb: **postmarks, postmarking, postmarked**)

postmaster »*noun* a person in charge of a post office.

postmen

postmistress (plural **postmistresses**)

postmodernism »*noun* a style and movement in the arts that features a deliberate mixing of different styles and draws attention to artistic traditions.
postmodern
postmodernist

post-mortem »*noun* ❶ an examination of a dead body to find out the cause of death. ❷ a detailed discussion of an event made after it has occurred.

> ✓ the ending is **em** not **um**: post-mortem (literally 'after death' in Latin)

post-natal »*adjective* having to do with the period after childbirth.

postpone (verb: **postpones, postponing, postponed**)
postponement

> ✓ **-pone** not **-phone**: postpone

postprandial »*adjective* having to do with the period after a meal.

posts

postscript »*noun* an additional remark at the end of a letter, following the signature.

post-traumatic stress disorder »*noun* a condition of persistent stress occurring as a result of injury or severe psychological shock.

postulant »*noun* a candidate who wishes to enter a religious order.
– **SAY** **poss**-tyuu-luhnt

postulate »*verb* (**postulates, postulating, postulated**) suggest or accept that something is true, as a basis for a theory or discussion.
– **SAY** **poss**-tyuu-layt
postulation

posture »*noun* ❶ a particular position of the body. ❷ the usual way in which a person holds their body. ❸ an approach or attitude towards something.
»*verb* (**postures, posturing, postured**) behave in a way that is meant to impress or mislead others.
postural

postwoman (plural **postwomen**)

posy »*noun* (plural **posies**) a small bunch of flowers.

the ending is **y** not **ey**: **posy**
plural: drop the **y** and add **ies**: **posies**

pot (verb: **pots**, **potting**, **potted**)

double the **t** in **potting** and **potted**

potable »*adjective* safe to drink.
– SAY poh-tuh-b'l

potash »*noun* an alkaline compound of potassium, used in making soap and fertilizers.

potassium »*noun* a soft silvery-white reactive metallic element.

single **t**, double **s**: **potassium**

potato (plural **potatoes**)

there is no **e** on the end in the singular, but the plural has **oes** not **os**: **potato** and **potatoes**

potboiler »*noun* a book, film, etc. produced purely to make the writer or artist a living by appealing to popular taste.

poteen »*noun* (in Ireland) whisky that is made illegally.
– SAY po-**teen**

potent »*adjective* ❶ having great power, influence, or effect. ❷ (of a man) able to achieve an erection or to reach an orgasm.
potency
potently

 ent not **ant**: **potent**

potentate »*noun* a monarch or ruler.

potential »*adjective* capable of becoming or developing into something.
» *noun* ❶ qualities or abilities that may be developed and lead to future success. ❷ (often **potential for** or **to do**) the possibility of something happening. ❸ (in physics) the difference in voltage between two points in an electric field or circuit.
potentiality
potentially

potentiometer »*noun* an instrument for measuring or adjusting an electromotive force.
– SAY poh-ten-shi-**om**-i-ter

pothole »*noun* ❶ a deep underground cave formed by water eroding the rock. ❷ a hole in a road surface.
potholed
potholing

potion »*noun*

pot-pourri »*noun* (plural **pot-pourris**) ❶ a mixture of dried petals and spices placed in a bowl to perfume a room. ❷ a mixture of things.
– SAY poh-**poor**-i or poh-puh-**ree**

 pot-pourri is French for 'rotten pot'

pots

potshot »*noun* a shot aimed unexpectedly or at random.

pottage »*noun* (an old word) soup or stew.

potted »*adjective* ❶ grown or preserved in a pot. ❷ put into a short, understandable form: *a potted history of Australia.*

potter (verb: **potters**, **pottering**, **pottered**)

pottery (plural **potteries**)

plural: drop the **y** and add **ies**: **potteries**

potties

potting

potty[1] »*adjective* (in informal English) ❶ foolish; crazy. ❷ extremely enthusiastic about someone or something.

potty[2] »*noun* (plural **potties**) a bowl for a child to use as a toilet.

plural: drop the **y** and add **ies**: **potties**

pouch

pouffe »*noun* a large firm cushion used as a seat or stool.
– SAY poof

pouffe (a French word) can also be spelled **pouf**

poulterer »*noun* a person who sells poultry.

terer not **trer**: **poulterer**

poultice »*noun* a soft moist mass of flour, plant material, etc., put on the skin to reduce inflammation.
– SAY pohl-tiss

poultry

try not **tery**: **poultry**

pounce (verb: **pounces**, **pouncing**, **pounced**)

pound[1] »*noun* ❶ the basic unit of money of the UK, equal to 100 pence. ❷ a unit of weight equal to sixteen ounces (0.4536 kg).

pound[2] (verb: **pounds**, **pounding**, **pounded**) [hit heavily again and again, walk or run with heavy steps]

pound[3] [a place holding stray dogs or illegally parked vehicles]

poundage »*noun* ❶ a charge made for every pound in weight of something, or

for every pound sterling in value.
② weight.

pounded

pounding

pounds

pour (verb: **pours**, **pouring**, **poured**) [flow or cause to flow in a steady stream]

> ℹ do not confuse **pour** with **pore**, which means 'study or read something with close attention'

pout (verb: **pouts**, **pouting**, **pouted**)
pouty

poverty

poverty trap »*noun* a situation where if someone earns more money they will lose state benefits and so be no better off.

POW »*abbreviation* prisoner of war.

powder (verb: **powders**, **powdering**, **powdered**)
powdery

powder blue »*noun* a soft, pale blue.

powdered

powdering

powder keg »*noun* a situation which is likely to suddenly become dangerous or violent.

powders

powdery

power (verb: **powers**, **powering**, **powered**)

powerboat

powered

powerful
powerfully

> ✓ **-ful** not **-full**: **powerful**

powerhouse »*noun* a person or thing having great energy or power.

powering

powerless
powerlessly
powerlessness

powers

powwow »*noun* **①** (in informal English) a meeting for discussion. **②** a North American Indian ceremony involving feasting and dancing.

> ✓ double **w** in the middle and single **w** at the end: **powwow**

pox »*noun* **①** a disease caused by a virus and producing a rash of pus-filled pimples that leave pockmarks on healing. **②** (**the pox**) (in informal English) syphilis.

poxy »*adjective* (in informal English) of poor quality.

PR »*abbreviation* **①** proportional representation. **②** public relations.

practicable »*adjective* able to be done successfully.
practicability
practicably

> ℹ **practicable** and **practical** do not mean exactly the same thing: **practicable** means 'able to be done successfully', while **practical** means 'not theoretical', 'likely to be successful or useful', 'skilled at making or doing things'

practical [not theoretical; likely to be successful or useful; skilled at making or doing things]
practically

practicality (plural **practicalities**)

> ✓ plural: drop the **y** and add **ies**: **practicalities**

practically

practice [the action of doing something rather than the theories about it]

> ✓ do you mean **practice** or **practise**? **Practice** is the spelling for the noun (as in *good technique only comes with practice* or *modern child-rearing practices*), **practise** for the verb (as in *they were practising for the Olympics*). Americans use the spelling **practice** for the verb as well as the noun.

practise (verb: **practises**, **practising**, **practised**) [do something repeatedly to improve your skill; do something regularly]

practitioner »*noun* a person who practises a profession or activity.

> ✓ two **t**'s in the middle: **practitioner**

pragmatic »*adjective* dealing with things in a practical way.
pragmatically

pragmatism »*noun* the attitude or policy of approaching matters in a practical way.
pragmatist

prairie »*noun* (in North America) a large open area of grassland.

> ✓ **air** not **ar** in the middle: **prairie**

praise (verb: **praises**, **praising**, **praised**)

praiseworthy

praising

praline »*noun* a filling for chocolates made from nuts boiled in sugar.
– SAY prah-leen or pray-leen

pram

prance (verb: **prances, prancing, pranced**)

prang »*verb* (**prangs, pranging, pranged**) (in informal English) crash a motor vehicle or aircraft.

prank

prankster »*noun* a person fond of playing pranks.

praseodymium »*noun* a silvery-white metallic element.
– **SAY** pray-zi-oh-**di**-mi-uhm

prat

prate »*verb* (**prates, prating, prated**) talk too much in a foolish or boring way.

pratfall »*noun* a fall where a person lands on their bottom.

prating

prattle (verb: **prattles, prattling, prattled**)

prawn

praxis »*noun* practice as opposed to theory.
– **SAY** **prak**-siss

> ℹ️ **praxis** is a Greek word meaning 'doing'

pray (verb: **prays, praying, prayed**) [say a prayer]

> ℹ️ do not confuse **pray** with **prey**, which means 'hunt and kill something for food'

prayer

prayerful »*adjective* ❶ having to do with praying or prayers. ❷ liking to pray; devout.

> ✓ **-ful** not **-full: prayerful**

praying

praying mantis see the note at **MANTIS**.

prays

preach (verb: **preaches, preaching, preached**)
preacher

preachy »*adjective* giving moral advice in a boring or overbearing way.

preamble »*noun* an introduction; an opening statement.

pre-arrange (verb: **pre-arranges, pre-arranging, pre-arranged**)

prebendary »*noun* (plural **prebendaries**) (in the Christian Church) an honorary canon.
– **SAY** pre-buhn-duh-ri

> ✓ plural: drop the **y** and add **ies**: **prebendaries**

Precambrian »*adjective* relating to the earliest geological period of the earth's history, ending about 570 million years ago.
– **SAY** pree-**kam**-bri-uhn

precarious »*adjective* ❶ likely to fall or to cause someone to fall. ❷ uncertain.
precariously
precariousness

precast »*adjective* (of concrete) made into a form that is ready for use in building.

precaution »*noun* something done in advance to avoid problems or danger.
precautionary

precede »*verb* (**precedes, preceding, preceded**) ❶ come or go before something in time or order. ❷ (**precede with**) introduce something with.

> ✓ **cede** not **ceed: precede**

precedence »*noun* the state of coming before others in order or importance: *his desire for power took precedence over everything else.*
– **SAY** **press**-i-duhnss or **pree**-si-duhnss

precedent »*noun* an earlier event, action, or legal case that is taken as an example to be followed in a similar situation.
– **SAY** **press**-i-d'nt

> ✓ **ent** not **ant: precedent**

precedes
preceding

precentor »*noun* a person who leads the singing or (in a synagogue) the prayers in a religious service.
– **SAY** pri-**sen**-ter

> ✓ **-or** not **-er: precentor**

precept »*noun* a general rule about how to behave or what to think.

> ✓ **cept** not **sept: precept**

precession »*noun* ❶ the slow movement of the axis of a spinning body around another axis. ❷ (in astronomy) the earlier occurrence of equinoxes each year.

precinct »*noun* ❶ an area in a town that is closed to traffic. ❷ the area around a place or building, often enclosed by a wall. ❸ (in American English) one of the districts into which a city or town is divided for elections or policing purposes.

precious
preciously
preciousness

precipice »*noun* a tall and very steep rock face or cliff.

there are no **s**'s in **precipice**

precipitate »*verb* (**precipitates, precipitating, precipitated**) ❶ cause something bad to happen suddenly or too soon. ❷ cause something to move suddenly and with force. ❸ (in chemistry) cause a substance to be deposited in solid form from a solution. ❹ cause moisture in the atmosphere to condense and fall as rain, snow, etc.
» *adjective* done or occurring suddenly or without careful thought.
» *noun* (in chemistry) a substance precipitated from a solution.
– SAY pri-**sip**-i-tayt [verb and noun], pri-**sip**-i-tuht [adjective and noun]
precipately

precipitation »*noun* ❶ rain, snow, sleet, or hail. ❷ (in chemistry) the action of precipitating a substance from a solution.

precipitous »*adjective* ❶ dangerously high or steep. ❷ sudden and considerable: *a precipitous decline in exports.*
– SAY pri-**sip**-i-tuhss
precipitously

precis »*noun* (plural **precis**) a summary.
» *verb* (**precises, precising, precised**) make a precis of something.
– SAY **pray**-si [singular], **pray**-si or **pray**-seez [plural]

 precis can also be written **précis**, with an acute accent on the **e** (as in the original French). The **s** is silent, and the verb forms are pronounced **pray**-seez (*precises*), **pray**-see-ing (*precising*), **pray**-seed (*precised*).

precise
precisely

ℹ strictly speaking, **precise** does not mean the same as **accurate**. **Precise** contains the idea of trying to specify details exactly, while **accurate** means 'correct in all details'. If you say 'It's 4.04 and 12 seconds' you are being *precise*, but not necessarily *accurate* (your watch might be slow).

precised
precisely
precises
precising

precision »*noun* the state of being precise.
» *adjective* very accurate: *a precision instrument.*

preclude »*verb* (**precludes, precluding, precluded**) prevent something from happening or someone from doing something.

precocious »*adjective* having developed certain abilities or tendencies at an earlier age than usual.
precociously
precociousness

precocity »*noun* the state of being precocious.
– SAY pri-**koss**-i-ti

 city not **sity**: **precocity**

precognition »*noun* knowledge of an event before it happens, gained by paranormal means.
– SAY pree-kog-**ni**-sh'n

preconceived »*adjective* (of an idea or opinion) formed before full knowledge or evidence is available.

 remember, **i** before **e**, except after **c**: **preconceived**

preconception »*noun* a preconceived idea or opinion.

precondition »*noun* something that must exist or happen before other things can happen or be done.

precursor »*noun* a person or thing that comes before another of the same kind.

 -or not **-er**: **precursor**

pre-date »*verb* (**pre-dates, pre-dating, pre-dated**) exist or occur at a date earlier than something else.

predator »*noun* an animal that hunts and kills others for food.
– SAY **pred**-uh-ter
predation

 -or not **-er**: **predator**

predatory »*adjective* ❶ (of an animal) killing others for food. ❷ taking advantage of others.

predecease »*verb* (**predeceases, predeceasing, predeceased**) die before another person.

predecessor »*noun* ❶ a person who held a job or office before the current holder. ❷ a thing that has been followed or replaced by another.

 double **s** and **-or**, not **-er** at the end: **predecessor**

predestination »*noun* the Christian belief that everything that happens has been decided in advance by God or fate.

predestine »*verb* (**predestines, predestining, predestined**) (of God or fate) decide in advance that something will happen.

predetermine »*verb* (**predetermines, predetermining, predetermined**) establish or decide something in advance.
predetermination

predicament »*noun* a difficult situation.

predicate »*verb* (**predicates, predicating, predicated**) (**predicate on**) found or base something on.
– say pred-i-kayt

predict (verb: **predicts, predicting, predicted**)
predictive
predictor

predictable
predictability
predictably

 -able not -ible: **predictable**

predicted

predicting

prediction

predictive

predictor

predicts

predilection »*noun* a preference or special liking for something.
– say pree-di-**lek**-sh'n

 the ending is **-dilection** not **-deliction**: **predilection**

predispose »*verb* (**predisposes, predisposing, predisposed**) make someone likely to be, do, or think something: *certain people are predisposed to become drug abusers.*
predisposition

predominant »*adjective* ① present as the main part of something: *the bird's predominant colour was white.* ② having the greatest control or power.
predominance
predominantly

 ant not **ent**: **predominant**

predominate »*verb* (**predominates, predominating, predominated**) ① be the main part of something. ② have control or power.

pre-eminent »*adjective* better than all others; outstanding.
pre-eminence
pre-eminently

 words made up of **pre** followed by another word which begins with **e** need a hyphen: **pre-eminent, pre-existing**, etc.

pre-empt »*verb* (**pre-empts, pre-empting, pre-empted**) ① take action so as to prevent something happening or someone from doing something. ② stop someone from saying something by speaking first.
pre-emption

pre-emptive »*adjective* done to prevent something happening or someone from doing something.
pre-emptively

pre-empts

preen »*verb* (**preens, preening, preened**) ① (of a bird) tidy and clean its feathers with its beak. ② attend to and admire your appearance. ③ (**preen yourself**) feel very pleased with yourself.

pre-existing »*adjective* existing from an earlier time.

prefab »*noun* a prefabricated building.

prefabricated »*adjective* (of a building) made in previously constructed sections that can be easily put together on site.
prefabrication

preface »*noun* an introduction to a book, stating its subject or aims.
»*verb* (**prefaces, prefacing, prefaced**) (**preface with** or **by**) say or do something to introduce a book, speech, or event.
– say pref-uhss
prefatory

prefect »*noun* ① a senior pupil in a school who has some authority over younger pupils. ② a chief officer, magistrate, or regional governor in certain countries.

prefecture »*noun* a district administered by a prefect.

prefer (verb: **prefers, preferring, preferred**)

 double the **r** to spell **preferring** and **preferred**

preferable
preferably

 -able not -ible: **preferable**

preference

 ence not **ance**: **preference**

preferential »*adjective* favouring a particular person or group.
preferentially

preferment »*noun* promotion to a job or position.

preferred

preferring

prefers

prefigure »*verb* (**prefigures, prefiguring, prefigured**) be an early sign or version of

p

something: *this passage prefigures her mature writing.*

prefix *»noun* (plural **prefixes**) ❶ a word, letter, or number placed before another. ❷ a letter or group of letters placed at the beginning of a word to alter its meaning (e.g. *non-*).
» verb (**prefixes, prefixing, prefixed**) add a prefix to something.

pregnancy (plural **pregnancies**)

> ✓ plural: drop the **y** and add **ies**: **pregnancies**

pregnant
pregnantly

> ✓ ant not ent: pregn**ant**

prehensile *»adjective* (of an animal's limb or tail) capable of grasping things.
– **say** pri-**hen**-syl

prehistoric

prehistory *»noun* ❶ the period of time before written records. ❷ the early stages of the development of something.

pre-industrial

prejudge *»verb* (**prejudges, prejudging, prejudged**) make a judgement about someone or something before you have all the necessary information.

prejudice *»noun* ❶ an opinion about someone or something that is not based on reason or experience. ❷ unfair reactions or behaviour based on such opinions.
» verb (**prejudices, prejudicing, prejudiced**) ❶ influence someone so that they form an opinion that is not based on reason or experience. ❷ cause harm to something: *delay is likely to prejudice the child's welfare.*

> ✓ there is no **d** before the **j**: prejudice

prejudicial *»adjective* harmful to someone or something.

prelate *»noun* a bishop or other high-ranking minister in the Christian church.
– **say** prel-uht

preliminary *»adjective* taking place before a main action or event.
» noun (plural **preliminaries**) a preliminary action or event.

> ✓ plural: drop the **y** and add **ies**: **preliminaries**

prelude *»noun* ❶ an action or event acting as an introduction to something more important. ❷ a piece of music acting as an introduction to a longer piece.

premarital *»adjective* occurring before marriage.
premaritally

premature *»adjective* ❶ occurring or done before the proper time. ❷ (of a baby) born before the normal length of pregnancy is completed.
prematurely

premeditated *»adjective* (of a bad action or crime) planned in advance.
premeditation

premenstrual *»adjective* occurring or experienced in the time of the month before menstruation.

premier *»adjective* first in importance, order, or position.
» noun a Prime Minister or other head of government.
premiership

> ⓘ do not confuse **premier** with **premiere**, which means 'the first performance or showing of something'

premiere *»noun* the first performance or showing of a play, film, ballet, etc.
» verb (**premieres, premiering, premiered**) give the premiere of something.
– **say** prem-i-air

> ✓ **premiere** can also be spelled **première**, with a grave accent over the **e** (as in the original French)

premiership

premise *»noun* a statement or idea that forms the basis for a theory, argument, or line of reasoning.
– **say** prem-iss

> ✓ **premise** can also be spelled **premiss**

premises *»plural noun* a building and land occupied by a business.

premiss another way of spelling **PREMISE**.

premium *»noun* (plural **premiums**) ❶ an amount paid for an insurance policy. ❷ an extra sum added to a basic price or other payment.
» adjective (of a product) of high quality and more expensive.

Premium Bond *»noun* (in the UK) a government certificate that pays no interest but is entered in regular draws for cash prizes.

premolar *»noun* a tooth between the canines and molar teeth.

premonition *»noun* a strong feeling that something is going to happen.
– **say** pre-muh-**ni**-sh'n or pree-muh-**ni**-sh'n
premonitory

prenatal »*adjective* before birth.
prenatally

preoccupation »*noun* ❶ the state of being preoccupied. ❷ a matter that preoccupies someone.

preoccupy »*verb* (**preoccupies, preoccupying, preoccupied**) completely fill someone's mind.

preordained »*adjective* decided or determined beforehand.

prep »*noun* (especially in a private school) school work done outside lessons.

pre-packaged

pre-packed

prepaid past and past participle of PREPAY.

preparation

preparatory »*adjective* done in order to prepare for something.

> ☑ ory not ery: preparatory

preparatory school »*noun* ❶ (in the UK) a private school for pupils aged seven to thirteen. ❷ (in the US) a private school that prepares pupils for college or university.

prepare (verb: **prepares, preparing, prepared**)
preparer

preparedness »*noun* readiness.

preparer

prepares

preparing

prepay »*verb* (**prepays, prepaying, prepaid**) pay for something in advance.
prepayment

preponderance »*noun* a greater number or incidence of something: *the preponderance of women among older people.*

> ☑ ance not ence: preponderance

preponderant »*adjective* greater in number or importance.
preponderantly

> ☑ ant not ent: preponderant

preponderate »*verb* (**preponderates, preponderating, preponderated**) be greater in number or importance.

preposition »*noun* a word used with a noun or pronoun to show place, position, time, or method (such as *from, to, on,* or *after*).
– SAY pre-puh-**zi**-sh'n
prepositional

> ℹ️ some people believe that a preposition should never end a sentence, as in *where do you come from?*, and that you should say *from where do you come?* instead. However, this can result in English that sounds very awkward, and is not a rule that has to be followed as long as the meaning of what you are saying is clear.

prepossessing »*adjective* attractive or appealing in appearance.

preposterous »*adjective* completely ridiculous or outrageous.
preposterously
preposterousness

prep school »*noun* a preparatory school.

pre-pubescent »*adjective* having to do with the period before puberty.

prepuce »*noun* = FORESKIN.
– SAY pree-pyooss

prequel »*noun* a story or film about events which happen before those of an existing work.

Pre-Raphaelite »*noun* a member of a group of English 19th-century artists who painted in the style of Italian artists from before the time of Raphael.
» *adjective* relating to the Pre-Raphaelites.
– SAY pree-**ra**-fuh-lyt

pre-recorded

prerequisite »*noun* a thing that must exist or happen before something else can exist or happen.
» *adjective* required before something else can happen or exist.
– SAY pree-**rek**-wi-zit

> ℹ️ do not confuse **prerequisite** with **perquisite**, which means 'a special privilege'

prerogative »*noun* a right or privilege belonging to a particular person or group.
– SAY pri-**rog**-uh-tiv

> ☑ note that the beginning of the word is **pre** not **per**: prerogative

presage »*verb* (**presages, presaging, presaged**) be a sign or warning of something.
» *noun* an omen.
– SAY press-ij

Presbyterian »*adjective* relating to a Protestant Church governed by elders who are all of equal rank.
» *noun* a member of a Presbyterian Church.
– SAY prez-bi-**teer**-i-uhn
Presbyterianism

> ☑ note the **y** in the middle of the word: **Presbyterian**

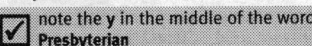

presbytery »*noun* (plural **presbyteries**)
❶ an administrative body in a Presbyterian Church. ❷ the house of a Roman Catholic parish priest. ❸ the eastern part of a church near the altar.
– SAY prez-bi-tuh-ri

prescient »*adjective* knowing about things before they happen.
– SAY press-i-uhnt
prescience
presciently

prescribe »*verb* (**prescribes**, **prescribing**, **prescribed**) ❶ recommend and permit the use of a medicine or treatment. ❷ state officially that something should be done.

ℹ️ do not confuse **prescribe** with **proscribe**, which means either 'officially forbid something' or 'criticize or condemn someone'

prescription »*noun* ❶ a piece of paper on which a doctor states that a patient may be supplied with a medicine or treatment. ❷ the action of prescribing a medicine or treatment.

prescriptive »*adjective* stating what should be done.

presence

present (verb: **presents**, **presenting**, **presented**)

presentable

presentation
presentational
presentationally

presented

presenter

presentiment »*noun* a feeling that something unpleasant is going to happen.
– SAY pri-zen-ti-muhnt

presenting

presently

present participle »*noun* (in grammar) the form of a verb, ending in -*ing*, which is used in forming tenses describing continuous action (e.g. *I'm thinking*), as a noun (e.g. *good thinking*), and as an adjective (e.g. *running water*).

presents

present tense »*noun* (in grammar) a tense that expresses an action or state now happening or existing.

preservation
preservationist

preservative »*noun* a substance used to prevent food or wood from decaying.

preserve (verb: **preserves**, **preserving**, **preserved**)
preserver

preset »*verb* (**presets**, **presetting**, **preset**) set the controls of an electrical device before it is used.

✅ double the **t** to spell **presetting**

preside »*verb* (**presides**, **presiding**, **presided**) lead or be in charge of a meeting or event.

presidency »*noun* (plural **presidencies**) the job of president or the period of time this is held.

✅ **ency** not **ancy**: **presidency**

president
presidential

✅ **ent** not **ant**: **president**

presides

presiding

press (verb: **presses**, **pressing**, **pressed**; plural **presses**)

press conference »*noun* a meeting with journalists in order to make an announcement or answer questions.

pressed

presses

press gang »*noun* (a historical term) a body of men employed to force men to serve in the army or navy.
»*verb* (**press-gangs**, **press-ganging**, **press-ganged**) force someone into doing something.

✅ add a hyphen if you use this word as a verb, as in *we press-ganged him into playing*

pressing »*adjective* ❶ needing urgent action. ❷ strongly expressed and difficult to refuse or ignore.
»*noun* an object made by moulding under pressure.

press release »*noun* a statement or piece of publicity issued to journalists.

press stud »*noun* a small fastener with two parts that fit together when pressed.

press-up

pressure (verb: **pressures**, **pressuring**, **pressured**)

pressurize »*verb* (**pressurizes**, **pressurizing**, **pressurized**) ❶ persuade or force someone into doing something. ❷ keep the air pressure in an aircraft

cabin the same as it is at ground level.
pressurization

✓ many people prefer the alternative spellings **pressurise, pressurises,** etc.: both **s** and **z** spellings are correct

prestidigitation »*noun* magic tricks performed as entertainment.
– SAY press-ti-di-ji-**tay**-sh'n

prestige »*noun* respect and admiration resulting from what someone has achieved or the high quality of something.

prestigious »*adjective* having or bringing prestige.
– SAY pre-**sti**-juhss

presto »*adverb & adjective* (in music) in a quick tempo.

prestressed »*adjective* (of concrete) strengthened by means of rods or wires inserted under tension before setting.

presumably

presume (verb: **presumes, presuming, presumed**)

ℹ **presume** and **assume** both mean 'suppose something to be true'. However **assume** is used where something is taken for granted without proof, while **presume** is used when the supposition is based on evidence.

presumption »*noun* ❶ something that is thought to be true or probable. ❷ an act of supposing that something is true. ❸ behaviour that is too confident, such as doing something without asking permission.

presumptuous »*adjective* behaving with disrespectful boldness.
presumptuously
presumptuousness

✓ **uous** not **ious**, and do not forget the second **p: presumptuous**

presuppose »*verb* (**presupposes, presupposing, presupposed**) ❶ need something to happen in order to exist or be true. ❷ assume, without knowing for sure, that something exists or is true and act on that basis.
presupposition

pretence

✓ the ending is **ce** not **se: pretence** (the spelling **pretense** is American)

pretend (verb: **pretends, pretending, pretended**)
pretender

pretense American spelling of **PRETENCE**.

pretension »*noun* ❶ the act of trying to appear more important or better than you actually are in order to impress other people. ❷ a claim to have or be something.

pretentious »*adjective* trying to appear more important or better than you actually are so as to impress other people.
pretentiously
pretentiousness

preternatural »*adjective* beyond what is normal or natural.
– SAY pree-ter-**na**-chuh-ruhl
preternaturally

pretext »*noun* a false reason used to justify an action.

prettier

prettiest

prettify »*verb* (**prettifies, prettifying, prettified**) try to make something look pretty.
prettification

pretty (adjective: **prettier, prettiest**)
prettily
prettiness

✓ drop the **y** and add **ier** or **iest** to spell **prettier** or **prettiest**

pretzel »*noun* a crisp salty biscuit in the shape of a knot or stick.

prevail »*verb* (**prevails, prevailing, prevailed**) ❶ be more powerful than someone or something. ❷ (**prevail on**) persuade someone to do something. ❸ be widespread or current.

prevailing wind »*noun* a wind from the direction that is most usual at a particular place or time.

prevails

prevalent »*adjective* widespread in a particular area.
– SAY **prev**-uh-luhnt
prevalence

prevaricate »*verb* (**prevaricates, prevaricating, prevaricated**) avoid giving a direct answer to a question.
– SAY pri-**va**-ri-kayt
prevarication
prevaricator

ℹ the verbs **prevaricate** and **procrastinate** have similar but not identical meanings: **prevaricate** means 'act or speak in an evasive way', whereas **procrastinate** means 'put off doing something'

prevent (verb: **prevents, preventing, prevented**)
preventable
preventer
prevention

preventative »*adjective* = PREVENTIVE.

preventer

prevention

preventive »*adjective* designed to prevent something from occurring.
» *noun* a preventive medicine or other treatment.

prevents

preview »*noun* ❶ a viewing or showing of something before it becomes generally available. ❷ a review of a forthcoming film, book, or performance.
» *verb* (previews, previewing, previewed) ❶ present something for a preview. ❷ write a preview of something.

previous
previously

prey »*noun* ❶ an animal that is hunted and killed by another for food. ❷ a person who is harmed or deceived by someone or something: *she fell prey to Will's charms.*
» *verb* (preys, preying, preyed) (prey on or upon) ❶ hunt and kill something for food. ❷ take advantage of or cause distress to someone.

> i do not confuse **prey** with **pray**, which means 'say a prayer'

priapic »*adjective* (of a man) have a strong sexual appetite.
– SAY pry-**ap**-ik

price (verb: prices, pricing, priced)

priceless

prices

pricey (adjective: pricier, priciest)

pricing

prick (verb: pricks, pricking, pricked)
pricker

prickle (verb: prickles, prickling, prickled)

prickly

prickly pear »*noun* a cactus which produces prickly, pear-shaped fruits.

pricks

pride (verb: prides, priding, prided)

pried [past of PRY]

pries

priest
priesthood
priestly

> ✓ i before e except after c: **priest** follows the usual rule

priestess (plural priestesses)

priesthood

priestly

prig »*noun* a person who behaves as if they are superior to others.
priggish

prim »*adjective* very formal and correct and disapproving of anything rude.
primly
primness

prima ballerina »*noun* the chief female dancer in a ballet or ballet company.
– SAY pree-muh bal-luh-**ree**-nuh

> i from an Italian phrase which means 'first ballerina'

primacy »*noun* the fact of being most important.
– SAY **pry**-muh-si

prima donna »*noun* ❶ the chief female singer in an opera or opera company. ❷ a very temperamental and self-important person.

> i from an Italian phrase which means 'first lady'

primaeval another way of spelling PRIMEVAL.

prima facie »*adjective & adverb* (in law) accepted as correct until proved otherwise.
– SAY pry-muh **fay**-shi-ee

> i from a Latin phrase which means 'at first sight'

primal »*adjective* ❶ having to do with early human life; primeval. ❷ basic; fundamental.

primarily »*adverb* for the most part; mainly.

primary »*adjective* ❶ of chief importance. ❷ earliest in time or order. ❸ relating to education for children between the ages of about five and eleven.
» *noun* (plural primaries) (in the US) a preliminary election to appoint delegates to a party conference or to select candidates for an election.

primary care »*noun* health care provided by general practitioners rather than in hospitals.

primary colours »*plural noun* the colours blue, red, and yellow, from which all other colours can be obtained by mixing.

primary industry »*noun* an industry concerned with obtaining or providing raw materials, such as mining or agriculture.

primate »*noun* ❶ an animal belonging to a group that includes monkeys, apes, and humans. ❷ (in the Christian Church) an archbishop.

prime[1] *» adjective* **①** of chief importance. **②** of the highest quality; excellent. **③** (of a number) that can be divided only by itself and one (e.g. 2, 3, 5). *» noun* **①** the time in a person's life when they are the strongest and most successful. **②** a prime number.

prime[2] *» verb* (**primes, priming, primed**) **①** make something ready for use or action. **②** prepare someone for a situation by giving them information. **③** cover a surface with primer.

prime minister

primer *» noun* **①** a substance painted on a surface as a base coat. **②** a book for teaching children to read or giving a basic introduction to a subject.

primes

primeval *» adjective* relating to the earliest times in history.
– **say** pry-**mee**-vuhl

> ☑ **primeval** can also be spelled with an **ae** in the middle: **primaeval**

priming

primitive
primitively
primitiveness

primly

primness

primogeniture *» noun* **①** the state of being the firstborn child. **②** the system by which the eldest son inherits all his parents' property.
– **say** pry-moh-**jen**-i-cher

primordial *» adjective* existing at the beginning of time.
– **say** pry-**mor**-di-uhl

primp *» verb* (**primps, primping, primped**) make small adjustments to your appearance.

primrose *» noun* a plant of woods and hedges with pale yellow flowers.

primula *» noun* a plant of a group that includes primroses and cowslips.
– **say** prim-**yuu**-luh

Primus *» noun* (plural **Primuses**) (trademark) a portable cooking stove that burns oil.
– **say** pry-muhss

prince

prince consort *» noun* the husband of a reigning queen who is himself a prince.

princeling *» noun* **①** the ruler of a small or unimportant country. **②** a young prince.

princely *» adjective* **①** relating to or suitable for a prince. **②** (of a sum of money) generous.

princess (plural **princesses**)

principal *» adjective* most important; main. *» noun* **①** the most important person in an organization or group. **②** the head of a school or college. **③** a sum of money lent or invested, on which interest is paid. **④** a person for whom someone else acts as a representative.
principally

> ℹ do not confuse **principal** with **principle**, which means 'a law, rule, or theory that something is based on'

principal boy *» noun* a woman who takes the leading male role in a pantomime.

principality *» noun* (plural **principalities**) **①** a state ruled by a prince. **②** (**the Principality**) Wales.

> ☑ plural: drop the **y** and add **ies**: **principalities**

principle *» noun* **①** a law, rule, or theory that something is based on. **②** (**principles**) rules or beliefs that govern your actions or personal behaviour. **④** a scientific theorem or natural law that explains why something happens or how it works.

> ℹ do not confuse **principle** with **principal**, which means 'main or most important'

principled *» adjective* acting according to strong beliefs about what is right and wrong.

print (verb: **prints, printing, printed**)
printable

printed circuit *» noun* an electronic circuit based on thin strips of a conducting material on an insulating board.

printer

printing

printout *» noun* a page of printed material from a computer's printer.

prints

prion *» noun* a protein particle believed to be the cause of certain brain diseases such as BSE and CJD.
– **say** pree-on

prior[1] *» adjective* **①** coming before in time, order, or importance. **②** (**prior to**) before.

> ☑ -or not -er: **prior**

prior[2] *» noun* **①** (in an abbey) the person next in rank below an abbot. **②** the head of a house of friars.

prioress *» noun* (plural **prioresses**) **①** (in an abbey) the person next in rank below an abbess. **②** the head of a house of nuns.

priories

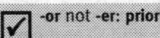

priorities

prioritize »*verb* (**prioritizes, prioritizing, prioritized**) ❶ treat something as being more important than other things. ❷ decide the order of importance of a number of tasks.
prioritization

> ✓ many people prefer the alternative spellings **prioritise, prioritises**, etc.: both **s** and **z** spellings are correct

priority »*noun* (plural **priorities**) ❶ the condition of being more important than other things. ❷ a thing seen as more important than others. ❸ the right to go before other traffic.

> ✓ plural: drop the **y** and add **ies**: **priorities**

priory »*noun* (plural **priories**) a monastery or nunnery governed by a prior or prioress.

> ✓ plural: drop the **y** and add **ies**: **priories**

prise »*verb* (**prises, prising, prised**) force something open or apart.

> ✓ note that the spelling is **ise**: **prise, prises**, etc. (the spellings **prize, prizes**, etc. are either American spellings of **prise**, or the word meaning 'reward for winning something')

prism »*noun* ❶ a piece of faceted glass or other transparent material of regular shape, used to separate white light into a spectrum of colours. ❷ a solid geometric figure whose two ends are parallel and of the same size and shape, and whose sides are parallelograms.

prismatic »*adjective* ❶ relating to a prism. ❷ (of colours) formed by a prism.

prison

prisoner

prisoner of conscience »*noun* a person imprisoned for their political or religious views.

prissy »*adjective* too concerned with behaving in a correct and respectable way.
prissily
prissiness

pristine »*adjective* ❶ in its original condition. ❷ clean and fresh as if new.
– SAY priss-teen

privacy

private
privately

private company »*noun* a company whose shares may not be offered to the public for sale.

privateer »*noun* (a historical term) a privately owned armed ship, authorized by a government for use in war.
– SAY pry-vuh-**teer**

privately

private means »*plural noun* income from investments, property, etc., rather than from employment.

private member »*noun* a member of a parliament who does not hold a government office.

private school »*noun* an independent school supported mainly by fees paid by pupils.

private secretary »*noun* ❶ a secretary who deals with the personal matters of their employer. ❷ a civil servant acting as an aide to a senior government official.

private sector »*noun* the part of the national economy not under direct state control.

privation »*noun* a state in which you do not have the basic things you need, such as food and warmth.
– SAY pry-**vay**-sh'n

privatize »*verb* (**privatizes, privatizing, privatized**) transfer a business or industry from ownership by the state to private ownership.
privatization

> ✓ many people prefer the alternative spellings **privatise, privatises**, etc., and **privatisation**: both **s** and **z** spellings are correct

privet »*noun* a shrub with small white flowers.
– SAY pri-vit

> ✓ **-et** not **-it**: **privet**

privies plural of PRIVY.

privilege

> ✓ there is no **d** in **privilege**

privileged

privy »*adjective* (**privy to**) sharing in the knowledge of something secret.
» *noun* (plural **privies**) a toilet in a small shed outside a house.
– SAY pri-vi

Privy Council »*noun* a body of politicians appointed to advise a king or queen.

prix fixe »*noun* (plural **prix fixes**) a meal of several courses costing a fixed price.
– SAY pree feeks [singular and plural]

> ⓘ **prix fixe** is French for 'fixed price'

prize (verb: **prizes, prizing, prized**) [reward for a winner or achievement; value something highly]

> ℹ️ do not confuse **prize** with **prise**, which means 'force something open or apart' (the use of the spelling **prize** to mean this is American)

prizefight »*noun* a boxing match for prize money.
prizefighter

prizes

prizing

pro (plural **pros**)

proactive »*adjective* creating or controlling a situation rather than just responding to it.
proactively

probability (plural **probabilities**)

> ✓ plural: drop the **y** and add **ies**: **probabilities**

probable

probably

probate »*noun* the official process of proving that a will is valid.

probation »*noun* ❶ the release of an offender from prison, subject to a period of good behaviour under supervision. ❷ the process of testing the abilities of a person in a certain role.
probationary

probationer »*noun* ❶ a person serving a probationary period in a job or position. ❷ an offender on probation.

probation officer »*noun* a person who supervises offenders on probation.

probe »*noun* ❶ a blunt-ended surgical instrument for exploring a wound or part of the body. ❷ a small measuring or testing device. ❸ an investigation. ❹ an unmanned exploratory spacecraft.
»*verb* (**probes, probing, probed**) ❶ physically explore or examine something. ❷ enquire into something closely.
probing

probity »*noun* honesty and decency.
– say proh-bi-ti

problem

problematic
problematical
problematically

proboscis »*noun* (plural **proboscises**) ❶ the nose of a mammal, especially when long and mobile like an elephant's trunk. ❷ an elongated sucking organ or mouthpart of an insect or worm.
– say pruh-**boss**-iss

> ✓ the plural of **proboscis** is **proboscises**, but you may also find **proboscides** (as in the original Greek)

procedure »*noun* ❶ an established or official way of doing something. ❷ a series of actions conducted in a certain manner.
procedural

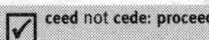

> ✓ **ced** not **ceed**: procedure

proceed (verb: **proceeds, proceeding, proceeded**)

> ✓ **ceed** not **cede**: proceed

proceedings »*plural noun* ❶ an event or a series of activities with a set procedure. ❷ action taken in a law court to settle a dispute.

proceeds

process[1] (plural: **processes**; verb: **processes, processing, processed**) [a series of steps towards achieving a particular end; perform a series of operations]

process[2] »*verb* (**processes, processing, processed**) walk in procession.
– say pruh-**sess**

procession

> ✓ one **c**, two **s**'s: procession

processor

> ✓ **-or** not **-er**: processor

pro-choice »*adjective* supporting the right of a woman to choose to have an abortion.

proclaim »*verb* (**proclaims, proclaiming, proclaimed**) ❶ announce something officially or publicly. ❷ show something clearly.

proclamation »*noun* a public or official announcement.

> ✓ **-clam-** in the middle, not **-claim-**: proclamation

proclivity »*noun* (plural **proclivities**) a tendency to do or choose something regularly; an inclination.
– say pruh-**kli**-vi-ti

> ✓ plural: drop the **y** and add **ies**: proclivities

procrastinate »*verb* (**procrastinates, procrastinating, procrastinated**) put off doing something.
– say proh-**krass**-ti-nayt
procrastination
procrastinator

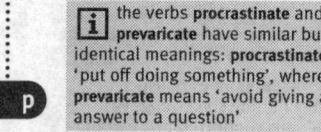

the verbs **procrastinate** and **prevaricate** have similar but not identical meanings: **procrastinate** means 'put off doing something', whereas **prevaricate** means 'avoid giving a direct answer to a question'

procreate »*verb* (**procreates**, **procreating**, **procreated**) produce young.
procreation
procreative

proctor »*noun* an officer in charge of discipline at certain universities.

procurator fiscal »*noun* (plural **procurators fiscal** or **procurator fiscals**) (in Scotland) a local coroner and public prosecutor.

> ✓ as **fiscal** is an adjective, the plural should strictly be **procurators fiscal**

procure »*verb* (**procures**, **procuring**, **procured**) obtain something.
procurement

prod (verb: **prods**, **prodding**, **prodded**)

> ✓ double the **d** in **prodding** and **prodded**

prodigal »*adjective* ❶ wastefully extravagant. ❷ lavish.
» *noun* ❶ a prodigal person. ❷ (also **prodigal son**) a person who leaves home to lead an extravagant life but returns feeling sorry.

> ✓ **gal** not **gle**: **prodigal**

prodigies

prodigious »*adjective* impressively large. – SAY pruh-di-juhşs
prodigiously

prodigy »*noun* (plural **prodigies**) ❶ a young person with exceptional abilities. ❷ an amazing or unusual thing.

> ✓ **d** before **g**: **prodigy**
> plural: drop the **y** and add **ies**: **prodigies**

prods

produce (verb: **produces**, **producing**, **produced**)
producer

product

production

productive »*adjective* ❶ producing or able to produce large amounts of goods or crops. ❷ achieving or producing a significant amount or result.
productively

productivity »*noun* ❶ the state of being productive. ❷ the efficiency with which things are produced.

profane »*adjective* ❶ not religious: *topics both sacred and profane.* ❷ not showing respect for God or holy things.
» *verb* (**profanes**, **profaning**, **profaned**) treat something with a lack of respect.

profanity »*noun* (plural **profanities**) ❶ profane language or behaviour. ❷ a swear word.

> ✓ plural: drop the **y** and add **ies**: **profanities**

profess »*verb* (**professes**, **professing**, **professed**) ❶ claim that you have a quality or feeling. ❷ declare your faith in a religion.

professed »*adjective* ❶ (of a quality or feeling) claimed openly but often falsely. ❷ openly declared.
professedly

professes

professing

profession

> ✓ one f, two **s**'s: **profession**

professional
professionalism
professionally

professor
professorial
professorship

> ✓ **-or** not **-er**: **professor**

proffer »*verb* (**proffers**, **proffering**, **proffered**) offer something for acceptance.

> ✓ double f: **proffer**

proficient »*adjective* competent; skilled.
proficiency
proficiently

profile »*noun* ❶ an outline of something as seen from one side. ❷ a short descriptive article about someone. ❸ the extent to which a person or organization attracts public notice.
» *verb* (**profiles**, **profiling**, **profiled**) ❶ describe someone in a short article. ❷ (**be profiled**) appear in outline.
profiler

profit (verb: **profits**, **profiting**, **profited**) [financial gain]

> ✓ do not double the **t** in **profiting** and **profited**

profitable
profitability
profitably

profited

profiteering »*noun* the making of a large profit in an unfair way.

profiterole »*noun* a small ball of choux pastry filled with cream and covered with chocolate sauce.

> 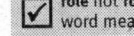 **role** not **roll**: **profiterole** is a French word meaning literally 'small profit'

profiting

profit margin »*noun* the difference between the cost of producing something and the price for which it is sold.

profits

profligate »*adjective* ❶ recklessly extravagant or wasteful. ❷ indulging excessively in physical pleasures.
» *noun* a profligate person.
– SAY prof-li-guht
profligacy

pro forma »*adverb & adjective* as a matter of form or politeness.
» *noun* a standard document or form.
– SAY proh for-muh

> i **pro forma** is a Latin phrase meaning 'as a matter of form'

profound »*adjective* (**profounder**, **profoundest**) ❶ very great: *profound social change.* ❷ showing great knowledge or insight. ❸ demanding deep study or thought.
profoundly
profundity

> drop the second o to spell **profundity**

profuse »*adjective* done or appearing in large quantities; abundant.
profusely
profuseness

profusion »*noun* an abundance or large quantity of something.
– SAY pruh-fyoo-zh'n

progenitor »*noun* ❶ an ancestor or parent. ❷ the originator of an artistic, political, or intellectual movement.
– SAY proh-jen-i-ter

> ✓ -or not -er: **progenitor**

progeny »*noun* offspring.
– SAY proj-uh-ni

progesterone »*noun* a hormone that stimulates the womb to prepare for pregnancy.
– SAY pruh-jess-tuh-rohn

progestogen »*noun* a hormone that maintains pregnancy and prevents further ovulation.
– SAY proh-jess-tuh-juhn

prognosis »*noun* (plural **prognoses**) a forecast, especially of the likely course of an illness.
– SAY prog-noh-siss [singular], prog-noh-seez [plural]

> ✓ make the plural by changing the **-is** ending to **-es** (as in Latin): **prognoses**

prognostic »*adjective* predicting the likely course of an illness.

prognosticate »*verb* (**prognosticates**, **prognosticating**, **prognosticated**) make a forecast about something.
prognostication
prognosticator

program see the note at **PROGRAMME**.

programmable

programmatic »*adjective* having to do with a programme or method.

programme (verb: **programmes**, **programming**, **programmed**)
programmable
programmer

> ✓ the usual British spelling of **programme** has **mme** at the end and there is also a double **m** in **programming** and **programmed**. However in computing, the American spellings **program** (for the noun) and **programs, programing, programed** (for the verb) are usual.

progress (verb: **progresses**, **progressing**, **progressed**)

progression »*noun* ❶ a gradual movement or development towards a destination or a more advanced state. ❷ a number of things coming one after the other.

progressive »*adjective* ❶ proceeding gradually or in stages. ❷ favouring new ideas or social reform.
» *noun* a person who supports social reform.
progressively
progressiveness

prohibit »*verb* (**prohibits**, **prohibiting**, **prohibited**) ❶ formally forbid something by law or a rule. ❷ make something impossible; prevent something.

prohibition »*noun* ❶ the action of prohibiting something. ❷ an order that forbids something. ❸ (**Prohibition**) the prevention by law of the manufacture and sale of alcohol in the US from 1920 to 1933.

prohibitive »*adjective* ❶ forbidding or restricting something. ❷ (of a price or charge) excessively high.
prohibitively
prohibitiveness

p

prohibits

project »*noun* ❶ an enterprise carefully planned to achieve a particular aim. ❷ a piece of research work by a student.
» *verb* (**projects, projecting, projected**)
❶ predict something on the basis of what is happening now. ❷ plan. ❸ extend outwards beyond something else. ❹ throw or cause something to move forward or outward. ❺ cause light, shadow, or an image to fall on a surface. ❻ present a particular image to others.

projectile »*noun* a missile fired or thrown at a target.

projecting

projection »*noun* ❶ a prediction about something based on what is happening now. ❷ the projecting of an image, sound, etc. ❸ a thing that sticks out.
projectionist

projector »*noun* an apparatus for projecting slides or film on to a screen.

 -or not -er: **projector**

projects

prolapse »*noun* a condition in which a part of the body has slipped from its normal position.
– SAY proh-laps

prole »*noun* (used in an insulting way) a member of the working class.

proletarian »*adjective* relating to the proletariat.
» *noun* a member of the proletariat.
– SAY proh-li-**tair**-i-uhn

proletariat »*noun* workers or working-class people.

pro-life »*adjective* seeking to ban abortion and euthanasia.
pro-lifer

proliferate »*verb* (**proliferates, proliferating, proliferated**) reproduce rapidly; increase rapidly in number.
– SAY pruh-**lif**-uh-rayt
proliferation

 one **l**, one **f**: **proliferate**

prolific »*adjective* ❶ producing much fruit or foliage or many offspring. ❷ (of an artist, author, etc.) producing many works.
prolifically

prolix »*adjective* (of speech or writing) long and tedious.
– SAY proh-liks or pruh-**liks**
prolixity

prologue »*noun* ❶ an introductory section or scene in a book, play, or musical work. ❷ an event or action leading to another.

 gue at the end: **prologue** (the spelling **prolog** is American)

prolong »*verb* (**prolongs, prolonging, prolonged**) make something last longer.
prolongation

prolonged »*adjective* continuing for a long time.

prolonging

prolongs

prom »*noun* ❶ (in British English) = PROMENADE (in sense 'paved walk by the sea'). ❷ (in British English) a promenade concert. ❸ (in American English) a formal dance at a high school or college.

promenade »*noun* ❶ a paved public walk, especially one along a seafront. ❷ a leisurely walk, ride, or drive in a public place.
» *verb* (**promenades, promenading, promenaded**) take a leisurely walk, ride, or drive.

 one m, one n: **promenade**

promenade concert »*noun* (in the UK) a concert of classical music at which part of the audience stands in an area without seating.

promenaded

promenades

promenading

Promethean »*adjective* daring or skilful, like Prometheus in Greek mythology who stole fire from the gods and gave it to the human race.
– SAY pruh-**mee**-thi-uhn

prominence »*noun* the state of being prominent.

prominent »*adjective* ❶ important; famous. ❷ bulging: *a man with big, prominent eyes*. ❸ particularly noticeable.
prominently

 ent not **ant**: **prominent**

promiscuous »*adjective* having many brief sexual relationships.
– SAY pruh-**miss**-kyuu-uhss
promiscuity
promiscuously

promise (verb: **promises, promising, promised**)

promising
promisingly

promissory note »*noun* a signed document containing a written promise to pay a stated sum.

> ☑ double the **s** in promi**ss**ory

promo »*noun* (plural **promos**) (in informal English) a promotional film, video, etc.
– SAY proh-moh

> ☑ the plural of promo has os not oes: promos

promontory »*noun* (plural **promontories**) a point of high land jutting out into the sea or a lake.
– SAY prom-uhn-tuh-ri

> ☑ **tory** not try: promon**tory** plural: drop the **y** and add **ies**: promontor**ies**

promote »*verb* (**promotes, promoting, promoted**) ❶ help the progress of a cause, venture, or aim. ❷ publicize a product or celebrity. ❸ raise someone to a higher position or rank. ❹ transfer a sports team to a higher division.
promoter

promotion »*noun* ❶ activity that supports or encourages. ❷ the publicizing of a product or celebrity. ❸ movement to a higher position or rank.
promotional

prompt (verb: **prompts, prompting, prompted**) »*verb* ❶ make something happen. ❷ (**prompt to**) make someone take a course of action. ❸ encourage someone to speak. ❹ tell an actor a word that they have forgotten.
»*noun* ❶ an act of prompting. ❷ a symbol on a computer screen to show that more input is needed. ❸ a word or phrase used to prompt an actor.
»*adjective* done without delay.
»*adverb* (in British English) exactly or punctually: *12 o'clock prompt.*
prompter
promptly
promptness

> ☑ remember the second **p**: prompt

promulgate »*verb* (**promulgates, promulgating, promulgated**) ❶ make an idea widely known. ❷ officially declare the introduction of a new law.
– SAY prom-uhl-gayt
promulgation

prone »*adjective* ❶ (**prone to** or **to do**) likely to suffer from, do, or experience something unfortunate. ❷ lying flat and face downwards (the opposite of *supine*).
proneness

prong »*noun* ❶ one of two or more long pointed parts on a fork. ❷ one of the separate parts of an attack or operation.

pronominal »*adjective* having to do with a pronoun.
– SAY proh-nom-i-nuhl

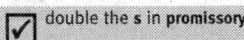

pronoun »*noun* a word used instead of a noun to indicate someone or something already mentioned or known, e.g. *I, this.*

pronounce (verb: **pronounces, pronouncing, pronounced**)

pronounced »*adjective* very noticeable: *a pronounced squint.*

pronouncement »*noun* a formal public statement.

pronounces

pronouncing

pronto »*adverb* (in informal English) promptly.

pronunciation »*noun* the way in which a word is pronounced.
– SAY pruh-nun-si-ay-sh'n

> ☑ unlike pronounce, pronunciation has no **o** in the middle

proof

proof-read »*verb* (**proof-reads, proof-reading, proof-read**) read a text and mark any errors.
proof-reader

prop (verb: **props, propping, propped**)

> ☑ double the **p** in pro**pp**ing and pro**pp**ed

propaganda »*noun* information, often biased or misleading, used to promote a political cause or point of view.

> ☑ propa not propo: propaganda

propagandist »*noun* a person who spreads propaganda.
»*adjective* consisting of or spreading propaganda.

propagate »*verb* (**propagates, propagating, propagated**) ❶ grow a new plant from a parent plant. ❷ promote an idea, knowledge, etc. widely.
propagation
propagator

> ☑ propa not propo: propagate

propane »*noun* a flammable gas present in natural gas and used as bottled fuel.
– SAY proh-payn

propel »*verb* (**propels, propelling, propelled**) drive or push something forwards.

☑ double the **l** in **propelling** and **propelled**

propellant »*noun* ❶ a compressed gas that forces out the contents of an aerosol. ❷ a substance used to provide thrust in a rocket engine.

☑ **ant** not **ent**: **propellant**

propelled

propeller

☑ **-er** not **-or**: **propeller**

propelling

propels

propensity »*noun* (plural **propensities**) a tendency to behave in a certain way.

☑ plural: drop the **y** and add **ies**: **propensities**

proper

proper fraction »*noun* a fraction that is less than one, with the numerator less than the denominator.

properly

proper name »*noun* = PROPER NOUN.

proper noun »*noun* a name for an individual person, place, or organization, having an initial capital letter.

property (plural **properties**)

☑ plural: drop the **y** and add **ies**: **properties**

prophecy »*noun* (plural **prophecies**) ❶ a prediction about what will happen in the future. ❷ the power or practice of prophesying.
– SAY prof-i-si

☑ plural: drop the **y** and add **ies**: **prophecies**

prophesy »*verb* (**prophesies**, **prophesying**, **prophesied**) predict that something will happen in the future.
– SAY prof-i-sI

☑ the ending is **esy**: **prophesy** (**ecy** is the ending of the noun)

prophet »*noun* ❶ a person sent by God to teach people about his intentions. ❷ a person who predicts the future.

prophetess (plural **prophetesses**)

prophetic »*adjective* ❶ accurately predicting the future. ❷ having to do with a prophet or prophecy.
– SAY pruh-**fet**-ik
prophetical
prophetically

prophylactic »*adjective* intended to prevent disease.
» *noun* a preventive medicine or course of action.
– SAY pro-fi-**lak**-tik

propinquity »*noun* nearness in time or space.
– SAY pruh-**ping**-kwi-ti

propitiate »*verb* (**propitiates**, **propitiating**, **propitiated**) win or regain someone's favour.
– SAY pruh-**pi**-shi-ayt
propitiation
propitiatory

propitious »*adjective* favourable.
– SAY pruh-**pi**-shuhss
propitiously
propitiousness

proponent »*noun* a person who proposes a theory, proposal, or project.
– SAY pruh-**poh**-nuhnt

☑ **ent** not **ant**: **proponent**

proportion »*noun* ❶ a part, share, or number considered in relation to a whole. ❷ the relationship of one thing to another in terms of size or quantity. ❸ the correct relation between things. ❹ (**proportions**) dimensions; size.
» *verb* (**proportions**, **proportioning**, **proportioned**) adjust something so that it has a particular relationship to something else.

proportional »*adjective* corresponding in size or amount to something else.
proportionality
proportionally

proportional representation »*noun* a system in which parties in an election gain seats in proportion to the number of votes cast for them.

proportionate »*adjective* = PROPORTIONAL.
proportionately

proportioned

proportioning

proportions

proposal

propose (verb: **proposes**, **proposing**, **proposed**)
proposer

proposition »*noun* ❶ a statement expressing a judgement or opinion. ❷ a proposed scheme or plan. ❸ a matter or person to be dealt with.
» *verb* (**propositions**, **propositioning**, **propositioned**) ask someone to have sex with you.

propound »*verb* (**propounds, propounding, propounded**) put forward an idea or theory for consideration.
– SAY pruh-**pownd**

propped

propping

proprietary »*adjective* ❶ having to do with an owner or ownership. ❷ (of a product) marketed under a registered trade name.

 etary not atery: **proprietary**

proprietary name »*noun* a name of a product or service registered as a trademark.

proprieties

proprietor »*noun* ❶ the owner of a business. ❷ a holder of property.

 -or not -er: **proprietor**

proprietorial »*adjective* ❶ relating to an owner. ❷ possessive.
– SAY pruh-pry-uh-**tor**-i-uhl
proprietorially

proprietress (plural **proprietresses**)

propriety »*noun* (plural **proprieties**)
❶ correctness of behaviour or morals.
❷ the quality of being appropriate.
❸ (**proprieties**) the rules of generally accepted behaviour.

 plural: drop the **y** and add **ies**: **proprieties**

props

propulsion »*noun* the action of propelling or driving forward.
propulsive

pro rata »*adjective* proportional.
» *adverb* proportionally.

 pro rata is a Latin word meaning 'according to the rate'

pros plural of PRO.

prosaic »*adjective* ❶ having the style of prose. ❷ ordinary; unromantic.
– SAY proh-**zay**-ik
prosaically

proscenium »*noun* (plural **prosceniums** or **proscenia**) ❶ the part of a stage in front of the curtain. ❷ (also **proscenium arch**) an arch framing the opening between the stage and the part of the theatre in which the audience sits.
– SAY pruh-**see**-ni-uhm

the plural of **proscenium** can be **prosceniums** or (as in Latin) **proscenia**

proscribe »*verb* (**proscribes, proscribing, proscribed**) ❶ officially forbid something.

❷ criticize or condemn someone.
proscription
proscriptive

i do not confuse **proscribe** with **prescribe**, which means either 'recommend and permit the use of a medicine or treatment' or 'state officially that something should be done'

prose »*noun* ordinary written or spoken language.

prosecute »*verb* (**prosecutes, prosecuting, prosecuted**) ❶ take legal proceedings against someone or with reference to a crime. ❷ continue a course of action with the intention to complete it.

prose- not prosa-: **prosecute**

prosecution »*noun* ❶ the prosecuting of someone in respect of a criminal charge.
❷ (**the prosecution**) the party prosecuting someone in a lawsuit.

prosecutor »*noun* ❶ a person who prosecutes someone. ❷ a lawyer who conducts the case against a person accused of a crime.

-or not -er: **prosecutor**

proselyte »*noun* a person who has converted from one opinion, religion, or party to another.
– SAY **pross**-i-lyt

proselytize »*verb* (**proselytizes, proselytizing, proselytized**) convert someone from one religion, belief, or opinion to another.
– SAY **pross**-i-li-tyz

many people prefer the alternative spellings **proselytise, proselytises**, etc.: both **s** and **z** spellings are correct

prosody »*noun* ❶ the patterns of rhythm and sound used in poetry. ❷ the study of these patterns, or the rules governing them.
– SAY **pross**-uh-di
prosodic

prospect »*noun* ❶ the possibility of something happening. ❷ a mental picture of what will happen in the future.
❸ (**prospects**) chances of being successful.
❹ a person who is likely to be successful.
» *verb* (**prospects, prospecting, prospected**) search for mineral deposits.
prospector

prospective »*adjective* likely to happen or be in the future.
prospectively

prospector

prospects

prospectus »*noun* (plural **prospectuses**) a printed booklet advertising a school or university or giving details of a share offer.

prosper (verb: **prospers, prospering, prospered**)

prosperous
  prosperously
  prosperity

prospers

prostate »*noun* a gland surrounding the neck of the bladder in male mammals that produces a component of semen.
– SAY pross-**tayt**

> ✓ **tate** not **trate**: prostate (**prostrate** means 'lying face downwards')

prosthesis »*noun* (plural **prostheses**) an artificial body part.
– SAY pross-**thee**-siss [singular], pross-**thee**-seez [plural]
  prosthetic

> ✓ make the plural by changing the **-is** ending to **-es** (as in Latin): **prostheses**

prosthetics »*plural noun* artificial body parts.
– SAY pross-**thet**-iks

prostitute »*noun* a person who has sex for money.
»*verb* (**prostitutes, prostituting, prostituted**) ❶ offer someone as a prostitute. ❷ put your talents to an unworthy use for money.
  prostitution

prostrate »*adjective* ❶ lying stretched out on the ground with your face downwards. ❷ completely overcome with distress or exhaustion.
»*verb* (**prostrates, prostrating, prostrated**) ❶ (**prostrate yourself**) throw yourself flat on the ground. ❷ (**be prostrated**) be completely overcome with stress or exhaustion.
– SAY pross-**trayt** [adjective], pross-**trayt** [verb]
  prostration

> ✓ **trate** not **tate**: prostrate (the **prostate** is a gland at the neck of the bladder in males)

protactinium »*noun* a rare radioactive metallic chemical element.
– SAY proh-tak-**tin**-i-uhm

protagonist »*noun* ❶ the leading character in a drama, film, or novel. ❷ an important person in a real event. ❸ a person who actively supports a cause or idea.

protean »*adjective* able to change or adapt.
– SAY proh-ti-uhn or proh-**tee**-uhn

> ℹ from the name of the Greek sea god *Proteus*, who was able to change shape at will

protect (verb: **protects, protecting, protected**)

protection

protectionism »*noun* (in economics) the theory or practice of shielding a country's own industries from foreign competition by taxing imports.
  protectionist

protective »*adjective* serving, intended, or wishing to protect.
  protectively
  protectiveness

protector

> ✓ **-or** not **-er**: protector
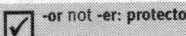

protectorate »*noun* a state that is controlled and protected by another.

protects

protege »*noun* a person who is guided and supported by an older and more experienced person.
– SAY pro-ti-*zhay* or proh-ti-*zhay*

> ✓ **protege** and the feminine form **protegee** can also be spelled with acute accents on the first and second **e**'s (as in the original French): **protégé** and **protégée**

protegee

protein »*noun* one of a group of organic compounds forming part of body tissues and making up an important part of the diet.

> ✓ **e** before **i**: **protein** does not follow the usual rule

pro tem »*adverb & adjective* for the time being.

> ℹ short for Latin *pro tempore*

protest (verb: **protests, protesting, protested**)
  protester

Protestant »*noun* a member or follower of one of the Western Christian Churches that are separate from the Roman Catholic Church.
»*adjective* relating to or belonging to one of the Protestant Churches.
– SAY pro-**tiss**-tuhnt
  Protestantism

> ✓ **ant** not **ent**: Protestant
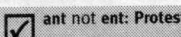

protestation »*noun* ❶ a firm declaration that something is or is not the case. ❷ an objection or protest.
– SAY pro-ti-**stay**-sh'n

protested

protester

protesting

protests

protocol »*noun* ❶ the official system of rules governing affairs of state or diplomatic occasions. ❷ the accepted code of behaviour in a particular situation.

proton »*noun* (in physics) a subatomic particle with a positive electric charge, occurring in all atomic nuclei.

protoplasm »*noun* (in biology) the material making up the living part of a cell.
– SAY **proh**-tuh-pla-z'm

prototype »*noun* a first form from which other forms are developed or copied.
prototypical

protozoan »*noun* a single-celled microscopic animal such as an amoeba.
» *adjective* relating to protozoans.
– SAY proh-tuh-**zoh**-uhn

protract »*verb* (**protracts**, **protracting**, **protracted**) prolong; draw out.
protracted

protractor »*noun* an instrument for measuring angles, in the form of a flat semicircle marked with degrees.

✓ -or not -er: protractor

protracts

protrude »*verb* (**protrudes**, **protruding**, **protruded**) stick out beyond or above a surface.
protrusion

protuberance »*noun* a thing that protrudes.
– SAY pruh-**tyoo**-buh-ruhnss

✓ -tube- not -trube-: protuberance

protuberant »*adjective* bulging.

proud (adjective: **prouder**, **proudest**)
proudly

prove (verb: **proves**, **proving**, **proved**; past participle **proved** or **proven**)
provable

 prove has two past participles, **proved** and **proven**. You can use either in sentences such as *this hasn't been proved yet* or *this hasn't been proven yet.* However, you should always use **proven** when the word is an adjective coming before the noun: *a proven talent*, not *a proved talent.*

provenance »*noun* the place where something originally comes from.
– SAY pro-vuh-**nuhnss**

Provencal »*noun* ❶ a person from Provence in south-eastern France. ❷ the language of Provence.
» *adjective* relating to Provence.
– SAY pro-von-**sahl**

✓ Provencal can also be written Provençal, with a cedilla on the **c** (as in French)

provender »*noun* animal fodder.
– SAY pro-**vin**-der

proverb

proverbial
proverbially

proves

provide (verb: **provides**, **providing**, **provided**)

provided »*conjunction* on the condition or understanding that.

providence »*noun* the protective care of God or of nature.

provident »*adjective* careful in planning for the future.
providently

providential »*adjective* happening by chance and at a favourable time.

providently

provider

provides

providing »*conjunction* = PROVIDED.

province »*noun* ❶ a main administrative division of a country or empire. ❷ (**the provinces**) the whole of a country outside the capital.

provincial
provincialism
provincially

proving

provision »*noun* ❶ the action of providing. ❷ something provided. ❸ (**provision for** or **against**) arrangements for possible future events or requirements. ❹ (**provisions**) supplies of food, drink, or equipment. ❺ a condition in a legal document.
» *verb* (**provisions**, **provisioning**, **provisioned**) supply with provisions.

provisional »*adjective* arranged for the present, possibly to be changed later.
provisionally

provisioned

provisioning

provisions

proviso »*noun* (plural **provisos**) a condition attached to an agreement.
- SAY pruh-**vy**-zoh

> [i] **proviso** comes from the Latin phrase *proviso quod*, which means 'it being provided that'
> the plural has **os** not **oes: provisos**

provocation

provocative
provocatively
provocativeness

provoke (verb: **provokes, provoking, provoked**)

provost »*noun* ❶ a person in charge of certain university colleges and public schools. ❷ (in Scotland) a mayor.
- SAY **pro**-vuhst

prow »*noun* the pointed front part of a ship.

prowess »*noun* skill or expertise in a particular activity.

prowl (verb: **prowls, prowling, prowled**)
prowler

proxies

proximate »*adjective* closest in space, time, or relationship.

proximity »*noun* nearness in space, time, or relationship.

proxy »*noun* (plural **proxies**) ❶ the authority to represent someone else, especially in voting. ❷ a person authorized to act on behalf of another.

Prozac »*noun* (trademark) a drug which is taken to treat depression.

prude »*noun* a person who is easily shocked by matters relating to sex.
prudery
prudish

prudent »*adjective* acting with or showing care and thought for the future.
prudence
prudently

prudential »*adjective* prudent.

prudently

prudery

prudish

prune[1] »*noun* a dried plum.

prune[2] »*verb* (**prunes, pruning, pruned**)
❶ trim a tree or bush by cutting away dead or overgrown branches. ❷ remove unwanted parts from.
» *noun* an instance of pruning.

prurient »*adjective* having or encouraging too much interest in sexual matters.
- SAY **proor**-i-uhnt
prurience
pruriently

pry »*verb* (**pries, prying, pried**) enquire too eagerly about a person's private life.
prying

PS »*abbreviation* postscript.

psalm »*noun* a song or poem in praise of God, found in the biblical Book of Psalms.
- SAY sahm
psalmist

> [✓] don't forget the **l** before the **m: psalm**

psalter »*noun* a book containing the biblical Psalms.
- SAY **sawl**-ter or **sol**-ter

psephology »*noun* the statistical study of elections and trends in voting.
- SAY se-**fol**-uh-ji
psephologist

pseud »*noun* (in informal English) a person who tries to impress others by pretending to have knowledge or expertise they do not really possess.
- SAY syood

pseudo »*adjective* not genuine.
- SAY **syoo**-doh

pseudo- »*prefix* false; not genuine: *pseudoscience*.

pseudonym »*noun* a false name, especially one used by an author.
- SAY **syoo**-duh-nim

> [✓] **nym** not **nim: pseudonym**

pseudonymous »*adjective* writing or written under a false name.
- SAY syoo-**don**-i-muhss
pseudonymously

pseudoscience »*noun* beliefs or practices which may appear scientific but actually are not.
pseudoscientific

psi »*noun* the twenty-third letter of the Greek alphabet (Ψ, ψ).
- SAY psI or sI

psoriasis »*noun* a skin disease marked by red, itchy, scaly patches.
- SAY suh-**ry**-uh-siss

> [✓] remember, **psoriasis** begins with a silent **p**, and the ending is **asis**

psych »*verb* (**psychs, psyching, psyched**)
❶ (**psych up**) prepare someone mentally for a difficult task. ❷ (**psych out**) intimidate an opponent by appearing very confident or aggressive.
- SAY syk

psyche »*noun* the human soul, mind, or spirit.
– SAY sy-ki

 e at the end, not y: **psyche**

psyched

psychedelic »*adjective* ❶ (of drugs) producing hallucinations. ❷ having bright colours or a swirling pattern.
– SAY sy-kuh-**del**-ik

✓ psyche- not psycho- or pyscha-: **psychedelic**

psychiatrist »*noun* a doctor specializing in the treatment of mental illness.

psychiatry »*noun* the branch of medicine concerned with mental illness.
– SAY sy-**ky**-uh-tri
psychiatric
psychiatrically

psychic »*adjective* ❶ relating to abilities or events that apparently cannot be explained by natural laws. ❷ (of a person) appearing to be telepathic or clairvoyant.
»*noun* a person claiming to have psychic powers.
– SAY sy-kik
psychical
psychically

psyching

psycho »*noun* (plural **psychos**) (in informal English) a psychopath.

✓ the plural of **psycho** has os not oes: **psychos**

psychoanalyse »*verb* (**psychoanalyses, psychoanalysing, psychoanalysed**) treat using psychoanalysis.

✓ lyse not lyze: the spelling **psychoanalyze** is American

psychoanalysis »*noun* a method of treating mental disorders by investigating the conscious and unconscious elements in the mind.
psychoanalyst
psychoanalytic

psychoanalyze American spelling of **PSYCHOANALYSE**.

psychological »*adjective* ❶ having to do with the mind. ❷ relating to psychology.
psychologically

psychology »*noun* ❶ the scientific study of the human mind and its functions. ❷ the mental characteristics or attitude of a person.
psychologist

✓ psy, not pys, at the beginning of **psychology** and related words

psychometrics »*plural noun* the science of measuring mental abilities and processes.

psychopath »*noun* a person having a serious mental illness that causes them to behave violently.
psychopathic

psychos

psychosis »*noun* (plural **psychoses**) a serious mental illness in which a person loses contact with external reality.
– SAY sy-**koh**-siss [singular], sy-**koh**-seez [plural]

✓ make the plural by changing the -is ending to -es: **psychoses**

psychosomatic »*adjective* ❶ (of a physical illness) caused or made worse by a mental factor such as stress. ❷ relating to the relationship between mind and body.
– SAY sy-koh-suh-**mat**-ik

psychotherapy »*noun* the treatment of mental disorder by psychological rather than medical means.
psychotherapist

psychotic »*adjective* relating to or suffering from a psychosis.
»*noun* a psychotic person.
– SAY sy-**kot**-ik
psychotically

psychs

PTA »*abbreviation* parent–teacher association.

ptarmigan »*noun* a grouse of northern mountains and the Arctic, having grey and black plumage which changes to white in winter.
– SAY **tar**-mi-guhn

pterodactyl »*noun* a pterosaur of the late Jurassic period, with a long slender head and neck.
– SAY te-ruh-**dak**-til

✓ ptero not ptera: **pterodactyl**

pterosaur »*noun* a fossil flying reptile of the Jurassic and Cretaceous periods.
– SAY te-ruh-sor

PTO »*abbreviation* please turn over.

pub

pube »*noun* (in informal English) a pubic hair.

puberty »*noun* the period during which adolescents reach sexual maturity and become able to have children.

pubes »*noun* ❶ (plural **pubes**) the lower part of the abdomen at the front of the pelvis, covered with hair from puberty. ❷ plural of **PUBIS**.

– SAY pyoo-beez

pubescence »*noun* the time when puberty begins.

– SAY pyuu-**bess**-uhnss
pubescent

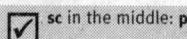 sc in the middle: **pubescence**

pubic »*adjective* relating to the pubes or pubis.

pubis »*noun* (plural **pubes**) one of a pair of bones forming the two sides of the pelvis.

– SAY **pyoo**-biss [singular], **pyoo**-beez [plural]

✓ make the plural by changing the **-is** ending to **-es** (as in Latin): **pubes**

public
publicly

publican »*noun* a person who owns or manages a pub.

publication

public company »*noun* a company whose shares are traded freely on a stock exchange.

publicise another way of spelling **PUBLICIZE**.

publicist »*noun* a person responsible for publicizing a product or celebrity.

publicity

publicize (verb: **publicizes**, **publicizing**, **publicized**)

✓ many people prefer the alternative spellings **publicise**, **publicises**, etc.: both **s** and **z** spellings are correct

public limited company »*noun* (in the UK) a company with shares offered to the public subject to conditions of limited legal responsibility for any company debts.

publicly

✓ the ending is **-ly** not **-ally**: **publicly**

public sector »*noun* the part of an economy that is controlled directly by the state.

public servant »*noun* a person who works for the state or for local government.

public utility »*noun* an organization supplying the community with electricity, gas, water, or sewerage.

publish (verb: **publishes**, **publishing**, **published**)
publishable
publisher
publishing

puce »*noun* a dark red or purple-brown colour.

– SAY pyooss

puck »*noun* a black disc made of hard rubber, used in ice hockey.

pucker »*verb* (**puckers**, **puckering**, **puckered**) tightly gather into wrinkles or small folds.
» *noun* a wrinkle or small fold.

puckish »*adjective* playful and mischievous.

pudding
puddingy

puddle

pudendum »*noun* (plural **pudenda**) a person's external genitals, especially a woman's.

– SAY pyoo-**den**-duhm [singular], pyoo-**den**-duh [plural]

✓ like many other words ending in **um** derived from Latin, **pudendum** has a plural ending in **a**: **pudenda**

pudgy »*adjective* (**pudgier**, **pudgiest**) (in informal English) fat or flabby.
pudginess

puerile »*adjective* childishly silly.

– SAY **pyoor**-yl

✓ don't forget the **e** in the middle: **puerile**

puerility »*noun* (plural **puerilities**) childish behaviour.

– SAY pyoor-**il**-i-ti

puerperal fever »*noun* fever caused by infection of the uterus following childbirth.

puff (verb: **puffs**, **puffing**, **puffed**)
puffer

puffa jacket »*noun* a type of thick padded jacket.

puffball »*noun* a fungus with a large round head that bursts to release its seeds.

puffed

puffer

puffery »*noun* exaggerated praise.

puffier

puffiest

puffin »*noun* a seabird with a large brightly coloured triangular bill.

puffiness

puffing

puffs

puffy (adjective: **puffier**, **puffiest**)
puffiness

pug »*noun* a very small dog with a broad flat nose and deeply wrinkled face.

pugilist »*noun* (old-fashioned) a boxer.

623

– **SAY** pyoo-ji-list
  pugilism
  pugilistic

pugnacious »*adjective* eager or quick to argue or fight.
– **SAY** pug-**nay**-shuhss
  pugnaciously
  pugnacity

pug nose »*noun* a short nose with an upturned tip.

puke (verb: pukes, puking, puked)

pukka »*adjective* ❶ genuine. ❷ socially acceptable. ❸ excellent.

> ℹ️ **pukka** is a Hindi word meaning 'cooked, ripe, substantial'

pulchritude »*noun* beauty.
– **SAY** pul-kri-tyood

> ☑️ remember the h: **pulchritude**

pule »*verb* (pules, puling, puled) cry in a complaining or weak way.
– **SAY** pyool

pull (verb: pulls, pulling, pulled)
  puller

pullet »*noun* a young hen.

pulley (plural pulleys)

pulling

pullover

pulls

pullulate »*verb* (pullulates, pullulating, pullulated) ❶ reproduce or spread so as to become very widespread. ❷ be full of activity.
– **SAY** pul-yuu-layt

> ☑️ double l then single l: **pullulate**

pulmonary »*adjective* relating to the lungs.
– **SAY** pul-muh-nuh-ri

pulp (verb: pulps, pulping, pulped)
  pulpy

pulpit

pulps

pulpy

pulsar »*noun* a type of star that gives off regular rapid pulses of radio waves.

pulsate »*verb* (pulsates, pulsating, pulsated) ❶ expand and contract with strong regular movements. ❷ produce a regular throbbing sensation or sound. ❸ (pulsating) very exciting.
  pulsation

pulse[1] (verb: pulses, pulsing, pulsed) [regular throbbing of the arteries; pulsate]

pulse[2] »*noun* the edible seeds of various plants, such as lentils or beans.

pulverize »*verb* (pulverizes, pulverizing, pulverized) ❶ crush something to fine particles. ❷ (in informal English) defeat utterly.

> ☑️ many people prefer the alternative spellings **pulverise, pulverises**, etc.: both s and z spellings are correct

puma »*noun* a large American wild cat with a yellowish-brown or grey coat.

pumice »*noun* a very light rock formed from lava, used to remove hard skin.
– **SAY** pum-iss

> ☑️ -ice not -is at the end: **pumice**

pummel »*verb* (pummels, pummelling, pummelled) strike someone or something repeatedly, especially with the fists.

> ☑️ double the l in **pummelling** and **pummelled** (the spellings **pummeling** and **pummeled** are American)

pump (verb: pumps, pumping, pumped)

pumpernickel »*noun* dark, heavy German bread made from wholemeal rye.

pumping

pumpkin

pumps

pun »*noun* a joke that uses a word with more than one meaning or words with different meanings that sound the same.
»*verb* (puns, punning, punned) make a pun.

> ☑️ double the n in **punning** and **punned**

punch (verb: punches, punching, punched)
  puncher

punchbag

punchball

punchbowl

punch-drunk

punched

puncher

punches

punchier

punchiest

punching

punchline »*noun* the final part of a joke, providing the humour.

punch-up

punchy (adjective: punchier, punchiest)

punctilio »*noun* (plural punctilios) a fine or petty point of conduct or procedure.
– **SAY** pungk-**ti**-li-oh

punctilious »*adjective* showing great attention to detail or correct behaviour.

- **say** pungk-**ti**-li-uhss
  punctiliously
  punctiliousness

> ✓ one **l** followed by **ious: punctilious**

punctual
  punctuality
  punctually

punctuate »*verb* (**punctuates**, **punctuating**, **punctuated**) ❶ interrupt something at intervals. ❷ add punctuation marks to a piece of writing.
- **say** pungk-**tyuu**-ayt

punctuation »*noun* the marks, such as full stop, comma, and brackets, used in writing to separate sentences and to make meaning clear.

puncture (verb: **punctures**, **puncturing**, **punctured**)

> ✓ **c** not **k** in the middle: **puncture**

pundit »*noun* a person who frequently gives opinions about a subject in public.
  punditry

pungent »*adjective* ❶ having a sharply strong taste or smell. ❷ (of remarks or humour) sharp.
- **say** pun-**juhnt**
  pungency
  pungently

punier

puniest

punily

puniness

punish (verb: **punishes**, **punishing**, **punished**)
  punishable

punishment

punitive »*adjective* intended as punishment.
- **say** **pyoo**-ni-tiv
  punitively

Punjabi »*noun* (plural **Punjabis**) ❶ a person from Punjab, a region of NW India and Pakistan. ❷ the language of Punjab.

> ✓ plural: simply add **s: Punjabis**
> **Punjabi** can also be spelled with **a** instead of u: **Panjabi** (**say** pan-**jah**-bi)

punk »*noun* ❶ (also **punk rock**) a loud, fast form of rock music with aggressive lyrics and behaviour. ❷ (also **punk rocker**) an admirer or player of punk music. ❸ (in informal English) a worthless person or criminal.

> »*adjective* relating to punk rock.
  punkish
  punky

punned

punnet »*noun* a small light basket or other container for fruit or vegetables.

> ✓ two **n**'s in **punnet**

punning

puns

punt (verb: **punts**, **punting**, **punted**)

punter (in informal English) »*noun* ❶ a person who places a bet. ❷ a customer or client.

punting

punts

puny (adjective: **punier**, **puniest**)
  punily
  puniness

pup (verb: **pups**, **pupping**, **pupped**)

pupa »*noun* (plural **pupae**) an insect in the form between larva and adult.
- **say** **pyoo**-puh [singular], **pyoo**-pee [plural]
  pupal

> ✓ the plural of **pupa** is **pupae** (as in Latin)

pupate »*verb* (**pupates**, **pupating**, **pupated**) become a pupa.
  pupation

pupil

pupped

puppet
  puppeteer
  puppetry

> ✓ **eer** not simply **er** at the end: **puppeteer**

puppies

pupping

puppy (plural **puppies**)
  puppyish

> ✓ plural: drop the **y** and add **ies: puppies**

pups

purblind »*adjective* ❶ partially sighted. ❷ lacking awareness or understanding.
- **say** per-**blynd**

purchase (verb: **purchases**, **purchasing**, **purchased**)
  purchaser

> ✓ the ending is **ase** not **ace: purchase**

purdah »*noun* the practice in certain Muslim and Hindu societies of screening women from men or strangers.
– **say** per-duh

 don't forget the **h** at the end: **purdah**

pure (adjective: **purer**, **purest**)
purely

pure-bred

puree »*noun* a soft, wet mass of crushed fruit or vegetables.
»*verb* (**purees**, **pureeing**, **pureed**) make a puree of.
– **say** pyoor-ay

 often written with an acute accent on the first **e**: **purée** (as in the original French)

purely

purer

purest

purgation »*noun* purification.
– **say** per-gay-sh'n

purgative »*adjective* strongly laxative in effect.
»*noun* a laxative.
– **say** per-guh-tiv

purgatory »*noun* (in Roman Catholic belief) a place inhabited by the souls of sinners who are making up for their sins before going to heaven.
– **say** per-guh-tuh-ri
purgatorial

purge »*verb* (**purges**, **purging**, **purged**) ❶ rid someone or something of people or things considered undesirable or harmful. ❷ empty your bowels, especially as a result of taking a laxative.
»*noun* ❶ an act of purging. ❷ (old-fashioned) a laxative.

purify (verb: **purifies**, **purifying**, **purified**)
purification
purifier

purist »*noun* a person who insists on following traditional rules, especially in language or style.
purism

puritan »*noun* ❶ (**Puritan**) a member of a group of English Protestants in the 16th and 17th centuries who wanted to simplify forms of worship. ❷ a person with strong moral beliefs who is critical of the behaviour of others.
»*adjective* ❶ (**Puritan**) relating to the Puritans. ❷ characteristic of a puritan.
puritanical
puritanism

purity

purl »*adjective* (of a knitting stitch) made by putting the needle through the front of the stitch from right to left.
»*verb* (**purls**, **purling**, **purled**) knit with a purl stitch.

purler »*noun* (in informal English) a headlong fall.

purlieus »*plural noun* the area near or surrounding a place.
– **say** per-lyoo

purling

purloin »*verb* (**purloins**, **purloining**, **purloined**) steal.
– **say** per-**loyn**

purls

purple (adjective: **purpler**, **purplest**)
purplish
purply

 drop the **e** to spell **purplish** and **purply**

purple patch »*noun* a run of success or good luck.

purple prose »*noun* writing that is too elaborate or ornate.

purpler

purplest

purplish

purply

purport »*verb* (**purports**, **purporting**, **purported**) appear to be or do.
»*noun* ❶ the meaning of something. ❷ the purpose of something.
– **say** per-**port** [verb], **per**-port [noun]
purported
purportedly

purpose (verb: **purposes**, **purposing**, **purposed**)

purposeful
purposefully

 -ful not **-full**: **purposeful**

purposeless

purposely

purposes

purposing

purposive »*adjective* having or done with a purpose.

purr (verb: **purrs**, **purring**, **purred**)

purse (verb: **purses**, **pursing**, **pursed**)

purser »*noun* a ship's officer who keeps the accounts.

purses

pursing

pursuance »*noun* the carrying out of a plan or action.

> ✓ ance not ence: pursuance

pursuant »*adverb* (**pursuant to**) in accordance with.
– SAY puh-**syoo**-uhnt

> ✓ ant not ent: pursuant

pursue (verb: **pursues, pursuing, pursued**)
pursuer

> ✓ pur not per: pursue

pursuit

purulent »*adjective* containing or giving out pus.
– SAY **pyoor**-uu-luhnt

purvey »*verb* (**purveys, purveying, purveyed**) provide or supply food or drink as a business.
purveyor

purview »*noun* ❶ the range of the influence or concerns of something. ❷ a range of experience or thought.

pus »*noun* a thick yellowish or greenish liquid produced in infected tissue.

> ✓ only a single s in pus

push (verb: **pushes, pushing, pushed**)
pusher

pushbike

pushchair

pushed

pusher

pushes

pushier

pushiest

pushiness

pushing

pushover

pushy (adjective: **pushier, pushiest**)
pushiness

pusillanimous »*adjective* lacking courage.
– SAY pyoo-si-**lan**-i-muhss
pusillanimity
pusillanimously

puss (plural **pusses**)

> ✓ double s for puss meaning 'cat'; single s for pus referring to the liquid produced by infection

pussy (plural **pussies**)

> ✓ plural: drop the y and add ies: pussies

pussyfoot »*verb* (**pussyfoots, pussyfooting, pussyfooted**) act very cautiously.

pussy willow »*noun* a willow with soft fluffy catkins that appear before the leaves.

pustule »*noun* a small blister on the skin containing pus.
– SAY **puss**-tyool
pustular

put (verb: **puts, putting, put**)

> ✓ double the t to spell putting

putative »*adjective* generally thought to be.
– SAY **pyoo**-tuh-tiv
putatively

put-down

putrefy »*verb* (**putrefies, putrefying, putrefied**) decay or rot and produce a very unpleasant smell.
– SAY **pyoo**-tri-fI
putrefaction

> ✓ efy not ify: putrefy

putrescent »*adjective* rotting.
– SAY pyoo-**tress**-uhnt

> ✓ -scent not -sent: putrescent

putrid »*adjective* ❶ decaying or rotting and producing a very unpleasant smell. ❷ very unpleasant.

puts

putsch »*noun* a violent attempt to overthrow a government.

> ✓ putsch is a Swiss German word meaning 'a thrust or blow'

putt »*verb* (**putts, putting, putted**) strike a golf ball gently so that it rolls into or near a hole.
» *noun* a stroke of this kind.

puttee »*noun* a long strip of cloth wound round the leg from ankle to knee for protection and support.
– SAY **pu**-tee

putter[1] »*noun* a golf club designed for putting.

putter[2] »*noun* the rapid irregular sound of a small petrol engine.
» *verb* (**putters, puttering, puttered**) move with or make such a sound.

putti plural of PUTTO.

putting

putto »*noun* (plural **putti**) a representation of a naked child, especially a cherub or a cupid.
– SAY **puut**-toh [singular], **puut**-ti [plural]

☑ the plural of **putto** is **putti** (it is an Italian word which means 'boy')

putts

putty »*noun* a soft paste that hardens as it sets, used for sealing glass in window frames.

puzzle (verb: **puzzles, puzzling, puzzled**)
puzzlement
puzzler

PVC »*abbreviation* polyvinyl chloride, a sort of plastic.

pygmy »*noun* (plural **pygmies**) ❶ a member of a race of very short people living in parts of Africa. ❷ a very small person or thing. ❸ a person who is lacking in a particular respect: *intellectual pygmies.*
»*adjective* very small.

☑ **pygmy** can also be spelled **pigmy** plural: drop the **y** and add **ies**:
pigmies

pyjamas

☑ the word begins **py**: **pyjamas** (the spelling **pajamas** is American)

pylon »*noun* a tall tower-like structure for carrying electricity cables.

pyracantha »*noun* a thorny evergreen shrub with white flowers and bright red or yellow berries.
– say py-ruh-**kan**-thuh

pyramid »*noun* a very large stone structure with a square or triangular base and sloping sides that meet in a point at the top.
pyramidal

pyre »*noun* a large pile of wood for the ritual burning of a dead body.

Pyrex »*noun* (trademark) a hard heat-resistant type of glass.

pyrites »*noun* a shiny yellow mineral that is a compound of iron and sulphur.
– say py-**ry**-teez

ℹ geologists also refer to this mineral as **pyrite** (say py-rīt)

pyromania »*noun* a very strong desire to set fire to things.
pyromaniac

pyrotechnic »*adjective* ❶ relating to fireworks. ❷ brilliant or spectacular.
– say py-ruh-**tek**-nik

pyrotechnics »*plural noun* ❶ a firework display. ❷ the art of making fireworks or staging firework displays. ❸ a spectacular performance or display: *vocal pyrotechnics.*

pyrrhic »*adjective* (of a victory) won at too great a cost to have been worthwhile.
– say **pir**-rik

ℹ named after *Pyrrhus*, an ancient king of Epirus in Greece, whose victory over the Romans cost very heavy losses

Pythagoras' theorem »*noun* the theorem that the square on the hypotenuse of a right-angled triangle is equal in area to the sum of the squares on the other two sides.

ℹ named after the Greek philosopher and mathematician *Pythagoras*

python »*noun* a large snake which crushes its prey.

☑ **-on** not **-en**: **python**

pzazz another way of spelling **pizzazz**.

Qq

Qatari (plural **Qataris**) [of Qatar]
– say kuh-**tah**-ri

☑ no **u** in **Qatar** or **Qatari**

QC »*abbreviation* (in law) Queen's Counsel.

QED »*abbreviation* used to say that something proves the truth of your claim.

ℹ QED is an abbreviation of *quod erat demonstrandum*, a Latin phrase which means 'which was to be demonstrated'

quack¹ (verb: **quacks, quacking, quacked**) [sound of a duck]

quack² »*noun* ❶ an unqualified person who falsely claims to have medical knowledge. ❷ (in informal English) a doctor.
quackery

quad »*noun* ❶ a quadrangle. ❷ a quadruplet.

quad bike »*noun* a motorcycle with four large tyres, for off-road use.

quadrangle »*noun* ❶ a four-sided geometrical figure. ❷ a square or rectangular courtyard enclosed by buildings.
quadrangular

quadrant »*noun* ❶ a quarter of a circle or of a circle's circumference. ❷ (a historical term) an instrument for measuring angles in astronomy and navigation.

quadraphonic »*adjective* (of sound reproduction) transmitted through four channels.
– **SAY** kwod-ruh-**fon**-ik

> ✓ **quadraphonic** can also be spelled with an **o** in the middle: **quadrophonic**

quadrate »*adjective* roughly square or rectangular.
– **SAY** kwod-ruht

quadratic »*adjective* (in mathematics) involving the second but no higher power of an unknown quantity.
– **SAY** kwod-**rat**-ik

quadrennial »*adjective* lasting for or happening every four years.

quadriceps »*noun* (plural **quadriceps**) a large muscle at the front of the thigh.
– **SAY** kwod-ri-seps

quadrilateral »*noun* a four-sided figure. »*adjective* having four straight sides.

quadrille »*noun* a square dance performed by four couples.
– **SAY** kwod-**ril**

> ✓ **-drille** not **-drill**: **quadrille** is a French word

quadriplegia »*noun* paralysis of all four limbs.
– **SAY** kwod-ri-**plee**-juh
quadriplegic

quadrophonic another way of spelling **QUADRAPHONIC**.

quadruped »*noun* an animal which has four feet.
– **SAY** kwod-ruu-ped
quadrupedal

> ✓ **quadru** not **quadra**: **quadruped**

quadruple »*adjective* ❶ consisting of four parts. ❷ four times as much or as many. »*verb* (**quadruples, quadrupling, quadrupled**) multiply something by four. »*noun* a quadruple number or amount.

quadruplet »*noun* one of four children born at one birth.

quadrupling

quaff »*verb* (**quaffs, quaffing, quaffed**) drink heartily.
– **SAY** kwoff
quaffable

quagga »*noun* an extinct South African zebra with a yellowish-brown coat with darker stripes.
– **SAY** kwag-guh

quagmire »*noun* ❶ a soft boggy area of land that gives way underfoot. ❷ a complicated or difficult situation: *a legal quagmire.*
– **SAY** kwag-myr or kwog-myr

quail[1] »*noun* (plural **quail** or **quails**) a small short-tailed game bird.

quail[2] »*verb* (**quails, quailing, quailed**) feel or show fear or worry.

quaint »*adjective* (**quainter, quaintest**) attractively unusual or old-fashioned.
quaintly
quaintness

quake (verb: **quakes, quaking, quaked**)

Quaker »*noun* a member of the Religious Society of Friends, a Christian movement devoted to peaceful principles and rejecting all set forms of worship.
Quakerism

quakes

quaking

qualification

qualified

qualifier »*noun* ❶ a person or team that qualifies for a competition. ❷ a match or contest to decide which individuals or teams qualify for a competition. ❸ (in grammar) a word or phrase used to qualify another word.

qualify (verb: **qualifies, qualifying, qualified**)

qualitative »*adjective* relating to or measured by quality (as opposed to quantity).
– **SAY** kwol-i-tuh-tiv
qualitatively

quality (plural **qualities**)

> ✓ plural: drop the **y** and add **ies**: **qualities**

quality control »*noun* a system of maintaining standards in manufactured products by testing a sample to see if it meets the required standard.

qualm »*noun* a feeling of doubt about what you are doing.
– **SAY** kwahm

quandary »*noun* (plural **quandaries**) a state of uncertainty.
– SAY kwon-duh-ri

> ✓ **dary** not **dry: quandary**

quango »*noun* (plural **quangos**) (used in a disapproving way) an organization that works independently but with support from the government.
– SAY kwang-goh

> i **quango** is an acronym from *quasi non-governmental organization*

> ✓ the plural of **quango** has **os** not **oes: quangos**

quanta plural of QUANTUM.

quantify »*verb* (**quantifies, quantifying, quantified**) express or measure the quantity of something.
quantifiable

quantise another way of spelling QUANTIZE.

quantitative »*adjective* relating to or measured by quantity.
– SAY kwon-ti-tuh-tiv or kwon-ti-tay-tiv
quantitatively

> ✓ remember the **-at-** in the middle: **quantitative** has four syllables, not three

quantity (plural **quantities**)

> ✓ plural: drop the **y** and add **ies: quantities**

quantity surveyor »*noun* a person who calculates the amount and cost of materials needed for building work.

quantize »*verb* (**quantizes, quantizing, quantized**) ❶ (in physics) divide something into quanta. ❷ (in electronics) represent a continuously varying signal by one whose strength is restricted to prescribed values.
quantization

> ✓ many people prefer the alternative spellings **quantise, quantises,** etc.: both **s** and **z** spellings are correct

quantum »*noun* (plural **quanta**) (in physics) a distinct quantity of energy corresponding to that involved in the absorption or emission of energy by an atom.
– SAY kwon-tuhm

> ✓ the plural of **quantum** is **quanta** (as in Latin)

quantum leap »*noun* a sudden large increase or advance.

quantum mechanics »*plural noun* the branch of physics concerned with describing the behaviour of subatomic particles in terms of quanta.

quarantine »*noun* a period of time when an animal or person that may have a disease is kept in isolation.
» *verb* (**quarantines, quarantining, quarantined**) put an animal or person in quarantine.

quark »*noun* (in physics) one of a group of subatomic particles which carry a very small electric charge and are believed to form protons, neutrons, and other particles.
– SAY kwark

quarrel (verb: **quarrels, quarrelling, quarrelled**)

> ✓ double the **l** to spell **quarrelling** and **quarrelled** (the spellings **quareling** and **quareled** are American)

quarrelsome

quarry¹ »*noun* (plural **quarries**) a place where stone or other materials are dug out of the earth.
» *verb* (**quarries, quarrying, quarried**) dig out stone or other materials from a quarry.

> ✓ plural: drop the **y** and add **ies: quarries**

quarry² »*noun* (plural **quarries**) an animal or person that is being hunted or chased.

quart »*noun* a unit of volume for liquid measures equal to a quarter of a gallon or two pints (in Britain, 1.13 litres).

quarter (verb: **quarters, quartering, quartered**)

quarterback »*noun* a player in American Football who directs a team's attacking play.

quarterdeck »*noun* the part of a ship's upper deck near the stern.

quartered

quarter-final

quarter-hour

quartering

quarter-light »*noun* a window in the side of a motor vehicle other than a main door window.

quarterly »*adjective & adverb* produced or occurring once every quarter of a year.
» *noun* (plural **quarterlies**) a publication produced four times a year.

quartermaster »*noun* ❶ a regimental officer in charge of accommodation and supplies. ❷ a naval petty officer responsible for steering and signals.

quarters

quarterstaff »*noun* a stout pole 6–8 feet long, formerly used as a weapon.

q

quarter tone »*noun* (in music) half a semitone.

quartet »*noun* ❶ a group of four people playing music or singing together. ❷ a composition for a quartet. ❸ a set of four.

quartile »*noun* one of four equal groups into which a population can be divided for statistical purposes.
– SAY kwor-tyl

quarto »*noun* (plural **quartos**) ❶ a page or paper size resulting from folding a sheet into four leaves. ❷ a book of this size.
– SAY kwor-toh

☑ the plural of **quarto** has **os** not **oes**: **quartos**

quartz »*noun* a hard mineral consisting of silica.

quasar »*noun* (in astronomy) a kind of galaxy which gives off enormous amounts of energy.
– SAY kway-zar

quash »*verb* (**quashes, quashing, quashed**) ❶ officially reject a decision as invalid. ❷ put an end to something.

quasi- »*prefix* seemingly or apparently but perhaps not really: *quasi-legal* | *a quasi-religion.*
– SAY kway-zI or kway-sI or kwah-zi

quaternary »*adjective* fourth in order or rank.
»*noun* (**Quaternary**) the most recent geological period, from about 1.64 million years ago to the present.
– SAY kwuh-**ter**-nuh-ri

quatrain »*noun* a group of four lines of poetry, typically with alternate rhymes.
– SAY kwot-rayn

quatrefoil »*noun* an ornamental design of four leaves.
– SAY ka-truh-foyl

quaver »*verb* (**quavers, quavering, quavered**) (of a voice) tremble.
»*noun* ❶ a tremble in a voice. ❷ (in music) a musical note that lasts as long as half a crotchet.
quavery

quay »*noun* a platform in a harbour for loading and unloading ships.
– SAY kee

quayside »*noun* a quay and the area around it.

queasy »*adjective* (**queasier, queasiest**) feeling sick.
queasily
queasiness

queen
queenly

queen mother »*noun* the widow of a king and mother of the king or queen.

Queensberry Rules »*plural noun* the standard rules of boxing.

 named after the 8th Marquess of *Queensberry*

Queen's Counsel »*noun* a senior barrister appointed on the recommendation of the Lord Chancellor.

Queen's evidence »*noun* (in English law) evidence for the prosecution given by someone involved in the crime being tried.

queen-sized »*adjective* of a larger size than the standard but smaller than king-sized.

Queen's Speech »*noun* (in the UK) a statement read by the sovereign at the opening of parliament, giving details of what the government plans to do.

queer (adjective: **queerer, queerest**)
queerly
queerness

quell »*verb* (**quells, quelling, quelled**) ❶ put an end to a rebellion by force. ❷ suppress a feeling.

quench »*verb* (**quenches, quenching, quenched**) ❶ satisfy thirst by drinking. ❷ satisfy a desire. ❸ put out a fire.

queried

queries

quern »*noun* a simple hand mill for grinding grain.

querulous »*adjective* complaining in a bad-tempered manner.
– SAY kwe-ruu-luhss
querulously
querulousness

☑ queru not quera: querulous

query »*noun* (plural **queries**) a question, especially one expressing doubt about something.
»*verb* (**queries, querying, queried**) ask a query.

☑ plural: drop the **y** and add **ies**: **queries**

quest »*noun* a long or difficult search.
»*verb* (**quests, questing, quested**) search for something.

question (verb: **questions, questioning, questioned**)
questioner

questionable
questionably

questioned

questioner

questioning

questionnaire

> ✓ note that there are two **n**'s, and an **e** at the end: **questionnaire** (a French word)

questions

quests

queue (verb: **queues**, **queuing** or **queueing**, **queued**) [line of people waiting; wait in a queue]

> ℹ do not confuse **queue** with **cue**, which means 'a signal for something to happen' or 'a rod for striking a snooker ball'

> ✓ note that there are two **u**'s: **queue**

quibble »*noun* a slight objection or criticism.
» *verb* (**quibbles**, **quibbling**, **quibbled**) argue about a trivial matter.

quiche »*noun* a baked flan with a savoury filling thickened with eggs.
– SAY keesh

quick (adjective: **quicker**, **quickest**)
quickly
quickness

quicken »*verb* (**quickens**, **quickening**, **quickened**) make or become quicker.

quicker

quickest

quick-fire

quickie

quicklime »*noun* a white caustic alkaline substance consisting of calcium oxide, obtained by heating limestone.

quickly

quickness

quicksand

quicksilver »*noun* liquid mercury.
» *adjective* moving or changing rapidly.

quickstep »*noun* a fast foxtrot.

quick-tempered

quick-witted
quick-wittedly

quid[1] »*noun* (plural **quid**) (in informal English) one pound sterling.

quid[2] »*noun* a lump of chewing tobacco.

quid pro quo »*noun* (plural **quid pro quos**) a favour given in return for something.
– SAY kwid proh **kwoh**

> ℹ **quid pro quo** is a Latin phrase which means 'something for something'

quiescent »*adjective* not active.
– SAY kwi-**ess**-uhnt
quiescence
quiescently

> ✓ -**scent** not -**sent**: quiescent

quiet (adjective: **quieter**, **quietest**; verb: **quiets**, **quieting**, **quieted**)
quietly
quietness

quieten »*verb* (**quietens**, **quietening**, **quietened**) make or become quiet and calm.

quieter

quietest

quieting

quietism »*noun* calm acceptance of things as they are.

quietly

quietness

quiets

quietude »*noun* a state of calmness and quiet.

quiff »*noun* a tuft of hair, brushed upwards and backwards from a man's forehead.

quill »*noun* ❶ a main wing or tail feather of a bird. ❷ the hollow shaft of a feather. ❸ a pen made from a quill. ❹ a hollow sharp spine of a porcupine, hedgehog, etc.

quilt »*noun* ❶ a warm bed covering made of padding enclosed between layers of fabric. ❷ a bedspread with decorative stitching.
» *verb* (**quilts**, **quilting**, **quilted**) join layers of fabric or padding with stitching to form a quilt or a garment.
quilting

quin »*noun* a quintuplet.

quince »*noun* the hard, acid, pear-shaped fruit of an Asian shrub or small tree.

quinine »*noun* a bitter drug made from the bark of a South American tree.
– SAY kwi-neen

quinquennial »*adjective* lasting for or happening every five years.
– SAY kwing-**kwen**-ni-uhl

quintessence »*noun* ❶ the perfect example of something. ❷ the most important aspect of something. ❸ a refined extract of a substance.
– SAY kwin-**tess**-uhnss

quintessential »*adjective* representing the most perfect or typical example.
– SAY kwin-ti-**sen**-sh'l
quintessentially

q

quintet »*noun* ❶ a group of five people playing music or singing together. ❷ a composition for a quintet. ❸ a set of five.

quintuple »*adjective* ❶ consisting of five parts or elements. ❷ five times as much or as many.
» *verb* (**quintuples, quintupling, quintupled**) increase or be increased fivefold.
– SAY **kwin**-tyuu-p'l or kwin-**tyoo**-p'l

quintuplet »*noun* one of five children born at one time.
– SAY kwin-tyuu-plit or kwin-**tyoo**-plit

quintupling

quip »*noun* a witty remark.
» *verb* (**quips, quipping, quipped**) make a quip.

✓ double the **p** to spell **quipping** and **quipped**

quire »*noun* ❶ four sheets of paper or parchment folded to form eight leaves. ❷ 25 sheets of paper; one twentieth of a ream.
– SAY *rhymes with* choir

ℹ **quire** is pronounced the same as **choir**, and you sometimes come across the old spelling **quire** used to mean **choir**

quirk »*noun* ❶ a peculiar habit. ❷ a strange thing that happens by chance: *a quirk of fate.*
quirkily
quirkiness

quirky (adjective: **quirkier, quirkiest**)

quisling »*noun* a traitor who collaborates with an occupying enemy force.
– SAY **kwiz**-ling

ℹ from Major Vidkun *Quisling*, who ruled Norway during the Second World War on behalf of the German occupying forces

quit (verb: **quits, quitting, quitted** or **quit**)

✓ double the **t** in **quitting** and **quitted**

quite [completely; moderately]

ℹ do not confuse **quite** with **quiet**, which means 'making little or no noise'

quits »*adjective* on equal terms because a debt or score has been settled.

quitted

quitter »*noun* a person who gives up easily.

quitting

quiver[1] (verb: **quivers, quivering, quivered**) [shake or vibrate]

quiver[2] »*noun* a case for carrying arrows.

quixotic »*adjective* unrealistic and impractical.
– SAY kwik-**sot**-ik
quixotically

ℹ from Don *Quixote*, hero of a book by the Spanish writer Cervantes

quiz (plural **quizzes**; verb: **quizzes, quizzing, quizzed**)

✓ double the **z** in the plural **quizzes**, in **quizzes, quizzing**, and **quizzed**, and in **quizzical**

quizzical »*adjective* showing mild or amused puzzlement.
quizzically

quizzing

quoin »*noun* ❶ an external angle of a wall or building. ❷ a cornerstone.
– SAY koyn or kwoyn

quoit »*noun* a ring of iron, rope, or rubber thrown in a game to land over or as near as possible to an upright peg.
– SAY koyt or kwoyt

quondam »*adjective* former.
– SAY **kwon**-dam

ℹ **quondam** is a Latin word meaning 'formerly'

quorate »*adjective* (of a meeting) having a quorum.
– SAY **kwor**-uht

quorum »*noun* (plural **quorums**) the minimum number of members that must be present at a meeting to make its business valid.
– SAY **kwor**-uhm

ℹ **quorum** is a Latin word meaning 'of whom'

quota »*noun* ❶ a limited quantity of a product which may be produced, exported, or imported. ❷ a share that you are entitled to receive or have to contribute. ❸ a fixed number of a group of people allowed to do something.

quotable »*adjective* suitable for or worth quoting.

quotation

quote (verb: **quotes, quoting, quoted**)

quoth »*verb* (an old word) said.
– SAY kwohth

quotidian »*adjective* ❶ daily. ❷ ordinary or everyday.
– SAY kwuh-**tid**-i-uhn

quotient »*noun* ❶ (in mathematics) a result obtained by dividing one quantity by another. ❷ a degree of a quality: *my coolness quotient evaporated on the spot.*
– SAY **kwoh**-shuhnt

quoting

Qur'an another way of spelling **KORAN**.
– SAY kuh-**rahn**

> ✓ Qur'an can also be spelled **Quran**, without the apostrophe in the middle

q.v. »*abbreviation* used to direct a reader to another part of a book for further information.

> ℹ️ q.v. is short for the Latin phrase *quod vide*, which means 'which see'

Rr

rabbi »*noun* (plural **rabbis**) a Jewish religious leader or teacher of Jewish law.
– SAY **rab**-bI

> ✓ rabbi is a Hebrew word meaning 'my master'. The plural has **-is** not **-ies**: **rabbis**.

rabbinic »*adjective* relating to rabbis or to Jewish law or teachings.
– SAY ruh-**bin**-ik
rabbinical

rabbis

rabbit (verb: **rabbits, rabbiting, rabbited**)
rabbity

> ✓ do not double the t in **rabbiting, rabbited**, and **rabbity**

rabble »*noun* **❶** a disorderly crowd. **❷** (**the rabble**) ordinary people seen as common or uncouth.

rabble-rouser »*noun* a person who stirs up popular opinion for political reasons.

Rabelaisian »*adjective* like the works of the French writer François Rabelais, especially in being highly imaginative and full of earthy humour.
– SAY ra-buh-**lay**-zi-uhn

rabid »*adjective* **❶** extreme; fanatical: *a rabid feminist.* **❷** affected with rabies.
– SAY **ra**-bid or **ray**-bid
rabidly

rabies »*noun* a dangerous disease of dogs and other mammals, caused by a virus that can be transmitted through the saliva to humans, causing madness and convulsions.
– SAY **ray**-beez or **ray**-biz

> ✓ only one b: rabies

RAC »*abbreviation* (in the UK) Royal Automobile Club.

raccoon »*noun* a greyish-brown American mammal with a black face and striped tail.

– SAY ruh-**koon**

> ✓ raccoon can also be spelled **racoon**, with only one c

race (verb: **races, racing, raced**)
racer

racecourse

raced

racehorse

racer

races

racetrack

racial »*adjective* having to do with race, or to relations or differences between races.
racially

racialism »*noun* racism.
racialist

racially

racier

raciest

racily

raciness

racing

racism »*noun* **❶** the belief that certain races are better than others. **❷** discrimination against or hostility towards other races.
racist

> ✓ rac not rasc: racism, racist

rack (verb: **racks, racking, racked**)

> ✓ rack can also be spelled **wrack** when it means 'cause great physical or mental pain to someone' (as in *he was racked/wracked with guilt*) and in the phrase *rack/wrack and ruin*.

rack-and-pinion »*adjective* (of a mechanism) using a fixed bar or rail with cogs or teeth that engage with a smaller cog.

racked

racket[1] [a bat]

✓ racket can also be spelled **racquet**

racket[2] *»noun* ❶ a loud unpleasant noise.
❷ a dishonest scheme for obtaining money.
rackety

racketeer *»noun* a person who makes money through dishonest activities.
racketeering

rackety

racking

racks

raconteur *»noun* a person who tells stories in an interesting and amusing way.
– SAY ra-kon-**ter**

✓ **eur** not **er**: **raconteur** is a French word

raconteuse *»noun* a female raconteur.
– SAY ra-kon-**terz**

racoon another way of spelling **RACCOON**.

racquet another way of spelling **RACKET**[1].

racy *»adjective* (**racier**, **raciest**) lively and exciting, especially in a sexual way.

✓ drop the **y** and add **ier** or **iest** to spell **racier** or **raciest**

RADA *»abbreviation* (in the UK) Royal Academy of Dramatic Art.
– SAY **rah**-duh

radar *»noun* a system for finding the position and speed of aircraft, ships, etc., by sending out pulses of radio waves which are reflected back off the object.

ℹ **radar** is an acronym from *radio detection and ranging*

raddled *»adjective* showing signs of age or exhaustion.

radial *»adjective* ❶ arranged in lines coming out from a central point to the edge of a circle. ❷ (also **radial-ply**) (of a tyre) in which the layers of fabric have their cords running at right angles to the circumference of the tyre.
radially

radian *»noun* an angle of 57.3 degrees, equal to the angle at the centre of a circle formed by an arc equal in length to the radius.
– SAY **ray**-di-uhn

radiant *»adjective* ❶ shining or glowing brightly. ❷ showing great joy, love, or health. ❸ (of heat) transmitted by radiation.

radiance
radiantly

✓ **ant** not **ent**: **radiant**

radiate *»verb* (**radiates**, **radiating**, **radiated**) ❶ (with reference to light, heat, or other energy) send out or be sent out in rays or waves. ❷ show a strong feeling or quality. ❸ spread out from something or as if from a central point.

radiation *»noun* ❶ the action of radiating. ❷ energy sent out as electromagnetic waves or subatomic particles.

radiator

✓ **-or** not **-er**: **radiator**

radical *»adjective* ❶ having to do with the basic nature of something; fundamental. ❷ supporting complete political or social reform. ❸ departing from tradition; new. ❹ (in mathematics) relating to the root of a number or quantity. ❺ relating to the root or stem base of a plant.
» noun ❶ a supporter of radical political or social reform. ❷ (in chemistry) a group of atoms behaving as a unit in a number of compounds.
radicalism
radically

✓ **al** not **le**: **radical**
radically ends in **cally** not **cly**

radicchio *»noun* (plural **radicchios**) a variety of chicory with dark red leaves.
– SAY ra-**dee**-ki-oh

✓ the plural of **radicchio**, an Italian word, has **os** not **oes**: **radicchios**

radices plural of **RADIX**.

radicle *»noun* the part of a plant embryo that develops into the primary root.
– SAY ra-di-k'l

✓ **le** not **al**: **radicle**

radii plural of **RADIUS**.

radio (plural **radios**; verb: **radioes**, **radioing**, **radioed**)

✓ the plural of **radio** has **os** not **oes**: **radios**. As a verb, there is an **e** in **radioes** and **radioed**, but not in **radioing**.

radioactive *»adjective* giving out harmful radiation or particles.
radioactively

radioactivity *»noun* ❶ the sending out of harmful radiation or particles, caused when atomic nuclei break up spontaneously. ❷ radioactive particles.

radiocarbon »*noun* a radioactive isotope of carbon used in carbon dating.

radioed

radioes

radiogram »*noun* (old-fashioned) a combined radio and record player.

radiography »*noun* the production of images by X-rays or other radiation.
radiographer

radioing

radioisotope »*noun* a radioactive isotope.

radiology »*noun* the study and use of X-rays and similar radiation in medicine.
radiological
radiologist

radiophonic »*adjective* having to do with sound produced electronically.

radiotelephone »*noun* a telephone using radio transmission.

radio telescope »*noun* an instrument used to detect radio waves from space.

radiotherapy »*noun* the treatment of cancer or other disease using X-rays or similar radiation.

radish »*noun* the crisp, hot-tasting, red root of a plant, eaten raw.

radium »*noun* a reactive, radioactive metallic element.
– **say** ray-di-uhm

radius »*noun* (plural **radii** or **radiuses**) ❶ a straight line from the centre to the circumference of a circle or sphere. ❷ a specified distance from a centre in all directions: *pubs within a two-mile radius*. ❸ the thicker and shorter of the two bones in the human forearm.
– **say** ray-di-uhss [singular], ray-di-I [plural]

> ☑ the plural of **radius** can be either **radii** (as in the original Latin) or **radiuses**

radix »*noun* (plural **radices**) (in mathematics) the base of a system of calculation.
– **say** ray-diks [singular], ray-di-seez [plural]

> ☑ the plural of **radix** is **radices** (as in the original Latin)

radon »*noun* a rare radioactive gaseous element produced by the radioactive decay of radium.
– **say** ray-don

RAF »*abbreviation* (in the UK) Royal Air Force.

raffia »*noun* fibre from the leaves of a tropical palm tree, used for making hats, baskets, etc.

> ☑ double f: **raffia**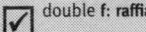

raffish »*adjective* slightly disreputable, but in an attractive way.
raffishly
raffishness

raffle (verb: **raffles**, **raffling**, **raffled**)

raft »*noun* ❶ a flat structure used as a boat or floating platform. ❷ a small inflatable boat. ❸ a large amount of something.

rafter »*noun* a beam forming part of the internal framework of a roof.

rag¹ [a piece of old cloth]

rag² »*noun* a programme of entertainments organized by students to raise money for charity.
» *verb* (**rags**, **ragging**, **ragged**) tease or play practical jokes on someone.

ragamuffin »*noun* a person in ragged, dirty clothes.

> ☑ **ragamuffin** can also be spelled **raggamuffin**, with a double g

rag-and-bone man »*noun* a person who goes from door to door, collecting second-hand items to sell.

ragbag »*noun* a collection of widely different things.

rage (verb: **rages**, **raging**, **raged**)

raggamuffin another way of spelling **RAGAMUFFIN**.

ragged
raggedly
raggedness

ragging

raging

raglan »*adjective* (of a sleeve) continuing in one piece up to the neck of a garment.

> ℹ named after Lord *Raglan*, a British commander in the Crimean War

ragout »*noun* a spicy stew of meat and vegetables.
– **say** ra-goo

> ☑ don't forget the silent t at the end: **ragout** is a French word

rags

ragtag »*adjective* disorganized and very varied: *a ragtag force of men*.

ragtime »*noun* an early form of jazz music played especially on the piano.

rag trade »*noun* (in informal English) the clothing or fashion industry.

ragwort »*noun* a plant with yellow flowers and ragged leaves.

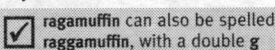

raid (verb: raids, raiding, raided)
raider

rail (verb: rails, railing, railed)

> ✓ do not double the l in **railing** and **railed**

railcard

railed

railhead »*noun* a point on a railway from which roads and other transport routes begin.

railing

raillery »*noun* good-humoured teasing.
– sᴀʏ rayl-luh-ri

> ✓ double l: **raillery**

railroad »*noun* (in American English) a railway.
»*verb* (railroads, railroading, railroaded) (in informal English) rush or force someone into doing something.

railway

raiment »*noun* (an old word) clothing.
– sᴀʏ ray-muhnt

> ✓ **raim** not **rainm** or **raym**: **raiment**

rain (verb: rains, raining, rained) [drops of water falling from clouds]

rainbow

rain check »*noun* (take a rain check) refuse an offer but imply that you may take it up later.

> ℹ️ an American phrase referring to a ticket given for later use when an outdoor event is interrupted or postponed by rain

raincoat

raindrop

rained

rainfall

rainforest

rainier

rainiest

raining

rains

rainstorm

rainwater

rainy (adjective: rainier, rainiest)

raise (verb: raises, raising, raised) [lift or move upwards]
raiser

> ℹ️ do not confuse **raise** with **raze**, which means 'completely destroy a building, town, etc.'

raisin »*noun* a partially dried grape.

> ✓ the ending is **-in** not **-on**: **raisin**

raising

raison d'etre »*noun* (plural raisons d'etre) the most important reason for someone or something's existence.
– sᴀʏ ray-zon det-ruh [singular and plural]

> ✓ **raison d'etre** can also be spelled **raison d'être**, with a circumflex accent above the **e** (as in the original French phrase meaning 'reason for being')
> make the plural by adding **s** after **raison** only: **raisons d'etre**

Raj »*noun* (a historical term) the period of British rule in India.
– sᴀʏ rahj

> ✓ **Raj** is a Hindi word meaning 'reign'

raja »*noun* (a historical term) an Indian king or prince.
– sᴀʏ rah-juh

> ✓ **raja** can also be spelled **rajah**, with an h on the end

rake (verb: rakes, raking, raked)

rakish »*adjective* having a dashing, jaunty, or slightly disreputable appearance.
rakishly
rakishness

rally (plural rallies; verb: rallies, rallying, rallied)
rallying

> ✓ plural: drop the y and add **ies**: **rallies**

RAM »*abbreviation* (in computing) random-access memory.

ram »*noun* ❶ an adult male sheep. ❷ a battering ram. ❸ a striking or plunging device in a machine.
»*verb* (rams, ramming, rammed) ❶ roughly force something into place. ❷ hit something or be hit with force.

> ✓ double the m in **ramming** and **rammed**

Ramadan »*noun* the ninth month of the Muslim year, during which Muslims fast from sunrise to sunset.
– sᴀʏ ram-uh-dan

> ✓ an Arabic word, **Ramadan** can also be spelled **Ramadhan** (sᴀʏ ram-uh-zan)

ramble (verb: rambles, rambling, rambled)
rambler

rambutan »*noun* the red fruit of a tropical tree, with soft spines and a slightly sour taste.

– **say** ram-**byoo**-tuhn

ramekin »*noun* a small dish for baking and serving an individual portion of food.
– **say** ra-mi-kin

 single m, and **mek** not **meck** or **mik**: **ramekin**

ramifications »*plural noun* complex results of an action or event: *any change is bound to have legal ramifications.*

ramify »*verb* (**ramifies, ramifying, ramified**) form parts that branch out.
– **say** ra-mi-fI

rammed

ramming

ramp

rampage »*verb* (**rampages, rampaging, rampaged**) rush around in a wild and violent way.
» *noun* a period of wild and violent behaviour.

rampant »*adjective* ❶ flourishing or spreading in an uncontrolled way. ❷ (in heraldry) (of an animal) shown standing on its left hind foot with its forefeet in the air: *two lions rampant.*
rampantly

 ant not **ent**: **rampant**

rampart »*noun* a wall built to defend a castle or town, having a broad top with a walkway.

ramrod »*noun* (a historical term) a straight rod used to ram down the charge of a gun.

rams

ramshackle »*adjective* in a very bad condition.

ran past of **RUN**.

ranch »*noun* a large farm, especially in the western US and Canada, where cattle or other animals are bred.
» *verb* (**ranches, ranching, ranched**) run a ranch.
rancher

rancid »*adjective* (of foods containing fat or oil) smelling or tasting unpleasant as a result of being stale.
rancidity

rancour »*noun* bitter feeling or resentment.
rancorous

☑ **-our** not **-or** (except in **rancorous**): **rancour** (the spelling **rancor** is American)

rand »*noun* the basic unit of money of South Africa.

R & B »*abbreviation* rhythm and blues.

R & D »*abbreviation* research and development.

randier

randiest

randiness

random »*adjective* done or happening without a definite or deliberate order, purpose, or choice.
randomly
randomness

random access »*noun* the process of storing or finding information on a computer without having to read through items in a particular sequence.

randomly

randomness

randy »*adjective* (**randier, randiest**) sexually aroused or excited.
randiness

rang past of **RING**[2].

range (verb: **ranges, ranging, ranged**)

rangefinder »*noun* an instrument for estimating the distance of an object.

ranger »*noun* a keeper of a park, forest, or area of countryside.

ranges

ranging

rangy »*adjective* (of a person) tall and slim with long limbs.
– **say** rayn-ji

rank[1] (verb: **ranks, ranking, ranked**) [a position within the armed forces or an organization; a row of people or things; give or hold a rank]

rank[2] »*adjective* (**ranker, rankest**) ❶ having a very unpleasant smell. ❷ (of vegetation) growing too thickly. ❸ absolute: *a rank amateur.*
rankly
rankness

ranking

rankle »*verb* (**rankles, rankling, rankled**) (of a comment or fact) cause continuing annoyance or resentment.

rankly

rankness

ranks

ransack »*verb* (**ransacks, ransacking, ransacked**) ❶ go hurriedly through a place stealing things and causing damage. ❷ search a place thoroughly or without care.

ransom »*noun* a sum of money demanded or paid for the release of someone who is held captive.

r

» verb (ransoms, ransoming, ransomed) obtain someone's release by paying a ransom.

☑ there is no **e** at the end: **ransom**

rant (verb: **rants, ranting, ranted**) **»verb** (**rants, ranting, ranted**) speak in a loud, angry, and forceful way.
ranter

rap (verb: **raps, rapping, rapped**)
rapper

☑ double the **p** in **rapping, rapped,** and **rapper**

rapacious **»adjective** very greedy.
– sᴀʏ ruh-**pay**-shuhss
rapaciously
rapaciousness

rapacity **»noun** greed.
– sᴀʏ ruh-**pa**-si-ti

rape[1] (verb: **rapes, raping, raped**) [force someone to have sex against their will; an act of raping someone]

rape[2] **»noun** a plant with bright yellow flowers, grown for its oil-rich seed.

rapid
rapidity
rapidly

rapids **»plural noun** a part of a river where the water flows very fast, often over rocks.

rapier **»noun** a thin, light sword used for thrusting.

rapine **»noun** (mainly a historical term) the violent seizure of property.
– sᴀʏ **ra**-pyn

raping

rapist **»noun** a man who commits rape.

rapped

rapper

rapping

rapport **»noun** a close relationship in which people understand each other and communicate well.
– sᴀʏ rap-**por**

☑ note the double **p** and the silent **t** at the end: **rapport** (a French word)

rapprochement **»noun** a renewal of friendly relations between two countries or groups.
– sᴀʏ ra-**prosh**-mon

☑ note the **ment** ending: **rapprochement** is a French word

raps

rapscallion **»noun** (an old word) a mischievous person.
– sᴀʏ rap-**skal**-li-uhn

rapt **»adjective** completely interested or absorbed in someone or something.
raptly
raptness

raptor **»noun** a bird of prey.

rapture **»noun** ❶ great pleasure or joy. ❷ (**raptures**) the expression of great pleasure or enthusiasm.

rapturous **»adjective** very pleased or enthusiastic.
rapturously
rapturousness

rare (adjective: **rarer, rarest**)

rarebit **»noun** a dish of melted cheese on toast.

rarefied **»adjective** ❶ (of air) of lower pressure than usual; thin. ❷ understood by a limited group of people.
– sᴀʏ **rair**-i-fyd
rarefaction

☑ **ref** not **rif**: **rarefied**

rarely

rarer

rarest

raring **»adjective** (**raring to do**) very eager to do something.

rarity **»noun** (plural **rarities**) ❶ the state of being rare. ❷ a rare thing.

☑ there is no **e**: **rarity** plural: drop the **y** and add **ies**: **rarities**

rascal
rascally

☑ **rascal** has a single **l** which is doubled in **rascally**

rash[1] **»adjective** acting or done without careful consideration of the possible results.
rashly
rashness

rash[2] **»noun** ❶ an area of red spots or patches on a person's skin. ❷ a series of unpleasant things happening within a short time.

rasher **»noun** a thin slice of bacon.

rashly

rashness

rasp **»noun** ❶ a coarse file for use on metal, wood, etc. ❷ a harsh, grating noise.
» verb (rasps, rasping, rasped) ❶ file something with a rasp. ❷ scrape something roughly. ❸ make a harsh, grating noise.
raspy

raspberry (plural **raspberries**)

✓ remember the **p** in the middle: **raspberry**

rasped

rasping

rasps

raspy

Rasta »*noun & adjective* (in informal English) a Rastafarian.

Rastafarian »*noun* a member of a Jamaican religious movement which worships Haile Selassie, the former Emperor of Ethiopia.
» *adjective* relating to Rastafarians or their beliefs.
– **say** rass-tuh-**fair**-i-uhn or rass-tuh-**fah**-ri-uhn
Rastafarianism

rat (verb: **rats, ratting, ratted**)

✓ double the **t** to spell **ratting** and **ratted**

ratable another way of spelling RATEABLE.

ratatouille »*noun* a vegetable dish of stewed onions, courgettes, tomatoes, etc.
– **say** ra-tuh-**too**-i

✓ note the **oui** in **ratatouille**: this is a French word

ratchet »*noun* a device with a set of angled teeth in which a cog, tooth, or bar fits, allowing movement in one direction only.
» *verb* (**ratchets, ratcheting, ratcheted**) (**ratchet up** or **down**) cause something to rise or fall as a step in a steady process.

✓ do not double the **t** in **ratcheting** and **ratcheted**

rate (verb: **rates, rating, rated**)

rateable »*adjective* able to be rated.

✓ **rateable** can also be spelled without the first **e**: **ratable**

rateable value »*noun* (in the UK) a value given to a business property, used to calculate how much tax must be paid on it to the local authority.

rated

rate payer

rates

rather

ratify »*verb* (**ratifies, ratifying, ratified**) make a treaty, contract, etc. valid by signing or agreeing to it.
ratification

rating

ratio »*noun* (plural **ratios**) an indication of the relationship between two amounts, showing the number of times one contains the other.

✓ the plural of **ratio** has **os** not **oes**: **ratios**

ratiocination »*noun* the process of thinking in a logical way; reasoning.
– **say** ra-ti-oss-i-**nay**-sh'n or ra-shi-oss-i-**nay**-sh'n

ration »*noun* ➊ a fixed amount of food, fuel, etc., officially allowed to each person. ➋ (**rations**) a regular allowance of food supplied to members of the armed forces.
» *verb* (**rations, rationing, rationed**) limit the supply of food, fuel, etc.

rational »*adjective* ➊ based on reason or logic. ➋ able to think sensibly or logically. ➌ (in mathematics) (of a number or quantity) able to be expressed as a ratio of whole numbers.
rationality
rationally

rationale »*noun* the reasons for a course of action or a belief.
– **say** ra-shuh-**nahl**

rationalise another way of spelling RATIONALIZE.

rationalism »*noun* the belief that opinions and actions should be based on reason rather than on religious belief or emotions.
rationalist

rationality

rationalize »*verb* (**rationalizes, rationalizing, rationalized**) ➊ try to find a logical reason for an action or attitude. ➋ reorganize a system to make it more logical. ➌ make a company more efficient by disposing of unwanted staff or equipment.
rationalization

✓ many people prefer the alternative spellings **rationalise, rationalises**, etc., and **rationalisation**: both **s** and **z** spellings are correct

rationally

ratios

rats

rattan »*noun* the thin, pliable stems of a tropical climbing palm, used to make furniture.
– **say** ruh-**tan**

ratted

ratting

rattle (verb: **rattles, rattling, rattled**)
rattler
rattly

rattlesnake

rattling

rattly

ratty

raucous »*adjective* sounding loud and harsh.
- SAY raw-kuhss
raucously
raucousness

raunchy »*adjective* (raunchier, raunchiest) sexually exciting or direct.
raunchily
raunchiness

ravage »*verb* (ravages, ravaging, ravaged) cause great damage to something.

ravages »*noun* the destruction caused by something.

ravaging

rave (verb: raves, raving, raved)
raver

ravel »*verb* (ravels, ravelling, ravelled) (ravel out) untangle.

> ✓ double the l to spell **ravelling** and **ravelled** (the spellings **raveling** and **raveled** are American)

raven »*noun* a large black crow.
» *adjective* (of hair) of a glossy black colour.

ravening »*adjective* very hungry.

ravenous
ravenously

raver

raves

ravine »*noun* a deep, narrow gorge with steep sides.
- SAY ruh-**veen**

raving

ravings

ravioli »*plural noun* small pasta cases containing minced meat, cheese, or vegetables.
- SAY ra-vi-**oh**-li

> ✓ single **v** and single **l**: **ravioli**

ravish »*verb* (ravishes, ravishing, ravished) (an old word) ❶ seize someone and carry them off by force. ❷ rape someone.

ravishing »*adjective* very beautiful.

raw (adjective: rawer, rawest)
rawly
rawness

ray

rayon »*noun* a synthetic fabric made from viscose.

raze »*verb* (razes, razing, razed) completely destroy a building, town, etc.

> ℹ️ do not confuse **raze** with **raise**, which means 'lift or move upwards'

razor

> ✓ -or not -er: **razor**

razor wire »*noun* metal wire with sharp edges or studded with small sharp blades, used as a barrier.

razzamatazz another way of spelling RAZZMATAZZ.

razzle »*noun* (on the razzle) out celebrating or enjoying yourself.

razzmatazz »*noun* noisy and exciting activity, designed to attract attention.

> ✓ a variant form of this word is **razzamatazz**

RE »*abbreviation* religious education (as a school subject).

re »*preposition* with regard to; about.
- SAY ree or ray

re- »*prefix* once more; again or anew: re-elect | reshuffle.

> ✓ words formed with **re-** are usually spelled without a hyphen (react). However, if the word to which **re-** is attached begins with **e**, then a hyphen is used to make it clear (re-examine, re-enter). You should also use a hyphen when the word formed with **re-** would be exactly the same as a word that already exists; so you should use **re-cover** to mean 'cover again' and **recover** to mean 'get well again'.

reach (verb: reaches, reaching, reached)
reachable

react (verb: reacts, reacting, reacted)

reactant »*noun* (in chemistry) a substance that undergoes change during a reaction.

reacted

reacting

reaction

reactionary »*adjective* opposing political or social progress or reform.
» *noun* (plural reactionaries) a person holding reactionary views.

> ✓ ary not ery: **reactionary**

reactivate »*verb* (reactivates, reactivating, reactivated) bring something back into action.
reactivation

reactive »*adjective* ❶ showing a reaction. ❷ having a tendency to react chemically.
reactivity

reactor »*noun* an apparatus in which material is made to undergo a controlled nuclear reaction that releases energy.

> ☑ -or not -er: reactor

reacts

read (verb: **reads, reading, read**)
  readable

reader

readership

readied

readier

readies

readiest

readily »*adverb* ❶ willingly. ❷ easily.

readiness

reading

reading age »*noun* a child's ability to read, measured by comparing it with the average ability of a child of that age.

readjust (verb: **readjusts, readjusting, readjusted**)
  readjustment

read-only memory »*noun* computer memory which can be read at high speed but which cannot be changed.

reads

ready (adjective: **readier, readiest**; verb: **readies, readying, readied**)
  readiness

> ☑ drop the **y** and add **ier** or **iest** to spell **readier** or **readiest**

ready-made

reagent »*noun* a substance that produces a chemical reaction, used to detect the presence of another substance.
– SAY ri-ay-juhnt

real [actual; genuine]
  really
  realness

real estate »*noun* property in the form of land or buildings.

realign »*verb* (**realigns, realigning, realigned**) change something to a different position or state.
  realignment

> ☑ single l: realign

realise another way of spelling **REALIZE**.

realism »*noun* ❶ the acceptance of a situation as it is. ❷ (in art or literature) the presentation of things in a way that is accurate and true to life.
  realist

realistic
  realistically

reality (plural **realities**)

> ☑ plural: drop the **y** and add **ies**: realities

realize (verb: **realizes, realizing, realized**)
  realizable
  realization

> ☑ many people prefer the alternative spellings **realise, realises**, etc., **realisable**, and **realisation**: both **s** and **z** spellings are correct

really

realm »*noun* ❶ a kingdom. ❷ a field of activity or interest.

> ☑ real- not rel-: realm

realness

real tennis »*noun* the original form of tennis, played with a solid ball on an enclosed court.

real-time »*adjective* (of a computer system) in which input data is processed almost immediately.

ream »*noun* ❶ 500 sheets of paper. ❷ (**reams**) a large quantity of something.

reap »*verb* (**reaps, reaping, reaped**) ❶ gather in a crop or harvest. ❷ receive a reward or benefit as a result of your actions.

reaper »*noun* ❶ a person or machine that harvests a crop. ❷ (**the Grim Reaper**) death, shown as a cloaked skeleton holding a scythe.

reaping

reappear »*verb* (**reappears, reappearing, reappeared**) appear again.
  reappearance

reappoint (verb: **reappoints, reappointing, reappointed**)

reappraisal »*noun* a new or different appraisal.

reaps

rear (verb: **rears, rearing, reared**)

rear admiral »*noun* a naval rank above commodore and below vice admiral.

reared

rearguard »*noun* a body of troops protecting the rear of the main force.

rearguard action »*noun* a defensive action carried out by a retreating army.

rearing

rearm (verb: **rearms, rearming, rearmed**)
  rearmament

rearmost »*adjective* furthest back.

rearms

rearrange (verb: **rearranges, rearranging, rearranged**)
rearrangement

rears

rearward »*adjective* directed towards the back.
» *adverb* towards the back.

rearwards

reason (verb: **reasons, reasoning, reasoned**)
reasoned

reasonable
reasonableness
reasonably

reasoned

reasoning

reasons

reassemble (verb: **reassembles, reassembling, reassembled**)
reassembly

reassert (verb: **reasserts, reasserting, reasserted**)
reassertion

reassess (verb: **reassesses, reassessing, reassessed**)
reassessment

> ☑ double s twice: **reassess**

reassign (verb: **reassigns, reassigning, reassigned**)
reassignment

reassure »*verb* (**reassures, reassuring, reassured**) make someone feel less worried or afraid.
reassurance
reassuring

rebarbative »*adjective* unpleasant.
– SAY ri-**bar**-buh-tiv

rebate »*noun* ❶ a partial refund to someone who has paid too much for tax, rent, etc. ❷ a discount on a sum that is due.
– SAY ree-bayt

rebel (verb: **rebels, rebelling, rebelled**)

> ☑ double the l to spell **rebelling** and **rebelled**

rebellion

rebellious
rebelliously
rebelliousness

rebels

rebirth »*noun* ❶ a return to life or activity: *a rebirth of faith in the old values.* ❷ the process of being born again.

reborn

rebound »*verb* (**rebounds, rebounding, rebounded**) ❶ bounce back after hitting a hard surface. ❷ increase again.
❸ (**rebound on**) have an unexpected and unpleasant effect on someone.
» *noun* a ball or shot that rebounds.

rebuff »*verb* (**rebuffs, rebuffing, rebuffed**) reject something in an abrupt or unkind way.
» *noun* an abrupt or unkind rejection.

rebuild (verb: **rebuilds, rebuilding, rebuilt**)

rebuke »*verb* (**rebukes, rebuking, rebuked**) criticize someone sharply.
» *noun* a sharp criticism.

rebus »*noun* (plural **rebuses**) a puzzle in which words are represented by combinations of pictures and letters.
– SAY **ree**-buhss

rebut »*verb* (**rebuts, rebutting, rebutted**) claim or prove something to be false.
– SAY ri-**but**

> ☑ double the t to spell **rebutting** and **rebutted**

rebuttal »*noun* a claim or proof that something is false.

rebutted

rebutting

recalcitrant »*adjective* unwilling to cooperate; disobedient.
– SAY ri-**kal**-si-truhnt
recalcitrance
recalcitrantly

recall »*verb* (**recalls, recalling, recalled**) ❶ remember. ❷ make someone think of something; bring something to mind.
❸ officially order someone to return.
❹ (of a manufacturer) ask for faulty products to be returned.
» *noun* ❶ the action of remembering. ❷ an official order for someone to return.

recant »*verb* (**recants, recanting, recanted**) withdraw a former opinion or belief.
– SAY ri-**kant**
recantation

recap »*verb* (**recaps, recapping, recapped**) recapitulate.
» *noun* a recapitulation.

> ☑ double the p in **recapping** and **recapped**

recapitulate »*verb* (**recapitulates, recapitulating, recapitulated**) give a summary or repeat the main points of something.
– SAY ree-kuh-**pit**-yuu-layt
recapitulation

recapped

recapping

recaps

recapture (verb: **recaptures**, **recapturing**, **recaptured**)

recast »*verb* (**recasts**, **recasting**, **recast**) present something in a different form.

recce (in informal English) »*noun* reconnaissance.
» *verb* (**recces**, **recceing**, **recced**) reconnoitre.
– SAY rek-ki

recede »*verb* (**recedes**, **receding**, **receded**)
❶ move back or further away.
❷ gradually become weaker or smaller.
❸ (**receding**) (of part of the face) sloping backwards.

> ✓ **-cede** not **-ceed** or **-seed**: **recede**

receipt »*noun* ❶ the action of receiving something. ❷ a written statement confirming that something has been paid for or received. ❸ (**receipts**) the amount of money received over a period by a business.

> ✓ **receipt** includes a silent **p**, and follows the usual rule **i** before **e** except after **c**

receive (verb: **receives**, **receiving**, **received**)
receivable

> ✓ the usual rule is **i** before **e** except after **c**: **receive**

received pronunciation »*noun* a standard form of British English pronunciation based on educated speech in southern England.

receiver »*noun* ❶ a person or thing that receives something. ❷ a radio or television apparatus that converts broadcast signals into sound or images. ❸ the part of a telephone that converts electrical signals into sounds. ❹ (also **official receiver**) a person appointed to manage the financial affairs of a bankrupt business.

receivership »*noun* the state of being managed by an official receiver.

receives

receiving

recent [shortly before the present]
recently

receptacle »*noun* an object used to contain something.

reception »*noun* ❶ the action of receiving. ❷ the way in which people react to something: *an enthusiastic reception.* ❸ a formal social occasion held to welcome someone or celebrate an event. ❹ the area

in a hotel, office, etc. where visitors are greeted. ❺ the quality with which broadcast signals are received.

receptionist

receptive »*adjective* ❶ able or willing to receive something. ❷ willing to consider new ideas.
receptivity

receptor »*noun* a nerve ending in the body that responds to a stimulus such as light.

recess »*noun* (plural **recesses**) ❶ a small space set back in a wall or in a surface. ❷ (**recesses**) remote or hidden places. ❸ a break between sessions of a parliament, law court, etc.
» *verb* (**recesses**, **recessing**, **recessed**) fit something so that it is set back into a surface.

> ✓ single **c** but double **s**: **recess**

recession »*noun* a period during which trade and industrial activity in a country are reduced.
recessionary

recessive »*adjective* (of a gene) appearing in offspring only if a contrary gene is not also inherited.

recharge (verb: **recharges**, **recharging**, **recharged**)
rechargeable

recherche »*adjective* unusual and not easily understood.
– SAY ruh-**shair**-shay

> ✓ **recherche** is often written **recherché**, with an acute accent on the final **e** (it is a French word which means 'carefully sought out')

recidivist »*noun* a person who constantly commits crimes, despite being punished.
– SAY ri-**sid**-i-vist
recidivism

recipe

recipient »*noun* a person who receives something.
– SAY ri-**sip**-i-uhnt

reciprocal »*adjective* ❶ given or done in return. ❷ affecting two parties equally.
» *noun* (in mathematics) the quantity obtained by dividing the number one by a given quantity.
– SAY ri-**sip**-ruh-k'l
reciprocally

reciprocate »*verb* (**reciprocates**, **reciprocating**, **reciprocated**) respond to an action or emotion with a similar one.

reciprocity »*noun* a situation in which two parties provide the same help or advantages to each other.
– SAY re-si-**pross**-i-ti

recital »*noun* ❶ the performance of a programme of music by a soloist or small group. ❷ a long account of a series of facts or events.

recitation »*noun* ❶ the action of reciting something. ❷ something that is recited.
– SAY re-si-**tay**-sh'n

recitative »*noun* a passage in an opera which is sung in a rhythm like that of ordinary speech.
– SAY re-si-tuh-**teev**

recite (verb: **recites, reciting, recited**)

reckless »*adjective* without thought or care for the results of an action.
recklessly
recklessness

reckon (verb: **reckons, reckoning, reckoned**)

reckoning »*noun* ❶ the action of calculating something. ❷ a person's opinion. ❸ punishment for past actions.

reckons

reclaim (verb: **reclaims, reclaiming, reclaimed**)
reclamation

recline »*verb* (**reclines, reclining, reclined**) lean or lie back in a relaxed position.
reclinable
recliner

recluse »*noun* a person who avoids others and lives alone.
– SAY ri-**klooss**
reclusion

reclusive »*adjective* avoiding the company of other people.

recognise another way of spelling RECOGNIZE.

recognition

recognize (verb: **recognizes, recognizing, recognized**)
recognizable

> ✓ many people prefer the alternative spellings **recognise, recognises**, etc., and **recognisable**: both **s** and **z** spellings are correct

recoil »*verb* (**recoils, recoiling, recoiled**)
❶ suddenly move back in fear, horror, or disgust. ❷ (of a gun) suddenly move backwards as a reaction on being fired. ❸ (**recoil on**) have an unpleasant effect on.
» *noun* the action of recoiling.

recollect »*verb* (**recollects, recollecting, recollected**) remember.

– SAY rek-uh-**lekt**
recollection

recommence »*verb* (**recommences, recommencing, recommenced**) begin again.

recommend (verb: **recommends, recommending, recommended**)
recommendation

> ✓ one **c** and double **m**: **recommend, recommendation**

recompense »*verb* (**recompenses, recompensing, recompensed**)
❶ compensate someone for loss or harm suffered. ❷ pay or reward someone for effort or work.
» *noun* compensation or reward.
– SAY **rek**-uhm-penss

reconcile »*verb* (**reconciles, reconciling, reconciled**) ❶ make two people or groups friendly again. ❷ find a satisfactory way of dealing with (opposing facts, ideas, etc.). ❸ (**reconcile to**) make someone accept something unwelcome.
– SAY **rek**-uhn-syl
reconcilable

reconciliation »*noun* ❶ the end of a disagreement and the return to friendly relations. ❷ the action of reconciling opposing ideas, facts, etc.
– SAY rek-uhn-si-li-**ay**-sh'n

reconciling

recondite »*adjective* obscure and little known.
– SAY **rek**-uhn-dyt or ri-**kon**-dyt

recondition »*verb* (**reconditions, reconditioning, reconditioned**) bring back to a good condition; renovate.

reconnaissance »*noun* military observation of an area to gain information.
– SAY ri-**kon**-ni-suhnss

> ✓ **ance** not **ence: reconnaissance**

reconnoitre »*verb* (**reconnoitres, reconnoitring, reconnoitred**) make a military observation of an area.
– SAY rek-uh-**noy**-ter

> ✓ the ending is **re** not **er: reconnoitre** (the spelling **reconnoiter** is American)

reconsider (verb: **reconsiders, reconsidering, reconsidered**)
reconsideration

reconstitute »*verb* (**reconstitutes, reconstituting, reconstituted**) ❶ change the form of an organization. ❷ restore dried food to its original state by adding water.
reconstitution

reconstruct (verb: **reconstructs, reconstructing, reconstructed**)
reconstruction
reconstructive

reconvene »*verb* (**reconvenes, reconvening, reconvened**) meet again after a break.

record (verb: **records, recording, recorded**)
recordable
recordist

recorder

recording

recordist

records

recount[1] »*verb* (**recounts, recounting, recounted**) tell someone about something.
– SAY ri-**kownt**

recount[2] (verb: **recounts, recounting, recounted**) [count again]
– SAY ree-**kownt**

recoup »*verb* (**recoups, recouping, recouped**) recover a loss.

recourse »*noun* ❶ a source of help in a difficult situation. ❷ (**recourse to**) the use of a particular source of help.

recover »*verb* (**recovers, recovering, recovered**) ❶ return to a normal state of health, mind, or strength. ❷ regain possession or control of. ❸ regain an amount of money that has been spent or lent.
recoverable

recovery (plural **recoveries**)

> ✓ plural: drop the **y** and add **ies**: **recoveries**

recreate »*verb* (**recreates, recreating, recreated**) make or do again.

recreation »*noun* enjoyable leisure activity.
– SAY rek-ri-**ay**-sh'n
recreational

recrimination »*noun* an accusation in response to one from someone else.

recruit »*verb* (**recruits, recruiting, recruited**) ❶ take on someone to serve in the armed forces or work for an organization. ❷ persuade someone to do something.
»*noun* a newly recruited person.
recruiter
recruitment

> ✓ **uit** not **ute**: **recruit**

recta plural of **RECTUM**.

rectal

rectangle
rectangular

rectify »*verb* (**rectifies, rectifying, rectified**) ❶ put right; correct. ❷ convert alternating current to direct current.
rectification
rectifier

rectilinear »*adjective* having or moving in a straight line or lines.
– SAY rek-ti-**lin**-i-er

rectitude »*noun* morally correct behaviour.

recto »*noun* (plural **rectos**) a right-hand page of an open book, or the front of a loose document (the opposite of *verso*).

> ✓ the plural of **recto** has **os** not **oes**: **rectos**

rector »*noun* ❶ a Christian priest in charge of a parish. ❷ the head of certain universities, colleges, and schools.

> ✓ **-or** not **-er** at the end: **rector**

rectory »*noun* (plural **rectories**) the house of a rector.

> ✓ plural: drop the **y** and add **ies**: **rectories**

rectos

rectum »*noun* (plural **rectums** or **recta**) the final section of the large intestine, ending at the anus.
rectal

> ✓ the plural can be either **recta** (like the original Latin) or **rectums**

recumbent »*adjective* lying down.
– SAY ri-**kum**-buhnt
recumbency

recuperate »*verb* (**recuperates, recuperating, recuperated**) ❶ recover from illness or tiredness. ❷ get back something that has been lost.
– SAY ri-**koo**-puh-rayt
recuperation
recuperative

recur »*verb* (**recurs, recurring, recurred**) happen again or repeatedly.
recurrence

> ✓ double the **r** in **recurring, recurred,** and **recurrence**

recurrent »*adjective* happening often or repeatedly.
recurrently

recurring

recurring decimal »*noun* a decimal fraction in which a figure or group of figures is repeated indefinitely, as in *0.666 …*

recurs

recusant »*noun* a person who refuses to obey an authority or a regulation.

– SAY rek-yuu-zuhnt

recycle (verb: **recycles, recycling, recycled**)
recyclable
recycler

 no e before the a in **recyclable**

red (adjective: **redder, reddest**)
reddish
redness

red-blooded »*adjective* (of a man) full of energy, especially sexual energy.

red-brick »*adjective* (of a British university) founded in the late 19th or early 20th century and with buildings of red brick, as distinct from the older universities.

redcoat »*noun* (a historical term) a British soldier.

redcurrant »*noun* a small edible red berry.

redden »*verb* (**reddens, reddening, reddened**) make or become red.

redder

reddest

reddish

redecorate (verb: **redecorates, redecorating, redecorated**)
redecoration

redeem »*verb* (**redeems, redeeming, redeemed**) ❶ make up for the faults or bad aspects of. ❷ save someone from sin or evil. ❸ fulfil a promise. ❹ regain possession of something in exchange for payment. ❺ exchange a coupon for goods or money. ❻ pay a debt.
redeemable
redeemer

redemption »*noun* the action of redeeming.
redemptive

 don't forget the p: **redemption**

redeploy »*verb* (**redeploys, redeploying, redeployed**) move troops, resources, etc. to a new place or task.
redeployment

redevelop (verb: **redevelops, redeveloping, redeveloped**)
redeveloper
redevelopment

red-handed

redhead

red herring »*noun* a thing that draws attention away from something important.

red-hot

redid past of REDO.

Red Indian »*noun* (old-fashioned) = AMERICAN INDIAN.

🛈 avoid using the term **Red Indian**: it is associated with the stereotypes of cowboys and Indians and the Wild West, and may cause offence. The normal terms in current use are **American Indian** and **Native American** or, if appropriate, the name of the specific people (**Cherokee, Iroquois**, and so on).

redirect (verb: **redirects, redirecting, redirected**)
redirection

rediscover (verb: **rediscovers, rediscovering, rediscovered**)
rediscovery

redistribute (verb: **redistributes, redistributing, redistributed**)
redistribution

red lead »*noun* a red form of lead oxide used as a pigment.

red-letter day »*noun* an important or memorable day.

🛈 so called from the practice of highlighting a festival in red on a calendar

redneck »*noun* (used in an insulting way) a working-class white person from the southern US, with politically conservative views.

redness

redo (verb: **redoes, redoing, redid**; past participle **redone**)

redolent »*adjective* (**redolent of** or **with**) ❶ strongly calling something to mind. ❷ strongly smelling of.
– SAY red-uh-luhnt
redolence

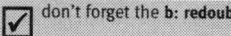 **ent** not **ant**: **redolent**

redone past participle of REDO.

redouble (verb: **redoubles, redoubling, redoubled**)

redoubt »*noun* a temporary or additional fortification.

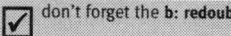 don't forget the b: **redoubt**

redoubtable »*adjective* worthy of respect or fear; formidable.

redound »*verb* (**redounds, redounding, redounded**) (**redound to**) be to someone's credit.
– SAY ri-**downd**

redress »*verb* (**redresses, redressing, redressed**) put right something unfair or wrong.

» *noun* payment or action to make amends for a wrong.

red tape »*noun* complicated official rules which hinder progress.

reduce (verb: **reduces, reducing, reduced**)
reducer
reducible

 -ible not **-able** at the end of **reducible**

reduction

reductive »*adjective* presenting something in an over-simplified form.

redundancy (plural **redundancies**) »*noun*
❶ the state of being no longer needed or useful. ❷ the state of being unemployed because your job is no longer needed.

 plural: drop the **y** and add **ies**: **redundancies**

redundant »*adjective* ❶ no longer needed or useful. ❷ unemployed because your job is no longer needed.
redundantly

redwood »*noun* a giant American coniferous tree with reddish wood.

reed »*noun* ❶ a tall, slender plant that grows in water or on marshy ground. ❷ a piece of thin cane or metal in musical instruments such as the clarinet, which vibrates when air is blown over it and produces sound.

reediness

re-educate »*verb* (**re-educates, re-educating, re-educated**) educate or train to behave or think differently.
re-education

reedy »*adjective* ❶ (of a sound or voice) high and thin in tone. ❷ full of reeds. ❸ (of a person) tall and thin.
reediness

reef »*noun* ❶ a ridge of jagged rock or coral just above or below the surface of the sea. ❷ one of several strips across a sail that can be drawn in so as to reduce the area exposed to the wind.
» *verb* (**reefs, reefing, reefed**) make a sail smaller by taking in a reef.

reefer »*noun* (in informal English) a cannabis cigarette.

reefer jacket »*noun* a thick close-fitting double-breasted jacket.

reefing

reef knot »*noun* a type of double knot that is very secure.

reefs

reek »*verb* (**reeks, reeking, reeked**) have a very unpleasant smell.

» *noun* a very unpleasant smell.

reel »*noun* ❶ a cylinder on which film, wire, thread, etc. can be wound. ❷ a lively Scottish or Irish folk dance.
» *verb* (**reels, reeling, reeled**) ❶ (**reel in**) bring something towards you by turning a reel. ❷ (**reel off**) recite something rapidly and with ease. ❸ stagger. ❹ feel giddy or bewildered.

re-elect (verb: **re-elects, re-electing, re-elected**)
re-election

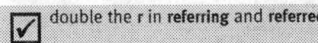 remember the hyphen in **re-elect** and words such as **re-educate** and **re-enter**, where the prefix **re-** is added to a word beginning with **e**

reeled

reeling

reels

re-emerge (verb: **re-emerges, re-emerging, re-emerged**)
re-emergence

re-enact »*verb* (**re-enacts, re-enacting, re-enacted**) act out a past event.
re-enactment

re-enter (verb: **re-enters, re-entering, re-entered**)
re-entry

reeve »*noun* the chief magistrate of a town or district in Anglo-Saxon England.

re-examine (verb: **re-examines, re-examining, re-examined**)
re-examination

ref »*noun* (in sports) a referee.

refectory »*noun* (plural **refectories**) a room used for meals in an educational or religious institution.

 ory not **ery** or **ary** at the end: **refectory**

refer »*verb* (**refers, referring, referred**) (**refer to**) ❶ write or say something about; mention. ❷ (of a word or phrase) describe. ❸ consult a person, book, etc. for information. ❹ pass a person or matter on to someone else for help or a decision.
referable

 double the **r** in **referring** and **referred**

referee (verb: **referees, refereeing, refereed**)

reference »*noun* ❶ the action of referring to something. ❷ a mention of a source of information in a book or article. ❸ a letter from a previous employer giving information about how suitable someone is for a new job.

referendum »*noun* (plural **referendums** or **referenda**) a vote by the people of a country on a single political issue.

> ✓ the plural can be either **referenda** (like the original Latin) or **referendums**

referral »*noun* the action of referring someone or something to a specialist or higher authority.

> ✓ double r in **referral**

referred

referring

refers

refill (verb: **refills**, **refilling**, **refilled**)
refillable

refine » *verb* (**refines**, **refining**, **refined**)
❶ make something pure by removing unwanted substances. ❷ improve something by minor changes. ❸ (**refined**) well educated, elegant, and having good taste.
refinement

refinery »*noun* (plural **refineries**) a factory where oil or another substance is refined.

> ✓ **ery** not **ary** at the end: **refinery** plural: drop the **y** and add **ies**: **refineries**

refines

refining

refit »*verb* (**refits**, **refitting**, **refitted**) replace or repair equipment and fittings in a ship, building, etc.
» *noun* an act of refitting.
– SAY ree-**fit** [verb], **ree**-fit [noun]

> ✓ double the t in **refitting** and **refitted**

reflect »*verb* (**reflects**, **reflecting**, **reflected**)
❶ throw back heat, light, or sound from a surface. ❷ (of a mirror) show an image of. ❸ show in a realistic or appropriate way. ❹ (**reflect well** or **badly on**) give a good or bad impression of. ❺ (**reflect on**) think seriously about.

reflection

reflective
reflectively
reflectivity

reflector

> ✓ -**or** at the end, not -**er**: **reflector**

reflects

reflex »*noun* (plural **reflexes**) an action done without conscious thought as a response to something.

» *adjective* ❶ done as a reflex. ❷ (of an angle) more than 180 degrees.

reflex camera »*noun* a camera in which the image given by the lens is reflected by an angled mirror to the viewfinder.

reflexive »*adjective* (in grammar) referring back to the subject of a clause or verb, e.g. *myself* in the clause *I hurt myself*.
reflexively
reflexivity

reflexology »*noun* a system of massage used to relieve tension and treat illness.
reflexologist

refocus (verb: **refocuses**, **refocusing**, **refocused**)

> ✓ do not double the s in **refocusing** and **refocused**

reform »*verb* (**reforms**, **reforming**, **reformed**)
❶ change something to improve it.
❷ make someone improve their behaviour.
» *noun* an act of reforming.
reformer

re-form »*verb* (**re-forms**, **re-forming**, **re-formed**) form again.

> ✓ don't forget the hyphen in **re-form** (**reform** means 'change something to improve it')

reformation »*noun* ❶ the action of reforming. ❷ (**the Reformation**) a 16th-century movement for reforming the Roman Catholic Church, that ended in the establishment of the Protestant Churches.

reformed

re-formed

Reformed Church »*noun* a Church that has accepted the principles of the Reformation, especially a Calvinist Church.

reformer

reforming

re-forming

reformist »*adjective* supporting gradual political or social reform.
» *noun* a supporter of such a policy.
reformism

reforms

re-forms

refract »*verb* (**refracts**, **refracting**, **refracted**) (of water, air, or glass) make a ray of light change direction when it enters at an angle.
refraction

refractive »*adjective* having to do with refraction.

refractor »*noun* a lens or other object which causes refraction.

refractory »*adjective* ❶ stubborn or difficult to control. ❷ (of an illness) not responding to treatment.

refracts

refrain[1] »*verb* (**refrains, refraining, refrained**) (**refrain from**) stop yourself from doing something.

refrain[2] »*noun* the part of a song that is repeated at the end of each verse.

refresh »*verb* (**refreshes, refreshing, refreshed**) give new strength or energy to.
refresher

refreshing
refreshingly

refreshment

refrigerant »*noun* a substance used for keeping things cold.

refrigerate (verb: **refrigerates, refrigerating, refrigerated**)
refrigeration

> ✓ there is no **d** in **refrigerate**, **refrigerates**, etc., or **refrigerator**

refrigerator

> ✓ **-or** not **-er** at the end: **refrigerator**

refuel (verb: **refuels, refuelling, refuelled**)

> ✓ double the **l** in **refuelling** and **refuelled** (the spellings **refueling** and **refueled** are American)

refuge »*noun* ❶ shelter from danger or trouble. ❷ a safe place.

refugee »*noun* a person who has been forced to leave their country because of a war or disaster or because they are being persecuted.

refulgent »*adjective* (a poetic term) shining very brightly.
– say ri-**ful**-juhnt
refulgence

refund (verb: **refunds, refunding, refunded**)
refundable

refurbish »*verb* (**refurbishes, refurbishing, refurbished**) redecorate and improve a building or room.
refurbishment

refuse[1] (verb: **refuses, refusing, refused**) [say no to; decline]
refusal

refuse[2] »*noun* things thrown away; rubbish.
– say ref-yooss

refute »*verb* (**refutes, refuting, refuted**) prove a statement or person to be wrong.
refutation

> ℹ strictly speaking, **refute** means 'prove wrong', although many people use it to mean 'deny'. If someone *refutes an allegation*, they don't simply deny it, they show it to be untrue.

regain (verb: **regains, regaining, regained**)

regal »*adjective* having to do with a king or queen, especially in being magnificent or dignified.
regality
regally

regale »*verb* (**regales, regaling, regaled**) ❶ entertain someone with conversation. ❷ supply someone generously with food or drink.

regalia »*noun* ❶ objects such as the crown and sceptre that are used at coronations or other state occasions. ❷ the distinctive clothing and objects of an order, rank, or office.
– say ri-**gay**-li-uh

regaling

regality

regally

regard »*verb* (**regards, regarding, regarded**) ❶ think of in a particular way. ❷ look steadily at.
»*noun* ❶ concern or care. ❷ high opinion; respect. ❸ a steady look. ❹ (**regards**) best wishes.

regarding »*preposition* about; concerning.

regardless »*adverb* ❶ (**regardless of**) without regard for. ❷ despite what is happening.

regards

regatta »*noun* a sporting event consisting of a series of boat or yacht races.

regency »*noun* (plural **regencies**) ❶ a period of government by a regent. ❷ (**the Regency**) the period when George, Prince of Wales, acted as regent in Britain (1811–20).
– say **ree**-juhn-si

> ✓ plural: drop the **y** and add **ies**: **regencies**

regenerate »*verb* (**regenerates, regenerating, regenerated**) ❶ bring new life or strength to. ❷ grow new tissue.
– say ri-**jen**-uh-rayt
regeneration
regenerative

regent »*noun* a person appointed to rule a state because the monarch is too young or unfit to rule, or is absent.

reggae »*noun* a style of popular music originating in Jamaica.
– SAY reg-gay

☑ **ae** not **ay** at the end: **reggae**

regicide »*noun* ❶ the killing of a king. ❷ a person who kills a king.
– SAY rej-i-syd

regime »*noun* ❶ a government, especially one that controls a state strictly. ❷ an ordered way of doing something; a system.
– SAY ray-zheem

☑ **regime** is sometimes written **régime**, with an acute accent over the first **e** (as in French)

regimen »*noun* a course of medical treatment, diet, or exercise.
– SAY rej-i-muhn

regiment »*noun* ❶ a permanent unit of an army. ❷ a large number of people or things.
»*verb* (**regiments**, **regimenting**, **regimented**) organize according to a strict system.
regimental
regimentation

Regina »*noun* the reigning queen.
– SAY ri-jy-nuh

ℹ **Regina** is Latin for 'queen', and is used mainly to refer to the Crown as a party in a legal case, e.g. *Regina v. Jones*, the Crown versus Jones

region

regional
regionally

regionalism »*noun* loyalty to your own region in cultural and political terms, rather than to central government.
regionalist

regionally

register »*noun* ❶ an official list or record. ❷ a particular part of the range of a musical instrument or voice. ❸ the level and style of a piece of writing or speech (e.g. informal, formal).
»*verb* (**registers**, **registering**, **registered**) ❶ enter in a register. ❷ put your name on a register. ❸ express an opinion or emotion. ❹ become aware of something. ❺ (of a measuring instrument) show a reading.

register office »*noun* (in the UK) a local government building where civil marriages are performed and births, marriages, and deaths are recorded.

ℹ the official term is **register office**, although the form **registry office** is commonly used in non-official contexts

registers

registrar »*noun* ❶ an official responsible for keeping official records. ❷ (in the UK) a hospital doctor undergoing training to be a specialist.

☑ don't forget the **r** before the **a**: **registrar**

registration »*noun* ❶ the action of registering. ❷ (also **registration number**) (in British English) the series of letters and figures shown on a vehicle's number plate.

registry »*noun* (plural **registries**) ❶ a place where registers are kept. ❷ registration.

☑ plural: drop the **y** and add **ies**: **registries**

registry office »*noun* a register office.

ℹ see the note at **REGISTER OFFICE**

Regius professor »*noun* (in the UK) the holder of a university chair founded by a sovereign or appointed by the Crown.
– SAY ree-ji-uhss

ℹ **Regius** is Latin for 'royal'

regress »*verb* (**regresses**, **regressing**, **regressed**) return to an earlier or less advanced state.
regression

regressive »*adjective* ❶ returning to an earlier or less advanced state. ❷ (of a tax) taking a proportionally greater amount from those on lower incomes.

regret (verb: **regrets**, **regretting**, **regretted**)

☑ double the **t** in **regretted** and **regretting**

regretful »*adjective* feeling or showing regret.
regretfully
regretfulness

ℹ do not confuse **regretful** with **regrettable**, which means 'giving rise to regret; undesirable'

☑ **-ful** not **-full**: **regretful**

regrettable »*adjective* giving rise to regret; undesirable.
regrettably

ℹ do not confuse **regrettable** with **regretful**, which means 'feeling or showing regret'

☑ double **t** in **regrettable**

regretted

regretting

regroup (verb: **regroups**, **regrouping**, **regrouped**)

regular
regularly

regularise another way of spelling REGULARIZE.

regularity (plural **regularities**)

> ☑ plural: drop the **y** and add **ies**: **regularities**

regularize »*verb* (**regularizes**, **regularizing**, **regularized**) ❶ make regular. ❷ make a temporary situation legal or official.
regularization

> ☑ many people prefer the alternative spellings **regularise**, **regularises**, etc., and **regularisation**: both **s** and **z** spellings are correct

regularly

regulate »*verb* (**regulates**, **regulating**, **regulated**) ❶ control the rate or speed of a machine or process. ❷ control or supervise by means of rules.

regulation »*noun* ❶ a rule made by an authority. ❷ the action of regulating.
» *adjective* of a familiar or expected type.

regulator

> ☑ **-or** not **-er** at the end: **regulator**

regulatory »*adjective* acting to regulate something: *a regulatory authority.*
– SAY reg-yuh-luh-tuh-ri or reg-yuh-**lay**-tuh-ri

regulo »*noun* (trademark) used before a number to indicate a setting on a temperature scale in a gas oven.
– SAY **reg**-yuu-loh

regurgitate »*verb* (**regurgitates**, **regurgitating**, **regurgitated**) ❶ bring swallowed food up again to the mouth. ❷ repeat information without understanding it.
– SAY ri-**ger**-ji-tayt
regurgitation

rehabilitate »*verb* (**rehabilitates**, **rehabilitating**, **rehabilitated**) ❶ help someone to get back to normal life after imprisonment or illness. ❷ restore the reputation of someone previously out of favour.
rehabilitation

> ☑ only one **l** in **rehabilitate**

rehash »*verb* (**rehashes**, **rehashing**, **rehashed**) reuse old ideas or material.

» *noun* a reuse of old ideas or material.

rehearsal

rehearse (verb: **rehearses**, **rehearsing**, **rehearsed**)

reheat (verb: **reheats**, **reheating**, **reheated**)

rehouse (verb: **rehouses**, **rehousing**, **rehoused**)

rehydrate »*verb* (**rehydrates**, **rehydrating**, **rehydrated**) add moisture to something dehydrated.
rehydration

reign »*verb* (**reigns**, **reigning**, **reigned**) ❶ rule as king or queen. ❷ be the dominant quality or aspect: *confusion reigned.* ❸ (**reigning**) currently holding a particular title in sport.
» *noun* ❶ the period of rule of a king or queen.

> ☑ remember the **g** in **reign** (**rein** refers to the strap used to control a horse)

reimburse »*verb* (**reimburses**, **reimbursing**, **reimbursed**) repay money to a person who has spent it.
– SAY ree-im-**berss**
reimbursement

rein »*noun* (usually **reins**) ❶ long, narrow straps used to control a horse. ❷ the power to direct and control something.
» *verb* (**reins**, **reining**, **reined**) ❶ control a horse by pulling on its reins. ❷ (**rein in** or **back**) restrain.

> ☑ there is no **g** in **rein** (**reign** means 'rule as king or queen')

reincarnate »*verb* (**be reincarnated**) be born again in another body.
– SAY ree-in-**kar**-nayt

reincarnation »*noun* ❶ the rebirth of a soul in a new body. ❷ a person in whom a soul is believed to have been born again.

reindeer (plural **reindeer** or **reindeers**)

reined

reinforce »*verb* (**reinforces**, **reinforcing**, **reinforced**) ❶ make stronger. ❷ strengthen a military force with additional personnel.
reinforcement

reinforced concrete »*noun* concrete in which metal bars or wire are embedded to strengthen it.

reinforcement

reinforces

reinforcing

reining

reins

reinstate »*verb* (**reinstates**, **reinstating**, **reinstated**) restore to a former position or

state.
reinstatement

reinterpret (verb: **reinterprets,
reinterpreting, reinterpreted**)
reinterpretation

reintroduce (verb: **reintroduces,
reintroducing, reintroduced**)
reintroduction

reinvent (verb: **reinvents, reinventing,
reinvented**)

reinvigorate »*verb* (**reinvigorates,
reinvigorating, reinvigorated**)give new
energy or strength to.

reissue (verb: **reissues, reissuing, reissued**)

> ☑ there is no **e** after the **u** in **reissuing**

reiterate »*verb* (**reiterates, reiterating,
reiterated**) say something again or
repeatedly.
reiteration

reject (verb: **rejects, rejecting, rejected**)
rejection

rejig »*verb* (**rejigs, rejigging, rejigged**)
rearrange.

> ☑ double **g** in **rejigging** and **rejigged**

rejoice (verb: **rejoices, rejoicing, rejoiced**)

rejoin[1] (verb: **rejoins, rejoining, rejoined**)
[join again]

rejoin[2] »*verb* (**rejoins, rejoining, rejoined**)
say in reply; retort.

rejoinder »*noun* a quick or witty reply.

rejoined

rejoining

rejoins

rejuvenate »*verb* (**rejuvenates,
rejuvenating, rejuvenated**) make someone
or something look younger or more
lively.
– **SAY** ri-joo-vuh-nayt
rejuvenation

rekindle »*verb* (**rekindles, rekindling,
rekindled**) ❶ relight a fire. ❷ revive
something.

relaid

relapse »*verb* (**relapses, relapsing,
relapsed**) ❶ become ill again after a
period of improvement. ❷ (**relapse into**)
return to a worse state.
» *noun* a return to ill health after a
temporary improvement.

relate (verb: **relates, relating, related**)
related
relatedness
relates

relating

relation

relationship

relative
relatively

relativism »*noun* the idea that truth,
morality, etc. exist in relation to other
things and are not absolute.
relativist

relativity »*noun* ❶ the state of being
relative; ability to be judged only in
comparison with something else. ❷ (in
physics) a description of matter, energy,
space, and time according to Albert
Einstein's theories.

relaunch (verb: **relaunches, relaunching,
relaunched**)

relax (verb: **relaxes, relaxing, relaxed**)

relaxant »*noun* a drug or other thing that
promotes relaxation.

relaxation

relaxed

relaxes

relaxing

relay[1] »*noun* ❶ a group of people or
animals that do something for a period of
time and are then replaced by a similar
group. ❷ a race between teams of
runners, each team member in turn
covering part of the total distance. ❸ an
electrical device which opens or closes a
circuit in response to a current in another
circuit. ❹ a device which receives,
strengthens, and transmits a signal again.
» *verb* (**relays, relaying, relayed**) ❶ receive
and pass on information. ❷ broadcast
something by means of a relay.

relay[2] »*verb* (**relays, relaying, relaid**) lay
something again or differently.

release (verb: **releases, releasing, released**)

relegate »*verb* (**relegates, relegating,
relegated**) ❶ place in a lower rank or
position. ❷ transfer a sports team to a
lower division of a league.
relegation

relent »*verb* (**relents, relenting, relented**)
❶ stop behaving in a harsh or cruel way.
❷ become less strong or severe.

relentless »*adjective* ❶ never ending;
oppressively constant. ❷ harsh or
inflexible.
relentlessly
relentlessness

relents

relevant »*adjective* closely connected or
appropriate to the current subject.

relevance
relevancy
relevantly

☑ ant not ent: **relevant**

reliable
reliability
reliableness
reliably

reliance »*noun* dependence on or trust in someone or something.
reliant

☑ ance not ence: **reliance**

relic »*noun* ❶ an object, custom, etc. that survives from an earlier time. ❷ a part of a holy person's body or belongings kept and considered holy after their death.

relict »*noun* an organism or other thing which has survived from an earlier period.
– SAY rel-ikt

☑ note the **t** on the end: **relict**

relied

relief

☑ the usual rule is **i** before **e** except after **c**: **relief**

relief map »*noun* a map indicating hills and valleys by shading.

relies

relieve (verb: **relieves, relieving, relieved**)

☑ like **relief, relieve** follows the usual rule: **i** before **e** except after **c**

religion

religiose »*adjective* excessively religious.
– SAY ri-lij-i-ohss
religiosity

religious
religiously
religiousness

relinquish »*verb* (**relinquishes, relinquishing, relinquished**) give up something, especially unwillingly.

reliquary »*noun* (plural **reliquaries**) a container for holy relics.
– SAY rel-i-kwuh-ri

relish »*noun* ❶ great enjoyment. ❷ pleasant anticipation. ❸ a highly flavoured sauce or pickle eaten with plain food to add flavour.
» *verb* (**relishes, relishing, relished**) ❶ enjoy something greatly. ❷ look forward to something.

relive »*verb* (**relives, reliving, relived**) live through an experience or feeling again in your mind.

reload (verb: **reloads, reloading, reloaded**)

relocate »*verb* (**relocates, relocating, relocated**) move your home or business to a new place.
relocation

reluctant »*adjective* unwilling and hesitant.
reluctance
reluctantly

☑ ant not ent: **reluctant**

rely »*verb* (**relies, relying, relied**) (**rely on**) ❶ depend on someone or something; trust someone or something. ❷ need or be dependent on someone or something.

remade past and past participle of REMAKE.

remain (verb: **remains, remaining, remained**)

remainder »*noun* ❶ a part, number, or amount that is left over. ❷ a part that is still to come. ❸ the number which is left over when one quantity does not exactly divide another.

remained

remaining

remains

remake (verb: **remakes, remaking, remade**)

remand »*verb* (**remands, remanding, remanded**) send a defendant to wait for their trial, either on bail or in jail.
» *noun* the state of being placed in custody.

remark (verb: **remarks, remarking, remarked**)

remarkable
remarkably

remarked

remarking

remarks

remaster »*verb* (**remasters, remastering, remastered**) make a new or improved sound recording from which other copies are made.

rematch

remedial »*adjective* ❶ intended as a remedy. ❷ provided for children with learning difficulties.

remedy »*noun* (plural **remedies**) ❶ a medicine or treatment for a disease or injury. ❷ a means of dealing with something undesirable.
» *verb* (**remedies, remedying, remedied**) put right an undesirable situation.

plural: drop the **y** and add **ies**: **remedies**

remember (verb: **remembers**, **remembering**, **remembered**)

remembrance

 br not **ber**, and **ance** not **ence**: **remembrance**

remind (verb: **reminds**, **reminding**, **reminded**)
reminder

reminisce »*verb* (**reminisces**, **reminiscing**, **reminisced**) think or talk about the past for enjoyment.
– SAY re-mi-**niss**

 isce not **iss**: **reminisce**

reminiscence »*noun* ❶ an account of something that you remember. ❷ the enjoyable remembering of past events.

reminiscent »*adjective* ❶ (**reminiscent of**) tending to remind you of something. ❷ absorbed in memories.
reminiscently

 the ending is **-scent** not **-sent**: **reminiscent**

reminisces

reminiscing

remiss »*adjective* not paying proper attention to duty.
– SAY ri-miss

remission »*noun* ❶ the cancellation of a debt, penalty, etc. ❷ the reduction of a prison sentence. ❸ a temporary lessening of the severity of disease. ❹ forgiveness of sins.

 single **m** but double **s**: **remission**

remit »*verb* (**remits**, **remitting**, **remitted**) ❶ cancel a debt or punishment. ❷ send money in payment. ❸ refer a matter for decision to an authority.
» *noun* the task officially given to an individual or organization.
– SAY ri-**mit** [verb], ree-mit [noun]

 double the **t** to spell **remitting** and **remitted**

remittance »*noun* ❶ a sum of money sent as payment. ❷ the action of remitting money.

remitted

remitting

remix »*verb* (**remixes**, **remixing**, **remixed**) produce a different version of a musical recording by altering the balance of the separate tracks.

» *noun* (plural **remixes**) a remixed recording.

remnant »*noun* ❶ a small remaining quantity of something. ❷ a piece of cloth left when the greater part has been used or sold.

 note the **mn** in the middle, and the ending is **ant** not **ent**: **remnant**

remonstrate »*verb* (**remonstrates**, **remonstrating**, **remonstrated**) make a strongly critical protest.
– SAY rem-uhn-strayt

remorse »*noun* deep regret or guilt for something wrong you have done.

remorseful »*adjective* filled with remorse or repentance.
remorsefully

 -ful not **-full**: **remorseful**

remorseless »*adjective* ❶ without remorse. ❷ (of something unpleasant) relentless.
remorselessly
remorselessness

remortgage »*verb* (**remortgages**, **remortgaging**, **remortgaged**) take out another or a different mortgage on a property.
» *noun* a different or additional mortgage.

 -gage not **-gauge**, and remember the **t**: **remortgage**

remote (adjective: **remoter**, **remotest**)
remotely
remoteness

remote control »*noun* ❶ control of a machine from a distance by means of signals transmitted from a radio or electronic device. ❷ a device that controls a machine in this way.
remote-controlled

remotely

remoteness

remoter

remotest

remould »*noun* a tyre which has had a new tread put on.

removable

removal

remove (verb: **removes**, **removing**, **removed**)
removable
remover

remunerate »*verb* (**remunerates**, **remunerating**, **remunerated**) pay someone for work they have done.
– SAY ri-**myoo**-nuh-rayt
remunerative

remuneration »*noun* money paid for work done.
remunerative

Renaissance »*noun* ❶ the revival of art and literature in the 14th–16th centuries. ❷ (**renaissance**) a period of renewed interest in something.
– SAY ri-**nay**-suhnss or ri-**nay**-sonss

> ✓ **renaissance** is a French word meaning 'rebirth': it has a single **n** before the **ai** and double **s** after it

Renaissance man »*noun* a man with a wide range of talents.

renal »*adjective* having to do with the kidneys.
– SAY **ree**-n'l

rename (verb: **renames, renaming, renamed**)

renascent »*adjective* becoming active again.
renascence

rend »*verb* (**rends, rending, rent**) (a poetic term) ❶ tear something to pieces. ❷ cause someone great emotional pain.

render »*verb* (**renders, rendering, rendered**) ❶ provide or give a service, help, etc. ❷ hand over for inspection, consideration, or payment. ❸ cause something or someone to be or become: *rendered speechless*. ❹ interpret or perform something artistically. ❺ melt down fat to separate out its impurities. ❻ cover a wall with a coat of plaster.

rendering »*noun* ❶ a performance of a piece of music or drama. ❷ a translation.
renders

rendezvous »*noun* (plural **rendezvous**) ❶ a meeting at an agreed time and place. ❷ a meeting place.
» *verb* (**rendezvouses, rendezvousing, rendezvoused**) meet at an agreed time and place.
– SAY **ron**-day-voo [singular], **ron**-day-voo or **ron**-day-vooz [plural], **ron**-day-vooz [rendezvouses], **ron**-day-voo-ing [rendezvousing], **ron**-day-vood [rendezvoused]

> ℹ **rendezvous** comes from a French phrase which means 'present yourselves!'

rending

rendition »*noun* a performance or version of a piece of music or drama.

rends

renegade »*noun* a person who deserts and betrays an organization, country, or set of principles.

» *adjective* having treacherously changed sides in a conflict.
– SAY **ren**-i-gayd

> ✓ **neg** not **nig**: **renegade**

renege »*verb* (**reneges, reneging, reneged**) go back on a promise, contract, etc.
– SAY ri-**nayg** or ri-**neeg**

> ✓ there is no **u** in **renege**, and the final **e** is dropped to spell **reneging**

renegotiate (verb: **renegotiates, renegotiating, renegotiated**)
renegotiable
renegotiation

renew (verb: **renews, renewing, renewed**)
renewable
renewal

rennet »*noun* curdled milk from the stomach of a calf, used in making cheese.
– SAY **ren**-nit

renounce »*verb* (**renounces, renouncing, renounced**) ❶ formally gives up a title, possession, etc. ❷ state that you no longer have a particular belief, allegiance, etc. ❸ abandon a cause, habit, etc.

renovate »*verb* (**renovates, renovating, renovated**) restore something old to a good state; repair.
– SAY **ren**-uh-vayt
renovation

> ✓ single **n**: **renovate**

renown »*noun* the state of being famous.
renowned

rent[1] (verb: **rents, renting, rented**) [payment to a landlord; pay rent for]

rent[2] »*noun* a large tear in a piece of fabric.

rent[3] past and past participle of **REND**.

rental

rented

renting

rents

renunciation »*noun* the action of renouncing or giving up something.

reoccupy (verb: **reoccupies, reoccupying, reoccupied**)

reoccur (verb: **reoccurs, reoccurring, reoccurred**)
reoccurrence

> ✓ double the **r** to spell **reoccurring**, **reoccurred**, and **reoccurrence**

reopen (verb: **reopens, reopening, reopened**)

r

reorder (verb: **reorders, reordering, reordered**)

reorganize (verb: **reorganizes, reorganizing, reorganized**)
reorganization

> ✓ many people prefer the alternative spellings **reorganise, reorganises**, etc., and **reorganisation**: both **s** and **z** spellings are correct

reorient »*verb* (**reorients, reorienting, reoriented**) ❶ change the focus or direction of something. ❷ (**reorient yourself**) find your bearings again.
reorientate
reorientation

rep »*noun* ❶ a representative. ❷ a repertory theatre or company.

repaid past and past participle of **REPAY**.

repair (verb: **repairs, repairing, repaired**)
repairable
repairer

repairman (plural **repairmen**)

repairs

reparable »*adjective* able to be repaired or put right.
– SAY rep-uh-ruh-b'l

> ✓ **par** not **pair**: reparable

reparation »*noun* ❶ something done to make up for a wrong. ❷ (**reparations**) compensation for war damage paid by a defeated country.
– SAY rep-uh-**ray**-sh'n

repartee »*noun* quick, witty comments or conversation.
– SAY rep-ar-**tee**

repast »*noun* a meal.
– SAY ri-**pahst**

repatriate »*verb* (**repatriates, repatriating, repatriated**) send someone back to their own country.
– SAY ree-**pat**-ri-ayt or ree-**pay**-tri-ayt
repatriation

repay (verb: **repays, repaying, repaid**)
repayable
repayment

repeal »*verb* (**repeals, repealing, repealed**) make a law or act of parliament no longer valid.
» *noun* the action of repealing.

repeat (verb: **repeats, repeating, repeated**)
repeatable
repeated
repeatedly
repeater

repel »*verb* (**repels, repelling, repelled**) ❶ drive back or away. ❷ be repulsive or distasteful to someone. ❸ force away something with a similar magnetic charge. ❹ (of a substance) resist mixing with something else: *good quality leather uppers to resist moisture.*

> ✓ double the **l** to spell **repelling** and **repelled**

repellent »*adjective* ❶ able to repel a particular thing: *water-repellent nylon.* ❷ causing disgust or distaste.
» *noun* ❶ a substance that deters insects. ❷ a substance used to treat something to make it repel water.
repellently

> ✓ **repellent** can also be spelled **repellant**

repelling

repels

repent »*verb* (**repents, repenting, repented**) feel sorry for something bad that you have done.
repentance
repentant

repercussions »*plural noun* the consequences of an event or action.

repertoire »*noun* the material known or regularly performed by a performer or company.
– SAY **rep**-er-twar

> ✓ remember the **r** in the middle, and the ending is **oire**: **repertoire** is a French word

repertory »*noun* (plural **repertories**) ❶ the performance by a company of various plays, operas, etc. at regular short intervals. ❷ a repertoire.
– SAY **rep**-er-tuh-ri

repetition

> ✓ **pet** not **pit**: repetition

repetitious »*adjective* having too much repetition; repetitive.
repetitiously
repetitiousness

repetitive
repetitively
repetitiveness

repetitive strain injury »*noun* a condition in which carrying out repetitive actions over long period of time causes pain in the muscles involved.

rephrase »*verb* (**rephrases, rephrasing, rephrased**) express something differently.

repine »*verb* (**repines, repining, repined**) be unhappy; fret.

replace (verb: **replaces, replacing, replaced**)
replaceable
replacement

replay (verb: **replays, replaying, replayed**)

replenish »*verb* (**replenishes, replenishing, replenished**) fill up a supply again after using some of it.
replenishment

replete »*adjective* ❶ (**replete with**) filled or well-supplied with. ❷ very full with food.
– **SAY** ri-**pleet**
repletion

replica »*noun* an exact copy or model of something.
– **SAY** rep-li-kuh

replicate »*verb* (**replicates, replicating, replicated**) make an exact copy of something.
– **SAY** rep-li-kayt
replication

reply (verb: **replies, replying, replied**; plural **replies**)

> ☑ plural: drop the **y** and add **ies: replies**

report (verb: **reports, reporting, reported**)

reportage »*noun* ❶ the reporting of news by the press and the broadcasting media. ❷ factual, journalistic presentation in a book.
– **SAY** rep-or-**tahzh** or ri-**por**-tij

reported

reported speech »*noun* a speaker's words reported by someone else who makes certain changes (e.g. *he said that he would go*, based on *I will go*), as opposed to *direct speech*.

reporter

reporting

reports

repose »*noun* a state of restfulness, peace, or calm.
»*verb* (**reposes, reposing, reposed**) ❶ rest. ❷ have confidence or trust in someone.

reposition »*verb* (**repositions, repositioning, repositioned**) adjust or alter the position of something.

repository »*noun* (plural **repositories**) ❶ a place or container for storage. ❷ a place where a lot of something is found.
– **SAY** ri-**poz**-i-tuh-ri

repossess »*verb* (**repossesses, repossessing, repossessed**) retake possession of something when a buyer fails to make the required payments.
repossession

> ☑ double **s** twice: **repossess**

reprehensible »*adjective* wrong or bad and deserving condemnation.
reprehensibly

> ☑ **-ible** not **-able: reprehensible**

represent (verb: **represents, representing, represented**)

representation »*noun* ❶ the action of representing. ❷ an image, model, etc. of something. ❸ (**representations**) statements or protests made to an authority.

representational »*adjective* ❶ relating to representation. ❷ (of art) depicting the physical appearance of things.

representative
representatively
representativeness

represented

representing

represents

repress »*verb* (**represses, repressing, repressed**) ❶ bring something under control by force. ❷ restrain, prevent, or inhibit something. ❸ suppress a thought or feeling.
repression

repressed »*adjective* ❶ oppressed. ❷ (of a thought or feeling) kept suppressed and unconscious in the mind. ❸ tending to suppress feelings and desires.

represses

repressing

repression

repressive »*adjective* obstructing or restraining personal freedom.
repressively
repressiveness

reprieve »*verb* (**reprieves, reprieving, reprieved**) cancel someone's punishment.
»*noun* ❶ the cancellation of a punishment. ❷ a short rest from difficulty or danger.

> ☑ the usual rule is **i** before **e** except after **c: reprieve**

reprimand »*noun* a formal expression of disapproval.
»*verb* (**reprimands, reprimanding, reprimanded**) formally express disapproval of someone; tell someone off.
– **SAY** rep-ri-mahnd

reprint (verb: **reprints, reprinting, reprinted**)

reprisal »*noun* an act of retaliation.
– **SAY** ri-**pry**-z'l

reprise »*noun* ❶ a repeated passage in music. ❷ a further performance of something.
» *verb* (**reprises, reprising, reprised**) repeat a piece of music or a performance.
– SAY ri-**preez**

> ✓ **reprise** cannot be spelled with an **ize** ending

reproach »*verb* (**reproaches, reproaching, reproached**) ❶ express disapproval of or disappointment with someone. ❷ (**reproach with**) accuse someone of something: *his wife reproached him with cowardice.*
» *noun* an expression of disapproval or disappointment.

reproachful »*adjective* expressing disapproval or disappointment.
reproachfully

> ✓ **-ful** not **-full**: reproachful

reproaching

reprobate »*noun* a person without moral principles.
» *adjective* unprincipled.
– SAY **rep**-ruh-bayt

reproduce (verb: **reproduces, reproducing, reproduced**)

reproduction
reproductive

reprographics »*plural noun* = REPROGRAPHY.

reprography »*noun* the science and practice of reproducing documents and graphic material.
– SAY ri-**prog**-ruh-fi

reproof »*noun* a criticism or reprimand.
– SAY ri-**proof**

reprove »*verb* (**reproves, reproving, reproved**) criticize or reprimand someone; tell someone off.

reptile
reptilian

republic »*noun* a state in which supreme power is held by the people and their elected representatives, and which has a president rather than a king or queen.

republican »*adjective* ❶ belonging to or characteristic of a republic. ❷ in favour of organizing a state as a republic. ❸ (**Republican**) (in the US) supporting the Republican Party.
» *noun* ❶ a person in favour of republican government. ❷ (**Republican**) (in the US) a member or supporter of the Republican Party. ❸ (**Republican**) a person who wants Ireland to be one republic.
republicanism

> in particular contexts, such as American or Irish politics, spell **Republican** with a capital **R**

repudiate »*verb* (**repudiates, repudiating, repudiated**) ❶ refuse to accept or be associated with someone or something. ❷ deny that something is true or valid.
– SAY ri-**pyoo**-di-ayt
repudiation

repugnance »*noun* great disgust.
– SAY ri-**pug**-nuhnss
repugnancy

repugnant »*adjective* extremely distasteful or unpleasant.

> ✓ **ant** not **ent**: repugnant

repulse »*verb* (**repulses, repulsing, repulsed**) ❶ drive back an attacking enemy by force. ❷ reject or refuse to accept something. ❸ make someone feel intense distaste or disgust.
» *noun* the action of repulsing.

repulsion »*noun* ❶ a feeling of intense distaste or disgust. ❷ a force by which objects tend to move push each other away.

repulsive »*adjective* ❶ arousing strong distaste or disgust. ❷ relating to repulsion between physical objects.
repulsively
repulsiveness

reputable »*adjective* having a good reputation.
– SAY **rep**-yuu-tuh-b'l
reputably

reputation »*noun* the beliefs or opinions that people generally hold about someone or something.

repute »*noun* ❶ the opinion that people have of someone or something. ❷ good reputation.
» *verb* ❶ (**be reputed**) have a particular reputation. ❷ (**reputed**) generally believed to exist: *the reputed flatness of the country.*
reputedly

request (verb: **requests, requesting, requested**)

requiem »*noun* ❶ a Christian Mass for the souls of dead people. ❷ a musical composition based on such a Mass.
– SAY **rek**-wi-uhm

require (verb: **requires, requiring, required**)
requirement
requires
requiring

requisite »*adjective* made necessary by circumstances or regulations.

» *noun* a thing that is needed for a particular purpose.
– SAY rek-wi-zit

requisition *»noun* ❶ an official order allowing property or materials to be taken or used. ❷ the taking of goods for military or public use.
» *verb* (**requisitions, requisitioning, requisitioned**) officially take possession of something, especially during a war.
– SAY rek-wi-**zi**-sh'n

reran past of RERUN.

reredos *»noun* (plural **reredos**) an ornamental screen at the back of an altar in a church.
– SAY reer-doss

re-release (verb: **re-releases, re-releasing, re-released**)

rerun (verb: **reruns, rerunning, reran**; past participle **rerun**)

resat past and past participle of RESIT.

reschedule (verb: **reschedules, rescheduling, rescheduled**)

rescind *»verb* (**rescinds, rescinding, rescinded**) cancel or repeal a law, etc.
– SAY ri-sind

rescue (verb: **rescues, rescuing, rescued**)
rescuer

☑ drop the **e** to spell **rescuing**

research (verb: **researches, researching, researched**)
researcher

research and development *»noun* (in industry) work directed towards new ideas and improvement of products and processes.

researched

researcher

researches

researching

resell (verb: **resells, reselling, resold**)

resemblance *»noun* ❶ the fact of resembling someone or something. ❷ a way in which things resemble each other.

☑ **ance** not **ence: resemblance**

resemble *»verb* (**resembles, resembling, resembled**) look like or be similar to something.

resent (verb: **resents, resenting, resented**) [feel bitter about something]

resentful
resentfully

☑ **-ful** not **-full: resentful**

resenting
resentment
resents
reservation
reserve (verb: **reserves, reserving, reserved**)

reserved *»adjective* slow to reveal emotion or opinions.
reservedly
reservedness

reserve price *»noun* the price named as the lowest acceptable by the seller for an item sold at auction.

reserves
reserving

reservist *»noun* a member of a military reserve force.

reservoir *»noun* ❶ a large lake used as a source of water supply. ❷ a place where fluid collects. ❸ a supply or source of something.

☑ remember the **r** before the **v: reservoir**

reset (verb: **resets, resetting, reset**)

☑ double the **t** to spell **resetting**

resettle (verb: **resettles, resettling, resettled**)
resettlement

reshuffle *»verb* (**reshuffles, reshuffling, reshuffled**) ❶ change around the positions of members of a team, especially government ministers. ❷ rearrange something.
» *noun* an act of reshuffling.

reside *»verb* (**resides, residing, resided**) ❶ live in a particular place. ❷ (of a right or legal power) belong to a person or group. ❸ (of a quality) be naturally present in something.

residence

☑ **ence** not **ance: residence**

residency *»noun* (plural **residencies**) ❶ the fact of living in a place. ❷ the time that an artist, musician, etc. spends working for a particular institution.

resident

residential *»adjective* ❶ designed for or relating to residence. ❷ providing accommodation in addition to other services. ❸ occupied by private houses.

resides
residing

residual »*adjective* remaining after the greater part has gone or been taken away.

residue »*noun* a small amount of something that remains after the main part has gone or been taken.

resign (verb: **resigns, resigning, resigned**)

resignation

resigned

resigning

resigns

resilient »*adjective* ❶ able to spring back into shape after bending, stretching, or being compressed. ❷ able to withstand or recover quickly from difficult conditions.
resilience
resiliently

> ✓ ent not ant: resili**ent**

resin »*noun* ❶ a sticky substance produced by some trees. ❷ a synthetic polymer used as the basis of plastics, adhesives, varnishes, etc.
– **SAY** rez-in
resinous

resist (verb: **resists, resisting, resisted**)

resistance »*noun* ❶ the action of resisting. ❷ a secret organization that fights against an enemy or authority. ❸ the impeding effect exerted by one thing on another. ❹ the ability not to be affected by something. ❺ the degree to which a material or device opposes the passage of an electric current.
resistant

> ✓ **ance** and **ant**, not **ence** and **ent**: resist**ance** and resist**ant**

resisted

resisting

resistor »*noun* (in physics) a device having resistance to the passage of an electric current.

> ✓ -or not -er: resist**or**

resists

resit »*verb* (**resits, resitting, resat**) take an examination again after failing.
» *noun* an examination held for this purpose.

> ✓ double the t in resi**tt**ing

resold

resolute »*adjective* determined.
– **SAY** rez-uh-loot
resolutely
resoluteness

resolution »*noun* ❶ a firm decision. ❷ a formal statement of opinion or intention by a law-making body. ❸ the quality of being resolute. ❹ the resolving of a problem or dispute. ❺ the process of reducing or separating something into its individual parts.

resolve »*verb* (**resolves, resolving, resolved**) ❶ settle or find a solution to a problem. ❷ decide firmly on a course of action. ❸ (of a law-making body) take a decision by a formal vote. ❹ (**resolve into**) reduce into separate elements.
» *noun* firm determination.

resonance »*noun* the quality of being resonant.

resonant »*adjective* ❶ (of sound) deep, clear, and ringing. ❷ (of a room, musical instrument, or hollow body) tending to prolong sounds. ❸ (**resonant with**) filled with. ❹ suggesting images, memories, or emotions.
resonantly

> ✓ ant not ent: reson**ant**

resonate »*verb* (**resonates, resonating, resonated**) make a deep, clear, ringing sound.
resonator

resort »*verb* (**resorts, resorting, resorted**) (**resort to**) adopt a strategy or course of action so as to resolve a difficult situation.
» *noun* ❶ a place visited for holidays or recreation. ❷ the action of resorting to something. ❸ a strategy or course of action.

resound »*verb* (**resounds, resounding, resounded**) ❶ fill or be filled with a ringing, booming, or echoing sound. ❷ (**resounding**) definite; unmistakable: *a resounding success.*
– **SAY** ri-zownd

resource »*noun* ❶ (**resources**) a stock or supply of materials or assets that can be drawn on when needed. ❷ (**resources**) a country's means of supporting itself, as represented by its minerals, land, and other assets. ❸ (**resources**) personal qualities that allow you to cope with difficult circumstances.
» *verb* (**resources, resourcing, resourced**) provide a person or place with resources.
– **SAY** ri-sorss or ri-zorss

> ✓ remember the u in the middle: reso**u**rce

resourceful »*adjective* able to find quick and clever ways to overcome difficulties.
resourcefully
resourcefulness

-ful not **-full: resourceful**

resources

resourcing

respect (verb: **respects, respecting, respected**)
respecter

respectable
respectability
respectably

respected

respecter

respectful
respectfully

 -ful not **-full: respectful**

respecting »*preposition* with reference to.

respective »*adjective* belonging or relating separately to each of two or more people or things.

respectively »*adverb* separately or individually and in the order already mentioned.

respects

respiration »*noun* ❶ the action of breathing. ❷ a single breath. ❸ (in biology) a process in living organisms involving the production of energy, typically with the intake of oxygen and the release of carbon dioxide.

respirator »*noun* ❶ an apparatus worn over the face to prevent the breathing in of dust, smoke, or other harmful substances. ❷ an apparatus used to provide artificial respiration.

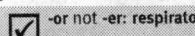 **-or** not **-er: respirator**

respiratory »*adjective* relating to respiration or the organs of respiration.
– SAY ri-**spi**-ruh-tuh-ri or **ress**-puh-ruh-tuh-ri

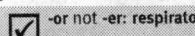 **tory** not **try: respiratory**

respiratory tract »*noun* the passage formed by the mouth, nose, throat, and lungs, through which air passes during breathing.

respire »*verb* (**respires, respiring, respired**)
❶ breathe. ❷ (of a plant) carry out respiration.

respite »*noun* a short period of rest or relief from something difficult or unpleasant.
– SAY **ress**-pyt or **ress**-pit

respite care »*noun* temporary care of a sick, elderly, or disabled person, providing relief for the person who usually looks after them.

resplendent »*adjective* attractive and impressive through being richly colourful or expensive-looking.
– SAY ri-**splen**-duhnt
resplendently

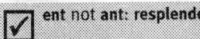 **ent** not **ant: resplendent**

respond (verb: **responds, responding, responded**)

respondent »*noun* ❶ an accused person in a lawsuit. ❷ a person who responds to a questionnaire or an advertisement.

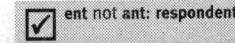 **ent** not **ant: respondent**

responding

responds

response

responsibility (plural **responsibilities**)

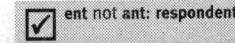 plural: drop the **y** and add **ies**: **responsibilities**

responsible
responsibly

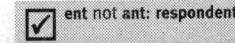 the ending is **-ible** not **-able**: **responsible** (and so also **responsibility**)

responsive »*adjective* responding readily and with enthusiasm.
responsively
responsiveness

rest (verb: **rests, resting, rested**)

restart (verb: **restarts, restarting, restarted**)

restaurant

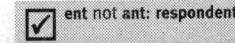 **taurant** not **traunt: restaurant**

restaurateur »*noun* a person who owns and manages a restaurant.
– SAY ress-tuh-ruh-**ter**

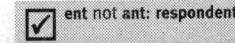 there is no **n** in **restaurateur** (it is a French word)

rested

restful
restfully

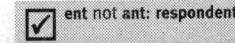 **-ful** not **-full: restful**

rest home »*noun* an institution where old or frail people live and are cared for.

resting

restitution »*noun* ❶ the restoration of something lost or stolen to its proper owner. ❷ payment for injury or loss.

restive »*adjective* unable to keep still or silent; restless.

restively
restiveness

restless
restlessly
restlessness

restoration »*noun* ❶ the returning of something to a former condition, place, or owner. ❷ the repair or renovation of a building, work of art, etc. ❸ the reinstatement of a previous practice, right, or situation. ❹ the return of a monarch to a throne, a head of state to government, or a regime to power. ❺ (**the Restoration**) the re-establishment of Charles II as King of England in 1660, or the period following this.

restorative »*adjective* having the ability to restore health, strength, or a feeling of well-being.
» *noun* a medicine or drink that restores health, strength, or well-being.

restore (verb: **restores, restoring, restored**)
restorer

restrain »*verb* (**restrains, restraining, restrained**) ❶ keep something under control or within limits. ❷ stop someone moving or acting as they wish.

restrained »*adjective* ❶ reserved or unemotional. ❷ not richly decorated or brightly coloured.

restraining

restrains

restraint »*noun* ❶ the action of restraining. ❷ a measure or condition that restrains. ❸ a device which limits or prevents freedom of movement. ❹ unemotional or controlled behaviour.

restrict (verb: **restricts, restricting, restricted**)

restricted »*adjective* ❶ limited in extent, number, or scope. ❷ not made public for reasons of national security.

restricting

restriction

restrictive »*adjective* preventing freedom of action or movement.
restrictively
restrictiveness

restricts

restroom »*noun* (in American English) a toilet in a public building.

restructure »*verb* (**restructures, restructuring, restructured**) ❶ organize something differently. ❷ convert a debt into another debt that is repayable at a later time.

rests

result (verb: **results, resulting, resulted**)

resultant »*adjective* occurring or produced as a result.

resulted

resulting

results

resume¹ »*verb* (**resumes, resuming, resumed**) ❶ begin again or continue after a pause or interruption. ❷ return to a seat or place.

resume² »*noun* ❶ a summary. ❷ (in American English) a curriculum vitae.
– SAY rez-yuu-may

> ✓ resume can also be spelled résumé, with acute accents on the **e**'s (as in the original French)

resumption »*noun* the action of beginning something again after an interruption.

resurface (verb: **resurfaces, resurfacing, resurfaced**)

resurgent »*adjective* becoming stronger or more popular again.
resurgence

> ✓ ent and ence, not ant and ance: resurgent and resurgence

resurrect »*verb* (**resurrects, resurrecting, resurrected**) ❶ restore someone to life. ❷ revive a practice, belief, etc.

> ✓ one s and two r's in the middle: resurrect

resurrection »*noun* ❶ the action of resurrecting. ❷ (**the Resurrection**) (in Christian belief) the time when Jesus rose from the dead.

resuscitate »*verb* (**resuscitates, resuscitating, resuscitated**) ❶ revive someone from unconsciousness. ❷ make something active or vigorous again.
– SAY ri-**suss**-i-tayt
resuscitation

> ✓ susc not suss: resuscitate

retail »*noun* the sale of goods to the general public.
» *adverb* being sold to the general public.
» *verb* (**retails, retailing, retailed**) ❶ sell goods by retail. ❷ (**retail at** or **for**) be sold by retail for a specified price.
retailer

retain »*verb* (**retains, retaining, retained**) ❶ keep possession of something. ❷ absorb and continue to hold a substance. ❸ keep something in place.

retainer »*noun* ❶ a thing that holds something in place. ❷ a fee paid in advance to a barrister to secure their services.

retaining

retains

retake »*verb* (**retakes, retaking, retook;** past participle **retaken**) ❶ take a test or examination again. ❷ regain possession of something.
» *noun* a test or examination that is retaken.

retaliate »*verb* (**retaliates, retaliating, retaliated**) make an attack or assault in return for a similar attack.
– SAY ri-**tal**-i-ayt
retaliation
retaliatory

retard »*verb* (**retards, retarding, retarded**) hold back the development or progress of someone or something.
» *noun* (used in an insulting way) a person with learning difficulties.
– SAY ri-**tard** [verb], ree-taard [noun]
retardation

retardant »*adjective* preventing or inhibiting: *fire-retardant polymers*.

 ant not ent: retardant

retarded »*adjective* (used in an insulting way) less developed mentally than is usual at a particular age.

retarding

retards

retch (verb: **retches, retching, retched**) [make the sound and movement of vomiting]

ℹ️ do not confuse **retch** with **wretch**, which means 'an unfortunate person'

retention »*noun* ❶ the action of retaining. ❷ failure to remove a substance from the body.

retentive »*adjective* (of a person's memory) effective in retaining facts and impressions.
retentively
retentiveness

rethink (verb: **rethinks, rethinking, rethought**)

reticent »*adjective* not revealing your thoughts or feelings readily.
– SAY **ret**-i-suhnt
reticence

 -cent not -sent: reticent

reticulated »*adjective* arranged or marked like a net or network.

retina »*noun* (plural **retinas** or **retinae**) a layer at the back of the eyeball containing cells that are sensitive to light and from which impulses are sent to the brain.
– SAY ret-i-nuh [singular], ret-i-nee [plural]

✓ the plural of **retina** can be **retinas** or **retinae** (as in the original Latin)

retinue »*noun* a group of advisers or assistants accompanying an important person.
– SAY **ret**-i-nyoo

 nue not new: retinue

retire (verb: **retires, retiring, retired**)
retired
retirement

retiring »*adjective* tending to avoid company; shy.

retook past of RETAKE.

retort[1] »*verb* (**retorts, retorting, retorted**) say something sharp or witty in answer to a remark or accusation.
» *noun* a sharp or witty reply.

retort[2] »*noun* ❶ a container or furnace for carrying out a chemical process on a large scale. ❷ (a historical term) a glass container with a long neck, used in distilling liquids and other chemical operations.

retouch »*verb* (**retouches, retouching, retouched**) improve or repair a painting, photograph, etc. by making slight additions or alterations.

retrace »*verb* (**retraces, retracing, retraced**) ❶ go back over the same route that you have just taken. ❷ discover and follow a route or course taken by someone else. ❸ trace something back to its source or beginning.

retract »*verb* (**retracts, retracting, retracted**) ❶ draw or be drawn back. ❷ withdraw a statement or accusation as untrue or unjustified. ❸ withdraw or go back on an undertaking or promise.
retractable
retraction

retrain »*verb* (**retrains, retraining, retrained**) teach or learn new skills.

retreat »*verb* ❶ (of an army) withdraw from confrontation with enemy forces. ❷ move back from a difficult situation. ❸ withdraw to a quiet or secluded place.
» *noun* ❶ an act of retreating. ❷ a quiet or secluded place. ❸ a quiet place where people go for a time to pray and meditate.

retrench »*verb* (**retrenches, retrenching, retrenched**) reduce costs or spending in response to economic difficulty.

retrial »*noun* a second or further trial.

retribution »*noun* severe punishment in revenge for something.
– SAY ret-ri-**byoo**-sh'n
retributive

retrieve »*verb* (retrieves, retrieves, retrieving) ❶ get or bring back something. ❷ (of a dog) find and bring back game that has been shot. ❸ find or extract information stored in a computer. ❹ rescue someone or something from a state of difficulty or collapse.
retrieval

> ✓ remember, **i** before **e**, except after **c**: **retrieve** follows the usual rule

retriever »*noun* a dog of a breed used for retrieving game.

retrieves

retrieving

retro »*adjective* imitative of a style from the recent past.

retroactive »*adjective* (especially of a law) taking effect from a date in the past.
retroactively

retrograde »*adjective* ❶ directed or moving backwards. ❷ making a situation worse.

retrogress »*verb* (retrogresses, retrogressing, retrogressed) go back to an earlier and typically inferior state.
– SAY ret-ruh-**gress**
retrogression

retrorocket »*noun* a small rocket on a spacecraft or missile, fired in the direction of travel to slow it down.

retrospect »*noun* (in retrospect) when looking back on a past event.

retrospective »*adjective* ❶ looking back on or dealing with past events or situations. ❷ (of an exhibition) showing the development of an artist's work over a period of time.
» *noun* a retrospective exhibition.
retrospectively

retrousse »*adjective* (of a person's nose) turned up at the tip.
– SAY ruh-**troo**-say

> ✓ **retrousse** can also be spelled **retroussé**, with an acute accent above the final **e** (as in the original French word meaning 'tucked up')

return (verb: returns, returning, returned)
returnable
returner

returnee »*noun* a person returning to work after a long absence.

returner

returning

returns

reunify »*verb* (reunifies, reunifying, reunified) restore political unity to a country.
reunification

reunion

reunite (verb: reunites, reuniting, reunited)

reuse »*verb* (reuses, reusing, reused) use something again or more than once.
– SAY ree-**yooz**
reusable

rev »*noun* (revs) the number of revolutions of an engine per minute.
» *verb* (revs, revving, revved) increase the running speed of an engine by pressing the accelerator.

> ✓ double the **v** in **revving** and **revved**

revamp »*verb* (revamps, revamping, revamped) give new and improved form, structure, or appearance to something.
» *noun* a new and improved version.

reveal (verb: reveals, revealing, revealed)

revealing
revealingly

reveals

reveille »*noun* a military waking signal sounded on a bugle, drum, etc.
– SAY ri-**val**-li

> ✓ **e** before **i** in the middle, and **ille** at the end: **reveille** (a French word)

revel »*verb* (revels, revelling, revelled) ❶ enjoy yourself in a lively and noisy way. ❷ (revel in) gain great pleasure from something.
» *noun* (revels) lively and noisy festivities.
reveller

> ✓ double the **l** in **revelling**, **revelled**, and **reveller** (the spellings **reveling**, **reveled**, and **reveler** are American)

revelation »*noun* ❶ the revealing of something previously unknown. ❷ a surprising or remarkable thing.

revelatory »*adjective* revealing something previously unknown.
– SAY rev-uh-**lay**-tuh-ri or rev-uh-luh-**tuh**-ri

revelled

reveller

revelling

revelry »*noun* (plural revelries) lively and noisy celebrations.

> ✓ plural: drop the **y** and add **ies**: **revelries**

revels

revenge (verb: **revenges, revenging, revenged**)

revengeful »*adjective* eager for revenge.

 -ful not -full: revengeful

revenges

revenging

revenue »*noun* ❶ the income received by an organization. ❷ a state's annual income, received from taxes.

 nue not new: revenue

reverberate »*verb* (**reverberates, reverberating, reverberated**) ❶ (of a loud noise) be repeated as an echo. ❷ have continuing serious effects.
reverberation

revere »*verb* (**reveres, revering, revered**) respect or admire someone deeply.
– SAY ri-**veer**

reverence »*noun* deep respect.

reverend »*adjective* a title or form of address to members of the Christian clergy.

reverent »*adjective* showing deep respect.
reverential
reverently

 ent not ant: reverent

reveres

reverie »*noun* a daydream.
– SAY rev-uh-ri

 ie not y: reverie

revering

revers »*noun* (plural **revers**) the turned-back edge of a garment which reveals the underside.
– SAY ri-**veer** [singular], ri-**veer** or ri-**veerz** [plural]

 no e at the end: revers is a French word

reversal

reverse (verb: **reverses, reversing, reversed**)
reverser
reversible

reversion »*noun* a return to a previous state.

revert »*verb* (**reverts, reverting, reverted**) return to a previous state or condition.

review (verb: **reviews, reviewing, reviewed**) [formal examination or critical assessment of something]
reviewer

i do not confuse a **review** with a **revue**, which is a light theatrical show

revile »*verb* (**reviles, reviling, reviled**) criticize someone in a rude or scornful way.

revise »*verb* (**revises, revising, revised**) ❶ examine and alter text. ❷ reconsider and change an opinion. ❸ reread previous work in order to prepare for an examination.

✓ revise cannot be spelled with an ize ending

revision

revitalize »*verb* (**revitalizes, revitalizing, revitalized**) give new life and vitality to someone or something.
revitalization

✓ many people prefer the alternative spellings **revitalise, revitalises**, etc., and **revitalisation**: both s and z spellings are correct

revival

revive »*verb* (**revives, reviving, revived**) ❶ restore someone to or regain life, consciousness, or strength. ❷ restore interest in or the popularity of something.

revivify »*verb* (**revivifies, revivifying, revivified**) give new life or vigour to someone or something.
– SAY ri-**viv**-i-fI

reviving

revoke »*verb* (**revokes, revoking, revoked**) make a decree, law, etc. no longer valid.
revocation

✓ change the k in revoke to a c in revocation

revolt »*verb* (**revolts, revolting, revolted**) ❶ rebel against or defy an authority. ❷ cause someone to feel disgust.
» *noun* an act of rebellion or defiance.

revolting
revoltingly

revolts

revolution »*noun* ❶ the overthrow of a government or social order by force, in favour of a new system. ❷ a dramatic and far-reaching change. ❸ motion in orbit or in a circular course around a central point. ❹ the single completion of an orbit or rotation.

revolutionary »*adjective* ❶ involving or causing dramatic change. ❷ engaged in, promoting, or relating to political revolution.
» *noun* (plural **revolutionaries**) a person who introduces a major change or who starts or supports a political revolution.

☑ **ary** not **ery: revolutionary**
plural: drop the **y** and add **ies:**
revolutionaries

revolutionize »*verb* (**revolutionizes,
revolutionizing, revolutionized**) change
something completely or fundamentally.

☑ many people prefer the alternative
spellings **revolutionise, revolutionises,**
etc.: both **s** and **z** spellings are correct

revolve (verb: **revolves, revolving, revolved**)

revolver »*noun* a pistol with revolving
chambers enabling several shots to be
fired without reloading.

revolves

revolving

revs

revue »*noun* a light theatrical
entertainment of short sketches, songs,
and dances.

ℹ do not confuse a **revue** with a **review,**
which is a formal examination or
critical assessment of something

revulsion »*noun* a sense of disgust and
loathing.

revved

revving

reward (verb: **rewards, rewarding, rewarded**)

rewarding
rewardingly

rewards

rewind (verb: **rewinds, rewinding, rewound**)

rewire (verb: **rewires, rewiring, rewired**)

rework »*verb* (**reworks, reworking,
reworked**) alter, revise, or reshape
something.

rewound past and past participle of
REWIND.

rewrite (verb: **rewrites, rewriting, rewrote;**
past participle **rewritten**)

rhapsodic

rhapsodies

rhapsodize »*verb* (**rhapsodizes,
rhapsodizing, rhapsodized**) express great
enthusiasm about someone or something.

☑ many people prefer the alternative
spellings **rhapsodise, rhapsodises,**
etc.: both **s** and **z** spellings are correct

rhapsody »*noun* (plural **rhapsodies**) ❶ an
expression of great enthusiasm or joy.
❷ an emotional piece of music in one
extended movement.
rhapsodic

☑ remember that **rhapsody** begins with
rha, not **ra**
plural: drop the **y** and add **ies: rhapsodies**

rhea »*noun* a large flightless South
American bird, resembling a small ostrich
with greyish-brown plumage.
– SAY ree-uh

rhenium »*noun* a rare silvery-white
metallic element.
– SAY ree-ni-uhm

rheostat »*noun* an instrument used to
control the current in an electrical circuit
by varying the amount of resistance in it.
– SAY ree-uh-stat

rhesus factor »*noun* a substance occurring
on red blood cells which can cause disease
in a newborn baby whose blood contains
the factor while the mother's blood does
not.
– SAY ree-suhss

rhesus monkey »*noun* a kind of small
brown monkey with red skin on the face
and rump.

rhetoric »*noun* ❶ the art of effective or
persuasive speaking or writing.
❷ persuasive language that is empty or
insincere.
– SAY **ret**-uh-rik

rhetorical »*adjective* ❶ relating to or
concerned with rhetoric. ❷ intended to
persuade or impress. ❸ (of a question)
asked for effect or to make a statement
rather than to obtain an answer.
– SAY ri-**torr**-i-k'l
rhetorically

rheumatic »*adjective* relating to or
suffering from rheumatism.
– SAY roo-**mat**-ik

rheumatic fever »*noun* an acute fever
with inflammation and pain in the joints.

rheumatism »*noun* a disease with
inflammation and pain in the joints and
muscles.

rheumatoid »*adjective* relating to or like
rheumatism.
– SAY **roo**-muh-toyd

rhinestone »*noun* an imitation diamond.

rhino (plural **rhino** or **rhinos**)

rhinoceros (plural **rhinoceros** or
rhinoceroses)

☑ **rhin** not **rin, ros** not **rous: rhinoceros**

rhinoplasty »*noun* (plural **rhinoplasties**)
plastic surgery performed on the nose.
– SAY **ry**-noh-plass-ti

rhinos

rhizome »*noun* a horizontal underground plant stem bearing both roots and shoots.
– SAY ry-zohm

rho »*noun* the seventeenth letter of the Greek alphabet (Ρ, ρ).

rhodium »*noun* a hard, dense silvery-white metallic element.
– SAY roh-di-uhm

rhododendron »*noun* a shrub with large clusters of showy trumpet-shaped flowers.
– SAY roh-duh-**den**-druhn

 rhodo not rhoda: rhododendron

rhombi plural of RHOMBUS.

rhombohedron »*noun* (plural **rhombohedra** or **rhombohedrons**) a three-dimensional shape whose faces are six equal rhombuses.
– SAY rom-buh-**hee**-druhn

the plural can be either **rhombohedra** (like the original Greek) or **rhombohedrons**

rhomboid »*adjective* having or resembling the shape of a rhombus.
»*noun* a quadrilateral of which only the opposite sides and angles are equal.
– SAY rom-boyd

rhombus »*noun* (plural **rhombuses** or **rhombi**) a shape like the diamond on a playing card, having four straight sides of equal length forming two opposite acute angles and two opposite obtuse angles.
– SAY rom-buhss [singular], rom-bI [plural]

the plural of **rhombus** can be **rhombuses** or **rhombi** (as in Latin)

rhubarb

 rhu not roo: rhubarb

rhumba another way of spelling RUMBA.

rhyme (verb: **rhymes, rhyming, rhymed**) [word ending with the same sound as another; short poem]

do not confuse **rhyme** with **rime**, which is a poetic word for 'hoar frost'

rhyming slang »*noun* a type of slang that replaces words with rhyming words, often with the rhyming element omitted (e.g. *butcher's*, short for *butcher's hook*, meaning 'look').

rhythm

remember the first **h**, following the **r**, and place the **y** before the **th**, not after: **rhythm**. The word has no normal vowels.

rhythmic »*adjective* ❶ having or relating to rhythm. ❷ happening regularly.

rhythmical
rhythmically

rib (verb: **ribs, ribbing, ribbed**)

 double the **b** in **ribbing** and **ribbed**

ribald »*adjective* humorous in a coarse way.
– SAY **ri**-buhld or **ry**-bawld
ribaldry

only one **b**: **ribald**

riband »*noun* (an old word) a ribbon.
– SAY **ri**-buhnd

ribbed

ribbing

ribbon

ribcage

ribonucleic acid »*noun* = RNA.
– SAY ry-boh-nyoo-**klay**-ik

ribs

rice

ricepaper »*noun* thin edible paper made from the pith of a shrub, used in oriental painting and in baking biscuits and cakes.

rich (adjective: **richer, richest**)
richly
richness

riches

richest

richly

richness

Richter scale »*noun* a scale for expressing the severity of an earthquake.
– SAY **rik**-ter

named after the American geologist Charles F. *Richter*

rick[1] »*noun* a stack of hay, corn, or straw.

rick[2] »*noun* a slight sprain or strain.
»*verb* (**ricks, ricking, ricked**) strain part of your body slightly.

rickets »*noun* a disease of children in which the bones become soft and distorted.

rickety

ricking

ricks

rickshaw »*noun* a light two-wheeled vehicle pulled by a person walking or riding a bicycle, chiefly used in Asian countries.

ricochet »*verb* (**ricochets, ricocheting, ricocheted**) (of a bullet or other fast-moving object) rebound off a surface.

» **noun ❶** a shot or hit that ricochets. **❷** the action of ricocheting.
– **SAY** ri-kuh-shay [noun], ri-kuh-shayz [ricochets], ri-kuh-shay-ing [ricocheting], ri-kuh-shayd [richocheted]

> ✓ do not double the **t** to spell **ricocheting** or **ricocheted**

ricotta »**noun** a soft white Italian cheese.
– **SAY** ri-kot-tuh

> ✓ single **c** but double **t**: **ricotta** is an italian word which means 'cooked twice'

rictus »**noun** (plural **rictuses**) a fixed grimace or grin.
– **SAY** rik-tuhss

rid (verb: **rids, ridding, rid**)

> ✓ double the **d** to spell **ridding** the past tense is **rid**, not **ridded**, which is old-fashioned

riddance

> ✓ **ance** not **ence**: **riddance**

ridden past participle of RIDE.

ridding [as in *ridding himself of bad habits*]

riddle[1] »**noun ❶** a cleverly worded question that is asked as a game. **❷** a puzzling person or thing.

riddle[2] »**verb** (**riddles, riddling, riddled**) **❶** make a lot of holes in something. **❷** (**riddled**) filled with something undesirable.
» **noun** a large coarse sieve.

ride (verb: **rides, riding, rode**; past participle **ridden**)

rider
    riderless

rides

ridge
    ridged

ridgeway »**noun** a road or track along a ridge.

ridicule (verb: **ridicules, ridiculing, ridiculed**)

ridiculous
    ridiculously
    ridiculousness

riding [as in *riding horses*]

rids

Riesling »**noun ❶** a variety of grape grown especially in Germany and Austria. **❷** a dry white wine made from this grape.
– **SAY** reez-ling or reess-ling

> ✓ **i** before **e**: **Riesling**. The spelling with **Rei**, and the corresponding

pronunciation of the first syllable as *rye*, is incorrect.

rife »**adjective ❶** (especially of something undesirable) widespread. **❷** (**rife with**) full of.
    rifeness

riff »**noun** a short repeated phrase in popular music or jazz.

riffle »**verb** (**riffles, riffling, riffled**) **❶** turn over pages quickly and casually. **❷** (**riffle through**) search through something quickly.
» **noun** an act of riffling.

riff-raff

rifle »**noun** a gun with a long spirally grooved barrel.
» **verb** (**rifles, rifling, rifled**) **❶** search through something hurriedly to find or steal something. **❷** hit or kick a ball hard and straight.

rifleman (plural **riflemen**)

rifles

rifling

rift »**noun ❶** a crack, split, or break. **❷** a serious break in friendly relations.

rig »**verb** (**rigs, rigging, rigged**) **❶** fit sails and rigging on a boat. **❷** set up a device or structure. **❸** (**rig out**) provide with clothes of a particular type. **❹** secretly arrange something in a dishonest way to gain an advantage.
» **noun ❶** an apparatus or device for a particular purpose. **❷** a large piece of equipment for extracting oil or gas from the ground. **❸** the arrangement of a boat's sails and rigging.

rigger »**noun** a ship rigged in a particular way: *a square-rigger*.

rigging »**noun ❶** the system of ropes or chains supporting a ship's masts. **❷** the ropes and wires supporting the structure of an airship, biplane, parachute, etc.

right (verb: **rights, righting, righted**)
    rightmost
    rightness
    rightwards

right angle »**noun** an angle of 90 degrees, as in a corner of a square.
    right-angled

right ascension »**noun** (in astronomy) the position of a point in the sky equivalent to longitude on the earth.

righted

righteous »**adjective** morally right or good.
– **SAY** ry-chuhss

> ✓ **eous** not **ious**: **righteous**

rightful
  rightfully
  rightfulness

> -ful not -full: rightful

right-handed

right-hander

righting

rightly

right-minded »*adjective* having sound views and principles.

rightmost

rightness

right of way »*noun* ❶ the legal right to go through someone's property along a specific route. ❷ a public path through someone's property. ❸ the right to proceed before another vehicle.

rights

rightward

rightwards

right wing »*noun* a conservative or reactionary section of a political party or system.
  right-winger

rigid »*adjective* ❶ unable to bend or be forced out of shape. ❷ (of a person) stiff and unmoving. ❸ not able to be changed or adapted.
  rigidity
  rigidly

> ✓ the only d in rigid is at the end

rigmarole »*noun* a lengthy and complicated procedure.
– SAY rig-muh-rohl

> ✓ the ending is -role not -roll: rigmarole

rigor American spelling of RIGOUR.

rigor mortis »*noun* stiffening of the joints and muscles a few hours after death.
– SAY ri-ger mor-tiss

> ℹ️ rigor mortis is a Latin phrase which means 'stiffness of death'

rigorous »*adjective* ❶ extremely thorough or accurate. ❷ (of a rule, system, etc.) strictly applied or adhered to. ❸ harsh or severe: *rigorous military training.*
  rigorously
  rigorousness

> ✓ there is no u after the first o in rigorous (but there is one in rigour)

rigour »*noun* ❶ the quality of being rigorous. ❷ (**rigours**) difficult or extreme conditions.

> ✓ -our not -or: rigour (the spelling rigor is American)

rigs

rile »*verb* (**riles, riling, riled**) annoy or irritate someone.

Riley »*noun* (**the life of Riley**) a luxurious or carefree existence.

riling

rill »*noun* a small stream.

rim (verb: **rims, rimming, rimmed**)
  rimless
  rimmed

> ✓ double the m to spell rimming and rimmed

rime »*noun* (a poetic term) hoar frost.
– SAY rym
  rimy

> ℹ️ do not confuse rime with rhyme referring to the rhyming of word in poetry

rimless

rimmed

rimming

rims

rimy

rind
  rinded
  rindless

ring[1] (verb: **rings, ringing, ringed**) [circular band; surround]
  ringed

> ✓ see the note at WRING

ring[2] (verb: **rings, ringing, rang**; past participle **rung**) [make a clear sound; an act of ringing]

ring binder »*noun* a binder with ring-shaped clasps that can be opened to pass through holes in paper.

ringed

ringer »*noun* (in informal English) a person's or thing's double.

ring-fence »*verb* (**ring-fences, ring-fencing, ring-fenced**) guarantee that funds for a particular purpose will not be spent on anything else.

ringing
  ringingly

ringleader »*noun* a person who leads a forbidden activity.

ringlet »*noun* a corkscrew-shaped curl of hair.

ringmaster »*noun* the person who directs a circus performance.

ring pull »*noun* a ring on a can that you pull to open it.

ring road »*noun* a road encircling a town.

rings

ringside »*noun* the area beside a boxing ring or circus ring.

ringworm »*noun* a skin disease that causes small, itchy circular patches, caused by various fungi.

rink »*noun* ❶ an enclosed area of ice for skating, ice hockey, or curling. ❷ an enclosed floor for roller skating. ❸ the strip of a bowling green used for a match.

rinse (verb: **rinses**, **rinsing**, **rinsed**)

> ✓ **se** not **ce**: **rinse**

riot (verb: **riots**, **rioting**, **rioted**)
rioter

riotous »*adjective* ❶ involving public disorder. ❷ involving wild and uncontrolled behaviour.
riotously
riotousness

riots

RIP »*abbreviation* rest in peace.

> ℹ **RIP** was originally short for the Latin phrase *requiescat in pace* (often used on gravestones)

rip (verb: **rips**, **ripping**, **ripped**) [tear; a long tear]
ripper

> ✓ double the **p** to spell **ripping**, **ripped**, and **ripper**

riparian »*adjective* of or on the banks of a river.
– **SAY** ri-**pair**-i-uhn

ripcord »*noun* a cord that is pulled to open a parachute.

> ✓ -**cord** not -**chord**: **ripcord**

ripe (adjective: **riper**, **ripest**)
ripely
ripeness

ripen (verb: **ripens**, **ripening**, **ripened**)

ripeness

ripening

ripens

riper

ripest

rip-off

riposte »*noun* a quick clever reply.
– **SAY** ri-**posst**

> ✓ note the **e** at the end: **riposte**

ripped

ripper

ripping

ripple (verb: **ripples**, **rippling**, **rippled**)
ripply

rip-roaring »*adjective* full of energy.

rips

rise (verb: **rises**, **rising**, **rose**; past participle **risen**; plural **rises**)
riser

risible »*adjective* causing laughter.
– **SAY** **ri**-zi-b'l
risibility
risibly

rising

rising damp »*noun* moisture absorbed from the ground into a wall.

risk (verb: **risks**, **risking**, **risked**)

risky (adjective: **riskier**, **riskiest**)
riskily
riskiness

> ✓ drop the **y** and add **ier** or **iest** to spell **riskier** or **riskiest**

risotto »*noun* (plural **risottos**) an Italian dish of rice cooked in stock with ingredients such as meat or seafood.
– **SAY** ri-**zot**-toh

> ✓ single **s** but double **t**: **risotto** the plural of **risotto** has **os** not **oes**: **risottos**

risque »*adjective* slightly indecent or rude.
– **SAY** riss-**kay** or **riss**-kay

> ✓ **risque** can also be spelled **risqué**, with an acute accent over the **e** (as in the original French)

rissole »*noun* a mixture of meat and spices, coated in breadcrumbs and fried.

rite »*noun* ❶ a religious or other solemn procedure. ❷ a set religious act characteristic of a Church.

ritual »*noun* ❶ a ceremony that involves a series of actions performed in a set order. ❷ something that is habitually done in the same way.
» *adjective* relating to or done as a ritual.
ritualistic
ritually

ritzy »*adjective* (**ritzier**, **ritziest**) (in informal English) expensively stylish.

> ℹ from *Ritz*, a name associated with luxury hotels

rival (verb: **rivals**, **rivalling**, **rivalled**)
rivalrous
rivalry

double the **l** to spell **rivalling** and **rivalled**

riven »*adjective* torn apart.

river

riverbank

rivet »*noun* a short metal pin or bolt for holding together two metal plates.
» *verb* (**rivets**, **riveting**, **riveted**) ❶ join or fasten something with a rivet or rivets. ❷ (**be riveted**) be completely intent or absorbed.
– SAY **ri**-vit
   riveter

 do not double the **t** to spell **riveting** or **riveted**

riviera »*noun* a coastal area of a warm country, especially that of southern France and northern Italy.
– SAY ri-vi-**air**-uh

ℹ️ **riviera** is an Italian word which means 'seashore'

rivulet »*noun* a very small stream.
– SAY **riv**-yuu-lit

RNA »*noun* a substance in living cells which carries instructions from DNA.

ℹ️ **RNA** is short for *ribonucleic acid*

roach[1] »*noun* (plural **roach**) a common freshwater fish of the carp family.

roach[2] »*noun* (plural **roaches**) (in informal English) a cockroach.

road

roadblock

roadholding »*noun* the ability of a moving vehicle to remain stable.

roadhouse »*noun* a pub, club, or restaurant on a country road.

roadie »*noun* a person who sets up and maintains equipment for a pop or rock group.

road rage »*noun* violent anger caused by conflict with the driver of another vehicle.

roadrunner »*noun* a fast-running long-tailed bird found from the southern US to Central America.

roadshow »*noun* ❶ a show broadcast from a different place each day. ❷ a touring political or promotional campaign.

roadside

roadster »*noun* an open-top car with two seats.

roadway

roadworks

roadworthy
   roadworthiness

roam (verb: **roams**, **roaming**, **roamed**)

roan »*adjective* (of a horse) having a bay, chestnut, or black coat with hairs of another colour.
» *noun* a roan horse.

roar (verb: **roars**, **roaring**, **roared**)

roaring
   roaringly

roars

roast (verb: **roasts**, **roasting**, **roasted**)
   roasting

rob (verb: **robs**, **robbing**, **robbed**)
   robber

 double the **b** to spell **robbing**, **robbed**, and **robber**

robbery (plural **robberies**)

 plural: drop the **y** and add **ies**: **robberies**

robbing

robe (verb: **robes**, **robing**, **robed**)

robin

✓ there is only one **b**: **robin**

robing

robot »*noun* a machine capable of carrying out a complex series of actions automatically.

robotic
   robotically

robotics »*plural noun* the science of designing, constructing, and using robots.

robs

robust »*adjective* ❶ sturdy or able to withstand difficult conditions. ❷ strong and healthy. ❸ uncompromising and forceful.
   robustly
   robustness

rock (verb: **rocks**, **rocking**, **rocked**)

rockabilly »*noun* a type of popular music that combines rock and roll and country music.

rock-bottom

rock crystal »*noun* transparent quartz.

rocked

rocker

rockery »*noun* (plural **rockeries**) an arrangement of rocks in a garden with plants growing between them.

 plural: drop the **y** and add **ies**: **rockeries**

r

rocket[1] (verb: **rockets, rocketing, rocketed**) [projectile that can be launched to great height; increase very rapidly]

> ✓ do not double the **t** to spell **rocketing** and **rocketed**

rocket[2] »*noun* a plant similar to lettuce, eaten in salads.

rocketry »*noun* the branch of science and technology concerned with rockets.

rockets

rockier

rockiest

rocking

rock 'n' roll

rocks

rock salt »*noun* ordinary salt occurring naturally as a mineral.

rocky (adjective: **rockier, rockiest**)

rococo »*adjective* in a highly decorated style of European furniture or architecture of the 18th century.
– SAY ruh-**koh**-koh

> ✓ there are two single **c**'s: **rococo**

rod

rode past of RIDE.

rodent »*noun* a mammal of a large group including rats, mice, and squirrels.

rodeo »*noun* (plural **rodeos**) a contest or entertainment in which cowboys show their skills.
– SAY roh-di-oh or roh-**day**-oh

> ✓ the plural of **rodeo** (a Spanish word) has **os** not **oes**: **rodeos**

roe »*noun* the eggs or sperm of a fish, used as food.

roebuck »*noun* a male roe deer.

roe deer »*noun* a small deer with a coat that is reddish in summer.

roentgen »*noun* a unit of ionizing radiation.
– SAY runt-yuhn or rernt-yuhn

> ✓ **roentgen** can also be spelled **röntgen**, with an umlaut over the **o** (it is named after the German physicist Wilhelm Conrad *Röntgen*, who discovered X-rays)

roger »*exclamation* your message has been received and understood (used in radio communication).
» *verb* (**rogers, rogering, rogered**) (vulgar) (of a man) have sex with someone.

rogue

rogues' gallery »*noun* a collection of photographs of known criminals.

roguish
   roguishly
   roguishness

roil »*verb* (**roils, roiling, roiled**) ❶ make a liquid muddy by disturbing the sediment. ❷ (of a liquid) move in a turbulent way.

roister »*verb* (**roisters, roistering, roistered**) enjoy yourself a noisy, lively way.
– SAY **roy**-ster

role [an actor's part]

> ℹ do not confuse **role** with **roll**, which means 'move by turning over and over; a rolling movement'

> ✓ **role** can also be spelled **rôle**, with a circumflex accent over the **o** (as in French)

role model »*noun* a person looked to by others as an example to be imitated.

roll (verb: **rolls, rolling, rolled**) [move by turning over and over; a rolling movement]

> ℹ do not confuse **roll** with **role**, which means 'an actor's part in a play'

roll-call

rolled

roller

rollerball »*noun* a ballpoint pen using a thin ink.

Rollerblade »*noun* (trademark) an in-line skate.
   rollerblader

roller coaster

roller skate
   roller skating

rollicking »*adjective* cheerfully lively and amusing.
» *noun* a severe telling-off.

> ✓ **rollicking** can also be spelled **rollocking** when it means 'a telling-off'

rolling

rolling stock »*noun* locomotives, carriages, or other vehicles used on a railway.

rollmop »*noun* a rolled uncooked pickled herring fillet.

rollocking see ROLLICKING.

roll-on

roll-on roll-off »*adjective* referring to a ferry in which vehicles are driven directly on at the start of the voyage and driven off at the end of it.

rollover

rolls

roly-poly »*noun* a hot pudding made of suet pastry covered with jam and rolled up.

» *adjective* round and plump.

ROM »*abbreviation* (in computing) read-only memory.

Roman

Roman Catholic »*adjective* having to do with the Christian Church which has the pope as its head.

» *noun* a member of the Roman Catholic Church.

Roman Catholicism

Romance »*noun* French, Spanish, Italian, and other languages descended from Latin.

romance (verb: romances, romancing, romanced)

romancer »*noun* a person who tends to exaggerate wildly or tell elaborate lies.

romances

romancing

Romanesque »*adjective* of a style of architecture common in Europe 900–1200, with massive vaulting and round arches.

– SAY roh-muh-**nesk**

 que at the end: **Romanesque**

Romanian

the older spellings **Rumanian** and **Roumanian** are still sometimes used

Romanies

Roman numerals »*plural noun* the letters representing numbers in the Roman numerical system: I = 1, V = 5, X = 10, L = 50, C = 100, D = 500, M = 1,000.

romantic »*adjective* ❶ having to do with love or romance. ❷ thinking about or showing life in an idealized rather than realistic way. ❸ (**Romantic**) relating to the artistic and literary movement of Romanticism.

» *noun* ❶ a person with romantic beliefs or attitudes. ❷ (**Romantic**) a writer or artist of the Romantic movement.

romantically

romanticise another way of spelling **ROMANTICIZE**.

romanticism »*noun* a literary and artistic movement which began in the late 18th century and emphasized creative inspiration and individual feeling.

romanticize »*verb* (**romanticizes, romanticizing, romanticized**) make something seem more attractive and

inspiring than it really is.

romanticization

many people prefer the alternative spellings **romanticise, romanticises,** etc., and **romanticisation**: both **s** and **z** spellings are correct

Romany »*noun* (plural **Romanies**) ❶ the language of the gypsies. ❷ a gypsy.

plural: drop the **y** and add **ies**: **Romanies**

Romeo »*noun* (plural **Romeos**) an attractive, passionate male lover.

i **Romeo** is the hero of Shakespeare's *Romeo and Juliet*

romp (verb: romps, romping, romped)

rompers »*plural noun* a young child's one-piece outer garment.

romping

romps

rondeau »*noun* (plural **rondeaux**) a poem of ten or thirteen lines with only two rhymes throughout and with the opening words used twice as a refrain.

– SAY ron-doh [singular and plural] or ron-dohz [plural]

the plural of **rondeau** is **rondeaux** (as in the original French)

rondo »*noun* (plural **rondos**) a piece of music with a recurring leading theme.

– SAY ron-doh

röntgen another way of spelling **ROENTGEN**.

rood »*noun* a crucifix.

rood screen »*noun* a screen of wood or stone separating the nave from the chancel of a church.

roof (plural **roofs**; verb: **roofs, roofing, roofed**)

i although the plural **rooves** is sometimes used, the form **roofs** is now much more common

roofer »*noun* a person who builds or repairs roofs.

roofing

roofless

roofs

rooftop

rook[1] »*noun* a kind of crow that nests in colonies in treetops.

rook[2] »*noun* a chess piece that can move in any direction along a rank or file on which it stands.

rookery »*noun* (plural **rookeries**) ❶ a collection of rooks' nests high in a clump of trees. ❷ a breeding place of seabirds.

rookie »*noun* a new recruit or member.

> ✓ **ie** not **y** at the end: **rookie**

room (verb: **rooms, rooming, roomed**)
roomier
roomiest
roominess
rooming
room-mate
rooms
roomy (adjective: **roomier, roomiest**)
  roominess
roost (verb: **roosts, roosting, roosted**)
rooster
roosting
roosts
root (verb: **roots, rooting, rooted**)
  rootless
root canal »*noun* a cavity in the root of a tooth.
rooted
rooting
rootless
root mean square »*noun* (in mathematics) the square root of the arithmetic mean of the squares of a set of values.
roots
rootstock »*noun* ❶ a rhizome. ❷ a plant on to which another variety is grafted.
rooves see ROOF.
rope (verb: **ropes, roping, roped**)
ropy »*adjective* (**ropier, ropiest**)
  ❶ resembling a rope. ❷ (in informal English) poor in quality or health.
  ropiness

> ✓ **ropy** can also be spelled with an **e**: **ropey**

rorqual »*noun* one of a group of whales including the blue whale.
– SAY ror-kwuhl
rosary »*noun* (plural **rosaries**) a string of beads used by some Roman Catholics for keeping count of how many prayers they have said.
– SAY roh-zuh-ri
rose[1] [flower]
rose[2] past of RISE.
rose[3] »*noun* light pink wine made from red grapes, coloured by only brief contact with the skins.
– SAY roh-zay

> ✓ often written with an acute accent on the final **e**: **rosé** (as in French)

rosebud
rose-coloured
rose hip »*noun* = HIP[2].
rosemary »*noun* an evergreen shrub with sweet-smelling leaves which are used as a herb in cooking.
rose-tinted
rosette »*noun* ❶ a rose-shaped decoration made of ribbon, worn by supporters of a sports team or political party or awarded as a prize. ❷ a design or object resembling a rose.

> ✓ **tte** at the end: **rosette** is a French word meaning 'little rose'

rose water »*noun* scented water made with rose petals.
rose window »*noun* a circular window with a branching rose-like pattern.
rosewood »*noun* the wood of a tropical tree used for making furniture and musical instruments.
Rosh Hashana »*noun* the Jewish New Year festival.
– SAY rosh huh-**shah**-nuh

> ✓ **Rosh Hashana** can also be written with an **h** at the end: **Rosh Hashanah**

rosier
rosiest
rosin »*noun* a kind of resin that is rubbed on the bows of stringed instruments.
roster »*noun* ❶ a list of people's names and the jobs they have to do at a particular time. ❷ a list of sports players available for team selection.
  »*verb* (**rosters, rostering, rostered**) put a person's name on a roster.
rostrum »*noun* (plural **rostra** or **rostrums**) a platform on which a person stands to make a speech, receive a prize, or conduct an orchestra.
– SAY ross-truhm [singular], ross-truh [plural]

> ✓ the plural can be either **rostra** (like the original Latin) or **rostrums**

rosy (adjective: **rosier, rosiest**)
rot (verb: **rots, rotting, rotted**)
rota »*noun* a list of names and days or times, given to people who are to share a task or tasks.
Rotarian »*noun* a member of Rotary.
  »*adjective* relating to Rotary.
rotary »*adjective* ❶ revolving around a centre or axis. ❷ having a rotating part or parts.

» *noun* (**Rotary**) a worldwide charitable society of business and professional people organized into local Rotary clubs.

rotate (verb: **rotates**, **rotating**, **rotated**)

rotation
rotational

rotator

 -**or** not -**er**: **rotator**

rotatory

rotavator »*noun* (trademark) a machine with rotating blades for breaking up or tilling the soil.

rote »*noun* regular repetition of something to be learned.

rotisserie »*noun* a rotating spit for roasting meat.
– SAY roh-**tiss**-uh-ri

rotor »*noun* ❶ the rotating part of a turbine, electric motor, or other device. ❷ a hub with a number of blades spreading out from it that is rotated to provide the lift for a helicopter.

 -**or** at the end, not -**er**: **rotor**

rots

rotted

rotten
rottenness

 do not forget to double the **n** in **rottenness**

rotten borough »*noun* (a historical term) (before the Reform Act of 1832) a borough that was able to elect an MP though having very few voters.

rottenness

rotter »*noun* (old-fashioned) an unkind or unpleasant person.

rotting

Rottweiler »*noun* a large, powerful breed of dog.
– SAY rot-vy-ler or rot-wy-ler

 ei not **ie**: **Rottweiler** (named after the town of *Rottweil* in Germany)

rotund »*adjective* rounded and plump.
– SAY roh-**tund**
rotundity

rotunda »*noun* a round building or room.
– SAY roh-**tun**-duh

rotundity

rouble »*noun* the basic unit of money of Russia.
– SAY **roo**-b'l

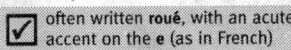 **rouble** can also be spelled **ruble**

roue »*noun* a man who leads an immoral life.
– SAY **roo**-ay

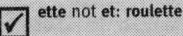 often written **roué**, with an acute accent on the **e** (as in French)

rouge »*noun* a red powder or cream used for colouring the cheeks.
– SAY roo*zh*

rough (adjective: **rougher**, **roughest**; verb: **roughs**, **roughing**, **roughed**)
roughly
roughness

roughage »*noun* material in cereals, fruit, and vegetables that cannot be digested and that helps to keep the bowels working.

roughcast »*noun* plaster of lime, cement, and gravel, used on outside walls.

roughed

roughen (verb: **roughens**, **roughening**, **roughened**)

rougher

roughest

rough-hewn »*adjective* (of a person) impolite or uncultured.

roughing

roughly

roughneck »*noun* ❶ (in informal English) a rough, impolite person. ❷ a person who works on an oil rig.

roughness

roughs

roughshod »*adjective* (**ride roughshod over**) take action without considering someone's needs or wishes.

ℹ️ **roughshod** is an old word referring to horses having shoes with nail heads projecting to prevent slipping

roulade »*noun* a piece of meat, sponge, etc., spread with a filling and rolled up.
– SAY roo-**lahd**

✓ **ade** at the end: **roulade**

roulette »*noun* a gambling game in which a ball is dropped on to a revolving wheel with numbered compartments.

✓ **ette** not **et**: **roulette**

Roumanian older spelling of **ROMANIAN**.

round (adjective: **rounder**, **roundest**; verb: **rounds**, **rounding**, **rounded**)
roundish

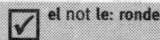 there is a difference in use between **round** and **around**: **round** tends to be used for definite, specific movement, as in *she turned round*, whereas **around** is used in contexts which are less definite (as in *she wandered around for ages* or *costing around £3,000*). Either word can be used in sentences such as *she put her arm round him* and *she put her arm around him*. In American English **around** is the normal form in most contexts.

roundabout

rounded

roundel »*noun* a small disc or circular design.
– SAY rown-d'l

✓ **el** not **le**: **rondel**

rounder

rounders

roundest

Roundhead »*noun* (a historical term) a supporter of the Parliamentary party in the English Civil War.

rounding

roundish

roundly »*adverb* ❶ in a firm or thorough way. ❷ in a circular shape.

round robin »*noun* ❶ a tournament in which each competitor plays in turn against every other. ❷ a petition.

rounds

round-table »*adjective* (of talks or a meeting) at which parties meet on equal terms for discussion.

round-up »*noun* ❶ an orderly gathering together of people or things. ❷ a summary of facts or events.

roundworm »*noun* a parasitic worm found in the intestines of animals.

rouse »*verb* (**rouses, rousing, roused**) ❶ wake someone up. ❷ stir someone to action or excitement.
– SAY rowz

rousing »*adjective* stirring.
rousingly

roustabout »*noun* an unskilled or casual labourer.
– SAY rowsst-uh-bowt

rout »*noun* ❶ a disorderly retreat of defeated troops. ❷ a decisive defeat.
» *verb* (**routs, routing, routed**) ❶ defeat utterly and force to retreat. ❷ cut a groove in a surface. ❸ rummage.
– SAY rowt

route (verb: **routes, routeing** or **routing, routed**) [way taken in getting from a starting point to a destination; send along a specified course]

✓ remember the **e** at the end of **route** (**rout** refers to a disorderly retreat of defeated troops)

routed

router »*noun* a power tool with a shaped cutter, used in carpentry.
– SAY row-ter

routes

routine
routinely

routing

routs

roux »*noun* (plural **roux**) a mixture of butter and flour used in making sauces.
– SAY roo

✓ remember the **x** at the end: **roux** is a French word

rove »*verb* (**roves, roving, roved**) ❶ travel constantly without a fixed destination. ❷ (of eyes) look around in all directions.
rover

row¹ [a number of people or things in a more or less straight line.]

row² (verb: **rows, rowing, rowed**) [move a boat through water with oars]
rower

row³ (verb: **rows, rowing, rowed**) [an angry quarrel; have an angry quarrel]

rowan »*noun* a small tree with white flowers and red berries.
– SAY roh-uhn or row-uhn

rowdy (adjective: **rowdier, rowdiest**; plural **rowdies**)
rowdily
rowdiness
rowdyism

rowed

rowing

rowlock »*noun* a fitting on the side of a boat for holding an oar.
– SAY rol-luhk

rows

royal
royally

Royal Commission »*noun* (in the UK) a commission of inquiry appointed by the Crown on the recommendation of the government.

royalist »*noun* ❶ a person who supports the system of having a king or queen. ❷ (a historical term) a supporter of the King

against Parliament in the English Civil War.
royalism

royal jelly *»noun* a substance produced by honeybee workers and fed by them to larvae which are being raised as potential queen bees.

royally

royalty *»noun* (plural **royalties**) ❶ the members of a royal family. ❷ the status or power of a king or queen. ❸ a sum paid for the use of a patent or to an author or composer for each copy of a work sold or each time it is performed.

> ✓ plural: drop the **y** and add **ies**: **royalties**

RSVP *»abbreviation* please reply.

> ℹ short for the French phrase *répondez s'il vous plaît*

rub (verb: **rubs, rubbing, rubbed**)

rubato *»noun* (plural **rubatos** or **rubati**) (in music) temporary disregard for strict tempo to allow an expressive quickening or slackening.
– **SAY** ruu-**bah**-toh [singular], ruu-**bah**-ti [plural]

> ✓ the plural can be either **rubati** (as in Italian) or **rubatos**

rubbed

rubber
  rubbery

rubberneck (in informal English) *»noun* a person who turns to look at something as they pass it.
»verb (**rubbernecks, rubbernecking, rubbernecked**) turn to look at something.

rubber plant *»noun* an evergreen tree of SE Asia with large dark green shiny leaves.

rubber-stamp *»verb* (**rubber-stamps, rubber-stamping, rubber-stamped**) approve automatically without proper consideration.

rubbery

rubbing

rubbish (verb: **rubbishes, rubbishing, rubbished**)
  rubbishy

rubble

rubella *»noun* a disease that is spread by a virus, with symptoms like mild measles.
– **SAY** ruu-**bel**-luh

Rubicon *»noun* a point of no return.
– **SAY** **roo**-bi-k'n or **roo**-bi-kon

> ℹ the *Rubicon* was a stream marking a boundary between Italy and Gaul; by

leading his army across it, Julius Caesar caused a civil war

rubicund *»adjective* having a red complexion.
– **SAY** roo-bi-kuhnd

rubidium *»noun* a rare soft silvery reactive metallic element.
– **SAY** ruu-**bid**-i-uhm

rubies

Rubik's cube *»noun* (trademark) a puzzle in the form of a plastic cube covered with multicoloured squares.
– **SAY** **roo**-biks

> ✓ **bik** not **brik**: Rubik (named after its Hungarian inventor, Erno *Rubik*)

ruble another way of spelling **ROUBLE**.

rubric *»noun* ❶ a heading on a document. ❷ a set of instructions or rules.
– **SAY** roo-**brik**

> ✓ remember the **r** after the **b**: rubric. Nothing to do with *Rubik's cube*.

rubs

ruby (plural **rubies**)

> ✓ plural: drop the **y** and add **ies**: **rubies**

ruby wedding *»noun* the fortieth anniversary of a wedding.

ruche *»noun* a frill or pleat of fabric.
– **SAY** roosh
  ruched

ruck *»noun* ❶ (in rugby) a loose scrum formed around a player with the ball on the ground. ❷ a crowd of people. ❸ (in British English) a noisy fight. ❹ a crease.
»verb (**rucks, rucking, rucked**) ❶ (in rugby) take part in a ruck. ❷ (often **ruck up**) form creases or folds.

ruckle (verb: **ruckles, ruckling, ruckled**)

rucks

rucksack

ruckus *»noun* (plural **ruckuses**) a row or commotion.
– **SAY** **ruk**-uhss

ruction *»noun* (in informal English) ❶ a disturbance or quarrel. ❷ (**ructions**) trouble.

rudder

rudderless *»adjective* lacking direction; not knowing what to do.

ruddy (adjective: **ruddier, ruddiest**)

rude (adjective: **ruder, rudest**)
  rudely
  rudeness

rudimentary *»adjective* ❶ involving only basic matters or facts. ❷ undeveloped.

– SAY roo-di-**men**-tuh-ri

> ✓ ary not ery: rudimentary

rudiments »*plural noun* ❶ the essential matters or facts relating to a subject. ❷ a basic form of something.
– SAY **roo**-di-muhntz

rue »*verb* (rues, rueing or ruing, rued) bitterly regret a past event or action.

> ✓ rueing can also be spelled without an e: ruing

rueful »*adjective* expressing regret.
ruefully

> ✓ -ful not -full: rueful

rueing

rues

ruff »*noun* ❶ a frill worn round the neck. ❷ a ring of feathers or hair round the neck of a bird or mammal.

ruffian »*noun* a rough or lawless person.

ruffle (verb: ruffles, ruffling, ruffled)

rufous »*adjective* reddish brown in colour.
– SAY **roo**-fuhss

> ✓ ous at the end: rufous

rug

rugby

rugged »*adjective* ❶ having a rocky surface. ❷ tough and determined. ❸ (of a man) having attractively masculine features.
ruggedly
ruggedness

rugger »*noun* (in informal English) rugby.

ruin (verb: ruins, ruining, ruined)

ruination »*noun* the process of ruining something.

ruined

ruing see the note at RUE.

ruining

ruinous »*adjective* ❶ disastrous or destructive. ❷ in ruins.
ruinously

ruins

rule (verb: rules, ruling, ruled)
ruler

rum¹ [an alcoholic spirit]

rum² »*adjective* (rummer, rummest) (old-fashioned) peculiar.

> ✓ double the m in rummer and rummest

Rumanian older spelling of ROMANIAN.

rumba »*noun* a rhythmic dance with Spanish and African elements, or a ballroom dance based on it.

> ✓ rumba can also be spelled with an h before the u: rhumba

rumble (verb: rumbles, rumbling, rumbled)

rumble strip »*noun* one of a series of raised strips set in a road to warn drivers to slow down.

rumbling

rumbustious »*adjective* (in informal English) high-spirited or difficult to control.
– SAY rum-**buss**-chuhss

> ✓ tious not tous at the end: rumbustious

ruminant »*noun* an animal that chews the cud, such as a cow, sheep, deer, or giraffe.

ruminate »*verb* (ruminates, ruminating, ruminated) ❶ think deeply about something. ❷ (of an animal) chew the cud.

ruminative »*adjective* thinking deeply about things.
– SAY **roo**-mi-nuh-tiv

rummage (verb: rummages, rummaging, rummaged)

rummer [more rum]

rummest

rummy »*noun* a card game in which the players try to form sets and sequences of cards.

rumour »*noun* a piece of information spread among a number of people which is unconfirmed or may be false.
» *verb* (be rumoured) be spread as a rumour.

> ✓ there are two u's in rumour (the spelling rumor is American)

rump »*noun* ❶ the hind part of the body of a mammal. ❷ a small piece left over from something larger.

rumple (verb: rumples, rumpling, rumpled)
rumpled

rumpus »*noun* (plural rumpuses) a noisy disturbance.

run (verb: runs, running, ran; past participle run)

> ✓ double the n in running

runabout »*noun* a small car.

runaround »*noun* (give someone the runaround) treat someone badly by giving them misleading information.

runaway

rundown »*noun* a brief summary.

» *adjective* (**run-down**) **①** in a poor or neglected state. **②** tired and rather unwell.

rune »*noun* **①** a letter of an ancient Germanic alphabet. **②** a symbol with mysterious or magical significance.
– say roon
runic

rung[1] [a horizontal support on a ladder]
rung[2] past participle of RING[2].

runic

run-in

runnel »*noun* **①** a gutter. **②** a stream.

runner

runner bean »*noun* a climbing bean plant with scarlet flowers and long green edible pods.

runner-up (plural **runners-up**)

> ✓ make the plural by adding **s** after **runner**, not after **up**: runners-up

runnier

runniest

running

running battle »*noun* a battle which does not occur at a fixed place.

running board »*noun* a footboard extending along the side of a vehicle.

running head »*noun* a heading printed at the top of each page of a book or chapter.

runny (adjective: **runnier**, **runniest**)

> ✓ drop the **y** and add **ier** or **iest** to spell **runnier** or **runniest**

run-off »*noun* a further contest after a clear winner has not emerged in a previous one.

run-of-the-mill »*adjective* ordinary.

runs

runt »*noun* the smallest animal in a litter.
runtish

run-through

runtish

run-up

runway

rupee »*noun* the basic unit of money of India, Pakistan, and some other countries.

rupture »*verb* (**ruptures**, **rupturing**, **ruptured**) **①** break or burst suddenly. **②** (**be ruptured** or **rupture yourself**) suffer a hernia in the abdomen. **③** disturb good relations.
» *noun* **①** an instance of rupturing. **②** a hernia in the abdomen.

rural »*adjective* having to do with the countryside rather than the town.

ruse »*noun* an action intended to deceive someone.
– say rooz

rush[1] (verb: **rushes**, **rushing**, **rushed**) [dash, hurry; a sudden quick movement]

rush[2] »*noun* a marsh or waterside plant, some kinds of which are used for matting, baskets, etc.

rusk »*noun* a dry biscuit eaten by babies.

russet »*adjective* reddish brown.
» *noun* **①** a reddish-brown colour. **②** a variety of dessert apple with a slightly rough greenish-brown skin.

Russian

rust (verb: **rusts**, **rusting**, **rusted**)

rustic »*adjective* **①** having to do with life in the country. **②** simple and charming in a way seen as typical of the countryside. **③** (of furniture) made of rough branches or timber.
» *noun* (mainly used in an insulting way) an unsophisticated country person.
rustically
rusticity

rusticate »*verb* (**rusticates**, **rusticating**, **rusticated**) **①** suspend a student from a university as a punishment. **②** shape stonework in large blocks with sunken joints and a roughened surface.
– say russ-ti-kayt

rusticity

rustier [more rusty]

rustiest

rustily

rustiness

rusting

rustle (verb: **rustles**, **rustling**, **rustled**)
rustler

rustproof »*adjective* not able to be corroded by rust.
» *verb* (**rustproofs**, **rustproofing**, **rustproofed**) make something rustproof.

rusts

rusty (adjective: **rustier**, **rustiest**)
rustily
rustiness

rut[1] [deep track made by wheels of passing vehicles]

rut[2] »*noun* an annual period of sexual activity in some animals, during which the males fight each other for access to the females.
» *verb* (**ruts**, **rutting**, **rutted**) engage in such activity.

> double the **t** in **rutting** and **rutted**

ruthenium »*noun* a hard silvery-white metallic chemical element.
– SAY ruu-**thee**-ni-uhm

ruthless »*adjective* having no sympathy or pity.
ruthlessly
ruthlessness

ruts
rutted
rutting

Rwandan [of Rwanda]

 Rw not **Ru:** Rwanda, Rwandan

rye »*noun* **❶** a cereal plant which grows in poor soils and low temperatures. **❷** whisky in which much of the grain used in producing it is rye.

ryegrass »*noun* a grass used for fodder and lawns.

Ss

sabbatarian »*noun* a strict observer of the sabbath.
» *adjective* relating to the observance of the sabbath.
– SAY sa-buh-**tair**-i-uhn
sabbatarianism

sabbath »*noun* a day intended for rest and religious worship, kept by Jews from Friday evening to Saturday evening, and by most Christians on Sunday.

 sabbath is a Hebrew word meaning 'to rest'

sabbatical »*noun* a period of paid leave granted to a university teacher for study or travel.
– SAY suh-**bat**-i-k'l

saber American spelling of SABRE.

sable »*noun* **❶** a weasel-like forest animal native to Japan and Siberia. **❷** the dark brown fur of the sable.
» *adjective* (an old term) black.
– SAY rhymes with table

sabotage »*verb* (sabotages, sabotaging, sabotaged) deliberately destroy or damage something.
» *noun* the action of sabotaging.
– SAY sab-uh-tah*zh*

 one **b**, one **t:** sabotage

saboteur »*noun* a person who sabotages something.
– SAY sab-uh-**ter**

 eur not **er:** saboteur is a French word

sabre »*noun* **❶** a heavy sword with a curved blade and a single cutting edge.

❷ a light fencing sword with a tapering curved blade.
– SAY **say**-ber

 re not **er:** sabre (the spelling **saber** is American)

sabretooth »*noun* (plural sabretooths) a large extinct member of the cat family with massive curved upper canine teeth.
sabre-toothed

sac »*noun* a hollow, flexible structure in the body or a plant, resembling a bag or pouch and containing liquid or air.

saccharin »*noun* a sweet-tasting synthetic substance used as a low-calorie substitute for sugar.
– SAY **sak**-kuh-rin

 cch in the middle: saccharin

saccharine »*adjective* **❶** sweet or sentimental. **❷** relating to or containing sugar.
– SAY **sak**-kuh-rin or **sak**-kuh-reen

sacerdotal »*adjective* relating to priests.
– SAY sass-er-**doh**-t'l or sak-er-**doh**-t'l

sachet »*noun* a small sealed bag or packet containing a small quantity of something.
– SAY **sa**-shay

 do not confuse **sachet** (originally a French word meaning 'little bag') with **sashay**, which means 'swing the hips from side to side when walking'

sack[1] (verb: sacks, sacking, sacked) [a large bag; dismiss someone from employment]
sackable

sack² »*verb* (**sacks, sacking, sacked**) (in the past) enter by force, rob, and destroy a place.
» *noun* the sacking of a town or city.

sackcloth »*noun* a coarse fabric woven from flax or hemp.

sacked

sacking

sacks

sacra plural of **sacrum**.

sacral »*adjective* (in anatomy) relating to the sacrum.
– **SAY** say-kruhl or sak-ruhl

sacrament »*noun* ❶ (in the Christian Church) a religious ceremony in which the participants receive the grace of God, such as baptism and the Eucharist. ❷ (also **the Blessed Sacrament**(or **the Holy Sacrament**) (in Catholic use) bread and wine used in the Eucharist.
– **SAY** sak-ruh-muhnt
sacramental

☑ **sacra** not **sacre: sacrament**

sacred »*adjective* ❶ connected with a god or goddess and treated as holy. ❷ (of a text) having to do with the teachings of a religion. ❸ religious: *sacred music*.
– **SAY** say-krid
sacredly
sacredness

sacred cow »*noun* a long-standing idea, custom, or institution that is thought to be above criticism.

ℹ️ with reference to the respect of Hindus for the cow as a sacred animal

sacredly

sacredness

sacrifice »*noun* ❶ the killing of an animal or person or giving up of a possession as an offering to a god or goddess. ❷ an animal, person, or object offered in this way. ❸ an act of giving up something you value for the sake of something that is more important.
» *verb* (**sacrifices, sacrificing, sacrificed**) give something as a sacrifice.
sacrificial

sacrilege »*noun* the treating of something sacred or highly valued with great disrespect.
– **SAY** sak-ri-lij
sacrilegious

☑ **rilege** not **relige** or **rilige: sacrilege**

sacristan »*noun* a person in charge of a sacristy.
– **SAY** sak-ri-stuhn

sacristy »*noun* (plural **sacristies**) a room in a church where a priest prepares for a service, and where things used in worship are kept.
– **SAY** sak-ri-sti

sacrosanct »*adjective* seen as too important or valuable to be changed or questioned.
– **SAY** sak-ruh-sangkt

sacrum »*noun* (plural **sacra** or **sacrums**) a triangular bone in the lower back between the two hip bones of the pelvis.
– **SAY** say-kruhm [singular], say-kruh [plural]

☑ the plural of **sacrum** can be either **sacra** (as in Latin) or **sacrums**

sad (adjective: **sadder, saddest**)
sadly
sadness

sadden (verb: **saddens, saddening, saddened**)

sadder

saddest

saddle (verb: **saddles, saddling, saddled**)

saddleback »*noun* ❶ a hill with a ridge along the top that dips in the middle. ❷ a pig of a black breed with a white stripe across the back.

saddlebag

saddled

saddler »*noun* a person who makes, repairs, or deals in equipment for horses.

saddlery »*noun* (plural **saddleries**) ❶ saddles and other equipment for horses. ❷ a saddler's business or premises.

saddles

saddle-sore

saddling

sadhu »*noun* a Hindu holy man.
– **SAY** sah-doo

sadism »*noun* sexual or other pleasure that is gained from hurting or humiliating other people.
– **SAY** say-di-z'm
sadist
sadistic
sadistically

ℹ️ **sadism** is named after the French writer the Marquis de *Sade*

sadly
sadness

S

sadomasochism »*noun* a sexual practice which is a combination of sadism and masochism.
– SAY say-doh-**mass**-uh-ki-z'm
sadomasochist
sadomasochistic

sae »*abbreviation* stamped addressed envelope.

safari (plural **safaris**)

> ✓ the plural of **safari** has **-is** not **-ies**: **safaris**

safe (adjective: **safer**, **safest**)
safely

safeguard (verb: **safeguards**, **safeguarding**, **safeguarded**)

safekeeping

safely

safer

safest

safety

saffron »*noun* an orange-yellow spice used in cooking, made from the dried stigmas of a crocus.

sag (verb: **sags**, **sagging**, **sagged**)
saggy

saga »*noun* ❶ a long traditional story describing heroic adventures. ❷ a long, involved account or series of incidents.

sagacious »*adjective* having good judgement; wise.
– SAY suh-**gay**-shuhss
sagaciously
sagacity

sage[1] »*noun* a Mediterranean plant with greyish-green leaves that are used as a herb in cookery.

sage[2] »*noun* a very wise man.
» *adjective* wise: *sage remarks*.
sagely

sagged

sagging

saggy

Sagittarius »*noun* a constellation and sign of the zodiac (the Archer, 22 November–20 December).
– SAY saj-i-**tair**-i-uhss

> ✓ one g, two t's: **Sagittarius**

sago »*noun* flour or starchy granules obtained from a palm, often cooked with milk to make a pudding.
– SAY **say**-goh

sags

sahib »*noun* (in Indian English) a polite form of address for a man.

– SAY sahb or suh-**heeb**

> ℹ️ **sahib** is an Arabic word meaning 'friend, lord'

said past and past participle of SAY.

sail (verb: **sails**, **sailing**, **sailed**)

sailboard »*noun* a board with a mast and a sail, used in windsurfing.

sailcloth »*noun* ❶ strong fabric used for making sails. ❷ a similar fabric used for making hard-wearing clothes.

sailed

sailing

sailor

> ✓ -or not -er: **sailor**

sailplane »*noun* a glider designed to be able to fly for a long time.

sails

saint
sainthood

St Bernard »*noun* a breed of very large dog originally kept to rescue travellers by monks of a hospice on the Great St Bernard, a pass across the Alps.

sainted »*adjective* (old-fashioned) very good or kind, like a saint.

St Elmo's fire »*noun* a luminous electrical discharge sometimes seen on a ship or aircraft during a storm.

sainthood

St Lucian [of St Lucia in the Caribbean]
– SAY suhnt **loo**-shuhn

saintly »*adjective* very holy or good.
saintliness

St Swithin's day »*noun* 15 July, a Church festival honouring St Swithin and believed to be a day on which, if it rains, it will continue raining for the next forty days.

sake[1] [as in *for the sake of*]

sake[2] »*noun* a Japanese alcoholic drink made from rice.
– SAY **sah**-ki or **sa**-kay

salaam »*noun* a low bow with the hand touching the forehead, made as a gesture of greeting or respect in Arabic-speaking and Muslim countries.
» *verb* (**salaams**, **salaaming**, **salaamed**) make a salaam.
– SAY suh-**lahm**

> ℹ️ **salaam** is an Arabic word meaning 'peace'

salable another way of spelling SALEABLE.

salacious »*adjective* having too much interest in sexual matters.

– **SAY** suh-**lay**-shuhss
 salaciously
 salaciousness

salad

salad days »*plural noun* (your salad days)
 the period when you are young and
 inexperienced.

salamander »*noun* an animal with bright
 markings resembling a newt, that can live
 in water and on land.
– **SAY** **sal**-uh-man-der

> ☑ **er** not **ar** at the end: **salamander**

salami »*noun* (plural **salami** or **salamis**) a
 type of spicy preserved sausage.
– **SAY** suh-**lah**-mi

> ☑ one **l**, one **m**: **salami** is an Italian
> word

salaried »*adjective* earning or offering a
 salary: *a salaried job*.

salary »*noun* (plural **salaries**) a fixed
 regular payment made by an employer to
 an employee.

> ☑ plural: drop the **y** and add **ies**:
> **salaries**

sale [selling]

saleable »*adjective* good enough to be
 sold.

> ☑ **saleable** can also be spelled **salable**,
> without the **e** in the middle

saleroom »*noun* a room in which auctions
 are held.

salesman (plural **salesmen**)
 salesmanship

salesperson (plural **salespeople**)

saleswoman (plural **saleswomen**)

salient »*adjective* ❶ most important: *the
 salient points of the case*. ❷ (of an angle)
 pointing outwards.
 »*noun* a piece of land or a fortified building
 that juts out to form an angle.
– **SAY** **say**-li-uhnt
 salience
 saliently

> ☑ **ent** not **ant**: **salient**

saline »*adjective* containing salt.
– **SAY** **say**-lyn
 salinity

saliva »*noun* a watery liquid in the mouth
 produced by glands, that helps chewing,
 swallowing, and digestion.
 salivary

> ☑ one **l**, one **v**: **saliva**

salivate »*verb* (**salivates, salivating,
 salivated**) ❶ produce saliva. ❷ show great
 excitement at the prospect of something.
– **SAY** **sal**-i-vayt
 salivation

sallied

sallies

sallow »*adjective* (of a person's
 complexion) yellowish in colour.
 sallowness

sally »*noun* (plural **sallies**) ❶ a sudden
 charge out of a place surrounded by an
 enemy. ❷ a witty or lively reply.
 »*verb* (**sallies, sallying, sallied**) (**sally forth**
 or **out**) set out.

> ☑ plural: drop the **y** and add **ies**: **sallies**

salmon (plural **salmon** or **salmons**)

> ☑ **lm** not **mm**: **salmon**

salmonella »*noun* (plural **salmonellae**) a
 bacterium that occurs mainly in the gut
 and can cause food poisoning.
– **SAY** sal-muh-**nel**-luh [singular], sal-muh-
 nel-lee [plural]

> ℹ the plural of **salmonella** is **salmonellae**
> (as in Latin). It is named after the
> American veterinary surgeon Daniel E.
> *Salmon*.

salon »*noun* ❶ a place where a hairdresser,
 beautician, or clothes designer carries out
 their work. ❷ a reception room in a large
 house. ❸ (a historical term) a regular
 gathering of writers, artists, etc., held in a
 fashionable household.

saloon »*noun* ❶ a lounge bar in a pub. ❷ a
 large public lounge on a ship. ❸ (in
 American English) a bar. ❹ a car having a
 closed body and separate boot.

salopettes »*plural noun* padded trousers
 with a high waist and shoulder straps,
 worn for skiing.
– **SAY** sal-uh-**pets**

> ☑ **ttes** at the end: **salopettes** is a French
> word

salsa »*noun* ❶ a type of Latin American
 dance music containing elements of jazz
 and rock. ❷ a dance performed to this
 music. ❸ a spicy tomato sauce.
– **SAY** **sal**-suh

> ℹ **salsa** is a Spanish word meaning
> 'sauce'

salsify »*noun* a plant with a long edible
 root like that of a parsnip.
– **SAY** **sal**-si-fi

salt (verb: **salts, salting, salted**)

salt cellar »*noun* a container for salt.

salted

saltier [more salty]

saltiest

saltiness

salting

saltire »*noun* (in heraldry) an X-shaped cross.
– SAY sawl-tyr or sol-tyr

salt pan »*noun* a hollow in the ground in which salt water evaporates to leave a deposit of salt.

saltpetre »*noun* potassium nitrate.
– SAY sawlt-**pee**-ter or solt-**pee**-ter

> ✓ petre not peter: saltpetre (the spelling saltpeter is American)

salts

saltwater

salty (adjective: **saltier**, **saltiest**)
saltiness

salubrious »*adjective* good for your health: *a salubrious district*.
– SAY suh-**loo**-bri-uhss
salubriously
salubriousness

salutary »*adjective* (of something unpleasant) beneficial because it allows you to learn from experience.
– SAY **sal**-yuu-tuh-ri

salutation »*noun* a greeting.

salute (verb: **salutes**, **saluting**, **saluted**)

Salvadorean [of El Salvador]

> ✓ ean not ian: Salvadorean

salvage »*verb* (**salvages**, **salvaging**, **salvaged**) ❶ rescue a ship or its cargo from loss at sea. ❷ save something from being lost or destroyed.
» *noun* ❶ the action of salvaging. ❷ cargo rescued from a wrecked ship.
salvageable

salvage yard »*noun* a place where disused machinery and vehicles are broken up and parts salvaged.

salvaging

salvation »*noun* ❶ (in Christian belief) the state of being saved from sin, believed to be brought about by faith in Jesus. ❷ a means of protecting someone from harm or loss.

Salvationist »*noun* a member of the Salvation Army, a Christian evangelical organization.

salve »*noun* ❶ an ointment used to soothe or heal the skin. ❷ something that reduces guilty feelings: *the idea provided a salve for his guilt*.
» *verb* (**salves**, **salving**, **salved**) (**salve your conscience**) do something to feel less guilty.

salver »*noun* a tray.

salves

salvia »*noun* a plant grown for its bright scarlet flowers.

salving

salvo »*noun* (plural **salvos** or **salvoes**) ❶ a shooting of a number of guns at the same time in a battle. ❷ a sudden series of aggressive statements or acts.

> ✓ the plural of salvo can have os or oes: salvos or salvoes

Samaritan »*noun* ❶ a member of a people living in Samaria, an ancient city and land of Palestine. ❷ (**good Samaritan**) a kind or helpful person.

> ℹ the use of good Samaritan to mean 'a kind person' refers to the parable told by Jesus (Luke's gospel)

samarium »*noun* a hard silvery-white metallic chemical element.
– SAY suh-**mair**-i-uhm

samba »*noun* a Brazilian dance of African origin.
» *verb* (**sambas**, **sambaing**, **sambaed**) dance the samba.

same
sameness
samey

samizdat »*noun* (in the former Soviet Union) the secret publishing of literature banned by the state.
– SAY **sam**-iz-dat

Samoan [of Samoa]

samosa »*noun* a triangular fried Indian pastry containing spiced vegetables or meat.
– SAY suh-**moh**-suh

> ✓ sam not som: samosa

samovar »*noun* a decorated Russian tea urn.
– SAY **sam**-uh-var

sampan »*noun* a small boat propelled with an oar at the stern, used in the Far East.

sample (verb: **samples**, **sampling**, **sampled**)

sampler »*noun* ❶ a piece of fabric decorated with a number of different embroidery stitches, used in the past to demonstrate someone's skill. ❷ a device for sampling music.

samples

sampling

samurai »*noun* (plural **samurai**) (a historical term) a member of a powerful Japanese military class.
– **SAY** sam-uh-ry

> ✓ note that the ending is **ai**, not simply **i**: **samurai**

sanatorium »*noun* (plural **sanatoriums** or **sanatoria**) ❶ a place like a hospital where people who have a long-term illness or who are recovering from an illness are treated. ❷ a place in a boarding school for children who are unwell.

> ✓ the plural of **sanatorium** can either be **sanatoriums** or (as in Latin) **sanatoria**

sanctify »*verb* (**sanctifies, sanctifying, sanctified**) ❶ make something holy. ❷ make something legal or right.
sanctification

sanctimonious »*adjective* making a show of being morally better than other people.
– **SAY** sangk-ti-**moh**-ni-uhss
sanctimoniously
sanctimoniousness
sanctimony

sanction »*noun* ❶ a penalty for disobeying a law or rule. ❷ (**sanctions**) measures taken by a state to try to force another to do something. ❸ official permission or approval.
»*verb* (**sanctions, sanctioning, sanctioned**) give official permission for something.

sanctity »*noun* ❶ the state of being holy. ❷ the state of being very important and worthy of great respect: *the sanctity of human life.*

sanctuary »*noun* (plural **sanctuaries**) ❶ a place of safety. ❷ a nature reserve. ❸ a place where injured or unwanted animals are cared for. ❹ a holy place. ❺ the part of the chancel of a church containing the high altar.

> ✓ plural: drop the **y** and add **ies**: **sanctuaries**

sanctum »*noun* (plural **sanctums**) ❶ a sacred place. ❷ a private place.

sand (verb: **sands, sanding, sanded**)

sandal

> 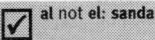 ✓ **al** not **el**: **sandal**

sandalwood »*noun* the sweet-smelling wood of an Indian or SE Asian tree.

sandbag

sandbank »*noun* a deposit of sand forming a shallow area in the sea or a river.

sandbar »*noun* a long, narrow sandbank.

sandblast »*verb* (**sandblasts, sandblasting, sandblasted**) roughen or clean a surface with a jet of sand.

sandboy

sandcastle

sanded

sander »*noun* a power tool used for smoothing a surface.

sandier

sandiest

sandiness

sanding

sandpaper (verb: **sandpapers, sandpapering, sandpapered**)
sandpapery

sandpiper »*noun* a wading bird with a long bill and long legs.

sandpit

sands

sandstone »*noun* rock formed from grains of sand tightly pressed together.

sandstorm

sandwich (plural **sandwiches**; verb: **sandwiches, sandwiching, sandwiched**)

> ✓ **sand** not **san** or **sam**, and the ending is **-wich** not **-witch** or **-which**: **sandwich**. Sandwiches were named after the 4th Earl of *Sandwich*.

sandwich course »*noun* a training course with alternate periods of study and work in business or industry.

sandwiched

sandwiches

sandwiching

sandy (adjective: **sandier, sandiest**)
sandiness

sane »*adjective* (**saner, sanest**) ❶ having a normal mind; not mad. ❷ sensible: *sane advice.*
sanely
saneness

sang past of **SING**.

sangfroid »*noun* cool courage in difficult circumstances.
– **SAY** song-**frwah**

> ⓘ **sangfroid** is a French word which means 'cold blood'

sangria »*noun* a Spanish drink of red wine, lemonade, fruit, and spices.
– **SAY** sang-**gree**-uh

sanguinary »*adjective* involving much bloodshed.
– **SAY** sang-gwi-nuh-ri

sanguine »*adjective* cheerful and confident about things that are going to happen.
– SAY sang-gwin

sanitarium (plural **sanitariums** or **sanitaria**) American spelling of SANATORIUM.

sanitary »*adjective* ❶ relating to sanitation. ❷ hygienic.

sanitaryware »*noun* toilet bowls, cisterns, and other fittings.

sanitation »*noun* arrangements to protect public health, such as the providing of clean drinking water and the disposal of sewage.

sanitize »*verb* (**sanitizes**, **sanitizing**, **sanitized**) ❶ make something hygienic. ❷ make something unpleasant seem more acceptable.
sanitization

> ✓ many people prefer the alternative spellings **sanitise**, **sanitises**, etc., and **sanitisation**: both s and z spellings are correct

sanity »*noun* ❶ the condition of being sane. ❷ reasonable behaviour.

sank past of SINK.

> ℹ on the use of **sank**, **sunk**, and **sunken**, see the note at SINK

sans »*preposition* (a poetic term) without: *she plays her role sans accent.*
– SAY sanz

Sanskrit »*noun* an ancient language of India.
– SAY san-skrit

Santa Claus

sap »*noun* the liquid that circulates in plants, carrying food to all parts.
»*verb* (**saps**, **sapping**, **sapped**) gradually weaken a person's strength.

> ✓ double the **p** to spell **sapping** and **sapped**

sapient »*adjective* wise or intelligent.
– SAY say-pi-uhnt
sapience

sapling »*noun* a young, slender tree.

sapped

sapper »*noun* a military engineer who lays or finds and defuses mines.

sapphic »*adjective* (a poetic term) relating to lesbians.
– SAY saf-fik

> ✓ two p's in **sapphic**. The word comes from the name of *Sappho*, an ancient Greek poet who is associated with lesbianism.

sapphire »*noun* ❶ a transparent blue precious stone. ❷ a bright blue colour.
– SAY saf-fyr

> ✓ double **p** followed by **h**: **sapphire**
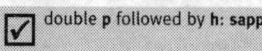

sapping

saprophyte »*noun* a plant or fungus that lives on and gets nutrition from decaying matter.
– SAY sap-ruh-fyt
saprophytic

saps

saraband »*noun* a slow, dignified Spanish dance.
– SAY sa-ruh-band

> ✓ **saraband** can also be spelled **sarabande**, with an **e** on the end

Saracen »*noun* an Arab or Muslim at the time of the Crusades.
– SAY sa-ruh-suhn

sarcasm »*noun* a way of using words which say the opposite of what you mean, as a way of hurting or mocking someone.

sarcastic »*adjective* using sarcasm.
sarcastically

sarcoma »*noun* (plural **sarcomas** or **sarcomata**) (in medicine) a cancerous tumour of a kind found chiefly in connective tissue.
– SAY sar-koh-muh [singular], sar-koh-muh-tuh [plural]

> ✓ in medicine the Latin or Greek plural **sarcomata** is often used, but the form with s is also correct

sarcophagus »*noun* (plural **sarcophagi**) a stone coffin.
– SAY sar-kof-fuh-guhss [singular], sar-kof-fuh-gy [plural]

sardine »*noun* a young pilchard or other small herring-like fish.

sardonic »*adjective* mocking.
– SAY sar-**don**-ik
sardonically

sardonyx »*noun* onyx in which white layers alternate with yellow or reddish ones.
– SAY sar-duh-niks or sar-**don**-iks

saree another way of spelling SARI.

sari »*noun* (plural **saris**) a length of fabric wrapped around the body, traditionally worn by women from the Indian subcontinent.
– SAY sah-ri

> ✓ **sari** can also be spelled **saree**

sarky »*adjective* (in informal English) sarcastic.
sarkily

sarong »*noun* a long piece of cloth wrapped round the body and tucked at the waist or under the armpits.
– SAY suh-**rong**

sarsaparilla »*noun* ❶ the dried roots of various plants, used as a flavouring. ❷ a sweet drink flavoured with this.
– SAY sar-suh-puh-**ril**-luh

> ☑ be careful spelling this word: the beginning is **sarsa** not **sasp** or **sarsp**:
> **sarsaparilla**

sartorial »*adjective* having to do with the way a person dresses.
– SAY sah-**tor**-i-uhl
sartorially

sash »*noun* ❶ a long strip of cloth worn over one shoulder or round the waist. ❷ a frame holding the glass in a window.

sashay »*verb* (**sashays, sashaying, sashayed**) swing the hips from side to side when walking.
– SAY sa-**shay**

> ☑ do not confuse **sashay** with **sachet**, which is a small packet of something

sash window »*noun* a window with one or two sashes which can be slid up and down to open it.

Sassenach (used in an insulting way) »*noun* an English person.
»*adjective* English.
– SAY sass-uh-nakh

sassy »*adjective* (**sassier, sassiest**) (in informal English) confident or cheeky.

SAT »*abbreviation* standard assessment task.

sat past and past participle of **SIT**.

> ℹ on the use of the participles **sitting** and **sat**, see the note at **SIT**

Satan »*noun* the Devil.

satanic »*adjective* having to do with Satan or the worship of Satan.

satanism »*noun* the worship of Satan.
satanist

satchel

> ☑ remember the **t**: **satchel**

sated »*adjective* having had as much or more of something than you want.

sateen »*noun* a cotton fabric woven like satin with a glossy surface.
– SAY sa-**teen**

satellite »*noun* ❶ an artificial object placed in orbit round the earth or another planet to collect information or for communication. ❷ a natural object that orbits a planet.
»*adjective* (of a country, community, etc.) dependent on or controlled by a larger or more powerful one.

> ☑ there are two single **t**'s but double **l**:
> **satellite**

satiate »*verb* (**satiates, satiating, satiated**) give someone as much or more than they want.
– SAY **say**-shi-ayt
satiation

satiety »*noun* the state of being fully satisfied or of having had too much of something.
– SAY suh-**ty**-i-ti

satin »*noun* a smooth, glossy fabric.
»*adjective* having a smooth, glossy surface or finish.
satiny

satinwood »*noun* the glossy yellowish wood of a tropical tree, used in making furniture.

satiny

satire »*noun* ❶ the use of humour, irony, exaggeration, or ridicule to reveal and criticize people's bad points. ❷ a play or other piece of writing that uses satire.
– SAY **sat**-yr
satirist

> ℹ do not confuse **satire** with a **satyr**, a lustful god in Greek mythology

satirical »*adjective* containing or using satire.
satirically

satirize »*verb* (**satirizes, satirizing, satirized**) mock and criticize someone or something using satire.
– SAY **sat**-i-ryz

> ☑ many people prefer the alternative spellings **satirise, satirises,** etc.: both **s** and **z** spellings are correct

satisfaction

satisfactory
satisfactorily

satisfy (verb: **satisfies, satisfying, satisfied**)

satsuma »*noun* a variety of tangerine with a loose skin.
– SAY sat-**soo**-muh

saturate »*verb* (**saturates, saturating, saturated**) ❶ soak something thoroughly with a liquid. ❷ make a substance combine with, dissolve, or hold the greatest possible quantity of another substance. ❸ fully magnetize or charge something. ❹ put more than is needed of a particular product into the market.

saturated »*adjective* ❶ thoroughly soaked with liquid. ❷ (in chemistry) (of a solution) containing the largest possible amount of a substance dissolved in it. ❸ (in chemistry) (of organic molecules) having only single bonds between carbon atoms.

saturates

saturating

saturation

Saturday

Saturn

saturnine »*adjective* ❶ (of a person or their manner) gloomy. ❷ (of looks) dark and brooding.
– **SAY** sat-er-nyn

satyr »*noun* (in Greek Mythology) a lustful god of the woods, with a man's face and body and a horse's or goat's ears, tail, and legs.
– **SAY** sat-er

> ℹ️ do not confuse **satyr** with **satire**, which is the use of humour to criticize people

sauce

saucepan

saucer

saucy (adjective: **saucier, sauciest**)
saucily
sauciness

> ✅ drop the **y** and add **ier** or **iest** to spell **saucier** or **sauciest**

Saudi »*noun* (plural **Saudis**) a person from Saudi Arabia.
» *adjective* relating to Saudi Arabia.
– **SAY** sow-di

sauerkraut »*noun* a German dish of chopped pickled cabbage.
– **SAY** sow-er-krowt

sauna »*noun* ❶ a small room used as a hot-air or steam bath for cleaning and refreshing the body. ❷ a session in a sauna.
– **SAY** saw-nuh

saunter »*verb* (**saunters, sauntering, sauntered**) walk in a slow, relaxed way.
» *noun* a leisurely stroll.

saurian »*adjective* having to do with or like a lizard.
– **SAY** saw-ri-uhn

sausage

saute »*adjective* fried quickly in shallow fat or oil.

» *noun* a dish cooked in such a way.
» *verb* (**sautes, sauteing, sauteed** or **sauted**) cook something in such a way.
– **SAY** soh-tay

> ✅ **saute, sautes,** etc. can also be spelled **sauté, sautès,** etc., with an acute accent on the **e** (**sauté** is a French word which means 'jumped')

savage (verb: **savages, savaging, savaged**)
savagely
savageness
savagery

savannah »*noun* a grassy plain in hot regions, with few trees.

> ✅ double n: **savannah**. It can also be spelled **savanna**, without the final **h**.

savant »*noun* a wise and knowledgeable person.
– **SAY** sav-uhnt

save (verb: **saves, saving, saved**)

saveloy »*noun* a smoked pork sausage.
– **SAY** sav-uh-loy

saver

saves

saving

saviour »*noun* ❶ a person who saves someone or something from danger or harm. ❷ (**the Saviour**) (in Christianity) God or Jesus.

> ✅ the ending is **-our** not **-or**: **saviour** (the spelling **savior** is American)

savoir faire »*noun* the ability to act appropriately in social situations.
– **SAY** sav-war **fair**

> ✅ **oir** not **ior**: **savoir faire** is a French phrase which means 'know how to do'

savor American spelling of **SAVOUR**.

savory[1] »*noun* a sweet smelling plant used as a herb in cookery.

savory[2] American spelling of **SAVOURY**.

savour (verb: **savours, savouring, savoured**)

> ✅ note that the ending is **-our** not **-or**: **savour** (the spelling **savor** is American)

savoury »*adjective* ❶ (of food) salty or spicy rather than sweet. ❷ morally acceptable or respectable: *the less savoury aspects of the story.*
» *noun* (plural **savouries**) a savoury snack.

> ✅ plural: drop the **y** and add **ies**: **savouries**

savoy »*noun* a cabbage of a variety with wrinkled leaves.

i from *Savoy*, an area of SE France

savvy (in informal English) »*noun* sharp awareness and good judgement.
» *adjective* (**savvier**, **savviest**) showing sharp awareness and good judgement.

saw[1] (verb: **saws**, **sawing**, **sawed**; past participle **sawn**) [cutting tool; cut with a saw]

saw[2] past of **see**[1].

saw[3] »*noun* a proverb or wise saying.

sawdust

sawed

sawing

sawmill »*noun* a place where logs are sawn by machine.

sawn past participle of **saw**[1].

sawn-off

saws

sawtooth »*adjective* shaped like the teeth of a saw.

sawyer »*noun* a person who saws timber.

sax »*noun* (in informal English) a saxophone.

saxifrage »*noun* a low-growing plant of rocky or stony ground.
– say saks-i-frayj

Saxon »*noun* a member of a people from Germany that conquered and settled in much of southern England in the 5th and 6th centuries.

☑ -on not -en: Saxon

saxophone
saxophonist

☑ saxo not saxa: the saxophone was named after the Belgian instrument-maker Adolphe *Sax*

say (verb: **says**, **saying**, **said**)

saying

says

scab
scabby

scabbard »*noun* a cover for the blade of a sword or dagger.
– say skab-berd

☑ ard not erd: scabbard

scabby

scabies »*noun* a skin disease that causes itching and small red spots.
– say skay-beez

scabious »*noun* a plant with blue, pink, or white pincushion-shaped flowers.
– say skay-bi-uhss

scabrous »*adjective* ❶ covered with scabs. ❷ indecent or sordid.
– say skay-bruhss or skab-ruhss

scaffold »*noun* ❶ a raised wooden platform on which people used to stand when they were to be executed by hanging. ❷ a structure made using scaffolding.
scaffolder

scaffolding »*noun* a temporary structure made of wooden planks and metal poles, used while building, repairing, or cleaning a building.

scalable »*adjective* ❶ able to be climbed. ❷ able to be changed in size or scale.

☑ scal- not scale-: scalable

scald (verb: **scalds**, **scalding**, **scalded**)

scale (verb: **scales**, **scaling**, **scaled**)

scalene »*adjective* (of a triangle) having sides which are unequal in length.
– say skay-leen

scales

scaling

scallion »*noun* (in American English) a spring onion.
– say skal-li-uhn

scallop »*noun* ❶ an edible shellfish with two hinged fan-shaped shells. ❷ one of a series of small curves like the edge of a scallop shell, forming a decorative edging.
» *verb* (**scallops**, **scalloping**, **scalloped**) decorate something with scallops.
– say skol-luhp or skal-luhp

☑ scall not scoll, with double l but single p: scallop

scallywag

scalp »*noun* ❶ the skin covering the top and back of the head. ❷ (in the past, among certain American Indians) the scalp and the hair belonging to it cut away from an enemy's head as a battle trophy.
» *verb* (**scalps**, **scalping**, **scalped**) take the scalp of an enemy.

scalpel »*noun* a knife with a small sharp blade, used by a surgeon.

scalping

scalps

scaly

scam »*noun* (in informal English) a dishonest scheme for making money.

scamp

scamper (verb: **scampers**, **scampering**, **scampered**)

scampi »*plural noun* small lobster-like creatures prepared for eating.

S

scan »*verb* (**scans**, **scanning**, **scanned**)
❶ look at something quickly in order to find relevant features or information.
❷ move a detector or beam across something. ❸ convert a document or picture into digital form for storing or processing on a computer. ❹ analyse the metre of a line of verse. ❺ (of verse) follow metrical rules.
» *noun* ❶ an act of scanning. ❷ a medical examination using a scanner. ❸ an image obtained by scanning.

> ✓ double the **n** to spell **scanning** and **scanned**

scandal »*noun* ❶ an action or event seen as wrong or unacceptable and causing general outrage. ❷ outrage or gossip arising from this.

scandalize »*verb* (**scandalizes**, **scandalizing**, **scandalized**) shock other people by acting in an improper or immoral way.

> ✓ many people prefer the alternative spellings **scandalise**, **scandalises**, etc.: both **s** and **z** spellings are correct

scandalmonger

scandalous
scandalously

Scandinavian

scandium »*noun* a soft silvery-white metallic chemical element.
– SAY skan-di-uhm

scanned

scanner »*noun* ❶ a machine that examines the body through the use of radiation, ultrasound, etc. ❷ a device that scans documents and converts them into digital data.

scanning

scans

scansion »*noun* ❶ the action of scanning a line of verse to find out its rhythm. ❷ the rhythm of a line of verse.
– SAY skan-sh'n

scant »*adjective* hardly any; not enough: *she gave it scant attention.*

scanty »*adjective* (**scantier**, **scantiest**) too little in size or amount for what is needed.
scantily

scapegoat »*noun* a person who is blamed for the things other people do wrong.
» *verb* (**scapegoats**, **scapegoating**, **scapegoated**) make someone a scapegoat.

scapula »*noun* (plural **scapulae** or **scapulas**) = SHOULDER BLADE.
– SAY skap-yuu-luh [singular], skap-yuu-lee [plural]

> ✓ the plural of **scapula** can either be **scapulae** (as in Latin) or **scapulas**

scapular »*adjective* relating to the shoulder or shoulder blade.
» *noun* a short cloak worn by monks, covering the shoulders.
– SAY skap-yuu-ler

scapulas

scar (verb: **scars**, **scarring**, **scarred**) [mark of an injury]

> ✓ double the **r** in **scarring** and **scarred**

scarab »*noun* ❶ a large dung beetle, considered sacred in ancient Egypt. ❷ an ancient Egyptian gem in the form of a scarab beetle.
– SAY ska-ruhb

scarce »*adjective* (**scarcer**, **scarcest**) ❶ (of a resource) available in quantities that are too small to meet the demand for it. ❷ rarely found.
scarcely
scarceness
scarcity

scare (verb: **scares**, **scaring**, **scared**) [frighten]

scarecrow

scared

scaremonger

scares

scarf (plural **scarves** or **scarfs**)

scarier

scariest

scarify[1] »*verb* (**scarifies**, **scarifying**, **scarified**) ❶ rake out unwanted material from a lawn. ❷ break up the surface of soil or a road or pavement. ❸ make shallow cuts in the skin. ❹ criticize someone hurtfully.
– SAY ska-ri-fy
scarification

scarify[2] »*verb* (**scarifies**, **scarifying**, **scarified**) (in informal English) frighten.
– SAY skair-i-fy

scarily

scariness

scaring

scarlatina »*noun* = SCARLET FEVER.
– SAY skar-luh-tee-nuh

> ✓ scarlat- not scarlet-: scarlatina

scarlet »*noun* a bright red colour.

scarlet fever »*noun* an infectious disease among children, causing fever and a scarlet rash.

scarp »*noun* a very steep bank or slope.

scarper »*verb* (**scarpers, scarpering, scarpered**) (in informal English) run away.

scarred

scarring

scars

scarves plural of **SCARF**.

scary (adjective: **scarier, scariest**)
scarily
scariness

✓ drop the **y** and add **ier** or **iest** to spell **scarier** or **scariest**

scat »*noun* improvised jazz singing in which the voice is used in imitation of an instrument.

scathing »*adjective* harshly critical.
– SAY skay-*thing*
scathingly

scatological »*adjective* obsessed with excrement and excretion.
scatology

scatter (verb: **scatters, scattering, scattered**)

scatterbrained

scattered

scattering

scatters

scatty »*adjective* absent-minded and disorganized.
scattiness

scavenge »*verb* (**scavenges, scavenging, scavenged**) ❶ search for and collect anything usable from waste. ❷ (of an animal or bird) search for dead animals as food.
– SAY ska-vinj
scavenger

✓ **enge** not **inge: scavenge**

scenario »*noun* (plural **scenarios**) ❶ a written outline of a film, novel, or stage work. ❷ a possible sequence of future events.
– SAY si-**nah**-ri-oh

✓ the plural of **scenario** (an Italian word) has **os** not **oes: scenarios**

scene

scenery

scenic »*adjective* (of natural scenery) impressive or beautiful.
scenically

scent (verb: **scents, scenting, scented**)
scented

scepter American spelling of **SCEPTRE**.

sceptic »*noun* a person who questions accepted beliefs or statements.
– SAY skep-tik
scepticism

✓ **scep** not **skep** in **sceptic** and related words (the spellings **skeptic, skeptical,** etc. are American)

sceptical »*adjective* not easily convinced; having doubts.
sceptically

sceptre »*noun* a staff carried by a king or queen on ceremonial occasions.
– SAY sep-ter

✓ **tre** not **ter: sceptre** (the spelling **scepter** is American)

Schadenfreude »*noun* pleasure felt at the misfortune of another.
– SAY shah-d'n-froy-duh

ⅈ **Schadenfreude** is German, from words meaning 'damage' and 'joy'

schedule (verb: **schedules, scheduling, scheduled**)
scheduler

scheduled »*adjective* ❶ forming part of a schedule. ❷ (of an airline or flight) forming part of a regular service rather than specially chartered.

scheduler

schedules

scheduling

schema »*noun* (plural **schemata** or **schemas**) an outline of a plan or theory.
– SAY skee-muh [singular], skee-muh-tuh [plural]

✓ the plural of **schema** can be **schemata** (as in the original Greek) or **schemas**

schematic »*adjective* ❶ (of a diagram) outlining the main features; simplified. ❷ (of thought, ideas, etc.) formulaic.
schematically

schematize »*verb* (**schematizes, schematizing, schematized**) arrange or show something in a schematic form.

✓ many people prefer the alternative spellings **schematise, schematises,** etc.: both **s** and **z** spellings are correct

scheme (verb: **schemes, scheming, schemed**)
schemer

scherzo »*noun* (plural **scherzos** or **scherzi**) a short lively movement in a symphony or sonata.
– SAY skair-tsoh [singular], skair-tsi [plural]

✓ the plural of **scherzo** (an Italian word meaning 'jest') can be **scherzos** or **scherzi** (as in the Italian)

schism »*noun* ❶ a deep disagreement between two groups. ❷ the formal separation of a Church into two Churches, owing to differences in belief.
– SAY si-z'm or ski-z'm

schismatic »*adjective* having to do with schism.

schist »*noun* a metamorphic rock which consists of layers of different minerals.
– SAY shist

schizoid »*adjective* having a mental condition similar to schizophrenia.
– SAY skit-soyd

schizophrenia »*noun* a long-term mental disorder whose symptoms include inappropriate actions and feelings and withdrawal from reality into fantasy.
– SAY skit-suh-free-ni-uh

schizophrenic »*adjective* ❶ suffering from schizophrenia. ❷ (in informal English) having contradictory elements.
» *noun* a person suffering from schizophrenia.
– SAY skits-uh-fren-ik

schlock »*noun* (in informal American English) cheap or poor quality goods.
– SAY shlok

schmaltz »*noun* excessive sentimentality.
– SAY shmawlts
schmaltzy

schmuck »*noun* (in informal American English) a stupid person.
– SAY shmuk

schnapps »*noun* a strong alcoholic drink resembling gin.
– SAY shnaps

> ✓ don't forget the **c**, and the double **p**: **schnapps**

schnitzel »*noun* a thin slice of veal, coated in breadcrumbs and fried.
– SAY shnit-z'l

> ℹ **schnitzel** is a German word meaning 'slice'

scholar

scholarly »*adjective* ❶ relating to serious academic study. ❷ having knowledge or learning.

scholarship »*noun* ❶ serious academic study. ❷ a grant made to support a student's education, awarded on the basis of achievement.

scholastic »*adjective* having to do with schools and education.

scholasticism »*noun* the system of theology and philosophy taught in medieval universities.

school (verb: **schools**, **schooling**, **schooled**)

schoolboy

schoolchild (plural **schoolchildren**)

schooled

schoolgirl

schoolhouse

schooling

schoolmarm »*noun* a schoolmistress, especially one who is prim and strict.

schoolmaster

schoolmate

schoolmistress (plural **schoolmistresses**)

schools

schoolteacher

schooner »*noun* ❶ a sailing ship with two or more masts. ❷ a large glass for sherry.
– SAY skoo-ner

schtum another way of spelling **SHTUM**.

sciatic »*adjective* ❶ having to do with the hip. ❷ affecting the sciatic nerve.
– SAY sy-at-ik

sciatica »*noun* pain affecting the back, hip, and outer side of the leg, caused by pressure on the sciatic nerve.

sciatic nerve »*noun* a major nerve extending from the lower end of the spinal cord down the back of the thigh.

science

> ✓ **i** before **e**, even though it is after **c**: **science** does not follow the usual rule

science fiction »*noun* fiction set in the future, often in space, and showing imagined scientific advances.

science park »*noun* an area devoted to scientific research or the development of science-based industries.

scientific
scientifically

scientist

Scientology »*noun* (trademark) a religious system based on the seeking of self-knowledge and spiritual fulfilment through courses of study and training.
Scientologist

sci-fi »*noun* = SCIENCE FICTION.

scimitar »*noun* a short sword with a curved blade, used in Eastern countries.
– SAY sim-i-ter

> ✓ don't forget the **c** after the **s**, and **ar** not **er** at the end: **scimitar**

scintilla »*noun* a tiny trace or amount.
– SAY sin-til-luh

> ✓ **sc**, and double **l**: **scintilla** is a Latin word meaning 'spark'

scintillate »*verb* (**scintillates, scintillating, scintillated**) give off flashes of light; sparkle.
– SAY sin-ti-layt
scintillation

 double **l** in **scintillate**

scintillating »*adjective* ❶ sparkling. ❷ brilliant and exciting.
scintillation

scion »*noun* ❶ a young shoot or twig of a plant that is cut off to create a new plant. ❷ a descendant of a notable family.
– SAY sy-uhn

scissors

 sc, and double **s**: **scissors**

sclerosis »*noun* ❶ abnormal hardening of body tissue. ❷ (in full **multiple sclerosis**) a disease involving damage to the sheaths of nerve cells and leading to partial or complete paralysis.
– SAY skleer-**oh**-siss or skluh-**roh**-siss

sclerotic »*adjective* ❶ of or having sclerosis. ❷ rigid; unable to adapt.
– SAY skleer-**oh**-tik or skluh-**roh**-tik

scoff (verb: **scoffs, scoffing, scoffed**)

scold (verb: **scolds, scolding, scolded**)

sconce »*noun* a candle holder attached to a wall with an ornamental bracket.

scone

scoop (verb: **scoops, scooping, scooped**)

scoot (verb: **scoots, scooting, scooted**)

scooter

scooting

scoots

scope »*noun* ❶ the extent of the area or subject matter that something deals with or to which it is relevant. ❷ the opportunity or possibility for doing something.

scorbutic »*adjective* relating to or affected with scurvy.
– SAY skor-**byoo**-tik

scorch (verb: **scorches, scorching, scorched**)
scorcher

score (verb: **scores, scoring, scored**)
scorer

scoreboard

scorebook

scorecard

scored

scoreless

scoreline

scorer

scores

scoresheet

scoring

scorn »*noun* the feeling that someone or something is worthless; contempt.
» *verb* (**scorns, scorning, scorned**) ❶ express scorn for someone or something. ❷ reject someone or something in a contemptuous way.

scornful »*adjective* showing or feeling scorn.
scornfully

☑ **-ful** not **-full**: **scornful**

scorning

scorns

Scorpio »*noun* a sign of the zodiac (the Scorpion, 23 October–21 November).

ℹ in astronomy, the corresponding constellation is called *Scorpius*

scorpion

Scot

Scotch »*adjective* (old-fashioned) = **SCOTTISH**.
» *noun* whisky made in Scotland.

ℹ the use of the adjective **Scotch** is now considered rather old-fashioned, and is mainly found in certain fixed phrases, such as *Scotch broth* and *Scotch whisky*. Elsewhere, use **Scottish** or **Scots** instead.

scotch »*verb* (**scotches, scotching, scotched**) put an end to something.

Scotch broth »*noun* a traditional Scottish soup made from meat stock with pearl barley and vegetables.

scotched

Scotch egg »*noun* a hard-boiled egg coated in sausage meat, rolled in breadcrumbs, and fried.

scotches

scotching

scot-free »*adverb* without suffering any punishment or injury.

Scots »*adjective* = **SCOTTISH**.
» *noun* the form of English used in Scotland.

Scotsman (plural **Scotsmen**)

Scots pine »*noun* a pine tree grown for timber and other products.

Scotswoman (plural **Scotswomen**)

Scottish

ℹ for the use of **Scottish** and **Scotch**, see the note at **SCOTCH**

scoundrel »*noun* a dishonest person.

scour »*verb* (scours, scouring, scoured)
❶ clean or brighten something by rubbing with something rough or a detergent.
❷ search a place thoroughly.
scourer

scourge »*noun* ❶ a person or thing causing great trouble or suffering. ❷ (a historical term) a whip used for punishment.
» *verb* (scourges, scourging, scourged)
❶ cause great suffering to someone. ❷ (a historical term) whip someone with a scourge.

scouring

scours

Scouse (in informal English) »*noun* ❶ the dialect or accent of people from Liverpool. ❷ (also **Scouser**) a person from Liverpool.
» *adjective* relating to Liverpool.
– SAY skowss

scout »*noun* ❶ a person sent ahead of a main force to gather information about the enemy. ❷ (also **Scout**) a member of the Scout Association, a boys' organization. ❸ a talent scout. ❹ an instance of scouting.
» *verb* (scouts, scouting, scouted) ❶ make a detailed search to find or discover something. ❷ act as a scout.

scoutmaster

scouts

scow »*noun* a flat-bottomed sailing dinghy.
– SAY skow

scowl (verb: scowls, scowling, scowled)

scrabble (verb: scrabbles, scrabbling, scrabbled)

scrag »*verb* (scrags, scragging, scragged) (in informal English) handle roughly; beat up.

☑ double the **g** in **scragging** and **scragged**

scraggy »*adjective* thin and bony.

scrags

scram (verb: scrams, scramming, scrammed)

☑ double the **m** in **scramming** and **scrammed**

scramble (verb: scrambles, scrambling, scrambled)

scrambler »*noun* a device for putting a broadcast transmission or telephone conversation into a form that can only be understood by using a decoding device.

scrambles

scrambling

scrammed

scramming

scrams

scrap (verb: scraps, scrapping, scrapped)
scrapper

☑ double the **p** in **scrapping**, **scrapped**, and **scrapper**

scrapbook

scrape (verb: scrapes, scraping, scraped)
scraper

scrapie »*noun* a disease of sheep involving the central nervous system, characterized by a lack of coordination causing affected animals to rub against objects for support.

scraping

scrapped

scrapper

scrappier

scrappiest

scrapping

scrappy »*adjective* (scrappier, scrappiest) disorganized, untidy, or incomplete.

scraps

scrapyard

scratch (verb: scratches, scratching, scratched)

scratchy »*adjective* (scratchier, scratchiest)
❶ causing scratching. ❷ (of a voice or sound) rough.

scrawl »*verb* (scrawls, scrawling, scrawled) write something in a hurried, careless way.
» *noun* hurried, careless handwriting.

scrawny »*adjective* (scrawnier, scrawniest) unattractively thin and bony.

scream (verb: screams, screaming, screamed)
screamer

scree »*noun* a mass of small loose stones that form or cover a slope on a mountain.

screech (verb: screeches, screeching, screeched)
screechy

screed »*noun* ❶ a long speech or piece of writing. ❷ a layer of material applied to level a floor.

screen (verb: screens, screening, screened)

screenplay »*noun* the script of a film, including acting instructions and scene directions.

screen-print »*verb* (screen-prints, screen-printing, screen-printed) force ink on to a surface through a screen of fine material so as to create a picture or pattern.
» *noun* (screen print) a picture or design produced by screen-printing.

screens

screen saver »*noun* a moving image displayed by a computer screen when not in use.

screen test »*noun* a filmed test to discover whether an actor is suitable for a film role.

screenwriter »*noun* a person who writes a screenplay.
screenwriting

screw (verb: **screws**, **screwing**, **screwed**)

screwball (in informal English) »*noun* a crazy or eccentric person.
» *adjective* crazy; absurd.

screwdriver

screwed

screwing

screws

screwy »*adjective* (in informal English) rather odd or eccentric.

scribal »*adjective* having to do with a scribe.
– say skry-b'l

scribble (verb: **scribbles**, **scribbling**, **scribbled**) [write carelessly]
scribbler

scribe »*noun* (a historical term) a person who copied out documents.

scrim »*noun* strong, coarse fabric used for heavy-duty lining or upholstery.

scrimmage »*noun* a confused struggle or fight.

> double m: **scrimmage**

scrimp »*verb* (**scrimps**, **scrimping**, **scrimped**) be very careful with money; economize.

scrip »*noun* a provisional certificate of money subscribed to a bank or company, entitling the holder to dividends.

script »*noun* ❶ the written text of a play, film, or broadcast. ❷ handwriting as distinct from print. ❸ a candidate's written answers in an examination.
» *verb* (**scripts**, **scripting**, **scripted**) write a script for a play, film, or broadcast.

scriptural »*adjective* having to do with scripture.

scripture »*noun* ❶ the sacred writings of Christianity contained in the Bible. ❷ the sacred writings of another religion.

scriptures

scriptwriter
scriptwriting

scrivener »*noun* (a historical term) a clerk or scribe.

– say skriv-uh-ner

scrofula »*noun* (a historical term) a disease causing glandular swellings.
– say skrof-yuu-luh
scrofulous

scroll »*noun* ❶ a roll of parchment or paper for writing or painting on. ❷ an ornamental design or carving resembling a partly unrolled scroll.
» *verb* (**scrolls**, **scrolling**, **scrolled**) move displayed text or graphics on a computer screen in order to view different parts of them.

scrollwork »*noun* decoration consisting of spiral lines or patterns.

Scrooge »*noun* a person who is mean with money.

> ℹ️ from Ebenezer *Scrooge*, a miser in Charles Dickens's story *A Christmas Carol*

scrotum »*noun* (plural **scrota** or **scrotums**) the pouch of skin containing the testicles.
scrotal

> ✓ the plural of **scrotum** can be **scrota** (as in the original Latin) or **scrotums**

scrounge »*verb* (**scrounges**, **scrounging**, **scrounged**) try to get something from others without having to pay or work for it.
scrounger

scrub[1] (verb: **scrubs**, **scrubbing**, **scrubbed**) [rub hard so as to clean]
scrubber

> ✓ double the **b** in **scrubbing** and **scrubbed**

scrub[2] »*noun* ❶ vegetation consisting mainly of brushwood or stunted trees. ❷ land covered with such vegetation.
scrubby

scruff

scruffy (adjective: **scruffier**, **scruffiest**)
scruffily
scruffiness

scrum »*noun* ❶ (in rugby) a formation of players in which the forwards of each team push against each other with heads down and the ball is thrown in. ❷ (in informal English) a disorderly crowd.

scrummage »*noun* = **SCRUM**.

> 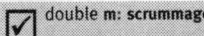 double m: **scrummage**

scrummy

scrump »*verb* (**scrumps**, **scrumping**, **scrumped**) (in informal English) steal fruit from an orchard or garden.

scrumptious

✓ don't forget the p: **scrumptious**

scrumpy »*noun* rough strong cider, as made in the West Country of England.

scrunch (verb: **scrunches**, **scrunching**, **scrunched**)

scrunchy »*noun* (plural **scrunchies**) a circular band of fabric-covered elastic used for fastening the hair.

✓ **scrunchy** can also be spelled **scrunchie**

scruple »*noun* a feeling of doubt as to whether an action is morally right.
» *verb* (**scruples**, **scrupling**, **scrupled**) (**not scruple to do**) not hesitate to do something, even if it may be wrong.

scrupulous »*adjective* ❶ very careful and thorough. ❷ very concerned to avoid doing wrong.
scrupulously
scrupulousness

scrutineer »*noun* a person who ensures that an election is organized correctly.

scrutinies

scrutinize »*verb* (**scrutinizes**, **scrutinizing**, **scrutinized**) examine something closely and thoroughly.

✓ many people prefer the alternative spellings **scrutinise**, **scrutinises**, etc.: both **s** and **z** spellings are correct

scrutiny »*noun* (plural **scrutinies**) close and critical examination.

scuba »*noun* a breathing apparatus for divers.
– SAY skoo-buh

ℹ **scuba** is an acronym from *self-contained underwater breathing apparatus*

scuba-diving

scud »*verb* (**scuds**, **scudding**, **scudded**) move fast because driven by the wind.

✓ double the **d** in **scudding** and **scudded**

scuff (verb: **scuffs**, **scuffing**, **scuffed**)

scuffle (verb: **scuffles**, **scuffling**, **scuffled**)

scuffs

scull »*noun* ❶ one of a pair of small oars used by a single rower. ❷ an oar placed over the back of a boat to propel it with a side to side motion. ❸ a light, narrow boat propelled with a scull or a pair of sculls.
» *verb* (**sculls**, **sculling**, **sculled**) propel a boat with sculls.
sculler

✓ do not confuse **scull** with **skull**, which refers to the bony structure surrounding the brain

scullery »*noun* (plural **sculleries**) a small room at the back of a house, used for washing dishes and other dirty household work.

✓ **ery** not **ary**: **scullery**

sculling

scullion »*noun* (a historical term) a servant who did the most menial kitchen tasks.
– SAY skul-li-uhn

sculls

sculpt »*verb* (**sculpts**, **sculpting**, **sculpted**) create or represent by sculpture.

sculptor

✓ **-or** not **-er**: **sculptor**

sculptress (plural **sculptresses**)

sculpts

sculpture »*noun* ❶ the art of making three-dimensional figures and shapes by carving stone or wood or casting metal. ❷ a work of such a kind.
» *verb* (**sculptures**, **sculpturing**, **sculptured**) ❶ make or represent by sculpture. ❷ (**sculptured**) pleasingly shaped, with strong lines.
sculptural

scum
scummy

scumbag

scummy

scupper »*noun* a hole in a ship's side to allow water to run away from the deck.
» *verb* (**scuppers**, **scuppering**, **scuppered**) ❶ sink a ship deliberately. ❷ prevent something from working or succeeding.

scurf »*noun* flakes on the surface of the skin, occurring as dandruff.

scurried

scurries

scurrility »*noun* the quality of being insulting and abusive.

scurrilous »*adjective* insulting and abusive and likely to damage a person's reputation.
– SAY skur-ri-luhss

✓ two **r**'s, one **l**: **scurrilous**

scurry (verb: **scurries**, **scurrying**, **scurried**)

scurvy »*noun* a disease caused by a lack of vitamin C, characterized by bleeding gums and the opening of previously healed wounds.

scut »*noun* the short tail of a hare, rabbit, or deer.

scutter »*verb* (**scutters, scuttering, scuttered**) move hurriedly with short steps.

scuttle[1] »*noun* a metal container with a lid and a handle, used to store coal for a domestic fire.

scuttle[2] »*verb* (**scuttles, scuttling, scuttled**) run hurriedly or secretively with short quick steps.

scuttle[3] »*verb* (**scuttles, scuttling, scuttled**) ❶ sink your own ship deliberately. ❷ deliberately cause a scheme to fail.

scuzzy »*adjective* (in informal English) dirty and unpleasant.

scythe »*noun* a tool used for cutting crops such as grass or corn, with a long curved blade at the end of a long pole.
»*verb* (**scythes, scything, scythed**) ❶ cut crops with a scythe. ❷ move through something rapidly and forcefully.

> ✓ don't forget the **c**, and the **e** at the end: **scythe**

sea

sea anemone »*noun* a sea creature with a tube-shaped body which bears a ring of stinging tentacles around the mouth.

sea bass »*noun* a sea fish resembling the freshwater perch.

seabed

seabird

seaboard »*noun* a region bordering the sea.

sea change »*noun* a great or remarkable transformation.

sea dog »*noun* (in informal English) an old or experienced sailor.

seafaring »*adjective* travelling by sea.
»*noun* travel by sea.
   seafarer

seafood

seafront

seagoing »*adjective* ❶ (of a ship) suitable for voyages on the sea. ❷ relating to sea travel.

seagull

sea horse »*noun* a small sea fish with an upright posture and a head and neck suggestive of a horse.

seal (verb: **seals, sealing, sealed**)

sealant »*noun* material used to make something airtight or watertight.

sealed

sealer

sealing

sealing wax »*noun* a type of wax used to make seals for letters and documents.

sea lion »*noun* a large seal with a mane on the neck and shoulders.

seals

seam »*noun* ❶ a line where two pieces of fabric are sewn together. ❷ an underground layer of a mineral such as coal or gold.

> ✓ **ea** not **ee**: **seam** (**seem** is a verb meaning 'give the impression of being')

seaman »*noun* (plural **seamen**) a sailor, especially one below the rank of officer.
   seamanship

seamed »*adjective* having a seam or seams: *seamed stockings*.

seamen plural of SEAMAN.

seamier

seamiest

sea mile »*noun* a nautical mile.

seamless »*adjective* smooth and without seams or obvious joins.
   seamlessly

seamstress »*noun* (plural **seamstresses**) a woman who sews, especially as a job.

seamy »*adjective* (**seamier, seamiest**) sordid.

seance »*noun* a meeting at which people attempt to make contact with the dead.
– SAY say-onss

seaplane

seaport

sear »*verb* (**sears, searing, seared**) ❶ burn or scorch with a sudden intense heat. ❷ (of pain) be experienced as a sudden burning sensation.

search (verb: **searches, searching, searched**)
   searchable
   searcher

search engine »*noun* (in computing) a program for finding data, files, or documents on a database or network.

searcher

searches

searching

searchlight

seared

searing

sears

seascape »*noun* a view or picture of an expanse of sea.

seashell

seashore

seasick
  seasickness

seaside

season (verb: seasons, seasoning, seasoned)

seasonable »*adjective* usual or appropriate for a particular season.

> i do not confuse **seasonable** and **seasonal**, which can be used to mean 'changing according to the season', as in *seasonal employment*

seasonal »*adjective* ❶ relating to or characteristic of a particular season of the year. ❷ changing according to the season: *seasonal rainfall*.
  seasonally

seasoned

seasoning

seasons

seat (verb: seats, seating, seated)
  seated
  seating

sea urchin »*noun* a small sea creature which has a shell covered in spines.

sea wall »*noun* a wall built to prevent the sea advancing on to an area of land.

seaward

seawards

seawater

seaway »*noun* a waterway or channel used by or capable of accommodating ships.

seaweed

seaworthy »*adjective* (of a boat) in a good enough condition to sail on the sea.
  seaworthiness

sebaceous »*adjective* producing oil or fat.
– SAY si-bay-shuhss

> ceous not cious: sebaceous

sec »*noun* (in informal English) a very short time.

secant »*noun* ❶ (in mathematics) (in a right-angled triangle) the ratio of the hypotenuse to the shorter side adjacent to an acute angle. ❷ (in geometry) a straight line that cuts a curve in two or more parts.
– SAY see-kuhnt or sek-uhnt

secateurs »*plural noun* a pair of pruning clippers for use with one hand.
– SAY sek-uh-**terz**

> seca not seco; eurs not ers: secateurs

secede »*verb* (secedes, seceding, seceded) withdraw formally from an organization or a federation of states.
– SAY si-seed

> ✓ cede not ceed: secede

secession »*noun* the action of seceding.
– SAY si-sesh-uhn

secluded »*adjective* (of a place) sheltered and private.

seclusion »*noun* the state of being private and away from other people.

second[1] (verb: seconds, seconding, seconded) [that is number two in a sequence; formally support a nomination]
  secondly

second[2] [unit of time]

second[3] »*verb* (seconds, seconding, seconded) temporarily move a worker to another position or role.
– SAY si-**kond**
  secondment

secondary »*adjective* ❶ coming after, or less important than, something else. ❷ (of education) for children from the age of eleven to sixteen or eighteen.
  secondarily

secondary industry »*noun* industry that converts raw materials into commodities and products; manufacturing industry.

second-class

second-degree »*adjective* (in medicine) (of burns) that cause blistering but not permanent scars.

seconded

second-guess »*verb* (second-guesses, second-guessing, second-guessed) predict someone's actions or thoughts by guesswork.

second-hand

seconding

secondly

secondment

second nature »*noun* a habit that has become instinctive.

second person »*noun* the form of a pronoun or verb used to refer to the person to whom you are speaking.

second-rate

seconds

second sight »*noun* the supposed ability to foretell the future.

second wind »*noun* fresh energy enabling you to continue with an activity after being tired.

secret
secrecy
secretly

secretarial

secretariat »*noun* a government office or department.
– SAY sek-ri-**tair**-i-uht

secretary (plural **secretaries**)
secretarial

✓ ary not ery: secretary
plural: drop the y and add ies:
secretaries

secretary bird »*noun* a slender long-legged African bird of prey, with a crest like a quill pen stuck behind the ear.

Secretary General »*noun* (plural **Secretaries General**) the principal administrator of some organizations.

Secretary of State »*noun* ❶ (in the UK) the head of a major government department. ❷ (in the US) the government official responsible for foreign affairs.

secrete »*verb* (**secretes, secreting, secreted**) ❶ (of a cell, gland, or organ) produce and discharge a substance. ❷ hide an object.
– SAY si-**kreet**
secretory

✓ ete at the end, not eet: secrete

secretion »*noun* ❶ a process by which substances are produced and discharged from a cell, gland, or organ. ❷ a substance discharged in such a way.

secretive
secretively
secretiveness

secretly

secretory

sect »*noun* a small religious group with different beliefs from those of the larger group that they belong to.

sectarian »*adjective* having to do with a sect or a group.
sectarianism

section (verb: **sections, sectioning, sectioned**)
sectional

sector »*noun* ❶ a distinct area or part. ❷ a part of a circle between two lines drawn from its centre to its circumference.

secular »*adjective* not religious or spiritual.

– SAY sek-yuu-ler
secularism
secularity

secure (verb: **secures, securing, secured**)
securely

security »*noun* (plural **securities**) ❶ the state of being or feeling secure. ❷ the safety of a state or organization. ❸ a valuable item offered as a guarantee that you will repay a loan.

✓ plural: drop the y and add ies:
securities

sedan »*noun* ❶ an enclosed chair carried between two horizontal poles. ❷ (in American English) a car for four or more people.
– SAY si-**dan**

sedate »*adjective* ❶ calm and unhurried. ❷ respectable and rather dull.
»*verb* (**sedates, sedating, sedated**) give someone a sedative drug.
sedately
sedateness

sedation »*noun* the action of giving someone drugs to calm them or make them sleep.

sedative »*adjective* having the effect of making someone calm or sleepy.
»*noun* a sedative drug.

sedentary »*adjective* ❶ sitting; seated. ❷ sitting down a lot; taking little exercise. ❸ staying in the same place for much of the time.
– SAY sed-uhn-tri

✓ tary not try: sedentary

sedge »*noun* a grass-like plant that grows in wet ground.

sediment »*noun* ❶ matter that settles to the bottom of a liquid. ❷ (in geology) material carried by water or wind and deposited on land.

sedimentary »*adjective* (of rock) that has formed from sediment.

sedition »*noun* things that are done or said to stir up rebellion against a ruler or government.
seditious

seduce »*verb* (**seduces, seducing, seduced**) ❶ persuade someone to do something unwise. ❷ persuade someone to have sex with you.
seducer
seduction

seductive
seductively
seductiveness

seductress (plural **seductresses**)

sedulous »*adjective* dedicated and careful.
– SAY sed-yuu-luhss
 sedulously

sedum »*noun* a plant of a large group having fleshy leaves.
– SAY see-duhm

see[1] (verb: **sees**, **seeing**, **saw**; past participle **seen**) [become aware of with the eyes]

see[2] »*noun* the district or position of a bishop or archbishop.

seed (verb: **seeds**, **seeding**, **seeded**) [thing which grows into a plant]

> do not confuse **seeding** with **ceding**, which means 'giving up power or territory'

seedbed »*noun* a bed of fine soil in which seeds are grown.

seeded

seedier

seediest

seediness

seeding

seedless

seedling »*noun* a young plant raised from seed.

seeds

seedsman »*noun* (plural **seedsmen**) a person who deals in seeds as a profession.

seedy »*adjective* (**seedier**, **seediest**) unpleasant because dirty or immoral.
 seediness

seeing

seek (verb: **seeks**, **seeking**, **sought**)
 seeker

seem (verb: **seems**, **seeming**, **seemed**) [give the impression of being]

> ee not ea: **seem** (**seam** refers to a line where two pieces of fabric are sewn together)

seeming »*adjective* appearing to be real or true; apparent.
 seemingly

seemly »*adjective* respectable or in good taste.

seems

seen past participle of SEE[1].

seep »*verb* (**seeps**, **seeping**, **seeped**) (of a liquid) flow or leak slowly through a substance.

seepage »*noun* the slow escape of a liquid or gas through a material.

seeped

seeping

seeps

seer »*noun* a person supposedly able to see visions of the future.
– SAY *rhymes with* beer

seersucker »*noun* a fabric with a crinkled surface.

sees

see-saw (verb: **see-saws**, **see-sawing**, **see-sawed**)

seethe »*verb* (**seethes**, **seething**, **seethed**)
❶ (of a liquid) boil or churn. ❷ be very angry but try not to show it. ❸ be filled with a crowd that is moving about.

see-through

segment »*noun* one of the parts into which something is divided.
» *verb* (**segments**, **segmenting**, **segmented**) divide into segments.
– SAY seg-muhnt [noun], seg-**ment** [verb]
 segmental
 segmentation

segregate »*verb* (**segregates**, **segregating**, **segregated**) ❶ keep separate from the rest or from each other. ❷ keep people of different races, sexes, or religions separate.
– SAY seg-ri-gayt
 segregation

segue »*verb* (**segues**, **seguing**, **segued**) move without interruption from one song or film scene to another.
» *noun* an instance of seguing.
– SAY seg-way

> be careful in writing this word which is pronounced and spelled very differently: **segue**

seine »*noun* a fishing net which hangs vertically in the water, with floats at the top.
– SAY *rhymes with* rain

seismic »*adjective* ❶ having to do with earthquakes. ❷ enormous in size or effect.
– SAY syz-mik
 seismically

> e before i: **seismic** does not follow the usual rule

seismograph »*noun* an instrument that measures and records details of earthquakes.
– SAY syz-muh-grahf

seismology »*noun* the branch of science concerned with earthquakes.
– SAY syz-**mol**-uh-ji
 seismologist

seize (verb: **seizes**, **seizing**, **seized**)

> e before i: **seize** does not follow the usual rule

seizure »*noun* ❶ the action of seizing. ❷ a sudden attack of illness, especially a stroke or an epileptic fit.

seldom »*adverb* not often.

select (verb: **selects**, **selecting**, **selected**)
selectable
selector

select committee »*noun* a small parliamentary committee appointed for a special purpose.

selected

selecting

selection

selective »*adjective* ❶ involving selection. ❷ tending to choose carefully. ❸ affecting some things and not others.
selectively
selectivity

selector

 ✓ -or not -er: **selector**

selects

selenium »*noun* a grey crystalline chemical element.
– SAY si-lee-ni-uhm

self (plural **selves**)

self-absorbed »*adjective* obsessed with your own emotions, interests, etc.
self-absorption

self-addressed

self-adhesive »*adjective* sticking without requiring moistening.

self-appointed »*adjective* having taken up a position or role without the approval of others.

self-assembly »*noun* the construction of a piece of furniture from materials sold in kit form.

self-assertion »*noun* confidence in expressing your views.

self-assessment

self-assurance »*noun* confidence in your own abilities or character.
self-assured

self-aware
self-awareness

self-catering

self-centred

self-confessed »*adjective* openly admitting to having certain qualities.

self-confidence
self-confident

self-congratulation »*noun* excessive pride in your achievements or qualities.
self-congratulatory

self-conscious »*adjective* nervous or awkward through being worried about what other people think of you.
self-consciously
self-consciousness

self-contained »*adjective* ❶ complete in itself. ❷ not depending on or influenced by others.

self-control

self-deception

self-defeating »*adjective* making things worse rather than achieving the desired aim.

self-defence

self-denial

self-deprecating »*adjective* modest about or critical of yourself.
self-deprecation

self-destruct (verb: **self-destructs**, **self-destructing**, **self-destructed**)
self-destructive

self-determination »*noun* the right or ability of a country or person to manage their own affairs.

self-discipline »*noun* the ability to control your feelings and actions.
self-disciplined

self-effacing »*adjective* not wanting to attract attention.

self-employed
self-employment

self-esteem »*noun* confidence in your own worth or abilities.

self-evident »*adjective* obvious.
self-evidently

self-explanatory »*adjective* not needing explanation; clearly understood.

self-expression »*noun* the expression of your feelings or thoughts, especially in an art form.

self-fertilization »*noun* the fertilization of plants and some invertebrate animals by their own pollen or sperm.

✓ the alternative spelling **self-fertilisation** is also correct

self-fulfilling »*adjective* (of a prediction) bound to come true because people behave in a way that makes it happen.

self-governing
self-governed
self-government

self-help »*noun* reliance on your own efforts and resources to achieve things.

self-image »*noun* noun the idea you have of your own abilities, appearance, and personality.

self-importance
self-important

self-improvement

self-induced »*adjective* brought about by yourself.

self-indulgent »*adjective* indulging your desires excessively.
self-indulgence

self-inflicted »*adjective* (of a wound or other harm) inflicted on yourself by your own actions.

self-interest »*noun* your personal interest or advantage.
self-interested

selfish
selfishly
selfishness

selfless »*adjective* concerned more with the needs and wishes of others than with your own.
selflessly
selflessness

self-made

self-opinionated »*adjective* having an excessively high regard for yourself or your own opinions.

self-parody »*noun* the intended or unintended parodying of your own behaviour, style, etc.

self-perpetuating »*adjective* able to make itself continue indefinitely without outside intervention.

self-pity »*noun* excessive concern with and unhappiness over your own troubles.
self-pitying

self-pollination »*noun* the pollination of a flower by pollen from the same plant.

self-portrait

self-possessed »*adjective* calm, confident, and in control of your feelings.
self-possession

self-preservation »*noun* the protection of yourself from harm or death.

self-proclaimed »*adjective* proclaimed to be such by yourself, without the agreement of others: *self-proclaimed experts.*

self-raising flour »*noun* flour that has baking powder already added.

self-regard »*noun* ❶ consideration for yourself. ❷ vanity.
self-regarding

self-regulating
self-regulation
self-regulatory

self-reliance »*noun* reliance on your own powers and resources.
self-reliant

self-respect
self-respecting

self-restraint

self-righteous »*adjective* certain that you are totally correct or morally superior.
self-righteously
self-righteousness

self-sacrifice »*noun* the giving up of your own interests or wishes in order to help others.
self-sacrificing

selfsame »*adjective* the very same.

self-satisfied
self-satisfaction

self-seeking »*adjective* concerned only with your own welfare and interests.

self-service

self-serving »*adjective* = SELF-SEEKING.

self-starter »*noun* an ambitious person who acts on their own initiative.

self-styled »*adjective* using a description or title that you have given yourself: *self-styled experts.*

self-sufficient »*adjective* able to satisfy your basic needs, especially for food, without outside help.
self-sufficiency

self-tapping »*adjective* (of a screw) able to cut a thread in the material into which it is inserted.

self-taught

self-worth »*noun* = SELF-ESTEEM.

sell (verb: **sells, selling, sold**) [hand over in exchange for money]
seller

sell-by date

seller [person who sells]

 er not **ar: seller** (a **cellar** is a room below ground level)

selling

Sellotape »*noun* (trademark) transparent adhesive tape.

sell-out »*noun* ❶ the selling of an entire stock of something. ❷ an event for which all tickets are sold. ❸ a sale of a business or company. ❹ a betrayal.

sells

selvedge »*noun* an edge on woven fabric that prevents it from unravelling.
– SAY sel-vij

 don't forget the **d: selvedge**

selves plural of **SELF**.

semantic »*adjective* having to do with meaning.
– SAY si-**man**-tik
  semantically

semantics »*plural noun* ❶ the study of the meaning of words and phrases. ❷ the meaning of words, phrases, etc.

semaphore »*noun* a system of sending messages by holding the arms or two flags in positions that represent letters of the alphabet.

 ✓ ph in the middle: **semaphore**

semblance »*noun* the way that something looks or seems.

semen »*noun* a fluid containing sperm that is produced by men and male animals.
– SAY see-muhn

semester »*noun* a half-year term in a school or university, especially in North America.
– SAY si-**mess**-ter

semi »*noun* (plural **semis**) (in informal English) ❶ a semi-detached house. ❷ a semi-final.

semi-annual »*adjective* occurring twice a year.

semiaquatic »*adjective* ❶ (of an animal) living partly on land and partly in water. ❷ (of a plant) growing in very wet ground.

semi-automatic »*adjective* (of a gun) able to load bullets automatically but not fire continuously.

semibreve »*noun* a musical note that lasts as long as two minims or four crotchets.
– SAY sem-i-breev

 ✓ eve not eev at the end: **semibreve**

semicircle
  semicircular

semicolon »*noun* a punctuation mark (;) indicating a more noticeable pause than that indicated by a comma.
– SAY sem-i-**koh**-luhn

semiconductor »*noun* a solid which conducts electricity, but to a smaller extent than a metal.

semi-conscious »*adjective* partially conscious.

semi-detached »*adjective* (of a house) joined to another house on one side by a common wall.

semi-final
  semi-finalist

seminal »*adjective* ❶ strongly influencing later developments. ❷ referring to semen.

seminar »*noun* ❶ a meeting for discussion or training. ❷ a university class for discussion of topics with a teacher.

seminary »*noun* (plural **seminaries**) a training college for priests or rabbis.
– SAY sem-i-**nuh**-ri
  seminarian

semiotics »*noun* the study of signs and symbols.
– SAY sem-i-**ot**-iks
  semiotic
  semiotician

semipermeable »*adjective* (of a membrane) allowing small molecules to pass through it but not large ones.

semi-precious »*adjective* (of minerals) used as gems but less valuable than precious stones.

semiquaver »*noun* a musical note lasting half as long as a quaver.

semi-retired
  semi-retirement

semis plural of **SEMI**.

semi-skilled »*adjective* (of work or a worker) having or needing some, but not full, training.

semi-skimmed »*adjective* (of milk) having had some of the cream removed.

Semite »*noun* a member of a people speaking a Semitic language, in particular the Jews and Arabs.
– SAY see-myt

 ✓ only one m: **Semite**

Semitic »*noun* a family of languages that includes Hebrew and Arabic.
» *adjective* relating to these languages or their speakers.
– SAY si-**mit**-ik

semitone »*noun* the smallest interval used in classical Western music, equal to half a tone.

semolina »*noun* the hard grains left after the milling of flour, used in puddings and in pasta.

✓ one m, one l, one n: **semolina**

Semtex »*noun* a plastic explosive that is easily moulded.

senate »*noun* ❶ the smaller but higher law-making body in the US, US states, France, and other countries. ❷ the governing body of a university or college. ❸ the state council of the ancient Roman republic and empire.

senator »*noun* a member of a senate.
senatorial

> ☑ **-or** not **-er: senator**

send (verb: **sends**, **sending**, **sent**)
sender

send-off

sends

send-up

Senegalese (plural **Senegalese**)

senescence »*noun* the deterioration of an organism with age.
– SAY si-**ness**-uhnss
senescent

senile »*adjective* having a loss of mental abilities because of old age.
– SAY see-nyl
senility

senile dementia »*noun* severe mental deterioration in old age, with loss of memory and lack of control of bodily functions.

senility

senior
seniority

senna »*noun* a laxative prepared from the dried pods of a tree of warm climates.

senor »*noun* (plural **senores**) (in Spanish-speaking countries) a form of address for a man, corresponding to *Mr* or *sir*.
– SAY sen-**yor** [singular], sen-**yor**-ayz [plural]

> ☑ **senor, senora,** and **senorita** can be spelled **señor, señora, señorita**, with a tilde accent over the **n** (as in the original Spanish)

senora »*noun* (in Spanish-speaking countries) a form of address for a woman, corresponding to *Mrs* or *madam*.
– SAY sen-**yor**-uh

senorita »*noun* (in Spanish-speaking countries) a form of address for an unmarried woman, corresponding to *Miss*.
– SAY sen-yuh-**ree**-tuh

sensation

sensational
sensationally

sensationalise another way of spelling SENSATIONALIZE.

sensationalism »*noun* (in the media) the use of exciting or shocking stories or language at the expense of accuracy.
sensationalist

sensationalize »*verb* (**sensationalizes**, **sensationalizing**, **sensationalized**) present information in an exaggerated way, so as to make it seem more exciting.

> ☑ many people prefer the alternative spellings **sensationalise, sensationalises,** etc.: both **s** and **z** spellings are correct

sensationally

sense (verb: **senses**, **sensing**, **sensed**)

senseless
senselessly
senselessness

senses

sensibility »*noun* (plural **sensibilities**)
❶ the ability to appreciate and respond to emotion or art. ❷ (**sensibilities**) a person's feelings which might be easily offended or shocked.

> ☑ plural: drop the **y** and add **ies: sensibilities**

sensible
sensibly

> ☑ **-ible** not **-able: sensible**

sensing

sensitise another way of spelling SENSITIZE.

sensitive »*adjective* ❶ quick to detect something or be affected by slight changes. ❷ appreciating the feelings of others. ❸ easily offended or upset. ❹ secret or controversial.
sensitively

sensitivity (plural **sensitivities**)

> ☑ plural: drop the **y** and add **ies: sensitivities**

sensitize »*verb* (**sensitizes**, **sensitizing**, **sensitized**) make someone or something sensitive or aware.

> ☑ many people prefer the alternative spellings **sensitise, sensitises,** etc.: both **s** and **z** spellings are correct

sensor »*noun* a device which detects or measures a physical property.

> ☑ **-or** not **-er: sensor**

sensory »*adjective* relating to sensation or the senses.

sensual »*adjective* relating to the senses as a source of pleasure.
sensuality
sensually

> ⓘ **sensual** and **sensuous** do not mean exactly the same thing. **Sensual** is used to refer to the senses as a source of pleasure or sexual gratification, while **sensuous** is used less specifically to mean

'relating to the senses rather than the intellect'.

sensuous »*adjective* ❶ relating to the senses rather than the intellect. ❷ attractive or pleasing physically.
sensuously
sensuousness

sent past and past participle of **send**.

sentence (verb: **sentences, sentencing, sentenced**)

 ence not ance: **sentence**

sententious »*adjective* given to making pompous comments on moral issues.
– SAY sen-**ten**-shuhss
sententiously
sententiousness

sentient »*adjective* able to perceive or feel things.
– SAY sen-shuhnt
sentience
sentiently

sentiment »*noun* ❶ an opinion or feeling. ❷ excessive feelings of tenderness, sadness, or nostalgia.

sentimental »*adjective* prone to or causing excessive feelings of tenderness, sadness, or nostalgia.
sentimentality
sentimentally

sentimentalize »*verb* (**sentimentalizes, sentimentalizing, sentimentalized**) present something in a sentimental way.

 many people prefer the alternative spellings **sentimentalise, sentimentalises**, etc.: both **s** and **z** spellings are correct

sentimentally

sentinel »*noun* a soldier or guard whose job is to stand and keep watch.
– SAY sen-ti-nuhl

 only one **l** at the end: **sentinel**

sentry »*noun* (plural **sentries**) a soldier stationed to keep guard or to control access to a place.

 plural: drop the **y** and add **ies**: **sentries**

sepal »*noun* one of the leaf-like parts of a flower that surround the petals.
– SAY sep-uhl or see-puhl

separable »*adjective* able to be separated or treated separately.

separate (verb: **separates, separating, separated**)

separately
separator

 remember, the middle syllable of **separate** is par not per

separation

separatist »*noun* a member of a group within a country who want to separate from the rest of the country to form an independent state.
separatism

separator

sepia »*noun* ❶ a reddish-brown colour, associated with early photographs. ❷ a brown pigment prepared from cuttlefish ink.
– SAY see-pi-uh

 only one **p**: **sepia**

sepoy »*noun* (a historical term) an Indian soldier serving under British or other European orders.
– SAY see-poy or si-poy

seppuku »*noun* = **hara-kiri**.
– SAY sep-**poo**-koo

sepsis »*noun* (in medicine) the presence in tissues of harmful bacteria, through infection of a wound.
– SAY sep-siss

septa plural of **septum**.

septal

September

septet »*noun* a group of seven people playing music or singing together.

septic »*adjective* (of a wound or a part of the body) infected with bacteria.

septicaemia »*noun* blood poisoning caused by bacteria.
– SAY sep-ti-**see**-mi-uh

 caem not cem: **septicaemia** (the spelling **septicemia** is American)

septic tank »*noun* a underground tank in which sewage is allowed to decompose through the activity of bacteria before being drained.

septuagenarian »*noun* a person who is between 70 and 79 years old.
– SAY sep-tyuu-uh-ji-**nair**-i-uhn

 septua not septa: **septuagenarian**

septum »*noun* (plural **septa**) a partition separating two cavities in the body, such as that between the nostrils.
septal

 the plural of **septum** is **septa** (as in the original Latin)

septuple »*adjective* ❶ consisting of seven parts. ❷ seven times as many or as much.

septuplet »*noun* one of seven children born at one birth.
– **SAY** sep-tyuu-plit or sep-**tyoo**-plit

sepulchral »*adjective* ❶ having to do with a tomb or burial. ❷ gloomy.
– **SAY** si-**pul**-kruhl
sepulchrally

sepulchre »*noun* a stone tomb.
– **SAY** sep-uhl-ker

> ✓ chre nor cher: sepulchre (the spelling sepulcher is American)

sequel »*noun* ❶ a book, film, or programme that continues the story of an earlier one. ❷ something that takes place after or as a result of an earlier event.

> ✓ the ending is el not al: sequel

sequence »*noun* ❶ a particular order in which things follow each other. ❷ a set of things that follow each other in a particular order.
» *verb* (sequences, sequencing, sequenced) arrange things in a sequence.

sequential »*adjective* following in a logical order or sequence.
sequentially

sequester »*verb* (sequesters, sequestering, sequestered) ❶ isolate something or hide something away. ❷ = SEQUESTRATE.
– **SAY** si-**kwess**-ter

sequestrate »*verb* (sequestrates, sequestrating, sequestrated) take legal possession of assets until a debt has been paid.
– **SAY** si-**kwess**-trayt or see-kwi-strayt
sequestration

sequin »*noun* a small, shiny disc sewn on to clothing for decoration.
sequinned

> ✓ sequinned can also be spelled sequined, with only one n

sequoia »*noun* a redwood tree.
– **SAY** si-**kwoy**-uh

> ✓ the ending is oia: sequoia. The trees are named after a Cherokee Indian, *Sequoya*, who invented written characters for the Cherokee language.

sera plural of SERUM.

seraglio »*noun* (plural seraglios) ❶ the women's apartments in a Muslim house or palace. ❷ a harem.
– **SAY** si-**rah**-li-oh

> ⓘ the plural of seraglio (an Italian word) has os not oes: seraglios

seraph »*noun* (plural seraphim or seraphs) a type of angel associated with light and purity.
– **SAY** se-ruhf [singular], se-ruh-fim [plural]
seraphic

> ✓ the plural of seraph can be seraphim (as in the original Hebrew) or seraphs

Serb »*noun* a person from Serbia.
Serbian

Serbo-Croat »*noun* the language spoken in Serbia, Croatia, and elsewhere in the former Yugoslavia.
– **SAY** ser-boh **kroh**-at

serenade »*noun* a piece of music sung or played in the open air at night, especially by a man under the window of his lover.
» *verb* (serenades, serenading, serenaded) entertain someone with a serenade.

> ✓ ren not ran in the middle: serenade

serendipity »*noun* the occurrence of events by chance in a fortunate way.
– **SAY** se-ruhn-**dip**-i-ti
serendipitous
serendipitously

serene »*adjective* calm and peaceful.
serenely
serenity

> ✓ rene not rine: serene

serf »*noun* (in the feudal system) an agricultural labourer who was tied to working on a particular estate.
serfdom

serge »*noun* a hard-wearing woollen or worsted fabric.
– **SAY** *rhymes with* urge

sergeant »*noun* ❶ a rank of non-commissioned officer in the army or air force above corporal. ❷ (in the UK) a police officer ranking below an inspector.
– **SAY** sar-juhnt

> ✓ geant not gant: sergeant. The old spelling serjeant still appears in some traditional contexts.

sergeant major »*noun* a warrant officer in the British army who assists with administrative duties.

serial »*adjective* ❶ consisting of or taking place in a series. ❷ repeatedly committing the same offence: *a serial killer.*
» *noun* a story or play published or broadcast in regular instalments.
serially

> ⓘ do not confuse serial with cereal, which refers to an edible grass such as wheat

serialize »*verb* (**serializes**, **serializing**, **serialized**) publish or broadcast a story or play in regular instalments.
serialization

> ✓ many people prefer the alternative spellings **serialise**, **serialises**, etc., and **serialisation**: both **s** and **z** spellings are correct

serially

serial number »*noun* an identification number showing the position of a manufactured item in a series.

series (plural **series**)

serious
seriously
seriousness

serjeant see the note at **SERGEANT**.

sermon »*noun* a religious or moral talk, especially one given in church.

sermonize »*verb* (**sermonizes**, **sermonizing**, **sermonized**) give moral advice to someone.

> ✓ many people prefer the alternative spellings **sermonise**, **sermonises**, etc.: both **s** and **z** spellings are correct

serology »*noun* the scientific study or diagnostic examination of blood serum.
– sᴀʏ si-**rol**-uh-ji
serological
serologist

serotonin »*noun* a compound present in blood which constricts the blood vessels and is involved in the sending of nerve impulses.
– sᴀʏ se-ruh-**toh**-nin

serpent »*noun* (a poetic term) a large snake.

serpentine »*adjective* winding or twisting.
– sᴀʏ **ser**-puhn-tyn

serrated »*adjective* having a jagged edge like the teeth of a saw.

> ✓ double **r**: **serrated**

serration »*noun* a tooth or point of a serrated edge.

serried »*adjective* (of rows of people or things) standing close together.

serum »*noun* (plural **sera** or **serums**) the thin liquid which separates out when blood clots.
– sᴀʏ **seer**-uhm [singular], **seer**-uh [plural]

> ✓ the plural of **serum** can be **sera** (as in the original Latin) or **serums**

servant

> 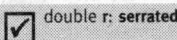 ✓ **ant** not **ent**: **servant**

serve (verb: **serves**, **serving**, **served**)

server »*noun* ❶ a person or thing that serves. ❷ a computer or computer program which manages access to a centralized resource or service in a network.

servery »*noun* (plural **serveries**) a counter, hatch, or room from which meals are served.

serves

service (verb: **services**, **servicing**, **serviced**)

serviceable »*adjective* ❶ usable or in working order. ❷ useful and hard-wearing rather than attractive.

> ✓ don't forget the **e** before -**able**: **serviceable**

serviced

service industry »*noun* a business that provides a service for a customer, but is not involved in manufacturing.

serviceman »*noun* (plural **servicemen**) a person serving in the armed forces.

service provider »*noun* (in computing) a company which provides access to the Internet.

service road »*noun* a road running parallel to a main road and giving access to houses, shops, or businesses.

services

servicewoman (plural **servicewomen**)

servicing

serviette »*noun* a table napkin.

> ✓ **ette** at the end: **serviette** is derived from French

servile »*adjective* ❶ too willing to serve or please others. ❷ having to do with a slave or slaves.
servility

serving

servitude »*noun* ❶ the state of being a slave. ❷ the state of being completely controlled by someone more powerful.
– sᴀʏ **ser**-vi-tyood

servomechanism »*noun* a powered mechanism producing motion or forces at a higher level of energy than the input level, e.g. in the brakes and steering of large motor vehicles.

sesame »*noun* a tall plant of tropical and subtropical areas, grown for its oil-rich seeds.
– sᴀʏ **sess**-uh-mi

> 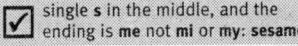 ✓ single **s** in the middle, and the ending is **me** not **mi** or **my**: **sesame**

sesquicentenary »*noun* (plural **sesquicentenaries**) the one-hundred-and-fiftieth anniversary of a significant event.
– **SAY** sess-kwi-sen-**tee**-nuh-ri
sesquicentennial

session [period for a particular activity]

> **i** do not confuse **session** with **cession**, which means 'the formal giving up of rights or territory by a state'

session musician »*noun* a freelance musician hired to play on recording sessions.

set (verb: **sets, setting, set**)

> ☑ double the **t** in **setting**

set-aside »*noun* ❶ the policy of taking land out of production to reduce crop surpluses. ❷ land taken out of production in this way.

setback

set piece »*noun* ❶ part of a novel, film, etc. that is arranged for maximum effect. ❷ a carefully organized move in a team game.

sets

set square »*noun* a right-angled triangular plate for drawing lines at particular angles.

sett »*noun* the earth or burrow of a badger.

settee

setter »*noun* a dog of a large long-haired breed trained to stand rigid when scenting game.

setting

settle (verb: **settles, settling, settled**)

settlement

settler

settles

settling

set-to »*noun* (plural **set-tos**) (in informal English) a fight or argument.

set-up

seven
  sevenfold

seventeen
  seventeenth

seventh
  seventhly

seventy (plural **seventies**)
  seventieth

sever »*verb* (**severs, severing, severed**)
❶ cut off or divide something by cutting. ❷ put an end to a connection or relationship.

several
  severally

> ☑ **ver** not **var** in the middle, and only one **l** at the end: **several**

severance »*noun* ❶ the action of ending a connection or relationship. ❷ the state of being separated or cut off.

> ☑ **ance** not **ence**: **severance**

severance pay »*noun* money paid to an employee on the early ending of a contract.

severe (adjective: **severer, severest**)
  severely
  severity

severed

severely

severer [more severe]

severest

severing

severity

severs

Seville orange »*noun* a bitter orange used for marmalade.

> **i** named after the city of *Seville* in Spain

sew (verb: **sews, sewing, sewed**; past participle **sewn** or **sewed**) [join by stitching]

sewage »*noun* waste water and excrement conveyed in sewers.

sewed

sewer[1] »*noun* an underground pipe for carrying off drainage water and waste matter.
– **SAY** soo-er

sewer[2] »*noun* a person who sews.
– **SAY** soh-uh

sewerage »*noun* ❶ the provision of drainage by sewers. ❷ (in American English) = **SEWAGE**.

sewing

sewn past participle of **SEW**.

sews

sex (plural **sexes**)

> **i** **sex** usually refers to biological differences, whereas **gender** usually refers to cultural or social ones

sexagenarian »*noun* a person between 60 and 69 years old.
– **SAY** seks-uh-ji-**nair**-i-uhn

sexed »*adjective* having specified sexual appetites: *highly sexed.*

sexes

sexier

sexiest

sexily

sexiness

sexism »*noun* prejudice or discrimination on the basis of sex.
sexist

sexless »*adjective* ❶ not sexually attractive or active. ❷ neither male nor female.

sextant »*noun* an instrument used for measuring the angular distances between objects, used in navigation and surveying.
-- SAY seks-tuhnt

> ☑ **ant** not **ent: sextant.** Do not confuse **sextant** with **sexton,** which means 'a person who looks after a church and churchyard'.

sextet »*noun* ❶ a group of six people playing music or singing together. ❷ a composition for a sextet. ❸ a set of six.

sexton »*noun* a person who looks after a church and churchyard.

> ☑ **-on** not **-en: sexton.** Do not confuse **sexton** with **sextant,** which refers to an instrument used in navigation.

sextuple »*adjective* ❶ made up of six parts. ❷ six times as much or as many.

sextuplet »*noun* one of six children born at one birth.
- SAY seks-tyuu-plit or seks-**tyoo**-plit

sexual
sexually

sexuality (plural sexualities)

sexually

sexual politics »*plural noun* relations between the sexes regarded in terms of power.

sexy (adjective: sexier, sexiest)
sexily
sexiness

shabby (adjective: shabbier, shabbiest)
shabbily
shabbiness

> ☑ double b: shabby

shack (verb: shacks, shacking, shacked)

shackle »*noun* ❶ (shackles) a pair of rings connected by a chain, used to fasten a prisoner's wrists or ankles together. ❷ (shackles) restraints: *the shackles of racism and colonialism.* ❸ a metal link or loop, closed by a bolt and used to secure a chain or rope to something.

» *verb* (shackles, shackling, shackled)
❶ chain someone with shackles.
❷ restrain or limit something.

shacks

shad »*noun* (plural shad or shads) an edible herring-like sea fish that enters rivers to spawn.

shade (verb: shades, shading, shaded)

shadier

shadiest

shadiness

shading

shadow (verb: shadows, shadowing, shadowed)

shadow-boxing »*noun* boxing against an imaginary opponent as a form of training.

shadowed

shadowing

shadows

shadowy

shads plural of SHAD.

shady (adjective: shadier, shadiest)
shadiness

shaft (verb: shafts, shafting, shafted)

shag[1] »*noun* coarse tobacco.
» *adjective* (of pile on a carpet) long and rough.

shag[2] »*noun* a cormorant with greenish-black plumage.

shag[3] (vulgar) »*verb* (shags, shagging, shagged) have sexual intercourse with someone.
» *noun* an act of sexual intercourse.

shaggy (adjective: shaggier, shaggiest)
shagginess

shagreen »*noun* ❶ sharkskin used for decoration. ❷ untanned leather with a rough surface.
- SAY sha-**green**

> ☑ do not confuse **shagreen** with **chagrin,** which means 'a feeling of annoyance or shame at having failed'

shags

shah »*noun* (a historical term) a title of the former monarch of Iran.

shake (verb: shakes, shaking, shook; past participle shaken)

shaker

shakes

Shakespearean

> ☑ **Shakespearean** can also be spelled with an **ian** ending: **Shakespearian**

shake-up

shakier

shakiest

shakily

shakiness

shaking

shaky (adjective: **shakier**, **shakiest**)
shakily
shakiness

shale »*noun* soft rock formed from compressed mud or clay, that splits easily into thin layers.
shaley

shall

> ℹ️ there are traditional rules as to when to use **shall** and when to use **will**. These state that when forming the future tense, **shall** should be used with **I** and **we** (*I shall be late*), while **will** should be used with **you**, **he**, **she**, **it**, and **they** (*he will not be there*). However, when you want to tell someone what to do or show that you are determined, this rule is reversed: **will** is used with **I** and **we** (*I will not tolerate this*), and **shall** is used with **you**, **he**, **she**, **it**, and **they** (*you shall go to school*). Nowadays, people do not follow these rules so strictly and are more likely to use the shortened forms **I'll**, **she'll**, etc.

shallot »*noun* a vegetable resembling a small onion (to which it is related).
– SAY shuh-**lot**

> ✅ note the double **l**: **shallot**

shallow (adjective: **shallower**, **shallowest**)
shallowly
shallowness

shallows »*noun* a shallow area of water.

shalom »*exclamation* said by Jews at meeting or parting.
– SAY shuh-**lom**

> ℹ️ **shalom** is a Hebrew word which means 'peace'

sham »*noun* ❶ a thing that is not what it appears to be or is not as good as it seems. ❷ a person who pretends to be something they are not.
» *adjective* not genuine; false.
» *verb* (**shams**, **shamming**, **shammed**) pretend.

> ✅ double the **m** to spell **shamming** and **shammed**

shaman »*noun* (plural **shamans**) (in some societies) a person believed to be able to contact good and evil spirits.

– SAY shay-muhn or sha-muhn
shamanic
shamanism

shamble »*verb* (**shambles**, **shambling**, **shambled**) walk in a slow, shuffling, awkward way.

shambles

shambling

shambolic

shame (verb: **shames**, **shaming**, **shamed**)

shamefaced
shamefacedly
shamefacedness

shameful
shamefully
shamefulness

> ✅ -**ful** not -**full**: **shameful**

shameless
shamelessly
shamelessness

shames

shaming

shammed

shammies

shamming

shammy »*noun* (plural **shammies**) chamois leather.

shampoo (verb: **shampoos**, **shampooing**, **shampooed**)

shamrock »*noun* a clover-like plant with three leaves on each stem, the national emblem of Ireland.

shams

shandy »*noun* (plural **shandies**) beer mixed with lemonade or ginger beer.

> ✅ plural: drop the **y** and add **ies**: **shandies**

shanghai »*verb* (**shanghais**, **shanghaiing**, **shanghaied**) (in informal English) force or trick someone into doing something.
– SAY shang-**hy**

> ℹ️ from the Chinese seaport of *Shanghai*. The **i** is doubled in **Shanghaiing**.

Shangri-La »*noun* an earthly paradise.

> ℹ️ the name **Shangri-La** was invented by James Hilton in his book *Lost Horizon* (1933), later filmed. **La** is Tibetan for 'mountain pass'.

shank »*noun* ❶ the lower part of the leg. ❷ the shaft of a tool.

shan't [shall not]

☑ be careful to put the apostrophe where the **o** has been left out, that is between the **n** and **t** of not: **shan't**

shanties

shantung »*noun* a type of silk fabric with a coarse surface.

shanty »*noun* (plural **shanties**) **❶** a small roughly built hut. **❷** a song with alternating solo and chorus, sung by sailors when working.

☑ plural: drop the **y** and add **ies**: **shanties**

shanty town »*noun* a settlement in or near a town where poor people live in shanties.

shape (verb: **shapes, shaping, shaped**)
shaper

shapeless
shapelessly
shapelessness

shapely (adjective: **shapelier, shapeliest**)
shapeliness

shaper

shapes

shaping

shard »*noun* a sharp piece of broken pottery, glass, etc.

share (verb: **shares, sharing, shared**)
sharer

shareholder

share option »*noun* an option for an employee to buy shares in their company at a discount or at a stated fixed price.

sharer

shares

sharia »*noun* Islamic law, based on the teachings of the Koran and the traditions of Muhammad.
– **SAY** shuh-**ree**-uh

sharing

shark

sharkskin »*noun* a stiff, slightly shiny synthetic fabric.

sharp (adjective: **sharper, sharpest**)
sharply
sharpness

sharpen »*verb* (**sharpens, sharpening, sharpened**) make or become sharp.
sharpener

sharper

sharpest

sharpish

sharply

sharpness

sharp practice »*noun* dishonest business dealings.

sharpshooter »*noun* a person skilled in shooting.

sharp-tongued

sharp-witted

shat past and past participle of **SHIT**.

shatter (verb: **shatters, shattering, shattered**)

shave (verb: **shaves, shaving, shaved**)
shaven
shaver

shaving

shawl

shaykh another way of spelling **SHEIKH**.

she

sheaf »*noun* (plural **sheaves**) **❶** a bundle of grain stalks tied together after reaping. **❷** a bundle of papers.

☑ the plural of **sheaf** drops the **f** and adds **ves**: **sheaves**

shear »*verb* (**shears, shearing, sheared**; past participle **shorn** or **sheared**) **❶** cut the wool off a sheep. **❷** cut off something such as wool or grass with shears. **❸** (**be shorn of**) have something taken away from you. **❹** tear or break off under pressure.
shearer

ℹ do not confuse **shear** with **sheer**, which means 'swerve or change course quickly', as in *the boat sheers off the bank*

shears »*plural noun* a cutting implement like very large scissors.

shearwater »*noun* a long-winged seabird related to the petrels, often flying low over the water.

☑ shear- not sheer-: **shearwater**

sheath »*noun* (plural **sheaths**) **❶** a cover for the blade of a knife or sword. **❷** a condom. **❸** a close-fitting covering. **❹** a close-fitting dress.
– **SAY** sheeth [singular], shee*th*z or sheeths [plural]

sheathe »*verb* (**sheathes, sheathing, sheathed**) **❶** put a knife or sword into a sheath. **❷** encase something in a close-fitting or protective covering.
– **SAY** shee*th*
sheathing

sheath knife »*noun* a short knife similar to a dagger, carried in a sheath.

sheaths

sheaves plural of **SHEAF**.

shebang »*noun* (**the whole shebang**) (in informal English) the whole thing; everything.
– SAY shi-**bang**

shed[1] [building for storage]

shed[2] »*verb* (**sheds, shedding, shed**)
❶ allow leaves, hair, skin, etc. to fall off naturally. ❷ get rid of something. ❸ take off clothes. ❹ give off light.
❺ accidentally drop or spill something.
❻ allow something to spill out.

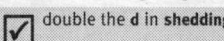 double the **d** in **shedding**

she'd [she had; she would]

shedding

sheds

sheen »*noun* a soft shine on a surface.

sheep (plural **sheep**)

sheepdog

sheepish
sheepishly
sheepishness

sheepshank »*noun* a kind of knot used to shorten a rope temporarily.

sheepskin

sheer[1] »*adjective* (**sheerer, sheerest**)
❶ nothing but; absolute: *sheer hard work.*
❷ (of a cliff, wall, etc.) vertical or almost vertical. ❸ (of a fabric) very thin.
»*adverb* vertically.
sheerly
sheerness

sheer[2] »*verb* (**sheers, sheering, sheered**)
❶ (especially of a boat) change course quickly. ❷ move away from an unpleasant topic.

ℹ️ do not confuse **sheer** with **shear**, which means 'cut the wool off a sheep' or 'cut or break off'

sheet

sheet anchor »*noun* ❶ an additional anchor for use in emergencies. ❷ a person or thing that can be relied on if all else fails.

sheeting

sheet music »*noun* music published on loose sheets of paper and not bound into a book.

sheikh »*noun* ❶ the leader of an Arab tribe, family, or village. ❷ a leader in a Muslim community or organization.
– SAY shayk
sheikhdom

✓ **sheikh** (remember the final **h**) is an Arabic word which means 'old man' or 'leader'. It is sometimes written **shaykh**: both spellings are correct.

shekel »*noun* the basic unit of money of modern Israel.
– SAY *rhymes with* heckle

✓ **kel** not **kle: shekel**

shelduck »*noun* a large goose-like duck with boldly marked plumage.

shelf (plural **shelves**)

✓ the plural of **shelf** drops the **f** and adds **ves**

shelf life »*noun* the length of time for which an item in a shop remains able to be eaten, used, or sold.

shell (verb: **shells, shelling, shelled**)

she'll [she shall; she will]

shellac »*noun* lac resin melted into thin flakes, used for making varnish.
– SAY shuh-**lak**

shelled

shellfire

shellfish

shelling

shells

shell shock »*noun* a mental illness resembling a state of shock, that can affect soldiers who have been in battle for a long time.
shell-shocked

shell suit »*noun* a casual outfit consisting of a loose jacket and trousers with a soft lining and a shiny outer layer.

shelter (verb: **shelters, sheltering, sheltered**)

sheltered housing »*noun* accommodation for elderly or disabled people consisting of private units with some shared facilities and a warden.

sheltering

shelters

shelve »*verb* (**shelves, shelving, shelved**)
❶ place something on a shelf. ❷ decide not to continue with a plan for the time being. ❸ (of ground) slope downwards.

shelves plural of **SHELF**.

shelving

shemozzle »*noun* (in informal English) a muddle.

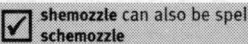 **shemozzle** can also be spelled **schemozzle**

shenanigans »*plural noun* ❶ secret or dishonest activity. ❷ high-spirited behaviour.

shepherd (verb: **shepherds, shepherding, shepherded**)

> ✓ note the single **p** and the **h** in the middle, and that the ending is **erd** not **ard**: **shepherd**

shepherdess (plural **shepherdesses**)

shepherding

shepherds

shepherd's pie »*noun* a dish of minced meat under a layer of mashed potato.

sherbet »*noun* ❶ a sweet fizzing powder eaten alone or made into a drink. ❷ (in Arab countries) a drink of sweet diluted fruit juices.

> ✓ **bet** not **bert**: **sherbet**

sheriff »*noun* ❶ (also **high sheriff**) (in England and Wales) the chief executive officer in a county, working on behalf of the king or queen. ❷ (in Scotland) a judge. ❸ (in the US) an elected officer in a county, responsible for keeping the peace.

> ✓ single **r** but double **f**: **sheriff**

Sherpa »*noun* (plural **Sherpa** or **Sherpas**) a member of a Himalayan people living on the borders of Nepal and Tibet.

sherry »*noun* (plural **sherries**) a strong wine originally from southern Spain.

> ⓘ named after the city of *Xeres*, now called Jerez de la Frontera

> ✓ plural: drop the **y** and add **ies**: **sherries**

she's [she is; she has]

Shetland pony »*noun* a small pony with a rough coat.

Shia »*noun* (plural **Shia** or **Shias**) ❶ one of the two main branches of Islam. ❷ a Muslim who follows this branch of Islam.
– SAY shi-uh

shiatsu »*noun* a medical treatment from Japan in which pressure is applied with the hands to points on the body.
– SAY shi-**at**-soo

shibboleth »*noun* a long-standing belief or principle held by a group of people.
– SAY shib-buh-leth

> ⓘ **shibboleth** is a Hebrew word which was used as a test of nationality in biblical times because foreigners were thought not to be able to pronounce it

shied past and past participle of SHY.

shield (verb: **shields, shielding, shielded**)

> ✓ the usual rule is **i** before **e**, except after **c**: **shield**

shies

shift (verb: **shifts, shifting, shifted**)
shifter

shiftier

shiftiest

shiftily

shiftiness

shifting

shiftless »*adjective* lazy and lacking ambition.
shiftlessness

shifts

shifty »*adjective* (**shiftier, shiftiest**) seeming dishonest or untrustworthy.
shiftily
shiftiness

Shiite »*noun* a follower of the Shia branch of Islam.
– SAY shee-yt
Shiism

> ✓ note the double **i** in **Shiite** and **Shiism**

shilling »*noun* a former British coin worth one twentieth of a pound or twelve pence.

shilly-shally »*verb* (**shilly-shallies, shilly-shallying, shilly-shallied**) be unable to make up your mind.

shimmer »*verb* (**shimmers, shimmering, shimmered**) shine with a soft wavering light.
» *noun* a soft wavering light or shine.
shimmery

shimmy »*verb* (**shimmies, shimmying, shimmied**) move swiftly and smoothly.

shin »*noun* ❶ the front of the leg below the knee. ❷ a cut of beef from the lower part of a cow's leg.
» *verb* (**shins, shinning, shinned**) (**shin up** or **down**) climb quickly up or down by gripping with your arms and legs.

shindig »*noun* (in informal English) a large, lively party.

shine (verb: **shines, shining, shone** or **shined**)
shiner

shingle[1] »*noun* a mass of small rounded pebbles on a seashore.

shingle[2] »*noun* a rectangular wooden tile used on walls or roofs.
shingled

shingles »*noun* a disease with painful blisters forming along the path of a nerve or nerves.

shinier

shiniest

shinily

shininess

shining [as in *the sun was shining*]

shinned

shinning [as in *children shinning up trees*]

shins

Shinto »*noun* a Japanese religion involving the worship of ancestors.
Shintoism

shinty »*noun* a Scottish game resembling hockey, played with curved sticks and taller goalposts.

shiny (adjective: shinier, shiniest)
shinily
shininess

> ✓ drop the **y** and add **ier** or **iest** to spell **shinier** or **shiniest**

ship (verb: ships, shipping, shipped)
shipload
shipper

shipboard

shipbuilder
shipbuilding

shipload

shipmate

shipment

shipped

shipper

shipping

ships

shipshape »*adjective* orderly and neat.

shipwreck (verb: shipwrecks, shipwrecking, shipwrecked)

shipwright »*noun* a shipbuilder.

shipyard

shire »*noun* ❶ a county in England. ❷ (the Shires) the rural areas of England, regarded as strongholds of traditional country life.

shire horse »*noun* a heavy powerful breed of horse, used for pulling loads.

shirk »*verb* (shirks, shirking, shirked) avoid work or a duty.
shirker

shirred »*adjective* (of fabric) gathered by means of threads in parallel rows.
– say *rhymes with* bird

shirt

shirtier

shirtiest

shirtily

shirtiness

shirtsleeves
shirtsleeved

shirty »*adjective* (shirtier, shirtiest) (in informal English) bad-tempered or annoyed.
shirtily
shirtiness

shish kebab »*noun* a dish of pieces of meat and vegetables cooked and served on skewers.

shit (verb: shits, shitting, shitted or shit or shat)

shitty (adjective: shittier, shittiest)

shiver[1] (verb: shivers, shivering, shivered) [shake slightly]
shivery

shiver[2] »*noun* a splinter or fragment.
» *verb* (shivers, shivering, shivered) break into shivers.

shoal »*noun* ❶ a large number of fish swimming together. ❷ an area of shallow water. ❸ a submerged sandbank that can be seen at low tide.

shock (verb: shocks, shocking, shocked)
shockable
shockproof

shock absorber »*noun* a device for absorbing jolts and vibrations on a vehicle.

shocked

shocker

shocking
shockingly

shockproof

shocks

shock troops »*plural noun* troops trained to carry out sudden attacks.

shock wave »*noun* a moving wave of very high pressure caused by explosion or by a body travelling faster than sound.

shod past and past participle of **SHOE**.

shoddy »*adjective* (shoddier, shoddiest) ❶ badly made or done. ❷ dishonest or immoral.
shoddily
shoddiness

> ✓ drop the **y** and add **ier** or **iest** to spell **shoddier** or **shoddiest**

shoe (verb: shoes, shoeing, shod) [covering for the foot; fit a horse with shoes]

shoebox

shoehorn »*noun* a curved piece of metal or plastic, used for easing your heel into a shoe.
» *verb* (**shoehorns, shoehorning, shoehorned**) force something into a tight space.

shoeing

shoelace

shoemaker

shoes

shoestring »*noun* (**on a shoestring**) with only a very small amount of money.

shoe tree »*noun* a shaped block put into a shoe when it is not being worn to keep it in shape.

shogun »*noun* (in the past, in Japan) a hereditary leader of the army.
– SAY shoh-guhn

shone past and past participle of SHINE.

shoo-in »*noun* a person or thing that is certain to succeed or win.

shook past of SHAKE.

shoot (verb: **shoots, shooting, shot**)
 shooter
 shooting

shooting star »*noun* a small, rapidly moving meteor that burns up on entering the earth's atmosphere.

shooting stick »*noun* a walking stick with a handle that unfolds to form a seat.

shoot-out

shoots

shop (verb: **shops, shopping, shopped**)

> ☑ double the **p** in **shopping** and **shopped**

shopaholic »*noun* (in informal English) a person with an uncontrollable urge to go shopping.

shopfitter »*noun* a person whose job it is to fit the counters, shelves, etc. with which a shop is equipped.

shop floor »*noun* the area in a factory where things are made or put together by the workers.

shopkeeper

shoplifting
 shoplifter

shopped

shopper

shopping

shops

shop-soiled »*adjective* (of an article) dirty or damaged from being displayed or handled in a shop.

shop steward »*noun* a person elected by workers in a factory to represent them in dealings with management.

shore[1] [land along the edge of the sea]

shore[2] »*verb* (**shores, shoring, shored**) (**shore up**) ❶ hold something up with a prop or beam. ❷ support or strengthen something.

shore leave »*noun* leisure time spent ashore by a sailor.

shoreline

shores

shoreward

shorewards

shoring

shorn past participle of SHEAR.

short (adjective: **shorter, shortest**; verb: **shorts, shorting, shorted**)
 shortish
 shortness

shortage

shortbread »*noun* a rich, crumbly type of biscuit made with butter, flour, and sugar.

shortcake »*noun* = SHORTBREAD.

short-change »*verb* (**short-changes, short-changing, short-changed**) cheat someone by giving them less than the correct change.

short circuit »*noun* a faulty connection in an electrical circuit in which the current flows along a shorter route than it should do.
» *verb* (**short-circuits, short-circuiting, short-circuited**) cause or have a short circuit.

shortcoming »*noun* a fault in someone's character or in a plan or system.

shortcrust pastry »*noun* crumbly pastry made with flour, fat, and a little water.

shorted

shorten (verb: **shortens, shortening, shortened**)

shortening »*noun* fat used for making pastry.

shortens

shorter

shortest

shortfall »*noun* a situation in which something amounts to less than is required.

shorthand »*noun* a way of writing very quickly when recording what someone is saying, by using abbreviations and symbols.

short-handed »*adjective & adverb* having fewer staff than you need or than is usual.

S

short head »*noun* (in horse racing) a distance less than the length of a horse's head.

shorting

shortish

shortlist »*noun* a list of selected candidates from which a final choice is made.
» *verb* (**shortlists, shortlisting, shortlisted**) put someone on a shortlist.

short-lived

shortly

shortness

short-range

shorts

short shrift »*noun* abrupt and unsympathetic treatment.

short-sighted »*adjective* ❶ unable to see things clearly unless they are close to your eyes. ❷ not thinking carefully about the consequences of something.
short-sightedly
short-sightedness

short-staffed »*adjective* = SHORT-HANDED.

short-tempered

short wave »*noun* a radio wave of a wavelength between about 10 and 100 metres (and a frequency of about 3 to 30 megahertz).

shot

shotgun

shotgun marriage »*noun* (in informal English) a wedding that has to take place quickly because the bride is pregnant.

shot put »*noun* an athletic contest in which a very heavy round ball is thrown as far as possible.
shot-putter

should

> ℹ️ there are traditional rules as to when to use **should** and when to use **would**. These say that **should** is used with I and **we** (*I said I should be late*), while **would** is used with **you, he, she, it,** and **they** (*you didn't say you would be late*). Nowadays, these rules are no longer strictly followed and it is usually acceptable to use **would** instead.

shoulder (verb: **shoulders, shouldering, shouldered**)

shoulder blade »*noun* either of the large, flat, triangular bones at the top of the back; the scapula.

shouldered

shouldering

shoulders

shouldn't [should not]

> ✅ be careful to put the apostrophe where a letter has been left out, that is between the **n** and **t** of **not**: **shouldn't**

shout (verb: **shouts, shouting, shouted**)

shove (verb: **shoves, shoving, shoved**)

shovel (verb: **shovels, shovelling, shovelled**)

> ✅ double the **l** in **shovelling** and **shovelled** (the spellings **shoveling** and **shoveled** are American)

shoves

shoving

show (verb: **shows, showing, showed**; past participle **shown** or **showed**)

showbiz

showboat »*noun* (in the US) a river steamer on which theatrical performances are given.
» *verb* (**showboats, showboating, showboated**) (in informal English) show off.

showcase »*noun* ❶ a glass case used for displaying articles in a shop or museum. ❷ an occasion for presenting something favourably.
» *verb* (**showcases, showcasing, showcased**) put something on display.

showdown »*noun* a final meeting or test intended to settle a dispute.

showed

shower (verb: **showers, showering, showered**)
showerproof

showery

showgirl »*noun* an actress who sings and dances in musicals, variety shows, etc.

showground »*noun* an area of land on which a show takes place.

showier

showiest

showily

showiness

showing

showjumping »*noun* the sport of riding horses over a course of obstacles in an arena.
showjumper

showman »*noun* (plural **showmen**) ❶ the manager or presenter of a circus, fair, etc. ❷ a person who is skilled at entertaining people or getting their attention.
showmanship

shown past participle of SHOW.

show-off

showpiece »*noun* something which attracts attention as an outstanding example of its type.

showplace »*noun* a place of beauty or interest that attracts many visitors.

showroom

shows

show-stopper »*noun* (in informal English) a very impressive performance that receives prolonged applause.
show-stopping

show trial »*noun* a public trial that is held to influence or satisfy public opinion, rather than to ensure that justice is done.

showy »*adjective* (**showier**, **showiest**) very bright or colourful and attracting much attention.
showily
showiness

> ✓ drop the y and add **ier** or **iest** to spell **showier** or **showiest**

shrank past of **SHRINK**.

shrapnel »*noun* small metal fragments thrown out by the explosion of a shell or bomb.

> ℹ named after General Henry *Shrapnel*, the British inventor

shred (verb: **shreds**, **shredding**, **shredded**)
shredder

> ✓ double the d in **shredding**, **shredded**, and **shredder**

shrew »*noun* ❶ a small mammal resembling a mouse, with a long pointed snout. ❷ a bad-tempered woman.

shrewd »*adjective* (**shrewder**, **shrewdest**) having or showing good judgement.
shrewdly
shrewdness

shrewish »*adjective* (of a woman) bad-tempered or nagging.
shrewishly
shrewishness

shriek (verb: **shrieks**, **shrieking**, **shrieked**)

> ✓ i before e, except after c: **shriek** follows the usual rule

shrike »*noun* a songbird with a hooked bill, that impales its prey on thorns.

shrill »*adjective* (**shriller**, **shrillest**) (of a voice or sound) high-pitched and piercing.
» *verb* (**shrills**, **shrilling**, **shrilled**) make a shrill noise.
shrillness
shrilly

shrimp (plural **shrimp** or **shrimps**)

shrine »*noun* ❶ a place believed to be holy because it is connected to a holy person or event. ❷ a niche containing a religious statue or object.

shrink (verb: **shrinks**, **shrinking**, **shrank**; past participle **shrunk** or **shrunken**)

shrinkage »*noun* the process of shrinking or the amount by which something has shrunk.

shrinking

shrinking violet »*noun* (in informal English) a very shy person.

shrinks

shrink-wrap »*verb* (**shrink-wraps**, **shrink-wrapping**, **shrink-wrapped**) enclose something in clinging plastic film.

shrive »*verb* (**shrives**, **shriving**, **shrove**; past participle **shriven**) (an old word) (of a priest) hear a person's confession, give them a religious duty, and declare them free from sin.
– **SAY** rhymes with drive

shrivel (verb: **shrivels**, **shrivelling**, **shrivelled**)

> ✓ double the l in **shrivelling** and **shrivelled** (the spellings **shriveling** and **shriveled** are American)

shriven past participle of **SHRIVE**.

shrives

shriving

shroud »*noun* ❶ a length of cloth in which a dead person is wrapped for burial. ❷ a thing that surrounds or hides something. ❸ (**shrouds**) a set of ropes supporting the mast of a sailing boat.
» *verb* (**shrouds**, **shrouding**, **shrouded**) cover or hide.

shrove past of **SHRIVE**.

Shrove Tuesday »*noun* the day before Ash Wednesday.

shrub
shrubby

shrubbery »*noun* (plural **shrubberies**) an area in a garden planted with shrubs.

shrubby

shrug (verb: **shrugs**, **shrugging**, **shrugged**)

> ✓ double the g in **shrugging** and **shrugged**

shrunk past participle of **SHRINK**.

shrunken past participle of **SHRINK**.

shtick »*noun* (in informal English) an attention-getting or theatrical routine, gimmick, or talent.

shtum »*adjective* (in informal English) (**keep shtum**) stay silent.

✓ shtum can also be spelled schtum

shudder (verb: shudders, shuddering, shuddered)

shuffle (verb: shuffles, shuffling, shuffled)
shuffler

shufti »*noun* (plural shuftis) (in informal English) a quick look.
– SAY shuuf-ti

shun (verb: shuns, shunning, shunned)

✓ double the n in shunning and shunned

shunt »*verb* (shunts, shunting, shunted)
❶ push or pull a railway vehicle or vehicles from one set of tracks to another.
❷ move something or someone to a different position, especially a less important one.
shunter

shut (verb: shuts, shutting, shut)

✓ double the t in shutting

shutdown

shut-eye »*noun* (in informal English) sleep.

shuts

shutter (verb: shutters, shuttering, shuttered)

shutting

shuttle »*noun* ❶ a form of transport that travels regularly between two places.
❷ (in weaving) a bobbin for carrying the weft thread across the cloth, between the warp threads. ❸ a bobbin carrying the lower thread in a sewing machine.
» *verb* (shuttles, shuttling, shuttled) ❶ travel regularly between places. ❷ transport people in a shuttle.

shuttlecock »*noun* a light cone-shaped object consisting of a rounded piece of cork or plastic with feathers attached, struck with rackets in badminton.

shuttled

shuttles

shuttling

shy »*adjective* (shyer, shyest) ❶ timid in the company of other people. ❷ (shy of or about) unwilling or reluctant to do.
❸ (shy of) short of.
» *verb* (shies, shying, shied) ❶ (of a horse) suddenly turn aside in fright. ❷ (shy from) avoid through nervousness or lack of confidence. ❸ throw something at a target.
shyly
shyness

shyster »*noun* (in informal English) a dishonest person, especially a lawyer.

Siamese »*noun* (plural Siamese) a breed of cat that has short pale fur with darker face, ears, feet, and tail.

Siamese twins »*plural noun* twins whose bodies are joined at birth.

Siberian [of Siberia]

sibilant »*adjective* (a poetic term) making a hissing sound.
» *noun* a speech sound made with a hissing effect, e.g. *s*, *sh*.

sibling »*noun* a brother or sister.

sibyl »*noun* (in ancient Greece and Rome) a woman supposedly able to pass on messages from a god.
sibylline

✓ i then y: sibyl

sic »*adverb* (after a copied or quoted word that appears odd or wrong) written exactly as it stands in the original.
– SAY sik

✓ sic is a Latin word meaning 'thus'

Sicilian [of Sicily]

sick (adjective: sicker, sickest)

sickbay »*noun* a room or building in a school or on a ship that is set aside for sick people.

sickbed

sicken (verb: sickens, sickening, sickened)
sickener
sickening
sickeningly

sicker

sickest

sickle »*noun* a short-handled farming tool with a semicircular blade, used for cutting corn.

sickly (adjective: sicklier, sickliest)
sickliness

sickness

side (verb: sides, siding, sided)
sideward
sidewards

sidebar »*noun* a short piece of additional information placed alongside a main article in a newspaper or magazine.

sideboard »*noun* ❶ a flat-topped piece of furniture with cupboards and drawers, used for storing crockery, glasses, etc.
❷ (sideboards) (in British English) sideburns.

sideburns

sidecar

sided

side effect »*noun* a secondary, usually bad effect of a drug.

sidekick

sidelight

sideline »*noun* ❶ something you do in addition to your main job. ❷ one of the two lines along the longer sides of a football field, basketball court, etc. ❸ (**the sidelines**) a position of watching a situation rather than being directly involved in it.
» *verb* (**sidelines, sidelining, sidelined**) remove someone from a team, game, or influential position.

sidelong

side-on

sidereal »*adjective* relating to the distant stars or their apparent positions in the sky.
– SAY sy-**deer**-i-uhl

sides

side-saddle »*adverb* (of a woman rider) sitting with both feet on the same side of the horse.

sideshow

side-splitting »*adjective* very amusing.

sidestep (verb: **sidesteps, sidestepping, sidestepped**)

> ✓ double the **p** in **sidestepping** and **sidestepped**

sideswipe »*noun* a critical remark made while discussing another matter.

sidetrack (verb: **sidetracks, sidetracking, sidetracked**)

sidewalk »*noun* (in American English) a pavement.

sideward

sidewards

sideways

sidewinder »*noun* a kind of rattlesnake that moves sideways over sand by throwing its body into S-shaped curves.

siding

sidle »*verb* (**sidles, sidling, sidled**) walk in a secretive or timid way.

siege »*noun* ❶ a military operation in which enemy forces try to capture a town or building by surrounding it and cutting off its supplies. ❷ a similar operation by a police team to force an armed person to surrender.

> ✓ remember, **i** before **e**, except after **c**: **siege** follows the usual rule

sienna »*noun* a kind of earth used as a pigment in painting, normally yellowish-brown (**raw sienna**) or deep reddish-brown when roasted (**burnt sienna**).

> ✓ double n: **sienna**

sierra »*noun* (in Spanish-speaking countries or the western US) a long jagged mountain chain.

Sierra Leonean

siesta »*noun* an afternoon rest or nap, especially in hot countries.
– SAY si-**ess**-tuh

sieve »*noun* a utensil consisting of a mesh held in a frame, used for straining solids from liquids or separating coarser from finer particles.
» *verb* (**sieves, sieving, sieved**) put something through a sieve.
– SAY siv

> ✓ remember, **i** before **e**, except after **c**: **sieve** follows the usual rule

sift »*verb* (**sifts, sifting, sifted**) ❶ put a substance through a sieve. ❷ examine something thoroughly to sort out what is important or useful.
sifter

sigh (verb: **sighs, sighing, sighed**)

sight (verb: **sights, sighting, sighted**)
[ability to see; manage to see or glimpse]

> ℹ do not confuse **sight** with **site**, which means 'a place where something happens or is located'

sighted »*adjective* ❶ having the ability to see; not blind. ❷ having a particular kind of sight: *keen-sighted*.

sighting

sightless

sight-read »*verb* (**sight-reads, sight-reading, sight-read**) read and perform music at sight, without preparation.

sights

sightseeing
sightseer

sight unseen »*adverb* without the opportunity to look at the object in question beforehand.

sigma »*noun* the eighteenth letter of the Greek alphabet (Σ, σ, or at the end of a word ς).
– SAY **sig**-muh

sign (verb: **signs, signing, signed**)
signer

> ℹ on the medical use of **sign**, see the note at SYMPTOM

S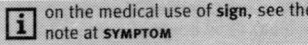

signal[1] (verb: **signals, signalling, signalled**) [action or sound giving information or an instruction; give a signal]
signaller

> ✓ double the **l** in **signalling** and **signalled** (the spellings **signaling** and **signaled** are American)

signal[2] »*adjective* noteworthy; striking.
signally

signalled

signaller

signalling

signally

signalman »*noun* (plural **signalmen**) a railway worker responsible for operating signals and points.

signals

signal-to-noise ratio »*noun* the ratio of the strength of an electrical or other signal carrying information to that of unwanted interference, generally expressed in decibels.

signatory »*noun* (plural **signatories**) a person that has signed an agreement.
– SAY sig-nuh-tuh-ri

> ✓ plural: drop the **y** and add **ies**: **signatories**

signature

> ✓ **nat** not **net** or **nit** in the middle: **signature**

signature tune »*noun* a special tune used to announce a particular television or radio programme.

signboard »*noun* a board displaying the name or logo of a business or product.

signed

signer

signet »*noun* (a historical term) a small seal used to authorize an official document.

> ℹ do not confuse **signet** with **cygnet**, which means 'a young swan'

signet ring »*noun* a ring with letters or a design set into it.

significance

significant
significantly

> ✓ **ant** not **ent**: **significant**

significant figures »*plural noun* (in mathematics) the digits used to express a number to a specified degree of accuracy.

significantly

signify »*verb* (**signifies, signifying, signified**) **❶** be a sign of or mean something. **❷** make known a feeling or intention.
signification

signing

sign language »*noun* a system of communication used among and with deaf people, consisting of signs made by the hands and face.

signor »*noun* (plural **signori**) a title or form of address for an Italian-speaking man, corresponding to *Mr* or *sir*.
– SAY see-**nyor** [singular], see-**nyor**-ee [plural]

signora »*noun* a title or form of address for an Italian-speaking married woman, corresponding to *Mrs* or *madam*.
– SAY see-**nyor**-uh

signori plural of SIGNOR.

signorina »*noun* a title or form of address for an Italian-speaking unmarried woman, corresponding to *Miss*.
– SAY see-nyuh-**ree**-nuh

signpost (verb: **signposts, signposting, signposted**)

signs

signwriter »*noun* a person who paints commercial signs and advertisements.
signwriting

Sikh »*noun* a member of a religion that developed from Hinduism, based on the belief that there is only one God.
»*adjective* relating to Sikhs or Sikhism.
– SAY seek
Sikhism

> ✓ **k** before **h**: **Sikh**. It is a Punjabi word meaning 'disciple'.

silage »*noun* grass or other green crops that are stored in a silo without being dried, used as animal feed in the winter.

silence (verb: **silences, silencing, silenced**)

silencer »*noun* a device for reducing the noise made by a gun or exhaust system.

silences

silencing

silent
silently

silhouette »*noun* **❶** the dark shape and outline of someone or something seen against a lighter background. **❷** a picture that shows someone or something as a black shape on a light background.
»*verb* (**silhouettes, silhouetting, silhouetted**) show something as a silhouette: *the castle was silhouetted against the sky.*
– SAY si-luu-et

✓ don't forget the **h** after the **l**: **silhouette**. The word comes from the name of the French author and politician Étienne de *Silhouette*.

silica »*noun* a compound of silicon and oxygen that occurs as quartz and is found in sandstone and many other rocks.
– SAY si-li-kuh

silica gel »*noun* silica in a granular form that absorbs moisture, used as a drying agent.

silicate »*noun* a compound of silica combined with a metal oxide.

silicon »*noun* a grey, non-metallic chemical element that is a semiconductor, used in making electronic circuits.
– SAY si-li-k'n

silicon chip »*noun* a microchip.

silicone »*noun* a synthetic substance made from silicon, used to make plastics, rubber, paints, etc.
– SAY si-li-kohn

✓ remember the final **e** to distinguish **silicone** from **silicon**. **Silicon** is a chemical element used in electronic circuits and microchips, while **silicone** is the material used in cosmetic implants and in polishes and lubricants.

silicosis »*noun* a lung disease caused by breathing in dust that contains silica.
– SAY si-li-**koh**-siss

silk

silken

silkier

silkiest

silkily

silkiness

silkworm »*noun* a caterpillar that spins a silk cocoon from which silk fibre is produced.

silky (adjective: **silkier**, **silkiest**)
silkily
silkiness

sill »*noun* a shelf or slab of stone, wood, or metal at the foot of a window or doorway.

✓ the correct spelling is considered to be **sill**, but you may sometimes find it spelled with a **c**, **cill**

silly (adjective: **sillier**, **silliest**)
silliness

✓ drop the **y** and add **ier** or **iest** to spell **sillier** or **silliest**

silo »*noun* (plural **silos**) ❶ a tower on a farm, used to store grain. ❷ a pit or airtight structure in which green crops are stored as silage. ❸ an underground chamber in which a guided missile is kept ready for firing.
– SAY sy-loh

✓ the plural of **silo** has **os** not **oes**: **silos**

silt »*noun* fine sand or clay carried by running water and deposited as a sediment.
» *verb* (**silts**, **silting**, **silted**) (**silt up**) fill or block something with silt.
silty

Silurian »*adjective* relating to the geological period from about 439 to 409 million years ago.
– SAY sy-**lyoor**-i-uhn

silver (verb: **silvers**, **silvering**, **silvered**)
silvery

silverfish »*noun* a small silvery wingless insect that lives in buildings.

silvering

silver jubilee »*noun* the twenty-fifth anniversary of an important event.

silver plate »*noun* ❶ a thin layer of silver applied as a coating to another metal. ❷ plates, dishes, etc. made of or plated with silver.

silvers

silver service »*noun* a style of serving food at formal meals in which the server uses a silver spoon and fork in one hand to place food on the diner's plate.

silverside »*noun* the upper side of a round of beef from the outside of the leg.

silversmith »*noun* a person who makes silver articles.

silver-tongued »*adjective* persuasive in speaking; eloquent.

silver wedding »*noun* the twenty-fifth anniversary of a wedding.

silvery

silviculture »*noun* the growing and cultivation of trees.
– SAY sil-vi-kul-cher
silvicultural

simian »*adjective* relating to or like apes or monkeys.
» *noun* an ape or monkey.
– SAY sim-i-uhn

similar
similarity
similarly

ℹ use **similar to** in sentences such as *I've had problems similar to yours*; it is not good English to say **similar as**, as in *I've had similar problems as yourself*

simile »*noun* a figure of speech in which one thing is compared to another of a different kind, using the words *as* or *like* (e.g. *the family was as solid as a rock*).
– SAY sim-i-li

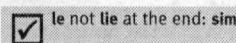 **le** not **lie** at the end: **simile**

similitude »*noun* the quality of being similar.
– SAY si-mil-i-tyood

simmer »*verb* (**simmers, simmering, simmered**) ❶ stay or cause to stay just below boiling point. ❷ be in a state of anger or excitement which you only just keep under control. ❸ (**simmer down**) become calmer and quieter.
»*noun* a state or temperature just below boiling point.

simnel cake »*noun* a rich fruit cake with a layer of marzipan on top, eaten especially at Easter or during Lent.

simoom »*noun* a hot, dry, dust-laden wind blowing in the desert.
– SAY si-**moom**

 simoom (an Arabic word) ends with **m** although it is sometimes written with a final **n** (**simoon**)

simper »*verb* (**simpers, simpering, simpered**) smile in a coy and silly way.
»*noun* a coy and silly smile.
simpering

simple (adjective: **simpler, simplest**)
simpleness
simply

simple-minded

simpleness

simpler

simplest

simpleton »*noun* a person with poor judgement or low intelligence.

simplicity

simplify (verb: **simplifies, simplifying, simplified**)
simplification

simplistic »*adjective* treating complex issues and problems as more simple than they really are.
simplistically

simply

simulacrum »*noun* (plural **simulacra** or **simulacrums**) something that looks like or is similar to something else.
– SAY sim-yuu-**lay**-kruhm

the plural of **simulacrum** can be either **simulacra** (as in Latin) or **simulacrums**

simulate »*verb* (**simulates, simulating, simulated**) ❶ imitate the appearance or nature of something. ❷ use a computer to create a model of something or conditions that are like those in real life. ❸ pretend to have or feel a particular emotion.
simulation

simulator »*noun* a machine that imitates the controls and conditions of a real vehicle, process, etc., used for training or testing.

-or not **-er**: **simulator**

simulcast »*noun* a broadcast of the same programme on radio and television at the same time.
– SAY sim-uhl-kahst

simultaneity »*noun* the quality of being simultaneous.
– SAY sim-uhl-tuh-**nay**-i-ti

simultaneous »*adjective* occurring or done at the same time.
– SAY sim-uhl-**tay**-ni-uhss
simultaneously
simultaneousness

eous not **ious**: **simultaneous**

sin »*noun* ❶ an act that breaks a religious or moral law. ❷ an act that causes strong disapproval.
»*verb* (**sins, sinning, sinned**) commit a sin.
sinless
sinner

double the **n** to spell **sinning, sinned,** and **sinner**

since

sincere »*adjective* (**sincerer, sincerest**) not pretending anything or deceiving anyone; genuine and honest.
sincerely

sincerity »*noun* the quality of being sincere.

sine »*noun* (in a right-angled triangle) the ratio of the side opposite a particular acute angle to the hypotenuse.
– SAY *rhymes with* line

sine not **sign**

sinecure »*noun* a job for which you are paid but which requires little or no work.
– SAY syn-i-kyoor or sin-i-kyoor

sine die »*adverb* (with reference to an adjournment or suspension) with no date set for being restarted or reversed.
– SAY see-nay dee-ay

sine die is a Latin phrase which means 'without a day'

sine qua non »*noun* a thing that is absolutely necessary.
– **SAY** see-nay kwah **nohn**

 sine qua non is a Latin phrase which means 'without which not'

sinew »*noun* a band of strong tissue that joins muscle to bone.
– **SAY** sin-yoo
sinewy

sinful »*adjective* ❶ wicked. ❷ disgraceful.
sinfully
sinfulness

✓ -ful not -full: sinful

sing (verb: **sings**, **singing**, **sang**; past participle **sung**)
singable
singer

singalong

Singaporean

singe »*verb* (**singes**, **singeing**, **singed**) burn the surface of something slightly.
»*noun* a slight burn.

singer

singing

single (verb: **singles**, **singling**, **singled**)
singly
singleness

single-breasted »*adjective* (of a jacket or coat) fastened by one row of buttons at the centre of the front.

singled

single file »*noun* a line of people arranged one behind another.

single-handed
single-handedly

single-lens reflex »*adjective* denoting a reflex camera in which the lens that forms the image on the film also provides the image in the viewfinder.

single-minded
single-mindedly
single-mindedness

singleness

singles

singlet »*noun* a vest or similar sleeveless garment.

singleton »*noun* a single person or thing.

singling

singly

sings

sing-song

singular »*adjective* ❶ exceptionally good or interesting; remarkable. ❷ (in grammar) (of a word or form) referring to just one person or thing. ❸ strange or eccentric.
»*noun* (in grammar) the singular form of a word.
singularity
singularly

Sinhalese »*noun* (plural **Sinhalese**) ❶ a member of an Indian people forming the majority of the population of Sri Lanka. ❷ the language of this people.
»*adjective* relating to the Sinhalese.
– **SAY** sin-huh-**leez** or sin-uh-**leez**

✓ no g in **Sinhalese**

sinister »*adjective* seeming evil or dangerous.

sink (verb: **sinks**, **sinking**, **sank**; past participle **sunk**)

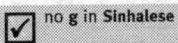 the past tense of **sink** is **sank**, as in *the boat sank*, and the past participle is **sunk**, as in *the boat had already sunk*. The form **sunken** is an adjective, as in *sunken garden*.

sinker »*noun* a weight used to keep a fishing line beneath the water.

sinkhole »*noun* a hole in the ground caused by water erosion and providing a route for surface water to disappear underground.

sinking

sinks

sinless

sinned

sinner

sinning

sinology »*noun* the study of Chinese language, history, and culture.
– **SAY** sy-**nol**-uh-ji or si-**nol**-uh-ji
sinologist

sins

sinuous »*adjective* ❶ having many curves and turns. ❷ moving in a graceful, swaying way.
– **SAY** sin-yuu-uhss
sinuosity
sinuously

✓ there are two **u**'s in **sinuous** but only one in **sinuosity**

sinus »*noun* (plural **sinuses**) a hollow space within the bones of the face that connects with the nostrils.
– **SAY** sy-**nuhss**

sinusitis »*noun* inflammation of a sinus.
– **SAY** si-nuh-**sy**-tiss

Sioux »*noun* (plural **Sioux**) a member of a North American Indian people living in the northern Mississippi valley area.
– SAY soo

sip (verb: **sips, sipping, sipped**)

> ☑ double the **p** to spell **sipping** and **sipped**

siphon »*noun* a tube used to move liquid from one container to another, using air pressure to maintain the flow.
» *verb* (**siphons, siphoning, siphoned**)
❶ draw off or move liquid by means of a siphon. ❷ (**siphon off**) take small amounts of money from a person or organization over a period of time.

> ☑ **siphon** can also be spelled sy: **syphon**

sipped
sipping
sips
sir

sire »*noun* ❶ the male parent of an animal. ❷ (a poetic term) a father or other male ancestor. ❸ (an old word) a respectful form of address to a king.
» *verb* (**sires, siring, sired**) be the male parent of someone.
– SAY *rhymes with* fire

siren »*noun* ❶ a device that makes a loud prolonged warning sound. ❷ (in Greek Mythology) one of a group of creatures who were part woman, part bird, whose singing lured sailors on to rocks. ❸ a woman who is considered to be attractive but also dangerous.

sirloin »*noun* the best part of a loin of beef.

sirocco »*noun* (plural **siroccos**) a hot wind blowing from North Africa to southern Europe.
– SAY si-**rok**-koh

> ☑ single **r** and double **c: sirocco**
> the plural of **sirocco** has **os** not **oes**: **siroccos**

sirup American spelling of **SYRUP**.

sisal »*noun* fibre made from the leaves of a tropical Mexican plant, used for ropes or matting.
– SAY sy-z'l

siskin »*noun* a small yellowish-green finch.

sissy (plural **sissies**)

> ☑ plural: drop the **y** and add **ies: sissies**

sister
  sisterly
sisterhood

sister-in-law (plural **sisters-in-law**)

> ☑ plural: the **s** goes after **sister** not **law: sisters-in-law**

sisterly

sit (verb: **sits, sitting, sat**)

> ⓘ in more formal contexts, use **sitting** rather than **sat** with the verb 'to be': say *we were sitting there for hours* rather than *we were sat there for hours*

sitar »*noun* a large, long-necked Indian lute.
– SAY si-tar

sitcom

> ⓘ **sitcom** is short for *situation comedy*

site »*noun* a place where something is located or happens.
» *verb* (**sites, siting, sited**) build or establish something in a particular place.

> ⓘ do not confuse **site** with **sight**, which means 'ability to see; manage to see' or **cite**, which means 'make a quotation from a book or author'

sits
sitter
sitting

sitting duck »*noun* a person or thing that is easy to attack.

situate »*verb* (**situates, situating, situated**)
❶ put something in a particular place.
❷ (**be situated**) in a particular set of circumstances.

situation
  situational

sit-up »*noun* an exercise designed to strengthen the abdominal muscles, in which a person sits up from a horizontal position without using the arms.

six
  sixfold

six-pack »*noun* ❶ a pack of six cans of beer. ❷ (in informal English) a set of well-developed stomach muscles.

sixpence »*noun* a former coin worth six old pence (2½ p).

six-shooter »*noun* a revolver with six chambers.

sixteen
  sixteenth
sixth
  sixthly
sixth-form college

sixth sense »*noun* a supposed ability to know things by intuition rather than using your sight, hearing, etc.

sixty (plural **sixties**)
  sixtieth

> ☑ plural: drop the **y** and add **ies: sixties**

sizable another way of spelling **SIZEABLE**.

size[1] (verb: **sizes, sizing, sized**) [overall extent; group according to size]

size[2] »*noun* a sticky solution used to glaze paper, stiffen textiles, and prepare plastered walls for decoration.
» *verb* (**sizes, sizing, sized**) treat something with size.

sizeable
  sizeably

> ☑ **sizeable** can also be spelled without the first **e: sizable**

sized

sizes

sizing

sizzle (verb: **sizzles, sizzling, sizzled**)
  sizzler

ska »*noun* a style of fast popular music originating in Jamaica.

skate (verb: **skates, skating, skated**)
  skater
  skating

skateboard (verb: **skateboards, skateboarding, skateboarded**)
  skateboarder

skated

skater

skates

skating

skedaddle (verb: **skedaddles, skedaddling, skedaddled**)

skein »*noun* a length of thread or yarn, loosely coiled and knotted.
 – **SAY** skayn

> ☑ **e** before **i: skein** does not follow the usual rule

skeletal »*adjective* ❶ having to do with a skeleton. ❷ looking like a skeleton. ❸ (of a plan) existing only in outline.
 – **SAY** skel-i-t'l or skuh-**lee**-t'l
  skeletally

skeleton

> ☑ **skele** not **skela** (or **skelling**): **skeleton**

skeleton key »*noun* a key designed to fit a number of locks.

skeptic American spelling of **SCEPTIC**.

sketch (verb: **sketches, sketching, sketched**)

sketchbook

sketched

sketches

sketchier

sketchiest

sketchily

sketchiness

sketching

sketchy (adjective: **sketchier, sketchiest**)
  sketchily
  sketchiness

skew »*noun* a bias towards one particular group or subject.
» *verb* (**skews, skewing, skewed**) ❶ suddenly change direction or move at an angle. ❷ make something biased or distorted.

skewbald »*adjective* (of a horse) with irregular patches of white and brown.

skewed

skewer »*noun* a long piece of metal or wood used for holding pieces of food together during cooking.
» *verb* (**skewers, skewering, skewered**) pierce something with a pin or skewer.

skewing

skews

skew-whiff »*adverb & adjective* (in informal English) not straight; askew.

ski (plural **skis**; verb: **skis, skiing, skied**)
  skier
  skiing

> ☑ note the double **i** in **skiing**
> the plural of **ski** is **skis** (without an **e**)

skid (verb: **skids, skidding, skidded**)

> ☑ double the **d** to spell **skidding** and **skidded**

skied

skier

skies plural of **SKY**.

skiff »*noun* a light rowing boat.

skiffle »*noun* a kind of 1950s British popular music, often using improvised instruments such as washboards.

skiing

skilful
  skilfully
  skilfulness

> ☑ **-ful** not **-full,** and there is only one **l** in the middle: **skilful** (the spelling **skillful** is American)

skill

skilled

skillet »*noun* a frying pan.

skillful American spelling of **SKILFUL**.

skim (verb: skims, skimming, skimmed)

> ☑ double the **m** to spell **skimming** and **skimmed**

skimp »*verb* (skimps, skimping, skimped) spend less money or use less of something than is really needed in an attempt to economize.

skimpy »*adjective* (skimpier, skimpiest) **❶** less than is necessary; meagre. **❷** (of clothes) short and revealing.

skims

skin (verb: skins, skinning, skinned)
skinless
skinned

> ☑ double the **n** to spell **skinning** and **skinned**

skincare

skin-deep

skin diving »*noun* the activity of swimming under water without a diving suit, using an aqualung and flippers.
skin-diver

skinflint

skinhead

skink »*noun* a smooth-bodied lizard with short or absent limbs.

skinless

skinned

skinnier

skinniest

skinniness

skinning

skinny (adjective: skinnier, skinniest)
skinniness

skins

skint »*adjective* (in informal English) having little or no money.

skintight

skip (verb: skips, skipping, skipped)

> ☑ double the **p** to spell **skipping** and **skipped**

skipper »*noun* **❶** the captain of a ship, boat, or aircraft. **❷** the captain of a sports team.
»*verb* (skippers, skippering, skippered) be captain of a boat, aircraft, or team.

skipping

skips

skirl »*noun* a shrill sound made by bagpipes.

skirmish »*noun* a short spell of unplanned fighting.

»*verb* (skirmishes, skirmishing, skirmished) take part in a skirmish.
skirmisher

skirt (verb: skirts, skirting, skirted)

skirting »*noun* a wooden board running along the base of the walls of a room.

skirts

skis plural of SKI.

skit »*noun* a short comedy sketch or piece of humorous writing that makes fun of something by imitating it.

skitter »*verb* (skitters, skittering, skittered) move lightly and quickly.

skittery »*adjective* restless; skittish.

skittish »*adjective* **❶** (of a horse) nervous and tending to shy. **❷** lively or changeable.
skittishly
skittishness

skittle »*noun* **❶** (skittles) a game played with wooden pins set up to be bowled down with a wooden ball. **❷** a pin used in the game of skittles.

skive »*verb* (skives, skiving, skived) (in informal English) avoid work or a duty by staying away or leaving early.
– SAY rhymes with dive
skiver

skivvy »*noun* (plural skivvies) a female domestic servant.

> ☑ note the double **v**: skivvy plural: drop the **y** and add **ies**: skivvies

skua »*noun* a large predatory seabird like a gull.
– SAY skyoo-uh

skulduggery »*noun* underhand or dishonest behaviour.

> ☑ the usual spelling is with a single **l**: skulduggery, but the spelling skullduggery also occurs

skulk »*verb* (skulks, skulking, skulked) hide or move around in a stealthy way.
skulker

skull

skullcap »*noun* a small close-fitting cap without a peak.

skullduggery another way of spelling SKULDUGGERY.

skunk »*noun* an animal with black-and-white stripes that can spray foul-smelling liquid at attackers.

sky (plural skies)
skyward
skywards

☑ plural: drop the **y** and add **ies: skies**

skydiving »*noun* the sport of jumping from an aircraft and performing acrobatic movements in the air before landing by parachute.
skydiver

sky-high

skylark »*noun* a lark that sings while in flight.
» *verb* (**skylarks, skylarking, skylarked**) play about light-heartedly.

skylight »*noun* a window set in a roof or ceiling.

skyline

skyrocket (verb: **skyrockets, skyrocketing, skyrocketed**)

skyscraper

skyward

skywards

slab

slack (verb: **slacks, slacking, slacked**)
slacker
slackly
slackness

slacken (verb: **slackens, slackening, slackened**)

slacker

slacking

slackly

slackness

slacks

slack water »*noun* the state of the tide when it is turning.

slag »*noun* ❶ stony waste matter that is left when metal has been separated from ore by smelting or refining. ❷ (used in an insulting way) a woman who has many sexual partners.
» *verb* (**slags, slagging, slagged**) (**slag off**) (in informal English) criticize someone in a rude or harsh way.

slag heap »*noun* a mound of waste material from a mine.

slags

slain past participle of SLAY.

slake »*verb* (**slakes, slaking, slaked**) satisfy a desire, thirst, etc.

slaked lime »*noun* calcium hydroxide, a soluble substance produced by combining quicklime with water.

slakes

slaking

slalom »*noun* a skiing or canoeing race following a winding course marked out by poles.
– SAY slah-luhm

slam (verb: **slams, slamming, slammed**)

☑ double the **m** to spell **slamming** and **slammed**

slammer »*noun* (in informal English) prison.

slamming

slams

slander »*noun* the crime of saying something untrue that harms a person's reputation.
» *verb* (**slanders, slandering, slandered**) say something untrue and damaging about someone.
slanderer
slanderous

slang »*noun* very informal words and phrases that are more common in speech than in writing and are used by a particular group of people.
slangy

slanging match »*noun* a long exchange of insults.

slangy

slant (verb: **slants, slanting, slanted**)
slantwise

slap (verb: **slaps, slapping, slapped**)
slapper

☑ double the **p** to spell **slapping** and **slapped**

slapdash »*adjective* done too hurriedly and carelessly.

slapped

slapper

slapping

slaps

slapstick »*noun* comedy based on deliberately clumsy actions and humorously embarrassing situations.

slap-up »*adjective* (in informal English) (of a meal) large and extravagant.

slash (verb: **slashes, slashing, slashed**)
slasher

slat »*noun* one of a series of thin, narrow pieces of wood, metal, etc., arranged so as to overlap or fit into each other.
slatted

slate »*noun* a dark grey rock that is easily split into smooth, flat plates, used in building and in the past for writing on.
» *verb* (**slates, slating, slated**) (in informal English) severely criticize.

slather »*verb* (**slathers**, **slathering**, **slathered**) spread or smear a substance thickly over something.

slating

slatted

slattern »*noun* (old-fashioned) a dirty, untidy woman.
slatternly

slaughter »*noun* ❶ the killing of farm animals for food. ❷ the killing of a large number of people in a cruel or violent way.
» *verb* (**slaughters**, **slaughtering**, **slaughtered**) ❶ kill animals for food. ❷ kill a number of people in a cruel or violent way.
slaughterer

slaughterhouse

slaughtering

slaughters

Slav »*noun* a member of a group of peoples in central and eastern Europe.

slave (verb: **slaves**, **slaving**, **slaved**)

slave-driver

slaver[1] »*noun* (a historical term) a person dealing in or owning slaves.
– SAY slay-ver

slaver[2] »*verb* (**slavers**, **slavering**, **slavered**) let saliva run from the mouth.
» *noun* saliva running from the mouth.
– SAY sla-ver or slay-ver

slavery

slaves

Slavic »*noun* the group of languages that includes Russian, Polish, and Czech.
» *adjective* relating to these languages or their speakers.
– SAY slah-vik

slaving

slavish »*adjective* ❶ showing no originality. ❷ excessively obedient.
slavishly

Slavonic »*noun & adjective* = SLAVIC.
– SAY sluh-von-ik

slay »*verb* (**slays**, **slaying**, **slew**; past participle **slain**) (an old word) kill someone in a violent way.
slayer

> ℹ️ do not confuse **slay** with **sleigh**, which is a sledge drawn by horses

sleaze »*noun* immoral or dishonest behaviour, especially in politics.

sleazy »*adjective* (**sleazier**, **sleaziest**)
❶ immoral or dishonest. ❷ (of a place) dirty and seedy.

sleazily
sleaziness

> ✅ drop the **y** and add **ier** or **iest** to spell **sleazier** or **sleaziest**

sled »*noun* (in American English) = SLEDGE.

sledge »*noun* ❶ a vehicle on runners for travelling over snow or ice, sometimes pulled by dogs. ❷ a toboggan.
» *verb* (**sledges**, **sledging**, **sledged**) ride or carry on a sledge.

sledgehammer

sledges

sledging

sleek »*adjective* ❶ (of hair or fur) smooth and glossy. ❷ having a wealthy and smart appearance. ❸ elegant and streamlined.
sleekly
sleekness

sleep (verb: **sleeps**, **sleeping**, **slept**)
sleeper
sleepless

sleepier

sleepiest

sleepily

sleepiness

sleeping

sleeping partner »*noun* a partner who does not share in the actual work of a firm.

sleeping sickness »*noun* a tropical disease marked by extreme tiredness.

sleepless

sleepover »*noun* an occasion of spending the night away from home.

sleeps

sleepwalk (verb: **sleepwalks**, **sleepwalking**, **sleepwalked**)
sleepwalker

sleepy (adjective: **sleepier**, **sleepiest**)
sleepily
sleepiness

sleet »*noun* rain containing some ice, or snow melting as it falls.
» *verb* (**sleets**, **sleeting**, **sleeted**) sleet falls.
sleety

sleeve
sleeved
sleeveless

sleigh »*noun* a sledge drawn by horses or reindeer.

> ✅ **ei** followed by **gh**: **sleigh** (**slay** is a verb meaning 'violently kill')

sleight »*noun* (**sleight of hand**) skilful use of the hands, especially when performing magic tricks.

– **say** rhymes with slight

> ✓ remember the **e**: **sleight** (**slight** is an adjective meaning 'small in degree')

slender »*adjective* (**slenderer**, **slenderest**) ❶ gracefully thin. ❷ barely sufficient.
slenderly
slenderness

slept past and past participle of SLEEP.

sleuth (in informal English) »*noun* a detective.
– **say** rhymes with truth
sleuthing

slew[1] »*verb* turn or slide violently or uncontrollably.

slew[2] past of SLAY.

slice (verb: **slices**, **slicing**, **sliced**)
slicer

slick »*adjective* ❶ impressively smooth and efficient. ❷ self-confident but insincere. ❸ (of skin or hair) smooth and glossy. ❹ (of a surface) smooth, wet, and slippery.
» *noun* a smooth patch of oil.
» *verb* (**slicks**, **slicking**, **slicked**) make hair smooth and glossy with water, oil, or cream.
slickly
slickness

slide (verb: **slides**, **sliding**, **slid**)

slide rule »*noun* a ruler with a sliding central strip, used for making calculations.

slides

sliding

sliding scale »*noun* a scale of fees, wages, etc., that varies according to some other factor.

slight »*adjective* ❶ small in degree. ❷ lacking depth; trivial. ❸ not sturdy and strongly built.
» *verb* insult someone by treating them without proper respect or attention.
» *noun* an insult.
slightly
slightness

> ✓ there is no **e** in **slight** (**sleight**, as in **sleight of hand**, refers to the skilful use of the hands)

slim (adjective: **slimmer**, **slimmest**; verb: **slims**, **slimming**, **slimmed**)
slimmer
slimness

> ✓ double the **m** in **slimmer**, **slimmest**, **slimming**, and **slimmed**

slime

slimier

slimiest

slimline »*adjective* ❶ slender in design. ❷ (of food or drink) low in calories.

slimmed

slimmer

slimmest

slimming

slimness

slims

slimy (adjective: **slimier**, **slimiest**)

> ✓ there is no **e** in **slimy**

sling (verb: **slings**, **slinging**, **slung**)

slingback »*noun* a shoe held in place by a strap around the ankle.

slinging

slings

slingshot »*noun* a hand-held catapult.

slink »*verb* (**slinks**, **slinking**, **slunk**) move quietly in a secretive way.

slinky (adjective: **slinkier**, **slinkiest**)

slip (verb: **slips**, **slipping**, **slipped**)
slippage

> ✓ double the **p** in **slipping**, **slipped**, and **slippage**

slip knot »*noun* a knot that can be undone by a pull, or that can slide along the rope on which it is tied.

slip-on »*adjective* (of shoes or clothes) having no fastenings.

slippage

slipped

slipped disc »*noun* a displaced disc in the spine that that presses on nearby nerves and causes pain.

slipper »*noun* a comfortable slip-on shoe that is worn indoors.

slipperiness

slippery

slippier

slippiest

slipping

slippy »*adjective* (**slippier**, **slippiest**) (in informal English) slippery.

slip road »*noun* a road entering or leaving a motorway.

slips

slipshod »*adjective* careless, thoughtless, or disorganized.

slipstream »*noun* ❶ a current of air or water driven back by a propeller or jet engine. ❷ the partial vacuum created in the wake of a moving vehicle.

slip-up

slipway »*noun* a slope leading into water, used for launching and landing boats and ships.

slit (verb: **slits, slitting, slit**)

slither »*verb* (**slithers, slithering, slithered**) ❶ move smoothly over a surface with a twisting motion. ❷ slide unsteadily on a loose or slippery surface.
  slithery

slits

slitting

sliver »*noun* a small, narrow, sharp piece cut or split off a larger piece.
– **say** *rhymes with* river *or* diver

Sloane »*noun* (in informal English) a fashionable upper-class young woman.
  Sloaney

> [i] the full term is **Sloane Ranger**, from *Sloane Square* in London and *Lone Ranger*, a fictitious cowboy hero

slob

slobber (verb: **slobbers, slobbering, slobbered**)
  slobbery

slobbish
  slobbishness

sloe »*noun* the small bluish-black sharp-tasting fruit of the blackthorn.
– **say** *rhymes with* slow

slog (verb: **slogs, slogging, slogged**)

slogan »*noun* a short, memorable phrase used in advertising or associated with a political group.

slogged

slogging

slogs

sloop »*noun* a type of sailing boat with one mast.

slop (verb: **slops, slopping, slopped**) [(of a liquid) spill over the edge of a container]

> [✓] double the **p** in **slopping** and **slopped**

slope (verb: **slopes, sloping, sloped**) [a surface with one side higher than another; slant up or down]

> [✓] only one **p** in **sloping** and **sloped**

slopped

sloppier

sloppiest

sloppily

sloppiness

slopping

sloppy (adjective: **sloppier, sloppiest**)
  sloppily
  sloppiness

slops

slosh (verb: **sloshes, sloshing, sloshed**)

sloshed »*adjective* (in informal English) drunk.

sloshes

sloshing

slot (verb: **slots, slotting, slotted**)
  slotted

sloth »*noun* ❶ laziness. ❷ a slow-moving mammal that hangs upside down from branches.
– **say** slohth
  slothful

slots

slotted

slotting

slouch (verb: **slouches, slouching, slouched**)
  slouchy

slouch hat »*noun* a hat with a wide flexible brim.

slouching

slouchy

slough[1] »*noun* ❶ a swamp. ❷ a situation without progress or activity.
– **say** *rhymes with* plough

slough[2] »*verb* (**sloughs, sloughing, sloughed**) (of an animal) cast off (an old skin).
– **say** *rhymes with* rough

Slovak »*noun* ❶ a person from Slovakia. ❷ the language of Slovakia.
  Slovakian

Slovene »*noun* ❶ a person from Slovenia. ❷ the language of Slovenia.
  Slovenian

slovenly
  slovenliness

slow (adjective: **slower, slowest**; verb: **slows, slowing, slowed**)
  slowly
  slowness

slowcoach

slowed

slower

slowest

slowing

slowly

slowness

slows

slow-worm »*noun* a small lizard without legs.

SLR »*abbreviation* single-lens reflex.

slub »*noun* ❶ a lump in yarn or thread. ❷ fabric woven from yarn with such a texture.

sludge
 sludgy

> there is no **e** in **sludgy**

slug (verb: **slugs**, **slugging**, **slugged**)

sluggard »*noun* a lazy, inactive person.

slugged

slugging

sluggish
 sluggishly
 sluggishness

slugs

sluice »*noun* ❶ (also **sluice gate**) a sliding device for controlling the flow of water. ❷ a channel for carrying off surplus water.
 »*verb* (**sluices**, **sluicing**, **sluiced**) wash or rinse with water.
 – **say** slooss

> don't forget the **i**: **sluice**

slum (verb: **slums**, **slumming**, **slummed**)

slumber (a poetic term) »*verb* (**slumbers**, **slumbering**, **slumbered**) sleep.
 »*noun* a sleep.

slummed

slumming

slump (verb: **slumps**, **slumping**, **slumped**)

slums

slung past and past participle of **SLING**.

slunk past and past participle of **SLINK**.

slur »*verb* (**slurs**, **slurring**, **slurred**) ❶ speak in an unclear way. ❷ (in music) perform a group of two or more notes in a smooth, flowing way.
 »*noun* ❶ an insult or accusation intended to damage someone's reputation. ❷ a curved line indicating that notes are to be slurred.

> ✓ double the **r** in **slurred** and **slurring**

slurp (verb: **slurps**, **slurping**, **slurped**)

slurred

slurries

slurring

slurry »*noun* (plural **slurry**) a semi-liquid mixture of manure, cement, or coal and water.

slurs

slush
 slushy

slush fund »*noun* a reserve of money used for something illegal.

slushy

slut
 sluttish

sly »*adjective* (**slyer**, **slyest**) ❶ cunning and deceitful. ❷ (of a remark, glance, or expression) suggesting secret knowledge.
 slyly
 slyness

smack (verb: **smacks**, **smacking**, **smacked**)

smacker »*noun* ❶ a loud kiss. ❷ (in British English) one pound sterling. ❸ (in American English) one dollar.

smacking

smacks

small (adjective: **smaller**, **smallest**)
 smallness

small arms »*plural noun* guns that can be carried in the hands.

smaller

smallest

small fry »*plural noun* ❶ young or small fish. ❷ young or unimportant people or things.

smallholding »*noun* a piece of agricultural land that is smaller than a farm.
 smallholder

small-minded

smallness

smallpox »*noun* a serious disease spread by a virus, which causes blisters that usually leave permanent scars.

small print »*noun* details printed so that they are not easily noticed in an agreement or contract.

small-scale

small-time »*adjective* unimportant.

smarmy »*adjective* excessively polite and friendly in an insincere way.
 smarminess

smart (adjective: **smarter**, **smartest**; verb: **smarts**, **smarting**, **smarted**)
 smartly
 smartness

smart alec »*noun* (in informal English) a person who irritates others by always having a clever answer to a question.

> ✓ **smart alec** can also be written with a **k**: **smart aleck**

smart card »*noun* a plastic card on which information is stored in electronic form.

smarted

smarten »*verb* (**smartens, smartening, smartened**) (**smarten up**) make or become smarter.

smarter

smartest

smarting

smartish

smartly

smartness

smarts

smash (verb: **smashes, smashing, smashed**)
smasher

smash-and-grab

smashed

smasher

smashes

smashing

smattering »*noun* ❶ a small amount. ❷ a slight knowledge of a language or subject.

smear (verb: **smears, smearing, smeared**)
smeary

smear test »*noun* a test to detect signs of cervical cancer.

smeary

smell (verb: **smells, smelling, smelt or smelled**)

smellier

smelliest

smelliness

smelling

smelling salts »*plural noun* a strong-smelling substance formerly sniffed by people who felt faint.

smells

smelly (adjective: **smellier, smelliest**)
smelliness

smelt[1] »*verb* (**smelts, smelting, smelted**) extract metal from its ore by heating and melting it.
smelter

smelt[2] past and past participle of **SMELL**.

smelt[3] »*noun* (plural **smelt or smelts**) a small silvery fish.

smidgen »*noun* a tiny amount.

> ✓ **smidgen** can also be spelled with an o before the n: **smidgeon**

smile (verb: **smiles, smiling, smiled**)

smiley »*adjective* (in informal English) smiling and cheerful.

smiling

smirch »*verb* (**smirches, smirching, smirched**) ❶ make dirty. ❷ discredit a person or their reputation.
– SAY smerch

smirk »*verb* (**smirks, smirking, smirked**) smile in an irritatingly smug or silly way. »*noun* a smug or silly smile.

smite »*verb* (**smites, smiting, smote; past participle smitten**) ❶ (an old word) strike with a firm blow. ❷ (an old word) defeat or conquer. ❸ (**be smitten**) be affected severely by a disease. ❹ (**be smitten**) be strongly attracted to someone or something.

smith »*noun* ❶ a person who works in metal. ❷ a blacksmith.

smithereens »*plural noun* small pieces.

smithy »*noun* (plural **smithies**) a blacksmith's workshop.
– SAY smi-*thi*

> ✓ plural: drop the y and add ies: **smithies**

smiting

smitten past participle of **SMITE**.

smock »*noun* ❶ a loose dress or blouse with the upper part gathered into decorative stitched pleats. ❷ a loose overall worn to protect your clothes.

smocking »*noun* decoration on a garment created by gathering a section of the material into tight pleats and holding them together with decorative parallel stitches.

smog »*noun* fog or haze made worse by pollution in the atmosphere.
smoggy

smoke (verb: **smokes, smoking, smoked**)
smokeless
smoker

smokescreen »*noun* ❶ a cloud of smoke created to conceal military operations. ❷ something designed to disguise someone's real intentions or activities.

smokestack »*noun* a chimney or funnel that discharges smoke from a locomotive, ship, factory, etc.

smokier

smokiest

smoking

smoking gun »*noun* a piece of evidence that proves without doubt that someone is guilty of wrongdoing.

smoking jacket »*noun* a man's comfortable jacket, formerly worn while smoking after dinner.

smoky (adjective: **smokier, smokiest**)

✓ there is no **e** in **smoky**

smolder American spelling of **SMOULDER**.

smolt »*noun* a young salmon or trout after the parr stage, when it migrates to the sea for the first time.

smooch (verb: **smooches, smooching, smooched**)
smoochy

smooth (adjective: **smoother, smoothest**; verb: **smooths, smoothing, smoothed**)
smoothly
smoothness

✓ the verb **smooth** sometimes has an **e** at the end: **smoothe** and **smoothes**

smoothie »*noun* ❶ (in informal English) a man with a smooth, confident manner. ❷ a thick, smooth drink of fresh fruit pureed with milk, yogurt, or ice cream.

smoothing

smoothly

smoothness

smooths

smooth-talk (verb: **smooth-talks, smooth-talking, smooth-talked**)

smooth-tongued »*adjective* insincerely flattering.

smorgasbord »*noun* a meal consisting of a range of open sandwiches and savoury items.
– SAY smor-guhz-bord

✓ -**bord** not -**board**: **smorgasbord** is a Swedish word meaning literally 'bread and butter table'

smote past of **SMITE**.

smother (verb: **smothers, smothering, smothered**)

smoulder (verb: **smoulders, smouldering, smouldered**)

✓ don't forget the **u**: **smoulder** (the spelling **smolder** is American)

smudge (verb: **smudges, smudging, smudged**)
smudgy

smug (adjective: **smugger, smuggest**)
smugly
smugness

smuggle (verb: **smuggles, smuggling, smuggled**)
smuggler
smuggling

smugly

smugness

smut
smutty

snack (verb: **snacks, snacking, snacked**)

snaffle »*noun* a bit on a horse's bridle.
»*verb* (**snaffles, snaffling, snaffled**) secretly take something.

snag (verb: **snags, snagging, snagged**)

snaggle »*verb* (**snaggles, snaggling, snaggled**) become knotted or tangled.

snaggle-toothed »*adjective* having irregular or projecting teeth.

snaggling

snags

snail

snake (verb: **snakes, snaking, snaked**)

snakebite

snaked

snakes

snakeskin

snakier

snakiest

snaking

snaky »*adjective* (**snakier, snakiest**) ❶ long and curvy. ❷ cold and cunning.

✓ there is no **e** in **snaky**

snap (verb: **snaps, snapping, snapped**)

✓ double the **p** in **snapping** and **snapped**

snapdragon »*noun* a plant with brightly coloured flowers which have a mouth-like opening.

snapped

snapper »*noun* a marine fish noted for snapping its jaws.

snappier

snappiest

snappily

snappiness

snapping

snappish »*adjective* irritable.
snappishly
snappishness

snappy (adjective: **snappier, snappiest**)
snappily
snappiness

snaps

snapshot

snare »*noun* ❶ a trap for catching small animals, consisting of a loop of wire that pulls tight. ❷ a situation that is likely to lure someone into trouble. ❸ a drum with a length of wire stretched across the head to produce a rattling sound.

S

» *verb* (**snares, snaring, snared**) catch in a snare or trap.

snarl (verb: **snarls, snarling, snarled**)
snarly

snarl-up »*noun* (in informal English) a traffic jam.

snarly

snatch (verb: **snatches, snatching, snatched**)
snatcher

snazzy »*adjective* (**snazzier, snazziest**) (in informal English) smart and stylish.

sneak (verb: **sneaks, sneaking, sneaked**)

> ℹ️ the usual past tense of **sneak** is **sneaked**: **snuck** is American

sneaker »*noun* a soft shoe worn for sports or casual occasions.

sneakily

sneaking

sneaks

sneaky »*adjective* guiltily secretive or sly.
sneakily

sneer (verb: **sneers, sneering, sneered**)

sneeze (verb: **sneezes, sneezing, sneezed**)
sneezy

snick »*verb* (**snicks, snicking, snicked**) cut a small notch in.
» *noun* a small notch or cut.

snicker (verb: **snickers, snickering, snickered**)

snicking

snicks

snide »*adjective* disrespectful or mocking in an indirect way.
snidely

sniff (verb: **sniffs, sniffing, sniffed**)
sniffer

sniffily

sniffing

sniffle (verb: **sniffles, sniffling, sniffled**)
sniffly

sniffs

sniffy »*adjective* (in informal English) scornful.
sniffily

snifter »*noun* (in informal English) a small quantity of an alcoholic drink.

snigger (verb: **sniggers, sniggering, sniggered**)

snip (verb: **snips, snipping, snipped**)

> ✓ double the p in **snipping** and **snipped**

snipe »*noun* (plural **snipe** or **snipes**) a brown wading bird with a long straight bill.
» *verb* (**snipes, sniping, sniped**) ❶ shoot at someone from a hiding place at long range. ❷ criticize in a sly or petty way.
sniper

snipped

snippet »*noun* a small piece or brief extract.

snipping

snips

snitch (in informal English) »*verb* (**snitches, snitching, snitched**) ❶ steal. ❷ inform on someone.
» *noun* an informer.

snivel »*verb* (**snivels, snivelling, snivelled**) ❶ cry and sniffle. ❷ complain in a whining or tearful way.

> ✓ double the l in **snivelling** and **snivelled** (the spellings **sniveling** and **sniveled** are American)

snob
snobbery
snobbism
snobby

snobbish
snobbishly

snobbism

snobby

snog (verb: **snogs, snogging, snogged**)

snood »*noun* a hairnet worn at the back of a woman's head.

snook »*noun* (**cock a snook**) (in informal English) openly show contempt or disrespect for.

snooker (verb: **snookers, snookering, snookered**)

snoop (verb: **snoops, snooping, snooped**)
snooper

snooty (adjective: **snootier, snootiest**)
snootily

snooze (verb: **snoozes, snoozing, snoozed**)

snore (verb: **snores, snoring, snored**)
snorer

snorkel »*noun* a tube for a swimmer to breathe through while under water.
» *verb* (**snorkels, snorkelling, snorkelled**) swim using a snorkel.

> ✓ double the l in **snorkelling** and **snorkelled** (the spellings **snorkeling** and **snorkeled** are American)

snort (verb: **snorts, snorting, snorted**)
snorter

snot

snotty (adjective: **snottier**, **snottiest**)

snout

snow (verb: **snows**, **snowing**, **snowed**)

snowball (verb: **snowballs**, **snowballing**, **snowballed**)

snowboard
snowboarder
snowboarding

snowbound »*adjective* ❶ unable to travel or go out because of the snow. ❷ (of a place) cut off by snow.

snowdrift

snowdrop

snowed

snowfall »*noun* ❶ a fall of snow. ❷ the quantity of snow falling within a particular area in a given time.

snowfield »*noun* a permanent wide expanse of snow in mountainous or polar regions.

snowflake

snowier

snowiest

snowing

snowline »*noun* the altitude above which some snow remains on the ground throughout the year.

snowman (plural **snowmen**)

snowmobile »*noun* a motor vehicle for travelling over snow.

snowplough »*noun* a device or vehicle for clearing roads of snow.

snows

snowshoe »*noun* a flat device attached to the sole of a boot and used for walking on snow.

snowstorm

snowy (adjective: **snowier**, **snowiest**)

snub (verb: **snubs**, **snubbing**, **snubbed**)

> ☑ double the **b** in **snubbing** and **snubbed**

snuck American past and past participle of SNEAK.

snuff »*verb* (**snuffs**, **snuffing**, **snuffed**)
❶ put out a candle. ❷ (**snuff out**) abruptly put an end to something. ❸ (**snuff it**) (in informal English) die. ❹ sniff at something.
» *noun* powdered tobacco that is sniffed up the nostril.

snuffer »*noun* a small metal cone on the end of a handle, used to snuff a candle.

snuffing

snuffle (verb: **snuffles**, **snuffling**, **snuffled**)
snuffly

snuffs

snug (adjective: **snugger**, **snuggest**)
snugly
snugness

> ☑ double the **g** in **snugger** and **snuggest**

snuggery »*noun* (plural **snuggeries**) a cosy place.

snuggest

snuggle (verb: **snuggles**, **snuggling**, **snuggled**)

snugly

snugness

so

soak (verb: **soaks**, **soaking**, **soaked**)

soakaway »*noun* a pit through which waste water drains slowly out into the surrounding soil.

soaked

soaking

soaks

so-and-so (plural **so-and-sos**)

soap (verb: **soaps**, **soaping**, **soaped**)

soapbox »*noun* (plural **soapboxes**) ❶ a box used as a makeshift stand for public speaking. ❷ an opportunity for someone to air their views publicly.

soaped

soapier [more soapy]

soapiest

soaping

soap opera

> ℹ️ so named because television and radio programmes of this sort in America were originally sponsored by soap manufacturers

soaps

soapstone »*noun* a soft rock consisting largely of talc.

soapsuds

soapy (adjective: **soapier**, **soapiest**)

soar (verb: **soars**, **soaring**, **soared**)

sob (verb: **sobs**, **sobbing**, **sobbed**)

> ☑ double the **b** in **sobbing** and **sobbed**

sober »*adjective* (**soberer**, **soberest**) ❶ not drunk. ❷ serious. ❸ (of a colour or clothes) not bright or likely to attract attention.
» *verb* (**sobers**, **sobering**, **sobered**) ❶ (**sober up**) make or become sober after drinking alcohol. ❷ make or become serious.
soberly

sobriety »*noun* the state of being sober.
– SAY suh-**bry**-uh-ti

sobriquet »*noun* a person's nickname.
– SAY soh-bri-kay

> ☑ a French word, **sobriquet** can also be
> spelled **soubriquet**

sobs

so-called

soccer

sociable »*adjective* ❶ willing to talk and
take part in activities with others.
❷ friendly and welcoming: *a very sociable
little village.*
sociability
sociably

> ℹ **sociable** and **social** do not mean quite
> the same thing. **Sociable** tends to
> mean 'willing to talk and take part in
> activities with others', while **social** means
> 'relating to society' or 'needing or done in
> the company of others'.

social »*adjective* ❶ having to do with
society and its organization. ❷ needing
the company of others: *we are social beings
as well as individuals.* ❸ (of an activity) in
which people meet each other for
pleasure. ❹ (of birds, insects, or
mammals) breeding or living in organized
communities.
»*noun* an informal social gathering.
socially

> ℹ see the note at SOCIABLE

social climber »*noun* (used in a
disapproving way) a person who is anxious
to improve their social status.

social contract »*noun* an unspoken
agreement among the members of a
society to cooperate for the benefit of all,
for example by giving up some individual
freedom in return for protection from the
state.

socialise another way of spelling SOCIALIZE.

socialism »*noun* a political and economic
theory which holds that a country's land,
transport, natural resources, and chief
industries should be owned or controlled
by the community as a whole.
socialist

socialite »*noun* a person who mixes in
fashionable society.

socialize »*verb* (**socializes, socializing,
socialized**) ❶ mix socially with others.
❷ make someone behave in a way that is
acceptable to society.

> ☑ many people prefer the alternative
> spellings **socialise, socialises,** etc.:
> both **s** and **z** spellings are correct

socially

social science »*noun* ❶ the scientific
study of human society and social
relationships. ❷ a subject within this field,
such as economics.

social security »*noun* (in the UK) money
provided by the state for people with an
inadequate or no income.

social services »*noun* services provided
by the state for the community, such as
education and medical care.

social studies »*noun* the study of human
society.

social work »*noun* work carried out by
people trained to help improve the
conditions of people who are poor, old,
etc.
social worker

society (plural **societies**)
societal

> ☑ plural: drop the **y** and add **ies**:
> **societies**

socio-economic »*adjective* relating to the
interaction of social and economic factors.

sociology »*noun* the study of the
development, structure, and functioning
of human society.
sociological
sociologist

sociopath »*noun* a person with a mental
disorder showing itself in extreme
antisocial attitudes and behaviour.
– SAY soh-si-oh-path or soh-shi-oh-path
sociopathic
sociopathy

sock (verb: **socks, socking, socked**)

socket

socking

socks

sod¹ »*noun* ❶ grass-covered ground. ❷ a
piece of turf.

sod² (verb: **sods, sodding, sodded**) [an
unpleasant person; used to express anger
or annoyance]

soda »*noun* ❶ (also **soda water**)
carbonated water. ❷ sodium carbonate.
❸ (in American English) a sweet fizzy
drink.

soda bread »*noun* bread leavened with
baking soda.

sodded

sodden »*adjective* ❶ soaked through. ❷ having drunk an excessive amount of an alcoholic drink: *whisky-sodden*.

sodding

sodium lamp »*noun* a lamp in which an electrical discharge in sodium vapour gives a yellow light.

sodomite »*noun* a person who engages in sodomy.
– SAY sod-uh-myt

sodomy »*noun* anal intercourse.

named after the city of *Sodom* in the Bible (Book of Genesis, chapter 19)

sods

Sod's Law »*noun* = MURPHY'S LAW.

sofa

soft (adjective: **softer**, **softest**)
softly
softness

softback »*noun* a paperback book.

softball »*noun* a form of baseball played on a smaller field with a larger, softer ball.

soft-boiled

soften (verb: **softens**, **softening**, **softened**)
softener

softer

softest

soft focus »*noun* deliberate slight blurring in a photograph or film.

soft furnishings »*plural noun* curtains, chair coverings, and other cloth items used to decorate a room.

soft-hearted

softie (plural **softies**)

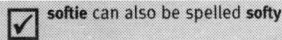 **softie** can also be spelled **softy**

softly

softly-softly »*adjective* cautious and patient.

softness

soft palate »*noun* the fleshy, flexible part towards the back of the roof of the mouth.

soft pedal »*noun* a pedal on a piano that can be pressed to soften the tone.
»*verb* (**soft-pedals**, **soft-pedalling**, **soft-pedalled**) play down the unpleasant aspects of.

soft sell »*noun* the selling of something in a gently persuasive way.

soft-soap »*verb* (**soft-soaps**, **soft-soaping**, **soft-soaped**) (in informal English) use flattery to persuade someone.

soft-top »*noun* a motor vehicle with a roof that can be folded back.

software »*noun* programs and other operating information used by a computer.

 **-ware** not **-wear**: **software**

softwood »*noun* the wood from a conifer as opposed to that of broadleaved trees.

softy another way of spelling SOFTIE.

soggy (adjective: **soggier**, **soggiest**)
soggily
sogginess

soi-disant »*adjective* self-styled: *soi-disant journalists*.
– SAY swah-**dee**-zon

soi-disant is a French word, from *soi* 'oneself' and *disant* 'saying'

soigne »*adjective* elegant and well groomed.
– SAY swun-yay

soigne can also be spelled **soigné**, with an acute accent on the **e** (as in the original French). When used to describe a woman, a second **e** is added at the end: **soignee** (or **soignée**).

soil (verb: **soils**, **soiling**, **soiled**)

soiree »*noun* an evening social gathering for conversation or music.
– SAY swah-ray

soiree can also be spelled **soirée**, with an acute accent on the first **e** (as in the original French)

sojourn »*noun* a temporary stay.
»*verb* (**sojourns**, **sojourning**, **sojourned**) stay somewhere temporarily.
– SAY so-juhn or so-jern

solace »*noun* comfort in time of distress.
»*verb* (**solaces**, **solacing**, **solaced**) give solace to someone.
– SAY sol-iss

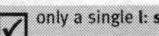 only a single l: **solace**

solar »*adjective* having to do with the sun or its rays.

solar cell »*noun* a device that converts the sun's radiation into electricity.

solarium »*noun* (plural **solariums** or **solaria**) ❶ a room equipped with sunlamps or sunbeds. ❷ a room with large areas of glass to let in sunlight.
– SAY suh-**lair**-i-uhm

the plural of **solarium** can be either **solariums** or **solaria** (as in Latin)

solar panel »*noun* a panel designed to absorb the sun's rays as a source of energy for generating electricity or heating.

solar plexus »*noun* a network of nerves at the pit of the stomach.

solar power »*noun* power obtained by harnessing the energy of the sun's rays.

solar system »*noun* the sun together with the planets, asteroids, comets, etc. in orbit around it.

solar wind »*noun* a continuous flow of charged particles from the sun, permeating the solar system.

sola topi »*noun* an Indian sun hat made from the pith of a marsh plant.

> ☑ **sola** not **solar**: the **sola topi** (or **topee**) is named after the *sola* plant

sold past and past participle of **SELL**.

solder »*noun* a soft alloy used for joining metals.
» *verb* (**solders, soldering, soldered**) join metals with solder.

soldering iron »*noun* an electrical tool for melting and applying solder.

solders

soldier (verb: **soldiers, soldiering, soldiered**)
soldierly

soldiery »*noun* ❶ soldiers as a group.
❷ military training or knowledge.

sole[1] (verb: **soles, soling, soled**) [the underside of a person's foot or shoe; have the sole of a shoe replaced]

sole[2] »*noun* an edible marine flatfish.

sole[3] [one and only]
solely

solecism »*noun* ❶ a grammatical mistake.
❷ an instance of bad manners or incorrect behaviour.
– **SAY** sol-i-si-z'm

soled

solely

> ☑ two **l**'s in **solely**

solemn »*adjective* ❶ formal and dignified: *a solemn procession.* ❷ serious. ❸ deeply sincere: *a solemn oath.*
solemnly

> ☑ don't forget the silent **n** at the end: **solemn**

solemnise another way of spelling **SOLEMNIZE**.

solemnity »*noun* (plural **solemnities**) ❶ the state of being solemn. ❷ (**solemnities**) solemn ceremonies or rites.
– **SAY** suh-**lem**-ni-ti

> ☑ plural: drop the **y** and add **ies**: **solemnities**

solemnize »*verb* (**solemnizes, solemnizing, solemnized**) duly perform a religious ceremony.
– **SAY** sol-uhm-nyz
solemnization

> ☑ many people prefer the alternative spellings **solemnise, solemnises**, etc., and **solemnisation**: both **s** and **z** spellings are correct

solemnly

solenoid »*noun* a coil of wire which becomes magnetic when an electric current is passed through it.
– **SAY** sol-uh-noyd or **soh**-luh-noyd

soles

soli plural of **SOLO**.

solicit »*verb* (**solicits, soliciting, solicited**)
❶ ask for or try to obtain something from someone. ❷ ask for something from someone. ❸ approach someone and offer them sex in return for money.
solicitation

> ☑ only a single **l** in **solicit** and **solicitor**

solicitor »*noun* a lawyer qualified to deal with property and wills, to advise clients and instruct barristers, and to represent clients in lower courts.

> ☑ **-or** not **-er**: **solicitor**

solicitous »*adjective* showing interest or concern about a person's well-being.
solicitously
solicitousness

solicits

solicitude »*noun* care or concern.

solid
solidity
solidly

> ⓘ the comparative and superlative are usually **more solid** and **most solid**, not **solider** and **solidest**

solidarity »*noun* agreement and support resulting from shared interests, feelings, or opinions.

solidify »*verb* (**solidifies, solidifying, solidified**) make something or become hard or solid.
solidification

solidity

solidly

solid-state »*adjective* (of an electronic device) using solid semiconductors, e.g. transistors, as opposed to valves.

soliloquy »*noun* (plural **soliloquies**) a speech in a play when a character speaks

their thoughts aloud when alone or regardless of hearers.
– **say** suh-**lil**-uh-kwi

soling

solipsism »*noun* the view that the self is all that can be known to exist.
– **say** sol-ip-siz-uhm

solitaire »*noun* ❶ a game for one player played by removing pegs from a board one at a time by moving others over them. ❷ the card game patience. ❸ a single gem in a piece of jewellery.

> ✓ remember the final **e**: **solitaire** is a French word

solitary »*adjective* ❶ done or existing alone. ❷ (of a place) secluded or isolated. ❸ single: *not a solitary shred of evidence*.
»*noun* (plural **solitaries**) ❶ a person living in solitude for personal or religious reasons. ❷ (in informal English) solitary confinement.

> ✓ plural: drop the **y** and add **ies**: **solitaries**

solitary confinement »*noun* the isolating of a prisoner in a separate cell as a punishment.

solitude »*noun* the state of being alone.

solo (plural **solos**; verb: **soloes**, **soloing**, **soloed**)

> ✓ the plural of **solo** is **solos**, but **soli** is occasionally used to refer to solo pieces of music, dance, etc.

soloist

Solomon's seal »*noun* a plant with arching stems and drooping green and white flowers.

solstice »*noun* one of the two times in the year, at midsummer and midwinter, when the sun reaches its highest or lowest point in the sky at noon, marked by the longest and shortest days.
– **say** sol-stiss

soluble »*adjective* ❶ (of a substance) able to be dissolved. ❷ (of a problem) able to be solved.
solubility

solute »*noun* a substance that is dissolved in another substance.
– **say** sol-yoot

solution

solve (verb: **solves**, **solving**, **solved**)
solver

solvency »*noun* the state of having more money than you owe.

solvent »*adjective* ❶ having more money than you owe. ❷ able to dissolve other substances.
»*noun* the liquid in which another substance is dissolved to form a solution.

> ✓ **ent** not **ant**: **solvent**

solvent abuse »*noun* the deliberate inhaling of the intoxicating fumes of certain solvents, e.g. glue.

solver

solves

solving

Somali (plural **Somali** or **Somalis**) [of Somalia]
Somalian

somatic »*adjective* having to do with the body rather than the mind.
– **say** suh-**mat**-ik
somatically

sombre »*adjective* ❶ dark or dull. ❷ very solemn or serious.
sombrely
sombreness

> ✓ **bre** not **ber**: **sombre** (the spelling **somber** is American)

sombrero »*noun* (plural **sombreros**) a broad-brimmed Mexican hat.
– **say** som-**brair**-oh

> ✓ the plural of **sombrero** has **os** not **oes**: **sombreros**

some

somebody

somehow

someone

someplace

somersault (verb: **somersaults**, **somersaulting**, **somersaulted**)

> ✓ **somer** not **summer**, and **-sault** not **-salt**: **somersault**

something

sometime

sometimes

somewhat

somewhere

somnambulism »*noun* sleepwalking.
– **say** som-**nam**-byuu-li-z'm
somnambulist

> ✓ **namb** not **nab** in the middle: **somnambulism**

somnolent »*adjective* ❶ sleepy. ❷ causing sleepiness: *a somnolent summer day*.
– **say** som-nuh-luhnt
somnolence

ent not **ant: somnolent**

son

sonar »*noun* ❶ a system for detecting objects under water by giving out sound pulses and measuring their return after being reflected. ❷ an apparatus used for this.
– SAY soh-nar

sonata »*noun* a classical composition for an instrumental soloist, often with a piano accompaniment.
– SAY suh-**nah**-tuh

 one n, one t: **sonata** is an Italian word meaning 'sounded'

son et lumiere »*noun* an entertainment held by night at a historic building, telling its history by the use of lighting effects and recorded sound.
– SAY son ay loo-my-air

 son et lumiere may also be spelled **son et lumière**, with a grave accent above the first **e** of **lumiere** (as in the original French phrase meaning 'sound and light')

song
songbird
songster »*noun* a person who sings.
songstress (plural **songstresses**)
songwriter
sonic »*adjective* relating to or using sound waves.
  sonically

sonic boom »*noun* an explosive noise caused by the shock wave from an object travelling faster than the speed of sound.

son-in-law (plural **sons-in-law**)

in the plural, the **s** goes after **son** not **law: sons-in-law**

sonnet »*noun* a poem of fourteen lines using a fixed rhyme scheme.

sonny »*noun* an informal form of address to a young boy.

sonogram »*noun* ❶ a graph showing the distribution of energy at different frequencies in a sound. ❷ a visual image produced from an ultrasound examination.

sonorous »*adjective* (of a sound) deep and full.
– SAY son-uh-ruhss
  sonority
  sonorously
  sonorousness

nor not **nour** in the middle: **sonorous**

soon (adverb: **sooner**, **soonest**)
  soonish

soot

sooth »*noun* (an old word) truth.

soothe (verb: **soothes**, **soothing**, **soothed**) [gently calm someone or relieve discomfort]
  soother

soothsayer »*noun* a person supposed to be able to foresee the future.
  soothsaying

sooty (adjective: **sootier**, **sootiest**)

sop »*noun* a thing given or done to calm or please someone who is angry or upset.
» *verb* (**sops**, **sopping**, **sopped**) (**sop up**) soak up liquid.

double the **p** in **sopping** and **sopped**

sophism »*noun* a false argument.
– SAY soff-i-z'm

sophist »*noun* a person who uses clever but false arguments.
– SAY soff-ist
  sophistic

sophisticate »*noun* a sophisticated person.

sophisticated »*adjective* ❶ (of a machine or system) highly developed and complex. ❷ having worldly experience and taste in matters of culture or fashion.
  sophisticatedly
  sophistication

sophistry »*noun* (plural **sophistries**) ❶ the use of false arguments. ❷ a false argument.
– SAY soff-iss-tri

sophomore »*noun* (in American English) a second-year university or high-school student.
– SAY soff-uh-mor

soporific »*adjective* causing drowsiness or sleep.
– SAY sop-uh-**ri**-fik
  soporifically

sopped
soppier
soppiest
soppily
soppiness
sopping

soppy (adjective: **soppier**, **soppiest**)
  soppily
  soppiness

soprano »*noun* (plural **sopranos**) the highest singing voice.

» *adjective* (of an instrument) of a high or
the highest pitch in its family: *a soprano
saxophone.*
– SAY suh-**prah**-noh

✓ the plural of **soprano**, an Italian word,
has **os** not **oes: sopranos**

sops

sorbet »*noun* a water ice.
– SAY **sor**-bay or **sor**-bit

✓ note the **et** ending: **sorbet** is a French
word

sorcerer »*noun* a person believed to
practise magic.
sorcery

sorceress (plural **sorceresses**)

sorcery

sordid »*adjective* ❶ involving dishonest or
immoral actions and motives.
❷ extremely dirty and unpleasant.
sordidly
sordidness

sore (adjective: **sorer**, **sorest**)
sorely
soreness

sorghum »*noun* a cereal found in warm
regions, grown for grain and animal feed.
– SAY **sor**-guhm

✓ don't forget the **h** after the **g:**
sorghum

sorority »*noun* (plural **sororities**) (in
American English) a society for female
students in a university or college.
– SAY suh-**ro**-ri-ti

sorrel[1] »*noun* an edible plant with arrow-
shaped leaves and a bitter flavour.

✓ two **r**'s, one **l: sorrel**

sorrel[2] »*noun* ❶ a light reddish-brown
colour. ❷ a horse with a sorrel coat.

sorrier

sorriest

sorrow

sorrowful
sorrowfully

✓ **-ful** not **-full: sorrowful**

sorry (adjective: **sorrier**, **sorriest**)

✓ drop the **y** and add **ier** or **iest** to spell
sorrier or **sorriest**

sort (verb: **sorts**, **sorting**, **sorted**)
sorted
sorter

ℹ when using **sort** to refer to a plural
noun, do not use *these sort*: say

these sorts of questions are not relevant
rather than *these sort of questions are not
relevant*

sortie »*noun* ❶ an attack by troops coming
out from a position of defence. ❷ a flight
by a single aircraft on a military
operation. ❸ a short trip.
» *verb* (**sorties**, **sortieing**, **sortied**) make a
sortie.

✓ do not drop the **e** in **sortieing**

sorting

sorts

SOS »*noun* (plural **SOSs**) ❶ an
international signal of extreme distress.
❷ an urgent appeal for help.

ℹ the letters were chosen as being
easily transmitted and recognized in
Morse code, but are often thought to be
short for *save our souls*

so-so

sot »*noun* a person who is regularly drunk.

sotto voce »*adverb & adjective* in a quiet
voice.
– SAY sot-toh **voh**-chay

ℹ **sotto voce** means 'under the voice' in
Italian

soubriquet another way of spelling
SOBRIQUET.

souffle »*noun* a light, spongy baked dish
made by mixing egg yolks and another
ingredient such as cheese or fruit with
stiffly beaten egg whites.

✓ **souffle** can also be spelled **soufflé**,
with an acute accent above the **e** (as
in the original French word meaning
'blown')

sought past and past participle of SEEK.

souk »*noun* an Arab market.
– SAY sook

✓ **souk** can also be spelled **suq**

soul

soul-destroying »*adjective* unbearably
dull and repetitive.

soulful »*adjective* expressing deep sadness
or love: *a soulful glance.*
soulfully

✓ **-ful** not **-full: soulful**

soulless »*adjective* ❶ lacking character or
interest. ❷ lacking human feelings:
soulless dark eyes.
soullessly
soullessness

S

double l: soulless

soulmate »*noun* a person ideally suited to another.

soul-searching

sound[1] (verb: sounds, sounding, sounded) [something that can be heard; make a sound]
soundless

sound[2] (adjective: sounder, soundest) [in good condition; based on solid judgement]
soundly
soundness

sound[3] »*verb* (sounds, sounding, sounded) ❶ find out the depth of water in the sea, a lake, etc. using a line, pole, or sound echoes. ❷ (sound out) question someone as to their opinions.

sound[4] »*noun* a narrow stretch of water forming an inlet or connecting two larger bodies of water.

sound barrier »*noun* the point at which an aircraft reaches the speed of sound.

sound bite »*noun* a short memorable extract from a speech or interview.

soundcheck »*noun* a test of sound equipment before a musical performance or recording.

sounded

sound effect »*noun* a sound other than speech or music made artificially for use in a play, film, etc.

sounder

soundest

sounding »*noun* ❶ a measurement of the depth of water, taken by sounding. ❷ (soundings) information found out before taking action.

sounding board »*noun* a person or group whose reactions to ideas or opinions are used to find out if they are valid or likely to succeed.

soundless

soundly

soundness

soundproof »*adjective* preventing sound getting in or out.
» *verb* (soundproofs, soundproofing, soundproofed) make something soundproof.

sounds

soundtrack

sound wave »*noun* a wave of alternate compression and reduction in density by which sound travels through air or water.

soup »*noun* a savoury liquid dish made by boiling meat, fish, or vegetables in stock or water.
» *verb* (soups, souping, souped) (soup up) (in informal English) increase the power and efficiency of an engine or other machine.
soupy

soupcon »*noun* a very small quantity.
– SAY soop-son

 soupcon can also be spelled **soupçon**, with a cedilla accent on the **c** (as in the original French)

souped

souping

soups

soupy

sour (adjective: sourer, sourest; verb: sours, souring, soured)
sourly
sourness

source »*noun* (sources, sourcing, sourced) ❶ a place, person, or thing from which something originates. ❷ a place where a river or stream starts. ❸ a person, book, or document that provides information.

sourdough »*noun* bread made from fermenting dough.

soured

sourer

sourest

souring

sourly

sourness

sourpuss »*noun* (plural sourpusses) (in informal English) a bad-tempered or sulky person.

sours

souse »*verb* (souses, sousing, soused) ❶ drench something with or soak it in liquid. ❷ (soused) pickled or marinaded: *soused herring.*
– SAY SOWSS

soutane »*noun* a type of cassock worn by Roman Catholic priests.
– SAY soo-**tahn**

south

South African

South American

southbound

south-east
south-easterly
south-eastern

south-eastward

south-eastwards

southerly

southern

southerner

Southern Lights »*plural noun* the aurora australis.

southpaw »*noun* a left-handed boxer who leads with the right hand.

south-south-east

south-south-west

southward

southwards

south-west
south-westerly
south-western

south-westward

south-westwards

souvenir

sou'wester »*noun* a waterproof hat with a broad brim that covers the back of the neck.
– **SAY** sow-**wess**-ter

sovereign »*noun* ❶ a king or queen who is the supreme ruler of a country. ❷ a former British gold coin worth one pound sterling.
» *adjective* ❶ possessing supreme power. ❷ (of a country) acting independently and without outside interference.

> ✓ e before i: **sovereign** does not follow the usual rule

sovereignty »*noun* (plural **sovereignties**) ❶ complete power or authority. ❷ a self-governing state.

Soviet »*noun* ❶ a citizen of the former Soviet Union. ❷ (**soviet**) an elected council in the former Soviet Union.
» *adjective* having to do with the former Soviet Union.
– **SAY** **soh**-vi-uht or **sov**-i-uht

> ✓ there is only one **v**: **Soviet**

sow[1] »*verb* (**sows**, **sowing**, **sowed**; past participle **sown** or **sowed**) ❶ plant seed by scattering it on or in the earth. ❷ plant an area with seed. ❸ spread or introduce something unwelcome.
sower

sow[2] »*noun* an adult female pig.
– **SAY** sow

sown past participle of **sow**[1].

sows

soy »*noun* ❶ a sauce made with fermented soya beans, used in Chinese and Japanese cooking. ❷ = **soya**.

soya »*noun* a plant which produces an edible bean that is high in protein.

sozzled »*adjective* (in informal English) very drunk.

spa »*noun* ❶ a mineral spring considered to have health-giving properties. ❷ a place with a mineral spring.

space (verb: **spaces**, **spacing**, **spaced**)
spacer
spacing

space age »*noun* the era that started when the exploration of space became possible.

> ✓ add a hyphen if you use this word as an adjective, as in *a space-age control room*

spacecraft

spaced

spaceman (plural **spacemen**)

spacer

spaces

spaceship

space shuttle »*noun* a rocket-launched spacecraft, used for journeys between earth and craft orbiting the earth.

space station »*noun* a large spacecraft used as a base for manned operations in space.

spacesuit

space–time »*noun* (in physics) the concepts of time and three-dimensional space seen as joined in a four-dimensional continuum.

spacey »*adjective* (**spacier**, **spaciest**) ❶ out of touch with reality. ❷ (of popular music) drifting and ethereal.

> ✓ **spacey** can also be spelled without the **e**: **spacy**

spacing

spacious
spaciously
spaciousness

spacy another way of spelling **spacey**.

spade

spadework

spaghetti

> ✓ note the **gh** in the middle and the double **t**: **spaghetti** is an Italian word which means 'little strings'

spaghetti Bolognese »*noun* a dish of spaghetti with a sauce of minced beef, tomato, onion, and herbs.
– **SAY** bol-uh-**nayz**

> ✓ **Bolognese** is an Italian word meaning 'of Bologna'; it ends in **ese** not **aise**

S

spake (an old word) past of **SPEAK**.

spam »*noun* ❶ (trademark) a canned meat product made mainly from ham. ❷ irrelevant or inappropriate messages sent on the Internet to a large number of users.

span »*noun* ❶ the width or extent of something from side to side. ❷ the length of time for which something lasts. ❸ a part of a bridge between the uprights supporting it. ❹ the maximum distance between the tips of the thumb and little finger.
» *verb* (spans, spanning, spanned) extend across or over something.

> ☑ double the n to spell **spanning** and **spanned**

spandex »*noun* (trademark) a type of stretchy polyurethane fabric.

spangle »*noun* ❶ a small piece of glittering material used to decorate a garment. ❷ a spot of bright colour or light.
spangled
spangly

Spaniard

> ☑ ard not erd: **Spaniard**

spaniel »*noun* a dog with a long silky coat and drooping ears.

Spanish

Spanish omelette »*noun* an omelette containing potatoes and onions, served open rather than folded.

spank (verb: spanks, spanking, spanked)
spanking

spanned

spanner

spanning

spans

spar[1] »*noun* a thick, strong pole used to support the sails on a ship.

spar[2] »*verb* (spars, sparring, sparred) ❶ make the motions of boxing without landing heavy blows, as a form of training. ❷ argue in a friendly way.

> ☑ double the r to spell **sparring** and **sparred**

spare (verb: spares, sparing, spared)
sparely
spareness

spare ribs »*noun* trimmed ribs of pork.

spares

sparing »*adjective* not wasteful; economical.
sparingly

spark (verb: sparks, sparking, sparked)
sparky

sparkle (verb: sparkles, sparkling, sparkled)
sparkler
sparkly

sparks

sparky

sparred

sparring

sparrow

sparrowhawk »*noun* a small hawk that preys on small birds.

spars

sparse »*adjective* (sparser, sparsest) thinly scattered.
sparsely
sparseness
sparsity

spartan »*adjective* not comfortable or luxurious.

> ℹ from the name of the ancient Greek city state of *Sparta*, where an austere lifestyle was favoured

spasm »*noun* ❶ a sudden involuntary contraction of a muscle. ❷ a sudden brief spell of an activity or a sensation.

spasmodic »*adjective* ❶ occurring or done in brief, irregular bursts. ❷ caused by a spasm or spasms.
spasmodically

spastic »*adjective* ❶ relating to or affected by muscle spasm. ❷ (old-fashioned) having to do with cerebral palsy.
» *noun* (old-fashioned) a person with cerebral palsy.
spasticity

> ℹ do not use the word **spastic** to refer to people because many now find it offensive; say *person with cerebral palsy* instead

spat[1] past and past participle of **SPIT**[1].

spat[2] »*noun* a cloth covering formerly worn by men over their ankles and shoes.

spat[3] »*noun* a petty quarrel.

spate »*noun* ❶ a large number of similar things coming quickly one after another. ❷ a sudden flood in a river.

spathe »*noun* a large sheath enclosing the flower cluster of certain plants.
– **SAY** spay*th*

spatial »*adjective* having to do with space.
– **SAY** spay-sh'l
spatially

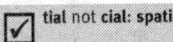

✓ tial not cial: spatial

spatter (verb: **spatters, spattering, spattered**)

spatula »*noun* an implement with a broad, flat, blunt blade, used for mixing or spreading.

spawn »*verb* (**spawns, spawning, spawned**) ❶ (of a fish, frog, etc.) release or deposit eggs. ❷ give rise to something: *the affair spawned a rash of publications.*
» *noun* the eggs of fish, frogs, etc.

spay »*verb* (**spays, spaying, spayed**) sterilize a female animal by removing the ovaries.

speak (verb: **speaks, speaking, spoke**; past participle **spoken**)

speakeasy »*noun* (plural **speakeasies**) (in the US during Prohibition) a secret illegal drinking club.

✓ plural: drop the **y** and add **ies**: **speakeasies**

speaker

speaking

speaks

spear (verb: **spears, spearing, speared**)

spearhead »*noun* ❶ the point of a spear. ❷ an individual or group leading an attack or movement.
» *verb* (**spearheads, spearheading, spearheaded**) lead an attack or movement.

spearing

spearmint »*noun* common garden mint, used in cooking.

spears

spec[1] »*noun* (**on spec**) without any specific preparation or plan.

spec[2] »*noun* (in informal English) a detailed working description.

special
    specialness

specialise another way of spelling **SPECIALIZE**.

specialist
    specialism

speciality (plural **specialities**)

✓ the normal spelling is **speciality**, but in American English and some medical uses it is spelled without the final **i**: **specialty**
plural: drop the **y** and add **ies**: **specialities**

specialize (verb: **specializes, specializing, specialized**)
    specialization

✓ many people prefer the alternative spellings **specialise, specialises,** etc., and **specialisation**: both **s** and **z** spellings are correct

specially »*adverb* ❶ for a special purpose. ❷ particularly.

ℹ for an explanation of the difference between **specially** and **especially**, see the note at **ESPECIALLY**

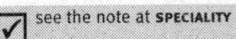

specialness

specialty »*noun* (plural **specialties**) (mainly in American English) = **SPECIALITY**.

✓ see the note at **SPECIALITY**

speciation »*noun* (in biology) the formation of new species in the course of evolution.
– **SAY** spee-shi-**ay**-sh'n or spee-si-**ay**-sh'n

specie »*noun* money in the form of coins rather than notes.
– **SAY** spee-shi

species »*noun* (plural **species**) ❶ a group of animals or plants that are capable of breeding with each other. ❷ a kind: *a species of criticism.*
– **SAY** spee-shiz or spee-sheez

✓ **i** before **e**, even though it is after **c**: **species** does not follow the usual rule

specifiable

specific »*adjective* ❶ clearly defined or identified. ❷ precise and clear. ❸ (**specific to**) belonging or relating only to.
» *noun* (**specifics**) precise details.
    specifically
    specificity
    specificness

✓ be careful to remember the **s** at the beginning of **specific**. Do not confuse it with **pacific,** which means 'peaceful'.

specification »*noun* ❶ the action of specifying. ❷ (also **specifications**) a detailed description of the design and materials used to make something. ❸ a standard of workmanship and materials required to be met in a piece of work.

specificity

specificness

specify (verb: **specifies, specifying, specified**)
    specifiable
    specifier

specimen »*noun* ❶ an example of an animal, plant, object, etc. used for study or display. ❷ a sample for medical testing. ❸ a typical example of something. ❹ a person of a specific type: *a sorry specimen.*

S

men not min: **specimen**

specious »*adjective* ❶ seeming reasonable, but actually wrong. ❷ misleading in appearance.
– SAY spee-shuhss
speciously
speciousness

speck (verb: **specks, specking, specked**)

speckle (verb: **speckles, speckling, speckled**)
speckled

specks

specs

spectacle »*noun* a visually striking performance or display.

✓ **acle** not **icle**: **spectacle**

spectacled »*adjective* wearing spectacles.
spectacles
spectacular
spectacularly

✓ **ular** not **uler** or **lier**: **spectacular**

spectate »*verb* (**spectates, spectating, spectated**) be a spectator.
spectator

✓ **-or** not **-er**: **spectator**

specter American spelling of SPECTRE.

spectra plural of SPECTRUM.

spectral »*adjective* ❶ like a spectre. ❷ having to do with the spectrum.
spectrally

spectre »*noun* ❶ a ghost. ❷ a possible unpleasant or dangerous occurrence: *the spectre of nuclear holocaust.*

✓ note that the ending is **re**: **spectre** (the spelling **specter** is American)

spectrometer »*noun* an apparatus used for recording and measuring spectra.
spectrometry

spectroscope »*noun* an apparatus for producing and recording spectra for examination.
spectroscopic

spectroscopy »*noun* the branch of science concerned with the measurement of spectra produced when matter interacts with or gives out electromagnetic radiation.
– SAY spek-**tross**-kuh-pi

spectrum »*noun* (plural **spectra**) ❶ a band of colours produced by separating light into elements with different wavelengths, e.g. in a rainbow. ❷ the entire range of wavelengths of light. ❸ a range of sound waves or different types of wave. ❹ a scale extending between two points.

✓ the plural of **spectrum** is **spectra** (as in the original Latin)

specula plural of SPECULUM.

speculate »*verb* (**speculates, speculating, speculated**) ❶ form a theory without firm evidence. ❷ invest in stocks, property, etc. in the hope of gain but with the risk of loss.
– SAY spek-yuu-layt
speculation
speculator

speculative »*adjective* ❶ based on theory or guesswork rather than knowledge. ❷ (of an investment) involving a high risk of loss.
speculatively
speculativeness

speculator

speculum »*noun* (plural **specula**) a metal instrument that is used to widen an opening or canal in the body so that it can be inspected.
– SAY spek-yuu-luhm

✓ the plural of **speculum** is **specula** (it is a Latin word which means 'mirror')

sped past and past participle of SPEED.

speech

speechify »*verb* (**speechifies, speechifying, speechified**) deliver a speech in a boring or pompous way.

speechless
speechlessly
speechlessness

speed (verb: **speeds, speeding, speeded** or **sped**)

speedboat

speeded

speedier

speediest

speedily

speediness

speeding

speedometer »*noun* an instrument on a vehicle's dashboard which shows its speed.

speeds

speedway »*noun* a form of motorcycle racing in which the riders race laps around an oval dirt track.

speedwell »*noun* a small creeping plant with blue or pink flowers.

speedy (adjective: **speedier**, **speediest**)
  speedily
  speediness

speleology »*noun* the study or exploration of caves.
– SAY spee-li-**ol**-uh-ji

spell (verb: **spells**, **spelling**, **spelled** or **spelt**)
  speller

spellbind »*verb* (**spellbinds**, **spellbinding**, **spellbound**) hold someone's complete attention.

spellchecker »*noun* a computer program which checks the spelling of words in text.

spelled

speller

spelling

spells

spelt past and past participle of SPELL.

spend (verb: **spends**, **spending**, **spent**)
  spender

spendthrift »*noun* a person who spends money in an extravagant, irresponsible way.

spent past and past participle of SPEND.

sperm »*noun* (plural **sperm** or **sperms**)
  ❶ semen. ❷ a spermatozoon.

spermatozoon »*noun* (plural **spermatozoa**) the male sex cell of an animal, that fertilizes the egg.
– SAY sper-muh-tuh-**zoh**-on

> ✓ the plural of **spermatozoon** is **spermatozoa** (it comes from Greek words meaning 'seed' and 'animal')

spermicide »*noun* a substance that kills spermatozoa, used as a contraceptive.
  spermicidal

sperms

sperm whale »*noun* a toothed whale that feeds largely on squid.

spew »*verb* (**spews**, **spewing**, **spewed**)
  ❶ pour out in large quantities rapidly and forcibly. ❷ (in informal English) vomit.

sphagnum »*noun* a kind of moss that grows in boggy areas.
– SAY sfag-nuhm

sphere »*noun* ❶ a round solid figure in which every point on the surface is at an equal distance from the centre. ❷ an area of activity, interest, or expertise.

spherical »*adjective* shaped like a sphere.
  spherically

spheroid »*noun* an object that is roughly the same shape as a sphere.

– SAY sfeer-oyd
  spheroidal

sphincter »*noun* a ring of muscle surrounding an opening such as the anus.
– SAY sfingk-ter

sphinx »*noun* an ancient Egyptian stone figure having a lion's body and a human or animal head.

> ✓ the vowel is **i** not **y**: **sphinx**

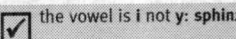

spice (verb: **spices**, **spicing**, **spiced**)

spicier

spiciest

spiciness

spicing

spick and span »*adjective* neat, clean, and well looked after.

spicy (adjective: **spicier**, **spiciest**)
  spiciness

> ✓ drop the **y** and add **ier** or **iest** to spell **spicier** or **spiciest**

spider

spidery

spied

spiel »*noun* (in informal English) an elaborate and insincere speech made in an attempt to persuade someone.
– SAY shpeel or speel

> ℹ **spiel** is a German word which means 'game'

spies

spiffing »*adjective* (old-fashioned) excellent.

spigot »*noun* ❶ a small peg or plug. ❷ (in American English) a tap. ❸ the end of a section of a pipe that fits into the socket of the next one.
– SAY spi-guht

spike (verb: **spikes**, **spiking**, **spiked**)

spikenard »*noun* a perfumed ointment made from the rhizome of a Himalayan plant.
– SAY spi-knahd

spikes

spikier

spikiest

spikily

spikiness

spiking

spiky (adjective: **spikier**, **spikiest**)
  spikily
  spikiness

spill (verb: **spills**, **spilling**, **spilt** or **spilled**)
  spillage

spilt past and past participle of **SPILL**.

spin (verb: **spins**, **spinning**, **spun**)
spinner

> ✓ double the **n** to spell **spinning** and **spinner**

spina bifida »*noun* a condition in which part of the spinal cord is exposed through a gap in the backbone, sometimes causing paralysis.
– SAY spy-nuh bi-fi-duh

spinach »*noun* a plant with large dark green leaves which are eaten as a vegetable.

> ✓ there is only one **n**, and the ending is **ach** not **age**: spinach

spinal »*adjective* relating to the spine.

spinal column »*noun* the spine.

spinal cord »*noun* the nerve fibres enclosed in the spine and connected to the brain.

spindle »*noun* ❶ a slender rod with tapered ends, used for spinning wool, flax, etc. by hand. ❷ a rod around which something revolves.

spindly

spin doctor »*noun* a person employed by a political party to give a favourable interpretation of events to the media.

spindrift »*noun* ❶ spray blown from the sea by the wind. ❷ driving snow.

spine

spine-chiller »*noun* a story or film that causes terror and excitement.
spine-chilling

spineless
spinelessly
spinelessness

spinet »*noun* a small kind of harpsichord.
– SAY spi-**net** or **spin**-it

spine-tingling

spinier

spiniest

spininess

spinnaker »*noun* a large three-cornered sail used on a racing yacht when the wind is coming from behind.
– SAY spin-nuh-ker

> ✓ double **n**: spinnaker

spinner

spinney »*noun* (plural **spinneys**) a small area of trees and bushes.

spinning

spin-off »*noun* something unexpected but useful resulting from an activity.

spins

spinster »*noun* a single woman beyond the usual age for marriage.
spinsterhood
spinsterish

spiny (adjective: **spinier**, **spiniest**)
spininess

spiral »*adjective* winding in a continuous curve around a central point or axis.
» *noun* ❶ a spiral curve, shape, or pattern. ❷ a continuous and dramatic rise or fall of prices, wages, etc.
» *verb* (**spirals**, **spiralling**, **spiralled**) ❶ follow a spiral course. ❷ show a continuous and dramatic increase or decrease.
spirally

> ✓ double the **l** to spell **spiralling** and **spiralled** (the spellings **spiraling** and **spiraled** are American)

spire »*noun* a pointed structure on the top of a church tower.

spirit (verb: **spirits**, **spiriting**, **spirited**)
spirited
spiritedly
spiritedness

spiriting

spiritless

spirit level »*noun* a glass tube partially filled with a liquid, containing an air bubble whose position reveals whether a surface is perfectly level.

spirits

spiritual
spirituality
spiritually

spiritualism »*noun* the belief that the spirits of the dead can communicate with the living.
spiritualist

spirituality

spiritually

spirogyra »*noun* a type of algae consisting of long green threads.
– SAY spy-ruh-jy-ruh

spit[1] (verb: **spits**, **spitting**, **spat** or **spit**) [eject saliva from the mouth; saliva]

spit[2] »*noun* ❶ a metal rod pushed through meat in order to hold and turn it while it is roasted. ❷ a narrow point of land projecting into the sea.

spite »*noun* a desire to hurt, annoy, or offend.
» *verb* (**spites**, **spiting**, **spited**) deliberately hurt, annoy, or offend.

spiteful
  spitefully
  spitefulness

   -ful not -full: spiteful

spites

spitfire »*noun* a person with a fierce temper.

spiting [as in *his selling the house was a way of spiting his family*]

spit-roasted

spits

spitting [as in *spitting is prohibited*]

spittle »*noun* saliva.

spittoon »*noun* a container for spitting into.

  ☑ double t and double o: spittoon

spiv »*noun* (in informal English) a flashily dressed man who makes a living by dishonest business dealings.

splash (verb: **splashes**, **splashing**, **splashed**)
  splasher
  splashy

splat

splatter (verb: **splatters**, **splattering**, **splattered**)

splay »*verb* (**splays**, **splaying**, **splayed**) spread something out or further apart.

spleen »*noun* ❶ an organ in the abdomen involved in the production and removal of blood cells and forming part of the immune system. ❷ bad temper.

splendid
  splendidly

splendour »*noun* magnificent and impressive appearance.

  ☑ -our not -or: splendour (the spelling splendor is American)

splenetic »*adjective* bad-tempered or spiteful.
  – SAY spli-**net**-ik

splice »*verb* (**splices**, **splicing**, **spliced**) ❶ join a rope or ropes by interweaving the strands at the ends. ❷ join pieces of timber, film, or tape at the ends.
  » *noun* a spliced join.

spliff »*noun* (in informal English) a cannabis cigarette.

spline »*noun* a rectangular key fitting into grooves in the hub and shaft of a wheel.

splint »*noun* a strip of rigid material for supporting a broken bone when it has been set.

splinter (verb: **splinters**, **splintering**, **splintered**)
  splintery

splinter group »*noun* a small organization that has broken away from a larger one.

splintering

splinters

splintery

split (verb: **splits**, **splitting**, **split**)
  splitter

  ☑ double the t in **splitting** and **splitter**

split infinitive »*noun* a construction consisting of an infinitive with an adverb or other word placed between *to* and the verb.

  ⓘ many people still think that splitting infinitives is wrong. They think that you should say *she used secretly to admire him* rather than *she used to secretly admire him*, although this can sound awkward or give a different emphasis to what is being said. For this reason, the rule about not splitting infinitives is not followed so strictly today, although it is best not to split them in writing or formal speech.

split-level

splits

split second »*noun* a very brief moment of time.

  ☑ add a hyphen when using **split second** as an adjective, as in *split-second timing*

splitter

splitting

splodge »*noun* a spot or smear.

splosh (verb: **sploshes**, **sploshing**, **sploshed**)

splotch »*noun* a spot or smear.
  splotchy

splurge »*noun* a sudden burst of extravagance.
  » *verb* (**splurges**, **splurging**, **splurged**) spend extravagantly.

splutter (verb: **splutters**, **spluttering**, **spluttered**)

spoil (verb: **spoils**, **spoiling**, **spoilt** or **spoiled**)

spoilage »*noun* the decay of food and other perishable goods.

spoiled

spoiler »*noun* ❶ a flap on an aircraft wing which can be raised to create drag and so reduce speed. ❷ a similar device on a motor vehicle intended to improve road-holding at high speeds.

spoiling

spoils

spoilsport

spoilt

spoke[1] *»noun* ❶ one of the bars or wire rods connecting the centre of a wheel to its rim. ❷ one of the metal rods in an umbrella to which the material is attached.

spoke[2] past of SPEAK.

spoken past participle of SPEAK.

spokeshave *»noun* a small plane with a handle on each side of its blade, used for shaping curved surfaces.

spokesman (plural **spokesmen**)

spokesperson (plural **spokespersons** or **spokespeople**)

spokeswoman (plural **spokeswomen**)

sponge (verb: **sponges**, **sponging** or **spongeing**, **sponged**)
sponger

spongier

spongiest

sponginess

sponging

spongy (adjective: **spongier**, **spongiest**)
sponginess

 the ending is **y** not **ey**: **spongy**

sponsor *»noun* ❶ a person or organization that pays for or contributes to the costs of an event or programme in return for advertising. ❷ a person who pledges an amount of money to a charity after another person has participated in a fund-raising event. ❸ a person who introduces and supports a proposal for a new law.
»verb (**sponsors**, **sponsoring**, **sponsored**) be a sponsor for something.
sponsorship

 -**or** not -**er**: **sponsor**

spontaneous *»adjective* ❶ performed or occurring as a result of an unplanned impulse. ❷ open, natural, and relaxed. ❸ (of a process or event) happening naturally, without being made to do so.
– SAY spon-**tay**-ni-uhss
spontaneity
spontaneously

 neous not **nious**: **spontaneous**

spoof *»noun* an imitation of something in which its characteristic features are exaggerated for comic effect.

spook (verb: **spooks**, **spooking**, **spooked**)

spooky (adjective: **spookier**, **spookiest**)
spookily
spookiness

spool *»noun* a cylindrical device on which thread, film, fishing line, etc. can be wound.
»verb (**spools**, **spooling**, **spooled**) wind something on to a spool.

spoon (verb: **spoons**, **spooning**, **spooned**)
spoonful

spoonbill *»noun* a tall wading bird having a long bill with a very broad flat tip.

spooned

spoonerism *»noun* a mistake in speech in which the initial sounds or letters of two or more words are accidentally swapped around, as in *you have hissed the mystery lectures.*

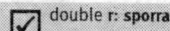 named after the Revd W. A. *Spooner*, who is supposed to have made such errors

spoon-feed *»verb* (**spoon-feeds**, **spoon-feeding**, **spoon-fed**) provide someone with so much help or information that they do not need to think for themselves.

spoonful

spooning

spoons

spoor *»noun* the track or scent of an animal.

sporadic *»adjective* occurring at irregular intervals or only in a few places.
– SAY spuh-**rad**-ik
sporadically

spore *»noun* a tiny reproductive cell produced by lower plants, fungi, and protozoans.

sporran *»noun* a small pouch worn around the waist so as to hang in front of the kilt as part of men's Scottish Highland dress.

 double **r**: **sporran**

sport (verb: **sports**, **sporting**, **sported**)

sportier

sportiest

sportiness

sporting *»adjective* ❶ connected with or interested in sport. ❷ fair and generous in your behaviour.
sportingly

sportive *»adjective* playful; light-hearted.

sports

sports car »*noun* a low-built fast car.

sports jacket »*noun* a man's informal jacket resembling a suit jacket.

sportsman (plural **sportsmen**)
  sportsmanlike
  sportsmanship

sportsperson »(plural **sportspersons** or **sportspeople**)

sportswear

sportswoman (plural **sportswomen**)

sporty (adjective: **sportier, sportiest**)
  sportiness

spot (verb: **spots, spotting, spotted**)
  spotted
  spotter

☑ double the **t** in **spotting, spotted,** and **spotter**

spot check »*noun* a test made without warning on a randomly selected subject.
  » *verb* (**spot-checks, spot-checking, spot-checked**) make a spot check on something.

spotless
  spotlessly
  spotlessness

spotlight (verb: **spotlights, spotlighting, spotlighted** or **spotlit**)

spots

spotted

spotter

spottier

spottiest

spottiness

spotting

spotty (adjective: **spottier, spottiest**)
  spottiness

spot-weld »*verb* (**spot-welds, spot-welding, spot-welded**) join two things by welding at a number of separate points.

spouse »*noun* a husband or wife.

spout (verb: **spouts, spouting, spouted**)

sprain »*verb* (**sprains, spraining, sprained**) wrench the ligaments of a joint so as to cause pain and swelling.
  » *noun* the result of such a wrench.

sprang past of **SPRING**.

sprat »*noun* a small edible sea fish of the herring family.

sprawl (verb: **sprawls, sprawling, sprawled**)

spray (verb: **sprays, spraying, sprayed**)

spread (verb: **spreads, spreading, spread**)
  spreader

spreadeagled »*adjective* stretched out with the arms and legs extended.

spreader

spreading

spreads

spreadsheet »*noun* a computer program in which figures arranged in a grid can be manipulated and used in calculations.

spree »*noun* a spell of unrestrained activity: *a shopping spree.*

sprig »*noun* a small stem bearing leaves or flowers, taken from a bush or plant.

sprightly »*adjective* (**sprightlier, sprightliest**) (especially of an old person) lively; energetic.
  sprightliness

☑ **sprightly** can also be spelled **spritely**

spring (verb: **springs, springing, sprang;** past participle **sprung**)

ℹ️ the standard past tense of **spring** is **sprang** (*the water tank sprang a leak*): **sprung** is American. However, the past participle is always **sprung** (*the tank has sprung a leak*).

springboard »*noun* ❶ a strong, flexible board from which a diver or gymnast may jump in order to push off more powerfully. ❷ a thing providing driving force to an action or enterprise.

springbok »*noun* a southern African gazelle that leaps when disturbed.

spring-clean (verb: **spring-cleans, spring-cleaning, spring-cleaned**)

springer »*noun* (also **springer spaniel**) a small spaniel of a breed originally used to flush game birds out of cover.

springier

springiest

springiness

springing

springlike

spring-loaded »*adjective* containing a compressed or stretched spring pressing one part against another.

springs

spring tide »*noun* a tide just after a new or full moon, when there is the greatest difference between high and low water.

springtime

springy (adjective: **springier, springiest**)
  springiness

sprinkle (verb: **sprinkles, sprinkling, sprinkled**)
  sprinkler

sprint »*verb* (**sprints, sprinting, sprinted**) run at full speed over a short distance.

s

» **noun** ❶ a spell of sprinting. ❷ a short, fast race.
sprinter

sprit »*noun* (in sailing) a small pole reaching diagonally from a mast to the upper outer corner of a sail.

sprite »*noun* an elf or fairy.

spritely another way of spelling **SPRIGHTLY**.

spritzer »*noun* a mixture of wine and soda water.

sprocket »*noun* one of several projections on the rim of a wheel that engage with the links of a chain or with holes in film, tape, or paper.

sprout »*verb* (**sprouts**, **sprouting**, **sprouted**) ❶ produce shoots. ❷ grow plant shoots or hair.
» **noun** ❶ a shoot of a plant. ❷ a Brussels sprout.

spruce[1] »*adjective* neat and smart.
» **verb** (**spruces**, **sprucing**, **spruced**) (**spruce up**) make something smarter.

spruce[2] »*noun* a coniferous tree with a conical shape and hanging cones.

sprue »*noun* ❶ a channel through which metal or plastic is poured into a mould. ❷ a piece of metal or plastic which has solidified in a sprue.

sprung past participle and (in American English) past of **SPRING**.

spry »*adjective* (**spryer**, **spryest**) (of an old person) lively.
spryly
spryness

spud

spume »*noun* (a poetic term) froth or foam that is found on waves.

spun past and past participle of **SPIN**.

spunk »*noun* ❶ (in informal English) courage and determination. ❷ (vulgar) semen.

spunky (adjective: **spunkier**, **spunkiest**)

spur »*noun* ❶ a device with a small spike or a spiked wheel, worn on a rider's heel for urging a horse forward. ❷ an encouragement. ❸ a projection from a mountain or mountain range. ❹ a slender projection from the base of a flower. ❺ a short branch road or railway line.
» **verb** (**spurs**, **spurring**, **spurred**) ❶ urge a horse forward with spurs. ❷ encourage someone.

> ✔️ double the **r** in **spurring** and **spurred**

spurge »*noun* a plant or shrub with milky latex and small greenish flowers.

spurious »*adjective* ❶ false or fake. ❷ (of a line of reasoning) apparently but not actually correct.
spuriously
spuriousness

spurn »*verb* (**spurns**, **spurning**, **spurned**) reject someone or something with contempt.

spurred

spurring

spurs

spurt (verb: **spurts**, **spurting**, **spurted**)

> ✔️ **pur** not **pir**: **spurt**

sputter »*verb* (**sputters**, **sputtering**, **sputtered**) ❶ make a series of soft explosive sounds. ❷ speak in a series of bursts that are hard to understand.

sputum »*noun* a mixture of saliva and mucus coughed up from the throat or lungs.

spy (plural **spies**; verb: **spies**, **spying**, **spied**)

> ✔️ plural: drop the **y** and add **ies**: **spies**

spyglass »*noun* (plural **spyglasses**) a small telescope.

spying

spymaster

squab »*noun* a young pigeon that is yet to leave the nest.

squabble (verb: **squabbles**, **squabbling**, **squabbled**)

> ✔️ double **b**: **squabble**

squad

squaddie »*noun* (plural **squaddies**) (in informal English) a private soldier.

squadron »*noun* ❶ an operational unit in an air force. ❷ a main division of an armoured or cavalry regiment. ❸ a group of warships on a particular duty.

> ✔️ **ron** not **ren**: **squadron**

squadron leader »*noun* a rank of officer in the RAF, above flight lieutenant and below wing commander.

squalid »*adjective* ❶ extremely dirty and unpleasant. ❷ very immoral or dishonest: *a squalid attempt to buy votes.*

> ✔️ only one **l**: **squalid**

squall »*noun* a sudden violent gust of wind or localized storm.

» *verb* (**squalls, squalling, squalled**) (of a baby) cry noisily and continuously.
squally

squalor »*noun* the state of being squalid.
– SAY rhymes with collar

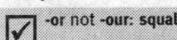
-or not -our: **squalor**

squander »*verb* (**squanders, squandering, squandered**) waste money, time, etc. in a reckless or foolish way.

square (adjective: **squarer, squarest**; verb: **squares, squaring, squared**)
squareness
squarish

square-bashing »*noun* (in informal English) military drill performed repeatedly on a barrack square.

squared

square dance »*noun* a country dance that starts with four couples facing one another in a square.

squarely »*adverb* in a straightforward way; directly.

squareness

square number »*noun* the product of a number multiplied by itself, e.g. 1, 4, 9.

squarer

square-rigged »*adjective* (of a sailing ship) having the main sails at right angles to the length of the ship.

square root »*noun* a number which produces a specified quantity when multiplied by itself.

squares

squarest

squaring

squarish

squash[1] (verb: **squashes, squashing, squashed**) [crush or squeeze something; a concentrated liquid diluted to make a drink]
squashy

squash[2] »*noun* (plural **squash** or **squashes**) a gourd with flesh that can be cooked and eaten as a vegetable.

squat »*verb* (**squats, squatting, squatted**)
❶ crouch or sit with the knees bent and the heels close to the bottom or thighs.
❷ unlawfully occupy an uninhabited building or area of land.
» *adjective* (**squatter, squattest**) short or low, and wide.
» *noun* ❶ a squatting position. ❷ a building occupied by squatters.
squatter

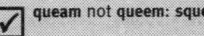
double the t in **squatting, squatted, squatter**, and **squattest**

squat thrust »*noun* an exercise in which the legs are thrust backwards to their full extent from a squatting position with the hands on the floor.

squatting

squawk (verb: **squawks, squawking, squawked**)

squeak (verb: **squeaks, squeaking, squeaked**)
squeaky

squeal (verb: **squeals, squealing, squealed**)
squealer

squeamish »*adjective* ❶ easily disgusted or made to feel sick. ❷ having very strong moral views.
squeamishly
squeamishness

queam not queem: **squeamish**

squeegee »*noun* a scraping implement with a rubber-edged blade, used for cleaning windows.
– SAY skwee-jee

squeeze (verb: **squeezes, squeezing, squeezed**)
squeezable
squeezer

squelch (verb: **squelches, squelching, squelched**)
squelchy

squib »*noun* a small firework that hisses before exploding.

squid »*noun* (plural **squid** or **squids**) a mollusc with a long body, eight arms, and two long tentacles.

squidge (verb: **squidges, squidging, squidged**)
squidgy

squiffy »*adjective* (in informal English) slightly drunk.

squiggle
squiggly

squint »*verb* (**squints, squinting, squinted**)
❶ look with partly closed eyes. ❷ partly close your eyes. ❸ have a squint affecting one eye.
» *noun* ❶ a permanent condition in which one eye does not look in the same direction as the other. ❷ (in informal English) a quick or casual look.

squire »*noun* ❶ a country gentleman. ❷ (in informal English) used as a friendly form of address by one man to another. ❸ (a historical term) a young nobleman acting

as an attendant to a knight before
becoming a knight himself.

squirm (verb: **squirms, squirming,
squirmed**)

squirrel »*noun* a bushy-tailed rodent which
lives in trees.
» *verb* (**squirrels, squirrelling, squirrelled**)
(**squirrel away**) hide money or valuables in
a safe place.

> ☑ double the **l** in **squirrelling** and
> **squirrelled** (the spellings **squirreling**
> and **squirreled** are American)

squirt (verb: **squirts, squirting, squirted**)

squish (verb: **squishes, squishing,
squished**)
squishy

Sri Lankan
– SAY sri **lang**-k'n or shri **lang**-k'n

St »*abbreviation* ❶ Saint. ❷ Street.

stab (verb: **stabs, stabbing, stabbed**)

> ☑ double the **b** in **stabbing** and **stabbed**

stabilise another way of spelling STABILIZE.
stability
stabilize (verb: **stabilizes, stabilizing,
stabilized**)
stabilization
stabilizer

> ☑ many people prefer the alternative
> spellings **stabilise, stabilises,** etc.,
> **stabilisation,** and **stabiliser:** both **s** and **z**
> spellings are correct

stable[1] »*adjective* ❶ not likely to give way
or overturn; firmly fixed. ❷ not worsening
in health after an injury or operation.
❸ emotionally well-balanced. ❹ not likely
to change or fail.
stably

> ⓘ the comparative and superlative are
> usually **more stable** and **most stable,**
> not **stabler** and **stablest**

stable[2] »*noun* ❶ a building for housing
horses. ❷ an establishment where
racehorses are kept and trained.
» *verb* (**stables, stabling, stabled**) put or
keep a horse in a stable.

stablemate »*noun* a horse from the same
stable as another.

stables

stabling

stably

staccato »*adverb & adjective* (in music)
with each sound or note sharply separated
from the others.

» *noun* (plural **staccatos**) ❶ (in music) a
staccato passage or performance. ❷ a
series of short, detached sounds or words.
– SAY stuh-**kah**-toh

> ☑ two **c**'s in the middle: **staccato** is an
> Italian word meaning 'detached'

stack (verb: **stacks, stacking, stacked**)
stackable
stacker

stadium (plural **stadiums** or **stadia**)

> ☑ the plural of **stadium** can be **stadia**
> (as in Latin) or **stadiums**

staff (verb: **staffs, staffing, staffed**)

staff nurse »*noun* an experienced hospital
nurse.

staff officer »*noun* a military officer
serving on the staff of a headquarters or
government department.

staffroom

staffs

stag »*noun* a fully adult male deer.

stag beetle »*noun* a large dark beetle, the
male of which has large antler-like jaws.

stage (verb: **stages, staging, staged**)
stager

stagecoach »*noun* a large closed horse-
drawn vehicle formerly used to carry
passengers along a regular route.

staged

stage direction »*noun* an instruction in a
play script indicating the position or tone
of an actor, or specifying sound effects,
lighting, etc.

stagehand »*noun* a person dealing with
scenery or props during a play.

stage-manage »*verb* (**stage-manages,
stage-managing, stage-managed**) ❶ be
responsible for lighting and other
technical arrangements for a stage play.
❷ arrange a situation carefully to create a
certain effect.
stage management
stage manager

stage name »*noun* a name taken for
professional purposes by an actor.

stager

stages

stage whisper »*noun* a loud whisper by
an actor on stage, intended to be heard by
the audience.

stagey another way of spelling STAGY.

stagger (verb: **staggers, staggering,
staggered**)

staggering
staggeringly

staggers

staghound »*noun* a large breed of dog used for hunting deer.

staging »*noun* ❶ a way of staging a play. ❷ a temporary platform for working on.

staging post »*noun* a place at which people or vehicles regularly stop during a journey.

stagnant »*adjective* ❶ (of water or air) not moving and often having an unpleasant smell. ❷ showing little activity.

 ant not ent: stagnant

stagnate »*verb* (**stagnates, stagnating, stagnated**) become stagnant.
stagnation

stagy »*adjective* excessively theatrical or exaggerated.

 stagy can also be spelled with an e before the y: stagey

staid »*adjective* (**staider, staidest**) respectable and unadventurous.

stain (verb: **stains, staining, stained**)

stainless »*adjective* unmarked by or resistant to stains.

stainless steel »*noun* a form of steel containing chromium, resistant to tarnishing and rust.

stains

stair [one of a set of fixed steps]

ℹ️ do not confuse stair with stare, which means 'look with great concentration'

staircase

stairway

stairwell »*noun* a shaft in which a staircase is built.

stake (verb: **stakes, staking, staked**) [a strong post; support with a stake; money gambled; gamble]

ℹ️ do not confuse stake with steak, which refers to a slice of beef

stakeholder »*noun* ❶ an independent party with whom money or counters wagered are deposited. ❷ a person with an interest or concern in something.

stake-out »*noun* a period of secret observation.

stakes

staking

stalactite »*noun* a column or similar structure hanging from the roof of a cave, made of calcium salts deposited by dripping water.

✓ stalactite is spelled with a c while stalagmite is spelled with a g. This can help you remember the difference between them: c for *ceiling* (a **stalactite** hanging down), g for *ground* (a **stalagmite** rising up).

stalagmite »*noun* a structure like a stalactite but rising from the floor of a cave.

stale »*adjective* (**staler, stalest**) ❶ (of food) no longer fresh or pleasant to eat. ❷ no longer new and interesting. ❸ no longer interested or motivated.
» *verb* (**stales, staling, staled**) make or become stale.
staleness

stalemate »*noun* ❶ (in chess) a position in which a player is not in check but can only move into check. ❷ a situation in which further progress by opposing parties seems impossible.

staleness

staler

stales

stalest

staling

Stalinism »*noun* the policies adopted by the Soviet Communist Party leader and head of state Joseph Stalin, based on dictatorial state control and the pursuit of communism.
Stalinist

stalk¹ »*noun* ❶ the stem of a plant or support of a leaf, flower, or fruit. ❷ a slender support or stem.

stalk² »*verb* (**stalks, stalking, stalked**) ❶ follow or approach stealthily. ❷ harass someone with unwanted and obsessive attention. ❸ walk in a proud, stiff, or angry manner.
stalker

stalking horse »*noun* a person or thing that is used to disguise the real purpose of something.

stalks

stall »*noun* ❶ a stand or booth where goods are sold in a market. ❷ a compartment for an animal in a stable or cowshed. ❸ a compartment in which a horse is held before the start of a race. ❹ a compartment in a set of toilets, shower cubicles, etc. ❺ (**stalls**) (in British English) the ground-floor seats in a theatre. ❻ a seat in the choir or chancel of a church.
» *verb* (**stalls, stalling, stalled**) ❶ (of a vehicle's engine) suddenly stop running. ❷ (of an aircraft) be moving at a speed

too low to allow effective operation of the controls. ❸ stop making progress. ❹ delay by putting something off until later.

stallholder

stalling

stallion »*noun* an adult male horse that has not been castrated.

stalls

stalwart »*adjective* loyal, reliable, and hard-working.
» *noun* a stalwart supporter or member of an organization.
– SAY stawl-wert or stol-wert

stamen »*noun* a male fertilizing organ of a flower.
– SAY stay-muhn

stamina »*noun* the ability to keep up physical or mental effort over a long period.

stammer (verb: stammers, stammering, stammered)
stammerer

stamp (verb: stamps, stamping, stamped)

stamp duty »*noun* a tax on some legal documents.

stamped

stampede (verb: stampedes, stampeding, stampeded)

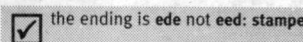 the ending is ede not eed: stampede

stamping

stamping ground »*noun* a place you regularly visit or spend time at.

stamps

stance »*noun* ❶ the way in which someone stands. ❷ an attitude or standpoint.

stanch American spelling of STAUNCH².

stanchion »*noun* an upright bar, post, or frame forming a support or barrier.
– SAY stan-shuhn

stand (verb: stands, standing, stood)

in more formal contexts, use **standing** rather than **stood** with the verb 'to be': say *we were standing there for hours* rather than *we were stood there for hours*

stand-alone »*adjective* (of computer hardware or software) able to operate independently of other hardware or software.

standard
standardly

standard-bearer

standard deviation »*noun* (in statistics) a quantity expressing by how much the members of a group differ from the mean value for the group.

standardize (verb: standardizes, standardizing, standardized)
standardization

 many people prefer the alternative spellings **standardise, standardising** etc., **standardisation**: both s and z spellings are correct

standard lamp »*noun* a lamp with a tall stem whose base stands on the floor.

standardly

standby (plural standbys)

plural: **bys** not **bies**: standbys

stand-in

standing

standing order »*noun* an instruction to a bank to make regular fixed payments to someone.

stand-off »*noun* a deadlock between two equally matched opponents.

stand-offish »*adjective* (in informal English) distant and cold in manner.

standpipe »*noun* a vertical pipe extending from a water supply, connecting a temporary tap to the mains.

standpoint »*noun* an attitude towards a particular issue.

stands

standstill »*noun* a situation without movement or activity.

stand-up »*adjective* (of comedy) performed by a comedian standing in front of an audience.

stank past of STINK.

stanza »*noun* a group of lines forming the basic unit in a poem; a verse.

staphylococcus »*noun* (plural staphylococci) a bacterium of a group including many kinds that cause pus to be formed.
– SAY staf-fi-luh-**kok**-kuhss [singular], staf-fi-luh-**kok**-ky [plural]
staphylococcal

single c, double c: **staphylococcus** make the plural by changing the **us** ending to **i** (as in Latin): **staphylococci**

staple¹ (verb: staples, stapling, stapled) [small U-shaped piece of wire used to fasten papers together]

staple² »*noun* ❶ a main item of trade or production. ❷ a main or important element.
» *adjective* main or important: *a staple food.*

stapler

staples

stapling

star (verb: **stars**, **starring**, **starred**)

> double the **r** in **starring** and **starred**

starboard »*noun* the side of a ship or aircraft that is on the right when you are facing forward (the opposite of *port*).

starburst »*noun* a pattern of lines or rays radiating from a central point.

starch »*noun* ❶ a carbohydrate which is obtained from cereals and potatoes and is an important part of the human diet. ❷ powder or spray used to stiffen fabric. » *verb* (**starches**, **starching**, **starched**) stiffen with starch.

starchy »*adjective* ❶ (of food) containing a lot of starch. ❷ stiff and formal.
starchily
starchiness

stardom

stardust »*noun* magical quality or feeling.

stare (verb: **stares**, **staring**, **stared**) [look with great concentration]

> **i** do not confuse **stare** with **stair**, which refers to one of a set of fixed steps

starfish »*noun* a sea creature having five or more arms extending from a central point.

stargazer

staring

stark »*adjective* (**starker**, **starkest**) ❶ severe or bare in appearance. ❷ unpleasantly or sharply clear. ❸ complete: *stark terror*.
starkly
starkness

starkers »*adjective* (in informal English) completely naked.

starkest

starkly

starkness

starlet »*noun* a promising young actress or performer.

starlight

starling »*noun* a bird with dark shining or iridescent plumage.

starlit

Star of David »*noun* a six-pointed figure made up of two equilateral triangles, used as a Jewish and Israeli symbol.

starred

starrier

starriest

starring

starry (adjective: **starrier**, **starriest**)

starry-eyed »*adjective* naively enthusiastic or idealistic.

stars

Stars and Stripes »*plural noun* the national flag of the US.

star shell »*noun* an explosive projectile which bursts in the air to light up an enemy's position.

starship

star-struck »*adjective* fascinated and greatly impressed by famous people.

star-studded »*adjective* featuring a number of famous people.

start (verb: **starts**, **starting**, **started**)
starter

starting price »*noun* the final odds at the start of a horse race.

startle (verb: **startles**, **startling**, **startled**)
startled

startling »*adjective* ❶ alarming. ❷ very surprising or remarkable.
startlingly

starts

starve (verb: **starves**, **starving**, **starved**)
starvation

stash (in informal English) »*verb* (**stashes**, **stashing**, **stashed**) store safely in a secret place. » *noun* a secret store of something.

stasis »*noun* a period or state when there is no activity or change.
– SAY stay-sis

state (verb: **states**, **stating**, **stated**)
statehood

stateless »*adjective* not recognized as a citizen of any country.

stately »*adjective* (**statelier**, **stateliest**) dignified or grand.
stateliness

stately home »*noun* a large and fine house occupied or formerly occupied by an aristocratic family.

statement

stateroom »*noun* ❶ a large room in a palace or public building, for use on formal occasions. ❷ a private compartment on a ship.

states

statesman (plural **statesmen**) »*noun* an experienced and respected political leader or figure.
statesmanlike
statesmanship

stateswoman (plural **stateswomen**)

static »*adjective* ❶ not moving, acting, or changing. ❷ (of an electric charge) acquired by objects that cannot conduct a current.
» *noun* ❶ static electricity. ❷ crackling or hissing on a telephone, radio, etc.
– SAY sta-tik
statically

stating

station (verb: **stations**, **stationing**, **stationed**)

stationary »*adjective* not moving or changing.

> ℹ️ do not confuse **stationary** with **stationery**, which means 'paper and other materials needed for writing'

stationed

stationer »*noun* a seller of stationery.

stationery »*noun* paper and other materials needed for writing.

> ℹ️ do not confuse **stationery** with **stationary**, which means 'not moving'

stationing

stationmaster »*noun* an official in charge of a railway station.

stations

station wagon »*noun* (in American English) an estate car.

statistic »*noun* a fact or piece of data obtained from a study of statistics.

statistical »*adjective* having to do with statistics.
statistically

statistics »the collection and analysis of large amounts of information shown in numbers.
statistician

statuary »*noun* statues as a whole.
– SAY stat-yoo-ri

> ℹ️ do not confuse **statuary** with **statutory**, which is an adjective meaning 'required or permitted by law'

statue

statuesque »*adjective* ❶ standing like a statue. ❷ (of a woman) attractively tall and dignified.
– SAY sta-tyuu-**esk** or sta-chuu-**esk**

> ✅ que at the end: **statuesque**

statuette »*noun* a small statue.

> ✅ ette at the end, not et: **statuette**

stature »*noun* ❶ a person's height when they are standing. ❷ importance or reputation.

status »*noun* ❶ the social or professional position of someone. ❷ high rank or social standing. ❸ the position of affairs at a particular time.

status quo »*noun* the existing state of affairs.
– SAY stay-tuhss kwoh

> ℹ️ a Latin phrase literally meaning 'the state in which'

status symbol »*noun* a possession which shows a person's wealth or high status.

statute »*noun* ❶ a written law. ❷ a rule of an organization or institution.

statute book »*noun* (**the statute book**) the body of a nation's laws.

statute law »*noun* the body of principles and rules of law laid down in statutes.

statutory »*adjective* required or permitted by law.

> ℹ️ do not confuse **statutory** with **statuary**, which refers to statues

staunch[1] »*adjective* (**stauncher**, **staunchest**) very loyal and committed.
– SAY stawnch
staunchly
staunchness

staunch[2] »*verb* (**staunches**, **staunching**, **staunched**) stop or slow down a flow of blood.
– SAY stawnch or stahnch

> ✅ au not just a: **staunch** (the spelling **stanch** is American)

stave »*noun* ❶ one of the lengths of wood fixed side by side to make a barrel, bucket, etc. ❷ a strong stick, post, or pole. ❸ (in music) a set of five parallel lines on or between which notes are written; a staff.
» *verb* (**staves**, **staving**, **staved** or **stove**)
❶ (**stave in**) break something by forcing it inwards. ❷ (**stave off**) stop or delay something bad or dangerous.

> ℹ️ the past tense or participle **stove** can only be used with **stave in**, 'break something by forcing it inwards'. The past of **stave off**, 'stop or delay something bad or dangerous', can only be **staved off**, and **staved in** is an allowed alternative to **stove in**. So you can say *the door was stove in* or *the door was staved in*, but you can only say *the attack was staved off*.

stay (verb: **stays**, **staying**, **stayed**)
stayer

staying power »*noun* endurance or stamina.

stays »*plural noun* (a historical term) a corset stiffened by strips of whalebone.

stead »*noun* (in someone's or something's stead) instead of someone or something.

steadfast »*adjective* determined and firm.
steadfastly
steadfastness

steady (adjective: **steadier**, **steadiest**; verb **steadies**, **steadying**, **steadied**)
steadily
steadiness

> ☑ drop the **y** and add **ier** or **iest** to spell **steadier** or **steadiest**

steak [thick slice of beef]

> ℹ do not confuse **steak** with **stake**, which means 'a strong post' or 'a sum of money gambled'

steakhouse

steal (verb: **steals**, **stealing**, **stole**; past participle **stolen**) [take something without permission; a bargain]

> ℹ do not confuse **steal** with **steel**, which refers to a hard, strong metal

stealth »*noun* cautious and secretive action or movement.

stealthy »*adjective* (**stealthier**, **stealthiest**) cautious and secretive.
stealthily

steam (verb: **steams**, **steaming**, **steamed**)

steamboat

steamed

steamer »*noun* ❶ a ship or boat powered by steam. ❷ a type of saucepan in which food can be steamed.

steamier

steamiest

steamily

steaming

steamroller (verb: **steamrollers**, **steamrollering**, **steamrollered**)

steams

steamy (adjective: **steamier**, **steamiest**)
steamily

stearin »*noun* a white crystalline substance which is the main constituent of tallow and suet.
– SAY steer-in

steatite »*noun* the mineral talc occurring in bulk form, especially as soapstone.
– SAY stee-uh-tyt

steed »*noun* (an old word) a horse.

steel »*noun* ❶ a hard, strong metal that is a mixture of iron and carbon. ❷ strength and determination.
»*verb* (**steels**, **steeling**, **steeled**) mentally prepare yourself for something difficult.

> ℹ do not confuse **steel** with **steal**, which means 'take something without permission'

steelier

steeliest

steeling

steels

steelworks

steely »*adjective* (**steelier**, **steeliest**) ❶ like steel. ❷ coldly determined.

steep[1] (adjective: **steeper**, **steepest**) [rising or falling sharply]
steeply
steepness

steep[2] »*verb* (**steeps**, **steeping**, **steeped**) ❶ soak in water or other liquid. ❷ (be **steeped in**) have a great deal of a particular quality or atmosphere.

steepen »*verb* (**steepens**, **steepening**, **steepened**) become or make steeper.

steeper

steepest

steeping

steeple

steeplechase »*noun* ❶ a horse race with ditches and hedges as jumps. ❷ a running race in which runners must clear hurdles and water jumps.
steeplechaser

steeplejack »*noun* a person who climbs tall structures such as chimneys and steeples to repair them.

steeply

steepness

steeps

steer[1] (verb: **steers**, **steering**, **steered**) [guide or control the movement of a vehicle]
steerable

steer[2] »*noun* a bullock.

steerage »*noun* (a historical term) the cheapest accommodation in a ship.

steered

steering

steering committee »*noun* a committee that decides on the priorities or order of business of an organization.

steering group »*noun* = STEERING COMMITTEE.

steers

steersman »*noun* (plural **steersmen**) a person who steers a boat or ship.

stegosaurus »*noun* (plural **stegosaurus**) a plant-eating dinosaur with a double row of large bony plates along the back.

stein »*noun* a large earthenware beer mug.
– SAY styn

stellar »*adjective* having to do with a star or stars.

> ☑ ar not er at the end: **stellar**

s

stem »*noun* ❶ the long, thin main part of a plant or shrub, or support of a fruit, flower, or leaf. ❷ a long, thin supporting part of a wine glass, tobacco pipe, etc. ❸ a vertical stroke in a letter or musical note. ❹ the root or main part of a word.
» *verb* (**stems, stemming, stemmed**) ❶ (**stem from**) come from or be caused by. ❷ stop or slow down the flow of something.

> ☑ double the **m** in **stemming** and **stemmed**

stench »*noun* a strong and very unpleasant smell.

stencil »*noun* a thin sheet with a pattern or letters cut out of it, used to produce a design by the application of ink or paint through the holes.
» *verb* (**stencils, stencilling, stencilled**) decorate with a stencil.

> ☑ double the **l** in **stencilling** and **stencilled** (the spellings **stenciling** and **stenciled** are American)

stenography »*noun* (in American English) the action of writing in shorthand and transcribing the shorthand on a typewriter.
– SAY sti-**nog**-ruh-fi
stenographer

stentorian »*adjective* (of a person's voice) loud and powerful.
– SAY sten-**tor**-i-uhn

step (verb: **steps, stepping, stepped**)

> ☑ double the **p** in **stepping** and **stepped**

stepbrother
stepchild
stepdaughter
stepfather
stephanotis »*noun* a climbing plant with waxy white flowers.
– SAY stef-fuh-**noh**-tiss
stepladder
stepmother
steppe »*noun* a large area of flat grassland in SE Europe or Siberia.
stepped

stepping
steps
stepsister
stepson
stepwise
stereo »*noun* (plural **stereos**)
❶ stereophonic sound. ❷ a stereophonic CD player, record player, etc.
» *adjective* stereophonic.
– SAY ste-ri-oh

stereophonic »*adjective* (of sound reproduction) using two or more channels so that the sound seems to come from more than one source.
stereophonically
stereophony

stereoscope »*noun* a device by which two photographs of the same object taken at slightly different angles are viewed together, creating an impression of depth and solidity.
stereoscopic

stereotype »*noun* an over-simplified idea of the typical characteristics of a person or thing.
» *verb* (**stereotypes, stereotyping, stereotyped**) view or represent as a stereotype.

stereotypical »*adjective* relating to a stereotype.
stereotypically

stereotyping

sterile »*adjective* ❶ not able to produce children, young, crops, or fruit. ❷ not imaginative, creative, or exciting. ❸ free from bacteria.
sterilely
sterility

sterilize »*verb* (**sterilizes, sterilizing, sterilized**) ❶ make sterile. ❷ make a person or animal unable to produce children or young.
sterilization

> ☑ many people prefer the alternative spellings **sterilise, sterilises,** and **sterilisation**: both **s** and **z** spellings are correct

sterling »*noun* British money.
» *adjective* ❶ excellent. ❷ (of silver) of at least 92¼ per cent purity.

stern[1] »*adjective* (**sterner, sternest**)
❶ grimly serious or strict. ❷ severe.
sternly
sternness

stern[2] »*noun* the rear end of a ship or boat.

sternum »*noun* (plural **sternums** or **sterna**) the breastbone.

✓ the plural can be either **sterna** (like the original Latin) or **sternums**

steroid »*noun* ❶ a type of organic compound produced in the body, e.g. certain hormones and vitamins. ❷ an anabolic steroid.
– SAY ste-royd or steer-oyd

stertorous »*adjective* (of breathing) noisy and laboured.
– SAY ster-tuh-ruhss
  stertorously

stethoscope »*noun* a device used by doctors for listening to the sound of someone's heart or breathing.
– SAY steth-uh-skohp

Stetson »*noun* (trademark in the US) a hat with a high crown and a very wide brim, worn by cowboys and ranchers in the US.

stevedore »*noun* a person employed at a dock to load and unload ships.
– SAY stee-vuh-dor

stew (verb: **stews, stewing, stewed**)

steward
  stewardship

stewardess (plural **stewardesses**)

stewardship

stewed

stewing

stews

stick (verb: **sticks, sticking, stuck**)

sticker

stickier

stickiest

stickiness

sticking

stick-in-the-mud »*noun* (in informal English) a person who resists change.

stickleback »*noun* a small fish with sharp spines along its back.

stickler »*noun* a person who insists on people behaving in a particular way.

sticks

sticky (adjective: **stickier, stickiest**)
  stickiness

✓ drop the y and add **ier** or **iest** to spell **stickier** or **stickiest**

sties plural of STY¹, STY².

stiff (adjective: **stiffer, stiffest**)
  stiffly
  stiffness

stiffen (verb: **stiffens, stiffening, stiffened**)
  stiffener

stiffer

stiffest

stiffly

stiffness

stifle »*verb* (**stifles, stifling, stifled**)
❶ prevent someone from breathing freely.
❷ smother or suppress something.

stifling »*adjective* unpleasantly hot and stuffy.
  stiflingly

stigma »*noun* (plural **stigmas** or **stigmata**)
❶ a mark or sign of disgrace.
❷ (**stigmata**) (in Christian tradition) marks on a person's body believed by some Christians to correspond to those left on Jesus's body by the Crucifixion.
❸ the part of a plant that receives the pollen during pollination.

ℹ when used in a religious sense, the plural of **stigma** is **stigmata** (SAY stig-mah-tuh), as in the original Greek, but in all other uses the plural is **stigmas**

stigmatic »*adjective* relating to a stigma or stigmas.
» *noun* a person bearing stigmata.

stigmatize »*verb* (**stigmatizes, stigmatizing, stigmatized**) regard or treat someone or something as shameful.
  stigmatization

✓ many people prefer the alternative spellings **stigmatise, stigmatises**, etc., and **stigmatisation**: both **s** and **z** spellings are correct

stile »*noun* an arrangement of steps in a fence or wall that allows people to climb over.

ℹ do not confuse **stile** and **style**, which means 'a way of doing something'

stiletto »*noun* (plural **stilettos**) ❶ a thin, high heel on a woman's shoe. ❷ a short dagger with a tapering blade.

✓ the plural of **stiletto** has **os** not **oes**: **stilettos** (it is an Italian word which means 'little dagger')

still¹ (verb: **stills, stilling, stilled**) [not moving; make still]
  stillness

still² »*noun* an apparatus for distilling alcoholic drinks such as whisky.

stillbirth »*noun* the birth of an infant that has died in the womb.

stillborn »*adjective* (of an infant) born dead.

stilled

stilling

still life »*noun* a painting or drawing of an arrangement of objects such as flowers or fruit.

stillness

stills

stilt »*noun* ❶ one of a pair of upright poles that are used to walk raised above the ground. ❷ one of a set of posts supporting a building.

stilted »*adjective* (of speech or writing) stiff and unnatural.
stiltedly
stiltedness

Stilton »*noun* (trademark) a kind of strong, rich blue cheese.

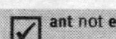 named after *Stilton* in Cambridgeshire

stimulant »*noun* something that stimulates.

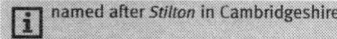 ant not ent: stimulant

stimulate »*verb* (stimulates, stimulating, stimulated) ❶ cause or provoke a reaction in the body. ❷ make more active, interested, or enthusiastic.
stimulation
stimulator
stimulatory

stimulus »*noun* (plural stimuli) something that stimulates.
– SAY stim-yuu-luhss [singular], stim-yuu-lee [plural]

> ✓ the plural of **stimulus** is **stimuli** (it is a Latin word which means 'incentive')

sting (verb: stings, stinging, stung)
stinger

stingier

stingiest

stingily

stinginess

stinging

stingray »*noun* a ray (flat sea fish) with a long poisonous spine at the base of the tail.

stings

stingy »*adjective* (stingier, stingiest) mean.
– SAY stin-ji
stingily
stinginess

stink (verb: stinks, stinking, stank or stunk; past participle stunk)
stinker
stinking

stinky (adjective: stinkier, stinkiest)

stint »*verb* (stints, stinting, stinted) restrict how much someone can have of something.
»*noun* a period spent working somewhere.

stipend »*noun* a fixed regular sum paid as a salary to a priest, teacher, or official.
– SAY sty-pend

stipendiary »*adjective* receiving a stipend; working for pay rather than voluntarily.
– SAY sty-pen-di-uh-ri

stipple »*verb* (stipples, stippling, stippled) mark a surface with many small dots.

stipulate »*verb* (stipulates, stipulating, stipulated) demand or specify something as part of an agreement.
– SAY stip-yuu-layt
stipulation

stir (verb: stirs, stirring, stirred)
stirrer

> ✓ double the r to spell **stirring, stirred,** and **stirrer**

stir-crazy »*adjective* (in informal English) mentally disturbed as a result of being confined or imprisoned.

stir-fry »*verb* (stir-fries, stir-frying, stir-fried) fry food quickly over a high heat while stirring.

stirred

stirrer

stirring »*adjective* causing great excitement or strong emotion.
»*noun* a first sign of activity, movement, or emotion.
stirringly

stirrup »*noun* one of a pair of loops attached to a horse's saddle to support the rider's foot.

> ✓ double r: **stirrup**

stirs

stitch (verb: stitches, stitching, stitched)
stitching

stitchwort »*noun* a plant with white starry flowers.

stoat »*noun* a small meat-eating mammal of the weasel family.

stochastic »*adjective* having a random probability pattern that can be analysed statistically but not predicted precisely.
– SAY stuh-kas-tik
stochastically

stock (verb: stocks, stocking, stocked)

stockade »*noun* a barrier or enclosure formed from upright wooden posts.

stockbreeder »*noun* a farmer who breeds livestock.

stockbroker »*noun* a broker who buys and sells stocks and shares on behalf of clients.

stocked

stock exchange »*noun* a place where stocks and shares are bought and sold.

stockier

stockiest

stockily

stockiness

stocking
  stockinged

stock-in-trade »*noun* the typical thing a person or company uses or deals in.

stockist »*noun* a retailer that sells goods of a particular type.

stockman »*noun* (plural **stockmen**) a person who looks after livestock.

stock market »*noun* a stock exchange.

stockmen

stockpile »*noun* a large stock of goods or materials that has been gathered together.
  »*verb* (**stockpiles, stockpiling, stockpiled**) gather together a large stock of something.

stockpot »*noun* a pot in which stock is prepared by long, slow cooking.

stocks

stock-still »*adverb* completely still.

stocktaking »*noun* the process of listing all the stock held by a business.

stocky »*adjective* (**stockier, stockiest**) (of a person) short and sturdy.
  stockily
  stockiness

> ✓ drop the **y** and add **ier** or **iest** to spell **stockier** or **stockiest**

stodge »*noun* food that is heavy and filling.
  stodginess
  stodgy

stoic »*noun* a stoical person.
  »*adjective* stoical.
  – SAY stoh-ik

stoical »*adjective* enduring pain and hardship without showing your feelings or complaining.
  stoically
  stoicism

stoke »*verb* (**stokes, stoking, stoked**)
  ❶ add coal to a fire, furnace, etc.
  ❷ encourage a strong emotion. ❸ (**stoke up**) eat a lot of food to gain energy.
  stoker

stole[1] »*noun* a woman's long scarf or shawl, worn loosely over the shoulders.

stole[2] past of STEAL.

stolen past participle of STEAL.

stolid »*adjective* calm, dependable, and unemotional.
  stolidity
  stolidly

stoma »*noun* (plural **stomas** or **stomata**) a tiny pore in a leaf or stem of a plant, allowing movement of gases in and out.
  – SAY stoh-muh [singular], stoh-muh-tuh [plural]

> ✓ the plural of **stoma** can be either **stomata** (as in the original Greek word meaning 'mouth') or **stomas**

stomach (verb: **stomachs, stomaching, stomached**)

stomata plural of STOMA.

stomp (verb: **stomps, stomping, stomped**)

stone (verb: **stones, stoning, stoned**)

Stone Age »*noun* a period that came before the Bronze Age, when weapons and tools were made of stone.

stonecrop »*noun* a plant with star-shaped yellow or white flowers which grows among rocks or on walls.

stoned

stoneground »*adjective* (of flour) ground with millstones.

stonemason »*noun* a person who prepares and builds with stone.

stones

stonewall »*verb* (**stonewalls, stonewalling, stonewalled**) refuse to answer questions, or give evasive replies.

stoneware »*noun* a hard, dense type of pottery.

stonewashed »*adjective* (of a garment or fabric) washed with small stones to give a worn or faded appearance.

stonework

stonier

stoniest

stonily

stoniness

stoning

stony (adjective: **stonier, stoniest**)
  stonily
  stoniness

> ✓ drop the **y** and add **ier** or **iest** to spell **stonier** or **stoniest**

stood past and past participle of STAND.

stooge »*noun* ❶ (used in an insulting way) a less important person used by another to do routine or unpleasant work. ❷ a performer whose act involves being the butt of a comedian's jokes.

stook »*noun* a group of sheaves of grain stood on end in a field.

stool

stool pigeon »*noun* a police informer.

stoop »*verb* (stoops, stooping, stooped)
❶ bend your head or body forwards and downwards. ❷ lower your standards to do something morally wrong.
» *noun* a stooping posture.

stop (verb: stops, stopping, stopped)

> ✓ double the p to spell **stopping** and **stopped**

stopcock »*noun* a valve which controls the flow of a liquid or gas through a pipe.

stopgap »*noun* a temporary solution or substitute.

stopover

stoppage

stopped

stopper (verb: stoppers, stoppering, stoppered)

> ✓ do not double the r to spell **stoppering** or **stoppered**

stopping

stop press »*noun* news added to a newspaper at the last minute.

stops

stopwatch

storage

> ✓ age not ege, and there is no e in the middle: **storage**

storage heater »*noun* an electric heater that stores up heat during the night and releases it during the day.

store (verb: stores, storing, stored)

storehouse

stores

storey »*noun* (plural storeys) a particular level of a building.

> ℹ do not confuse **storey** with **story**, which means 'a tale', although in American English the same spelling (**story**) is used for both words

stories

storing

stork »*noun* a tall long-legged bird with a long heavy bill.

storm (verb: storms, storming, stormed)

storm drain »*noun* a drain built to carry away excess water in times of heavy rain.

stormed

stormier

stormiest

stormily

storminess

storming

storms

storm troops »*plural noun* shock troops.
storm trooper

stormy (adjective: stormier, stormiest)
stormily
storminess

story (plural stories) [a tale]

> ℹ on the relationship between **story** and **storey**, see the note at **STORY**

> ✓ plural: drop the y and add **ies**: **stories**

storyboard »*noun* a sequence of drawings representing the shots planned for a film or television production.

storybook

storyline

storyteller
storytelling

stoup »*noun* a basin for holy water in a church.
– SAY stoop

stout »*adjective* (stouter, stoutest) ❶ rather fat or heavily built. ❷ (of an object) sturdy and thick. ❸ brave and determined: *a stout defence.*
» *noun* a kind of strong, dark beer.
stoutly
stoutness

stove[1] [cooking device]

stove[2] past and past participle of STAVE.

stovepipe

stow »*verb* (stows, stowing, stowed)
❶ pack or store an object tidily. ❷ (stow away) hide on a ship, aircraft, etc. to travel secretly or without paying.
stowage

stowaway

stowed

stowing

stows

strabismus »*noun* the condition of having a squint.
– SAY struh-biz-muhss

straddle »*verb* (straddles, straddling, straddled) ❶ sit or stand with one leg on either side of something. ❷ extend across both sides of something.

strafe »*verb* (strafes, strafing, strafed) attack with machine-gun fire or bombs from low-flying aircraft.
– SAY strahf or strayf

ℹ️ from the German First World War catchphrase *Gott strafe England* 'may God punish England'

straggle »*verb* (**straggles, straggling, straggled**) ❶ trail slowly behind the person or people in front. ❷ grow or spread out in an untidy way.
straggler
straggly

straight (adjective: **straighter, straightest**) [without a curve or bend]
straightness

ℹ️ do not confuse **straight** with **strait**, which means 'a narrow passage of water'

straighten (verb: **straightens, straightening, straightened**)

straighter

straightest

straightforward
straightforwardly
straightforwardness

straightjacket another way of spelling STRAITJACKET.

straight-laced another way of spelling STRAIT-LACED.

straightness

strain (verb: **strains, straining, strained**)
strained
strainer

strait »*noun* ❶ (also **straits**) a narrow passage of water connecting two other large areas of water. ❷ (**straits**) trouble or difficulty: *the economy is in dire straits*.

straitened »*adjective* ❶ characterized by poverty; poor: *straitened circumstances*. ❷ restricted or limited.

straitjacket »*noun* ❶ a strong garment with long sleeves which can be tied together to confine the arms of a violent prisoner or mental patient. ❷ a severe restriction.

✅ **straitjacket** can also be spelled **straightjacket**

strait-laced »*adjective* very strictly moral and conventional.

✅ **strait-laced** can also be spelled **straight-laced**

strake »*noun* ❶ a continuous line of planking or plates from the stem to the stern of a ship or boat. ❷ a protruding ridge fitted to an aircraft or other structure to improve aerodynamic stability.

strand »*verb* (**strands, stranding, stranded**) ❶ drive or leave a ship, whale, etc.

aground on a shore. ❷ leave someone unable to move from a place.
» *noun* ❶ a single thin length of thread, wire, etc. ❷ an element that forms part of a complex whole. ❸ (a poetic term) a beach or shore.

strange (adjective: **stranger, strangest**)
strangely
strangeness

stranger

strangest

strangle (verb: **strangles, strangling, strangled**)
strangler

stranglehold

strangler

strangles

strangling

strangulation

strap (verb: **straps, strapping, strapped**)
strapless
strappy

✅ double the **p** to spell **strapping** and **strapped**

strapping »*adjective* (of a person) big and strong.

strappy

straps

strata plural of STRATUM.

stratagem »*noun* a plan or scheme intended to outwit an opponent.
– SAY stra-tuh-juhm

strategic »*adjective* ❶ forming part of a long-term plan to achieve a specific purpose. ❷ relating to the gaining of long-term military advantage. ❸ (of weapons) for use against enemy territory rather than in battle.
– SAY struh-**tee**-jik
strategically

strategy »*noun* (plural **strategies**) ❶ a plan designed to achieve a long-term aim. ❷ the art of planning and directing military activity in a war or battle.
– SAY stra-ti-ji
strategist

✅ plural: drop the **y** and add **ies**: **strategies**

stratify »*verb* (**stratifies, stratifying, stratified**) ❶ form or arrange something into strata. ❷ arrange or classify something.
– SAY stra-ti-fy
stratification

stratosphere »*noun* ❶ the layer of the earth's atmosphere above the troposphere

and below the mesosphere. ❷ the very highest levels of something.
– SAY stra-tuh-sfeer
stratospheric

✓ strato not strata: stratosphere

stratum »*noun* (plural **strata**) ❶ a layer or a series of layers of rock. ❷ a level or class of society.
– SAY strah-tuhm [singular], strah-tuh [plural]

ℹ do not use **strata** as a singular or to create the form **stratas** as the plural. One layer is a **stratum** and more than one are **strata** (**stratum** is a Latin word which means 'something laid down').

stratus »*noun* cloud forming a continuous horizontal grey sheet.
– SAY strah-tuhss

straw

strawberry (plural **strawberries**)

✓ plural: drop the **y** and add **ies**: strawberries

strawberry blonde »*adjective* (of hair) light reddish-blonde.

straw poll »*noun* an unofficial test of opinion.

stray (verb: **strays, straying, strayed**)

streak (verb: **streaks, streaking, streaked**)
streaker
streaking

streaky (adjective: **streakier, streakiest**)
streakily
streakiness

stream (verb: **streams, streaming, streamed**)

streamer »*noun* a long, narrow strip of material used as a decoration or flag.

streaming

streamline (verb: **streamlines, streamlining, streamlined**)

streams

street

streetcar »*noun* (in American English) a tram.

street value »*noun* the price something, especially drugs, would fetch if sold illegally.

streetwalker »*noun* a prostitute who seeks clients in the street.

streetwise »*adjective* able to deal well with modern urban life.

strength

✓ remember the **g** in **strength** and strengthen

strengthen (verb: **strengthens, strengthening, strengthened**)
strengthener

strenuous »*adjective* requiring or using great exertion.
strenuously
strenuousness

streptococcus »*noun* (plural **streptococci**) a bacterium of a large group including those causing tooth decay and souring of milk as well as some serious infections.
– SAY strep-tuh-**kok**-kuhss [singular], strep-tuh-**kok**-ky [plural]
streptococcal

✓ single **c**, double **c**: streptococcus make the plural by changing the **us** ending to **i** (as in Latin): streptococci

stress »*noun* (plural **stresses**) ❶ pressure or tension exerted on an object. ❷ mental or emotional strain or tension. ❸ particular emphasis. ❹ emphasis given to a syllable or word in speech.
»*verb* (**stresses, stressing, stressed**) ❶ emphasize something. ❷ give emphasis to a syllable or word in speech. ❸ subject someone or something to pressure, tension, or strain.

stressful

✓ -ful not -full: stressful

stressing

stretch (verb: **stretches, stretching, stretched**)
stretchy

stretcher (verb: **stretchers, stretchering, stretchered**)

stretches

stretching

stretchy

strew »*verb* (**strews, strewing, strewed**; past participle **strewn** or **strewed**) ❶ scatter untidily over a surface or area. ❷ (**be strewn with**) be covered with untidily scattered things.

striated »*adjective* marked with a series of ridges or grooves.
– SAY stry-**ayt**-id
striation

stricken North American or old past participle of **STRIKE**. »*adjective* ❶ seriously affected by something unpleasant. ❷ showing great distress.

strict (adjective: **stricter, strictest**)
strictly
strictness

stricture »*noun* ❶ a rule restricting behaviour or action. ❷ a sternly critical remark.

stride (verb: **strides, striding, strode**)

strident »*adjective* ❶ loud and harsh. ❷ presenting a point of view in an excessively forceful way.
stridency
stridently

✓ ent not ant: stri**d**ent

strides

striding

strife »*noun* angry or bitter disagreement.

strike (verb: **strikes, striking, struck**)
striker

striking »*adjective* ❶ noticeable. ❷ dramatically good-looking or beautiful.
strikingly

string (verb: **strings, stringing, strung**)
stringed

stringent »*adjective* (of regulations or requirements) strict, precise, and demanding.
– SAY strin-juhnt
stringency
stringently

✓ ent not ant: strin**g**ent

stringier

stringiest

stringing

string quartet »*noun* a chamber music group made up of first and second violins, viola, and cello.

strings

stringy »*adjective* (**stringier, stringiest**) ❶ resembling string. ❷ tall, wiry, and thin. ❸ (of food) tough and fibrous.

strip (verb: **strips, stripping, stripped**)

✓ double the **p** in stri**pp**ing and stri**pp**ed

stripe (verb: **stripes, striping, striped**)
striped
stripy

stripey another way of spelling STRIPY.

strip light »*noun* a fluorescent lamp in the shape of a tube.

stripling »*noun* (an old word) a young man.

stripped

stripper

stripping

strips

strip-search (verb: **strip-searches, strip-searching, strip-searched**)

striptease

stripy

✓ stripy can also be spelled stripey

strive »*verb* (**strives, striving, strove** or **strived**; past participle **striven** or **strived**) ❶ make great efforts. ❷ (**strive against**) fight vigorously against something.

strobe »*noun* a stroboscope.
» *verb* (**strobes, strobing, strobed**) flash at rapid intervals.

stroboscope »*noun* an instrument which shines a bright light at rapid intervals so that a moving object appears stationary.
– SAY stroh-buh-skohp
stroboscopic

strode past of STRIDE.

stroke (verb: **strokes, stroking, stroked**)

stroll (verb: **strolls, strolling, strolled**)

strong (adjective: **stronger, strongest**)
strongly

strong-arm »*adjective* using force or violence.

strongbox »*noun* (plural **strongboxes**) a small lockable metal box in which valuables may be kept.

stronger

strongest

stronghold »*noun* ❶ a place that has been strengthened against attack. ❷ a place of strong support for a cause or political party.

strongly

strongman (plural **strongmen**)

strongroom »*noun* a room, typically one in a bank, designed to protect valuable items against fire and theft.

strontium »*noun* a soft silver-white metallic chemical element.
– SAY stron-ti-uhm

strop »*noun* ❶ a strip of leather for sharpening razors. ❷ (in informal English) a temper.

stroppy »*adjective* (in informal English) bad-tempered.

strove past of STRIVE.

struck past and past participle of STRIKE.

structural »*adjective* relating to or forming part of a structure.
structurally

structure (verb: **structures, structuring, structured**)

S

strudel »*noun* a dessert of thin pastry rolled up round a fruit filling and baked.
– SAY stroo-duhl

> one d, one l: **strudel** is a German word meaning 'whirlpool'

struggle (verb: **struggles, struggling, struggled**)
  struggler

strum »*verb* (**strums, strumming, strummed**) play a guitar or similar instrument by sweeping the thumb or a plectrum up or down the strings.

> ☑ double the **m** in **strumming** and **strummed**

strumpet »*noun* (an old word) a woman who has many sexual partners.

strums

strung past and past participle of STRING.

strut »*noun* ❶ a bar used to support or strengthen a structure. ❷ a strutting walk.
» *verb* (**struts, strutting, strutted**) walk in a proud way, with your back straight and head up.

> ☑ double the **t** in **strutting** and **strutted**

strychnine »*noun* a bitter and highly poisonous substance obtained from the fruit of an Asian tree.
– SAY strik-neen

stub (verb: **stubs, stubbing, stubbed**)

> ☑ double the **b** in **stubbing** and **stubbed**

stubbier

stubbiest

stubbing

stubble
  stubbly

stubborn
  stubbornly
  stubbornness

stubby (adjective: **stubbier, stubbiest**)

stubs

stucco »*noun* fine plaster used for coating wall surfaces or moulding into architectural decorations.
  stuccoed

> ☑ double **c**: **stucco** is an Italian word

stuck past participle of STICK.

stuck-up »*adjective* (in informal English) snobbishly aloof.

stud[1] (verb: **studs, studding, studded**) [a small projection fixed to a surface; decorate with studs]

> ☑ double the **d** in **studding** and **studded**

stud[2] »*noun* ❶ an establishment where horses are kept for breeding. ❷ a stallion. ❸ (in informal English) man who has many sexual partners or is considered sexually desirable.

student
  studentship

studied

studies

studio (plural **studios**)

> ☑ the plural of **studio** has **os** not **oes**: **studios**

studio flat »*noun* a flat containing one main room.

studios

studious »*adjective* ❶ spending a lot of time studying or reading. ❷ done deliberately or with great care.
  studiously
  studiousness

studs

study (plural **studies**; verb: **studies, studying, studied**)

> ☑ plural: drop the **y** and add **ies**: **studies**

stuff (verb: **stuffs, stuffing, stuffed**)

stuffier

stuffiest

stuffily

stuffiness

stuffing

stuffs

stuffy (adjective: **stuffier, stuffiest**)
  stuffily
  stuffiness

stultify »*verb* (**stultifies, stultifying, stultified**) cause someone to feel bored or drained of energy.
– SAY stul-ti-fy
  stultification

stumble (verb: **stumbles, stumbling, stumbled**)

stump (verb: **stumps, stumping, stumped**)

stumpy

stun (verb: **stuns, stunning, stunned**)

> ☑ double the **n** in **stunning** and **stunned**

stung past and past participle of STING.

stunk past and past participle of STINK.

stunned

stunner

stunning
stunningly

stuns

stunt (verb: stunts, stunting, stunted)

stuntman (plural stuntmen)

stunts

stuntwoman (plural stuntwomen)

stupefy »*verb* (stupefies, stupefying, stupefied) ❶ make someone unable to think or feel properly. ❷ astonish and shock someone.
– sᴀʏ styoo-pi-fy
stupefaction

 efy not **ify**: stupefy

stupendous »*adjective* extremely impressive.
– sᴀʏ styoo-pen-duhss
stupendously

stupid (adjective: stupider, stupidest)
stupidity
stupidly

stupor »*noun* a state of near-unconsciousness.
– sᴀʏ styoo-per

 -por not -pour: stupor

sturdy (adjective: sturdier, sturdiest)
sturdily
sturdiness

sturgeon »*noun* a very large fish with bony plates on the body, found in seas and rivers and important for its roe, from which caviar is made.
– sᴀʏ ster-juhn

stutter (verb: stutters, stuttering, stuttered)
stutterer

sty[1] »*noun* (plural sties) a pigsty.

 plural: drop the **y** and add **ies**: sties

sty[2] »*noun* (plural sties) an inflamed swelling on the edge of an eyelid.

✓ in this sense, **sty** can also be spelled **stye** (plural styes)

Stygian »*adjective* (a poetic term) very dark.
– sᴀʏ sti-ji-uhn

ℹ from the *Styx*, an underworld river in Greek mythology, over which dead souls were ferried

style (verb: styles, styling, styled) [a way of doing something; make or arrange something in a particular form]

ℹ do not confuse **style** with **stile**, which means 'an arrangement of steps in a fence, allowing people to climb over'

styli plural of sᴛʏʟᴜs.

styling

stylised another way of spelling sᴛʏʟɪᴢᴇᴅ.

stylish
stylishly
stylishness

stylist »*noun* a person who designs fashionable clothes or cuts hair.

stylistic »*adjective* having to do with style, especially literary style.
stylistically

stylized »*adjective* done or treated in an artificial style.
stylization

✓ **stylized** and **stylization** can also be spelled **stylised** and **stylisation**: both **s** and **z** spellings are correct

stylus »*noun* (plural styli) ❶ a pointed implement used for scratching or tracing letters or engraving. ❷ a pen-like device used to input handwriting directly into a computer. ❸ a hard point following a groove in a gramophone record and transmitting the recorded sound for reproduction.
– sᴀʏ sty-luhss [singular], sty-ly [plural]

✓ sty not **sti**: stylus. The plural is **styli** (as in Latin).

stymie »*adjective* (stymies, stymying or stymieing, stymied) (in informal English) prevent or slow down the progress of something.
– sᴀʏ sty-mi

styptic »*adjective* (in medicine) able to make bleeding stop.
– sᴀʏ stip-tik

styrene »*noun* (in chemistry) a liquid hydrocarbon obtained from petroleum and used to make plastics and resins.
– sᴀʏ sty-reen

styrofoam »*noun* (trademark in the US) a kind of expanded polystyrene, used for making food containers.

suave »*adjective* (suaver, suavest) (of a man) charming, confident, and elegant.
– sᴀʏ swahv
suavely
suavity

✓ u before **a**: suave

sub (in informal English) »*noun* ❶ a submarine. ❷ a substitute.
»*verb* (subs, subbing, subbed) act as a substitute.

sub- »*prefix* under; below; secondary: *sub-zero*

subaltern »*noun* an officer in the British army below the rank of captain.
– SAY sub-uhl-tern

sub-aqua »*adjective* relating to swimming or exploring under water, especially with an aqualung.

subatomic »*adjective* smaller than or occurring within an atom.

subbed

subbing

subcategory »*noun* (plural **subcategories**) a secondary category.

subconscious »*adjective* having to do with the part of the mind of which you are not fully aware but which influences your actions and feelings.
» *noun* this part of the mind.
subconsciously

subcontinent »*noun* a large part of a continent considered as a particular area, such as India.
subcontinental

subcontract »*verb* (**subcontracts, subcontracting, subcontracted**) employ a firm or person outside your company to do work.
subcontractor

subculture »*noun* a cultural group within a larger culture, having beliefs or interests that are different from those of the larger culture.

subcutaneous »*adjective* under the skin.
subcutaneously

> ✓ neous not nious: subcutaneous

subdivide »*verb* (**subdivides, subdividing, subdivided**) divide something into smaller parts.

subdivision »*noun* ❶ the action of subdividing. ❷ a secondary division.

subduction »*noun* (in geology) the gradual sideways and downward movement of a plate of the earth's crust into the mantle beneath another plate.

subdue »*verb* (**subdues, subduing, subdued**) ❶ overcome, quieten, or control someone. ❷ bring a country under control by force.

> drop the e in subduing

subdued »*adjective* ❶ quiet and rather thoughtful or depressed. ❷ (of colour or lighting) soft; muted.

subdues

subduing

subedit »*verb* (**subedits, subediting, subedited**) check and correct text before printing.
subeditor

subgroup »*noun* a small group that is part of a larger group.

sub-heading »*noun* a heading given to a subsection of a piece of writing.

subhuman »*adjective* not behaving like a human being or not fit for human beings.

subject (verb: **subjects, subjecting, subjected**)
subjection

subjective »*adjective* ❶ based on or influenced by personal opinions. ❷ (in grammar) relating to a case of nouns and pronouns used for the subject of a sentence.
subjectively
subjectivity

subjects

sub judice »*adjective* (in law) being considered by a court of law and therefore forbidden to be publicly discussed elsewhere.
– SAY sub joo-di-si

> ℹ️ sub judice means 'under a judge' in Latin

subjugate »*verb* (**subjugates, subjugating, subjugated**) bring someone under control by force.
– SAY sub-juu-gayt
subjugation

> ✓ subj not subd: subjugate

subjunctive »*adjective* (in grammar) (of a form of a verb) expressing what is imagined or wished or possible.
– SAY suhb-**jungk**-tiv

sublet » *verb* (**sublets, subletting, sublet**) lease to another person a property of which you are already a tenant.

> ✓ double the t in subletting

sub lieutenant »*noun* a rank of officer in the Royal Navy, above midshipman and below lieutenant.

sublimate »*verb* (**sublimates, sublimating, sublimated**) ❶ transform something into a purer or idealized form. ❷ (in chemistry) = SUBLIME.
– SAY sub-li-mayt
sublimation

sublime »*adjective* (**sublimer, sublimest**) ❶ of very high quality and causing great admiration. ❷ extreme: *the sublime confidence of youth.*

» *verb* (**sublimes, subliming, sublimed**) (in chemistry) (of a solid substance) change directly into vapour when heated, forming a solid deposit again on cooling.
sublimely
sublimity

subliminal » *adjective* (of a stimulus or mental process) affecting someone's mind without their being aware of it.
– say suhb-**lim**-i-n'l
subliminally

subliming

sublimity

sub-machine gun » *noun* a hand-held lightweight machine gun.

submarine
submariner

submerge » *verb* (**submerges, submerging, submerged**) ❶ push or hold something under water. ❷ go below the surface of water. ❸ completely cover or hide something.
submergence

submerse » *verb* (**submerses, submersing, submersed**) submerge.

submersible » *adjective* designed to operate under water.
» *noun* a small boat or craft that is submersible.

> ☑ **-ible** not **-able: submersible**

submersing

submersion » *noun* the action of submerging.

submicroscopic » *adjective* too small to be seen with an ordinary microscope.

submission » *noun* ❶ the action of submitting. ❷ a proposal or application submitted for consideration.

submissive » *adjective* very obedient or passive.
submissively
submissiveness

submit » *verb* (**submits, submitting, submitted**) ❶ accept or give in to a superior force or stronger person. ❷ present a proposal or application for consideration or judgement.

> ☑ double the **t** in **submitting** and **submitted**

subnormal » *adjective* lower or less than normal, especially with respect to intelligence.

subordinate » *adjective* ❶ lower in rank or position. ❷ less important.

» *noun* a person under the authority of another.
» *verb* (**subordinates, subordinating, subordinated**) treat someone or something as less important than someone or something else.
subordination

subordinate clause » *noun* a clause that forms part of and is dependent on a main clause (e.g. 'when it rang' in 'she answered the phone when it rang').

subordinated

subordinates

subordinating

subordination

suborn » *verb* (**suborns, suborning, suborned**) pay or persuade someone to commit an unlawful act such as perjury.
– say suh-**born**

sub-plot » *noun* a plot in a play, novel, etc. that is secondary to the main plot.

subpoena (in law) » *noun* a written order instructing a person to attend a court.
» *verb* (**subpoenas, subpoenaing, subpoenaed** or **subpoena'd**) summon a person with a subpoena.
– say suhb-**pee**-nuh

> ☑ remember the **b: subpoena** (from Latin *sub poena* meaning 'under penalty')

sub-post office » *noun* (in the UK) a small local post office.

subroutine » *noun* (in computing) a set of instructions designed to perform a frequently used operation within a program.

subs

sub-Saharan » *adjective* from or forming part of the African regions south of the Sahara desert.

subscribe » *verb* (**subscribes, subscribing, subscribed**) ❶ arrange to receive something regularly by paying in advance. ❷ (**subscribe to**) contribute a sum of money to a project or cause. ❸ apply to take part in something. ❹ (**subscribe to**) express agreement with an idea or proposal.
subscriber

subscript » *adjective* (of a letter, figure, or symbol) written or printed below the line.

subscription » *noun* ❶ the action of subscribing. ❷ a payment to subscribe to something.

subsection » *noun* a division of a section.

subsequent »*adjective* coming after something in time.
subsequently

✓ don't forget the **u** after the **q**:
subsequent

subservient »*adjective* ❶ excessively willing to obey others. ❷ less important.
subservience

✓ ent not ant: **subservient**

subset »*noun* ❶ a part of a larger group of related things. ❷ (in mathematics) a set of which all the elements are contained in another set.

subside »*verb* (**subsides, subsiding, subsided**) ❶ become less strong, violent, or severe. ❷ (of water) go down to a lower or the normal level. ❸ (of a building) sink lower into the ground. ❹ (of the ground) cave in; sink. ❺ (**subside into**) give way to a strong feeling.

subsidence »*noun* the gradual caving in or sinking of an area of land.
– **SAY** subh-sy-duhnss or sub-si-duhnss

✓ ence not ance: **subsidence**

subsides

subsidiaries

subsidiarity »*noun* (in politics) the principle that a central authority should only do those things which cannot be done at a more local level.
– **SAY** suhb-si-di-a-ri-ti

subsidiary »*adjective* ❶ related but less important. ❷ (of a company) controlled by another company.
» *noun* (plural **subsidiaries**) a subsidiary company.

✓ plural: drop the **y** and add **ies**:
subsidiaries

subsidies

subsiding

subsidize »*verb* (**subsidizes, subsidizing, subsidized**) ❶ support an organization or activity financially. ❷ pay part of the cost of producing something to reduce its price.
subsidization

✓ many people prefer the alternative spellings **subsidise, subsidises**, etc., and **subsidisation**: both **s** and **z** spellings are correct

subsidy »*noun* (plural **subsidies**) ❶ a sum of money granted from public funds to help an industry or business keep the price of a product or service low. ❷ a sum of money granted to support an undertaking that is in the public interest.

✓ plural: drop the **y** and add **ies**:
subsidies

subsist »*verb* (**subsists, subsisting, subsisted**) maintain or support yourself at a basic level.

subsistence »*noun* ❶ the action of subsisting. ❷ the means of doing this.
» *adjective* (of production) at a level which is enough only for a person's own use, without any surplus for trade: *subsistence agriculture*.

✓ ence not ance: **subsistence**

subsistence level »*noun* a standard of living that provides only the basic necessities of life.

subsisting

subsists

subsoil »*noun* the soil lying immediately under the surface soil.

subsonic »*adjective* relating to or flying at a speed or speeds less than that of sound.

substance

✓ ance not ence: **substance**

substandard »*adjective* below the usual or required standard.

substantial »*adjective* ❶ of considerable importance, size, or worth. ❷ strongly built or made.
substantially

substantiate »*verb* (**substantiates, substantiating, substantiated**) provide evidence to prove the truth of something.
– **SAY** suhb-**stan**-shi-ayt
substantiation

substantive »*adjective* dealing with real or important matters.
– **SAY** sub-**stuhn**-tiv or suhb-**stan**-tiv
substantively

substation »*noun* a set of equipment reducing the high voltage of electrical power transmission to that suitable for supply to consumers.

substitute (verb: **substitutes, substituting, substituted**)
substitution

substratum »*noun* (plural **substrata**) a layer of rock or soil beneath the surface of the ground.

✓ the plural of **substratum** is **substrata** (as in Latin)

S

subsume »*verb* (**subsumes, subsuming, subsumed**) include or absorb something in something else.

subtenant »*noun* a person who leases property from a tenant.

subtend »*verb* (**subtends, subtending, subtended**) (of a line, arc, etc.) form an angle at a particular point when straight lines from its extremities meet.

subterfuge »*noun* a trick or deception used in order to achieve your goal.
– SAY sub-ter-fyooj

> ☑ the middle syllable is **ter**: sub**ter**fuge

subterranean »*adjective* existing or happening under the earth's surface.
– SAY sub-tuh-**ray**-ni-uhn

> ☑ double r, and **ean** not **ian** at the end: subterr**ean**

subtext »*noun* an underlying theme in a piece of writing or speech.

subtitle (verb: **subtitles, subtitling, subtitled**)

subtle »*adjective* (**subtler, subtlest**) ❶ so delicate or precise as to be difficult to describe. ❷ good at noticing and understanding things. ❸ done in a clever but understated way: *subtle lighting.* ❹ using clever and indirect methods to achieve something.
subtlety
subtly

> ☑ don't forget the **b**, which is not pronounced: su**b**tle

subtotal »*noun* the total of one set of a larger group of figures to be added.

subtract (verb: **subtracts, subtracting, subtracted**)
subtraction
subtractive

subtropical »*adjective* having to do with the regions next to or bordering on the tropics.

suburb »*noun* an outlying residential district of a city.
suburban
suburbanite

> ☑ **sub** not **surb** in **suburb** and **suburban**

suburbia »*noun* suburbs and suburban life.

subvention »*noun* a grant of money, especially from a government.

subversion

subversive »*adjective* trying to undermine an established system or institution.

» *noun* a subversive person.
subversively
subversiveness

subvert »*verb* (**subverts, subverting, subverted**) undermine the power and authority of an established system or institution.
subversion

subway

sub-zero

succeed (verb: **succeeds, succeeding, succeeded**)

> ☑ double c, double e: su**cc**e**e**d

success (plural **successes**)
successful
successfully

> ☑ double c, double s, one l: su**cc**e**ss**ful

succession »*noun* ❶ a number of people or things following one after the other. ❷ the action or right of inheriting a position, title, etc.

> ☑ double c, double s: su**cc**e**ss**ion

successive »*adjective* following one another or following others.
successively

> ☑ double c, double s: su**cc**e**ss**ive

successor

> ☑ **-or** not **-er**: success**or**

succinct »*adjective* briefly and clearly expressed.
– SAY suhk-**singkt**
succinctly

> ☑ double c in the middle: su**cc**inct

succour »*noun* help and support in times of hardship and distress.
» *verb* (**succours, succouring, succoured**) give help to someone.
– SAY suk-ker

> ☑ **-our** not **-or**: succ**our** (the spelling **succor** is American)

succubus »*noun* (plural **succubi**) a female demon believed to have sex with sleeping men.
– SAY suk-kyuu-buhss [singular], suk-kyuu-by [plural]

> ☑ the plural of **succubus** is **succubi** (as in the original Latin, in which the word means 'prostitute')

S

succulent »*adjective* ❶ (of food) tender, juicy, and tasty. ❷ (of a plant) having thick fleshy leaves or stems adapted to storing water.
» *noun* a succulent plant.
succulence
succulently

> ✓ double **c**, and **ent** not **ant** at the end: **succulent**

succumb »*verb* (**succumbs**, **succumbing**, **succumbed**) ❶ give in to pressure, temptation, etc. ❷ die from the effect of a disease or injury.

> ✓ don't forget the final **b**, which is not pronounced: **succumb**

such

suchlike

suck (verb: **sucks**, **sucking**, **sucked**)
sucker

suckle »*verb* (**suckles**, **suckling**, **suckled**) (with reference to a baby or young animal) feed from the breast or teat.

suckling »*noun* a young child or animal that is still feeding on its mother's milk.

sucks

sucrose »*noun* a compound which is the chief component of cane or beet sugar.
– SAY syoo-krohz

suction »*noun* the process of removing air or liquid from a space or container, creating a partial vacuum that causes something else to be sucked in or surfaces to stick together.

Sudanese (plural **Sudanese**)

sudden
suddenly
suddenness

> ✓ remember that the ending is **en**: **sudden**
> double **n** in **suddenness**

suds
sudsy

sue »*verb* (**sues**, **suing**, **sued**) ❶ take legal action against a person or institution. ❷ (**sue for**) appeal formally to a person for something: *sue for peace*.

> ✓ drop the **e** in **suing**

suede »*noun* leather with one side rubbed to make a velvety nap.
– SAY swayd

sues

suet »*noun* the hard white fat on the kidneys and loins of cattle, sheep, and other animals, used in making puddings, pastry, etc.

suffer (verb: **suffers**, **suffering**, **suffered**)
sufferer

> ✓ double **f**: **suffer**

sufferance »*noun* lack of objection rather than actual approval; toleration.

> ✓ remember the **e** in the middle, and the ending is **ance** not **ence**: **sufferance**

suffered

sufferer

suffering

suffers

suffice »*verb* (**suffices**, **sufficing**, **sufficed**) ❶ be enough or adequate. ❷ meet someone's needs.
– SAY suh-**fyss**

sufficiency »*noun* (plural **sufficiencies**) ❶ the quality of being sufficient. ❷ an adequate amount.

sufficient »*adjective & determiner* enough; adequate.
sufficiently

> ✓ **i** before **e**, even though it is after **c**: **sufficient** does not follow the usual rule

sufficing

suffix »*noun* (plural **suffixes**) a letter or group of letters added at the end of a word to form a derivative (e.g. *-ation*).

suffocate »*verb* (**suffocates**, **suffocating**, **suffocated**) ❶ die or kill someone due to lack of air or inability to breathe. ❷ feel trapped.
suffocation

suffragan »*noun* a bishop appointed to help the bishop of a diocese.
– SAY suff-ruh-guhn

suffrage »*noun* the right to vote in political elections.
– SAY suf-frij

> ✓ **suffr-** not **suffer-**: **suffrage**

suffragette »*noun* (a historical term) a woman who campaigned for the right to vote in an election.
– SAY suf-fruh-**jet**

> ✓ **tte** at the end: **suffragette**

suffuse »*verb* (**suffuses**, **suffusing**, **suffused**) gradually spread through or over.
– SAY suh-**fyooz**
suffusion

Sufi »*noun* (plural **Sufis**) a member of a Muslim group leading a very religious, strict, and simple life.
– **SAY** soo-fi
Sufism

sugar (verb: **sugars, sugaring, sugared**)

sugar beet »*noun* a type of beet from which sugar is extracted.

sugar cane »*noun* a tropical grass with tall thick stems from which sugar is extracted.

sugared

sugaring

sugarloaf »*noun* a conical moulded mass of sugar.

sugars

sugary

suggest (verb: **suggests, suggesting, suggested**)

suggestible »*adjective* quick to accept other people's ideas or suggestions.
suggestibility

 -ible not **-able**: **suggestible**

suggesting

suggestion

suggestive »*adjective* ❶ making you think of a particular thing. ❷ hinting at sexual matters.
suggestively
suggestiveness

suggests

suicide
suicidal
suicidally

sui generis »*adjective* unique.
– **SAY** soo-i jen-uh-riss

ⓘ **sui generis** is a Latin phrase which means 'of its own kind'

suing

suit (verb: **suits, suiting, suited**)

suitable
suitability
suitably

suitcase

suite »*noun* ❶ a set of rooms. ❷ a set of furniture of the same design. ❸ (in music) a set of instrumental compositions to be played in succession.
– **SAY** sweet

ⓘ do not confuse **suite** with **sweet**, which means 'tasting like sugar' or 'a piece of confectionery'

suited

suiting

suitor »*noun* (old-fashioned) a man who takes a woman out and pays attention to her because he wants to marry her.

 -or not **-er**: **suitor**

suits

sulfur etc. American spelling of **SULPHUR** etc.

sulk (verb: **sulks, sulking, sulked**)

sulky (adjective: **sulkier, sulkiest**)
sulkily
sulkiness

sullen »*adjective* silent and bad-tempered.
sullenly
sullenness

sully »*verb* (**sullies, sullying, sullied**) spoil the purity or cleanliness of something.

sulphate »*noun* a salt or ester of sulphuric acid.

✓ **sulphur**, and all the words related to it such as **sulphate** and **sulphuric**, are spelled with an **f** in America: **sulfur, sulfate, sulfuric**, etc. The **f** spellings are also used elsewhere by scientists.

sulphide »*noun* (in chemistry) a compound of sulphur with another element or group.
– **SAY** sul-fyd

sulphur »*noun* a chemical element in the form of yellow crystals, which easily catches fire.

✓ the ending is **ur**, not **er**: **sulphur** the American spelling is **sulfur**: see the note at **SULPHATE**

sulphur dioxide »*noun* a colourless poisonous gas formed by burning sulphur.

sulphuric »*adjective* containing sulphur or sulphuric acid.
– **SAY** sul-**fyoor**-ik

✓ see the note at **SULPHATE**

sulphuric acid »*noun* a strong corrosive acid.

sulphurous »*adjective* containing or derived from sulphur.

✓ note the **ph** in the middle: **sulphurous** (the spelling **sulfurous** is American)

sultan »*noun* a Muslim ruler.

sultana »*noun* ❶ a seedless raisin. ❷ a wife of a sultan.

sultanate »*noun* a state ruled by a sultan.

sultry »*adjective* (**sultrier, sultriest**) ❶ (of the weather) hot and humid. ❷ suggesting sexual passion.

sum »*noun* ❶ a particular amount of money. ❷ the total amount resulting from

S

the addition of two or more numbers or amounts. ❸ a calculation in arithmetic.
» *verb* (**sums, summing, summed**) (**sum up**) ❶ concisely describe the nature or character of. ❷ summarize briefly.

> ☑ double the **m** to spell **summing** and **summed**

sumac »*noun* a shrub or small tree with conical clusters of fruits and bright autumn colours.

> ☑ the ending is **c** (or sometimes **ch**), not k: **sumac, sumach**

summarily

summarize »*verb* (**summarizes, summarizing, summarized**) give a summary of something.

> ☑ many people prefer the alternative spellings **summarise, summarises**, etc.: both **s** and **z** spellings are correct

summary »*noun* (plural **summaries**) a brief statement of the main points of something.
» *adjective* ❶ done immediately, without unnecessary details or formalities. ❷ (of a legal process or judgement) done or made immediately and without following the normal procedures.
summarily

> ☑ **a** in the middle: **summary** (**summery** is an adjective meaning 'like summer') plural: drop the **y** and add **ies**: **summaries**

summation »*noun* ❶ the process of adding things together. ❷ the action of summing up. ❸ a summary.
– SAY sum-**may**-sh'n

summed

summer
summery

summertime »*noun* ❶ the period of summer. ❷ (**summer time**) time as advanced one hour ahead of standard time to achieve longer evening daylight in summer.

summery [like summer]

summing

summing-up

summit »*noun* ❶ the highest point of a hill or mountain. ❷ the highest possible level of achievement. ❸ a meeting between heads of government.

summon (verb: **summons, summoning, summoned**)

summons »*noun* (plural **summonses**) ❶ an order to appear in a law court. ❷ an act of summoning.

sumo »*noun* Japanese wrestling in which a wrestler must not go outside a circle or touch the ground with any part of his body except the soles of his feet.

sump »*noun* the base of an internal-combustion engine, in which a reserve of oil is stored.

sumptuous »*adjective* splendid and expensive-looking.
sumptuously
sumptuousness

sums

sun (verb: **suns, sunning, sunned**)
sunless

> ☑ double the **n** to spell **sunning** and **sunned**

sun-baked

sunbathe (verb: **sunbathes, sunbathing, sunbathed**)
sunbather

sunbeam

sunbed

sunblock

sunburn (verb: **sunburns, sunburning, sunburned** or **sunburnt**)

suncream

sundae »*noun* a dish of ice cream with added fruit and syrup.

> ☑ **ae** not **ay**: **sundae**

Sunday

sunder »*verb* (**sunders, sundering, sundered**) (a poetic term) split apart.

sundial »*noun* an instrument showing the time by the shadow cast by a pointer.

sundown

sundress (plural **sundresses**)

sun-dried

sundries »*plural noun* various items not important enough be mentioned individually.

sundry »*adjective* of various kinds: *vol-au-vents and sundry other delicacies.*
– SAY sun-dri

sunflower

sung past participle of **SING**.

sunglasses

sunk past and past participle of **SINK**.

> ℹ️ on the use of **sunk, sunken,** and **sank**, see the note at **SINK**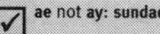

sunken
sunlamp
sunless

sunlight
> sunlit

sunned

Sunni »*noun* (plural **Sunni** or **Sunnis**) **❶** one of the two main branches of Islam. **❷** a Muslim who follows this branch of Islam.

sunnier

sunniest

sunning

sunny (adjective: **sunnier**, **sunniest**)

sunrise

sunrise industry »*noun* a new and growing industry.

sunroof (plural **sunroofs**)

suns

sunscreen

sunset

sunshade

sunshine

sunspot »*noun* (in astronomy) a temporary darker and cooler patch on the sun's surface.

sunstroke »*noun* heatstroke brought about by staying too long in the hot sun.

suntan
> suntanned

sunup »*noun* sunrise.

sup (old-fashioned) »*verb* (**sups**, **supping**, **supped**) **❶** take drink or liquid food by sips or spoonfuls. **❷** eat supper.
» *noun* a sip.

> double the **p** to spell **supping** and **supped**

super

superannuate »*verb* (**superannuates**, **superannuating**, **superannuated**) **❶** arrange for someone to retire with a pension. **❷** (**superannuated**) belonging to a superannuation scheme. **❸** (**superannuated**) too old to be effective or useful.

superannuation »*noun* regular payment made by an employee into a fund from which a future pension will be paid.

superb
> superbly

superbug »*noun* a bacterium, insect, etc. which has developed resistance to antibiotics or pesticides.

supercharge »*verb* (**supercharges**, **supercharging**, **supercharged**) **❶** provide with a supercharger. **❷** (**supercharged**) having powerful emotional associations.

supercharger »*noun* a device that make an engine more efficient by forcing extra air or fuel into it.

supercharges

supercharging

supercilious »*adjective* having a manner that shows you think you are better than other people.
> superciliously
> superciliousness

> **cil** not **sil**: **supercilious**

supercomputer »*noun* a particularly powerful mainframe computer.

superconductor »*noun* a substance which has zero electrical resistance at very low temperatures.
> superconducting
> superconductivity

super-duper

superego »*noun* (plural **superegos**) the part of the mind that acts as a conscience, reflecting social standards that have been learned.

superficial »*adjective* **❶** existing or happening at or on the surface. **❷** apparent rather than real. **❸** not thorough; cursory. **❹** lacking the ability to think deeply about things.
> superficiality
> superficially

> **super** not **supa**, and **cial** not **tial**: **superficial**

superfluous »*adjective* more than what is needed.
> superfluity
> superfluousness

superglue

superheat »*verb* (**superheats**, **superheating**, **superheated**) (in physics) **❶** heat a liquid under pressure above its boiling point without vaporization. **❷** heat steam or other vapour above the temperature of the liquid from which it was formed.

superhero »*noun* (plural **superheroes**) a fictional hero with superhuman powers.

> the plural of **superhero** has **oes** not **os**: **superheroes**

superhuman
> superhumanly

superimpose »*verb* (**superimposes**, **superimposing**, **superimposed**) lay one thing over another.
> superimposition

superintend »*verb* (**superintends, superintending, superintended**) manage or oversee something.

superintendent »*noun* ❶ a person who supervises and controls a team of people, an activity, or a place. ❷ a senior police officer.
superintendence

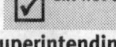 ☑ **ent** not **ant: superintendent**

superintending

superintends

superior »*adjective* ❶ higher in quality or status (the opposite of *inferior*). ❷ of high standard or quality. ❸ arrogant and conceited.
» *noun* a person who is higher in status than someone else, or who is better at doing something.
superiority

superlative »*adjective* ❶ of the highest quality or degree. ❷ (of an adjective or adverb) expressing the highest degree of a quality (e.g. *bravest*).
» *noun* an exaggerated expression of praise.
– SAY soo-**per**-luh-tiv
superlatively

superman (plural **supermen**)

supermarket

supermen

supermodel »*noun* a very successful and famous fashion model.

supernatural »*adjective* not able to be explained by the laws of nature.
» *noun* (**the supernatural**) supernatural events.
supernaturally

supernova »*noun* (plural **supernovae** or **supernovas**) a star that undergoes a catastrophic explosion, becoming suddenly very much brighter.
– SAY soo-per-**noh**-vuh [singular], soo-per-**noh**-vee [plural]

☑ the plural of **supernova** can be either **supernovae** (as in Latin) or **supernovas**

supernumerary »*adjective* ❶ present in more than the required number. ❷ not belonging to a regular staff but engaged for extra work.
» *noun* (plural **supernumeraries**) a supernumerary person or thing.
– SAY soo-puh-**nyoo**-muh-ruh-ri

superpose »*verb* (**superposes, superposing, superposed**) place something on or above something else, especially so that they coincide.
superposition

superpower »*noun* one of the few most powerful nations of the world.

superscript »*adjective* (of a letter, figure, or symbol) printed above the line.

supersede »*verb* (**supersedes, superseding, superseded**) take the place of something or someone.
– SAY soo-per-**seed**

☑ **-sede** not **-cede** or **-seed: supersede**

supersonic »*adjective* involving or referring to a speed greater than that of sound.
supersonically

superstar
superstardom

superstate »*noun* a large and powerful state formed from a federation or union of nations.

superstition »*noun* a belief in the supernatural, especially that particular things bring good or bad luck.

superstitious »*adjective* believing in the supernatural and in the power of particular things to bring good or bad luck.
superstitiously

☑ **-itious** not **-icious: superstitious**

superstore

superstructure »*noun* ❶ a structure that is built on top of something else. ❷ the part of a structure that is built above a supporting base or foundation.

supertanker »*noun* a very large oil tanker.

supervene »*verb* (**supervenes, supervening, supervened**) occur as an interruption or change to an existing situation.
– SAY soo-puh-**veen**

supervise (verb: **supervises, supervising, supervised**)
supervision
supervisor
supervisory

☑ unlike most verbs ending in **ise**, **supervise** cannot be spelled with an **ize** ending

superwoman (plural **superwomen**)

supine »*adjective* ❶ lying face upwards (the opposite of *prone*). ❷ passive or lazy.
– SAY syoo-**pyn**
supinely

supped

supper

supping

supplant »*verb* (supplants, supplanting, supplanted) take someone's place.

supple »*adjective* (suppler, supplest) able to move and bend parts of your body easily; flexible.
suppleness

supplement »*noun* ❶ a thing added to something else to improve or complete it. ❷ a separate section added to a newspaper or periodical. ❸ an additional charge payable for an extra service or facility.
»*verb* (supplements, supplementing, supplemented) provide a supplement for something.
supplemental
supplementation

supplementary »*adjective* completing or improving something.

 ary not ery: supplementary

supplementation

supplemented

supplementing

supplements

suppleness

suppler

supplest

suppliant »*noun* a person who makes a humble request.
»*adjective* making or expressing a humble request.
– SAY sup-pli-uhnt

supplicate »*verb* (supplicates, supplicating, supplicated) humbly ask or beg for something.
– SAY sup-pli-kayt
supplicant
supplication

supply (verb: supplies, supplying, supplied)
supplier

 remember the double p: supply, supplied, supplier, etc.

support (verb: supports, supporting, supported)
supportable

supporter

 -er not -or: supporter

supporting

supportive
supportively
supportiveness

supports

suppose (verb: supposes, supposing, supposed)

supposedly

supposes

supposing

supposition »*noun* a belief that something is likely to be true.

suppository »*noun* (plural suppositories) a solid medical preparation designed to dissolve after being inserted into the rectum or vagina.

suppress »*verb* (suppresses, suppressing, suppressed) ❶ forcibly put an end to something. ❷ stop something being expressed or published.
suppression
suppressor

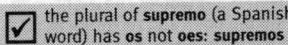 two p's and two s's: suppress, suppression

suppressant »*noun* a drug which acts to stop one of the body's functions from working.

suppressed

suppresses

suppressing

suppression

suppressor

suppurate »*verb* (suppurates, suppurating, suppurated) form pus.
– SAY sup-pyuh-rayt
suppuration

supranational »*adjective* having power or influence that goes beyond individual nations or governments.

supremacist »*noun* a person who believes that a particular group is superior to all others.
supremacism

supremacy »*noun* the state of being superior to all others in authority, power, or status.
– SAY soo-**prem**-uh-si

supreme
supremely

supremo »*noun* (plural supremos) ❶ a person in overall charge. ❷ a person with great authority or skill in a certain area.

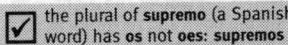 the plural of supremo (a Spanish word) has os not oes: supremos

sups

suq another way of spelling SOUK.

surcharge »*noun* an extra charge or payment.

sure
surely
sureness

sure-fire »*adjective* (in informal English) certain to succeed.

sure-footed

surely

sureness

surety »*noun* (plural **sureties**) ❶ a person who accepts responsibility for someone else should they fail to do something they have agreed to do or to pay a debt. ❷ money given as a guarantee that someone will do something.
– SAY shoor-i-ti or shoor-ti

> ✓ plural: drop the **y** and add **ies**: **sureties**

surf »*noun* the breaking of large waves on a seashore or reef.
»*verb* (**surfs**, **surfing**, **surfed**) ❶ stand or lie on a surfboard and ride on the crest of a wave towards the shore. ❷ occupy yourself by moving from site to site on the Internet.
surfer
surfing

surface (verb: **surfaces**, **surfacing**, **surfaced**)

surface tension »*noun* the force which acts within the surface of a liquid and tends to minimize surface area.

surfacing

surfboard

surfed

surfeit »*noun* an amount that is more than is needed or wanted.

> ✓ **e** before **i**: **surfeit** does not follow the usual rule

surfer

surfing

surfs

surge (verb: **surges**, **surging**, **surged**)

surgeon »*noun* ❶ a medical practitioner who is qualified to practise surgery. ❷ a doctor in the navy.

> ✓ **g** not **j** in **surgeon** and **surgery**

surgery »*noun* (plural **surgeries**) ❶ medical treatment that involves cutting open or entering the body and repairing or removing parts. ❷ a place where a doctor or nurse treats or advises patients.

> ✓ plural: drop the **y** and add **ies**: **surgeries**

surges

surgical »*adjective* ❶ relating to or used in surgery. ❷ worn to correct or relieve an injury or part of the body that is not functioning properly. ❸ done with great precision: *a surgical strike*.
surgically

surgical spirit »*noun* methylated spirit used for cleansing the skin before injections or surgery.

surging

surly »*adjective* (**surlier**, **surliest**) bad-tempered and unfriendly.
surlily
surliness

> ✓ drop the **y** and add **ier** or **iest** to spell **surlier** or **surliest**

surmise »*verb* (**surmises**, **surmising**, **surmised**) suppose something without having evidence.
»*noun* a guess.
– SAY ser-myz

> ✓ **surmise** cannot be spelled with an **ize** ending

surmount »*verb* (**surmounts**, **surmounting**, **surmounted**) ❶ overcome a difficulty or obstacle. ❷ stand or be placed on top of something.
surmountable

surname

> ✓ **sur** not **sir**: **surname**

surpass »*verb* (**surpasses**, **surpassing**, **surpassed**) be greater or better than something or someone.
surpassable

surplice »*noun* a white robe worn over a cassock by the minister and choir members at Christian church services.
– SAY ser-pliss

surplus »*noun* (plural **surpluses**) an amount left over when requirements have been met.
»*adjective* more than what is needed or used.

surprise (verb: **surprises**, **surprising**, **surprised**)
surprised
surprising
surprisingly

> ✓ **surp-** not **sup-**, and note also that **surprise** cannot be spelled with an **ize**

surreal »*adjective* strange and having the qualities of a dream.
surreality
surreally

double r: **surreal**

surrealism »*noun* an artistic movement which combined normally unrelated images in a bizarre way.
surrealist
surrealistic

surreality

surreally

surrender (verb: **surrenders, surrendering, surrendered**)

 double r in the middle: **surrender**

surreptitious »*adjective* done secretly.
– SAY sur-ruhp-ti-shuhss
surreptitiously

surrogate »*noun* a person who stands in for someone else.
– SAY sur-ruh-guht
surrogacy

surrogate mother »*noun* a woman who bears a child on behalf of another woman.

surround (verb: **surrounds, surrounding, surrounded**)

surroundings

surrounds

surtax »*noun* an extra tax on something already taxed.

surtitle »*noun* a caption projected on a screen above the stage in an opera, translating the text being sung.

surveillance »*noun* close observation, especially of a suspected spy or criminal.

 take care spelling this word, which has **e** before **i**, and double **l**: **surveillance**

survey (verb: **surveys, surveying, surveyed**)

surveyor »*noun* a person who surveys land or buildings as a profession.

 -**or** not -**er**: **surveyor**

surveys

survival

survive (verb: **survives, surviving, survived**)
survivable

survivor

 -**or** not -**er**: **survivor**

susceptibility »*noun* (plural **susceptibilities**) ❶ the state or fact of being easily influenced or hurt. ❷ (**susceptibilities**) sensitive feelings.

susceptible »*adjective* ❶ likely to be influenced or harmed by something.

❷ easily influenced by feelings or emotions.
– SAY suh-**sep**-ti-b'l
susceptibly

 remember the **c**, and the ending is -**ible** not -**able**: **susceptible**

sushi »*noun* a Japanese dish consisting of balls of cold rice with raw seafood, vegetables, etc.
– SAY soo-shi

suspect (verb: **suspects, suspecting, suspected**)

suspend (verb: **suspends, suspending, suspended**)

suspender »*noun* ❶ (in British English) an elastic strap attached to a belt or garter, fastened to the top of a stocking to hold it up. ❷ (**suspenders**) (in American English) braces for holding up trousers.

suspending

suspends

suspense
suspenseful

 -**ense** not -**ence**: **suspense**

suspension »*noun* ❶ the suspending of something. ❷ a system of springs and shock absorbers that supports a vehicle on its wheels and makes it more comfortable to ride in. ❸ a mixture in which particles are spread throughout a fluid.

 the ending is -**sion** not -**tion**: **suspension**

suspension bridge »*noun* a bridge which is suspended from cables running between towers.

suspicion

suspicious
suspiciously
suspiciousness

 -**cious** not -**tious**: **suspicious**

suss »*verb* (**susses, sussing, sussed**) (in informal English) realize or understand the true character or nature of something.

sustain (verb: **sustains, sustaining, sustained**)

sustainable »*adjective* ❶ able to be sustained. ❷ (of industry, development, or agriculture) avoiding using up natural resources.
sustainability
sustainably

sustained

sustaining

sustains

sustenance »*noun* ❶ the food and drink needed to keep someone alive. ❷ the process of keeping something going.

 ance not ence: **sustenance**

suture »*noun* ❶ a stitch holding together the edges of a wound or surgical cut. ❷ a thread used for this.
» *verb* (**sutures, suturing, sutured**) stitch a wound up with a suture.
– SAY soo-cher

suzerain »*noun* a ruler or state exercising suzerainty over another.
– SAY soo-zuh-rayn

suzerainty »*noun* the right of one country to rule over another country which has its own ruler but is not fully independent.
– SAY soo-zuh-rayn-ty

svelte »*adjective* (**svelter, sveltest**) slender and elegant.

 remember the final **e**: **svelte** (a French word based on Italian *svelto*)

Svengali »*noun* a person who exercises a controlling influence on another.
– SAY sven-gah-li

ⓘ from *Svengali*, a character in George du Maurier's novel *Trilby*

swab »*noun* ❶ a pad used for cleaning a wound or for taking liquid from the body for testing. ❷ a sample of liquid taken with a swab.
» *verb* (**swabs, swabbing, swabbed**) ❶ clean or take liquid from a wound with a swab. ❷ wash down a surface with water and a cloth or mop.

 double the **b** to spell **swabbing** and **swabbed**

swaddle »*verb* (**swaddles, swaddling, swaddled**) wrap someone or something in garments or cloth.

swaddling clothes »*plural noun* strips of cloth formerly wrapped round a baby to calm it.

swag »*noun* ❶ an ornamental garland of flowers, fruit, and greenery. ❷ a curtain hanging in a drooping curve. ❸ (in informal English) money or goods taken by a thief or burglar.

swagger (verb: **swaggers, swaggering, swaggered**)

Swahili »*noun* a language widely spoken in East Africa.

swain »*noun* (an old word) a young man.

swallow (verb: **swallows, swallowing, swallowed**)
swallower

swallowtail »*noun* ❶ a deeply forked tail. ❷ a brightly coloured butterfly with tail-like projections on the back wings.

swam past of **swim**.

swamp (verb: **swamps, swamping, swamped**)
swampy

swan (verb: **swans, swanning, swanned**)

✓ double the **n** to spell **swanning** and **swanned**

swanky »*adjective* (**swankier, swankiest**) (in informal English) ❶ stylishly luxurious and expensive. ❷ inclined to show off.

swanned

swanning

swans

swansong »*noun* the final performance or activity of a person's career.

ⓘ from the myth that a dying swan sings a song

swap (verb: **swaps, swapping, swapped**)

✓ **swap** can also be spelled with an **o**: **swop**
double the **p** to spell **swapping** and **swapped**

sward »*noun* an expanse of grass.
– SAY sword

swarf »*noun* fine chips or filings produced by machining.
– SAY swahf

swarm (verb: **swarms, swarming, swarmed**)

swarthy »*adjective* (**swarthier, swarthiest**) having a dark skin.
swarthiness

swash »*verb* (**swashes, swashing, swashed**) (of water) move with a splashing sound.
» *noun* the rush of seawater up the beach after the breaking of a wave.

swashbuckling »*adjective* engaging in or full of daring and romantic adventures.
swashbuckler

swashed

swashes

swashing

swastika »*noun* an ancient symbol in the form of a cross with its arms bent at a right angle, used in the twentieth century as the emblem of the Nazi party.
– SAY swoss-ti-kuh

ⓘ **swastika** comes from a Sanskrit word which means 'well-being'

S

swat (verb: **swats**, **swatting**, **swatted**) [hit something with a flat object]

> ℹ️ do not confuse **swat** with **swot**, which means 'study hard; a person who studies hard'

> ☑️ double the t to spell **swatting** and **swatted**

swatch »*noun* ❶ a piece of fabric used as a sample. ❷ a number of fabric samples bound together.

swathe¹ »*noun* ❶ a row or line of grass, corn, etc. as it falls when cut down. ❷ a broad strip or area: *vast swathes of countryside*.
– **SAY** swayth

> ☑️ note the **e** on the end: **swathe**. The alternative spelling **swath** (**SAY** swawth), plural **swaths**, is chiefly American.

swathe² »*verb* (**swathes**, **swathing**, **swathed**) wrap someone or something in several layers of fabric.
»*noun* a strip of material in which something is wrapped.
– **SAY** swayth

swats

swatted

swatting

sway »*verb* (**sways**, **swaying**, **swayed**) ❶ move slowly and rhythmically backwards and forwards or from side to side. ❷ make someone change their opinion: *he's easily swayed*.
»*noun* ❶ a swaying movement. ❷ influence or control over people.

Swazi (plural **Swazi** or **Swazis**) [of Swaziland]

swear (verb: **swears**, **swearing**, **swore**; past participle **sworn**)

sweat (verb: **sweats**, **sweating**, **sweated**)

> ℹ️ in America the past tense is **sweat**, not **sweated**

sweatband

sweated »*adjective* (of goods or workers) produced by or subjected to long hours under poor conditions.

sweater

sweatier

sweatiest

sweatily

sweatiness

sweating

sweatpants

sweats

sweatshirt

sweatshop »*noun* a factory or workshop employing workers for long hours in poor conditions.

sweaty (adjective: **sweatier**, **sweatiest**)
sweatily
sweatiness

Swede »*noun* a person from Sweden.

swede »*noun* a round yellow root vegetable.

Swedish

> ☑️ there is only one **e**: **Swedish**

sweep (verb: **sweeps**, **sweeping**, **swept**)
sweeper

sweeping »*adjective* ❶ extending or performed in a long, continuous curve. ❷ wide in range or effect. ❸ (of a statement) too general.
sweepingly

sweeps

sweepstake »*noun* a form of gambling in which all the stakes are divided among the winners.

sweet (adjective: **sweeter**, **sweetest**) [tasting like sugar; a piece of confectionery]
sweetish
sweetly
sweetness

> ℹ️ do not confuse **sweet** with **suite**, which means 'a set of rooms, furniture, or pieces of music'

sweet-and-sour

sweetbread »*noun* the thymus gland or pancreas of an animal, used for food.

sweetbriar »*noun* a wild rose with fragrant leaves and flowers.

sweetcorn

sweeten (verb: **sweetens**, **sweetening**, **sweetened**)
sweetener

sweeter

sweetest

sweetheart

sweetie

sweetish

sweetly

sweetmeat »*noun* (an old word) an item of confectionery or sweet food.

sweetness

sweet pea »*noun* a climbing plant of the pea family with colourful sweet-smelling flowers.

S

sweet potato »*noun* the pinkish-orange tuber of a tropical climbing plant, eaten as a vegetable.

sweet-talk (verb: **sweet-talks, sweet-talking, sweet-talked**)

sweet william »*noun* a fragrant plant with flattened clusters of vivid red, pink, or white flowers.

swell (verb: **swells, swelling, swelled**, past participle **swollen** or **swelled**)
swelling

swelter »*verb* (**swelters, sweltering, sweltered**) be uncomfortably hot.

swept past and past participle of **SWEEP**.

swerve (verb: **swerves, swerving, swerved**)

swift »*adjective* (**swifter, swiftest**)
❶ happening quickly or promptly.
❷ moving or able to move at high speed.
» *noun* a fast-flying bird with long, slender wings.
swiftly
swiftness

swig (verb: **swigs, swigging, swigged**)

> ☑ double the **g** to spell **swigging** and **swigged**

swill »*verb* (**swills, swilling, swilled**)
❶ rinse something out with large amounts of water. ❷ (of liquid) swirl round in a container or cavity.
» *noun* food waste mixed with water for feeding to pigs.

swim (verb: **swims, swimming, swam**; past participle **swum**)
swimmer

> ℹ note that the past tense of **swim** is **swam** (*she swam to the shore*) and the past participle is **swum** (*she had never swum there before*)

swimmingly »*adverb* smoothly and satisfactorily.

swims

swimsuit

swimwear

swindle »*verb* (**swindles, swindling, swindled**) cheat someone in order to get money or other possessions from them.
» *noun* a dishonest scheme to get money or possessions from someone.
swindler

swine »*noun* ❶ (plural **swine**) (mainly in American English) a pig. ❷ (plural **swine** or **swines**) an unpleasant person.
swinish

swine fever »*noun* an intestinal disease of pigs, caused by a virus.

swing (verb: **swings, swinging, swung**)
swinger

swingeing »*adjective* extreme or severe.
– SAY swin-jing

swinger

swinging

swings

swinish

swipe (verb: **swipes, swiping, swiped**)

swipe card »*noun* a plastic card such as a credit card carrying coded information which is read when the card is slid through an electronic device.

swiped

swipes

swiping

swirl (verb: **swirls, swirling, swirled**)
swirly

swish (verb: **swishes, swishing, swished**)

Swiss (plural **Swiss**) [of Switzerland]

switch (verb: **switches, switching, switched**)

switchback »*noun* ❶ a road or route with alternate sharp ascents and descents. ❷ a roller coaster.

switchblade »*noun* (in American English) a flick knife.

switchboard

switched

switched-on

switches

switchgear »*noun* electrical switching equipment.

switching

swivel (verb: **swivels, swivelling, swivelled**)

> ☑ double the **l** to spell **swivelling** and **swivelled** (the spellings **swiveling** and **swiveled** are American)

swizz »*noun* (in informal English) an instance of being mildly cheated or disappointed.

swizzle stick »*noun* a stick used for frothing up or taking the fizz out of drinks.

swollen past participle of **SWELL**.

swoon »*verb* (**swoons, swooning, swooned**) faint, especially from extreme emotion.
» *noun* an instance of swooning.

swoop (verb: **swoops, swooping, swooped**)

swop another way of spelling **SWAP**.

sword

swordfish »*noun* a large sea fish with a streamlined body and a sword-like snout.

swordplay »*noun* fencing with swords or foils.

swordsman (plural **swordsmen**)
  swordsmanship

swore past of **SWEAR**.

sworn past participle of **SWEAR**. »*adjective*
bound by an oath.

swot »*verb* (**swots, swotting, swotted**) study
hard.
»*noun* a person who spends a lot of time
studying.
  swotty

> ℹ️ do not confuse **swot** with **swat**, which
> means 'hit something with a flat
> object'

> ✓ double the t to spell **swotting** and
> **swotted**

swum past participle of **SWIM**.

swung past and past participle of **SWING**.

sybarite »*noun* a person who is very fond
of luxury.
– SAY **si**-buh-ryt
  sybaritic

> ℹ️ first referring to a person from
> *Sybaris*, an ancient Greek city in Italy

sycamore »*noun* ❶ a large maple native to
central and southern Europe. ❷ (in
American English) a plane tree.

sycophant »*noun* a person who tries to
gain favour with someone in a position of
importance by flattering them.
– SAY **si**-kuh-fant
  sycophancy
  sycophantic

> ✓ sy, c, o, and ph: **sycophant**

syllabi plural of **SYLLABUS**.

syllabic »*adjective* relating to or based on
syllables.
– SAY sil-**lab**-ik

syllable »*noun* a unit of pronunciation
having one vowel sound and forming all or
part of a word (e.g. *butter* has two
syllables).

> ✓ double l, and -able not -ible: **syllable**

syllabub »*noun* a whipped cream dessert,
typically flavoured with white wine or
sherry.

syllabus »*noun* (plural **syllabuses** or
syllabi) all the things covered in a course
of study or teaching.
– SAY **sil**-luh-buhss [singular], sil-luh-by
[plural]

> ✓ the plural of **syllabus** can be either
> **syllabi** (as in Latin) or **syllabuses**

syllogism »*noun* a form of reasoning in
which a conclusion is drawn from two
propositions (e.g. *all dogs are animals; all
animals have four legs; therefore all dogs
have four legs*).
– SAY **sil**-luh-ji-z'm

sylph »*noun* ❶ an imaginary spirit of the
air. ❷ a slender woman or girl.
– SAY silf
  sylphlike

sylvan »*adjective* (a poetic term) having to
do with woods; wooded.

symbiosis »*noun* (plural **symbioses**) (in
biology) a situation in which two different
organisms are connected with and
dependent on each other, to the
advantage of both.
– SAY sim-bi-**oh**-siss or sim-by-**oh**-siss
[singular], sim-bi-**oh**-seez or sim-by-
oh-seez [plural]
  symbiotic

> ✓ make the plural by changing the -**is**
> ending to -**es** (as in the original Latin)

symbol »*noun* ❶ an object, person, or
event that represents something else. ❷ a
letter, mark, or character used as a
standard representation of something.

> ℹ️ do not confuse **symbol** with **cymbal**,
> which is a musical instrument

symbolic »*adjective* ❶ serving as a symbol.
❷ involving the use of symbols or
symbolism.
  symbolically

symbolise another way of spelling
SYMBOLIZE.

symbolism »*noun* ❶ the use of symbols to
represent ideas or qualities. ❷ symbolic
meaning attached to objects.
  symbolist

symbolize »*verb* (**symbolizes, symbolizing,
symbolized**) ❶ be a symbol of something.
❷ represent something by means of
symbols.

> ✓ many people prefer the alternative
> spellings **symbolise, symbolises**, etc.:
> both **s** and **z** spellings are correct

symmetrical »*adjective* exactly the same
each side.
  symmetric
  symmetrically

symmetry »*noun* (plural **symmetries**) ❶ the
exact match in size or shape between two
halves, parts, or sides of something. ❷ a
pleasing balance or proportion. ❸ the
quality of being exactly the same or very
similar.
– SAY **sim**-mi-tri

✓ sy not si, and double m: symmetry

sympathetic
  sympathetically

sympathies

sympathize (verb: **sympathizes**,
  sympathizing, **sympathized**)
  sympathizer

✓ many people prefer the alternative
spellings **sympathise**, **sympathises**,
etc., and **sympathiser**: both **s** and **z**
spellings are correct

sympathy »*noun* (plural **sympathies**) ❶ the
feeling of being sorry for someone.
❷ understanding between people.
❸ support for or approval of something.
❹ (**in sympathy**) fitting in; in keeping.

ℹ on the difference between **sympathy**
and **empathy**, see the note at
EMPATHY

✓ plural: drop the **y** and add **ies**:
sympathies

symphonic »*adjective* relating to or having
the form or character of a symphony.

symphony »*noun* (plural **symphonies**) an
elaborate musical composition for full
orchestra.

✓ plural: drop the **y** and add **ies**:
symphonies

symposium »*noun* (plural **symposia** or
symposiums) a conference or meeting to
discuss a particular academic subject.
– SAY sim-**poh**-zi-uhm

✓ the plural of **symposium** can be either
symposia (as in Latin) or **symposiums**

symptom »*noun* ❶ a change in the body or
mind which indicates a disease. ❷ a sign
of an undesirable situation.

ℹ doctors distinguish between a
symptom (which is apparent to the
patient) and a **sign** (which is not)

symptomatic »*adjective* acting as a
symptom of something.

synagogue »*noun* a building where Jews
meet for worship and teaching.
– SAY **sin**-uh-gog

✓ **gogue** not **gog**: **synagogue**

synapse »*noun* a connection between two
nerve cells.
– SAY **sy**-naps or **si**-naps
  synaptic

sync »*noun* synchronization.

✓ remember that the vowel is **y** not **i**:
sync (as in **synchronize** and other

related words)
sync can also be spelled with an **h** at the
end: **synch**

synchromesh »*noun* a system of gear
changing in which the gearwheels are
made to revolve at the same speed during
engagement.

synchronicity »*noun* the occurrence of
events at the same time, which appear to
be related but have no obvious connection.

synchronize »*verb* (**synchronizes**,
synchronizing, **synchronized**) make things
happen or operate at the same time or rate.
synchronization

✓ many people prefer the alternative
spellings **synchronise**, **synchronises**,
etc., and **synchronisation**: both **s** and **z**
spellings are correct

synchronous »*adjective* existing or
occurring at the same time.
– SAY **sing**-kruh-nuhss
  synchronously

synchrony »*noun* simultaneous action,
development, or occurrence.
– SAY **sing**-kruh-ni

syncopated »*adjective* (of music or a
rhythm) having the beats or accents
altered so that strong beats become weak
and vice versa.
– SAY **sing**-kuh-payt-id
  syncopation

syncope »*noun* fainting caused by low
blood pressure.
– SAY **sing**-kuh-pi

syncretism »*noun* the combining of
different religions, cultures, or schools of
thought.
– SAY **sing**-kri-ti-z'm
  syncretic

syndicate »*noun* a group of individuals or
organizations who get together to
promote a common interest.
» *verb* (**syndicates**, **syndicating**, **syndicated**)
❶ control or manage an operation
through a syndicate. ❷ publish or
broadcast something in a number of
places at the same time.
syndication

✓ **syn** not **sin**: **syndicate**, **syndrome**, etc.

syndrome »*noun* a set of medical
symptoms which tend to occur together.

synecdoche »*noun* a figure of speech in
which a part is made to represent the
whole or vice versa, as in *England won by
six wickets* (meaning 'the English cricket
team').
– SAY si-**nek**-duh-ki

synergism »*noun* = SYNERGY.

synergy »*noun* the working together of two or more things to produce a combined effect greater than the sum of their separate effects.
– SAY sin-er-ji
synergistic

 synergy is also called **synergism**

synod »*noun* an official meeting of church ministers and members.
– SAY si-nod
synodical

synonym »*noun* a word or phrase that means the same as another word or phrase in the same language.
– SAY sin-uh-nim

✓ **nym** not **nim**: **synonym**

synonymous »*adjective* ❶ (of a word or phrase) having the same meaning as another word or phrase in the same language. ❷ closely associated with something.
– SAY si-**non**-i-muhss
synonymously

synopsis »*noun* (plural **synopses**) a brief summary or general survey.
– SAY si-**nop**-siss [singular], si-**nop**-seez [plural]

✓ make the plural by changing the **-is** ending to **-es** (as in Latin): **synopses**

synoptic »*adjective* ❶ having to do with a synopsis. ❷ (**Synoptic**) referring to the Gospels of Matthew, Mark, and Luke, which describe events from a similar point of view.

synovial »*adjective* relating to joints of the body enclosed in a flexible membrane containing a lubricating fluid.
– SAY sy-**noh**-vi-uhl

syntax »*noun* ❶ the way in which words and phrases are put together to form sentences. ❷ a set of rules for the forming of sentences.
syntactic
syntactical

synthesis »*noun* (plural **syntheses**) ❶ the combination of parts to form a connected whole. ❷ the production of chemical compounds by reaction from simpler materials.
– SAY sin-thuh-siss [singular], sin-thuh-seez [plural]

✓ make the plural by changing the **-is** ending to **-es** (as in Latin): **syntheses**

synthesize »*verb* (**synthesizes, synthesizing, synthesized**) ❶ make something by chemical synthesis. ❷ combine parts into a whole. ❸ produce sound with a synthesizer.

✓ many people prefer the alternative spellings **synthesise, synthesises**, etc.: both **s** and **z** spellings are correct

synthesizer »*noun* an electronic musical instrument producing sounds by generating and combining signals of different frequencies.

synthesizes

synthesizing

synthetic »*adjective* ❶ made by chemical synthesis, especially to imitate a natural product. ❷ not genuine.
»*noun* a synthetic textile.
synthetically

syphilis »*noun* a disease caused by bacteria that are passed on during sex.
– SAY si-fi-liss
syphilitic

syphon another way of spelling SIPHON.

Syrian [of Syria]

syringe »*noun* a tube with a nozzle and piston for sucking in and forcing out liquid in a thin stream, often fitted with a hollow needle for injecting drugs or for withdrawing blood.
»*verb* (**syringes, syringing, syringed**) clean something by spraying it with liquid using a syringe.
– SAY si-**rinj**

✓ **syringe** begins with **sy** not **si**

syrup

✓ note that the beginning is **sy**: **syrup** (the spelling **sirup** is American)

syrupy

system

systematic
systematically

systematize »*verb* (**systematizes, systematizing, systematized**) arrange things according to an organized system.

✓ many people prefer the alternative spellings **systematise, systematises**, etc.: both **s** and **z** spellings are correct

systemic »*adjective* relating to a system as a whole.
– SAY si-**stem**-ik or si-**steem**-ik

systems analyst »*noun* a person who studies a complex process or operation in order to improve its efficiency.

S

systole »*noun* the phase of the heartbeat when the heart muscle contracts and pumps blood into the arteries.
– SAY siss-tuh-li
  systolic

syzygy »*noun* (plural **syzygies**) ❶ (mainly in astrology) conjunction or opposition, especially of the moon with the sun. ❷ a pair of connected or corresponding things.
– SAY siz-i-ji

Tt

ta

tab (verb: **tabs, tabbing, tabbed**)

tabard »*noun* a sleeveless jacket consisting only of front and back pieces with a hole for the head.
– SAY tab-uhd

Tabasco »*noun* (trademark) a pungent sauce made from capsicums.
– SAY tuh-bas-koh

> ℹ️ named after the state of *Tabasco* in Mexico

tabbed

tabbies

tabbing

tabbouleh »*noun* a Middle Eastern salad of cracked wheat mixed with chopped tomatoes, onions, and parsley.
– SAY tuh-boo-lay

> ✓ **tabbouleh** (an Arabic word) is spelled with double **b**, **ou** in the middle, and the ending **eh**

tabby »*noun* (plural **tabbies**) a grey or brownish cat with dark stripes.

> ✓ plural: drop the **y** and add **ies**: **tabbies**

tabernacle »*noun* ❶ (in the Bible) a tent used by the Israelites to house the Ark of the Covenant during the Exodus. ❷ a place of worship for some religions.
– SAY tab-er-na-k'l

table (verb: **tables, tabling, tabled**)

tableau »*noun* (plural **tableaux**) a group of models or motionless figures representing a scene.
– SAY tab-loh [singular], tab-lohz [plural]

> ✓ the plural of **tableau** is **tableaux** (it is a French word meaning 'picture')

tablecloth

tabled

table d'hote »*noun* a restaurant menu or meal offered at a fixed price and with limited choices.
– SAY tah-bluh doht

> ✓ **table d'hote** can also be spelled **table d'hôte**, with a circumflex accent over the **o** (as in the original French phrase meaning 'host's table')

tableland »*noun* a broad, high, level region; a plateau.

tables

tablespoon
  tablespoonful

tablet

tableware

tabling

tabloid »*noun* a newspaper that has small pages and is written in a popular style.

taboo »*noun* (plural **taboos**) a social custom that prevents people from doing or talking about something, so that if they do it is offensive or embarrassing.
»*adjective* banned or restricted by social custom.

tabs

tabular »*adjective* (of facts or figures) arranged in columns or tables.
– SAY tab-yuu-ler

tabulate »*verb* (**tabulates, tabulating, tabulated**) arrange facts or figures in columns or tables.
  tabulation

tabulator »*noun* a facility in a word-processing program, or a device on a typewriter, for advancing to set positions in order to produce columns or tables.

> ✓ **-or** not **-er**: **tabulator**

tachograph »*noun* a tachometer used in commercial road vehicles to provide a record of engine speeds.

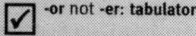

– **say** tak-uh-grahf

tachometer »*noun* an instrument which measures the working speed of an engine.
– **say** ta-**kom**-i-ter

tachycardia »*noun* an abnormally rapid heart rate.
– **say** ta-ki-**kah**-di-uh

tachyon »*noun* an imagined or theoretical subatomic particle that travels faster than light.
– **say** ta-ki-on

tacit »*adjective* understood or meant without being stated.
– **say** ta-sit
tacitly

taciturn »*adjective* saying little.
– **say** ta-si-tern
taciturnity
taciturnly

tack[1] »*noun* ❶ a small broad-headed nail. ❷ a long stitch used to fasten fabrics together temporarily. ❸ a course of action: *it is time to try a different tack*.
»*verb* (**tacks**, **tacking**, **tacked**) ❶ fasten something with tacks. ❷ (**tack on**) casually add something to something already existing. ❸ (in sailing) change course by turning a boat's head into and through the wind.

tack[2] »*noun* equipment used in horse riding.

tack[3] »*noun* (in informal English) cheap, shoddy, or tasteless material.

tackier

tackiest

tackily

tackiness

tacking

tackle (verb: **tackles**, **tackling**, **tackled**)
tackler

tacks

tacky »*adjective* (**tackier**, **tackiest**) ❶ (of glue, paint, etc.) slightly sticky because not fully dry. ❷ showing poor taste and quality.
tackily
tackiness

☑ drop the **y** and add **ier** or **iest** to spell **tackier** or **tackiest**

taco »*noun* (plural **tacos**) a Mexican dish consisting of a folded tortilla filled with spicy meat or beans.
– **say** ta-koh or **tah**-koh

☑ the plural of **taco** has **os** not **oes**: **tacos**

tact »*noun* sensitivity and skill in dealing with others or with difficult issues.

tactful »*adjective* having or showing tact.
tactfully
tactfulness

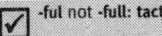
☑ **-ful** not **-full**: **tactful**

tactic »*noun* ❶ the method you use to achieve something. ❷ (**tactics**) the art of organizing and directing the movement of soldiers and equipment during a war.
tactician

tactical »*adjective* ❶ planned in order to achieve a particular end. ❷ (of weapons) for use in direct support of military or naval operations. ❸ (of voting) done to prevent the strongest candidate, whom you do not support, from winning, rather than indicating your true political choice.
tactically

tactician

tactile »*adjective* ❶ having to do with the sense of touch. ❷ fond of touching others in a friendly way.
tactility

tactless »*adjective* thoughtless and insensitive.
tactlessly
tactlessness

tad

tadpole

tae kwon do »*noun* a modern Korean martial art similar to karate.
– **say** ty kwon **doh**

ℹ **tae kwon do** means 'art of hand and foot fighting' in Korean

taffeta »*noun* a fine shiny silk or similar synthetic fabric.
– **say** taf-fi-tuh

☑ **eta** not **ita**: **taffeta**

taffrail »*noun* a rail round a ship's stern.

tag (verb: **tags**, **tagging**, **tagged**)

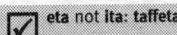
☑ double the **g** in **tagging** and **tagged**

tagliatelle »*plural noun* pasta in narrow ribbons.
– **say** tal-yuh-**tel**-li

☑ **e** not **i** at the end: **tagliatelle** is an Italian word

tags

tag wrestling »*noun* a form of wrestling involving pairs of wrestlers who fight as a team, each taking turns in the ring.

t'ai chi ch'uan »*noun* a Chinese martial art and system of callisthenics, consisting of sequences of very slow controlled movements.
– SAY ty chee **chwahn**

> ℹ **t'ai chi ch'uan**, also known simply as **t'ai chi**, means 'great ultimate boxing' in Chinese

taiga »*noun* swampy, cold, coniferous forest, especially that between the tundra and steppes of Siberia.
– SAY ty-**guh**

tail (verb: **tails**, **tailing**, **tailed**) [rear or end part]
tailless

> ℹ do not confuse **tail** with **tale**, which means 'a story'

tailback

tailcoat

tailed

tailgate »*noun* ❶ a hinged flap giving access to the back of a truck. ❷ the door at the back of an estate or hatchback car.

tailing

tailless

> ✓ two **l**'s: **tailless**

tailor (verb: **tailors**, **tailoring**, **tailored**)
tailored
tailoring

> ✓ -or not -er: **tailor**

tailor-made »*adjective* made or adapted for a particular purpose or person.

tailors

tailpiece »*noun* a part added to the end of a piece of writing.

tailpipe »*noun* the rear section of the exhaust pipe of a motor vehicle.

tailplane »*noun* a horizontal aerofoil at the tail of an aircraft.

tails

tailspin »*noun* a spin by an aircraft.

tailwind »*noun* a wind blowing in the direction of travel of a vehicle or aircraft.

taint (verb: **taints**, **tainting**, **tainted**)

Taiwanese (plural **Taiwanese**) [of Taiwan]

Tajik [of Tajikistan]

take (verb: **takes**, **taking**, **took**; past participle **taken**)
taker

takeaway

take-home pay

taken past participle of **TAKE**.

take-off

takeover

taker

takes

taking

takings

talc »*noun* ❶ talcum powder. ❷ a soft mineral that is a form of magnesium silicate.

talcum powder »*noun* a powder used on the skin to make it feel smooth and dry.

tale [a story]

> ℹ do not confuse **tale** with **tail**, which means 'rear or end part'

talent
talented
talentless

talisman »*noun* (plural **talismans**) an object thought to have magic powers and to bring good luck.
– SAY tal-iz-**muhn**
talismanic

talk (verb: **talks**, **talking**, **talked**)
talker

talkative
talkatively
talkativeness

talked

talker

talkie »*noun* (a historical term) a film with a soundtrack, as distinct from a silent film.

talkier

talkiest

talking

talking head »*noun* (used in a disapproving way) a person who appears on television addressing the camera and is viewed in close-up.

talking-to

talks

talky (adjective: **talkier**, **talkiest**)

tall (adjective: **taller**, **tallest**)
tallish
tallness

tallboy »*noun* a tall chest of drawers in two sections, one standing on the other.

taller

tallest

tallied

tallies

tallish

tallness

tallow »*noun* a hard substance made from animal fat, used in making candles and soap.

tall ship »*noun* a sailing ship with a high mast or masts.

tally »*noun* (plural **tallies**) ❶ a current score or amount. ❷ a record of a score or amount. ❸ (a historical term) a stick scored across with notches for the items of an account.
» *verb* (**tallies, tallying, tallied**) ❶ agree or correspond. ❷ calculate the total number of something.

> ☑ plural: drop the **y** and add **ies: tallies**

tally-ho »*exclamation* a huntsman's cry to the hounds on sighting a fox.

tallying

Talmud »*noun* a collection of ancient writings on Jewish civil and ceremonial law and legend.
– SAY **tal**-muud
Talmudic

> ⓘ **Talmud** is a Hebrew word meaning 'instruction'

talon »*noun* a claw of a bird of prey.

> ☑ **-on** not **-en: talon**

talus »*noun* (plural **tali**) the bone in the ankle that forms a movable joint with the shin bone.
– SAY **tay**-luhss [singular], **tay**-ly [plural]

> ☑ the plural of **talus** is **tali** (as in the original Latin)

talus² »*noun* (plural **taluses**) a sloping mass of rock fragments at the foot of a cliff.
– SAY **tay**-luhs

tamarin »*noun* a small forest-dwelling South American monkey.
– SAY **tam**-uh-rin

tamarind »*noun* sticky brown acidic pulp from the pod of a tropical African tree, used in Asian cookery.
– SAY **tam**-uh-rind

tamarisk »*noun* a shrub or small tree with tiny scale-like leaves on slender branches.
– SAY **tam**-uh-risk

tambourine »*noun* a shallow drum with metal discs around the edge, which you play by shaking or hitting with the hand.

> ☑ **bour** not **bor** in the middle: **tambourine**

tame (adjective: **tamer, tamest**; verb: **tames, taming, tamed**)
tamely

tameness
tamer

Tamil »*noun* ❶ a member of a people living in parts of South India and Sri Lanka. ❷ the language of the Tamils.

taming

tam-o'-shanter »*noun* a round Scottish cap with a bobble in the centre.

> ⓘ named after the hero of Robert Burns's poem *Tam o'Shanter*

tamp »*verb* (**tamps, tamping, tamped**) firmly ram or pack a substance down or into something.

tamper (verb: **tampers, tampering, tampered**)
tamperer

tamping

tampon »*noun* a plug of soft material inserted into the vagina to absorb menstrual blood.

tamps

tan (verb: **tans, tanning, tanned**)
tanner

> ☑ double the **n** in **tanning, tanned,** and **tanner**

tandem »*noun* a bicycle with seats and pedals for two riders, one behind the other.

tandoor »*noun* a clay oven of a type used originally in northern India and Pakistan.

tandoori »*adjective* (of Indian food) cooked in a tandoor.
– SAY tan-**door**-i

tang »*noun* ❶ a strong flavour or smell. ❷ the projection on the blade of a tool that holds it firmly in the handle.

tangent »*noun* ❶ a straight line that touches a curve but does not cross it at that point. ❷ (in mathematics) the ratio of the sides (other than the hypotenuse) opposite and adjacent to an angle in a right-angled triangle. ❸ a completely different line of thought or action: *her mind went off at a tangent.*
– SAY **tan**-juhnt

tangential »*adjective* ❶ relating to or along a tangent. ❷ only slightly connected or relevant.
– SAY tan-**jen**-sh'l
tangentially

tangerine

> ☑ **tange** not **tanga: tangerine**

tangible »*adjective* ❶ able to be perceived by touch. ❷ definite or real: *we need tangible results.*

– **SAY** tan-ji-b'l
tangibility
tangibly

 -ible not **-able**: **tangible**

tangier [more tangy]

tangiest

tanginess

tangle (verb: **tangles, tangling, tangled**)
tangly

tango »*noun* (plural **tangos**) a Latin American ballroom dance with marked rhythms and postures and abrupt pauses.
» *verb* (**tangoes, tangoing, tangoed**) dance the tango.

 the plural of **tango** has **os** not **oes**: **tangos**

tangy »*adjective* (**tangier, tangiest**) having a strong, sharp flavour or smell.
tanginess

tank (verb: **tanks, tanking, tanked**)
tankful

tankard »*noun* a tall beer mug with a handle and sometimes a hinged lid.

 ard not **erd**: **tankard**

tanked

tanker

tankful

 -ful not **-full**: **tankful**

tanking

tanks

tank top »*noun* a close-fitting sleeveless top worn over a shirt or blouse.

tanned

tanner

tannery »*noun* (plural **tanneries**) a place where animal hides are treated to make leather.

tannic acid »*noun* = **TANNIN**.

tannin »*noun* a bitter-tasting substance present in tea, some barks, grapes, etc.
tannic

tanning

tannoy »*noun* (trademark) a type of public address system.

tans

tantalize »*verb* (**tantalizes, tantalizing, tantalized**) tease someone with the sight or promise of something that they cannot have.
tantalization

 from *Tantalus* in Greek mythology, who was punished by being provided with fruit and water which moved away when he reached for them

 many people prefer the alternative spellings **tantalise, tantalises,** etc., and **tantalisation**: both **s** and **z** spellings are correct

tantalum »*noun* a hard silver-grey metallic chemical element.
– **SAY** tan-tuh-luhm

tantamount »*adjective* (**tantamount to**) equivalent in seriousness to.

tantra »*noun* a Hindu or Buddhist text dealing with mystical or magical practices.
– **SAY** tan-truh
tantric

tantrum »*noun* an uncontrolled outburst of anger and frustration.

Tanzanian [of Tanzania]
– **SAY** tan-zuh-**nee**-uhn

Taoiseach »*noun* the Prime Minister of the Irish Republic.
– **SAY** tee-shuhkh

 Taoiseach is an Irish word meaning 'chief, leader'

Taoism »*noun* a Chinese philosophy based on the Tao, or fundamental principle underlying the universe, incorporating the principles of yin and yang and emphasizing humility and religious piety.
– **SAY** tow-i-z'm
Taoist

 Tao means 'the right way' in Chinese

tap (verb: **taps, tapping, tapped**)

 double the **p** in **tapping** and **tapped**

tapas »*plural noun* small Spanish savoury dishes served with drinks at a bar.
– **SAY** tap-uhss

 tapas means 'lid' in Spanish (because the food was served on a dish balanced on the glass of a drink)

tap dance (verb: **tap-dances, tap-dancing, tap-danced**)
tap dancer
tap-dancing

 add a hyphen if you use this as a verb: **tap-dance, tap-dances,** etc.

tape (verb: **tapes, taping, taped**)

taper »*verb* (**tapers, tapering, tapered**)
❶ reduce in thickness towards one end.
❷ (**taper off**) gradually lessen.
» *noun* a slender candle.

tapes

tapestry »*noun* (plural **tapestries**) a piece of thick fabric with designs woven or embroidered on it.

> ✓ est not ist: tapestry
> plural: drop the **y** and add **ies**: tapestries

tapeworm »*noun* a long ribbon-like worm, the adult of which lives as a parasite in the intestines.

taping [as in *she was taping the show*]

tapioca »*noun* a starchy substance in the form of hard white grains used for puddings and other dishes.
– **SAY** ta-pi-**oh**-kuh

tapir »*noun* a pig-like animal with a long flexible snout.
– **SAY** **tay**-peer or **tay**-per

> ⓘ do not confuse **tapir** with **taper**, which means 'reduce in thickness towards one end'

tapped

tappet »*noun* a moving part in a machine which transmits motion in a straight line between a cam and another part.

tapping [as in *tapping your fingers*]

taproom »*noun* a room in which beer is available on tap.

taproot »*noun* a tapering root growing straight downwards and forming the centre from which other roots spring.

taps

tar¹ »*noun* ❶ a dark, thick flammable liquid distilled from wood or coal, used in road-making and for preserving timber. ❷ a similar substance formed by burning tobacco.
» *verb* (**tars, tarring, tarred**) cover something with tar.

> ✓ double the r in **tarring** and **tarred**

tar² »*noun* (old-fashioned) a sailor.

taramasalata »*noun* a Greek dip made from the roe of cod or other fish.
– **SAY** tuh-rah-mah-suh-**laa**-tuh

tarantula »*noun* ❶ a very large hairy spider found chiefly in tropical and subtropical America. ❷ a large black spider of southern Europe.
– **SAY** tuh-**ran**-tyuu-luh

tardy »*adjective* (**tardier, tardiest**) ❶ late. ❷ slow to act or respond.
tardily
tardiness

tare »*noun* ❶ the common vetch. ❷ (in the Bible) a weed.
– **SAY** tair

tare² »*noun* ❶ an allowance made for the weight of the packaging in determining the net weight of goods. ❷ the weight of a vehicle without its fuel or load.

target (verb: **targets, targeting, targeted**)

> ✓ do not double the t in **targeting** and **targeted**

tariff »*noun* ❶ a tax to be paid on a particular class of imports or exports. ❷ a table of the fixed charges made by a business such as a hotel or restaurant.

> ✓ one r, two f's: **tariff**

tarmac »*noun* (trademark in the UK) material used for surfacing roads or other outdoor areas, consisting of broken stone mixed with tar.
» *verb* (**tarmacs, tarmacking, tarmacked**) surface an area with tarmac.

> ✓ add a k in **tarmacking** and **tarmacked**

tarn »*noun* a small mountain lake.

tarnish »*verb* (**tarnishes, tarnishing, tarnished**) ❶ cause metal to lose its shine by exposure to air or damp. ❷ make someone or something less respected.
» *noun* a film or stain formed on an exposed surface of a mineral or metal.

tarot »*noun* a set of special playing cards used for fortune telling.
– **SAY** **ta**-roh

> ✓ don't forget the final t, which is not pronounced: **tarot** is a French word

tarpaulin »*noun* ❶ heavy-duty waterproof cloth. ❷ a covering of this.
– **SAY** tar-**por**-lin

tarragon »*noun* a plant with narrow leaves, used as a herb in cooking.
– **SAY** **ta**-ruh-guhn

> ✓ double r: **tarragon**

tarred

tarried

tarries

tarring

tarry¹ »*adjective* having to do with or covered with tar.
– **SAY** *rhymes with* starry

tarry² »*verb* (**tarries, tarrying, tarried**) (an old word) stay longer than intended.
– **SAY** *rhymes with* marry

tars

tarsal »*adjective* relating to the bones in the ankle.
» *noun* a bone in the ankle.

– **say** tar-s'l

tarsier »*noun* a small tree-dwelling primate with very large eyes, native to the islands of SE Asia.
– **say** tah-si-uh

tarsus »*noun* (plural **tarsi**) the group of small bones in the ankle and upper foot.
– **say** tar-suhss [singular], tar-sy [plural]

> ☑ make the plural by changing the **us** ending to **i** (as in Latin): **tarsi**

tart[1] [a filled pastry]
tartlet

tart[2] »*noun* ❶ (used in an insulting way) a woman who has many sexual partners. ❷ a prostitute.
»*verb* (**tarts, tarting, tarted**) ❶ (**tart yourself up**) make yourself look attractive with clothes or make-up. ❷ (**tart up**) improve the appearance of something.
tarty

tart[3] »*adjective* ❶ sharp or acid in taste. ❷ (of a remark or tone of voice) sharp or hurtful.
tartly
tartness

tartan

Tartar »*noun* ❶ (a historical term) a member of a group of central Asian peoples who conquered much of Asia and eastern Europe in the early 13th century. ❷ (**tartar**) a person who is fierce or difficult to deal with.

tartar »*noun* ❶ a hard deposit that forms on the teeth and contributes to their decay. ❷ a deposit formed during the fermentation of wine.

> ☑ **ar** not **er** at the end: **tartar**

tartare »*adjective* (of fish or meat) served raw, seasoned, and shaped into small cakes: *steak tartare.*
– **say** tah-**tah**

tartare sauce »*noun* a cold sauce consisting of mayonnaise mixed with chopped onions, gherkins, and capers.

tartaric acid »*noun* an organic acid found in unripe grapes and used in baking powders and as a food additive.

tarted

tarting

tartlet

tartly

tartness

tartrazine »*noun* a brilliant yellow synthetic dye made from tartaric acid and used to colour food, drugs, and cosmetics.

– **say** tah-truh-zeen

tarts

tarty

task (verb: **tasks, tasking, tasked**)

task force »*noun* ❶ an armed force organized for a special operation. ❷ a group of people specially organized for a task.

tasking

taskmaster »*noun* a person who imposes a demanding workload on someone.

tasks

Tasmanian devil »*noun* a heavily built aggressive marsupial with a large head, powerful jaws, and mainly black fur, found only in Tasmania.

tassel »*noun* a tuft of threads that are knotted together at one end, used for decorating furniture and clothing.

> ☑ **el** not **le**: **tassel**

taste (verb: **tastes, tasting, tasted**)

tasteful
tastefully
tastefulness

> **-ful** not **-full**: **tasteful**

tasteless
tastelessly
tastelessness

taster

tastes

tastier

tastiest

tastily

tastiness

tasting

tasty (adjective: **tastier, tastiest**)
tastily
tastiness

tat

tattered

tatters

tattier

tattiest

tattily

tattiness

tatting »*noun* ❶ a kind of knotted lace made by hand with a small shuttle. ❷ the process of making such lace.

tattle »*noun* gossip.
»*verb* (**tattles, tattling, tattled**) engage in gossip.

tattoo »*noun* (plural **tattoos**) ❶ a military display consisting of music, marching, and exercises. ❷ a rhythmic tapping or drumming. ❸ an evening drum or bugle signal calling soldiers back to their quarters. ❹ a permanent design made by inserting pigment into punctures in the skin.
» *verb* (**tattoos, tattooing, tattooed**) mark the skin by inserting pigment into punctures in it.
tattooist

tatty (adjective: **tattier, tattiest**)
tattily
tattiness

tau »*noun* the nineteenth letter of the Greek alphabet (T, τ).
– **SAY** tor or tow

taught past and past participle of **TEACH**.

taunt (verb: **taunts, taunting, taunted**)
taunter

taupe »*noun* a grey tinged with brown.
– **SAY** rhymes with rope

Taurus »*noun* a constellation and sign of the zodiac (the Bull, 21 April–20 May).
– **SAY** taw-ruhss

taut »*adjective* (**tauter, tautest**) ❶ stretched or pulled tight. ❷ (of muscles or nerves) tense.
tautly
tautness

tauten »*verb* (**tautens, tautening, tautened**) make something taut.

tauter

tautest

tautly

tautness

tautology »*noun* (plural **tautologies**) the saying of the same thing over again in different words, seen as a fault of style (e.g. *they arrived one after the other in succession*).
– **SAY** taw-**tol**-uh-ji
tautological
tautologous

 plural: drop the **y** and add **ies**: **tautologies**

tavern »*noun* (an old word) an inn or public house.

taverna »*noun* a small Greek restaurant.
– **SAY** tuh-**ver**-nuh

tawdry »*adjective* (**tawdrier, tawdriest**) ❶ showy but cheap and of poor quality. ❷ sleazy or unpleasant: *the tawdry business of politics*.
tawdriness

tawny »*adjective* (**tawnier, tawniest**) of an orange-brown or yellowish-brown colour.

tax (plural **taxes**; verb: **taxes, taxing, taxed**)
taxable

taxation »*noun* ❶ the imposing of tax. ❷ money paid as tax.

tax-deductible »*adjective* permitted to be deducted from income before the amount of tax to be paid is calculated.

taxed

taxes

tax exile »*noun* a wealthy person who chooses to live in a country with low taxes.

tax haven »*noun* a country or independent area where taxes are low.

taxi (plural **taxis**; verb: **taxies, taxiing, taxied**)

 double **i** in **taxiing**

taxicab

taxidermy »*noun* the art of preparing, stuffing, and mounting the skins of dead animals so that they look like living ones.
– **SAY** tak-si-der-mi
taxidermist

taxied

taxies

taxiing

taximeter »*noun* a device used in taxis that automatically records the distance travelled and the fare to be paid.

taxing

taxman (plural **taxmen**)

taxonomy »*noun* ❶ the branch of science concerned with classification. ❷ a system of classifying things.
– **SAY** taks-**on**-uh-mi
taxonomic
taxonomist

taxpayer

tax year »*noun* a year as reckoned for the purposes of taxation (in Britain from 6 April).

tayberry »*noun* (plural **tayberries**) a dark red soft fruit produced by crossing a blackberry and a raspberry.

TB »*abbreviation* tubercle bacillus; tuberculosis.

T-bone »*noun* a large piece of loin steak containing a T-shaped bone.

tea [drink]

do not confuse **tea** with **tee**, which refers to the place from which a golf ball is struck

teacake

teach (verb: **teaches**, **teaching**, **taught**)
  teachable
  teaching

teacher

teaches

teaching

teacup

teak »*noun* hard wood used in shipbuilding and for making furniture, obtained from a tree native to India and SE Asia.

teal »*noun* ❶ a small freshwater duck. ❷ a dark greenish-blue colour.

team (verb: **teams**, **teaming**, **teamed**) [group of people working or playing together]

 do not confuse **team** with **teem**, which means 'be full of or swarming with something'

teammate

teams

teamwork

teapot

tear[1] (verb: **tears**, **tearing**, **tore**; past participle **torn**) [rip a hole or split in; a hole or split caused by tearing]

tear[2] [a drop of clear salty liquid produced in a person's eye]
  teary

tearaway »*noun* a person who behaves in a wild or reckless way.

teardrop

tear duct »*noun* a passage through which tears pass from the glands which produce them to the eye or from the eye to the nose.

tearful
  tearfully
  tearfulness

 -ful not -full: **tearful**

tear gas »*noun* gas that causes severe irritation to the eyes, used in warfare and riot control.

tearing

tear-jerker »*noun* a very sad book, film, etc.

tears

teary

tease (verb: **teases**, **teasing**, **teased**)
  teaser

teasel »*noun* a tall prickly plant with spiny purple flower heads.

✓ **teasel** can also be spelled **teazle**

teaser

teases

teasing

teaspoon
  teaspoonful

teat »*noun* ❶ a nipple on a woman's breast or an animal's udder. ❷ (in British English) a plastic nipple-shaped device for sucking milk from a bottle.

teatime

teazle another way of spelling **TEASEL**.

technical
  technically

✓ remember the **h** in **technical** and related words

technicality »*noun* (plural **technicalities**) ❶ a small formal detail in a set of rules. ❷ (**technicalities**) small details of a particular field or activity. ❸ the use of technical terms or methods.

✓ plural: drop the **y** and add **ies**: **technicalities**

technically

technician »*noun* ❶ a person who looks after equipment or does practical work in a laboratory. ❷ an expert in a particular science or craft.

✓ **cian** not **tian**: **technician**

Technicolor »*noun* (trademark) ❶ a process of producing cinema films in colour. ❷ (**technicolor**) (in informal English) vivid colour.

✓ **-or** not **-our**: **Technicolor** follows the American spelling

technique »*noun* ❶ a particular way of carrying out a task. ❷ a person's level of skill in doing something.

✓ **que** at the end: **technique**

techno »*noun* a style of fast, loud electronic dance music.

technocracy »*noun* (plural **technocracies**) a social or political system in which scientific or technical experts hold a great deal of power.
– **say** tek-**nok**-ruh-si
  technocrat

technology
  technological
  technologically
  technologist

✓ plural: drop the **y** and add **ies**:
  technologies

technophobe »*noun* a person who dislikes or fears new technology.
technophobia
technophobic

tectonic »*adjective* (in geology) having to do with the structure of the earth's crust.
– SAY tek-**ton**-ik

teddy (plural **teddies**)

> ☑ plural: drop the **y** and add **ies**: **teddies**

Teddy boy »*noun* (in Britain during the 1950s) a young man of a group who had their hair slicked up in a quiff and liked rock-and-roll music.

tedious »*adjective* too long, slow, or dull.
tediously

tedium »*noun* the state of being tedious.

tee (verb: **tees**, **teeing**, **teed**) [place from which a golf ball is struck]

> ℹ do not confuse **tee** with **tea** (the drink)

teem »*verb* ❶ (**teem with**) be full of or swarming with. ❷ (of rain) fall heavily.

> ℹ do not confuse **teem** with **team**, which refers to a group of people working or playing together

teen »*adjective* relating to teenagers.
»*noun* a teenager.

teenage
teenaged

teenager

teenier

teeniest

teens

teensy

teensy-weensy

teeny (adjective: **teenier**, **teeniest**)

teeny-bopper

teeny-weeny

teepee another way of spelling **TEPEE**.

tees

tee shirt another way of spelling **T-SHIRT**.

teeter (verb: **teeters**, **teetering**, **teetered**)

teeth plural of **TOOTH**.

teethe »*verb* (**teethes**, **teething**, **teethed**) (of a baby) develop his or her first teeth.

teething troubles »*plural noun* short-term problems that occur in the early stages of a new project.

teetotal »*adjective* choosing not to drink alcohol.
teetotalism
teetotaller

Teflon »*noun* (trademark) a tough synthetic resin used to make seals and bearings and to coat non-stick cooking utensils.

telecast »*noun* a television broadcast.

telecommunications »*noun* communication over a distance by cable, telegraph, telephone, or broadcasting.

telecoms »*noun* telecommunications.

> ☑ **telecoms** can also be spelled with two **m**'s: **telecomms**

teleconference »*noun* a conference with participants in different locations linked by telecommunication devices.
teleconferencing

telegenic »*adjective* having an appearance or manner that is attractive on television.
– SAY teli-**jen**-ik

telegram »*noun* a message sent by telegraph and delivered in written or printed form.

telegraph »*noun* a system or device for transmitting messages from a distance along a wire.
»*verb* (**telegraphs**, **telegraphing**, **telegraphed**) send a message to someone by telegraph.
telegraphic
telegraphy

telegraphese »*noun* the abrupt, abbreviated style of language used in telegrams.

telegraphic

telegraphing

telegraphs

telekinesis »*noun* the supposed ability to move objects at a distance by mental power.
– SAY te-li-ki-**nee**-siss
telekinetic

telemarketing »*noun* the marketing of goods or services by telephone calls to potential customers.
telemarketer

telemessage »*noun* a message sent by telephone or telex and delivered in written form.

telemetry »*noun* the action of making measurements automatically and transmitting them by radio to a distant location.
– SAY ti-**lem**-i-tri

teleology »*noun* the philosophical theory that all things in nature have a purpose and happen because of that.
– SAY teli-**ol**-uh-ji or teel-**ol**-uh-ji
teleological

t

telepathy »*noun* the supposed communication of thoughts or ideas by means other than the known senses. **telepathic**

telephone (verb: **telephones, telephoning, telephoned**) **telephonic** **telephonically**

telephonist »*noun* an operator of a telephone switchboard.

telephony »*noun* the working or use of telephones. – **SAY** ti-**lef**-fuh-ni

telephoto lens »*noun* a lens that produces a magnified image of a distant object.

teleprinter »*noun* a device for transmitting telegraph messages as they are keyed.

telesales »*plural noun* the selling of goods or services over the telephone.

telescope (verb: **telescopes, telescoping, telescoped**) **telescopic**

teletext

telethon »*noun* a long television programme broadcast to raise money for a charity.

televise (verb: **televises, televising, televised**)

> ✓ **televise** cannot be spelled with an **ize** ending

television

televisual »*adjective* relating to or suitable for television. **televisually**

telex »*noun* (plural **telexes**) ❶ an international system in which printed messages are transmitted and received by teleprinters. ❷ a device used for this. ❸ a message sent by telex. » *verb* (**telexes, telexing, telexed**) send a message to someone by telex.

tell (verb: **tells, telling, told**)

teller »*noun* ❶ a person who deals with customers' transactions in a bank. ❷ a person who counts votes. ❸ a person who tells something.

tellies

telling »*adjective* having a striking or revealing effect. **tellingly**

telling-off »*noun* (plural **tellings-off**) a reprimand.

> ✓ make the plural by adding **s** to **telling**: **tellings-off**

tells

telltale »*adjective* revealing or betraying something. » *noun* a person who reports things that other people have done wrong.

tellurium »*noun* a silvery-white crystalline non-metallic element. – **SAY** tel-**lyoor**-i-uhm

telly »*noun* (plural **tellies**) (in informal English) a television set.

> ✓ plural: drop the **y** and add **ies: tellies**

temerity »*noun* excessive confidence or boldness. – **SAY** ti-**me**-ri-ti

temp »*noun* a person who is employed on a temporary basis. » *verb* (**temps, temping, temped**) work as a temp.

temper »*noun* ❶ a person's state of mind. ❷ a tendency to become angry easily. ❸ an angry state of mind. ❹ the degree of hardness of a metal. » *verb* (**tempers, tempering, tempered**) ❶ harden metal by heating and then cooling it. ❷ neutralize or counterbalance something.

tempera »*noun* a method of painting with powdered colours mixed with egg yolk. – **SAY** **tem**-puh-ruh

temperament »*noun* a person's nature in terms of the way it affects their behaviour.

> ✓ **era** not **re** in the middle: **temperament**

temperamental »*adjective* ❶ relating to or caused by temperament. ❷ tending to change mood in an unreasonable way. **temperamentally**

temperance »*noun* complete avoidance of drinking alcohol.

> ✓ **ance** not **ence: temperance**

temperate »*adjective* ❶ (of a region or climate) having mild temperatures. ❷ showing self-control.

temperature

> ✓ **temper-** not **tempr-**, and **-at-** not **-it-**: **temperature**

tempered

tempering

tempers

tempest »*noun* a violent windy storm.

tempestuous »*adjective* ❶ very stormy. ❷ characterized by strong and changeable emotion.

– SAY tem-**pess**-tyoo-uhss
tempestuously
tempestuousness

tempi plural of TEMPO.

temping

template »*noun* ❶ a shaped piece of rigid material used as a pattern for cutting out, shaping, or drilling. ❷ a model for others to copy.

temple[1] [a building for the worship of a god or gods]

temple[2] »*noun* the flat part either side of the head between the forehead and the ear.

tempo »*noun* (plural **tempos** or **tempi**) ❶ the speed at which a passage of music is played. ❷ the pace of an activity or process.
– SAY tem-poh [singular], tem-pi [plural]

> ✓ the plural can be either **tempi** (as in Italian) or **tempos**

temporal »*adjective* ❶ relating to time. ❷ relating to worldly affairs. ❸ (in anatomy) having to do with or situated in the temples of the head.
– SAY tem-puh-ruhl
temporally

> ✓ -or not -er: **temporal**

temporary »*adjective* lasting for only a short time.
temporarily

> ✓ note that the ending is -orary, not -ory or -ary: **temporary**

temporize »*verb* (**temporizes, temporizing, temporized**) delay making a decision or committing yourself.

> ✓ many people prefer the alternative spellings **temporise, temporises,** etc.: both **s** and **z** spellings are correct

tempos

temps

tempt »*verb* (**tempts, tempting, tempted**) ❶ try to persuade someone to do something appealing but wrong. ❷ (**be tempted to do**) have an urge or inclination to do. ❸ attract; charm.
temptation
tempter
tempting
temptingly

temptress (plural **temptresses**)

tempts

ten
tenfold

tenable »*adjective* ❶ able to be defended against attack or objection. ❷ (of a post, grant, etc.) able to be held or used for a specified period.

tenacious »*adjective* ❶ firmly holding on to something. ❷ continuing to exist or do something for longer than might be expected: *a tenacious belief.*
– SAY ti-**nay**-shuhss
tenaciously
tenacity

tenancy (plural **tenancies**) »*noun* possession of land or property as a tenant.

> ✓ plural: drop the **y** and add **ies**: **tenancies**

tenant »*noun* a person who rents land or property from a landlord.
» *verb* (**tenants, tenanting, tenanted**) occupy property as a tenant.

tench »*noun* (plural **tench**) a freshwater fish of the carp family.

tend »*verb* (**tends, tending, tended**) ❶ frequently behave in a particular way or have certain characteristics. ❷ go or move in a particular direction. ❸ care for or look after.

tendency »*noun* (plural **tendencies**) an inclination to behave in a particular way.

> ✓ ency not ancy: **tendency**

tendentious »*adjective* expressing a strong opinion; opinionated.
– SAY ten-**den**-shuhss
tendentiously
tendentiousness

> ✓ tious not cious: **tendentious**

tender[1] (adjective: **tenderer, tenderest**) [gentle and kind]
tenderly
tenderness

tender[2] »*verb* (**tenders, tendering, tendered**) ❶ offer or present formally. ❷ make a formal written offer to do work, supply goods, etc. for a stated fixed price. ❸ offer money as payment.
» *noun* a tendered offer.

tender[3] »*noun* ❶ a vehicle used by a fire service or the armed forces for carrying supplies. ❷ a wagon attached to a steam locomotive to carry fuel and water. ❸ a boat used to ferry people and supplies to and from a ship.

tender-hearted

tendering

tenderize »*verb* (**tenderizes, tenderizing, tenderized**) make meat more tender by beating or slow cooking.

many people prefer the alternative spellings **tenderise, tenderises,** etc.: both **s** and **z** spellings are correct

tenderloin »*noun* the tenderest part of a loin of beef, pork, etc., taken from under the short ribs in the hindquarters.

tenderly

tenderness

tenders

tending

tendinitis »*noun* inflammation of a tendon.
– SAY ten-di-**ny**-tiss

 tendinitis is sometimes spelled **tendonitis**

tendon »*noun* a strong band or cord of tissue attaching a muscle to a bone.

tendonitis another way of spelling TENDINITIS.

tendril »*noun* ❶ a thin curling stem of a climbing plant, which twines round any suitable support. ❷ a slender ringlet of hair.

 only one **l** at the end: **tendril**

tends

tenebrous »*adjective* (a poetic term) dark; shadowy.
– SAY ten-i-bruhss

tenement »*noun* ❶ a separate residence within a house or block of flats. ❷ a house divided into several separate residences.
– SAY ten-uh-muhnt

tenet »*noun* a central principle or belief.
– SAY ten-it

tenfold

ten-gallon hat »*noun* a large, broad-brimmed hat, traditionally worn by cowboys.

tenner [a ten-pound note]

tennis

tennis elbow »*noun* inflammation of the tendons of the elbow caused by overuse of the forearm muscles.

tenon »*noun* a projecting piece of wood that fits into a slot in another piece of wood.
– SAY ten-uhn

 single **n** in the middle: **tenon**

tenor »*noun* ❶ the male singing voice below alto or countertenor. ❷ the general meaning or character of something.

 one **n** and **-or** not **-er**: **tenor** (a **tenner** is a ten-pound note)

tenpin bowling

tense[1] »*adjective* (**tenser, tensest**) ❶ stretched tight or rigid. ❷ feeling, causing, or showing anxiety and nervousness.
» *verb* (**tenses, tensing, tensed**) make or become tense.
tensely
tenseness

tense[2] »*noun* (in grammar) a set of forms of a verb that indicate the time or completeness of the action referred to.

tensile »*adjective* ❶ relating to tension. ❷ capable of being drawn out or stretched.
– SAY ten-syl

tension
tensional

tent

tentacle
tentacled

tentative »*adjective* ❶ done without confidence. ❷ not certain or fixed.
tentatively
tentativeness

tenterhooks »*plural noun* (**on tenterhooks**) in a state of nervous suspense.

tenth
tenthly

tenuous »*adjective* ❶ very slight or weak. ❷ very slender or fine.
tenuously
tenuousness

 uous not just **ous**: **tenuous**

tenure »*noun* ❶ the conditions under which land or buildings are held or occupied. ❷ the holding of an office.
– SAY ten-yer

tenured »*adjective* having a permanent post.

tepee »*noun* a cone-shaped tent used by American Indians.
– SAY tee-pee

 tepee can also be spelled **teepee** or **tipi**

tepid »*adjective* ❶ lukewarm. ❷ unenthusiastic.
tepidity
tepidly

tequila »*noun* a clear Mexican alcoholic spirit.
– SAY tuh-kee-luh

terabyte »*noun* (in computing) a unit of information equal to one million million bytes.

terbium »*noun* a silvery-white metallic chemical element.
– SAY ter-bi-uhm

tercentenary »*noun* (plural **tercentenaries**) a three-hundredth anniversary.

tergiversation »*noun* the use of evasive or ambiguous language.
– SAY ter-ji-vuh-say-shun

term (verb: **terms**, **terming**, **termed**)
termly

termagant »*noun* a bad-tempered or bossy woman.
– SAY ter-muh-guhnt

> ✓ **ant** not **ent** at the end: term**ant**

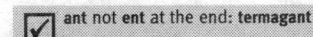

termed

terminable »*adjective* ❶ able to be terminated. ❷ coming to an end after a certain time.

terminal »*adjective* ❶ having to do with or situated at the end. ❷ (of a disease) predicted to lead to death.
»*noun* ❶ the station at the end of a railway or bus route. ❷ a departure and arrival building for passengers at an airport. ❸ a point at which connection can be made in an electric circuit. ❹ a keyboard and screen joined to a central computer system.
terminally

terminate »*verb* (**terminates**, **terminating**, **terminated**) ❶ bring or come to an end. ❷ (of a train or bus service) end its journey. ❸ end a pregnancy early by artificial means.
termination
terminator

terming

termini plural of **TERMINUS**.

terminology »*noun* (plural **terminologies**) the set of terms used in a subject, profession, etc.
terminological

terminus »*noun* (plural **termini** or **terminuses**) a railway or bus terminal.

> ✓ the plural of **terminus** can be either **termini** (as in Latin) or **terminuses**

termite »*noun* a small insect which eats wood and lives in colonies in large nests of earth.
– SAY ter-myt

termly

terms

tern »*noun* a white seabird with long pointed wings and a forked tail.

ternary »*adjective* composed of three parts.

– SAY ter-nuh-ri

terpsichorean »*adjective* relating to dancing.
– SAY terp-si-kuh-**ree**-uhn

terrace »*noun* ❶ one of a series of flat areas on a slope, used for growing plants and crops. ❷ a patio. ❸ a row of houses built in one block. ❹ a flight of wide, shallow steps for spectators in a stadium.
»*verb* (**terraces**, **terracing**, **terraced**) make or form into terraces.
terraced
terracing

terracotta »*noun* ❶ unglazed, brownish-red earthenware, used as a decorative building material and in modelling. ❷ a strong brownish-red colour.
– SAY te-ruh-**kot**-tuh

> ✓ double **r** and double **t**: terr**a**co**tt**a is from Italian *terra cotta*, 'baked earth'

terra firma »*noun* dry land; the ground.
– SAY te-ruh **fer**-muh

> ℹ **terra firma** is Latin for 'firm land'

terrain »*noun* a stretch of land seen in terms of its physical features.
– SAY te-**rayn**

terra incognita »*noun* unknown territory.
– SAY te-ruh in-**kog**-ni-tuh

> ℹ **terra incognita** is a Latin phrase, meaning 'unknown land'

terrapin »*noun* a small freshwater turtle.

terrarium »*noun* (plural **terrariums** or **terraria**) ❶ a glass-fronted case for keeping small reptiles, amphibians, etc. ❷ a sealed transparent container in which plants are grown.
– SAY ter-**rair**-i-uhm

> ✓ the plural can be either **terraria** (as in Latin) or **terrariums**

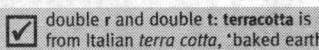

terrazzo »*noun* flooring material consisting of chips of marble or granite set in concrete and polished smooth.
– SAY te-**rat**-zoh

> ✓ double **r**, double **z**: terr**a**zz**o** (an Italian word meaning 'terrace')

terrestrial »*adjective* ❶ having to do with the earth or dry land. ❷ (of an animal or plant) living on or in the ground. ❸ (of television broadcasting) not using a satellite.
– SAY tuh-**ress**-tri-uhl

> ✓ double **r** in the middle, and **-trial** not **-tial** at the end: terres**trial**

terrible
terribly

terrier »*noun* a small, lively breed of dog.

terrific
terrifically

terrify (verb: **terrifies, terrifying, terrified**)
terrifying

terrine »*noun* a mixture of chopped savoury food that is pressed into a container and served cold.
– **say** tuh-**reen**

territorial »*adjective* ❶ relating to a territory or area. ❷ (of an animal) having a territory which it defends.
territoriality
territorially

Territorial Army »*noun* (in the UK) a military reserve force of volunteers.

territoriality

territorially

territorial waters »*plural noun* the waters under the control of a state, especially those within a stated distance from its coast.

territory »*noun* (plural **territories**) ❶ an area controlled by a ruler or state. ❷ a division of a country. ❸ an area defended by an animal against others. ❹ an area in which a person has rights, responsibilities, or knowledge.

> ✓ double r in the middle, and the ending is **ory: territory**

terror

terrorise another way of spelling **TERRORIZE**.

terrorist
terrorism

terrorize (verb: **terrorizes, terrorizing, terrorized**)

> ✓ many people prefer the alternative spellings **terrorise, terrorises**, etc.: both **s** and **z** spellings are correct

terry »*noun* a fabric with raised loops of thread on both sides.

terse »*adjective* (**terser, tersest**) using few words.
tersely
terseness

tertiary »*adjective* ❶ third in order or level. ❷ (of education) at a level beyond that provided by schools.
»*noun* (**Tertiary**) the geological period from about 65 to 1.64 million years ago.
– **say** ter-**shuh**-ri

tertiary industry »*noun* the service industries of a country.

terylene »*noun* (trademark) a polyester fibre used to make clothing, bed linen, etc.

TESSA »*noun* (formerly in the UK) a special savings account allowing savers to invest a certain amount without paying tax on the interest.

tessellated »*adjective* decorated with mosaics.
– **say tess**-uh-**lay**-tid
tessellation

> ✓ double **s**, double **l: tessellated**

tessera »*noun* (plural **tesserae**) a small block of stone, tile, etc. used in a mosaic.
– **say tess**-uh-ruh [singular], **tess**-uh-ree [plural]

> ✓ the plural is spelled with an **e** (as in Latin): **tesserae**

tessitura »*noun* (in music) the range within which most notes of a vocal part fall.
– **say** tess-i-**tyoor**-uh

test (verb: **tests, testing, tested**)
testable

testa »*noun* (plural **testae**) the protective outer covering of a seed.
– **say tess**-tuh [singular], **tess**-tee [plural]

> ✓ the plural is spelled with an **e** (as in Latin): **testae**

testable

testament »*noun* ❶ a person's will. ❷ something that provides evidence of a fact, event, or quality. ❸ (**Testament**) one of the two divisions of the Bible.
testamentary

testate »*adjective* having made a valid will before dying.

testator »*noun* (in law) a person who has made a will or given a legacy.
– **say** tess-**tay**-ter

> ✓ **-or** not **-er: testator**

testatrix »*noun* (plural **testatrices** or **testatrixes**) a female testator.
– **say** tess-**tay**-triks [singular], tess-**tay**-tri-seez or tess-**tay**-triks-iz [plural]

test case »*noun* (in law) a case setting an example for future cases.

test-drive »*verb* (**test-drives, test-driving, test-drove**; past participle **test-driven**) drive a motor vehicle to judge its performance and quality.

tested

tester

testes plural of **TESTIS**.

testicle »*noun* one of the two oval organs that produce sperm in male mammals, enclosed in the scrotum.
testicular

testier

testiest

testify »*verb* (**testifies, testifying, testified**)
❶ give evidence as a witness in a law
court. ❷ serve as evidence or proof:
luxurious villas testify to the wealth here.

testimonial »*noun* ❶ a formal statement
of a person's good character and
qualifications. ❷ a public tribute to
someone and to their achievements.
– SAY tess-ti-**moh**-ni-uhl

testimony »*noun* (plural **testimonies**) ❶ a
formal statement, especially one given in
a court of law. ❷ evidence or proof of
something.

testing

testis »*noun* (plural **testes**) an organ which
produces sperm.
– SAY tess-tiss [singular], tess-teez [plural]

> ☑ make the plural by changing the **-is**
> ending to **-es** (as in the original
> Latin): **testes**

testosterone »*noun* a steroid hormone
that stimulates the development of male
sexual characteristics at puberty.
– SAY tess-**toss**-tuh-rohn

tests

test tube

test-tube baby »*noun* (in informal English)
a baby conceived by in vitro fertilization.

testy »*adjective* (**testier, testiest**) easily
irritated.
testily
testiness

tetanus »*noun* a disease causing the
muscles to stiffen and go into spasms,
spread by bacteria.
– SAY tet-uh-nuhss

tetchy »*adjective* (**tetchier, tetchiest**) bad-
tempered and irritable.
tetchily
tetchiness

tete-a-tete »*noun* (plural **tete-a-tete** or
tete-a-tetes) a private conversation
between two people.
– SAY tayt-ah-**tayt** [singular and plural]

> ☑ **tete-a-tete** can also be spelled with
> circumflex accents on the first **e**'s of
> tete and a grave accent on the **a**: **tête-à-
> tête** (as in the original French phrase
> meaning 'head-to-head')

tether »*noun* a rope or chain used to tie an
animal to a post, fence, etc.
»*verb* (**tethers, tethering, tethered**) tie an
animal with a tether.

tetrahedron »*noun* (plural **tetrahedra** or
tetrahedrons) a solid having four plane
triangular faces.
– SAY tet-ruh-**hee**-druhn
tetrahedral

> ☑ the plural of **tetrahedron** can be
> **tetrahedra** (like the original Greek) or
> **tetrahedrons**

tetralogy »*noun* (plural **tetralogies**) a
group of four related literary or operatic
works.
– SAY ti-**tral**-uh-ji

tetrameter »*noun* a line of verse made up
of four metrical feet.
– SAY ti-**tram**-i-ter

tetrapod »*noun* an animal of a group
which includes all vertebrates apart from
fishes.
– SAY te-truh-pod

Teuton »*noun* a member of an ancient
Germanic people who lived in Jutland.
– SAY tyoo-tuhn

Teutonic »*adjective* ❶ relating to the
Teutons. ❷ displaying qualities thought to
belong to Germans.
– SAY tyoo-**ton**-ik

Texan [of Texas]

text

textbook

textile »*noun* a type of cloth or woven
fabric.
»*adjective* relating to fabric or weaving.

textual »*adjective* relating to a text or
texts.
textually

texture »*noun* the feel, appearance, or
consistency of a surface, substance, or
fabric.
»*verb* (**textures, texturing, textured**) give a
rough or raised texture to something.
textural

Thai »*noun* (plural **Thai** or **Thais**) ❶ a
person from Thailand. ❷ the official
language of Thailand.
– SAY *rhymes with* my

thalidomide »*noun* a drug formerly used
as a sedative, but found to cause
malformation of the fetus when taken in
early pregnancy.
– SAY thuh-**lid**-uh-myd

thallium »*noun* a soft silvery-white
metallic chemical element whose
compounds are very poisonous.
– SAY **thal**-li-uhm

than

> ⓘ some people insist that it is wrong to
> use *me* and *us* rather than *I* and *we*

after **than**: *she's younger than I* rather than *she's younger than me*. In modern English, however, the use with *me* and *us* is quite acceptable, while *I* and *we* are generally used only in formal situations.

thane »*noun* ❶ (in Anglo-Saxon England) a lesser nobleman granted land by the king or a higher-ranking nobleman. ❷ (in Scotland) a nobleman who held land from a Scottish king.
– SAY thayn

thank (verb: thanks, thanking, thanked)

thankful
thankfully
thankfulness

> ✓ -ful not -full: thankful

thanking

thankless »*adjective* ❶ (of a job or task) unpleasant and unlikely to be appreciated by others. ❷ not showing or feeling gratitude.

thanks

thanksgiving »*noun* ❶ the expression of gratitude to God. ❷ (**Thanksgiving**) (in North America) a national holiday commemorating a harvest festival celebrated by the Pilgrim Fathers, held in the US on the fourth Thursday in November and in Canada on the second Monday in October.

that

> ℹ when is it right to use **that** and when should you use **which**? When introducing clauses that define or identify something, it is acceptable to use **that** or **which**: *a book which aims to simplify scientific language* or *a book that aims to simplify scientific language*. You should use **which**, but never **that**, to introduce a clause giving additional information: *the book, which costs £15, has sold over a million copies* not *the book, that costs £15, has sold over a million copies*.

thatch »*noun* ❶ a roof covering of straw, reeds, or similar material. ❷ (in informal English) the hair on a person's head.
»*verb* (thatches, thatching, thatched) cover a roof with thatch.
thatcher

Thatcherism »*noun* the political and economic policies advocated by the British Conservative politician Margaret Thatcher, Prime Minister 1979–90.
Thatcherite

thatches
thatching

thaw »*verb* (thaws, thawing, thawed) ❶ make or become liquid or soft after being frozen. ❷ make or become friendlier.
»*noun* ❶ a period of warmer weather that thaws ice and snow. ❷ an increase in friendliness.

the

theatre

> ✓ tre not ter: theatre (the spelling theater is American)

theatrical »*adjective* ❶ having to do with acting, actors, or the theatre. ❷ exaggerated and excessively dramatic.
theatricality
theatrically

theatricals »*plural noun* theatrical performances or behaviour.

theatrics »*plural noun* theatricals.

thee »*pronoun* (an old word) you (as the singular object of a verb or preposition).

theft

their [belonging to them]

> ℹ do not confuse **their** and **there**. **Their** means 'belonging to them' (as in *I went round to their house*) while **there** means 'in, at, or to that place' (as in *it will take an hour to get there*).
> For an explanation of the use of **their** in the singular to mean 'his or her', see the note at **THEY**.

theirs [something belonging to them]

> ✓ no apostrophe: theirs. Do not confuse theirs with there's, the shortened form of *there is* or *there has*.

theism »*noun* belief in the existence of a creator who intervenes in the universe.
– SAY thee-i-z'm
theist
theistic

them

> ℹ for an explanation of the use of **them** in the singular to mean 'his or her', see the note at **THEY**

thematic »*adjective* arranged by subject or having to do with a subject.
thematically

theme

themselves

> ℹ the standard reflexive pronoun (word such as 'myself' or 'herself') corresponding to **they** and **them** is **themselves**, as in *they can do it themselves*. The singular form **themself** has been used recently to correspond to the singular use of **they** when referring to a

person whose sex is not specified, as in *helping someone to help themself.* However, **themself** is not good English, and you should use **themselves** instead.

then

thence »*adverb* ❶ from a place or source previously mentioned. ❷ as a consequence.

> ℹ **thence** means 'from that place', as in *he travelled across France to Spain and thence to England.* Strictly speaking, **from** is not needed before **thence**, but nevertheless **from thence** is usually accepted as good English, as in *they proceeded from thence to Scotland.*

thenceforth »*adverb* from that time, place, or point onward.

thenceforward »*adverb* thenceforth.

theocracy »*noun* (plural **theocracies**) a system of government in which priests rule in the name of God or a god.
– say thi-**ok**-ruh-si
theocratic

theodolite »*noun* an instrument with a rotating telescope used in surveying for measuring horizontal and vertical angles.
– say thi-**od**-uh-lyt

theologian »*noun* a person expert in or studying theology.
– say thi-uh-**loh**-juhn

theology »*noun* (plural **theologies**) ❶ the study of God and religious belief. ❷ a system of religious beliefs and theory: *Christian theology.*
theological
theologically
theologist

theorem »*noun* ❶ (in physics & mathematics) a general proposition or rule that can be proved by reasoning. ❷ (in mathematics) a rule expressed by symbols or formulae.
– say **theer**-uhm

theoretical »*adjective* ❶ concerned with the theory of a subject rather than its practical application. ❷ based on theory rather than experience or practice: *British players have a theoretical advantage.*
theoretically

theoretician »*noun* a person who develops or studies the theory of a subject.
– say theer-uh-**ti**-sh'hn

theories

theorise another way of spelling **THEORIZE**.

theorist »*noun* a theoretician.

theorize »*verb* (**theorizes**, **theorizing**, **theorized**) form a theory or theories about something.

> ✓ many people prefer the alternative spellings **theorise**, **theorises**, etc.: both **s** and **z** spellings are correct

theory »*noun* (plural **theories**) ❶ an idea or set of ideas that is intended to explain something. ❷ a set of principles on which an activity is based: *a theory of education.*

> ✓ plural: drop the **y** and add **ies**: **theories**

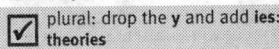

theosophy »*noun* a philosophy which believes that a knowledge of God may be achieved through such things as intuition, meditation, and prayer.
– say thi-**oss**-uh-fi
theosophical

therapeutic »*adjective* ❶ relating to the healing of disease. ❷ having a good effect on the body or mind.
– say the-ruh-**pyoo**-tik
therapeutically

> ✓ **peu** not **pu** in the middle: **therapeutic**

therapy »*noun* (plural **therapies**) ❶ treatment intended to relieve or heal a physical disorder or illness. ❷ the treatment of mental disorders or problems using psychological methods.
therapist

> ✓ plural: drop the **y** and add **ies**: **therapies**

there [in, at, or to that place]

> ℹ do not confuse **there** and **their**. **There** means 'in, at, or to that place' (as in *it will take an hour to get there*), while **their** means 'belonging to them' (as in *I went round to their house*). Do not confuse **there** and **they're**, the shortened form of *they are.*

thereabout

thereabouts

thereafter

thereat »*adverb* (an old word) ❶ at that place. ❷ on account of or after that.

thereby

therefore

therein »*adverb* (an old word) in that place, document, or respect.

thereof »*adverb* of the thing just mentioned.

thereon »*adverb* on or following from the thing just mentioned.

there's [there is; there has]

thereto »*adverb* (an old word) to that or that place.

thereupon »*adverb* immediately or shortly after that.

therewith »*adverb* (an old word) ❶ with or in the thing mentioned. ❷ soon or immediately after that.

thermal »*adjective* ❶ relating to heat. ❷ (of a garment) made of a fabric that keeps the body warm by stopping heat from escaping.
» *noun* ❶ an upward current of warm air, used by birds, gliders, and balloonists to gain height. ❷ (**thermals**) thermal underwear.
thermally

thermal imaging »*noun* the technique of using the heat given off by an object to produce an image of it or locate it.

thermionic valve »*noun* a vacuum tube in which a flow of electrons is produced from a hot electrode, used in rectifying a current and in radio reception.
– SAY ther-mi-**on**-ik

thermocouple »*noun* a device for measuring or sensing a temperature difference, consisting of two wires of different metals connected at two points, between which a voltage is developed in proportion to any temperature difference.

thermodynamics »*noun* the branch of science concerned with the relations between heat and other forms of energy involved in physical and chemical processes.
thermodynamic
thermodynamically

thermoelectric »*adjective* producing electricity by a difference of temperatures.

thermometer »*noun* an instrument for measuring temperature, typically consisting of a glass tube containing mercury or alcohol which expands when heated.

thermonuclear »*adjective* relating to or using nuclear fusion reactions that occur at very high temperatures.

thermopile »*noun* a set of thermocouples arranged for measuring small quantities of heat transmitted by radiation.
– SAY ther-moh-pyl

thermoplastic »*adjective* (of a substance) becoming plastic when heated.

thermoregulation »*noun* the regulation of bodily temperature.

Thermos »*noun* (trademark) a vacuum flask.

ℹ **Thermos** is a Greek word meaning 'hot'

thermosetting »*adjective* (of a substance) setting permanently when heated.

thermosphere »*noun* the upper region of the atmosphere above the mesosphere.

thermostat »*noun* a device that automatically regulates temperature or activates a device at a set temperature.
– SAY ther-muh-stat
thermostatic
thermostatically

thesaurus »*noun* (plural **thesauri** or **thesauruses**) a book containing lists of words which have the same, similar, or a related meaning.
– SAY thi-**saw**-ruhss [singular], thi-**saw**-ry [plural]

✓ the plural of **thesaurus** can be **thesauri** (as in Latin) or **thesauruses**

these plural of THIS.

thesis »*noun* (plural **theses**) ❶ a statement or theory put forward to be supported or proved. ❷ a long piece of written work involving personal research, written as part of a university degree.
– SAY **thee**-siss [singular], **thee**-seez [plural]

✓ make the plural by changing the **-is** ending to **-es** (as in Latin): **theses**

thespian »*adjective* relating to drama and the theatre.
» *noun* an actor or actress.
– SAY **thess**-pi-uhn

theta »*noun* the eighth letter of the Greek alphabet (Θ, θ).
– SAY **thee**-tuh

they

ℹ many people now think that the traditional use of **he** to refer to a person of either sex is outdated and sexist; the alternative, **he or she**, is rather clumsy. For this reason, **they** (with its counterparts **them** or **their**) has become acceptable instead, as in *anyone can join if they are a resident* and *each to their own*.

they'd [they had; they would]
they'll [they shall; they will]
they're [they are]
they've [they have]
thick (adjective: **thicker**, **thickest**)
thickly
thicken (verb: **thickens**, **thickening**, **thickened**)
thickener
thicker

thickest

thicket »*noun* a dense group of bushes or trees.

thickly

thickness (plural **thicknesses**)

thickset »*adjective* heavily or solidly built.

thief (plural **thieves**)

> ☑ remember, the usual rule is **i** before **e** except after **c**: **thief**

thieve (verb: **thieves**, **thieving**, **thieved**)
  thievery
  thievish

thieves

thieving

thievish

thigh

thigh bone »*noun* the femur.

thimble

thimbleful »*noun* a small quantity of something.

thin (adjective: **thinner**, **thinnest**; verb: **thins**, **thinning**, **thinned**)
  thinly
  thinness

> ☑ double the **n** in **thinning**, **thinned**, **thinner**, **thinnest**, and **thinness**

thine [belonging to thee]

thing

thingamabob

thingamajig

thingamy another way of spelling THINGUMMY.

thingies

thingummy (plural **thingummies**)

> ☑ **thingummy** can also be spelled **thingamy**

thingy (plural **thingies**)

think (verb: **thinks**, **thinking**, **thought**)
  thinker
  thinking

think tank »*noun* a body of experts providing advice and ideas on specific political or economic problems.

thinly

thinned

thinner

thinness

thinnest

thinning

thins

third
  thirdly

third-class

third-degree »*adjective* (of burns) of the most severe kind, affecting tissue below the skin.

» *noun* (**the third degree**) long and harsh questioning to obtain information or a confession.

thirdly

third party »*noun* a person or group besides the two main ones involved in a situation or dispute.

» *adjective* (**third-party**) (of insurance) covering damage or injury suffered by a person other than the insured.

third person »*noun* ❶ a third party. ❷ the form of a pronoun or verb used to refer to a third party (e.g. *he*, *she*, *they*).

third-rate »*adjective* of very poor quality.

Third Reich »*noun* the Nazi regime in Germany, 1933–45.

– SAY rykh

> ℹ **Reich** means 'empire' in German

third way »*noun* a political agenda which is moderate and based on general agreement rather than left- or right-wing.

Third World »*noun* the developing countries of Asia, Africa, and Latin America.

> ℹ originally called 'Third' in contrast to the capitalist and Communist blocs

thirst (verb: **thirsts**, **thirsting**, **thirsted**)

thirsty (adjective: **thirstier**, **thirstiest**)
  thirstily
  thirstiness

thirteen
  thirteenth

thirty (plural **thirties**)
  thirtieth

> ☑ plural: drop the **y** and add **ies**: **thirties**

this (plural **these**)

thistle

thistledown »*noun* the light fluffy down of thistle seeds, which enable them to be blown about in the wind.

thither »*adverb* (an old word) to or towards that place.

tho' »*conjunction & adverb* informal spelling of THOUGH.

thole »*noun* a pin fitted to the gunwale of a rowing boat, forming the point on which an oar turns.

– SAY thohl

thong »*noun* ❶ a narrow strip of leather or other material, used as a fastening or as the lash of a whip. ❷ a skimpy bathing garment or pair of knickers like a G-string.

thorax »*noun* (plural **thoraces** or **thoraxes**) ❶ the part of the body between the neck and the abdomen. ❷ the middle section of the body of an insect, bearing the legs and wings.
– **say** thor-aks [singular], thor-uh-seez [plural]
thoracic

> ✓ the plural of **thorax** can be **thoraces** (as in Latin) or **thoraxes**

thorium »*noun* a white radioactive metallic chemical element.
– **say** thor-i-uhm

thorn

thorny (adjective: **thornier**, **thorniest**)

thorough [complete with regard to every detail]
thoroughly
thoroughness

> ℹ do not confuse **thorough** with **through**, which means 'in one side and out the other side of something'

thoroughbred »*adjective* ❶ of pure breed. ❷ of outstanding quality.
»*noun* a thoroughbred animal.

thoroughfare »*noun* a road or path forming a route between two places.

thoroughgoing »*adjective* ❶ involving or dealing with every detail or aspect. ❷ complete; absolute.

thoroughly

thoroughness

those

thou[1] »*pronoun* (an old word) you (as the singular subject of a verb).

thou[2] »*noun* (plural **thou** or **thous**) ❶ (in informal English) a thousand. ❷ one thousandth of an inch.

though

thought

thoughtful
thoughtfully
thoughtfulness

> ✓ -ful not -full: thoughtful

thoughtless
thoughtlessly
thoughtlessness

thousand
thousandfold
thousandth

thrall »*noun* the state of being in another's power: *she was in thrall to her husband.*

thrash (verb: **thrashes**, **thrashing**, **thrashed**)
thrasher

thread (verb: **threads**, **threading**, **threaded**)
threader

threadbare »*adjective* thin and tattered with age.

threaded

threader

threading

threads

threadworm »*noun* a thin, thread-like worm, living as a parasite.

threat

threaten (verb: **threatens**, **threatening**, **threatened**)

three
threefold

three-dimensional »*adjective* having or appearing to have length, breadth, and depth.

threefold

three-line whip »*noun* (in the UK) a written notice, underlined three times to stress its urgency, to members of a political party to attend a vote in parliament.

threepence »*noun* the sum of three pence, especially before decimalization (1971).
– **say** threp-uhnss or thruu-puhnss

threepenny bit »*noun* (a historical term) a coin worth three old pence (1¼ p).
– **say** thri-puh-ni or thruu-puh-ni

three-piece

three-point turn »*noun* a method of turning a vehicle round in a narrow space by moving forwards, backwards, and forwards again in a sequence of arcs.

three-quarter

threescore »*cardinal number* (a poetic term) sixty.

threesome

threnody »*noun* (plural **threnodies**) a song, piece of music, or poem expressing grief or regret.
– **say** thren-uh-di

thresh »*verb* (**threshes**, **threshing**, **threshed**) separate grain from corn or other crops.
thresher

threshold »*noun* ❶ a strip of wood or stone forming the bottom of a doorway. ❷ a level or point at which something is about to begin: *she was on the threshold of a dazzling career.*

 there is only one **h** in the middle: **threshold**

threw past of **THROW**.

thrice »*adverb* (an old word) **❶** three times. **❷** extremely; very: *I was thrice blessed.*

thrift »*noun* **❶** carefulness and economy in the use of money and other resources. **❷** a plant with tufts of slender leaves and rounded pink flower heads, found on sea cliffs and mountains.

thriftier

thriftiest

thriftily

thriftless »*adjective* spending money in an extravagant and wasteful way.

thrifty »*adjective* (**thriftier, thriftiest**) careful and economical with money. **thriftily**

thrill (verb: **thrills, thrilling, thrilled**)

thriller »*noun* a novel, play, or film with an exciting plot, typically involving crime or spying.

thrilling

thrills

thrips »*noun* (plural **thrips**) a tiny black insect which sucks plant sap, noted for swarming on warm still summer days.

thrive »*verb* (**thrives, thriving, thrived** or **throve**; past participle **thrived** or **thriven**) **❶** grow or develop well or vigorously. **❷** prosper; flourish.

throat

throaty »*adjective* (**throatier, throatiest**) (of a voice or other sound) deep and husky. **throatily**
throatiness

throb (verb: **throbs, throbbing, throbbed**)

 double the **b** in **throbbing** and **throbbed**

throes »*plural noun* severe or violent pain and struggle.
– **SAY** throhz

 oes not **ows: throes**

thrombosis »*noun* (plural **thromboses**) the formation of a blood clot in a part of the circulatory system.
– **SAY** throm-**boh**-siss [singular], throm-**boh**-seez [plural]

 make the plural by changing the **-is** ending to **-es** (as in Latin): **thromboses**

throne

throng »*noun* a large, densely packed crowd.
» *verb* (**throngs, thronging, thronged**) gather in large numbers in a place.

throttle »*noun* a device controlling the flow of fuel or power to an engine.
» *verb* (**throttles, throttling, throttled**) **❶** attack or kill someone by choking or strangling them. **❷** control an engine or vehicle with a throttle.

 double **t** in the middle: **throttle**

through [moving in one side and out of the other side of something]

 do not confuse **through** with **thorough**, which means 'complete with regard to every detail'

throughout

throughput »*noun* the amount of material or items passing through a system or process.

throve past of **THRIVE**.

throw (verb: **throws, throwing, threw**; past participle **thrown**)

throwaway

throwback »*noun* a return to an earlier ancestral type or characteristic.

thrower

throw-in

throwing

thrown past participle of **THROW**.

throws

thru informal American spelling of **THROUGH**.

thrum »*verb* (**thrums, thrumming, thrummed**) make a continuous rhythmic humming sound.
» *noun* a continuous rhythmic humming sound.

 double the **m** in **thrumming** and **thrummed**

thrush »*noun* **❶** a songbird with a brown back and spotted breast. **❷** infection of the mouth and throat or the genitals by a yeast-like fungus.

thrust (verb: **thrusts, thrusting, thrust**)
thruster

thrusting »*adjective* aggressively ambitious.

thrusts

thud (verb: **thuds, thudding, thudded**)

 double the **d** in **thudding** and **thudded**

thug
   thuggery
   thuggish

thulium »*noun* a soft silvery-white metallic chemical element.
   – sᴀʏ thyoo-li-uhm

thumb (verb: **thumbs, thumbing, thumbed**)

> ☑ don't forget the **b**, which is not pronounced: **thumb**

thumbnail »*adjective* brief or concise: *a thumbnail sketch*.

thumbprint

thumbs

thumbscrew »*noun* an instrument of torture that crushes the thumbs.

thump (verb: **thumps, thumping, thumped**)
   thumper
   thumping

thunder (verb: **thunders, thundering, thundered**)
   thundery

thunderbolt »*noun* a flash of lightning with a crash of thunder at the same time.

thunderclap »*noun* a crash of thunder.

thundercloud »*noun* a cloud with a towering or spreading top, charged with electricity and producing thunder and lightning.

thundered

thunderflash »*noun* a noisy but harmless pyrotechnic device used especially in military exercises.

thundering

thunderous »*adjective* ❶ very loud. ❷ (of a person's expression) very angry or threatening.
   thunderously

thunders

thunderstorm

thunderstruck »*adjective* extremely surprised or shocked.

thundery

thurible »*noun* a container in which incense is burnt; a censer.
   – sᴀʏ thyoor-ib-uhl

Thursday

thus

thwack (verb: **thwacks, thwacking, thwacked**)

thwart »*verb* (**thwarts, thwarting, thwarted**) prevent someone from succeeding in or accomplishing something.
   – sᴀʏ thwort

thy »*possessive determiner* (an old word) your.

thyme »*noun* a low-growing plant of the mint family, used as a herb in cooking.
   – sᴀʏ *rhymes with* time

thymus »*noun* a gland in the neck which produces white blood cells for the immune system.
   – sᴀʏ thy-muhss

> ℹ the plural is either **thymus glands** or the Latin form **thymi** (sᴀʏ thy-my)

thyroid »*noun* a large gland in the neck which produces hormones regulating growth and development.
   – sᴀʏ thy-royd

thyself »*pronoun* (an old word) yourself.

tiara »*noun* a jewelled ornamental band worn above the forehead.

Tibetan [of Tibet]

tibia »*noun* (plural **tibiae**) the inner of the two bones between the knee and the ankle, parallel to the fibula.
   – sᴀʏ ti-bi-uh [singular], ti-bi-ee [plural]

> ☑ add an **e** to make the plural (as in the original Latin): **tibiae**

tic »*noun* a recurring spasm in the muscles of the face.

> ☑ no **k** at the end: **tic**

tich another way of spelling **ᴛɪᴛᴄʜ**.

tick (verb: **ticks, ticking, ticked**)

ticker »*noun* (in informal English) ❶ a watch. ❷ a person's heart.

ticker tape »*noun* a paper strip on which information is recorded in a machine.

ticket

ticking »*noun* a hard-wearing material used to cover mattresses.

tickle (verb: **tickles, tickling, tickled**)
   tickler
   ticklish
   tickly

ticks

tidal »*adjective* relating to or affected by tides.
   tidally

tidal wave »*noun* an exceptionally large ocean wave, caused by an earthquake, storm, etc.

tidbit American spelling of **ᴛɪᴛʙɪᴛ**.

tiddler »*noun* (in informal English) ❶ a small fish. ❷ a young or unusually small person or thing.

tiddly »*adjective* (**tiddlier, tiddliest**) (in informal English) ❶ slightly drunk. ❷ little; tiny.

tiddlywinks

tide (verb: **tides, tiding, tided**)

tideline »*noun* a line made by the sea on a beach at the highest point of a tide.

tidemark »*noun* a dirty mark left around the inside of a bath at the level reached by the water.

tides

tidewater »*noun* water brought or affected by tides.

tideway »*noun* a channel in which a tide runs.

tidied

tidier

tidies

tidiest

tidily

tidiness

tiding

tidings »*plural noun* (a poetic term) news; information.

tidy (adjective: **tidier, tidiest**; plural **tidies**; verb: **tidies, tidying, tidied**)
   tidily
   tidiness

✓ drop the **y** and add **ier** or **iest** to spell **tidier** or **tidiest**

tie (verb: **ties, tying, tied**; plural **ties**)

tie-break

tie-breaker

tied »*adjective* ❶ (of accommodation) rented by someone on condition that they work for its owner. ❷ (of a public house) owned and controlled by a brewery.

tie-dye »*noun* a method of producing textile patterns by tying parts of the fabric to shield it from the dye.

tie-in

tiepin

tier »*noun* one of a series of rows or levels placed one above and behind the other.
– **say** *rhymes with* rear
   tiered

ties

tie-up

tiff »*noun* (in informal English) a trivial quarrel.

tig

tiger

tiger lily »*noun* a tall Asian lily which has orange flowers spotted with black or purple.

tiger moth »*noun* a moth with boldly spotted and streaked wings.

tight (adjective: **tighter, tightest**)
   tightly
   tightness

tighten (verb: **tightens, tightening, tightened**)

tighter

tightest

tight-fisted

tight-knit »*adjective* (of a group of people) bound together by strong relationships and common interests.

tight-lipped

tightly

tightly knit »*adjective* = TIGHT-KNIT.

tightness

tightrope

tights

tigress (plural **tigresses**)

tikka »*noun* an Indian dish of small pieces of meat or vegetables marinated in a spice mixture.

 double **k**: **tikka** (a Punjabi word)

tilde »*noun* an accent (˜) placed over Spanish *n* or Portuguese *a* or *o* to change the way they are pronounced.
– **say** til-duh

tile (verb: **tiles, tiling, tiled**)
   tiler
   tiling

till[1] [until]

till[2] [cash register]

till[3] »*verb* (**tills, tilling, tilled**) prepare land for growing crops.
   tillage

tillage

tilled

tiller »*noun* a horizontal bar fitted to the head of a boat's rudder post and used for steering.

tilling

tills

tilt (verb: **tilts, tilting, tilted**)

tilth »*noun* ❶ cultivation of land. ❷ the condition of tilled soil.

tilting

tilts

timber [wood]
   timbered

timbre »*noun* the character of a musical sound or voice as distinct from its pitch and strength.
– **say** tam-ber

bre not **ber**: **timbre** (**timber** refers to wood prepared for use in building and carpentry)

time (verb: **times, timing, timed**)

time-and-motion study »*noun* a study of the efficiency of a company's working methods.

timed

time frame »*noun* a specified period of time.

time-honoured »*adjective* (of a custom or tradition) respected or valued because it has existed for a long time.

timekeeper
timekeeping

time-lapse »*adjective* (of a photographic technique) taking a sequence of frames at set intervals to record changes that take place slowly over time.

timeless »*adjective* not affected by the passage of time or changes in fashion.
timelessly
timelessness

timely »*adjective* done or occurring at a good or appropriate time.
timeliness

timepiece »*noun* an instrument for measuring time; a clock or watch.

timer

times

timescale »*noun* the time allowed for or taken by a process or sequence of events.

time-server »*noun* a person who makes very little effort at work because they are waiting to leave or retire.

timeshare »*noun* an arrangement in which joint owners use a property as a holiday home at different specified times.

time signature »*noun* (in music) an indication of rhythm following a clef.

timetable (verb: **timetables, timetabling, timetabled**)

time warp »*noun* an imaginary distortion of space and time whereby people or objects of one period exist in another.

time-worn »*adjective* impaired or made less striking as a result of age or long use.

timid »*adjective* lacking in courage or confidence.
timidity
timidly

ℹ️ the comparative and superlative are usually **more timid** and **most timid**, not **timider** and **timidest**

timing

timorous »*adjective* lacking in courage or confidence; nervous.
– SAY tim-uh-ruhss
timorously
timorousness

 mor not **mour**: **timorous**

timpani »*plural noun* kettledrums, especially in an orchestra.
– SAY tim-puh-ni
timpanist

☑️ **timpani** can also be spelled **tympani**

tin (verb: **tins, tinning, tinned**)

☑️ double the **n** in **tinning** and **tinned**

tincture »*noun* ❶ a medicine made by dissolving a drug in alcohol. ❷ a slight trace.
– SAY tingk-cher

tinder »*noun* dry material which burns easily, used for lighting a fire.

tinderbox »*noun* (a historical term) a box containing tinder, flint, a steel, and other items for lighting fires.

tine »*noun* a prong or sharp point, especially of a fork.
– SAY *rhymes with* line
tined

tinfoil

ting [clear ringing sound]

tinge »*verb* (**tinges, tinging** or **tingeing, tinged**) ❶ colour something slightly. ❷ give a small amount of a quality to something.
» *noun* a slight trace of a colour or quality.

tingle (verb: **tingles, tingling, tingled**)
tingly

tinier

tiniest

tinily

tininess

tinker »*noun* ❶ a travelling mender of pots, kettles, etc. ❷ (used in a disapproving way) a gypsy or other person living in a travelling community. ❸ an act of tinkering with something.
» *verb* (**tinkers, tinkering, tinkered**) (**tinker with**) try to repair or improve something by making many small changes.
tinkerer

tinkle (verb: **tinkles, tinkling, tinkled**)

tinned

tinniness

tinning

tinnitus »*noun* (in medicine) ringing or
buzzing in the ears.
– sᴀʏ tin-ni-tuhss or ti-ny-tuhss

 double **n** in the middle: **tinnitus**

tinny »*adjective* ❶ having a thin, metallic
sound. ❷ made of thin or poor-quality
metal.

tin-opener

tinplate »*noun* sheet steel or iron coated
with tin.

tinpot »*adjective* (in informal English) of
poor quality; worthless.

tins

tinsel

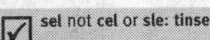 **sel** not **cel** or **sle**: **tinsel**

Tinseltown »*noun* the glamorous but
artificial world of Hollywood and its film
industry.

tinsmith »*noun* a person who makes or
repairs articles of tin or tinplate.

tinsnips »*plural noun* a pair of clippers for
cutting sheet metal.

tint (verb: **tints, tinting, tinted**)

tintinnabulation »*noun* a ringing or
tinkling sound.

tints

tiny (adjective: **tinier, tiniest**)
 tinily
 tininess

 drop the **y** and add **ier** or **iest** to spell
 tinier or **tiniest**

tip (verb: **tips, tipping, tipped**)

 double the **p** in **tipping** and **tipped**

tipi another way of spelling ᴛᴇᴘᴇᴇ.

tip-off

tipped

tipper

tipping

tipple »*verb* (**tipples, tippling, tippled**)
drink alcohol regularly.
 »*noun* (in informal English) an alcoholic
drink.
 tippler

tips

tipsier

tipsiest

tipsily

tipsiness

tipster »*noun* a person who gives tips as to
the likely winner of a race or contest.

tipsy »*adjective* (**tipsier, tipsiest**) slightly
drunk.
 tipsily
 tipsiness

 drop the **y** and add **ier** or **iest** to spell
 tipsier or **tipsiest**

tiptoe (verb: **tiptoes, tiptoeing, tiptoed**)

 do not drop the **e** in **tiptoeing**

tip-top

tirade »*noun* a long speech of angry
criticism.
– sᴀʏ ty-**rayd** or ti-**rayd**

tiramisu »*noun* an Italian dessert
consisting of layers of sponge cake soaked
in coffee and brandy or liqueur, with
powdered chocolate and cheese.
– sᴀʏ ti-ruh-mi-**soo**

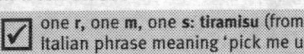 one **r**, one **m**, one **s**: **tiramisu** (from an
Italian phrase meaning 'pick me up')

tire[1] (verb: **tires, tiring, tired**) [make or
become tired]

tire[2] American spelling of ᴛʏʀᴇ.

tired
 tiredly
 tiredness

tireless »*adjective* having or showing great
effort or energy.
 tirelessly
 tirelessness

tires

tiresome »*adjective* causing you to feel
bored or impatient.
 tiresomely
 tiresomeness

tiring

'tis »*contraction* (a poetic term) it is.

tissue »*noun* ❶ one of the distinct types of
material of which animals or plants are
made, consisting of specialized cells and
their products. ❷ a piece of absorbent
paper used as a disposable handkerchief.

tit

Titan »*noun* ❶ one of a family of giant gods
in Greek mythology. ❷ (**titan**) a person
who is very strong or powerful.

titanic »*adjective* of very great strength,
size, or power.

titanium »*noun* a silver-grey metal used in
strong, corrosion-resistant alloys.
– sᴀʏ ti-**tay**-ni-uhm or ty-**tay**-ni-uhm

titbit

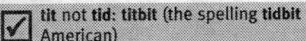 **tit** not **tid**: **titbit** (the spelling **tidbit** is
American)

titch »*noun* (in informal English) a small person.

 titch can also be spelled **tich**

titchy »*adjective* (in informal English) very small.

tithe »*noun* one tenth of what people produced or earned in a year, formerly taken as a tax to support the Church and clergy.
– SAY ty*th*

titillate »*verb* (titillates, titillating, titillated) make someone feel mildly interested or sexually excited.
– SAY ti-til-layt
titillation

i do not confuse **titillate** and **titivate**: titillate means 'excite', whereas titivate means 'adorn or smarten up'

 double l: **titillate**

titivate »*verb* (titivates, titivating, titivated) make something smarter or more attractive.
– SAY ti-ti-vayt
titivation

title (verb: titles, titling, titled)

titled »*adjective* having a title indicating nobility or rank.

title deed »*noun* a legal document giving evidence of a person's right to own a property.

titles

titling

titmouse »*noun* (plural titmice) a small songbird that searches for food among foliage and branches.

titrate »*verb* (titrates, titrating, titrated) (in chemistry) calculate the amount of a substance in a solution by measuring the volume of a standard reagent required to react with it.
– SAY ty-trayt
titration

titter (verb: titters, tittering, tittered)

tittle »*noun* a tiny amount or part of something.

tittle-tattle (verb: tittle-tattles, tittle-tattling, tittle-tattled)

titular »*adjective* ❶ relating to a title. ❷ holding a formal position or title without any real authority.
– SAY tit-yuu-ler
titularly

 ar not er: **titular**

tizz »*noun* (plural tizzes) = TIZZY.

tizzy »*noun* (plural tizzies) (in informal English) a state of nervous excitement or worry.

T-junction »*noun* a road junction at which one road joins another at right angles without crossing it.

TLC »*abbreviation* tender loving care.

TNT »*abbreviation* trinitrotoluene, a high explosive.

to [in the direction of]

i do not confuse **to** with **too** or **two**. To mainly means 'in the direction of' (as in *the next train to London*), while **too** means 'more than is desired, allowed, or possible' (as in *she was driving too fast*). **Two** is the number one less than three (as in *we met two years ago*).

toad »*noun* a tailless amphibian with a short stout body and short legs.

toadied

toadies

toad-in-the-hole »*noun* a dish consisting of sausages baked in batter.

toadstool

toady »*noun* (plural toadies) a person who behaves in an excessively respectful way towards others.
» *verb* (toadies, toadying, toadied) act in an excessively respectful way.

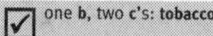 plural: drop the y and add **ies**: **toadies**

to and fro »*adverb* in a constant movement backwards and forwards or from side to side.
toing and froing

toast (verb: toasts, toasting, toasted)

toaster

toastie »*noun* a toasted sandwich or snack.

toasting

toastmaster »*noun* an official responsible for proposing toasts and making formal announcements at a large social event.

toastmistress (plural toastmistresses)

toasts

tobacco (plural tobaccos)

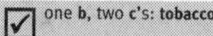 one b, two **c**'s: **tobacco**

tobacconist »*noun* a shopkeeper who sells cigarettes and tobacco.

tobaccos

toboggan »*noun* a light, narrow vehicle on runners, used for sliding downhill over

snow or ice.
tobogganist

> ☑ one **b**, two **g**: **toboggan**

toby jug »*noun* a beer jug or mug in the form of a seated old man wearing a three-cornered hat.

> ℹ said to come from a poem about *Toby Philpot*, a soldier who liked to drink

toccata »*noun* a musical composition for a keyboard instrument designed to show the performer's touch and technique.
– SAY tuh-**kah**-tuh

> ☑ double **c**: **toccata** is an Italian word meaning 'touched'

tocsin »*noun* (an old word) an alarm bell or signal.
– SAY **tok**-sin

tod »*noun* (**on your tod**) (in informal English) on your own.

> ℹ from rhyming slang *Tod Sloan*, an American jockey

today

> ☑ one word, without a hyphen: **today**

toddies

toddle (verb: **toddles, toddling, toddled**)
toddler

toddy »*noun* (plural **toddies**) a drink made of spirits with hot water and sugar.

> ☑ plural: drop the **y** and add **ies**: **toddies**

to-do »*noun* (in informal English) a commotion or fuss.

toe (verb: **toes, toeing, toed**) [digit at the end of the foot; push or touch with the toes]

> ☑ do not confuse **toe** with **tow**, which means 'use a vehicle to pull another along'
> the phrase *toe the line* meaning 'obey authority' contains the word **toe** not **tow**

toecap

toed

toehold »*noun* a small foothold.

toeing

toenail

toes

toff

toffee

> ☑ double **f**, double **e**: **toffee**

toffee-nosed »*adjective* (in informal English) snobbish.

tofu »*noun* curd made from mashed soya beans, used in Asian and vegetarian cookery.
– SAY **toh**-foo

> ℹ **tofu** is a Chinese word meaning 'rotten beans'

tog »*noun* a unit of thermal resistance used to express the insulating properties of clothes and quilts.

toga »*noun* a loose outer garment made of a single piece of cloth, worn by the citizens of ancient Rome.
– SAY **toh**-guh

together
togetherness

togged »*adjective* (**togged up** or **out**) (in informal English) fully dressed for a particular occasion or activity.

toggle »*noun* a narrow piece of wood or plastic attached to a garment, pushed through a loop to act as a fastener.

toggle switch »*noun* an electric switch operated by means of a projecting lever that is moved up and down.

Togolese (plural **Togolese**) [of Togo in West Africa]

togs »*plural noun* (in informal English) clothes.

toil »*verb* (**toils, toiling, toiled**) ❶ work extremely hard or without a rest. ❷ move somewhere slowly and with difficulty.
»*noun* exhausting work.
toiler

toilet

toiletries

toilet-train (verb: **toilet-trains, toilet-training, toilet-trained**)

toilet water »*noun* a diluted form of perfume.

toiling

toils

toilsome »*adjective* (an old word) involving hard work.

toing and froing

token

tokenism »*noun* the fact of doing something in an insincere way, so as to be seen to be obeying the law or satisfying a particular group of people.
tokenistic

told past and past participle of **TELL**.

tolerable »*adjective* ❶ able to be tolerated. ❷ fairly good.
tolerably

tolerance »*noun* ❶ the ability to accept things you dislike or disagree with. ❷ an allowable amount of variation in the dimensions of a machine or part.

 ance not ence: tolerance

tolerant »*adjective* ❶ showing tolerance. ❷ able to endure specified conditions or treatment: *rye is tolerant of drought.*
tolerantly

 single l, and ant not ent: tolerant

tolerate »*verb* (**tolerates, tolerating, tolerated**) ❶ allow something that you dislike or disagree with to exist or happen. ❷ patiently accept something unpleasant. ❸ able to be exposed to a drug, etc. without being harmed.
toleration

toll[1] »*noun* ❶ a charge payable to use a bridge or road or (in American English) for a long-distance telephone call. ❷ the number of deaths or casualties arising from an accident, disaster, etc. ❸ the cost or damage resulting from something.
– **SAY** tohl

toll[2] »*verb* (**tolls, tolling, tolled**) ❶ (of a bell) sound with a slow, even series of strokes. ❷ announce the time, a service, or a person's death in this way.
»*noun* a single ring of a bell.
– **SAY** tohl

tollbooth »*noun* a roadside kiosk where tolls are paid.

tolled

tolling

tolls

tom »*noun* the male of various animals, especially a domestic cat.

tomahawk »*noun* a light axe formerly used as a tool or weapon by American Indians.

 single m: tomahawk

tomato (plural **tomatoes**)

there is no **e** on the end in the singular, but the plural has **oes** not **os**: tomato and tomatoes

tomb

tombola »*noun* a game in which tickets are drawn from a revolving drum to win prizes.

tomboy »*noun* a girl who enjoys rough, noisy activities traditionally associated

with boys.
tomboyish

tombstone

tomcat

Tom, Dick, and Harry »*noun* ordinary people in general.

tome »*noun* (mainly used in a humorous way) a large, serious book.

tomfoolery »*noun* silly behaviour.

Tommy »*noun* (plural **Tommies**) (in informal English) a British private soldier.

from a use of the name *Thomas Atkins* in examples of completed official forms in the British army

tommy gun »*noun* (in informal English) a sub-machine gun.

tomography »*noun* a technique for displaying a cross section through a human body or other solid object using X-rays or ultrasound.
– **SAY** tuh-**mog**-ruh-fi
tomographic

tomorrow

 one **m**, two **r**'s: tomorrow

tom-tom »*noun* a drum beaten with the hands.

ton [unit of weight]

tonal »*adjective* ❶ relating to tone. ❷ (of music) written using traditional keys and harmony.
– **SAY** toh-n'l
tonally

tonality »*noun* (plural **tonalities**) the character of a piece of music as determined by the key in which it is played.

tonally

tone (verb: **tones, toning, toned**)
toneless

tone-deaf »*adjective* unable to notice differences of musical pitch accurately.

toneless

tonepad »*noun* a device generating specific tones to control another device at the other end of a telephone line.

toner »*noun* ❶ a liquid applied to the skin to reduce oiliness and improve its condition. ❷ a powder used in photocopiers.

tones

Tongan [of Tonga]

tongs

tongue (verb: **tongues, tonguing, tongued**)

817

tongue and groove »*noun* wooden boards which are placed next to each other and joined by means of interlocking ridges and hollows down their sides.

tongued

tongue-lashing »*noun* a loud or severe scolding.

tongues

tongue-tied »*adjective* too shy or embarrassed to speak.

tongue-twister »*noun* a sequence of words that are difficult to pronounce quickly.

tonguing

tonic »*noun* ❶ a drink taken as a medicine, to give a feeling of energy or well-being. ❷ something that makes a person feel happier or healthier. ❸ tonic water.

tonic water »*noun* a fizzy soft drink with a bitter flavour, used as a mixer with spirits.

tonight

toning

tonnage »*noun* ❶ weight in tons. ❷ the size or carrying capacity of a ship measured in tons.

tonne »*noun* = METRIC TON.
– SAY tun

tonsil »*noun* one of two small masses of tissue in the throat, on each side of the root of the tongue.

> ☑ single **l**, but double it in **tonsillectomy** and **tonsillitis**

tonsillectomy »*noun* (plural **tonsillectomies**) a surgical operation to remove the tonsils.
– SAY ton-sil-**lek**-tuh-mi

tonsillitis »*noun* inflammation of the tonsils.

tonsorial »*adjective* having to do with hairdressing.
– SAY ton-**sor**-i-uhl

tonsure »*noun* a part of a monk's or priest's head left bare on top by shaving off the hair.

too [more than is desirable, allowed, or possible]

> ℹ for an explanation of the difference between **too**, **to**, and **two**, see the note at **TO**

took past of TAKE.

tool (verb: **tools**, **tooling**, **tooled**)

toolbar »*noun* (in computing) a strip of icons used to perform certain functions.

toolbox (plural **toolboxes**)

tooled

tooling

toolmaker »*noun* a person who makes and repairs tools for use in a manufacturing process.

tools

toot (verb: **toots**, **tooting**, **tooted**)

tooth (plural **teeth**)
toothed
toothless

toothache

toothbrush

toothcomb see the note at **FINE-TOOTH COMB**.

toothed

toothier

toothiest

toothily

toothless

toothpaste

toothpick

toothsome »*adjective* ❶ (of food) temptingly tasty. ❷ attractive.

toothy »*adjective* (**toothier**, **toothiest**) having large noticeable teeth.
toothily

tooting

tootle »*verb* (**tootles**, **tootling**, **tootled**) casually make a series of sounds on a horn, trumpet, etc.

toots

tootsie »*noun* (plural **tootsies**) (in informal English) ❶ a person's foot. ❷ a young woman.

> ☑ **tootsie** can also be spelled **tootsy**

top (verb: **tops**, **topping**, **topped**)
topmost

> ☑ double the **p** in **topping** and **topped**

topaz »*noun* (plural **topazes**) a colourless, yellow, or pale blue precious stone.

> ☑ no **e** at the end of **topaz**

topcoat

top-drawer »*adjective* (in informal English) of the highest quality or social class.

tope »*verb* (**topes**, **toping**, **toped**) (an old word) frequently drink too much alcohol.
toper

topgallant »*noun* ❶ the section of a square-rigged sailing ship's mast immediately above the topmast. ❷ a sail set on such a mast.
– SAY top-**gal**-luhnt or tuh-**gal**-luhnt

top-heavy

topiary »*noun* (plural **topiaries**) ❶ the art of clipping shrubs or trees into attractive shapes. ❷ shrubs or trees clipped in such a way.
– SAY **toh**-pi-uh-ri

 ✓ ary not ery: top**iary**

topic

topical »*adjective* ❶ relating to or dealing with current affairs. ❷ relating to a particular subject.
 topicality
 topically

toping

topknot »*noun* ❶ a knot of hair arranged on the top of the head. ❷ a decorative knot or bow of ribbon worn on the top of the head. ❸ a tuft or crest of hair or feathers on the head of an animal or bird.

topless

topmast »*noun* the second section of a square-rigged sailing ship's mast, immediately above the lower mast.

topmost

top-notch »*adjective* (in informal English) of the highest quality.

topography »*noun* ❶ the arrangement of the physical features of an area. ❷ a detailed description or representation on a map of such features.
– SAY tuh-**pog**-ruh-fi
 topographic
 topographical

topology »*noun* (in mathematics) the study of shapes and their properties which are unaffected by changes in size and other parameters.
– SAY tuh-**pol**-uh-ji
 topological

topped

topping

topple (verb: **topples**, **toppling**, **toppled**)

tops

topsail »*noun* ❶ a sail set on a ship's topmast. ❷ a sail set lengthwise, above the gaff.
– SAY **top**-sayl or **top**-s'l

topside »*noun* the outer side of a round of beef.

topsoil »*noun* the top layer of soil.

topspin »*noun* a fast forward spin given to a moving ball, resulting in a curved path or a strong forward motion on rebounding.

topsy-turvy

tor »*noun* a steep hill or rocky peak.

Torah »*noun* (in Judaism) the law of God as revealed to Moses and recorded in the Pentateuch.
– SAY **tor**-uh or tor-**ah**

 ℹ️ **Torah** is a Hebrew word meaning 'instruction, law'

torch (verb: **torches**, **torching**, **torched**)

torchlight
 torchlit

tore past of TEAR[1].

toreador »*noun* a bullfighter, especially one on horseback.
– SAY to-ri-uh-dor

tori plural of TORUS.

Tories

torment »*noun* ❶ great physical or mental suffering. ❷ a cause of torment.
»*verb* (**torments**, **tormenting**, **tormented**) ❶ make someone suffer greatly. ❷ annoy or tease someone unkindly.
 tormentor

torn past participle of TEAR[1].

tornado »*noun* (plural **tornadoes** or **tornados**) a violently rotating wind storm having the appearance of a funnel-shaped cloud.

 ✓ the plural of **tornado** can have **oes** or **os**: tornad**oes** or tornad**os**

torpedo »*noun* (plural **torpedoes**) a long narrow self-propelled underwater missile fired from a ship, submarine, or an aircraft.
»*verb* (**torpedoes**, **torpedoing**, **torpedoed**) ❶ attack something with a torpedo or torpedoes. ❷ ruin a plan or project.

 ✓ the plural of **torpedo** has **oes** not **os**: torped**oes**

torpid »*adjective* inactive and lacking energy.
 torpidity
 torpidly

torpor »*noun* the state of being inactive and lacking in energy.
– SAY **tor**-per

  ✓ -**por** not -**pour**: tor**por**

torque »*noun* a force that tends to cause rotation.

torque wrench »*noun* a tool for tightening nuts and bolts by a set amount.

torrent »*noun* ❶ a strong and fast-moving stream of water or other liquid. ❷ an overwhelmingly large outpouring: *a torrent of abuse.*

✓ double r, and **ent** not **ant** at the end: **torrent**

torrential »*adjective* (of rain) falling rapidly and heavily.

torrid »*adjective* ❶ very hot and dry. ❷ full of sexual passion. ❸ full of difficulty.
torridly

torsion »*noun* the action of twisting or the state of being twisted.
– SAY tor-sh'n
torsional

torso »*noun* (plural **torsos**) the trunk of the human body.

✓ the plural of **torso** (an Italian word meaning 'stalk, stump') has **os** not **oes: torsos**

tort »*noun* (in law) a wrongful act or a violation of a right (other than under contract) leading to legal liability.

torte »*noun* (plural **torten** or **tortes**) a sweet cake or tart.
– SAY tor-tuh or tort

✓ the plural of **torte** can be **torten** (as in the original German) or **tortes**

tortellini »*noun* stuffed pasta parcels rolled and formed into small rings.
– SAY tor-tuhl-**lee**-ni

✓ two l's, one n: **tortellini** is an Italian word

torten plural of **TORTE**.

tortilla »*noun* ❶ (in Mexican cookery) a thin, flat maize pancake. ❷ (in Spanish cookery) a thick omelette containing potato.
– SAY tor-**tee**-yuh

ℹ **tortilla** is a Spanish word meaning 'little cake'

tortious »*adjective* (in law) constituting a tort; wrongful.
– SAY tor-shuhss

tortoise [reptile]

tortoiseshell »*noun* ❶ the semi-transparent mottled yellow and brown shell of certain turtles, used to make jewellery or ornaments. ❷ a domestic cat with markings resembling tortoiseshell. ❸ a butterfly with mottled orange, yellow, and black markings.

tortuous »*adjective* ❶ full of twists and turns. ❷ excessively lengthy and complex.
tortuosity
tortuously

ℹ do not confuse **tortuous** with **torturous**, which means 'characterized by pain or suffering'

torture (verb: **tortures, torturing, tortured**)
torturer

torturous »*adjective* characterized by pain or suffering.
torturously

ℹ do not confuse **torturous** with **tortuous**, which means 'full of twists and turns'

torus »*noun* (plural **tori** or **toruses**) an object or shape like a ring or doughnut.
– SAY tor-uhss [singular], tor-I [plural]

✓ the plural of **torus** can be either **tori** (as in Latin) or **toruses**

Tory »*noun* (plural **Tories**) a member or supporter of the British Conservative Party.
Toryism

✓ plural: drop the **y** and add **ies: Tories**

tosh »*noun* (in informal English) nonsense.

toss (verb: **tosses, tossing, tossed**)
tosser

toss-up

tot[1] »*noun* ❶ a very young child. ❷ a small drink of spirits.

tot[2] »*verb* (**tots, totting, totted**) (**tot up**) ❶ add up numbers or amounts. ❷ collect up over time.

✓ double the **t** in **totting** and **totted**

total (verb: **totals, totalling, totalled**)
totally

✓ double the **l** in **totalling** and **totalled** (the spellings **totaling** and **totaled** are American)

total eclipse »*noun* an eclipse in which the whole of the disc of the sun or moon is covered.

totalisator another way of spelling **TOTALIZATOR**.

totalitarian »*adjective* (of government) consisting of only one leader or party and having complete power and control.
» *noun* a person in favour of such a system.
– SAY toh-tal-i-**tair**-i-uhn
totalitarianism

totality »*noun* ❶ the whole of something. ❷ the time during which the sun or moon is totally covered during an eclipse.

totalizator »*noun* ❶ a device showing the number and amount of bets staked on a race. ❷ the betting system based on this.

✓ **totalizator** can also be spelled **totalisator**

totalled

totalling

totally

totals

tote[1] »*noun* the system of horse-race betting based on the use of the totalizator, in which winnings are calculated according to the amount staked rather than odds offered.

tote[2] »*verb* (**totes, toting, toted**) carry.

tote bag »*noun* a large bag for carrying a number of items.

toted

totem »*noun* a natural object or animal believed by a particular society to have spiritual meaning and adopted by it as an emblem.
– SAY toh-tuhm
  totemic

totem pole »*noun* a pole on which totems are hung or on which the images of totems are carved.

totes

toting

tots

totted

totter (verb: **totters, tottering, tottered**)

totting

totty »*noun* (in informal English) girls or women regarded as sexually desirable.

toucan »*noun* a tropical American bird with a massive bill and brightly coloured plumage.
– SAY too-kuhn

touch (verb: **touches, touching, touched**)

touch-and-go

touchdown

touche »*exclamation* **❶** (in fencing) used to acknowledge a hit by your opponent. **❷** used to acknowledge a good point made at your expense.
– SAY too-shay

> ✓ **touche** can also be spelled **touché**, with an acute accent above the **e** (as in the original French word meaning 'touched')

touched

touches

touchier

touchiest

touchily

touchiness

touching
  touchingly

touchline

touchpaper »*noun* a strip of paper treated with saltpetre, for setting light to fireworks or gunpowder.

touchstone »*noun* **❶** a piece of stone formerly used for testing alloys of gold by observing the colour of the mark which they made on it. **❷** a standard.

touch-tone »*adjective* (of a telephone) producing different sounds when different numbers are pushed.

touch-type »*verb* (**touch-types, touch-typing, touch-typed**) type using all of your fingers and without looking at the keys.

touchy (adjective: **touchier, touchiest**)
  touchily
  touchiness

touchy-feely »*adjective* openly expressing affection or other emotions.

tough (adjective: **tougher, toughest**)
  toughly
  toughness

toughen (verb: **toughens, toughening, toughened**)

tougher

toughest

toughly

toughness

toupee »*noun* a small wig or hairpiece worn to cover a bald spot.
– SAY too-pay

> ✓ **toupee** can also be spelled **toupée**, with an acute accent on the first **e** (as in the original French)

tour (verb: **tours, touring, toured**)

tour de force »*noun* (plural **tours de force**) a performance or achievement accomplished with great skill.
– SAY toor duh forss [singular and plural]

> ✓ make the plural of **tour de force** (a French phrase meaning 'feat of strength') by adding **s** after **tour** only: **tours de force**

toured

tourer »*noun* a car, caravan, or bicycle designed for touring.

touring

tourism

tourist
  touristy

tourmaline »*noun* a brittle grey or black mineral used as a gemstone and in electrical devices.
– SAY toor-muh-leen

tournament

tour- not **tor-**, and **-nam-** not **-nem-**: **tournament**

tournedos »*noun* (plural **tournedos**) a small round thick cut from a fillet of beef.
– SAY toor-nuh-doh

tourney »*noun* (plural **tourneys**) a medieval joust.
– SAY toor-ni or ter-ni

tourniquet »*noun* a cord or tight bandage which is tied around a limb to stop the flow of blood through an artery.
– SAY toor-ni-kay or tor-ni-kay

 tour- not **tor-** and the ending is **quet**: **tourniquet** (a French word)

tours

tousle »*verb* (**tousles, tousling, tousled**) make someone's hair untidy.

tout »*verb* (**touts, touting, touted**)
❶ attempt to sell something. ❷ attempt to persuade people of the worth of something. ❸ resell a ticket for a popular event at a price higher than the official one.
»*noun* a person who buys up tickets for an event to resell them at a profit.

tow¹ »*verb* (**tows, towing, towed**) use a vehicle or boat to pull another vehicle or boat along.
»*noun* an act of towing.
towable
towage

☑ do not confuse **tow** with **toe**, which refers to a digit on the end of the foot (and note the phrase meaning 'obey authority' is **toe the line** not **tow the line**)

tow² »*noun* short coarse fibres of flax or hemp, used for making yarn etc.

toward
towards
towed

towel (verb: **towels, towelling, towelled**)
towelling

☑ double the **l** in **towelling** and **towelled** (the spellings **toweling** and **toweled** are American)

tower (verb: **towers, towering, towered**)
towering

towing

towline »*noun* a rope, cable, etc., used in towing.

town

town crier »*noun* (a historical term) a person employed to make public announcements in the streets.

townie »*noun* (in informal English) a person who lives in a town.

townscape »*noun* an urban landscape.

townsfolk

township »*noun* (in South Africa) a suburb or city which is mainly occupied by black people.

townspeople

towpath »*noun* a path beside a river or canal, originally used as a pathway for horses towing barges.

tows

toxic »*adjective* ❶ poisonous. ❷ relating to or caused by poison.
toxicity

toxicology »*noun* the branch of science concerned with the nature, effects, and detection of poisons.
– SAY toks-i-kol-uh-ji
toxicological
toxicologist

toxin »*noun* a poison produced by a micro-organism or other organism, to which the body reacts by producing antibodies.

toy (verb: **toys, toying, toyed**)

toy boy »*noun* (in informal English) a male lover who is much younger than his partner.

toyed

toying

toys

toytown

trace (verb: **traces, tracing, traced**)
traceable

trace element »*noun* a chemical element present or required only in tiny amounts.

tracer »*noun* a bullet or shell whose course is made visible by a trail of flames or smoke, used to assist in aiming.

tracery »*noun* (plural **traceries**) ❶ a decorative design of holes and outlines in stone. ❷ a delicate branching pattern.

traces

trachea »*noun* (plural **tracheae** or **tracheas**) the tube carrying air between the larynx and the bronchial tubes; the windpipe.
– SAY truh-kee-uh or tray-ki-uh [singular], truh-kee-ee or tray-ki-ee [plural]

☑ the plural of **trachea** can be either **tracheae** (as in Latin) or **tracheas**

tracheotomy »*noun* (plural **tracheotomies**) a surgical incision in the windpipe, made to enable someone to breathe when the windpipe is blocked.
– SAY tra-ki-ot-uh-mi

☑ a **tracheotomy** is also known as a **tracheostomy** (SAY tra-ki-oss-tuh-mi)

tracing

track (verb: **tracks, tracking, tracked**)
  tracker
  trackless

trackball »*noun* a small ball set in a holder that can be rotated by hand to move a cursor on a computer screen.

trackbed »*noun* the foundation structure on which railway tracks are laid.

tracked

tracker

tracking

trackless

track record »*noun* the past achievements or performance of a person, organization, or product.

tracks

tracksuit

trackway »*noun* a path formed by the repeated treading of people or animals.

tract »*noun* ❶ a large area of land. ❷ a major passage in the body. ❸ a short piece of writing in the form of a pamphlet, typically on a religious subject.

tractable »*adjective* ❶ (of a person) easy to control or influence. ❷ (of a situation or problem) easy to deal with.
  tractability

> ✓ **-able** not **-ible: tractable**

traction »*noun* ❶ the action of pulling a thing along a surface. ❷ the power used for pulling. ❸ a way of treating a broken bone that gradually pulls the bone back into position. ❹ the grip of a tyre on a road or a wheel on a rail.

traction engine »*noun* a steam or diesel-powered road vehicle used for pulling very heavy loads.

tractor

> ✓ **-or** not **-er: tractor**

trad »*adjective* (especially of music) traditional.

trade (verb: **trades, trading, traded**)
  tradable

trade deficit »*noun* the amount by which the cost of a country's imports is more than the value of its exports.

trademark »*noun* ❶ a symbol, word, or words that are chosen to represent a company or product. ❷ a distinctive characteristic.

trade name »*noun* ❶ a name that has the status of a trademark. ❷ a name by which

something is known in a particular trade or profession.

trade-off »*noun* a compromise.

trader

trades

tradescantia »*noun* an American plant with triangular three-petalled flowers.
– **say** trad-i-**skan**-ti-uh

> ℹ named after the English botanist John *Tradescant*

tradesman (plural **tradesmen**)

trades union »*noun* = TRADE UNION.

trade surplus »*noun* the amount by which the value of a country's exports is more than the cost of its imports.

trade union »*noun* an association formed within an industry or particular workplace to protect the rights of workers.
  trade unionism
  trade unionist

> ✓ **trade union** can also be called **trades union**

trade wind »*noun* a wind blowing steadily towards the equator from the north-east in the northern hemisphere or the south-east in the southern hemisphere.

trading

tradition

traditional
  traditionally

traditionalism »*noun* the upholding of tradition, especially so as to resist change.
  traditionalist

traditionally

traduce »*verb* (**traduces, traducing, traduced**) say things about someone that are unpleasant or untrue.
– **say** truh-**dyooss**

traffic (verb: **trafficks, trafficking, trafficked**)
  trafficker

> ✓ add a **k** to spell **trafficking, trafficked,** and **trafficker**

tragedian »*noun* ❶ an actor or actress who plays tragic roles. ❷ a writer of tragedies.
– **say** truh-**jee**-di-uhn

tragedienne »*noun* an actress who plays tragic roles.

tragedy (plural **tragedies**)

> ✓ **ged** not **gid: tragedy**
> plural: drop the **y** and add **ies: tragedies**

tragic
  tragically

tragicomedy »*noun* (plural **tragicomedies**)
a play or novel containing elements of
both comedy and tragedy.
tragicomic

> ✓ plural: drop the **y** and add **ies**:
> **tragicomedies**

trail (verb: **trails, trailing, trailed**)

trailblazer »*noun* ❶ a person who makes a
new track through wild country. ❷ a
person who is the first to do something
new.
trailblazing

trailed

trailer

trailing

trailing edge »*noun* the rear edge of a
moving body, especially an aircraft wing
or propeller blade.

trails

train (verb: **trains, training, trained**)
training
trainload

trainee

trainer

training

trainload

trains

trainspotter
trainspotting

traipse »*verb* (**traipses, traipsing, traipsed**)
walk or move wearily or reluctantly.
»*noun* a tedious or tiring walk.

> ✓ remember the **i**, and the ending is **se**
> not **es**: **traipse**

trait »*noun* a distinguishing quality or
characteristic.
– **SAY** trayt or tray

traitor
traitorous

> ✓ -or not -er: **traitor**

trajectory »*noun* (plural **trajectories**) the
path followed by a moving object.
– **SAY** truh-**jek**-tuh-ri

> ✓ plural: drop the **y** and add **ies**:
> **trajectories**

tram »*noun* a passenger vehicle powered by
electricity and running on rails laid in a
road.

tramcar

tramlines

trammel »*verb* (**trammels, trammelling,
trammelled**) restrict or limit someone's
freedom to move or do something.

> ✓ double the **l** to spell **trammelling** and
> **trammelled** (the spellings **trammeling**
> and **trammeled** are American)

trammels »*plural noun* curbs to someone's
freedom; restrictions.

tramp (verb: **tramps, tramping, tramped**)

trample (verb: **tramples, trampling,
trampled**)

trampoline
trampolining

tramps

tramway

trance »*noun* a half-conscious state in
which someone does not respond to
things happening around them.

tranche »*noun* a portion, especially of
money.
– **SAY** rhymes with branch

tranquil »*adjective* free from disturbance;
calm.
tranquillity
tranquilly

> ✓ single **l** in **tranquil**, but double in
> **tranquillity** and other related words

tranquillize »*verb* (**tranquillizes,
tranquillizing, tranquillized**) give someone
a calming or sedative drug.

> ✓ many people prefer the alternative
> spellings **tranquillise, tranquillises,**
> etc., and **tranquilliser**: both **s** and **z**
> spellings are correct
> double **l**: **tranquillize** (the spelling
> **tranquilize** is American)

tranquillizer »*noun* a medicinal drug
taken to reduce tension or anxiety.

tranquilly

transact »*verb* (**transacts, transacting,
transacted**) conduct or carry out business.

transaction »*noun* ❶ an instance of
buying or selling. ❷ the action of
conducting business.

transacts

transatlantic »*adjective* ❶ crossing the
Atlantic. ❷ concerning countries on both
sides of the Atlantic, especially Britain and
the US. ❸ relating to or situated on the
other side of the Atlantic.

transceiver »*noun* a combined radio
transmitter and receiver.

> ✓ remember the **s** in the middle, and **e**
> before **i** after the **c**: **transceiver**

transcend »*verb* (**transcends, transcending,
transcended**) ❶ be or go beyond the range
or limits of something. ❷ be superior to
another person or thing.

✓ **-scend** not **-send**: transcend

transcendent »*adjective* ❶ going beyond normal or physical human experience. ❷ (of God) existing apart from the material world.
transcendence
transcendently

✓ **ent** not **ant**: transcendent

transcendental »*adjective* going beyond the limits of human knowledge, especially in a religious or spiritual way.
transcendentally

transcendently

transcending

transcends

transcontinental »*adjective* crossing or extending across a continent or continents.

transcribe »*verb* (transcribes, transcribing, transcribed) ❶ put thoughts, speech, or data into written form, or in a different form from the original. ❷ arrange a piece of music for a different instrument or voice.

transcript »*noun* a written or printed copy of material that was originally spoken or presented in another form.

transcription »*noun* ❶ a transcript. ❷ the action or process of transcribing. ❸ a piece of music transcribed for a different instrument or voice.

transducer »*noun* a device that converts variations in a physical quantity (such as pressure or brightness) into an electrical signal, or vice versa.
transduction

transept »*noun* (in a cross-shaped church) one of the two parts forming the arms of the cross, at right angles from the nave.

transfer (verb: transfers, transferring, transferred)
transferable
transferral

✓ double the **r** to spell **transferring**, **transferred**, and **transferral**

transference

✓ **ence** not **ance**: transference

transferral

transferred

transferring

transfers

transfigure »*verb* (be transfigured) be transformed into something more

beautiful or spiritual.
transfiguration

transfix »*verb* (transfixes, transfixing, transfixed) ❶ make someone motionless with horror, wonder, or astonishment. ❷ pierce something with a sharp object.

transform (verb: transforms, transforming, transformed)

transformation
transformational

transformed

transformer »*noun* a device for changing the voltage of an electric current.

transforming

transforms

transfuse »*verb* (transfuses, transfusing, transfused) transfer blood from one person or animal to another.
transfusion

transgenic »*adjective* (in biology) containing genetic material into which DNA from a different organism has been artificially added.

transgress »*verb* (transgresses, transgressing, transgressed) go beyond the limits set by a law or accepted standard.
transgression
transgressive
transgressor

tranship another way of spelling TRANS-SHIP.

transient »*adjective* ❶ lasting only for a short time. ❷ staying or working in a place for a short time only.
» *noun* a transient person.
transience
transiently

✓ **ent** not **ant**: transient

transistor »*noun* ❶ a silicon-based device which is able to amplify or rectify an electric current. ❷ (also **transistor radio**) a portable radio using circuits containing transistors.

✓ **-or** not **-er**: transistor

transit »*noun* ❶ the carrying of people or things from one place to another. ❷ an act of passing through or across a place.

transition »*noun* ❶ the process of changing from one state or condition to another. ❷ a period of such change.
transitional

transitive »*adjective* (of a verb) able to take a direct object, e.g. *saw* in *he saw the donkey*, as opposed to *intransitive*.

transitively
transitivity

transitory »*adjective* lasting only for a short time.
transitorily
transitoriness

 ory not **ery**: transit**ory**

translate »*verb* (translates, translating, translated) **❶** express the sense of words or text in another language. **❷** (translate into) convert or be converted into another form or medium.
translatable

translation

translator

 -or not **-er**: translat**or**

transliterate »*verb* (transliterates, transliterating, transliterated) write or print a letter or word using the corresponding letters of a different alphabet or language.
transliteration

translucent »*adjective* allowing light to pass through partially; semi-transparent.
translucence

 -cent not **-scent**: translu**cent**

transmigration »*noun* the passing of a person's soul after their death into another body.

transmissible

transmission »*noun* **❶** the passing of something from one place or person to another. **❷** a transmitted programme or signal. **❸** the mechanism by which power is passed from an engine to the axle in a motor vehicle.

transmit »*verb* (transmits, transmitting, transmitted) **❶** cause something to pass on from one place or person to another. **❷** broadcast or send out an electrical signal or a radio or television programme. **❸** allow heat, light, etc. to pass through a medium.
transmissible

 double the **t** to spell transmit**t**ing and transmit**t**ed

transmitter »*noun* a device used to produce and transmit electromagnetic waves carrying messages or signals, especially those of radio or television.

transmitting

transmogrify »*verb* (transmogrifies, transmogrifying, transmogrified) change into something else in a surprising or magical manner.
transmogrification

transmute »*verb* (transmutes, transmuting, transmuted) change in form, nature, or substance.
transmutation

transnational »*adjective* extending or operating across national boundaries.
» *noun* a multinational company.

transom »*noun* **❶** the flat surface forming the stern of a boat. **❷** a strengthening crossbar.

transparency »*noun* (plural transparencies) **❶** the condition of being transparent. **❷** a positive transparent photograph printed on plastic or glass, and viewed using a slide projector.

 plural: drop the **y** and add **ies**: transparenc**ies**

transparent »*adjective* **❶** allowing light to pass through so that objects behind can be distinctly seen. **❷** obvious or evident.
transparently

 ent not **ant**: transpar**ent**

transpire »*verb* (transpires, transpiring, transpired) **❶** come to be true. **❷** take place; happen. **❸** (of a plant or leaf) give off water vapour through pores in the surface layer.
transpiration

transplant »*verb* (transplants, transplanting, transplanted) **❶** transfer someone or something to another place or situation. **❷** take living tissue or an organ and put it in another part of the body or in another body.
» *noun* **❶** an operation in which an organ or tissue is transplanted. **❷** a person or thing that has been transplanted.
transplantation

transponder »*noun* a device for receiving a radio signal and automatically transmitting a different signal.

transport (verb: transports, transporting, transported)
transportation
transporter

transportable
transportability

transportation

transported

transporter

transporting

transports

transpose »*verb* (transposes, transposing, transposed) **❶** cause two or more things

to change places with each other. ❷ move something to a different place or context. ❸ write or play music in a different key from the original.
transposable
transposition

transsexual »*noun* a person born with the physical characteristics of one sex who emotionally and psychologically feels that they belong to the opposite sex.

✓ double s: transsexual

trans-ship »*verb* (trans-ships, trans-shipping, trans-shipped) transfer cargo from one ship or other form of transport to another.
trans-shipment

✓ trans-ship can also be spelled tranship, with no hyphen and only one s

transubstantiation »*noun* (in Christian belief) the doctrine that the bread and wine served in the Eucharist become the actual body and blood of Jesus after they have been blessed.

transverse »*adjective* placed or extending across something.
transversely

transvestite »*noun* a person who likes to dress in clothes usually worn by the opposite sex.
transvestism

trap (verb: traps, trapping, trapped)

✓ double the p to spell trapping and trapped

trapdoor

trapeze »*noun* a horizontal bar hanging by two ropes high above the ground, used by acrobats in a circus.

✓ eze, not eeze or ese: trapeze

trapezium »*noun* (plural trapezia or trapeziums) (in geometry) a quadrilateral with one pair of sides parallel.
– say truh-pee-zi-uhm

✓ the plural of trapezium can be either trapezia (as in the original Latin) or trapeziums

trapped

trapper

trapping

trappings »*plural noun* ❶ the signs or objects associated with a particular situation or role: *the trappings of success.* ❷ a horse's ornamental harness.

Trappist »*noun* a monk belonging to an order that takes a vow of silence.

traps

trash (verb: trashes, trashing, trashed)
trashy

trattoria »*noun* an Italian restaurant.
– say trat-tuh-ree-uh

✓ double t in the middle, followed by a single r: trattoria

trauma »*noun* (plural traumas) ❶ a deeply disturbing experience. ❷ (in medicine) physical injury. ❸ emotional shock following a stressful event.
– say traw-muh or trow-muh
traumatic
traumatically

traumatize »*verb* (traumatizes, traumatizing, traumatized) cause someone lasting shock as a result of a disturbing experience or injury.

✓ many people prefer the alternative spellings traumatise, traumatises, etc.: both s and z spellings are correct

travail »*noun* (also travails) (an old word) painful or laborious effort.
– say tra-vayl

travel (verb: travels, travelling, travelled)

✓ double the l to spell travelling and travelled (the spellings traveling and traveled are American)

traveller

✓ double l: traveller (the spelling traveler is American)

traveller's cheque »*noun* a cheque for a fixed amount that can be exchanged for cash in a foreign country.

travelling

travelogue »*noun* a film, book, or illustrated lecture about a person's travels.

✓ logue not log: travelogue

travels

travel-sick
travel-sickness

traverse »*verb* (traverses, traversing, traversed) travel or extend across or through.
– say tra-verss or truh-verss
traversal

travesty »*noun* (plural travesties) an absurd or shocking misrepresentation: *the trial was a travesty of justice.*
» *verb* (travesties, travestying, travestied) represent something in such a way.
– say tra-vi-sti

plural: drop the **y** and add **ies**:
travesties

trawl »*verb* (**trawls, trawling, trawled**)
❶ catch fish with a trawl net or seine.
❷ search through something thoroughly.
» *noun* ❶ an act of trawling. ❷ a large
wide-mouthed fishing net dragged by a
boat along the bottom of the sea or a lake.

trawler »*noun* a fishing boat used for
trawling.

trawling

trawls

tray

treacheries

treacherous
treacherously
treacherousness

 treach not **trech**: **treacherous**

treachery (plural **treacheries**)

treacle »*noun* ❶ molasses. ❷ golden syrup.
treacly

tread (verb: **treads, treading, trod**; past
participle **trodden** or **trod**)

treadle »*noun* a lever which you work with
your foot to operate a machine.

treadmill »*noun* ❶ a large wheel turned by
the weight of people or animals treading
on steps fitted into it, used in the past to
drive machinery. ❷ a device used for
exercise consisting of a continuous moving
belt on which to walk or run. ❸ a job or
situation that is tiring, boring, or
unpleasant.

treads

treason »*noun* the crime of betraying your
country.
treasonable
treasonous

treasure (verb: **treasures, treasuring,
treasured**)

treasurer »*noun* a person appointed to
manage the finances of a society,
company, etc.

treasures

treasure trove »*noun* an item that has
been found hidden and whose owner is
unknown (until 1996 declared to be royal
property).

treasuries

treasuring

treasury »*noun* (plural **treasuries**) ❶ the
funds or revenue of a state, institution, or
society. ❷ (**Treasury**) (in some countries)
the government department responsible

for the overall management of the
economy.

 plural: drop the **y** and add **ies**:
treasuries

treat (verb: **treats, treating, treated**)
treatable

treaties

treating

treatise »*noun* a formal piece of writing on
a particular subject.
– sᴀʏ **tree**-tiss or **tree**-tiz

treatment

treats

treaty »*noun* (plural **treaties**) a formal
agreement between states.

 plural: drop the **y** and add **ies**:
treaties

treble[1] »*adjective* ❶ consisting of three
parts. ❷ multiplied or occurring three
times.
» *pronoun* an amount which is three times
as large as usual.
» *verb* (**trebles, trebling, trebled**) make or
become treble.

treble[2] »*noun* ❶ a high-pitched voice,
especially a boy's singing voice. ❷ the
high-frequency output of a radio or audio
system.

trebled

trebles

trebling

tree
treeless

treecreeper »*noun* a small brown bird
which creeps about on the trunks of trees
to search for insects.

tree fern »*noun* a large palm-like fern with
a trunk-like stem.

treeless

treeline »*noun* the height up a mountain
above which no trees grow.

tree ring »*noun* one of a number of rings
in the cross section of a tree trunk,
representing a single year's growth.

tree surgeon »*noun* a person who treats
old or damaged trees in order to preserve
them.

trefoil »*noun* ❶ a small plant with yellow
flowers and clover-like leaves.
❷ architectural stonework in the form of
three rounded lobes like a clover leaf.
– sᴀʏ **tre**-foyl or **tree**-foyl

trek »*noun* a long difficult journey,
especially one made on foot.

» *verb* (**treks, trekking, trekked**) go on a trek.
trekker

> ☑ the ending is **k**, not **ck**: **trek** (a Dutch word introduced into English from South Africa)
> double the **k** to spell **trekking, trekked**, and **trekker**

trellis »*noun* a framework of bars used as a support for climbing plants.

> ☑ double **l**, and the ending is **-is** not **-iss** or **-ice**: **trellis**

tremble (verb: **trembles, trembling, trembled**)
trembly

tremendous
tremendously

tremolo »*noun* (plural **tremolos**) a wavering effect in singing or playing some musical instruments.

> ☑ **olo** not **elo**: **tremolo**
> the plural of **tremolo** has **os** not **oes**: **tremolos**

tremor »*noun* ❶ a quivering movement that one cannot control. ❷ a slight earthquake. ❸ a sudden feeling of fear or excitement.

> ☑ **-or** not **-our**: **tremor**

tremulous »*adjective* ❶ shaking or quivering slightly. ❷ nervous.
tremulously
tremulousness

trench »*noun* ❶ a long, narrow ditch. ❷ a ditch dug by troops to provide shelter from enemy fire. ❸ a long, deep depression in the ocean bed.

trenchant »*adjective* (of something said or written) expressed strongly and clearly.
– SAY tren-chuhnt
trenchantly

> ☑ **ant** not **ent**: **trenchant**

trench coat »*noun* a belted double-breasted raincoat.

trencher »*noun* (a historical term) a flat piece of wood from which food was served or eaten.

trend

trendier

trendiest

trendily

trendiness

trendsetter

trendy (adjective: **trendier, trendiest**)
trendily
trendiness

trepan »*noun* a saw used by surgeons for making holes in the skull.
» *verb* (**trepans, trepanning, trepanned**) make holes in a person's skull with a trepan.
– SAY tri-**pan**

> ℹ️ **trepan** is mainly a historical term. The modern term for this saw or its action is **trephine** (SAY tri-**fIn** or tri-**feen**).

trephine (verb: **trephines, trephining, trephined**) see the note at **TREPAN**.

trepidation »*noun* a feeling of fear or nervousness about something that may happen.

trespass (verb: **trespasses, trespassing, trespassed**)
trespasser

> ☑ single **s** first but double **s** at the end: **trespass**

tress »*noun* (plural **tresses**) a long lock of hair.

trestle »*noun* a framework made of a horizontal beam supported by two pairs of sloping legs, used in pairs to support a flat surface such as a table top.

trews »*plural noun* (mainly a Scottish word) trousers.
– SAY trooz

triad »*noun* a group or set of three connected people or things.
triadic

triage »*noun* (in a hospital) the assessment of the seriousness of wounds or illnesses to decide the order in which patients should be treated.
– SAY tree-ah*zh* or try-ij

trial (verb: **trials, trialling, trialled**)
triallist

> ☑ double the **l** to spell **trialling** and **trialled** (the spellings **trialing** and **trialed** are American)

triangle

triangular

> ☑ **ar** not **er**: **triangular**

triangulate »*verb* (**triangulates, triangulating, triangulated**) divide an area into triangles in order to survey it.
triangulation

Triassic »*adjective* referring to the geological period from about 245 to 208 million years ago.
– SAY try-**ass**-ik

triathlon »*noun* an athletic contest involving three different events, typically swimming, cycling, and long-distance running.
– **SAY** try-**ath**-lon
  triathlete

tribal »*adjective* having to do with a tribe or tribes.
  tribally

tribalism »*noun* behaviour and attitudes that are based on loyalty to a tribe or other social group.

tribally

tribe

> ℹ️ the word **tribe** can cause offence when used to refer to a community living within a traditional society today, and it is better to use alternative terms such as **people** or **community**

tribesman (plural **tribesmen**)

tribeswoman (plural **tribeswomen**)

tribulation »*noun* ❶ great trouble or suffering. ❷ a cause of this.

tribunal »*noun* ❶ a group of people established to settle certain types of dispute. ❷ a court of justice.
– **SAY** try-**byoo**-nuhl or tri-**byoo**-nuhl

tribune »*noun* (in ancient Rome) an official chosen by the ordinary people to protect their interests.

tributary »*noun* (plural **tributaries**) ❶ a river or stream flowing into a larger river or lake. ❷ (a historical term) a person or state that pays money to another more powerful state or ruler.
– **SAY** **trib**-yuu-tuh-ri

> ✅ plural: drop the **y** and add **ies**: **tributaries**

tribute »*noun* ❶ an act, statement, or gift that is intended to show gratitude, respect, or admiration. ❷ something resulting from and indicating the worth of something else: *his victory was a tribute to his persistence.* ❸ (a historical term) payment made periodically by a state to a more powerful one.

trice »*noun* (**in a trice**) in a moment.

triceps »*noun* (plural **triceps**) the large muscle at the back of the upper arm.
– **SAY** try-**seps**

> ℹ️ the plural of **triceps** is the same as the singular: **triceps**

triceratops »*noun* a large plant-eating dinosaur having a huge head with two large horns, a smaller horn on the snout, and a bony frill above the neck.
– **SAY** try-**se**-ruh-tops

trichology »*noun* the branch of medicine concerned with the hair and scalp.
– **SAY** tri-**kol**-uh-ji
  trichological
  trichologist

> ✅ **chol** not **col** in the middle: **trichology**

trick (verb: **tricks**, **tricking**, **tricked**)
  trickery

trickier

trickiest

trickily

trickiness

tricking

trickle (verb: **trickles**, **trickling**, **trickled**)

tricks

tricksier

tricksiest

trickster »*noun* a person who cheats or deceives people.

tricksy »*adjective* (**tricksier**, **tricksiest**) ❶ clever in an inventive or deceptive way. ❷ playful or mischievous.

tricky (adjective: **trickier**, **trickiest**)
  trickily
  trickiness

tricolour »*noun* a flag with three bands of different colours, especially the French national flag.
– **SAY** tri-**kuh**-ler or **try**-kul-er

> ✅ **-our** not **-or**: **tricolour** (the spelling **tricolor** is American)

tricorne »*noun* a hat with a brim turned up on three sides.
– **SAY** try-**korn**

> ✅ **tricorne** can also be spelled **tricorn**, without the **e**

tricycle

trident »*noun* a three-pronged spear.

tried past and past participle of **TRY**.

triennial »*adjective* lasting for or recurring every three years.
– **SAY** try-**en**-ni-uhl
  triennially

trier »*noun* a person who always makes an effort, however unsuccessful they may be.

> ✅ **trier** is spelled with an **i**, not a **y**

tries

trifle »*noun* ❶ a thing of little value or importance. ❷ a small amount. ❸ a cold dessert of sponge cake and fruit covered with layers of custard, jelly, and cream.

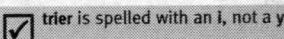

» *verb* (**trifles, trifling, trifled**) (**trifle with**) treat something without seriousness or respect.
trifler

trifling
triflingly

trigger (verb: **triggers, triggering, triggered**)

trigger-happy »*adjective* excessively willing to fire a gun or take other violent action.

triggering

triggers

trigonometry »*noun* the branch of mathematics concerned with the relationships between the sides and angles of triangles and with the functions of angles.
– **say** tri-guh-**nom**-i-tri
trigonometric

trike »*noun* (in informal English) a tricycle.

trilateral »*adjective* ❶ shared by or involving three parties: *trilateral talks*. ❷ (in geometry) on or with three sides.

trilby »*noun* (plural **trilbies**) a soft felt hat with a narrow brim and indented crown.

> ℹ from the heroine of George du Maurier's novel *Trilby*, in the stage version of which such a hat was worn

trilingual »*adjective* ❶ speaking three languages fluently. ❷ written or carried out in three languages.

trill »*noun* a quavering or vibrating sound.
» *verb* (**trills, trilling, trilled**) produce a quavering or warbling sound.

trillion »*cardinal number* ❶ a million million (1,000,000,000,000). ❷ (old-fashioned) a million million million (1,000,000,000,000,000,000).
trillionth

trills

trilobite »*noun* a fossil marine arthropod with a rear part divided into three segments.
– **say** try-loh-byt

trilogy »*noun* (plural **trilogies**) a group of three related novels, plays, or films.

> ✓ plural: drop the **y** and add **ies**: **trilogies**

trim (verb: **trims, trimming, trimmed**; adjective: **trimmer, trimmest**)
trimly
trimmer
trimness

> ✓ double the **m** in **trimming, trimmed, trimmer**, and **trimmest**

trimaran »*noun* a yacht with three hulls side by side.
– **say** try-muh-ran

trimester »*noun* ❶ a period of three months, as a division of the duration of pregnancy. ❷ (in American English) one of the three terms in an academic year.
– **say** try-**mess**-ter

trimly

trimmed

trimmer

trimmest

trimming

trimness

trims

Trinidadian

trinity »*noun* (plural **trinities**) ❶ (**the Trinity**(or **the Holy Trinity**) (in Christian belief) the three persons (Father, Son, and Holy Spirit) that together make up God. ❷ a group of three people or things.

trinket

trio (plural **trios**)

> ✓ the plural of **trio** has **os** not **oes: trios**

triode »*noun* an electrical device with three connections, typically allowing the flow of current in one direction only.
– **say** try-ohd

trioxide

trip (verb: **trips, tripping, tripped**)

> ✓ double the **p** in **tripping** and **tripped**

tripartite »*adjective* ❶ consisting of three parts. ❷ shared by or involving three parties.
– **say** try-**par**-tyt

tripe »*noun* ❶ the stomach of a cow or sheep, used as food. ❷ (in informal English) nonsense; rubbish.

triple (verb: **triples, tripling, tripled**)
triply

triple jump »*noun* an athletic event in which competitors attempt to jump as far as possible by performing a hop, a step, and a jump from a running start.

triples

triplet »*noun* ❶ one of three children or animals born at the same birth. ❷ (in music) a group of three equal notes to be performed in the time of two or four. ❸ a set of three rhyming lines of verse.

triplicate »*adjective* existing in three copies or examples.

» verb (triplicates, triplicating, triplicated)
❶ make three copies of something.
❷ multiply something by three.
  triplication

tripling

triply

tripod »noun a three-legged stand for
  supporting a camera or other apparatus.

tripped

tripper

tripping

trips

triptych »noun ❶ a picture or carving on
  three panels, hinged together vertically
  and used as an altarpiece. ❷ a set of three
  related artistic works.
– **SAY trip**-tik

 ych not ic: triptych

tripwire »noun a wire that is stretched
  close to the ground and sets off a trap,
  explosion, or alarm when disturbed.

trireme »noun an ancient Greek or Roman
  warship with three banks of oars.
– **SAY try**-reem

trisect »verb (trisects, trisecting, trisected)
  divide something into three parts.
– **SAY try**-**sekt**

trite »adjective (triter, tritest) (of a remark
  or idea) unoriginal and dull because of
  overuse.
  tritely
  triteness

triumph (verb: **triumphs, triumphing,
  triumphed**)

triumphal »adjective done or made to
  celebrate a victory.

ℹ️ on the difference between **triumphal**
  and **triumphant**, see the note at
  TRIUMPHANT

triumphalism »noun excessive rejoicing
  over your success or achievements.
  triumphalist

triumphant [victorious; joyful after a
  victory or achievement]
  triumphantly

ℹ️ do not confuse **triumphant** and
  triumphal: **triumphant** means
  'victorious' or 'joyful after a victory or
  achievement' (as in *a triumphant smile*),
  whereas **triumphal** means 'done or made
  to celebrate a victory' (as in *a triumphal
  procession*)

triumphed
triumphing

triumphs

triumvirate »noun ❶ a group of three
  powerful or important people or things.
  ❷ (in ancient Rome) a group of three men
  holding power.
– **SAY** try-**um**-vi-ruht

trivet »noun ❶ a metal stand on which hot
  dishes are placed. ❷ an iron tripod placed
  over a fire for a cooking pot or kettle to
  stand on.

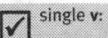 ✓ single **v: trivet**

trivia »plural noun unimportant details or
  pieces of information.
– **SAY tri**-vi-uh

trivial »adjective of little value or
  importance.
  trivially

trivialise another way of spelling **TRIVIALIZE**.

triviality (plural **trivialities**)

✓ plural: drop the **y** and add **ies:
  trivialities**

**trivialize »verb (trivializes, trivializing,
  trivialized)** make something seem less
  important or complex than it really is.
  trivialization

✓ many people prefer the alternative
  spellings **trivialise, trivialises**, etc.,
  and **trivialisation**: both **s** and **z** spellings
  are correct

trivially

trod past and past participle of **TREAD**.

trodden past participle of **TREAD**.

troglodyte »noun a person who lives in a
  cave.
– **SAY trog**-luh-dyt

✓ **dyte** not **dite: troglodyte**

troika »noun ❶ a Russian vehicle pulled by
  a team of three horses side by side. ❷ a
  group of three people working together.
– **SAY troy**-kuh

Trojan »noun an inhabitant of ancient Troy
  in Asia Minor.

Trojan Horse »noun something intended
  to weaken or defeat an enemy secretly.

ℹ️ from the hollow wooden statue of a
  horse in which the ancient Greeks
  are said to have hidden themselves in
  order to enter Troy

troll¹ »noun (in folklore) an ugly giant or
  dwarf that lives in a cave.

troll² »verb (trolls, trolling, trolled) fish by
  trailing a baited line along behind a boat.
  troller

trolley »*noun* (plural **trolleys**) ❶ a large metal basket with wheels, for transporting heavy or bulky items. ❷ a small table on wheels.

> **ey** not simply **y** at the end: **trolley**

trolleybus »*noun* a bus powered by electricity obtained from overhead wires.

trolleys

trolling

trollop »*noun* (old-fashioned) a woman who has many sexual partners.

trolls

trombone »*noun* a large brass wind instrument with a sliding tube which is moved to produce different notes.
trombonist

trompe l'oeil »*noun* (plural **trompe l'oeils**) a method of painting that creates the illusion of a three-dimensional object or space.
– *say* tromp loy [singular and plural]

> **trompe l'oeil**, which is a French phrase meaning 'deceives the eye', is sometimes printed with the **oe** as a ligature (**œ**): **trompe l'œil**

troop (verb: **troops**, **trooping**, **trooped**)

trooper »*noun* ❶ a private soldier in a cavalry or armoured unit. ❷ (in American and Australian English) a mounted police officer. ❸ (in American English) a state police officer.

trooping

troops

troopship

trope »*noun* a figurative or metaphorical use of a word or expression.
– *say* rhymes with rope

trophy (plural **trophies**)

> plural: drop the **y** and add **ies**: **trophies**

tropic »*noun* ❶ the line of latitude 23 degrees 26 minutes north (**tropic of Cancer**) or south (**tropic of Capricorn**) of the equator. ❷ (**the tropics**) the region between the tropics of Cancer and Capricorn.

tropical »*adjective* ❶ having to do with the tropics. ❷ very hot and humid.
tropically

tropism »*noun* (in biology) the turning of all or part of an organism in a particular direction in response to an external stimulus.
– *say* troh-pi-z'm or trop-i-z'm

troposphere »*noun* the lowest region of the atmosphere, extending from the earth's surface to the lower boundary of the stratosphere.
– *say* tro-puh-sfeer or troh-puh-sfeer

trot (verb: **trots**, **trotting**, **trotted**)

> double the **t** in **trotting** and **trotted**

troth »*noun* (**pledge** or **plight your troth**) (an old word) make a solemn promise to marry.
– *say* trohth or troth

trots

Trotskyism »*noun* the political or economic principles of the Russian revolutionary Leon Trotsky, especially the theory that socialism should be established throughout the world by continuing revolution.
Trotskyist
Trotskyite

trotted

trotter

trotting

troubadour »*noun* (in medieval France) a travelling poet who composed and sang in the Provencal language.
– *say* troo-buh-dor

> **-dour** not **-dor**: **troubadour**

trouble (verb: **troubles**, **troubling**, **troubled**)

troublemaker

troubles

troubleshooter »*noun* a person who investigates and solves problems in an organization.
troubleshooting

troublesome
troublesomeness

troubling

troublous »*adjective* (an old word) full of troubles: *troublous times*.

trough »*noun* ❶ a long, narrow open container for animals to eat or drink out of. ❷ a channel used to convey a liquid. ❸ (in weather forecasting) a long region of low pressure. ❹ a point of low activity or achievement.

trounce »*verb* (**trounces**, **trouncing**, **trounced**) defeat someone heavily in a contest.

troupe »*noun* a group of entertainers who tour to different venues.

trouper »*noun* ❶ an entertainer with long experience. ❷ a reliable and uncomplaining person.

t

trouser »*verb* (**trousers, trousering, trousered**) (in informal English) receive or take something for yourself.

trousers
trousered

trousseau »*noun* (plural **trousseaux** or **trousseaus**) the clothes, linen, and other belongings collected by a bride for her marriage.
– **say** troo-soh

 the plural of **trousseau** can be **trousseaux** (as in the original French) or **trousseaus**

trout (plural **trout** or **trouts**)

trove »*noun* a store of valuable or delightful things.

trowel »*noun* ❶ a small hand-held tool with a curved scoop for lifting plants or earth. ❷ a small hand-held tool with a flat, pointed blade, used to apply and spread mortar or plaster.

troy »*noun* a system of weights used for precious metals and gems, based on a pound of 12 ounces.

truant »*noun* a pupil who stays away from school without permission or explanation.
» *adjective* wandering; straying: *her truant husband.*
» *verb* (**truants, truanting, truanted**) (also **play truant**) (of a pupil) stay away from school without permission or explanation.
truancy

truce »*noun* an agreement between enemies to stop fighting for a certain time.

truck
trucker

truculent »*adjective* quick to argue or fight.
– **say** truk-yuu-luhnt
truculence
truculently

 ent not **ant: truculent**

trudge (verb: **trudges, trudging, trudged**)

true (adjective: **truer, truest**)
truly

truffle »*noun* ❶ an underground fungus that resembles a rough-skinned potato, eaten as a delicacy. ❷ a soft chocolate sweet.

trug »*noun* a shallow oblong wooden basket, used for carrying garden flowers, fruit, and vegetables.

truism »*noun* a statement that is obviously true and says nothing new or interesting.

 there is no **e** in **truism**

truly

 there is no **e** in **truly**

trump »*noun* ❶ (in card games) a card of the suit chosen to rank above the others. ❷ a valuable resource that may be used as a surprise to gain an advantage.
» *verb* (**trumps, trumping, trumped**) ❶ play a trump on a card of another suit. ❷ beat someone by saying or doing something better. ❸ (**trump up**) invent a false accusation or excuse.

trumpery »*noun* (plural **trumperies**) (an old word) articles, practices, or beliefs with superficial appeal but little real worth.

trumpet (verb: **trumpets, trumpeting, trumpeted**)
trumpeter

 do not double the second **t** in **trumpeting** and **trumpeted**

trumping
trumps

truncate »*verb* (**truncates, truncating, truncated**) shorten something by cutting off the top or the end.
truncation

truncheon »*noun* a short thick stick carried as a weapon by a police officer.
– **say** trun-chuhn

 -eon not **-en** or **-on: truncheon**

trundle (verb: **trundles, trundling, trundled**)

trunk

trunk call »*noun* (old-fashioned) a long-distance telephone call made within a country.

trunking »*noun* a system of shafts or conduits for cables or ventilation.

trunks

truss »*noun* (plural **trusses**) ❶ a framework of rafters, posts, and bars which supports a roof, bridge, or other structure. ❷ a padded belt worn to support a hernia. ❸ a compact cluster of flowers or fruit growing on one stalk.
» *verb* (**trusses, trussing, trussed**) ❶ support a framework with a truss or trusses. ❷ bind or tie something up tightly. ❸ tie up the wings and legs of a bird before cooking.

trust (verb: **trusts, trusting, trusted**)
trusted

trustee »*noun* a person given legal powers to hold and manage property for the benefit of one or more others.
trusteeship

trustful
  trustfully
  trustfulness

 -ful not -full: trustful

trust fund »*noun* a fund consisting of money or property that is held and managed for another person by a trust.

trusting
  trustingly
  trustingness

trusts

trustworthy
  trustworthiness

trusty »*adjective* (mainly used in a humorous way) reliable or faithful.

truth (plural **truths**)

truthful
  truthfully
  truthfulness

 -ful not -full: truthful

truths

try (verb: **tries, trying, tried**; plural **tries**)

 plural: drop the y and add ies: tries

trying »*adjective* difficult or annoying.

try square »*noun* an implement used to check and mark right angles in building work.

tryst »*noun* (a poetic term) a private, romantic meeting between lovers.
– SAY trist

tsar »*noun* an emperor of Russia before 1917.
– SAY zar or tsar
  tsarist

 tsar is often spelled **czar** in America, especially when used informally to mean 'person with authority'

tsarina »*noun* an empress of Russia before 1917.
– SAY zah-**ree**-nuh or tsah-**ree**-nuh

tsarist

tsetse »*noun* an African bloodsucking fly which transmits sleeping sickness and other diseases.
– SAY tet-si or tset-si

 tset not tet: tsetse (a word from the Setswana language of Southern Africa)

T-shirt

T-shirt can also be spelled tee shirt

T-square »*noun* a T-shaped instrument for drawing or testing right angles.

tsunami »*noun* (plural **tsunami** or **tsunamis**) a tidal wave caused by an earthquake or other disturbance.
– SAY tsoo-**nah**-mi

 tsunami is a Japanese word meaning 'harbour wave'

tub

tuba »*noun* a large low-pitched brass wind instrument.

tubby (adjective: **tubbier, tubbiest**)
  tubbiness

tube

tuber »*noun* ❶ a thick underground part of a stem or root of some plants, e.g. the potato, from which new plants grow. ❷ a thickened fleshy root, e.g. of the dahlia.

tubercle »*noun* ❶ a small lump on a bone or on the surface of an animal or plant. ❷ a small rounded swelling in the lungs or other tissues, characteristic of tuberculosis.
– SAY tyoo-ber-k'l

tubercle bacillus »*noun* the bacterium that causes tuberculosis.

tubercular »*adjective* ❶ relating to or affected with tuberculosis. ❷ having or covered with tubercles.
– SAY tyuu-**ber**-kyuu-ler

tuberculosis »*noun* an infectious disease in which tubercles (small swellings) appear in the tissues, especially the lungs.
– SAY tyuu-ber-kyuu-**loh**-siss

tuberculous »*adjective* = TUBERCULAR.
– SAY tyuu-**ber**-kyuu-luhss

tuberose »*noun* a Mexican plant with heavily scented white waxy flowers and a bulb-like base.
– SAY **tyoo**-buh-rohz

tuberous »*adjective* (of a plant) having or forming a tuber or tubers.
– SAY **tyoo**-buh-ruhss

tubing »*noun* a length or lengths of material in the form of tubes.

tub-thumping »*noun* (in informal English) the expression of opinions in a loud and aggressive way.
  tub-thumper

tubular »*adjective* ❶ long, round, and hollow like a tube. ❷ made from a tube or tubes.

 ar not er: tubular

tubular bells »*plural noun* an orchestral instrument consisting of a row of hanging metal tubes struck with a mallet.

tubule »*noun* a tiny tube.
– say tyoo-byool

TUC »*abbreviation* (in the UK) Trades Union Congress.

tuck (verb: **tucks**, **tucking**, **tucked**)

Tudor »*adjective* relating to the English royal dynasty which held the throne from 1485 to 1603.

Tuesday

tufa »*noun* ❶ a rock composed of calcium carbonate and formed as a deposit from mineral springs. ❷ = **TUFF**.
– say tyoo-fuh

tuff »*noun* rock formed from volcanic ash.

tuffet »*noun* ❶ a tuft or clump. ❷ a footstool or low seat.

tuft
  tufted
  tufty

tug (verb: **tugs**, **tugging**, **tugged**)

> ☑ double the **g** in **tugging** and **tugged**

tuition »*noun* teaching or instruction.

tulip

tulle »*noun* a soft, fine net material, used for making veils and dresses.
– say tyool

> ℹ from *Tulle*, a town in SW France

tumble (verb: **tumbles**, **tumbling**, **tumbled**)

tumbledown »*adjective* (of a building) falling or fallen into ruin.

tumble-dryer

tumbler

tumbles

tumbleweed »*noun* (in American & Australian English) a plant of dry regions which breaks off near the ground in late summer, forming light masses blown about by the wind.

tumbling

tumbril »*noun* (a historical term) an open cart of a kind used to take prisoners to the guillotine during the French Revolution.
– say tum-bril

> ☑ **tumbril** can also be spelled **tumbrel**

tumescent »*adjective* swollen or becoming swollen.
– say tyuu-mess-uhnt
  tumescence

> ☑ -scent not -sent: **tumescent**

tumid »*adjective* (of a part of the body) swollen.
– say tyoo-mid

tummy (plural **tummies**)

> ☑ plural: drop the **y** and add **ies**: **tummies**

tumour »*noun* a swelling of a part of the body caused by an abnormal growth of tissue.

> ☑ remember the **u**: **tumour** (the spelling **tumor** is American)

tumuli plural of **TUMULUS**.

tumult »*noun* ❶ a loud, confused noise. ❷ confusion or disorder.

tumultuous »*adjective* ❶ very loud or uproarious. ❷ excited, confused, or disorderly.
– say tyuu-**mul**-tyuu-uhss
  tumultuously

> ☑ **uous**, not **urous** or just **ous**, at the end: **tumultuous**

tumulus »*noun* (plural **tumuli**) an ancient burial mound.
– say tyoo-myuu-luhss [singular], tyoo-myuu-ly [plural]

> ☑ make the plural by changing the **us** ending to **i** (as in Latin): **tumuli**

tun »*noun* a large beer or wine cask.

> ℹ do not confuse **tun** with **ton** or **tonne** which refer to units of weight

tuna »*noun* (plural **tuna** or **tunas**) a large edible fish of warm seas.

tundra »*noun* a vast, flat, treeless region of Europe, Asia, and North America in which the soil under the surface is permanently frozen.

tune (verb: **tunes**, **tuning**, **tuned**)
  tunable

> ☑ **tunable** is sometimes spelled with an **e**: **tuneable**

tuneful
  tunefully
  tunefulness

> ☑ -ful not -full: **tuneful**

tuneless
  tunelessly
  tunelessness

tuner »*noun* ❶ a person or device that tunes musical instruments. ❷ a part of a stereo system that receives radio signals.

tunes

tungsten »*noun* a hard grey metallic element, used to make electric light filaments.
– SAY tung-stuhn

tunic »*noun* ❶ a loose sleeveless garment reaching to the thigh or knees. ❷ a close-fitting short coat worn as part of a uniform.

tuning

Tunisian

tunnel (verb: **tunnels**, **tunnelling**, **tunnelled**)
tunneller

> ✓ double n, single l: **tunnel**, but double the l in **tunnelling** and **tunnelled** (the spellings **tunneling** and **tunneled** are American)

tunnel vision »*noun* ❶ a condition in which things cannot be seen properly if they are not straight ahead. ❷ (in informal English) the tendency to focus only on a single situation or aspect.

tunny »*noun* (plural **tunny** or **tunnies**) a tuna.

> ✓ plural: drop the y and add **ies**: **tunnies**

tup »*noun* a ram.
»*verb* (**tups**, **tupping**, **tupped**) (of a ram) mate with a ewe.

> ✓ double the p in **tupping** and **tupped**

tuppence »*noun* = TWOPENCE.

tuppenny »*adjective* = TWOPENNY.

tupping

tups

turban »*noun* a long length of material wound round the head by Muslim and Sikh men.
turbaned

> ✓ **turbaned** is sometimes spelled with two n's: **turbanned**

turbid »*adjective* (of a liquid) cloudy or muddy; not clear.
– SAY ter-bid
turbidity

> ℹ do not confuse **turbid** with **turgid**, which means either 'swollen' or 'tediously pompous'

turbine »*noun* a machine in which a wheel or rotor is made to revolve by a fast-moving flow of water, air, gas, or other fluid.

turbo »*noun* (plural **turbos**) = TURBOCHARGER.

turbocharger »*noun* a supercharger driven by a turbine powered by the engine's exhaust gases.
turbocharged

turbofan »*noun* a jet engine in which a turbine-driven fan provides additional thrust.

turbojet »*noun* a jet engine in which the jet gases also operate a turbine-driven device for compressing the air drawn into the engine.

turboprop »*noun* a jet engine in which a turbine is used to drive a propeller.

turbos plural of TURBO.

turbot »*noun* (plural **turbot**) an edible flatfish which has large bony swellings on the body.

turbulence »*noun* ❶ violent or unsteady movement of air or water, or of some other fluid. ❷ conflict or confusion.

turbulent »*adjective* ❶ involving much conflict, disorder, or confusion. ❷ (of air or water) moving unsteadily or violently.
– SAY ter-byuu-luhnt
turbulently

> ✓ ent not ant: **turbulent**

turd

tureen »*noun* a deep covered dish from which soup is served.
– SAY tyuu-reen or tuh-reen

> ✓ one r, two e's: **tureen**

turf »*noun* (plural **turfs** or **turves**) ❶ grass and the surface layer of earth held together by its roots. ❷ a piece of such grass and earth cut from the ground. ❸ (**the turf**) horse racing or racecourses generally. ❹ (in informal English) a person's territory.
»*verb* (**turfs**, **turfing**, **turfed**) ❶ (**turf off** or **out**) (in informal English) force a person to leave somewhere. ❷ cover an area with turf.

turgid »*adjective* ❶ swollen or full. ❷ (of language or style) pompous and boring.
– SAY ter-jid
turgidity
turgidly

> ℹ do not confuse **turgid** with **turbid**, which means 'cloudy or muddy'

Turk »*noun* a person from Turkey.

turkey (plural **turkeys**)

turkeycock »*noun* a male turkey.

Turkish

turmeric »*noun* a bright yellow powder obtained from a plant of the ginger family, used as a spice in Asian cookery.

– say ter-muh-rik

 turm not tum: turmeric

turmoil »*noun* a state of great disturbance, confusion, or uncertainty.

turn (verb: **turns, turning, turned**)
turner

turnaround

turncoat »*noun* a person who deserts one party or cause in order to join an opposing one.

turned

turner

turning

turnip

turnkey »*noun* (plural **turnkeys**) (an old word) a jailer.

turn-off

turn-on

turnout »*noun* the number of people attending or taking part in an event.

turnover »*noun* **①** the amount of money taken by a business in a particular period. **②** the rate at which employees leave a workforce and are replaced. **③** the rate at which goods are sold and replaced in a shop. **④** a small pie made by folding a piece of pastry over on itself to enclose a filling.

turnpike »*noun* **①** (a historical term) a toll gate. **②** (a historical term) a road on which a toll was collected. **③** (in American English) a motorway on which a toll is charged.

turnround

turns

turnstile »*noun* a mechanical gate with revolving arms that allow only one person at a time to pass through.

 -stile not -style: turnstile

turntable »*noun* a circular revolving platform or support, e.g. for the record in a record-player.

turn-up

turpentine »*noun* a strong-smelling liquid derived from certain trees, used to thin paint and clean brushes.
– say ter-puhn-tyn

 tur not ter: turpentine

turpitude »*noun* wickedness.
– say ter-pi-tyood

turps »*noun* turpentine.

turquoise »*noun* **①** a greenish-blue or sky-blue semi-precious stone. **②** a greenish-blue colour.
– say ter-kwoyz or ter-kwahz

 quo not qo in the middle: turquoise

turret »*noun* **①** a small tower at the corner of a building or wall. **②** an armoured tower for a gun in a ship, aircraft, fort, or tank.
turreted

 double r in the middle and single t at the end: turret

turtle

turtle dove »*noun* a small dove with a soft purring call.

turtleneck »*noun* **①** a high, round, close-fitting neck on a knitted garment. **②** (in American English) = POLO NECK.

turves plural of TURF.

Tuscan »*adjective* relating to Tuscany in central Italy.

tusk »*noun* a long, pointed tooth which protrudes from a closed mouth, as in the elephant, walrus, or wild boar.
tusked

tussle »*noun* a vigorous struggle or scuffle.
»*verb* (**tussles, tussling, tussled**) engage in a tussle.

 double s in the middle, not st: tussle

tussock »*noun* a dense clump or tuft of grass.
tussocky

tutee »*noun* a student or pupil of a tutor.

tutelage »*noun* **①** protection of or authority over someone or something. **②** instruction; tuition.
– say tyoo-ti-lij

tutelary »*adjective* serving as a protector, guardian, or patron.
– say tyoo-ti-luh-ri

tutor »*noun* **①** a private teacher who teaches a single pupil or a very small group. **②** a university or college teacher responsible for students assigned to them. **③** a book of instruction in a particular subject.
»*verb* (**tutors, tutoring, tutored**) act as a tutor to someone.

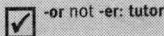 -or not -er: tutor

tutorial »*noun* **①** a period of tuition given by a university or college tutor. **②** a written account or explanation of a subject, intended for private study.

» *adjective* relating to a tutor.

tutoring

tutors

tutti »*adverb & adjective* (in music) with all voices or instruments together.
– SAY tuut-ti

tutti-frutti »*noun* (plural **tutti-fruttis**) a type of ice cream containing mixed fruits.
– SAY toot-ti-**froot**-ti

> ✓ **frutti** not **fruiti**: **tutti-frutti** (it is an Italian phrase meaning 'all fruits')

tutu »*noun* a female ballet dancer's very short, stiff skirt that sticks out from the waist.

Tuvaluan [of Tuvalu in the SW Pacific]
– SAY too-**val**-uu-uhn

tuxedo »*noun* (plural **tuxedos** or **tuxedoes**) **❶** a man's dinner jacket. **❷** a formal evening suit including such a jacket.
– SAY tuk-**see**-doh

> ✓ the plural of **tuxedo** can have either **os** or **oes**: **tuxedos** or **tuxedoes**. The word comes from *Tuxedo* Park, the site of a country club in New York.

TV

twaddle »*noun* (in informal English) trivial or foolish speech or writing.

twain »*cardinal number* (an old word) = **TWO**.

twang (verb: **twangs, twanging, twanged**)
twangy

'twas »*contraction* (an old word) it was.

twat

tweak »*verb* (**tweaks, tweaking, tweaked**) **❶** twist or pull something with a small but sharp movement. **❷** improve something by making fine adjustments.
» *noun* an act of tweaking.

> ✓ **ea** not **ee**: **tweak**
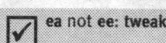

twee »*adjective* excessively quaint, pretty, or sentimental.
tweeness

tweed »*noun* **❶** a rough woollen cloth flecked with mixed colours. **❷** (**tweeds**) clothes made of tweed.
tweedy

tweeness

tweet (verb: **tweets, tweeting, tweeted**)

tweeter »*noun* a loudspeaker designed to reproduce high frequencies.

tweeting

tweets

tweeze (verb: **tweezes, tweezing, tweezed**)

tweezers

tweezes

tweezing

twelfth

Twelfth Night »*noun* **❶** 6 January, the feast of the Epiphany. **❷** the evening of 5 January, formerly the twelfth and last day of Christmas festivities.

twelve

twelvemonth »*noun* (an old word) a year.

twenty (plural **twenties**)
twentieth

> ✓ plural: drop the **y** and add **ies**: **twenties**

twenty-four-seven »*adverb* (in informal English) twenty-four hours a day, seven days a week; all the time.

> ✓ usually written as numbers: **24/7**

twenty-twenty »*adjective* (of vision) of normal sharpness.

> ✓ often written as numbers: **20/20**

'twere »*contraction* (an old word) it were.

twerp »*noun* (in informal English) a silly or annoying person.

twice

twiddle »*verb* (**twiddles, twiddling, twiddled**) play or fiddle with something in an aimless or nervous way.
» *noun* an act of twiddling.
twiddler
twiddly

twig (verb: **twigs, twigging, twigged**)
twiggy

> ✓ double the **g** in **twigging, twigged,** and **twiggy**

twilight »*noun* **❶** the soft glowing light from the sky when the sun is below the horizon. **❷** a period or state of gradual decline: *the twilight of his career.*

twilight zone »*noun* a state or area which does not have clear limits or meaning.

twilit »*adjective* dimly lit by twilight.

twill »*noun* a fabric woven so as to have a surface of diagonal parallel ridges.
twilled

twin (verb: **twins, twinning, twinned**)

> ✓ double the **n** in **twinning** and **twinned**
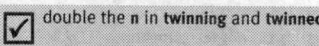

twine »*noun* strong string made of strands of hemp or cotton twisted together.
» *verb* (**twines, twining, twined**) wind round something.

twinge »*noun* ❶ a sudden, sharp pain in a part of the body. ❷ a brief, sharp pang of emotion.

twining

twinkle (verb: **twinkles, twinkling, twinkled**)
twinkly

twinkle-toed »*adjective* (in informal English) nimble and quick on your feet.

twinkling

twinkly

twinned

twinning

twins

twinset »*noun* a woman's matching cardigan and jumper.

twin-tub »*noun* a type of washing machine having two top-loading drums, one for washing and the other for spin-drying.

twirl (verb: **twirls, twirling, twirled**)
twirler
twirly

twist (verb: **twists, twisting, twisted**)
twister
twisty

twit (in informal English) »*noun* a silly person.
» *verb* (**twits, twitting, twitted**) tease someone good-humouredly.

 double the t in **twitting** and **twitted**

twitch (verb: **twitches, twitching, twitched**)

twitcher »*noun* (in informal English) a birdwatcher devoted to spotting rare birds.

twitches

twitchier

twitchiest

twitching

twitchy »*adjective* (**twitchier, twitchiest**) (in informal English) nervous.

twits

twitted

twitter »*verb* (**twitters, twittering, twittered**) ❶ (of a bird) make a series of short high sounds. ❷ talk rapidly in a nervous or trivial way.
» *noun* ❶ a twittering sound. ❷ (in informal English) an agitated or excited state.
twittery

twitting

'twixt »*contraction* betwixt.

two
twofold

 for an explanation of the difference between **two, to,** and **too,** see the note at **TO**

two-dimensional »*adjective* having or appearing to have length and breadth but no depth.

two-faced

twofold

twopence »*noun* ❶ the sum of two pence before decimalization (1971). ❷ (in informal English) anything at all: *he didn't care twopence.*
– **SAY** tup-puhnss

 twopence can also be spelled **tuppence**

twopenn'orth »*noun* an amount that is worth or costs twopence.

twopenny »*adjective* costing two pence before decimalization (1971).
– **SAY** tup-puh-ni

✓ **twopenny** can also be spelled **tuppenny**

twopenny-halfpenny »*adjective* (in informal English) insignificant or worthless.

two-piece

twosome

two-step »*noun* a round dance with a sliding step in march or polka time.

two-stroke »*adjective* (of an internal-combustion engine) having its power cycle completed in one up-and-down movement of the piston.

two-time »*verb* (**two-times, two-timing, two-timed**) be unfaithful to a lover or husband or wife.

two-way

tycoon »*noun* a wealthy, powerful person in business or industry.

tying present participle of **TIE**.

tyke

tympani another way of spelling **TIMPANI**.

tympanum »*noun* (plural **tympanums** or **tympana**) the eardrum.
– **SAY** tim-puh-nuhm

✓ the plural of **tympanum** can be **tympanums** or (as in Latin) **tympana**

Tynwald »*noun* the parliament of the Isle of Man.
– **SAY** tin-wuhld

type (verb: **types, typing, typed**)
typing

typecast »*adjective* (of an actor) repeatedly cast in the same type of role because their appearance is appropriate or they are known for such roles.

typed

typeface »*noun* (in printing) a particular design of type.

types

typescript »*noun* a typed copy of a text.

typeset »*verb* (**typeset**, **typesetting**, **typeset**) arrange or generate the type for text to be printed.
typesetter

> ✓ double the **t** in **typesetting** and **typesetter**

typewriter
typewriting
typewritten

typhoid »*noun* an infectious fever caused by bacteria, resulting in red spots on the chest and abdomen and severe irritation of the intestines.

typhoon »*noun* a tropical storm in the region of the Indian or western Pacific oceans.

typhus »*noun* an infectious disease caused by bacteria, resulting in a purple rash, headaches, fever, and usually delirium.

typical »*adjective* ❶ having the distinctive qualities of a particular type of person or thing: *it's a typical example of a small American town.* ❷ characteristic of a particular person or thing.
typically

typify »*verb* (**typifies**, **typifying**, **typified**) be typical of something.

typing

typist

typo »*noun* (plural **typos**) (in informal English) a small mistake in typed or printed text.

typography »*noun* ❶ the process of setting and arranging types and printing from them. ❷ the style and appearance of printed material.
– say ty-**pog**-ruh-fi
typographer
typographic
typographical

tyrannical »*adjective* using power over others in a cruel and unfair way.
tyrannically

> ✓ single **r** and double **n**: **tyrannical**

tyrannies

tyrannize »*verb* (**tyrannizes**, **tyrannizing**, **tyrannized**) dominate or treat someone cruelly.
– say ti-ruh-nyz

> ✓ many people prefer the alternative spellings **tyrannise**, **tyrannises**, etc.: both **s** and **z** spellings are correct

tyrannosaurus »*noun* (plural **tyrannosaurus**) a very large carnivorous dinosaur with powerful jaws and small claw-like front legs.
– say ti-ran-nuh-**sor**-uhss

> ✓ single **r**, double **n**: **tyrannosaurus**. **Tyrannosaurus rex** is the Latin name of one particularly large species.

tyranny »*noun* (plural **tyrannies**) ❶ cruel and oppressive government or rule. ❷ a state under such rule.
tyrannous

> ✓ one **r**, two **n**'s : **tyranny** plural: drop the **y** and add **ies**: **tyrannies**

tyrant »*noun* a cruel and oppressive person, especially a ruler.

> ✓ **ant** not **ent**: **tyrant**

tyre [rubber covering around a wheel]

> ✓ **y** not **i**: **tyre** (the spelling **tire** is American)

tyro »*noun* (plural **tyros**) a beginner or novice.
– say **ty**-roh

> ℹ **tyro** is a Latin word meaning 'recruit'

tzatziki »*noun* a Greek side dish of yogurt with cucumber, garlic, and often mint.
– say tsat-**tsee**-ki

Uu

UB40 »*noun* (in the UK) a card issued to a person registered as unemployed.

U-bend »*noun* a section of a waste pipe shaped like a U.

ubiquitous »*adjective* present, appearing, or found everywhere.
– **say** yoo-**bi**-kwi-tuhss
ubiquitously
ubiquity

> ☑ -**quit**- not -**qut**- in the middle:
> **ubiquitous**

U-boat »*noun* a German submarine of the First or Second World War.

udder »*noun* the bag-like milk-producing organ of female cattle, sheep, goats, horses, etc.

UEFA »*abbreviation* Union of European Football Associations.
– **say** yoo-**ay**-fuh

UFO »*noun* (plural **UFOs**) an unidentified flying object.
ufology **say** yoo-**fol**-uh-ji

Ugandan

uglier

ugliest

Ugli fruit »*noun* (trademark) a mottled green and yellow citrus fruit which is a hybrid of a grapefruit and tangerine.

ugly (adjective: **uglier**, **ugliest**)
ugliness

> ☑ drop the **y** and add **ier** or **iest** to spell
> **uglier** or **ugliest**

UHF »*abbreviation* ultra-high frequency.

UHT »*abbreviation* ultra heat treated (a process used to extend the shelf life of milk).

UK

Ukrainian [of Ukraine]

> ☑ remember the **i** in the middle:
> **Ukrainian**

ukulele »*noun* a small four-stringed guitar of Hawaiian origin.
– **say** yoo-kuh-**lay**-li

> ☑ **uku** not **uke**: **ukulele**

ulcer »*noun* an open sore on the body or on a bodily organ.
ulcerous

ulcerate »*verb* (**ulcerates**, **ulcerating**, **ulcerated**) develop into or become affected by an ulcer.
ulceration

ulcerous

ullage »*noun* ❶ the amount by which a container falls short of being full. ❷ loss of liquid by evaporation or leakage.
– **say** **ul**-lij

ulna »*noun* (plural **ulnae** or **ulnas**) the thinner and longer of the two bones in the human forearm.
– **say** **ul**-nuh [singular], **ul**-nee [plural]
ulnar

> ☑ the plural of **ulna** can be **ulnae** (as in
> the original Latin) or **ulnas**

ulster »*noun* a man's long, loose overcoat of rough cloth.

> ⓘ from *Ulster* in Ireland, where it was
> originally sold

Ulsterman (plural **Ulstermen**)

Ulsterwoman (plural **Ulsterwomen**)

ulterior »*adjective* other than what is obvious or admitted: *she had some ulterior motive in coming.*

ultimata plural of **ultimatum**.

ultimate »*adjective* ❶ being or happening at the end of a process; final. ❷ being the best or most extreme example of its kind. ❸ basic or fundamental.
»*noun* (**the ultimate**) the best imaginable of its kind: *the ultimate in decorative luxury.*
ultimately

ultimatum »*noun* (plural **ultimatums** or **ultimata**) a final warning that action will be taken against you if you do not agree to another party's demands.
– **say** ul-ti-**may**-tuhm [singular], ul-ti-**may**-tuh [plural]

> ☑ the plural of **ultimatum** can be
> **ultimatums** or (as in the original
> Latin) **ultimata**

ultra »*adverb* (in informal English) very: *ultra modern furniture.*

ultra-high frequency »*noun* a radio frequency in the range 300 to 3,000 megahertz.

ultramarine »*noun* a brilliant deep blue pigment and colour.

ultramicroscope »*noun* a microscope used to detect very small particles by observing light scattered from them.
ultramicroscopic

ultrasonic »*adjective* involving sound waves with a frequency above the upper limit of human hearing.
ultrasonically

ultrasonics »*plural noun* ❶ the science and application of ultrasonic waves. ❷ ultrasound.

ultrasound »*noun* sound or other vibrations having an ultrasonic frequency, used in medical scans.

ultraviolet »*noun* invisible electromagnetic radiation having a wavelength just shorter than that of violet light but longer than that of X-rays.
» *adjective* referring to such radiation.

ultra vires »*adjective & adverb* beyond a person's legal power or authority.
– **SAY** ul-truh **vy**-reez or uul-trah **veer**-ayz

> ℹ️ **ultra vires** means 'beyond the powers' in Latin

ululate »*verb* (**ululates, ululating, ululated**) howl or wail.
– **SAY** yoo-lyuu-layt or **ul**-yuu-layt
ululation

umbel »*noun* (in botany) a flower cluster in which stalks spring from a common centre and form a flat or curved surface, as in cow parsley.

umber »*noun* a brown or yellowish-brown colour.

umbilical »*adjective* having to do with the navel or umbilical cord.
– **SAY** um-**bil**-i-k'l or um-bi-**ly**-k'l
umbilically

umbilical cord »*noun* a flexible cord-like structure containing blood vessels, attaching a fetus to the placenta and nourishing it while it is in the womb.

umbilically

umbilicus »*noun* (plural **umbilici** or **umbilicuses**) the navel.
– **SAY** um-**bil**-li-kuhss or um-bi-**ly**-kuhss [singular], um-**bil**-li-sy or um-bi-**ly**-sy [plural]

> ✅ the plural of **umbilicus** can be either **umbilici** (as in the original Latin) or **umbilicuses**

umbra »*noun* (plural **umbrae** or **umbras**) the dark inner region of the shadow cast by an object.
– **SAY** um-bruh [singular], **um**-bree [plural]

> ✅ the plural of **umbra** can be **umbrae** (as in the original Latin) or **umbras**

umbrage »*noun* (**take umbrage**) take offence or become annoyed.
– **SAY** um-brij

umbrella

> ✅ umbr not umber: umbrella

umlaut »*noun* a mark (¨) used over a vowel in German and some other languages to indicate how it should be pronounced.
– **SAY** uum-lowt

umpire »*noun* (in certain sports) an official who supervises a game to ensure that players keep to the rules.
» *verb* (**umpires, umpiring, umpired**) act as an umpire.

umpteen »*cardinal number* (in informal English) very many.
umpteenth

UN »*abbreviation* United Nations.

unabashed »*adjective* not embarrassed or ashamed.
unabashedly

unabated »*adjective* without any reduction in intensity or strength.

unable

unabridged »*adjective* (of a text) not cut or shortened.

unacceptable
unacceptability
unacceptably

unaccompanied »*adjective* ❶ having no companion or escort. ❷ without instrumental accompaniment. ❸ without something specified occurring at the same time.

unaccountable »*adjective* ❶ unable to be explained. ❷ not responsible for or required to explain the outcome of something.
unaccountability
unaccountably

unaccounted »*adjective* (**unaccounted for**) not taken into consideration or explained.

unaccustomed »*adjective* ❶ not usual or customary. ❷ (**unaccustomed to**) not familiar with or used to.

unacknowledged »*adjective* ❶ existing or having taken place but not accepted or admitted to. ❷ (of a person or their work) deserving but not receiving recognition.

unacquainted »*adjective* ❶ (**unacquainted with**) having no experience of or familiarity with. ❷ not having met before.

> ☑ don't forget the **c** before the **q**: **unacquainted**

unadulterated »*adjective* ❶ not mixed with any different or inferior substances. ❷ complete; total: *pure, unadulterated jealousy.*

unadventurous
unadventurously

unadvisedly »*adverb* in an unwise or rash way.

unaffected »*adjective* ❶ feeling or showing no effects. ❷ (of a person) sincere and genuine.
unaffectedly
unaffectedness

unaffiliated »*adjective* not officially attached to or connected with an organization.

> ☑ two **f**'s, one **l**: **unaffiliated**

unaffordable
unafraid
unaided
unalike

unalloyed »*adjective* ❶ (of metal) not mixed with another metal to form an alloy. ❷ complete; total: *unalloyed delight.*

unalterable
unalterably

unaltered

unambiguous »*adjective* not open to more than one interpretation; clear in meaning.
unambiguously

unambitious

un-American »*adjective* ❶ not American in nature. ❷ (mainly a historical term) against the interests of the US and therefore treasonable.

unanimous »*adjective* ❶ fully in agreement. ❷ (of an opinion, decision, or vote) held or carried by everyone involved.
– **say** yoo-**nan**-i-muhss
unanimity
unanimously

unannounced
unanswerable
unanswered

unapologetic
unapologetically

unappealing
unappealingly

unappetizing »*adjective* not inviting or attractive.
unappetizingly

> ☑ **unappetizing** can also be spelled **unappetising**: both **s** and **z** spellings are correct

unappreciated

unappreciative »*adjective* not fully understanding or recognizing something.

unapproachable

unarguable »*adjective* not able to be disagreed with.
unarguably

unarmed »*adjective* not equipped with or carrying weapons.

unashamed
unashamedly

unasked

unassailable »*adjective* unable to be attacked, questioned, or defeated.
unassailability
unassailably

unassertive »*adjective* not having or showing a confident and forceful personality.

unassisted

unassuming »*adjective* not wanting to draw attention to yourself or your abilities.
unassumingly

unattached »*adjective* without a husband or wife or established lover.

> ☑ double **t**, and **ach** not **atch** in the middle: **unattached**

unattainable »*adjective* not able to be reached or achieved.
unattainably

unattended »*adjective* without the owner or a responsible person present; not being watched or looked after.

unattractive
unattractively
unattractiveness

unattributed »*adjective* (of a quotation, story, or work of art) of unknown or unpublished origin.
unattributable

unauthorized »*adjective* not having official permission or approval.

☑ **unauthorized** can also be spelled **unauthorised**: both **s** and **z** spellings are correct

unavailable
  unavailability

unavailing »*adjective* achieving little or nothing.
  unavailingly

unavoidable
  unavoidably

unaware
  unawareness

unawares

unbalance (verb: **unbalances, unbalancing, unbalanced**)

unbearable
  unbearably

unbeatable

unbeaten

unbecoming »*adjective* ❶ not flattering: *an unbecoming red dress.* ❷ (of behaviour) improper; unseemly.
  unbecomingly

unbeknown »*adjective* (**unbeknown to**) without the knowledge of.

ℹ️ **unbeknown** and **unbeknownst** mean the same thing, but **unbeknown** is the more common form in British English, while **unbeknownst** is more American

unbeknownst
unbelievable
  unbelievably

☑ **i** before **e**, except after **c**: **unbelievable** follows the usual rule

unbeliever »*noun* a person without religious belief.

unbend (verb: **unbends, unbending, unbent**)

unbending »*adjective* unwilling to change your mind; inflexible.

unbent

unbiased »*adjective* showing no prejudice.

☑ one **s**: **unbiased**

unbidden »*adjective* without having been invited.

unbleached

unblock (verb: **unblocks, unblocking, unblocked**)

unblushing »*adjective* not feeling or showing embarrassment or shame.
  unblushingly

unborn

unbound »*adjective* not bound or tied up.

unbounded »*adjective* having no limits.

unbowed »*adjective* not having been defeated.

unbreakable

unbridgeable »*adjective* (of a gap or difference between two people) not able to be closed or made less significant.

☑ don't forget the **e** in the middle: **unbridgeable**

unbridled »*adjective* uncontrolled: *unbridled lust.*

unbroken

unbuckle (verb: **unbuckles, unbuckling, unbuckled**)

unburden »*verb* (**unburdens, unburdening, unburdened**) (**unburden yourself**) confide in someone about a worry or problem.

unbutton (verb: **unbuttons, unbuttoning, unbuttoned**)

uncalled »*adjective* (**uncalled for**) undesirable and unnecessary.

uncanny »*adjective* strange or mysterious.
  uncannily

uncared »*adjective* (**uncared for**) not looked after properly.

uncaring
  uncaringly

unceasing
  unceasingly

unceremonious »*adjective* impolite or abrupt.
  unceremoniously

uncertain
  uncertainly

☑ don't forget the **a**: **uncertain**

uncertainty (plural **uncertainties**)

☑ plural: drop the **y** and add **ies**: **uncertainties**

unchallengeable
unchallenged
unchanged
unchanging
  unchangingly
uncharacteristic
  uncharacteristically
uncharitable
  uncharitably

uncharted »*adjective* (of an area of land or sea) not mapped or surveyed.

unchecked »*adjective* (of something undesirable) not controlled or restrained.

unchristian

uncivil »*adjective* not polite.

uncivilized

☑ **uncivilized** can also be spelled **uncivilised**: both **s** and **z** spellings are correct

unclaimed

unclasp (verb: **unclasps**, **unclasping**, **unclasped**)

unclassified

uncle

unclean

uncleanliness »*noun* the state of being dirty.

unclear

unclench (verb: **unclenches**, **unclenching**, **unclenched**)

Uncle Sam »*noun* the United States or its government, often shown as a tall man with a tall hat and white beard.

unclog (verb: **unclogs**, **unclogging**, **unclogged**)

☑ double the **g** in **unclogging** and **unclogged**

unclothed

unclouded »*adjective* **❶** (of the sky) not dark or overcast. **❷** not spoiled by anything: *unclouded happiness.*

uncluttered

uncoil (verb: **uncoils**, **uncoiling**, **uncoiled**)

uncoloured

☑ **oured** not **ored**: **uncoloured** (the spelling **uncolored** is American)

uncomfortable
 uncomfortably

uncommercial »*adjective* not making or intended to make a profit.

uncommon
 uncommonly

uncommunicative

uncompetitive

uncomplaining
 uncomplainingly

uncomplicated

uncomplimentary »*adjective* rude or insulting.

☑ **plim** not **plem** in the middle: **uncomplimentary**

uncomprehending »*adjective* unable to understand something.
 uncomprehendingly

uncompromising »*adjective* **❶** unwilling to change your mind or behaviour. **❷** harsh or relentless.
 uncompromisingly

unconcealed

unconcern
 unconcerned
 unconcernedly

unconditional
 unconditionally

unconfined »*adjective* **❶** not confined to a limited space. **❷** (of joy or excitement) very great.

unconfirmed

uncongenial »*adjective* **❶** not friendly or pleasant to be with. **❷** not suitable: *the atmosphere was uncongenial to good conversation.*

unconnected

unconscionable »*adjective* not right or reasonable.
– SAY un-kon-shuh-nuh-b'l
 unconscionably

unconscious
 unconsciously
 unconsciousness

unconstitutional »*adjective* not in accordance with the constitution of a country or the rules of an organization.
 unconstitutionally

unconstrained »*adjective* not restricted or limited.

unconsummated »*adjective* (of a marriage) not having been consummated.

☑ double **m**: **unconsummated**

uncontaminated

uncontentious »*adjective* not causing or likely to cause disagreement or controversy.

uncontested

uncontrollable
 uncontrollably

uncontrolled

uncontroversial
 uncontroversially

unconventional »*adjective* not following what is generally done or believed.
 unconventionality
 unconventionally

unconvinced

unconvincing
 unconvincingly

uncooked

uncool

uncooperative

uncoordinated

uncorroborated »*adjective* not supported or confirmed by evidence.

u

✓ double r, one b, then one r:
uncorroborated

uncountable »*adjective* too many to be counted.

uncouple »*verb* (**uncouples, uncoupling, uncoupled**) disconnect or become disconnected.

uncouth »*adjective* lacking good manners.

uncover (verb: **uncovers, uncovering, uncovered**)

uncritical
uncritically

uncross (verb: **uncrosses, uncrossing, uncrossed**)

uncrowned

unction »*noun* ❶ the smearing of someone with oil or ointment as a religious ceremony. ❷ excessive politeness or flattery.
– SAY ungk-sh'n

unctuous »*adjective* excessively flattering or friendly.
– SAY ungk-tyuu-uhss
unctuously
unctuousness

✓ tuous not tious: unctuous

uncultivated »*adjective* ❶ (of land) not used for growing crops. ❷ not highly educated.

uncultured »*adjective* not having good taste, manners, or education.

uncut

undamaged

undated

undaunted »*adjective* not discouraged by difficulty, danger, or disappointment.

undeceive »*verb* (**undeceives, undeceiving, undeceived**) tell someone that an idea or belief is mistaken.

✓ e before i, because it is after c:
undeceive follows the usual rule

undecided

undefeated

undefined
undefinable

undemanding

undemocratic
undemocratically

undemonstrative »*adjective* not tending to express feelings openly.

undeniable
undeniably

under

underachieve (verb: **underachieves, underachieving, underachieved**)
underachievement
underachiever

underarm

underbelly »*noun* (plural **underbellies**) ❶ the soft underside of an animal. ❷ a hidden unpleasant or criminal part of society.

undercarriage »*noun* ❶ a wheeled structure beneath an aircraft which supports the aircraft on the ground. ❷ the supporting frame under the body of a vehicle.

undercharge (verb: **undercharges, undercharging, undercharged**)

underclass »*noun* (plural **underclasses**) the lowest social class in a country or community, consisting of the poor and unemployed.

underclothes
underclothing

undercoat

undercover

undercurrent

undercut »*verb* (**undercuts, undercutting, undercut**) ❶ offer goods or services at a lower price than a competitor. ❷ cut or wear away the part under something. ❸ weaken; undermine: *the chairman's authority was being undercut.*

✓ double the t in **undercutting**

underdeveloped »*adjective* ❶ not fully developed. ❷ (of a country or region) not advanced economically.

underdog »*noun* a competitor thought to have little chance of winning a fight or contest.

underdone »*adjective* (of food) not cooked enough.

underdressed »*adjective* dressed too plainly or informally for a particular occasion.

underemployed »*adjective* not having enough work.
underemployment

underestimate (verb: **underestimates, underestimating, underestimated**)
underestimation

underfed

underfelt »*noun* felt laid under a carpet for protection or support.

underfoot

underfund (verb: **underfunds, underfunding, underfunded**)
underfunding

undergarment

undergo (verb: **undergoes, undergoing, underwent**; past participle **undergone**)

undergraduate »*noun* a student at a university who has not yet taken a first degree.

underground

undergrowth

underhand »*adjective* acting or done in a secret or dishonest way.

underlay[1] »*verb* (**underlays, underlaying, underlaid**) place something under something else to support or raise it.
» *noun* material laid under a carpet for protection or support.

underlay[2] past tense of **UNDERLIE**.

underlie »*verb* (**underlies, underlying, underlay**; past participle **underlain**) lie or be situated under.
underlying

underline (verb: **underlines, underlining, underlined**)

underling »*noun* a person of lower status.

underlining

underlying present participle of **UNDERLIE**.

underman »*verb* (**undermans, undermanning, undermanned**) fail to provide a place with enough workers.

> ☑ double the **n** in **undermanning** and **undermanned**

undermine »*verb* (**undermines, undermining, undermined**) ❶ damage or weaken: *this could undermine years of hard work.* ❷ wear away the base or foundation of a rock formation. ❸ dig beneath a building so as to make it collapse.

underneath

undernourished »*adjective* not having enough food or the right type of food for good health.
undernourishment

underpaid past and past participle of **UNDERPAY**.

underpants

underpart

underpass »*noun* (plural **underpasses**) a road or tunnel passing under another road or a railway.

underpay (verb: **underpays, underpaying, underpaid**)

underperform (verb: **underperforms, underperforming, underperformed**)
underperformance

underpin »*verb* (**underpins, underpinning, underpinned**) ❶ support a structure from below by laying a solid foundation or replacing weak materials with stronger ones. ❷ support or form the basis for an argument, claim, etc.

> ☑ double the **n** in **underpinning** and **underpinned**

underplay »*verb* (**underplays, underplaying, underplayed**) try to make something seem less important than it really is.

underprivileged »*adjective* not enjoying the same rights or standard of living as the majority of the population.

> ☑ **leged** not **ledged: underprivileged**

underrate »*verb* (**underrates, underrating, underrated**) fail to recognize the real extent, value, or importance of something.

> ☑ double **r: underrate**

underscore »*verb* (**underscores, underscoring, underscored**) = **UNDERLINE**.

undersea

undersecretary »*noun* (plural **undersecretaries**) (in the UK) a junior minister or senior civil servant.

undersell »*verb* (**undersells, underselling, undersold**) sell something at a lower price than a competitor.

undershirt

undershoot »*verb* (**undershoots, undershooting, undershot**) fall short of a point or target.

underside

undersigned »*noun* (**the undersigned**) the person or people who have signed the document in question.

undersize

undersized

underskirt

undersold past and past participle of **UNDERSELL**.

underspend (verb: **underspends, underspending, underspent**)

understaffed »*adjective* (of an organization) having too few members of staff to operate effectively.

understand (verb: **understands, understanding, understood**)

understandable
understandably

understanding
  understandingly

understands

understate »*verb* (**understates, understating, understated**) describe or represent something as being smaller or less important than it really is.
  understatement

understated »*adjective* expressed in an effectively subtle way.

understatement

understates

understating

understood past and past participle of **UNDERSTAND**.

understudy »*noun* (plural **understudies**) an actor who learns another's role in order to take their place if necessary.
  » *verb* (**understudies, understudying, understudied**) be an understudy for someone.

> ✓ plural: drop the **y** and add **ies**: **understudies**

undersubscribed »*adjective* (of a course or event) having more places available than applications.

undertake »*verb* (**undertakes, undertaking, undertook**; past participle **undertaken**)
  ❶ commit yourself to and begin an activity. ❷ formally guarantee or promise.
  undertaking

undertaker »*noun* a person whose business is preparing dead bodies for burial or cremation and making arrangements for funerals.

undertakes

undertaking

undertone »*noun* ❶ a subdued or muted tone of sound or colour. ❷ an underlying quality or feeling.

undertook past of **UNDERTAKE**.

undertow »*noun* = **UNDERCURRENT**.

underuse (verb: **underuses, underusing, underused**)

undervalue (verb: **undervalues, undervaluing, undervalued**)

underwater

underwear

underweight

underwent past of **UNDERGO**.

underwhelm »*verb* (**underwhelms, underwhelming, underwhelmed**) (mainly used in a humorous way) fail to impress someone.

underwired »*adjective* (of a bra) having a semicircular wire support stitched under each cup.

underworld »*noun* ❶ the world of criminals or of organized crime. ❷ (in myths and legends) the home of the dead, imagined as being under the earth.

underwrite »*verb* (**underwrites, underwriting, underwrote**; past participle **underwritten**) ❶ sign and accept legal responsibility for an insurance policy.
  ❷ finance or otherwise support or guarantee something.
  underwriter

undeserved
  undeservedly

undeserving

undesirable
  undesirability
  undesirably

undesired

undetectable
  undetectably

undetected

undetermined »*adjective* not firmly decided or settled.

undeterred »*adjective* persevering despite setbacks.

> ✓ one **t**, two **r**'s: **undeterred**

undeveloped

undeviating »*adjective* constant and steady.

undid past of **UNDO**.

undies

undifferentiated »*adjective* not different or recognized as different.

undigested

undignified »*adjective* appearing foolish.

undiluted

undiminished

undiplomatic »*adjective* insensitive and tactless.
  undiplomatically

undisciplined »*adjective* uncontrolled in behaviour or manner.

undisclosed »*adjective* not revealed or made known.

undiscovered

undiscriminating »*adjective* lacking good judgement or taste.

undisguised

undismayed

undisputed

undistinguished »*adjective* not very good or impressive.

undisturbed

undivided

undo (verb: **undoes, undoing, undid**; past participle **undone**)

undocumented »*adjective* not recorded in or proved by documents.

undoes

undoing »*noun* a person's ruin or downfall.

undone

undoubted
undoubtedly

undreamed »*adjective* (**undreamed of**) not previously thought to be possible.

 undreamed can also be written undreamt

undress (verb: **undresses, undressing, undressed**)
undressed

undrinkable

undue »*adjective* excessive or unreasonably great.

undulate »*verb* (**undulates, undulating, undulated**) ❶ move with a smooth wave-like motion. ❷ have a wavy form or outline.
– SAY un-dyuu-layt
undulation
undulatory

unduly »*adverb* excessively.

undyed

undying

unearned

unearth »*verb* (**unearths, unearthing, unearthed**) ❶ find something in the ground by digging. ❷ discover something by investigation or searching.

unearthly »*adjective* ❶ unnatural or mysterious. ❷ unreasonably early or inconvenient: *she couldn't call the doctor at such an unearthly hour.*

unearths

unease

uneasy (adjective: **uneasier, uneasiest**)
uneasily
uneasiness

uneatable

uneaten

uneconomic »*adjective* not profitable or making efficient use of resources.

uneconomical »*adjective* wasteful of money or other resources.
uneconomically

unedifying »*adjective* distasteful or unpleasant.

uneducated

unelectable »*adjective* very likely to be defeated at an election.

unelected

unembarrassed

 double r, double s: **unembarrassed**

unemotional
unemotionally

unemployable »*adjective* not able to get paid employment because of a lack of skills or qualifications.

unemployed

unemployment

unencumbered »*adjective* not burdened or held back.

unending

unendurable

unenlightened »*adjective* not reasonable and tolerant in outlook.

unenterprising »*adjective* lacking initiative or resourcefulness.

unenthusiastic
unenthusiastically

unenviable »*adjective* difficult, undesirable, or unpleasant.

unequal
unequally

unequalled »*adjective* better or greater than all others.

 double l: **unequalled** (the spelling **unequaled** is American)

unequally

unequivocal »*adjective* leaving no doubt; clear in meaning.
unequivocally

unerring »*adjective* always right or accurate.
unerringly

 double r: **unerring**

UNESCO »*abbreviation* United Nations Educational, Scientific, and Cultural Organization.
– SAY yoo-**ness**-koh

unethical »*adjective* not morally correct.
unethically

uneven
unevenly
unevenness

u

uneventful
uneventfully
uneventfulness

> ✓ -ful not -full: uneventful

unexceptionable »*adjective* not able to be objected to, but not particularly new or exciting.

> ℹ do not confuse **unexceptionable** and **unexceptional**: **unexceptionable** means 'not able to be objected to', while **unexceptional** means 'not out of the ordinary; usual'

unexceptional »*adjective* not out of the ordinary; usual.
unexceptionally

unexciting

> ✓ remember the **c** after the **x**: unexciting

unexpected
unexpectedly
unexpectedness

unexplained
unexplainable

unexploded

unexplored

unexposed »*adjective* ❶ not exposed. ❷ (**unexposed to**) not introduced to or knowing about.

unexpressed

unexpurgated »*adjective* (of a text) complete and containing all the original material.

unfailing
unfailingly

unfair
unfairly
unfairness

unfaithful
unfaithfully
unfaithfulness

> ✓ -ful not -full: unfaithful

unfamiliar
unfamiliarity

unfashionable
unfashionably

unfasten (verb: unfastens, unfastening, unfastened)

unfathomable »*adjective* ❶ too strange or difficult to be understood. ❷ impossible to measure the depth or extent of.
unfathomably

unfavourable
unfavourably

> ✓ **vour** not **vor**: unfavourable (the spelling **unfavorable** is American)

unfazed »*adjective* not surprised or worried by something unexpected.

unfeasible »*adjective* inconvenient or impractical.
unfeasibly

> ✓ -ible not -able: unfeasible

unfeeling

unfeigned »*adjective* genuine; sincere.

> ✓ **e** before **i**: unfeigned does not follow the usual rule

unfertilized

> ✓ **unfertilized** can also be spelled **unfertilised**: both **s** and **z** spellings are correct

unfettered »*adjective* unrestrained or uninhibited.

> ✓ double **t**: unfettered

unfilled

unfinished

unfit

unfitted »*adjective* unfit for something.

unfitting »*adjective* unsuitable or unbecoming.

unfixed

unflagging »*adjective* tireless or persistent.
unflaggingly

unflappable »*adjective* calm in a crisis.

unflattering
unflatteringly

unflinching »*adjective* not afraid or hesitant.
unflinchingly

unfocused

> ✓ **unfocused** can also be spelled **unfocussed**, with a double **s**

unfold (verb: unfolds, unfolding, unfolded)

unforced »*adjective* produced naturally and without effort.

unforeseen
unforeseeable

> ✓ **fores** not **fors** in the middle: unforeseen

unforgettable
unforgettably

> ✓ double the **t**: unforgettable

unforgivable
unforgivably

☑ no **e** in the middle of **unforgivable**

unforgiven

unforgiving

unformed »*adjective* ❶ without a definite form. ❷ not fully developed.

unforthcoming »*adjective* ❶ not willing to give out information. ❷ not available when needed.

unfortunate
unfortunately

unfounded »*adjective* having no basis in fact: *unfounded rumours.*

unfreeze (verb: **unfreezes, unfreezing, unfroze**; past participle **unfrozen**)

unfrequented »*adjective* visited only rarely.

unfriendly (adjective: **unfriendier, unfriendliest**)
unfriendliness

unfroze past of **UNFREEZE**.

unfrozen past participle of **UNFREEZE**.

unfulfilled
unfulfilling

unfunny

unfurl »*verb* (**unfurls, unfurling, unfurled**) spread out something that is rolled or folded.

unfurnished

ungainly »*adjective* clumsy; awkward.
ungainliness

ungenerous
ungenerously

ungentlemanly »*adjective* (of a man's behaviour) not well-mannered or pleasant.

ungodly »*adjective* ❶ disrespectful to God; wicked. ❷ (in informal English) inconveniently early or late: *calls at ungodly hours.*
ungodliness

ungovernable »*adjective* impossible to control or govern.
ungovernability

ungraceful
ungracefully

☑ -ful not -full: **ungraceful**

ungracious »*adjective* not polite, kind, or pleasant.
ungraciously

ungrammatical »*adjective* not following grammatical rules.
ungrammatically

ungrateful
ungratefully
ungratefulness

☑ -ful not -full: **ungrateful**

unguarded »*adjective* ❶ without protection or a guard. ❷ not well considered; careless: *an unguarded remark.*

unguent »*noun* a soft greasy or thick substance used as ointment or for lubrication.
– **SAY** ung-gwuhnt

☑ note the **ue** after the **g**: **unguent**

ungulate »*noun* (in zoology) a mammal with hoofs, such as a horse, cow, or pig.
– **SAY** ung-gyuu-luht or **ung**-gyuu-layt

unhand »*verb* (**unhands, unhanding, unhanded**) (an old word) release someone or something from your grasp.

unhappy (adjective: **unhappier, unhappiest**)
unhappily
unhappiness

unharmed

unhealthy (adjective: **unhealthier, unhealthiest**)
unhealthily

unheard

unheeded »*adjective* heard or noticed but ignored.

unheeding

unhelpful
unhelpfully
unhelpfulness

☑ -ful not -full: **unhelpful**

unheralded »*adjective* not previously announced, expected, or recognized.

unhesitating
unhesitatingly

unhinged »*adjective* mentally unbalanced.

unholy »*adjective* (**unholier, unholiest**) ❶ sinful; wicked. ❷ unnatural and likely to be harmful. ❸ dreadful: *an unholy row.*

unhook (verb: **unhooks, unhooking, unhooked**)

unhorse »*verb* (**unhorses, unhorsing, unhorsed**) drag or cause someone to fall from a horse.

unhurried
unhurriedly
unhurriedness

unhurt

unhygienic
unhygienically

uni »*noun* (plural **unis**) (in informal English) university.

unicameral »*adjective* (of a parliament) having only one main body.
– SAY yoo-ni-**kam**-uh-ruhl

UNICEF »*abbreviation* United Nations Children's Fund.
– SAY yoo-ni-sef

> ℹ the original title of the organization was the *United Nations International Children's Emergency Fund*

unicellular »*adjective* (in biology) consisting of a single cell.

unicorn »*noun* a mythical creature like a horse with a single horn on its forehead.

unicycle »*noun* a cycle with a single wheel.
unicyclist

unidentifiable

unidentified

unification »*noun* the process of being unified.

unified

unifies

uniform »*adjective* not varying in form or character; the same throughout.
»*noun* the distinctive clothing worn by members of the same organization or school.
uniformed
uniformity
uniformly

unify »*verb* (**unifies, unifying, unified**) make or become united or uniform.
– SAY yoo-ni-fy

unilateral »*adjective* done by or affecting only one person or group.
unilaterally

unimaginable »*adjective* impossible to imagine or understand.
unimaginably

unimaginative »*adjective* not using or showing imagination; dull.
unimaginatively

unimpaired »*adjective* not weakened or damaged.

unimpeachable »*adjective* beyond doubt or criticism: *an unimpeachable witness.*
unimpeachably

unimpeded »*adjective* not obstructed or hindered.

unimportant
unimportance

> ☑ ant not ent: unimportant

unimpressed

unimpressive

uninformed

uninhabitable

uninhabited »*adjective* having no people living there.

uninhibited »*adjective* saying or doing things without concern about what other people think.
uninhibitedly

uninitiated »*adjective* without special knowledge or experience of something.

uninjured

uninspired

uninspiring

unintelligent
unintelligently

unintelligible
unintelligibility
unintelligibly

> ☑ -**ible** not -**able**: unintelligible

unintended

unintentional
unintentionally

uninterested »*adjective* not interested or concerned.

> ℹ for an explanation of the difference between **uninterested** and **disinterested**, see the note at DISINTERESTED

uninteresting

uninterrupted »*adjective* not interrupted, stopped, or blocked; continuous.

> ☑ double r: uninterrupted

uninvited

uninviting

union

unionise another way of spelling UNIONIZE.

unionist »*noun* ➊ a member of a trade union. ➋ (**Unionist**) a person in Northern Ireland in favour of union with Great Britain.
unionism

unionize »*verb* (**unionizes, unionizing, unionized**) become or cause to become members of a trade union.
unionization

> ☑ many people prefer the alternative spellings **unionise, unionises,** etc., and **unionisation**: both **s** and **z** spellings are correct

Union Jack »*noun* the national flag of the United Kingdom.

unipolar »*adjective* having or relating to a single pole.

unique »*adjective* **①** being the only one of its kind. **②** (**unique to**) belonging or connected to one particular person, group, or place. **③** (in informal English) very special or unusual.
uniquely
uniqueness

> ℹ️ you should be careful in using **unique** in writing or formal speech. Strictly speaking, either a thing is unique or it isn't, so it cannot be described as *quite unique* or *very unique*.

unisex »*adjective* designed to be suitable for both sexes.

unison »*noun* the fact of two or more people saying or doing the same thing at exactly the same time.

unit

Unitarian »*noun* a member of a Christian Church that believes in the unity of God and rejects the idea of the Trinity.
– SAY yoo-ni-**tair**-i-uhn
Unitarianism

unitary »*adjective* **①** single; uniform. **②** relating to a unit or units.

unite »*verb* (**unites, uniting, united**) **①** join together with others in order to do something as a group. **②** bring things together to form a unit or whole.
united

unities

uniting

unit trust »*noun* a company that invests money in various different businesses on behalf of individuals, who can buy small units of investment.

unity »*noun* (plural **unities**) **①** the state of being united or forming a whole. **②** a thing forming a complex whole. **③** (in mathematics) the number one.

> ✓ plural: drop the **y** and add **ies: unities**

universal »*adjective* **①** affecting or done by all people or things in the world or in a particular group. **②** true or right in all cases.
universality
universally

universe

university (plural **universities**)

> ✓ plural: drop the **y** and add **ies: universities**

unjust »*adjective* unfair.
unjustly

unjustifiable
unjustifiably

unjustified

unjustly

unkempt »*adjective* having an untidy appearance.

> ✓ do not forget the **p: unkempt**

unkind
unkindly
unkindness

unknowable

unknowing
unknowingly

unknown

unknown quantity »*noun* a person or thing that is not known about and whose actions or effects are unpredictable.

unlabelled

> ✓ double **l** at the end: **unlabelled** (the spelling **unlabeled** is American)

unlace (verb: **unlaces, unlacing, unlaced**)

unladen »*adjective* not carrying a load.

unladylike

unlaid

unlamented »*adjective* not mourned or regretted.

unlatch »*verb* (**unlatches, unlatching, unlatched**) unfasten the latch of a door or gate.

unlawful
unlawfully
unlawfulness

> ℹ️ see the note at **LAWFUL**

> ✓ -**ful** not -**full: unlawful**

unleaded

unlearned[1] »*adjective* not well educated.
– SAY un-**ler**-nid

unlearned[2] »*adjective* not having been learned.
– SAY un-**lernd**

unleash »*verb* (**unleashes, unleashing, unleashed**) release something from a leash or restraint; set free.

unleavened »*adjective* (of bread) flat because made without yeast.
– SAY un-**lev**-uhnd

unless

unlettered »*adjective* poorly educated or unable to read and write.

unlicensed »*adjective* not having a licence for the sale of alcoholic drinks.

☑ **sed** not **ced: unlicensed**

unlike

ℹ it is not good English to use **unlike** as a word connecting parts of a sentence together, as in *she was behaving unlike she'd ever behaved before*. You should use **as** with a negative instead: *she was behaving as she'd never behaved before*.

unlikely (adjective: **unlikelier, unlikeliest**)
unlikelihood

unlimited

unlined

unlisted »*adjective* not included on a list, especially of stock exchange prices or telephone numbers.

unlit

unlived-in »*adjective* not appearing to be inhabited.

unload (verb: **unloads, unloading, unloaded**)

unlock (verb: **unlocks, unlocking, unlocked**)

unlooked »*adjective* (**unlooked for**) not planned or expected.

unloose »*verb* (**unlooses, unloosing, unloosed**) release something.

unloosen »*verb* (**unloosens, unloosening, unloosened**) release something.

unlooses

unloosing

unloved

unlovely

unlucky (adjective: **unluckier, unluckiest**)
unluckily

unmade

unman »*verb* (**unmans, unmanning, unmanned**) (a poetic term) deprive someone of manly qualities such as self-control or courage.

unmanageable
unmanageably

unmanned

unmannerly »*adjective* not well mannered.

unmanning

unmans

unmarked

unmarried

unmask (verb: **unmasks, unmasking, unmasked**)

unmatched

unmentionable

unmerciful
unmercifully

☑ **-ful** not **-full: unmerciful**

unmerited »*adjective* not deserved.

unmetalled »*adjective* (of a road) not having a hard surface.

☑ double **l: unmetalled**

unmindful »*adjective* (**unmindful of**) not conscious or aware of something.

☑ **-ful** not **-full: unmindful**

unmissable

unmistakable
unmistakably

☑ **unmistakable** can also be spelled with an **e** after the **k: unmistakeable**

unmitigated »*adjective* complete; absolute: *an unmitigated disaster*.

unmotivated

unmoved

unmoving

unmusical

unnatural
unnaturally
unnaturalness

☑ remember the double **n: unnatural**

unnavigable »*adjective* not safe for a ship or boat to sail on.

unnecessary
unnecessarily

☑ single **c** but double **s**, and **ary** not **ery** at the end: **unnecessary**

unnerve »*verb* (**unnerves, unnerving, unnerved**) make someone feel fearful or lacking in confidence.
unnerving

unnoticeable

unnoticed

unnumbered

unobserved

unobstructed

unobtainable

unobtrusive »*adjective* not conspicuous or attracting attention.
unobtrusively
unobtrusiveness

unoccupied

unofficial
unofficially

unopened

unopposed »*adjective* not opposed; unchallenged.

unorganized

✓ unorganized can also be spelled unorganised: both s and z spellings are correct

unoriginal
unoriginality
unoriginally

unorthodox »*adjective* different from what is usual, traditional, or accepted.
unorthodoxy

unostentatious »*adjective* not ostentatious; simple.
unostentatiously

unpack (verb: unpacks, unpacking, unpacked)

unpaid

unpalatable »*adjective* ❶ not pleasant to taste. ❷ difficult to accept.

unparalleled »*adjective* having no equal; exceptional.

✓ double l followed by a single l: unparalleled

unpardonable
unpardonably

unpasteurized

✓ unpasteurized can also be spelled unpasteurised: both s and z spellings are correct

unpatriotic
unpatriotically

unpaved

unperturbed »*adjective* not concerned or worried.

unpick (verb: unpicks, unpicking, unpicked)

unpin (verb: unpins, unpinning, unpinned)

✓ double the n to spell unpinning and unpinned

unpitying
unplanned
unplayable
unpleasant
unpleasantly
unpleasantness

unplug (verb: unplugs, unplugging, unplugged)

✓ double the g to spell unplugging and unplugged

unplumbed »*adjective* ❶ not provided with plumbing. ❷ not fully explored or understood.
unplumbable

unpolished
unpopular
unpopularity

unpopulated »*adjective* without inhabitants.

unpowered

unprecedented »*adjective* never done or known before.
unprecedentedly

unpredictable
unpredictability
unpredictably

unprejudiced

✓ prej not predj: unprejudiced

unpremeditated »*adjective* not planned beforehand.

unprepared

unprepossessing »*adjective* not attractive or interesting.

unpretentious »*adjective* not pretentious; modest.
unpretentiously
unpretentiousness

unprincipled »*adjective* not acting in accordance with moral principles.

unprintable

unproblematic »*adjective* not presenting a problem or difficulty.
unproblematically

unproductive
unprofessional
unprofessionally

✓ single f but double s: unprofessional, unprofessionally

unprofitable
unpromising
unpromisingly

unprompted »*adjective* without being prompted; spontaneous.

unpronounceable
unprotected
unproved
unproven
unprovoked
unpublished
unpunished

unputdownable »*adjective* (in informal English) (of a book) so absorbing that you cannot stop reading it.

unqualified

unquantifiable »*adjective* impossible to express or measure.

unquenchable »*adjective* not able to be quenched or satisfied.

u

unquestionable
unquestionably

unquestioned

unquiet »*adjective* ❶ unable to be still; restless. ❷ anxious.

unravel (verb: unravels, unravelling, unravelled)

> ✓ double the l to spell **unravelling** and **unravelled** (the spellings **unraveling** and **unraveled** are American)

unreachable

unreactive »*adjective* having little tendency to react chemically.

unread

unreadable
unreadably

unready

unreal
unreality
unreally

unrealised another way of spelling UNREALIZED.

unrealistic
unrealistically

unreality

unrealized »*adjective* ❶ not achieved or created. ❷ not converted into money.

> ✓ **unrealized** can also be spelled **unrealised**: both s and z spellings are correct

unreally

unreason »*noun* lack of reasonable thought.

unreasonable
unreasonableness
unreasonably

unreasoning »*adjective* not guided by or based on reason.

unrecognizable
unrecognizably

> ✓ **unrecognizable** can also be spelled **unrecognisable**: both s and z spellings are correct

unrecognized

> ✓ **unrecognized** can also be spelled **unrecognised**: both s and z spellings are correct

unrecorded

unrefined »*adjective* ❶ not processed to remove impurities. ❷ not elegant or cultured.

unregenerate »*adjective* not reforming; stubbornly wrong or bad.
– SAY un-ri-jen-uh-ruht

unregistered

unregulated

unrehearsed

unrelated

unreleased

unrelenting »*adjective* ❶ not stopping or becoming less severe. ❷ not giving in to other people's requests.
unrelentingly

unreliable
unreliability
unreliably

unrelieved »*adjective* lacking variation or change; boring.

unremarkable

unremarked

unremitting »*adjective* never relaxing or slackening.
unremittingly

> ✓ single m but double t: **unremitting**, **unremittingly**

unremunerative »*adjective* bringing little or no profit or income.

unrepeatable

unrepentant
unrepentantly

> ✓ ant not ent: **unrepentant**

unrepresentative »*adjective* not typical of a class, group, or body of opinion.

unrequited »*adjective* (of love) not given in return.

unreserved »*adjective* ❶ without doubts or reservations. ❷ honest and open. ❸ not set apart or booked in advance.
unreservedly

unresolved »*adjective* (of a problem, dispute, etc.) not resolved.

unresponsive
unresponsiveness

unrest »*noun* ❶ a situation in which people are feeling discontented and rebellious. ❷ a state of uneasiness.

unrestrained
unrestrainedly

unrestricted

unrewarding

unripe

unrivalled

> ✓ double l: **unrivalled** (the spelling **unrivaled** is American)

unroll (verb: unrolls, unrolling, unrolled)

unromantic

unruffled »*adjective* (of a person) calm and unconcerned.

unruly »*adjective* (unrulier, unruliest) difficult to control; disorderly.
unruliness

unsafe

unsaid

unsaleable »*adjective* not able to be sold.

> ☑ unsaleable can also be spelled without the e in the middle: unsalable

unsalted

unsanitary »*adjective* not hygienic.

unsatisfactory
unsatisfactorily

unsatisfied [not satisfied]

> ℹ the words unsatisfied and dissatisfied have different meanings: if you are unsatisfied you do not have enough of something you want or need; if you are dissatisfied you are unhappy because what you have is not what you want

unsatisfying
unsatisfyingly

unsaturated »*adjective* (in chemistry) (of organic molecules, especially fats) having double and/or triple bonds between carbon atoms. See also POLYUNSATURATED.

unsavoury »*adjective* ❶ unpleasant to taste, smell, or look at. ❷ not respectable: *an unsavoury reputation.*

> ☑ the ending is oury: unsavoury (the spelling unsavory is American)

unscarred

unscathed »*adjective* without suffering any injury, damage, or harm.

unscented

unscheduled

unschooled »*adjective* ❶ lacking schooling or training. ❷ natural and spontaneous.

unscientific
unscientifically

unscrew (verb: unscrews, unscrewing, unscrewed)

unscripted

unscrupulous »*adjective* without moral principles; dishonest or unfair.
unscrupulously
unscrupulousness

unsealed

unseasonable »*adjective* (of weather) unusual for the time of year.
unseasonably

unseasonal »*adjective* unusual or inappropriate for the time of year.

unseasoned

unseat (verb: unseats, unseating, unseated)

unsecured »*adjective* (of a loan) made without an asset given as security.

unseeded »*adjective* (of a competitor in a sports tournament) not seeded.

unseeing

unseemly »*adjective* (of behaviour or actions) not proper or appropriate.

unseen

unselfconscious
unselfconsciously

unselfish
unselfishly

unsentimental

unserviceable »*adjective* not in working order; unfit for use.

unsettled

unshackle (verb: unshackles, unshackling, unshackled)

unshakeable

> ☑ unshakeable can also be spelled without the e in the middle: unshakable

unshaken

unshaven

unsheathe »*verb* (unsheathes, unsheathing, unsheathed) draw out a knife or other object from a sheath.

> ☑ do not forget the e at the end of unsheathe

unsighted »*adjective* ❶ lacking the power of sight. ❷ (especially in sport) prevented from having a clear view.

unsightly »*adjective* unpleasant to look at; ugly.
unsightliness

unsigned

unsinkable

unskilful »*adjective* not having or showing skill.
unskilfully

> ☑ single l's before the f and at the end: unskilful (the spelling unskillful is American)

unskilled

unsmiling

unsociable »*adjective* ❶ not enjoying the company of others. ❷ not likely to produce friendly relations: *watching TV is an unsociable activity.*

> ℹ do not confuse unsociable with unsocial: unsociable means 'not enjoying the company of or engaging in

activities with others'; **unsocial** usually means 'socially inconvenient' and typically refers to the hours of work of a job

unsocial »*adjective* (of hours of work) not falling within the normal working day.

> ℹ️ do not confuse **unsocial** with **antisocial**, which means 'against accepted social customs and therefore annoying'

unsold

unsolicited »*adjective* not asked for.

unsolved

unsophisticated

unsound

unsparing
  unsparingly

unspeakable
  unspeakably

unspecific

unspecified

unspectacular

> ✓ ar not er: **unspectacular**

unspoilt

unspoken

unsporting
  unsportingly

unsportsmanlike

unsprung

unstable »*adjective* (**unstabler**, **unstablest**) ❶ likely to fall or collapse. ❷ likely to change; unsettled. ❸ prone to mental health problems or sudden changes of mood.

unstated

unsteady (adjective: **unsteadier**, **unsteadiest**)
  unsteadily
  unsteadiness

unstick (verb: **unsticks**, **unsticking**, **unstuck**)

unstinting »*adjective* given or giving freely or generously.
  unstintingly

unstoppable
  unstoppably

> ✓ -able not -ible: **unstoppable**

unstructured

unstuck past and past participle of **UNSTICK**.

unstudied »*adjective* spontaneous and natural.

unsubstantial

unsubstantiated »*adjective* not supported or proven by evidence.

unsubtle
  unsubtly

unsuccessful
  unsuccessfully
  unsuccessfulness

> ✓ -ful not -full: **unsuccessful**

unsuitable
  unsuitability
  unsuitably

unsuited

unsullied »*adjective* not spoiled.

unsung »*adjective* not celebrated or praised: *unsung heroes.*

unsupervised

> ✓ **unsupervised** cannot be spelled with an **ized** ending

unsupported

unsure

unsurfaced »*adjective* (of a road or path) not provided with a hard upper layer.

unsurpassed

unsurprising
  unsurprisingly

unsuspected

unsuspecting
  unsuspectingly

unsustainable
  unsustainably

unswayed

unsweetened

unswerving
  unswervingly

unsymmetrical

> ✓ double m: **unsymmetrical**

unsympathetic
  unsympathetically

unsystematic
  unsystematically

untainted

untameable

> ✓ **untameable** can also be spelled without the **e** in the middle: **untamable**

untangle (verb: **untangles**, **untangling**, **untangled**)

untapped

untarnished

untasted

untaught

untenable »*adjective* not able to be maintained or defended against criticism or attack.

untended

untested

unthinkable
unthinkably

> ✓ -able not -ible: unthinkable

unthinking
unthinkingly

unthreatening

untidy (adjective: untidier, untidiest)
untidily
untidiness

untie (verb: unties, untying, untied)

until

> ✓ single l in until, although till has two l's

untimely »*adjective* ❶ happening or done at an unsuitable time. ❷ (of a death or end) happening too soon or sooner than normal.

untiring

untitled

unto »*preposition* (an old word) ❶ = TO. ❷ = UNTIL.

untold

untouchable
untouchability

untouched

untoward »*adjective* unexpected and unwanted.

untraceable

untrained

untrammelled »*adjective* not restricted or hampered.

> ✓ double l at the end: untrammelled (the spelling untrammeled is American)

untranslatable

untreatable

untreated

untried »*adjective* not yet tested; inexperienced.

untrodden

untroubled

untrue

untrustworthy
untrustworthiness

untruth (plural untruths)

untruthful
untruthfully
untruthfulness

> ✓ -ful not -full: untruthful

untutored »*adjective* not formally taught.

untying

untypical
untypically

unusable

unused

unusual
unusually
unusualness

unutterable »*adjective* too great or bad to describe.
unutterably

unuttered

unvalued

unvaried

unvarnished

unvarying
unvaryingly

unveil (verb: unveils, unveiling, unveiled)

unverifiable

unverified

unversed »*adjective* (unversed in) not experienced or skilled in.

unviable

unvoiced

unwaged »*adjective* ❶ unemployed or doing unpaid work. ❷ (of work) unpaid.

unwanted

unwarily

unwariness

unwarrantable »*adjective* unjustifiable.
unwarrantably

unwarranted »*adjective* not warranted.

unwary »*adjective* not cautious.
unwarily
unwariness

unwashed

unwatchable

unwatched

unwavering
unwaveringly

unweaned

unwearied

unwearying

unwelcome

unwelcoming

unwell

u

unwholesome

unwieldy
unwieldiness

> ✓ i before e, and only one l: **unwieldy**

unwilling
unwillingly
unwillingness

unwind (verb: unwinds, unwinding, unwound)

unwinking »*adjective* (of a stare or light) unwavering.

unwise
unwisely

unwitting »*adjective* ❶ not aware of the full facts. ❷ unintentional.
unwittingly

unwonted »*adjective* unaccustomed or unusual.
– SAY un-**wohn**-tid
unwontedly

unworkable

unworldly »*adjective* ❶ having little awareness of the realities of life. ❷ not seeming to belong to this world.
unworldliness

unworried

unworthy (adjective: unworthier, unworthiest)
unworthily
unworthiness

unwound past and past participle of UNWIND.

unwrap (verb: unwraps, unwrapping, unwrapped)

> ✓ double the p in **unwrapping** and **unwrapped**

unwritten

unyielding

unzip (verb: unzips, unzipping, unzipped)

> ✓ double the p in **unzipping** and **unzipped**

up (verb: ups, upping, upped)

> ✓ double the p in **upping** and **upped**

up-and-coming »*adjective* likely to become successful.

upbeat »*noun* (in music) an unaccented beat coming before an accented beat.
» *adjective* cheerful.

upbraid »*verb* (upbraids, upbraiding, upbraided) scold or criticize.

upbringing

upcoming

upcountry »*adverb & adjective* inland.

update (verb: updates, updating, updated)

upend »*verb* (upends, upending, upended) set or turn something on its end or upside down.

upfield »*adverb* (in sport) in or to a position nearer to the opponents' end of a field.

upfront

upgrade »*verb* (upgrades, upgrading, upgraded) raise someone or something to a higher standard or rank.
» *noun* an act of upgrading or an upgraded version.

upgradeable

> ✓ **upgradeable** can also be spelled **upgradable**

upgraded

upgrades

upgrading

upheaval »*noun* a big change that causes a lot of upset or disruption.

upheld past and past participle of UPHOLD.

uphill

uphold »*verb* (upholds, upholding, upheld) ❶ confirm or support something which has been questioned. ❷ maintain a custom or practice.

upholster »*verb* (upholsters, upholstering, upholstered) provide furniture with a soft, padded covering.
upholsterer

upholstery »*noun* ❶ the soft, padded covering used to upholster furniture. ❷ the art or practice of upholstering furniture.

upkeep

upland »*noun* an area of high or hilly land.

uplift (verb: uplifts, uplifting, uplifted)

upload »*verb* (uploads, uploading, uploaded) transfer data to a larger computer system.

upmarket »*adjective & adverb* at or towards the more expensive and high quality end of the market.

upon

upped

upper

upper case »*noun* capital letters.

uppercut »*noun* a punch delivered with an upwards motion and the arm bent.

upper house »*noun* the higher house in a parliament with two chambers.

uppermost

upper school »*noun* a secondary school for children aged from about fourteen upwards.

upping

uppish »*adjective* (in informal English) self-assertive and arrogant.

uppity »*adjective* (in informal English) self-important.

upright
  uprightly
  uprightness

uprising »*noun* an act of rebellion.

upriver

uproar

uproarious »*adjective* ❶ very noisy; causing uproar. ❷ very funny.
  uproariously
  uproariousness

uproot »*verb* (**uproots, uprooting, uprooted**) ❶ pull a plant, tree, etc. out of the ground. ❷ move someone from their home or a familiar location.

ups

upset (verb: **upsets, upsetting, upset**)
  upsetting

> double the t in **upsetting**

upshot »*noun* the eventual outcome or conclusion.

upside down

upsilon »*noun* the twentieth letter of the Greek alphabet (Υ, υ).
– **SAY** uhp-sy-luhn

upstage »*adverb & adjective* at or towards the back of a stage.
» *verb* (**upstages, upstaging, upstaged**) divert attention from someone towards yourself.

upstairs

upstanding

upstart »*noun* a person who has suddenly become important and behaves arrogantly.

upstate »*adjective & adverb* (in American English) in or to a part of a state remote from its large cities.

upstream

upstroke »*noun* an upwards stroke.

upsurge »*noun* an increase.

upswing »*noun* an upward trend.

upsy-daisy

uptake

uptempo »*adjective & adverb* (in music) played with a fast or increased tempo.

upthrust »*noun* ❶ (in physics) the upward force that a fluid exerts on a body floating in it. ❷ (in geology) the upward movement of part of the earth's surface.

uptight

up-to-date

uptown »*adjective & adverb* in or into the residential area of a town or city.

upturn

upturned

upward
  upwardly

upwards

upwind »*adverb & adjective* into the wind.

uranium »*noun* a radioactive metallic chemical element used as a fuel in nuclear reactors.
– **SAY** yuu-**ray**-ni-uhm

Uranus [planet]
– **SAY** yoo-**ray**-nuhss or **yoo**-ruh-nuhss

urban »*adjective* having to do with a town or city.

urbane »*adjective* (of a man) confident, polite, and refined.
– **SAY** er-**bayn**
  urbanely

urbanise another way of spelling **URBANIZE**.

urbanite »*noun* (in informal English) a town or city dweller.

urbanity »*noun* an urbane quality or manner.

urbanize »*verb* (**urbanizes, urbanizing, urbanized**) make or become urban.
  urbanization

> ✓ many people prefer the alternative spellings **urbanise, urbanises,** etc., and **urbanisation**: both **s** and **z** spellings are correct

urban myth (also **urban legend**) »*noun* an entertaining story or piece of information of uncertain origin that is circulated as though true.

urchin »*noun* a poor child dressed in rags.

Urdu »*noun* a language of Pakistan and India, closely related to Hindi.
– **SAY** oor-doo or er-doo

urea »*noun* a colourless compound found in urine.
– **SAY** yuu-ree-uh

ureter »*noun* the duct by which urine passes from the kidney to the bladder.
– **SAY** yuu-**ree**-ter

urethra »*noun* the duct by which urine is conveyed out of the body, and which in males also carries semen.

– sᴀʏ yuu-**ree**-thruh
urethral

urge (verb: **urges, urging, urged**)

 drop the **e** to spell **urging**

urgent
  urgency
  urgently

urges

urging

urinal »*noun* a container into which men
  urinate, that is attached to the wall in a
  public toilet.
– sᴀʏ yuu-**ry**-nuhl or **yoor**-i-nuhl

urinary »*adjective* having to do with urine
  or its production in the body.

 ary not **ery**: **urinary**

urinate »*verb* (**urinates, urinating, urinated**)
  discharge urine.
  urination

urine

URL »*abbreviation* uniform (or universal)
  resource locator, the address of a World
  Wide Web page.

urn »*noun* ❶ a tall vase with a stem and
  base, especially one for storing a cremated
  person's ashes. ❷ a large metal container
  with a tap, in which tea or coffee is made
  and kept hot.

urology »*noun* the branch of medicine
  concerned with disorders of the urinary
  system.
– sᴀʏ yuu-**rol**-uh-ji
  urological
  urologist

ursine »*adjective* having to do with bears.
– sᴀʏ **er**-syn

urticaria »*noun* (in medicine) a rash of
  round, red, itchy patches on the skin,
  caused by an allergic reaction; nettlerash.
– sᴀʏ er-ti-**kair**-i-uh

Uruguayan
– sᴀʏ yoor-uh-**gwy**-uhn

 Uru not **Ura**: **Uruguay, Uruguayan**

US »*abbreviation* United States.

us

USA »*abbreviation* United States of
  America.

usable
  usability

 usable can also be spelled **useable**,
  with an **e** in the middle

usage

use (verb: **uses, using, used**)
  user

useable another way of spelling **USABLE**.

used

useful
  usefully
  usefulness

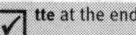 **-ful** not **-full**: **useful**

useless
  uselessly
  uselessness

user

user-friendly
  user-friendliness

uses

usher »*noun* ❶ a person who shows people
  to their seats in a theatre or cinema or in
  church. ❷ an official in a law court who
  swears in jurors and witnesses and keeps
  order.
  »*verb* (**ushers, ushering, ushered**) show or
  guide someone somewhere.

usherette »*noun* a woman who shows
  people to their seats in a cinema or
  theatre.

 tte at the end: **usherette**

ushering

ushers

using

USS »*abbreviation* United States Ship.

USSR »*abbreviation* (a historical term) Union
  of Soviet Socialist Republics.

usual
  usually

usurer »*noun* a person who lends money at
  unreasonably high rates of interest.
– sᴀʏ **yoo**zh-uh-ruh

usurious »*adjective* relating to usury.
– sᴀʏ yoo-**zhoor**-i-uhss

usurp »*verb* (**usurps, usurping, usurped**)
  take over someone's position or power
  when you haven't the right to do so.
– sᴀʏ yuu-**zerp**
  usurpation
  usurper

usury »*noun* the practice of lending money
  at unreasonably high rates of interest.
– sᴀʏ **yoo**-zhuh-ri

utensil »*noun* a tool or container,
  especially for household use.

 sil not **cil**: **utensil**

uteri plural of **UTERUS**.

uterine »*adjective* having to do with the uterus.
– SAY yoo-tuh-ryn

uterus »*noun* (plural **uteri**) the womb.
– SAY yoo-tuh-ruhss [singular], yoo-tuh-ry [plural]

> ✓ make the plural by changing the **us** ending to **i** (as in Latin): **uteri**

utilise another way of spelling **UTILIZE**.

utilitarian »*adjective* ❶ useful or practical rather than attractive. ❷ relating to utilitarianism.
– SAY yuu-ti-li-**tair**-i-uhn

utilitarianism »*noun* the belief that the greatest happiness of the greatest number should be the guiding principle of right behaviour.

utility »*noun* (plural **utilities**) ❶ the state of being useful or profitable. ❷ a public organization supplying electricity, gas, water, or sewerage.
» *adjective* having several functions or uses.

> ✓ plural: drop the **y** and add **ies**: **utilities**

utility room »*noun* a room where a washing machine and other domestic equipment is kept.

utilize »*verb* (**utilizes**, **utilizing**, **utilized**) make practical and effective use of something.
utilization

> ✓ many people prefer the alternative spellings **utilise**, **utilises**, etc., and **utilisation**: both **s** and **z** spellings are correct

utmost

Utopia »*noun* an imaginary place where everything is perfect.
– SAY yoo-**toh**-pi-uh

> ℹ **Utopia** was the title of a book by Sir Thomas More written in 1516

utopian »*adjective* idealistic.
» *noun* an idealistic reformer.
utopianism

utter[1] [complete; absolute]
utterly

utter[2] (verb: **utters**, **uttering**, **uttered**) [say something]

utterance

> ✓ **ance** not **ence**: **utterance**

uttered

uttering

utterly

uttermost »*adjective & noun* utmost.

utters

U-turn

UV »*abbreviation* ultraviolet.

uvula »*noun* (plural **uvulae**) a fleshy part of the soft palate which hangs above the throat.
– SAY yoo-**vyuu**-luh [singular], yoo-**vyuu**-lee [plural]

> ✓ add **e** to make the plural (as in the original Latin): **uvulae**

uxorious »*adjective* (of a man) very or excessively fond of his wife.
– SAY uk-**sor**-i-uhss
uxoriousness

Uzbek [of Uzbekistan]

Uzi »*noun* a type of sub-machine gun made in Israel.
– SAY **oo**-zi

Vv

vacancy (plural **vacancies**)

> ✓ plural: drop the **y** and add **ies**: **vacancies**

vacant »*adjective* ❶ empty. ❷ (of a position) not filled. ❸ showing no intelligence or interest.
vacantly

vacate »*verb* (**vacates**, **vacating**, **vacated**) ❶ leave a place. ❷ give up a position or job.

vacation (verb: **vacations**, **vacationing**, **vacationed**)
vacationer

vaccinate »*verb* (**vaccinates**, **vaccinating**, **vaccinated**) treat a person or animal with

a vaccine to produce immunity against a disease.
– SAY vak-si-nayt
vaccination

 double c: **vaccinate**

vaccine »*noun* a substance injected into the body to cause it to produce antibodies and so provide immunity against a disease.
– SAY vak-seen

vacillate »*verb* (**vacillates, vacillating, vacillated**) waver between different opinions or actions.
– SAY va-si-layt
vacillation

 one c, two l's: **vacillate**

vacua plural of VACUUM.

vacuity

vacuole »*noun* (in biology) a space inside a cell, enclosed by a membrane and containing fluid.
– SAY vak-yuu-ohl

vacuous »*adjective* showing a lack of thought or intelligence.
– SAY vak-yuu-uhss
vacuity
vacuously
vacuousness

vacuum »*noun* (plural **vacuums** or **vacua**) ❶ a space entirely empty of matter. ❷ a space from which the air has been completely or partly removed. ❸ a gap left by the loss of someone or something important. ❹ (plural **vacuums**) a vacuum cleaner.
»*verb* (**vacuums, vacuuming, vacuumed**) clean a surface with a vacuum cleaner.
– SAY vak-yoom [singular], vak-yuu-uh [plural]

once c, two u's: **vacuum**
the plural can be either **vacuums** or (as in the original Latin) **vacua**

vacuum flask »*noun* a container that keeps a substance hot or cold by means of a double wall enclosing a vacuum.

vacuuming

vacuum-pack »*verb* (**vacuum-packs, vacuum-packing, vacuum-packed**) seal a product in a pack or wrapping with the air removed.

vacuums

vacuum tube »*noun* a sealed glass tube containing a near vacuum which allows the free passage of electric current.

vade mecum »*noun* (plural **vade mecums**) a handbook or guide kept constantly at hand.
– SAY vah-di **may**-kuhm or vay-di **mee**-kuhm

vade mecum is a Latin phrase meaning 'go with me'

vagabond »*noun* a vagrant.
– SAY vag-uh-bond

vagary »*noun* (plural **vagaries**) an unexpected and mysterious change.
– SAY vay-guh-ri

vagina (plural **vaginas**)
vaginal

vagrant »*noun* a person without a home or job.
»*adjective* living like a vagrant.
– SAY vay-gruhnt
vagrancy

 ant not ent: **vagrant**

vague (adjective: **vaguer, vaguest**)
vaguely
vagueness

vain (adjective: **vainer, vainest**) [conceited]
vainly

do not confuse **vain** with **vane**, which refers to the blade of a windmill, propeller, etc., or **vein** 'a tube which carries blood through the body'

vainglory »*noun* (a poetic term) excessive vanity.
vainglorious
vaingloriously

vainly

valance »*noun* a length of fabric attached to the base of a bed beneath the mattress to cover the space below.
– SAY va-luhnss
valanced

 ance not ence: **valance**

vale »*noun* (a poetic term) a valley.

do not confuse with **veil**, which refers to a garment used to cover the face

valediction »*noun* ❶ the action of saying farewell. ❷ a farewell speech.
– SAY va-li-**dik**-sh'n

 vale- not **vali-**: **valediction**

valedictory »*adjective* serving as a farewell.
– SAY va-li-**dik**-tuh-ri

valence »*noun* (in chemistry) = VALENCY.
– SAY vay-luhnss

valency »*noun* (plural **valencies**) (in chemistry) the combining power of an element, as measured by the number of hydrogen atoms it can displace or combine with.
– SAY vay-luhn-si

valentine

valerian »*noun* ❶ a plant with clusters of small pink, red, or white flowers. ❷ a sedative drug obtained from a valerian root.
– SAY vuh-**leer**-i-uhn

valet »*noun* ❶ a man's personal male attendant, responsible for his clothes and appearance. ❷ a hotel employee performing such duties for guests. ❸ a person employed to clean or park cars.
» *verb* (**valets, valeting, valeted**) ❶ act as a valet to someone. ❷ clean a car.
– SAY va-lay or va-lit

> ☑ do not double the t in **valeting** and **valeted**

valetudinarian »*noun* a person who is in poor health or who worries too much about their health.
– SAY va-li-tyoo-di-**nair**-i-uhn

valiant »*adjective* showing courage or determination.
valiantly

> ☑ ant not ent: **valiant**

valid »*adjective* ❶ (of a reason, argument, etc.) sound or logical. ❷ legally binding or officially acceptable.
validity
validly

validate »*verb* (**validates, validating, validated**) ❶ check or prove the validity of something. ❷ make or declare something legally valid.
validation

validity

validly

valise »*noun* a small travelling bag or suitcase.
– SAY vuh-**leez**

Valium »*noun* (trademark) a tranquillizing drug used to relieve anxiety.
– SAY va-li-uhm

valley (plural **valleys**)

valor American spelling of **VALOUR**.

valorize »*verb* (**valorizes, valorizing, valorized**) give value or validity to something.
– SAY va-luh-ryz
valorization

> ☑ many people prefer the alternative spellings **valorise, valorises**, etc., and **valorisation**: both **s** and **z** spellings are correct

valour »*noun* courage in the face of danger.
valorous

> ☑ **-our** not **-or** (but not in **valorous**): **valour** (the spelling **valor** is American)

valuable
valuably

valuation »*noun* an estimate of how much something is worth.

value (verb: **values, valuing, valued**)
valueless
valuer

> ☑ drop the **e** in **valuing**

value added tax »*noun* a tax on the amount by which goods or services rise in value at each stage of production.

valued

valueless

valuer

values

valuing

valve »*noun* ❶ a device for controlling the passage of fluid through a pipe or duct. ❷ a cylindrical mechanism used to vary the length of the tube in a brass musical instrument. ❸ a structure in the heart or in a blood vessel that allows blood to flow in one direction only. ❹ one of the halves of the hinged shell of a bivalve mollusc.

valvular »*adjective* relating to or having a valve or valves.

vamoose »*verb* (**vamooses, vamoosing, vamoosed**) (in informal English) leave hurriedly.
– SAY vuh-**mooss**

vamp[1] »*noun* the upper front part of a boot or shoe.
» *verb* (**vamps, vamping, vamped**) (**vamp up**) (in informal English) improve something by adding something more interesting.

vamp[2] »*noun* (in informal English) a woman who uses her sexual attraction to control men.
vampish

vampire »*noun* ❶ (in stories) a dead person that leaves their grave at night to drink the blood of living people. ❷ (also **vampire bat**) a small blood-sucking bat, found mainly in tropical America.
vampiric
vampirism

vampish

vamps

van[1] [motor vehicle]

van[2] »*noun* the leading part of an advancing group.

vanadium »*noun* a hard grey metallic chemical element, used to make alloy steels.
– SAY vuh-**nay**-di-uhm

vandal
vandalism

vandalize (verb: **vandalizes**, **vandalizing**, **vandalized**)

✓ many people prefer the alternative spellings **vandalise**, **vandalises**, etc.: both **s** and **z** spellings are correct

vane »*noun* ❶ a broad blade attached to a rotating axis or wheel which is moved by wind or water, forming part of a windmill, propeller, or turbine. ❷ a weathervane.

ℹ do not confuse **vane** with **vain**, which means 'conceited', or **vein**, which means 'a tube which carries blood through the body'

vanguard »*noun* ❶ the leading part of an advancing army. ❷ a group of people leading the way in new developments or ideas.

vanilla »*noun* a substance obtained from the pods of a tropical plant, used as a flavouring or scent.

✓ one n, two l's: **vanilla**

vanish (verb: **vanishes**, **vanishing**, **vanished**)

vanishing point »*noun* the point in the distance at which receding parallel lines appear to meet.

vanity (plural **vanities**)

✓ plural: drop the **y** and add **ies**: **vanities**

vanquish »*verb* (**vanquishes**, **vanquishing**, **vanquished**) defeat someone or something thoroughly.
– SAY **vang**-kwish

vantage »*noun* a place or position giving a good view.
– SAY **vahn**-tij

Vanuatuan [of Vanuatu in the SW Pacific]
– SAY van-uu-**ah**-tuu-uhn

vapid »*adjective* offering nothing that is stimulating or challenging.
– SAY **vap**-id
vapidity
vapidly

vapor American spelling of **VAPOUR**.

vaporize »*verb* (**vaporizes**, **vaporizing**, **vaporized**) convert something into vapour.
vaporization

✓ many people prefer the alternative spellings **vaporise**, **vaporises**, etc., **vaporisation**, and **vaporiser**: both **s** and **z** spellings are correct

vaporizer »*noun* a device that is used to breathe in medicine in the form of a vapour.

vaporizes

vaporizing

vapour »*noun* ❶ moisture or another substance that is diffused or suspended in the air. ❷ (in physics) a gaseous substance that can be made into liquid by pressure alone.
vaporous

✓ **-our** not **-or** (but not in **vaporous**): **vapour** (the spelling **vapor** is American)

vapour trail »*noun* a trail of condensed water from an aircraft or rocket at high altitude, seen as a white streak against the sky.

variable
variability
variably

variance »*noun* the amount by which something changes or is different from something else.

variant »*noun* a form or version that varies from other forms of the same thing.

variation
variational

varicoloured »*adjective* consisting of several different colours.
– SAY **vair**-i-kul-erd

✓ **-oured** not **-ored**: **varicoloured** (the spelling **varicolored** is American)

varicose »*adjective* (of a vein) swollen, twisted, and lengthened, as a result of poor circulation.
– SAY **va**-ri-kohss or **va**-ri-kuhss

varied
variedly

variegated »*adjective* having irregular patches or streaks of different colours.
– SAY **vair**-i-gay-tid
variegation

✓ remember the **e** in the middle: **variegated**

varies

variety (plural **varieties**)
varietal

☑ plural: drop the **y** and add **ies**: **varieties**

varifocal »*adjective* (of a lens) having a number of focusing distances for near, intermediate, and far vision.
» *noun* (**varifocals**) varifocal glasses.
– SAY vair-i-**foh**-k'l

various
variously

varlet »*noun* ❶ (an old word) a rogue or rascal. ❷ (a historical term) a male servant.
– SAY var-lit

varnish (verb: **varnishes, varnishing, varnished**)

varsity »*noun* (plural **varsities**) ❶ (old-fashioned) university. ❷ (in American English) a sports team representing a university or college.

vary »*verb* (**varies, varying, varied**) ❶ differ in size, degree, or nature from something else of the same general class. ❷ change from one form or state to another. ❸ alter something to make it less uniform.

vascular »*adjective* referring to the system of vessels for carrying blood or (in plants) sap, water, and nutrients.
– SAY vass-**kyuu**-ler

☑ **ar** not **er**: **vascular**

vas deferens »*noun* one of the two ducts which convey sperm from the testicles to the urethra.
– SAY vass **def**-uh-renz

☑ you are unlikely to need a plural, but if you do it is **vasa deferentia** (as in the original Latin)

vase

vasectomy »*noun* (plural **vasectomies**) the surgical cutting and sealing of part of each vas deferens as a means of sterilization.
– SAY vuh-**sek**-tuh-mi

vaseline »*noun* (trademark) a type of petroleum jelly used as an ointment and lubricant.
– SAY vass-uh-leen

vassal »*noun* ❶ (a historical term) a man who promised to fight for a king or queen or lord in return for holding a piece of land. ❷ a country that is controlled by or dependent on another.
– SAY vass-uhl

vast (adjective: **vaster, vastest**)
vastly
vastness

VAT »*abbreviation* value added tax.

vat »*noun* a large tank or tub used to hold liquid.

Vatican »*noun* the official residence of the Pope in Rome.

vaudeville »*noun* a type of entertainment featuring a mixture of musical and comedy acts.
– SAY vaw-duh-vil or voh-duh-vil
vaudevillian

☑ remember the final **e**: **vaudeville** is a French word

vault[1] »*noun* ❶ a roof in the form of an arch or a series of arches. ❷ a large room used for storage, especially in a bank. ❸ a chamber beneath a church or in a graveyard used for burials.
vaulted

vault[2] »*verb* (**vaults, vaulting, vaulted**) jump over something in a single movement, using your hands or a pole to push yourself.
» *noun* an act of vaulting.

vaulting »*noun* the arrangement of vaults in a roof or ceiling.

vaulting horse »*noun* a padded wooden block used for vaulting over by gymnasts and athletes.

vaults

vaunted »*adjective* much praised or boasted about.
– SAY rhymes with haunted

VCR »*abbreviation* video cassette recorder.

VD »*abbreviation* venereal disease.

VDU »*abbreviation* visual display unit.

veal »*noun* meat from a young calf.

vector »*noun* ❶ (in mathematics & physics) a quantity having direction as well as magnitude. ❷ the carrier of a disease or infection.
vectorial

☑ **-or** not **-er**: **vector**

veer »*verb* (**veers, veering, veered**) ❶ change direction suddenly. ❷ (of the wind) change direction clockwise around the points of the compass.
» *noun* a sudden change of direction.

veg (in informal English) »*noun* (plural **veg**) a vegetable or vegetables.
» *verb* (**vegges, vegging, vegged**) (**veg out**) relax completely.
– SAY rhymes with hedge

☑ double the **g** to spell **vegges, vegging,** and **vegged**

vegan »*noun* a person who does not eat or use any animal products.
– SAY vee-guhn

vegetable

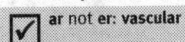

vege not **vega**: vegetable

vegetal »*adjective* relating to plants.
– say vej-i-tuhl

vegetarian »*noun* a person who does not eat meat.
»*adjective* eating or including no meat.
vegetarianism

vegetate »*verb* (**vegetates, vegetating, vegetated**) live or spend time in an inactive, unchallenging way.

vegetated »*adjective* covered with vegetation or plant life.

vegetation »*noun* plants.

vegetative »*adjective* ❶ relating to vegetation or the growth of plants. ❷ relating to reproduction or breeding by asexual means. ❸ (in medicine) alive but showing no sign of brain activity.
– say vej-i-tuh-tiv

vegged

vegges

vegging

vehement »*adjective* showing strong feeling.
– say vee-uh-muhnt
vehemence
vehemently

ent not **ant**: vehement

vehicle
vehicular

veil »*noun* ❶ a piece of fine material worn to protect or hide the face. ❷ the part of a nun's headdress that covers the head and shoulders. ❸ a thing that hides or disguises.
»*verb* (**veils, veiling, veiled**) ❶ cover with a veil. ❷ (**veiled**) partially hidden or disguised.

do not confuse a **veil** with a **vale**, which is a poetic term for a valley

vein [tube carrying blood through the body]
veined
veiny

do not confuse **vein** with **vain**, which means 'conceited', or **vane**, which is the blade of a windmill, propeller, etc.

Velcro »*noun* (trademark) a fastener consisting of two strips of fabric covered with tiny hooks.
Velcroed

veld »*noun* open, uncultivated country or grassland in southern Africa.
– say velt

veld can also be spelled with a final t: **veldt**. It is an Afrikaans word which means 'field'.

vellum »*noun* fine parchment made from animal skin.

velociraptor »*noun* a small meat-eating dinosaur.
– say vi-los-si-rap-ter

-or not **-er**: velociraptor

velocity »*noun* (plural **velocities**) speed in a particular direction.
– say vi-loss-i-ti

velodrome »*noun* a cycle-racing track with steeply banked curves.
– say vel-uh-drohm

velour »*noun* a thick soft fabric resembling velvet.
– say vuh-loor

velvet
velvety

velveteen »*noun* a cotton fabric resembling a thin velvet.

velvety

venal »*adjective* open to bribery.
– say vee-n'l
venality

do not confuse **venal** with **venial**, which is used in Christian theology to refer to a sin that is not regarded as depriving the soul of divine grace

vend »*verb* (**vends, vending, vended**) sell small items.

vendetta »*noun* a feud in which a family of a murdered person seeks vengeance on the murderer or the murderer's family.
– say ven-det-tuh

single **d** but double **t**: vendetta is an Italian word

vending

vending machine »*noun* a machine that dispenses small articles when you insert a coin.

vendor »*noun* ❶ a person or company offering something for sale. ❷ a person who is selling a property.

vends

veneer »*noun* ❶ a thin covering of fine wood applied to a cheaper wood or other material. ❷ an outward appearance that hides the true nature of someone or something.
– say vi-neer
veneered

venerable »*adjective* given great respect because of age, wisdom, or character.

venerate »*verb* (**venerates, venerating, venerated**) respect someone highly.
– SAY ven-uh-rayt
veneration

venereal disease »*noun* a disease caught by having sex with an infected person.

Venetian »*adjective* relating to Venice.
» *noun* a person from Venice.
– SAY vuh-**nee**-sh'n

venetian blind »*noun* a window blind consisting of horizontal slats which can be turned to control the amount of light that passes through.

Venezuelan

vengeance »*noun* an act of punishing or harming someone in return for what they have done to you or someone close to you.
– SAY ven-juhnss

 gean not gen: ven**gean**ce

vengeful »*adjective* wanting to harm someone in return for something they have done.
vengefully
vengefulness

 -ful not -full: venge**ful**

venial »*adjective* ❶ (in Christian belief) referring to a sin that will not deprive the soul of divine grace. ❷ (of a fault or offence) slight and pardonable.
– SAY vee-ni-uhl

 do not confuse **venial** with **venal**, which means 'open to bribery'

venison »*noun* meat from a deer.
– SAY ven-i-s'n

Venn diagram »*noun* a diagram representing mathematical sets as circles, with overlapping sections representing elements shared between sets.

 named after the English logician John Venn

venom »*noun* ❶ poisonous liquid produced by some animals that bite or sting, such as snakes and scorpions. ❷ a strong feeling of hatred or bitterness.

venomous »*adjective* ❶ producing venom. ❷ full of hatred or bitterness.
venomously

 venom- not venem-: **venom**ous

venous »*adjective* relating to a vein or the veins.
– SAY vee-nuhss

vent »*noun* ❶ an opening that allows air, gas, or liquid to pass out of or into a confined space. ❷ a slit in a garment.
» *verb* (**vents, venting, vented**) ❶ allow yourself to express a strong emotion. ❷ let air, gas, or liquid pass through a vent.

ventilate »*verb* (**ventilates, ventilating, ventilated**) cause air to enter and circulate freely in a room or building.
ventilation

ventilator »*noun* ❶ an opening or a machine for ventilating a room or building. ❷ a machine that pumps air in and out of a person's lungs to help them to breathe.

 only one **l**, and the ending is **-or** not **-er**: ventilat**or**

venting

ventral »*adjective* having to do with the underside or abdomen (the opposite of *dorsal*).

ventricle »*noun* one of the two larger and lower cavities of the heart.
– SAY ven-tri-k'l

ventriloquist »*noun* an entertainer who makes their voice seem to come from a dummy of a person or animal.
– SAY ven-**tril**-uh-kwist
ventriloquism
ventriloquy

vents

venture »*noun* ❶ a risky or daring journey or undertaking. ❷ a business enterprise involving considerable risk.
» *verb* (**ventures, venturing, ventured**) ❶ dare to do something dangerous or risky. ❷ dare to say something bold.
venturer

venture capital »*noun* capital invested in a project in which there is a large amount of risk.

ventured

venturer

ventures

venturesome »*adjective* willing to take on something difficult or risky.

venturing

venue »*noun* the place where an event or meeting is held.
– SAY ven-yoo

Venus

Venus's flytrap »*noun* a plant with hinged leaves that spring shut on and digest insects which land on them.

V

> ℹ️ also called a **Venus flytrap**

veracious »*adjective* truthful or speaking the truth.
– SAY vuh-**ray**-shuhss

> ℹ️ do not confuse **veracious** with **voracious**, which means 'wanting or eating great quantities of food'

veracity »*noun* accuracy and truthfulness.
– SAY vuh-**rass**-i-ti

veranda »*noun* a structure with an open front and roof, like a long porch, outside of a house.

> ☑️ **veranda** can also be spelled with an **h** on the end: **verandah**

verb »*noun* a word expressing an action or occurrence, such as *hear* or *happen*.

verbal »*adjective* ❶ relating to or in the form of words. ❷ spoken rather than written. ❸ relating to a verb.
verbally

verbalize »*verb* (**verbalizes**, **verbalizing**, **verbalized**) express something in words.
verbalization

> ☑️ many people prefer the alternative spellings **verbalise**, **verbalises**, etc., and **verbalisation**: both **s** and **z** spellings are correct

verbally

verbal noun »*noun* (in grammar) a noun formed as an inflection of a verb, such as *smoking* in *smoking is forbidden*.

verbatim »*adverb & adjective* in exactly the same words as were used originally.
– SAY ver-**bay**-tim

verbena »*noun* an ornamental plant with heads of bright showy flowers.
– SAY ver-**bee**-nuh

verbiage »*noun* excessively long or detailed speech or writing.
– SAY **ver**-bi-ij

verbose »*adjective* using more words than are needed.
– SAY ver-**bohss**
verbosely
verbosity

verdant »*adjective* green with grass or other lush vegetation.
– SAY **ver**-duhnt
verdantly

> ☑️ **ant** not **ent**: **verdant**

verdict »*noun* ❶ a decision made by a jury in a court of law as to whether a person is innocent or guilty. ❷ an opinion or judgement that you form after you have tried or tested something.

verdigris »*noun* a bright bluish-green substance formed on copper or brass by oxidation.
– SAY **ver**-di-gree or **ver**-di-greess

verdure »*noun* lush green vegetation.

verge (verb: **verges**, **verging**, **verged**)

verger »*noun* an official in a church who acts as a caretaker and attendant.

verges

verging

verify »*verb* (**verifies**, **verifying**, **verified**) make sure or show that something is true and accurate.
– SAY **ve**-ri-fy
verifiable
verification
verifier

verily »*adverb* (an old word) truly; certainly.

verisimilitude »*noun* the appearance of being true or real.
– SAY ve-ri-si-**mil**-i-tyood

> ☑️ **veri** not **vers**: **verisimilitude**

veritable »*adjective* genuine.
veritably

verity »*noun* (plural **verities**) truthfulness or a truth.

> ☑️ plural: drop the **y** and add **ies**: **verities**

vermicelli »*plural noun* ❶ pasta made in long slender threads. ❷ shreds of chocolate used to decorate cakes.
– SAY ver-mi-**chel**-li or ver-mi-**sel**-li

> ☑️ single **c** but double **l**: **vermicelli** is an Italian word which means 'little worms'

vermifuge »*noun* a medicine used to destroy parasitic worms.
– SAY **ver**-mi-fyooj

vermilion »*noun* a brilliant red pigment or colour.
– SAY ver-**mil**-yuhn

> ☑️ single **l**: **vermilion**

vermin »*noun* ❶ wild mammals or birds which carry disease or harm crops. ❷ parasitic worms or insects.
verminous

vermouth »*noun* a red or white wine flavoured with herbs.
– SAY **ver**-muhth or ver-**mooth**

vernacular »*noun* the language or dialect spoken by the ordinary people of a country or region.
– SAY ver-**nak**-yuu-ler

 ar not er: vernacular

vernal »*adjective* relating to the season of spring.
– SAY ver-n'l

vernier »*noun* a small movable scale for showing fractions of the main scale on a measuring device.
– SAY ver-ni-er

named after the French mathematician Pierre *Vernier*

verruca »*noun* (plural **verrucae** or **verrucas**) a contagious wart on the sole of the foot.
– SAY vuh-**roo**-kuh [singular], vuh-**roo**-kee [plural]

 double r but single c: verruca
the plural of verruca can either be verrucae (as in the original Latin) or verrucas

versatile »*adjective* able to adapt or be adapted to many different functions or activities.
versatility

verse

versed »*adjective* (**versed in**) experienced or skilled in; knowledgeable about.

versify »*verb* (**versifies, versifying, versified**) write verse or turn a piece of writing into verse.
versification
versifier

version

verso »*noun* (plural **versos**) a left-hand page of an open book, or the back of a loose document (the opposite of RECTO).

the plural of verso has os not oes: versos

versus

vertebra »*noun* (plural **vertebrae**) one of the series of small bones forming the backbone.
– SAY ver-ti-bruh [singular], ver-ti-bree [plural]
vertebral

the plural of vertebra is vertebrae (as in the original Latin)

vertebrate »*noun* an animal having a backbone, including mammals, birds, reptiles, amphibians, and fishes.
– SAY ver-ti-bruht

vertex »*noun* (plural **vertices** or **vertexes**) ❶ the highest point. ❷ a meeting point of two lines that form an angle.
– SAY ver-teks [singular], ver-ti-seez [plural]

the plural of vertex can be either vertices (as in the original Latin) or vertexes

vertical »*adjective* going straight up or down, at right angles to a horizontal line or surface.
»*noun* a vertical line or surface.
verticality
vertically

vertiginous »*adjective* extremely high or steep so as to give someone a feeling of vertigo.
– SAY ver-**tij**-i-nuhss
vertiginously

vertigo »*noun* a feeling of giddiness caused by looking down from a great height.
– SAY ver-ti-goh

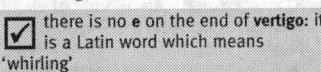 there is no e on the end of vertigo: it is a Latin word which means 'whirling'

vervain »*noun* a plant with small blue, white, or purple flowers, used in herbal medicine.
– SAY ver-vayn

verve »*noun* vigour, spirit, and style.

very

Very light »*noun* a flare fired into the air from a pistol for signalling or for temporary illumination.
– SAY veer-i or ve-ri

named after Edward *Very*, an American naval officer

vespers »*noun* a service of evening prayer.

vessel »*noun* ❶ a ship or large boat. ❷ a tube or duct carrying a liquid within the body or within a plant. ❸ (an old word) a bowl, cup, or other container for liquids.

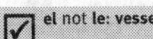 el not le: vessel

vest »*noun* ❶ (in British English) a sleeveless garment or undergarment worn on the upper part of the body. ❷ (in American & Australian English) a waistcoat or sleeveless jacket.
»*verb* (**vests, vesting, vested**) (**vest in**) give someone power or property, or the legal right to hold power or own property.

vestal virgin »*noun* (in ancient Rome) a virgin dedicated to the goddess Vesta and vowed to chastity.

vested

V

vested interest »*noun* a personal reason for wanting something to happen.

vestibule »*noun* a room or hall just inside the outer door of a building.
– SAY vess-ti-byool

vestige »*noun* ❶ a last remaining trace of something. ❷ the smallest amount.
– SAY vess-tij

vestigial »*adjective* forming a very small remaining part of something.
– SAY ve-sti-ji-uhl or ve-sti-juhl
   vestigially

vesting

vestment »*noun* a robe worn by ministers or members of a choir during services.

vestry »*noun* (plural **vestries**) a room in a church, used as an office and for changing into ceremonial robes.

vests

vet »*noun* a veterinary surgeon.
»*verb* (**vets**, **vetting**, **vetted**) find out about someone's background and past before employing them.

> ✅ double the **t** to spell **vetting** and **vetted**

vetch »*noun* a plant with purple, pink, or yellow flowers, grown for silage or fodder.

veteran »*noun* ❶ a person who has had long experience in a particular field. ❷ a person who used to serve in the armed forces.

veterinarian »*noun* (in American English) = VETERINARY SURGEON.

veterinary »*adjective* relating to the treatment of injuries and diseases in animals.
– SAY vet-ri-nuh-ri or vet-uhn-ri

> ✅ note the **-er-** before the **-in-**: **veterinary**

veterinary surgeon »*noun* a person qualified to treat diseased or injured animals.

veto »*noun* (plural **vetoes**) ❶ a right or power to reject a ruling or decision made by others. ❷ such a rejection.
»*verb* (**vetoes**, **vetoing**, **vetoed**) use a veto against something.
– SAY vee-toh

> ℹ️ **veto** is a Latin word which means 'I forbid'

> ✅ add an **e** to spell **vetoes** and **vetoed**, but not to spell **vetoing**

vets

vetted

vetting

vex »*verb* (**vexes**, **vexing**, **vexed**) make someone annoyed or worried.
   vexation

vexatious »*adjective* causing annoyance or worry.

vexed »*adjective* ❶ (of an issue) difficult to deal with and causing a lot of debate: *the vexed question of Europe*. ❷ annoyed or worried.

vexes

vexing

VHF »*abbreviation* very high frequency.

via »*preposition* ❶ travelling through a place on the way to somewhere else. ❷ by way of; through. ❸ by means of.

viable »*adjective* ❶ capable of working successfully. ❷ (of a plant, animal, or cell) able to live.
– SAY vy-uh-b'l
   viability
   viably

viaduct »*noun* a long bridge-like structure carrying a road or railway across a valley or other low ground.

Viagra »*noun* (trademark) a drug used to help a man achieve an erection.
– SAY vy-ag-ruh

vial »*noun* a small container used for holding liquid medicines.
– SAY vy-uhl

> ✅ do not confuse **vial** with **phial**, 'a small cylindrical glass bottle', or **vile** 'extremely unpleasant'

viands »*plural noun* (an old word) food.
– SAY vy-uhndz

vibe »*noun* (in informal English) the atmosphere of a place or a feeling passing between people.

vibrant »*adjective* ❶ full of energy and enthusiasm. ❷ (of sound) strong or resonant. ❸ (of colour) bright.
   vibrancy
   vibrantly

> ✅ **ant** not **ent**: **vibrant**

vibraphone »*noun* an electrical percussion instrument giving a vibrato effect.
– SAY vy-bruh-fohn

vibrate (verb: **vibrates**, **vibrating**, **vibrated**)
   vibratory

vibration
   vibrational

vibrato »*noun* a rapid, slight variation in pitch in singing or playing some musical instruments.
– SAY vi-brah-toh

vibrator »*noun* a vibrating device used for massage or sexual stimulation.

> ☑ -or not -er: **vibrator**

vibratory

viburnum »*noun* a shrub or small tree with clusters of small white flowers.
– SAY vy-**ber**-nuhm

vicar »*noun* (in the Church of England) a priest in charge of a parish.

vicarage »*noun* the house of a vicar.

vicarious »*adjective* (of a situation or feeling) that you feel as if you have experienced yourself, after hearing about it or seeing it.
– SAY vi-**kair**-i-uhss
vicariously

vice¹ »*noun* ❶ immoral or wicked behaviour. ❷ criminal activities that involve sex or drugs. ❸ a bad personal characteristic. ❹ a bad habit.

vice² »*noun* a metal tool with movable jaws which are used to hold an object firmly in place while work is done on it.
vice-like

> ☑ spelled **vise** in America

vice admiral »*noun* the naval rank above rear admiral and below admiral.

vice chancellor »*noun* a deputy chancellor in a British university, in charge of its administration.

vice-like

vice-president

viceroy »*noun* a person sent by a king or queen to govern a colony.

vice versa »*adverb* reversing the order of the items just mentioned.

> ⓘ **vice versa** is a Latin phrase which means 'in-turned position'

vichyssoise »*noun* a soup made with potatoes, leeks, and cream.
– SAY vee-shee-**swahz**

> ⓘ named after the town of *Vichy* in central France

vicinity »*noun* (plural **vicinities**) the area near or surrounding a place.

vicious
viciously
viciousness

vicious circle »*noun* a situation in which one problem leads to another, which then makes the first one worse.

viciously
viciousness

vicissitudes »*plural noun* the ups and downs and changes in your life.
– SAY vi-**siss**-i-tyoodz

victim

victimize »*verb* (**victimizes**, **victimizing**, **victimized**) single someone out for cruel or unfair treatment.
victimization

> ☑ many people prefer the alternative spellings **victimise**, **victimises**, etc., and **victimisation**: both **s** and **z** spellings are correct

victor

> ☑ -or not -er: **victor**

Victorian »*adjective* relating to the reign of Queen Victoria (1837–1901).

Victoriana »*plural noun* articles from the Victorian period.

victories

victorious
victoriously

victory (plural **victories**)

> ☑ plural: drop the **y** and add **ies**: **victories**

victualler »*noun* ❶ a person who is licensed to sell alcoholic liquor. ❷ (old-fashioned) a person providing or selling food or other provisions.
– SAY vi-**t'l**-er

> ☑ double **l**: **victualler** (the spelling **victualer** is American)

victuals »*plural noun* (an old word) food or provisions.
– SAY vi-**t'lz**

vicuna »*noun* ❶ a wild relative of the llama, having fine silky wool. ❷ cloth made from this wool.
– SAY vi-**koo**-nyuh

> ☑ **vicuna** can also be spelled **vicuña**, with a tilde over the **n** (as in Spanish)

video (plural **videos**; verb: **videoes**, **videoing**, **videoed**)

> ☑ the plural of **video** has **os** not **oes**: **videos**. However you must add an **e** when spelling parts of the verb: **videoes** (as in *he videoes the programme each week*) and **videoed**.

videoconference »*noun* an arrangement in which television sets linked to telephone lines are used to allow a group of people to see and talk to each other.
videoconferencing

videodisc »*noun* a CD-ROM or other disc used to store visual images.

videoed

videoes see the note at **VIDEO**.

videophone »*noun* a kind of telephone that sends and receives visual images as well as sound.

videotape (verb: **videotapes**, **videotaping**, **videotaped**)

vie »*verb* (**vies**, **vying**, **vied**) compete eagerly with others in order to do or achieve something.

Viennese (plural **Viennese**) [of Vienna]

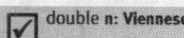 double n: **Viennese**

vies

Vietnamese (plural **Vietnamese**)

view (verb: **views**, **viewing**, **viewed**)
viewable

viewer

viewership »*noun* the audience for a particular television programme or channel.

viewfinder »*noun* a device on a camera showing the field of view of the lens, used in framing and focusing the picture.

viewing

viewpoint

views

vigil »*noun* a period of staying awake during the night to keep watch or pray.
– SAY **vi**-jil

vigilant »*adjective* keeping careful watch for possible danger or difficulties.
vigilance
vigilantly

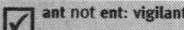 ant not ent: **vigilant**

vigilante »*noun* a member of a group of people who take it upon themselves to prevent crime or punish criminals in their community, without legal authority.
– SAY vi-ji-**lan**-ti
vigilantism

note the ending **-te**: **vigilante** (a Spanish word)

vigilantly

vignette »*noun* ❶ a brief vivid description or episode. ❷ a small illustration or portrait photograph which fades into its background without a definite border.
– SAY vee-**nyet**

note the **ette** ending: **vignette** is a French word

vigor American spelling of **VIGOUR**.

vigorous »*adjective* ❶ strong, healthy, and full of energy. ❷ involving physical strength, effort, or energy.
vigorously
vigorousness

vigour »*noun* ❶ physical strength and good health. ❷ effort, energy, and enthusiasm.

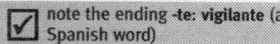 **-our** not **-or** (but not in **vigorous**): **vigour** (the spelling **vigor** is American)

Viking »*noun* a member of the Scandinavian seafaring people who settled in parts of Britain and NW Europe between the 8th and 11th centuries.

vile [extremely unpleasant]
vilely
vileness

do not confuse **vile** with **vial**, 'a small container for holding liquid medicines'

vilify »*verb* (**vilifies**, **vilifying**, **vilified**) speak or write about someone in a very unpleasant way.
– SAY **vil**-i-fy
vilification

villa

village
villager
villagey

villain [bad person]
villainous
villainy

double **l**, and **-ain** not **-an**: **villain**

villein »*noun* (in medieval England) a poor man who had to work for a lord in return for a small piece of land on which to grow food.
– SAY **vil**-luhn or **vil**-layn

vim »*noun* energy; enthusiasm.

vinaigrette »*noun* salad dressing of oil mixed with vinegar.
– SAY vi-ni-**gret** or vi-nay-**gret**

note the two **i**'s, and the **ette** ending: **vinaigrette** is a French word

vindaloo »*noun* a very hot Indian curry.

vindicate »*verb* (**vindicates**, **vindicating**, **vindicated**) ❶ clear someone of blame or suspicion. ❷ show something to be right or justified.
vindication

vindictive »*adjective* having a strong or inappropriate desire for revenge.
vindictively
vindictiveness

V

vine »*noun* ❶ a climbing plant, especially one that bears grapes. ❷ the thin stem of a climbing plant.

vinegar
vinegary

☑ ar not er: vine**gar**

vineyard »*noun* a plantation of grapevines, producing grapes used in winemaking.

vino »*noun* (plural **vinos**) (in informal English) wine.

vinous »*adjective* having to do with or like wine.
– SAY vy-nuhss

vintage »*noun* ❶ the year or place in which wine was produced. ❷ a wine of high quality made from the crop of a single identified district in a good year. ❸ the harvesting of grapes for winemaking. ❹ the grapes or wine of a particular season. ❺ the time that something was produced.
»*adjective* ❶ referring to vintage wine. ❷ referring to something from the past of high quality.

vintage car »*noun* an old car, specifically one made between 1919 and 1930.

vintner »*noun* a wine merchant.

vinyl »*noun* a strong flexible plastic or synthetic resin, used in making products such as paints, book covers and, especially in the past, gramophone records.
– SAY vy-n'l

viol »*noun* an early instrument like a violin, but with six strings.
– SAY vy-uhl

viola[1] »*noun* an instrument of the violin family, larger than the violin and tuned a fifth lower.
– SAY vi-**oh**-luh

viola[2] »*noun* a plant of a group that includes the pansies and violets.
– SAY vy-uh-luh

violate »*verb* (**violates, violating, violated**) ❶ break a rule or formal agreement. ❷ treat something with disrespect. ❸ rape or sexually assault someone.
violation
violator

violence

☑ ence not ance: viol**ence**

violent
violently

violet [plant; bluish-purple colour]

violin
violinist

violist »*noun* a viola player.
– SAY vi-**oh**-list

VIP »*abbreviation* very important person.

viper »*noun* ❶ a poisonous snake with large fangs and a patterned body. ❷ a spiteful or treacherous person.

virago »*noun* (plural **viragos** or **viragoes**) a domineering, violent, or bad-tempered woman.
– SAY vi-**rah**-goh

☑ the plural of **virago** can have either **os** or **oes**: vira**gos** or vira**goes**

viral »*adjective* having to do with or caused by a virus or viruses.
virally

virgin
virginal

virginity

Virgo »*noun* a constellation and sign of the zodiac (the Virgin, 23 August–22 September).

viridian »*noun* a bluish-green pigment or colour.
– SAY vi-**rid**-i-uhn

virile »*adjective* (of a man) strong, energetic, and having a strong sex drive.
virility

virology »*noun* the branch of science concerned with the study of viruses.
– SAY vy-**rol**-uh-ji
virologist

virtual »*adjective* ❶ almost or nearly the thing described, but not completely. ❷ (in computing) not existing in reality but made by software to appear to do so.
virtuality
virtually

virtual reality »*noun* a system in which images that look like real objects are created by computer and can be interacted with by using special electronic equipment.

virtue »*noun* ❶ behaviour showing high moral standards. ❷ a good or desirable personal quality. ❸ (an old word) virginity or chastity.

virtuoso »*noun* (plural **virtuosi** or **virtuosos**) a person highly skilled in music or another art.
– SAY ver-tyoo-**oh**-soh [singular], ver-tyoo-**oh**-si [plural]
virtuosic
virtuosity

☑ the plural of **virtuoso** can be **virtuosi** (as in the original Italian) or **virtuosos**

virtuous »*adjective* ❶ having high moral standards. ❷ (an old word) chaste.

V

virtuously
virtuousness

virulent »*adjective* ❶ (of a disease or poison) extremely harmful. ❷ (of a virus) spreading very quickly. ❸ bitterly hostile: *a virulent attack.*
– SAY vi-ruu-luhnt or vir-yuu-luhnt
virulence
virulently

> ✓ one r, one l, and ent not ant at the end: **virulent**

virus »*noun* (plural **viruses**) ❶ a very simple submicroscopic organism which can cause disease and is only able to reproduce inside the living cells of a host. ❷ an infection or disease caused by a virus. ❸ (also **computer virus**) a piece of code introduced secretly into a system in order to damage or destroy data.

visa »*noun* a note on a passport indicating that the holder is allowed to enter, leave, or stay for a specified period of time in a country.

visage »*noun* (a poetic term) a person's facial features or expression.
– SAY vi-zij

vis-a-vis »*preposition* in relation to.
– SAY veez-ah-**vee**

> ✓ **vis-a-vis** can also be spelled **vis-à-vis**, with a grave accent on the **a** (as in the original French phrase meaning 'face-to-face')

viscera »*plural noun* the internal organs of the body, especially those in the abdomen.
– SAY viss-uh-ruh

> ✓ the singular (rarely used) is **viscus** (a Latin word)

visceral »*adjective* ❶ relating to the viscera. ❷ relating to deep inward feelings rather than to the intellect.
viscerally

viscid »*adjective* sticky.
– SAY viss-id

viscose »*noun* ❶ a thick orange-brown solution obtained by treating cellulose with certain chemicals. ❷ rayon fabric made from this.

> ⓘ do not confuse **viscose** with **viscous**, which means 'having a thick, sticky consistency'

viscosity »*noun* (plural **viscosities**) the state of being viscous.
– SAY viss-**koss**-i-ti

viscount »*noun* a British nobleman ranking above a baron and below an earl.
– SAY vy-kownt

viscountess »*noun* (plural **viscountesses**) the wife or widow of a viscount, or a woman holding the rank of viscount in her own right.
– SAY vy-kown-tiss

viscous »*adjective* having a thick, sticky consistency between solid and liquid.
– SAY viss-kuhss

> ⓘ do not confuse **viscous** with **viscose**, which is a rayon fabric, and the substance from which such fabric is made

viscus singular form of **VISCERA**.

vise American spelling of **VICE²**.

visibility »*noun* ❶ the state of being able to see or be seen. ❷ the distance you can see depending on light and weather conditions.

visible
visibly

> ✓ -ible not -able: **visible**

vision

visionary »*adjective* ❶ thinking about the future with imagination or wisdom. ❷ relating to supernatural or dreamlike visions.
»*noun* (plural **visionaries**) a visionary person.

> ✓ plural: drop the y and add ies: **visionaries**

visit (verb: **visits**, **visiting**, **visited**)

> ✓ do not double the t in **visiting** and **visited**

visitant »*noun* ❶ (a poetic term) a supernatural being; a ghost. ❷ (an old word) a visitor.

visitation »*noun* ❶ an official or formal visit. ❷ the appearance of a god or goddess, or other supernatural being. ❸ a disaster or difficulty seen as a punishment from God: *a visitation of the plague.*

visited

visiting

visitor

> ✓ -or not -er: **visitor**

visits

visor »*noun* ❶ a movable part of a helmet that can be pulled down to cover the face. ❷ a screen for protecting the eyes from unwanted light. ❸ (in American English) a stiff peak at the front of a cap.
– SAY vy-zer

> ✓ **visor** can also be spelled **vizor**

vista »*noun* a pleasing view.

visual
   visually

visual display unit »*noun* a device for displaying information from a computer on a screen.

visualize »*verb* (visualizes, visualizing, visualized) form an image of something in the mind.
   visualization

> ✓ many people prefer the alternative spellings **visualise, visualises,** etc., and **visualisation**: both **s** and **z** spellings are correct

visually

vital »*adjective* ❶ absolutely necessary. ❷ essential for life: *the vital organs.* ❸ full of energy.
   » *noun* (vitals) the body's important internal organs.
   vitally

vitalise another way of spelling **VITALIZE**.

vitality »*noun* the state of being strong and active.

vitalize »*verb* (vitalizes, vitalizing, vitalized) give strength and energy to someone.

> ✓ many people prefer the alternative spellings **vitalise, vitalises,** etc.: both **s** and **z** spellings are correct

vitally

vital signs »*plural noun* measurements, specifically pulse rate, temperature, rate of breathing, and blood pressure, that indicate the state of a patient's essential body functions.

vitamin »*noun* one of a group of organic compounds which are present in many foods and are essential for normal nutrition.
   – **SAY** vi-tuh-min or vy-tuh-min

> ✓ **min** not **men**: **vitamin**

vitiate »*verb* (vitiates, vitiating, vitiated) make something less good or effective.
   – **SAY** vi-shi-ayt

viticulture »*noun* ❶ the cultivation of grapevines. ❷ the study of grape cultivation.
   – **SAY** vi-ti-kul-cher
   viticultural
   viticulturist

vitreous »*adjective* resembling or containing glass.
   – **SAY** vi-tri-uhss

> ✓ **eous** not **ious**: **vitreous**

vitrify »*verb* (vitrifies, vitrifying, vitrified) convert into glass or a glass-like substance by exposure to heat.
   – **SAY** vi-tri-fy
   vitrification

vitriol »*noun* ❶ (an old word) sulphuric acid. ❷ extreme bitterness or malice.
   – **SAY** vi-tri-uhl
   vitriolic
   vitriolically

vituperation »*noun* bitter and abusive language.

vituperative »*adjective* bitter and abusive.
   – **SAY** vi-**tyoo**-puh-ruh-tiv or vy-**tyoo**-puh-ruh-tiv

viva[1] »*noun* an oral examination for an academic qualification.
   – **SAY** vy-vuh

viva[2] »*exclamation* long live! (used to express acclaim or support).
   – **SAY** vee-vuh

vivace »*adverb & adjective* (in music) in a lively and brisk manner.
   – **SAY** vi-**vah**-chay

vivacious »*adjective* attractively lively.
   vivaciously
   vivacity

> ✓ **cious** not **tious**: **vivacious**

vivarium »*noun* (plural **vivaria**) a container or structure prepared for keeping animals in conditions similar to their natural environment for the purposes of study or as pets.
   – **SAY** vi-**vair**-i-uhm or vy-**vair**-i-uhm

> ✓ the plural of **vivarium** is **vivaria** (as in the original Latin word meaning 'warren, fish pond')

viva voce »*adjective* oral rather than written.
   » *noun* = **VIVA**[1].
   – **SAY** vy-vuh **voh**-chay or vy-vuh **voh**-chi

> ℹ **viva voce** is a Latin phrase meaning 'with the living voice'

vivid »*adjective* ❶ producing powerful feelings or strong, clear images in the mind. ❷ (of a colour) very deep or bright.
   vividly
   vividness

vivify »*verb* (vivifies, vivifying, vivified) make something more lively or interesting.
   – **SAY** vi-vi-fy

vivisection »*noun* the practice of performing operations on live animals for scientific research (used by people opposed to such work).

V

vixen »*noun* ❶ a female fox. ❷ a spiteful or quarrelsome woman.

Viyella »*noun* (trademark) a fabric made from a mixture of cotton and wool.
– SAY vy-**el**-luh

viz. »*adverb* that is to say; namely; in other words.

> ℹ️ **viz.** is a medieval abbreviation of the Latin *videlicet*

vizier »*noun* (a historical term) an important official in some Muslim countries.
– SAY vi-**zeer**

vizor another way of spelling **VISOR**.

V-neck
   V-necked

vocabulary »*noun* (plural **vocabularies**) ❶ all the words used in a particular language or activity. ❷ all the words known to a person. ❸ a list of words and their meanings, accompanying a text.
– SAY voh-**kab**-yuu-luh-ri

> ✅ plural: drop the **y** and add **ies**: **vocabularies**

vocal »*adjective* ❶ relating to the human voice. ❷ expressing opinions or feelings freely or loudly. ❸ (of music) consisting of or including singing.
» *noun* ❶ (also **vocals**) a musical performance involving singing. ❷ a part of a piece of music that is sung.
   vocally

vocal cords »*plural noun* folds of the lining of the larynx whose edges vibrate in the airstream to produce the voice.

> ✅ **cords** not **chords**

vocalise another way of spelling **VOCALIZE**.

vocalist »*noun* a singer.

vocalize »*verb* (**vocalizes, vocalizing, vocalized**) ❶ produce a sound or word. ❷ express something with words. ❸ (in music) sing with several notes to one vowel.
   vocalization

> ✅ many people prefer the alternative spellings **vocalise, vocalises**, etc., and **vocalisation**: both **s** and **z** spellings are correct

vocally

vocation »*noun* ❶ a strong feeling that you ought to pursue a particular career or occupation. ❷ a person's career or occupation.

vocational »*adjective* relating to or directed towards an occupation or employment.
   vocationally

vociferous »*adjective* vehement or loud.
– SAY vuh-**sif**-uh-ruhss
   vociferously

vodka »*noun* a clear Russian alcoholic spirit made from rye, wheat, or potatoes.

vogue »*noun* the fashion or style current at a particular time.
   voguish

voice (verb: **voices, voicing, voiced**)

voice box »*noun* the larynx.

voiced

voiceless »*adjective* (of a speech sound) produced without vibration of the vocal cords.

voicemail »*noun* a centralized electronic system which can store messages from telephone callers.

voice-over

voices

voicing

void »*adjective* ❶ not valid or legally binding. ❷ completely empty. ❸ (**void of**) free from; lacking.
» *noun* a completely empty space.
» *verb* (**voids, voiding, voided**) ❶ declare something to be no longer valid. ❷ discharge or empty water, gases, or waste matter.

voile »*noun* a thin, semi-transparent fabric of cotton, wool, or silk.
– SAY voyl or vwahl

> ℹ️ **voile** is a French word meaning 'veil'

volatile »*adjective* ❶ (of a substance) easily evaporated at normal temperatures. ❷ liable to change rapidly and unpredictably.
» *noun* a volatile substance.
– SAY **vol**-uh-tyl
   volatility

vol-au-vent »*noun* a small round case of puff pastry filled with a savoury mixture.
– SAY **vol**-oh-von

> ℹ️ **vol-au-vent** means 'flight in the wind' in French

volcanic
   volcanically

volcanism »*noun* (in geology) volcanic activity or phenomena.

> ✅ **volcanism** can also be spelled **vulcanism**

volcano (plural **volcanoes** or **volcanos**)

☑ the plural of **volcano** can have **oes** or **os**: **volcanoes** or **volcanos**

volcanology »*noun* the scientific study of volcanoes.
– SAY vol-kuh-**nol**-uh-ji
volcanologist

☑ **volcanology** can also be spelled **vulcanology**

vole »*noun* a small mouse-like rodent with a rounded muzzle.

volition »*noun* the power of choosing freely and making your own decisions.
– SAY vuh-**li**-sh'n
volitional

volley »*noun* (plural **volleys**) ❶ a number of bullets, arrows, or other missiles fired at one time. ❷ a series of questions, insults, etc. directed rapidly at someone. ❸ (in sport) a strike of the ball made before it touches the ground.
» *verb* (**volleys**, **volleying**, **volleyed**) strike the ball before it touches the ground.

volleyball

volleyed

volleying

volleys

volt »*noun* a basic unit of electrical potential or electromotive force.

ℹ named after the Italian physicist Alessandro *Volta*

voltage »*noun* an electromotive force or potential difference expressed in volts.

voltaic »*adjective* referring to electricity produced by chemical action in a primary battery.
– SAY vol-**tay**-ik

volte-face »*noun* an abrupt and complete reversal of attitude or policy.
– SAY volt-**fass**

ℹ **volte-face** is a French expression meaning 'turning to face the opposite way'

voltmeter »*noun* an instrument for measuring electric potential in volts.

voluble »*adjective* speaking easily and at length.
– SAY vol-**yuu**-b'l
volubility
volubly

volume »*noun* ❶ a book, especially one forming part of a larger work or series. ❷ the amount of space occupied by a substance or object or enclosed within a container. ❸ the amount or quantity of something. ❹ degree of loudness. ❺ fullness of the hair.

volumetric »*adjective* relating to the measurement of volume.
– SAY vol-yuu-**met**-rik
volumetrically

voluminous »*adjective* ❶ (of clothing) loose and full. ❷ (of writing) very lengthy.
– SAY vuh-**lyoo**-mi-nuhss
voluminously

volumize »*verb* (**volumizes**, **volumizing**, **volumized**) give volume or body to hair.

☑ many people prefer the alternative spellings **volumise**, **volumises**, etc.: both **s** and **z** spellings are correct

voluntary »*adjective* ❶ done or acting of your own free will. ❷ working or done without payment. ❸ under the conscious control of the brain.
» *noun* (plural **voluntaries**) an organ solo played before, during, or after a church service.
voluntarily

☑ **tary** not **try**: volun**tary**

volunteer (verb: **volunteers**, **volunteering**, **volunteered**)

voluptuary »*noun* (plural **voluptuaries**) a person devoted to luxury and sensual pleasure.

voluptuous »*adjective* ❶ giving sensual pleasure. ❷ (of a woman) curvaceous and sexually attractive.
voluptuously
voluptuousness

vomit (verb: **vomits**, **vomiting**, **vomited**)

☑ do not double the **t** in **vomiting** and **vomited**

voodoo »*noun* a religious cult practised in the Caribbean and the southern US, involving sorcery and possession by spirits.

voracious »*adjective* ❶ wanting or eating great quantities of food. ❷ eagerly consuming something: *his voracious reading of literature.*
– SAY vuh-**ray**-shuhss
voraciously
voracity

ℹ do not confuse **voracious** with **veracious**, which means 'truthful'

vortex »*noun* (plural **vortexes** or **vortices**) a whirling mass of water or air.
– SAY vor-teks [singular], **vor**-ti-seez [plural]

☑ the plural of **vortex** can be either **vortexes** or **vortices** (as in the original Latin)

votary »*noun* (plural **votaries**) a person who has taken vows to dedicate their life to God or religious service.
– SAY voh-tuh-ri

vote (verb: **votes, voting, voted**)
voter

votive »*adjective* offered to a god as a sign of gratitude.

vouch »*verb* (**vouches, vouching, vouched**) (**vouch for**) ❶ state or confirm the truth or accuracy of something. ❷ say that someone is reliable, honest, etc.

voucher
vouches
vouching

vouchsafe »*verb* (**vouchsafes, vouchsafing, vouchsafed**) give or say something in a gracious or superior way.

vow (verb: **vows, vowing, vowed**)
vowel

> ✓ the ending is **el** not **al**: **vowel**

vowing
vows

vox pop »*noun* popular opinion as represented by informal comments from members of the public.

> ℹ short for Latin *vox populi* 'the people's voice'

voyage (verb: **voyages, voyaging, voyaged**)
voyager

voyeur »*noun* ❶ a person who gains sexual pleasure from watching others when they are naked or having sex. ❷ a person who enjoys seeing the pain or distress of others.
– SAY vwa-**yer** or voy-**er**
voyeurism
voyeuristic
voyeuristically

> ✓ **eur** not **er**: **voyeur** is a French word meaning 'person who sees'

V-sign

vulcanise another way of spelling VULCANIZE.

vulcanism another way of spelling VOLCANISM.

vulcanite »*noun* hard black vulcanized rubber.

vulcanize »*verb* (**vulcanizes, vulcanizing, vulcanized**) harden rubber or rubber-like material by treating it with sulphur at a high temperature.
vulcanization

> ✓ many people prefer the alternative spellings **vulcanise, vulcanises,** etc., and **vulcanisation**: both **s** and **z** spellings are correct

vulcanology another way of spelling VOLCANOLOGY.

vulgar »*adjective* ❶ lacking sophistication or good taste. ❷ referring to sex or bodily functions in a rude way. ❸ (old-fashioned) having to do with ordinary people.
vulgarly

> ✓ **gar** not **ger**: **vulgar**

vulgar fraction »*noun* a fraction expressed by numerator and denominator, not as a decimal.

vulgarian »*noun* a person who lacks good taste and sophistication.
– SAY vul-**gair**-i-uhn

vulgarise another way of spelling VULGARIZE.

vulgarism »*noun* a vulgar word or expression.

vulgarity (plural **vulgarities**)

> ✓ plural: drop the **y** and add **ies**: **vulgarities**

vulgarize »*verb* (**vulgarizes, vulgarizing, vulgarized**) spoil something by making it ordinary or less refined.
vulgarization

> ✓ many people prefer the alternative spellings **vulgarise, vulgarises,** etc., and **vulgarisation**: both **s** and **z** spellings are correct

vulgarly

vulgar tongue »*noun* the language spoken by the ordinary people of a country.

vulnerable »*adjective* exposed to being attacked or harmed.
– SAY vul-nuh-ruh-b'l
vulnerability
vulnerably

> ✓ **vuln-** not **vun-**: **vulnerable**

vulpine »*adjective* having to do with or like a fox or foxes.
– SAY vul-pyn

vulture »*noun* ❶ a large bird of prey with the head and neck bare of feathers, that feeds on dead animals. ❷ a person who tries to benefit from the difficulties of others.

vulva »*noun* the female external genitals.

vying present participle of VIE.

Ww

wacky »*adjective* (**wackier**, **wackiest**) funny or amusing in a slightly odd way.
wackily
wackiness

✓ **wacky** can also be spelled **whacky**

wad »*noun* ❶ a lump or bundle of a soft material, as used for padding, stuffing, or wiping. ❷ a bundle of paper, banknotes, or documents. ❸ (in informal English) a large amount of something: *wads of money*.
wadded

wadding »*noun* soft, thick material, especially cotton wool, used to line garments or pack fragile items.

waddle (verb: **waddles**, **waddling**, **waddled**)

wade »*verb* (**wades**, **wading**, **waded**) ❶ walk through water or mud. ❷ (**wade through**) read through a long piece of writing with effort. ❸ (**wade in** or **into**) (in informal English) attack or intervene in a forceful way.

wader »*noun* ❶ a sandpiper, plover, or other wading bird. ❷ (**waders**) high waterproof boots, used by anglers.

wades

wadi »*noun* (plural **wadis**) (in Arabic-speaking countries) a valley, ravine, or channel that is dry except in the rainy season.
– SAY **wah**-di or **wod**-i

wading [as in *wading through mud*]

wads

wafer

wafer-thin

waffle[1] (verb: **waffles**, **waffling**, **waffled**) [prattle, ramble]
waffler
waffly

waffle[2] »*noun* a small crisp batter cake, eaten hot with butter or syrup.

waft »*verb* (**wafts**, **wafting**, **wafted**) pass easily or gently through the air.
»*noun* ❶ a gentle movement of air. ❷ a scent carried in the air.

wag (verb: **wags**, **wagging**, **wagged**)

✓ double the **g** in **wagging** and **wagged**

wage (verb: **wages**, **waging**, **wages**)

wager »*noun* a bet.
» *verb* (**wagers**, **wagering**, **wagered**) bet.

wages

wagged

wagging [as in *he was wagging his tail*]

waggish »*adjective* (in informal English) humorous or playful.
waggishly

waggle (verb: **waggles**, **waggling**, **waggled**)
waggly

waggon another way of spelling **WAGON**.

waging [as in *waging a war*]

wagon

✓ **wagon** can also be spelled **waggon**, with a double **g**

wagon-lit »*noun* (plural **wagons-lits**) a sleeping car on a train in continental Europe.
– SAY va-gon-**lee** [singular and plural]

✓ make the plural of **wagon-lit** (a French phrase) by adding **s** after **wagon** and after **lit**: **wagons-lits**

wags

wagtail »*noun* a slender songbird with a long tail that it often wags up and down.

waif »*noun* a poor and homeless child.

wail (verb: **wails**, **wailing**, **wailed**)

wain »*noun* (an old word) a wagon or cart.

wainscot »*noun* an area of wooden panelling on the lower part of the walls of a room.
wainscoting

✓ **wainscoting** can also be spelled **wainscotting**, with a double **t**

wainwright »*noun* (a historical term) a wagon-builder.

waist [middle part of the body]

waistband

waistcoat

W

waistline

wait (verb: **waits, waiting, waited**)

waiter

waiting

waitress (plural **waitresses**)
  waitressing

waits

waive »*verb* (**waives, waiving, waived**) refrain from insisting on or applying a right or claim.

> ℹ️ do not confuse **waive** with **wave**, which refers to a gesture with the hand or a ridge of water on the sea

waiver »*noun* ❶ an act of waiving a right or claim. ❷ a document recording this.

waives

waiving

wake¹ (verb: **wakes, waking, woke**; past participle **woken**) [emerge from sleep; a watch beside a body or party after a funeral]

wake² »*noun* a trail of disturbed water or air left by the passage of a ship or aircraft.

wakeful »*adjective* ❶ not sleeping, or unable to sleep. ❷ alert and aware of possible dangers.
  wakefulness

> ✓ -ful not -full: **wakeful**

waken (verb: **wakens, wakening, wakened**)

wakes

waking

wale »*noun* ❶ a ridge on a textured woven fabric such as corduroy. ❷ a horizontal wooden strip fitted to strengthen a boat's side.

walk (verb: **walks, walking, walked**)
  walker

walkabout »*noun* ❶ an informal stroll among a crowd conducted by an important visitor. ❷ a traditional journey on foot undertaken by an Australian Aboriginal.

walked

walker

walkie-talkie

walk-in

walking

Walkman »*noun* (plural **Walkmans** or **Walkmen**) (trademark) a type of personal stereo.

walk-on »*adjective* (of a part in a play or film) small and not involving any speaking.

walkout

walkover

walks

walkway

wall (verb: **walls, walling, walled**)

wallaby »*noun* (plural **wallabies**) an Australasian marsupial similar to but smaller than a kangaroo.

> ✓ plural: drop the **y** and add **ies**: **wallabies**

wallah »*noun* (in Indian or informal English) a person of a specified kind or having a specified role: *an office wallah.*
– SAY wol-luh

wallchart

wallcovering

walled

wallet

wall-eyed »*adjective* having eyes that show an abnormal amount of white, as caused by a squint.

wallflower »*noun* ❶ a plant with fragrant flowers that bloom in early spring. ❷ (in informal English) a girl who has no one to dance with at a dance or party.

wallies

walling

Walloon »*noun* ❶ a member of a people who speak a French dialect and live in southern and eastern Belgium and neighbouring parts of France. ❷ the French dialect spoken by this people.
– SAY wol-**loon**

wallop (verb: **wallops, walloping, walloped**)

wallow »*verb* (**wallows, wallowing, wallowed**) ❶ roll about or lie in mud or water. ❷ (of a boat or aircraft) roll from side to side. ❸ (**wallow in**) indulge without restraint in something pleasurable.
  »*noun* ❶ an act of wallowing. ❷ an area of mud or shallow water where mammals go to wallow.

wallpaper (verb: **wallpapers, wallpapering, wallpapered**)

walls

wally (plural **wallies**)

> ✓ plural: drop the **y** and add **ies**: **wallies**

walnut

> ✓ wal- not wall-: **walnut**

walrus »*noun* a large sea mammal with downward-pointing tusks.

waltz (verb: **waltzes, waltzing, waltzed**)

> ☑ note the **t** before the **z: waltz**

waltzer »*noun* a fairground ride in which cars are carried round a track that moves up and down.

waltzes

waltzing

wan »*adjective* ❶ (of a person) pale and appearing ill or exhausted. ❷ (of light) pale; weak. ❸ (of a smile) weak; strained.
– SAY won
wanly

wand

wander (verb: **wanders, wandering, wandered**) [move in a leisurely or aimless way]
wanderer

> ☑ do not confuse **wander** with **wonder**, which is a feeling of admiration or amazement

wanderlust »*noun* a strong desire to travel.

wanders

wane »*verb* (**wanes, waning, waned**) ❶ (of the moon) appear to decrease in size day by day. ❷ become weaker.

wanes

wangle »*verb* (**wangles, wangling, wangled**) (in informal English) obtain something by tricks or persuasion.

waning

wank (verb: **wanks, wanking, wanked**)
wanker

wanly

wannabe »*noun* (used in a disapproving way) a person who tries to be like someone else or to fit in with a particular group of people.
– SAY won-nuh-bee

want (verb: **wants, wanting, wanted**)

wanting »*adjective* ❶ not having something required or usual. ❷ absent; not provided.

wanton »*adjective* ❶ (of a cruel or violent action) deliberate and unprovoked. ❷ having many sexual partners.
– SAY won-t'n
wantonly
wantonness

wants

WAP »*abbreviation* Wireless Application Protocol, a means of enabling a mobile phone to browse the Internet and display data.

war (verb: **wars, warring, warred**)

> ☑ double the **r** to spell **warring** and **warred**

warble »*verb* (**warbles, warbling, warbled**) ❶ (of a bird) sing softly and with constantly changing notes. ❷ (of a person) sing in a trilling or quavering voice.
» *noun* a warbling sound.

warbler »*noun* a small songbird with a warbling song.

warbles

warbling

war chest »*noun* a reserve of funds used for fighting a war.

war crime »*noun* an action that violates accepted international rules of war.

ward »*noun* ❶ a room or division in a hospital for one or more patients. ❷ a division of a city or borough that is represented by a councillor or councillors. ❸ a young person looked after by a guardian appointed by their parents or a court. ❹ a ridge or bar in a lock that engages grooves on a key.
» *verb* (**wards, warding, warded**) (**ward off**) keep something from being harmful.
wardship

warden »*noun* a person supervising a particular place or procedure.

warder »*noun* a prison guard.

warding

ward of court »*noun* a young person for whom a guardian has been appointed by the Court of Chancery or who has become directly subject to the authority of that court.

wardress »*noun* (plural **wardresses**) a female prison guard.

wardrobe

wardroom »*noun* the room on a warship where the officers eat.

wards

wardship

ware »*noun* ❶ pottery of a specified type: *porcelain ware.* ❷ manufactured articles. ❸ (**wares**) articles offered for sale.

warehouse

warfare

war game »*noun* a military exercise carried out to test or improve tactics.

warhead »*noun* the explosive head of a missile, torpedo, or similar weapon.

warhorse »*noun* a soldier, politician, sports player, etc.

W

warier [more wary]

wariest

warily

wariness

warlike

warlock »*noun* a man who practises witchcraft.

warlord »*noun* a military commander, especially one controlling a region.

warm (adjective: **warmer**, **warmest**; verb: **warms**, **warming**, **warmed**)
 warmer
 warmly
 warmness

warm-blooded

warmed

warmer

warmest

warm-hearted

warming

warmly

warmness

warmonger »*noun* a person who tries to bring about war.

warms

warmth

warn (verb: **warns**, **warning**, **warned**)

warning
 warningly

warns

warp »*verb* (**warps**, **warping**, **warped**)
 ❶ make or become bent or twisted.
 ❷ make something abnormal or strange: *his hatred has warped his judgement.*
 »*noun* **❶** a distortion or twist in shape.
 ❷ the lengthwise threads on a loom over and under which the weft threads are passed to make cloth.

warpaint

warplane

warrant »*noun* **❶** an official authorization allowing police, soldiers, etc. to make an arrest, search premises, etc. **❷** a document that entitles you to receive goods, money, or services. **❸** justification or authority.
 »*verb* (**warrants**, **warranting**, **warranted**)
 ❶ justify or make something necessary.
 ❷ officially state or guarantee something.

 double **r**, and the ending is **ant** not **ent**: **warrant**

warranties

warranting

warrant officer »*noun* a rank of military officer below the commissioned officers.

warrants

warranty »*noun* (plural **warranties**) a written guarantee promising to repair or replace an article if necessary within a specified period.

 plural: drop the **y** and add **ies**: **warranties**

warred

warren »*noun* **❶** a network of interconnecting rabbit burrows. **❷** a complex network of paths or passages.

warring

warrior

 -**or** not -**er**: **warrior**

wars

warship

wart »*noun* a small, hard growth on the skin.
 warty

warthog »*noun* an African wild pig with warty lumps on the face.

wartime

warty

wary »*adjective* (**warier**, **wariest**) cautious about possible dangers or problems.
 warily
 wariness

 drop the **y** and add **ier** or **iest** to spell **warier** or **wariest**

was

wash (verb: **washes**, **washing**, **washed**)
 washable

washbasin

washboard »*noun* a ridged or corrugated board formerly used for scrubbing clothes when washing them.

washed

washed out »*adjective* **❶** faded by repeated washing. **❷** pale and tired.

washed-up »*adjective* (in informal English) no longer effective or successful.

washer »*noun* **❶** a person or device that washes. **❷** a small flat ring fixed between a nut and bolt.

washerwoman (plural **washerwomen**)

washes

washing

washing-up

washout »*noun* a disappointing failure.

washroom »*noun* (in American English) a room with washing and toilet facilities.

washstand »*noun* a piece of furniture formerly used to hold a bowl or basin for washing the hands and face.

wasn't [was not]

> ✓ be careful to put the apostrophe where a letter has been left out, that is between the **n** and **t** of **not**: **wasn't**

Wasp »*noun* (in American English) an upper- or middle-class American white Protestant, seen as a member of the most powerful social group.

> ℹ **Wasp** is an acronym from *white Anglo-Saxon Protestant*

wasp

waspish
  waspishly
  waspishness

wassail (an old word) »*noun* lively festivities involving the drinking of a lot of alcohol.
» *verb* (**wassails, wassailing, wassailed**)
  ❶ celebrate with a lot of alcohol. ❷ go carol-singing at Christmas.
– **SAY** wos-sayl or wos-s'l
  wassailer

wastage »*noun* ❶ the process of wasting. ❷ an amount wasted. ❸ (also **natural wastage**) the reduction in the size of a workforce through people willingly resigning or retiring rather than being made redundant.

waste (verb: **wastes, wasting, wasted**) [unwanted material; use carelessly]

wastebasket

wasted

waste-disposal unit

wasteful
  wastefully
  wastefulness

> ✓ **-ful** not **-full**: **wasteful**

wasteland

waster

wastes

wasting

wastrel »*noun* (a poetic term) a wasteful or worthless person.
– **SAY** way-struhl

watch (verb: **watches, watching, watched**)
  watchable
  watcher

watchdog

watched

watcher

watches

watchful
  watchfully
  watchfulness

> ✓ **-ful** not **-full**: **watchful**

watching

watchman (plural **watchmen**)

watchtower

watchword »*noun* a word or phrase expressing a central aim or belief.

water (verb: **waters, watering, watered**)
  waterless

water-based »*adjective* using or having water as a main ingredient.

waterbed »*noun* a bed with a water-filled mattress.

watercolour »*noun* ❶ artists' paint that is thinned with water rather than oil. ❷ a picture painted with watercolours.
  watercolourist

watercourse »*noun* a stream or artificial water channel.

watercress »*noun* a kind of cress which grows in running water.

watered

waterfall

waterfowl »*plural noun* ducks, geese, or other large birds living in water.

waterfront

waterhole »*noun* a hollow in which water collects, typically one at which animals drink.

watering

watering hole »*noun* (in informal English) a pub or bar.

waterless

waterline »*noun* ❶ the level normally reached by the water on the side of a ship. ❷ a line on a shore, riverbank, etc. marking the level reached by the sea or a river.

waterlogged

watermark »*noun* a faint design made in some paper that can be seen when held against the light.

watermelon

watermill »*noun* a mill worked by a waterwheel.

waterproof (verb: **waterproofs, waterproofing, waterproofed**)

water-resistant

waters

W

watershed »*noun* ❶ an area of land that separates waters flowing to different rivers, seas, etc. ❷ a turning point in a state of affairs. ❸ the time after which programmes that are unsuitable for children are broadcast on television.

waterside

waterski (plural **waterskis**; verb: **waterskis**, **waterskiing**, **waterskied**)
    waterskier

> ☑ double the **i** to spell **waterskiing**

waterspout »*noun* a column of water and spray formed by a whirlwind occurring over the sea.

water table »*noun* the level below which the ground is saturated with water.

watertight

waterway »*noun* a river, canal, or other route for travel by water.

waterweed

waterwheel »*noun* a large wheel driven by flowing water, used to work machinery or to raise water to a higher level.

waterworks

watery

watt »*noun* the basic unit of power.

> ℹ named after the Scottish engineer James *Watt*

wattage »*noun* an amount of electrical power expressed in watts.

wattle »*noun* ❶ rods interlaced with twigs or branches, used for making fences, walls, etc. ❷ a fleshy part hanging from the head or neck of the turkey and some other birds.

wattle and daub »*noun* wattle covered with mud or clay, formerly used in building walls.

wave (verb: **waves**, **waving**, **waved**) [move your hand as a greeting; ridge of water on the sea]

> ℹ do not confuse **wave** with **waive**, which means 'refrain from insisting on a right'

waveband »*noun* a range of wavelengths used in radio transmission.

waved

wavelength »*noun* ❶ (in physics) the distance between successive crests of a wave of sound, light, radio, etc. ❷ a person's way of thinking: *we weren't on the same wavelength.*

wavelet »*noun* a small wave.

waver »*verb* (**wavers**, **wavering**, **wavered**) ❶ move in a quivering way; flicker. ❷ begin to weaken; falter. ❸ be indecisive.
    waverer

waves

wavier

waviest

waviness

waving

wavy (adjective: **wavier**, **waviest**)

wax¹ (plural **waxes**; verb: **waxes**, **waxing**, **waxed**) [soft oily substance; polish with wax]
    waxed

wax² »*verb* (**waxes**, **waxing**, **waxed**) ❶ (of the moon) gradually appear to increase in size. ❷ (a poetic term) become larger or stronger. ❸ speak or write in the specified way: *they waxed lyrical.*

waxen »*adjective* ❶ looking like wax. ❷ (an old word) made of wax.

waxes

waxier

waxiest

waxiness

waxing

waxwork »*noun* ❶ a lifelike dummy made of wax. ❷ (**waxworks**) an exhibition of waxworks.

waxy (adjective: **waxier**, **waxiest**)
    waxiness

way

wayfarer »*noun* a person who travels on foot.
    wayfaring

waylay »*verb* (**waylays**, **waylaying**, **waylaid**) ❶ intercept someone in order to attack them. ❷ stop someone and talk to them.

waymark »*noun* a sign forming one of a series used to mark out a footpath.

way-out »*adjective* unconventional or experimental.

wayside

wayward »*adjective* unpredictable and hard to control.
    waywardly
    waywardness

WC »*abbreviation* water closet.

we

weak (adjective: **weaker**, **weakest**) [lacking strength]
    weakly

> ℹ do not confuse **weak** with **week**, 'a period of seven days'

weaken (verb: **weakens**, **weakening**, **weakened**)

weaker

weakest

weak-kneed

weakling »*noun* a weak person or animal.

weakly [in a weak manner]

weakness (plural **weaknesses**)

weal[1] »*noun* a red, swollen mark left on flesh by a blow or pressure.

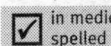 in medical use **weal** is sometimes spelled **wheal**

weal[2] »*noun* (an old word) that which is best for someone or something: *guardians of the public weal.*

wealth

wealthy (adjective: **wealthier**, **wealthiest**)

wean[1] »*verb* (**weans**, **weaning**, **weaned**) ❶ make a young mammal used to food other than its mother's milk. ❷ make someone give up a habit or addiction. ❸ (**be weaned on**) be strongly influenced by something from an early age.

wean[2] »*noun* (in Scottish and Northern English) a young child.

weapon
  weaponry

 weap not **wep**: **weapon**

wear (verb: **wears**, **wearing**, **wore**; past participle **worn**)
  wearable
  wearer

wearied

wearier

wearies

weariest

wearily

weariness

wearing

wearisome »*adjective* tiring or boring.

wears

weary (adjective: **wearier**, **weariest**; verb: **wearies**, **wearying**, **wearied**)
  wearily
  weariness

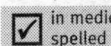 drop the **y** and add **ier** or **iest** to spell **wearier** or **weariest**

weasel »*noun* ❶ a small slender meat-eating mammal with reddish-brown fur. ❷ (in informal English) a deceitful or treacherous person.
  weaselly

 el not **le**: **weasel**

weather (verb: **weathers**, **weathering**, **weathered**)

 do not forget the **a** before the **th**: **weather**
do not confuse **weather** with **whether** (a conjunction, as used in *I'll see whether she's at home*) or **wether** (a castrated ram)

weather-beaten

weatherboard »*noun* ❶ a sloping board attached to the bottom of an outside door to keep out the rain. ❷ one of a series of horizontal boards nailed to outside walls with edges overlapping to keep out the rain.

weathercock »*noun* a weathervane in the form of a cockerel.

weathered

weathering

weatherman (plural **weathermen**)

weatherproof

weathers

weathervane »*noun* a revolving pointer to show the direction of the wind.

weatherwoman (plural **weatherwomen**)

weave[1] »*verb* (**weaves**, **weaving**, **wove**; past participle **woven** or **wove**) ❶ form fabric by interlacing long threads passing in one direction with others at a right angle to them. ❷ (**weave into**) make facts, events, etc. into a story.
» *noun* a particular way in which fabric is woven.

weave[2] »*verb* (**weaves**, **weaving**, **weaved**) move from side to side to get around obstructions.

weaver

weaves

weaving

web

webbed

webbing »*noun* strong, closely woven fabric used for making straps, belts, chairs, etc.

webcam »*noun* (trademark in the US) a video camera connected to a computer, so that the film produced may be viewed on the Internet.

webcast »*noun* a live video broadcast of an event transmitted across the Internet.

webmaster »*noun* (in computing) a person who is responsible for a particular server on the Internet.

W

web page »*noun* (in computing) a document that can be accessed via the Internet.

website »*noun* (in computing) a location on the Internet that maintains one or more web pages.

wed (verb: **weds**, **wedding**, **wedded** or **wed**)

☑ double the **d** to spell **wedding** and **wedded**

we'd [we had; we should; we could]

wedded

wedding

wedge (verb: **wedges**, **wedging**, **wedged**)

Wedgwood »*noun* (trademark) ceramic ware made by the English potter Josiah Wedgwood and his successors.

☑ there is no **e** after the **g**: **Wedgwood**

wedlock »*noun* the state of being married.

Wednesday

weds

wee[1] »*adjective* (in Scottish English) little.

wee[2] (verb: **wees**, **weeing**, **weed**) [act of urinating; urinate]

weed (verb: **weeds**, **weeding**, **weeded**)

weedier

weediest

weeding

weedkiller

weeds

weedy (adjective: **weedier**, **weediest**)

weeing

week [period of seven days]

ℹ️ do not confuse **week** with **weak**, 'lacking strength'

weekday

weekend
  weekender

weekly (plural **weeklies**) [every week]

weeny (adjective: **weenier**, **weeniest**)

weep (verb: **weeps**, **weeping**, **wept**)

weepie »*noun* (plural **weepies**) a sentimental or emotional film, novel, or song.

weepier

weepiest

weepily

weepiness

weeping

weeps

weepy »*adjective* (**weepier**, **weepiest**) (in informal English) ❶ tearful. ❷ sentimental.

weepily

weepiness

wees

weevil »*noun* a small beetle which eats crops or stored foodstuffs.

☑ **il** not **el**: **weevil**

weft »*noun* (in weaving) the threads that are passed over and under the warp threads to make cloth.

weigh (verb: **weighs**, **weighing**, **weighed**)

weighbridge »*noun* a machine on to which vehicles are driven to be weighed.

weighed

weigh-in »*noun* an official weighing, e.g. of boxers before a fight.

weighing

weighs

weight (verb: **weights**, **weighting**, **weighted**)

weightier

weightiest

weightily

weighting »*noun* ❶ adjustment made to take account of special circumstances. ❷ additional wages paid to allow for a higher cost of living in a particular area.

weightless
  weightlessly
  weightlessness

weightlifting
  weightlifter

weights

weighty »*adjective* (**weightier**, **weightiest**) ❶ heavy. ❷ very serious and important. ❸ very influential.
  weightily

weir »*noun* ❶ a low dam built across a river to raise the level of water upstream or regulate its flow. ❷ an enclosure of stakes set in a stream as a trap for fish.

☑ **e** before **i**: **weir** does not follow the usual rule

weird »*adjective* (**weirder**, **weirdest**) ❶ suggesting something supernatural. ❷ very strange.
  weirdly
  weirdness

☑ **e** before **i**: **weird** does not follow the usual rule

weirdo (plural **weirdos**)

Welch old spelling of **WELSH**.

welch another way of spelling **WELSH**.

W

welcome (verb: **welcomes, welcoming, welcomed**)
welcomer

weld »*verb* (**welds, welding, welded**) ❶ join together metal parts by heating the surfaces to the point of melting and pressing or hammering them together. ❷ make or shape an article in such a way. ❸ cause two things to combine and form a whole.
» *noun* a welded joint.
welder

welfare »*noun* ❶ the health, happiness, and fortunes of a person or group. ❷ organized efforts designed to promote the basic well-being of people in need. ❸ financial support given for this purpose.

> ☑ -fare not -fair: welfare

welfare state »*noun* a system under which the state undertakes to protect the health and well-being of its citizens by means of grants, pensions, and other benefits.

well[1] (adverb & adjective: **better, best**) [in a good way; in a satisfactory state]

> the adverb **well** is often used with a past participle (such as *known*) to form compound adjectives: **well known, well dressed,** and so on. Such adjectives should be written without a hyphen when they are used alone after a verb (*she is well known as a writer*) but with a hyphen when they come before a noun (*a well-known writer*).

well[2] (verb: **wells, welling, welled**) [shaft in the ground; hollow; rise up to the surface and spill]

we'll [we shall; we will]

well advised »*adjective* sensible; wise.

well appointed »*adjective* (of a building or room) having a high standard of equipment or furnishing.

well-being

well disposed »*adjective* having a positive, sympathetic, or friendly attitude.

welled

well endowed »*adjective* ❶ having plentiful supplies of a resource. ❷ (mainly used in a humorous way) having (of a man) large genitals or (of a woman) large breasts.

well-heeled »*adjective* (in informal English) wealthy.

well hung »*adjective* (mainly used in a humorous way) (of a man) having large genitals.

wellie another way of spelling **WELLY**.

welling

wellington

> ℹ️ the **wellington boot** is named after the British soldier and Prime Minister, the Duke of *Wellington*

well meaning »*adjective* having good intentions but not necessarily the desired effect.
well meant

well-nigh »*adverb* almost.

well off »*adjective* ❶ wealthy. ❷ in a favourable situation or circumstances.

well preserved »*adjective* (of an old person) showing little sign of ageing.

well rounded »*adjective* ❶ having a pleasing curved shape. ❷ (of a person) plump. ❸ (of a person) having a personality that is fully developed in all aspects.

wells

well spoken »*adjective* speaking in an educated and refined way.

wellspring »*noun* (a poetic term) ❶ the place where a spring comes out of the ground. ❷ an abundant source of something: *a wellspring of creativity*.

well thumbed »*adjective* (of a book) having been read often and bearing marks of frequent handling.

well-to-do »*adjective* wealthy; prosperous.

well travelled »*adjective* ❶ (of a person) having travelled widely. ❷ (of a route) much frequented by travellers.

well trodden »*adjective* much frequented by travellers.

well turned »*adjective* ❶ (of a phrase or compliment) elegantly expressed. ❷ (of a woman's ankle or leg) attractively shaped.

well-wisher

well worn »*adjective* ❶ showing signs of extensive use or wear. ❷ (of a phrase or idea) used or repeated so often that it no longer has interest or significance.

welly »*noun* (plural **wellies**) (in informal English) ❶ = **WELLINGTON**. ❷ power or vigour.

> ☑ welly can also be spelled wellie

Welsh
Welshness

> ☑ you sometimes come across the old spelling **Welch** in official names

welsh »*verb* (**welshes, welshing, welshed**) (**welsh on**) fail to honour a debt or obligation.

W

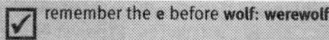
welsh can also be spelled **welch**

Welshman (plural **Welshmen**)

Welshness

Welsh rarebit »*noun* = RAREBIT.

Welshwoman (plural **Welshwomen**)

welt »*noun* ❶ a leather rim to which the sole of a shoe is attached. ❷ a ribbed, reinforced, or decorative border on a garment. ❸ a weal.

welter »*noun* a large number of items in no order.

welterweight »*noun* a boxing weight between lightweight and middleweight.

wen »*noun* a boil or other swelling or growth on the skin.

wench »*noun* (an old word) a girl or young woman.

wend »*verb* (**wends**, **wending**, **wended**) (**wend your way**) go slowly or by an indirect route.

Wendy house »*noun* a toy house large enough for children to play in.

ℹ️ named after the house built around *Wendy* in J.M. Barrie's play *Peter Pan*

Wensleydale »*noun* a type of white cheese with a crumbly texture.
– SAY wenz-li-dayl

went past of GO.

wept past and past participle of WEEP.

were [past of BE, as in *they were*.]

we're [we are]

weren't [were not]

☑️ be careful to put the apostrophe where a letter has been left out, that is between the **n** and **t** of *not*: **weren't**

werewolf »*noun* (plural **werewolves**) (in folklore) a person who periodically changes into a wolf, typically when there is a full moon.
– SAY wair-wuulf or weer-wuulf

☑️ remember the **e** before *wolf*: **werewolf**

Wesleyan »*adjective* having to do with the teachings of the English preacher John Wesley or the main branch of the Methodist Church which he founded.
»*noun* a follower of Wesley or of the main Methodist tradition.

west
    westbound

westerly

western

Western Church »*noun* the part of the Christian Church originating in the Western Roman Empire, including the Roman Catholic, Anglican, Lutheran, and Reformed Churches (as opposed to the *Orthodox Church*).

westerner

westernize »*verb* (**westernizes**, **westernizing**, **westernized**) bring or come under the influence of the cultural, economic, or political systems of Europe and North America.
westernization

☑️ many people prefer the alternative spellings **westernise**, **westernises**, etc., and **westernisation**: both **s** and **z** spellings are correct

West Indian

west-north-west

west-south-west

westward

westwards

wet (adjective: **wetter**, **wettest**; verb: **wets**, **wetting**, **wet** or **wetted**)
wetly
wetness

☑️ double the **t** in **wetting**, **wetted**, **wetter**, and **wettest**

wether »*noun* a castrated ram.

wetland »*noun* swampy or marshy land.

wetly

wetness

wet nurse »*noun* (mainly a historical term) a woman employed to breastfeed another woman's child.

wets

wetsuit »*noun* a close-fitting rubber garment covering the entire body, worn for warmth in water sports or diving.

wetted

wetter

wettest

wetting

we've [we have]

whack (verb: **whacks**, **whacking**, **whacked**)

whacked »*adjective* (in informal English) ❶ completely exhausted. ❷ under the influence of drugs.

whacking

whacks

whacky another way of spelling WACKY.

whale (plural **whale** or **whales**)

whalebone »*noun* an elastic horny substance which grows in a series of thin parallel plates in the upper jaw of some whales.

whaler »*noun* ❶ a whaling ship. ❷ a seaman engaged in whaling.

whaling »*noun* the practice or industry of hunting and killing whales for their oil, meat, or whalebone.

wham (verb: **whams, whamming, whammed**)

✓ double the **m** in **whamming** and **whammed**

whammy »*noun* (plural **whammies**) (in informal English) an event with a powerful and unpleasant effect; a blow.

✓ plural: drop the **y** and add **ies**: **whammies**

whams

whap another way of spelling **whop**.

wharf »*noun* (plural **wharves** or **wharfs**) a level quayside area to which a ship may be moored to load and unload.

what

whatever

whatnot

whatsit

whatsoever

wheal another way of spelling **weal**[1].

wheat

wheatear »*noun* a songbird with black and grey, buff, or white plumage and a white rump.

wheaten »*adjective* made of wheat.

wheatgerm »*noun* a nutritious foodstuff consisting of the extracted embryos of grains of wheat.

wheatmeal »*noun* flour made from wheat from which some of the bran and germ has been removed.

wheedle »*verb* (**wheedles, wheedling, wheedled**) use endearments or flattery to persuade someone to do something.

✓ **ee** not **ea** in the middle: **wheedle**

wheel (verb: **wheels, wheeling, wheeled**)

wheelbarrow

wheelbase »*noun* the distance between the front and rear axles of a vehicle.

wheelchair

wheeled

wheeler »*noun* a vehicle having a specified number of wheels: *a three-wheeler*.

wheeler-dealer »*noun* a person who takes part in commercial or political scheming.

wheelhouse »*noun* a shelter for the person at the wheel of a boat or ship.

wheelie »*noun* the action of riding a bicycle or motorcycle for a short distance with the front wheel raised off the ground.

wheelie bin »*noun* a large refuse bin set on wheels.

✓ **wheelie bin** can also be spelled **wheely bin**

wheeling

wheels

wheelspin »*noun* rotation of a vehicle's wheels without movement of the vehicle forwards or backwards.

wheelwright »*noun* (mainly a historical term) a person who makes or repairs wooden wheels.

wheeze (verb: **wheezes, wheezing, wheezed**)
wheezily
wheeziness
wheezy

whelk »*noun* a shellfish with a heavy pointed spiral shell, some kinds of which are eaten as food.

whelp »*noun* ❶ a puppy. ❷ (used in an insulting way) a boy or young man.
» *verb* (**whelps, whelping, whelped**) give birth to a puppy.

when

whence »*adverb* ❶ from what place or source? ❷ from which; from where. ❸ to the place from which. ❹ as a consequence of which.

ℹ **whence** means 'from what place', and therefore, strictly speaking **from** is not needed before **whence**. However, **from whence** is usually accepted as good English.

whenever

whensoever »*conjunction & adverb* (an old word) = **whenever**.

where [adverb, as in *where are you?*]

whereabouts

✓ remember, two **e**'s in **whereabouts** and **whereas**

whereas

whereat »*adverb & conjunction* (an old word) at which.

whereby

wherefore (an old word) »*adverb* for what reason?
» *adverb & conjunction* as a result of which.

wherein »*adverb* ❶ in which. ❷ in what place or respect?

whereof »*adverb* of what or which.

wheresoever »*adverb & conjunction* (an old word) = WHEREVER.

whereupon »*conjunction* immediately after which.

wherever

wherewithal »*noun* the money or other resources needed for a particular purpose.

> ✓ only one **l** at the end: **wherewithal**

wherry »*noun* (plural **wherries**) ❶ a light rowing boat used chiefly for carrying passengers. ❷ a large light barge.

> ✓ plural: drop the **y** and add **ies**: **wherries**

whet »*verb* (**whets**, **whetting**, **whetted**) ❶ sharpen the blade of a tool or weapon. ❷ excite or stimulate someone's desire, interest, or appetite.

> ℹ️ do not confuse with **wet**, meaning 'saturated with liquid'

> ✓ double the **t** in **whetting** and **whetted**

whether »*conjunction* ❶ expressing a doubt or choice between alternatives: *I'll see whether she's at home.* ❷ indicating that a statement applies whichever of the alternatives mentioned is the case: *I'm going whether you like it or not.*

> ✓ remember the first **h** (a **wether** is a castrated male sheep), and do not confuse **whether** with **weather** (the atmospheric conditions)

whets

whetstone »*noun* a fine-grained stone used for sharpening cutting tools.

whetted

whetting

whey »*noun* the watery part of milk that remains after curds have formed.

which [asking for more information specifying one or more people or things from a set]

> ℹ️ do not confuse **which** with **witch** 'a woman thought to have magic powers'

whichever

whiff

whiffy (adjective: **whiffier**, **whiffiest**)

Whig »*noun* (a historical term) a member of the British reforming party that sought the supremacy of Parliament, succeeded in the 19th century by the Liberal Party.

while (verb: **whiles**, **whiling**, **whiled**)

whilst

whim »*noun* a sudden desire or change of mind.

whimper (verb: **whimpers**, **whimpering**, **whimpered**)

whimsical »*adjective* ❶ playfully old-fashioned or fanciful. ❷ showing sudden changes of direction or behaviour.
whimsicality
whimsically

> ✓ remember the **h** in **whimsical** and **whimsy**

whimsy »*noun* (plural **whimsies**) ❶ playfully old-fashioned or fanciful behaviour or humour. ❷ a fanciful or odd thing. ❸ a whim.

whin »*noun* gorse.

whine (verb: **whines**, **whining**, **whined**) [long high-pitched sound]
whiny

whinge (verb: **whinges**, **whingeing**, **whinged**)
whinger

> ✓ remember the **h**: **whinge**

whining

whinny »*noun* (plural **whinnies**) a gentle, high-pitched neigh.
»*verb* (**whinnies**, **whinnying**, **whinnied**) (of a horse) make such a sound.

> ✓ plural: drop the **y** and add **ies**: **whinnies**

whiny

whip (verb: **whips**, **whipping**, **whipped**)

> ✓ double the **p** in **whipping** and **whipped**

whipcord »*noun* ❶ thin, tough, tightly twisted cord used for making the flexible end part of whips. ❷ a closely woven ribbed worsted fabric.

whiplash »*noun* ❶ the lashing action of a whip. ❷ the flexible part of a whip. ❸ injury caused by a severe jerk to the head.

whipped

whippersnapper »*noun* (in informal English) a young and inexperienced person who is bold and overconfident.

whippet »*noun* a dog of a small slender breed, bred for racing.

whippiness

whipping

whipping boy »*noun* a person who is blamed or punished for the faults or incompetence of others.

> ℹ️ first referring to a boy educated with a young prince and punished instead of him

whippoorwill »*noun* an American nightjar with a distinctive call.
– **say** wip-per-wil

whippy »*adjective* flexible; springy.
whippiness

whip-round »*noun* (in informal English) a collection of contributions of money for a particular purpose.

whips

whipsaw »*noun* a saw with a narrow blade and a handle at both ends.

whir another way of spelling **whirr**.

whirl (verb: **whirls**, **whirling**, **whirled**)

whirligig »*noun* ❶ a toy that spins round, e.g. a top or windmill. ❷ a roundabout in a children's playground.

whirling

whirlpool

whirls

whirlwind

whirr (verb: **whirrs**, **whirring**, **whirred**)

> ✅ **whirr** can also be spelled with a single **r**, **whir** (**whirs**, **whirring**, **whirred**)

whisk (verb: **whisks**, **whisking**, **whisked**)

whisker
whiskered
whiskery

whiskey see the note at **whisky**.

whisking

whisks

whisky »*noun* (plural **whiskies**) a spirit distilled from malted grain, especially barley or rye.

> ✅ Scotch **whisky**, but Irish **whiskey**. In America the spelling tends to be **whiskey**.

whisper (verb: **whispers**, **whispering**, **whispered**)
whisperer
whispery

whist »*noun* a card game in which points are scored according to the number of tricks won.

whistle (verb: **whistles**, **whistling**, **whistled**)
whistler

whistle-blower »*noun* a person who informs on someone engaged in a secret or illegal activity.

whistled

whistler

whistles

whistle-stop »*adjective* very fast and with only brief pauses.

whistling

whit »*noun* a very small part or amount.

white (adjective: **whiter**, **whitest**)
whitely
whiteness
whitish

white ant »*noun* = **termite**.

whitebait »*noun* the small silvery-white young of herrings, sprats, and similar marine fish as food.

whiteboard »*noun* a wipeable board with a white surface used for teaching or presentations.

white-collar »*adjective* relating to the work done or people who work in an office or other professional environment.

white elephant »*noun* a possession that is useless or troublesome.

> ℹ️ from the story that the kings of Siam gave such animals to courtiers they disliked, in order to ruin them financially by the great cost of looking after the animals

whitefish »*noun* a mainly freshwater fish of the salmon family, widely used as food.

whitefly »*noun* (plural **whitefly**) a tiny winged bug covered with powdery white wax, damaging plants by feeding on sap and coating them with honeydew.

whitehead »*noun* a pale or white-topped pimple on the skin.

white heat »*noun* the temperature or state of something that is so hot that it gives out white light.
white-hot

white hope »*noun* a person expected to bring much success to a team or organization.

white-hot

white-knuckle »*adjective* causing fear or nervous excitement.

whitely

whiten (verb: **whitens**, **whitening**, **whitened**)
whitener

whiteness

W

white noise »*noun* (in physics) noise containing many frequencies with equal intensities.

whitens

white-out »*noun* a dense blizzard.

White Paper »*noun* (in the UK) a government report giving information or proposals on an issue.

whiter

white spirit »*noun* a colourless liquid distilled from petroleum, used as a paint thinner and solvent.

whitest

white-van man »*noun* (in informal English) an aggressive male driver of a delivery or workman's van (typically white in colour).

whitewash »*noun* ❶ a solution of lime or chalk and water, used for painting walls white. ❷ a deliberate concealment of someone's mistakes or faults. ❸ a victory by the same side in every game of a series.
» *verb* (**whitewashes, whitewashing, whitewashed**) ❶ paint walls with whitewash. ❷ conceal mistakes or faults. ❸ defeat a side with a whitewash.

whither (an old word) »*adverb* ❶ to what place or state? ❷ what is the likely future of? ❸ to which (with reference to a place). ❹ to whatever place.

> ✓ remember the first **h**: whither (**wither** is a verb meaning 'become shrivelled or shrunken')

whiting »*noun* ❶ (plural **whiting**) a slender sea fish with white flesh eaten as food. ❷ ground chalk used for purposes such as whitewashing and cleaning metal plate.

whitish

whitlow »*noun* an abscess in the soft tissue near a fingernail or toenail.

Whitsun »*noun* Whitsuntide.

Whit Sunday »*noun* the seventh Sunday after Easter, a Christian festival commemorating the descent of the Holy Spirit on the Apostles at Pentecost.

Whitsuntide »*noun* the weekend or week including Whit Sunday.

whittle »*verb* (**whittles, whittling, whittled**) ❶ carve wood by repeatedly cutting small slices from it. ❷ make something by whittling. ❸ (**whittle away** or **down**) reduce something by a gradual series of steps.

> ✓ double **t**: whittle

whiz another way of spelling **whizz**.

whiz-kid another way of spelling **whizz-kid**.

whizz (verb: **whizzes, whizzing, whizzed**) **whizzy**

> ✓ whizz can also be spelled **whiz**, with only one **z**

whizz-kid »*noun* a young person who is very successful or highly skilled.

> ✓ whizz-kid can also be spelled **whiz-kid**

whizzy

WHO »*abbreviation* World Health Organization.

who

> ℹ️ when writing, **who** should be used as the subject of a verb (*who decided this?*) and **whom** should be used as the object of a verb or preposition (*whom do you think we should support?*). When speaking, however, most people think it is acceptable to use **who** instead of **whom**, as in *who do you think we should support?*

whoa »*exclamation* used as a command to a horse to stop or slow down.

who'd [who had; who would]

whodunnit »*noun* a story or play about a murder in which the identity of the murderer is not revealed until the end.

> ✓ double **n**: whodunnit (the spelling **whodunit** is American)

whoever

whole **wholeness**

wholefood »*noun* (also **wholefoods**) food that has been processed as little as possible and is free from additives.

wholegrain »*adjective* made with or containing whole unprocessed grains of something.

wholehearted **wholeheartedly**

wholemeal »*adjective* referring to flour or bread made from wholewheat, including the husk.

wholeness

whole number »*noun* a number without fractions; an integer.

wholesale »*noun* the selling of goods in large quantities to be sold to the public by others.
» *adverb* ❶ being sold in such a way. ❷ on a large scale.
» *adjective* done on a large scale.
» *verb* (**wholesales, wholesaling, wholesaled**) sell goods wholesale.
wholesaler

wholesome »*adjective* helping towards good health and physical or moral well-being.
wholesomely
wholesomeness

wholewheat »*noun* whole grains of wheat including the husk.

wholly »*adverb* entirely; fully.

> ✓ olly not olely: wholly

whom »*pronoun* used instead of 'who' as the object of a verb or preposition.

> ℹ on the use of who and whom, see the note at WHO

whomever »*pronoun* used instead of 'whoever' as the object of a verb or preposition.

whomp (in informal English) »*verb* (**whomps, whomping, whomped**) strike something heavily.
»*noun* a thump.

whomsoever »*relative pronoun* (an old word) used instead of 'whosoever' as the object of a verb or preposition.

whoop (verb: **whoops, whooping, whooped**)

whoopee

whooper swan »*noun* a large northern swan with a black and yellow bill and a loud trumpeting call.
– **SAY** hoo-per

whooping

whooping cough »*noun* a contagious disease chiefly affecting children, caused by bacteria and characterized by coughs followed by a rasping intake of breath.
– **SAY** hoo-ping

whoops

whoops-a-daisy

whoosh (verb: **whooshes, whooshing, whooshed**)

> ✓ whoosh can also be spelled woosh

whop (in informal English) »*verb* (**whops, whopping, whopped**) hit something hard.
»*noun* a heavy blow or its sound.

> ✓ whop can also be spelled whap. Double the p in whopping and whopped.

whopper

whopping

whops

whore »*noun* ❶ a prostitute. ❷ (used in an insulting way) a woman who has many sexual partners.
– **SAY** hor

whorehouse »*noun* (in informal English) a brothel.

whorl »*noun* ❶ one of the turns in the spiral shell of a mollusc. ❷ a coil of leaves, flowers, or branches encircling a stem. ❸ a complete circle in a fingerprint.
– **SAY** worl or werl

who's [who is; who has]

> ℹ do not confuse who's with whose. Who's is short for either who is or who has, as in *he has a son who's a doctor* or *who's done the reading?*, whereas whose means 'belonging to associated with which person' or 'of whom or which', as in *whose is this?* or *he's a man whose opinion I respect*.

whose [belonging to or associated with which person; of whom or which]

whosesoever »*relative pronoun & determiner* (an old word) whoever's.

whosever »*relative pronoun & determiner* belonging to or associated with whichever person; whoever's.

whosoever »*pronoun* (an old word) = WHOEVER.

whup »*verb* (**whups, whupping, whupped**) (in informal English) beat; thrash.

> ✓ double the p in whupping and whupped

why

Wicca »*noun* a modern religion based on pre-Christian pagan beliefs.
– **SAY** wik-kuh
Wiccan

wick »*noun* a length of cord in a candle, lamp, or lighter which carries liquid fuel to the flame.

wicked
wickedly
wickedness

> ℹ the comparative and superlative are usually more wicked and most wicked, not wickeder and wickedest

wicker »*noun* easily bent twigs plaited or woven to make items such as furniture and baskets.
wickerwork

> ✓ no h in wicker

wicket »*noun* ❶ (in cricket) one of the sets of three stumps with two bails across the top at either end of the pitch, defended by a batsman. ❷ a small door or gate.

wicketkeeper

widdle (verb: **widdles, widdling, widdled**)

W

wide (adjective: **wider**, **widest**)
  widely

wide-angle »*adjective* (of a lens) having a field covering a wide angle.

wide-eyed

widely

widen (verb: **widens**, **widening**, **widened**)

wider

widescreen »*adjective* referring to a cinema or television screen presenting a wide field of vision in relation to height.

widespread

widest

widgeon another way of spelling **WIGEON**.

widget »*noun* (in informal English) a small gadget or mechanical device.

widow
  widowed
  widowhood

widower »*noun* a man whose wife has died and who has not married again.

widowhood

widowing

widows

width

> ✓ remember the **d** before the **th**: width

widthways

widthwise

wield »*verb* (**wields**, **wielding**, **wielded**) ❶ hold and use a weapon or tool. ❷ have and be able to use power or influence.

> ✓ the usual rule is **i** before **e** except after **c**: wield

wife (plural **wives**)
  wifely

wig

wigeon »*noun* a duck with mainly reddish-brown and grey plumage.
– **say** rhymes with pigeon

> ✓ wigeon can also be spelled with a **d** in the middle: widgeon

wiggle (verb: **wiggles**, **wiggling**, **wiggled**)
  wiggly

wigwam »*noun* a tent consisting of animal skins fixed over a framework of poles, as lived in in the past by some North American Indian peoples.

wild (adjective: **wilder**, **wildest**)
  wildly
  wildness

wild card »*noun* ❶ a playing card that can take on any value, suit, or colour that the person holding it needs. ❷ a person or

thing whose qualities are uncertain. ❸ (in computing) a character that will match any character or sequence of characters in a search.

wildcat »*adjective* (of a strike) sudden and unofficial.

wildebeest »*noun* = **GNU**.
– **say** wil-duh-beest or vil-duh-beest

> ✓ **-beest** not **-beast**: wildebeest is an Afrikaans word which means 'wild beast'

wilder

wilderness (plural **wildernesses**)

wildest

wildfire

wildfowl »*plural noun* birds that are hunted as game.

wildlife

wildly

wildness

wiles »*plural noun* cunning plans.

> ✓ **wi** not **whi**: wiles

wilful »*adjective* ❶ deliberate. ❷ stubborn and determined.
  wilfully
  wilfulness

> ✓ both **l**'s are single: wilful. The American spelling is willful.

wilier

wiliest

wiliness

will[1] [expressing the future]

> ℹ for an explanation of the difference between **will** and **shall**, see the note at **SHALL**

will[2] (verb: **wills**, **willing**, **willed**) [the power to decide on something; legal document; intend to happen]

willful American spelling of **WILFUL**.

willie another way of spelling **WILLY**.

willies »*plural noun* (**the willies**) a feeling of uneasiness or fear.

willing
  willingly
  willingness

will-o'-the-wisp »*noun* a faint flickering light seen at night on marshy ground, thought to result from natural gases burning.

willow

willowherb »*noun* a plant with long narrow leaves and pink or pale purple flowers.

willowy »*adjective* (of a person) tall and slim.

wills

willy »*noun* (plural **willies**) (in informal English) a penis.

> ☑ willy can also be spelled **willie**
> plural: drop the **y** and add **ies: willies**

willy-nilly »*adverb* ❶ whether you like it or not. ❷ without any direction or plan.

wilt »*verb* (**wilts, wilting, wilted**) ❶ (of a plant) become limp through heat or lack of water. ❷ have no energy because you are hot and tired.

wily »*adjective* (**wilier, wiliest**) cunningly clever.
wiliness

> ☑ drop the **y** and add **ier** or **iest** to spell
> **wilier** or **wiliest**

wimp »*noun* (in informal English) a timid and weak person.
wimpish
wimpy

wimple »*noun* a cloth headdress covering the head, neck, and sides of the face, worn in the past by women and still today by some nuns.

wimpy

win (verb: **wins, winning, won**)
winnable

> ☑ double the **n** to spell **winning**

wince »*verb* (**winces, wincing, winced**) flinch slightly and have an expression of pain on your face, on feeling pain or distress.
» *noun* an instance of wincing.

winceyette »*noun* a soft brushed cotton fabric.
– SAY win-si-et

> ☑ note the **ette** ending: **winceyette**

winch »*noun* a hauling or lifting device consisting of a rope or chain winding around a horizontal rotating drum, turned by a crank or by motor.
» *verb* (**winches, winching, winched**) hoist or haul something with a winch.

wincing

wind¹ (verb: **winds, winding, winded**) [movement of the air; make someone have difficulty breathing]
windless

wind² (verb: **winds, winding, wound**) [move in a twisting course]

windbag

windbreak »*noun* a row of trees, wall, or screen providing shelter from the wind.

windcheater »*noun* a wind-resistant jacket with a close-fitting neck and cuffs.

wind chill »*noun* the cooling effect of wind on a surface.

winded

winder

windfall »*noun* ❶ an apple or other fruit blown from a tree by the wind. ❷ a piece of unexpected good fortune.

windfall tax »*noun* a tax levied on an unexpectedly large profit, especially one regarded to be excessive or unfairly obtained.

windier

windiest

windily

windiness

winding

winding sheet »*noun* a shroud.

wind instrument »*noun* ❶ a musical instrument which you play by blowing into it. ❷ a woodwind instrument as distinct from a brass instrument.

windlass »*noun* (plural **windlasses**) a winch used on a ship or in a harbour.

windless [without wind]

windmill

window
windowless

window dressing »*noun* ❶ the arrangement of a display in a shop window. ❷ the presentation of something in a superficially attractive way to give a good impression.

windowless

windowpane

window-shop (verb: **window-shops, window-shopping, window-shopped**)
window-shopper

windpipe »*noun* the tube carrying air down the throat and into the lungs; the trachea.

winds

windscreen

windshield

windsock »*noun* a light, flexible cylinder or cone mounted on a mast to show the direction and strength of the wind.

windsurfing »*noun* the sport of riding on water on a sailboard.
windsurfer

windswept

W

wind tunnel »*noun* a tunnel-like structure in which a strong current of air is created, to test the effect of air flow on various products.

wind-up »*noun* (in informal English) an attempt to tease or irritate someone.

windward »*adjective & adverb* facing the wind or on the side facing the wind.

windy[1] »*adjective* (windier, windiest) marked by or exposed to strong winds.
– SAY win-di
windily
windiness

windy[2] »*adjective* following a winding course.
– SAY wyn-di

wine [alcoholic drink]
winey

winemaker
winemaking

winery »*noun* (plural wineries) an establishment where wine is made.

> ☑ plural: drop the y and add ies: wineries

winey [like or containing wine]

wing (verb: wings, winging, winged)
winged
wingless

wingbeat

wing collar »*noun* a high stiff shirt collar with turned-down corners.

wing commander »*noun* a rank of RAF officer, above squadron leader and below group captain.

winged

winger »*noun* an attacking player on the wing in soccer, hockey, etc.

winging

wingless

wings

wingspan »*noun* the full extent from tip to tip of the wings of an aircraft, bird, etc.

wink (verb: winks, winking, winked)

winkle »*noun* a small edible shellfish with a spiral shell.
» *verb* (winkles, winkling, winkled) (winkle out) ❶ take something out from a tight or embedded position. ❷ get information from someone who is reluctant to give it.

winks

winnable

> ☑ double n: winnable

winner

winning
winningly

winnings

winnow »*verb* (winnows, winnowing, winnowed) blow air through grain in order to remove the chaff.

wino »*noun* (plural winos) (in informal English) a person who spends all day in the streets drinking alcohol.

> ☑ the plural of wino has os not oes: winos

wins

winsome »*adjective* appealing.
winsomely
winsomeness

winter (verb: winters, wintering, wintered)

wintergreen »*noun* ❶ a low-growing plant with white bell-shaped flowers. ❷ an American shrub whose leaves produce oil. ❸ a pungent oil obtained from these plants or from birch bark, used medicinally and as a flavouring.

wintering

winters

wintertime

wintry »*adjective* (wintrier, wintriest) very cold or bleak.

> ☑ no e in wintry

wipe (verb: wipes, wiping, wiped)
wipeable
wiper

wire (verb: wires, wiring, wired)

wired »*adjective* ❶ making use of computers and information technology to transfer or receive information. ❷ nervous or tense.

wireless »*noun* (old-fashioned) ❶ a radio. ❷ broadcasting using radio signals.

wires

wiretapping »*noun* the secret tapping of telephone lines in order to listen to other people's conversations.

wireworm »*noun* the worm-like larva of a beetle, which feeds on roots and can damage crops.

wirier

wiriest

wiring

wiry »*adjective* (wirier, wiriest) ❶ resembling wire in form and texture. ❷ lean, tough, and sinewy.

wisdom

wisdom tooth »*noun* one of the four molars at the back of the mouth which usually appear at about the age of twenty.

wise
  wisely

wiseacre »*noun* a person who affects wisdom or knowledge.
– SAY wyz-ay-ker

wisecrack (verb: **wisecracks**, **wisecracking**, **wisecracked**)

wisely

wish (verb: **wishes**, **wishing**, **wished**)

wishbone »*noun* a forked bone between the neck and breast of a bird.

wished

wishes

wishful
  wishfully

> ✓ -ful not -full: **wishful**

wish-fulfilment »*noun* the satisfying of wishes or desires in dreams or fantasies.

wishing

wishy-washy

wisp »*noun* a small thin bunch or strand of something.
  wispy

wisteria »*noun* a climbing plant with hanging clusters of pale bluish-lilac flowers.
– SAY wi-**steer**-i-uh or wi-**stair**-i-uh

> ✓ **wisteria** can also be spelled with an **a** in the middle: **wistaria**. It was named after the American anatomist Caspar *Wistar* or *Wister*. The correct botanical name is *Wisteria*.

wistful »*adjective* having a feeling of vague or regretful longing.
  wistfully

> ✓ no **h**, and the ending is -ful not -full: **wistful**

wit »*noun* ❶ (also **wits**) the capacity for inventive thought and quick understanding. ❷ a natural aptitude for using words and ideas in a quick and funny way. ❸ a person with this aptitude.

witch »*noun* ❶ a woman believed to have evil magic powers. ❷ a practitioner of Wicca.
  witchy

> ℹ do not confuse **witch** with **which** (as in *which one?* or *the house in which I was born*)

witchcraft

witchery

witch hazel »*noun* a shrub with yellow or orange flowers.

witch-hunt »*noun* a campaign against a person who holds unpopular views.

witching hour »*noun* midnight, regarded as the time when witches are supposedly active.

witchy

with

withdraw (verb: **withdraws**, **withdrawing**, **withdrew**; past participle **withdrawn**)

withdrawal

> ✓ -drawal not -drawl: **withdrawal**

withdrawing

withdrawn past participle of **WITHDRAW**. »*adjective* very shy or reserved.

withdraws

withdrew

wither (verb: **withers**, **withering**, **withered**)
  withering
  witheringly

> ✓ no **h**: **wither** (**whither** is an old word meaning primarily 'to what place or state')

withers »*plural noun* the highest part of a horse's back, at the base of the neck.

withhold (verb: **withholds**, **withholding**, **withheld**)
  withholder

> ✓ remember the double **h**: **withhold**

withies

within

without

withstand »*verb* (**withstands**, **withstanding**, **withstood**) ❶ remain undamaged by something. ❷ resist something.

withy »*noun* (plural **withies**) a tough flexible branch of a willow, used for making baskets or tying.

witless »*adjective* foolish; stupid.
  witlessly
  witlessness

witness (plural **witnesses**; verb: **witnesses**, **witnessing**, **witnessed**)

witter »*verb* (**witters**, **wittering**, **wittered**) talk for a long time about unimportant things.

witticism »*noun* a witty remark.

wittier

wittiest

wittily

wittiness

W

witting »*adjective* aware of what you are doing.
wittingly

witty (adjective: **wittier, wittiest**)
wittily
witiness

wives plural of **WIFE**.

wizard

☑ only one **z** in **wizard**, not two (*Wizzard* are a rock band who made 'I wish it could be Christmas every day')

wizardry

wizened »*adjective* shrivelled or wrinkled with age.
– SAY wi-zuhnd

woad »*noun* a plant whose leaves were used in the past to make blue dye.

wobble (verb: **wobbles, wobbling, wobbled**)
wobbler

wobbly (adjective: **wobblier, wobbliest**)
wobbliness

wodge »*noun* (in informal English) a large piece or amount.

woe »*noun* ❶ great sorrow or distress. ❷ (**woes**) troubles.

woebegone »*adjective* looking sad or miserable.
– SAY woh-bi-gon

woeful »*adjective* ❶ full of sadness or distress. ❷ very bad.
woefully

☑ -ful not -full: woeful

woggle »*noun* a loop or ring through which the ends of a Scout's neckerchief are threaded.

wok »*noun* a bowl-shaped frying pan used in Chinese cookery.

☑ there is no **c**: wok

woke past of **WAKE**¹.

woken past participle of **WAKE**¹.

wold »*noun* an area of high, open land.

wolf (plural **wolves**; verb: **wolfs, wolfing, wolfed**)
wolfish

☑ plural: drop the **f** and add **ves**: wolves

wolfhound »*noun* a large breed of dog originally used to hunt wolves.

wolfing

wolfish

wolfram »*noun* tungsten or its ore.
– SAY wuul-fruhm

wolfs

wolf whistle »*noun* a whistle with a rising and falling pitch.
»*verb* (**wolf-whistles, wolf-whistling, wolf-whistled**) whistle in such a way at someone.

wolverine »*noun* a heavily built meat-eating mammal found in cold northern areas.
– SAY wuul-vuh-reen

wolves plural of **WOLF**.

woman (plural **women**)

womanhood

womanize »*verb* (**womanizes, womanizing, womanized**) (of a man) regularly give women attention in the hope of forming sexual relationships.
womanizer

☑ many people prefer the alternative spellings **womanise, womanises**, etc., and **womaniser**: both **s** and **z** spellings are correct

womankind

womanly
womanliness

womb »*noun* the organ in a woman's body in which a baby develops before it is born.

wombat »*noun* an Australian burrowing animal resembling a small bear with short legs.

☑ single **m**: wombat

women plural of **WOMAN**.

womenfolk

womenswear

won past and past participle of **WIN**.

wonder (verb: **wonders, wondering, wondered**) [feeling of admiration or amazement; be interested to know about something]

☑ do not confuse **wonder** with **wander**, which means 'move in a leisurely or aimless way'

wonderful
wonderfully
wonderfulness

☑ -ful not -full: wonderful

wondering

wonderland

wonderment »*noun* a state of great admiration or respect.

wonders

wondrous »*adjective* (a poetic term) inspiring wonder.
wondrously

✓ there is no **e** between the **d** and the **r**: **wondrous**

wonky (adjective: **wonkier**, **wonkiest**)
wonkily
wonkiness

wont »*noun* (**your wont**) (mainly used in a humorous way) your normal behaviour.
– SAY wohnt

won't [will not]

✓ be careful to put the apostrophe where a letter has been left out, that is between the **n** and **t** of **not**: **won't**

wonted »*adjective* (an old word) usual.
– SAY wohn-tid

wonton »*noun* (in Chinese cookery) a small round dumpling with a savoury filling.
– SAY won-**ton**

woo »*verb* (**woos**, **wooing**, **wooed**) ❶ try to make someone love you. ❷ try to get someone's support or custom.
wooer

wood

woodbine »*noun* the common honeysuckle.

woodblock »*noun* ❶ a block of wood from which woodcut prints are made. ❷ a hollow wooden block used as a percussion instrument.

woodchip »*noun* wallpaper with small chips of wood in it, used to give a grainy texture.

woodchuck »*noun* a North American marmot with a heavy body and short legs.

woodcock »*noun* a long-billed woodland bird of the sandpiper family, with brown plumage.

woodcut »*noun* a print made with a block of wood in which a design has been cut.

woodcutter

wooded

wooden
woodenly
woodenness

woodier

woodiest

woodland

woodlouse »*noun* (plural **woodlice**) a small land insect-like creature with a grey segmented body.

woodpecker

wood pulp »*noun* wood fibre reduced chemically or mechanically to pulp and used in the manufacture of paper.

woodshed

woodsman »*noun* (plural **woodsmen**) a forester, hunter, or woodcutter.

woodturning »*noun* the activity of shaping wood with a lathe.
woodturner

woodwind »*noun* wind instruments other than brass instruments forming a section of an orchestra.

woodwork
woodworker
woodworking

woodworm »*noun* the larva of a kind of small brown beetle, that bores into wood.

woody (adjective: **woodier**, **woodiest**)

woodyard

wooed

wooer

woof[1] (verb: **woofs**, **woofing**, **woofed**) [bark]

woof[2] »*noun* = WEFT.

woofer »*noun* a loudspeaker designed to reproduce low frequencies.

woofing

woofs

wooing

wool

woollen

✓ double **l**: **woollen** (the spelling **woolen** is American)

woolly (adjective: **woollier**, **woolliest**; plural **woollies**)

✓ plural: drop the **y** and add **ies**: **woollies**

woos

woosh another way of spelling WHOOSH.

woozy »*adjective* (**woozier**, **wooziest**) unsteady, dizzy, or dazed.
woozily
wooziness

Worcester sauce »*noun* a tangy sauce containing soy sauce and vinegar.

word (verb: **words**, **wording**, **worded**)
wordless

wordier

wordiest

wordily

wordiness

wording

word-perfect

wordplay

W

word processor »*noun* a computer or program for creating, editing, storing, and printing a document or piece of text.

words

wordsmith »*noun* a skilled user of words.

wordy (adjective: **wordier, wordiest**)
wordily
wordiness

wore past of WEAR.

work (verb: **works, working, worked** or formerly **wrought**)
worker

workable »*adjective* ❶ able to be shaped, dug, etc. ❷ capable of producing the desired result.
workability

workaday »*adjective* ordinary.

workaholic »*noun* a person who works very hard and finds it difficult to stop working.
workaholism

 a not o after **work: workaholic**

workbench

worked

worker

work ethic »*noun* the idea that hard work is good in itself or brings rewards.

workforce

workhorse »*noun* a person or machine that works hard and reliably over a long period.

workhouse »*noun* (a historical term) (in the UK) a public institution in which poor people received board and lodging in return for work.

working

working party »*noun* a group appointed to study and report on a particular question and make recommendations.

workload

workman (plural **workmen**)

workmanlike »*adjective* showing efficient skill.

workmanship »*noun* the degree of skill with which a product is made or a job done.

workmate

workmen

workout

work permit »*noun* an official document giving a foreigner permission to take a job in a country.

workpiece »*noun* an object being worked on with a tool or machine.

workplace

works

worksheet

workshop

work-shy »*adjective* not inclined to work.

workspace »*noun* ❶ an area rented or sold for commercial purposes. ❷ (in computing) a memory storage facility for temporary use.

workstation »*noun* a desktop computer terminal, typically networked and more powerful than a personal computer.

worktop

world

world-beater »*noun* a person or thing that is better than all others in its field.

world-class

worldly »*adjective* (**worldlier, worldliest**) ❶ having to do with material things rather than spiritual ones. ❷ experienced and sophisticated.
worldliness

worldly-wise »*adjective* having enough experience not to be easily shocked or deceived.

world music »*noun* music from the developing world incorporating traditional and/or popular elements.

world-ranking

world-weary »*adjective* bored with or cynical about life.

worldwide

World Wide Web »*noun* an extensive information system on the Internet providing facilities for documents to be connected to other documents by hypertext links.

worm (verb: **worms, worming, wormed**)

worm cast »*noun* a small spiral of earth or sand thrown up at the surface by a burrowing worm.

wormed

wormhole »*noun* ❶ a hole made by a burrowing insect larva or worm in wood, fruit, etc. ❷ (chiefly in science fiction) a supposed connection between widely separated locations in space–time.

worming

worms

wormwood »*noun* ❶ a woody shrub with a bitter taste, used as an ingredient of vermouth and absinthe and in medicine. ❷ bitterness or grief, or a source of this.

W

wormy »*adjective* worm-eaten or full of worms.

worn past participle of **WEAR**.

worried
  worriedly

worrier

worries

worrisome »*adjective* causing anxiety or concern.

> ☑ **i** in the middle, not **y**: **worrisome**

worry (verb: **worries, worrying, worried**; plural **worries**)
  worrier

> ☑ plural: drop the **y** and add **ies**: **worries**

worse

> ☑ **i** **worse** already means 'more bad'. It is not good English to use *worser* or *worsest* for something even more bad.

worsen (verb: **worsens, worsening, worsened**)

worship (verb: **worships, worshipping, worshipped**)
  worshipper

> ☑ double the **p** in **worshipping, worshipped**, and **worshipper** (the spellings **worshiping, worshiped**, and **worshiper** are American)

worshipful »*adjective* feeling or showing great respect and admiration.

> ☑ -**ful** not -**full**: **worshipful**

worshipped

worshipper

worshipping

worships

worst »*adjective* most bad, severe, or serious.
» *adverb* ❶ most severely or seriously.
  ❷ least well.
» *noun* the worst part, event, or circumstance.
» *verb* (**worsts, worsting, worsted**) get the better of someone.

worsted »*noun* ❶ a fine smooth yarn spun from long strands of combed wool.
  ❷ fabric made from such yarn.
  – SAY wuus-tid

worsting

worsts

worth

worthier

worthies

worthiest

worthily

worthiness

worthless
  worthlessly
  worthlessness

worthwhile

> ☑ remember the second **h**: **worthwhile**

worthy (adjective: **worthier, worthiest**; plural **worthies**)
  worthily
  worthiness

> ☑ plural: drop the **y** and add **ies**: **worthies**

would

> ☑ **i** for an explanation of the difference between **would** and **should**, see the note at **SHOULD**

would-be »*adjective* desiring or hoping to be a specified type of person: *a would-be actress*.

wouldn't »*contraction* would not.

> ☑ be careful to put the apostrophe where a letter has been left out, that is between the **n** and **t** of **not**: **wouldn't**

wound¹ (verb: **wounds, wounding, wounded**) [an injury; injure]

wound² past and past participle of **WIND**².

wove past of **WEAVE**¹.

woven past participle of **WEAVE**¹.

wow (verb: **wows, wowing, wowed**)

wrack¹ (verb: **wracks, wracking, wracked**) another way of spelling **RACK**.

> ☑ **i** for an explanation of the relationship between **wrack** and **rack**, see the note at **RACK**

wrack² »*noun* a coarse brown seaweed which grows on the shoreline.

wraith »*noun* a ghost or ghostly image of someone, especially one seen shortly before or after their death.
  wraithlike

wrangle »*noun* a long and complicated dispute or argument.
» *verb* (**wrangles, wrangling, wrangled**) engage in a wrangle.
  wrangler

wrap (verb: **wraps, wrapping, wrapped**)
  wrapper
  wrapping

> ☑ double the **p** in **wrapping** and **wrapped**

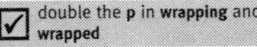

wrasse »*noun* (plural **wrasse** or **wrasses**) a brightly coloured marine fish with thick lips and strong teeth.
– SAY rass

wrath »*noun* extreme anger.
– SAY roth or rawth

wrathful »*adjective* (a poetic term) very angry.
wrathfully

> ☑ -ful not -full: **wrathful**

wreak »*verb* (**wreaks**, **wreaking**, **wreaked**)
❶ cause a large amount of damage or harm. ❷ inflict vengeance.

> ℹ the past tense of the verb **wreak** is **wreaked**, as in *torrential rainstorms wreaked havoc*, not **wrought**. When **wrought** is used in the phrase **wrought havoc**, it is in fact an old past tense of **work**.

wreath »*noun* (plural **wreaths**) ❶ an arrangement of flowers or leaves fastened in a ring. ❷ a curl or ring of smoke or cloud.
– SAY reeth [singular], reeths or ree*thz* [plural]

> ℹ do not confuse **wreath** and **wreathe**: **wreath** with no **e** at the end means 'arrangement of flowers', while **wreathe** with an **e** is a verb meaning 'surround or encircle'

wreathe »*verb* (**wreathes**, **wreathing**, **wreathed**) ❶ surround or encircle. ❷ (of smoke) move with a curling motion.
– SAY ree*th*

wreaths

wreck (verb: **wrecks**, **wrecking**, **wrecked**)
wrecker

wreckage »*noun* the remains of something that has been badly damaged or destroyed.

wrecked

wrecker

wrecking

wrecks

wren »*noun* a very small songbird with a cocked tail.

wrench »*verb* (**wrenches**, **wrenching**, **wrenched**) ❶ pull or twist something suddenly and violently. ❷ injure a part of the body as a result of a sudden twisting movement.
» *noun* ❶ a sudden violent twist or pull. ❷ a feeling of sudden pain and distress caused by a person's departure. ❸ an adjustable tool like a spanner, used for gripping and turning nuts or bolts.

wrest »*verb* (**wrests**, **wresting**, **wrested**)
❶ forcibly pull something from a person's grasp. ❷ take power or control after effort or resistance.
– SAY rest

wrestle (verb: **wrestles**, **wrestling**, **wrestled**)
wrestler
wrestling

> ☑ be careful to spell **wrestle** with **st**

wrests

wretch »*noun* ❶ an unfortunate person. ❷ (in informal English) a contemptible person.

wretched »*adjective* ❶ in a very unhappy or unfortunate state. ❷ of poor quality.
wretchedly
wretchedness

> ℹ the comparative and superlative are usually **more wretched** and **most wretched**, not **wretcheder** and **wretchedest**

wrier [more wry]

wriest

wriggle (verb: **wriggles**, **wriggling**, **wriggled**)
wriggler
wriggly

wright »*noun* (an old word) a maker or builder.

wring »*verb* (**wrings**, **wringing**, **wrung**)
❶ squeeze and twist something to force out liquid. ❷ break an animal's neck by twisting forcibly. ❸ squeeze someone's hand tightly. ❹ (**wring from** or **out of**) obtain something with difficulty or effort.
» *noun* an act of wringing.

> ☑ remember the **w** in **wring** (not *ring*) in phrases such as *wringing their hands* or *wring its neck*.

wringer »*noun* a device for wringing water from wet clothes or other objects.

wringing »*adjective* extremely wet.

wrings

wrinkle (verb: **wrinkles**, **wrinkling**, **wrinkled**)
wrinkled

wrinkly (adjective: **wrinklier**, **wrinkliest**)

wrist

wristband

wristwatch

writ[1] »*noun* ❶ an official written command issued by a court or other legal authority. ❷ (**your writ**) your power to enforce obedience.

writ[2] »*verb* old past participle of **WRITE**.

write (verb: **writes**, **writing**, **wrote**; past participle **written**)
　writer

write-off »*noun* something that is too badly damaged to be repaired.

writer

writerly »*adjective* ❶ having to do with a professional author. ❷ deliberately literary in style.

writer's block »*noun* the condition of being unable to think of what to write or how to write something.

writer's cramp »*noun* pain or stiffness in the hand caused by too much writing.

writes

write-up »*noun* a newspaper review of a recent event, performance, etc.

writhe »*verb* (**writhes**, **writhing**, **writhed**) twist or squirm in pain or as if in pain.

writing

written past participle of **WRITE**.

wrong (verb: **wrongs**, **wronging**, **wronged**)
　wrongly
　wrongness

wrongdoing
　wrongdoer

wronged

wrong-foot »*verb* (**wrong-foots**, **wrong-footing**, **wrong-footed**) ❶ (in a game) play so as to catch an opponent off balance. ❷ place someone in a difficult or embarrassing situation by saying or doing something unexpected.

wrongful
　wrongfully

> ✓ -ful not -full: wrongful

wrong-headed »*adjective* having or showing bad judgement.

wronging

wrongly

wrongness

wrongs

wrote past tense of **WRITE**.

wroth »*adjective* (an old word) angry.
– SAY rohth or roth

wrought »*adjective* ❶ (of metals) beaten out or shaped by hammering. ❷ made in the specified way: *well-wrought*.
– SAY *rhymes with* bought

> ℹ️ **wrought** is an old past participle of **work**. See the notes at **WORK** and **WREAK**.

wrought iron »*noun* a tough form of iron suitable for forging or rolling rather than casting.

wrung past and past participle of **WRING**.

wry »*adjective* (**wryer**, **wryest** or **wrier**, **wriest**) ❶ using or expressing dry, mocking humour. ❷ (of a person's face) twisted into an expression of disgust, disappointment, or annoyance. ❸ bending or twisted to one side.
– SAY ry
　wryly
　wryness

> ✓ the comparative and superlative of **wry** can be spelt with a **y** or with an **i**: **wryer** and **wryest** or **wrier** and **wriest**

wryneck »*noun* a brown bird of the woodpecker family, with a habit of twisting its head backwards.

wunderkind »*noun* (plural **wunderkinds** or **wunderkinder**) a person who achieves great success when young.
– SAY vuun-der-kind

> ✓ the plural of **wunderkind** can be either **wunderkinds** or (as in the original German) **wunderkinder**

Wurlitzer »*noun* (trademark) a large pipe organ or electric organ.
– SAY wer-lit-ser

> ℹ️ named after the American instrument-maker Rudolf *Wurlitzer*

wuss »*noun* (in informal American English) a feeble person.

WWF »*abbreviation* ❶ World Wide Fund for Nature. ❷ World Wrestling Federation.

WWW »*abbreviation* World Wide Web.

xenon »*noun* an inert gaseous chemical element, present in tiny amounts in the air and used in some kinds of electric light.
– SAY zen-on or zee-non

xenophobia »*noun* strong dislike or fear of people from other countries.
– SAY zen-uh-**foh**-bi-uh
xenophobe
xenophobic

✓ note that **xenophobia** and related words begin with an **x** not a **z**

xerography »*noun* a dry copying process in which powder sticks to electrically charged parts of a surface which has been exposed to light from an image of the document to be copied.
– SAY zeer-og-ruh-fi
xerographic

Xerox »*noun* (trademark) ❶ a xerographic copying process. ❷ a copy made using such a process.
»*verb* (**xeroxes, xeroxing, xeroxed**) copy a document by such a process.
– SAY zeer-oks or ze-roks

xi »*noun* the fourteenth letter of the Greek alphabet (Ξ, ξ).
– SAY ksy or zy

Xmas

X-rated

X-ray »*noun* ❶ an electromagnetic wave of very short wavelength, able to pass through many solids and make it possible to see into or through them. ❷ an image of the internal structure of an object produced by passing X-rays through it.
»*verb* (**X-rays, X-raying, X-rayed**) photograph or examine something with X-rays.

xylem »*noun* the tissue in plants which carries water and nutrients upwards from the root and also helps to form the woody part of the stem.
– SAY zy-luhm

xylophone »*noun* a musical instrument played by striking a row of wooden bars of graduated length with small beaters.

✓ **xylo** not **xyla: xylophone**

yacht »*noun* ❶ a medium-sized sailing boat equipped for cruising or racing. ❷ a powered boat equipped for cruising.
– SAY yot
yachting

✓ be careful to spell the last three letters in the correct order, **cht: yacht**

yachtsman (plural **yachtsmen**)

yack another way of spelling **YAK²**.

yahoo »*noun* (in informal English) a rude, coarse, or violent person.

ⓘ the *Yahoos* were an imaginary people in Jonathan Swift's *Gulliver's Travels*

yak¹ »*noun* a large ox with shaggy hair and large horns, found in Tibet and central Asia.

yak² (in informal English) »*verb* (**yaks, yakking, yakked**) talk at length about trivial or boring subjects.
»*noun* a trivial or lengthy conversation.

✓ with reference to talking, **yak** can also be spelled with a **c: yack**

Yale »*noun* (trademark) a type of lock with a latch bolt and a flat key with a serrated edge.

yam »*noun* the starchy tuber of a tropical climbing plant, eaten as a vegetable.

yammer (in informal English) »*verb* (**yammers, yammering, yammered**) talk loudly and without pausing.
» *noun* loud and sustained noise.

yang »*noun* (in Chinese philosophy) the active male principle of the universe (the opposite of *yin*).

Yank »*noun* (in informal English) an American.

yank (verb: **yanks, yanking, yanked**)

Yankee »*noun* (in informal English) ❶ an American. ❷ a person from New England or one of the northern states. ❸ (a historical term) a Federal soldier in the Civil War.

yanking

yanks

yap (verb: **yaps, yapping, yapped**)

yappy

> ☑ double the **p** in **yapping, yapped,** and **yappy**

yard

yardage »*noun* a distance or length measured in yards.

yardarm »*noun* either end of a ship's yard supporting a sail.

Yardie (in informal English) »*noun* ❶ (among Jamaicans) a fellow Jamaican. ❷ (in the UK) a member of a Jamaican or West Indian gang of criminals.

yardstick »*noun* ❶ a measuring rod a yard long. ❷ a standard used for comparison.

yarn »*noun* ❶ spun thread used for knitting, weaving, or sewing. ❷ a long or rambling story.

yarrow »*noun* a plant with feathery leaves and heads of small white or pale pink flowers, used in herbal medicine.

yashmak »*noun* a veil concealing all of the face except the eyes, worn by some Muslim women in public.
– SAY yash-mak

yaw »*verb* (**yaws, yawing, yawed**) (of a moving ship or aircraft) turn to one side or from side to side.
» *noun* yawing movement of a ship or aircraft.

yawl »*noun* a kind of sailing boat with two masts.

yawn (verb: **yawns, yawning, yawned**)

yawp (verb: **yawps, yawping, yawped**)

yaws »*noun* a contagious tropical disease caused by a bacterium that enters cuts on the skin and causes small lesions which may develop into deep ulcers.

ye[1] »*pronoun* plural of **THOU**[1].

ye[2] old form of **THE**.

> the **y** in **ye** meaning 'the' (as in *Ye Olde Cock Tavern*) originally represented the Anglo-Saxon letter þ, which is known as a *thorn* and was formerly used to write *Th*. It was not pronounced as a *y*.

yea »*adverb* (an old word) yes.

yeah

> ☑ **yeah** can also be spelled **yeh**

year

yearbook »*noun* an annual publication giving current information about and listing events of the previous year.

yearling »*noun* an animal of a year old, or in its second year.

yearly

yearn »*verb* (**yearns, yearning, yearned**) have a strong feeling of loss and longing for something.

year-on-year »*adjective* (of figures, prices, etc.) as compared with the corresponding ones from a year earlier.

year-round

yeast »*noun* ❶ a fungus capable of converting sugar into alcohol and carbon dioxide. ❷ a greyish-yellow substance formed from this, used to make bread rise and to ferment beer.

yeasty

yell (verb: **yells, yelling, yelled**)

yellow (adjective: **yellower, yellowest**; verb: **yellows, yellowing, yellowed**)

yellowish

yellowness

yellowy

yellow fever »*noun* a tropical disease caused by a virus transmitted by mosquitoes, causing fever and jaundice and often death.

yellowhammer »*noun* a common brown songbird, the male of which has a yellow head, neck, and breast.

yellowing

yellowish

yellowness

yellows

yellowy

yells

yelp (verb: **yelps, yelping, yelped**)

Yemeni [of Yemen]

– **SAY** yem-uh-ni

yen[1] »*noun* (plural **yen**) the basic unit of money of Japan.

yen[2] »*noun* (in informal English) a longing or yearning.

yeoman »*noun* (plural **yeomen**) (a historical term) ❶ a man owning a house and a small area of farming land. ❷ a servant in a royal or noble household.

– **SAY** yoh-muhn

Yeoman of the Guard »*noun* a member of the British king or queen's bodyguard (now having only ceremonial duties).

yeomanry »*noun* (a historical term) yeomen as a group.

Yeoman Warder »*noun* a warder at the Tower of London.

yeomen

yes

yes-man »*noun* (plural **yes-men**) (in informal English) a person who always agrees with their superiors.

yesterday

yesteryear »*noun* (a poetic term) last year or the recent past.

yet

> ℹ️ avoid the unnecessarily long phrase *as of yet: as yet* is the proper form

yeti »*noun* a large hairy manlike creature said to live in the highest part of the Himalayas.

– **SAY** yet-i

yew »*noun* a coniferous tree with poisonous red berry-like fruit and springy wood.

Yiddish »*noun* a language used by Jews from central and eastern Europe, originally a German dialect with words from Hebrew and several modern languages.

»*adjective* relating to this language.

yield »*verb* (**yields**, **yielding**, **yielded**) ❶ produce or provide a natural or industrial product. ❷ produce a result or gain. ❸ give way to demands or pressure. ❹ give up possession of something. ❺ (of a mass or structure) give way under force or pressure.

»*noun* an amount or result yielded.

> ✅ **i** before **e** except after **c**: **yield** follows the usual rule

yin »*noun* (in Chinese philosophy) the passive female principle of the universe (the opposite of *yang*).

yippee

ylang-ylang »*noun* a sweet-scented essential oil obtained from the flowers of a tropical tree, used in perfumery and aromatherapy.

– **SAY** ee-lang-ee-lang

YMCA »*abbreviation* Young Men's Christian Association.

yob
yobbery
yobbish

yobbo (plural **yobbos** or **yobboes**)

yodel »*verb* (**yodels**, **yodelling**, **yodelled**) sing or call in a style in which you alternate rapidly between your normal voice and a very high voice.

»*noun* a song or call delivered in such a way.

yodeller

> ✅ double the l in **yodelling**, **yodelled**, and **yodeller** (the spellings **yodeling**, **yodeled**, and **yodeler** are American)

yoga »*noun* a Hindu spiritual discipline, a part of which, including simple meditation, breathing exercises, and specific body positions, is widely practised for health and relaxation.

yogic

> ℹ️ **yoga** is a Sanskrit word meaning 'union'

yoghourt another way of spelling **YOGURT**.

yoghurt another way of spelling **YOGURT**.

yogi »*noun* (plural **yogis**) a person who is skilled in yoga.

yogic

yogis

yogurt »*noun* a semi-solid slightly sour food prepared from milk with bacteria added.

> ✅ **yogurt** can also be spelled **yoghurt** or **yoghourt**

yoke »*noun* ❶ a piece of wood fastened over the necks of two animals and attached to a plough or cart in order for them to pull it. ❷ (plural **yoke** or **yokes**) a pair of yoked animals. ❸ a frame fitting over the neck and shoulders of a person, used for carrying pails or baskets. ❹ something that restricts freedom or is a burden. ❺ a part of a garment that fits over the shoulders and to which the main part of the garment is attached.

»*verb* (**yokes**, **yoking**, **yoked**) ❶ join animals with a yoke. ❷ bring two people or things into a close relationship.

> ℹ️ do not confuse **yoke** with **yolk**, which refers to the yellow part of an egg

yokel »*noun* an unsophisticated country person.
– SAY yoh-k'l

yokes

yoking

yolk [yellow part of an egg]

> ℹ️ do not confuse **yolk** with **yoke**, whose chief meaning is 'a piece of wood fastened over the necks of two animals'

Yom Kippur »*noun* the most solemn religious fast of the Jewish year, the last of the ten days of penitence that begin with Rosh Hashana (the Jewish New Year).
– SAY yom kip-**poor** or yom **kip**-per

> ℹ️ **Yom Kippur** means 'day of atonement' in Hebrew

yon (old-fashioned or dialect) »*determiner & adverb* yonder; that.
» *pronoun* yonder person or thing.

yonder (old-fashioned or dialect) »*adverb* over there.
» *determiner* that or those (referring to something situated at a distance).

yonks »*plural noun* (in informal English) a very long time.

yore »*noun* (**of yore**) (a poetic term) of former times or long ago.

Yorkshire pudding »*noun* a baked batter pudding typically eaten with roast beef.

you

you'd [you had; you would]

you'll [you will; you shall]

young (adjective: **younger**, **youngest**)
youngish

youngster

your [belonging to you]

> ℹ️ do not confuse the **your** meaning 'belonging to you' (as in *let me talk to your daughter*) with **you're**, which is short for **you are** (as in *you're a good cook*)

you're [you are]

yours

> ✅ there is no apostrophe in **yours**

yourself (plural **yourselves**)

youth (plural **youths**)

youthful
youthfully
youthfulness

> ✅ -ful not -full: **youthful**

youth hostel »*noun* a place providing cheap accommodation, aimed mainly at young people on holiday.

youths

you've [you have]

yowl (verb: **yowls**, **yowling**, **yowled**)

yo-yo »*noun* (plural **yo-yos**) (trademark in the UK) a toy consisting of a pair of joined discs with a deep groove between them in which string is attached and wound, which can be spun down and up as the string unwinds and rewinds.
» *verb* (**yo-yoes**, **yo-yoing**, **yo-yoed**) move up and down repeatedly.

YTS »*abbreviation* Youth Training Scheme.

ytterbium »*noun* a silvery-white metallic chemical element.
– SAY it-**ter**-bi-uhm

yttrium »*noun* a greyish-white metallic chemical element.
– SAY it-tri-uhm

yuan »*noun* (plural **yuan**) the basic unit of money of China.
– SAY yuu-**ahn**

yucca »*noun* a plant with sword-like leaves, native to warm regions of the US and Mexico.
– SAY yuk-kuh

> ✅ double **c**: **yucca**

yuck
yucky

> ✅ **yuck** can also be spelled **yuk**, without the **c**

Yugoslav [of Yugoslavia]
Yugoslavian

Yule »*noun* (an old word) Christmas.

yule log »*noun* ❶ a large log traditionally burnt in the hearth on Christmas Eve. ❷ a log-shaped chocolate cake eaten at Christmas.

Yuletide »*noun* = YULE.

yummy (adjective: **yummier**, **yummiest**)

yuppie »*noun* (plural **yuppies**) (used in a disapproving way) a well-paid young middle-class professional working in a city.

> ✅ **yuppie** can also be spelled **yuppy**. The word comes from the acronym *young urban professional*.

YWCA »*abbreviation* Young Women's Christian Association.

Zz

zabaglione »*noun* an Italian dessert made of whipped egg yolks, sugar, and wine.
– SAY za-ba-**lyoh**-ni

✓ ne not **ni** at the end: **zabaglione**

Zambian [of Zambia]

zany »*adjective* (**zanier**, **zaniest**) amusingly unconventional and individual.
zanily
zaniness

zap (verb: **zaps**, **zapping**, **zapped**)

✓ double the **p** in **zapping** and **zapped**

zeal »*noun* great energy or enthusiasm for a cause or aim.

zealot »*noun* an excessively enthusiastic and strict follower of a religion or policy.
– SAY zel-uht
zealotry

zealous »*adjective* having or showing zeal.
– SAY zel-uhss
zealously
zealousness

zebra

zeitgeist »*noun* the characteristic spirit or mood of a particular period of history.
– SAY zyt-gysst

✓ e before **i** twice: **zeitgeist** is a German word

Zen »*noun* a type of Buddhism emphasizing the value of meditation and intuition.

zenith »*noun* ❶ (in astronomy) the point in the sky directly overhead (the opposite of *nadir*). ❷ the highest point in the sky reached by the sun or moon. ❸ the time at which something is most powerful or successful.
– SAY zen-ith

zephyr »*noun* (a poetic term) a soft gentle breeze.
– SAY zef-fer

Zeppelin »*noun* (a historical term) a large German airship of the early 20th century.
– SAY zep-puh-lin

✓ double p, single l: **Zeppelin**. It was named after Ferdinand, Count von *Zeppelin*, German airship pioneer.

zero (plural **zeros**; verb: **zeroes**, **zeroing**, **zeroed**)

zero hour »*noun* the time at which a military or other operation is set to begin.

zeroing

zeros

zero tolerance »*noun* strict enforcement of the law regarding any form of anti-social behaviour.

zest »*noun* ❶ great enthusiasm and energy. ❷ the quality of being exciting or interesting. ❸ the outer coloured part of the peel of citrus fruit, used as flavouring.
zestful
zesty

zester »*noun* a kitchen utensil for scraping or peeling zest from citrus fruit.

zestful

✓ -ful not -full: **zestful**

zesty

zeta »*noun* the sixth letter of the Greek alphabet (Z, ζ).
– SAY zee-tuh

zigzag (verb: **zigzags**, **zigzagging**, **zigzagged**)

✓ double the **g** in **zigzagging** and **zigzagged**

zilch »*pronoun* (in informal English) nothing.

zillion »*cardinal number* (in informal English) an extremely large number of people or things.
zillionth

Zimbabwean [of Zimbabwe]

Zimmer »*noun* (trademark) a kind of walking frame.

ℹ from *Zimmer* Orthopaedic Limited, the name of the manufacturer

zinc »*noun* a silvery-white metallic chemical element which is used in making brass and for coating iron and steel as a protection against corrosion.

zing (in informal English) »*noun* energy or excitement.
»*verb* (**zings**, **zinging**, **zinged**) move swiftly.
zingy

zinnia »*noun* a plant of the daisy family with bright showy flowers.
– SAY zin-ni-uh

Zion »*noun* **❶** the hill of Jerusalem on which the city of David was built. **❷** the Jewish people or religion. **❸** (in Christian thought) the heavenly city or kingdom of heaven.
– SAY zy-uhn

Zionism »*noun* a movement for the development and protection of a Jewish nation in Israel.
– SAY zy-uh-ni-z'm
Zionist

zip (verb: **zips**, **zipping**, **zipped**)

> ✓ double the **p** in **zipping** and **zipped**

zip code »*noun* (in American English) a postcode.

> ✓ **zip code** is often written **ZIP code**: it is an acronym from *zone improvement plan*

zipped
zipper (verb: **zippers**, **zippering**, **zippered**)
zippier
zippiest
zipping
zippy »*adjective* (**zippier**, **zippiest**) (in informal English) **❶** bright, fresh, or lively. **❷** speedy.
zips
zip-up

zircon »*noun* a brown or semi-transparent mineral, used as a gem and in industry.

zirconium »*noun* a hard silver-grey metallic chemical element, of which zircon is a compound.
– SAY zer-koh-ni-uhm

zit »*noun* (in informal English) a pimple.

zither »*noun* a musical instrument with numerous strings stretched across a flat box, placed horizontally and played with the fingers and a plectrum.

zodiac »*noun* an area of the sky in which the sun, moon, and planets appear to lie, divided by astrologers into twelve equal divisions or signs.
– SAY zoh-di-ak
zodiacal

zombie »*noun* **❶** a corpse supposedly brought back to life by witchcraft. **❷** (in informal English) a lifeless or completely unresponsive person.

zone (verb: **zones**, **zoning**, **zoned**)
zonal

zonk (verb: **zonks**, **zonking**, **zonked**)

zoo

zookeeper

zoology »*noun* **❶** the scientific study of animals. **❷** the animal life of a particular area or time.
– SAY zoo-ol-uh-ji or zoh-ol-uh-ji
zoological
zoologically
zoologist

zoom (verb: **zooms**, **zooming**, **zoomed**)

Zoroastrianism »*noun* a religion of ancient Persia based on the worship of a single god, founded by the prophet Zoroaster (also called Zarathustra) in the 6th century BC.
– SAY zo-roh-ass-tri-uh-ni-z'm
Zoroastrian

zucchini »*noun* (plural **zucchini** or **zucchinis**) (in American English) a courgette.
– SAY zuu-kee-ni

> ✓ double **c** followed by **h**: **zucchini** is an Italian word meaning 'little gourds'

Zulu »*noun* **❶** a member of a South African people. **❷** the language of this people.

zygote »*noun* (in biology) a cell resulting from the joining of two gametes in sexual reproduction.
– SAY zy-goht

Z